The Longman Anthology of World Literature

VOLUME B

THE MEDIEVAL ERA

David Damrosch

COLUMBIA UNIVERSITY

The Ancient Near East; Mesoamerica

David L. Pike

AMERICAN UNIVERSITY

Rome and the Roman Empire; Medieval Europe

⣷

April Alliston

PRINCETON UNIVERSITY

The Age of the Enlightenment

Marshall Brown

UNIVERSITY OF WASHINGTON

The Nineteenth Century

Page duBois

UNIVERSITY OF CALIFORNIA, SAN DIEGO

Classical Greece

Sabry Hafez

UNIVERSITY OF LONDON

Arabic and Islamic Literatures

Ursula K. Heise

STANFORD UNIVERSITY

The Twentieth Century

Djelal Kadir

PENNSYLVANIA STATE UNIVERSITY

The Twentieth Century

Sheldon Pollock

COLUMBIA UNIVERSITY

South Asia

Bruce Robbins

COLUMBIA UNIVERSITY

The Nineteenth Century

Haruo Shirane

COLUMBIA UNIVERSITY

Japan

Jane Tylus

NEW YORK UNIVERSITY

Early Modern Europe

Pauline Yu

AMERICAN COUNCIL OF LEARNED SOCIETIES

China

The Longman Anthology of World Literature

SECOND EDITION

David Damrosch

David L. Pike

General Editors

VOLUME B

THE MEDIEVAL ERA

David L. Pike

Sabry Hafez

Haruo Shirane

Pauline Yu

with contributions by

David Damrosch and Sheldon Pollock

PEARSON

Longman

New York   San Francisco   Boston
London   Toronto   Sydney   Tokyo   Singapore   Madrid
Mexico City   Munich   Paris   Cape Town   Hong Kong   Montreal

Editor-in-Chief: *Joseph Terry*
Associate Development Editor: *Erin Reilly*
Executive Marketing Manager: *Joyce Nilsen*
Senior Supplements Editor: *Donna Campion*
Production Manager: *Ellen MacElree*
Project Coordination, Text Design, and Page Makeup: *GGS Book Services PMG*
Senior Cover Design Manager: *Nancy Danahy*
On the Cover: Detail from *Portrait of Murasaki Shikibu*, c. 978–1014, by Ogata Kōrin
    (1658–1716)
Image Permission Coordinator: *Joanne Dippel*
Senior Manufacturing Buyer: *Alfred C. Dorsey*
Printer and Binder: *Quebecor-World/Taunton*
Cover Printer: *The Lehigh Press, Inc.*

For permission to use copyrighted material, grateful acknowledgment is made to the copyright
holders on pages 1167–1173, which are hereby made part of this copyright page.

Library of Congress Cataloging-in-Publication Data

The Longman anthology of world literature / David Damrosch, David L. Pike, general
editors.—2nd ed.
    p.   cm.
    Includes bibliographical references and index.
    Contents: v. A. The ancient world—v. B. The medieval era—v. C. The early
modern period—v. D. The seventeenth and eighteenth centuries—v. E. The
nineteenth century—v. F. The twentieth century.
    ISBN 978-0-205-62595-6 (v. A).—ISBN 978-0-205-62596-3 (v. B).— 978-0-205-62597-0
(v. C).— 978-0-205-62590-1 (v. D).— 978-0-205-62591-8 (v. E).— 978-0-205-62594-9 (v. F).
    1. Literature—Collections.   2. Literature—History and criticism.
I. Damrosch, David.   II. Pike, David L. (David Lawrence), 1963–
PN6013.L66 2009
808.8—dc22

                                                                        2008015921

Please visit us at http://www.ablongman.com/damrosch.

To place your order, please use the following ISBN numbers:

Volume One Package *The Ancient World to The Early Modern Period*
(includes Volumes A, B, and C): **ISBN 13: 978-0-205-62593-2; ISBN 10: 0-205-62593-2**

Volume Two Package *The Seventeenth Century to The Twentieth Century*
(includes Volumes D, E, and F): **ISBN 13: 978-0-205-62592-5; ISBN 10: 0-205-62592-4**

Or, to order individual volumes, please use the following ISBN numbers:

Volume A, *The Ancient World:* ISBN 13: 978-0-205-62595-6; ISBN 10: 0-205-62595-9
Volume B, *The Medieval Era:* ISBN 13: 978-0-205-62596-3; ISBN 10: 0-205-62596-7
Volume C, *The Early Modern Period:* ISBN 13: 978-0-205-62597-0; ISBN 10: 0-205-62597-5
Volume D, *The Seventeenth and Eighteenth Centuries:* ISBN 13: 978-0-205-62590-1;
    ISBN 10: 0-205-62590-8
Volume E, *The Nineteenth Century:* ISBN 13: 978-0-205-62591-8; ISBN 10: 0-205-62591-6
Volume F, *The Twentieth Century:* ISBN 13: 978-0-205-62594-9; ISBN 10: 0-205-62594-0

1 2 3 4 5 6 7 8 9 10—QWT—11 10 09 08

CONTENTS

The Medieval Era   1

Medieval China   11

LIU XIANG (c. 79–8 B.C.E.)   23

BAN ZHAO (c. 45–120)   26

⇥ PERSPECTIVES ⇤
What Is Literature?   101

Japan   125

MAN'YŌSHŪ (COLLECTION OF MYRIAD LEAVES) (c. 702–c. 785)   134

MURASAKI SHIKIBU (c. 978–c. 1014)   146

⇒ PERSPECTIVES ⇐
Courtly Women   237

NOH: DRAMA OF GHOSTS, MEMORIES, AND SALVATION   282

Classical Arabic and Islamic Literatures   315

Illustration. Calligraphy of the name of the Prophet Muhammad 314
Map. The Abbasid Caliphate in 850 C.E. 325
Illustration. Mosque of Muhammad Ali, Cairo 327

On the Cover

Detail from Ogata Kōrin, *Portrait of Murasaki Shikibu,* c. 1710. This imaginary portrait testifies to the enduring importance of Heian-era Japan's greatest writer, Lady Murasaki. Born in Kyoto, where he lived most of his life, Kōrin inherited a fortune from his cloth merchant father but squandered it in a life of luxury, indulging his love of painting and Noh drama. By the late 17th century he was almost bankrupt and decided to pursue a career as a painter. He became one of the most influential painters of his generation, working in the highly decorative Rinpa style, which combined flat and simplified shapes with colorful, flamboyant, and visually stunning images, and which often drew on themes (such as birds and plants or scenes from classical literature) from traditional Japanese painting scrolls. In Kōrin's portrait, Murasaki Shikibu sits on the floor in traditional Japanese fashion, in front of a low writing table, pondering a blank scroll for writing. In the manner of 11th century aristocratic women at court, she has long flowing hair and eyebrows painted high on her forehead, and she wears multiple layers of robes, each in a different color with designs of flowers and plants. These long multilayered robes, with their large, flowing sleeves, trail on the floor behind the woman when she is walking. Murasaki Shikibu appears like one of her own characters on a stage, with a curtain drawn aside for the spectator to observe her.

ADDITIONAL AUDIO AND ONLINE RESOURCES

VOICES OF WORLD LITERATURE, DISK 1 (ISBN: 0-321-22517-1)

An audio CD to accompany *The Longman Anthology of World Literature,* Volume 1. Throughout most of history, literature was created to be read, recited, or sung aloud. The selections on this CD, which can be ordered/packaged with the anthology, present a range of the many voices of world literature from its beginnings to the end of the early modern period and open up a range of cultural contexts for student discussion and writing. The following selections are available for Volume B.

THE MEDIEVAL ERA

12. Reminiscence Song: from Tang Dynasty China
Performed by the Chinese Cultural Theater Group (2:28)

> *Orchestral music was highly developed during the Tang dynasty, with as many as a thousand musicians playing on state occasions. Notes of the pentatonic (five-tone) scale were given names and recorded with indications of tempo, allowing for contemporary reconstructions of how the music may have sounded.*

13. Kengyo Yaezaki: from Yugao: Music based on *The Tale of Genji*
Performed by Shinichi Yuize (2:28)

> *Written in the early 1600s, this piece dramatizes a scene in which Genji and one of his lovers are visited at night by the vengeful ghost of a dead lover. The thirteen-stringed koto echoes the singer's voice and suggests the ghost's presence.*

14. Zeami: from the Prelude to *Kagekiyo*
Performed by the Kanze Kaikan Noh Theater Company (1:54)

> *This opening to a Noh play by the great dramatist Zeami sets the stage for a drama of heartbreak. The story, derived from* Tales of the Heike, *concerns an exiled warrior, Kagekiyo the Hot-Tempered, about to part forever from his daughter.*

15. Al-Adhan: The Muslim Call to Prayer
Performed by an anonymous *muezzin* (crier) at a London mosque (2:32)

> *The call begins "Allahu akbar" (God is great), repeated four times, and continues: "I testify that there is no god by God. I testify that Muhammad is the Messenger of God. Come to the Prayer! Come to prosperity! God is most great. There is no god by God."*

16. Muwwal Kamil: Raqqat Hawashiha
Performed by the Ensemble Ibn Baya and the Cofradia Shushtari (4:23)

> *This Sufi chant (muwwal) combines song and patterned breathing with dance to induce a trancelike state of union with the divine. The Moroccan chanters perform a mystic poem by the Andalusian poet Ibn al-Arabi: "Soft were its sides*

and soft its breeze, and the clouds were flashing and thundering / And the
raindrops were descending from the crevices of the clouds like tears shed by
a passionate lover. / Listen rapturously to a singer who chants: / "O the pure
wine that in Adam's time related an authentic tradition of the Garden of Eden!"

17. Alyawm: A Byzantine-Arab hymn
Performed by the Saraband Ensemble (2:08)

The medieval Maronite Church of Syria and Lebanon conveyed Christian themes in
Arabic language and style. This hymn for Good Friday recalls that "Today, He who
had raised the earth from the waters was crucified on a piece of wood. / . . . We kneel
before your pain, Messiah. / Let us also be witnesses to Your glorious resurrection."

18. Ibn Arabi: Ala ya nasima: The Secret Encounter
Performed by the Ensemble Ibn Baya (3:09)

Like Dante, the Andalusian poet Ibn al-Arabi wrote poems envisioning divine love
reflected in an ideal passion for a mortal woman. This poem refers both to God
and to Ibn al-Arabi's beloved Nizam: "O breeze, bear this message to the gazelles
of Najd: / I am faithful to the covenant which you know. / And if her words be true
and she feel the same tormenting desire for me as I feel / For her, then we shall
meet secretly in the heat of noon / at her tent with the most inviolable truth."

19. Sephardic Song: Nochez nochez
Performed by Voice of the Turtle (2:41)

The poetic traditions of Andalusian Spain continued among Jews driven out of
Spain after 1492. In this seventeenth-century Judeo-Spanish song from the
Balkans, an emperor's daughter, "Sleepless Melisenda," is advised by her sisters
to go to her lover: "Beautiful nights, / nights are for love; / ah, nights are for
love. / Restless, tossing in bed, / all three as one, / ah, like the fishes in the sea. /
There were three sisters, / all three move as one, / all three move as one."

20. Carmina Burana: *Tempus est jocundum*
Performed by Ensemble Anonymous (3:24)

This lively Latin song from "Carmina Burana" celebrates the pleasure of love in
the springtime: "How fine this weather is, my fair damsels. / Oh! Oh! Oh! I feel
myself blossoming! . . . / Spring forth, O song, from my heart; / in winter pa-
tience, in spring licentious."

21. Hildegard von Bingen: from *O Magne Pater*
Performed by the Saraband Ensemble (3:39)

The great medieval abbess and mystic Hildegard von Bingen composed music and
poems to record her divine visions, using a melodic range and harmonies unusual
for the time. This prayer entreats: "O great Father, we are in great distress . . .
Turn toward us, O Father . . . and help us that we may not perish and that thy
name will not become dark within us. Help us for thy name's sake!"

22. Codex Las Huelgas De Burgos: *Rex virginum amator*
Performed by the Saraband Ensemble (2:19)

The convent of Las Huelgas was favored by the daughters of the Castilian aristoc-
racy, and became known for its music. Written around 1300, the parchment
Codex Las Huelgas records pieces for daily use, including this Latin hymn to

Father, Son, and Holy Spirit, which begins: "O King, lover of the Virgin,
privileged God of Mary, have mercy upon us."

23. Geoffrey Chaucer: From the General Prologue to *The Canterbury Tales,* lines
447–478
Read by J. B. Bessinger Jr. (1:58)

> *This passage gives Chaucer's vivid description of the Wife of Bath in a rich Middle*
> *English dialect.*

Companion Website for *The Longman Anthology of World Literature,*
Second Edition

www.ablongman.com/damrosch

Our Companion Website for the second edition has been enhanced with the addition
of an interactive timeline, practice quizzes for major periods and authors, author biographies, research links, a glossary of literary terms, an audio glossary that provides
the accepted pronunciations of author, character, and selection names from the anthology, audio recordings of our Translations features, and sample syllabi.

RESOURCES FOR VOLUME B

Practice Quizzes

Period Quizzes
- Medieval China
- Japan
- Classical Arabic and Islamic Literatures
- Medieval Europe

Quizzes on Major Texts
- The poetry of Li Bo
- *Man'Yoshu (Collection of*
  Myriad Leaves)
- *The Tale of Genji*
- *Tales of the Heike*
- The Qur'an
- *The Thousand and One Nights*
- *The Epic of Son-Jara*
- Beowulf
- *Sir Gawain and the Green Knight*
- *The Divine Comedy*
- *The Canterbury Tales*

Author Biographies

- Li Bo
- Murasaki Shikibu
- Confucius
- Abelard and Heloise
- Dante Alighieri
- Geoffrey Chaucer

Research Links

Authors and Major Texts
- Abelard and Heloise
- Dante Alighieri
- Ban Zhao
- *Beowulf*
- Bo Juyi
- Geoffrey Chaucer
- Confucius
- Du Fu
- *The Epic of Son-Jara*
- Firdawsi
- Hafiz
- Han-shan
- Ibn Battuta
- Li Bo

- *Man'yoshu (Collection of Myriad Leaves)*
- Marie de France
- Murasaki Shikibu
- Noh Drama
- *The Play of Adam*
- *The Poem of the Cid*
- Poetry of the Tang dynasty
- Pre-Islamic poetry
- *The Qur'an*
- *Sir Gawain and the Green Knight*
- *Tales of the Heike*
- Tao Qian
- *The Thousand and One Nights*
- Voices of women
- Wang Wei
- Women in early China
- Yuan Cai
- Yuan Zhen
- Zeami

Perspectives

- What Is "Literature"?
- Courtly Women
- Poetry, Wine, and Love
- Asceticism, Sufism, and Wisdom
- Iberia, The Meeting of Three Worlds

Translations

- *The Thousand and One Nights*
- Dante Alighieri's *Divine Comedy*

PREFACE

Our world today is both expanding and growing smaller at the same time. Expanding, through a tremendous increase in the range of cultures that actively engage with each other; and yet growing smaller as well, as people and products surge across borders in the process known as globalization. This double movement creates remarkable opportunities for cross-cultural understanding, as well as new kinds of tensions, miscommunications, and uncertainties. Both the opportunities and the uncertainties are amply illustrated in the changing shape of world literature. A generation ago, when the term "world literature" was used in North America, it largely meant masterworks by European writers from Homer onward, together with a few favored North American writers, heirs to the Europeans. Today, however, it is generally recognized that Europe is only part of the story of the world's literatures, and only part of the story of North America's cultural heritage. An extraordinary range of exciting material is now in view, from the earliest Sumerian lyrics inscribed on clay tablets to the latest Kashmiri poetry circulated on the Internet. Many new worlds—and newly visible *older* worlds of classical traditions around the globe—await us today.

How can we best approach such varied materials from so many cultures? Can we deal with this embarrassment of riches without being overwhelmed by it, and without merely giving a glancing regard to less familiar traditions? This anthology has been designed to help readers successfully navigate "the sea of stories"—as Salman Rushdie has described the world's literary heritage.

The enthusiastic reception of the first edition attests to the growing relevance of a truly global approach to world literature. Drawing from the insight of instructors across the country, we have updated and further improved our anthology. We've gone about this challenging, fascinating task in several ways.

NEW TO THIS EDITION

- In our new Translations features, a brief selection is presented in the original language accompanied by two or three translations, chosen to show differing strategies translators have used to convey the sense of the original in new and powerful ways.
- Each of the Perspectives sections is now followed by our new Crosscurrents feature, which will highlight additional connections for students to explore.
- In response to reviewer requests, we have reevaluated each selection and streamlined our coverage to focus on the readings most frequently taught in the world literature course. We have also added several important works in their entirety, including Sophocles' *Antigone,* Shakespeare's *Othello,* Moliere's *Tartuffe,* Tolstoy's *The Death of Ivan Ilych,* and Silko's "Yellow Woman."

- Pull-out quotations in our period introductions and new headings in our author introductions have been added to help draw student interest and highlight important information.
- We have enhanced our Companion Website with the addition of a multitude of resources, including an interactive timeline, practice quizzes for major periods and authors, author biographies, research links, a glossary of literary terms, an audio glossary that provides the accepted pronunciations of author, character, and selection names from the anthology, audio recordings of our translations features, and sample syllabi. Visit www.ablongman.com/damrosch to explore these and other resources.
- We have improved our table of contents through the addition of a new media index—enabling you to locate all available resources quickly.

CONNECTING DISTINCTIVE TRADITIONS

Works of world literature engage in a double conversation: with their culture of origin and with the varied contexts into which they travel away from home. To look broadly at world literature is therefore to see patterns of difference as well as points of contact and commonality. The world's disparate traditions have developed very distinct kinds of literature, even very different ideas as to what should be called "literature" at all. This anthology uses a variety of means to showcase what is most distinctive and also what is commonly shared among the world's literatures. Throughout the anthology, we employ two kinds of grouping:

☞ **PERSPECTIVES: Groupings that provide cultural context for major works, illuminating issues of broad importance.**

☞ **RESONANCES: Sources for a specific text or responses to it, often from a different time and place.**

Throughout the anthology, our many "Perspectives" sections provide cultural context for the major works around them, giving insight into such issues as the representation of death and immortality (in the ancient Near East); the meeting of Christians, Muslims, and Jews in medieval Iberia; the idea of the national poet in the nineteenth century; and "modernist memory" in the twentieth. Perspectives sections give a range of voices and views, strategies and styles, in highly readable textual groupings. The Perspectives groupings serve a major pedagogical as well as intellectual purpose in making these selections accessible and useful within the time constraints of a survey course. New to the second edition is "Crosscurrents," a feature that concludes each "Perspectives" section with connections to related selections within the same volume and in other volumes of the anthologies. "Crosscurrents" opens up the focused grouping of the "Perspectives," facilitating the study of specific themes and issues across cultures and across time.

Our "Resonances" perform the crucial function of linking works across time as well as space. For Homer's *Iliad,* a Resonance shows oral composition as it is still practiced today north of Greece, while for the *Odyssey* we have Resonances giving modern responses to Homer by Franz Kafka, Derek Walcott, and the Greek poet George Seferis. Accompanying the traditional Navajo "Story of the Emergence" (Volume E) is an extended selection from *Black Elk Speaks* which shows how ancient imagery infused the dream visions of the Sioux healer and warrior Nicholas Black Elk, helping him deal with the crises of lost land and independence that his people were facing. Resonances for Conrad's *Heart of Darkness* (Volume F) give selections from Conrad's diary of his own journey upriver in the Congo, and a speech by Henry Morton Stanley, the explorer-journalist who was serving as publicist for King Leopold's exploitation of his colony in the years just before Conrad went there. Stanley's surreal speech—in which he calculates how much money the Manchester weavers can make providing wedding dresses and burial clothes for the Congolese—gives a vivid instance of the outlook, and the rhetoric, that Conrad grimly parodies in Mr. Kurtz and his associates.

PRINCIPLES OF SELECTION

Beyond our immediate groupings, our overall selections have been made with an eye to fostering connections across time and space: a Perspectives section on "Courtly Women" in medieval Japan (Volume B) introduces themes that can be followed up in "Court Culture and Female Authorship" in Enlightenment-era Europe (Volume D), while the ancient Mediterranean creation myths at the start of Volume A find echoes in later cosmic-creation narratives from Mesoamerica (Volume C) and indigenous peoples today (Volume E). Altogether, we have worked to create an exceptionally coherent and well-integrated presentation of an extraordinary variety of works from around the globe, from the dawn of writing to the present.

Recognizing that different sorts of works have counted as literature in differing times and places, we take an inclusive approach, centering on poems, plays, and fictional narratives but also including selections from rich historical, religious, and philosophical texts like Plato's *Apology* and the Qur'an that have been important for much later literary work, even though they weren't conceived as literature themselves. We present many complete masterworks, including *The Epic of Gilgamesh* (in a beautiful verse translation), Homer's *Odyssey*, Dante's *Inferno*, and Chinua Achebe's *Things Fall Apart*, and we have extensive, teachable selections from such long works as *The Tale of Genji, Don Quixote*, and both parts of Goethe's *Faust*.

Along with these major selections we present a great array of shorter works, some of which have been known only to specialists and only now are entering into world literature. It is our experience as readers and as teachers that the established classics themselves can best be understood when they're set in a varied literary landscape. Nothing is included here, though, simply to make a point: whether world-renowned or recently rediscovered, these are compelling works to read. Throughout our work on this book, we've tried to be highly inclusive in principle and yet carefully selective in practice, avoiding tokenism and also its inverse, the piling up of an unmanageable array of heterogeneous material. If we've succeeded as we hope, the result will be coherent as well as capacious, substantive as well as stimulating.

LITERATURE, ART, AND MUSIC

One important way to understand literary works in context is to read them in conjunction with the broader social and artistic culture in which they were created. Literature has often had a particularly close relation to visual art and to music. Different as the arts are in their specific resources and techniques, a culture's artistic expressions often share certain family resemblances, common traits that can be seen across different media—and that may even come out more clearly in visual or musical form than in translations of literature itself. This anthology includes dozens of black-and-white illustrations and a suite of color illustrations in each volume, chosen to work in close conjunction with our literary selections. Some of these images directly illustrate literary works, while others show important aspects of a culture's aesthetic sensibility. Often, writing actually appears on paintings and sculptures, with represented people and places sharing the space with beautifully rendered Mayan hieroglyphs, Arabic calligraphy, or Chinese brushstrokes.

Music too has been a close companion of literary creation and performance. Our very term "lyric" refers to the lyres or harps with which the Greeks accompanied poems as they were sung. In China, the first major literary work is the *Book of Songs*. In Europe too, until quite recent times poetry was often sung and even prose was usually read aloud. We have created two audio CDs to accompany the anthology, one for Volumes A through C and one for Volumes D through F. These CDs give a wealth of poetry and music from the cultures we feature in the anthology; they are both a valuable teaching resource and also a pure pleasure to listen to.

AIDS TO UNDERSTANDING

A major emphasis of our work has been to introduce each culture and each work to best effect. Each major period and section of the anthology, each grouping of works, and each individual author has an introduction by a member of our editorial team. Our goal has been to write introductions informed by deep knowledge worn lightly. Neither talking down to our readers nor overwhelming them with masses of unassimilable information, our introductions don't seek to "cover" the material but instead try to uncover it, to provide ways in and connections outward. Similarly, our footnotes and glosses are concise and informative, rather than massive or interpretive. Time lines for each volume, and maps and pronunciation guides throughout the anthology, all aim to foster an informed and pleasurable reading of the works. The second edition of *The Longman Anthology of World Literature* has added highlighted quotations in the period introductions and additional headings to the author introductions to help draw student interest and clarify key ideas.

GOING FURTHER

The second edition makes connections beyond its covers as well as within them. Bibliographies at the end of each volume point the way to historical and critical readings for students wishing to go into greater depth for term papers. The Companion Website we've developed for the course (www.ablongman.com/damrosch) gives a wealth of links to excellent Web resources on all our major texts and many related historical and cultural movements and events. The Website includes an audio version of our printed pronunciation guides: you can simply click on a name to hear it pronounced. Each of our new Translations features is also available on the Website, where you can listen to readings of works in their original language and in translation. This rich resource will give you extensive exposure to the aural dimension of many of the languages represented in the anthology. We have also enhanced the Website for this edition, with the addition of practice quizzes for each period and for major selections, an interactive timeline, author biographies, a searchable glossary of literary terms, and sample syllabi. For instructors, we have also created an extensive instructor's manual, written directly by the editors themselves, drawing on years of experience in teaching these materials. Finally, our audio CDs remain available, providing a library of music and readings to augment your world literature course.

TRANSLATION ACROSS CULTURES

The circulation of world literature is always an exercise in cultural translation, and one way to define works of world literature is that they are the works that gain in translation. Some great texts remain so intimately tied to their point of origin that they never read well abroad; they may have an abiding importance at home, but don't play a role in the wider world. Other works, though, gain in resonance as they move out into new contexts, new conjunctions. Edgar Allan Poe found his first really serious readers in France, rather than in the United States. *The Thousand and One Nights,* long a marginal work in Arabic traditions oriented toward poetry rather than popular prose, gained new readers and new influence abroad, and Scheherazade's intricately nested tales now help us in turn to read the European tales of Boccaccio and Marguerite de Navarre with new attention and appreciation. A Perspectives section on "*The Thousand and One Nights* in the Twentieth Century" (Volume F) brings together a range of Arab, European, and American writers who have continued to plumb its riches to this day.

As important as cultural translation in general is the issue of actual translation from one language to another. We have sought out compelling translations for all our foreign-language works, and periodically we offer our readers the opportunity to think directly about the issue of translation. Sometimes we offer distinctively different translations of differing works from a single author or source: for the Bible, for example, we give Genesis 1–11 in Robert Alter's lively, oral-style translation, while we give selected psalms in the magnificent King James Version and the Joseph story in the lucid New International Version. Our selections from Homer's *Iliad* appear in Richmond Lattimore's stately older translation, while Homer's *Odyssey* is given in Robert Fagles's eloquent new version.

At other times, we give alternative translations of a single work. So we have Chinese lyrics translated by the modernist poet Ezra Pound and by a contemporary scholar; and we have Petrarch sonnets translated by the Renaissance English poet Thomas Wyatt and also by contemporary translators. These juxtapositions can show some of the varied ways in which translators over the centuries have sought to carry works over from one time and place to another—not so much by mirroring and reflecting an unchanged meaning, as by refracting it, in a prismatic process that can add new highlights and reveal new facets in a classic text. At times, when we haven't found a translation that really satisfies us, we've translated the work ourselves—an activity we recommend to all who wish to come to know a work from the inside.

To help focus on the many issues involved in translation, we have incorporated a new Translations feature into the second edition. In each volume of the anthology, two major works are followed by a selection in the original language and in several different translations. By studying the different choices made by translators in different times and cultural contexts, we not only discover new meaning in the original work but in the ways in which literature is transformed as it is translated for each generation of readers.

We hope that the results of our years of work on this project will be as enjoyable to use as the book has been to create. We welcome you now inside our pages.

David Damrosch
David L. Pike

ACKNOWLEDGMENTS

In the extended process of planning and preparing the second edition of this anthology, the editors have been fortunate to have the support, advice, and assistance of many people. Our editor, Joe Terry, and our publisher, Roth Wilkofsky, have supported our project in every possible way and some seemingly impossible ones as well, helping us produce the best possible book despite all challenges to budgets and well-laid plans in a rapidly evolving field. Their associates Mary Ellen Curley and Joyce Nilsen have shown unwavering enthusiasm and constant creativity in developing the book and its related Web site and audio CDs and in introducing the results to the world. Our development editors, first Adam Beroud and then Erin Reilly, have shown a compelling blend of literary acuity and quiet diplomacy in guiding thirteen far-flung editors through the many stages of work. Peter Meyers brought great energy and creativity to work on our CDs. Donna Campion and Dianne Hall worked diligently to complete the instructor's manual. A team of permission editors cleared hundreds and hundreds of text permissions from publishers in many countries.

Once the manuscript was complete, Ellen MacElree, the production manager, oversaw the simultaneous production of six massive books on a tight and shifting schedule. Valerie Zaborski, managing editor in production, also helped and, along the way, developed a taste for the good-humored fatalism of Icelandic literature. Our copyeditor, Stephanie Magean, and then Doug Bell and his colleagues at GGS Book Services PMG, worked overtime to produce beautiful books accurate down to the last exotic accent.

Our plans for this edition have been shaped by the comments, suggestions, and thoughtful advice of our reviewers. Charles Bane (University of Central Arkansas); Laurel Bollinger (University of Alabama in Huntsville); Patricia Cearley (South Plains College); Ed Eberhart (Troy University); Fidel Fajardo-Acosta (Creighton University); Gene C. Fant (Union University); Kathy Flann (Eastern Kentucky University); Katona D. Hargrave (Troy University); Nainsi J. Houston (Creighton University); Marta Kvande (Valdosta State University); Wayne Narey (Arkansas State University); Kevin R. Rahimzadeh (Eastern Kentucky University); Elizabeth L. Rambo (Campbell University); Gavin Richardson (Union University); Joseph Rosenblum (University of North Carolina at Greensboro); Douglass H. Thomson (Georgia Southern University); and Tomasz Warchol (Georgia Southern University).

We remain grateful as well for the guidance of the many reviewers who advised us on the creation of the first edition: Roberta Adams (Fitchburg State College); Adetutu Abatan (Floyd College); Magda al-Nowaihi (Columbia University); Nancy Applegate (Floyd College); Susan Atefat-Peckham (Georgia College and State University); Evan Balkan (CCBC-Catonsville); Michelle Barnett (University of Alabama, Birmingham); Colonel Bedell (Virginia Military Institute); Thomas Beebee (Pennsylvania State University); Paula Berggren (Baruch College); Mark Bernier (Blinn College); Ronald Bogue (University of Georgia); Terre Burton (Dixie State College); Patricia Cearley (South Plains College); Raj Chekuri (Laredo Community College); Sandra Clark (University of Wyoming); Thomas F. Connolly (Suffolk University); Vilashini Cooppan (Yale University); Bradford Crain (College of the Ozarks); Robert W. Croft (Gainesville College); Frank Day (Clemson University); Michael Delahoyde (Washington State University); Elizabeth Otten Delmonico (Truman State University); Jo Devine (University of Alaska Southeast); Gene Doty (University of Missouri—Rolla); James Earle (University of Oregon); R. Steve Eberly (Western Carolina

University); Walter Evans (Augusta State University); Fidel Fajardo-Acosta (Creighton University); Mike Felker (South Plains College); Janice Gable (Valley Forge Christian College); Stanley Galloway (Bridgewater College); Doris Gardenshire (Trinity Valley Community College); Jonathan Glenn (University of Central Arkansas); Dean Hall (Kansas State University); Dorothy Hardman (Fort Valley State University); Elissa Heil (University of the Ozarks); David Hesla (Emory University); Susan Hillabold (Purdue University North Central); Karen Hodges (Texas Wesleyan); David Hoegberg (Indiana University-Purdue University—Indianapolis); Sheri Hoem (Xavier University); Michael Hutcheson (Landmark College); Mary Anne Hutchinson (Utica College); Raymond Ide (Lancaster Bible College); James Ivory (Appalachian State University); Craig Kallendorf (Texas A & M University); Bridget Keegan (Creighton University); Steven Kellman (University of Texas—San Antonio); Roxanne Kent-Drury (Northern Kentucky University); Susan Kroeg (Eastern Kentucky University); Tamara Kuzmenkov (Tacoma Community College); Robert Lorenzi (Camden County College—Blackwood); Mark Mazzone (Tennessee State University); David Mc-Cracken (Coker College); George Mitrenski (Auburn University); James Nicholl (Western Carolina University); Roger Osterholm (Embry-Riddle University); Joe Pellegrino (Eastern Kentucky University); Linda Lang-Peralta (Metropolitan State College of Denver); Sandra Petree (University of Arkansas); David E. Phillips (Charleston Southern University); Terry Reilly (University of Alaska); Constance Relihan (Auburn University); Nelljean Rice (Coastal Carolina University); Colleen Richmond (George Fox University); Gretchen Ronnow (Wayne State University); John Rothfork (West Texas A & M University); Elise Salem-Manganaro (Fairleigh Dickinson University); Asha Sen (University of Wisconsin Eau Claire); Richard Sha (American University); Edward Shaw (University of Central Florida); Jack Shreve (Allegany College of Maryland); Jimmy Dean Smith (Union College); Floyd C. Stuart (Norwich University); Eleanor Sumpter-Latham (Central Oregon Community College); Ron Swigger (Albuquerque Technical Vocational Institute); Barry Tharaud (Mesa State College); Theresa Thompson (Valdosta State College); Teresa Thonney (Columbia Basin College); Charles Tita (Shaw University); Scott D. Vander Ploeg (Madisonville Community College); Marian Wernicke (Pensacola Junior College); Sallie Wolf (Arapahoe Community College); and Dede Yow (Kennesaw State University).

We also wish to express our gratitude to the reviewers who gave us additional advice on the book's companion Web site: Nancy Applegate (Floyd College); James Earl (University of Oregon); David McCracken (Coker College); Linda Lang-Peralta (Metropolitan State College of Denver); Asha Sen (University of Wisconsin—Eau Claire); Jimmy Dean Smith (Union College); Floyd Stuart (Norwich University); and Marian Wernicke (Pensacola Junior College).

The editors were assisted in tracking down texts and information by wonderfully able research assistants: Kerry Bystrom, Julie Lapiski, Katalin Lovasz, Joseph Ortiz, Laura B. Sayre, and Lauren Simonetti. April Alliston wishes to thank Brandon Lafving for his invaluable comments on her drafts and Gregory Maertz for his knowledge and support. Marshall Brown would like to thank his research assistant Françoise Belot for her help and Jane K. Brown for writing the Goethe introduction. Sheldon Pollock would like to thank Whitney Cox, Rajeev Kinra, Susanne Mrozik, and Guriqbal Sahota for their assistance and Haruo Shirane thanks Michael Brownstein for writing the introduction to Hozumi Ikan, and Akiko Takeuchi for writing the introductions to the Noh drama.

It has been a great pleasure to work with all these colleagues both at Longman and at schools around the country. This book exists for its readers, whose reactions and suggestions we warmly welcome, as the second edition of *The Longman Anthology of World Literature* moves out into the world.

ABOUT THE EDITORS

David Damrosch (Columbia University). His books include *The Narrative Covenant: Transformations of Genre in the Growth of Biblical Literature* (1987), *Meetings of the Mind* (2000), *What Is World Literature?* (2003), and *How to Read World Literature* (2009). He has been president of the American Comparative Literature Association (2001–2003) and is founding general editor of *The Longman Anthology of British Literature* (third edition, 2006).

David L. Pike (American University). Author of *Passage Through Hell: Modernist Descents, Medieval Underworlds* (1997), *Subterranean Cities: The World Beneath Paris and London, 1800–1945* (2005), and *Metropolis on the Styx: The Underworlds of Modern Urban Culture* (2007). He is co-author of the forthcoming *A World of Writing: Poems, Stories, Drama, Essays*.

April Alliston (Princeton University). Author of *Virtue's Faults: Correspondences in Eighteenth-Century British and French Women's Fiction* (1996), and editor of Sophia Lee's *The Recess* (2000). Her book on concepts of character, gender, and plausibility in Enlightenment historical narratives is forthcoming.

Marshall Brown (University of Washington). Author of *The Shape of German Romanticism* (1979), *Preromanticism* (1991), *Turning Points: Essays in the History of Cultural Expressions* (1997), *The Gothic Text* (2005), and *The Tooth That Nibbles at the Soul: Essays on Music and Poetry* (forthcoming). Editor of *Modern Language Quarterly: A Journal of Literary History,* and the *Cambridge History of Literary Criticism,* Vol. 5: Romanticism.

Page duBois (University of California, San Diego). Her books include *Centaurs and Amazons* (1982), *Sowing the Body* (1988), *Torture and Truth* (1991), *Sappho Is Burning* (1995), *Trojan Horses* (2001), and *Slaves and Other Objects* (2003).

Sabry Hafez (University of London). Author of several books in Arabic on poetry, drama, the novel, and on a number of major Arab writers, including works on Mahfouz, Idris, and Mahmoud Darwish. His books in English include *The Genesis of Arabic Narrative Discourse* (1993), *The Quest for Identities: The Arabic Short Story* (2007), and the edited volumes *A Reader of Modern Arabic Short Stories* and *Modern Arabic Criticism*. He is the editor of the on-line bilingual Arabic/English monthly journal, *Al-Kalimah/The World*.

Ursula K. Heise (Stanford University). Author of *Chronoschisms: Time, Narrative, and Postmodernism* (1997) and of *Sense of Place and Sense of Planet: The Environmental Imagination of the Global* (2008).

Djelal Kadir (Pennsylvania State University). His books include *Columbus and the Ends of the Earth* (1992), *The Other Writing: Postcolonial Essays in Latin America's Writing Culture* (1993), and *Other Modernisms in an Age of Globalizations* (2002). He served in the 1990s as editor of *World Literature Today* and is coeditor of the *Comparative History of Latin America's Literary Cultures* (2004). He is the founding president of the International American Studies Association.

Sheldon Pollock (Columbia University). His books include *The Language of the Gods in the World of Men* (2006). He recently edited *Literary Cultures in History: Reconstructions from South Asia* (2003). He is general editor of the Clay Sanskrit Library.

Bruce Robbins (Columbia University). His books include *The Servant's Hand: English Fiction from Below* (1986), *Secular Vocations* (1993), *Feeling Global: Internationalism in Distress* (1999), and *Upward Mobility and the Common Good: Toward a Literary History of the Welfare State* (2007). Edited volumes include *Cosmopolitics: Thinking and Feeling Beyond the Nation* (1998).

Haruo Shirane (Columbia University). Author of *The Bridge of Dreams: A Poetics of "The Tale of Genji"* (1987) and of *Traces of Dreams: Landscape, Cultural Memory, and the Poetry of Bashō* (1998). He is coeditor of *Inventing the Classics: Modernity, National Identity, and Japanese Literature* (2000) and has recently edited *Early Modern Japanese Literature: An Anthology 1600–1900*.

Jane Tylus (New York University). Author of *Writing and Vulnerability in the Late Renaissance* (1993), coeditor of *Epic Traditions in the Contemporary World* (1999), and editor and translator of Lucrezia Tornabuoni de' Medici's *Sacred Narratives* (2001). Her study on late medieval female spirituality and the origins of humanism is forthcoming.

Pauline Yu (American Council of Learned Societies). President of the American Council of Learned Societies, she is the author of *The Poetry of Wang Wei* (1980) and *The Reading of Imagery in the Chinese Poetic Tradition* (1987), the editor of *Voices of the Song Lyric in China* (1994), and coeditor of *Culture and State in Chinese History* (1997) and *Ways with Words: Writing about Reading Texts from Early China* (2000).

King Arthur and His Knights, from a manuscript of the *Prose Lancelot*, France, 13th century. In this illustration from a collection of Arthurian romances, King Arthur is majestically enthroned, and in keeping with his royal stature he towers over his knights. He is shown requesting a central commodity in the Arthurian stories—more stories. "Now tell the tales," he commands, "that have befallen you since the day of Pentecost before all the companions of the Quest returned."

The Medieval Era

The term "medieval" was coined long after the close of the period to which it refers, as people looking back from early modern times sought a name for the thousand years or so between their day and classical antiquity; "medieval" comes from the Latin for "middle era." Originally applied specifically to Europe, the term has come to be used for a "middle" period in a range of cultures around the world. The beginnings of this middle era vary from place to place, but each of the literary cultures presented in Volume A, *The Ancient World,* went through a major time of transition in late antiquity, roughly between the first and fourth centuries C.E. By that point, a body of ancient works had been established as foundational for the later culture: the Confucian classics in China and Indochina; the Vedas and early epics of India; the Bible and the Greek and Roman classics in the Mediterranean world. These and other classic works continued to have a lasting influence, yet many more texts were lost in the upheavals of late antiquity; only a small fraction of Sappho's and Sophocles's output survived, for example, and some entire civilizations vanished, such as those of Mesopotamia and ancient Egypt.

Even as one era was passing away, another was coming into being. Distinctly new literatures were created in many areas, sometimes in languages that had never been written before, such as Japanese, Arabic, and German, sometimes through creative transformation of classical languages such as Chinese, Sanskrit, and Latin. This volume presents a varied selection of the rich literatures produced in many regions of the world from around the fourth through the fourteenth centuries C.E.

LORDS AND LADIES, KNIGHTS AND SAMURAI

The vast majority of the medieval world's population consisted of peasantry: farmers tilling small plots of land (or fishing, in coastal areas), often as virtual or outright slaves of powerful lords who controlled the land. In Europe and sometimes elsewhere, authority and land ownership were organized feudally, a system in which an overlord held title to all land in his domain, and granted it to noble vassals in exchange for their loyalty and support; the vassals in turn controlled the lives of the serfs who worked their lands. Monarchs often tried to gather the nobility round them, to enhance the glory of their courts and to keep a watchful eye on their powerful underlings. Royal courts in China, Japan, India, Persia, Iraq, and Europe were sites of feasting and of seduction, where court poets celebrated noble deeds in heroic epics and romances, and sang the sorrows of love in enticing lyrics.

Women weren't only the idealized objects of poetic devotion; increasingly, they were poets themselves as well. Court life, and the convents to which women might withdraw from court life, provided new opportunities for women to become writers. With a few important exceptions such as Sappho, women in antiquity had had little access to literacy and no opportunity to record their stories and songs. In the medieval era, women began to play important roles in patronizing and also creating literature and other works of art. The pre-Islamic woman poet al-Khansa' became a founding figure for Arabic

Women weren't only the idealized objects of poetic devotion; increasingly, they were poets themselves as well.

1

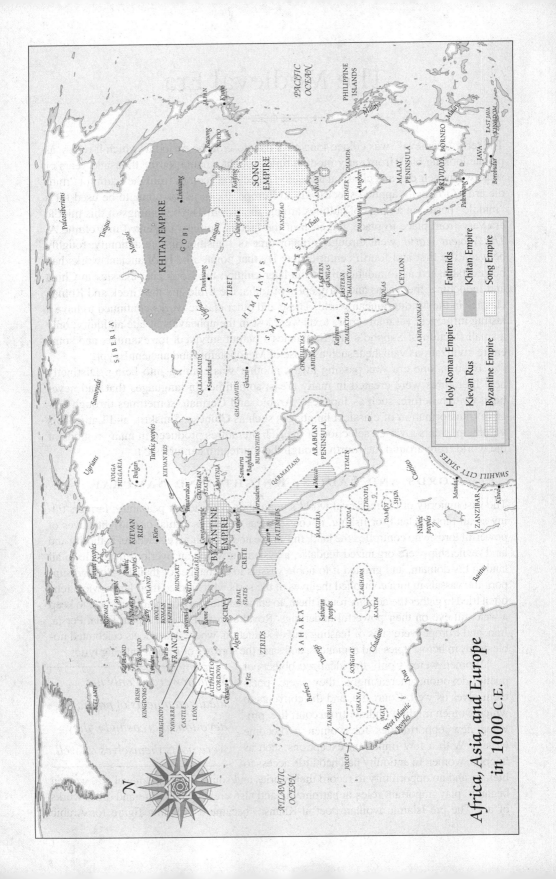

Africa, Asia, and Europe in 1000 C.E.

Plate 1   Liang King, *Scholar of the Eastern Fence*, China, c. 13th century. This portrait of the poet and scholar Tao Qian (page 68) identifies him with the eastern fence of his property, against which his beloved chrysanthemums thrived. The poet-recluse is framed by pines, emblematic of consistency and integrity, and by red-leaved trees suggesting autumnal decline and old age. *(National Palace Museum, Taipei, Taiwan, Republic of China.)*

Plate 2 *Portrait of Empress Chabi,*
China, late 13th century. The favorite
wife of the Mongol Emperor Kubilai
Khan, Chabi is a picture of calm good
humor and opulent order in the tasteful
display of wealth; her portrait, and a
parallel portrait of her husband, enroll
them in the age-old lineage of imperial
Chinese rule, countering the tensions of
Kubilai's Mongol heritage. In unifying
China and seeking to maintain his hold
over an empire stretching through Mon-
golia to Persia and into Russia, Kubilai
Khan welcomed foreigners to his court
and promoted religious tolerance. The
Venetian traveler Marco Polo, who
worked for him, describes him as curious
to learn more about Christianity (see
page 1072), but in China as well as
Persia there had long been communities
of Nestorian Christians (a sect originating
in Syria); Chabi herself, in fact, was
Christian. *(National Palace Museum,
Taipei, Taiwan, Republic of China.)*

Plate 3 Kosho, *The Priest Kuya,*
Japan, c. 1200. This wooden sculpture,
four feet high, portrays a wandering
Buddhist monk. Kuya (903–972)
advocated a life of complete simplicity.
He went through the countryside
teaching people to chant the phrase
Namu Amida Bu(tsu). "Hail to Amida
Buddha." As Kuya walks forward,
putting his soul into his chant, each
syllable emerges from his mouth as
a tiny, perfect Buddha. (*Asanuma
Photo Studios / Rokuhara Mitsu-ji.*)

Plate 4 *Genji Holding the Newborn Kaoru,* Japan, early 1100s. This scene comes from a set of scrolls that originally illustrated all 54 chapters of *The Tale of Genji* (page 147). Focusing on mood rather than plot, these illustrations reflect the interests of the noblewomen who were the tale's primary audience, and the delicate rhythms of the image suggest the style known as *onna-e,* "painting in the feminine manner." In this scene from the middle of the tale, Genji tenderly holds his supposed son Kaoru, privately aware that the father is actually his own nephew Kashiwagi. Genji's sorrow and remorse aren't directly revealed by his impassive features but are suggested symbolically in the faded lavender of his robe (a color associated with his first love Murasaki, who has been subordinated to Genji's new wife, the Third Princess), and Genji's robe further contrasts with the deep, passionate crimson of the kimono worn by the lady-in-waiting in front of him. *(The Tokugawa Art Museum, Nagoya.)*

Plate 5 *Jesus Watching Muhammad Leave Mecca,* from a medieval Persian manuscript. Muhammad leaves Mecca on camelback in the *hijrah* or emigration in the year 622 that became the founding moment of Islam, escaping the wrath of the polytheistic Meccans who rejected his message of faith in the one true God. Regarded in Islam as one of Muhammad's prophetic predecessors, Jesus is shown looking on approvingly, in an image that both suggests continuity and also shows Muhammad about to go beyond the religious understandings of his day. *(Edinburgh University Library.)*

Plate 6   Limbourg Brothers, *February,* from *Les Très Riches Heures du Duc de Berry,* France, 1416. The medieval European nobility used "books of hours" (prayers and psalms to be said at set hours of the day) in their private devotions; beautifully illustrated, these books became treasured works of art. Created by three artist brothers for Jean, Duc de Berry, the *Très Riches Heures* ("very rich hours") included a calendar with an illustration for each month of the year. Above, the chariot of the Sun proceeds through the months and the signs of the zodiac; below is shown an entertaining scene of peasant life. People hike their clothing up to warm their feet at the fire in their hut (its wall conveniently cut away for our viewing), the woman taking care not to expose herself as much as the men do. Outside, sheep huddle for warmth in their pen and a peasant hurries across the barnyard holding his cloak across his face, while in the background a man chops firewood and another takes bundles of wood into town. Only nine by eight inches, this painting gives an entire and very earthly world in miniature. *(Réunion des Musées Nationaux / Art Resource, New York.)*

Plate 7 Prayer hall in the Great Mosque, Córdoba, Spain, begun 786 C.E. A masterpiece of Moorish architecture in al-Andalus (Muslim Spain), this mosque incorporates elements from a range of cultures, including Roman arches, Greek-style Corinthian columns, and Byzantine mosaics. Soft light from side doors and shadows from flickering oil lamps help to create an otherworldly space of worship amid the forest of columns. *(Gary Conner / Photolibrary.com. Royalty Free.)*

Plate 8 Upper chapel, Sainte-Chapelle, Paris, 1240s. Following the sacking of Constantinople by Frankish crusaders, King Louis IX of France acquired a group of sacred relics that included wood supposed to have come from Christ's cross and his Crown of Thorns. Ordinarily, relics would be kept in an ornate chest or reliquary, but these relics were so special that Louis decided to commission an entire building in their honor. The Sainte-Chapelle has the feel of a great jewel box, soaring into the sky thanks to buttresses outside that support the delicate tracery of its stained glass (see page 566 for an outside view of nearby Notre Dame Cathedral, with its prominent flying buttresses). Like the mosque in Córdoba (Plate 7), the Sainte-Chapelle creates a self-enclosed space of connection between human and divine worlds, in this case emphasizing radiant light rather than shadow, in keeping with the theological emphasis on Christ as the *verum lumen,* true Light of the World. *(Giraudon / Art Resource, New York.)*

Plate 9 Sandro Botticelli, illustration to Dante's *Commedia*, Italy, c. 1492. One of the great Florentine painters, Botticelli became famous for richly colored scenes from classical myth, such as the Birth of Venus. Later in life, he turned to religious scenes. His later work included an unfinished series of some one hundred drawings illustrating Dante's *Divine Comedy*. This scene, from the start of Canto 15 of the *Inferno* (page 954), shows Virgil (in blue) and Dante (in red, and once in white not yet colored in), walking precariously along the edge of the River of Boiling Blood. The scorching desert beside the river holds the Violent against Nature: blasphemers, sodomites, and usurers. In a kind of stop-action pattern, Dante and Virgil are shown more than once as they proceed downward. Near the top, Brunetto Latini grabs the hem of Dante's garment. Dante reacts with astonishment to see his old friend and fellow poet, then proceeds, talking with Brunetto. This dramatic action is confined to the left side of the image, the rest of which shows the tormented souls in their eternal suffering and remorse, sand-colored like the burning ground beneath them and sprinkled with drops of bloody fire. *(Biblioteca Apostolica Vaticana.)*

poetry, and in several regions aristocratic women in particular gained a new stature as writers. In Japan, a remarkable series of courtly women wrote poetry and became pioneers in prose writing. *The Tale of Genji,* by the noblewoman known as Murasaki Shikibu, has long been recognized as one of the greatest narratives ever written. In Europe, women mystics like Hildegard von Bingen and Mechthild von Magdeburg wrote compelling poems as well as theological works, Marie de France became a major writer of Arthurian verse romance, and at the close of the fourteenth century Christine de Pizan became perhaps the first woman in the world to support herself by her writing.

Medieval knights in Europe, and their Japanese counterparts the samurai, sought fame as much as wealth, and became the subjects of great poems and prose tales concerning their exploits battling one another or dragons and other monsters. Writers including Marie de France and the anonymous author of *Sir Gawain and the Green Knight* celebrated the adventures of the legendary King Arthur's knights, while the great Japanese samurai clans had their deeds commemorated in the *Tales of the Heike* and many later works, even starring in very recent times in such movies as Kurosawa's *The Seven Samurai.* The common folk sang songs and told stories, but they were rarely literate and their oral traditions generally went unmarked. Yet folk songs and tales survived when they were recorded for upper-class consumption, as notably happened with the stories included in *The Thousand and One Nights.* That text actually dramatizes this process of transmission, in tales in which the Caliph Haroun al-Rashid goes out into Baghdad dressed as a common merchant, accompanied by his vizier and his executioner, to seek adventure and hear marvelous stories; back home in his palace, he regularly has the best of these stories recorded in letters of gold.

Medieval writers typically portray their royal patrons as vastly wise, powerful, and generous, yet the reality was often a good deal less glorious. In many regions, transportation was poor and long-distance communication was awkward, rendering central control difficult, and subsistence-level farming didn't produce very great surpluses that could support both a local aristocracy and the royal household in the style to which both aspired. There were frequent struggles for position and ascendency, both between the lords of neighboring regions and between vassals and their overlords. Feuding and open warfare are constant themes in medieval literature. A partial exception to this pattern was China. Unified in ancient times under the feudal Han dynasty (202 B.C.E.–220 C.E.), early medieval China experienced a long phase of conflict and division, but was then reunified under the Sui dynasty in the late sixth century. A period of great prosperity ensued, with much of central China linked by canals as well as rivers, and older feudal patterns were replaced by a national bureaucracy controlled by the emperor and his administration. The Tang dynasty (618–907) became the golden age of Chinese poetry as of several other arts, and in this sense China's "middle" period became its *central* period in the eyes of later historians, writers, and artists.

> *Medieval writers typically portray their royal patrons as vastly wise, powerful, and generous, yet the reality was often a good deal less glorious.*

TRAVEL, TRADE, AND CONQUEST

The medieval period saw steadily increasing contacts across regions, promoted especially by two kinds of travelers: merchants and missionaries or pilgrims. The Italian merchant Marco Polo and the North African judge and religious scholar Ibn Battuta typify these dual motives, and both Polo and Ibn Battuta traveled tens of thousands of miles through dozens of countries, almost certainly farther than anyone in history had gone before them. They were captivating writers as well as exceptionally ambitious travelers, but many less-famous pilgrims and traders traveled widely as well. A "Silk Road" was established from East Asia to the shores of the Mediterranean, and Constantinople and Venice became major connecting links between Europe and points east. Armies were on the move as well, often fueled by religious fervor as well as political ambition. Following the establishment of Islam in Arabia in the early seventh century, a wave of conversion and consolidation spread westward across North Africa, and north and east into Mesopotamia and Turkey. Baghdad became a major cultural as well as political center, and by the eighth century much of Spain had come under Muslim control. Regional empires waxed and waned elsewhere as well, particularly in Europe, in South Asia, and among the Maya in what is now Mexico and Guatemala; in East Asia, Japan and Korea became consolidated as unified and strong countries, and China influenced many regions around its borders directly or indirectly.

THE GROWTH OF WORLD RELIGIONS

Every aspect of medieval life was profoundly marked by religion, and several faiths gained an increasingly global scope during the period. Buddhism spread from India to China, Tibet, Korea, Japan, and beyond; Islam spread far beyond the boundaries of any one empire, reaching as far east as Indonesia, west to Spain, and south into central Africa. Christianity pressed back against the advance of Islam, and Christian missionaries began to fan out across the known world (a process that accelerated at the start of the early modern period with the European discovery of the "New World"). The intermingling of old and new forms of belief produced conflict but also gave people new options in orienting themselves toward the universe and the social world. Medieval literature often registers these intermixtures: in the Anglo-Saxon *Beowulf* and the Norse *Njal's Saga,* both written in Christian times but set in pagan times; in the mixing of pre-Islamic and Islamic motifs in *The Thousand and One Nights* and in the Mali *Epic of Son-Jara;* in the interplay of Buddhist and Confucian elements in Chinese poetry.

> *Every aspect of medieval life was profoundly marked by religion, and several faiths gained an increasingly global scope during this period.*

The need to define one's religion against alternatives also stimulated the growth of organized theological reflection: theologians in Paris and Rome, in Baghdad and Mecca, and in the courts of India and elsewhere debated proper modes of understanding, forms of worship, and ethical behavior. Closely connected to these theological and philosophical issues were debates on the role of literature: aesthetic, social, and religious concerns intertwined in these discussions, which appear in this volume in Perspectives groupings on literature and art in the sections devoted to China and Europe.

Building on these philosophical discussions, many medieval works of literature join theological and aesthetic themes, from the haunting poetry of the Buddhist Han Shan, to the comic, mystical *Conference of the Birds* by the Persian poet Farid ud-Din al'Attar, to Dante's transcendent vision blending earthly life and afterlife in his *Divine Comedy.* The medieval world was both resolutely worldly and thoroughly otherworldly as well. "The medieval world" was many worlds, in fact, including the many richly imaginative worlds unfolded in the following pages.

THE MEDIEVAL ERA

YEAR	THE WORLD	LITERATURE
200s		
	220 End of Han dynasty in China	
	220–265 Three Kingdoms period in China	
	265–419 Chin dynasty in China	
300s		
	335–470 Gupta dynasty in northern India	
		365–427 Life of Chinese poet Tao Qian
400s		
	c. 400 Unification of Japan	**c. 400** *Mahabharata* achieves established form
	410 Visigoths sack Rome	
	420 China divided between Southern and Northern dynasties (to 589)	
	450 Anglo-Saxons invade England	
500s		
		524 Boethius, *The Consolation of Philosophy*
	530 Justinian Code	
	c. 550 Buddhism introduced to Japan	
	c. 570–632 Life of the Prophet Muhammad	
	588 Lombards invade Italy	
	589 Sui dynasty in China (to 618)	
600s		
		c. 600–646 Life of pre-Islamic woman poet al-Khansa'
	618 Tang dynasty in China (to 907)	
	622 Hegira of Muhammad from Mecca; foundation of Islam	
	638 Arab conquest of Jerusalem	
		651–652 Text of Qur'an established
		c. 658–680 Caedmon's dream hymn
	698 Arabs take Carthage	
700s		
	700 Benedictine missionaries complete the Christianization of England begun by Gregory the Great	**701** Birth of Chinese poets Wang Wei (d. 761) and Li Bo (d. 762)
	710–784 Nara period in Japan	
	711–715 Arabs arrive in Spain and in western India	
		712–770 Life of poet Du Fu
		731 The Venerable Bede, *Ecclesiastical History of the English Nation*
	732 Charles Martel halts Arab invasion at Poitiers	
	750 Abbasid dynasty in Middle East and North Africa (to 1258)	**c. 750** Irish monks produce the *Book of Kells;* Ibn Ishaq writes *The Biography of the Prophet*
		c. 750–950 *Beowulf*
		753 The Venerable Bede dies
		759 *Manyōshū,* collection of Japanese court poetry
	763 Tibetans invade Tang China	
	772–804 Saxon Wars	
	786–809 Haroun al-Rashid is Caliph in Baghdad	
	794–1185 Heian period in Japan	

YEAR	THE WORLD	LITERATURE
800s		
	800s Fujiwara clan achieves dominance in Japan (to 12th century) **800** Charlemagne is crowned Holy Roman Emperor (dies in 814)	
		810–850 Writings by al-Jahiz, Arabic prose master **868** *The Diamond Sutra;* World's oldest surviving printed book
	819 Samanid dynasty in Persia (to 1005) **870** Vikings discover Iceland	
	899 Alfred the Great of England dies	
900s		
	907 Five Dynasties period in China (to 959)	
	960 Song dynasty in China (to 1279) **979** Paper money introduced in China	
1000		
	1000 Sweden begins to be converted to Christianity; Iceland converted to Christianity **c. 1000** Vikings reach North America	**10th century** First mozarabic *kharjas* in Spain **1002** Sei Shōnagon, *The Pillow Book* **c. 1000–1019** Murasaki Shikibu, *The Tale of Genji*
1010		
		1010 Firdawsi's Persian epic, the *Shah-nama*
	1018 Choles conquer Sri Lanka	
1020		
		1027 Ibn Hazm, *The Dove's Neckring*
1030		
	1031 Christian reconquest of Spain begins	
1040		
	c. 1045 Chinese invent movable type printing	
1050		
	1054 Great Schism between the Eastern and Western Churches	
1060		
	1066 Battle of Hastings: William the Conqueror and Normans begin their rule over the British Isles	**1063–1078** Anselm of Canterbury, *Proslogion*
1070		
	1071 Seljuk Turks defeat Byzantines at Manzikert	**1071–1127** William of Aquitaine, the first known troubadour **1075–1141** Yehuda ha-Levi, author of poems and *The Book of the Khazars*
1080		
	1085 Yorimoto becomes first shogun of Japan; Christians recapture Toledo, Spain	
1090		
	1095 Pope Urban II preaches the First Crusade **1099** Fall of Jerusalem to Christian crusaders	
1100		
	c. 1100 Anasazi build cliff dwellings at Mesa Verde and Chaco Canyon	
1110		

YEAR	THE WORLD	LITERATURE
1120		
	c. 1122–1204 Eleanor of Aquitaine, queen consort of Louis VII of France (1137–1152) and of Henry II of England (1152–1204)	
1130		
	1130 Song move capital to Huangzhou	**1130–1145** Bernard of Clairvaux, *Sermons on the Song of Songs*
		c. 1133–1140 Letters of Abelard and Heloise
1140		
	1147–1149 Second Crusade	**1141–1152** Hildegard von Bingen, *Scivias*
		1146–1174 *The Play of Adam*
1150		
		c. 1150 Geoffrey of Monmouth, *History of the Kings of Britain*
	1152 Temple of Ankor Wat completed	
1160		
	1163 Foundation stone laid for the cathedral of Notre-Dame de Paris	**1160–1180** Marie de France, *Lais*
	1167 Foundation of Oxford University	**1165–1180** Chrétien de Troyes, Arthurian romances
		1169–1196 Ibn Rushd (Averroës), summaries and commentaries on Aristotle
1170		
	1170 Death of Thomas Becket ordered by Henry II	**1177** Farid ud-Din al'Attar, *The Conference of the Birds*
1180		
	1187 Saladin retakes Jerusalem from the Christians	**1180–1194** Bertran de Born, *Songs*
	1189–1192 Third Crusade led by Richard I the Lion-Heart and Frederick Barbarossa	**1186–1196** Andreas Capellanus, *The Art of Courtly Love*
1190		
	1198 Innocent III founds the Papal State and organizes the Fourth Crusade to recapture Jerusalem from the Arabs	**1190–1230** Walther von der Vogelweide, *Songs*
1200		
	1206 Genghis Khan unites Mongols	**late 12th–early 13th century** *The Poem of the Cid*
	1208 Innocent III proclaims the Albigensian Crusade	**1207–1283** Life of Persian mystical poet Jalaloddin Rumi
1210		
	1215 Magna Carta	**c. 1210** Gottfried von Strassburg, *Tristan*
	1216 Dominican order founded by St. Dominic of Spain	**1212** Kamo no Chomei, *An Account of My Ten-Foot-Square Hut*
		1218 First version of *Tales of Heike*
1220		
	1222–1242 Mongols invade Europe, rule Russia for two centuries	**c. 1225** Guillaume de Lorris, *The Romance of the Rose*
	1227 Death of Genghis Khan	
	1228 Francis of Assisi dies	
1230		
		early 13th century Ibn 'Arabi, *Gentle Now, Doves*
1240		
	1244 Muslims capture Jerusalem; West doesn't recapture Jerusalem until 1917	**c. 1240** Snorri Sturluson, *The Prose Edda*
	1248 Construction of the Alhambra begins in Granada	**mid-13th century** Martin Codax, *Songs*

YEAR	THE WORLD	LITERATURE
1250		c. 1250 Alfonso the Wise, *Cantigas of Santa Maria*
	1258 Mongols sack Baghdad and end Abbasid dynasty	c. 1250–1275 Mechthild von Magdeburg, *A Flowing Light of the Godhead*
1260		
	1260 Consecration of Chartres Cathedral	c. 1265–1273 Thomas Aquinas, *Summa Theologica*
	1267 Giotto begins his school of painting in Florence	1267 Brunetto Latini, *Book of the Treasure*
1270		
	1270 Eighth Crusade	
	1279 The Mongols under Kublai Khan crush final Song resistance	
1280		
	1280 Yuan (Mongol) dynasty in China (to 1368)	c. 1280 *Njal's Saga*
	1281 Beginning of Ottoman power in Turkey	c. 1284 Ramon Llull, *Blanquerna*
1290		
	1292 Marco Polo returns from travels	1295 Dante Alighieri, *La Vita Nuova*
		1298 Marco Polo, *The Book of Marvels*
1300		
	1309–1377 Papacy at Avignon	late 13th century Jean de Meun's continuation of *The Romance of the Rose*
		c. 1300–1325 *Songs* by Dom Dinis, King of Portugal
		1307–1321 Dante, *La Commedia*
1310		
1320		
	1324 Pilgrimage to Mecca of Mansa Musa of Mal	1321 Dante Alighieri dies
1330		
	1337 Hundred Years' War begins	
	1338 Beginning of Muromachi period in Japan (to 1573)	
1340		
	1345–1346 Ibn Battuta travels in Southeast Asia and China	1340–1374 Francis Petrarch, *Scattered Rhymes*
	1347–1351 Black Death in Europe	1343 Juan Ruiz, *The Book of Good Love*
		1349 Giovanni Boccaccio, *The Decameron*
1350		
	1354 Ottomans begin conquest of the Balkan Peninsula	
1360		
	1365 First German university is opened at Heidelberg; the universities of Bologna and Oxford date from the 12th century	
	1368 Ming dynasty in China (to 1644)	
1370		
		1374 Francis Petrarch dies
		1378 Death of Muslim world traveler Ibn Battuta
1380		
	c. 1380 Ottomans found Janissary corps	c. 1388–1400 Geoffrey Chaucer, *The Canterbury Tales*
1390		
	1398 Tamerlone sacks Delhi	late 14th century *Sir Gawain and the Green Knight*

YEAR	THE WORLD	LITERATURE
1400		**1400** Geoffrey Chaucer dies
	1405 Zheng He's first voyage to the Indian Ocean	**1404–1405** Christine de Pizan, *The Book of the City of Ladies*
1410		
1420		
1430		
	1431 Joan of Arc dies	
	1434 Medici family gains control over government of Florence	
1440		
	1441 Portuguese capture slaves in Africa; start of Atlantic Slave Trade	**1444** Juan de Mena, *The Labyrinth of Fortune*
1450		
	1450 Gutenberg invents the printing press	
	1453 Fall of Constantinople; Ottoman Turks end the Eastern Empire	
	1455 Henry VI wages the Wars of the Roses (between Lancaster and York)	
1460		
	1469 Ferdinand of Aragon marries Isabella of Castile and unites the kingdom of Spain	**1461** François Villon, *The Testament*
1470		
1480		
1490		
	1492 Ferdinand and Isabella annex Granada and expel Jews from Spain; discovery of America	

Sakyamuni Buddha, Yungang, Shanxi Province, c. 460. The non-Chinese rulers of the Northern Wei dynasty adopted Buddhism, foreign like themselves, with enthusiasm. They carved a series of shrines and figures out of some twenty caves in the cliffs of Yungang, as monuments to both their faith and power. Here a 15-meter-high sandstone statue of the historical Buddha sits impassively next to another deity, probably Maitreya, who was worshiped as a future Buddha and especially popular during the Northern Wei dynasty. The masklike demeanor of these figures may have been modeled on the older colossi at Gandhara, Afghanistan, destroyed by the Taliban in 2001.

Medieval China

As was the case in Western Europe, what is often referred to as the medieval period in China followed upon the collapse of the first great empire, the Han. In 184 C.E. two uprisings led by Daoist messianic cults rattled a state already weakened by internal and external pressures and natural disasters. Its future became even more uncertain when the generals dispatched to subdue the rebels chose instead to establish themselves as regional warlords. During the ensuing struggle for power, three generals based in different states emerged as the primary contenders for the throne, and when the Han emperor finally abdicated in 220, each proclaimed himself ruler but none succeeded in winning uncontested dominion. The fragile state of subsequent governments left the empire vulnerable to outside attack, and by 311 non-Chinese tribes managed to invade the capital of Luoyang and sent its rulers and officials to exile in southeastern China, along the Yangzi River near modern-day Nanjing. For almost three centuries thereafter, relatively short-lived regimes followed one another on parallel courses in the north and south, and the epoch is therefore known variously as the Northern and Southern Dynasties, or the Period of Division. "Barbarians" in the north ruled over populations that were still largely Chinese, although gradually permeated by foreign customs and institutions, and aristocratic resettlement to the south took advantage of the region's rich resources to maintain and enhance the traditions of the civilization.

Unlike its Western counterpart, China's middle ages also include the eventual reunification of the empire under the Sui rulers from the north in 589, almost immediately followed by the Tang dynasty, which lasted from 618 to 907. Mirroring the relationship between the Qin and Han dynasties centuries earlier, the brief rule of the Sui was instrumental in laying the institutional foundation for the centralized control exercised at much greater length by its successor. The medieval period in China also differs in having bequeathed a cultural legacy whose significance was never subject to question. Indeed, in many areas its accomplishments came to be regarded as pinnacles that later generations dared not even hope to scale.

INDIVIDUALS IN RETREAT

The political instability that marked the centuries from the downfall of the Han to the reunification of the Sui hindered the engagement in public life that Confucius had sought to foster and that had gradually become institutionalized during the Han. During this period the Confucian ethic of official service grew as endangered as the governments it was meant to support, and the attractions of life in retreat became increasingly compelling during the period of disunion. There are many literary indications of the real precariousness of bureaucratic life: the considerable number of poet-officials who died untimely deaths, often executed on trumped-up charges of treason; the obviously diminished size of the literary corpus that has survived compared with its original state; and the burgeoning of such poetic subgenres as "poems written on the way to execution" or "songs for coffin-pullers." The best-known poet of the early medieval period, Tao Qian (365–427), wrestles with many of these issues in his writings.

An anonymous poem in the sixth-century B.C.E. *Book of Songs* provides the following advice:

> Don't take the big carriage:
> You'll just get dusty.
> Don't ponder a hundred worries:
> You'll just become ill.

Although the context for the work is unclear, it could well be read as a recommendation to retreat from public engagement. Even Confucius had allowed that certain circumstances might favor a withdrawal from active participation in government service, advising his students to "Enter not a state that is in peril; stay not in a state that is in danger. Show yourself when the Way prevails in the Empire, but hide yourself when it does not." More systematic arguments for attention to individual, as opposed to collective, needs were provided by Daoist and Buddhist doctrines that attracted increasing numbers of adherents at this time. Daoist sects seized upon the concern with self-preservation inherent in the more philosophically oriented founding texts and indulged in experiments with herbs, potions, magic, and exercise as means of prolonging one's life. A Daoist alchemical text published in the second century C.E. may in fact be the world's oldest book on the topic. The cultivation of unorthodox behavior recorded in tales of often hedonistic eccentrics like the Seven Sages of the Bamboo Grove also characterized the retreat from public life inspired by Daoist values. As the impact of Buddhism began to register on the Chinese landscape, Daoist groups adopted many of its features, building temples in the mountains and constructing an elaborate pantheon of deities.

The first mention of Buddhism's arrival in China can be dated to the first century C.E.: according to a later legend, the Han emperor Ming dreamed of a flying golden figure and was told by his advisors that it was the Buddha; he then sent a mission to India that brought back two monks and a sūtra (scripture spoken by the Buddha). A more likely vehicle was the growing merchant trade across the desert on what was to become known as the Silk Road. The religion had already developed over the course of several centuries since the death of the historical Buddha in 483 B.C.E., with a focus on the Four Noble Truths he had realized: first, that all existence is suffering; second, that suffering has a cause (the craving for existence and pleasure); third, that this suffering can be eliminated; and fourth, that the path toward this goal is eightfold, involving wisdom, morality, and concentration. Various traditions or sects arose that promoted the superior doctrinal merits of one of the many sūtras attributed to him or emphasized one practice over another. Some promoted the importance of textual study, others the efficacy of meditation, chanting, faith, or good works, but all promised a personal salvation and release from the suffering of endless rebirth and karmic retribution to which all sentient beings were believed to be subject.

The Buddhist focus on the individual's renunciation of the duties and rewards of this world marked a radical departure from Confucianism's emphasis on social and ethical responsibility.

The Buddhist focus on the individual's renunciation of the duties and rewards of this world marked a radical departure from Confucianism's emphasis on social and ethical responsibility. Although at first confused with Daoism because of similar interests in breathing and meditation techniques, Buddhism made significant inroads in both northern and southern China during the period of division. The non-Chinese rulers of the north appreciated its shared "barbarian" origins and provided substantial government support to Buddhist missionaries. Well-educated but unconnected to powerful local families, they could offer service to the government without posing a political threat. In the south Buddhism proved equally appealing to both the relatively weaker rulers and the stronger aristocratic clans, who, in contrast to the more pietistic, devotional practice of the north, preferred to indulge in the abstruse and often witty discussion inspired by Buddhism's sophisticated metaphysics. Monasteries and retreats soon came to dot the landscape in both northern and southern dynasties. Many sūtras were translated from Sanskrit into Chinese by monks from India in state-sponsored schools, and the resulting attention to features of both languages led to systematic analysis of the tonal structure of Chinese and also to the development of poetic forms that exploited differences among the tones.

Lively debates between Chinese intellectuals and Buddhist monks focused on the striking disparities between indigenous Confucian values and those of the new foreign religion. Buddhism's otherworldliness and attention to the salvation of the individual challenged the integrity of a structure built on filial piety and strong familial obligations in this world. The requirement to shave one's head if entering the clergy ran directly counter to Confucian beliefs that harming any part of one's body meant disrespect to one's parents, from whom it was a gift. Similarly, celibacy and the continuity of the family line were mutually exclusive values. An early Buddhist writer named Mouzi had an answer for such complaints:

> Wives, children and property are luxuries of the world, and simple living and doing nothing are wonders of the Way. . . . The monk practices the Way and substitutes it for the pleasures of disporting himself in the world. He accumulates goodness and wisdom in exchange for the joys of wife and children.

As an import from India, the religion also threatened China's political integrity, since the early Buddhist populations were largely foreign, and monks did not consider themselves subject to Chinese law. Buddhist monasteries, moreover, were exempt from taxation, a fact that became increasingly irritating as they became more lavishly furnished. While these issues were being thrashed out during the period, the attractions of the Buddhist faith continued nonetheless to exert their power; given the number of adherents in China gained from the fourth through eighth centuries, in fact, it is fair to say that half of the entire world's population at the time was Buddhist. An attempt was made to ban Buddhism in the middle of the ninth century, leading to widespread destruction of temples and confiscation of lands and goods, yet its influence continued to be felt, particularly in

. . . it is fair to say that half of the entire world's population at the time was Buddhist.

the uniquely Chinese tradition of Chan or Zen that was less dependent on institutional structures. Native religions may have been wary of Buddhism's economic, social, and political challenges, but they were not governed by jealous gods, which opened up the possibility for an often peaceful, complementary coexistence. The Indian religion took a decidedly less ascetic, monastic turn when transplanted into China, and its

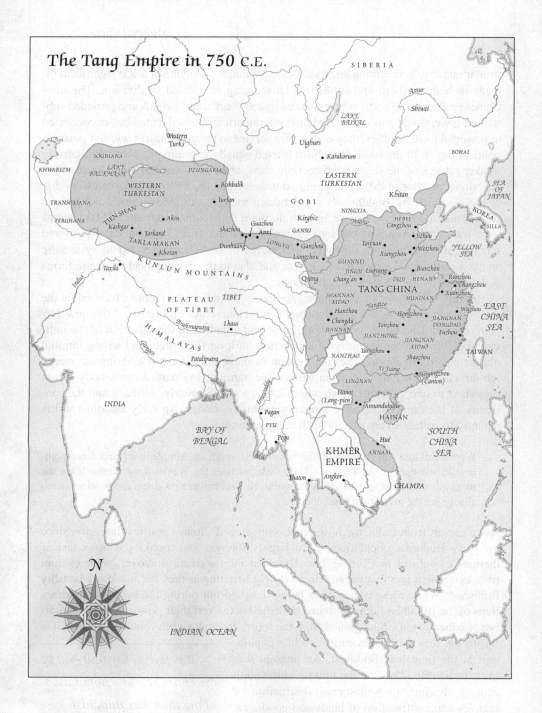

The Tang Empire in 750 C.E.

commitment to charity and compassion beyond the boundaries of familial relationships fostered the establishment of warmly welcomed free medical dispensaries and inexpensive travel hostels. Its monasteries became repositories of some of the most important works of art produced during the middle ages, and for centuries thereafter Buddhist rituals would mark milestones such as birth, marriage, and death in the lives of both commoners and the imperial household.

THE EMPIRE REUNIFIED

The succession of dynasties on the Yangzi River in the south regarded themselves as the principal custodians of the civilization's legacy, even as it was being infused with new Buddhist elements. Poetry, painting, and calligraphy flourished, as well as numerous theories about these cultural practices and their significance. These regional courts in the south also sponsored the compilation of numerous important anthologies that helped both to preserve and to evaluate what had been transmitted from the past. It was a northern ruler, however, who finally succeeded in reuniting the divided Chinese empire, but his Sui dynasty fell within thirty years to the Tang, which managed to govern the country for the next three centuries.

Reunification of China returned the center of the government to the northern capital of Chang'an. Rebuilt several times since the beginning of the Han dynasty, the city was laid out in checkerboard fashion and covered an area of some thirty square miles. The city wall was punctuated on each of its four sides by three large gates, each topped with a watch tower and wide enough to allow the simultaneous passage of four carriages. The central government administration constituted a virtual city within the city, as did the emperor's three lavish palace compounds.

Approximately a million people resided within the city walls of Chang'an during the dynasty's most prosperous period, the reign of Emperor Xuanzong (712–756). Foreign influences became increasingly visible, both because the city was located at the end of the Silk Road, but also because Tang military campaigns sought continually to expand the empire's boundaries in all directions. Diplomats, students, and Buddhist monks from Japan and Korea stayed for extended periods in the capital, as did artists, musicians, nomads, and merchants from In-

Diplomats, students, and Buddhist monks from Japan and Korea stayed for extended periods in the capital, as did artists, musicians, nomads, and merchants from India, Persia, and the Middle East.

dia, Persia, and the Middle East. The introduction of instruments and melodies from central Asia eventually inspired the development of new genres of prose and poetry whose first audiences were more popular than elite. What must have been a rich and lively flow of cultural goods has been confirmed by the large cache of manuscripts and art preserved in the caves sealed up by desert sands at Dunhuang, at the western extremity of the Great Wall.

Governing an empire that extended a thousand miles from the Great Wall to the north to Hainan Island in the south, with a registered population of nearly fifty million, required a complex system of taxation, state monopolies, and forced labor, as well as an elaborate structure of provincial and county administration staffed by educated bureaucrats. As had always been the case, aristocratic birth offered the easiest entry into government office, but the civil service examination now began to vie in importance as a means of qualification. Implemented in rudimentary form at the beginning of the Sui dynasty, this competition was refined and institutionalized during the Tang and presented a significant challenge to the entrenched political power exerted by the early medieval hereditary families.

Five major examinations, which conferred five different degrees, were offered throughout the Tang, but the one requiring the most sophisticated literary talent quickly became the most prestigious one; it led to the degree of "presented scholar" (*jinshi*), someone suitable for presentation to the emperor. Only about one percent of the

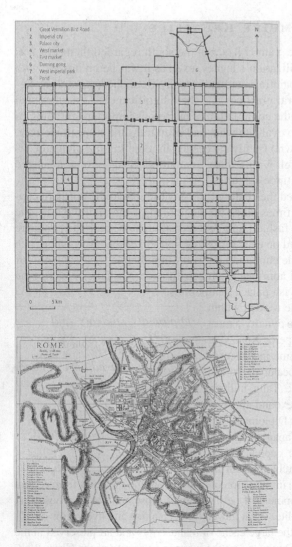

1 Great Vermilion Bird Road
2 Imperial city
3 Palace city
4 West market
5 East market
6 Daming gong
7 West imperial park
8 Pond

0   5 km

ROME.

The urban plans of imperial Chang'an and of imperial Rome. From earliest times Chinese imperial cities were laid out in a highly regulated fashion, in striking contrast, for example, with the sprawling extension of Rome, spread over seven hills. Chang'an, the cosmopolitan metropolis of the Tang Empire, covered an area of over 80 square kilometers, bisected by a broad avenue that led due north to the administrative center of the government (Imperial City) and the Emperor's main palace. Each of the 110 blocks created by the grid of avenues was walled and had its own name. Two large markets, east and west, provided the city's population with a large variety of products and entertainments.

candidates sitting for this exam would pass. Slightly less esteemed, because it relied more on rote memorization, was a version "elucidating the classics," and even less difficult were those calling upon what were regarded as the more technical skills of law, mathematics, and calligraphy. Success on an examination did not guarantee official appointment, for a second set of hurdles involved further tests of writing ability and an oral interview, which introduced an element of flexibility into the evaluation process.

The civil service examination system wasn't the only channel of official recruitment for the Tang court, and personal connections continued to be exercised. Families of established wealth were also clearly in the best position to support their sons' pursuit of office. Nonetheless, it did succeed in opening a door to men of relatively humble background and fulfilled in large measure the Confucian mandate for government based on merit. Many who could have called upon other routes to office in fact often chose to be validated by success on the examination, and its institutionalized curriculum served as an important unifying force intellectually as well.

POETRY AND OFFICIAL LIFE

The range of knowledge tested on the *jinshi* examination was relatively broad; its basic curriculum included literature, the classics, current affairs, and administrative issues, thereby approaching fairly closely the Confucian ideal of a liberal education. During the Tang, furthermore, a test of poetic composition was included at various times on the *jinshi* examination, providing testimony not only to the stature of poetry as a literary form during the dynasty but also an index of its deep embeddedness in official life. Court appointees had to be prepared to write at the command of a member of the ruling family. If the emperor composed a poem inspired by some outing or memorable event, courtiers would be expected to "respond respectfully," using the same form and rhyme

> *. . . a member of the ruling family might simply set the topic, with officials in attendance composing poems at his command . . .*

scheme. Or a member of the ruling family might simply set the topic, with officials in attendance composing poems at his command or to a rhyme assigned by him.

Poems composed at court typically indicated relevant details about the context, as in the title of a work by the major court poet Wang Wei (701–761): "Written at Imperial Command to Harmonize with His Majesty's Poem, 'On the Double Ninth Festival the Ministers and Assembled Officials Offer Their Wishes for Longevity.'" The poem's opening lines sound a note of praise for the emperor that was equally characteristic:

> Within the four seas there are no untoward affairs;
> In autumn's third month the harvest has been abundant.
> A hundred officials come together this day
> To wish their ruler a life of a myriad years.

Anecdotes surviving from such events typically record who finished his poem first and whose was judged of the highest quality.

Other rhythms of public life were marked in poetic form as well. Officials regularly exchanged poems among themselves while in the capital, and wrote rueful poems of parting when leaving for postings to remote parts of the country (commonly used to prevent administrators from building up a power base). Another example from Wang Wei, "Farewell to Shen Zifu Returning East of the Yangzi," expresses his emotions in a typically understated way:

> By willows at the edge of the ford, travelers are few.
> The fisherman swings his oar toward the winding shore.
> There are only thoughts of you like the colors of spring:
> South of the Yangzi, north of the Yangzi, sending you home.

Such works fill many chapters of all major poets' collections. Homecomings were correspondingly joyous, and there are also countless examples of poems recording visits to acquaintances of all sorts; if the friend wasn't at home, a poem might be written on his wall by the disappointed visitor. Meetings with individuals like Daoist or Buddhist monks who were situated outside the sphere of the court typically called for expressions of envy for their life in reclusion. Such protestations also, of course, provide as much evidence of the bureaucratic ethic's pervasiveness as do compositions openly written to fulfill it.

Like the Tang emperor, officials in other regions of the empire also took delight in sponsoring poetic activity. When relegated to positions remote from the central government, poets often formed literary salons under the patronage of local governors, where they cultivated styles and themes different from those dominant in the capi-

> *For later generations . . . the achievements of Tang poetry established the standard to be emulated.*

tal, thus expanding the repertoire and scope of the tradition. Many of the foremost Tang poets benefited from the patronage of these provincial officials, and after Xuanzong's reign the imperial court could no longer be said to be the center of poetic activity. For later generations, however, the achievements of Tang poetry established the standard to be emulated.

THE ART OF THE TANG POEM

The practices of court poetry were honed to perfection by poets of the Tang in nonofficial contexts as well. Among other virtues, the short length and prescriptive rules facilitated swift composition, which was demanded by both the civil service examination and the numerous courtly and social occasions in which officials would find themselves. Older forms permitted greater metrical freedom and maintained their popularity, and all forms of Chinese poetry, whether old or new, could take advantage of features of the classical language itself, which seems spare and sometimes ambiguous when compared to Western European languages, owing to its lack of inflection and characteristic omission of indications of person, tense, and other grammatical relationships. To an experienced reader familiar with the conventions, a typical poem would not—as has been argued by some—be read as "telegraphic," but it also left much unspecified in the text. A good example is the following quatrain by Li Bo (701–762) that is still memorized by Chinese schoolchildren today. A word-for-word rendering is shown beneath the Chinese characters:

靜 夜 思
Quiet Night Thought

床 前 明 月 光

Bed front bright moon radiance

疑 是 地 上 霜

Suspect is ground upon frost

舉 頭 望 明 月

Raise head gaze bright moon

低 頭 思 故 鄉

Lower head think old province

Thoughts on a Quiet Night

Before my bed the bright moon's gleam
I take to be frost on the ground.
Lifting my head I gaze at the bright moon;
Lowering my head I think of home.

Readers have long appreciated the way in which these twenty words convey a powerful sense of a traveler's longing without making any overt emotional reference.

Li Bo's poem is written in an older and relatively simple style; newer forms refined in the Tang (called "recent-style" or regulated verse) demanded even greater manipulation of variables and concentration of expression. In addition to restrictions on length (four or eight lines) and number of words per line (generally five or seven), they required adherence to one rhyme on even-numbered lines throughout the poem, parallelism of syntax and meaning within the middle couplets, and conformity to set patterns of alternation of the tones characteristic of all Chinese words. The following regulated verse by Du Fu (712–770) observes all of these rules. For the purposes of poetic composition, tones were divided into two large categories, "level" and "deflected," which are indicated below by the minus (–) and plus (+) signs, respectively, next to the romanizations; (r) denotes the rhyming words.

春　　望

chun–wang+

Spring Gaze

國　破　山　河　在

guo+   po+   shan–   he–zai+

nation broken mountain river exist

城　　春　草　木　沈

cheng – chun–cao+ mu+ shen–(r)

city-wall spring grass tree deep

感　時　花　濺　淚

gan+ shi– hua– jian+ lei+

feel time flower sprinkle tear

恨　別　鳥　驚　心

hen+   bie+ niao+ jing– xin–(r)

hate parting bird alarm heart

烽　火　連　三　月

feng–huo+ lian–   san– yue+

beacon fire consecutive three months

家　書　抵　萬　金
jia-　shu-　di+　wan+　jin-(r)
family letter worth 10,000 gold

白　頭　搔　更　短
bai+　tou-　sao-　geng+duan+
white hair scratch more short

渾　欲　不　勝　簪
hun-　yu+　bu+　sheng-zan-(r)
all about-to not bear hatpin

Spring Prospect

The country shattered, mountains and rivers remain.
Spring in the city—grasses and trees are dense
Feeling the times, flowers draw forth tears.
Hating to part, birds alarm the heart.
Beacon fires for three months in a row:
A letter from home worth ten thousand in gold.
White hairs scratched grow even shorter—
Soon too few to hold a hatpin on.

More than any other Tang poet, Du Fu excelled in his ability to manipulate the many requirements of the regulated verse forms in the service of nuanced expression and evocative description.

WOMEN AND MEN

Not all poets during the Tang could aspire to a career in government service. In the middle of the ninth century a woman named Yu Xuanji (fl. 844–868) encountered a list of successful examination candidates posted on a tower and lamented in a poem:

> Bitterly I regret that skirts of lace veil the lines of my poems.
> I lift my head in vain to covet a publicly posted name.

An accomplished courtesan, Yu Xuanji enjoyed at best the access to influence afforded by her position as a concubine to a prominent official. Other women from medieval China whose poetry has been recorded were similarly dependent on such relationships to develop their literary talents, and very few of their works have survived. During the Tang, however, upper-class women enjoyed an unprecedented equality and status that even later epochs sometimes failed to match. They socialized with relative freedom, could walk freely in the streets and indulged in traditionally male activities like riding and playing polo. Even political power was not necessarily foreclosed to them. During the seventh century one of the first Tang emperor's concubines succeeded in becoming the power behind the throne of his successor, usurping

Female polo-player, lead-glazed earthenware, Tang dynasty, c. 695–715. As this tomb figurine suggests, women of the Tang dynasty partook enthusiastically in vigorous activity. The slender figure of this polo player reflects an aesthetic that yielded to one of fashionable plumpness by the middle of the 8th century.

the place of his rightful consort and even taking control of the government after his death. She proclaimed herself empress of a new Zhou dynasty that—though short-lived and castigated for its impropriety by Confucian critics—was judged by less partisan observers as an effectively governed regime.

Such meteoric rises to prominence were exceptional, of course, and the fate of the tens of thousands of palace women at court was more commonly a less happy one. For most of them the only male they were allowed to see—with the exception of eunuchs and young boys—was the emperor, and many lived out their lives without ever having been "favored" by him. Physically isolated and emotionally deprived, neglected palace women were a favorite subject for poets, as in the "Song of the Rear Palace" by Bo Juyi (772–846):

Tears wet her gauze scarf, she cannot sleep.
Deep in the night, she taps to music from the front palace.
Her rosy complexion youthful, yet favor is of the past;
Next to the incense burner she sits until the dawn.

Bo Juyi also recounted the tragic tale of Emperor Xuanzong's own most favored palace woman, Yang Guifei (Precious Consort Yang), which marked a turning point in his reign, and in the course of the dynasty as well. One of his son's concubines, she caught the ruler's attention and was immediately brought into the center of court activity. The plumpness of her figure displaced an earlier fashion for slender beauties, and she was also said to have popularized a hair style known as "just fallen off a horse," inadvertently created when her lofty coiffure came loose on one side after a minor riding accident. The story goes that Xuanzong was so captivated by Yang Guifei that he both ignored his duties and also agreed to promote the careers of her relatives. One of her cousins rose to prominence as chief minister but became involved in a feud with a frontier general, An Lushan, who proceeded to launch a rebellion against the government in 755. His forces invaded the capital and sent the emperor and his entourage fleeing to the southwest. Along the way, however, his palace guards, blaming the empire's troubles on Yang Guifei and her cousin, demanded their death; Xuanzong was forced to comply and then abdicated in favor of one of his sons. Although the rebellion was quelled in 757, with the Tang rulers reinstated in the capital for the next century and a half, the dynasty never regained the stability and prosperity that had supported a wealth of cultural activities during its golden age.

WOMEN IN EARLY CHINA

Women in twentieth-century China were exhorted to remember that they held up half the sky, but such was not the vision of their capabilities in the premodern world. In the sixth century B.C.E. the philosopher Confucius had articulated an influential set of assumptions in his *Analects* regarding the aspirations and places of all individuals in society and the body politic, focusing on an understanding of proper roles and responsibilities in any relationship. Primarily concerned about the mutual obligations of father and son, ruler and minister, he had little to say specifically about the position and participation of women. What he did observe was rarely positive, as is evident in this well-known observation: "In one's household, it is the women and the small men that are difficult to deal with. If you let them get too close, they become insolent. If you keep them at a distance, they complain." Keeping women in their place, in other words, was quite literally the problem.

Where was that place? Women were expected to understand that "Three Obeyings"—as daughters, wives, and mothers—structured their lives, which unfolded in the private space of the domestic household, largely separated from the public realms within which males operated. Within those roles, however, they could in fact exercise profound influence on the men in their family. As mothers, after all, they were expected to be their sons' first teachers, and as wives they could also exert a certain intellectual and moral authority, although this agency may have diminished over time as the power of Confucian orthodoxy became more entrenched. The higher up the political hierarchy, the more significant their potential impact, and anecdotes therefore abound extolling the sage counsel of exemplary royal consorts or, conversely, the pernicious effects of their misbehavior. Disorder or chaos was the consequence of transgressing boundaries; women who violated the norm could "topple kingdoms," and they would surely suffer great personal misfortune as well. Small wonder, then, that a rich literature of exemplary tales and conduct books burgeoned to promote proper behavior.

The place of women in the Chinese literary tradition is a complex one, and the line between historical reality and literary representation is often difficult to draw. Within the ancient anthology of poetry, the *Book of Songs* (Volume A, page 1027), a substantial number of poems focus on typical activities and preoccupations of women, but whether they were actually composed by them cannot be determined for certain. The poems were in fact claimed by males as their production, and varieties of allegorical interpretation purported to demonstrate how, for example, the women in the poems were actually figures for male officials. Indeed, although modern readers are quite willing to assume the female authorship of many songs in this early anthology, it wasn't acknowledged as a fount of women's poetry until the seventeenth century. And as the poetic tradition evolved, male writers frequently did employ women as personae for their own frustrated and unhappy selves or as figures of desire onto which their fantasies could be projected.

What did women write? In early China their literary training was informal at best, since the purported natural order excluded them from significant public, intellectual activity. Within many aristocratic households, however, their responsibility for early childhood education led them to acquire and transmit skills that were often, as in the case of Ban Zhao, taken beyond the limits of any expected mastery. Literary compositions by such women were, however, a largely private business and rarely preserved until later dynasties. The most significant body of early writing by women that has survived, therefore, has been attributed to a rather different social group—of courtesans and other female entertainers. As marginal figures who didn't maintain the mandated domestic separation of space, they had the opportunity to socialize with men and develop relationships within which writings circulated as freely and publicly as did the exchange of personal favors. During the later imperial period the literary possibilities expanded for gentry women in more socially sanctioned contexts; the numbers of women reading and writing burgeoned tremendously from the sixteenth century onward, but a tension persisted between self-expression and the risks of self-exposure. Indeed, as one often-repeated saying in the Ming dynasty put it, "Only a woman without talents can be virtuous." Recent scholarship on the explosion of literary activity among women in the Ming and Qing dynasties, however, has revealed how successfully this statement was tested.

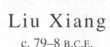

Liu Xiang

c. 79–8 B.C.E.

Born into the ruling family of the Han dynasty, Liu Xiang overcame early setbacks in his political career that twice landed him in prison; he was finally appointed Collator of Secret Documents at court in 26 B.C.E. Charged with collecting and editing all important canonical, philosophical, and literary texts, he became known for his ingenious editorial techniques and extensive bibliographical expertise. In addition to playing a role in the compilation of three volumes of political tales and arguments, he is said to have collected the 125 *Memoirs of Women* (*Lienü zhuan*) in 16 B.C.E., presenting them to the emperor as didactic illustrations of the positive and negative influences of women on individuals and the state.

For Liu Xiang virtue began at home, and the first of the eight chapters in the *Memoirs* therefore presents exemplars of "maternal rectitude," starting with the mother of Mencius, the fourth-century B.C.E. follower of Confucius and most important proponent of the sage's thought. The four biographical anecdotes graphically illustrate the extent of her commitment to the importance of learning and understanding proper behavior toward members of the family. Other chapters celebrate the wisdom, chastity, benevolence, and obedience of female paragons,

Mencius and His Mother, from an illustrated version of the *Memoirs of Women,* preface dated 1552, reprinted in a later Qing dynasty collection. An exemplar of "maternal rectitude," Mencius's mother prepares to slash her day's weavings on learning that Mencius has abandoned his studies. Numerous illustrated editions of these *Memoirs* were published from the Song dynasty on; in one version Mencius is represented as an adult, an indication of his future sagehood.

with one chapter presenting counterexamples of "pernicious and depraved" influences. The *Memoirs* were widely read in courtly circles and frequently published in illustrated versions for the illiterate as well.

PRONUNCIATION:
   Liu Xiang: lee-OH she-AHNG

from Memoirs of Women[1]
The Mother of Mencius

The mother of Mencius lived in Tsou in a house near a cemetery. When Mencius was a little boy he liked to play burial rituals in the cemetery, happily building tombs and grave mounds. His mother said to herself, "This is no place to bring up my son."

   She moved near the marketplace in town. Mencius then played merchant games of buying and selling. His mother again said, "This is no place to bring up my son."

   So once again she moved, this time next to a schoolhouse. Mencius then played games of ancestor sacrifices and practiced the common courtesies between students

---

1. Translated by Nancy Gibbs.

and teachers. His mother said, "At last, this is the right place for my son!" There they remained.

When Mencius grew up he studied the six arts of propriety, music, archery, charioteering, writing, and mathematics. Later he became a famous Confucian scholar. Superior men commented that Mencius' mother knew the right influences for her sons. The *Book of Songs* says, "That admirable lady, what will she do for them!"

When Mencius was young, he came home from school one day and found his mother was weaving at the loom. She asked him, "Is school out already?"

He replied, "I left because I felt like it."

His mother took her knife and cut the finished cloth on her loom. Mencius was startled and asked why. She replied, "Your neglecting your studies is very much like my cutting the cloth. The superior person studies to establish a reputation and gain wide knowledge. He is calm and poised and tries to do no wrong. If you do not study now, you will surely end up as a menial servant and will never be free from troubles. It would be just like a woman who supports herself by weaving to give it up. How long could such a person depend on her husband and son to stave off hunger? If a woman neglects her work or a man gives up the cultivation of his character, they may end up as common thieves if not slaves!"

Shaken, from then on Mencius studied hard from morning to night. He studied the philosophy of the Master and eventually became a famous Confucian scholar. Superior men observed that Mencius' mother understood the way of motherhood. The *Book of Songs* says, "That admirable lady, what will she tell them!"

After Mencius was married, one day as he was going into his private quarters, he encountered his wife not fully dressed. Displeased, Mencius stopped going into his wife's room. She then went to his mother, begged to be sent home, and said, "I have heard that the etiquette between a man and a woman does not apply in their private room. But lately I have been too casual, and when my husband saw me improperly dressed, he was displeased. He is treating me like a stranger. It is not right for a woman to live as a guest; therefore, please send me back to my parents."

Mencius' mother called him to her and said, "It is polite to inquire before you enter a room. You should make some loud noise to warn anyone inside, and as you enter, you should keep your eyes low so that you will not embarrass anyone. Now, you have not behaved properly, yet you are quick to blame others for their impropriety. Isn't that going a little too far?"

Mencius apologized and took back his wife. Superior men said that his mother understood the way to be a mother-in-law.

When Mencius was living in Ch'i, he was feeling very depressed. His mother saw this and asked him, "Why are you looking so low?"

"It's nothing," he replied.

On another occasion when Mencius was not working, he leaned against the door and sighed. His mother saw him and said, "The other day I saw that you were troubled, but you answered that it was nothing. But why are you leaning against the door sighing?"

Mencius answered, "I have heard that the superior man judges his capabilities and then accepts a position. He neither seeks illicit gains nor covets glory or high salary. If the Dukes and Princes do not listen to his advice, then he does not talk to them. If they listen to him but do not use his ideas, then he no longer frequents their courts. Today my ideas are not being used in Ch'i, so I wish to go somewhere else. But I am worried because you are getting too old to travel about the country."

His mother answered, "A woman's duties are to cook the five grains, heat the wine, look after her parents-in-law, make clothes, and that is all! Therefore, she cultivates the skills required in the women's quarters and has no ambition to manage affairs outside of the house. The *Book of Changes* says, 'In her central place, she attends to the preparation of the food.' The *Book of Songs* says, 'It will be theirs neither to do wrong nor to do good, / Only about the spirits and the food will they have to think.' This means that a woman's duty is not to control or to take charge. Instead she must follow the 'three submissions.' When she is young, she must submit to her parents. After her marriage, she must submit to her husband. When she is widowed, she must submit to her son. These are the rules of propriety. Now you are an adult and I am old; therefore, whether you go depends on what you consider right, whether I follow depends on the rules of propriety."

Superior men observed that Mencius' mother knew the proper course for women. The *Book of Songs* says, "Serenely she looks and smiles, / Without any impatience she delivers her instructions."

⊷ ⊰✧⊱ ⊶

Ban Zhao
c. 45–120

Ban Zhao was the daughter and sister of two eminent Han dynasty scholars, and she was a learned figure in her own right. Known for her "widowly rectitude" after the death of her husband, Ban Zhao was asked to complete the official history of the Former Han dynasty on which her brother had been working when he died. Supervising an imperial staff, she was responsible for a number of chronological tables and the treatise on astronomy and may also have lent an editorial hand to the rest of the history. She also provided instruction to the empress and other female occupants of the palace and tutored several male courtiers who were to become distinguished scholars. Tradition has it that she edited Liu Xiang's *Memoirs of Women* as well.

The author of several memorials to the throne and poetic rhapsodies, Ban Zhao is best known for her *Lessons for Women (Nü jie)*, the oldest female conduct book. Although she states that the work was written for her "daughters"—i.e., the female members of her extended family—it is possible that it was also intended to reach a wider audience. Its seven chapters draw on canonical and ritual texts to provide protocols for the correct conduct of wives on a very practical level. Ban Zhao emphasizes the importance of distinctions between men and women, their separate natures and correspondingly separate spheres. Her reading of yin-yang cosmology and the complementary differences between male and female lead her to stress the naturally superior nature of men and deferential obligations of women, which in later conservative dynasties was used to repress the cultivation and display of any but domestic talents by women. At the same time, however, the second chapter of the *Lessons* makes the earliest known argument in China that girls should receive the same education as boys, and Ban Zhao's own career served as an inspiring example of the impressive extent to which such erudition could be exercised.

A number of other texts providing protocols for women followed in later dynasties, some targeting members of a family clan, others defining themselves as female versions of earlier male-oriented texts, such as the *Classic of Filial Piety for Women* and the *Analects for Women*. Like Ban Zhao's *Lessons,* these instruction books both insist on a hierarchical separation of spheres between men and women and also encourage the development of female literacy and talent, a balance whose delicate equilibrium stimulated considerable discussion in later imperial China.

Lessons for Women[1]
Introduction

I, the unworthy writer, am unsophisticated, unenlightened, and by nature unintelligent, but I am fortunate both to have received not a little favor from my scholarly father, and to have had a cultured mother and instructresses upon whom to rely for a literary education as well as for training in good manners. More than forty years have passed since at the age of fourteen I took up the dustpan and the broom in the Ts'ao family.[2] During this time with trembling heart I feared constantly that I might disgrace my parents, and that I might multiply difficulties for both the women and the men of my husband's family. Day and night I was distressed in heart, but I labored without confessing weariness. Now and hereafter, however, I know how to escape from such faults.

Being careless, and by nature stupid, I taught and trained my children without system. Consequently I fear that my son Ku may bring disgrace upon the Imperial Dynasty by whose Holy Grace he has unprecedentedly received the extraordinary privilege of wearing the Gold and the Purple,[3] a privilege for the attainment of which by my son, I a humble subject never even hoped. Nevertheless, now that he is a man and able to plan his own life, I need not again have concern for him. But I do grieve that you, my daughters,[4] just now at the age for marriage, have not at this time had gradual training and advice; that you still have not learned the proper customs for married women. I fear that by failure in good manners in other families you will humiliate both your ancestors and your clan. I am now seriously ill, life is uncertain. As I have thought of you all in so untrained a state, I have been uneasy many a time for you. At hours of leisure I have composed in seven chapters these instructions under the title *Lessons for Women*. In order that you may have something wherewith to benefit your persons, I wish every one of you, my daughters, each to write out a copy for yourself.

From this time on, every one of you strive to practice these lessons.

Chapter 1: Humility

On the third day after the birth of a girl the ancients observed three customs: first to place the baby below the bed;[5] second to give her a potsherd with which to play;[6] and third to announce her birth to her ancestors by an offering. Now to lay the baby below the bed plainly indicated that she is lowly and weak, and should regard it as her primary duty to humble herself before others. To give her potsherds with which to play indubitably signified that she should practice labor and consider it her primary duty to be industrious. To announce her birth before her ancestors clearly meant that she ought to esteem as her primary duty the continuation of the observance of worship in the home.

These three ancient customs epitomize a woman's ordinary way of life and the teachings of the traditional ceremonial rites and regulations. Let a woman modestly yield to others; let her respect others; let her put others first, herself last. Should she do something good, let her not mention it; should she do something bad, let her not

1. Translated by Nancy Lee Swann.
2. That is, joined the household in the subordinate role of daughter-in-law.
3. The gold seal and purple robe were symbols of high nobility.
4. Referring to the girls of her family as a whole.

5. On the floor.
6. Alluding to the *Book of Songs,* poem 189 ("The Beck," included in Volume A), which says that boys shall be given scepters and girls loom-whorls as toys. Potsherds were used as loom-whorls, or spindle-weights.

deny it. Let her bear disgrace; let her even endure when others speak or do evil to her. Always let her seem to tremble and to fear. When a woman follows such maxims as these, then she may be said to humble herself before others.

Let a woman retire late to bed, but rise early to duties; let her not dread tasks by day or by night. Let her not refuse to perform domestic duties whether easy or difficult. That which must be done, let her finish completely, tidily, and systematically. When a woman follows such rules as these, then she may be said to be industrious.

Let a woman be correct in manner and upright in character in order to serve her husband. Let her live in purity and quietness of spirit, and attend to her own affairs. Let her love not gossip and silly laughter. Let her cleanse and purify and arrange in order the wine and the food for the offerings to the ancestors. When a woman observes such principles as these, then she may be said to continue ancestral worship.

No woman who observes these three fundamentals of life has ever had a bad reputation or has fallen into disgrace. If a woman fails to observe them, how can her name be honored; how can she but bring disgrace upon herself?

Chapter 2: Husband and Wife

The Way of husband and wife is intimately connected with yin and yang, and relates the individual to gods and ancestors. Truly it is the great principle of Heaven and Earth, and the great basis of human relationships. Therefore the *Rites* honor union of man and woman; and in the *Classic Book of Poetry,* the "First Ode" manifests the principle of marriage.[7] For these reasons the relationship cannot but be an important one.

If a husband be unworthy, then he possesses nothing by which to control his wife. If a wife be unworthy, then she possesses nothing with which to serve her husband. If a husband does not control his wife, then the rules of conduct manifesting his authority are abandoned and broken. If a wife does not serve her husband, then the proper relationship between men and women and the natural order of things are neglected and destroyed. As a matter of fact, the purpose of these two, the controlling of women by men and the serving of men by women, is the same.

Now examine the gentlemen of the present age. They only know that wives must be controlled and that the husband's rules of conduct manifesting his authority must be established. They therefore teach their boys to read books and study histories. But they do not in the least understand that husbands and masters must also be served, and that the proper relationship and the rites should be maintained.

Yet only to teach men and not to teach women—is that not ignoring the essential relation between them? According to the *Rites,* it is the rule to begin to teach children to read at the age of eight years, and by the age of fifteen years they ought then to be ready for cultural training.[8] Only why should it not be that girls' education as well as boys' be according to this principle?

Chapter 3: Respect and Caution

As yin and yang are not of the same nature, so man and woman have different characteristics. The distinctive quality of the yang is rigidity; the function of the yin is yield-

---

7. As seen in the Preface and the first poem in the *Book of Songs* (Volume A).

8. This would include all of the accomplishments of a gentleman: ritual, music, archery, charioteering, writing, and mathematics.

ing. Man is honored for strength; a woman is beautiful on account of her gentleness. Hence there arose the common saying: "A man though born like a wolf may, it is feared, become a weak monstrosity; a woman though born like a mouse may, it is feared, become a tiger."

Now for self-culture nothing equals respect for others. To counteract firmness nothing equals compliance. Consequently it can be said that the Way of respect and acquiescence is woman's most important principle of conduct. So respect may be defined as nothing other than holding on to that which is permanent; and acquiescence nothing other than being liberal and generous. Those who are steadfast in devotion know that they should stay in their proper places; those who are liberal and generous esteem others, and honor and serve them.

If husband and wife have the habit of staying together, never leaving one another, and following each other around within the limited space of their own rooms, then they will lust after and take liberties with one another. From such action improper language will arise between the two. This kind of discussion may lead to licentiousness. Out of licentiousness will be born a heart of disrespect to the husband. Such a result comes from not knowing that one should stay in one's proper place.

Furthermore, affairs may be either crooked or straight; words may be either right or wrong. Straightforwardness cannot but lead to quarreling; crookedness cannot but lead to accusation. If there are really accusations and quarrels, then undoubtedly there will be angry affairs. Such a result comes from not esteeming others, and not honoring and serving them.

If wives suppress not contempt for husbands, then it follows that such wives rebuke and scold their husbands. If husbands stop not short of anger, then they are certain to beat their wives. The correct relationship between husband and wife is based upon harmony and intimacy, and conjugal love is grounded in proper union. Should actual blows be dealt, how could matrimonial relationship be preserved? Should sharp words be spoken, how could conjugal love exist? If love and proper relationship both be destroyed, then husband and wife are divided.

Chapter 4: Womanly Qualifications

A woman ought to have four qualifications: (1) womanly virtue, (2) womanly words, (3) womanly bearing, and (4) womanly work. Now what is called womanly virtue need not be brilliant ability, exceptionally different from others. Womanly words need be neither clever in debate nor keen in conversation. Womanly appearance requires neither a pretty nor a perfect face and form. Womanly work need not be work done more skillfully than that of others.

To guard carefully her chastity, to control circumspectly her behavior, in every motion to exhibit modesty, and to model each act on the best usage—this is womanly virtue.

To choose her words with care, to avoid vulgar language, to speak at appropriate times, and not to weary others with much conversation may be called the characteristics of womanly words.

To wash and scrub filth away, to keep clothes and ornaments fresh and clean, to wash the head and bathe the body regularly, and to keep the person free from disgraceful filth may be called the characteristics of womanly bearing.

With wholehearted devotion to sew and to weave, to love not gossip and silly laughter, in cleanliness and order to prepare the wine and food for serving guests may be called the characteristics of womanly work.

These four qualifications characterize the greatest virtue of a woman. No woman can afford to be without them. In fact they are very easy to possess if a woman only treasures them in her heart. The ancients had a saying: "Is Love far off? If I desire love, then love is at hand!"[9] So can it be said of these qualifications.

Chapter 5: Wholehearted Devotion

Now in the *Rites* is written the principle that a husband may marry again, but there is no canon that authorizes a woman to be married the second time. Therefore it is said of husbands as of Heaven, that as certainly as people cannot run away from Heaven, so surely a wife cannot leave a husband's home.

If people in action or character disobey the spirits of Heaven and of Earth, then Heaven punishes them. Likewise if a woman errs in the rites and in the proper mode of conduct, then her husband esteems her lightly. The ancient book, *A Pattern for Women*,[1] says: "To obtain the love of one man is the crown of a woman's life; to lose the love of one man is to miss the aim in woman's life." For these reasons a woman cannot but seek to win her husband's heart. Nevertheless, the beseeching wife need not use flattery, coaxing words, and cheap methods to gain intimacy.

Decidedly nothing is better to gain the heart of a husband than wholehearted devotion and correct manners. In accordance with the rites and the proper mode of conduct, let a woman live a pure life. Let her have ears that hear not licentiousness and eyes that see not depravity. When she goes outside her own home, let her not be conspicuous in dress and manners. When at home let her not neglect her dress. Women should not assemble in groups, not gather together, for gossip and silly laughter. They should not stand watching in the gateways. If a woman follows these rules, she may be said to have wholehearted devotion and correct manners.

If, in all her actions, she is frivolous, she sees and hears only that which pleases herself. At home her hair is disheveled and her dress is slovenly. Outside the home she emphasizes her femininity to attract attention; she says what ought not to be said; and she looks at what ought not to be seen. If a woman does such as these, she may be said to be without wholehearted devotion and correct manners.

Chapter 6: Implicit Obedience

Now "to win the love of one man is the crown of a woman's life; to lose the love of one man is her eternal disgrace." This saying advises a fixed will and a wholehearted devotion for a woman. Ought she then to lose the hearts of her father- and mother-in-law?

There are times when love may lead to differences of opinion between individuals; there are times when duty may lead to disagreement. Even should the husband say that he loves something, when the parents-in-law say "no," this is called a case of duty leading to disagreement. This being so, then what about the hearts of the parents-in-law? Nothing is better than an obedience that sacrifices personal opinion.

Whenever the mother-in-law says, "Do not do that," and if what she says is right, unquestionably the daughter-in-law obeys. Whenever the mother-in-law says, "Do that," even if what she says is wrong, still the daughter-in-law submits unfailingly to the command.

---

9. Quoting *Analects* (7.29) of Confucius. The word translated here as "love" means something like "humaneness."

1. *Nü xian,* thought to be the title of a long-lost book.

Let a woman not act contrary to the wishes and opinions of parents-in-law about right and wrong; let her not dispute with them what is straight and what is crooked. Such docility may be called obedience that sacrifices personal opinion. Therefore the ancient book, *A Pattern for Women,* says: "If a daughter-in-law who follows the wishes of her parents-in-law is like an echo and a shadow, how could she not be praised?"

Chapter 7: Harmony with Younger Brothers- and Sisters-in-law

In order for a wife to gain the love of her husband, she must win for herself the love of her parents-in-law. To win for herself the love of her parents-in-law, she must secure for herself the good will of younger brothers- and sisters-in-law. For these reasons the right and the wrong, the praise and the blame of a woman alike depend upon younger brothers- and sisters-in-law. Consequently it will not do for a woman to lose their affection.

They are stupid both who know not that they must not lose the hearts of younger brothers- and sisters-in-law, and who cannot be in harmony with them in order to be intimate with them. Excepting only the Holy Men, few are able to be faultless. Now Yen Tzu's[2] greatest virtue was that he was able to reform. Confucius praised him for not committing a misdeed the second time. In comparison with him a woman is the more likely to make mistakes.

Although a woman possesses a worthy woman's qualifications and is wise and discerning by nature, is she able to be perfect? Yet if a woman lives in harmony with her immediate family, unfavorable criticism will be silenced within the home. But if a man and woman disagree, then this evil will be noised abroad. Such consequences are inevitable. The *Classic of Changes* says:

> Should two hearts harmonize,
> The united strength can cut gold.
> Words from hearts which agree,
> Give forth fragrance like the orchid.

This saying may be applied to harmony in the home.

Though a daughter-in-law and her younger sisters-in-law are equal in rank, nevertheless they should respect each other; though love between them may be sparse, their proper relationship should be intimate. Only the virtuous, the beautiful, the modest, and the respectful young women can accordingly rely upon the sense of duty to make their affection sincere, and magnify love to bind their relationships firmly.

Then the excellence and the beauty of such a daughter-in-law becomes generally known. Moreover, any flaws and mistakes are hidden and unrevealed. Parents-in-law boast of her good deeds; her husband is satisfied with her. Praise of her radiates, making her illustrious in district and in neighborhood; and her brightness reaches to her own father and mother.

But a stupid and foolish person as an elder sister-in-law uses her rank to exalt herself;[3] as a younger sister-in-law, because of parents' favor, she becomes filled with arrogance. If arrogant, how can a woman live in harmony with others? If love and proper relationships be perverted, how can praise be secured? In such instances the wife's

---

2. Yan Hui, Confucius's favorite disciple.   3. The eldest daughter-in-law had authority over the other sons' wives.

good is hidden and her faults are declared. The mother-in-law will be angry, and the husband will be indignant. Blame will reverberate and spread in and outside the home. Disgrace will gather upon the daughter-in-law's person, on the one hand to add humiliation to her own father and mother, and on the other to increase the difficulties of her husband.

Such then is the basis for both honor and disgrace, the foundation for reputation or for ill-repute. Can a woman be too cautious? Consequently, to seek the hearts of young brothers- and sisters-in-law decidedly nothing can be esteemed better than modesty and acquiescence.

Modesty is virtue's handle; acquiescence is the wife's most refined characteristic. All who possess these two have sufficiency for harmony with others. In the *Classic of Poetry* it is written that "Here is no evil; there is no dart." So it may be said of these two, modesty and acquiescence.

—✦—

Yuan Cai
fl. 1140–1195

Born in southeastern China to a landowning family, Yuan Cai passed the most literary of the civil service examinations in 1163 and held a number of government offices in the provinces and the capital. He was the author of eight books providing advice to fellow magistrates, none of which has survived, and is therefore best known for his *Precepts for Social Life* of 1178, which shares with those lost texts a wide-ranging pragmatic impulse. Such manuals of family instructions were modeled on canonical texts and rooted in the Confucian assumption that morality, social harmony, and political order begin in the home and, more specifically, in an understanding of the proper duties and behaviors attendant upon all family members. The typical advice was extremely detailed and practical, vividly conveying the sense of a Chinese family as a complex corporate unit requiring highly sophisticated management to ensure its preservation.

Yuan Cai's *Precepts for Social Life* was addressed to the educated public and consists of three chapters: Getting Along with Relatives, Improving Personal Conduct, and Managing Family Affairs. Taking for granted a hierarchical authority based on age and sex, he directs his advice to men and covers topics ranging from birth and childrearing to death and the division of family property. Although the domain of women in his view was a limited and highly dependent one, it is also clear that he considered them entitled to both common sense and compassion.

PRONUNCIATION:
Yuan Cai: YUEN TSIGH

from Precepts for Social Life[1]

WOMEN SHOULD NOT TAKE PART IN AFFAIRS OUTSIDE THE HOME

Women do not take part in extra-familial affairs. The reason is that worthy husbands and sons take care of everything for them, while unworthy ones can always find ways to hide their deeds from the women.

---

1. Translated by Patricia Ebrey.

Many men today indulge in pleasure and gambling; some end up mortgaging their lands, and even go so far as to mortgage their houses without their wives' knowledge. Therefore, when husbands are bad, even if wives try to handle outside matters, it is of no use. Sons must have their mothers' signatures to mortgage their family properties, but there are sons who falsify papers and forge signatures, sometimes borrowing money at high interest from people who would not hesitate to bring their claim to court. Other sons sell illicit tea and salt to get money, which, if discovered by the authorities, results in fines. Mothers have no control in such matters. Therefore, when sons are bad, it is useless for mothers to try to handle matters relating to the outside world.

For women, these are grave misfortunes, but what can they do? If husbands and sons could only remember that their wives and mothers are helpless and suddenly repent, would that not be best?

WOMEN'S SYMPATHIES SHOULD BE INDULGED

Without going overboard, people should marry their daughters with dowries appropriate to their family's wealth. Rich families should not consider their daughters outsiders but should give them a share of the property. Sometimes people have incapable sons and so have to entrust their affairs to their daughters' families; even after their deaths, their burials and sacrifices are performed by their daughters. So how can people say that daughters are not as good as sons?[2]

Generally speaking, a woman's heart is very sympathetic. If her parents' family is wealthy and her husband's family is poor, she wants to take her parents' wealth to help her husband's family prosper. If her husband's family is wealthy but her parents' family is poor, then she wants to take from her husband's family to enable her parents to prosper. Her parents and husband should be sympathetic toward her feelings and indulge some of her wishes. When her own sons and daughters are grown and married, if either her son's family or her daughter's family is wealthy while the other is poor, she wishes to take from the wealthy one to give to the poor one. Her sons and daughters should understand her feelings and be somewhat indulgent. But taking from the poor to make the rich richer is unacceptable, and no one should ever go along with it.

ORPHANED GIRLS SHOULD HAVE THEIR MARRIAGES ARRANGED EARLY

When a widow remarries she sometimes has an orphaned daughter not yet engaged. In such cases she should try to get a respectable relative to arrange a marriage for her daughter. She should also seek to have her daughter reared in the house of her future in-laws, with the marriage to take place after the girl has grown up. If the girl were to go along with the mother to her step-father's house, she would not be able to clear herself if she were subjected to any humiliations.[3]

FOR WOMEN OLD AGE IS PARTICULARLY HARD TO BEAR

People say that, though there may be a hundred years allotted to a person's life, only a few reach seventy, for time quickly runs out. But for those destined to be poor, old age is hard to endure. For them, until about the age of fifty, the passage of twenty years seems like only ten; but after that age, ten years can feel as long as twenty. For women

---

2. This phrase appears often in epitaphs for women and may have been something of a proverb.

3. Living in her stepfather's house she would be at risk, since men unrelated to her would not be subject to an incest taboo.

who live a long life, old age is especially hard to bear, because most women must rely on others for their existence. Before a woman's marriage, a good father is even more important than a good grandfather; a good brother is even more important than a good father; a good nephew is even more important than a good brother. After her marriage, a good husband is even more important than a good father-in-law; a good son is even more important than a good husband; and a good grandson is even more important than a good son. For this reason women often enjoy comfort in their youth but find their old age difficult to endure. It would be well for their relatives to keep this in mind.

It Is Difficult for Widows to Entrust Their Financial Affairs to Others

Some wives with stupid husbands are able to manage the family's finances, calculating the outlays and receipts of money and grain, without being cheated by anyone. Of those with degenerate husbands, there are also some who are able to manage the finances with the help of their sons without ending in bankruptcy. Even among those whose husbands have died and whose sons are young, there are occasionally women able to raise and educate their sons, keep the affection of all their relatives, manage the family business, and even prosper. All of these are wise and worthy women. But the most remarkable are the women who manage a household after their husbands have died leaving them with young children. Such women could entrust their finances to their husbands' kinsmen or their own kinsmen, but not all relatives are honorable, and the honorable ones are not necessarily willing to look after other people's business.

When wives themselves can read and do arithmetic, and those they entrust with their affairs have some sense of fairness and duty with regard to food, clothing, and support, then things will usually work out all right. But in most of the rest of the cases, bankruptcy is what happens.

Beware of Future Difficulties in Taking in Female Relatives

You should take into your own house old aunts, sisters, or other female relatives whose children and grandchildren are unfilial and do not support them. However, take precautions. After a woman dies, her unfilial sons or grandsons might make outrageous accusations to the authorities, claiming that the woman died from hunger or cold or left valuables in trunks. When the authorities receive such complaints, they have to investigate and trouble is unavoidable. Thus, while the woman is alive, make it clear to the public and to the government that the woman is bringing nothing with her but herself. Generally, in performing charitable acts, it is best to make certain that they will entail no subsequent difficulties.

Before Buying a Servant Girl or Concubine, Make Sure of the Legality

When buying a female servant or concubine, inquire whether it is legal for her to be indentured or sold before closing the deal. If the girl is impoverished and has no one to rely on, then she should be brought before the authorities to give an account of her past. After guarantors have been secured and an investigation conducted, the transaction can be completed. But if she is not able to give an account of her past, then the agent who offered her for sale should be questioned. Temporarily she may be hired on a salaried basis. If she is ever recognized by her relatives, she should be returned to them.

Hired Women Should Be Sent Back When Their Period of Service Is Over

If you hire a man's wife or daughter as a servant, you should return her to her husband or father on completion of her period of service. If she comes from another district, you should send her back to it after her term is over. These practices are the most humane and are widely carried out by the gentry in the Southeast. Yet there are people who do not return their hired women to their husbands but wed them to others instead; others do not return them to their parents but marry them off themselves. Such actions are the source of many lawsuits.

How can one not have sympathy for those separated from their relatives, removed from their hometowns, who stay in service for their entire lives with neither husbands nor sons? Even in death these women's spirits are left to wander all alone. How pitiful they are!

Voices of Women

What are traditionally regarded as the first poems by women in China are all anonymous, the many untitled pieces in the sixth century B.C.E. classic, the *Book of Songs,* that speak of women's lives or in their voices. Whether they were actually composed by women is unknown, and the authorship of most of the likely poetic compositions by women over the course of the next millennium is similarly uncertain. A handful of poems has been attributed to historically prominent figures, but the most substantial plausible body of writing by women until well into the eighth century is ascribed to unknown singers and courtesans of indeterminate social status.

Most of these works originated in the commercial centers south of the Yangzi River and belong to a genre called "Music Bureau songs," after a Han dynasty office charged with composing court music and collecting popular folk songs. Whether framed in the voice of women or as dialogues between couples, they were probably composed to set tunes, now lost, and were eventually performed by female entertainers at local courts. They speak of desire and love in disarmingly direct and often quite erotic terms, with frequent recourse to wit and puns. Best known among this group is a set of forty-two songs attributed to a famous fourth-century professional singer named Midnight, whose playful and poignant lyrics were said to have been set to profoundly anguished music.

In addition to these short lyrics, most of which are quatrains, a number of anonymous longer narrative Music Bureau songs also focus on the lives and fates of female characters. Both "A Peacock Southeast Flew" and "The Ballad of Mulan" tell stories that have striking resonances with legends in other cultures. Set in southeastern China, the tragic ballad of the faithful spouses suggests how real were the challenges of adhering to protocols prescribed for dutiful daughters-in-law. The heroics of Mulan's story, in contrast, reflect its likely origin in the northern nomadic borderlands.

Here's a Willow Bough: Songs of the Thirteen Months[1]

1. FIRST MONTH OF SPRING[2]

And still the spring wind is gloomy and cold
Out with the old and in with the new

---

1. Translated by Joseph R. Allen. Thanks to a play between the word for "willow" and the verb "to stay" in classical Chinese, a willow branch given as a token to a departing friend was a message to "please stay." These anonymous poems adopt the voice of an upper-class woman.
2. On the lunar calendar, the first month marked the beginning of spring.

Our troubles are more than a morning's worry
    Here's a willow bough
5   Sad thoughts tangle my heart in knots
There's no knowing their number or profusion

2. MIDDLE MONTH OF SPRING

Into the village the crows swing on tireless wings
On the road I meet swallows flying two by two[3]
Look, we are now in the height of spring
10   Here's a willow bough
To send a message to the one I love
Come back soon, stay away no longer

3. LAST MONTH OF SPRING

As the boat floats through the curved pool
We lift our eyes to the spring flowers
15   The cry of the nightjar threads the woods[4]
        Here's a willow bough
They come two by two, fluttering here and there
My love and I shall have each other

4. FIRST MONTH OF SUMMER

When the lotus is just coming to bud[5]
20   Where would I find a kindred soul to love
To share our lives in the Buddha's presence
        Here's a willow bough
Offering incense and these fine flowers
We shall have each other, each other forever

5. MIDDLE MONTH OF SUMMER

25   Wild rice standing three or four feet high
For whom will this pure body be a jewel?
Lovely it is in full growth
        Here's a willow bough
With it I'll make sweet buns[6]
30   Intending them for my love's own hand

---

3. Harbingers of spring and a cliché for lovers.
4. According to legend, the ancient ruler Du Yu was infatuated with the wife of a court official; he died of lovesickness and was transformed into the nightjar, sometimes translated as "cuckoo." In some versions of the story the bird spits blood while emitting its cry, coloring red azaleas, which are thus known as "nightjar flowers."
5. An erotic symbol for a beautiful woman, the lotus was also associated with Buddhism's ability to bring forth purity from defilement.
6. These "nine-seed" (or nine son) buns are meant to suggest fertility.

6. LAST MONTH OF SUMMER

Midsummer burns like fire
The lattice is open on the north window
I sit on a couch across from my man
    Here's a willow bough
35   Cool hydromel stored in a bronze jar[7]
We drink it straight and undiluted

7. FIRST MONTH OF AUTUMN

The Weaving Girl wanders beside her river
On the other side the Herd Boy watches and sighs[8]
Meeting only once with each turn of the year
40   Here's a willow bough
Knotting together the flowers of long life
Kindred souls will not fail each other

8. MIDDLE MONTH OF AUTUMN

I make clothes to welcome my love
Days and nights flow on like water
45   Sparkling dew freezes into courtyard frost
    Here's a willow bough
At night hearing the washing blocks pound
Whose wife is this lovely lady?

9. LAST MONTH OF AUTUMN

Sweet mums burst into yellow flower[9]
50   It's not that we have no cups for wine
Ah, but what about the cold
    Here's a willow bough
I give my love these silken clothes
He says no, but with a smile

10. FIRST MONTH OF WINTER

55   The great trees turn lonely and stark
The sky is dark but the rain does not come
A heavy frost builds in the middle of the night

7. A drink made of fermented honey.
8. The Weaving Girl and Herd Boy were legendary ill-fated lovers who were transformed into stars separated by the Milky Way, known in Chinese as the Silver River. They were allowed to meet once a year, on the seventh day of the seventh month, when magpies formed a bridge over the river.
9. Because chrysanthemums bloom late in the year they were a traditional symbol of longevity; steeped in wine they were a tonic to ensure a healthy old age.

Here's a willow bough
In the woods with pine and cypress[1]
60 The year grows cold; we shall not fail each other

11. MIDDLE MONTH OF WINTER

Again the snow is in wind-blown drifts
The branches of the tree turn barren
But pine and cypress have no need to worry
     Here's a willow bough
65 Bundled in winter clothes, I tread on thin ice
Will my love recognize me like this?

12. LAST MONTH OF WINTER

The sky is cold, the year about to close
Spring and fall, winter and summer too
Let's put these troubles to rest
70   Here's a willow bough
Sunk between pillow and mat
Sweetly entangled, time passes us by

13. INTERCALARY MONTH[2]

The intercalary comes in the heat and the cold
Spring and fall rounded out by a lesser month
75 But there's no time that I don't think of you
     Here's a willow bough
The flux of *yin* and *yang* presses me to leave
How will I ever get a steady one to care for me?

Midnight Songs[1]

1

The sun sinks low. I
go to my front gate,
and look long, and see
you passing by.

Seductive face,
so many charms,
such hair!

---

1. According to Confucius, "Only when the season turns cold do we note that the pine and cypress are the last to lose their leaves" (*Analects* 9.28).
2. A 13th, or intercalary, month was inserted seven times in every 19 years to align the lunar and solar calendars.

1. Translated by Jeanne Larsen. Most likely the work of many female entertainers writing lyrics to the same plaintive melody in the late 4th century, these are attributed to one well-known singer named Midnight.

—and sweet perfume
that spills
in from the road.

2

My perfume?
No more
than incense leaves.
Seductive face?
You really think I'd dare?

But heaven doesn't rob us
of desires:
that's why it's sent me
here, why I've
seen you.

3

Night after night, I do not
comb my hair. Silky
tangles hang
across my shoulders.

I stretch my limbs
around that young man's
hips. Is there any
place on him
I could not
love?

7

When I started wanting
to know that man,
I hoped our coupled hearts
would be like one.

Silk thoughts threaded[2]
on a broken loom—
who'd have known
the tangled snarls to come?

9

So soon. Today, love, we
part. And our re-
union—when
will that time come?

2. In some of the several puns throughout this series, the word "silk" resembles the word for "thoughts [of love]," and "mate" resembles "length of cloth."

A bright lamp
shines on an empty place,
in sorrow and longing:
not yet, not yet, not
yet.

12

Through the front gate,
my morning thoughts
take off; from river-
isles out back,
at twilight, they return.

Talk and
laughter—who
shall I share them with?
Deep in my belly, dark and
damp, I think of you.

16

Seize the moment!—
while you're still young.
Miss your chance—
one day, and you've grown old.

If you don't
believe my words, just look
out at those grasses
underneath the frost.

28

Night so
long. Can't get
to sleep. Turn
on my side, and hear
the nightwatch drum.

No reason for it, love,
and yet we met:
it leaves a bitter taste
down in my guts.

33

Night so
long. Can't get
to sleep. Bright
moon blazes into bloom.

In thought, I hear
a call from a windblown
voice. And to the empty
sky, make hollow answer,
yes.

42

Morning's sun
shines through windows draped
in brocade sewn
with coins. Light
breezes move those pure
white silks.

An artful smile: a pair
of lush, curved, crimson
horns.
Lovely eyes: soft
moth-brows fall
and rise.

A Peacock Southeast Flew[1]
Preface

At the close of the Han Dynasty, during the years of 196–220 C.E., the wife of Chiao Chung-ch'ing, the magistrate of Luchiang prefecture, whose maiden name was Liu, was dismissed from home by her husband's mother. She swore to herself that she would never remarry, but her own parents and family brought a great deal of pressure to bear on her. So she committed suicide by drowning herself. When her husband, Chung-ch'ing, learned of this, he also committed suicide by hanging himself from a tree in the garden. A contemporary poet felt deep sympathy for these two and composed a poem about them. It goes as follows:

A peacock southeast flew,[2]
After five leagues it faltered.

"At thirteen I could weave white silk,
At fourteen I learned to make clothes.
5   At fifteen I played the many-stringed lute,
At sixteen recited *Odes* and *History*.[3]
At seventeen I became your wife
And my heart was full of constant pain and sorrow.

"You became a government clerk,
10 I kept chaste, my love never straying.

---

1. Translated by Anne Birrell. This ballad, unusual in the tradition for its length, probably dates from the 5th century, with a preface composed at a later date.
2. The image of a bird's becoming separated from its mate or flock was a popular opening for folk songs.
3. Two of the Confucian classics, the *Book of Songs* and the *Book of Documents*.

At cockcrow I went in to weave at the loom,
Night after night found no rest.
In three days I cut five lengths of cloth,
Mother-in-law still nagged at my sloth.
15   It wasn't my weaving that was too slow,
But it's hard to be a wife in your home.
I don't want to be driven out,
But there's no way I can stay on here.
So please speak with your mother
20   To let me be sent home in good time."

The clerk heard these words
And up in the hall spoke with his mother.
"As a boy my physiognomy chart was unlucky,
I was fortunate to get such a wife as she.
25   We bound our hair,[4] shared pillow and mat,
Vowed to be lovers till Yellow Springs.[5]
We both have served you two years or three,
From the start not so long a time,
Yet the girl's conduct is not remiss,
30   Why do you treat her so unkindly?"

His mother said to the clerk,
"How can you be so soft!
This wife has no sense of decorum,
Whatever she does she goes her own way.
35   I've borne my anger for a long time now,
You must not just suit yourself!
Our east neighbors have a good daughter,
Her name is Ch'in Lofu.[6]
So pretty her body, beyond compare,
40   Your mother will seek her for your wife.
It's best to dismiss this one as soon as we can,
Dismiss her, we won't let her stay!"

The government clerk knelt down in reply,
"Now I only have this to say, Mother.
45   If you dismiss this wife today,
For the rest of my life I will not remarry!"
His mother heard these words,
Thumped her bed, then in a fierce rage:
"My son, have you no respect?
50   How dare you speak in your wife's defense!
I have lost all feeling for you,
On no account will I let you disobey me!"

4. Boys and girls bound their hair at puberty, and the phrase came to mean marriage.
5. The land of the dead, beneath the earth.
6. A stock character from other folk songs and a model of female decorum for having resisted the advances of a high official and composing instead a song in praise of her husband.

The government clerk silent, without a word,
Bowed twice and went back within their doors.
55   He started to speak to his new wife,
Stammered, unable to talk.
"I myself would not drive you away,
But there's my mother, scolding and nagging.
You just go home for a little while,
60   Today I must report to the office.
It won't be for long, I'll soon be coming home,
And when I come back I'll be sure to fetch you.
So let this put your mind at rest.
Please don't contradict me!"

65   His new wife said to the clerk:
"No more of this nonsense!
Long ago in early springtime
I left home to come to your gates.
Whatever I did I obeyed your mother,
70   In my behavior never dared do as I pleased.
Day and night I tried hard at my work.
Brought low I am caught in a vice of misery.
My words have been blameless,
I fulfilled my duties diligently.
75   Why then, as I'm being summarily dismissed,
Do you still talk of my coming back here?
I have embroidered tunics,
Gorgeous they shine with a light of their own;
Red silk funnel bedcurtains,
80   At the four corners hang scent sachets;
Dressing cases sixty or seventy,
Green jasper, green silk cord;
Many, many things, each of them different,
All sorts of things in these boxes.
85   I am despised, and my things also worthless,
Not worth offering your next wife,
But I'll leave them here as gifts.
From now on we'll never meet again,
But it will be a constant comfort for me,
90   If you never, never forget me!"

The cock crew, outside it was getting light.
The new wife got up and carefully dressed.
She puts on her broidered lined gown
And four or five different things.
95   On her feet she slips silk shoes;
On her head tortoise-shell combs gleam;
Round her waist she wears flowing silk white,
On her ears wears bright moon pendants.
Her hands are like pared onion stems,
100   Her mouth seems rich scarlet cinnabar.

Svelte, svelte she walks with tiny steps,
Perfect, matchless in all the world.

She went up the high hall, bowed to Mother.
The mother heard she was leaving, didn't stop her.
105   "Long ago when I was a child,
I grew up in the countryside.
I had no schooling from the start,
On both counts would shame the man of a great house.
I received from you, Mother, much money and silk,
110   I do not want to be summarily dismissed;
Today, though, I am going back home.
I am afraid I have brought trouble to your house,"

She withdrew and took leave of her sister-in-law.
Tears fell, beads of pearl.
115   "When I first came as a bride
You were beginning to lean on the bed.
Now as I am being dismissed,
You are as tall as I, sister.
Care for Mother with all your heart,
120   Be nice and help all you can.
On the first, seventh, and last ninth of the month,[7]
When you're enjoying yourself, don't forget me!"

She left the gates, climbed the coach, departed,
Tears fell in more than a hundred streams.
125   The clerk's horse was in front,
The new wife's coach behind.
Clatter-clatter, how it rumbled, rumbled!
They met at the mouth of the main road,
He dismounted, got into her coach.
130   With bowed head he whispered these words in her ear:
"I swear I won't be parted from you,
Just go home for a little while.
Today I am going to the office,
But I'll return before long.
135   I swear by Heaven I'll not betray you!"

His new wife said to the clerk:
"I feel you love me fondly,
And you seem to hold me in high esteem.
Before long I hope you will come for me.
140   You must be rock firm,
I must be a pliant reed.
The pliant reed is supple as silk,
The firm rock will not be rolled away.
I have my father and brothers,

---

7. Women were allowed to rest from their work on the 7th and 29th days of each lunar month.

145 Their temper is wild as thunder;
  I fear they will not abide by my wishes,
  But oppose me, destroy my hopes."
  They raised their hands in a long, long farewell,
  For both loves the same wistful longing.

150 She entered the gates, went up the family hall,
  Approaching, withdrawing with expressionless face.
  Her mother beat her fist loud:
  "We didn't plan for you to return on your own!
  At thirteen I taught you to weave,
155 At fourteen you could make clothes,
  At fifteen you played the many-stringed lute,
  At sixteen you knew ceremonial rites,
  At seventeen I sent you off in marriage,
  Telling you to swear not to give offense.
160 What have you done wrong now that
  Uninvited you come home yourself!"
  "I, Lanchih, have brought shame on my mother,
  But your child has truly done no wrong."
  Her mother's heart was broken with deep sorrow.

165 She had been home more than ten days
  When the district magistrate sent a matchmaker.
  He said, "We have a third young master,
  Charming beyond compare in all the world!
  He is barely eighteen or nineteen,
170 Eloquent, very talented he is!"

  Mother said to daughter:
  "Go, you may answer 'yes.'"
  Her daughter choked back the tears:
  "When I, Lanchih, first came home,
175 The clerk showed me great kindness,
  Swore on oath he'd never desert me.
  If I were now to betray our love,
  I fear this act would be wrong.
  Let's break off the betrothal talks.
180 In good time we'll discuss the matter again."

  Her mother explained to the matchmaker:
  "In all humility, I do have such a daughter,
  She went away in marriage, but is returned to our gates.
  She was reluctant to be an official's wife,
185 How would she please a fine gentleman's son?
  I hope you will be successful with other inquiries.
  We cannot at present give permission."

  The matchmaker was gone many days,
  Then a deputy was sent for, asked to reconsider.
190 "They say they have a daughter, Lanchih,

Whose forefathers for generations have held office.
Say, 'My master says he has a fifth son,
Elegant, refined, not yet married.
My deputy I've sent as matchmaker,
195   And a secretary to bring his message.'"
Immediately they put their case: "The prefect's family
Has such a fine son,
He wishes to take solemn vows of marriage
And so we are sent to your house."

200   The mother refused the matchmaker:
"My daughter has already sworn an oath.
What dare a mother say?"
When her brother learned of this
He was disappointed and furious in his heart.
205   He broached the matter, telling his sister:
"In these arrangements, why are you so unreasonable?
First you married a government clerk,
Later you might marry a squire.
Fortune is like Heaven and Earth,
210   It can bring glory to your person.
Not to wed this lord now,
What will happen in the future?"

Lanchih looked up and replied:
"In fact what my brother says is right.
215   I left home to serve my bridegroom.
Midway I returned to my brother's gates.
It's my place to follow my brother's wishes,
Why would I do as I please?
Though I made a vow with the government clerk,
220   I may never chance to meet him again.
Tell them straight away I agree to marry,
They may arrange a betrothal."

The matchmaker got down from the ritual couch:
"Yes, yes!" and "Quite, quite!"
225   He went back to the office and explained to the prefect:
"Your servant has carried out your command.
Our discussion has met with great success!"
When the prefect heard this
He rejoiced in his heart.
230   He scanned the calendar, opened the almanac:
"It will be auspicious this month,
The Six Cardinal Points[8] are in conjunction.
The luckiest day is the thirtieth,
Today it's now the twenty-seventh,
235   You may go and conclude the nuptials."

8. North, east, south, west, zenith, and nadir.

Discussions on both sides hastened the wedding gifts,
In succession like floating clouds.
A green sparrow and white swan boat,
At the four corners were dragon banners
240   Softly curling in the wind.
A gold coach of jade its wheels,
Prancing piebald horses,
Colored silk threads and gold stitched saddles.
A wedding gift of three million cash,
245   All strung on green cord.
Assorted silks, three hundred bolts,
From Chiaokuang[9] a purchase of fine fish.
A retinue of four or five hundred men
Densely massed set out to the palace.

250   Mother said to daughter:
"I have just received a letter from the prefect,
Tomorrow he will come to invite you in marriage.
Why aren't you making your clothes?
Don't fail to start now!"
255   Her daughter, silent, without a word,
Sobbed with her kerchief stifling her mouth.
Tears fell as if poured.
She moved her seat of lapis lazuli,
Set it near the window.
260   Her left hand held shears and rule,
Her right hand took the sheer silk.
By morning she finished an embroidered robe,
Later she finished an unlined dress of silk.
Dim, dim, the sun was about to darken,
265   With sad thoughts she left the gates and wept.

When the government clerk heard of this affair
He asked for furlough to go home a while.
Before he had come two or three leagues
His wearisome horse sadly whinnied.
270   His new wife recognized his horse's whinny,
Slipped on her shoes and met him.
Sadly from a distance they gazed at each other,
She knew it was her long lost one coming.
She raised her hand, patted his horse's saddle,
275   Her loud sighs tore his heart.

"Since you parted from me
Unimaginable things have happened!
Things have turned out not as we once wished,
Nor could I make you understand.
280   I have had my parents—father and mother,

---

9. On the far southern seacoast.

Bringing pressure to bear joined by my brother,
To make me consent to marry another man.
You have come back, what do you hope for?"

The government clerk said to his new wife:
285 "Congratulations for winning such high promotion!
The firm rock square and strong
Could have endured a thousand years.
The pliant reed, once so supple,
Is reduced to this in the space of dawn to dusk!
290 You may reign supreme like the sun,
I will face Yellow Springs alone."

His new wife said to the government clerk:
"What do you mean by such words?
Together we have suffered this great crisis,
295 First you, and then your wife.
Down in Yellow Springs we will meet,
Don't betray our vow made this day!"
They held hands, then went their separate ways,
Each returning to their different gates.
300 For the living to make a parting unto death
Is more hateful than words can tell.
They think of their farewell from this world,
Never in a million years to be brought back to life.

The government clerk went back home,
305 Up in the hall he bowed to his mother:
"Today the great wind is cold,
Cold winds have crushed a tree,
Harsh frosts grip the garden orchid.
Your son today goes to darkness,
310 Leaving Mother to survive alone.
For I must carry out a most unhappy plan;
Torment our souls no more!
May your life be like South Mountain's rock,[1]
Your four limbs healthy and strong!"

315 When his mother heard these words
Teardrops fell with each word:
"You are the son of a great family,
With official position at galleried courts.
Don't die for the sake of that wife!
320 About noble and base are you so naive?
Our east neighbor has a good daughter,
Meek and mild, the loveliest in town.
Your mother will seek her for your wife,
All will be arranged between dawn and dusk."

---

1. A traditional symbol of longevity, the mountain was located south of the Han dynasty capital of Chang'an.

325   The government clerk bowed twice and went back
        Sighing long sighs in his empty rooms.
        The plan he made was fixed as ever.
        He turned his head toward the door,
        Slowly he watched, grief's oppressive rage.

330   That day horses and cattle lowed,
        His new wife goes into her green hut.
        After dusk had fallen
        A quiet hush, people start to settle down.
        "My life will end today,
335   My soul will vanish, my corpse will linger a while."
        She lifts her skirt, removes her silk shoes,
        Stands up and goes toward the clear lake.

        When the government clerk hears of this act,
        His heart knows it is the long separation.
340   He hesitates under a garden tree,
        Hangs himself from a southeast branch.

        The two families asked for a joint burial,
        A joint burial on the side of Mount Hua.[2]
        East and west were planted pine and cypress,
345   Left and right catalpa were set.
        Branch with branch joins to form a canopy,
        Leaf with leaf meets in wedlock.
        Among them is a pair of flying birds,
        Called mandarin ducks, drake and hen,
350   Lifting their heads they call to each other,
        Night after night until the fifth watch.[3]
        Passersby stay their steps to listen,
        Widows get out of bed and pace to and fro.
        Be warned, men of the future,
355   Learn this lesson and never forget!

The Ballad of Mulan[1]

        Click, click, forever click, click;
        Mulan sits at the door and weaves.
        Listen, and you will not hear the shuttle's sound,
        But only hear a girl's sobs and sighs.
5   "Oh tell me, lady, are you thinking of your love,
        Oh tell me, lady, are you longing for your dear?"
        "Oh no, oh no, I am not thinking of my love,
        Oh no, oh no, I am not longing for my dear.
        But last night I read the battle-roll;
10   The Khan has ordered a great levy of men.
        The battle-roll was written in twelve books,

2. One of five sacred mountains.   1. Translated by Arthur Waley.
3. Just before dawn, between 3 and 5 A.M.

And in each book stood my father's name.
My father's sons are not grown men,
And of all of my brothers, none is older than me.
15   Oh let me to the market to buy saddle and horse,
And ride with the soldiers to take my father's place."
In the eastern market she's bought a gallant horse,
In the western market she's bought saddle and cloth.
In the southern market she's bought snaffle and reins,
20   In the northern market she's bought a tall whip.
In the morning she stole from her father's and mother's house;
At night she was camping by the Yellow River's side.
She could not hear her father and mother calling to her by her name,
But only the song of the Yellow River as its hurrying waters hissed and
        swirled through the night.
25   At dawn they left the River and went on their way;
At dusk they came to the Black Water's side.
She could not hear her father and mother calling to her by her name,
She could only hear the muffled voices of Scythian horsemen riding on the
        hills of Yen.
A thousand leagues she tramped on the errands of war,
30   Frontiers and hills she crossed like a bird in flight.
Through the northern air echoed the watchman's tap;
The wintry light gleamed on coats of mail.
The captain had fought a hundred fights, and died;
The warriors in ten years had won their rest.
35   They went home; they saw the Emperor's face;
The Son of Heaven was seated in the Hall of Light.
To the strong in battle lordships and lands he gave;
And of prize money a hundred thousand strings.
Then spoke the Khan and asked her what she would take.
40   "Oh, Mulan asks not to be made
        A Counsellor at the Khan's court;
She only begs for a camel that can march
        A thousand leagues a day,
        To take her back to her home."

45   When her father and mother heard that she had come,
They went out to the wall and led her back to the house.
When her little sister heard that she had come,
She went to the door and rouged her face afresh.
When her little brother heard that his sister had come,
50   He sharpened his knife and darted like a flash
Toward the pigs and sheep.

She opened the gate that leads to the eastern tower,
She sat on her bed that stood in the western tower.
She cast aside her heavy soldier's cloak,
55   And wore again her old-time dress.
She stood at the window and bound her cloudy hair;

She went to the mirror and fastened her yellow combs.
She left the house and met her messmates in the road;
Her messmates were startled out of their wits.
60   They had marched with her for twelve years of war
And never known that Mulan was a girl.
For the male hare has a lilting, lolloping gait,
And the female hare has a wild and roving eye;
But set them both scampering side by side,
65   And who so wise could tell you "This is he"?

—◦—⟨◦⟩—◦—

Yuan Zhen
779–831

Born into a family that had ruled northern China during the fifth and sixth centuries but had subsequently fallen on hard times, Yuan Zhen passed a series of highly selective civil service examinations that, in 806, yielded him an appointment at court. Charged with offering proposals for policy reforms to the emperor, he took his responsibility seriously enough to be banished almost immediately from the capital. When he was appointed to another provincial post three years later, his critique of local corruption resulted in a second, ten-year removal from office. Although he eventually secured another position in 822 and continued to hold high offices until his death, his career as a government bureaucrat intent on effecting political reform was frustrating at best. As a writer, however, he enjoyed greater success. With his lifelong friend Bo Juyi (772–846), Yuan Zhen spearheaded a movement to revive and imitate older folk songs. Their hope was both to liberate poetry from prosodic regulations that had come to shackle most poets and to reinstill it with the mission, ascribed to the canonical *Book of Songs,* of social and political critique and change. He wrote prolifically and was the first editor of his own collected works and those of his friend Bo Juyi.

"The Story of Ying-ying" circulated at the capital around the time when Yuan Zhen was preparing for his last examination in 804; it may in fact have served as a "warming scroll" that candidates distributed informally in hopes of impressing prospective employers or patrons with their literary talents. It is the best-known example of the classical tale (*chuanqi,* literally "transmitted marvel"), a narrative genre that flourished during the Tang dynasty (618–907) and typically claims to recount, in terse classical language, an actual event that may contain supernatural elements. The story presented in "Ying-ying"—that of an aspiring scholar's seduction and abandonment of his distant cousin—is probably also the most famous love story in the Chinese literary tradition; it inspired over seventy later retellings in other genres, many of which, however, altered the story line considerably. From the twelfth century on, "Ying-ying" has been read as thinly veiled autobiography, and a number of correspondences between Yuan Zhen's own life and details of the story support such a view. What continues to perplex modern readers, however, are the conclusions to be drawn from the tale, owing to the tension between the student's behavior and the narrator's apparently unqualified approval of it. Is it meant to be self-critical or self-justifying, ironic or righteous? Is Ying-ying an innocent victim or just another demonic female whose potential for disorder is compounded by her ability to write?

The Story of Ying-ying[1]

During the Cheng-yüan period [785–805] of the T'ang dynasty there lived a man called Chang. His nature was gentle and refined, and his person of great beauty. But his deeper feelings were absolutely held in restraint, and he would indulge in no license. Sometimes his friends took him to a party and he would try to join in their frolics; but when the rest were shouting and scuffling their hardest, Chang only pretended to take his share. For he could never overcome his shyness. So it came about that though already twenty-three, he had not yet enjoyed a woman's beauty. To those who questioned him he answered, "It is not such as Master Teng-t'u who are true lovers of beauty, for they are merely profligates. I consider myself a lover of beauty, who happens never to have met with it. And I am of this opinion because I know that, in other things, whatever is beautiful casts its spell upon me; so that I cannot be devoid of feeling." His questioners only laughed.

About this time Chang went to Puchow. Some two miles east of the town there is a temple called the P'u-chiu-ssu, and here he took up his lodging. Now it happened that at this time the widow of a certain Ts'ui was returning to Ch'ang-an. She passed through Puchow on the way and stayed at the same temple.

This lady was born of the Cheng family and Chang's mother was also a Cheng. He unravelled their relationship and found that they were second-cousins.

This year General Hun Chan died at Puchow. There was a certain Colonel Ting Wen-ya who ill-treated his troops. The soldiers accordingly made Hun Chan's funeral the occasion of a mutiny, and began to plunder the town. The Ts'ui family had brought with them much valuable property and many slaves. Subjected to this sudden danger when far from home, they had no one from whom they could seek protection.

Now it happened that Chang had been friendly with the political party to which the commander at Puchow belonged. At his request a guard was sent to the temple and no disorder took place there. A few days afterwards the Civil Commissioner Tu Chio was ordered by the emperor to take over the command of the troops. The mutineers then laid down their arms.

The widow Cheng was very sensible of the service which Chang had rendered. She therefore provided dainties and invited him to a banquet in the middle hall. At table she turned to him and said, "I, your cousin, a lonely and widowed relict, had young ones in my care. If we had fallen into the hands of the soldiery, I could not have helped them. Therefore the lives of my little boy and young daughter were saved by your protection, and they owe you eternal gratitude. I will now cause them to kneel before you, their merciful cousin, that they may thank you for your favours." First she sent for her son, Huan-lang, who was about ten years old, a handsome and gentle child. Then she called to her daughter, Ying-ying: "Come and bow to your cousin. Your cousin saved your life." For a long while she would not come, saying that she was not well. The widow grew angry and cried, "Your cousin saved your life. But for his help, you would now be a prisoner. How can you treat him so rudely?"

At last the girl came in, dressed in everyday clothes, with a look of deep unhappiness on her face. She had not put on any ornaments. Her hair hung down in coils, the black of her two eyebrows joined, her cheeks were not rouged. But her features were of exquisite beauty and shone with an almost dazzling lustre.

1. Translated by Arthur Waley.

Chang bowed to her, amazed. She sat down by her mother's side and looked all the time towards her, turning from him with a fixed stare of aversion, as though she could not endure his presence.

He asked how old she was. The widow answered, "She was born in the year of the present emperor's reign that was a year of the Rat, and now it is the year of the Dragon in the period Cheng-yüan [800]. So she must be seventeen years old."

Chang tried to engage her in conversation, but she would not answer, and soon the dinner was over. He was passionately in love with her and wanted to tell her so, but could find no way.

Ying-ying had a maid-servant called Hung-niang, whom Chang sometimes met and greeted. Once he stopped her and was beginning to tell her of his love for her mistress, but she was frightened and ran away. Then Chang was sorry he had not kept silence.

Next day he met Hung-niang again, but was embarrassed and did not say what was in his mind. But this time the maid herself broached the subject and said to Chang, "Master, I dare not tell her what you told me, or even hint at it. But since your mother was a kinswoman of the Ts'ui, why do you not seek my mistress's hand on that plea?"

Chang said, "Since I was a child in arms, my nature has been averse to intimacy. Sometimes I have idled with wearers of silk and gauze, but my fancy was never once detained. I little thought that in the end I should be entrapped.

"Lately at the banquet I could scarcely contain myself; and since then, when I walk, I forget where I am going and when I eat, I forget to finish my meal, and do not know how to endure the hours from dawn to dusk.

"If we were to get married through a matchmaker and perform the ceremonies of Sending Presents and Asking Names, it would take many months, and by that time you would have to look for me 'in the dried-fish shop.' What is the use of giving me such advice as that?"

The maid replied, "My mistress clings steadfastly to her chastity, and even an equal could not trip her with lewd talk. Much less may she be won through the stratagems of a maid-servant. But she is skilled in composition, and often when she has made a poem or essay, she is restless and dissatisfied for a long while after. You must try to provoke her with a love-poem. There is no other way."

Chang was delighted and at once composed two Spring Poems to send her. Hung-niang took them away and came back the same evening with a coloured tablet, which she gave to Chang, saying, "This is from my mistress." It bore the title "The Bright Moon of the Fifteenth Night." The words ran:

> To wait for the moon I am sitting in the western parlour;
> To greet the wind, I have left the door ajar.
> When a flower's shadow stirred and brushed the wall,
> For a moment I thought it the shadow of a lover coming.

Chang could not doubt her meaning. That night was the fourth after the first decade of the second month. Beside the eastern wall of Ying-ying's apartments there grew an apricot-tree; by climbing it one could cross the wall. On the next night (which was the night of the full moon) Chang used the tree as a ladder and crossed the wall. He went straight to the western parlour and found the door ajar. Hung-niang lay asleep on the bed. He woke her, and she cried in a voice of astonishment, "Master Chang, what are you doing here?" Chang answered, half-truly: "Your mistress's letter invited me. Tell her I have come." Hung-niang soon returned, whispering, "She is coming, she is coming." Chang was both delighted and surprised, thinking that his salvation was indeed at hand.

At last Ying-ying entered.

Her dress was sober and correct, and her face was stern. She at once began to reprimand Chang, saying, "I am grateful for the service which you rendered to my family. You gave support to my dear mother when she was at a loss how to save her little boy and young daughter. How came you then to send me a wicked message by the hand of a low maid-servant? In protecting me from the license of others, you acted nobly. But now that you wish to make me a partner to your own licentious desires, you are asking me to accept one wrong in exchange for another.

"How was I to repel this advance? I would gladly have hidden your letter, but it would have been immoral to harbour a record of illicit proposals. Had I shown it to my mother, I should ill have requited the debt we owe you. Were I to entrust a message of refusal to a servant or concubine, I feared it might not be truly delivered. I thought of writing a letter to tell you what I felt; but I was afraid I might not be able to make you understand. So I sent those trivial verses, that I might be sure of your coming. I have no cause to be ashamed of an irregularity which had no other object but the preservation of my chastity."

With these words she vanished. Chang remained for a long while petrified with astonishment. At last he climbed back over the wall and went home in despair.

Several nights after this he was lying asleep near the verandah, when someone suddenly woke him. He rose with a startled sigh and found that Hung-niang was there, with bed-clothes under her arm and a pillow in her hand. She shook Chang, saying, "She is coming, she is coming. Why are you asleep?" Then she arranged the bedclothes and pillow and went away.

Chang sat up and rubbed his eyes. For a long while he thought he must be dreaming. But he assumed a respectful attitude and waited.

Suddenly Hung-niang came back, bringing her mistress with her. Ying-ying, this time, was languid and flushed, yielding and wanton in her air, as though her strength could scarcely support her limbs. Her former severity had utterly disappeared.

That night was the eighth of the second decade. The crystal beams of the sinking moon twinkled secretly across their bed. Chang, in a strange exaltation, half-believed that a fairy had come to him, and not a child of mortal men.

At last the temple bell sounded, dawn glimmered in the sky and Hung-niang came back to fetch her mistress away. Ying-ying turned on her side with a pretty cry, and followed her maid to the door.

The whole night she had not spoken a word.

Chang rose when it was half-dark, still thinking that perhaps it had been a dream. But when it grew light, he saw her powder on his arm and smelt her perfume in his clothes. A tear she had shed still glittered on the mattress.

For more than ten days afterwards he did not see her again. During this time he began to make a poem called "Meeting a Fairy," in thirty couplets. It was not yet finished, when he chanced to meet Hung-niang in the road. He asked her to take the poem to Ying-ying.

After this Ying-ying let him come to her, and for a month or more he crept out at dawn and in at dusk, the two of them living together in that western parlour of which I spoke before.

Chang often asked her what her mother thought of him. Ying-ying said, "I know she would not oppose my will. So why should we not get married at once?"

Soon afterwards, Chang had to go to the capital. Before starting he tenderly informed her of his departure. She did not reproach him, but her face showed pitiable distress. On the night before he started, he was not able to see her.

After spending a few months in the west, Chang returned to Puchow and again lodged for several months in the same building as the Ts'ui family. He made many attempts to see Ying-ying alone, but she would not let him do so. Remembering that she was fond of calligraphy and verse, he frequently sent her his own compositions, but she scarcely glanced at them.

It was characteristic of her that when any situation was at its acutest point, she appeared quite unconscious of it. She talked glibly, but would seldom answer a question. She expected absolute devotion, but herself gave no encouragement.

Sometimes when she was in the depth of despair, she would affect all the while to be quite indifferent. It was rarely possible to know from her face whether she was pleased or sorry.

One night Chang came upon her unawares when she was playing on the zither, with a touch full of passion. But when she saw him coming, she stopped playing. This incident increased his infatuation.

Soon afterwards, it became time for him to compete in the Literary Examinations, and he was obliged once more to set out for the western capital.

The evening before his departure, he sat in deep despondency by Ying-ying's side, but did not try again to tell her of his love. Nor had he told her that he was going away, but she seemed to have guessed it, and with submissive face and gentle voice she said to him softly, "Those whom a man leads astray, he will in the end abandon. It must be so, and I will not reproach you. You deigned to corrupt me and now you deign to leave me. That is all. And your vows of 'faithfulness till death'—they too are cancelled. There is no need for you to grieve at this parting, but since I see you so sad and can give you no other comfort—you once praised my zither-playing; but I was bashful and would not play to you. Now I am bolder, and if you choose, I will play you a tune."

She took her harp and began the prelude to "Rainbow Skirts and Feather Jackets." But after a few bars the tune broke off into a wild and passionate dirge.

All who were present caught their breath; but in a moment she stopped playing, threw down her harp and, weeping bitterly, ran to her mother's room.

She did not come back.

Next morning Chang left. The following year he failed in his examinations and could not leave the capital. So, to unburden his heart, he wrote a letter to Ying-ying. She answered him somewhat in this fashion:

> I have read your letter and cherish it dearly. It has filled my heart half with sorrow, half with joy. You sent with it a box of garlands and five sticks of paste, that I may decorate my head and colour my lips.
>
> I thank you for your presents; but there is no one now to care how I look. Seeing these things only makes me think of you and grieve the more.
>
> You say that you are prospering in your career at the capital, and I am comforted by that news. But it makes me fear you will never come back again to one who is so distant and humble. But *that* is settled forever, and it is no use talking of it.
>
> Since last autumn I have lived in a dazed stupor. Amid the clamour of the daytime, I have sometimes forced myself to laugh and talk; but alone at night I have done nothing but weep. Or, if I have fallen asleep my dreams have always been full of the sorrows of parting.

Often I dreamt that you came to me as you used to do, but always before the moment of our joy your phantom vanished from my side. Yet, though we are still bedfellows in my dreams, when I wake and think of it the time when we were together seems very far off. For since we parted, the old year has slipped away and a new year has begun. . . .

Ch'ang-an is a city of pleasure, where there are many snares to catch a young man's heart. How can I hope that you will not forget one so sequestered and insignificant as I? And indeed, if you were to be faithful, so worthless a creature could never requite you. But our vows of unending love—those *I* at least can fulfil.

Because you are my cousin, I met you at the feast. Lured by a maid-servant, I visited you in private. A girl's heart is not in her own keeping. You "tempted me by your ballads" and I could not bring myself to "throw the shuttle" to repulse you.[2]

Then came the sharing of pillow and mat, the time of perfect loyalty and deepest tenderness. And I, being young and foolish, thought it would never end.

Now, having "seen my Prince," I cannot love again; nor, branded by the shame of self-surrender, am I fit to perform the "service of towel and comb," to become your wife; and of the bitterness of the long celibacy which awaits me, what need is there to speak?

The good man uses his heart; and if by chance his gaze has fallen on the humble and insignificant, till the day of his death he continues the affections of his life. The cynic cares nothing for people's feelings. He will discard the small to follow the great, look upon a former mistress merely as an accomplice in sin, and hold that the most solemn vows are made only to be broken. He will reverse all natural laws—as though Nature should suddenly let bone dissolve, while cinnabar resisted the fire. The dew that the wind has shaken from the tree still looks for kindness from the dust; and such, too, is the sum of *my* hopes and fears.

As I write, I am shaken by sobs and cannot tell you all that is in my heart. My darling, I am sending you a jade ring that I used to play with when I was a child. I want you to wear it at your girdle, that you may become firm and flawless as this jade, and, in your affections, unbroken as the circuit of this ring.

And with it I am sending a skein of thread and a tea-trough of flecked bamboo. There is no value in these few things. I send them only to remind you to keep your heart pure as jade and your affection unending as this round ring. The bamboo is mottled as if with tears, and the thread is tangled as the thoughts of those who are in sorrow. By these tokens I seek no more than that, knowing the truth, you may think kindly of me for ever.

Our hearts are very near, but our bodies are far apart. There is no time fixed for our meeting; yet a secret longing can unite souls that are separated by a thousand miles.

Protect yourself against the cold spring wind, eat well—look after yourself in all ways and do not worry too much about your worthless handmaid,

TS'UI YING-YING

Chang showed this letter to his friends and so the story became known to many who lived at that time. All who heard it were deeply moved; but Chang, to their disappointment, declared that he meant to break with Ying-ying. Yüan Chen, of Honan, who knew Chang well, asked him why he had made this decision.

Chang answered: "I have observed that in Nature whatever has perfect beauty is either itself liable to sudden transformations or else is the cause of them in others. If Ying-ying were to marry a rich gentleman and become his pet, she would forever be changing, as the clouds change to rain, or as the scaly dragon turns into the horned dragon. I, for one, could never keep pace with her transformations.

---

2. The poet Sima Xiangru succeeded in stirring his lover by playing his harp, whereas the object of Xie Kun's affections rebuffed his advances by throwing the shuttle of her loom at him.

"Of old, Hsin of the Yin dynasty and Yu of the Chou dynasty ruled over kingdoms of many thousand chariots, and their strength was very great. Yet a single woman brought each to ruin, dissipating their hosts and leading these monarchs to the assassin's knife, so that to this day they are a laughingstock to all the world. I know that my constancy could not withstand such spells, and that is why I have curbed my passion."

At these words all who were present sighed deeply.

A few years afterwards Ying-ying married someone else and Chang also found a wife. Happening once to pass the house where Ying-ying was living, he called on her husband and asked to see her, saying he was her cousin. The husband sent for her, but she would not come. Chang's vexation showed itself in his face. Someone told Ying-ying of this and she secretly wrote the poem:

> Since I have grown so lean, my face has lost its beauty.
> I have tossed and turned so many times that I am too tired to leave my bed.
> It is not that I mind the others seeing
> How ugly I have grown;
> It is *you* who have caused me to lose my beauty,
> Yet it is *you* I am ashamed should see me!

Chang went away without meeting her, and a few days afterwards, when he was leaving the town, wrote a poem of final farewell, which said:

> You cannot say that you are abandoned and deserted;
> For you have found someone to love you.
> Why do you not convert your broodings over the past
> Into kindness to your present husband?

After that they never heard of one another again. Many of Chang's contemporaries praised the skill with which he extricated himself from this entanglement.

⁓⁓⁓

RESONANCE

Wang Shifu: from The Story of the Western Wing[1]

[*Clown, costumed as a bald one, enters and speaks:*] I, Dharma Wit, am a disciple of the abbot, Dharma Source, of this Monastery of Universal Salvation. Today my teacher has gone out to a vegetarian meal and has made me stay here in the monastery. I am supposed to take note of anyone who comes looking for him and then report to my teacher as soon as he comes home, so I am standing in front of the temple gate to see if anyone will come by. [*Male lead enters and speaks:*] Well, I'm here already. [*He meets clown. Clown asks him:*] Where are you from traveler? [*Male lead*

---

1. Translated by Stephen H. West and Wilt L. Idema. One of the many reworkings of the story of Ying-ying, this play adopts an earlier significant revision of the original story that changed the ending of the story to allow for the happy marriage of Ying-ying ("female lead") with the Student Zhang. In addition, the dramatic version substantially enlarges the role of Ying-ying's maid Hongniang (Crimson) as both ingenious agent of the action and witty commentator on it.

About the playwright little is known, other than that he lived during the second half of the 13th century in Beijing and is credited with over a dozen other plays. *The Story of the Western Wing* was to become the most popular romantic comedy in China. Its rendition of the "scholar meets beauty" theme served as an important vernacular model for many other works, of which the best-known example is the Qing dynasty masterpiece, Cao Xueqin's *The Story of the Stone*. Indeed, its reputed usefulness as a kind of lover's handbook, as can be seen in the excerpt from the novel included in Volume D, conferred upon it considerable notoriety and appeal.

speaks:] Well, I've come from Western Luo. I have heard that your ashram is elegant and secluded, pure and refreshing, and so I have come partly to gaze upon the Buddha image and partly to pay my respects to your abbot. May I ask whether the abbot is here? [*Clown speaks:*] My teacher is not in the monastery. I am his poor disciple Dharma Wit. May I invite you, sir, to our ten-foot-square for some tea? [*Male lead speaks:*] Since the abbot isn't here, there's no need to drink tea. Could I trouble you, my monk, to guide me around the monastery so I may gaze upon its wonders? [*Clown speaks:*] I'll go get the keys and open up the Buddha hall, the bell tower, the pagoda court, the arhat hall, the refectory; and when we have made our tour, my teacher should be back. [*Male lead speaks:*] The architecture is really fine.

[*Student Zhang enters the monastery.*]

STUDENT [*sings*]: Having gladdened my heart by visiting the Buddha hall above,
       Here I am already at the monks' court below.
       We pass close by the west end of the kitchen,
       The north of the dharma hall, the front of the bell tower.
       I've strolled through the grotto cells,
       Climbed the precious pagoda,
       And wound my way along twisting corridors.
       I've finished counting the arhats,
       Paid my respects to the bodhisattvas,
       Made my obeisances to the Holy One—

[*Female lead enters, leading Crimson and twirling a flowering sprig.*]

FEMALE LEAD: Crimson, let's go and play around in the Buddha hall.
MALE LEAD [*acts out seeing her*]: Wow!
STUDENT [*sings*]: And now I run smack into my alluring karmic sentence from five centuries ago!

STUDENT [*sings*]: Stunning knockouts—I've seen a million;
       But a lovely face like this is rarely seen!
       It dazzles a man's eyes, stuns him speechless,
       And makes his soul fly away into the heavens.
       She there, without a thought of teasing, fragrant shoulders bare,
       Simply twirls the flower, smiling.

       This is Tushita Palace,
       Don't guess it to be the heaven of Separation's Regret.
       Ah, who would ever have thought that I would meet a divine sylph?
       I see her spring-breeze face, fit for anger, fit for joy,
       Just suited to those flowered pins pasted with kingfisher feathers.

       See her palace-style eyebrows, curved like crescent moons,
       Invading the borders of her clouds of locks.

FEMALE LEAD: Crimson, look:

       Lonely, lonely monks' chambers where no one goes;
       Filling the steps, padded by moss, the red of fallen flowers.

STUDENT: I'm dying.

STUDENT [*sings*]: Bashful in front of others before she even speaks:
>Cherry fruits split apart their redness,
>Jade grains reveal their whiteness.
>Time passes before she speaks.

"Reprise"
>Just like the warbling sound of an oriole twittering beyond the flowers,
>Each step she takes makes me tingle:
>A waist just made for dancing, lovely and lithe,
>A thousand kinds of alluring charms,
>Myriad kinds of graceful motions,
>Just like a weeping willow before the evening breeze.

* * *

MALE LEAD [*enters and speaks*]: I've just moved into the temple and am living quite close to the western wing. The monks told me that missy burns incense in the flower garden every night. The flower garden is right next to the temple. Before missy comes out I'll hide myself near the Taihu rocks at the corner of the wall. When she appears, I'll get an eyeful of her. All of the monks in the twin corridors are sound asleep, the night is deep, people are still. The moon is bright, the breeze is fresh. Ah, what lovely weather!

[*He recites a poem:*]

>In leisure I seek the abbot's cell for the noble monk's conversation;
>When depressed, I face the western wing to chant under the hoary moon. * * *

FEMALE LEAD [*enters and speaks*]: Crimson, go on up, and when you've opened the corner door, bring the incense table out.

STUDENT [*sings*]: Of a sudden I hear the corner door creak;
>Where the breeze passes, flower's perfume is lightly borne.
>Standing on tiptoe, I fix my eyes carefully:
>Her face is even more chic than when I first saw her.

FEMALE LEAD: Set that incense table down closer to the Taihu rocks.

MALE LEAD [*acts out watching her and speaks, first reciting*]:

>It must be that this springtime beauty is fed up with confinement
>And has flown freely out of her Palace of Spreading Frigidity.

Her whole face still covered with powder, draping gown baring one shoulder, she lets her fragrant sleeves fall without word and trails her river-goddess skirts without talking—she's just like the Consorts of the Xiang Tomb, leaning against the red doors of Shun's temple, or like Chang'e in the Moon Hall, barely visible in the Golden Hall of the Ecliptic Toad. What a fine girl!

STUDENT [*sings*]: I've just seen her lithe gracefulness
>And compare her to Chang'e in the Moon Hall, who is not so fine a piece.
>Now blocked from view, now hidden, she threads the fragrant path;
>I can imagine how hard it is for her to walk on such tiny feet.
>A hundred seductions spring from the face of this delightful lass—
>Oh, it steals a man's soul away!

FEMALE LEAD: Give me the incense.

MALE LEAD: I'll pay attention to what she prays for.

FEMALE LEAD: With this first stick of incense I pray for my deceased father's rebirth in heaven's realm. With this second stick of incense I pray that my old mother will stay healthy. And with this third stick . . .

[*She acts out falling silent.*]

CRIMSON: Sister, don't utter a prayer with this stick of incense; I'll do it for you—I pray that my sister will soon find a husband who will take Crimson along too.

[*Female lead sticks the incense (into a censer) on the table and makes obeisance and speaks (in verse):*]

FEMALE LEAD: The unending heartbreaks in my heart
    All lie in these two deep, deep bows.

[*Female lead heaves a deep sigh.*]

MALE LEAD: The young miss leans against the balustrade and heaves a deep sigh. It seems as if her feelings have been stirred.

STUDENT [*sings*]: In night's depth mists of incense disperse through the empty courtyard,
    The curtains of the door are stilled in the eastern breeze.
    Her bows finished, she leans on the curving balustrade
    And sighs deeply three or four times.
    The perfectly round moon is like a mirror suspended:
    This is neither the slightest cloud nor thinnest haze;
    But is all smoke of incense and human breath,
    Wafting inseparably upward together.

MALE LEAD: Though I'm no match for Sima Xiangru, I can see that the little miss certainly has the mind of Wenjun. I'll sing a quatrain to see what she has to say. [*He recites a poem:*]

> *A night bathed in moonlight,*
> *A spring desolated by flowers' shadows;*
> *Why, under the hoary sickle,*
> *Do I not see the lady in the moon?*

FEMALE LEAD: Someone's chanting a poem by the corner of the wall.

CRIMSON: Why, it's the voice of that twenty-three-year-old, as-yet-unmarried, addle-pated jerk!

FEMALE LEAD: What a fresh and original poem. I'll make up one on the same rhyme.

CRIMSON: The two of you make a nice couple—couplet.

FEMALE LEAD [*recites a matching poem*]:

> *Long has my orchid chamber been lonely,*
> *No way to pass the fragrant spring;*
> *I reckon that he who walks and chants*
> *Will take pity on the one who heaves a sigh.*

MALE LEAD: That was a snappy response.

STUDENT [*sings*]: Already struck by a vexing loveliness redundant upon her face,
    I'm now perplexed by the quick intelligence stored away in her mind:

She has matched, oh, so well the meter of my new poem;
Each word, one by one, tells true feelings—what a pleasure to hear.

The lyrics are fresh,
The prosody flows easily—
No accident that she has been given Oriole as a name.
If she were to fix her eyes on me,
We would banter verses across the wall until dawn.
Now rings true the saying, "Since ancient days the bright have loved the bright."

MALE LEAD: I'll rush out here and see what she'll say.
STUDENT [*sings*]: I pluck my gown up, about to walk—

[*Female lead acts out seeing him.*]

She welcomes me with a smile on her face;
But that unhelpful Crimson is just too unfeeling,
Even though she only follows orders.

CRIMSON: Missy, someone's here. Let's go inside; otherwise, the madam will take us to task.

[*Female lead looks back as she leaves.*] * * *

MALE LEAD: How will sleep ever come to my eyes tonight?
STUDENT [*sings*]: Facing that single flickering blue lamp on its short stand,
Leaning against that chilling, cold screen with its old panels,
Neither does the lamp give light, nor do my dreams coalesce.
At the window, the freezing, chilling wind penetrates the widely spaced stiles;
Flapping and fluttering, the paper shreds chatter.
Alone on my pillow,
Desolate in my quilted burrow.
If you were a man with a heart of stone—
A man with a heart of stone would still be moved.

"Reprise"
Resent, I cannot,
Hate, I will not;
I sit, but unsteadily,
I sleep, but unquietly.
A day will come when—blocked by willows and shielded by flowers,
Obstructed by mists and screened by clouds,
When night is deep and people are quiet,
With ocean promises and mountain covenants—
Then, at that time,
In romantic and happy celebration,
With a future like a strip of brocade,
With our love wonderfully fulfilled,
Spring will blossom forth in our painted hall.

The happiness of that day has now been fixed:
A single poem is clear evidence.

Never again will I seek in dreams the blue palace gates
But only wait beneath the peach flower tree.

[*He leaves.*]

* * *

MALE LEAD: There's someone outside the window. It must be missy. I'll retune my strings, do another tune, and sing a song entitled "The Phoenix Seeks Its Mate." Long ago Xiangru carried off his affair because of this song. I may not be a match for Sima Xiangru, but I hope that missy has the intentions of Wenjun.

[*He sings the song:*]

> *There is a beautiful woman, oh,*
> *Seeing her, I cannot forget.*
> *If I don't see her for a single day,*
> *I long for her as though crazed.*
> *The phoenix flies, soaring, soaring, oh,*
> *Seeking its mate within the four seas.*
> *Alas, that wonderful person, oh,*
> *Is not at the eastern wall.*
> *I string my zither to take words' place, oh,*
> *So I may spell out my subtlest feelings.*
> *When will I be accepted, oh,*
> *And my vacillations eased?*
> *Oh, to be a match to her virtue, oh,*
> *And lead each other by the hand.*
> *If we cannot fly together, oh,*
> *It will destroy me utterly.*

FEMALE LEAD: How well he plays! The words are sorrowful, the intention is keen, chilling and cold as a crane's cry in the sky. It makes me weep all unawares.
STUDENT [*sings*]: This is to make her ears keenly perceptive
  As I give plaint to my innermost feelings.
  One who loves music—a fragrant heart will naturally understand;
  One moved by feeling—a heart will be broken by pain. * * *

FEMALE LEAD [*enters and speaks*]: I haven't seen Student Zhang since I listened to him play the zither last night. I'll send Crimson now to his study to see what he has to say.

[*She acts out calling Crimson. Crimson enters.*]

CRIMSON: Missy is calling me. I don't know why, but I'd better go and see. * * *
FEMALE LEAD: Go and find out what Student Zhang has to say and then come tell me.
CRIMSON: I won't go! If the madam finds out, it will be no laughing matter.
FEMALE LEAD: Dearest sister, I'll bow to you twice if only you'll go.
CRIMSON: Rise up my governess; I'll go, I'll go. I'll say, "Student Zhang, your illness is surely grave, but sister suffers no less."

[*Crimson recites:*]

> Because of a zither-playing hand at midnight,
> A moon-loving heart has been aroused in spring chambers.
> Needlework my sister has no mind to take in hand;

Fragrance of powder and rouge dissipated, too listless is she to apply them again;
Spring grief weighs down the tips of her brows.
Her lingering illness would be cured
If only the smallest groove were opened down the divine rhinoceros horn.

[*Crimson leaves.*]

FEMALE LEAD: Crimson is gone. I'll see what she has to say when she comes back, and then I'll make up my mind.

[*Female lead leaves.*]

* * *

CRIMSON [*enters and speaks*]: My missy ordered me to deliver a letter today to Student Zhang. She put on all kinds of airs in front of me but all the time in that poem of hers had secretly made a tryst with him. She didn't say anything to me, so I'll pretend ignorance and ask her to come out to burn incense. Tonight she made her evening toilet differently from on other days. I'll see how she deceives me when the moment actually arrives!

[*Calling, Crimson acts out something and continues:*]

Sister, let's go and burn incense!
FEMALE LEAD [*enters and recites*]:

Flowers' perfume thickly layered, gentle breezes soft;
No one in the courtyard, the pale moon is full.

CRIMSON: Sister, tonight the moon is bright, the breeze is fresh. What a wonderful starry sky!

[*Sings:*]

The evening breeze, cold and piercing, penetrates the window's gauze;
Latched with golden hooks, the embroidered screens are furled.
On the door shutters freeze the evening mists;
On the tower corner collects lingering sunset rosiness.
Willow skeins and flower clusters unfurl their screens,
Green sedge unrolls a pad of embroidered couch.

[*Crimson explains female lead to student, singing:*]

The fine night goes on and on,
The quiet courtyard is deserted and still,
Flower stems bend low and rustle.
She's a young girl:
You should pamper her temper,
Massage her with words,
Blend with her moods.
Don't suppose her a broken willow or tattered blossom.

She's an, oh, so lovable, beautiful jade without flaw:
Her powdered face engenders spring,
Her cloudy locks are like piled-up raven feathers.
She's, oh, so timid, oh, so fearful,
And she does not scheme for free wine or idler's tea.

But once between the sheets, you should give it your all:
When your fingertips report back from duty worn out,
Then you can stack away your moans and sighs;
And when you are finished with your concerns and anxieties,
When you have cleared away frustrations and sorrows,
Then be prepared to be happily stuffed.

[*Student acts out jumping across the wall.*]

FEMALE LEAD: Who is that?

MALE LEAD: Me, your student.

FEMALE LEAD [*angrily*]: Student Zhang—what kind of person are you? Here I am burning incense, and you come without any reason. If the madam should hear of this, what kind of explanation could you give?

MALE LEAD: Ai—she has changed her stripes! * * *

[THEN LATER THAT NIGHT . . .]

CRIMSON [*enters and speaks*]: Missy, I'll go over; you stay here.

[*Crimson acts out knocking on the door.*]

MALE LEAD: Who is it?

CRIMSON: Your mother from your former life.

STUDENT: Missy, come on, I'm waiting.

[*Female lead greets male lead. Male lead acts out opening the door. Male lead kneels and speaks:*]

MALE LEAD: What abilities do I, Zhang Gong, have that a divine sylph should trouble herself to descend from heaven? Am I sleeping or dreaming? * * *

STUDENT [*sings*]: Her embroidered shoes, barely half a span,
Her willowy waist just fills a single armful;
Bashful and embarrassed, she refuses to lift her head
But keeps grasping the mandarin-duck pillow.
Her cloudy coif seems to let slip its golden hairpins:
How it suits her, the bun at her nape awry.

I loosen the knotted buttons,
Untie her silken waistwrap;
Orchid musk spreads through my secluded study.
O cruel one, you can really make me suffer.
Ai,
Why aren't you willing to turn your face to me?

Here to my breast I press her pliant jade and warm perfume—
Ai,
Ruan Zhao has reached Mount Tiantai.
Spring has come to the realm of men, flowers sport their color!
Gently she adjusts her willowy waist
And lightly splits the flower's heart:
Dew drips; the peony opens.

I just wet the tip, and she becomes numb all over:
Fish and water find harmonious concord;

From the lovely fragrance of the tender pistil the butterfly collects at will.
Partly resistant, partly eager to give,
Now alarmed, now full of love—
A sandalwood mouth kisses fragrant cheeks.

MALE LEAD [*kneels*]: Thank you, missy, for not rejecting Zhang Gong. Tonight I was allowed to share your pillow and mat, and on another day I shall repay this favor like a devoted servant.

FEMALE LEAD: In a single second I have thrown away my body, precious as a thousand pieces of gold. My body and my life I entrust to you forever. May you never disdain me in the future and make me lament my white hair.

MALE LEAD: How would I ever dare such a thing! ✳ ✳ ✳

STUDENT [*sings*]: I will treasure you as my own precious heart,
    Since I've sullied your pure whiteness.
    I forgot to eat, neglected to sleep, vented heart's suffering;
    But if I had not endured it with a true heart and struggled through with sincerity,
    Would it have been possible that from the bitterness of our love-longing such
        sweetness would come?

✳ ✳ ✳

[*Old lady and abbot enter.*]

OLD LADY: Today we are sending Student Zhang off to the capital. I've arranged for a banquet at the ten-mile pavilion. The abbot and I have gone ahead. What's keeping Student Zhang and missy?

[*Female lead, leading Crimson, and male lead, leading lute boy, enter together.*]

FEMALE LEAD: Today I'm seeing Student Zhang off to the capital to take the examinations. Already upset by emotions of separation, I encounter now this atmosphere of late autumn. How vexing! ✳ ✳ ✳

[*They greet old lady.*]

OLD LADY: Student Zhang, you sit with the abbot. Missy, you sit over here. Crimson, you bring the wine. Come forward, Student Zhang. You are a member of the family now. Don't keep such a distance! Today I give Oriole to you. Don't disgrace my child in the capital. Put all your energies into becoming the head of the list.

MALE LEAD: Relying on your ample support and on the talents in my heart, I will find obtaining official position no more than picking up a mustard seed.

BALD ONE: Madam, you've made the right decision. Student Zhang is not one to fall behind others.

[*After offering a cup of wine, he sits down. Female lead heaves a sigh.*]

FEMALE LEAD [*sings*]: Felled by western winds, yellow leaves fly in confusion;
    Tinged by cold mists, sere grass spreads afar.
    At the feast mat he sits stuck at the side,
    Wrinkling sorrowed brows, as if nearly dead and buried.

    I see him stop his welling tears, daring not let them fall
    Lest others know.
    Suddenly seeing each other, we bow our heads,
    Heave heavy sighs,

Rearrange our garments of plain silk.

Even though later we'll become a fine couple,
How can we keep now from grievous weeping?
My mind's like a fool's,
My heart as if drunk—
Last night and today
Pare away the small round of my waist.

OLD LADY: Missy, offer a cup of wine. [*After Crimson has passed her the wine, female lead acts out offering a cup. She heaves a heavy sigh.*]

CRIMSON: Please drink this wine.

FEMALE LEAD [*sings*]: Before the joy of our union ended,
The sorrow of separation had taken over.
I call to mind our secret passion of earlier evenings,
Our marriage of last night,
And our separation of today.
I have known full well, these last few days,
The flavor of love's longing;
But it turns out nothing when compared to the grief of separation—
That is tenfold more!

Those young in years
Lightly part for distant places.
Those shallow in feeling
Easily discard their partners,
Never thinking of thigh pressing thigh,
Face hugging face,
Hand holding hand.
For you to be the son-in-law of Chancellor Cui
Means glory for the wife, honor for the husband.
For me, finding a double-headed lotus
Far outstrips passing the examinations as head of the list!

* * *

[*Student, leading servant, enters.*]

STUDENT: Since taking leave of missy in late autumn, half a year has flashed by. Thanks to the protection of my ancestors, I passed the examinations on my first try and attained the highest rank, head of the list! I am now waiting in the hostel for a formal appointment by imperial decree. I am afraid that missy may be worrying about me, so I've composed a letter and will have the lute boy take it to her. I'll inform the madam that this small student did succeed, so she can put her mind at ease. Lute boy! Come here!

[*Servant enters.*]

MALE LEAD: Bring me the perfect treasures of the literary studio. I will write a letter home; I want you to take it with all dispatch to Hezhong Prefecture. When you see missy, tell her, "My master was afraid that you might be anxious and so especially dispatched me ahead of him to deliver this letter. Please let me have a letter of reply as soon as possible." Oh, how swiftly have the days and months gone by.

* * *

FEMALE LEAD [*acts out reciting the letter*]:

> I, Gong, with a hundred obeisances, present this letter
> To the dressing table of the fragrant one.

Since our separation in late autumn, half a year has gone in a flash. Thanks to the protection of my ancestors and the virtue of you, my worthy wife, I have passed the examinations in the highest category. At present I am housed in the Hostel for Gathering Worthies to wait upon my formal appointment by imperial decree. Precisely because I have feared that the madam and you, my worthy wife, would be anxious about me, I specifically ordered my lute boy to deliver this letter with all due haste. I hope that this will free you from worry. Even though my body may be far away, my heart is always near. Alas, that we cannot fly like two birds on a single wing or nest together like orioles. As one who esteems fortune and fame over favor and love, I am truly guilty of shortsighted greed. When in the future we meet face-to-face, I must offer my apologies for my inadequacies. Here below I have completed a quatrain for your inspection.

> *He who plucked a flower in the fairy precincts of the jade capital*
> *Sends word to the modest and retiring lady of East of Pu:*
> *In a day I will bow to imperial grace and be clothed in daytime brocade;*
> *Do not, for any reason, affect to lean by the gate.* * * *

FEMALE LEAD [*sings*]: On that day he hid in moonlight by the western wing,
     But on this day he shines at the banquet in the Jasper Forest.
     Who could have hoped that the feet that leapt the eastern wall would dominate
          the tortoise's head?
     Who would have said that the heart that loved flowers could nurture a hand that
          plucks the cassia branch?
     In a thicket of rouge and powder was hidden brocade and embroidery.
     From now on, the evening dressing loft will become the Loft of Impartiality.

* * *

STUDENT [*sings*]: At the gate we welcome the four-horse chariot;
     At the door are displayed eight pepperwood pictures.
     A fourfold virtuous, threefold obedient chancellor's daughter—
     My life's desire is fulfilled!
     Thanks to all you relatives and friends!

MALE LEAD and FEMALE LEAD [*sing in unison*]:
     If our great benefactor had not drawn his blade to help us,
     How could this fine couple be like fish in water?
     Achieved it is, the original inscription on the pillar;
     Rightly paired are husband and wife in this life.
     As of old, the girl has been physiognomized as a husband's fit mate—
     A new head of the list, flowers fill the road!

STUDENT [*sings*]: Nothing untoward in the wide world:
     Each calls himself a loyal minister or subject;
     All nations come to pay court,
     Wishing our emperor myriad years.

His deeds surpass Xi and Xuan,
His virtue exceeds that of Shun and Yu:
Sage plans and divine tactics,
Humane culture and righteous might!
At court the prime minister is wise;
Throughout the realm citizens are prosperous.
For ten thousand miles the Yellow River runs clear;
All five grains mature at harvest.
Door after door lives in peace,
From place to place stretches a happy land.
Phoenix couples come to preen;
The unicorn repeatedly appears.

MALE LEAD and FEMALE LEAD [*sing in unison*]:
We thank the present sagely and enlightened sage ruler of Tang,
Who bestowed on us a decree making us man and wife:
For all eternity without separation,
For all infinity forever united.
May lovers of the whole world all be thus united in wedlock!

Because they matched couplets by the light of the moon,
A frustrated girl and unmarried man have been brought together. * * *

FEMALE LEAD: I am grateful, Mother, for your management as head of the house.
OLD LADY: The husband is glorious, the wife is noble, this day brings satisfaction.
EXTRA FEMALE LEAD: May you be together in the mandarin-duck bedcurtains for a
     hundred years!

End

[END OF WOMEN IN EARLY CHINA]

⚘

⊷━❈⬥❈━⊷

Tao Qian

365–427

One of the best-loved poets in the Chinese tradition, Tao Qian (also known as Tao Yuanming),
has left much in the way of anecdote and self-representation but little certain knowledge of his
life. The great-grandson of a noted statesman and general, Tao led a brief and undistinguished official career spanning thirteen years that took him in and out of a number of positions, of which
the final one lasted fewer than three months. According to biographies in dynastic histories, he
was serving as magistrate of Pengze, the county seat some thirty miles from his home, in 405
when the arrival of a provincial dignitary required a greeting with appropriate ceremony. Having
deemed the visitor unworthy of the necessary protocol, Tao is said to have declared that he would
not bend his waist for "five pecks of rice" and resigned the post. In a preface to his poetic rhapsody entitled "The Return" he further explains that he had decided to cease "mortgaging" his life
to his "mouth and belly" and to follow instead his true inclinations. He returned to his family farm
and a life of genteel poverty until his death. (See his portrait, Color Plate 1.)

Tao Qian's decision to retreat from government service resonated with the intellectual currents of his time, a period when northern China had been taken over by non-Chinese invaders and the political and cultural leadership of the country had relocated south of the Yangzi River. Buddhism had already taken root since its introduction from India at the beginning of the millennium, and interest in Daoism had burgeoned as well, providing both religious and philosophical support for arguments in favor of withdrawal from the engagement in public life mandated by Confucianism. The lush and gentle landscape of the south enhanced the appeal of an unconstrained life amid the tranquil beauties of nature. For Tao what mattered was the chance to return to what he considered his basic nature, and he shares the details of his daily life with a humor and apparent candor unprecedented in the work of earlier poets. The pleasures of wine and desultory reading were, however, always tempered by constant poverty, strong intimations of mortality, and ideals of Confucian duty that were difficult to relinquish.

That Tao Qian chose nonetheless to sacrifice advancement for the sake of principles earned him great respect for his personal integrity, but admiration for his poetry came later. Contemporary taste preferred an ornateness of imagery, parallelism, and allusion rarely found in the relatively simple, straightforward diction of his poems. Poets of the Tang and Song dynasties like Wang Wei, Du Fu, and Su Shi, however, found great inspiration in both his themes and language, and his position in the canon has been secure ever since.

Biography of the Gentleman of the Five Willows[1]

We do not know of what place the gentleman is a native, nor do we know his family or his courtesy-name. Around his house there are five willows and from these he took his literary name. Quiet and of few words, he does not desire glory or profit. He delights in study but does not seek abstruse explanations. Whenever there is something of which he apprehends the meaning, then in his happiness he forgets to eat.[2]

By nature he is fond of wine, but his family is poor and he cannot usually get it. His relatives and friends know that this is so, and sometimes set out wine and invite him. Whenever he goes to a party, he will drink to the end. He expects that he will certainly get drunk. When he is drunk, he will withdraw, but never regret that he must go.

His house "with surrounding walls only a few paces long"[3] is lonely and does not shelter him from wind and sun. His short coarse robe is torn and mended. His dishes and gourds are "often empty."[4] Yet he is at peace. He constantly delights himself with writing in which he widely expresses his own ideals. He is unmindful of gain or loss, and thus he will be to the end.

The Appraisal:[5] Ch'ien Lou[6] had a saying: "One does not grieve over poverty and low position, one is not concerned about riches and high rank." May we think he was speaking of this sort of man? Drinking wine and writing poems to please his own will, is he not a man of the time of Lord Wu-huai or Lord Ko-t'ien?[7]

---

1. Translated by A. R. Davis. This brief essay is one of the earliest and best-known autobiographies in the Chinese tradition, and largely responsible for the image Tao Qian succeeded in constructing of himself as a modest and carefree person of integrity.

2. An allusion to Confucius (*Analects* 7.18).

3. The classical description of a poor scholar's house.

4. Like the gourds of Confucius's favorite—and impoverished—disciple, Yan Hui.

5. Biographies in dynastic histories typically concluded with an appraisal of the subject's character.

6. A figure from the ancient state of Lu who was said to have turned down offers of wealth and high office with alacrity.

7. Legendary rulers of high antiquity.

The Peach Blossom Spring[1]

During the T'ai-yuan period of the Chin dynasty a fisherman of Wuling once rowed upstream, unmindful of the distance he had gone, when he suddenly came to a grove of peach trees in bloom. For several hundred paces on both banks of the stream there was no other kind of tree. The wild flowers growing under them were fresh and lovely, and fallen petals covered the ground—it made a great impression on the fisherman. He went on for a way with the idea of finding out how far the grove extended. It came to an end at the foot of a mountain whence issued the spring that supplied the stream. There was a small opening in the mountain and it seemed as though light was coming through it. The fisherman left his boat and entered the cave, which at first was extremely narrow, barely admitting his body; after a few dozen steps it suddenly opened out onto a broad and level plain where well-built houses were surrounded by rich fields and pretty ponds. Mulberry, bamboo and other trees and plants grew there, and criss-cross paths skirted the fields. The sounds of cocks crowing and dogs barking could be heard from one courtyard to the next.[2] Men and women were coming and going about their work in the fields. The clothes they wore were like those of ordinary people. Old men and boys were carefree and happy.

When they caught sight of the fisherman, they asked in surprise how he had got there. The fisherman told the whole story, and was invited to go to their house, where he was served wine while they killed a chicken for a feast. When the other villagers heard about the fisherman's arrival they all came to pay him a visit. They told him that their ancestors had fled the disorders of Ch'in times and, having taken refuge here with wives and children and neighbors, had never ventured out again; consequently they had lost all contact with the outside world. They asked what the present ruling dynasty was, for they had never heard of the Han, let alone the Wei and the Chin. They sighed unhappily as the fisherman enumerated the dynasties one by one and recounted the vicissitudes of each. The visitors all asked him to come to their houses in turn, and at every house he had wine and food. He stayed several days. As he was about to go away, the people said, "There's no need to mention our existence to outsiders."

After the fisherman had gone out and recovered his boat, he carefully marked the route. On reaching the city, he reported what he had found to the magistrate, who at once sent a man to follow him back to the place. They proceeded according to the marks he had made, but went astray and were unable to find the cave again.

A high-minded gentleman of Nan-yang named Liu Tzu-chi heard the story and happily made preparations to go there, but before he could leave he fell sick and died. Since then there has been no one interested in trying to find such a place.

> The Ying clan[3] disrupted Heaven's ordinance
> And good men withdrew from such a world.
> Huang and Ch'i[4] went off to Shang Mountain
> And these people too fled into hiding.
> 5   Little by little their tracks were obliterated

---

1. Translated by James Robert Hightower. This narrative "record" became far more celebrated than the poem for which it was designed to serve as a preface.
2. I.e., the population is content and at peace, perhaps an echo of Chapter 30 of the *Dao de Jing* (Volume A).
3. The family name of the first emperor of the Qin dy-

nasty, whose unification of the country was achieved at considerable expense to classical values.
4. Two of four recluses known as the "Four White-hairs," who withdrew from society in protest against the first Qin emperor.

The paths they followed overgrown at last.
By agreement they set about farming the land
When the sun went down each rested from his toil.
Bamboo and mulberry provided shade enough,
10   They planted beans and millet, each in season.
From spring silkworms came the long silk thread
On the fall harvest no king's tax was paid.
No sign of traffic on overgrown roads,
Cockcrow and dogsbark within each other's earshot.
15   Their ritual vessels were of old design,
And no new fashions in the clothes they wore.
Children wandered about singing songs,
Greybeards went paying one another calls.
When grass grew thick they saw the time was mild,
20   As trees went bare they knew the wind was sharp.
Although they had no calendar to tell,
The four seasons still filled out a year.
Joyous in their ample happiness
They had no need of clever contrivance.
25   Five hundred years this rare deed stayed hid,
Then one fine day the fay retreat was found.
The pure and the shallow belong to separate worlds:
In a little while they were hidden again.
Let me ask you who are convention-bound,
30   Can you fathom those outside the dirt and noise?
I want to tread upon the thin thin air
And rise up high to find my own kind.

❧

RESONANCE

Wang Wei: Song of Peach Blossom Spring[1]

The fisherman's boat follows the water; he loves spring in the mountains.
On both banks peach blossoms enclose the ancient ford.
Sitting he looks at the rosy trees, unaware of distance.
Traveling to the green creek's end he does not see any men.
5   At the mountain valley a hidden path begins to twist and turn.
From the mountain a broad view opens out: suddenly, flat land.
Afar he looks at a whole expanse of gathered clouds and trees;
He nears and enters—a thousand homes, scattered flowers and bamboo.
Woodcutters have just passed on the names of the Han,
10   And residents have not yet altered Qin dynasty clothes.
The residents lived together at Wuling Spring,
And yet from beyond this world started fields and gardens.

---

1. Translated by Pauline Yu. The Tang poet Wang Wei (701–761), like many of his contemporaries, looked back with great interest at the writings of Tao Qian. Notice how this poem, composed when Wang Wei was 19, adds a spiritual dimension to Tao's political utopia.

The moon shines beneath the pines on houses and windows at peace.
The sun rises within the clouds as cocks and dogs clamor.
15 Startled to hear of the worldly guest, they rush and gather together,
Vying to bring him home with them to ask about their districts.
At dawn on the village lanes, they sweep the flowers away,
Toward evening woodsmen and fishermen enter along the water.
At first to escape from disaster, they left the midst of men.
20 Then, it's heard, they became immortal and so did not return.
Amid these gorges who knows that human affairs exist?
Within the world one gazes afar at empty clouded mountains.
Not suspecting that ethereal realms are hard to hear of and see,
His dusty heart has not yet ceased to long for his native home.
25 He goes out of the grotto, not thinking of the mountains and water between,
Then leaves his family, planning at last a long, leisurely journey.
Telling himself that what he passed through before cannot be lost,
How can he know that valleys and peaks when he comes today have
     changed?
Of that time all he remembers is entering mountains deep.
30 How many times does the green creek arrive at a cloudy forest?
When spring comes, everywhere are peach-blossomed waters:
Not distinguishing the faery spring, where can he seek?

❦

The Return[1]

I was poor, and what I got from farming was not enough to support my family. The house was full of children, the rice-jar was empty, and I could not see any way to supply the necessities of life. Friends and relatives kept urging me to become a magistrate, and I had at last come to think I should do it, but there was no way for me to get such a position. At the time I happened to have business abroad and made a good impression on the grandees as a conciliatory and humane sort of person. Because of my poverty an uncle offered me a job in a small town, but the region was still unquiet and I trembled at the thought of going away from home. However, P'eng-tse was only thirty miles from my native place, and the yield of the fields assigned the magistrate was sufficient to keep me in wine, so I applied for the office. Before many days had passed, I longed to give it up and go back home. Why, you may ask. Because my instinct is all for freedom, and will not brook discipline or restraint. Hunger and cold may be sharp, but this going against myself really sickens me. Whenever I have been involved in official life I was mortgaging myself to my mouth and belly, and the realization of this greatly upset me. I was deeply ashamed that I had so compromised my principles, but I was still going to wait out the year, after which I might pack up my clothes and slip away at night. Then my sister who had married into the Ch'eng family died in Wu-ch'ang, and my only desire was to go there as quickly as possible. I gave up my office and left of my own accord. From mid-autumn to winter I was altogether some eighty days in office, when

---

1. Translated by James Robert Hightower. Introduced by a prose preface, this is an example of a *fu* or rhymeprose, a hybrid form usually directed toward descriptive or elegiac purposes but employed by Tao Qian here for more personal ends.

events made it possible for me to do what I wished. I have entitled my piece "The Return"; my preface is dated the eleventh moon of the year *i-ssu* (405).

> To get out of this and go back home!
> My fields and garden will be overgrown with weeds—I must go back.
> It was my own doing that made my mind my body's slave
> Why should I go on in melancholy and lonely grief?
> 5   I realize that there's no remedying the past
> But I know that there's hope in the future.
> After all I have not gone far on the wrong road
> And I am aware that what I do today is right, yesterday wrong.
> My boat rocks in the gentle breeze
> 10 Flap, flap, the wind blows my gown;
> I ask a passerby about the road ahead,
> Grudging the dimness of the light at dawn.
> Then I catch sight of my cottage—
> Filled with joy I run.
> 15 The servant boy comes to welcome me
> My little son waits at the door.
> The three paths are almost obliterated[2]
> But pines and chrysanthemums are still here.
> Leading the children by the hand I enter my house
> 20   Where there is a bottle filled with wine.
> I draw the bottle to me and pour myself a cup;
> Seeing the trees in the courtyard brings joy to my face.
> I lean on the south window and let my pride expand,
> I consider how easy it is to be content with a little space.
> 25 Every day I stroll in the garden for pleasure,
> There is a gate there, but it is always shut.
> Cane in hand I walk and rest
> Occasionally raising my head to gaze into the distance.
> The clouds aimlessly rise from the peaks,
> 30 The birds, weary of flying, know it is time to come home.
> As the sun's rays grow dim and disappear from view
> I walk around a lonely pine tree, stroking it.
>
> Back home again!
> May my friendships be broken off and my wanderings come to an end.
> 35 The world and I shall have nothing more to do with one another.
> If I were again to go abroad, what should I seek?
> Here I enjoy honest conversation with my family
> And take pleasure in books and cither to dispel my worries.
> The farmers tell me that now spring is here
> 40 There will be work to do in the west fields.
> Sometimes I call for a covered cart
> Sometimes I row a lonely boat
> Following a deep gully through the still water

2. The "three paths" on which a famous earlier hermit walked with two friends had become part of the vocabulary of reclusion.

Or crossing the hill on a rugged path.
45 The trees put forth luxuriant foliage,
The spring begins to flow in a trickle.
I admire the seasonableness of nature
And am moved to think that my life will come to its close.
It is all over—
50 So little time are we granted human form in the world!
Let us then follow the inclinations of the heart:
Where would we go that we are so agitated?
I have no desire for riches
And no expectation of Heaven.
55 Rather on some fine morning to walk alone
Now planting my staff to take up a hoe,
Or climbing the east hill and whistling long
Or composing verses beside the clear stream:
So I manage to accept my lot until the ultimate homecoming.
60 Rejoicing in Heaven's command, what is there to doubt?

Returning to the Farm to Dwell[1]

1

From early days I have been at odds with the world;
My instinctive love is hills and mountains.
By mischance I fell into the dusty net
And was thirteen years away from home.
5 The migrant bird longs for its native grove.
The fish in the pond recalls the former depths.
Now I have cleared some land to the south of town,
Simplicity intact, I have returned to farm.
The land I own amounts to a couple of acres
10 The thatched-roof house has four or five rooms.
Elms and willows shade the eaves in back,
Peach and plum stretch out before the hall.
Distant villages are lost in haze,
Above the houses smoke hangs in the air.
15 A dog is barking somewhere in a hidden lane,
A cock crows from the top of a mulberry tree.
My home remains unsoiled by worldy dust
Within bare rooms I have my peace of mind.
For long I was a prisoner in a cage
20 And now I have my freedom back again.

2

Here in the country human contacts are few
On this narrow lane carriages seldom come.

1. Translated by James Robert Hightower. Two from a series of five poems traditionally thought to have been written after Tao's retirement from his post as magistrate of Pengze.

In broad daylight I keep my rustic gate closed,
From the bare rooms all dusty thoughts are banned.
25   From time to time through the tall grass
Like me, village farmers come and go;
When we meet we talk of nothing else
Than how the hemp and mulberry are growing.
Hemp and mulberry grow longer every day
30   Every day the fields I have plowed are wider;
My constant worry is that frost may come
And my crops will wither with the weeds.

from On Reading the *Seas and Mountains Classic*[1]
1

In early summer when the grasses grow
And trees surround my house with greenery,
The birds rejoice to have a refuge there
And I too love my home.
5   The fields are plowed and the new seed planted
And now is time again to read my books.
This out-of-the-way lane has no deep-worn ruts
And tends to turn my friends' carts away.
With happy face I pour the spring-brewed wine
10   And in the garden pick some greens to cook.
A gentle shower approaches from the east
Accompanied by a temperate breeze.
I skim through the *Story of King Mu*[2]
And view the pictures in the *Seas and Mountains Classic*.
15   A glance encompasses the ends of the universe—
Where is there any joy, if not in these?

The Double Ninth, in Retirement[1]

Living in retirement, I rejoice in the name of the Double Ninth. This autumn the chrysanthemums fill the courtyard, but I have no way to come by wine. So I have to be content with drinking the blossoms of the Ninth and expressing my feelings in words.

Life is short but our desires are many;
And all mankind finds joy in living long.
When day and month reach this auspicious time
Everyone rejoices in its name.

1. Translated by James Robert Hightower. An early text of uncertain date that purports to be a travelogue of the legendary king Yu and is an important repository of ancient Chinese myth and marvel. The illustrated version perused by Tao Qian is no longer extant. This is the first of a series of 13 poems.
2. Another ancient text that recounts the travels of King Mu, the fifth Zhou ruler, and is recognized as more fantasy than history.
1. Translated by James Robert Hightower. This is the first of many poems in the tradition marking the festival of the Ninth Day of the Ninth Month, an opportunity to appreciate wine, chrysanthemums, and mountain-climbing and to express hopes for longevity, since "nine" in Chinese is a homonym for "long-lasting."

5   The dew is chill, the summer wind has ceased,
The air is clear and all the sky is bright.
No trace remains of departed swallows,
The honking still echoes from passing geese.
Wine serves to exorcise all our concerns,

10   Chrysanthemum keeps us from growing old.
But what is the thatched-hut gentleman to do
Who helpless views time's revolutions?
The dusty cup shames the empty wine cask,
The cold flower blooms uncelebrated.

15   Drawing tight my robe, I sing to myself,
In my reverie deepest feelings stir.
There are many joys in living here,
And just to see it through is something gained.

In the Sixth Month of 408, Fire[1]

I built my thatched hut in a narrow lane,
Glad to renounce the carriages of the great.
In midsummer, while the wind blew long and sharp,
Of a sudden grove and house caught fire and burned.

5   In all the place not a roof was left to us
And we took shelter in the boat by the gate.

Space is vast this early autumn evening,
The moon, nearly full, rides high above.
The vegetables begin to grow again

10   But the frightened birds still have not returned.
Tonight I stand a long time lost in thought;
A glance encompasses the Nine Heavens.[2]
Since youth I've held my solitary course
Until all at once forty years have passed.

15   My outward form follows the way of change
But my heart remains untrammelled still.
Firm and true, it keeps its constant nature,
No jadestone is as strong, adamantine.
I think back to the time when East-Gate[3] ruled

20   When there was grain left out in the fields
And people, free of care, drummed full bellies,
Rising mornings and coming home to sleep.
Since I was not born in such a time,
Let me just go on watering my garden.

1. Translated by James Robert Hightower.
2. This refers to the sky in all eight directions plus the center.

3. A legendary ruler whose subjects enjoyed such plenty that objects dropped on the road weren't picked up and grain could be left in the fields.

Begging for Food[1]

Hunger came and drove me out
To go I had no notion where.
I walked until I reached this town,
Knocked at a door and fumbled for words
5   The owner guessed what I was after
And gave it, but not just the gift alone.
We talked together all day long,
And drained our cups as the bottle passed.
Happy in our new acquaintance
10   We sang old songs and wrote new poems.
You are as kind as the washerwoman,
But to my shame I lack Han's talent.[2]
I have no way to show my thanks
And must repay you from the grave.

Finding Fault with My Sons[1]

Over my temples the white hair hangs,
My wrinkled skin is past filling out.
Although five sons belong to me
Not one is fond of brush and paper.
5   Already Shu is twice times eight—
For laziness he has no match.
At A-hsüan's age one should study,[2]
But love of letters is not in him.
Both Yung and Tuan count thirteen years
10   And cannot add up six and seven.
T'ung-tzu is getting on toward nine
And all he wants are pears and chestnuts.
If this is the way it is fated to be,
Just let me reach for the Thing in the Cup.

from Twenty Poems After Drinking Wine[1]
Preface

Living in retirement here I have few pleasures, and now the nights are growing longer; so, as I happen to have some excellent wine, not an evening passes without a drink. All alone with my shadow I empty a bottle until suddenly I find myself drunk. And once I am drunk I write a few verses for my own amusement. In the course of time the pages have multiplied, but there is no particular sequence in what I have written. I have had a friend make a copy, with no more in mind than to provide a diversion.

1. Translated by James Robert Hightower. Scholars disagree on whether Tao Qian was asking literally for a meal or rather for an appointment.
2. Han Xin, who was to become one of the Han dynasty's most distinguished generals, was fed by a washerwoman for several weeks while an impoverished youth and repaid her handsomely when circumstances allowed.
1. Translated by James Robert Hightower.
2. I.e., 15, the age at which Confucius said his "heart was bent on study" (*Analects* 2.4).
1. Translated by James Robert Hightower.

5

I built my hut beside a traveled road
Yet hear no noise of passing carts and horses.
You would like to know how it is done?
With the mind detached, one's place becomes remote.
5   Picking chrysanthemums by the eastern hedge[2]
I catch sight of the distant southern hills:[3]
The mountain air is lovely as the sun sets
And flocks of flying birds return together.
In these things is a fundamental truth
10   I would like to tell, but lack the words.[4]

Han-shan
7th–9th centuries

About the authorship of the poems attributed to Han-shan ("Cold Mountain") little is known for certain. From the group of 311 poems attached to this name we can surmise the following: that he had once been an educated gentleman farmer, with a wife and family, who held minor office; that he had, at age thirty (or, according to some readings, thirty years before) retired to Cold Mountain in the Tiantai range of southeastern China, taking his pen name from his new home; that he enjoyed poking fun at Confucian officious self-righteousness and Daoist quests for immortality; that, whether layman or monk, he didn't spare Buddhist clergy his ridicule either; and that his embrace of Buddhism could express itself in both didactic sermonizing and evocative metaphors. From his poems it would appear that he spent much of his life in reclusion, but Buddhist legends depict him as an irreverent monk associated with an equally eccentric sidekick, Shide, and their master Fenggan. Linguistic analysis has determined that the poems were written during at least two different periods of the Tang dynasty (the seventh and ninth centuries), indicating that what we have is a tradition that multiple writers added to, rather than the work of one hand.

Whether these authors were Buddhist monks or not, much of their language draws on vocabulary and concepts central to the Chan (Zen) tradition in particular. Many religious figures in China dropped their family name for that of a place, but Cold Mountain refers not only to a person and a place, but to a state of mind as well. Is Han-shan sitting on a mountaintop or practicing meditation? Is he clambering up a rocky path or embarking on a journey of the spirit? Does enlightenment require arduous effort or simply being able to see into what has always been there, one's true Buddha-nature? Has he succeeded in realizing it or is he still beset with anxieties?

Although the landscape and religious poems have attracted the greatest interest from readers, it is important to note that Han-shan wrote on a variety of other themes as well. The poems employ five-syllable verse forms favored by Tang dynasty poets but with a colloquial diction, unconventional imagery, and sense of humor rare at the time. Perhaps for this reason the Han-shan poems weren't collected in contemporary Chinese anthologies of poetry, although they

2. Most likely for use in preparing a wine infusion as a tonic for long life.
3. A reference both to an established literary embodiment of longevity (South Mountain, from the *Book of Songs*)

and, literally, to a mountain to the south on which Tao Qian expected to locate his grave.
4. See Zhuangzi's discussion of the virtues of forgetting words, in Volume A.

were enormously popular and were often imitated. In Japan, however, Zen monks studied them seriously and produced numerous commentaries as well.

Men ask the way to Cold Mountain[1]

Men ask the way to Cold Mountain
Cold Mountain: there's no through trail.
In summer, ice doesn't melt
The rising sun blurs in swirling fog.
5   How did I make it?
My heart's not the same as yours.
If your heart was like mine
You'd get it and be right here.

Spring-water in the green creek is clear[1]

Spring-water in the green creek is clear
Moonlight on Cold Mountain is white
Silent knowledge—the spirit is enlightened of itself
Contemplate the void: this world exceeds stillness.

When men see Han-shan[1]

When men see Han-shan
They all say he's crazy
And not much to look at—
Dressed in rags and hides.
5   They don't get what I say
& I don't talk their language.
All I can say to those I meet:
"Try and make it to Cold Mountain."

I climb the road to Cold Mountain[1]

I climb the road to Cold Mountain,
The road to Cold Mountain that never ends.
The valleys are long and strewn with stones;
The streams broad and banked with thick grass.
5   Moss is slippery, though no rain has fallen;
Pines sigh, but it isn't the wind.
Who can break from the snares of the world
And sit with me among the white clouds?

Wonderful, this road to Cold Mountain

Wonderful, this road to Cold Mountain—
Yet there's no sign of horse or carriage.

1. Translated by Gary Snyder.
1. Translated by Gary Snyder.
1. Translated by Gary Snyder.

1. This and the following poems are translated by Burton Watson.

In winding valleys too tortuous to trace,
On crags piled who knows how high,
5   A thousand different grasses weep with dew
And pines hum together in the wind.
Now it is that, straying from the path,
You ask your shadow, "What way from here?"

Cold cliffs, more beautiful the deeper you enter

Cold cliffs, more beautiful the deeper you enter—
Yet no one travels this road.
White clouds idle about the tall crags;
On the green peak a single monkey wails.
5   What other companions do I need?
I grow old doing as I please.
Though face and form alter with the years,
I hold fast to the pearl of the mind.[1]

Men these days search for a way through the clouds

Men these days search for a way through the clouds,
But the cloud way is dark and without sign.
The mountains are high and often steep and rocky;
In the broadest valleys the sun seldom shines.
5   Green crests before you and behind,
White clouds to east and west—
Do you want to know where the cloud way lies?
There it is, in the midst of the Void!

Today I sat before the cliff

Today I sat before the cliff,
Sat a long time till mists had cleared.
A single thread, the clear stream runs cold;
A thousand yards the green peaks lift their heads.
5   White clouds—the morning light is still;
Moonrise—the lamp of night drifts upward;
Body free from dust and stain,
What cares could trouble my mind?

Have I a body or have I none?

Have I a body or have I none?
Am I who I am or am I not?
Pondering these questions,
I sit leaning against the cliff while the years go by,
5   Till the green grass grows between my feet
And the red dust settles on my head,
And the men of the world, thinking me dead,
Come with offerings of wine and fruit to lay by my corpse.

1. The Buddha-nature each person carries within.

My mind is like the autumn moon

My mind is like the autumn moon
Shining clean and clear in the green pool.
No, that's not a good comparison.
Tell me, how shall I explain?

Do you have the poems of Han-shan in your house?

Do you have the poems of Han-shan in your house?
They're better for you than sutra-reading!
Write them out and paste them on a screen
Where you can glance them over from time to time.

RESONANCE

Lüqiu Yin: from *Preface to the Poems of Han-shan*[1]

No one knows just what sort of man Han-shan was. There are old people who knew him: they say he was a poor man, a crazy character. He lived alone seventy li west of the T'ang-hsing district of T'ien-t'ai at a place called Cold Mountain (Han-shan). He often went down to the Kuo-ch'ing Temple. At the temple lived Shih-te, who ran the dining hall. He sometimes saved leftovers for Han-shan, hiding them in a bamboo tube. Han-shan would come and carry it away, walking the long veranda, calling and shouting happily, talking and laughing to himself. Once the monks followed him, caught him, and made fun of him. He stopped, clapped his hands, and laughed greatly—Ha Ha!—for a spell, then left.

He looked like a tramp. His body and face were old and beat. Yet in every word he breathed was a meaning in line with the subtle principles of things, if only you thought of it deeply. Everything he said had a feeling of the Tao in it, profound and arcane secrets. His hat was made of birch bark, his clothes were ragged and worn out, and his shoes were wood. Thus men who have made it hide their tracks: unifying categories and interpenetrating things. On that long veranda calling and singing, in his words of reply—Ha Ha!—the three worlds revolve.[2] Sometimes at the villages and farms he laughed and sang with the cowherds. Sometimes intractable, sometimes agreeable, his nature was happy of itself. But how could a person without wisdom recognize him?

I once received a position as a petty official at Tan-ch'iu. The day I was to depart, I had a bad headache. I called a doctor, but he couldn't cure me and it turned worse. Then I met a Buddhist Master named Feng-kan, who said he came from the Kuo-ch'ing Temple of T'ien-t'ai especially to visit me. I asked him to rescue me from my illness. He smiled and said, "The four realms[3] are within the body; sickness comes from illusion. If you want to do away with it, you need pure water." Someone brought water to the Master, who spat it on me. In a moment the disease was rooted out. He then said, "There are

---

1. Translated by Gary Snyder. This undated preface—written in a style uncharacteristic of a bureaucrat—may be fictitious but it illustrates the legends that grew up around the name of Han-shan.

2. In Buddhist thought, these are the worlds of desires, of forms, and of formlessness.
3. Of earth, water, fire, and wind.

miasmas in T'ai prefecture, when you get there take care of yourself." I asked him, "Are there any wise men in your area I could look on as Master?" He replied, "When you see him you don't recognize him, when you recognize him you don't see him. If you want to see him, you can't rely on appearances. Then you can see him. Han-shan is a Manjusri hiding at Kuo-ch'ing. Shih-te is a Samantabhadra.[4] They look like poor fellows and act like madmen. Sometimes they go and sometimes they come. They work in the kitchen of the Kuo-ch'ing dining hall, tending the fire." When he was done talking, he left.

I proceeded on my journey to my job at Tan-ch'iu, not forgetting this affair. I arrived three days later, immediately went to a temple, and questioned an old monk. It seemed the Master had been truthful, so I gave orders to see if T'ang-hsing really contained a Han-shan and Shih-te. The District Magistrate reported to me: "In this district, seventy li west, is a mountain. People used to see a poor man heading from the cliffs to stay awhile at Kuo-ch'ing. At the temple dining hall is a similar man named Shih-te." I made a bow, and went to Kuo-ch'ing. I asked some people around the temple, "There used to be a Master named Feng-kan here. Where is his place? And where can Han-shan and Shih-te be seen?" A monk named Tao-ch'iao spoke up: "Feng-kan the Master lived in back of the library. Nowadays nobody lives there; a tiger often comes and roars. Han-shan and Shih-te are in the kitchen." The monk led me to Feng-kan's yard. Then he opened the gate: all we saw were tiger tracks. I asked the monks Tao-ch'iao and Pao-te, "When Feng-kan was here, what was his job?" The monks said, "He pounded and hulled rice. At night he sang songs to amuse himself." Then we went to the kitchen, before the stoves. Two men were facing the fire, laughing loudly. I made a bow. The two shouted HO! at me. They struck their hands together— Ha Ha!—great laughter. They shouted. Then they said, "Feng-kan—loose-tongued, loose-tongued. You don't recognize Amitabha,[5] why be courteous to us?" The monks gathered round, surprise going through them. "Why has a big official bowed to a pair of clowns?" The two men grabbed hands and ran out of the temple. I cried, "Catch them"—but they quickly ran away. Han-shan returned to Cold Mountain. I asked the monks, "Would those two men be willing to settle down at this temple?" I ordered them to find a house, and to ask Han-shan and Shih-te to return and live at the temple.

I returned to my district and had two sets of clean clothes made, got some incense and such, and sent it to the temple—but the two men didn't return. So I had it carried up to Cold Mountain. The packer saw Han-shan, who called in a loud voice, "Thief! Thief!" and retreated into a mountain cave. He shouted, "I tell you, man, strive hard!"—entered the cave and was gone. The cave closed of itself and they weren't able to follow. Shih-te's tracks disappeared completely.

I ordered Tao-ch'iao and the other monks to find out how they had lived, to hunt up the poems written on bamboo, wood, stones and cliffs—and also to collect those written on the walls of people's houses. There were more than three hundred. On the wall of the Earth-shrine Shih-te had written some short poems, *gatha*. It was all brought together and made into a book.

I hold to the principle of the Buddha-mind. It is fortunate to meet with men of Tao, so I have made this eulogy.

---

4. Manjusri and Samantabhadra were two Buddhist deities (bodhisattvas) who embodied the virtues of devotion and wisdom, respectively.

5. The Buddha of the Western Paradise, in which devotees of the Pure Land tradition hoped to be reborn.

POETRY OF THE TANG DYNASTY

Chinese literature began with the lyric, whose period of greatest flowering, by common agreement, was the Tang dynasty (618–907). Artistic achievement of all sorts benefited from the reunification of the country that had been accomplished during the preceding, short-lived Sui dynasty (581–618) and the political consolidation and expansion that followed for over a century until the brief but disruptive rebellion led by An Lushan between 755 and 757. The imperial capital of Chang'an thrived, thanks to elaborate transportation systems that brought goods in from the provinces, as well as equally sophisticated administrative structures that dispatched bureaucrats in all directions to manage them. Government policies fostered the institutional growth of both Buddhism and Daoism, while still maintaining a commitment to Confucian texts and values, encouraging an atmosphere of pluralism that was further enlivened by the many influences generated by rich contacts with foreign cultures, especially those of central Asia.

The earliest theories of poetry in China regarded it as a spontaneous, if crafted, response to an external stimulus, a form of writing of unquestioned value as a means of communication, instruction, and critique. Poetic composition was a skill that any scholar/bureaucrat would be expected to display, on occasions both serious and trivial. The standard collection of Tang poetry contains almost 49,000 works by 2,200 poets and testifies in its variety to its deep integration in the daily life of the educated class, for whom poetry was a widely accepted currency of personal, social, and political exchange. It is difficult to imagine how depleted the collections of the past would be had such circumstances not inspired, or compelled, the composition of a poem. In particular, the typically peripatetic career of government bureaucrats is responsible for the thick chapters of farewell and keepsake poems in almost all individual collections. The cultural importance of poetry was further institutionalized during the Tang by the introduction of a test of poetic composition on the most prestigious imperial civil service examination that, when passed, conferred on the successful candidate the most prestigious degree, that of the *jinshi,* or "presented scholar." This requirement was in fact removed at various points during the dynasty, and debates raged almost immediately regarding its reliability as an indicator of future administrative competence and its influence on the quality of poetic production in general. Its presence does certainly attest, nonetheless, to the stature and popularity of poetry during the Tang and confirms that it was a means of articulating the relationship between an individual and the body politic.

Chinese literary historians have long been fond of demarcating periods and categories, and the Tang was no exception to this practice. The history of Tang poetry has thus typically been divided into four periods—Early, High, Middle, and Late—with its peak, unsurprisingly, during the High Tang, or the first half of the eighth century. The three most esteemed poets of the period—Wang Wei, Li Bo, and Du Fu—were also conveniently associated with the three major belief systems of the epoch, Buddhism, Daoism, and Confucianism, respectively. Their works together epitomize the varied creativity of this central period of Chinese poetry.

Wang Wei
701–761

One of the most prominent poets of his time, Wang Wei was born into a distinguished family and earned youthful renown as poet, painter, and musician. After passing the most literary of the imperial civil service examinations in 721, he enjoyed a slow but steady rise through government ranks that took him through various offices at the capital, to several provincial posts, and finally in 759 back to court in a high-ranking position with few duties. A minor infraction and the death of his mother briefly interrupted his progress, but the most important setback occurred when he was captured by the rebel general An Lushan, who took over the Tang capital of Chang'an from 755 to 757 and forced Wang Wei to serve under his puppet government. Only the intercession of Wang Wei's powerful younger brother led to his pardon and rehabilitation upon the imperial family's return to the capital.

Wang Wei was an accomplished master of both old and new poetic forms and was especially admired for his quatrains in regulated verse. His poetry displays the hallmarks of the urbane courtly style—impersonal, witty, and decorous—whose mastery is best revealed, perhaps paradoxically, in his limpid evocations of life in retreat, and especially scenes from his country estate on the Wang River outside the capital. After his mother's death in 730, he converted part of this property to a monastery, and his poetry demonstrates his commitment to Buddhism, sometimes in its themes, but even more so in language and style. Wang Wei was also an influential painter, and in one poem in fact declares that he was "mistakenly a poet" and in an earlier life "must have been a painter." His depictions of landscape, however, are noteworthy not for elaborate descriptive detail but rather for their apparently artless language and tranquil mood. In accord with Chan (Zen) doctrine, he appears to accept both the simple and concrete reality of nature and its ultimate illusoriness, and his poetry conveys this dual awareness in a tone of contemplative, dispassionate detachment.

from The Wang River Collection[1]
Preface

My retreat is in the Wang River mountain valley. The places to walk to include: Meng Wall Cove, Huazi Hill, Grained Apricot Lodge, Clear Bamboo Range, Deer Enclosure, Magnolia Enclosure, Dogwood Bank, Sophora Path, Lakeside Pavilion, Southern Hillock, Lake Yi, Willow Waves, Luan Family Shallows, Gold Powder Spring, White Rock Rapids, Northern Hillock, Bamboo Lodge, Magnolia Bank, Lacquer Tree Garden, and Pepper Tree Garden. When Pei Di and I were at leisure, we each composed the following quatrains.

1. Meng Wall Cove

A new home at the mouth of Meng Wall:
Ancient trees, the last withered willows.
The one who comes again—who will it be?
Grieving in vain for former men's possessions.

5. Deer Enclosure

Empty mountain, no man is seen.
Only heard are echoes of men's talk.
Reflected light enters the deep wood
And shines again on blue-green moss.

---

1. Translated by Pauline Yu. Inspired by sites on his country estate in Lantian, outside the capital of Chang'an, Wang Wei composed a series of 20 quatrains that were matched by a set written by his close friend Pei Di (b. 716). Wang also painted a long handscroll depicting the same scenic spots; the scroll has been lost, though numerous imitations exist.

8. Sophora Path

The bypath is shaded by sophoras;
In secluded shadows, green moss is thick.
But the gatekeeper sweeps it in welcome
In case the mountain monk should come.

11. Lake Yi

Blowing flutes cross to the distant shore.
At day's dusk I bid farewell to you.
On the lake with one turn of the head:
Mountain green rolls into white clouds.

17. Bamboo Lodge

Alone I sit amid the dark bamboo,
Play the zither and whistle[2] loud again.
In the deep wood men do not know
The bright moon comes to shine on me.

Bird Call Valley[1]

Man at leisure, cassia flowers fall.
The night still, spring mountain empty.
The moon emerges, startling mountain birds:
At times they call within the spring valley.

Farewell

Dismounting I give you wine to drink,
And inquire where you are going.
You say you did not achieve your wishes
And return to rest at the foot of Southern Mountain.

5   But go—do not ask again:
White clouds have no ending time.

Farewell to Yuan the Second on His Mission to Anxi[1]

In Wei City morning rain dampens the light dust.
By the travelers' lodge, green upon green—the willows' color is new.
I urge you to drink up yet another glass of wine:
Going west from Yang Pass, there are no old friends.

---

2. This was probably a combination of Daoist breathing techniques and whistling, and was said to express feelings while harmonizing with nature and facilitating the achievement of immortality.
1. The first of a series of five quatrains composed at a friend's estate, "Miscellaneous Poems Written at

Huangfu Yue's Cloud Valley."
1. One of many poems to often unidentified fellow officials setting off to distant posts. The city of Wei was in Shaanxi Province, near the imperial capital, whereas Anxi was located far to the northwest in Xinjiang. This quatrain was set to music and became a popular farewell tune.

Visiting the Temple of Gathered Fragrance[1]

I do not know the Temple of Gathered Fragrance,
For several miles, entering cloudy peaks.
Ancient trees, paths without people;
Deep in the mountains, where is the bell?
5   Noise from the spring swallows up lofty rocks;
The color of the sun chills green pines.
Toward dusk by the curve of an empty pond,
Peaceful meditation controls poison dragons.[2]

Zhongnan Retreat

In middle years I am rather fond of the Dao;
My late home is at the foot of Southern Mountain.
When the feeling comes, each time I go there alone.
That splendid things are empty, of course, I know.
5   I walk to the place where the water ends
And sit and watch the time when clouds rise.
Meeting by chance an old man of the forest,
I chat and laugh without a date to return.

In Response to Vice-Magistrate Zhang

In late years I care for tranquility alone—
A myriad affairs do not concern my heart.
A glance at myself: there are no long-range plans.
I only know to return to the old forest.
5   Pine winds blow, loosening my belt;
The mountain moon shines as I pluck my zither.
You ask about reasons for success and failure:
A fisherman's song enters the shore's deeps.[1]

Li Bo
701–762

About Li Bo's family little is known for certain, despite the richness of legends concerning his background—for which the poet himself was probably largely responsible. Possibly of Turkish origin, he was raised in what is now Sichuan province and appears to have treated his birth in the wild west of China as a license to flout accepted norms of behavior. Unlike most of his

1. A Buddhist monastery located south of Chang'an.
2. Most likely referring to illusions or passions that serve as obstacles to enlightenment.
1. Among other things, Wang Wei is alluding to an anonymous fisherman's song included in an anthology of poetry from the southern kingdom of Chu. Responding to

the lament of a political exile about having been banished for his high moral principles, the fisherman's gently mocking song speaks of the greater wisdom of being able to adapt to circumstances: "If the waters are clear, I'll wash my hat, / If they're muddy I'll wash my feet."

peers he never attempted the civil service examination, thus sparing himself the humiliation of failure. But his career aspirations were no less ambitious, perhaps owing to his claim of kinship with the imperial family, also surnamed Li. Thanks to a friendship he cultivated with a powerful Daoist adept, in 742 he succeeded in securing a post in the court bureau responsible for producing official documents, where he initially attracted favorable attention from the emperor and his entourage, but then his drunken audacity led to his expulsion two years later. Lamenting the alleged failure of those in power to appreciate him, he wandered for over a decade and finally provided the emperor with a legitimate reason to mistrust him by becoming involved in a minor revolt. For this he was arrested for treason, and though he was eventually pardoned he died without having secured the patronage he had sought. A popular legend tells of his drowning while trying to embrace the reflection of the moon in the water, although overindulgence in alcohol and long-life elixirs (typically containing mercury) were more likely to blame.

Li Bo traveled extensively to Daoist retreats, and he became known as the "Poet-Immortal." Although he clearly didn't spurn political engagement, his outsider image entitled him to excesses and eccentricities that also characterize his poetry, and his poems often display a playful fantasy that can have the poet, for example, engaging in conversation with the moon. Of his nearly one thousand poems, the majority consist not of the newer regulated verse patterns but of older forms that allowed greater liberties of expression. Li Bo especially enjoyed imitating folk songs, and the colloquial diction and bold expression of longer examples like "The Road to Shu Is Hard" are especially distinctive. As was true for all Tang poets, much of his work consists of responses to occasions like visits and farewells. Li Bo made much of the spontaneity and facility with which he composed, and the disarming simplicity of his diction and imagery in these occasional pieces can suggest deep feeling with extraordinary effectiveness.

Reasonably well known during his lifetime, Li Bo was singled out by later generations as an inspired genius and complement to the more serious and sober Du Fu. Comparative evaluations of the two figures have occupied critics for centuries, but they are generally agreed to be the two most important poets of the Tang dynasty.

Drinking Alone with the Moon[1]

A pot of wine among the flowers.
I drink alone, no friend with me.
I raise my cup to invite the moon.
He and my shadow and I make three.

5   The moon does not know how to drink;
My shadow mimes my capering;
But I'll make merry with them both—
And soon enough it will be Spring.

I sing—the moon moves to and fro.
10   I dance—my shadow leaps and sways.
Still sober, we exchange our joys.
Drunk—and we'll go our separate ways.

Let's pledge—beyond human ties—to be friends,
And meet where the Silver River ends.

1. Translated by Vikram Seth.

Liang Kai, *Li Bo Chanting a Poem,* hanging scroll, 13th century. An honored member of the imperial painting academy, Liang Kai chose, for unknown reasons, to retreat to a Chan Buddhist monastery outside Hangzhou. The spare brushwork of this imaginary portrait captures the nonchalant abandon that Li Bo (701–762) sought to convey in his poetry.

Fighting South of the Ramparts[1]

Last year we were fighting at the source of the Sang-kan;
This year we are fighting on the Onion River road.
We have washed our swords in the surf of Parthian seas;
We have pastured our horses among the snows of the T'ien Shan.
5 The King's armies have grown grey and old
Fighting ten thousand leagues away from home.
The Huns have no trade but battle and carnage;
They have no fields or ploughlands,
But only wastes where white bones lie among yellow sands.
10 Where the house of Ch'in built the Great Wall that was to keep away the
        Tartars,
There, in its turn, the House of Han lit beacons of war.
The beacons are always alight, fighting and marching never stop.
Men die in the field, slashing sword to sword;
The horses of the conquered neigh piteously to Heaven.
15 Crows and hawks peck for human guts,
Carry them in their beaks and hang them on the branches of withered trees.
Captains and soldiers are smeared on the bushes and grass;
The general schemed in vain.
Know therefore that the sword is a cursed thing
20 Which the wise man uses only if he must.

The Road to Shu Is Hard[1]

Ah! it's fearsome—oh! it's high!
The road to Shu is hard, harder than climbing to the sky.
        The kings Can Cong and Yu Fu
        Founded long ago the land of Shu,
5   Then for forty-eight thousand years
        Nothing linked it to the Qin frontiers.
        White Star Peak blocked the western way.
A bird-track tried to cut across to Mount Emei—
And only when the earth shook, hills collapsed, and brave men died
10 Did cliff-roads and sky-ladders join it to the world outside.
Above—high peaks turn back the dragon-chariot of the sun.
Below—great whirlpools turn around the waves that rush and stun.
        Not even yellow cranes can fly across—
        Even the clambering apes are at a loss.
15   At Green Mud Ridge the path coils to and fro:
Nine twists for every hundred steps—up a sheer cliff we go.
The traveller, touching the stars, looks upwards, scared out of his wits.
He clutches his heart with a deep sigh—down on the ground he sits!
Sir, from this journey to the West, will you return some day?
20 How can you hope to climb the crags along this fearful way?
Mournful birds in ancient trees—you'll hear no other sound

---

1. Translated by Arthur Waley.   1. Translated by Vikram Seth.

Of life: the male bird follows his mate as they fly round and round.
　　You'll hear the cuckoo call in the moonlight,
　　Sad that the mountain's bare at night.
25　The road to Shu is hard, harder than climbing to the sky.
Just speak these words to someone's face—you'll see its colour fly.
A hand's breadth from the sky peaks join to crown a precipice
Where withered pines, bent upside down, lean over the abyss.
Swift rapids, wrestling cataracts descend in roaring spasms,
30　Pound cliffs, boil over rocks, and thunder through ten thousand chasms.
　　To face such danger and such fear,
　　Alas, from such a distance, Sir, what could have brought you here?
　　Dagger Peak is high and steep—
　　Even a single man can keep
　　The pass from thousands—though he may
　　Become a wolf or jackal—and betray.
By day we dread the savage tiger's claws,
By night the serpent's jaws,
Its sharp, blood-sucking fangs bared when
It mows down like hemp stalks the lives of men.
　　Though Chengdu is a pleasure dome,
　　Better to quickly turn back home.
The road to Shu is hard, harder than climbing to the sky.
Leaning, I stare into the west and utter a long sigh.

Bring in the Wine[1]

The waters of the Yellow River come down from the sky,
Never once returning as towards the sea they flow.
The mirrors of high palaces are sad with once-bright hair:
Though silken-black at morning it has changed by night to snow.
5　Fulfil your wishes in this life, exhaust your every whim
And never raise an empty golden goblet to the moon.
Fate's loaded me with talent and it must be put to use!
Scatter a thousand coins—they'll all come winging homeward soon.
Cook a sheep, slaughter an ox—and for our further pleasure
10　Let's drink three hundred cups of wine down in a single measure.
　　So here's to you, Dan Qiu—
　　And Master Cen, drink up.
　　Bring in, bring in the wine—
　　Pour on, cup after cup.
15　　I'll sing a song for you—
　　So lend your ears and hear me through.
Bells and drums and feasts and jade are all esteemed in vain:
Just let me be forever drunk and never be sober again.
The sages and the virtuous men are all forgotten now.

1. Translated by Vikram Seth.

20 It is the drinkers of the world whose names alone remain.
Chen Wang, the prince and poet,[2] once at a great banquet paid
Ten thousand for a cask of wine with laughter wild and free.
How can you say, my host, that you have fallen short of cash?
You've got to buy more wine and drink it face to face with me.
25   My furs so rare—
    My dappled mare—
Summon the boy to go and get the choicest wine for these
And we'll dissolve the sorrows of a hundred centuries.

The Jewel Stairs' Grievance[1]

The jewelled steps are already quite white with dew,
It is so late that the dew soaks my gauze stockings,
And I let down the crystal curtain
And watch the moon through the clear autumn.

The River Merchant's Wife: A Letter[1]

While my hair was still cut straight across my forehead
I played about the front gate, pulling flowers.
You came by on bamboo stilts, playing horse,
You walked about my seat, playing with blue plums.
5 And we went on living in the village of Chokan:
Two small people, without dislike or suspicion.

At fourteen I married My Lord you.
I never laughed, being bashful.
Lowering my head, I looked at the wall.
10 Called to, a thousand times, I never looked back.

At fifteen I stopped scowling,
I desired my dust to be mingled with yours
Forever and forever and forever.
Why should I climb the look out?

15 At sixteen you departed,
You went into far Ku-to-yen, by the river of swirling eddies,
And you have been gone five months.
The monkeys make sorrowful noise overhead.

You dragged your feet when you went out.
20 By the gate now, the moss is grown, the different mosses,
Too deep to clear them away!
The leaves fall early this autumn, in wind.
The paired butterflies are already yellow with August
Over the grass in the West garden;

---

2. Chen Wang (Prince Chen) was Cao Zhi (192–232).
1. Translated by Ezra Pound. Pound didn't know classical Chinese, but he worked from the notes to poems of Ernest Fenellosa, a scholar of Japanese culture. With his first volume of these translations, *Cathay* (1915), Pound was said by T. S. Eliot to have become "the inventor of Chinese poetry for our time."
1. Translated by Ezra Pound.

25   They hurt me. I grow older.
       If you are coming down through the narrows of the river Kiang,
       Please let me know beforehand,
       And I will come out to meet you

                                                   As far as Cho-fu-Sa.

Listening to a Monk from Shu Playing the Lute[1]

The monk from Shu with his green lute-case walked
Westward down Emei Shan, and at the sound
Of the first notes he strummed for me I heard
A thousand valleys' rustling pines resound.
5   My heart was cleansed, as if in flowing water.
In bells of frost I heard the resonance die.
Dusk came unnoticed over the emerald hills
And autumn clouds layered the darkening sky.

Farewell to a Friend[1]

Verdant mountains behind the northern ramparts.
White waters wind around the east city wall.
From this place once parting has ended,
The lone tumbleweed flies a myriad miles.
5   Floating clouds: a traveler's thoughts.
Setting sun: an old friend's feelings.
Waving hands, you go from here—
Horses neigh gently as they leave.

In the Quiet Night[1]

The floor before my bed is bright:
Moonlight—like hoarfrost—in my room.
I lift my head and watch the moon.
I drop my head and think of home.

Sitting Alone by Jingting Mountain[1]

The flocks of birds have flown high and away,
A solitary cloud goes off calmly alone.
We look at each other and never get bored—
Just me and Ching-t'ing Mountain.

Question and Answer in the Mountains[1]

They ask me why I live in the green mountains.

1. Translated by Vikram Seth.   1. Translated by Stephen Owen.
1. Translated by Pauline Yu.   1. Translated by Vikram Seth.
1. Translated by Vikram Seth.

I smile and don't reply; my heart's at ease.
Peach blossoms flow downstream, leaving no trace—
And there are other earths and skies than these.

—◦—✠◦✠—◦—

Du Fu
712–770

By common consensus Du Fu wears the heavy mantle of China's greatest poet, but during his lifetime he struggled unsuccessfully for recognition of another sort. The grandson of a prominent court poet, he took the most literary and difficult civil service examination twice to qualify for a position in the central government but failed both times. He attracted the emperor's attention by sending him examples of his literary work and passed a special examination set for him, but when he eventually secured a court position his forthrightness led to dismissal within days. Offered minor provincial posts, he soon opted to resign and embarked on what was to be a lifetime of travel in search of better employment. The separation and hardship he and his family endured were great; one young son died of starvation, and Du Fu himself suffered from chronic and often severe illness and died never having attained his goal.

A failure as a public man, Du Fu nonetheless produced a body of poetry whose concerns and compassion have been seen to embody the highest Confucian ideals. He was the first poet to write directly and often critically about contemporary political and social conditions in China, on a scale both large and small, and has been dubbed as a consequence both the "Poet-Sage" and the "Poet-Historian." He was deeply affected by the devastating effect of the rebellion of general An Lushan in 755, even after the recapture of the capital by imperial troops in 757. The government never regained its past stability or glory, and a sense of irrevocable loss is developed especially powerfully in Du Fu's eight-poem sequence "Autumn Meditations," written while he was in Kuizhou, Sichuan, frustratingly far from the center of activity. What has impressed later readers is his ability to situate his own personal fate within the grand course of events. No poet before him had written so extensively about himself and his own family and with such detail about his daily existence. Du Fu further intertwines this history with that of the nation with great poignancy, the frequent image of a solitary figure in the landscape conveying both his aspirations and his agony at not being able to translate his compassion into broader action.

Du Fu was also the first poet to speak extensively of his own writing, and his work expresses the hope that his poetry could play the role that eluded him in public service. Highly conscious of his craft, he preferred the newer regulated verse forms that allowed him to test the limits of poetic expression under technically demanding conditions. In a poem of eight five- or seven-word lines, a poet would be expected to introduce a topic in the first couplet, provide illustrative descriptive imagery in the next two couplets, and then finish with a witty or enigmatic closure, while conforming to established tonal patterns and observing syntactic and semantic parallelism. The poems written during the last decade of his life are especially noteworthy for their densely packed, ambiguous, and allusive language, and his constant concern with the effort of his art made him the poet's poet for succeeding generations and, by the eleventh century, afforded him an undisputed place at the top of the literary hierarchy.

Ballad of the Army Carts[1]

Carts rattle and squeak,
Horses snort and neigh—
Bows and arrows at their waists, the conscripts march away.
Fathers, mothers, children, wives run to say goodbye.
5   The Xianyang Bridge in clouds of dust is hidden from the eye.
They tug at them and stamp their feet, weep, and obstruct their way.
    The weeping rises to the sky.
    Along the road a passer-by
    Questions the conscripts. They reply:

10 They mobilize us constantly. Sent northwards at fifteen
To guard the River, we were forced once more to volunteer,
Though we are forty now, to man the western front this year.
The headman tied our headcloths for us when we first left here.
We came back white-haired—to be sent again to the frontier.
15 Those frontier posts could fill the sea with the blood of those who've died,
But still the Martial Emperor's aims remain unsatisfied.
In county after county to the east, Sir, don't you know,
In village after village only thorns and brambles grow.
Even if there's a sturdy wife to wield the plough and hoe,
20 The borders of the fields have merged, you can't tell east from west.
It's worse still for the men from Qin, as fighters they're the best—
And so, like chickens or like dogs, they're driven to and fro.

    Though you are kind enough to ask,
    Dare we complain about our task?
25 Take, Sir, this winter. In Guanxi
The troops have not yet been set free.
The district officers come to press
The land tax from us nonetheless.
But, Sir, how can we possibly pay?
30 Having a son's a curse today.
Far better to have daughters, get them married—
A son will lie lost in the grass, unburied.
Why, Sir, on distant Qinghai shore
The bleached ungathered bones lie year on year.
35 New ghosts complain, and those who died before
Weep in the wet gray sky and haunt the ear.

Moonlit Night[1]

In Fuzhou, far away, my wife is watching
The moon alone tonight, and my thoughts fill
With sadness for my children, who can't think
Of me here in Changan; they're too young still.
5   Her cloud-soft hair is moist with fragrant mist.

---

1. Translated by Vikram Seth.   1. Translated by Vikram Seth.

In the clear light her white arms sense the chill.
When will we feel the moonlight dry our tears,
Leaning together on our window-sill?

Spring Prospect[1]

The country shattered, mountains and rivers remain.
Spring in the city—grasses and trees are dense.
Feeling the times, flowers draw forth tears.
Hating to part, birds alarm the heart.
5   Beacon fires for three months in a row:
A letter from home worth ten thousand in gold.
White hairs scratched grow even shorter—
Soon too few to hold a hatpin on.[2]

Traveling at Night[1]

Slender grass, a faint wind on the shore.
Tall mast, a lonely night on the boat.
Stars hang down on the flat plain's expanse.
The moon surges up in the great river, flowing.
5   A name—how can writing make it known?
An office—for age and sickness given up.
Fluttering, floating, what is there for likeness?
On heaven and earth, one sandy gull.

Autumn Meditations[1]

1

Gems of dew wilt and wound the maple trees in the wood:
From Wu mountains, from Wu gorges, the air blows desolate.
The waves between the river banks merge in the seething sky,
Clouds in the wind above the passes touch their shadows on the ground.
5   Clustered chrysanthemums have opened twice, in tears of other days:
The forlorn boat, once and for all, tethers my homeward thoughts.
    In the houses quilted clothes speed scissors and ruler.
The washing blocks pound, faster each evening, in Pai Ti[2] high on the hill.

2

On the solitary walls of K'uei-chou the sunset rays slant,
10   Each night guided by the Dipper I gaze towards the capital.
It is true then that tears start when we hear the gibbon cry thrice:[3]
Useless my mission adrift on the raft which came by this eighth month.[4]
Fumes of the censers by the pictures in the ministry elude my sickbed pillow,
The whitewashed parapets of turrets against the hills dull the mournful bugles.

---

1. Translated by Pauline Yu.
2. Used to anchor the cap of an official.
1. Translated by Pauline Yu.
1. Translated by A. C. Graham. Du Fu wrote this sequence in 766 while in exile in Kuizhou, on the middle Yangzi River far south of the capital of Chang'an.

2. White Emperor City, adjacent to Kuizhou.
3. According to a traditional fishermen's song, the gibbon's three cries in the Wu gorges sounded so mournful they could not but elicit tears.
4. In two separate legends, a fisherman and a Han dynasty official were carried on rafts to the Milky Way.

15   Look! On the wall, the moon in the ivy
       Already, by the shores of the isle, lights the blossoms on the reeds.

                                    3

       A thousand houses rimmed by the mountains are quiet in the morning light,
       Day after day in the house by the river I sit in the blue of the hills.
       Two nights gone the fisher-boats once more come bobbing on the waves,
20   Belated swallows in cooling autumn still flit to and fro. . . .
       A disdained K'uang Heng, as a critic of policy:
       As promoter of learning, a Liu Hsiang who failed.[5]
           Of the school-friends of my childhood, most did well.
       By the Five Tombs[6] in light cloaks they ride their sleek horses.

                                    4

25   Well said Ch'ang-an looks like a chess-board:[7]
       A hundred years of the saddest news.
       The mansions of princes and nobles all have new lords:
       Another breed is capped and robed for office.
       Due north on the mountain passes the gongs and drums shake,
30   To the chariots and horses campaigning in the west the winged dispatches
           hasten.
           While the fish and the dragons fall asleep and the autumn river turns cold
       My native country, untroubled times, are always in my thoughts.

                                    5

       The gate of P'eng-lai Palace faces the South Mountain:
       Dew collects on the bronze stems out of the Misty River.
35   See in the west on Jasper Lake the Queen Mother descend:
       Approaching from the east the purple haze fills the Han-ku pass.[8]
       The clouds roll back, the pheasant-tail screens open before the throne:
       Scales ringed by the sun on dragon robes! I have seen the majestic face.
           I lay down once by the long river, wake left behind by the years,
40   Who so many times answered the roll of court by the blue chain-patterned
           door.

                                    6

       From the mouth of Ch'üt-t'ang gorges here, to the side of Crooked River
           there,
       For ten thousand miles of mist in the wind the touch of pallid autumn.
       Through the walled passage from Calyx Hall the royal splendour coursed,
       To Hibiscus Park the griefs of the frontier came.
45   Pearl blinds and embellished pillars closed in the yellow cranes,
       Embroidered cables and ivory masts startled the white seagulls.
           Look back and pity the singing, dancing land!
       Ch'in from most ancient times was the seat of princes.

5. A famous statesman and a famous editor of the Han dynasty. Between 757 and 758, Du Fu held a position charged with "reminding" the emperor of oversights, but fell out of favor owing to critical memorials.
6. Imperial tombs outside the capital.
7. Recently invaded by rebel troops, Chang'an's streets were also laid out as a symmetrical grid (see page 16).
8. Du Fu refers variously to the Penglai Palace in Chang'an, named after one of the fairy islands in the Eastern sea; the copper pans raised on pillars which the Emperor Wu (140–87 B.C.E.) made to collect dew for the elixir; the Misty River is the empyrean; the Western Queen Mother (Xiwangmu) who banqueted King Mu (1001–947 B.C.E.) at Jasper Lake in her country far to the west, an incident which the poet fuses with her later descent from the sky to teach the arts of immortality to the Emperor Wu; the philosopher Laozi coming through the passes preceded by a purple cloud on his final journey to the west [translator's note].

7

K'un-ming Pool was the Han time's monument,
50 The banners of the Emperor Wu are here before my eyes.[9]
Vega threads her loom in vain by night under the moon,
And the great stone fish's plated scales veer in the autumn wind.
The waves toss a zizania seed, over sunken clouds as black:
Dew on the calyx chills the lotus, red with dropped pollen.
55   Over the pass, all the way to the sky, a road for none but the birds.
On river and lakes, to the ends of the earth, one old fisherman.

8

The K'un-wu road by Yü-su river ran its meandering course,
The shadow of Purple Turret Peak fell into Lake Mei-p'i,
Grains from the fragrant rice-stalks, pecked and dropped by the parrots;
60 On the green *wu-t'ung* tree branches which the perching phoenix aged.
Beautiful girls gathered kingfisher feathers for spring gifts:
Together in the boat, a troop of immortals, we set forth again in the
        evening. . . .
This brush of many colours once forced the elements.
Chanting, peering into the distance, in anguish my white head droops.

Yangtse and Han[1]

By Yangtse and Han, a stranger who thinks of home,
One withered pedant between the Ch'ien and K'un.[2]
Under as far a sky as that streak of cloud,
The moon in the endless night no more alone.
5   In sunset hale of heart still:
In the autumn wind, risen from sickness.
There's always a place kept for an old horse
Though it can take no more to the long road.

Bo Juyi
772–846

Born into a scholar-official family of limited means, Bo Juyi passed the most rigorous civil service examination in 800 and held government posts fairly steadily thereafter, although only
briefly in the capital. Appointed to relatively powerful positions in the provinces as prefect, he
became attracted to Buddhism later in life and thus grew increasingly remote spiritually, as
well as geographically, from the center of political activity. Reacting against tendencies toward
increasingly difficult and obscure poetic styles, Bo wrote prolifically and cultivated a plain
style that he hoped would be accessible even to a peasant woman. Much of his poetry deals

9. Kunming Pool near Chang'an was made by Wu of Han
for naval exercises. Near it was a statue of the Weaving
Girl (the star Vega) and in it a stone whale with movable
fins and tail [translator's note].

1. Translated by A. C. Graham.
2. Ch'ien (qian) and K'un (kun) represent heaven and
earth in the divination system of the *Book of Changes*.

with surprising frankness with details of his daily life, ranging from topics like eating bamboo shoots to the aggravations of child-rearing and the virtues of baldness.

Bo Juyi also took seriously the Confucian mandate to employ poetry as a vehicle of social and political protest. With his lifelong friend Yuan Zhen, he promoted a revival of folk song traditions based on those collected by the Han dynasty Music Bureau, but whose subject matter, unlike that of those predecessors, would focus resolutely on contemporary bureaucratic abuses. But his best-loved work, somewhat to his chagrin, was the tragic story of the Tang emperor Minghuang (or Xuanzong, r. 713–755) and his prized consort, Yang Guifei. She was blamed for preparing the way for the disastrous rebellion of An Lushan, owing both to her infatuating beauty and to the seditious behavior of her relatives. When the emperor was forced to flee the capital with her, his soldiers reportedly refused to protect him unless she was first executed. This anguished tale of conflict between the affairs of the heart and the interests of the state was the subject of numerous other poems, stories, and dramas as well.

A Song of Unending Sorrow[1]

China's Emperor, craving beauty that might shake an empire,
Was on the throne, for many years, searching, never finding,
Till a little child of the Yang clan, hardly even grown,
Bred in an inner chamber, with no one knowing her,
5   But with graces granted by heaven and not to be concealed,
At last one day was chosen for the imperial household.
If she but turned her head and smiled, there were cast a hundred spells,
And the powder and paint of the Six Palaces faded into nothing. . . .
It was early spring. They bathed her in the Flower-Pure Pool,
10   Which warmed and smoothed the creamy-tinted crystal of her skin,
And, because of her languor, a maid was lifting her
When first the Emperor noticed her and chose her for his bride.
The cloud of her hair, petal of her cheek, gold ripples of her crown when
         she moved,
Were sheltered on spring evenings by warm hibiscus-curtains;
15   But nights of spring were short and the sun arose too soon,
And the Emperor, from that time forth, forsook his early hearings
And lavished all his time on her with feasts and revelry,
His mistress of the spring, his despot of the night.
There were other ladies in his court, three thousand of rare beauty,
20   But his favors to three thousand were concentered in one body.
By the time she was dressed in her Golden Chamber, it would be almost
         evening;
And when tables were cleared in the Tower of Jade, she would loiter, slow
         with wine.
Her sisters and brothers all were given titles;
And, because she so illumined and glorified her clan,
25   She brought to every father, every mother through the empire,
Happiness when a girl was born rather than a boy. . . .
High rose Li Palace, entering blue clouds,
And far and wide the breezes carried magical notes
Of soft song and slow dance, of string and bamboo music.

---

1. Translated by Witter Bynner.

30 The Emperor's eyes could never gaze on her enough—
Till war-drums, booming from Yü-yang, shocked the whole earth
And broke the tunes of "The Rainbow Skirt and the Feathered Coat."
The Forbidden City, the nine-tiered palace, loomed in the dust
From thousands of horses and chariots headed southwest.
35 The imperial flag opened the way, now moving and now pausing—
But thirty miles from the capital, beyond the western gate,
The men of the army stopped, not one of them would stir
Till under their horses' hoofs they might trample those moth-eyebrows . . .
Flowery hairpins fell to the ground, no one picked them up,
40 And a green and white jade hair-tassel and a yellow-gold hair-bird.
The Emperor could not save her, he could only cover his face.
And later when he turned to look, the place of blood and tears
Was hidden in a yellow dust blown by a cold wind. . . .
At the cleft of the Dagger-Tower Trail they crisscrossed through a cloud-
          line
45 Under O-mei Mountain. The last few came.
Flags and banners lost their color in the fading sunlight . . .
But as waters of Shu are always green and its mountains always blue,
So changeless was his majesty's love and deeper than the days.
He stared at the desolate moon from his temporary palace,
50 He heard bell-notes in the evening rain, cutting at his breast.
And when heaven and earth resumed their round and the dragon-car faced
          home,
The Emperor clung to the spot and would not turn away
From the soil along the Ma-wei slope, under which was buried
That memory, that anguish. Where was her jade-white face?
55 Ruler and lords, when eyes would meet, wept upon their coats
As they rode, with loose rein, slowly eastward, back to the capital. . . .
The pools, the gardens, the palace, all were just as before,
The Lake T'ai-yi hibiscus, the Wei-yang Palace willows;
But a petal was like her face and a willow-leaf her eyebrow—
60 And what could he do but cry whenever he looked at them? . . .
Peach-trees and plum-trees blossomed, in the winds of spring;
Lakka-foliage fell to the ground, after autumn rains;
The Western and Southern Palaces were littered with late grasses,
And the steps were mounded with red leaves that no one swept away.
65 Her Pear-Garden Players became white-haired
And the eunuchs thin-eyebrowed in her Court of Pepper-Trees;
Over the throne flew fireflies, while he brooded in the twilight.
He would lengthen the lamp-wick to its end and still could never sleep.
Bell and drum would slowly toll the dragging night-hours
70 And the River of Stars grow sharp in the sky, just before dawn,
And the porcelain mandarin-ducks on the roof grow thick with morning
          frost
And his covers of kingfisher-blue feel lonelier and colder
With the distance between life and death year after year;
And yet no beloved spirit ever visited his dreams. . . .
75 At Ling-ch'ün lived a Taoist priest who was a guest of heaven,

Able to summon spirits by his concentrated mind.
And people were so moved by the Emperor's constant brooding
That they besought the Taoist priest to see if he could find her.
He opened his way in space and clove the ether like lightning
80   Up to heaven, under the earth, looking everywhere.
Above, he searched the Green Void, below, the Yellow Spring;
But he failed, in either place, to find the one he looked for.
And then he heard accounts of an enchanted isle at sea,
A part of the intangible and incorporeal world,
85   With pavilions and fine towers in the five-colored air,
And of exquisite immortals moving to and fro,
And of one among them—whom they called The Ever True—
With a face of snow and flowers resembling hers he sought.
So he went to the West Hall's gate of gold and knocked at the jasper door
90   And asked a girl, called Morsel-of-Jade, to tell The Doubly-Perfect.
And the lady, at news of an envoy from the Emperor of China,
Was startled out of dreams in her nine-flowered canopy.
She pushed aside her pillow, dressed, shook away sleep,
And opened the pearly shade and then the silver screen.
95   Her cloudy hair-dress hung on one side because of her great haste,
And her flower-cap was loose when she came along the terrace,
While a light wind filled her cloak and fluttered with her motion
As though she danced "The Rainbow Skirt and the Feathered Coat."
And the tear-drops drifting down her sad white face
100   Were like a rain in spring on the blossom of the pear.
But love glowed deep within her eyes when she bade him thank her liege,
Whose form and voice had been strange to her ever since their parting—
Since happiness had ended at the Court of the Bright Sun,
And moons and dawns had become long in Fairy-Mountain Palace.
105   But when she turned her face and looked down toward the earth
And tried to see the capital, there were only fog and dust.
So she took out, with emotion, the pledges he had given
And, through his envoy, sent him back a shell box and gold hairpin,
But kept one branch of the hairpin, and one side of the box,
110   Breaking the gold of the hairpin, breaking the shell of the box;
"Our souls belong together," she said, "like this gold and this shell—
Somewhere, sometime, on earth or in heaven, we shall surely meet."
And she sent him, by his messenger, a sentence reminding him
Of vows which had been known only to their two hearts:
115   "On the seventh day of the Seventh-month, in the Palace of Long Life,
We told each other secretly in the quiet midnight world
That we wished to fly in heaven, two birds with the wings of one,
And to grow together on the earth, two branches of one tree." . . .
Earth endures, heaven endures; sometime both shall end,
120   While this unending sorrow goes on and on forever.

[END OF POETRY OF THE TANG DYNASTY]

⟞⟝ PERSPECTIVES ⟞⟝
What Is Literature?

In classical Chinese the word for writing, *wen,* embraces a multitude of meanings beyond that of "literature" alone, among them culture, civilization, learning, pattern, refinement, and embellishment. The notion of literature as a primarily aesthetic phenomenon, or belles lettres, arose only very late in China, as in the West, and never took deep or exclusive root in the tradition. Not only did *wen* embrace pragmatic forms such as epitaphs, dispatches, and memorials to the throne, but any individual work was rarely seen as an end in itself, to be read independently of its context and tradition. Much more compelling were the presumptions that literature was an integral element of the cosmos and of the sociopolitical world, and that in writing of the self one inevitably spoke to and of society as well; the forms and patterns of one's writing corresponded naturally with those of the universe itself.

These assumptions played a powerful role in shaping ideas about writing and habits of reading in China. What are now taken as early theoretical statements also often appear embedded in more general discussions or commentaries and introductions to anthologies, rather than as independent, discrete works. The notion that a poem, for example, was a critical response to an external stimulus motivates the most important commentaries on the first anthology of poetry, the *Book of Songs,* and when applied to other works led to a de-emphasis on ideas of purely imaginative creation, originality, and uniqueness in favor of the search for the concrete historical circumstances that produced a given poem. This impulse to contextualize the elements of a literary work was a persistent one. A poem could serve to construct a biography, and known biographical facts, conversely, could explicate the poetry; extended works of narrative would similarly be construed less as fiction than as chronicles—no matter how disguised—of the author and his personal circumstances. Critical attention was also paid to other more ineffable sources of inspiration, for which Daoism provided important images, as well as to the technical and aesthetic dimensions of the craft of writing itself. But the belief in the didactic function of all writing and the obsession with the political dimension of expression remained paramount and distinguishes the Chinese tradition notably from that of Japan, with which it otherwise shares several basic ideas.

Cao Pi
187–226

Cao Pi ascended to the throne of the Wei dynasty in 220 after the abdication of the last Han emperor, thanks to the successful inroads on the emperor's mandate to rule made by Cao Pi's father, Cao Cao (155–220). His right to the throne continued to be contested by two other warlords (the period is therefore known as that of the Three Kingdoms), and his rule was further threatened by the claims made on behalf of his two brothers, one of whom was also a talented poet. Though emperor for only six years, Cao Pi was the first to be known as a man of letters, though only a handful of his poems and rhapsodies have survived. The "Discourse on Literature" (*Lun wen*) is the only surviving chapter of a longer series of essays entitled "Classical Discourses" (*Dian lun*) and may itself be incomplete. Cao Pi comments on the most prominent writers of the age and on popular literary genres, but his most important statements address the ways in which a writer's character, thanks to his spirit or *qi,* informs literature and in which literature itself can transcend mere utilitarian purposes and the ravages of mortality.

from A Discourse on Literature[1]

Literary men disparage one another—it's always been that way. The relation between Fu Yi and Pan Ku was nothing less than the relation of a younger brother to an elder brother.[2] Yet Pan Ku belittled him, writing in a letter to his elder brother Pan Chao: "Wu-chung [Fu Yi] became Imperial Librarian through his facility in composition: whenever he used his writing brush, he couldn't stop himself."

People are good at [or fond of] making themselves known; but since literature (*wen*) is not of one form alone, few can be good at everything. Thus each person disparages that in which he is weak by the criterion of those things in which he is strong. There is a village saying: "The worn-out broom that belongs to my own household is worth a thousand in gold." Such is the ill consequence of a lack of self-awareness.

The literary men of this day * * * have omitted nothing in their learning, have no borrowed colors in their diction. Yet they have found it most difficult to all gallop together a thousand leagues, side by side with equal pace on their mighty steeds, and thus to pay one another due respect.

A superior person examines himself to measure others; and thus he is able to avoid such entanglements [e.g., envy and blindness to the worth of others]. Thus I have written a discourse on literature.

Ordinary people value what is far away and feel contempt for what is close at hand. They favor repute and turn their backs on substance. Moreover, they suffer the ill consequences of ignorance in self-awareness, claiming to be men of great worth.

Literature is the same at the root, but differs in its branches [a "branch tip," the later stages of a process]. Generally speaking, memorials and disquisitions should have dignity; letters and memorials should be based on natural principle; inscriptions and eulogy value the facts; poetry and poetic exposition aspire to beauty. Each of these four categories is different, so that a writer's ability will favor some over others. Only a comprehensive talent can achieve the full complement of these forms.

In literature *ch'i*[3] is the dominant factor. *Ch'i* has its normative forms—clear and murky. It is not to be brought by force. Compare it to music: though melodies be equal and though the rhythms follow the rules, when it comes to an inequality in drawing on a reserve of *ch'i*, we have grounds to distinguish skill and clumsiness. Although it may reside in a father, he cannot transfer it to his son; nor can an elder brother transfer it to the younger.

I would say that literary works are the supreme achievement in the business of state, a splendor that does not decay. A time will come when a person's life ends; glory and pleasure go no further than this body. To carry both to eternity, there is nothing to compare with the unending permanence of the literary work.

---

1. Translated by Stephen Owen.
2. Fu Yi and Pan Ku (Ban Gu) were the most eminent writers of the later 1st century. The sibling metaphor may refer either to their personal friendship or the comparison of quality.

3. Literally "breath" or spirit, *ch'i* (*qi*) is what animates and unifies the elements of a literary work.

So writers of ancient times entrusted their persons to ink and the brush, and let their thoughts be seen in their compositions; depending neither on a good historian nor on momentum from a powerful patron, their reputations were handed down to posterity on their own force.

The Earl of the West [later made King Wen of the Chou], when imprisoned, amplified the *Book of Changes;* the Duke of Chou, though in his glory, prescribed the Rites. The former did not ignore this [the importance of literary work] in spite of hardship; the latter was not distracted by health and pleasure. From this we can see how the ancients thought nothing of large jade disks [marks of wealth], but valued each moment, fearful lest their time pass them by.

Yet people usually do not exert themselves: in poverty and low station they fear the hunger and cold; amid wealth and honor they drift with the distractions of pleasure. They busy themselves with the demands of what lies right before their eyes, and neglect an accomplishment lasting a thousand years. Overhead, the days and months pass away from us; here below, face and body waste away. Suddenly we will move off into transformation with all the other things of the world—this is the greatest pain for a person with high aspirations.

Lu Ji
261–303

Having gained early renown for his literary talents, Lu Ji became a well-known statesman as well as a general, but he was implicated in an unsuccessful revolt against the Jin dynasty and was therefore executed on charges of treason at a relatively young age. A prolific poet, he owes his reputation to a single work, the *Rhymeprose on Literature* (*Wen fu*), the earliest sustained and systematic discussion of literature. Its date of composition has been disputed for some time; Tang dynasty poets thought the work was written when Lu Ji was twenty, whereas other sources suggest a date two decades later.

Like other early theorists, Lu Ji addresses the sources, forms, processes, and effects of literature, with less attention than others to its didactic function and greater focus on the agonies and mysteries of inspiration and composition. His special interest in exploring the engagement of the writer's mind with ideas and nature reflects contemporary neo-Daoist debates about the relationship between words and meaning and provides us with notions worth comparing to Western theories of the imagination. Lu Ji's choice of genre accounts for significant stylistic features of his work: variously translated as "rhapsody," "prose poem," and "exposition," the *fu* alternates sections of rhymed verse with passages of prose and is characterized by balanced parallel constructions, frequent enumeration, lush description, and a profusion of metaphors.

from Rhymeprose on Literature[1]
Preface
(in Unrhymed Prose)

Each time I study the works of great writers, I flatter myself I know how
their minds worked.

1. Translated by Achilles Fang.

Certainly expression in language and the charging of words with meaning can be done in various ways.

Nevertheless, we may speak of beauty and ugliness, of good and bad in each literary work.

Whenever I write myself, I obtain greater and greater insight.

5   Our constant worry is that our ideas may not equal their objects and our style may fall short of our ideas.[2]

The difficulty, then, lies not so much in knowing as in doing.

I have written this rhymeprose on literature to expatiate on the consummate artistry of writers of the past and to set forth the whence and why of good and bad writings as well.

May it be considered, someday, an exhaustive treatment.

Now, it is true, I am hewing an ax handle with an ax handle in my hand: the pattern is not far to seek.[3]

10   However, the conjuring hand of the artist being what it is, I cannot possibly make my words do the trick.

Nevertheless, what I am able to say I have put down here.

Text

1: PREPARATION

Taking his position at the hub of things, [the writer] contemplates the mystery of the universe; he feeds his emotions and his mind on the great works of the past.

Moving along with the four seasons, he sighs at the passing of time; gazing at the myriad objects, he thinks of the complexity of the world.

He sorrows over the falling leaves in virile autumn; he takes joy in the delicate bud of fragrant spring.

With awe at heart, he experiences chill; his spirit solemn, he turns his gaze to the clouds.

5   He declaims the superb works of his predecessors; he croons the clean fragrance of past worthies.

He roams in the Forest of Literature, and praises the symmetry of great art.

Moved, he pushes his books away and takes the writing brush, that he may express himself in letters.

2: PROCESS

At first he withholds his sight and turns his hearing inward; he is lost in thought, questioning everywhere.

His spirit gallops to the eight ends of the universe;[4] his mind wanders along vast distances.

---

2. This notion became a commonplace of Chinese literary criticism and goes back to a Confucian commentary on the *Book of Changes* that states: "Writing does not exhaust language, and language does not exhaust meaning."
3. An allusion to poem 158 in the *Book of Songs,* which begins: "How does one hew an ax-handle? / Without an ax it can't be done."
4. The extremes of the eight compass directions: north, east, south, west, northeast, etc.

10   In the end, as his mood dawns clearer and clearer, objects, now clean-cut in
      outline, shove one another forward.

He sips the essence of letters; he rinses his mouth with the extract of the Six
      Arts.[5]

Floating on the heavenly lake, he swims along; plunging into the nether
      spring, he immerses himself.

Thereupon, submerged words wriggle up, as when a darting fish, with the
      hook in its gills, leaps from a deep lake; floating beauties flutter down, as
      when a high-flying bird, with the harpoon-string around its wings, drops
      from a crest of cloud.

He gathers words never used in a hundred generations; he picks rhythms
      never sung in a thousand years.

15   He spurns the morning blossom, now full blown; he plucks the evening bud,
      which has yet to open.

He sees past and present in a moment; he touches the four seas in the twin-
      kling of an eye.

3: WORDS, WORDS, WORDS

Now he selects ideas and fixes them in their order; he examines words and
      puts them in their places.

He taps at the door of all that is colorful; he chooses from among everything
      that rings.

Now he shakes the foliage by tugging the twig; now he follows the waves to
      the fountainhead of the stream.

20   Sometimes he brings out what was hidden; sometimes, looking for an easy
      prey, he bags a hard one.

Now the tiger puts on new stripes, to the consternation of other beasts; now
      the dragon emerges, and terrifies all the birds.

Sometimes things fit together, and are easy to manage; sometimes they jar
      each other, and are awkward to manipulate.

He empties his mind completely to concentrate his thoughts; he collects his
      wits before he puts words together.

He traps heaven and earth in the cage of form; he crushes the myriad objects
      against the tip of his brush.

25   At first they hesitate upon his parched lips; finally they flow through the
      well-moistened brush.

Reason, supporting the matter [of the poem], stiffens the trunk; style, de-
      pending from it, spreads luxuriance around.

Emotion and expression never disagree: all changes [in his mood] are be-
      trayed on his face.

If the thought touches on joy, a smile is inevitable; no sooner is sorrow spo-
      ken of than a sigh escapes.

Sometimes words flow easily as soon as he grasps the brush; sometimes he
      sits vacantly, nibbling at it.

5. Either the six arts of the *Rituals of Zhou* (ceremonies, music, archery, charioteering, calligraphy, and mathematics) or
the six Confucian "arts" or classics (*Book of Songs, Book of Changes, Book of Documents, Book of Music* [long since lost],
Record of Rituals, and *Spring and Autumn Annals*).

4: VIRTUE

30   There is joy in this vocation; all sages esteem it.

We [poets] struggle with Non-Being to force it to yield Being; we knock
upon Silence for an answering Music.

We enclose boundless space in a square foot of paper; we pour out a deluge
from the inch-space of the heart.

Language spreads wider and wider; thought probes deeper and deeper.

The fragrance of delicious flowers is diffused; exuberant profusion of green
twigs is budding.

35   A laughing wind will fly and whirl upward; dense clouds will arise from the
Forest of Writing Brushes.

5: DIVERSITY

The Poet's Aim

Forms vary in a thousand ways; objects are not of one measure.

Topsy-turvy and fleeting, shapes are hard to delineate.

Words vie with words for display, but it is mind that controls them.

Confronted with bringing something into being or leaving it unsaid, he
groans; between the shallow and the deep, he makes his choice
resolutely.

40   He may depart from the square and deviate from the compasses; for he is
bent on exploring the shape and exhausting the reality.

Hence, he who would dazzle the eyes makes much of the gorgeous; he who
intends to convince the mind values cogency.

If persuasion is your aim, do not be a stickler for details; when your discourse is lofty, you may be free and easy in your language.

Genres

Shih (lyric poetry) traces emotions daintily; *fu* (rhymeprose) embodies objects brightly.

Pei (epitaph) balances substance with style; *lei* (dirge) is tense and mournful.

45   *Ming* (inscription) is comprehensive and concise, gentle and generous;
chen (admonition), which praises and blames, is clear-cut and
vigorous.

Sung (eulogy) is free and easy, rich and lush; *lun* (disquisition) is rarefied
and subtle, bright and smooth.

Tsou (memorial to the throne) is quiet and penetrating, genteel and decorous; *shuo* (discourse) is dazzling bright and extravagantly bizarre.

Different as these forms are, they all forbid deviation from the straight, and
interdict unbridled license.

Essentially, words must communicate, and reason must dominate; prolixity
and long-windedness are not commendable.

6: Multiple Aspects

50   As an object, literature puts on numerous shapes; as a form, it undergoes diverse changes.

Ideas should be cleverly brought together; language should be beautifully commissioned.

And the mutation of sounds and tones should be like the five colors of embroidery sustaining each other.

It is true that your moods, which come and go without notice, embarrass you by their fickleness,

But if you can rise to all emergencies and know the correct order, it will be like opening a channel from a spring of water.

55   If, however, you have missed the chance and reach the sense belatedly, you will be putting the tail at the head.

The sequence of dark and yellow being deranged, the whole broidery will look smudged and blurred.

7: Revision

Now you glance back and are constrained by an earlier passage; now you look forward and are coerced by some anticipated line.

Sometimes your words jar though your reasoning is sound; sometimes your language is smooth while your ideas make trouble.

Such collisions avoided, neither suffers; forced together, both suffer.

60   Weigh merit or demerit by the milligram; decide rejection or retention by a hairbreadth.

If your idea or word has not the correct weight, it has to go, however comely it may look.

8: Key Passages

Maybe your language is already ample and your reasoning rich, yet your ideas do not round out.

If what must go on cannot be ended, what has been said in full cannot be added to.

Put down terse phrases here and there at key positions; they will invigorate the entire piece.

65   Your words will acquire their proper values in the light of these phrases.

This clever trick will spare you the pain of deleting and excising.

9: Plagiarism

It may be that language and thought blend into damascened gauze—fresh, gay, and exuberantly lush;

Glowing like many-colored broidery, mournful as multiple chords;

But assuredly there is nothing novel in my writing, if it coincides with earlier masterpieces.

70   True, the arrow struck my heart; what a pity, then, that others were struck
        before me.
      As plagiarism will impair my integrity and damage my probity, I must re-
        nounce the piece, however fond I am of it.

10: PURPLE PATCHES

      It may be that one ear of the stalk buds, its tip standing prominent, solitary
        and exquisite.
      But shadows cannot be caught; echoes are hard to bind.
      Standing forlorn, your purple passage juts out conspicuously; it cannot be
        woven into ordinary music.
75   Your mind, out of step, finds no mate for it; your ideas, wandering hither
        and thither, refuse to throw away that solitary passage.
      When the rock embeds jade, the mountain glows; when the stream is im-
        pregnated with pearls, the river becomes alluring.
      When the hazel and arrow-thorn bush is spared from the sickle, it will glory
        in its foliage.
      We will weave the market ditty into the classical melody; perhaps we may
        thus rescue what is beautiful.

11: FIVE IMPERFECTIONS

1: In Vacuo

      Maybe you have entrusted your diction to an anemic rhythm; living in a
        desert, you have only yourself to talk to.
80   When you look down into silence, you see no friend; when you lift your
        gaze to space, you hear no echo.
      It is like striking a single chord—it rings out, but there is no music.

2: Discord

      Maybe you fit your words to a frazzled music; merely gaudy, your language
        lacks charm.
      As beauty and ugliness are commingled, your good stuff suffers.
      It is like the harsh note of a wind instrument in the courtyard below; there is
        music, but no harmony.

3: Novelty for Novelty's Sake

85   Maybe you forsake reason and strive for the bizarre; you are merely search-
        ing for inanity and pursuing the trivial.
      Your language lacks sincerity and is poor in love; your words wash back
        and forth and never come to the point.
      They are like a thin chord violently twanging—there is harmony, but it is
        not sad.

4: License

Maybe by galloping unbridled, you make your writing sound good; by using luscious tunes, you make it alluring.
Merely pleasing to the eye, it mates with vulgarity—a fine voice, but a nondescript song.
90   It reminds one of Fang-lu and Sang-chien,[6]—it is sad, but not decorous.

5: Insipidity

Or perhaps your writing is simple and terse, all superfluities removed—
So much so that it lacks even the lingering flavor of a sacrificial broth;[7] it
rather resembles the limpid tune of the "vermilion chord."
"One man sings, and three men do the refrain";[8] it is decorous, but it lacks
beauty.

12: VARIABILITY

As to whether your work should be loose or constricted, whether you should
mold it by gazing down or looking up,
95   You will accommodate necessary variation, if you would bring out all the
overtones.
Maybe your language is simple, whereas your conceits are clever; maybe
your reasoning is plain, but your words fall too lightly.
Maybe you follow the beaten track to attain greater novelty; maybe you immerse yourself in the muddy water—to reach true limpidity.
Well, perspicacity may come after closer inspection; subtlety may ensue
from more polishing.
It is like dancers flinging their sleeves in harmony with the beat or singers
throwing their voices in tune with the chord.
100   All this is what the wheelwright Pien despaired of ever explaining;[9] it certainly is not what mere language can describe.

13: MASTERPIECES

I have been paying tribute to laws of words and rules of style.
I know well what the world blames, and I am familiar with what the wor-
thies of the past praised.
Originality is a thing often looked at askance by the fixed eye.
The *fu*-gems and jade beads, they say, are as numerous as the "pulse in the
middle of the field,"[1]

6. Most likely, titles of "indecorous" songs from a fallen
state.
7. Sacrificial broth was purposefully bland.
8. The vermilion chord refers to zithers played in ancestral temples, which were either so understated or so
evocative that one note would require or elicit a refrain
(or sigh) of three others.

9. The wheelwright Pien is the master craftsman in
Zhuangzi's "The Way of Heaven" who cannot transmit
through words the secret of his art.
1. Alluding to a poem from the *Book of Songs* (no. 196)
that speaks of the easy availability to commoners of pulse
(large beans) growing in the fields.

105   As inexhaustible as the space between heaven and earth, and growing co-
          eternally with heaven and earth themselves.
       The world abounds with masterpieces; and yet they do not fill my two
          hands.

14: THE POET'S DESPAIR

       How I grieve that the bottle is often empty; how I sorrow that Elevating
          Discourse is hard to continue.
       No wonder I limp along with trivial rhythms and make indifferent music to
          complete the song.
       I always conclude a piece with a lingering regret; can I be smug and self-
          satisfied?
110   I fear to be a drummer on an earthen jug; the jinglers of jade pendants will
          laugh at me.

15: INSPIRATION

       As for the interaction of stimulus and response, and the principle of the
          flowing and ebbing of inspiration,
       You cannot hinder its coming or stop its going,
       It vanishes like a shadow, and it comes like echoes.
       When the Heavenly Arrow[2] is at its fleetest and sharpest, what confusion is
          there that cannot be brought to order?
115   The wind of thought bursts from the heart; the stream of words rushes
          through the lips and teeth.
       Luxuriance and magnificence wait the command of the brush and the paper.
       Shining and glittering, language fills your eyes; abundant and overflowing,
          music drowns your ears.

       When, on the other hand, the Six Emotions[3] become sluggish and foul, the
          mood gone but the psyche remaining,
       You will be as forlorn as a dead stump, as empty as the bed of a dry river.
120   You probe into the hidden depth of your soul; you rouse your spirit to
          search for yourself.
       But your reason, darkened, is crouching lower and lower; your thought must
          be dragged out by force, wriggling and struggling.
       So it is that when your emotions are exhausted you produce many faults;
          when your ideas run freely you commit fewer mistakes.
       True, the thing lies in me, but it is not in my power to force it out.
       And so, time and again, I beat my empty breast and groan; I really do not
          know the causes of the flowing and the not flowing.

---

2. The beginning impulses of a natural process.   3. Variously defined, but always paired, as in pleasure
                                                          and anger, joy and sorrow, love and hate.

16: Coda—Encomium

125   The function of style is, to be sure, to serve as a prop for your ideas. (Yet allow me to expatiate on the art of letters:)

It travels over endless miles, removing all obstructions on the way; it spans innumerable years, taking the place, really, of a bridge.

Looking down, it bequeaths patterns to the future; gazing up, it contemplates the examples of the ancients.

It preserves the way of Wen and Wu,[4] about to fall to the ground; and it propagates good ethos, never to perish.

No path is too far for it to tread; no thought is too subtle for it to comprehend.

130   It is a match for clouds and rain in yielding sweet moisture; it is like spirits and ghosts in bringing about metamorphoses.

It inscribes bronze and marble to make virtue known; it breathes through flutes and strings, and is new always.

Liu Xie
c. 465–522

About the details of Liu Xie's life little is known. He was a lay scholar of Buddhism who spent considerable time studying with monks and eventually entered a monastery himself. His sole critical work, the *Wenxin Diaolong,* was probably written around 501. It was the first—and, indeed, only—comprehensive book on literature in all of its aspects and manifestations and gained for him, before he took his Buddhist vows, a series of minor posts in one of the princely courts in southern China, where literary issues were debated with genteel fervor during the fifth and sixth centuries. Although it never vanished from scholarly view, it wasn't celebrated as a major theoretical work until the eighteenth century. Modern Western scholars have continued to appreciate its broad and systematic approach, which is unusual in the Chinese critical tradition.

The title of Liu Xie's work, *Wenxin Diaolong,* has been the subject of much discussion. It may be translated, among various possibilities, as *The Literary Mind: Dragon-Carvings,* referring perhaps to two major components of writing, mind and craft, or to the book's presentation of crafted elaborations on the essence of literature. Of its forty-nine chapters and afterword, the first half discusses origins and types of writing and the second analyzes specific relations among writer, work, and world. The two chapters included here head each section; in Chapter 1, Liu Xie plays on the multiple meanings of the word *wen* to establish literature as a natural form of expression premised on correlations between the individual and the cosmos; Chapter 26, like Lu Ji's *Rhymeprose on Literature,* reflects Liu's debt to Daoist metaphors in understanding the process of writing.

PRONUNCIATION:
    Liu Xie: lee-OH she-EH

---

4. The founders of the Zhou dynasty, whose ways, according to Confucius, had not yet fallen to the ground.

from The Literary Mind[1]

Chapter 1

ITS SOURCE IN THE WAY

As an inner power, pattern (*wen*) is very great indeed, born together with Heaven and Earth. And how is this? All colors are compounded of two primary colors, the purple that is Heaven and the brown that is Earth. All forms are distinguished through two primary forms, Earth's squareness and Heaven's circularity.[2] The sun and moon are successive disks of jade, showing to those below images that cleave to Heaven. Rivers and mountains are glittering finery, unrolling forms that give order to Earth. These are the pattern of the Way.

Considering the radiance emitted above, and reflecting on the loveliness that in-hered below, the positions of high and low were determined, and the two standards were generated.[3] Only the human being, endowed with the divine spark of consciousness, ranks as a third with this pair. And they were called the Triad [Heaven, Earth, and human beings]. The human being is the flower of the elements: in fact, the mind of Heaven and Earth. When mind came into being, language was established; and with the establish-ment of language, pattern became manifest. This is the natural course of things, the Way.

If we consider further the thousands of categories of things, each plant and animal has its own pattern. Dragon and phoenix display auspicious omens by their intricacy and bright colors; the visual appearance of a tiger is determined by its stripes, and that of a leopard, by its spots. The sculpted forms and colors of the clouds possess a sub-tlety that transcends the painter's craft; the intricate luxuriance of trees and plants does not depend upon the wondrous skill of an embroiderer. These are in no way ex-ternal adornments: they are of Nature. And when we consider the resonances created by the vents in the forest,[4] they blend like zithers and ocarinas; the tones stirred by streams running over stones have a harmony like that of chimes and bells. Thus when shape is established, a unit is complete; when sound emerges, pattern is generated. Given the fact that these things which lack the power of recognition may still possess such lush colors, how can this vessel of mind lack a pattern appropriate to it?

The origins of human pattern began in the Primordial.[5] The Images of the *Book of Changes* were first to bring to light spiritual presences that lie concealed. Fu Hsi marked out the initial stages [by producing the trigrams of the *Changes*], and Confu-cius added the Wings [exegetical and cosmological tracts accompanying the *Changes*] to bring the work to a conclusion. Only for the two positions of Ch'ien and K'un did Confucius make the "Patterned Words."[6] For is not pattern in words "the mind of Heaven and Earth"?! And then it came to pass that the "Yellow River Diagram" became imprinted with the eight trigrams;[7] and the "Lo River Writing"

1. Translated by Stephen Owen.
2. The earth is square because it was presumed to be at rest, whereas heaven was a circle that rotated.
3. The "two standards" are Heaven and Earth, whose large categorical difference became manifest through the investigation of the patterns inhering in each [translator's note].
4. I.e., winds blowing through the empty spaces of the earth associated with the "piping of earth" in the "Dis-cussion on Making All Things Equal" in the *Zhuangzi*

[translator's note].
5. The undifferentiated state from which all distinct things came into being.
6. A commentary on the first two hexagrams in the *Book of Changes,* said to have been written by Confucius.
7. There was a legend that the trigrams, the core elements of the hexagrams of the *Book of Changes*, first appeared in a diagram carried by a dragon that emerged from the Yellow River [translator's note].

contained the Nine Divisions.[8] No person was responsible for these, which are the fruit of jade tablets inlaid with gold, the flower of green strips with red writing (*wen*): they came from the basic principle of spirit.

When the "tracks of birds" took the place of knotted cords,[9] the written word first appeared in its glory. The events that occurred in the reigns of Yen-ti and Shen-nung were recorded in the "Three Monuments";[1] but that age is murky and remote, and its sounds and colors cannot be sought. It was in the literary writings of Yao and Shun that the first splendid flourishing occurred. The song of "The Leader" [a verse in the *Book of Documents*] initiated singing intent [the origin of poetry]. The expostulation offered in the *Yi-chi* [chapter of the *Book of Documents*] handed down to us the custom of memorials to the throne. Then rose up the Lords of Hsia [the dynasty before the Shang], whose achievements were towering and whose merit was vast; when "the nine sequences were put into song,"[2] their deeds and virtue were even more fully elaborated. When it reached the dynasties of Shang and Chou, patterning became greater than substance. Whatever the *Ya* and *Sung* [of the *Book of Songs*] covered is daily renewed in all its splendor. The "Comments" [to the *Book of Changes* composed] by King Wen of Chou in the time of his troubles [when imprisoned by the Shang] still gleam, like streaked jade, multifarious and cryptic, the essential principles firm and deep. In addition to this there was the Duke of Chou with his great talent, who displayed his goodness and endeavors in fashioning *Songs* and compiling the Hymns (*Sung,* of the *Book of Songs*), master of intricate wordcraft. Then came Confucius, successor of the Sages, uniquely outstanding among former wise men; he molded the Six Classics so that they would ring like metal and jade and would sculpt human nature in the interweaving of their words. The sound of the wooden bell-clapper arose,[3] and was answered from a thousand leagues around; the treasures at his table [his writings] flow forth and resound for ten thousand generations: he delineated the radiance of Heaven and Earth, and opened up the eyes and ears of all the people.

From Fu Hsi, the mysterious Sage who founded the canon, up to the time of Confucius, the uncrowned king who transmitted the teaching, all took for their source the mind of the Way to set forth their writings, and they investigated the principle of spirit to establish their teaching. They took the Images from the Yellow River Diagram and the Lo River Writing, and they consulted both milfoil and tortoise carapaces about fate [methods of divination]. They observed the pattern of the heavens to know the full range of mutations; and they investigated human pattern to perfect their transforming [i.e., to civilize the people]. Only then could they establish the warp and woof of the cosmos, completing and unifying its great ordinances, and they accomplished a patrimony of great deeds, leaving truths shining in their words.

8. Another legend had it that when Yü was controlling the great flood, a sacred tortoise appeared in the Lo River, which carried the "Nine Divisions," nine sets of enumerated categories which comprehended the operations of nature and the state [translator's note].

9. Cang Jie, the "recorder" of the Yellow Emperor, came up with the idea for written characters by observing the tracks of birds; prior to this, knotted cords had been used for keeping records [translator's note].

1. Both Yen-ti and Shen-nung were mythical Sage Emperors of high antiquity. The "Three Monuments" were legendary lost texts of antiquity.

2. A quotation from the *Book of Documents*, referring to the history of the Xia rulers.

3. In the *Analects* 3.24, Confucius is described as "wooden bell-clapper" whom Heaven intends to use to show the world the Way that has been lost.

Thus we know that the Way sent down its pattern through the Sages, and that the Sages made the Way manifest in their patterns. It extends everywhere with no obstruction, and is applied every day and never found wanting. The *Book of Changes* says, "That which stirs the world into movement is preserved in language." That by which language can stir all the world into movement is the pattern of the Way.

SUPPORTING VERSE

The mind of the Way is subtle,
The principle of spirit establishes teaching.
Luminous is that Primal Sage,
In whom fellow-feeling and fillal piety gleam.
The diagram on the Yellow River dragon offered the form;
The writing on the tortoise showed its appearance.
Here the pattern of Heaven can be observed,
For all the people to emulate.

Chapter 26

SPIRIT THOUGHT

Long ago someone spoke of "the physical form's being by the rivers and lakes, but the mind's remaining at the foot of the palace towers of Wei."[4] This is what is meant by spirit thought. And spirit goes far indeed in the thought that occurs in writing (*wen*). When we silently focus our concerns, thought may reach to a thousand years in the past; and as our countenance stirs ever so gently, our vision may cross ten thousand leagues. The sounds of pearls and jade are given forth while chanting and singing; right before our eyelashes, the color of windblown clouds unfurls. This is accomplished by the basic principle of thought.

When the basic principle of thought is at its most subtle, the spirit wanders with things. The spirit dwells in the breast; intent and *ch'i*[5] control the bolt to its gate [to let it out]. Things come in through the ear and eye; in this, language controls the hinge and trigger. When hinge and trigger permit passage, no things have hidden appearance; when the bolt to the gate is closed, then spirit is concealed.

Thus in shaping and turning [as on a potter's wheel] literary thought, the most important thing is emptiness and stillness within. Dredge clear the inner organs and wash the spirit pure.[6] Amass learning to build a treasure house; consult principle to enrich talent; investigate and experience to know all that appears [literally "exhaust

---

4. In the *Zhuangzi*, this line refers to a ruler's inability to detach himself from political involvement even while living in retirement, but Liu Xie disregards this original context here.

5. *Ch'i* (qi) is the animating force that may actualize the direction of one's interest, or intent.
6. A similar passage describing inner purification for spiritual events appears in the *Zhuangzi*.

what shines"]; guide it along to spin the words out. Only then can the butcher, who cuts things apart mysteriously, set the pattern according to the rules of sound; and the uniquely discerning carpenter wield his ax with his eye to the concept-image.[7] This is the foremost technique in directing the course of *wen,* the major point for planning a piece.

When spirit thought is set in motion, ten thousand paths sprout before it; rules and regulations are still hollow positions; and the cutting or carving as yet has no form. If one climbs a mountain, one's affections are filled by the mountain; if one contemplates the sea, one's concepts are brought to brimming over by the sea. And, according to the measure of talent in the self, one may speed off together with the wind and clouds.

Whenever a person grasps the writing brush, the *ch'i* is doubled even before the words come. But when a piece is complete, it goes no further than half of that with which the mind began. Why is this? When concepts soar across the empty sky, they easily become wondrous; but it is hard to be artful by giving them substantial expression in words. Thus concept is received from thought, and language in turn is received from concept. These [language and concept] may be so close that there is no boundary between them, or so remote that they seem a thousand leagues from one another. Sometimes the principle lies within the speck of mind, yet one seeks it far beyond the world; sometimes a truth is only a foot away, but thought goes beyond mountains and rivers in pursuit of it. Thus if one grasps the mind and nourishes its techniques, it will not be requisite to brood painfully. If you retain the design within and retain control of the creditor's half of the contract,[8] you need not force the affections to suffer.

People are endowed with different allotments of talent, some swift and some slow. And the forms of literary work differ in the achievement, some of large magnitude and some small. * * *

The mind of a sharp-witted person combines all the essential techniques; and his very quickness preempts reflection, making instant decisions in response to the demands of the moment. The state of mind of someone who broods deeply is filled with forking paths: he sees clearly only after uncertainties and makes his determination only after thoughtful reflection. When one is quick of mind in response to the demands of the moment, the accomplishment is brought about hastily; when reflection is full of uncertainties, it takes a much longer time to achieve one's goals.

Although ease and difficulty differ, both depend on perfecting oneself on a broad scope. If learning is shallow, the latter type is slow in vain; if talent is diffuse, the former type is swift to no good end. One never hears of great accomplishment by the likes of these. There are two sources of danger as you approach a piece and compose your reflections: if principle remains blocked, there is poverty [of content]; if language

---

7. The "butcher" is Cook Ting (Ding) in "The Secret of Caring for Life" in the *Zhuangzi,* who carves an ox effortlessly thanks to unselfconscious operations of the spirit. Carpenter Shi appears in another anecdote from the *Zhuangzi* as a craftsman of similarly marvelous skills.

8. Contractual arrangements were formalized by assigning each party matching halves of a round tally.

gets bogged down, there is confusion. In such cases, broad experience is the provision that can feed poverty [of content], and continuity is the medicine that can save one from confusion. To have breadth and still to be able to provide continuity aids the force of mind.

The variety of states of mind may be peculiar and mixed; the mutations of normative form shift just as often. Plain and simple diction may be made pregnant by some artful truth; commonplace matters may be brought to sprout by fresh concepts. Compare hempen cloth to threads of hemp—though some might say the latter are of little value, when shuttle and loom set their achievement before us, it is prized for its glittering brightness.

But when it comes to those tenuous implications beyond the reach of thought, the fine variations in sentiment beyond the text (*wen*), these are things that language cannot pursue, and where the writing brush knows well to halt. That subtlety can be brought to light only by reaching ultimate essence; that order can be comprehended only by reaching the ultimate in mutation. Yi Yin could not tell of the art of the cauldron; Wheelwright Pien could not speak of the ax.[9] These are the real fine points.

SUPPORTING VERSE

> Spirit gets through by images,
> Giving birth to mutations of the affections.
> Things are sought by their outer appearance,
> But the response of mind is for basic principle.
> Craftsmanship is given to the rules of sound,
> It sprouts in comparisons and affective images:
> Drawing one's thoughts together, take the creditor's half of the contract,
> And behind hanging tent-flaps determine victories.[1]

Wang Changling
c. 690–c. 756

Despite his birth into an eminent family and success on the most difficult civil service examination, Wang Changling didn't enjoy a distinguished career as a government official, perhaps owing to his relatively late start in the mid-730s. He served briefly in the capital of Chang'an until posted to the provinces. While serving as a county administrator, he was executed for unknown reasons during the An Lushan rebellion of 755–757.

Wang Changling's literary career was a happier one. Judging by his generous representation in extant Tang dynasty anthologies, he was highly regarded by his contemporaries, who especially appreciated his mastery of the quatrain and his poems set on the frontier and in palace boudoirs. A brief theoretical work by Wang entitled *Forms of Poetry* (*Shi ge*) disappeared from

---

9. Yi Yin, who was to become the minister of King Tang of the Shang dynasty, was originally a cook and, by legend, is said to have been unable to explain the secrets of his art [translator's note]. Similarly, the Wheelwright Pien in the *Zhuangzi's* "The Way of Heaven" could not transmit the secrets of his skill in language.

1. The reference here is to General Zhang Liang, who won great victories by staying in his tent and planning [translator's note].

China after the Tang but was preserved, along with other texts that would not otherwise have survived, by the Japanese monk Kūkai (774–835), who brought them back to Japan along with the Buddhist treatises that had been his primary reason for traveling to China. Kūkai rearranged and collected them in a volume designed to provide both Buddhists and courtiers in Japan with the information they would be expected to possess about Chinese language and poetry. "A Discussion of Literature and Meaning" (*Lun wen yi*) is his heading for a section from Wang's *Forms of Poetry* that presents well-accepted ideas about the sources, composition, and critique of poetry in often concrete and colorful terms.

from A Discussion of Literature and Meaning[1]

It has been said that writing arose from the kingly way and only existed after the men of old drew the character "one." The kingly way is that which the first rulers transmitted; without words, the world was self-ruled; without teaching, the world was itself. This is the kingly way.

The kingly way is in accord with the nature of matter, and the nature of matter is in accord with heavenly principle. Thus, the myriad things are endowed by it, and living beings are ruled by it. Yao put it into practise and Shun was an example of it. Under his pure and simple teaching, the people did not know they had a ruler. But the knowledge of later men declined. The sages knew of it, and so they drew the eight trigrams and passed down a shallow teaching for later men to rely on.

Thus we know that the one gave rise to names, that names gave rise to teachings, and that afterwards the teaching of names (Confucianism)[2] arose therefrom. If we regard the teaching of names as its forebear, then literature arises from the kingly way and starts with the "Songs of the States."[3]

From ancient times literature has arisen from non-action and started from nature, forming itself in response to stimulus, without ornament or selection. We produce words to be fitting. When they fit their objects, then they are appropriate.

* * *

Poetry is basically the intent of the heart. When a poet has an intent in his heart, he utters words to make a poem. His feelings move inside and become manifest in words; then he writes them on paper. When a superior talent works, he creates a new meaning in each line; failing this, in two lines. His meaning is like billowing smoke rising from earth to the skies; it gets gradually higher toward the end, so high that one cannot ascend higher. An inferior talent's later lines are weaker than his earlier ones; he doesn't look back and doesn't establish a central meaning. No one can bear to read them.

* * *

Writing is neither difficult nor toilsome. * * * In writing, just have lots of ideas, letting the one penetrate the other, until your mind is tired and your intelligence exhausted. You must forget yourself and be unrestrained. If no thought comes, then relax your feelings, step back and be patient, and allow the world to create thoughts. Thereafter illuminate them with the world. If thoughts come, then write. But if thoughts of the world don't come, then you can't work.

---

1. Translated by Richard W. Bodman.
2. The "Teaching of Names" refers to the largely Confucian articulation of the moral responsibility of persons engaged in public life. Daoism, by contrast, was known as the "Nameless Teaching."
3. The first section of the *Book of Songs*, folk songs assigned to various feudal states of the Zhou dynasty.

Now when you have an idea for making a poem, you must concentrate your mind's eye and attack its object. When you attack it with your mind, then you deeply penetrate its world. It's like climbing to the summit of a tall mountain and looking down; the myriad things seem as if in the palm of your hand. When you see things in this way, you see clearly in your mind. When you put this into practise, it's as if there's nothing in the poem which doesn't resemble what you see.

Then one applies the rules of harmony. When this is all set, then one writes the poem out on paper, capping it with a title. The mountains, forests, sun and moon are the true scene, and when one praises them in song, it's like seeing the sun or moon reflected in water. Writing is the reflection, the scene is the original. When one illuminates it (the scene) one must clearly see its objects.[4]

When writing is inspired, it first excites the spirit. The spirit is born in the mind; the mind is uttered in words, is heard by the ear, seen by the eye, and recorded on paper. Its idea must surpass the world of ordinary men, and look toward the men of old while standing in the present. It compresses the sea of heaven into a square inch.[5] Here is where the poet must exert every effort.

The head of a poem discusses its meaning. When that meaning is exhausted, its belly broadens; when its belly broadens, then the poem can be easy and comfortable. The physical world is written down helter-skelter, and when the tail is reached, one steps back and embraces the original meaning. Each verse must have its place.

There are several ways of using words. There are light words and heavy, medium-heavy words and medium-light words. There are cases in which although the heavy and muddy words can be used, the light and pure cannot be used. Everything requires a detailed rule.

* * *

Everyone who writes must always create ideas. Concentrate your mind beyond the sea of heaven, let your imagination roam before the beginning of the world. Cleverly revolve words and phrases, skillfully train your ideas and soul. In the words and lines you write, never use archaic language. Nowadays people forge words with old meanings, revise old language, move the head and change the tail. Such people will never advance far. That's because they have no character of their own. If you can't concentrate your mind, belaboring your mind for insight will not work.

A poet places a bright lamp at the head of his bed at night. If sleep comes, then he lets himself sleep. After he has slept and gotten up again, then inspiration comes and an idea grows, his spirits are cheerful, clear and bright. You must always place yourself in the midst of your idea. If there is no self in the poem, then how can there be a poem? If you don't write about your own mind, then how can you make a poem? Therefore poetry is the vehicle by which we write out our own minds and which sets in order our present enthusiasm. For if enthusiasm should come which is not appropriate, our mind's concern may not succeed.

These concerns may be to criticize superiors, to reform inferiors, to express one's mind, or to narrate events in order. In each case, no one will understand me unless my

---

4. This section contains perhaps the earliest use in Chinese literary criticism of the analogy between literature and a mirror [translator's note].

5. Alluding to a passage from Lu Ji's "Rhymeprose on Literature": "We enclose boundless space in a square foot of paper; we pour out a deluge from the inch-space of the heart." The same allusion recurs below.

mind is made up. Speaking of it from this point of view, we recognize at last the basics of the men of old.

All those who write poems copy out for themselves the good parts of poetic language from past to present, in what are called "pocket notebooks," in order to ward off depression. When the impulse to write doesn't come, then you must glance through your pocket notebook to elicit that impulse.

* * *

Whenever you write, you must observe how the masters of the past and present use their imagination, and study whatever new and remarkable tunes there may be.

Poetry values melting the ideas in the title into the poem without remainder. Make sure that you mention the places that you see in connection with the ideas that you have.

If you state your intent right off, the poem will be ordinary and tasteless. If there is too much talk about the scene, not closely connected with your idea, it will also be without savor, even though it may be well-said. When scenes of dusk and dawn or the climate of the four seasons are matched with ideas and given an order; when you speak of them at the same moment as meaning—that's marvelous.

At the first light of the sun, rivers, mountains, forests, peaks, cliffs and walls are separated by night mist and sunny clouds; but wherever the sun's rays strike, they open up. The reason why each object the sun touches emits light is that when the sun illuminates each place that the mist has moistened, the water reflects the light. Towards noon, although the sunny clouds are used up, the force of yang is at its height, and everything is hidden and obscured, so that the poet can't bear to use it. But at dawn, when sunny clouds have not yet lifted, the force of yang is slight, and everything is pure. When the poet looks at this, then he can bear to use it. Whenever any object becomes shining, then he can use it. His thoughts and the objects in the scene that he speaks of must conform to the appropriate season. Spring, summer, fall and winter each in their own time create their own meaning, which the poet should select and use. When he uses these meanings, he must quiet his soul and make tranquil his anxieties. As his eye observes an object, it enters his mind. His mind penetrates it and when the object is penetrated, he speaks. When he speaks of its form, what he says must resemble its image. His speech must be such that the contents of the sea of heaven are gathered within a square inch. At clear dawn, that which he sees—scenes near and far, dark places, and scenic spots—must each be allowed to give thought free rein and give rise to their own meaning.

If you want to write, take advantage of imagination and then set to work. But if it seems tedious, then stop, and don't allow your mind to become tired. If you always do it this way, your inspiration will not cease and your soul will never be exhausted.

* * *

Whenever your soul is uneasy, it makes you joyless and uninspired. When uninspired, let yourself sleep; sleep greatly restores your soul. You must always put out your lamp at night and let yourself wake up naturally. You must not force yourself to get up. If you force yourself to get up, you will be muddled, and what you see will be of no profit. Paper, brush, and ink must always accompany you, so that when inspiration strikes, you can record it. For if you're without paper and brush as you travel, your idea will get tangled. After a trip by boat, you must sleep peacefully. After you've had enough sleep, then many clear vistas, rivers and mountains will fill your breast and combine to give birth to inspiration. You must wall off business affairs and concentrate on letting your feelings go. Thus you will create, even to excess.

If you see that your inspiration is flagging a little and your poem is yet unfinished, then wait until later for inspiration to finish it. You must not forcibly harm your spirit.

Imitate old writings, but don't follow their old ideas, or you will never advance far. In all cases you must criss-cross and zig-zag, transform and appropriate the material in a hundred ways. At the head and in each section you must let your idea lead the way, then afterwards return and gather up the original idea.

* * *

Whenever you have an idea for a poem, masterful and startling lines rise up. It's as if no one is by your side. You shouldn't be afraid.

Sikong Tu
837–908

Born into a family with a distinguished record of public service, Sikong Tu himself passed the highest civil service examination in 869. His government career, however, was a short one, owing to the social instability and rebellions that disrupted the waning decades of the Tang dynasty. Having retired to his mountain estate and the contemplative attractions of Buddhism and Daoism, Sikong Tu resisted later attempts to reengage him in political struggles and, according to legend, starved himself to death when he heard that the last Tang emperor had been murdered.

The author of some four hundred poems and two often-cited letters articulating influential notions of poetic effect, Sikong Tu is best known for a series of poems entitled *The Twenty-four Classes of Poetry* (*Ershisi shi pin*), although this attribution has been questioned in recent years. Written in an archaic four-syllable verse form and employing elusive imagery and elliptical statement, the series presents twenty-four "classes" (the word *pin* referred most commonly to bureaucratic ranks), but in no apparent sequence or hierarchy. They are probably best thought of as "modes" or "moods," whether of the poet, the poem, the reader's experience, or all of them at once. The important influence of Daoism is evident in the series' emphasis on the transcendence of worldly distinctions, a nonassertion of the self, and an ideal of natural and spontaneous creation.

from The Twenty-four Classes of Poetry[1]
1. POTENT AND GRAND

> Great power manifested without,
> Full of spiritual substance within;
> Return to the void, enter the All
> And gathered vigor becomes grandeur.
> 5   It contains a myriad phenomena,
> Extends across the great emptiness,

---

1. Translated by Pauline Yu (sections 1, 2, 20, and 24) and Stephen Owen (sections 11 and 14).

Vast as the flowing clouds,
Lonely as the distant wind.
Leap beyond the external appearance
10 To reach the circle's center[2]—
Hold it without coercion,
It will come without end.

2. PLACID AND CALM

By nature it dwells in silence,
Its mysterious essence so subtle;
It drinks of celestial harmony
And flies alone with the crane.
5   It's like the kindly breeze,
Gently blowing through clothes,
Sound passing through beautiful bamboo,
Bringing beauty back home.
Encountering it is not difficult,
10 Pursue it and it grows more scarce.
If it has a shape,
Grasp with the hand—it escapes.

11. RESERVE/ACCUMULATION WITHIN

It does not inhere in any single word
Yet the utmost flair is attained.
Though the words do not touch on oneself,
It is as if there were unbearable melancholy.
5   In this there is that "someone in control,"[3]
Floating or sinking along with them.
It is like straining the thickest wine,
Or the season of flowers reverting to autumn.
Far, far away, specks of dust in the sky;
10 Passing in a flash, bubbles on the ocean.
Shallow and deep, clustering, scattering,
Thousands of grains are gathered into one.

14. CLOSE-WOVEN AND DENSE

This does possess genuine traces,
But it is as though they cannot be known.
As the concept-image is about to emerge,
The process of creation is already wondrous.

---

2. In the *Zhuangzi*, the center of the circle, or empty space around which a wheel turns, refers to unrealized transformative powers.

3. An allusion to a passage on human identity from the "Discussion on Making All Things Equal" in the *Zhuangzi* (Volume A).

5   Water flowing, flowers opening,
     The clear dew not yet dried away,
     The strategic road getting ever farther,
     The slowness of passage through secluded places.
     The words should not come to redundancy,
10   The thought should not tend to naïveté.
     It is like the spring in greenness,
     Or bright moonlight where there is snow.

20. DESCRIPTION

     Solely gather spiritual simplicity
     And soon will return the pure truth,
     Like seeking the shadows in water
     Or writing the glories of spring.
5   Winds' and clouds' shifting shapes,
     Flowers' and grasses' vividness,
     Oceans' rolling billows,
     Mountains' precipitous crags—
     All resemble the great Dao
10   Mysteriously bonded even to dust.
     Leave the substance to reach the image
     To approximate this kind of poet.

24. FLUX

     Like a receiving water wheel,
     Like a revolving round pearl,
     How can one speak of it?
     It borrows substance to speak to the dull.
5   Extensive as the earth's pivot,
     Distant as the heaven's axis;
     Seek its principles
     And harmonize with it.
     Ever transcending spirit's brightness,
10   Ever returning to dark nothingness,
     Coming and going for a thousand years,
     This is what can be said of it.

❀ CROSSCURRENTS: WHAT IS "LITERATURE"? ❀

- Poetry was the preeminent literary genre in medieval China, an integral part of public life both official and nonofficial. In what ways do the poems of the Tang dynasty (page 83) provide information about the authors' theories and beliefs about the function of literature? What do the poems of Tao Qian (page 68) and Han-shan (page 78) suggest about the tensions between the official and the less official roles of the poet?

- Much of medieval Japanese poetry was written by members of the aristocracy rather than civil servants, as in medieval China. What do the poems of the *Man'yōshū* or in the Perspectives section on courtly women suggest about attitudes toward poetry in the imperial court in Japan? How do these ideas about poetry compare with those in medieval China?

- Several Perspectives sections in other volumes of the anthology also focus on theories of literature. What similarities and differences in assumptions about the nature and function of literature are found in "What Is Literature?" in Early South Asia (Volume A), "Lyric Sequences and Self-Definition" in Early Modern Europe (Volume C), "The National Poet" in the nineteenth century (Volume E), and "The Art of the Manifesto" and "Poetry About Poetry" in the twentieth century (Volume F)?

↔ END OF PERSPECTIVES: WHAT IS LITERATURE? ↔

Shusetsu Dōjin, landscape painting, Japan, 15th century. Shusetsu
Dōjin was the disciple of Shūbun, a noted Zen priest-painter. The towering cliffs recede in the mist, while in the foreground a contemplative
man reads in his lightly sketched house.

Japan

ANCIENT PERIOD (TO 794)

From the fourth century onward, a number of powerful clans dominated the Japanese archipelago. Each clan traced its origins to an ancestral deity and built large key-shaped tombs. Gradually the Yamato clan, whose clan deity was the Sun Goddess (Amaterasu) and which was based in the Yamato basin, in present-day Nara City (southeast of Kyoto), conquered the other clans. The Yamato clan formed an imperial court centered on a sovereign who claimed descent from the Sun Goddess and eventually incorporated the heads of the other clans into a state administrative system. The Yamato clan became the imperial clan that was to rule Japan or stand as a figurehead for political authority for many centuries up until the present.

The *Kojiki* (*Record of Ancient Matters*), one of the earliest works of Japanese literature, was originally written in order to legitimize this new imperial order by providing an account of how the islands of Japan and its gods came into being. The *Kojiki* later became the bible of Shintō (the way of the gods), the native folk religion that saw the divine in nature (trees, mountains, rivers, and so on), stressed ancestral worship, and focused on issues of bounty, purification/pollution, exorcism, and spirit pacification. Besides being an important historical chronicle, the *Kojiki* is valued today as the primary source for understanding Japanese myths and narrative archetypes such as the exile of the young noble, which appears in *The Tale of Genji* and other later narratives.

Buddhism—named after the teachings of Shakyamuni, the historical Buddha born in India—was introduced to Japan from China in the middle of the sixth century, and it became a major carrier of Chinese civilization. Because Buddhism was first thought to cure disease and ward off plagues, it was adapted by the ruling Yamato clan as a means of protecting the state, but it eventually had a far more profound impact in shaping Japanese views of life and death. If the animistic folk beliefs later called Shintō focused on fertility and life in this world, Buddhism focused on suffering and death. For Buddhism, the primary consequence of suffering in this world was attachment to the phenomenal world, which was by nature impermanent and illusory. Attachment and craving resulted in an endless cycle of life, death, and rebirth. The primary means of overcoming that suffering was through the Buddhist path, which was interpreted in various ways in the coming centuries but which stressed, above all, detachment and the realization of the impermanent and illusory nature of all things.

Confucianism, which came from China as well, also had a major impact on Japan. The seventh and eighth centuries were a period of great Chinese cultural influence, introducing a writing system based on Chinese graphs, Chinese literature, and Chinese philosophy, particularly Confucianism, which established a social-political and moral code based on the family, with filial piety as the highest virtue. Chinese became the official language of government and religion in Japan, creating a double system of spoken Japanese and written Chinese. The Japanese had only an oral tradition prior to contact with the Chinese writing system. In China, the two great literary genres had been poetry and history, a tradition continued by the Japanese. The *Kojiki* is an attempt to imitate the Chinese dynastic histories, and the *Man'yōshū* is the first major attempt to assemble an anthology of poetry in the manner of Chinese anthologies.

The latter half of the seventh century witnessed a blossoming of Japanese poetry, particularly long poems (*chōka*) and short poems (*tanka*), employing *man'yōgana,* a system of using Chinese graphs to record Japanese words and sounds. For the next five hundred years, poetry played a key role in the life of the aristocracy. It had an important public role, functioning much like speeches made today by dignitaries and heads of state, celebrating political or military accomplishments, paying respects to the deceased, or commemorating the occasion of imperial visits. Poetry also had a key private role, functioning as the chief form of communication between men and women, who were normally physically separated from each other. Hitomaro, the most famous poet of his time, served as court poet to three sovereigns, particularly Jitō (r. 690–697), in the late seventh century, writing poems such as the Ōmi poem which glorified the imperial family and nostalgically remembered a lost past. Equally important were Hitomaro's love poems about the lover's absence or death. These poems mark one of the important beginnings of a long lyrical tradition in which love, the four seasons, and bereavement became the central themes of Japanese poetry. The four seasons not only became one of the major topics of Japanese poetry, they provided the primary metaphors for expressing a range of human emotions.

> *. . . poetry played a key role in the life of the aristocracy . . . functioning much like speeches made today by dignitaries and heads of state . . .*

Occasions and topics for Japanese poetry, or *waka,* ranged from the seasons to love to celebration, mourning, separation, and travel, all separate chapters in the *Kokinshū.* Poems were composed for public functions, at poetry contests and poetry parties, and for illustrated screens. Privately *waka* functioned as a social medium, for greetings, courtship, and farewell, as well as a monologic form of self-reflection. These poems were sometimes collected together in large, public anthologies such as the *Kokinshū,* the first imperial anthology of *waka.* At other times poets edited private collections, which in turn could become travel diaries which commemorated and highlighted the experience of travel, as is evident in the *Sarashina Diary.* Private poetry collections could also provide the seed and core for a confessional autobiography such as *The Kagerō Diary,* which probably began as a private collection of poems by Michitsuna's Mother. Poetry, indeed, was everywhere. As a preface to the *Kokinshū* poetry collection put it:

> Japanese poetry has the human heart as seed and myriads of words as leaves. It comes into being when men use the seen and the heard to give voice to feelings aroused by the innumerable events in their lives. The song of the warbler among the blossoms, the voice of the frog dwelling in the water—these teach us that every living creature sings. It is song that moves heaven and earth without effort, stirs emotions in the invisible spirits and gods, brings harmony to the relations between men and women, and calms the hearts of fierce warriors.

Japanese society from the late seventh century through the twelfth century revolved around a court-centered aristocracy that prized elegance and refinement. In 710 the capital moved to present-day Nara, modeled after the Tang capital, and it grew to a population of 200,000 with about 60,000 aristocrats. It is the writing of this segment of society, particularly mid-level aristocrats such as the poets Yamanoue Okura, Yamanobe Akahito, and Ōtomo Yakamochi, that is remembered today. Yakamochi compiled the *Man'yōshū,* with roughly 4,500 poems. It was during the Nara period that a state university was established, with the Confucian classics at the core.

THE HEIAN PERIOD (794–1185)

In 794, the capital moved to Heian, present-day Kyoto, marking the beginning of four centuries of cultural efflorescence centered on the imperial court and aristocratic life. Culturally, Japan continued to absorb influence from the continent, but it gradually developed its own native cultural forms. Complex Chinese graphs were supplemented by the invention of a simplified phonetic syllabary (*kana*) in the early tenth century, making possible the growth of vernacular literature, particularly the thirty-one syllable classical poem, which was practiced by both sexes. Writing in Chinese, particularly Chinese poetry, was held in the highest esteem from the ancient period. The *Kokinshū* (c. 905), the first imperial anthology of classical poetry, however, marked the recognition of vernacular poetry as equal to Chinese poetry. The emergence of women's literature in the tenth century can partly be attributed to the fact that men continued to write in Chinese, the public language, while women devoted themselves to the native syllabary, which proved to be a rich medium for poetry, prose, and narrative fiction.

> *... men continued to write in Chinese, the public language, while women devoted themselves to the native syllabary, which proved to be a rich medium for poetry, prose, and narrative fiction.*

The Fujiwara clan came to the fore in the Heian period. During the late ninth century, Emperor Uda (r. 887–897) and then his son Emperor Daigo (r. 897–930), with the aid of Sugawara no Michizane (845–903) and other ministers, managed to hold off the Fujiwara, and their reigns were later considered to be a golden age of imperial rule and cultural efflorescence. It was Emperor Daigo who ordered the compilation of the *Kokinshū.* But by the latter half of the tenth century, the Fujiwara took firm control of the throne through a regent system in which a Fujiwara regent ruled in place of a child emperor. The Fujiwara married their daughters to the emperor, thereby becoming the uncles of future emperors, and placing a clan member in the position to be the ruling chancellor. The Fujiwara poured vast resources into the entourages and residences of these imperial consorts, enabling women's court literature to flourish at this time. The most powerful of these regents was Fujiwara Michinaga (966–1027), whose eldest daughter Shōshi became the empress and consort of Emperor Ichijō (r. 986–1011). Murasaki Shikibu, Japan's most noted woman writer, probably wrote much of *The Tale of Genji* while serving as a lady in waiting to Empress Shōshi, while Sei Shōnagon, the author of *The Pillowbook,* the other great vernacular work of this period, was a lady in waiting to Empress Teishi, a consort of Emperor Ichijō and Shōshi's rival. *The Pillowbook,* a witty commentary on court life and aesthetics, is a paean to the cultural achievements of Empress Teishi and her entourage. Women writers appear as early as Princess Nukata in the *Man'yōshū,* but never in the concentration and quality that we find in this period.

But these women writers were not in positions of social or political domination. Almost all of the vernacular literature of this period (such as the *Kagerō Diary, The Tale of Genji,* and the *Sarashina Diary*) was written by daughters of men in the provincial governor class, the middle level of the aristocracy, who were sent to the provinces and who were frequently in unstable political and economic positions. Many of these provincial governors, having failed to rise in the court hierarchy, had a critical, outsider's perspective on court politics and aristocratic society. One consequence was that while women's court literature paid homage to their imperial patrons and the powerful Fujiwara clan (as in *The Pillowbook* and the *Diary of Murasaki Shi-kibu*) it also expressed deep disillusionment with court life and the unstable and vulnerable position of women, particularly as a result of the polygamous marriage system in which men commuted to the residences of women. *The Tale of Genji*, widely considered to be the world's first novel, reveals the high level of cultural accomplishment of the imperial court—in such diverse fields as calligraphy, painting, poetry, incense, dance, and music—even as it focuses on the vicissitudes of a wide range of very distinctive women. In a Buddhist twist, the sin of transgression (of having an illegitimate son by one's stepmother) is revisited on the protagonist, the shining Genji, at the height of courtly glory. Equally important, in a larger aesthetic that reflects the influence of the Buddhist notion of impermanence and that is embodied in the fleeting cherry blossoms, many of the most moving, powerfully emotional scenes are those that are the result of the sorrowful and fleeting nature of things.

> The Tale of Genji, *widely considered to be the world's first novel, reveals the high level of cultural accomplishment of the imperial court . . .*

Much of vernacular literature from the Heian period through the medieval period exists in a larger Buddhist context that regards excessive attachments—especially deep emotions such as resentment, hatred, and love—as the cause for suffering and a serious deterrent to individual salvation. By the mid-Heian period, the Japanese believed strong attachments, particularly at the point of death, would impede progress of the soul to the next world, which, hopefully, would be the Pure Land, or Western Paradise. However, Heian women's vernacular works such as *The Tale of Genji* and the *Sarashina Diary* do not engage in religious didacticism; instead they take a highly ambivalent view of Buddhist ideals—focusing on the difficulty of attaining detachment in a world of passion, complex family ties, and secular concerns.

THE MEDIEVAL PERIOD (1185–1600)

At the end of the twelfth century, two major warrior clans, the Heike (Taira) and the Genji (Minamoto), engaged in an extended war for control of the capital and the court, ushering in the age of the samurai. The Heike clan initially displaced the ruling Fujiwara clan as the *de facto* rulers of the country, but they imitated the Fujiwara aristocrats and were soon defeated by the Genji, who were warriors from the East and who established a military government in Kamakura, southeast of present-day Tokyo. The result was two political centers, a court government in Kyoto and a military government in the East. The military government in the East gradually increased in power to the point where the court government in Kyoto was completely hollowed out. The aristocrats in Kyoto, who saw their fortunes waning, occasionally attempted to restore power to the imperial court, but the struggle between the two courts in the fourteenth century (1336–1392) ended any more such attempts, destroying the capital and dispersing the nobility, with the power permanently shifting to the military. The impact of the new warrior culture—the

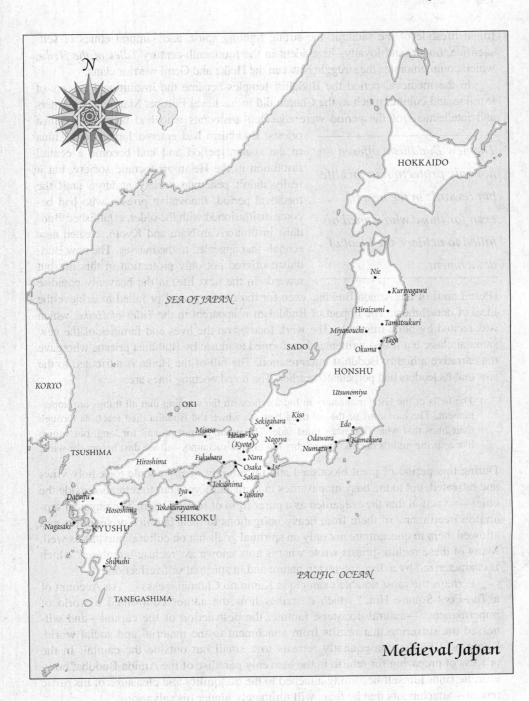

Medieval Japan

HOKKAIDO

SEA OF JAPAN

Nie
Kuriyagawa
Hiraizumi
Tamatsukuri
Miyanouchi
Okuma
Taga

SADO

HONSHU

KORYO

Utsunomiya

OKI

Sekigahara
Kiso
Edo
Misasa
Heian-kyo
(Kyoto)
Nagoya
Odawara
Kamakura
Numazu

TSUSHIMA

Hiroshima
Fukuhara
Nara
Osaka
Ise
Sakai

Dazaifu
Iya
Yashiro
Hososhima
Tokushima

Nagasaki
Yokokurayama
SHIKOKU

KYUSHU

Shibushi

PACIFIC OCEAN

TANEGASHIMA

frugal lifestyle of the samurai, the strong fighting spirit, and samurai ethics of self-sacrifice, honor, and loyalty—is evident in the fourteenth-century *Tales of the Heike,* which commemorates the struggle between the Heike and Genji warrior clans.

In the medieval period the Buddhist temples became the institutional centers of learning and culture, much as the Church did in medieval Europe. Many of the writers and intellectuals of the period were educated aristocrats who had become Buddhist priests. Buddhism had entered Japan from China in the ancient period and had become a central institution in the Heian aristocratic society, but it really didn't penetrate society at large until the medieval period. Innovative priests, who had become disillusioned with the older, established Buddhist institutions in Nara and Kyoto, created new schools that appealed to the masses. The new Buddhism offered not only protection in this life but rewards in the next life, in the heavenly paradise (Pure Land) of the Amida Buddha, even for those who sinned or failed to achieve the ideal of detachment. The impact of Buddhism is apparent in the *Tales of Heike,* which was recited by blind minstrels. The work focuses on the lives and families of the new samurai class, but it was written and performed to music by Buddhist priests, who gave the narrative a highly Buddhist interpretation. The fall of the Heike is attributed to the sins that its leaders had perpetuated earlier. The noted opening lines are:

> The bells of the Gion monastery in India echo with the warning that all things are impermanent. The blossoms of the sal trees beneath which the Buddha died teach us through their hues that what flourishes must fade. The proud do not prevail for long, but vanish like a spring night's dream. The mighty too in time succumb—all are dust before the wind.

During this period of great bloodshed and uncertainty, many people took holy vows and retreated, not to the busy monasteries in Nara and Kyoto but to retreats outside the cities—an action that they regarded as a purer form of renunciation. The physical separation freed many of them from heavy obligations to their families or superiors and allowed them to concentrate not only on spiritual goals but on cultural pursuits as well. Many of these recluse-priests wrote what is now known as "recluse literature," which is characterized by a deep interest in nature and in spiritual self-reflection.

Perhaps the most notable example is Kamo no Chōmei's essay, "An Account of a Ten-Foot-Square Hut," which describes how the author confronted a world of impermanence—natural disasters, famine, the destruction of the capital—and witnessed the suffering that results from attachment to the material and social world. Kamo no Chōmei consequently retreats to a small hut outside the capital. In the process of preparing for rebirth in the heavenly paradise of the Amida Buddha, however, he finds himself becoming attached to the tranquility and pleasures of his rustic retreat—attachments that he fears will ultimately hinder his salvation.

In the late medieval period, from 1336 to 1572, generally referred to as the Muromachi age, the political center shifted back to Kyoto. The Ashikaga shogunate, or military government, which was to rule over Japan for almost two and a half centuries, located its headquarters in Kyoto (rather than in the East). It came of age with the third shogun, Ashikaga Yoshimitsu (r. 1368–1394), who unified the rival imperial courts, took control of the imperial court in Kyoto, and became a great patron of the arts.

Mutō Shūi, *Portrait of the Monk Musō Soseki*. On completing their studies with a spiritual leader, Zen monks would ask for a portrait of their master, who would often write a symbolic poem above the image. This portrait of the Zen master Musō Soseki (1275–1351) was painted by his disciple Mutō Shūi, who captures his teacher's spiritual concentration in a style of rhythmic, harmonious simplicity.

The fusion of samurai patronage and court culture is evident in the maturation of Noh drama, particularly under the leadership of Zeami (1363–1443), the foremost playwright of Japan. Noh drama originated from performances by groups of entertainers and actors attached to large temples and shrines in the provinces around Kyoto. A number of Noh plays tell about the origins of the local gods in these temples and shrines. But in its mature phase Noh was patronized by the Ashikaga military elite, which was situated in the capital of Kyoto and had assimilated court and aristocratic culture. Zeami elevated Noh by incorporating Heian court poetry and aesthetics into his drama, creating, for example, plays centered on women such as *Pining Wind* (*Matsukaze*), which re-creates the elegant Heian aristocratic and courtly past through a character (Yukihira) who is exiled and closely associated with the exiled protagonist of *The Tale of Genji*. Zeami also appealed directly to his powerful warrior patrons by creating warrior plays such as *Atsumori*, which reenacts the psychological trauma of a fallen warrior in the *Tales of the Heike*, which became the main source for warrior plays.

Buddhism continues to play a key role. In Noh plays such as *Pining Wind* and *Atsumori* the protagonists are the spirits of the dead who linger in this world as a result of attachments to it. In a typical Noh play by Zeami, the protagonist is caught in one of the lower realms—often as a wandering ghost or a person suffering in hell—as a result of some deep attachment or resentment. For the warrior, the attachment is often the bitterness or ignominy of defeat; and for women, the jealousy or the failure of love. In Zeami's so-called dream plays, such as *Atsumori*, the warrior protagonist appears in the dream of the traveling monk and reenacts the source of his attachment to the priest, who offers prayers for his salvation and spiritual release.

A major characteristic of the later medieval literature is a focus on commoner life in the provinces, as evident in kyōgen, or comic drama. With the establishment of the seat of the military government in Kamakura, at the beginning of the medieval period, cultural activity continued to center on Kyoto, as it had before, but a new cultural community gathered in the east. The spreading of culture outside the capital increased dramatically after the Ōnin War (1467–1477), which took place mainly in Kyoto and destroyed the capital, causing aristocrats and cultural leaders to flee to the provinces. The resulting interaction of elite and popular forms is evident in the relationship between Noh drama and kyōgen, the comic drama that was performed side-by-side with Noh. Zeami had transformed Noh drama from a commoner, provincial form of entertainment into a refined theater that drew on the Heian court classics, but kyōgen maintained its commoner and comic roots, focusing on the bottom of the social ladder. In *Delicious Poison*, the most famous of kyōgen plays today, the clever servants outwit the master who has tried to deceive them, implicitly inverting the social hierarchy.

GENERAL CHARACTERISTICS OF JAPANESE LITERATURE

Japanese literature often stresses brevity, condensation, and overtones. The paring down of form and expression occurs in a wide variety of forms: poetry, Noh drama, gardens, bonsai, tea ceremony, and ink painting, to mention only the most obvious. Historically, Japanese poetry evolved from the long poem found in the *Man'yōshū* to the thirty-one syllable classical short poem, the central form of the

Japanese literature often stresses brevity, condensation, and overtones.

Kokinshū and the Heian period, to the seventeen-syllable haiku, probably the shortest poetic form in world literature.

A similar condensation of form can be found in Noh drama. Under Zeami, the greatest Noh playwright, it evolved into a drama of elegance, restraint, and suggestion. Human actions were reduced to the bare essentials, to highly symbolic movements such as tilting the mask to express joy or sweeping the hand to represent weeping. In one essay (*Kakyō*), Zeami writes that "if what the actor feels in the heart is ten, what appears in movement should be seven." Zeami stresses that the point at which physical movement becomes minute and then finally stops is the point of greatest intensity. The physical and visual restrictions—the fixed mask, the slow body movement, the almost complete absence of props or scenery—create a drama that must occur as much in the mind of the audience as on the stage. In other words, a great deal is left to the imagination, like the open white space on ink paintings such as the one that opens this section (page 124).

> *. . . a great deal is left to the imagination, like the open white space on ink paintings . . .*

In *Essays in Idleness,* written in the mid-fourteenth century, often considered the ultimate compendium of classical aesthetics, Yoshida Kenkō argues that what is not stated, cannot be seen by the eyes, and is incomplete in expression is more moving, alluring, and memorable than what is directly presented. From ancient times, the Japanese have prized the social capacity for indirection and suggestion. Classical poetry was recognized for connotations, subtle allegory, and metaphor, rather than for what was explicitly stated.

Heian vernacular fiction has a strong lyrical quality in which the exploration and intensification of mood or emotion often becomes more important than the unfolding of conflict or plot. Japanese drama and prose fiction, while sometimes possessing elaborate and complex plot structures, are usually concerned with the elaboration of a particular mood or state of mind. In vernacular fiction, the poetic diary, and Noh drama, one of the most popular scenes is the parting, a poetic topic that can be traced back to the poetry of the *Man'yōshū. The Tale of Genji* is highlighted by a series of partings, including the deaths and departures of major characters throughout the book. The same can be said of the *Tales of the Heike,* which repeatedly focuses on the terrible partings that war forces on human beings. The closeness of traditional social ties—between parent and child, lord and retainer, husband and wife, individual and group—make the parting an emotionally explosive situation, which is often presented in highly poetic language.

The lyrical character of Japanese vernacular literature derives in significant part from the fusion of genres and media that in European literature are generally thought of as being separate. In Japan, prose fiction and prose writing are extensively interwoven with poetry and poetic diction. Except for some folk literature, it is hard to find a work of premodern Japanese prose literature that doesn't include poetry. A more obvious fusion of media occurs in Japanese drama. Since the Renaissance, European theater has generally been split into three basic forms—drama, opera, and ballet—whereas traditional Japanese theater has combined these elements (acting, music, and dance) in Noh drama, jōruri (puppet theater), and kabuki. Of the major dramatic forms, only kyōgen doesn't depend on music. One of the central principles of Noh and jōruri is the *jo/ha/kyū* (introduction, development, and finale), which refers to the rhythm and tempo of the play, particularly in relationship to dance and song. This multimedia quality often makes the drama more performative than mimetic; instead of emphasizing the represented world, the work calls attention to itself as a performative medium.

Japanese fiction and drama also tend to have a strong narrational voice: one or more narrators describe and comment on the action from a subjective point of view. The conventions of oral storytelling are evident in almost all prose fiction, including such highly sophisticated, stream-of-consciousness narratives as *The Tale of Genji*. In Japanese traditional drama, this type of narrational voice flows over the action, dialogue, and scenery. In the Noh, for example, the dialogue alternates with descriptive passages narrated by both the chorus and the protagonist. The position of the narrator is most prominent in jōruri, where the chanter, on a dais separate from the puppet stage, performs both the puppet dialogue and the narration. This double structure—action accompanied by overriding narration—lends itself to extremely powerful lyric tragedy, in which the tone is elegant, poetic, and uplifting even as the subject matter or situation is tragic and sorrowful. The same can be said of climactic scenes in *The Tale of Genji* or in the final chapter of the *Tales of the Heike,* when Kenreimon'in reflects on the destruction of her clan. In most of these scenes the poetic descriptions of nature and seasons, so central to Japanese poetry, suggest that death is not an end but a return to nature.

Like the structure of the prose narratives, Japanese literary forms tend to be accretionary. Every major historical era gave birth to new literary and artistic genres, but usually without destroying or abandoning the earlier forms. The thirty-one-syllable classical poem emerged in the Nara and Heian periods, linked verse in the medieval period, the seventeen-syllable haiku in the Edo period, and free verse in the modern period (under the influence of Western poetry). With the exception of linked verse, all of these poetic genres continue to flourish today in Japan. The same is true of Japanese drama. Noh and its comic counterpart, kyōgen, emerged in the Muromachi period; jōruri (puppet theater) and kabuki became dominant in the Edo period; and modern theater came to the fore in the twentieth century. These dramatic forms have continued to coexist even today. The early masterpieces presented in this section are ongoing presences in Japanese literature in the twenty-first century.

→ ≕✦≕ ←

Man'yōshū (Collection of Myriad Leaves)
c. 702–c. 785

The *Man'yōshū (Collection of Myriad Leaves)* is Japan's oldest anthology of poetry.[1] It has twenty volumes containing 4,516 poems (*uta*), most of which were composed from the mid-seventh to the mid-eighth centuries. The first half of the first volume was probably compiled at the beginning of the eighth century, and the finished product was perhaps completed sometime between 770 and 785.

The three main poetic categories of the *Man'yōshū* are *zōka*, *sōmon*, and *banka*. *Zōka* literally means "miscellaneous poems" and includes poems composed on imperial excursions, on seasonal topics, and on a variety of other themes. *Sōmon*, which literally means "exchanges," focuses on poems of love and to a lesser extent other personal and family relationships. *Banka*, which literally means "coffin pulling songs," originally referred to poems that were performed

1. Introductions to the *Man'yōshū* are by Torquil Duthie.

at the site of the temporary burial of sovereigns and princes, but when this ritual practice was abolished at the end of the seventh century, *banka* simply came to refer to poems on death, something like "elegy" in English.

The two main poetic forms of the *Man'yōshū* are the *tanka* (short poem), and the *chōka* (long poem). When a *tanka* is placed after a *chōka* it is sometimes referred to as a *hanka* (envoy). The short poem consists of five lines in a 5, 7, 5, 7, 7 syllabic pattern. The *chōka* can be of varied length and alternates 5 and 7 syllabic lines, closing with three lines that are usually in a 5, 7, 7 syllabic pattern. Most of the poems in the *Man'yōshū* are short poems, with the long form tending to be composed by professional poets on specific themes.

The main rhetorical figures of the poetry of the *Man'yōshū* are the pillow-phrase, the preface-phrase, and the binary measures. The pillow-phrases are formulaic epithets that are placed before words as modifiers. In many cases they are used before place names, but also before words such as "palace," "gods," and other terms of special significance. Some pillow-phrases are words of praise, others are simply descriptive, and many are of obscure meaning and origin. Part of the function of the pillow-phrase appears to have been rhythmic, producing a 5-7 / 5-7-7 rhythm in the short poem, or a 5-7 / 5-7 / 5-7 . . . rhythm in the long poem, since the pillow-phrase (5) and the modified phrase (7) have to be read together as a unit. Originally they may have lent a sacred significance to the words they modified. Some may also be references to legends, particularly those that modify place names.

The preface-phrase usually consists of two or three measures and introduces the main topic of the poem, or a particular section of a long poem. In general, the preface-phrase connects with the main statement of the poem through a pun or through metaphoric association. In contrast to the pillow-phrases, the preface-phrases aren't formulaic epithets and are often unique to a particular poem. Most prefaces are translated with an explanatory word such as "like" or "as." Binary measures are a Chinese-influenced style of rhetoric most often used in long poems. The most common binary measures set up some kind of spatial or temporal framework, such as day/night, morning/evening, spring/autumn, land/sea, and heaven/earth. Many of them are formulaic phrases that are employed in a variety of different contexts.

The *Man'yōshū* is a vast anthology, compiled over a period of some seventy-five years, and including a variety of poetry composed over a period of more than a century. The *Man'yōshū* is generally divided into four historical periods. The First Period, which includes the poetry of Yūryaku, Jomei, and Princess Nukata, covers poetry produced before the Jinshin War (672). The Second Period, which contains the poetry of Kakinomoto no Hitomaro, begins after the Jinshin War and ends with the move of the capital to Nara (710). The Third Period, which includes the work of Yamabe no Akahito and Yamanoue no Okura, spans poetry produced from 710 to 733 (the date of the poet Yamanoue no Okura's death). The Fourth Period concludes in 759, which is the date of the last poem in the *Man'yōshū*.

The *Man'yōshū* as an anthology began to be produced in and around the imperial court during the Second Period. In the Third Period, with the move of the capital to Nara and the expansion of the Ritsuryō State, poetic circles also emerged outside the capital, as courtiers were sent to the provinces as governors. By the Fourth Period, the process of compilation of the *Man'yōshū* appears to have become more of a private production of Ōtomo no Yakamochi and his circle. The *Man'yōshū* was a cultural production of the aristocracy, and therefore sovereigns and high-ranking aristocrats are well represented. However, with the exception of the Ōtomo clan poets such as Yakamochi, most of the major poets of the *Man'yōshū* seem to have been lower-ranking aristocrats, such as Hitomaro, Akahito, and Okura.

Looking at the *Man'yōshū* as a whole, it is clear that poetry was a very versatile practice: it was used to record myth-historical narrative, to describe the political order, to express mourning, to tell tales and legends, to depict both real and fictional social interaction and correspondence, to mark public occasions at court, and to entertain. In addition, and perhaps most important of all, it was something to be collected and classified in encyclopedic fashion. The

Man'yōshū was thus compiled not only as a definitive guide to poetic practice but also as a monument of poetic knowledge.

PRONUNCIATIONS:

Man'yōshū: mun-yoh-sheu
Yūryaku: yeu-rya-koo
Jomei: jo-mey
Nukata: noo-ka-ta
Hitomaro: hee-to-mah-ro
Yakamochi: ya-ka-mo-chee

─ ⊰◆⊱ ─

Emperor Yūryaku
r. 456–479

The first poem in the *Man'yōshū* is attributed to Emperor Yūryaku (r. 456–479). Historians believe that it was during Yūryaku's reign that the Yamato clan, which would eventually rule all of Japan and became the present imperial family, extended its influence to the Kantō area in Eastern Japan and down to Kyūshū in the South. Yūryaku is also given particular importance in the *Kojiki* (c. 712), where he is described as a great lover. In this sense, it is fitting that the first half of the poem appears to be a courtship song. The speaker calls out to the girl "picking herbs" (a spring activity which was associated with fertility rites and courtship rituals) and asks her "house" (family, lineage) and her name, which was equivalent to proposing marriage. In the second half of the poem, however, this "suitor" describes himself in solemn terms as the ruler of Yamato.

Scholars agree that the poem cannot possibly date from Yūryaku's reign in the fifth century. It is probably an adaptation dating after 710 of what may have been an old courtship song. The choice of this poem to begin the anthology was perhaps due to its combination of the themes of courtship and power (which are two of the main themes of the poetry of the *Man'yōshū*), as well as to its attribution to a model lover/ruler of the ancient age such as Yūryaku.

I: 1

A poem by the Emperor[1]

> Your basket, with your lovely basket,
> your trowel, with your lovely trowel,
> Girl, you who pick herbs on this hill,
> Speak of your house. Speak of your name.
> In the Land of Yamato, so full of the sky,[2]
> It is I who conquer and reign,
> It is I who conquer and rule.
> Let it be me who speaks
> of my house and of my name.

---

1. Translated by Torquil Duthie.

2. "So full of the sky" (*sora mitsu*) is a pillow-phrase for the place name Yamato.

Emperor Jomei
r. 629–641

The second poem in the *Man'yōshū* is usually read as a "land-viewing" ritual in which the lord climbs a mountain to look over the land and affirm its prosperity as well as his own power over it. The sea can't actually be seen from the top of Mount Kagu, in the Nara basin, which suggests that Jomei's power of "looking" goes much further than that of actual eyesight. Indeed, "looking" in this context is a metaphor for "ruling," for the "scope" of Jomei's power. There are two senses to the place-name "Yamato." The first is the province of Yamato (present day Nara), where Mount Kagu is and where the capital was situated. The second sense, the "land of Yamato" of the last phrase of the poem, refers to the whole of Japan. Another interpretation is that the "smoke" suggests the spirits of the land, and that the "birds" are not normal birds but some kind of mythical flying creatures. This would suggest that Jomei has a connection to the other world of gods and spirits.

I: 2

A poem by the Emperor at the time of climbing Kagu mountain and looking on the land[1]

> In Yamato, amidst a ring of hills
> stands Mt. Kagu of Heaven,[2]
> and when I climb up to look on the land,
> from the plain of the land, smoke rises and rises,
> from the plain of the sea, birds rise and rise;
> a splendid land, the dragonfly island,
> the land of Yamato.

Princess Nukata
c. 638–fl. until 690s

Princess Nukata is a somewhat mysterious figure. Little is known of her lineage. She was a consort of Prince Ōama (later Emperor Tenmu, r. 672–686), by whom she had a daughter, but then later became a consort of Ōama's elder brother Emperor Tenchi (r. 662–671). Many of her poems in the *Man'yōshū* are also attributed to Empress Saimei (r. 655–661), suggesting that she may have composed poems on the Empress Saimei's behalf, perhaps in the role of some kind of medium or priestess.

The following is Princess Nukata's most famous poem, and indeed perhaps one of the most famous poems in the *Man'yōshū*. The poem compares spring and autumn, or more precisely, the hills in spring and the hills in autumn. This emphasis on spring and autumn (versus summer and winter) was originally due to the importance of these seasons in the agricultural year, but here they become seasons of change and transition. The prominence of spring and autumn anticipates the major role they would play in subsequent Japanese poetry, beginning with the *Kokinshū* (c. 905).

---

1. Translated by Torquil Duthie.
2. In the *Kojiki* there is an account of how Mt. Kagu descended from heaven to the earth and settled in the midst of the Asuka hills in Yamato. For this reason this mountain is almost invariably accompanied by the epithet "of Heaven."

I: 16

When the Emperor [Tenchi] commanded the Palace Minister, Fujiwara no Asomi, to match the radiance of the myriad blossoms of the spring mountains against the colors of the thousand leaves of the autumn mountains, Princess Nukata decided the question with this poem:[1]

<blockquote>
When spring comes forth
That lay in hiding all the winter through,
The birds that did not sing
Come back and sing to us once more;
5   The flowers that did not bloom
Have blossomed everywhere again.
    Yet so rife the hills
We cannot make our way to pick,
And so deep the grass
10   We cannot pluck the flowers to see.
    But when on autumn hills
We gaze upon the leaves of trees,
    It is the yellow ones
We pluck and marvel for sheer joy,
15   And the ones still green,
Sighing, leave upon the boughs—
    Those are the ones I hate to lose.
For me, it is the autumn hills.
</blockquote>

⊷ ⊱◇⊰ ⊶

Kakinomoto no Hitomaro
fl. 689–700

Kakinomoto no Hitomaro is regarded as the greatest poet in the *Man'yōshū*. His dates are unknown, and there are no extant references to him outside of the prose headnotes to his poems. For this reason, he is thought to have been a courtier whose rank was too low to get mentioned in the official histories. In addition to poems that are described in the *Man'yōshū* as "composed by Hitomaro," there is also a corpus of poetry referred to as the "Hitomaro poem collection," whose exact relationship to Hitomaro is uncertain. The poems "composed by Hitomaro" mostly consist of *chōka* (long poems) accompanied by envoys in the *tanka* (short poem) form, and the earliest of these can be dated to the year 689. Hitomaro may have been active to some extent during the reign of Tenmu (r. 672–686), but he appears to have played a major role as a court poet during the reign of Jitō (r. 687–696).

    Hitomaro's poems are often divided into two types: "public poems," in honor of the emperor and members of the ruling family, and "private poems" such as his poem on the death of his wife. Hitomaro's long poems are far longer and more elaborate than anything written before his time, and his use of pillow-phrases, preface-phrases, and binary measures is more complex

---

1. Translated by Edwin Cranston.

than that of previous poets. He composed many laments for the deaths of princes of the imperial family, and was responsible for the poetic deification of Emperor Tenmu (r. 672–686) and Empress Jitō (r. 690–697). In addition, his poetry is characterized by the use of certain unique metaphors and comparisons such as the analogy between swaying seaweed and a woman lying down in the poem on the death of his wife.

Not long after his death, the persona of Hitomaro appears to have become legendary. In the preface to the *Kokinshū* (Collection of Ancient and Modern Poems, c. 905) he is described as "the sage of poetry."

I: 29–31

The following poem is Hitomaro's first appearance in the *Man'yōshū*. Many scholars believe it to date from the year 689. The occasion of the poem is a journey, on which the travelers pass by the ruined capital of Ōmi. In 668, Emperor Tenchi (r. 662–671) moved the capital from its historical location in Asuka (in the province of Yamato) to the province of Ōmi, to the north. This was an unprecedented move. According to the *Nihon Shoki* (c. 720), Tenchi had named his brother Prince Ōama his successor, but shortly before he died Tenchi appears to have changed his mind and transferred the succession to his son Prince Ōtomo. After Tenchi's death, a conflict known as the Jinshin War (672) broke out between the forces of Ōtomo, based in the Ōmi capital, and Ōama, who was based in Yoshino, close to the old Asuka capital in Yamato. Ōama won the war and moved the capital back to Asuka, reigning as Emperor Tenmu (r. 672–686). Tenmu was then succeeded by his wife (Tenchi's daughter) Empress Jitō (r. 687–696). Thus, for the Jitō court, for whom Hitomaro was writing, the Ōmi capital was a problematic topic. On the one hand, the present court was the product of a war that had been waged on the Ōmi capital. On the other, the Jitō court had many ties with the Ōmi court, not the least of which was the fact that the Ōmi Emperor, Tenchi, was the present Empress's father.

Hitomaro's poem on the Ōmi capital has often been read as an attempt to ritually pacify the spirits of the dead courtiers of the Ōmi capital. Many of the expressions, which also appear in elegies, suggest that the poem is also a lament on the ruins. By definition, the capital was the center of the realm by virtue of being situated directly beneath "heaven." The present capital and all capitals (except Ōmi) were in Asuka in the province of Yamato. Thus it follows that, from this Yamato-centered point of view, Ōmi was "a barbarous place, far from heaven." And yet, it was from Ōmi that Tenchi "ruled all beneath heaven." In other words, during Tenchi's reign it was Ōmi that was the center of the realm.

Passing by the ruined capital of Ōmi, a poem composed by Kakinomoto no Asomi Hitomaro[1]

> Since the glorious age of the Kashiwara
> sun-ruler,[2] by Mt. Unebi of the jeweled-cords,[3]
> each and every of the gods that have appeared
> like the winding spruce one after the next
> 5   have reigned and ruled all beneath heaven,

1. Translated by Torquil Duthie.
2. According to the *Kojiki* (c. 712) and *Nihon Shoki* (c. 720), the legendary first emperor, known as Emperor Jinmu, reigned from the palace of Kashiwara.
3. A pillow-phrase for Unebi. The "cords" may refer to an item of ceremonial attire when praying to or celebrating in honor of the gods. Since the cords were worn over the shoulders, perhaps the pillow-phrase modifies the place name Unebi because of a pun on *une*, "the back of the neck." Unebi is one of the Three Mountains of Yamato (the other two being Mt. Kagu and Mt. Miminashi), which were in the vicinity of the Asuka capital.

but to leave Yamato, so full of heaven,[4]
and cross the Nara hills, so rich in green,[5]
—what designs were in his mind,[6]
that in a barbarous place, far from heaven,[7]
10   in the land of Ōmi of the racing rocks,[8]
in the palace of Ōtsu of the lively waves,[9]
he[1] reigned and ruled all beneath heaven?
The heavenly lord, divine sovereign,
though I have heard here was his glorious palace,
15   though it is said here were his glorious halls,
now all is overgrown by the spring grass,
and clouded by the haze of the spring sun,
the site of the glorious palace of stone
we feel sad to see.

ENVOYS

20   Oh Cape of Kara in Shiga,
in Sasanami of the lively waves,
though you are unchanged,
in vain we wait
for the courtiers' boats.

25   Oh Shore of Shiga
in Sasanami of the lively waves,
though your waters are still,[2]
how can we meet the people of the past?

II: 135–137

The poetic category of personal exchanges tends to include mostly short poems. However, the following long poem (with two envoys) by Hitomaro is the most renowned exception to this rule. The poem has often been taken to be autobiographical, but the male protagonist was probably originally a non-specific figure with whom courtiers who had to travel from the provinces up to the capital could identify. The heading of the poem, which names Hitomaro himself as the protagonist, was probably a later addition by the *Man'yōshū* compilers who fictionalized Hitomaro's life.

The metaphor in the extended preface-phrase that compares the woman to swaying seaweed is unique to Hitomaro and has fascinated (mostly male) Japanese poets in the modern period. This poem is remarkable for its use of imagery that in some of Hitomaro's other poems is used in reference to death (the moon covered by clouds, the sun setting) to describe parting.

---

4. The traditional pillow-phrase for Yamato is "full of the sky," but in this poem "sky" is written with the character for "heaven," which produces a contrast with the "barbarous place, far from heaven."
5. A pillow-phrase for Nara.
6. In Emperor Tenchi's mind.
7. A pillow-phrase for "barbarous." Since heaven was by definition situated directly above the palace and the surrounding capital, anywhere far from the capital was also

"far from heaven."
8. "Of the racing rocks" is a pillow-phrase for Ōmi.
9. "Of the lively waves" is a pillow-phrase for Ōtsu and other place-names in Ōmi. It is also a place-name (Sasanami).
1. Emperor Tenchi.
2. Flowing water is a metaphor for time passing; in this case, "though your waters are still" has the connotation of "although time does not seem to pass."

Poem by Kakinomoto no Hitomaro when he parted from his wife, coming up to the capital from the province of Iwami, with short poems[1]

In the sea of Iwami,
By the cape of Kara,
There amid the stones under the sea
Grows the deep-sea miru weed;
5   There along the rocky strand
Grows the sleek sea-tangle.
Like the swaying sea-tangle,
Unresisting would she lie beside me—
My wife whom I love with a love
10   Deep as the miru-growing ocean.
But few are the nights
We two have lain together.
Away I have come, parting from her
Even as the creeping vines[2] do part.
15   My heart aches within me;
I turn back to gaze—
But because of the yellow leaves
Of Watari Hill
Flying and fluttering in the air,
20   I cannot see plainly
My wife waving her sleeve to me.
Now as the moon, sailing through the cloud rift
Above the mountain of Yakami,
Disappears, leaving me full of regret,
25   So vanishes my love out of sight;
Now sinks at last the sun,
Coursing down the western sky.
I thought myself a strong man,
But the sleeves of my garment
30   Are wetted through with tears.

ENVOYS

My black steed
Galloping fast,
Away have I come,
Leaving under distant skies
35   The dwelling place of my love.

Oh, yellow leaves
Falling on the autumn hill,
Cease a while
To fly and flutter in the air
40   That I may see my love's dwelling-place!

---

1. Translated by Nippon Gakujutsu Shinkōkai.   2. A pillow-phrase for "part."

II: 207–209

In addition to composing laments in honor of members of the imperial family, Hitomaro also composed two laments on the death of his wife, the first of which is translated here. The poem may be fictional. The opening of the poem suggests that the relationship is a secret or forbidden one, and that the two lovers find it hard to meet. Then
the "messenger" (through whom they correspond) comes to tell the protagonist that his
wife has died. The death is described in a series of natural metaphors of passing (the
sun setting, the autumn leaves) that are characteristic of Hitomaro. In the second half of
the poem the protagonist goes to the Karu market, not in search of the woman herself,
but of her spirit. And yet, since he cannot hear the cries of the birds on Unebi mountain
(the dead were thought to manifest themselves in birds shortly after death), and she
does not appear to him in the faces of passers-by either, he can do nothing but call her
name and wave his sleeves (a ritual to summon the spirits of the dead).

*A poem by Kakinomoto no Hitomaro as he shed tears of blood in his grief following
the death of his wife, with short poems.*[1]

On the Karu Road
is the village of my wife,
and I desired to meet her intimately,
but if I went there too much
5   the eyes of others would cluster around us,
and if I went there too often
others would find us out.
And so I hoped
that later we would meet like
10   tangling vines,
trusted that we would
as I would trust a great ship,[2]
and hid my love:
faint as jewel's light,
15   a pool walled in by cliffs.
Then came the messenger,
his letter tied
to a jewelled catalpa twig,
to tell me,
20   in a voice
like the sound
of a catalpa bow,
that my girl,
who had swayed to me in sleep
25   like seaweed of the offing,
was gone
like the coursing sun
gliding into dusk,
like the radiant moon
30   secluding itself behind the clouds,
gone like the scarlet leaves of autumn.

---

1. Translated by Ian Levy.   2. A pillow-phrase for "trust."

I did not know what to say,
what to do,
but simply could not listen
35   and so, perhaps to solace
a single thousandth
of my thousand-folded longing,
I stood at the Karu market
where often she had gone,
40   and listened,
but could not even hear
the voices of the birds
that cry on Unebi Mountain,
where the maidens
45   wear strands of jewels,
and of the ones who passed me
on that road
straight as a jade spear,[3]
not one resembled her.
50   I could do nothing
but call my wife's name
and wave my sleeves.

ENVOYS

Too dense the yellowed leaves
on the autumn mountain:
55   my wife is lost
and I do not know the path
to find her by.

With the falling away
of the yellowed leaves,
60   I see the messenger
with his jeweled catalpa staff,
and I recall the days I met her.

⊷ ⊰◇⊱ ⊶

Yamabe no Akahito
fl. 724–736

Yamabe no Akahito's dates are unknown. Like Hitomaro, there are no references to him out-side of the prose headnotes to his poems, and for this reason he is thought to have been of low rank. The date of his earliest poem in the *Man'yōshū*, on Mount Fuji (translated below), is usu-ally estimated to be somewhere between 720 and 724. His last poem dates from 736. Akahito is

3. A pillow-phrase for "road."

thought to have been at the forefront of a revival of court poetry in the reign of Shōmu (r. 724–749). He wrote many poems of praise on imperial excursions and was strongly influenced by Hitomaro's poetry. One characteristic that is particular to Akahito is his description of landscape. For this reason, it is often said that Hitomaro is a poet of sound and Akahito is a poet of images.

III: 317–318

The poem included here is the first mention of Mount Fuji in the Japanese poetic tradition. While the mountain, situated some seventy miles from Tokyo, has now become the symbol of Japan, in the eighth century it was in what were referred to as "the eastern lands" (*Azuma*), far from the Nara capital in Yamato. Some have read the poem autobiographically, believing that Akahito was describing what he saw on a voyage to the eastern lands, and others see a connection to the tradition of "land-looking" (*kunimi*) poems (such as the poem by Jomei on page 137).

The poem opens by announcing Mount Fuji's mythical origins. Then the power of Mount Fuji is described spatially (hiding the light of the sun and the moon) and temporally (permanently covered in snow). The poem closes with an exhortation to transmit the glory of Mount Fuji to future generations. The envoy, which is one of the most famous poems in the Japanese literary tradition, redescribes the sight of Mount Fuji, forever covered in snow.

A poem by Yamabe no Sukune Akahito on looking at Mt. Fuji, with short poem[1]

> Since the heavens
> and earth were parted,
> it has stood, godlike,
> lofty and noble,
> 5   the high peak of Fuji
> in Suruga;
> when I look up to see it
> in heaven's high plain,
> hidden is the light
> 10   of the sky-crossing sun,
> invisible the glow
> of the shining moon;
> even the white clouds
> fear to move over it,
> 15   and for all time
> the snows are falling;
> let us tell about it,
> and pass on the word
> of Fuji's high peak.

ENVOY

> 20   Going out on Tago Bay,
> when I look

---

1. Translated by Anne Commons.

it is pure white;
on the high peak of Fuji,
snow is falling.

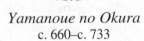

Yamanoue no Okura
c. 660–c. 733

Perhaps because of his low rank, nothing is known of the first half of Okura's life. However, in 701, at age forty-two, he was selected to join a government mission to the Tang Court in China, where he spent seven years. In 721 he was appointed as one of Emperor Shōmu's tutors, and in 728, probably as a reward for a lifetime of service to the court, he was appointed governor of Chikuzen, in northern Tsukushi (Kyūshū), where he organized a poetic circle with the governor of Tsukushi, Ōtomo no Tabito. The fifth volume of the *Man'yōshū*, which is thought to have been compiled by Okura, is dedicated to the poetry of this circle in Tsukushi. Okura is one of the most idiosyncratic poets in the *Man'yōshū*. Although all the poets in the *Man'yōshū* could read and were familiar with the Chinese classics, in Okura's case, almost all the topics of his poems are drawn from Chinese texts and many of his poems include long prefaces in Chinese. His poetry has a strong philosophical content (Buddhist, Confucianist, Daoist), and his choice of themes, such as old age, or "loving one's children," was often unusual.

V: 802–803

The poem included here is the second of a series of three poems on the theme of "longing for one's children" that Okura wrote in the district of Kama in Chikuzen in 728. In the preface to the poem, Okura quotes from a Buddhist sutra that, in the context of cautioning against attachment to the world, warns "there is no love surpassing that for a child." Okura, however, deliberately misreads this in a positive sense. The long poem focuses on the attachment to his children which does not let him sleep (i.e, does not let him achieve enlightenment). However, the envoy then states that children are more valuable than any treasure, implying that children are also more important than the "seven treasures" of Buddhist scripture. It is possible to interpret the poem as a conflict between the Buddhist doctrine of nonattachment and the Confucian ideal of parent-child relations.

A poem of longing for his children; with preface[1]

The Buddha preached truly with his golden mouth that he had equal compassion for all beings, even as for Rahula. He also preached that there is no love surpassing that for a child. The greatest sage still had the feeling of love for his child. Who then of the green grass of the world would not love his children?

When I eat melons
My children come to my mind;
When I eat chestnuts
The longing is even worse.

1. Translated by Edwin Cranston.

5   Where do they come from,
         Flickering before my eyes,
         Making me helpless
         Incessantly night after night,
         Not letting me sleep in peace?

                         ENVOY

10   What are they to me,
         Silver, or gold, or jewels?
         How could they ever
         Equal the greater treasure
         That is a child?

         [END OF MAN'YŌSHŪ (COLLECTION OF MYRIAD LEAVES)]

—◆—

Murasaki Shikibu
c. 978–c. 1014

Murasaki Shikibu belonged to the Northern Branch of the Fujiwara clan, the same branch that produced the Regent family. Both sides of her family can in fact be traced back to Fujiwara no Fuyutsugu (775–826), whose son Yoshifusa became the first regent. Murasaki Shikibu's family line, however, subsequently declined, and by her grandfather's generation had settled at the provincial governor level. Murasaki Shikibu's father, Fujiwara no Tametoki (d. 1029), while eventually receiving the governorships of Echizen and Echigo provinces, had an undistinguished and uncertain career as a bureaucrat. He was, however, able to distinguish himself as a scholar of Chinese literature and as a poet.

In 996 Murasaki Shikibu accompanied her father to his new post as provincial governor in Echizen, on the north side of Japan. A year or two later she returned to the capital to marry Fujiwara no Nobutaka, who was old enough to be her father and who came from the same middle tier of the aristocracy. Murasaki Shikibu bore a daughter named Kenshi, probably in 999, and Nobutaka died only a few years later, in 1001.

It is generally believed that Murasaki Shikibu started writing *The Tale of Genji* (*Genji monogatari*) after her husband's death, perhaps in response to the sorrow it caused her, and it was probably the reputation of the early chapters that resulted in her being summoned to the imperial court around 1005–1006. She became a lady-in-waiting to Empress Shōshi, the consort of Emperor Ichijō and the eldest daughter of Fujiwara no Michinaga (966–1027), who had become regent. At least half of the *Diary of Murasaki Shikibu* is devoted to a long-awaited event in Michinaga's career—the birth of a son to Empress Shōshi in 1008—which would make Michinaga the grandfather of a future emperor. Murasaki Shikibu was the sobriquet given to her as a lady-in-waiting at the imperial court and is not her actual name, which remains unknown. "Shikibu" probably comes from the position in the Shikibu-shō (Ministry of Ceremonial) occupied by her father, while "Murasaki" may refer to the lavender color of the flower of her clan (Fujiwara, Wisteria Fields) or it may be that her nickname came from the heroine of *The Tale of Genji*.

THE TALE OF GENJI

The title of *The Tale of Genji* comes from the surname of the hero, the son of the reigning emperor at the beginning of the narrative. *The Tale of Genji* is generally divided into three parts: the first thirty-three chapters follow Genji's career, from his birth to exile to triumphant return to his rise to the pinnacle of society, focusing equally, if not more, on the fate of the various women that he becomes involved with. The second part, Chapters 34 to 41, explores the darkness that gathers over Genji's private life and that of his great love Murasaki, who eventually succumbs and dies, and ends with Genji's own death. The third part consists of the thirteen chapters following Genji's death, which are primarily concerned with the affairs of Kaoru, Genji's supposed son, and with three sisters (particularly Oigimi and Ukifune) with whom Kaoru becomes involved. A significant shift of focus occurs in the third part: from the capital and court to the countryside, and from a society concerned with refinement, elegance, and the various arts, to an otherworldly, ascetic perspective—a shift that anticipates the movement of mid-Heian court culture toward the religious literature of the medieval period, focused on hermits who withdrew from the world.

The Tale of Genji both follows and works against a common plot convention of the Heian vernacular tale (*monogatari*) in which the heroine, whose family has declined or disappeared, is discovered and loved by an illustrious noble. This association of love and inferior social status appears from the opening line of the *Genji* and extends to the last relationship between Kaoru and Ukifune. In the opening chapter, the reigning emperor, like all Heian emperors, was expected to devote himself to his principal consort (the Kokiden lady), the lady of the highest rank, and yet he dotes on a woman of considerably lower status—a social and political violation that eventually results in the woman's death. Like his monogatari predecessor, Ariwara no Narihira, the hero of *The Tales of Ise,* and like his father, Genji pursues love where it is forbidden and most unlikely to be found or attained. In "Lavender," the fifth chapter, Genji discovers his future wife, the young Murasaki, who has lost her mother and is in danger of losing her only guardian when Genji takes her into his home.

In Murasaki Shikibu's day, it would have been unheard of for a man of Genji's high rank to take a girl of Murasaki's low position into his own residence and marry her. In the upper levels of Heian aristocratic society, the man usually lived in his wife's residence, either in the house of her parents or in a dwelling nearby (as Genji does with Aoi, his principal wife). The prospective groom had high stakes in marriage, for the bride's family provided not only a residence but other forms of support as well. When Genji takes a girl (such as the young Murasaki) with no backing or social support into his house, he openly flouts the conventions of marriage as they were known to Murasaki Shikibu's audience. In the monogatari tradition, however, this action becomes a sign of excessive, romantic love.

A number of other sequences in the story—those of Yūgao, the Akashi lady, Oigimi, and Ukifune—start on a similar note. All of these women come from upper- or middle-rank aristocratic families (much like that of the author herself) that have, for various reasons, fallen into social obscurity and must struggle to survive. The appearance of the highborn hero implies, at least for the attendants surrounding the woman, an opportunity for social redemption. However, Murasaki Shikibu focuses on the difficulties that the woman subsequently encounters, either in dealing with the man, or failing to make the social transition between her own social background and that of the highborn hero. The woman may, for example, be torn between pride and material need, or between emotional dependence and a desire to be more independent, or she may feel abandoned and betrayed—all conflicts explored in *The Tale of Genji.* In classical Japanese poetry, such as that of Ono no Komachi (page 237), love has a similar fate: it is never about happiness or the blissful union of souls. Instead, it dwells on unfulfilled hopes, regretful partings, fears of abandonment, and lingering resentment.

The Tale of Genji is remarkable for the manner in which it absorbs the exploration of identity and social position found in earlier women's diaries, the social romance of the early monogatari, and the poetry and imagery of The Tales of Ise, blending these strands into a deeply psychological narrative that evolves around distinctive characters. But while bearing a striking resemblance to the modern psychological novel, The Tale of Genji wasn't conceived and written as a single work and then published and distributed to a mass audience as novels are today. Instead, it was issued in limited installments, chapter by chapter or sequence by sequence, to an circumscribed, aristocratic audience over an extended period of time. As a result The Tale of Genji can be appreciated as a closely interrelated series of texts that can be read either individually or as a whole and that is the product of an author whose attitudes, interests, and techniques evolved significantly with time and experience. For example, the reader of the Ukifune narrative can appreciate this sequence both independently and as an integral part of the previous narrative. The Genji can also be understood as a kind of multiple bildungsroman or novel of the development of a character through time and experience. Yet in this work, the development occurs not only in the life of a single hero or heroine but over different generations, with two or more characters. Genji, for example, attains an awareness of death, mutability, and the illusory nature of the world through repeated suffering. By contrast, Kaoru, his supposed son, begins his life, or rather his narrative, with a profound grasp and acceptance of these darker aspects of life. In the second part, in the "New Herbs" chapters, the heroine Murasaki has long assumed that she can monopolize Genji's affections and act as his principal wife. Genji's unexpected marriage to the Third Princess, however, crushes these assumptions, causing Murasaki to fall mortally ill. In the third part, the Uji sequence, Oigimi never suffers the way Murasaki does, but she quickly comes to a similar awareness of the inconstancy of men, love, and marriage, even though Kaoru appears to be an ideal companion.

Murasaki Shikibu probably first wrote a short sequence of chapters, perhaps beginning with "Lavender," and then, in response to reader demand, wrote a sequel or another related series of chapters, and so forth. Certain sequences, which appear to have been inserted later, focus on women of the middle and lower aristocracy, as opposed to the main chapters of the first part which deal with Fujitsubo and other upper-rank women related to the throne. The only chapters in which authorship has been questioned are three chapters following the death of Genji at the end of the second part. The following selections condense this extended narrative by leaving out those chapters and sections that were later additions, of questionable authorship, or tangential to the lives of the central characters.

PRONUNCIATIONS:
Murasaki Shikibu: moo-ra-sa-ki shi-ki-boo
Genji: gen-jee
Aoi: ah-oh-ee
Rokujō: ro-koo-joh

The Tale of Genji[1]

from *Chapter 1. The Paulownia Court*

In a certain reign there was a lady not of the first rank whom the emperor loved more than any of the others. The grand ladies with high ambitions thought her a presumptuous upstart, and lesser ladies were still more resentful. Everything she did offended someone. Probably aware of what was happening, she fell seriously ill and came to

---

1. Translated by Edward Seidensticker and with notes adapted from Seidensticker.

spend more time at home than at court. The emperor's pity and affection quite passed bounds. No longer caring what his ladies and courtiers might say, he behaved as if intent upon stirring gossip.

His court looked with very great misgiving upon what seemed a reckless infatuation. In China just such an unreasoning passion had been the undoing of an emperor and had spread turmoil through the land. As the resentment grew, the example of Yang Kuei-fei[2] was the one most frequently cited against the lady.

She survived despite her troubles, with the help of an unprecedented bounty of love. Her father, a grand councilor, was no longer living. Her mother, an old-fashioned lady of good lineage, was determined that matters be no different for her than for ladies who with paternal support were making careers at court. The mother was attentive to the smallest detail of etiquette and deportment. Yet there was a limit to what she could do. The sad fact was that the girl was without strong backing, and each time a new incident arose she was next to defenseless.

It may have been because of a bond in a former life that she bore the emperor a beautiful son, a jewel beyond compare. The emperor was in a fever of impatience to see the child, still with the mother's family; and when, on the earliest day possible, he was brought to court, he did indeed prove to be a most marvelous babe. The emperor's eldest son was the grandson of the Minister of the Right. The world assumed that with this powerful support he would one day be named crown prince; but the new child was far more beautiful. On public occasions the emperor continued to favor his eldest son. The new child was a private treasure, so to speak, on which to lavish uninhibited affection.

The mother was not of such a low rank as to attend upon the emperor's personal needs. In the general view she belonged to the upper classes. He insisted on having her always beside him, however, and on nights when there was music or other entertainment he would require that she be present. Sometimes the two of them would sleep late, and even after they had risen he would not let her go. Because of his unreasonable demands she was widely held to have fallen into immoderate habits out of keeping with her rank.

With the birth of the son, it became yet clearer that she was the emperor's favorite. The mother of the eldest son began to feel uneasy. If she did not manage carefully, she might see the new son designated crown prince. She had come to court before the emperor's other ladies, she had once been favored over the others, and she had borne several of his children. However much her complaining might trouble and annoy him, she was one lady whom he could not ignore.

Though the mother of the new son had the emperor's love, her detractors were numerous and alert to the slightest inadvertency. She was in continuous torment, feeling that she had nowhere to turn. Her quarters were in the Kiritsubo.[3] The emperor had to pass the apartments of other ladies to reach hers, and it must be admitted that their resentment at his constant comings and goings was not unreasonable. Her visits to the royal chambers were equally frequent. The robes of her women were in a scandalous state from trash strewn along bridges and galleries. Once some women conspired to have both doors of a gallery she must pass bolted shut, and so she found herself unable to advance or retreat. Her anguish over the mounting list of insults was presently more

---

2. The beautiful concubine of the Tang emperor Hsüan Tsung. The emperor's infatuation with her was viewed as the cause of the An Lu-shan rebellion, and led to her execution.

3. The Paulownia Court, in the northeast corner of the residential compound of the palace. The distance of the Kiritsubo lady's quarters from the emperor's, near the middle of the compound, is a reflection of her relatively low rank.

than the emperor could bear. He moved a lady out of rooms adjacent to his own and assigned them to the Kiritsubo lady and so, of course, aroused new resentment.

When the young prince reached the age of three,[4] the resources of the treasury and the stewards' offices were exhausted to make the ceremonial bestowing of trousers as elaborate as that for the eldest son. Once more there was malicious talk; but the prince himself, as he grew up, was so superior of mien and disposition that few could find it in themselves to dislike him. Among the more discriminating, indeed, were some who marveled that such a paragon had been born into this world.

In the summer the boy's mother, feeling vaguely unwell, asked that she be allowed to go home. The emperor would not hear of it. Since they were by now used to these indispositions, he begged her to stay and see what course her health would take. It was steadily worse, and then, suddenly, everyone could see that she was failing. Her mother came pleading that he let her go home. At length he agreed.

Fearing that even now she might be the victim of a gratuitous insult, she chose to go off without ceremony, leaving the boy behind. Everything must have an end, and the emperor could no longer detain her. It saddened him inexpressibly that he was not even permitted to see her off. A lady of great charm and beauty, she was sadly emaciated. She was sunk in melancholy thoughts, but when she tried to put them into words her voice was almost inaudible. The emperor was quite beside himself, his mind a confusion of things that had been and things that were to come. He wept and vowed undying love, over and over again. The lady was unable to reply. She seemed listless and drained of strength, as if she scarcely knew what was happening. Wanting somehow to help, the emperor ordered that she be given the honor of a hand-drawn carriage. He returned to her apartments and still could not bring himself to the final parting.

"We vowed that we would go together down the road we all must go. You must not leave me behind."

She looked sadly up at him. "If I had suspected that it would be so—" She was gasping for breath.

> "I leave you, to go the road we all must go.
> The road I would choose, if only I could, is the other."

It was evident that she would have liked to say more; but she was so weak that it had been a struggle to say even this much.

The emperor was wondering again if he might not keep her with him and have her with him to the end.

But a message came from her mother, asking that she hurry. "We have obtained the agreement of eminent ascetics to conduct the necessary services, and I fear that they are to begin this evening."

So, in desolation, he let her go. He passed a sleepless night.

He sent off a messenger and was beside himself with impatience and apprehension even before there had been time for the man to reach the lady's house and return. The man arrived to find the house echoing with laments. She had died at shortly past midnight. He returned sadly to the palace. The emperor closed himself up in his private apartments. He would have liked at least to keep the boy with him, but no precedent could be found for having him away from his mother's house through the mourning.

---

4. All ages are by the Asian count, not of the full years but of the number of years in which one has lived, therefore one or two years above the full count: someone born near the end of a year would turn "two" at New Year's.

The boy looked in bewilderment at the weeping courtiers, at his father too, the tears streaming over his face. The death of a parent is sad under any circumstances, and this one was indescribably sad.

But there must be an end to weeping, and orders were given for the funeral. If only she could rise to the heavens with the smoke from the pyre, said the mother between her sobs. She rode in the hearse with several attendants, and what must her feelings have been when they reached Mount Otaki?[5] It was there that the services were conducted with the utmost solemnity and dignity.

She looked down at the body. "With her before me, I cannot persuade myself that she is dead. At the sight of her ashes I can perhaps accept what has happened."

The words were rational enough, but she was so distraught that she seemed about to fall from the carriage. The women had known that it would be so and did what they could for her.

A messenger came from the palace with the news that the lady had been raised to the Third Rank, and presently a nunciary arrived to read the official order. For the emperor, the regret was scarcely bearable that he had not had the courage of his resolve to appoint her an imperial consort, and he wished to make amends by promoting her one rank. There were many who resented even this favor. Others, however, of a more sensitive nature, saw more than ever what a dear lady she had been, simple and gentle and difficult to find fault with. It was because she had been excessively favored by the emperor that she had been the victim of such malice. The grand ladies were now reminded of how sympathetic and unassuming she had been. It was for just such an occasion, they remarked to one another, that the phrase "how well one knows" had been invented.

The days went dully by. The emperor was careful to send offerings for the weekly memorial services. His grief was unabated and he spent his nights in tears, refusing to summon his other ladies. His serving women were plunged into dew-drenched autumn.

There was one lady, however, who refused to be placated. "How ridiculous," said the lady of the Kokiden Pavilion, mother of his eldest son, "that the infatuation should continue even now."

The emperor's thoughts were on his youngest son even when he was with his eldest. He sent off intelligent nurses and serving women to the house of the boy's grandmother, where he was still in residence, and made constant inquiry after him.

The autumn tempests blew and suddenly the evenings were chilly. Lost in his grief, the emperor sent off a note to the grandmother. His messenger was a woman of middle rank called Myōbu, whose father was a guards officer. It was on a beautiful moonlit night that he dispatched her, a night that brought memories. On such nights he and the dead lady had played the koto for each other. Her koto had somehow had overtones lacking in other instruments, and when she would interrupt the music to speak, the words too carried echoes of their own. Her face, her manner—they seemed to cling to him, but with "no more substance than the lucent dream."

[Myōbu visits the Kiritsubo lady's grieving mother, and delivers a letter in which the emperor hints that he would like his young son to return to the palace.]

Myōbu was much moved to find the emperor waiting up for her. Making it seem that his attention was on the small and beautifully planted garden before him, now in

5. To the east of the city.

full autumn bloom, he was talking quietly with four or five women, among the most sensitive of his attendants. He had become addicted to illustrations by the emperor Uda for "The Song of Everlasting Sorrow"[6] and to poems by Ise and Tsurayuki on that subject, and to Chinese poems as well.

He listened attentively as Myōbu described the scene she had found so affecting. He took up the letter she had brought from the grandmother.

"I am so awed by this august message that I would run away and hide; and so violent are the emotions it gives rise to that I scarcely know what to say.

> The tree that gave them shelter has withered and died.
> One fears for the plight of the hagi[7] shoots beneath."

A strange way to put the matter, thought the emperor; but the lady must still be dazed with grief. He chose to overlook the suggestion that he himself could not help the child.

He sought to hide his sorrow, not wanting these women to see him in such poor control of himself. But it was no use. He reviewed his memories over and over again, from his very earliest days with the dead lady. He had scarcely been able to bear a moment away from her while she lived. How strange that he had been able to survive the days and months since on memories alone. He had hoped to reward the grandmother's sturdy devotion, and his hopes had come to nothing.

"Well," he sighed, "she may look forward to having her day, if she will only live to see the boy grow up."

Looking at the keepsakes Myōbu had brought back, he thought what a comfort it would be if some wizard were to bring him, like that Chinese emperor, a comb from the world where his lost love was dwelling. He whispered:

> "And will no wizard search her out for me,
> That even he may tell me where she is?"

There are limits to the powers of the most gifted artist. The Chinese lady in the paintings did not have the luster of life. Yang Kuei-fei was said to have resembled the lotus of the Sublime Pond, the willows of the Timeless Hall. No doubt she was very beautiful in her Chinese finery. When he tried to remember the quiet charm of his lost lady, he found that there was no color of flower, no song of bird, to summon her up. Morning and night, over and over again, they had repeated to each other the lines from "The Song of Everlasting Sorrow":

> In the sky, as birds that share a wing.
> On earth, as trees that share a branch.

It had been their vow, and the shortness of her life had made it an empty dream.

Everything, the moaning of the wind, the humming of autumn insects, added to the sadness. But in the apartments of the Kokiden lady matters were different. It had been some time since she had last waited upon the emperor. The moonlight being so beautiful, she saw no reason not to have music deep into the night. The emperor muttered something about the bad taste of such a performance at such a time, and those who saw his distress agreed that it was an unnecessary injury. Kokiden was of an arrogant and intractable nature and her behavior suggested that to her the emperor's grief was of no importance.

6. By Po Chü-i, describing the grief of the Tang emperor Hsüan Tsung upon the death of his concubine Yang Kuei-fei. Uda reigned in the late 9th century and died in 931.

Tsurayuki and Ise (one of Uda's concubines) were active in the early 10th century.
7. A kind of clover.

The moon set. The wicks in the lamps had been trimmed more than once and presently the oil was gone. Still he showed no sign of retiring. His mind on the boy and the old lady, he jotted down a verse:

> Tears dim the moon, even here above the clouds.[8]
> Dim must it be in that lodging among the reeds.

Calls outside told him that the guard was being changed. It would be one or two in the morning. People would think his behavior strange indeed. He at length withdrew to his bedchamber. He was awake the whole night through, and in dark morning, his thoughts on the blinds that would not open,[9] he was unable to interest himself in business of state. He scarcely touched his breakfast, and lunch seemed so remote from his inclinations that his attendants exchanged looks and whispers of alarm.

Not all voices were sympathetic. Perhaps, some said, it had all been foreordained, but he had dismissed the talk and ignored the resentment and let the affair quite pass the bounds of reason; and now to neglect his duties so—it was altogether too much. Some even cited the example of the Chinese emperor who had brought ruin upon himself and his country.

The months passed and the young prince returned to the palace. He had grown into a lad of such beauty that he hardly seemed meant for this world—and indeed one almost feared that he might only briefly be a part of it. When, the following spring, it came time to name a crown prince, the emperor wanted very much to pass over his first son in favor of the younger, who, however, had no influential maternal relatives. It did not seem likely that the designation would pass unchallenged. The boy might, like his mother, be destroyed by immoderate favors. The emperor told no one of his wishes. There did after all seem to be a limit to his affections, people said; and Kokiden regained her confidence.

The boy's grandmother was inconsolable. Finally, because her prayer to be with her daughter had been answered, perhaps, she breathed her last. Once more the emperor was desolate. The boy, now six, was old enough to know grief himself. His grandmother, who had been so good to him over the years, had more than once told him what pain it would cause her, when the time came, to leave him behind.

He now lived at court. When he was seven he went through the ceremonial reading of the Chinese classics, and never before had there been so fine a performance. Again a tremor of apprehension passed over the emperor—might it be that such a prodigy was not to be long for this world?

"No one need be angry with him now that his mother is gone." He took the boy to visit the Kokiden Pavilion. "And now most especially I hope you will be kind to him."

Admitting the boy to her inner chambers, even Kokiden was pleased. Not the sternest of warriors or the most unbending of enemies could have held back a smile. Kokiden was reluctant to let him go. She had two daughters, but neither could compare with him in beauty. The lesser ladies crowded about, not in the least ashamed to show their faces, all eager to amuse him, though aware that he set them off to disadvantage. I need not speak of his accomplishments in the compulsory subjects, the classics and the like. When it came to music his flute and koto made the heavens echo—but to recount all his virtues would, I fear, give rise to a suspicion that I distort the truth.

---

8. Even here in the palace.
9. Referring to a poem by Ise on "The Song of Everlasting Sorrow": "The jeweled blinds are drawn, the morning is dark. / I had not thought I would not even dream."

An embassy came from Korea. Hearing that among the emissaries was a skilled physiognomist, the emperor would have liked to summon him for consultation. He decided, however, that he must defer to the emperor Uda's injunction against receiving foreigners, and instead sent this favored son to the Kōro mansion,[1] where the party was lodged. The boy was disguised as the son of the grand moderator, his guardian at court. The wise Korean cocked his head in astonishment.

"It is the face of one who should ascend to the highest place and be father to the nation," he said quietly, as if to himself. "But to take it for such would no doubt be to predict trouble. Yet it is not the face of the minister, the deputy, who sets about ordering public affairs."

The moderator was a man of considerable learning. There was much of interest in his exchanges with the Korean. There were also exchanges of Chinese poetry, and in one of his poems the Korean succeeded most skillfully in conveying his joy at having been able to observe such a countenance on this the eve of his return to his own land, and sorrow that the parting must come so soon. The boy offered a verse that was received with high praise. The most splendid of gifts were bestowed upon him. The wise man was in return showered with gifts from the palace.

Somehow news of the sage's remarks leaked out, though the emperor himself was careful to say nothing. The Minister of the Right, grandfather of the crown prince and father of the Kokiden lady, was quick to hear, and again his suspicions were aroused. In the wisdom of his heart, the emperor had already analyzed the boy's physiognomy after the Japanese fashion and had formed tentative plans. He had thus far refrained from bestowing imperial rank on his son, and was delighted that the Korean view should so accord with his own. Lacking the support of maternal relatives, the boy would be most insecure as a prince without court rank, and the emperor could not be sure how long his own reign would last. As a commoner he could be of great service. The emperor therefore encouraged the boy in his studies, at which he was so proficient that it seemed a waste to reduce him to common rank. And yet—as a prince he would arouse the hostility of those who had cause to fear his becoming emperor. Summoning an astrologer of the Indian school, the emperor was pleased to learn that the Indian view coincided with the Japanese and the Korean; and so he concluded that the boy should become a commoner with the name Minamoto or Genji.

The months and the years passed and still the emperor could not forget his lost love. He summoned various women who might console him, but apparently it was too much to ask in this world for one who even resembled her. He remained sunk in memories, unable to interest himself in anything. Then he was told of the Fourth Princess, daughter of a former emperor, a lady famous for her beauty and reared with the greatest care by her mother, the empress. A woman now in attendance upon the emperor had in the days of his predecessor been most friendly with the princess, then but a child, and even now saw her from time to time.

"I have been at court through three reigns now," she said, "and never had I seen anyone who genuinely resembled my lady. But now the daughter of the empress dowager is growing up, and the resemblance is most astonishing. One would be hard put to find her equal."

Hoping that she might just possibly be right, the emperor asked most courteously to have the princess sent to court. Her mother was reluctant and even fearful, however.

---

1. In the southern part of the city.

One must remember, she said, that the mother of the crown prince was a most willful lady who had subjected the Kiritsubo lady to open insults and presently sent her into a fatal decline. Before she had made up her mind she followed her husband in death, and the daughter was alone. The emperor renewed his petition. He said that he would treat the girl as one of his own daughters.

Her attendants and her maternal relatives and her older brother, Prince Hyōbu, consulted together and concluded that rather than languish at home she might seek consolation at court; and so she was sent off. She was called Fujitsubo. The resemblance to the dead lady was indeed astonishing. Because she was of such high birth (it may have been that people were imagining things) she seemed even more graceful and delicate than the other. No one could despise her for inferior rank, and the emperor need not feel shy about showing his love for her. The other lady had not particularly encouraged his attentions and had been the victim of a love too intense; and now, though it would be wrong to say that he had quite forgotten her, he found his affections shifting to the new lady, who was a source of boundless comfort. So it is with the affairs of this world.

Since Genji never left his father's side, it was not easy for this new lady, the recipient of so many visits, to hide herself from him. The other ladies were disinclined to think themselves her inferior, and indeed each of them had her own merits. They were all rather past their prime, however. Fujitsubo's beauty was of a younger and fresher sort. Though in her childlike shyness she made an especial effort not to be seen, Genji occasionally caught a glimpse of her face. He could not remember his own mother and it moved him deeply to learn, from the lady who had first told the emperor of Fujitsubo, that the resemblance was striking. He wanted to be near her always.

"Do not be unfriendly," said the emperor to Fujitsubo. "Sometimes it almost seems to me too that you are his mother. Do not think him forward, be kind to him. Your eyes, your expression: you are really so uncommonly like her that you could pass for his mother."

Genji's affection for the new lady grew, and the most ordinary flower or tinted leaf became the occasion for expressing it. Kokiden was not pleased. She was not on good terms with Fujitsubo, and all her old resentment of Genji came back. He was handsomer than the crown prince, her chief treasure in the world, well thought of by the whole court. People began calling Genji "the shining one." Fujitsubo, ranked beside him in the emperor's affections, became "the lady of the radiant sun."

It seemed a pity that the boy must one day leave behind his boyish attire; but when he reached the age of twelve he went through his initiation ceremonies and received the cap of an adult. Determined that the ceremony should be in no way inferior to the crown prince's, which had been held some years earlier in the Grand Hall, the emperor himself bustled about adding new details to the established forms. As for the banquet after the ceremony, he did not wish the custodians of the storehouses and granaries to treat it as an ordinary public occasion.

The throne faced east on the east porch, and before it were Genji's seat and that of the minister who was to bestow the official cap. At the appointed hour in midafternoon Genji appeared. The freshness of his face and his boyish coiffure were again such as to make the emperor regret that the change must take place. The ritual cutting of the boy's hair was performed by the secretary of the treasury. As the beautiful locks fell the emperor was seized with a hopeless longing for his dead lady. Repeatedly he found himself struggling to keep his composure. The ceremony over, the boy withdrew to change to adult trousers and descended into the courtyard for ceremonial thanksgiving. There was not a person in the assembly who did not feel his eyes misting over. The emperor was stirred by the deepest of emotions. He had on brief occasions been able to forget the past, and now it all came back again. Vaguely apprehensive lest the initiation of so young a boy bring a sudden aging, he was astonished to see that his son delighted him even more.

The Minister of the Left, who bestowed the official cap, had only one daughter, named Aoi, his chief joy in life. Her mother, the minister's first wife, was a princess of the blood. The crown prince had sought the girl's hand, but the minister thought rather of giving her to Genji. He had heard that the emperor had similar thoughts. When the emperor suggested that the boy was without adequate sponsors for his initiation and that the support of relatives by marriage might be called for, the minister quite agreed.

* * *

The nuptial observances were conducted with great solemnity. The groom seemed to the minister and his family quite charming in his boyishness. The bride was older, and somewhat ill at ease with such a young husband.

The minister had the emperor's complete confidence, and his principal wife, the girl's mother, was the emperor's sister. Both parents were therefore of the highest standing. And now they had Genji for a son-in-law. The Minister of the Right, who as grandfather of the crown prince should have been without rivals, was somehow eclipsed. The Minister of the Left had numerous children by several ladies. One of the sons, named Tō no Chūjō, a very handsome lad by his principal wife, was already a guards lieutenant. Relations between the two ministers were not good but the Minister of the Right found it difficult to ignore such a talented youth, to whom he offered the hand of his fourth and favorite daughter. His esteem for his new son-in-law rivaled the other minister's esteem for Genji. To both houses the new arrangements seemed ideal.

Constantly at his father's side, Genji spent little time at the Sanjō mansion of his bride. Fujitsubo was for him a vision of sublime beauty. If he could have someone like her—but in fact there was no one really like her. His bride too was beautiful, and she had had the advantage of every luxury; but he was not at all sure that they were meant for each other. The yearning in his young heart for the other lady was agony. Now that he had come of age, he no longer had his father's permission to go behind her curtains. On evenings when there was music, he would play the flute to her koto and so communicate something of his longing, and take some comfort from her voice, soft through the curtains. Life at court was for him much preferable to life at Sanjō. Two or three days at Sanjō would be followed by five or six days at court. For the minister, youth seemed sufficient excuse for this neglect. He continued to be delighted with his son-in-law.

The minister selected the handsomest and most accomplished of ladies to wait upon the young pair and planned the sort of diversions that were most likely to interest Genji. At the palace the emperor assigned him the apartments that had been his mother's and took care that her retinue was not dispersed. Orders were handed down to the offices of repairs and fittings to remodel the house that had belonged to the lady's family. The results were magnificent. The plantings and the artificial hills had always been remarkably tasteful, and the grounds now swarmed with workmen widening the lake. If only, thought Genji, he could have with him the lady he yearned for.

The sobriquet "the shining Genji," one hears, was bestowed upon him by the Korean.

from *Chapter 2. The Broom Tree*

"The shining Genji": it was almost too grand a name. Yet he did not escape criticism for numerous little adventures. It seemed indeed that his indiscretions might give him a name for frivolity, and he did what he could to hide them. But his most secret affairs (such is the malicious work of the gossips) became common talk. If, on the other hand, he were to go through life concerned only for his name and avoid all these interesting and amusing little affairs, then he would be laughed to shame by the likes of the lieutenant of Katano.[1]

Still a guards captain, Genji spent most of his time at the palace, going infrequently to the Sanjō mansion of his father-in-law. The people there feared that he might have been stained by the lavender of Kasugano.[2] Though in fact he had an instinctive dislike for the promiscuity he saw all around him, he had a way of sometimes turning against his own better inclinations and causing unhappiness.

The summer rains came, the court was in retreat, and an even longer interval than usual had passed since his last visit to Sanjō. Though the minister and his family were much put out, they spared no effort to make him feel welcome. The minister's sons were more attentive than to the emperor himself. Genji was on particularly good terms with Tō no Chūjō. They enjoyed music together and more frivolous diversions as well. Tō no Chūjō was of an amorous nature and not at all comfortable in the apartments which his father-in-law, the Minister of the Right, had at great expense provided for him. At Sanjō with his own family, on the other hand, he took very good care of his rooms, and when Genji came and went the two of them were always together. They were a good match for each other in study and at play. Reserve quite disappeared between them.

It had been raining all day. There were fewer courtiers than usual in the royal presence. Back in his own palace quarters, also unusually quiet, Genji pulled a lamp near and sought to while away the time with his books. He had Tō no Chūjō with him. Numerous pieces of colored paper, obviously letters, lay on a shelf. Tō no Chūjō made no attempt to hide his curiosity.

"Well," said Genji, "there are some I might let you see. But there are some I think it better not to."

"You miss the point. The ones I want to see are precisely the ones you want to hide. The ordinary ones—I'm not much of a hand at the game, you know, but even I am up to the ordinary give and take. But the ones from ladies who think you are not doing right by them, who sit alone through an evening and wait for you to come—those are the ones I want to see."

It was not likely that really delicate letters would be left scattered on a shelf, and it may be assumed that the papers treated so carelessly were the less important ones.

"You do have a variety of them," said Tō no Chūjō, reading the correspondence through piece by piece. This will be from her, and this will be from her, he would say. Sometimes he guessed correctly and sometimes he was far afield, to Genji's great amusement. Genji was brief with his replies and let out no secrets.

"It is I who should be asking to see your collection. No doubt it is huge. When I have seen it I shall be happy to throw my files open to you."

1. Evidently the hero of a romance that has been lost.
2. *Tales of Ise* 1: "Kasugano lavender stains my robe / in deep disorder, like my secret loves." Kasugano is on the outskirts of Nara. Here as elsewhere lavender (*murasaki*) suggests a romantic affinity.

"I fear there is nothing that would interest you." Tō no Chūjō was in a contemplative mood. "It is with women as it is with everything else: the flawless ones are very few indeed. This is a sad fact which I have learned over the years. All manner of women seem presentable enough at first. Little notes, replies to this and that, they all suggest sensibility and cultivation. But when you begin sorting out the really superior ones you find that there are not many who have to be on your list. Each has her little tricks and she makes the most of them, getting in her slights at rivals, so broad sometimes that you almost have to blush. Hidden away by loving parents who build brilliant futures for them, they let word get out of this little talent and that little accomplishment and you are all in a stir. They are young and pretty and amiable and carefree, and in their boredom they begin to pick up a little from their elders, and in the natural course of things they begin to concentrate on one particular hobby and make something of it. A woman tells you all about it and hides the weak points and brings out the strong ones as if they were everything, and you can't very well call her a liar. So you begin keeping company, and it is always the same. The fact is not up to the advance notices."

Tō no Chūjō sighed, a sigh clearly based on experience. Some of what he had said, though not all, accorded with Genji's own experience. "And have you come upon any," said Genji, smiling, "who would seem to have nothing at all to recommend them?"

"Who would be fool enough to notice such a woman? And in any case, I should imagine that women with no merits are as rare as women with no faults. If a woman is of good family and well taken care of, then the things she is less than proud of are hidden and she gets by well enough. When you come to the middle ranks, each woman has her own little inclinations and there are thousands of ways to separate one from another. And when you come to the lowest—well, who really pays much attention?"

He appeared to know everything. Genji was by now deeply interested.

"You speak of three ranks," he said, "but is it so easy to make the division? There are well-born ladies who fall in the world and there are people of no background who rise to the higher ranks and build themselves fine houses as if intended for them all along. How would you fit such people into your system?"

At this point two young courtiers, a guards officer and a functionary in the ministry of rites, appeared on the scene, to attend the emperor in his retreat. Both were devotees of the way of love and both were good talkers. Tō no Chūjō, as if he had been waiting for them, invited their views on the question that had just been asked. The discussion progressed, and included a number of rather unconvincing points.

"Those who have just arrived at high position," said one of the newcomers, "do not attract the same sort of notice as those who were born to it. And those who were born to the highest rank but somehow do not have the right backing—in spirit they may be as proud and noble as ever, but they cannot hide their deficiencies. And so I think that they should both be put in your middle rank.

"There are those whose families are not quite of the highest rank but who go off and work hard in the provinces. They have their place in the world, though there are all sorts of little differences among them. Some of them would belong on anyone's list. So it is these days. Myself, I would take a woman from a middling family over one who has rank and nothing else. Let us say someone whose father is almost but not quite a councilor. Someone who has a decent enough reputation and comes from a decent enough family and can live in some luxury. Such people can be very pleasant. There is nothing wrong with the household arrangements, and indeed a daughter can sometimes be set out in a way that dazzles you. I can think of several such women it would be hard to find fault with. When they go into court service, they are the ones the unexpected favors have a way of falling on. I have seen cases enough of it, I can tell you."

Genji smiled. "And so a person should limit himself to girls with money?"

"That does not sound like you," said Tō no Chūjō.

"When a woman has the highest rank and a spotless reputation," continued the other, "but something has gone wrong with her upbringing, something is wrong in the way she puts herself forward, you wonder how it can possibly have been allowed to happen. But when all the conditions are right and the girl herself is pretty enough, she is taken for granted. There is no cause for the least surprise. Such ladies are beyond the likes of me, and so I leave them where they are, the highest of the high. There are surprisingly pretty ladies wasting away behind tangles of weeds, and hardly anyone even knows of their existence. The first surprise is hard to forget. There she is, a girl with a fat, sloppy old father and boorish brothers and a house that seems common at best. Off in the women's rooms is a proud lady who has acquired bits and snatches of this and that. You get wind of them, however small the accomplishments may be, and they take hold of your imagination. She is not the equal of the one who has every-thing, of course, but she has her charm. She is not easy to pass by."

He looked at his companion, the young man from the ministry of rites. The latter was silent, wondering if the reference might be to his sisters, just then coming into their own as subjects for conversation. Genji, it would seem, was thinking that on the highest levels there were sadly few ladies to bestow much thought upon. He was wearing sev-eral soft white singlets with an informal court robe thrown loosely over them. As he sat in the lamplight leaning against an armrest, his companions almost wished that he were a woman. Even the "highest of the high" might seem an inadequate match for him.

[*Although Genji remains aloof from the discussion, the other young men continue trading notes about desirable and undesirable qualities in women they have known. Tō no Chūjō describes an affair he had with a reticent, undemanding woman (Yūgao) by whom he had a child, but who was eventually driven off by his principal wife. Throughout, Genji's thoughts remain on Fujitsubo, who seems to him without flaw.*]

from *Chapter 5. Lavender*

[*Genji falls ill and goes to the Northern Hills, where he is treated by a Sage and remains to recover.*]

The evening was long. Genji took advantage of a dense haze to have a look at the house behind the wattle fence. Sending back everyone except Koremitsu, he took up a position at the fence. In the west room sat a nun who had a holy image before her. The blinds were slightly raised and she seemed to be offering flowers. She was leaning against a pillar and had a text spread out on an armrest. The effort to read seemed to take all her strength. Perhaps in her forties, she had a fair, delicate skin and a pleas-antly full face, though the effects of illness were apparent. The features suggested breeding and cultivation. Cut cleanly at the shoulders, her hair seemed to him far more pleasing than if it had been permitted to trail the usual length. Beside her were two attractive women, and little girls scampered in and out. Much the prettiest was a girl of perhaps ten in a soft white singlet and a russet robe. She would one day be a real beauty. Rich hair spread over her shoulders like a fan. Her face was flushed from weeping.

"What is it?" The nun looked up. "Another fight?" He thought he saw a resemblance. Perhaps they were mother and daughter.

"Inuki let my baby sparrows loose." The child was very angry. "I had them in a basket."

"That stupid child," said a rather handsome woman with rich hair who seemed to be called Shōnagon and was apparently the girl's nurse. "She always manages to do the wrong thing, and we are forever scolding her. Where will they have flown off to? They were getting to be such sweet little things too! How awful if the crows find them." She went out.

"What a silly child you are, really too silly," said the nun. "I can't be sure I will last out the day, and here you are worrying about sparrows. I've told you so many times that it's a sin to put birds in a cage. Come here."

The child knelt down beside her. She was charming, with rich, unplucked eyebrows and hair pushed childishly back from the forehead. How he would like to see her in a few years! And a sudden realization brought him close to tears: the resemblance to Fujitsubo, for whom he so yearned, was astonishing.

The nun stroked the girl's hair. "You will not comb it and still it's so pretty. I worry about you, you do seem so very young. Others are much more grown up at your age. Your poor dead mother: she was only ten when her father died, and she understood everything. What will become of you when I am gone?"

She was weeping, and a vague sadness had come over Genji too. The girl gazed attentively at her and then looked down. The hair that fell over her forehead was thick and lustrous.

> "Are these tender grasses to grow without the dew
> which holds itself back from the heavens that would receive it?"

There were tears in the nun's voice, and the other woman seemed also to be speaking through tears:

> "It cannot be that the dew will vanish away
> ere summer comes to these early grasses of spring."

The bishop came in. "What is this? Your blinds up? And today of all days you are out on the veranda? I have just been told that General Genji is up at the hermitage being treated for malaria. He came in disguise and I was not told in time to pay a call."

"And what a sight we are. You don't suppose he saw us?" She lowered the blinds.

"The shining one of whom the whole world talks. Wouldn't you like to see him? Enough to make a saint throw off the last traces of the vulgar world, they say, and feel as if new years had been added to his life. I will get off a note."

He hurried away, and Genji too withdrew. What a discovery! It was for such unforeseen rewards that his amorous followers were so constantly on the prowl. Such a rare outing for him, and it had brought such a find! She was a perfectly beautiful child. Who might she be? He was beginning to make plans: the child must stand in the place of the one whom she so resembled.

[After Genji has retired to his quarters, the bishop, the brother of Murasaki's grandmother, arrives and invites him to pay a visit.]

The bishop talked of this ephemeral world and of the world to come. His own burden of sin was heavy, thought Genji, that he had been lured into an illicit and profitless affair. He would regret it all his life and suffer even more terribly in the life to come. What joy to withdraw to such a place as this! But with the thought came thoughts of the young face he had seen earlier in the evening.

"Do you have someone with you here? I had a dream that suddenly begins to make sense."

"How quick you are with your dreams, sir! I fear my answer will disappoint you. It has been a very long time since the Lord Inspector died. I don't suppose you will even have heard of him. He was my brother-in-law. His widow turned her back on the world and recently she has been ill, and since I do not go down to the city she has come to stay with me here. It was her thought that I might be able to help her."

"I have heard that your sister had a daughter. I ask from no more than idle curiosity, you must believe me."

"There was an only daughter. She too has been dead these ten years and more. He took very great pains with her education and hoped to send her to court; but he died before that ambition could be realized, and the nun, my sister, was left to look after her. I do not know through whose offices it was that Prince Hyōbu began visiting the daughter in secret. His wife is from a very proud family, you know, sir, and there were unpleasant incidents, which finally drove the poor thing into a fatal decline. I saw before my own eyes how worry can destroy a person."

So the child he had seen would be the daughter of Prince Hyōbu and the unfortunate lady; and it was Fujitsubo, the prince's sister, whom she so resembled. He wanted more than ever to meet her. She was an elegant child, and she did not seem at all spoiled. What a delight if he could take her into his house and make her his ideal!

"A very sad story." He wished to be completely sure. "Did she leave no one behind?"

"She had a child just before she died, a girl, a great source of worry for my poor sister in her declining years."

There could be no further doubt. "What I am about to say will, I fear, startle you—but might I have charge of the child? I have rather good reasons, for all the suddenness of my proposal. If you are telling yourself that she is too young—well, sir, you are doing me an injustice. Other men may have improper motives, but I do not."

"Your words quite fill me with delight. But she is indeed young, so very young that we could not possibly think even in jest of asking you to take responsibility for her. Only the man who is presently to be her husband can take that responsibility. In a matter of such import I am not competent to give an answer. I must discuss the matter with my sister." He was suddenly remote and chilly.

Genji had spoken with youthful impulsiveness and could not think what to do next.

[Genji spends the night at the bishop's and engages in an exchange of poetry with the nun, making his interest in the girl known, much to the consternation of the nun and the attendants. The bishop and the nun agree that Genji's proposal is rather precipitate, and suggest that he wait until the girl grows up. Genji returns to the city and grudgingly accedes to his father-in-law's request that he spend some time at Sanjō to continue his recuperation.]

At the minister's Sanjō mansion everything was in readiness. It had been polished and refitted until it was a jeweled pavilion, perfect to the last detail. As always,

Genji's wife Aoi secluded herself in her private apartments, and it was only at her father's urging that she came forth; and so Genji had her before him, immobile, like a princess in an illustration for a romance. It would have been a great pleasure, he was sure, to have her comment even tartly upon his account of the mountain journey. She seemed the stiffest, remotest person in the world. How odd that the aloofness seemed only to grow as time went by.

"It would be nice, I sometimes think, if you could be a little more wifely. I have been very ill, and I am hurt, but not really surprised, that you have not inquired after my health."

"Like the pain, perhaps, of awaiting a visitor who does not come?"

She cast a sidelong glance at him as she spoke, and her cold beauty was very intimidating indeed.

"You so rarely speak to me, and when you do you say such unpleasant things. 'A visitor who does not come'—that is hardly an appropriate way to describe a husband, and indeed it is hardly civil. I try this approach and I try that, hoping to break through, but you seem intent on defending all the approaches. Well, one of these years, perhaps, if I live long enough."

He withdrew to the bedchamber. She did not follow. Though there were things he would have liked to say, he lay down with a sigh. He closed his eyes, but there was too much on his mind to permit sleep.

He thought of the little girl and how he would like to see her grown into a woman. Her grandmother was of course right when she said that the girl was still too young for him. He must not seem insistent. And yet—was there not some way to bring her quietly to Nijō and have her beside him, a comfort and a companion? Prince Hyōbu was a dashing and stylish man, but no one could have called him remarkably handsome. Why did the girl so take after her aunt? Perhaps because aunt and father were children of the same empress. These thoughts seemed to bring the girl closer, and he longed to have her for his own.

* * *

Fujitsubo was ill and had gone home to her family. Genji managed a sympathetic thought or two for his lonely father, but his thoughts were chiefly on the possibility of seeing Fujitsubo. He quite halted his visits to other ladies. All through the day, at home and at court, he sat gazing off into space, and in the evening he would press Omyōbu to be his intermediary. How she did it I do not know; but she contrived a meeting. It is sad to have to say that his earlier attentions, so unwelcome, no longer seemed real, and the mere thought that they had been successful was for Fujitsubo a torment. Determined that there would not be another meeting, she was shocked to find him in her presence again. She did not seek to hide her distress, and her efforts to turn him away delighted him even as they put him to shame. There was no one else quite like her. In that fact was his undoing: he would be less a prey to longing if he could find in her even a trace of the ordinary. And the tumult of thoughts and feelings that now assailed him—he would have liked to consign it to the Mountain of Obscurity.[1] It might have been better, he sighed, so short was the night, if he had not come at all.

> "So few and scattered the nights, so few the dreams,
> Would that the dream tonight might take me with it."

---

1. Kurabunoyama, thought to have been in present-day Kyoto.

He was in tears, and she did, after all, have to feel sorry for him.

> "Were I to disappear in the last of dreams
> Would yet my name live on in infamy?"

She had every right to be unhappy, and he was sad for her. Omyōbu gathered his clothes and brought them out to him.

Back at Nijō he spent a tearful day in bed. He had word from Omyōbu that her lady had not read his letter. So it always was, and yet he was hurt. He remained in distraught seclusion for several days. The thought that his father might be wondering about his absence filled him with terror.

Lamenting the burden of sin that seemed to be hers, Fujitsubo was more and more unwell, and could not bestir herself, despite repeated messages summoning her back to court. She was not at all her usual self—and what was to become of her? She took to her bed as the weather turned warmer. Three months had now passed and her condition was clear; and the burden of sin now seemed to have made it necessary that she submit to curious and reproving stares. Her women thought her behavior very curious indeed. Why had she let so much time pass without informing the emperor? There was of course a crucial matter of which she spoke to no one. Ben, the daughter of her old nurse, and Omyōbu, both of whom were very close to her and attended her in the bath, had ample opportunity to observe her condition. Omyōbu was aghast. Her lady had been trapped by the harshest of fates. The emperor would seem to have been informed that a malign spirit had possession of her, and to have believed the story, as did the court in general. He sent a constant stream of messengers, which terrified her and allowed no pause in her sufferings.

Genji had a strange, rather awful dream. He consulted a soothsayer, who said that it portended events so extraordinary as to be almost unthinkable.

"It contains bad omens as well. You must be careful."

"It was not my own dream but a friend's. We will see whether it comes true, and in the meantime you must keep it to yourself."

What could it mean? He heard of Fujitsubo's condition, thought of their night together, and wondered whether the two might be related. He exhausted his stock of pleas for another meeting. Horrified that matters were so out of hand, Omyōbu could do nothing for him. He had on rare occasions had a brief note, no more than a line or two, but now even these messages ceased coming.

Fujitsubo returned to court in the Seventh Month. The emperor's affection for her had only grown in her absence. Her condition was now apparent to everyone. A slight emaciation made her beauty seem if anything nearer perfection, and the emperor kept her always at his side. The skies as autumn approached called more insistently for music. Keeping Genji too beside him, the emperor had him try his hand at this and that instrument. Genji struggled to control himself, but now and then a sign of his scarcely bearable feelings did show through, to remind the lady of what she wanted more than anything to forget. * * *

In the autumn evening, his thoughts on his unattainable love, he longed more than ever, unnatural though the wish may have seemed, for the company of the little girl who sprang from the same roots. The thought of the evening when the old nun had described herself as dew holding back from the heavens made him even more impatient—and at the same time he feared that if he were to bring the girl to Nijō he would be disappointed in her.

I long to have it, to bring it in from the moor,
The lavender[2] that shares its roots with another.

In the Tenth Month the emperor was to visit the Suzaku Palace. From all the great families and the middle and upper courtly ranks the most accomplished musicians and dancers were selected to go with him, and grandees and princes of the blood were busy at the practice that best suited their talents. Caught up in the excitement, Genji was somewhat remiss in inquiring after the nun.

When, finally, he sent off a messenger to the northern hills, a sad reply came from the bishop: "We lost her toward the end of last month. It is the way of the world, I know, and yet I am sad."

If the news shocked even him into a new awareness of evanescence, thought Genji, how must it be for the little girl who had so occupied the nun's thoughts? Young though she was, she must feel utterly lost. He remembered, though dimly, how it had been when his mother died, and he sent off an earnest letter of sympathy. Shōnagon's answer seemed rather warmer. He went calling on an evening when he had nothing else to occupy him, some days after he learned that the girl had come out of mourning and returned to the city. The house was badly kept and almost deserted. The poor child must be terrified, he thought. He was shown to the same room as before. Sobbing, Shōnagon told him of the old lady's last days. Genji too was in tears.

"My young lady's father would seem to have indicated a willingness to take her in, but she is at such an uncomfortable age, not quite a child and still without the discernment of an adult; and the thought of having her in the custody of the lady who was so cruel to her mother is too awful. Her sisters will persecute her dreadfully, I know. The fear of it never left my lady's mind, and we have had too much evidence that the fear was not groundless. We have been grateful for your expressions of interest, though we have hesitated to take them seriously. I must emphasize that my young lady is not at all what you must think her to be. I fear that we have done badly by her, and that our methods have left her childish even for her years."

"Must you continue to be so reticent and apologetic? I have made my own feelings clear, over and over again. It is precisely the childlike quality that delights me most and makes me think I must have her for my own. You may think me complacent and self-satisfied for saying so, but I feel sure that we were joined in a former life. Let me speak to her, please.

> Rushes hide the sea grass at Wakanoura.
> Must the waves that seek it out turn back to sea?

"That would be too much to ask of her."

> "The grass at Wakanoura were rash indeed
> To follow waves that go it knows not whither.

"It would be far, far too much to ask."

---

2. *Murasaki*, a millet from the roots of which a lavender dye is extracted. Lavender, in general the color of affinity or intimacy, suggests more specifically the *fuji* of Fujitsubo, "Wisteria Court." It is because of this poem that the girl is presently to be called Murasaki. The name Murasaki Shikibu also derives from it.

The easy skill with which she turned her poem made it possible for him to forgive its less than encouraging significance. "After so many years," he whispered, "the gate still holds me back."[3]

The girl lay weeping for her grandmother. Her playmates came to tell her that a gentleman in court dress was with Shōnagon. Perhaps it would be her father?

She came running in. "Where is the gentleman, Shōnagon? Is Father here?"

What a sweet voice she had!

"I'm not your father, but I'm someone just as important. Come here."

She saw that it was the other gentleman, and child though she was, she flushed at having spoken out of turn. "Let's go." She tugged at Shōnagon's sleeve. "Let's go. I'm sleepy."

"Do you have to keep hiding yourself from me? Come here. You can sleep on my knee."

"She is really very young, sir." But Shōnagon urged the child forward, and she knelt obediently just inside the blinds.

He ran his hand over a soft, rumpled robe, and, a delight to the touch, hair full and rich to its farthest ends. He took her hand. She pulled away—for he was, after all, a stranger.

"I said I'm sleepy." She went back to Shōnagon.

He slipped in after her. "I am the one you must look to now. You must not be shy with me."

"Please, sir. You forget yourself. You forget yourself completely. She is simply not old enough to understand what you have in mind."

"It is you who do not understand. I see how young she is, and I have nothing of the sort in mind. I must again ask you to be witness to the depth and purity of my feelings."

It was a stormy night. Sleet was pounding against the roof.

"How can she bear to live in such a lonely place? It must be awful for her." Tears came to his eyes. He could not leave her. "I will be your watchman. You need one on a night like this. Come close to me, all of you."

Quite as if he belonged there, he slipped into the girl's bedroom. The women were astounded, Shōnagon more than the rest. He must be mad! But she was in no position to protest. Genji pulled a singlet over the girl, who was trembling like a leaf. Yes, he had to admit that his behavior must seem odd; but, trying very hard not to frighten her, he talked of things he thought would interest her.

"You must come to my house. I have all sorts of pictures, and there are dolls for you to play with."

She was less frightened than at first, but she still could not sleep. The storm blew all through the night, and Shōnagon quite refused to budge from their side. They would surely have perished of fright, whispered the women, if they had not had him with them. What a pity their lady was not a little older!

It was still dark when the wind began to subside and he made his departure, and all the appearances were as of an amorous expedition. "What I have seen makes me very sad and convinces me that she must not be out of my sight. She must come and live with me and share my lonely days. This place is quite impossible. You must be in constant terror."

---

3. Fujiwara Koretada, *Gosenshū* 732: "Alone, in secret, I hurry to Meeting Hill. / After so many years, the gate still holds me back."

"Her father has said that he will come for her. I believe it is to be after the memorial services."

"Yes, we must think of him. But they have lived apart, and he must be as much of a stranger as I am. I really do believe that in this very short time my feelings for her are stronger than his." He patted the girl on the head and looked back smiling as he left.

[Genji decides to retrieve the young Murasaki before her father, Prince Hyōbu, comes to pick her up.]

He went into her bedroom, where the women were too surprised to cry out. He took her in his arms and smoothed her hair. Her father had come for her, she thought, only half awake.

"Let's go. I have come from your father's." She was terrified when she saw that it was not after all her father. "You are not being nice. I have told you that you must think of me as your father." And he carried her out.

A chorus of protests now came from Shōnagon and the others.

"I have explained things quite well enough. I have told you how difficult it is for me to visit her and how I want to have her in a more comfortable and accessible spot; and your way of making things easier is to send her off to her father. One of you may come along, if you wish."

"Please, sir." Shōnagon was wringing her hands. "You could not have chosen a worse time. What are we to say when her father comes? If it is her fate to be your lady, then perhaps something can be done when the time comes. This is too sudden, and you put us in an extremely difficult position."

"You can come later if you wish."

His carriage had been brought up. The women were fluttering about helplessly and the child was sobbing. Seeing at last that there was nothing else to be done, Shōnagon took up several of the robes they had been at work on the night before, changed to presentable clothes of her own, and got into the carriage.

It was still dark when they reached Nijō, only a short distance away. Genji ordered the carriage brought up to the west wing and took the girl inside.

"It is like a nightmare," said Shōnagon. "What am I to do?"

"Whatever you like. I can have someone see you home if you wish."

Weeping helplessly, poor Shōnagon got out of the carriage. What would her lady's father think when he came for her? And what did they now have to look forward to? The saddest thing was to be left behind by one's protectors. But tears did not augur well for the new life. With an effort she pulled herself together.

Since no one was living in this west wing, there was no curtained bedchamber. Genji had Koremitsu put up screens and curtains, sent someone else to the east wing for bedding, and lay down. Though trembling violently, the girl managed to keep from sobbing aloud.

"I always sleep with Shōnagon," she said softly in childish accents.

"Imagine a big girl like you still sleeping with her nurse."

Weeping quietly, the girl lay down.

Shōnagon sat up beside them, looking out over the garden as dawn came on. The buildings and grounds were magnificent, and the sand in the garden was like jewels. Not used to such affluence, she was glad there were no other women in this west wing. It was here that Genji received occasional callers. A few guards beyond the blinds were the only attendants.

They were speculating on the identity of the lady he had brought with him. "Someone worth looking at, you can bet."

Water pitchers and breakfast were brought in. The sun was high when Genji arose. "You will need someone to take care of you. Suppose you send this evening for the ones you like best." He asked that children be sent from the east wing to play with her. "Pretty little girls, please." Four little girls came in, very pretty indeed.

The new girl, his Murasaki, still lay huddled under the singlet he had thrown over her.

"You are not to sulk, now, and make me unhappy. Would I have done all this for you if I were not a nice man? Young ladies should do as they are told." And so the lessons began.

She seemed even prettier here beside him than from afar. His manner warm and fatherly, he sought to amuse her with pictures and toys he had sent for from the east wing. Finally she came over to him. Her dark mourning robes were soft and un-starched, and when she smiled, innocently and unprotestingly, he had to smile back. She went out to look at the trees and pond after he had departed for the east wing. The flowers in the foreground, delicately touched by frost, were like a picture. Streams of courtiers, of the medium ranks and new to her experience, passed back and forth. Yes, it was an interesting place. She looked at the pictures on screens and elsewhere and (so it is with a child) soon forgot her troubles. * * *

Presently Murasaki had all her women with her. She was a bright, lively child, and the boys and girls who were to be her playmates felt quite at home with her. Sometimes on lonely nights when Genji was away she would weep for her grand-mother. She thought little of her father. They had lived apart and she scarcely knew him. She was by now extremely fond of her new father. She would be the first to run out and greet him when he came home, and she would climb on his lap, and they would talk happily together, without the least constraint or embarrassment. He was delighted with her. A clever and watchful woman can create all manner of difficulties. A man must be always on his guard, and jealousy can have the most unwelcome con-sequences. Murasaki was the perfect companion, a toy for him to play with. He could not have been so free and uninhibited with a daughter of his own. There are restraints upon paternal intimacy. Yes, he had come upon a remarkable little treasure.

from *Chapter 7. An Autumn Excursion*

Fujitsubo had gone home to her family. Looking restlessly, as always, for a chance to see her, Genji was much criticized by his father-in-law's people at Sanjō. And rumors of the young Murasaki were out. Certain of the women at Sanjō let it be known that a new lady had been taken in at Nijō. Genji's wife was intensely displeased. It was most natural that she should be, for she did not of course know that the "lady" was a mere child. If she had complained to him openly, as most women would have done, he might have told her everything, and no doubt eased her jealousy. It was her arbitrary judgments that sent him wandering. She had no specific faults, no vices or blemishes, which he could point to. She had been the first lady in his life, and in an abstract way he admired and treasured her. Her feelings would change, he felt sure, once she was more familiar with his own. She was a perceptive woman, and the change was certain to come. She still occupied first place among his ladies.

Murasaki was by now thoroughly comfortable with him. She was maturing in appearance and manner, and yet there was artlessness in her way of clinging to him.

Thinking it too early to let the people in the main hall know who she was, he kept her in one of the outer wings, which he had had fitted to perfection. He was constantly with her, tutoring her in the polite accomplishments and especially calligraphy. It was as if he had brought home a daughter who had spent her early years in another house. He had studied the qualifications of her stewards and assured himself that she would have everything she needed. Everyone in the house, save only Koremitsu, was consumed with curiosity. Her father still did not know of her whereabouts. Sometimes she would weep for her grandmother. Her mind was full of other things when Genji was with her, and often he stayed the night; but he had numerous other places to look in upon, and he was quite charmed by the wistfulness with which she would see him off in the evening. Sometimes he would spend two and three days at the palace and go from there to Sanjō. Finding a pensive Murasaki upon his return, he would feel as if he had taken in a little orphan. He no longer looked forward to his nocturnal wanderings with the same eagerness. Her granduncle the bishop kept himself informed of her affairs, and was pleased and puzzled. Genji sent most lavish offerings for memorial services.

Longing for news of Fujitsubo, still with her family, he paid a visit. Omyōbu, Chūnagon, Nakatsukasa, and others of her women received him, but the lady whom he really wanted to see kept him at a distance. He forced himself to make conversation. Prince Hyōbu, her brother and Murasaki's father, came in, having heard that Genji was on the premises. He was a man of great and gentle elegance, someone, thought Genji, who would interest him enormously were they of opposite sexes. Genji felt very near this prince so near the two ladies, and to the prince their conversation seemed friendly and somehow significant as earlier conversations had not. How very handsome Genji was! Not dreaming that it was a prospective son-in-law he was addressing, he too was thinking how susceptible (for he was a susceptible man) he would be to Genji's charms if they were not of the same sex.

When, at dusk, the prince withdrew behind the blinds, Genji felt pangs of jealousy. In the old years he had followed his father behind those same blinds, and there addressed the lady. Now she was far away—though of course no one had wronged him, and he had no right to complain.

"I have not been good about visiting you," he said stiffly as he got up to leave. "Having no business with you, I have not wished to seem forward. It would give me great pleasure if you would let me know of any services I might perform for you."

Omyōbu could do nothing for him. Fujitsubo seemed to find his presence even more of a trial than before, and showed no sign of relenting. Sadly and uselessly the days went by. What a frail, fleeting union theirs had been!

Shōnagon, Murasaki's nurse, continued to marvel at the strange course their lives had taken. Perhaps some benign power had arranged it, the old nun having mentioned Murasaki in all her prayers. Not that everything was perfect. Genji's wife at Sanjō was a lady of the highest station, and other affairs, indeed too many of them, occupied him as well. Might not the girl face difficult times as she grew into womanhood? Yet he did seem fond of her as of none of the others, and her future seemed secure. The period of mourning for a maternal grandmother being set at three months, it was on New Year's Eve that Murasaki took off her mourning weeds. The old lady had been for her both mother and grandmother, however, and so she chose to limit herself to pale, unfigured pinks and lavenders and yellows. Pale colors seemed to suit her even better than rich ones.

"And do you feel all grown up, now that a new year has come?" Smiling, radiating youthful charm, Genji looked in upon her. He was on his way to the morning festivities at court.

She had already taken out her dolls and was busy seeing to their needs. All manner of furnishings and accessories were laid out on a yard-high shelf. Dollhouses threatened to overflow the room.

"Inuki knocked everything over chasing out devils last night and broke this." It was a serious matter. "I'm gluing it."

"Yes, she really is very clumsy, that Inuki. We'll ask someone to repair it for you. But today you must not cry. Crying is the worst way to begin a new year."

And he went out, his retinue so grand that it overflowed the wide grounds. The women watched from the veranda, the girl with them. She set out a Genji among her dolls and saw him off to court.

"This year you must try to be just a little more grown up," said Shōnagon. "Ten years old, no, even more, and still you play with dolls. It will not do. You have a nice husband, and you must try to calm down and be a little more wifely. Why, you fly into a tantrum even when we try to brush your hair." A proper shaming was among Shōnagon's methods.

So she had herself a nice husband, thought Murasaki. The husbands of these women were none of them handsome men, and hers was so very young and handsome. The thought came to her now for the first time, evidence that, for all this play with dolls, she was growing up. It sometimes puzzled her women that she should still be such a child. It did not occur to them that she was in fact not yet a wife.

From the palace Genji went to Sanjō. His wife, as always, showed no suggestion of warmth or affection; and as always he was uncomfortable.

"How pleasant if this year you could manage to be a little friendlier."

But since she had heard of his new lady she had become more distant than ever. She was convinced that the other was now first among his ladies, and no doubt she was as uncomfortable as he. But when he jokingly sought to make it seem that nothing was amiss, she had to answer, if reluctantly. Everything she said was uniquely, indefinably elegant. She was four years his senior and made him feel like a stripling. Where, he asked, was he to find a flaw in this perfection? Yet he seemed determined to anger her with his other affairs. She was a proud lady, the single and treasured daughter, by a princess, of a minister who overshadowed the other grandees, and she was not prepared to tolerate the smallest discourtesy. And here he was behaving as if these proud ways were his to make over. They were completely at cross purposes, he and she.

* * *

Genji did not pay many New Year calls. He called upon his father, the crown prince, the old emperor,[1] and, finally, Fujitsubo, still with her family. Her women thought him handsomer than ever. Yes, each year, as he matured, his good looks produced a stronger shudder of delight and foreboding. Fujitsubo was assailed by innumerable conflicting thoughts.

The Twelfth Month, when she was to have been delivered of her child, had passed uneventfully. Surely it would be this month, said her women, and at court everything was in readiness; but the First Month too passed without event. She was greatly troubled by rumors that she had fallen under a malign influence. Her worries had made her

---

1. Perhaps the father of the reigning emperor, he is mentioned nowhere else. The reign of the present emperor seems to have been preceded by that of Fujitsubo's father, now dead.

physically ill and she began to wonder if the end was in sight. More and more certain as time passed that the child was his, Genji quietly commissioned services in various temples. More keenly aware than most of the evanescence of things, he now found added to his worries a fear that he would not see her again. Finally toward the end of the Second Month she bore a prince, and the jubilation was unbounded at court and at her family palace. She had not joined the emperor in praying that she be granted a long life, and yet she did not want to please Kokiden, an echo of whose curses had reached her. The will to live returned, and little by little she recovered.

The emperor wanted to see his little son the earliest day possible. Genji, filled with his own secret paternal solicitude, visited Fujitsubo at a time when he judged she would not have other visitors.

"Father is extremely anxious to see the child. Perhaps I might have a look at him first and present a report."

She refused his request, as of course she had every right to do. "He is still very shriveled and ugly."

There was no doubt that the child bore a marked, indeed a rather wonderful, resemblance to Genji. Fujitsubo was tormented by feelings of guilt and apprehension. Surely everyone who saw the child would guess the awful truth and damn her for it. People were always happy to seek out the smallest and most trivial of misdeeds. Hers had not been trivial, and dreadful rumors must surely be going the rounds. Had ever a woman been more sorely tried?

Genji occasionally saw Omyōbu and pleaded that she intercede for him; but there was nothing she could do.

"This insistence, my lord, is very trying," she said, at his constant and passionate pleas to see the child. "You will have chances enough later." Yet secretly she was as unhappy as he was.

"In what world, I wonder, will I again be allowed to see her?" The heart of the matter was too delicate to touch upon.

> "What legacy do we bring from former lives that
> Loneliness should be our lot in this one?"

"I do not understand. I do not understand at all."

His tears brought her to the point of tears herself. Knowing how unhappy her lady was, she could not bring herself to turn him brusquely away.

> "Sad at seeing the child, sad at not seeing.
> The heart of the father, the mother, lost in darkness."[2]

And she added softly: "There seems to be no lessening of the pain for either of you."

She saw him off, quite unable to help him. Her lady had said that because of the danger of gossip she could not receive him again, and she no longer behaved toward Omyōbu with the old affection. She behaved correctly, it was true, and did nothing that might attract attention, but Omyōbu had done things to displease her. Omyōbu was very sorry for them.

In the Fourth Month the little prince was brought to the palace. Advanced for his age both mentally and physically, he was already able to sit up and to right himself when he rolled over. He was strikingly like Genji. Unaware of the truth, the emperor

---

2. Fujiwara Kanesuke, *Gosenshū* 1103: "The heart of a parent is not darkness, / and yet he wanders lost in thoughts upon his child."

would say to himself that people of remarkable good looks did have a way of looking alike. He doted upon the child. He had similarly doted upon Genji, but, because of strong opposition—and how deeply he regretted the fact—had been unable to make him crown prince. The regret increased as Genji, now a commoner, improved in looks and in accomplishments. And now a lady of the highest birth had borne the emperor another radiant son. The infant was for him an unflawed jewel, for Fujitsubo a source of boundless guilt and foreboding.

One day, as he often did, Genji was enjoying music in Fujitsubo's apartments. The emperor came out with the little boy in his arms.

"I have had many sons, but you were the only one I paid a great deal of attention to when you were this small. Perhaps it is the memory of those days that makes me think he looks like you. Is it that all children look alike when they are very young?" He made no attempt to hide his pleasure in the child.

Genji felt himself flushing crimson. He was frightened and awed and pleased and touched, all at the same time, and there were tears in his eyes. Laughing and babbling, the child was so beautiful as to arouse fears that he would not be long in this world. If indeed he resembled the child, thought Genji, then he must be very handsome. He must take better care of himself. (He seemed a little self-satisfied at times.) Fujitsubo was in such acute discomfort that she felt herself breaking into a cold sweat. Eager though he had been to see the child, Genji left in great agitation.

[*In "The Festival of the Cherry Blossoms," the next chapter, Genji has his first encounter with Oborozukiyo, the daughter of the powerful Minister of the Right and sister of the Kokiden lady, who is slated to become the consort of the crown prince (the future Suzaku emperor). "Heartvine," the following chapter, opens with a change of guard: Genji's father, the Kiritsubo emperor, has abdicated, bringing to the throne the Suzaku emperor, son of the Kokiden lady and the Minister of the Right. Fujitsubo's son (and secretly that of Genji), the future Reizei emperor, is made the heir apparent.*]

from *Chapter 9. Heartvine*

With the new reign Genji's career languished, and since he must be the more discreet about his romantic adventures as he rose in rank, he had less to amuse him. Everywhere there were complaints about his aloofness.

As if to punish him, there was one lady who continued to cause him pain with her own aloofness. Fujitsubo saw more of the old emperor, now abdicated, than ever. She was always at his side, almost as if she were a common housewife. Annoyed at this state of affairs, Kokiden did not follow the old emperor when he left the main palace. Fujitsubo was happy and secure. The concerts in the old emperor's palace attracted the attention of the whole court, and altogether life was happier for the two of them than while he had reigned. Only one thing was lacking: he greatly missed the crown prince, Fujitsubo's son, and worried that he had no strong backers. Genji, he said, must be the boy's adviser and guardian. Genji was both pleased and embarrassed.

And there was the matter of the lady at Rokujō. With the change of reigns, her daughter, who was also the daughter of the late crown prince, had been appointed high priestess of the Ise Shrine. No longer trusting Genji's affections, the Rokujō lady had been thinking that, making the girl's youth her excuse, she too would go to Ise.

The old emperor heard of her plans. "The crown prince was so very fond of her," he said to Genji, in open displeasure. "It is sad that you should have made light of her, as if she were any ordinary woman. I think of the high priestess as one of my own children, and you should be good to her mother, for my sake and for the sake of the dead prince. It does you no good to abandon yourself to these affairs quite as the impulse takes you."

It was perfectly true, thought Genji. He waited in silence.

"You should treat any woman with tact and courtesy, and be sure that you cause her no embarrassment. You should never have a woman angry with you."

What would his father think if he were to learn of Genji's worst indiscretion? The thought made Genji shudder. He bowed and withdrew.

The matter his father had thus reproved him for did no good for either of them, the woman or Genji himself. It was a scandal, and very sad for her. She continued to be very much on his mind, and yet he had no thought of making her his wife. She had grown cool toward him, worried about the difference in their ages. He made it seem that it was because of her wishes that he stayed away. Now that the old emperor knew of the affair the whole court knew of it. In spite of everything, the lady went on grieving that he had not loved her better. * * *

At Sanjō, his wife and her family were even unhappier about his infidelities, but, perhaps because he did not lie to them, they for the most part kept their displeasure to themselves. His wife was with child and in considerable distress mentally and physically. For Genji it was a strange and moving time. Everyone was delighted and at the same time filled with apprehension, and all manner of retreats and abstinences were prescribed for the lady. Genji had little time to himself. While he had no particular wish to avoid the Rokujō lady and the others, he rarely visited them.

At about this time the high priestess of Kamo resigned. She was replaced by the old emperor's third daughter, whose mother was Kokiden. The new priestess was a favorite of both her brother, the new emperor, and her mother, and it seemed a great pity that she should be shut off from court life; but no other princess was qualified for the position. The installation ceremonies, in the austere Shinto tradition, were of great dignity and solemnity. Many novel details were added to the Kamo festival in the Fourth Month, so that it was certain to be the finest of the season. Though the number of high courtiers attending the princess at the lustration was limited by precedent, great care was taken to choose handsome men of good repute. Similar care was given to their uniforms and to the uniform trappings of their horses. Genji was among the attendants, by special command of the new emperor. Courtiers and ladies had readied their carriage far in advance, and Ichijō was a frightening crush, without space for another vehicle. The stands along the way had been appointed most elaborately. The sleeves that showed beneath the curtains fulfilled in their brightness and variety all the festive promise.

Genji's wife seldom went forth on sightseeing expeditions and her pregnancy was another reason for staying at home.

But her young women protested. "Really, my lady, it won't be much fun sneaking off by ourselves. Why, even complete strangers—why, all the country folk have come in to see our lord! They've brought their wives and families from the farthest provinces. It will be too much if you make us stay away."

Her mother, Princess Omiya, agreed. "You seem to be feeling well enough, my dear, and they will be very disappointed if you don't take them."

And so carriages were hastily and unostentatiously decked out, and the sun was already high when they set forth. The waysides were by now too crowded to admit the elegant Sanjō procession. Coming upon several fine carriages not attended by grooms and footmen, the Sanjō men commenced clearing a space. Two palm-frond carriages remained, not new ones, obviously belonging to someone who did not wish to attract attention. The curtains and the sleeves and aprons to be glimpsed beneath them, some in the gay colors little girls wear, were in very good taste.

The men in attendance sought to defend their places against the Sanjō invaders. "We aren't the sort of people you push around."

There had been too much drink in both parties, and the drunken ones were not responsive to the efforts of their more mature and collected seniors to restrain them.

The palm-frond carriages were from the Rokujō house of the high priestess of Ise. The Rokujō lady had come quietly to see the procession, hoping that it might make her briefly forget her unhappiness. The men from Sanjō had recognized her, but preferred to make it seem otherwise.

"They can't tell us who to push and not to push," said the more intemperate ones to their fellows. "They have General Genji to make them feel important."

Among the newcomers were some of Genji's men. They recognized and felt a little sorry for the Rokujō lady, but, not wishing to become involved, they looked the other way. Presently all the Sanjō carriages were in place. The Rokujō lady, behind the lesser ones, could see almost nothing. Quite aside from her natural distress at the insult, she was filled with the bitterest chagrin that, having refrained from display, she had been recognized. The stools for her carriage shafts had been broken and the shafts propped on the hubs of perfectly strange carriages, a most undignified sight. It was no good asking herself why she had come. She thought of going home without seeing the procession, but there was no room for her to pass; and then came word that the procession was approaching, and she must, after all, see the man who had caused her such unhappiness. How weak is the heart of a woman! Perhaps because this was not "the bamboo by the river Hinokuma,"[1] he passed without stopping his horse or looking her way; and the unhappiness was greater than if she had stayed at home.

Genji seemed indifferent to all the grandly decorated carriages and all the gay sleeves, such a flood of them that it was as if ladies were stacked in layers behind the carriage curtains. Now and again, however, he would have a smile and a glance for a carriage he recognized. His face was solemn and respectful as he passed his wife's carriage. His men bowed deeply, and the Rokujō lady was in misery. She had been utterly defeated.

She whispered to herself:

> "A distant glimpse of the River of Lustration.
> His coldness is the measure of my sorrow."

She was ashamed of her tears. Yet she thought how sorry she would have been if she had not seen that handsome figure set off to such advantage by the crowds.

The high courtiers were, after their several ranks, impeccably dressed and caparisoned and many of them were very handsome; but Genji's radiance dimmed the strongest lights. Among his special attendants was a guards officer of the Sixth Rank, though attendants of such standing were usually reserved for the most splendid royal processions. His retinue made such a fine procession itself that every tree and blade of grass along the way seemed to bend forward in admiration.

It is not on the whole considered good form for veiled ladies of no mean rank and even nuns who have withdrawn from the world to be jostling and shoving one another

---

1. Anonymous, *Kokinshū* 1080: "In the bamboo by the river Hinokuma, / stop that your horse may drink, and I may see you."

in the struggle to see, but today no one thought it out of place. Hollow-mouthed women of the lower classes, their hair tucked under their robes, their hands brought respectfully to their foreheads, were hopping about in hopes of catching a glimpse. Plebeian faces were wreathed in smiles which their owners might not have enjoyed seeing in mirrors, and daughters of petty provincial officers of whose existence Genji would scarcely have been aware had set forth in carriages decked out with the most exhaustive care and taken up posts which seemed to offer a chance of seeing him. There were almost as many things by the wayside as in the procession to attract one's attention.

And there were many ladies whom he had seen in secret and who now sighed more than ever that their station was so out of keeping with his. Prince Shikibu viewed the procession from a stand. Genji had matured and did indeed quite dazzle the eye, and the prince thought with foreboding that some god might have noticed, and was making plans to spirit the young man away. His daughter, Princess Asagao, having over the years found Genji a faithful correspondent, knew how remarkably steady his feelings were. She was aware that attentions moved ladies even when the donor was a most ordinary man; yet she had no wish for further intimacy. As for her women, their sighs of admiration were almost deafening.

No carriages set out from the Sanjō mansion on the day of the festival proper.

Genji presently heard the story of the competing carriages. He was sorry for the Rokujō lady and angry at his wife. It was a sad fact that, so deliberate and fastidious, she lacked ordinary compassion. There was indeed a tart, forbidding quality about her. She refused to see, though it was probably an unconscious refusal, that ladies who were to each other as she was to the Rokujō lady should behave with charity and forbearance. It was under her influence that the men in her service flung themselves so violently about. Genji sometimes felt uncomfortable before the proud dignity of the Rokujō lady, and he could imagine her rage and humiliation now.

He called upon her. The high priestess, her daughter, was still with her, however, and, making reverence for the sacred sakaki tree[2] her excuse, she declined to receive him.

She was right, of course. Yet he muttered to himself: "Why must it be so? Why cannot the two of them be a little less prickly?" * * *

For the Rokujō lady the pain was unrelieved. She knew that she could expect no lessening of his coldness, and yet to steel herself and go off to Ise with her daughter— she would be lonely, she knew, and people would laugh at her. They would laugh just as heartily if she stayed in the city. Her thoughts were as the fisherman's bob at Ise.[3] Her very soul seemed to jump wildly about, and at last she fell physically ill.

Genji discounted the possibility of her going to Ise. "It is natural that you should have little use for a reprobate like myself and think of discarding me. But to stay with me would be to show admirable depths of feeling."

These remarks did not seem very helpful. Her anger and sorrow increased. A hope of relief from this agony of indecision had sent her to the river of lustration, and there she had been subjected to violence.

At Sanjō, Genji's wife seemed to be in the grip of a malign spirit. It was no time for nocturnal wanderings. Genji paid only an occasional visit to his own Nijō mansion.

2. A glossy-leafed tree related to the camellia. Its branches are used in Shinto ritual.

3. Anonymous, *Kokinshū* 509: "Has my heart become the fisherman's bob at Ise? / It jumps and bobs and knows not calm or resolve."

His marriage had not been happy, but his wife was important to him and now she was carrying his child. He had prayers read in his Sanjō rooms. Several malign spirits were transferred to the medium and identified themselves, but there was one which quite refused to move. Though it did not cause great pain, it refused to leave her for so much as an instant. There was something very sinister about a spirit that eluded the powers of the most skilled exorcists. The Sanjō people went over the list of Genji's ladies one by one. Among them all, it came to be whispered, only the Rokujō lady and the lady at Nijō seemed to have been singled out for special attentions, and no doubt they were jealous. The exorcists were asked about the possibility, but they gave no very informative answers. Of the spirits that did announce themselves, none seemed to feel any deep enmity toward the lady. Their behavior seemed random and purposeless. There was the spirit of her dead nurse, for instance, and there were spirits that had been with the family for generations and had taken advantage of her weakness.

The confusion and worry continued. The lady would sometimes weep in loud wailing sobs, and sometimes be tormented by nausea and shortness of breath.

The old emperor sent repeated inquiries and ordered religious services. That the lady should be worthy of these august attentions made the possibility of her death seem even more lamentable. Reports that they quite monopolized the attention of court reached the Rokujō mansion, to further embitter its lady. No one can have guessed that the trivial incident of the carriages had so angered a lady whose sense of rivalry had not until then been strong.

Not at all herself, she left her house to her daughter and moved to one where Buddhist rites would not be out of place.[4] Sorry to hear of the move, Genji bestirred himself to call on her. The neighborhood was a strange one and he was in careful disguise. He explained his negligence in terms likely to make it seem involuntary and to bring her forgiveness, and he told her of Aoi's illness and the worry it was causing him.

"I have not been so very worried myself, but her parents are beside themselves. It has seemed best to stay with her. It would relieve me enormously if I thought you might take a generous view of it all." He knew why she was unwell, and pitied her.

They passed a tense night. As she saw him off in the dawn she found that her plans for quitting the city were not as firm as on the day before. Her rival was of the highest rank and there was this important new consideration; no doubt his affections would finally settle on her. She herself would be left in solitude, wondering when he might call. The visit had only made her unhappier. In upon her gloom, in the evening, came a letter.

"Though she had seemed to be improving, she has taken a sudden and drastic turn for the worse. I cannot leave her."

The usual excuses, she thought. Yet she answered:

> "I go down the way of love and dampen my sleeves,
>   and go yet further, into the muddy fields.

A pity the well is so shallow."[5]

The hand was the very best he knew. It was a difficult world, which refused to give satisfaction. Among his ladies there was none who could be dismissed as completely beneath consideration and none to whom he could give his whole love.

---

4. They were out of place in the house of a Shinto priestess.
5. Anonymous, *Kokin Rokujō, Zoku Kokka Taikan* 31863:

"A pity the mountain well should be so shallow. / I seek to take water and only wet my sleeves."

Despite the lateness of the hour, he got off an answer: "You only wet your sleeves—what can this mean? That your feelings are not of the deepest, I should think.

> You only dip into the shallow waters,
> And I quite disappear into the slough?

"Do you think I would answer by letter and not in person if she were merely indisposed?"

The malign spirit was more insistent, and Aoi was in great distress. Unpleasant rumors reached the Rokujō lady, to the effect that it might be her spirit or that of her father, the late minister. Though she had felt sorry enough for herself, she had not wished ill to anyone; and might it be that the soul of one so lost in sad thoughts went wandering off by itself? She had, over the years, known the full range of sorrows, but never before had she felt so utterly miserable. There had been no release from the anger since the other lady had so insulted her, indeed behaved as if she did not exist. More than once she had the same dream: in the beautifully appointed apartments of a lady who seemed to be a rival she would push and shake the lady, and flail at her blindly and savagely. It was too terrible. Sometimes in a daze she would ask herself if her soul had indeed gone wandering off. The world was not given to speaking well of people whose transgressions had been far slighter. She would be notorious. It was common enough for the spirits of the angry dead to linger on in this world. She had thought them hateful, and it was her own lot to set a hateful example while she still lived. She must think no more about the man who had been so cruel to her. But so to think was, after all, to think.

The high priestess, her daughter, was to have been presented at court the year before, but complications had required postponement. It was finally decided that in the Ninth Month she would go from court to her temporary shrine. The Rokujō house was thus busy preparing for two lustrations, but its lady, lost in thought, seemed strangely indifferent. A most serious state of affairs—the priestess's attendants ordered prayers. There were no really alarming symptoms. She was vaguely unwell, no more. The days passed. Genji sent repeated inquiries, but there was no relief from his worries about another invalid, a more important one.

It was still too early for Aoi to be delivered of her child. Her women were less than fully alert; and then, suddenly, she was seized with labor pains. More priests were put to more strenuous prayers. The malign spirit refused to move. The most eminent of exorcists found this stubbornness extraordinary, and could not think what to do. Then, after renewed efforts at exorcism, more intense than before, it commenced sobbing as if in pain.

"Stop for a moment, please. I want to speak to General Genji."

It was as they had thought. The women showed Genji to a place at Aoi's curtains. Thinking—for she did seem on the point of death—that Aoi had last words for Genji, her parents withdrew. The effect was grandly solemn as priests read from the Lotus Sutra in hushed voices. Genji drew the curtains back and looked down at his wife. She was heavy with child, and very beautiful. Even a man who was nothing to her would have been saddened to look at her. Long, heavy hair, bound at one side, was set off by white robes, and he thought her lovelier than when she was most carefully dressed and groomed.

He took her hand. "How awful. How awful for you." He could say no more.

Usually so haughty and forbidding, she now gazed up at him with languid eyes that were presently filled with tears. How could he fail to be moved? This violent weeping, he thought, would be for her parents, soon to be left behind, and perhaps, at this last leave-taking, for him too.

"You mustn't fret so. It can't be as bad as you think. And even if the worst comes, we will meet again. And your good mother and father: the bond between parents and children lasts through many lives. You must tell yourself that you will see them again."

"No, no. I was hurting so, I asked them to stop for a while. I had not dreamed that I would come to you like this. It is true: a troubled soul will sometimes go wandering off." The voice was gentle and affectionate.

> "Bind the hem of my robe, to keep it within,
> the grieving soul that has wandered through the skies."[6]

It was not Aoi's voice, nor was the manner hers. Extraordinary—and then he knew that it was the voice of the Rokujō lady. He was aghast. He had dismissed the talk as vulgar and ignorant fabrication, and here before his eyes he had proof that such things did actually happen, he was horrified and repelled.

"You may say so. But I don't know who you are. Identify yourself."

It was indeed she. "Aghast"—is there no stronger word? He waved the women back.

Thinking that these calmer tones meant a respite from pain, her mother came with medicine; and even as she drank it down she gave birth to a baby boy. Everyone was delighted, save the spirits that had been transferred to mediums. Chagrined at their failure, they were raising a great stir, and all in all it was a noisy and untidy scene. There was still the afterbirth to worry about. Then, perhaps because of all the prayers, it too was delivered. The grand abbot of Hiei and all the other eminent clerics departed, looking rather pleased with themselves as they mopped their foreheads. Sure that the worst was past after all the anxious days, the women allowed themselves a rest.

The prayers went on as noisily as ever, but the house was now caught up in the happy business of ministering to a pretty baby. It hummed with excitement on each of the festive nights.[7] Fine and unusual gifts came from the old emperor and from all the princes and high courtiers. Ceremonies honoring a boy baby are always interesting.

The Rokujō lady received the news with mixed feelings. She had heard that her rival was critically ill, and now the crisis had passed. She was not herself. The strangest thing was that her robes were permeated with the scent of the poppy seeds burned at exorcisms. She changed clothes repeatedly and even washed her hair, but the odor persisted. She was overcome with self-loathing. And what would others be thinking? It was a matter she could discuss with no one. She could only suffer in distraught silence.

Somewhat calmer, Genji was still horrified at the unsolicited remarks he had had from the possessive spirit. He really must get off a note to the Rokujō lady. Or should he have a talk with her? He would find it hard to be civil, and he did not wish to hurt her. In the end he made do with a note.

Aoi's illness had been critical, and the strictest vigil must be continued. Genji had been persuaded to stop his nocturnal wanderings. He still had not really talked to his wife, for she was still far from normal. The child was so beautiful as to arouse forebodings, and preparations were already under way for a most careful and elaborate education. The minister was pleased with everything save the fact that his daughter had still not recovered. But he told himself that he need not worry. A slow convalescence was to be expected after so serious an illness.

---

6. Tying the skirt of a robe was a device for keeping an errant spirit at home.

7. There were celebrations on the third, fifth, seventh, and ninth nights.

Especially around the eyes, the baby bore a strong resemblance to the crown prince, whom Genji suddenly felt an intense longing to see. He could not sit still. He had to be off to court.

"I have been neglecting my duties," he said to the women, "and am feeling rather guilty. I think today I will venture out. It would be good if I might see her before I go. I am not a stranger, you know."

"Quite true, sir. You of all people should be allowed near. She is badly emaciated, I fear, but that is scarcely a reason for her to hide herself from you."

And so a place was set out for him at her bedside. She answered from time to time, but in a very weak voice. Even so little, from a lady who had been given up for dead, was like a dream. He told her of those terrible days. Then he remembered how, as if pulling back from a brink, she had begun talking to him so volubly and so eagerly. A shudder of revulsion passed over him.

"There are many things I would like to say to you, but you still seem very tired."

He even prepared medicine for her. The women were filled with admiration. When had he learned to be so useful?

She was sadly worn and lay as if on the border of death, pathetic and still lovely. There was not a tangle in her lustrous hair. The thick tresses that poured over her pillows seemed to him quite beyond compare. He gazed down at her, thinking it odd that he should have felt so dissatisfied with her over the years.

"I must see my father, but I am sure I will not be needed long. How nice if we could always be like this. But your mother is with you so much, I have not wanted to seem insistent. You must get back your strength and move back to your own rooms. Your mother pampers you too much. That may be one reason why you are so slow getting well."

As he withdrew in grand court dress she lay looking after him as she had not been in the habit of doing.

There was to be a conference on promotions and appointments. The minister too set off for court, in procession with all his sons, each of them with a case to plead and determined not to leave his side.

The Sanjō mansion was almost deserted. Aoi was again seized with a strangling shortness of breath; and very soon after a messenger had been sent to court she was dead. Genji and the others left court, scarcely aware of where their feet were taking them. Appointments and promotions no longer concerned them. Since the crisis had come at about midnight there was no possibility of summoning the grand abbot and his suffragans. Everyone had thought that the worst was over, and now of course everyone was stunned, dazed, wandering aimlessly from room to room, hardly knowing a door from a wall. Messengers crowded in with condolences, but the house was in such confusion that there was no one to receive them. The intensity of the grief was almost frightening. Since malign spirits had more than once attacked the lady, her father ordered the body left as it was for two or three days in hopes that she might revive. The signs of death were more and more pronounced, however, and, in great anguish, the family at length accepted the truth. Genji, who had private distress to add to the general grief, thought he knew as well as anyone ever would what unhappiness love can bring. Condolences even from the people most important to him brought no comfort. The old emperor, himself much grieved, sent a personal message; and so for the minister there was new honor, happiness to temper the sorrow. Yet there was no relief from tears.

Every reasonable suggestion was accepted toward reviving the lady, but, the ravages of death being ever more apparent, there was finally no recourse but to see her to

Toribe Moor. There were many heartrending scenes along the way. The crowds of mourners and priests invoking the holy name quite overflowed the wide moor. Messages continued to pour in, from the old emperor, of course, and from the empress and crown prince and all the great houses as well.

The minister was desolate. "Now in my last years to be left behind by a daughter who should have had so many years before her." No one could see him without sharing his sorrow.

Grandly the services went on through the night, and as dawn came over the sky the mourners turned back to the city, taking with them only a handful of ashes. Funerals are common enough, but Genji, who had not been present at many, was shaken as never before. Since it was late in the Eighth Month a quarter moon still hung in a sky that would have brought melancholy thoughts in any case; and the figure of his father-in-law, as if groping in pitch darkness, seemed proper to the occasion and at the same time indescribably sad.

A poem came to his lips as he gazed up into the morning sky:

> "Might these clouds be the smoke that mounts from her pyre?
> They fill my heart with feelings too deep for words."

[Genji remains in seclusion at Sanjō for seven weeks, grieving for Aoi. At last he takes leave of his in-laws, leaving his newborn son Yūgiri in their care, and returns to his own Nijō mansion.]

The Nijō mansion had been cleaned and polished for his return. The whole household assembled to receive him. The higher-ranking ladies had sought to outdo one another in dress and grooming. The sight of them made him think of the sadly dejected ladies at Sanjō. Changing to less doleful clothes, he went to the west wing. The fittings, changed to welcome the autumn, were fresh and bright, and the young women and little girls were all very pretty in autumn dress. Shōnagon had taken care of everything.

Murasaki too was dressed to perfection. "You have grown," he said, lifting a low curtain back over its frame.

She looked shyly aside. Her hair and profile seemed in the lamplight even more like those of the lady he so longed for.

He had worried about her, he said, coming nearer. "I would like to tell you everything, but it is not a very lucky sort of story. Maybe I should rest awhile in the other wing. I won't be long. From now on you will never be rid of me. I am sure you will get very bored with me."

Shōnagon was pleased but not confident. He had so many wellborn ladies, another demanding one was certain to take the place of the one who was gone. She was a dry, unsentimental sort.

Genji returned to his room. Asking Chūjō to massage his legs, he lay down to rest. The next morning he sent off a note for his baby son. He gazed on and on at the answer, from one of the women, and all the old sadness came back.

It was a tedious time. He no longer had any enthusiasm for the careless night wanderings that had once kept him busy. Murasaki was much on his mind. She seemed peerless, the nearest he could imagine to his ideal. Thinking that she was no longer too young for marriage, he had occasionally made amorous overtures; but she had not seemed to understand. They had passed their time in games of Go and *hentsugi.*[8] She was clever and she had many delicate ways of pleasing him in the most trivial diversions. He had not seriously thought of her as a wife. Now he could not restrain himself. It would be a shock, of course.

What had happened? Her women had no way of knowing when the line had been crossed. One morning Genji was up early and Murasaki stayed on and on in bed. It was not at all like her to sleep so late. Might she be unwell? As he left for his own rooms, Genji pushed an inkstone inside her bed curtains.

At length, when no one else was near, she raised herself from her pillow and saw beside it a tightly folded bit of paper. Listlessly she opened it. There was only this verse, in a casual hand:

> Many have been the nights we have spent together
> Purposelessly, these coverlets between us.

She had not dreamed he had anything of the sort on his mind. What a fool she had been, to repose her whole confidence in so gross and unscrupulous a man.

It was almost noon when Genji returned. "They say you're not feeling well. What can be the trouble? I was hoping for a game of Go."

She pulled the covers over her head. Her women discreetly withdrew. He came up beside her.

"What a way to behave, what a very unpleasant way to behave. Try to imagine, please, what these women are thinking."

He drew back the covers. She was bathed in perspiration and the hair at her forehead was matted from weeping.

"Dear me. This does not augur well at all." He tried in every way he could think of to comfort her, but she seemed genuinely upset and did not offer so much as a word in reply.

"Very well. You will see no more of me. I do have my pride."

He opened her writing box but found no note inside. Very childish of her—and he had to smile at the childishness. He stayed with her the whole day, and he thought the stubbornness with which she refused to be comforted most charming.

Boar-day sweets[9] were served in the evening. Since he was still in mourning, no great ceremony attended upon the observance. Glancing over the varied and tastefully arranged foods that had been brought in cypress boxes to Murasaki's rooms only, Genji went out to the south veranda and called Koremitsu.

"We will have more of the same tomorrow night," he said, smiling, "though not in quite such mountains. This is not the most propitious day."

Koremitsu had a quick mind. "Yes, we must be careful to choose lucky days for our beginnings." And, solemnly and deliberately: "How many rat-day sweets am I asked to provide?"[1]

"Oh, I should think one for every three that we have here."

Koremitsu went off with an air of having informed himself adequately. A clever and practical young fellow, thought Genji.

Koremitsu had the nuptial sweets prepared at his own house. He told no one what they signified.

---

8. Guessing concealed parts of Chinese characters.
9. Eaten on the first Day of the Boar in the Tenth Month, to ensure good health, and perhaps too by way of prayer for a fruitful marriage, the wild boar being a symbol of fertility.

1. There were no "rat-day sweets." The words for "rat" and "sleep" sound the same, and the Day of the Rat follows the Day of the Boar; Koremitsu is referring obliquely to the nuptial bed.

Genji felt like a child thief. The role amused him and the affection he now felt for the girl seemed to reduce his earlier affection to the tiniest mote. A man's heart is a very strange amalgam indeed! He now thought that he could not bear to be away from her for a single night.

The sweets he had ordered were delivered stealthily, very late in the night. A man of tact, Koremitsu saw that Shōnagon, an older woman, might make Murasaki uncomfortable, and so he called her daughter.

"Slip this inside her curtains, if you will," he said, handing her an incense box. "You must see that it gets to her and to no one else. A solemn celebration. No carelessness permitted."

She thought it odd. "Carelessness? Of that quality I have had no experience."

"The very word demands care. Use it sparingly."

Young and somewhat puzzled, she did as she was told. It would seem that Genji had explained the significance of the incense box to Murasaki.

The women had no warning. When the box emerged from the curtains the next morning, the pieces of the puzzle began to fall into place. Such numbers of dishes—when might they have been assembled?—and stands with festooned legs, bearing sweets of a most especial sort. All in all, a splendid array. How very nice that he had gone to such pains, thought Shōnagon. He had overlooked nothing. She wept tears of pleasure and gratitude.

"But he really could have let us in on the secret," the women whispered to one another. "What can the gentleman who brought them have thought?"

When he paid the most fleeting call on his father or put in a brief appearance at court, he would be impossibly restless, overcome with longing for the girl. Even to Genji himself it seemed excessive. He had resentful letters from women with whom he had been friendly. He was sorry, but he did not wish to be separated from his bride for even a night. He had no wish to be with these others and let it seem that he was indisposed.

from *Chapter 10. The Sacred Tree*

The Rokujō lady was more and more despondent as the time neared for her daughter's departure. Since the death of Aoi, who had caused her such pain, Genji's visits, never frequent, had stopped altogether. They had aroused great excitement among her women and now the change seemed too sudden. Genji must have very specific reasons for having turned against her—there was no explaining his extreme coldness otherwise. She would think no more about him. She would go with her daughter. There were no precedents for a mother's accompanying a high priestess to Ise, but she had as her excuse that her daughter would be helpless without her. The real reason, of course, was that she wanted to flee these painful associations.

In spite of everything, Genji was sorry when he heard of her decision. He now wrote often and almost pleadingly, but she thought a meeting out of the question at this late date. She would risk disappointing him rather than have it all begin again.

She occasionally went from the priestess's temporary shrine[1] to her Rokujō house, but so briefly and in such secrecy that Genji did not hear of the visits. The temporary shrine did not, he thought, invite casual visits. Although she was much on his mind, he let the days and months go by. His father, the old emperor, had begun to

---

1. In the western part of the city.

suffer from recurrent aches and cramps, and Genji had little time for himself. Yet he did not want the lady to go off to Ise thinking him completely heartless, nor did he wish to have a name at court for insensitivity. He gathered his resolve and set off for the shrine.

It was on about the seventh of the Ninth Month. The lady was under great tension, for their departure was imminent, possibly only a day or two away. He had several times asked for a word with her. He need not go inside, he said, but could wait on the veranda. She was in a torment of uncertainty but at length reached a secret decision: she did not want to seem like a complete recluse and so she would receive him through curtains.

It was over a reed plain of melancholy beauty that he made his way to the shrine. The autumn flowers were gone and insects hummed in the wintry tangles. A wind whistling through the pines brought snatches of music to most wonderful effect, though so distant that he could not tell what was being played. Not wishing to attract attention, he had only ten outrunners, men who had long been in his service, and his guards were in subdued livery. He had dressed with great care. His more perceptive men saw how beautifully the melancholy scene set him off, and he was having regrets that he had not made the journey often. A low wattle fence, scarcely more than a suggestion of an enclosure, surrounded a complex of board-roofed buildings, as rough and insubstantial as temporary shelters.

The shrine gates, of unfinished logs, had a grand and awesome dignity for all their simplicity, and the somewhat forbidding austerity of the place was accentuated by clusters of priests talking among themselves and coughing and clearing their throats as if in warning. It was a scene quite unlike any Genji had seen before. The fire lodge[2] glowed faintly. It was all in all a lonely, quiet place, and here away from the world a lady already deep in sorrow had passed these weeks and months. Concealing himself outside the north wing, he sent in word of his arrival. The music abruptly stopped and the silence was broken only by a rustling of silken robes.

Though several messages were passed back and forth, the lady herself did not come out.

"You surely know that these expeditions are frowned upon. I find it very curious that I should be required to wait outside the sacred paling. I want to tell you everything, all my sorrows and worries."

He was right, said the women. It was more than a person could bear, seeing him out there without even a place to sit down. What was she to do? thought the lady. There were all these people about, and her daughter would expect more mature and sober conduct. No, to receive him at this late date would be altogether too undignified. Yet she could not bring herself to send him briskly on his way. She sighed and hesitated and hesitated again, and it was with great excitement that he finally heard her come forward.

"May I at least come up to the veranda?" he asked, starting up the stairs.

The evening moon burst forth and the figure she saw in its light was handsome beyond describing.

Not wishing to apologize for all the weeks of neglect, he pushed a branch of the sacred tree[3] in under the blinds.

---

2. There are several theories about the use of this building. The most likely are that it was for preparing offerings and that it was for lighting torches and flares.

3. *Sakaki,* related to the camellia.

"With heart unchanging as this evergreen,
this sacred tree, I enter the sacred gate."

She replied:

"You err with your sacred tree and sacred gate.
No beckoning cedars stand before my house."[4]

And he:

"Thinking to find you here with the holy maidens,
I followed the scent of the leaf of the sacred tree."

Though the scene did not encourage familiarity, he made bold to lean inside the blinds.

He had complacently wasted the days when he could have visited her and perhaps made her happy. He had begun to have misgivings about her, his ardor had cooled, and they had become the near strangers they were now. But she was here before him, and memories flooded back. He thought of what had been and what was to be, and he was weeping like a child.

She did not wish him to see her following his example. He felt even sadder for her as she fought to control herself, and it would seem that even now he urged her to change her plans. Gazing up into a sky even more beautiful now that the moon was setting, he poured forth all his pleas and complaints, and no doubt they were enough to erase the accumulated bitterness. She had resigned herself to what must be, and it was as she had feared. Now that she was with him again she found her resolve wavering.

Groups of young courtiers came up. It was a garden which aroused romantic urges and which a young man was reluctant to leave.

Their feelings for each other, Genji's and the lady's, had run the whole range of sorrows and irritations, and no words could suffice for all they wanted to say to each other. The dawn sky was as if made for the occasion. Not wanting to go quite yet, Genji took her hand, very gently.

"A dawn farewell is always drenched in dew,
But sad is the autumn sky as never before."

A cold wind was blowing, and a pine cricket seemed to recognize the occasion. It was a serenade to which a happy lover would not have been deaf. Perhaps because their feelings were in such tumult, they found that the poems they might have exchanged were eluding them.

At length the lady replied:

"An autumn farewell needs nothing to make it sadder.
Enough of your songs, O crickets on the moors!"

It would do no good to pour forth all the regrets again. He made his departure, not wanting to be seen in the broadening daylight. His sleeves were made wet along the way with dew and with tears.

The lady, not as strong as she would have wished, was sunk in a sad reverie. The shadowy figure in the moonlight and the perfume he left behind had the younger women in a state only just short of swooning.

---

4. Anonymous, *Kokinshū 982:* "Should you seek my house at the foot of Mount Miwa, / you need only look for the cedars by the gate."

"What kind of journey could be important enough, I ask you," said one of them, choking with tears, "to make her leave such a man?"

His letter the next day was so warm and tender that again she was tempted to reconsider. But it was too late: a return to the old indecision would accomplish nothing. Genji could be very persuasive even when he did not care a great deal for a woman, and this was no ordinary parting. He sent the finest travel robes and supplies, for the lady and for her women as well. They were no longer enough to move her. It was as if the thought had only now come to her of the ugly name she seemed fated to leave behind.

[*In the Tenth Month of the same year, Genji's father the old emperor dies. On his deathbed, he instructs his son, the Suzaku emperor, to look to Genji for advice in public affairs, and to be good to the crown prince (the future Reizei emperor). The following year Genji makes further overtures to Fujitsubo, driving her to become a nun after the anniversary of the old emperor's death. In the summer of the next year the Minister of the Right discovers Genji with Oborozukiyo, now a favored concubine of the Suzaku emperor. The Kokiden faction uses this episode as a pretext to destroy Genji politically.*]

from *Chapter 12. Suma*

[*In the Third Month of the year following his scandal with Oborozukiyo, Genji, now twenty-five, opts to go into voluntary exile in Suma, an isolated area to the southwest of the capital, near the sea, rather than face further adversity in the capital. He is accompanied by only a few close associates.*]

At Suma, melancholy autumn winds were blowing. Genji's house was some distance from the sea, but at night the wind that blew over the barriers, now as in Yukihira's day, seemed to bring the surf to his bedside. Autumn was hushed and lonely at a place of exile. He had few companions. One night when they were all asleep he raised his head from his pillow and listened to the roar of the wind and of the waves, as if at his ear. Though he was unaware that he wept, his tears were enough to set his pillow afloat.[1] He plucked a few notes on his koto, but the sound only made him sadder.

> The waves on the strand, like moans of helpless longing.
> The winds—like messengers from those who grieve?

He had awakened the others. They sat up, and one by one they were in tears.

This would not do. Because of him they had been swept into exile, leaving families from whom they had never before been parted. It must be very difficult for them, and his own gloom could scarcely be making things easier. So he set about cheering them. During the day he would invent games and make jokes, and set down this and that poem on multicolored patchwork, and paint pictures on fine specimens of figured Chinese silk. Some of his larger paintings were masterpieces. He had long ago been told of this Suma coast and these hills and had formed a picture of them in his mind, and he found now that his imagination had fallen short of the actuality. What a pity, said his men, that they could not summon Tsunenori and Chieda[2] and other famous painters of the day to add colors to Genji's monochromes. This resolute cheerfulness

---

1. This extravagant figure of speech is to be found in *Kokin Rokujō, Zoku Kokka Taikan* 34087.

2. Tsunenori seems to have been active some three quarters of a century before; so too, presumably, was Chieda.

had the proper effect. His men, four or five of whom were always with him, would not have dreamed of leaving him.

There was a profusion of flowers in the garden. Genji came out, when the evening colors were at their best, to a gallery from which he had a good view of the coast. His men felt chills of apprehension as they watched him, for the loneliness of the setting made him seem like a visitor from another world. In a dark robe tied loosely over singlets of figured white and aster-colored trousers, he announced himself as "a disciple of the Buddha" and slowly intoned a sutra, and his men thought that they had never heard a finer voice. From offshore came the voices of fishermen raised in song. The barely visible boats were like little seafowl on an utterly lonely sea, and as he brushed away a tear induced by the splashing of oars and the calls of wild geese overhead, the white of his hand against the jet black of his rosary was enough to bring comfort to men who had left their families behind.

*　*　*

It was the day of the serpent, the first such day in the Third Month.

"The day when a man who has worries goes down and washes them away," said one of his men, admirably informed, it would seem, in all of the annual observances.

Wishing to have a look at the seashore, Genji set forth. Plain, rough curtains were strung up among the trees, and a soothsayer who was doing the circuit of the province was summoned to perform the lustration.

Genji thought he could see something of himself in the rather large doll being cast off to sea, bearing away sins and tribulations.

> "Cast away to drift on an alien vastness,
> I grieve for more than a doll cast out to sea."

The bright, open seashore showed him to wonderful advantage. The sea stretched placid into measureless distances. He thought of all that had happened to him, and all that was still to come.

> "You eight hundred myriad gods must surely help me,
> For well you know that blameless I stand before you."

Suddenly a wind came up and even before the services were finished the sky was black. Genji's men rushed about in confusion. Rain came pouring down, completely without warning. Though the obvious course would have been to return straightway to the house, there had been no time to send for umbrellas. The wind was now a howling tempest, everything that had not been tied down was scuttling off across the beach. The surf was biting at their feet. The sea was white, as if spread over with white linen. Fearful every moment of being struck down, they finally made their way back to the house.

"I've never seen anything like it," said one of the men. "Winds do come up from time to time, but not without warning. It is all very strange and very terrible."

The lightning and thunder seemed to announce the end of the world, and the rain to beat its way into the ground; and Genji sat calmly reading a sutra. The thunder subsided in the evening, but the wind went on through the night.

"Our prayers seem to have been answered. A little more and we would have been carried off. I've heard that tidal waves do carry people off before they know what is happening to them, but I've not seen anything like this."

Towards dawn sleep was at length possible. A man whom he did not recognize came to Genji in a dream.

"The court summons you." He seemed to be reaching for Genji. "Why do you not go?"

It would be the king of the sea, who was known to have a partiality for handsome men. Genji decided that he could stay no longer at Suma.

from *Chapter 13. Akashi*

The days went by and the thunder and rain continued. What was Genji to do? People would laugh if, in this extremity, out of favor at court, he were to return to the city. Should he then seek a mountain retreat? But if it were to be noised about that a storm had driven him away, then he would cut a ridiculous figure in history.

His dreams were haunted by that same apparition. Messages from the city almost entirely ceased coming as the days went by without a break in the storms. Might he end his days at Suma? No one was likely to come calling in these tempests.

A messenger did come from Murasaki, a sad, sodden creature. Had they passed in the street, Genji would scarcely have known whether he was man or beast, and of course would not have thought of inviting him to come near. Now the man brought a surge of pleasure and affection—though Genji could not help asking himself whether the storm had weakened his moorings.

Murasaki's letter, long and melancholy, said in part: "The terrifying deluge goes on without a break, day after day. Even the skies are closed off, and I am denied the comfort of gazing in your direction.

> What do they work, the sea winds down at Suma?
> At home, my sleeves are assaulted by wave after wave."

Tears so darkened his eyes that it was as if they were inviting the waters to rise higher.

The man said that the storms had been fierce in the city too, and that a special reading of the Prajñāpāramitā Sutra had been ordered. "The streets are all closed and the great, gentlemen can't get to court, and everything has closed down."

The man spoke clumsily and haltingly, but he did bring news. Genji summoned him near and had him questioned.

"It's not the way it usually is. You don't usually have rain going on for days without a break and the wind howling on and on. Everyone is terrified. But it's worse here. They haven't had this hail beating right through the ground and thunder going on and on and not letting a body think." The terror written so plainly on his face did nothing to improve the spirits of the people at Suma.

Might it be the end of the world? From dawn the next day the wind was so fierce and the tide so high and the surf so loud that it was as if the crags and the mountains must fall. The horror of the thunder and lightning was beyond description. Panic spread at each new flash. For what sins, Genji's men asked, were they being punished? Were they to perish without another glimpse of their mothers and fathers, their dear wives and children?

Genji tried to tell himself that he had been guilty of no misdeed for which he must perish here on the seashore. Such were the panic and confusion around him, however, that he bolstered his confidence with special offerings to the god of Sumiyoshi.

"O you of Sumiyoshi who protect the lands about: if indeed you are an avatar of the Blessed One, then you must save us."

His men were of course fearful for their lives; but the thought that so fine a gentleman (and in these deplorable circumstances) might be swept beneath the waters seemed altogether too tragic. The less distraught among them prayed in loud voices to this and that favored deity, Buddhist and Shinto, that their own lives be taken if it meant that his might be spared.

They faced Sumiyoshi and prayed and made vows: "Our lord was reared deep in the fastnesses of the palace, and all blessings were his. You who, in the abundance of your mercy, have brought strength through these lands to all who have sunk beneath the weight of their troubles: in punishment for what crimes do you call forth these howling waves? Judge his case if you will, you gods of heaven and earth. Guiltless, he is accused of a crime, stripped of his offices, driven from his house and city, left as you see him with no relief from the torture and the lamentation. And now these horrors, and even his life seems threatened. Why? we must ask. Because of sins in some other life, because of crimes in this one? If your vision is clear, O you gods, then take all this away."

Genji offered prayers to the king of the sea and countless other gods as well. The thunder was increasingly more terrible, and finally the gallery adjoining his rooms was struck by lightning. Flames sprang up and the gallery was destroyed. The confusion was immense; the whole world seemed to have gone mad. Genji was moved to a building out in back, a kitchen or something of the sort it seemed to be. It was crowded with people of every station and rank. The clamor was almost enough to drown out the lightning and thunder. Night descended over a sky already as black as ink.

Presently the wind and rain subsided and stars began to come out. The kitchen being altogether too mean a place, a move back to the main hall was suggested. The charred remains of the gallery were an ugly sight, however, and the hall had been badly muddied and all the blinds and curtains blown away. Perhaps, Genji's men suggested somewhat tentatively, it might be better to wait until dawn. Genji sought to concentrate upon the holy name, but his agitation continued to be very great.

He opened a wattled door and looked out. The moon had come up. The line left by the waves was white and dangerously near, and the surf was still high. There was no one here whom he could turn to, no student of the deeper truths who could discourse upon past and present and perhaps explain these wild events. All the fisherfolk had gathered at what they had heard was the house of a great gentleman from the city. They were as noisy and impossible to communicate with as a flock of birds, but no one thought of telling them to leave.

"If the wind had kept up just a little longer," someone said, "absolutely everything would have been swept under. The gods did well by us."

There are no words—"lonely" and "forlorn" seem much too weak—to describe his feelings.

> "Without the staying hand of the king of the sea
> the roar of the eight hundred waves would have taken us under."

Genji was as exhausted as if all the buffets and fires of the tempest had been aimed at him personally. He dozed off, his head against some nondescript piece of furniture.

The old emperor came to him, quite as when he had lived. "And why are you in this wretched place?" He took Genji's hand and pulled him to his feet. "You must do as the god of Sumiyoshi tells you. You must put out to sea immediately. You must leave this shore behind."

"Since I last saw you, sir," said Genji, overjoyed, "I have suffered an unbroken series of misfortunes. I had thought of throwing myself into the sea."

"That you must not do. You are undergoing brief punishment for certain sins. I my-self did not commit any conscious crimes while I reigned, but a person is guilty of trans-gressions and oversights without his being aware of them. I am doing penance and have no time to look back towards this world. But an echo of your troubles came to me and I could not stand idle. I fought my way through the sea and up to this shore and I am very tired; but now that I am here I must see to a matter in the city." And he disappeared.

Genji called after him, begging to be taken along. He looked around him. There was only the bright face of the moon. His father's presence had been too real for a dream, so real that he must still be here. Clouds traced sad lines across the sky. It had been clear and palpable, the figure he had so longed to see even in a dream, so clear that he could almost catch an afterimage. His father had come through the skies to help him in what had seemed the last extremity of his sufferings. He was deeply grateful, even to the tempests; and in the aftermath of the dream he was happy.

Quite different emotions now ruffled his serenity. He forgot his immediate trou-bles and only regretted that his father had not stayed longer. Perhaps he would come again. Genji would have liked to go back to sleep, but he lay wakeful until daylight.

A little boat had pulled in at the shore and two or three men came up.

"The revered monk who was once governor of Harima has come from Akashi. If the former Minamoto councillor, Lord Yoshikiyo, is here, we wonder if we might trouble him to come down and hear the details of our mission."

Yoshikiyo pretended to be surprised and puzzled. "He was once among my closer acquaintances here in Harima, but we had a falling out and it has been some time since we last exchanged letters. What can have brought him through such seas in that little boat?"

Genji's dream had given intimations. He sent Yoshikiyo down to the boat imme-diately. Yoshikiyo marveled that it could even have been launched upon such a sea.

These were the details of the mission, from the mouth of the old governor: "Early this month a strange figure came to me in a dream. I listened, though somewhat incred-ulously, and was told that on the thirteenth there would be a clear and present sign. I was to ready a boat and make for this shore when the waves subsided. I did ready a boat, and then came this savage wind and lightning. I thought of numerous foreign sov-ereigns who have received instructions in dreams on how to save their lands, and I con-cluded that even at the risk of incurring his ridicule I must on the day appointed inform your lord of the import of the dream. And so I did indeed put out to sea. A strange jet blew all the way and brought us to this shore. I cannot think of it except as divine inter-vention. And might I ask whether there have been corresponding manifestations here? I do hate to trouble you, but might I ask you to communicate all of this to your lord?"

Yoshikiyo quietly relayed the message, which brought new considerations. There had been these various unsettling signs conveyed to Genji dreaming and waking. The possibility of being laughed at for having departed these shores under threat now seemed the lesser risk. To turn his back on what might be a real offer of help from the gods would be to ask for still worse misfortunes. It was not easy to reject ordinary ad-vice, and personal reservations counted for little when the advice came from great em-inences. "Defer to them; they will cause you no reproaches," a wise man of old once said.[1] He could scarcely face worse misfortunes by deferring than by not deferring, and he did not seem likely to gain great merit and profit by hesitating out of concern for his brave name. Had not his own father come to him? What room was there for doubts?

---

1. Lao-tze, say early commentaries; but the advice is not to be found in his extant writings.

He sent back his answer: "I have been through a great deal in this strange place, and I hear nothing at all from the city. I but gaze upon a sun and moon going I know not where as comrades from my old home; and now comes this angler's boat, happy tidings on an angry wind.[2] Might there be a place along your Akashi coast where I can hide myself?

The old man was delighted. Genji's men pressed him to set out even before sunrise. Taking along only four or five of his closest attendants, he boarded the boat. That strange wind came up again and they were at Akashi as if they had flown. It was very near, within crawling distance, so to speak; but still the workings of the wind were strange and marvelous.

The Akashi coast was every bit as beautiful as he had been told it was. He would have preferred fewer people, but on the whole he was pleased. Along the coast and in the hills the old monk had put up numerous buildings with which to take advantage of the four seasons: a reed-roofed beach cottage with fine seasonal vistas; beside a mountain stream a chapel of some grandeur and dignity, suitable for rites and meditation and invocation of the holy name; and rows of storehouses where the harvest was put away and a bountiful life assured for the years that remained. Fearful of the high tides, the old monk had sent his daughter and her women off to the hills. The house on the beach was at Genji's disposal.

The sun was rising as Genji left the boat and got into a carriage. This first look by daylight at his new guest brought a happy smile to the old man's lips. He felt as if the accumulated years were falling away and as if new years had been granted him. He gave silent thanks to the god of Sumiyoshi. He might have seemed ridiculous as he bustled around seeing to Genji's needs, as if the radiance of the sun and the moon had become his private property; but no one laughed at him.

I need not describe the beauty of the Akashi coast. The careful attention that had gone into the house and the rocks and plantings of the garden, the graceful line of the coast—it was infinitely pleasanter than Suma, and one would not have wished to ask a less than profoundly sensitive painter to paint it. The house was in quiet good taste. The old man's way of life was as Genji had heard it described, hardly more rustic than that of the grandees at court. In sheer luxury, indeed, he rather outdid them.

[Genji remains in Akashi for nearly a year and a half, during which the Akashi priest succeeds in bringing about a union between Genji and his daughter, the Akashi lady. The same violent storm that hit Suma also hit the capital, bringing other omens and disturbances with it: the Kiritsubo emperor appears to his son, the reigning Suzaku emperor, in a dream, reproving him for his treatment of Genji. The Suzaku emperor suffers subsequently a painful eye ailment, the Kokiden lady falls ill, and the Minister of the Right dies. Finally, a year later, Suzaku grants Genji a pardon, summoning him back to the capital in the Seventh Month. Early the following year, Suzaku yields the throne to Reizei, and Genji returns to power. His liaison with the Akashi lady results in a daughter, who is eventually brought to the capital to be raised by Murasaki. Shortly thereafter, Fujitsubo dies. Reizei is informed of his true parentage, and tries to abdicate in favor of his father Genji. Genji refuses but rises rapidly in political rank, eventually being appointed Chancellor. In his thirty-fourth year, Genji constructs a lavish residence, the Rokujō mansion, a virtual court where he gathers all of*

---

2. Ki no Tsurayuki, *Gosenshū* 1225: "An angler's boat upon the waves that pound us, / happy tidings on an angry wind."

his women around him. Among these women is Tamakazura, a lost daughter of Tō no Chūjō whom Genji has discovered, adopted, and treats as though she were his own daughter. The following passage from the Tamakazura sequence is known as the "defense of fiction."]

from *Chapter 25. Fireflies*

The rains of early summer continued without a break, even gloomier than in most years. The ladies at Rokujō amused themselves with illustrated romances. The Akashi lady, a talented painter, sent pictures to her daughter.

Tamakazura was the most avid reader of all. She quite lost herself in pictures and stories and would spend whole days with them. Several of her young women were well informed in literary matters. She came upon all sorts of interesting and shocking incidents (she could not be sure whether they were true or not), but she found little that resembled her own unfortunate career. There was *The Tale of Sumiyoshi,* popular in its day, of course, and still well thought of. She compared the plight of the heroine, within a hairbreadth of being taken by the chief accountant,[1] with her own escape from the Higo person.[2]

Genji could not help noticing the clutter of pictures and manuscripts. "What a nuisance this all is," he said one day. "Women seem to have been born to be cheerfully deceived. They know perfectly well that in all these old stories there is scarcely a shred of truth, and yet they are captured and made sport of by the whole range of trivialities and go on scribbling them down, quite unaware that in these warm rains their hair is all dank and knotted."

He smiled. "What would we do if there were not these old romances to relieve our boredom? But amid all the fabrication I must admit that I do find real emotions and plausible chains of events. We can be quite aware of the frivolity and the idleness and still be moved. We have to feel a little sorry for a charming princess in the depths of gloom. Sometimes a series of absurd and grotesque incidents which we know to be quite improbable holds our interest, and afterwards we must blush that it was so. Yet even then we can see what it was that held us. Sometimes I stand and listen to the stories they read to my daughter, and I think to myself that there certainly are good talkers in the world. I think that these yarns must come from people much practiced in lying. But perhaps that is not the whole of the story?"

She pushed away her inkstone. "I can see that that would be the view of someone much given to lying himself. For my part, I am convinced of their truthfulness."

He laughed. "I have been rude and unfair to your romances, haven't I? They have set down and preserved happenings from the age of the gods to our own. *The Chronicles of Japan* and the rest are a mere fragment of the whole truth. It is your romances that fill in the details.

"We are not told of things that happened to specific people exactly as they happened; but the beginning is when there are good things and bad things, things that happen in this life which one never tires of seeing and hearing about, things which one cannot bear not to tell of and must pass on for all generations. If the storyteller wishes to speak well, then he chooses the good things; and if he wishes to hold the reader's attention he chooses bad things, extraordinarily bad things. Good things and bad things alike, they are things of this world and no other.

---

1. There is no such incident in the version which survives today.

2. A rustic man who had pursued her in Kyūshu, before her arrival in the capital and adoption by Genji.

"Writers in other countries approach the matter differently. Old stories in our own are different from new. There are differences in the degree of seriousness. But to dismiss them as lies is itself to depart from the truth. Even in the writ which the Buddha drew from his noble heart are parables, devices for pointing obliquely at the truth. To the ignorant they may seem to operate at cross purposes. The Greater Vehicle is full of them, but the general burden is always the same. The difference between enlightenment and confusion is of about the same order as the difference between the good and the bad in a romance. If one takes the generous view, then nothing is empty and useless."

He now seemed bent on establishing the uses of fiction.

"But tell me: is there in any of your old stories a proper, upright fool like myself?" He came closer. "I doubt that even among the most unworldly of your heroines there is one who manages to be as distant and unnoticing as you are. Suppose the two of us set down our story and give the world a really interesting one."

"I think it very likely that the world will take notice of our curious story even if we do not go to the trouble." She hid her face in her sleeves.

"Our curious story? Yes, incomparably curious, I should think." Smiling and playful, he pressed nearer.

"Beside myself, I search through all the books,
and come upon no daughter so unfilial."

"You are breaking one of the commandments."

He stroked her hair as he spoke, but she refused to look up. Presently, however, she managed a reply:

"So too it is with me. I too have searched,
and found no cases quite so unparental."

Somewhat chastened, he pursued the matter no further. Yet one worried. What was to become of her?

Murasaki too had become addicted to romances. Her excuse was that Genji's little daughter insisted on being read to.

"Just see what a fine one this is," she said, showing Genji an illustration for *The Tale of Kumano*.[3] The young girl in tranquil and confident slumber made her think of her own younger self. "How precocious even very little children seem to have been. I suppose I might have set myself up as a specimen of the slow, plodding variety. I would have won that competition easily."

Genji might have been the hero of some rather more eccentric stories.

"You must not read love stories to her. I doubt that clandestine affairs would arouse her unduly, but we would not want her to think them commonplace."

What would Tamakazura have made of the difference between his remarks to her and these remarks to Murasaki?

"I would not of course offer the wanton ones as a model," replied Murasaki, "but I would have doubts too about the other sort. Lady Atemiya in *The Tale of the Hollow Tree,* for instance. She is always very brisk and efficient and in control of things, and she never makes mistakes; but there is something unwomanly about her cool manner and clipped speech."

"I should imagine that it is in real life as in fiction. We are all human and we all have our ways. It is not easy to be unerringly right. Proper, well-educated parents go

3. Or *The Tale of Komano*. It does not survive.

to great trouble over a daughter's education and tell themselves that they have done well if something quiet and demure emerges. It seems a pity when defects come to light one after another and people start asking what her good parents can possibly have been up to. Yet the rewards are very great when a girl's manner and behavior seem just right for her station. Even then empty praise is not satisfying. One knows that the girl is not perfect and looks at her more critically than before. I would not wish my own daughter to be praised by people who have no standards."

He was genuinely concerned that she acquit herself well in the tests that lay before her.

Wicked stepmothers are of course standard fare for the romancers, and he did not want them poisoning relations between Murasaki and the child. He spent a great deal of time selecting romances he thought suitable, and ordered them copied and illustrated.

from *Chapter 34. New Herbs (Part 1)*

[*Genji is now forty years old. His daughter by the Akashi lady has gone to court as a consort to the crown prince. He has retired as Chancellor, and been accorded benefices equivalent to those of a retired emperor. Meanwhile, the Suzaku emperor falls ill, and is worried about the future of his favorite daughter, the Third Princess. Although he considers Genji's son Yūgiri, Tō no Chūjō's son Kashiwagi, and Genji's half brother Prince Hotaru as potential husbands for her, he asks Genji to take care of her. Despite his fear of hurting Murasaki, Genji agrees to marry the girl (spurred on, perhaps, by the fact that like Murasaki the Third Princess is a niece of Fujitsubo).*]

And so the contract was made.

In the evening there was a banquet for Genji's party and the Suzaku household. The priest's fare was unpretentious but beautifully prepared and served. The tableware and the trays of light aloeswood also suggested the priestly vocation and brought tears to the eyes of the guests. The melancholy and moving details were innumerable, but I fear that they would clutter my story.

It was late in the night when Genji and his men departed, the men bearing lavish gifts. The Fujiwara councilor was among those who saw them off. There had been a fall of snow and the Suzaku emperor had caught cold. But he was happy. The future of the Third Princess seemed secure.

Genji was worried. Murasaki had heard vague rumors, but she had told herself that it could not be. Genji had once been very serious about the high priestess of Ise, it seemed, but in the end he had held himself back. She had not worried a great deal, and asked no questions.

How would she take this news? Genji knew that his feelings towards her would not change, or if they did it would be in the direction of greater intensity. But only time could assure her of that fact, and there would be cruel uncertainty in the meantime. Nothing had been allowed to come between them in recent years, and the thought of having a secret from her for even a short time made him very unhappy.

He said nothing to her that night.

The next day was dark, with flurries of snow.

"I went yesterday to call on the Suzaku emperor. He is in very poor health indeed." It was in the course of a leisurely conversation that Genji brought the matter up. "He said many sad things, but what seems to trouble him most as he goes off to his retreat is the future of the Third Princess." And he described that part of the interview. "I was really so extremely sorry for him that I found it impossible to refuse. I suppose people will make a great thing of it. The thought of taking a bride at my age has seemed so utterly preposterous that I have tried through this and that intermediary to suggest a certain want of ardor. But to see him in person and have it directly from him—I simply could not bring myself to refuse. Do you think that when the time does finally come for him to go off into the mountains we might have her come here? Would that upset you terribly? Please do not let it. Trust me, and tell yourself what is the complete truth, that nothing is going to change. She has more right to feel insecure than you do. But I am sure that we can arrange things happily enough for her too."

She was always torturing herself over the smallest of his affairs, and he had dreaded telling her of this one.

But her reply was quiet and unassertive, "Yes, it is sad for her. The only thing that worries me is the possibility that she might feel less than completely at home. I shall be very happy if our being so closely related persuades her that I am no stranger."

"How silly that this very willingness to accept things should bother me. But it does. It makes me start looking for complications, and I am sure I will feel guiltier as the two of you get used to each other. You must pay no attention to what people say. Rumors are strange things. It is impossible to know where they come from, but there they are, like living creatures bent on poisoning relations between a man and a woman. You must listen only to yourself and let matters take their course. Do not start imagining things, and do not torture yourself with empty jealousies."

It was a tempest out of the blue which there was no escaping. Murasaki was determined that she would not complain or give any hint of resentment. She knew that neither her wishes nor her advice would have made any difference. She did not want the world to think that she had been crushed by what had to come. There was her sharp-tongued stepmother, so quick to blame and to gloat. . . . She was certain to gloat over this, and to say that Murasaki deserved exactly what had come to her. Though very much in control of herself, Murasaki was prey to these worries. The very durability of her relations with Genji was sure to make people laugh harder. But she gave no hint of her unhappiness.

The New Year came, and at the Suzaku Palace the Third Princess's wedding plans kept people busy. Her several suitors were deeply disappointed. The emperor, who had let it be known that he would welcome her at court, was among them.

[*In due course, the Third Princess is installed in the Rokujō mansion.*]

It was an unsettling time for Murasaki. No doubt Genji was giving an honest view of the matter when he said that she would not be overwhelmed by the Third Princess. Yet for the first time in years she felt genuinely threatened. The new lady was young and, it would seem, rather showy in her ways, and of such a rank that Murasaki could not ignore her. All very unsettling; but she gave no hint of her feelings, and indeed helped with all the arrangements. Genji saw more than ever that there was really no one like her.

The Third Princess was, as her father had said, a mere child. She was tiny and immature physically, and she gave a general impression of still greater, indeed quite extraordinary, immaturity. He thought of Murasaki when he had first taken her in. She had even then been interesting. She had had a character of her own. The Third Princess was like a baby. Well, thought Genji, the situation had something to recommend it: she was not likely to intrude and make Murasaki unhappy with fits of jealousy. Yet he did think he might have hoped for someone a *little* more interesting. For the first three nights he was faithfully in attendance upon her. Murasaki was unhappy but said nothing. She gave herself up to her thoughts and to such duties, now performed with unusual care, as scenting his robes. He thought her splendid. Why, he asked himself, whatever the pressures and the complications, had he taken another wife? He had been weak and he had given an impression of inconstancy, and brought it all upon himself. Yūgiri had escaped because the Suzaku emperor had seen what an unshakable pillar of fidelity he was.

Genji was near tears. "Please excuse me just this one more night. I have no alternative. If after this I neglect you, then you may be sure that I will be angrier with myself than you can ever be with me. We do have to consider her father's feelings."

"Do not ask us bystanders," she said, a faint smile on her lips, "to tell you how to behave."

He turned away, chin in hand, to hide his confusion.

> "I had grown so used to thinking it would not change,
> and now, before my very eyes, it changes."

He took up the paper on which she had jotted down old poems that fitted her mood as well as this poem of her own. It was not the most perfect of poems, perhaps, but it was honest and to the point.

> "Life must end. It is a transient world.
> The one thing lasting is the bond between us."

He did not want to leave, but she said that he was only making things more difficult for her. He was wearing the soft robes which she had so carefully scented. She had over the years seen new threats arise only to be turned away, and she had finally come to think that there would be no more. Now this had happened, and everyone was talking. She knew how susceptible he had been in his earlier years, and now the whole future seemed uncertain. It was remarkable that she showed no sign of her disquiet.

Her women were talking as of the direst happenings.

"Who would have expected it? He has always kept himself well supplied with women, but none of them has seemed the sort to raise a challenge. So things have been quiet. I doubt that our lady will let them defeat her—but we must be careful. The smallest mistake could make things very difficult."

Murasaki pretended that nothing at all was amiss. She talked pleasantly with them until late in the night. She feared that silence on the most important subject might make it seem more important than it was.

"I am so glad that she has come to us. We have had a full house, but I sometimes think he has been a little bored with us, poor man. None of us is grand enough to be really interesting. I somehow hope that we will be the best of friends. Perhaps it is because they say that she is still a mere child. And here you all are digging a great chasm between us. If we were of the same rank, or perhaps if I had some slight reason to think myself a little her superior, then I would feel that I had to be careful. But as it is—you may think it impertinent of me to say so—I only want to be friendly."

Nakatsukasa and Chūjō exchanged glances. "Such kindness," one of them, I do not know which, would seem to have muttered. They had once been recipients of Genji's attentions but they had been with Murasaki for some years now, and they were among her firmer allies.

Inquiries came from the ladies in the other quarters, some of them suggesting that they who had long ago given up their ambitions might be the more fortunate ones. Murasaki sighed. They meant to be kind, of course, but they were not making things easier. Well, there was no use in tormenting herself over things she could not change, and the inconstancy of the other sex was among them.

Her women would think it odd if she spent the whole night talking with them. She withdrew to her boudoir and they helped her into bed. She was lonely, and the presence of all these women did little to disguise the fact. She thought of the years of his exile. She had feared that they would not meet again, but the agony of waiting for word that he was still alive was in itself a sort of distraction from the sorrow and longing. She sought to comfort herself now with the thought that those confused days could so easily have meant the end of everything.

The wind was cold. Not wanting her women to know that she could not sleep, she lay motionless until she ached from the effort. Still deep in the cold night, the call of the first cock seemed to emphasize the loneliness and sorrow.

She may not have been in an agony of longing, but she was deeply troubled, and perhaps for that reason she came to Genji in his dreams. His heart was racing. Might something have happened to her? He lay waiting for the cock as if for permission to leave, and at its first call rushed out as if unaware that it would not yet be daylight for some time. Still a child, the princess kept her women close beside her. One of them saw him out through a corner door. The snow caught the first traces of dawn, though the garden was still dark. "In vain the spring's darkness,"[1] whispered her nurse, catching the scent he had left behind.

The patches of snow were almost indistinguishable from the white garden sands. "There is yet snow by the castle wall,"[2] he whispered to himself as he came to Murasaki's wing of the house and tapped on a shutter. No longer in the habit of accommodating themselves to nocturnal wanderings, the women let him wait for a time.

"How slow you are," he said, slipping in beside her. "I am quite congealed, as much from terror as from cold. And I have done nothing to deserve it."

He thought her rather wonderful. She did nothing at all, and yet, hiding her wet sleeves, she somehow managed to keep him at a distance. Not even among ladies of the highest birth was there anyone quite like her. He found himself comparing her with the little princess he had just left.

He spent the day beside her, going over their years together, and charging her with evasion and deviousness.

He sent a note saying that he would not be calling on the princess that day. "I seem to have caught a chill from the snow and think I would be more comfortable here."

Her nurse sent back tartly by word of mouth that the note had been passed on to her lady. Not a very amiable sort, thought Genji.

He did not want the Suzaku emperor to know of his want of ardor, but he did not seem capable even of maintaining appearances. Things could scarcely have been worse. For her part, Murasaki feared that the Suzaku emperor would hold her responsible.

---

1. Oshikōchi Mitsune, *Kokinshū* 40: "In vain the spring night's darkness accosts the plum, / destroying the color but not the scent of its blossoms."

2. Po Chü-i, Collected Works 16, "Dawn from *Yü Hsin's Tower*."

Waking this time in the familiar rooms, he got off another note to the princess. He took great trouble with it, though he was not sure that she would notice. He chose white paper and attached it to a sprig of plum blossom.

> "Not heavy enough to block the way between us,
> the flurries of snow this morning yet distress me."

He told the messenger that the note was to be delivered at the west gallery.[3] * * *

An answer did presently come. It was on red tissue paper and folded neatly in an envelope. He opened it with trepidation, hoping that it would not be too irredeemably childish. He did not want to have secrets from Murasaki, and yet he did not want her to see the princess's hand, at least for a time. To display the princess in all her immaturity seemed somehow insulting. But it would be worse to make Murasaki yet unhappier. She sat leaning against an armrest. He laid the note half open beside her.

> "You do not come. I fain would disappear,
> a veil of snow upon the rough spring winds."

It was every bit as bad as he had feared, scarcely even a child's hand—and of course in point of years she was not a child at all. Murasaki glanced at it and glanced away as if she had not seen it. He would have offered it up for what it was, evidence of almost complete uselessness, had it been from anyone else.

"So you see you have nothing to worry about," he said.

He paid his first daytime call upon the princess. He had dressed with unusual care and no doubt his good looks had an unusually powerful effect on women not used to them. For the older and more experienced of them, the nurse, for instance, the effect was of something like apprehension. He was so splendid that they feared complications. Their lady was such a pretty little child of a thing, reduced to almost nothing at all by the brilliance of her surroundings. It was as if there were no flesh holding up the great mounds of clothing. She did not seem shy before him, and if it could have been said that her openness and freedom from mannerism were for purposes of putting him at ease, then it could also have been said that they succeeded very well. Her father was not generally held to be a virile sort of man, but no one denied his superior taste and refinement, and the mystery was that he had done so little by way of training her. And of course Genji, like everyone else, knew that she was his favorite, and that he worried endlessly about her. It all seemed rather sad. The other side of the matter was that she did undeniably have a certain girlish charm. She listened quietly and answered with whatever came into her mind. He must be good to her. In his younger days his disappointment would have approached contempt, but he had become more tolerant. They all had their ways, and none was enormously superior to the others. There were as many sorts of women as there were women. A disinterested observer would probably have told him that he had made a good match for himself. Murasaki was the only remarkable one among them all, more remarkable now than ever, he thought, and he had known her very well for a very long time. He had no cause for dissatisfaction with his efforts as guardian and mentor. A single morning or evening away from her and the sense of deprivation was so intense as to bring a sort of foreboding.

* * *

A frequenter of the Suzaku Palace, Kashiwagi had known all about the Third Princess and the Suzaku emperor's worries. He had offered himself as a candidate for

---

3. His reasons are not clear. There is a theory that he doesn't want Murasaki to see, but it is not very tenable.

her hand. His candidacy had not been dismissed, and then, suddenly and to his very great disappointment, she had gone to Genji. He still could not reconcile himself to what had happened. He seems to have taken some comfort in exchanging reports with women whom he had known in her maiden days. He of course heard what everyone else heard, that she was no great competitor for Genji's affection.

He was forever complaining to Koji.

[*On a pleasant day in the Third Month, a number of young men, including Yūgiri (Genji's son by Aoi) and Kashiwagi (Tō no Chūjō's son), assemble at Rokujō and engage in a game of kickball* (kemari), *while Genji looks on.*]

Taking their places under a fine cherry in full bloom, Yūgiri and Kashiwagi were very handsome in the evening light. Genji's less than genteel sport—such things do happen—took on something of the elegance of the company and the place. Spring mists enfolded trees in various stages of bud and bloom and new leaf. The least subtle of games does have its skills and techniques, and each of the players was determined to show what he could do. Though Kashiwagi played only briefly, he was clearly the best of them all. He was handsome but retiring, intense and at the same time lively and expansive. Though the players were now under the cherry directly before the south stairs, they had no eye for the blossoms. Genji and Prince Hotaru were at a corner of the veranda.

Yes, there were many skills, and as one inning followed another a certain abandon was to be observed and caps of state were pushed rather far back on noble foreheads. Yūgiri could permit himself a special measure of abandon, and his youthful spirits and vigor were infectious. He had on a soft white robe lined with red. His trousers were gently taken in at the ankles, but by no means untidy. He seemed very much in control of himself despite the abandon, and cherry petals fell about him like a flurry of snow. He broke off a twig from a dipping branch and went to sit on the stairs.

"How quick they are to fall," said Kashiwagi, coming up behind him. "We much teach the wind to blow wide and clear."[4]

He glanced over toward the Third Princess's rooms. They seemed to be in the usual clutter. The multicolored sleeves pouring from under the blinds and through openings between them were like an assortment of swatches to be presented to the goddess of spring. Only a few paces from him a woman had pushed her curtains carelessly aside and looked as if she might be in a mood to receive a gentleman's addresses. A Chinese cat, very small and pretty, came running out with a larger cat in pursuit. There was a noisy rustling of silk as several women pushed forward to catch it. On a long cord which had become badly tangled, it would not yet seem to have been fully tamed. As it sought to free itself the cord caught in a curtain, which was pulled back to reveal the women behind. No one, not even those nearest the veranda, seemed to notice. They were much too worried about the cat.

A lady in informal dress stood[5] just inside the curtains beyond the second pillar to the west. Her robe seemed to be of red lined with lavender, and at the sleeves and throat the colors were as bright and varied as a book of paper samples. Her cloak was of white figured satin lined with red. Her hair fell as cleanly as sheaves of thread and fanned out towards the neatly trimmed edges some ten inches beyond her feet. In the

---

4. Fujiwara Yoshikaze, *Kokinshū* 85: "Blow wide and clear, spring wind, of the cherry blossoms. / Let us see if they will fall of their own accord."

5. The verb is important. Well-behaved ladies did not permit themselves to be seen standing.

rich billowing of her skirts the lady scarcely seemed present at all. The white profile framed by masses of black hair was pretty and elegant—though unfortunately the room was dark and he could not see her as well in the evening light as he would have wished. The women had been too delighted with the game, young gentlemen heedless of how they scattered the blossoms, to worry about blinds and concealment. The lady turned to look at the cat, which was mewing piteously, and in her face and figure was an abundance of quiet, unpretending young charm.

Yūgiri saw and strongly disapproved, but would only have made matters worse by stepping forward to lower the blind. He coughed warningly. The lady slipped out of sight. He too would have liked to see more, and he sighed when, the cat at length disengaged, the blind fell back into place. Kashiwagi's regrets were more intense. It could only have been the Third Princess, the lady who was separated from the rest of the company by her informal dress. He pretended that nothing had happened, but Yūgiri knew that he had seen the princess, and was embarrassed for her. Seeking to calm himself, Kashiwagi called the cat and took it up in his arms. It was delicately perfumed. Mewing prettily, it brought the image of the Third Princess back to him (for he had been ready to fall in love).

from *Chapter 35. New Herbs (Part 2)*

The royal cat had had a large litter of kittens, which had been put out here and there. One of them, a very pretty little creature, was scampering about the crown prince's rooms. Kashiwagi was of course reminded of the Rokujō cat.

"The Third Princess has a really fine cat. You would have to go a very long way to find its rival. I only had the briefest glimpse, but it made a deep impression on me."

Very fond of cats, the crown prince asked for all the details. Kashiwagi perhaps made the Rokujō cat seem more desirable than it was.

"It is a Chinese cat, and Chinese cats are different. All cats have very much the same disposition, I suppose, but it does seem a little more affectionate than most. A perfectly charming little thing."

The crown prince made overtures through the Akashi princess and presently the cat was delivered. Everyone was agreed that it was a very superior cat. Guessing that the crown prince meant to keep it, Kashiwagi waited a few days and paid a visit. He had been a favorite of the Suzaku emperor's and now he was close to the crown prince, to whom he gave lessons on the koto and other instruments.

"Such numbers of cats as you do seem to have. Where is my own special favorite?"

The Chinese cat was apprehended and brought in. He took it in his arms.

"Yes, it is a handsome beast," said the crown prince, "but it does not seem terribly friendly. Maybe it is not used to us. Do you really think it so superior to our own cats?"

"Cats do not on the whole distinguish among people, though perhaps the more intelligent ones do have the beginnings of a rational faculty. But just look at them all, such swarms of cats and all of them such fine ones. Might I have the loan of it for a few days?"

He was afraid that he was being rather silly. But he had his cat. He kept it with him at night, and in the morning would see to its toilet and pet it and feed it. Once the initial shyness had passed it proved to be a most affectionate animal. He loved its way of sporting with the hem of his robe or entwining itself around a leg. Sometimes when he was sitting at the veranda lost in thought it would come up and speak to him.

"What an insistent little beast you are." He smiled and stroked its back. "You are here to remind me of someone I long for, and what is it you long for yourself? We must have been together in an earlier life, you and I."

He looked into its eyes and it returned the gaze and mewed more emphatically. Taking it in his arms, he resumed his sad thoughts.

"Now why should a cat all of a sudden dominate his life?" said one of the women. "He never paid much attention to cats before."

The crown prince asked to have the cat back, but in vain. It had become Kashiwagi's constant and principal companion.

[*Several years pass. The Akashi princess has since given birth to several children, one of whom will be the next crown prince. Although Murasaki and Genji remain happily married, she has begun asking him to allow her to become a nun, but he refuses.*]

Murasaki was now busy being grandmother to the royal children. She did nothing that might have left her open to charges of bad judgment. Hers was a perfection, indeed, that was somehow ominous. It aroused forebodings. The evidence is that such people are not meant to have long lives. Genji had known many women and he knew what a rarity she was. She was thirty-seven this year.[1]

He was thinking over the years they had been together. "You must be especially careful this year. You must overlook none of the prayers and services. I am very busy and sometimes careless, and I must rely on you to keep track of things. If there is something that calls for special arrangements I can give the orders. It is a pity that your uncle, the bishop, is no longer living. He was the one who really knew about these things.

"I have always been rather spoiled and there can be few precedents for the honors I enjoy. The other side of the story is that I have had more than my share of sorrow. The people who have been fond of me have left me behind one after another, and there have been events in more recent years that I think almost anyone would call very sad. As for nagging little worries, it almost seems as if I were a collector of them. I sometimes wonder if it might be by way of compensation that I have lived a longer life than I would have expected to. You, on the other hand—I think that except for our years apart you have been spared real worries. There are the troubles that go with the glory of being an empress or one of His Majesty's other ladies. They are always being hurt by the proud people they must be with and they are engaged in a competition that makes a terrible demand on their nerves. You have lived the life of a cloistered maiden, and there is none more comfortable and secure. It is as if you had never left your parents. Have you been aware, my dear, that you have been luckier than most? I know that it has not been easy for you to have the princess move in on us all of a sudden. We sometimes do not notice the things that are nearest to us, and you may not have noticed that her presence has made me fonder of you. But you are quick to see these things, and perhaps I do you an injustice."

"You are right, of course. I do not much matter, and it must seem to most people that I have been more fortunate than I deserve. And that my unhappiness should sometimes have seemed almost too much for me—perhaps that is the prayer that has sustained me." She seemed to be debating whether to go on. He thought her splendid.

---

1. She should be 39 or 40. The thirty-seventh year by the Asian count was thought to be a dangerous one. It was then that Fujitsubo died.

"I doubt that I have much longer to live. Indeed, I have my doubts about getting through this year if I pretend that no changes are needed. It would make me very happy if you would let me do what I have so long wanted to do."

"Quite out of the question. Do you think I could go on without you? Not very much has happened these last years, I suppose, but knowing that you are here has been the most important thing. You must see to the end how very much I have loved you."

It was the usual thing, all over again.

A very little more and she would be in tears, he could see. He changed the subject.

"I have not known enormous numbers of women, but I have concluded that they all have their good points, and that the genuinely calm and equable ones are very rare indeed.

"There was Yūgiri's mother. I was a mere boy when we were married and she was one of the eminences in my life, someone I could not think of dismissing. But things never went well. To the end she seemed very remote. It was sad for her, but I cannot convince myself that the fault was entirely mine. She was an earnest lady with no faults that one would have wished to single out, but it might be said that she was the cold intellectual, the sort you might turn to for advice and find yourself uncomfortable with.

"There was the Rokujō lady, Akikonomu's mother. I remember her most of all for her extraordinary subtlety and cultivation, but she was a difficult lady too, indeed almost impossible to be with. Even when her anger seemed justified it lasted too long, and her jealousy was more than a man could be asked to endure. The tensions went on with no relief, and the reservations on both sides made easy companionship quite impossible. I stood too much on my dignity, I suppose. I thought that if I gave in she would gloat and exult. And so it ended. I could see how the gossip hurt her and how she condemned herself for conduct which she thought unworthy of her position, and I could see that difficult though she might be I was at fault myself. It is because I have so regretted what finally happened that I have gone to such trouble for her daughter. I do not claim all the credit, of course. It is obvious that she was meant all along for important things. But I made enemies for myself because of what I did for her, and I like to think that her mother, wherever she is, has forgiven me. I have on the impulse of the moment done many things I have come to regret. It was true long ago and it is true now." By fits and starts, he spoke of his several ladies.

"There is the Akashi lady. I looked down upon her and thought her no more than a plaything. But she has depths. She may seem docile and uncomplicated, but there is a firm core underneath it all. She is not easily slighted."

"I was not introduced to the other ladies and can say nothing about them," replied Murasaki. "I cannot pretend to know very much about the Akashi lady either, but I have had a glimpse of her from time to time, and would agree with you that she has very great pride and dignity. I often wonder if she does not think me a bit of a simpleton. As for your daughter, I should imagine that she forgives me my faults."

It was affection for the Akashi princess, thought Genji, that had made such good friends of Murasaki and a lady she had once so resented. Yes, she was splendid indeed.

"You may have your little blank spots," he said, "but on the whole you manage things as the people and the circumstances demand. I have as I have said known numbers of ladies and not one of them has been quite like you. Not"—he smiled—"that you always keep your feelings to yourself."

In the evening he went off to the main hall. "I must commend the princess for having carried out her instructions so faithfully."

Immersed in her music, she was as youthful as ever. It did not seem to occur to her that anyone might be less than happy with her presence.

"Let me have a few days off," said Genji, "and you take a few off too. You have quite satisfied your teacher. You worked hard and the results were worthy of the effort. I have no doubts now about your qualifications." He pushed the koto aside and lay down.

As always when he was away, Murasaki had her women read stories to her. In the old stories that were supposed to tell what went on in the world, there were men with amorous ways and women who had affairs with them, but it seemed to be the rule that in the end the man settled down with one woman. Why should Murasaki herself live in such uncertainty? No doubt, as Genji had said, she had been unusually fortunate. But were the ache and the scarcely endurable sense of deprivation to be with her to the end? She had much to think about and went to bed very late, and towards daylight she was seized with violent chest pains. Her women were immediately at her side. Should they call Genji? Quite out of the question, she replied. Presently it was daylight. She was running a high fever and still in very great pain. No one had gone for Genji. Then a message came from the Akashi princess and she was informed of Murasaki's illness, and in great trepidation sent word to Genji. He immediately returned to Murasaki's wing of the house, to find her still in great pain.

"And what would seem to be the matter?" He felt her forehead. It was flaming hot.

He was in terror, remembering that only the day before he had warned her of the dangerous year ahead. Breakfast was brought but he sent it back. He was at her side all that day, seeing to her needs. She was unable to sit up and refused even the smallest morsel of fruit.

The days went by. All manner of prayers and services were commissioned. Priests were summoned to perform esoteric rites. Though the pain was constant, it would at times be of a vague and generalized sort, and then, almost unbearable, the chest pains would return. An endless list of abstinences was drawn up by the soothsayers, but it did no good. Beside her all the while, Genji was in anguish, looking for the smallest hopeful sign, the barely perceptible change that can brighten the prospects in even the most serious illness. She occupied the whole of his attention. Preparations for the visit to the Suzaku emperor, who sent frequent and courteous inquiries, had been put aside.

The Second Month was over and there was no improvement. Thinking that a change of air might help, Genji moved her to his Nijō mansion. Anxious crowds gathered there and the confusion was enormous. The Reizei emperor was much troubled and Yūgiri even more so. There were others who were in very great disquiet. Were Murasaki to die, then Genji would almost certainly follow through with his wish to retire from the world. Yūgiri saw to the usual sort of prayers and rites, of course, and extraordinary ones as well.

"Do you remember what I asked for?" Murasaki would say when she was feeling a little more herself. "May I not have it even now?"

"I have longed for many years to do exactly that," Genji would reply, thinking that to see her even briefly in nun's habit would be as painful as to know that the final time had come. "I have been held back by the thought of what it would mean to you if I were to insist on having my way. Can you now think of deserting me?"

But it did indeed seem that the end might be near. There were repeated crises, each of which could have been the last. Genji no longer saw the Third Princess. Music had lost all interest and koto and flute were put away. Most of the Rokujō household moved to Nijō. At Rokujō, where only women remained, it was as if the fires had gone out. One saw how much of the old life had depended on a single lady.

The Akashi princess was at Genji's side.

"But whatever I have might take advantage of your condition," said Murasaki, weak though she was. "Please go back immediately."

The princess's little children were with them, the prettiest children imaginable. Murasaki looked at them and wept. "I doubt that I shall be here to see you grow up. I suppose you will forget all about me"

The princess too was weeping.

"You must not even think of it," said Genji. "Everything will be all right if only we manage to think so. When we take the broad, easy view we are happy. It may be the destiny of the meaner sort to rise to the top, but the fretful and demanding ones do not stay there very long. It is the calm ones who survive. I could give you any number of instances."

He described her virtues to all the native and foreign gods and told them how very little she had to atone for. The venerable sages entrusted with the grander services and the priests in immediate attendance as well, including the ones on night duty, were sorry that they seemed to be accomplishing so little. They turned to their endeavors with new vigor and intensity. For five and six days there would be some improvement and then she would be worse again, and so time passed. How would it all end? The malign force that had taken possession of her refused to come forth. She was wasting away from one could not have said precisely what ailment, and there was no relief from the worry and sorrow.

I have been neglecting Kashiwagi. Now a councilor of the middle rank, he enjoyed the special confidence of the emperor and was one of the more promising young officials of the day. But fame and honor had done nothing to satisfy the old longing. He took for his bride the Second Princess, daughter of the Suzaku emperor by a low-ranking concubine. It must be admitted that he thought her less than the very best he could have found. She was an agreeable lady whose endowments were far above the ordinary, but she was not capable of driving the Third Princess from his thoughts. He did not, to be sure, treat her like one of the old women who are cast out on mountainsides to die, but he was not as attentive as he might have been.

The Kojijū[2] to whom he went with the secret passion he was unable to quell was a daughter of Jijū, the Third Princess's nurse. Jijū's elder sister was Kashiwagi's own nurse, and so he had long known a great deal about the princess. He had known when she was still a child that she was very pretty and that she was her father's favorite. It was from these early beginnings that his love had grown.

Guessing that the Rokujō mansion would be almost deserted, he called Kojijū and warmly pleaded his case. "My feelings could destroy me, I fear. You are my tie with her and so I have asked you about her and hoped that you might let her know something of my uncontrollable longing. You have been my hope and you have done nothing. Someone was saying to her royal father that Genji had many ladies to occupy his attention and that one of them seemed to have monopolized it, and the Third Princess was spending lonely nights and days of boredom. It would seem that her father might have been having second thoughts. If his daughters had to marry commoners, he said, it would be nice if they were commoners who had a little time for them. Someone told me that he might even think the Second Princess the more fortunate of the two. She is the one who has long years of comfort and

---

2. One of the Third Princess's attendants, through whom Kashiwagi had in the past had messages delivered to the princess.

security ahead of her. I cannot tell you how it all upsets me." He sighed. "They are daughters of the same royal father, but the one is the one and the other is the other."

"I think, sir, that you might be a little more aware of your place in the world. You have one princess and you want another? Your greed seems boundless."

He smiled. "Yes, I suppose so. But her father gave me some encouragement and so did her brother. Though it may be, as you say, that I am not as aware of my place in the world as I should be, I have let myself think of her. Both of them found occasion to say that they did not consider me so very objectionable. You are the one who is at fault—you should have worked just a little harder."

"It was impossible. I have been told that there is such a thing as fate. It may have been fate which made Genji ask for her so earnestly and ceremoniously. Do you really think His Majesty's affection for you such that, had you made similar overtures, they would have prevailed over His Lordship's? It is true that you have a little more dignity and prestige now than you had then."

He did not propose to answer this somewhat intemperate outburst. "Let us leave the past out of the matter. The present offers a rare opportunity. There are very few people around her and you can, if you will, contrive to admit me to her presence and let me tell her just a little of what has been on my mind. As for the possibility of my doing anything improper—look at me, if you will, please. Do I seem capable of anything of the sort?"

"This is preposterous, utterly preposterous. The very thought of it terrifies me. Why did I even come?"

"Not entirely preposterous, I think. Marriage is an uncertain arrangement. Are you saying that these things never under any circumstances happen to His Majesty's own ladies? I should think that the chances might be more considerable with someone like the princess. On the surface everything may seem to be going beautifully, but I should imagine that she has her share of private dissatisfactions. She was her father's favorite and now she is losing out to ladies of no very high standing. I know everything. It is an uncertain world we live in and no one can legislate to have things exactly as he wants them."

"You are not telling me, are you, that she is losing out to others and so she must make fine new arrangements for herself? The arrangements she has already made for herself are rather fine, I should think, and of a rather special nature. Her royal father would seem to have thought that with His Lordship to look after her as if she were his daughter she would have no worries. I should imagine that they have both of them accepted the relationship for what it is. Do you think it is quite your place to suggest changes?"

He must not let her go away angry. "You may be sure that I am aware of my own inadequacy and would not dream of exposing myself to the critical eye of a lady who is used to the incomparable Genji. But it would not be such a dreadful thing, I should think, to approach her curtains and speak with her very briefly? It is not considered such a great sin, I believe, for a person to speak the whole truth to the powers above."

He seemed prepared to swear by all the powers, and she was young and somewhat heedless, and when a man spoke as if he were prepared to throw his life away she could not resist forever.

"I will see what I can do if I find what seems the right moment. On nights when His Lordship does not come the princess has swarms of women in her room, and always several of her favorites right beside her, and I cannot imagine what sort of moment it will be."

Frowning, she left him.

He was after her constantly. The moment finally came, it seemed, and she got off a note to him. He set out in careful disguise, delighted but in great trepidation. It did not occur to him that a visit might only add to his torments. He wanted to see a little more of her whose sleeves he had glimpsed that spring evening. If he were to tell her what was in his heart, she might pity him, she might even answer him briefly.

It was about the middle of the Fourth Month, the eve of the lustration for the Kamo festival. Twelve women from the Third Princess's household were to be with the high priestess, and girls and young women of no very high rank who were going to watch the procession were busy at their needles and otherwise getting ready. No one had much time for the princess. Azechi, one of her most trusted intimates, had been summoned by the Minamoto captain with whom she was keeping company and had gone back to her room. Only Kojijū was with the princess. Sensing that the time was right, she led him to a seat in an east corner of the princess's boudoir. And was that not a little extreme?

The princess had gone serenely off to bed. She sensed that a man was in her room and thought that it would be Genji. But he seemed rather too polite—and then suddenly he put his arms around her and took her from her bed. She was terrified. Had some evil power seized her? She forced herself to look up and saw that it was a stranger. And here he was babbling complete nonsense. She called for her women, but no one came. She was trembling and bathed in perspiration. Though he could not help feeling sorry for her, he thought this agitation rather charming.

"I know that I am nothing, but I would not have expected quite such unfriendliness. I once had ambitions that were perhaps too grand for me. I could have kept them buried in my heart, I suppose, eventually to die there, but I spoke to someone of a small part of them and they came to your father's attention. I took courage from the fact that he did not seem to consider them entirely beneath his notice, and I told myself that the regret would be worse than anything if a love unique for its depth and intensity should come to nothing, and my low rank and only that must be held responsible. It was a very deep love indeed, and the sense of regret, the injury, the fear, the yearning, have only grown stronger as time has gone by. I know that I am being reckless and I am very much ashamed of myself that I cannot control my feelings and must reveal myself to you as someone who does not know his proper place. But I vow to you that I shall do nothing more. You will have no worse crimes to charge me with."

She finally guessed who he was, and was appalled. She was speechless.

"I know how you must feel; but it is not as if this sort of thing had never happened before. Your coldness is what has no precedent. It could drive me to extremes. Tell me that you pity me and that will be enough. I will leave you."

He had expected a proud lady whom it would not be easy to talk to. He would tell her a little of his unhappiness, he had thought, and say nothing he might later regret. But he found her very different. She was pretty and gentle and unresisting, and far more graceful and elegant, in a winsome way, than most ladies he had known. His passion was suddenly more than he could control. Was there no hiding place to which they might run off together?

He presently dozed off (it cannot be said that he fell asleep) and dreamed of the cat of which he had been so fond. It came up to him mewing prettily. He seemed to be dreaming that he had brought it back to the princess. As he awoke he was asking himself why he should have done that. And what might the dream have meant?

The princess was still in a state of shock. She could not believe that it had all happened.

"You must tell yourself that there were ties between us which we could not escape. I am in as much of a daze as you can possibly be."

He told her of the surprising event that spring evening, of the cat and the cord and the raised blind. So it had actually happened! Sinister forces seemed to preside over her affairs. And how could she face Genji? She wept like a little child and he looked on with respectful pity. Brushing away her tears, he let them mingle with his own.

There were traces of dawn in the sky. He felt that he had nowhere to go and that it might have been better had he not come at all. "What am I to do? You seem to dislike me most extravagantly, and I find it hard to think of anything more to say. And I have not even heard your voice."

He was only making things worse. Her thoughts in a turmoil, she was quite unable to speak.

"This muteness is almost frightening. Could anything be more awful? I can see no reason for going on. Let me die. Life has seemed to have some point and so I have lived, and even now it is not easy to think that I am at the end of it. Grant me some small favor, some gesture, anything at all, and I will not mind dying."

He took her in his arms and carried her out. She was terrified. What could he possibly mean to do with her? He spread a screen in a corner room and opened the door beyond. The south door of the gallery, through which he had come the evening before, was still open. It was very dark. Wanting to see her face, even dimly, he pushed open a shutter.

"This cruelty is driving me mad. If you wish to still the madness, then say that you pity me."

She did want to say something. She wanted to say that his conduct was outrageous. But she was trembling like a frightened child. It was growing lighter.

"I would like to tell you of a rather startling dream I had, but I suppose you would not listen. You seem to dislike me very much indeed. But I think it might perhaps mean something to you."

The dawn sky seemed sadder than the saddest autumn sky.

> "I arise and go forth in the dark before the dawn.
> I know not where, nor whence came the dew on my sleeve."

He showed her a moist sleeve.

He finally seemed to be leaving. So great was her relief that she managed an answer:

> "Would I might fade away in the sky of dawn,
> and all of it might vanish as a dream."

She spoke in a tiny, wavering voice and she was like a beautiful child. He hurried out as if he had only half heard, and felt as if he were leaving his soul behind.

He went quietly off to his father's house, preferring it to his own and the company of the Second Princess. He lay down but was unable to sleep. He did not know what if anything the dream had meant. He suddenly longed for the cat—and he was frightened. It was a terrible thing he had done. How could he face the world? He remained in seclusion and his secret wanderings seemed to be at an end. It was a terrible thing for the Third Princess, of course, and for himself as well. Supposing he had seduced the emperor's own lady and the deed had come to light—could the punishment be worse? Even if he were to avoid specific punishment he did not know how he could face a reproachful Genji.

There are wellborn ladies of strongly amorous tendencies whose dignity and formal bearing are a surface that falls away when the right man comes with the right overtures. With the Third Princess it was a matter of uncertainty and a want of firm principles. She was a timid girl and she felt as vulnerable as if one of her women had already broadcast her secret to the world. She could not face the sun. She wanted to brood in darkness.

She said that she was unwell. The report was passed on to Genji, who came hurrying over. He had thought that he already had worries enough. There was nothing emphatically wrong with her, it would seem, but she refused to look at him. Fearing that she was out of sorts because of his long absence, he told her about Murasaki's illness.

"It may be the end. At this time of all times I would not want her to think me unfeeling. She has been with me since she was a child and I cannot abandon her now. I am afraid I have not had time these last months for anyone else. It will not go on forever, and I know that you will presently understand."

She was ashamed and sorry. When she was alone she wept a great deal.

For Kashiwagi matters were worse. The conviction grew that it would have been better not to see her. Night and day he could only lament his impossible love. A group of young friends, in a hurry to be off to the Kamo festival, urged him to go with them, but he pleaded illness and spent the day by himself. Though correct in his behavior toward the Second Princess, he was not really fond of her. He passed the tedious hours in his own rooms. The little girl came in with a sprig of aoi, the heartvine of the Kamo festival.

> "In secret, without leave, she brings this heartvine.
> A most lamentable thing, a blasphemous thing."

He could think only of the Third Princess. He heard the festive roar in the distance as if it were no part of his life and passed a troubled day in a tedium of his own making.

The Second Princess was used to these low spirits. She did not know what might be responsible for them, but she felt unhappy and inadequate. She had almost no one with her, most of the women having gone off to the festival. In her gloom she played a sad, gentle strain on a koto. Yes, she was very beautiful, very delicate and refined; but had the choice been his he would have taken her sister. He had not, of course, been fated to make the choice.

> "Laurel branches twain, so near and like.
> Why was it that I took the fallen leaf?"[3]

It was a poem he jotted down to while away the time—and not very complimentary to the Second Princess.

Though Genji was in a fever of impatience to be back at Nijō, he so seldom visited Rokujō that it would be bad manners to leave immediately.

A messenger came. "Our lady has expired."

He rushed off. The road was dark before his eyes, and ever darker. At Nijō the crowds overflowed into the streets. There was weeping within. The worst did indeed seem to have happened. He pushed his way desperately through.

"She had seemed better these last few days," said one of the women, "and now this."

---

3. The Second Princess is often called Ochiba, "Fallen Leaf." The name comes from this poem.

The confusion was enormous. The women were wailing and asking her to take them with her. The altars had been dismantled and the priests were leaving, only the ones nearest the family remaining behind. For Genji it was like the end of the world.

He set about quieting the women. "Some evil power has made it seem that she is dead. Nothing more. Certainly this commotion does not seem called for."

He made vows more solemn and detailed than before and summoned ascetics known to have worked wonders.

"Even if her time has come and she must leave us," they said, "let her stay just a little longer. There was the vow of the blessed Fudō.[4] Let her stay even that much longer."

So intense and fevered were their efforts that clouds of black smoke seemed to coil over their heads.

Genji longed to look into her eyes once more. It had been too sudden, he had not even been allowed to say goodbye. There seemed a possibility—one can only imagine the dread which it inspired—that he too was on the verge of death.

Perhaps the powers above took note. The malign spirit suddenly yielded after so many tenacious weeks and passed from Murasaki to the little girl who was serving as medium, and who now commenced to thresh and writhe and moan. To Genji's joy and terror Murasaki was breathing once more.

The medium was now weeping and flinging her hair madly about. "Go away, all of you. I want a word with Lord Genji and it must be with him alone. All these prayers and chants all these months have been an unrelieved torment. I have wanted you to suffer as I have suffered. But then I saw that I had brought you to the point of death and I pitied you, and so I have come out into the open. I am no longer able to seem indifferent, though I am the wretch you see. It is precisely because the old feelings have not died that I have come to this. I had resolved to let myself be known to no one."

He had seen it before. The old terror and anguish came back. He took the little medium by the hand lest she do something violent.

"Is it really you? I have heard that foxes and other evil creatures sometimes go mad and seek to defame the dead. Tell me who you are, quite plainly. Or give me a sign, something that will be meaningless to others but unmistakable to me. Then I will try to believe you."

Weeping copiously and speaking in a loud wail, the medium seemed at the same time to cringe with embarrassment.

"I am horribly changed, and you pretend not to know me. You are the same. Oh dreadful, dreadful."

Even in these wild rantings there was a suggestion of the old aloofness. It added to the horror. He wanted to hear no more.

But there was more. "From up in the skies I saw what you did for my daughter and was pleased. But it seems to be a fact that the ways of the living are not the ways of the dead and that the feeling of mother for child is weakened. I have gone on thinking you the cruelest of men. I heard you tell your dear lady what a difficult and unpleasant person you once found me, and the resentment was worse than when you insulted me to my face and finally abandoned me. I am dead, and I hoped that you had forgiven me and would defend me against those who spoke ill of me and say that it was none of it true. The hope was what twisted a twisted creature more cruelly and brought this horror. I do not hate her; but the powers have shielded you and only let me hear your voice in the distance. Now this has happened. Pray for me. Pray that my

4. Early commentaries say that Fudō vowed to give six more months of life to those of the faithful who wished it.

sins be forgiven. These services, these holy texts, they are an unremitting torment, they are smoke and flames, and in the roar and crackle I cannot hear the holy word. Tell my child of my torments. Tell her that she is never to fall into rivalries with other ladies, never to be a victim of jealousy. Her whole attention must go to atoning for the sins of her time at Ise, far from the Good Law. I am sorry for everything."

It was not a dialogue which he wished to pursue. He had the little medium taken away and Murasaki quietly moved to another room.

The crowds swarming through the house seemed themselves to bode ill. All the high courtiers had been off watching the return procession from the Kamo Shrine and it was on their own way home that they heard the news.

"What a really awful thing," said someone, and there was no doubting the sincerity of the words. "A light that should for every reason have gone on shining has been put out, and we are left in a world of drizzling rain."

But someone else whispered: "It does not do to be too beautiful and virtuous. You do not live long. 'Nothing in this world would be their rival,' the poet said.[5] He was talking about cherry blossoms, of course, but it is so with her too. When such a lady lives to know all the pleasures and successes, her fellows must suffer. Maybe now the Third Princess will enjoy some of the attention that should have been hers all along. She has not had an easy time of it, poor thing."

Not wanting another such day, Kashiwagi had ridden off with several of his brothers to watch the return procession. The news of course came as a shock. They turned towards Nijō.

"Nothing is meant in this world to last forever,"[6] he whispered to himself. He went in as if inquiring after her health, for it had after all been only a rumor. The wailing and lamenting proclaimed that it must be true.

Prince Hyōbu had arrived and gone inside and was too stunned to receive him. A weeping Yūgiri came out.

"How is she? I heard these awful reports and was unable to believe them, though I had of course known of her illness."

"Yes, she has been very ill for a very long time. This morning at dawn she stopped breathing. But it seems to have been a possession. I am told that although she has revived and everyone is enormously relieved the crisis has not yet passed. We are still very worried."

His eyes were red and swollen. It was his own unhappy love, perhaps, that made Kashiwagi look curiously at his friend, wondering why he should grieve so for a stepmother of whom he had not seen a great deal.

"She was dangerously ill," Genji sent out to the crowds. "This morning quite suddenly it appeared that she had breathed her last. The shock, I fear, was such that we were all quite deranged and given over to loud and unbecoming grief. I have not myself been as calm and in control of things as I ought to have been. I will thank you properly at another time for having been so good as to call."

It would not have been possible for Kashiwagi to visit Rokujō except in such a crisis. He was in acute discomfort even so—evidence, no doubt, of a very bad conscience.

Genji was more worried than before. He commissioned numberless rites of very great dignity and grandeur. The Rokujō lady had done terrible things while she lived,

---

5. Anonymous, *Kokinshū* 70: "If cherry blossoms waited at our command / nothing in this world would be their rival."

6. *Tales of Ise* 82: "The cherry blossom is dearest when it falls. / Nothing is meant in this world to last forever."

and what she had now become was utterly horrible. He even felt uncomfortable about his relations with her daughter, the Reizei empress. The conclusion was inescapable: women were creatures of sin. He wanted to be done with them. He could not doubt that it was in fact the Rokujō lady who had addressed him. His remarks about her had been in an intimate conversation with Murasaki overheard by no one. Disaster still seemed imminent. He must do what he could to forestall it. Murasaki had so earnestly pleaded to become a nun. He thought that tentative vows might give her strength and so he permitted a token tonsure and ordered that the five injunctions be administered. There were noble and moving phrases in the sermon describing the admirable power of the injunctions. Weeping and hovering over Murasaki quite without regard for appearances, Genji too invoked the holy name. There are crises that can unsettle the most superior of men. He wanted only to save her, to have her still beside him, whatever the difficulties and sacrifices. The sleepless nights had left him dazed and emaciated.

Murasaki was better, but still in pain through the Fourth Month. It was now the rainy Fifth Month, when the skies are their most capricious. Genji commissioned a reading of the Lotus Sutra in daily installments and other solemn services as well towards freeing the Rokujō lady of her sins. At Murasaki's bedside there were continuous readings by priests of good voice. From time to time the Rokujō lady would make dolorous utterances through the medium, but she refused all requests that she go away.

Murasaki was troubled with a shortness of breath and seemed even weaker as the warm weather came on. Genji was in such a state of distraction that Murasaki, ill though she was, sought to comfort him. She would have no regrets if she were to die, but she did not want it to seem that she did not care. She forced herself to take broth and a little food and from the Sixth Month she was able to sit up. Genji was delighted but still very worried. He stayed with her at Nijō.

The Third Princess had been unwell since that shocking visitation. There were no specific complaints or striking symptoms. She felt vaguely indisposed and that was all. She had eaten very little for some weeks and was pale and thin. Unable to contain himself, Kashiwagi would sometimes come for visits as fleeting as dreams. She did not welcome them. She was so much in awe of Genji that to rank the younger man beside him seemed almost blasphemous. Kashiwagi was an amiable and personable young man, and people who were no more than friends were quite right to think him superior; but she had known the incomparable Genji since she was a child and Kashiwagi scarcely seemed worth a glance. She thought herself very badly treated indeed that he should be the one to make her unhappy. Her nurse and a few others knew the nature of her indisposition and grumbled that Genji's visits were so extremely infrequent. He did finally come to inquire after her.

It was very warm. Murasaki had had her hair washed and otherwise sought renewal. Since she was in bed with her hair spread about her, it was not quick to dry. It was smooth and without a suggestion of a tangle to the farthest ends. Her skin was lovely, so white that it almost seemed iridescent, as if a light were shining through. She was very beautiful and as fragile as the shell of a locust.

The Nijō mansion had been neglected and was somewhat run-down, and compared to the Rokujō mansion it seemed very cramped and narrow. Taking advantage of a few days when she was somewhat more herself, Genji sent gardeners to clear the brook and restore the flower beds, and the suddenly renewed expanse before her made Murasaki marvel that she should be witness to such things. The lake was very cool, a carpet of lotuses. The dew on the green of the pads was like a scattering of jewels.

"Just look, will you," said Genji. "As if it had a monopoly on coolness. I cannot tell you how pleased I am that you have improved so." She was sitting up and her pleasure in the scene was quite open. There were tears in his eyes. "I was almost afraid at times that I too might be dying."

She was near tears herself.

> "It is a life in which we cannot be sure of lasting
>   as long as the dew upon the lotus."

And he replied:

> "To be as close as the drops of dew on the lotus
>   must be our promise in this world and the next."

Though he felt no eagerness to visit Rokujō, it had been some time since he had learned of the Third Princess's indisposition. Her brother and father would probably have heard of it too. They would think his inability to leave Murasaki rather odd and his failure to take advantage of a break in the rains even odder.

The princess looked away and did not answer his questions. Interpreting her silence as resentment at his long absence, he set about reasoning with her.

He called some of her older women and made detailed inquiries about her health.

"She is in an interesting condition, as they say."

"Really, now! And at this late date! I couldn't be more surprised."

It was his general want of success in fathering children that made the news so surprising. Ladies he had been with for a very long while had remained childless. He thought her sweet and pathetic and did not pursue the matter. Since it had taken him so long to collect himself for the visit, he could not go back to Nijō immediately. He stayed with her for several days. Murasaki was always on his mind, however, and he wrote her letter after letter.

"He certainly has thought of a great deal to say in a very short time," grumbled a woman who did not know that the lady was the more culpable party. "It does not seem like a marriage with the firmest sort of foundations."

Kojijū was frantic with worry.

Hearing that Genji was at Rokujō, Kashiwagi was a victim of a jealousy that might have seemed out of place. He wrote a long letter to the Princess describing his sorrows. Kojijū took advantage of a moment when Genji was in another part of the house to show her the letter.

"Take it away. It makes me feel worse." She lay down and refused to look at it.

"But do just glance for a minute at the beginning here." Kojijū unfolded the letter. "It is very sad."

Someone was coming. She pulled the princess's curtains closed and went off.

It was Genji. In utter confusion, the princess had time only to push it under the edge of a quilt.

He would be going back to Rokujō that evening, said Genji. "You do not seem so very ill. The lady in the other house is very ill indeed and I would not want her to think I have deserted her. You are not to pay any attention to what they might be saying about me. You will presently see the truth."

So cheerful and even frolicsome at other times, she was subdued and refused to look at him. It must be that she thought he did not love her. He lay down beside her and as they talked it was evening. He was awakened from a nap by a clamor of evening cicadas.

"It will soon be dark," he said, getting up to change clothes.

"Can you not stay at least until you have the moon to guide you?"[7]

She seemed so very young. He thought her charming. At least until then—it was a very small request.

"The voice of the evening cicada says you must leave.
'Be moist with evening dews,' you say to my sleeves?"

Something of the cheerful innocence of old seemed to come back. He sighed and knelt down beside her.

"How do you think it sounds in yonder village,
the cicada that summons me there and summons me here?"

He was indeed pulled in two directions. Finally deciding that it would be cruel to leave, he stayed the night. Murasaki continued to be very much on his mind. He went to bed after a light supper.

He was up early, thinking to be on his way while it was still cool.

"I left my fan somewhere. This one is not much good." He searched through her sitting room, where he had had his nap the day before.

He saw a corner of pale-green tissue paper at the edge of a slightly disarranged quilt. Casually he took it up. It was a note in a man's hand. Delicately perfumed, it somehow had the look of a rather significant document. There were two sheets of paper covered with very small writing. The hand was without question Kashiwagi's.

The woman who opened the mirror for him paid little attention. It would of course be a letter he had every right to see. But Kojijū noted with horror that it was the same color as Kashiwagi's of the day before. She quite forgot about breakfast. It could not be. Nothing so awful could have been permitted to happen. Her lady absolutely must have hidden it.

The princess was still sleeping soundly. What a child she was, thought Genji, not without a certain contempt. Supposing someone else had found the letter. That was the thing: the heedlessness that had troubled him all along.

He had left and the other women were some distance away. "And what did you do with the young gentleman's letter?" asked Kojijū. "His Lordship was reading a letter that was very much the same color."

The princess collapsed in helpless weeping.

Kojijū was sorry for her, of course, but shocked and angry too. "Really, my lady—where did you put it? There were others around and I went off because I did not want him to think we were conspiring. That was how I felt. And you had time before he came in. Surely you hid it?"

"He came in on me while I was reading it. I didn't have time. I slipped it under something and forgot about it."

Speechless, Kojijū went to look for the letter. It was of course nowhere to be found.

"How perfectly, impossibly awful. The young gentleman was terrified of His Lordship, terrified that the smallest word might reach him. And now this has happened, and in no time at all. You are such a child, my lady. You let him see you, and he could not forget you however many years went by, and came begging to me. But that we should lose control of things so completely—it just did not seem possible. Nothing could be worse for either of you."

7. Oyakeme of Buzen, *Manyōshū* 709, with variations in other anthologies: "Dark the way and dangerous. / Can you not stay at least until you have the moon to guide you?"

She did not mince words. The princess was too good-natured and still too much of a child to argue back. Her tears flowed on.

She quite lost her appetite. Her women thought Genji cruel and unfeeling. "She is so extremely unwell, and he ignores her. He gives all his attention to a lady who has quite recovered."

Genji was still puzzled. He read the letter over and over again. He tested the hypothesis that one of her women had deliberately set about imitating Kashiwagi's hand. But it would not do. The idiosyncrasies were all too clearly Kashiwagi's. He had to admire the style, the fluency and clear detail with which Kashiwagi had described the fortuitous consummation of all his hopes, and all his sufferings since. But Genji had felt contemptuous of the princess and he must feel contemptuous of her young friend too. A man simply did not set these matters down so clearly in writing. Kashiwagi was a man of discernment and some eminence, and he had written a letter that could easily embarrass a lady. Genji himself had in his younger years never forgotten that letters have a way of going astray. His own letters had always been laconic and evasive even when he had longed to make them otherwise. Caution had not always been easy.

And how was he to behave towards the princess? He understood rather better the reasons for her condition. He had come upon the truth himself, without the aid of informers. Was there to be no change in his manner? He would have preferred that there be none but feared that things could not be the same again. Even in affairs which he had not from the outset taken seriously, the smallest evidence that the lady might be interested in someone else had always been enough to kill his own interest; and here he had more, a good deal more. What an impertinent trifler the young man was! It was not unknown for a young man to seduce even one of His Majesty's own ladies, but this seemed different. A young man and lady might in the course of their duties in the royal service find themselves favorably disposed towards each other and do what they ought not to have done. Such things did happen. Royal ladies were, after all, human. Some of them were not perhaps as sober and careful as they might be and they made mistakes. The man would remain in the court service and unless there was a proper scandal the mistake might go undetected. But this—Genji snapped his fingers in irritation. He had paid more attention to the princess than the lady he really loved, the truly priceless treasure, and she had responded by choosing a man like Kashiwagi!

He thought that there could be no precedent for it. Life had its frustrations for His Majesty's ladies when they obediently did their duty. There might come words of endearment from an honest man and there might be times when silence seemed impossible, and in a lady's answers would be the start of a love affair. One did not condone her behavior but one could understand it. But Genji thought himself neither fatuous nor conceited in wondering how the Third Princess could possibly have divided her affections between him and a man like Kashiwagi.

Well, it was all very distasteful. But he would say nothing. He wondered if his own father had long ago known what was happening and said nothing. He could remember his own terror very well, and the memory told him that he was hardly the one to reprove others who strayed from the narrow path.

Despite his determined silence, Murasaki knew that something was wrong. She herself had quite recovered, and she feared that he was feeling guilty about the Third Princess.

"I really am very much better. They tell me that Her Highness is not well. You should have stayed with her a little longer."

"Her Highness—it is true that she is indisposed, but I cannot see that there is a great deal wrong with her. Messenger after messenger has come from court. I gather that there was one just today from her father. Her brother worries about her because her father worries about her, and I must worry about both of them."

"I would worry less about them than about the princess herself if I thought she was unhappy. She may not say very much, but I hate to think of all those women giving her ideas."

Genji smiled and shrugged his shoulders. "You are the important one and you have no troublesome relatives, and you think of all these things. I think about her important brother and you think about her women. I fear I am not a very sensitive man." But of her suggestion that he return to Rokujō he said only: "There will be time when you are well enough to go with me."

"I would like to stay here just a little while longer. Do please go ahead and make her happy. I won't be long."

And so the days went by. The princess was of course in no position to charge him with neglect. She lived in dread lest her father get some word of what had happened.

Letter after passionate letter came from Kashiwagi. Finally, pushed too far, Kojijū told him everything. He was horrified. When had it happened? It had been as if the skies were watching him, so fearful had he been that something in the air might arouse Genji's suspicions. And now Genji had irrefutable evidence. It was a time of still, warm weather even at night and in the morning, but he felt as if a cold wind were cutting through him. Genji had singled him out for special favors and made him a friend and adviser, and for all this Kashiwagi had been most grateful. How could he now face Genji—who must think him an intolerable upstart and interloper! Yet if he were to avoid Rokujō completely people would notice and think it odd, and Genji would of course have stronger evidence than before. Sick with worry, Kashiwagi stopped going to court. It was not likely that he would face specific punishment, but he feared that he had ruined his life. Things could not be worse. He hated himself for what he had let happen.

[*Tormented by guilt, and fearful of Genji's displeasure, Kashiwagi falls seriously ill.*]

from *Chapter 36. The Oak Tree*

The New Year came and Kashiwagi's condition had not improved. He knew how troubled his parents were and he knew that suicide was no solution, for he would be guilty of the grievous sin of having left them behind. He had no wish to live on. Since his very early years he had had high standards and ambitions and had striven in private matters and public to outdo his rivals by even a little. His wishes had once or twice been thwarted, however, and he had so lost confidence in himself that the world had come to seem unrelieved gloom. A longing to prepare for the next world had succeeded his ambitions, but the opposition of his parents had kept him from following the mendicant way through the mountains and over the moors. He had delayed, and time had gone by. Then had come events, and for them he had only himself to blame, which had made it impossible for him to show his face in public. He did not blame the gods. His own deeds were working themselves out. A man does not have the thousand years of the pine, and he wanted to go now, while there were still those who might mourn for him a little, and perhaps even a sigh from her would be the reward for his burning passion. To die now and perhaps win the forgiveness of the man who must feel so aggrieved would be far preferable to living on and bringing sorrow and dishonor upon the lady and upon himself. In his last moments everything must disappear. Perhaps, because he had no other sins to atone for, a part of the affection with which Genji had once honored him might return.

The same thoughts, over and over, ran uselessly through his mind. And why, he asked himself in growing despair, had he so deprived himself of alternatives? His pillow threatened to float away on the river of his woes.

He took advantage of a slight turn for the better, when his parents and the others had withdrawn from his bedside, to get off a letter to the Third Princess.

"You may have heard that I am near death. It is natural that you should not care very much, and yet I am sad." His hand was so uncertain that he gave up any thought of saying all that he would have wished to say.

> "My thoughts of you: will they stay when I am gone
> like smoke that lingers over the funeral pyre?

One word of pity will quiet the turmoil and light the dark road I am taking by my own choice."

Unchastened, he wrote to Kojijū of his sufferings, at considerable length. He longed, he said, to see her lady one last time. She had from childhood been close to his house, in which she had near relatives. Although she had strongly disapproved of his designs upon a royal princess who should have been far beyond his reach, she was extremely sorry for him in what might be his last illness.

"Do answer him, please, my lady," she said, in tears. "You must, just this once. It may be your last chance."

"I am sorry for him, in a general sort of way. I am sorry for myself too. Any one of us could be dead tomorrow. But what happened was too awful. I cannot bear to think of it. I could not possibly write to him."

She was not by nature a very careful sort of lady, but the great man to whom she was married had terrorized her with hints, always guarded, that he was displeased with her.

Kojijū insisted and pushed an inkstone towards her, and finally, very hesitantly, she set down an answer which Kojijū delivered under cover of evening.

Tō no Chūjō had sent to Mount Katsuragi for an ascetic famous as a worker of cures, and the spells and incantations in which he immersed himself might almost have seemed overdone. Other holy men were recommended and Tō no Chūjō's sons would go off to seek in mountain recesses men scarcely known in the city. Mendicants quite devoid of grace came crowding into the house. The symptoms did not point to any specific illness, but Kashiwagi would sometimes weep in great, racking sobs. The soothsayers were agreed that a jealous woman had taken possession of him. They might possibly be right, thought Tō no Chūjō. But whoever she was she refused to withdraw, and so it was that the search for healers reached into these obscure corners. The ascetic from Katsuragi, an imposing man with cold, forbidding eyes, intoned mystic spells in a somewhat threatening voice.

"I cannot stand a moment more of it," said Kashiwagi. "I must have sinned grievously. These voices terrify me and seem to bring death even nearer."

Slipping from bed, he instructed the women to tell his father that he was asleep and went to talk with Kojijū. Tō no Chūjō and the ascetic were conferring in subdued tones. Tō no Chūjō was robust and youthful for his years and in ordinary times much given to laughter. He told the holy man how it had all begun and how a respite always seemed to be followed by a relapse.

"Do please make her go away, whoever she might be," he said entreatingly.

A hollow shell of his old self, Kashiwagi was meanwhile addressing Kojijū in a faltering voice sometimes interrupted by a suggestion of a laugh.

"Listen to them. They seem to have no notion that I might be ill because I misbehaved. If, as these wise men say, some angry lady has taken possession of me, then I would expect her presence to make me hate myself a little less. I can say that others have done much the same thing, made mistakes in their longing for ladies beyond their reach, and ruined their prospects. I can tell myself all this, but the torment goes on. I cannot face the world knowing that he knows. His radiance dazzles and blinds me. I would not have thought the misdeed so appalling, but since the evening when he set upon me I have so lost control of myself that it has been as if my soul were wandering loose. If it is still around the house somewhere, please lay a trap for it."[1]

She told him of the Third Princess, lost in sad thoughts and afraid of prying eyes. He could almost see the forlorn little figure. Did unhappy spirits indeed go wandering forth disembodied?

"I shall say no more of your lady. It has all passed as if it had never happened at all. Yet I would be very sorry indeed if it were to stand in the way of her salvation. I have only one wish left, to know that the consequences of the sad affair have been disposed of safely. I have my own interpretation of the dream I had that night and have had very great trouble keeping it to myself."

Kojijū was frightened at the inhuman tenacity which these thoughts suggested. Yet she had to feel sorry for him. She was weeping bitterly.

He sent for a lamp and read the princess's note. Though fragile and uncertain, the hand was interesting. "Your letter made me very sad, but I cannot see you. I can only think of you. You speak of the smoke that lingers on, and yet

> I wish to go with you, that we may see
> whose smoldering thoughts last longer, yours or mine."

That was all, but he was grateful for it.

"The smoke—it will follow me from this world. What a useless, insubstantial affair it was!"

Weeping uncontrollably, he set about a reply. There were many pauses and the words were fragmentary and disconnected and the hand like the tracks of a strange bird.

> "As smoke I shall rise uncertainly to the heavens,
> and yet remain where my thoughts will yet remain.

Look well, I pray you, into the evening sky. Be happy, let no one reprove you; and, though it will do no good, have an occasional thought for me."

Suddenly worse again, he made his way tearfully back to his room. "Enough. Go while it is still early, please, and tell her of my last moments. I would not want anyone who already thinks it odd to think it even odder. What have I brought from other lives, I wonder, to make me so unhappy?"

Usually he kept her long after their business was finished, but today he dismissed her briefly. She was very sorry for him and did not want to go.

His nurse, who was her aunt, told Kojijū of his illness, weeping all the while.

Tō no Chūjō was in great alarm. "He had seemed better these last few days. Why the sudden change?"

---

1. *Tales of Ise* 110: "In longing my soul has ventured forth alone. / If you see it late in the night, please seek to trap it."

"I cannot see why you are surprised," replied his son. "I am dying. That is all."

That evening the Third Princess was taken with severe pains.

Guessing that they were birth pangs, her women sent for Genji in great excitement. He came immediately. How vast and unconditional his joy would be, he thought, were it not for his doubts about the child. But no one must be allowed to suspect their existence. He summoned ascetics and put them to continuous spells and incantations, and he summoned all the monks who had made names for themselves as healers. The Rokujō mansion echoed with mystic rites. The princess was in great pain through the night and at sunrise was delivered of a child. It was a boy. Most unfortunate, thought Genji. It would not be easy to guard the secret if the resemblance to the father was strong. There were devices for keeping girls in disguise and of course girls did not have to appear in public as did boys. But there was the other side of the matter: given these nagging doubts from the outset, a boy did not require the attention which must go into rearing a girl.

But how very strange it all was! Retribution had no doubt come for the deed which had terrified him then and which he was sure would go on terrifying him to the end. Since it had come, all unexpectedly, in this world, perhaps the punishment would be lighter in the next.

Unaware of these thoughts, the women quite lost themselves in ministering to the child. Because it was born of such a mother in Genji's late years, it must surely have the whole of his affection.

[*Kashiwagi dies, and after the Third Princess gives birth to his son, Kaoru, she immediately takes Buddhist vows despite Genji's protests. Kaoru, a beautiful little boy, is thought by the world to be Genji's son, and is raised in the Rokujō mansion.*]

from *Chapter 40. The Rites*

[*Three years have passed. Murasaki has continued to be in uncertain health since her great illness, and again seeks permission from Genji to take Buddhist vows, but Genji stubbornly refuses. The Akashi daughter, who was raised by Murasaki and has since been named empress, visits her sickbed.*]

Murasaki had always found the heat very trying. This summer she was near prostration. Though there were no marked symptoms and though there was none of the unsightliness that usually goes with emaciation, she was progressively weaker. Her women saw the world grow dark before their eyes as they contemplated the future.

Distressed at reports that there was no improvement, the empress visited Nijō. She was given rooms in the east wing and Murasaki waited to receive her in the main hall. Though there was nothing unusual about the greetings, they reminded Murasaki, as indeed did everything, that the empress's little children would grow up without her. The attendants announced themselves one by one, some of them very high courtiers. A familiar voice, thought Murasaki, and another. She had not seen the empress in a very long while and hung on the conversation with fond and eager attention.

Genji looked in upon them briefly. "You find me disconsolate this evening," he said to the empress, "a bird turned away from its nest. But I shall not bore you with my complaints." He withdrew. He was delighted to see Murasaki out of bed, but feared that the pleasure must be a fleeting one.

"We are so far apart that I would not dream of troubling you to visit me, and I fear that it will not be easy for me to visit you."[1]

After a time the Akashi lady came in. The two ladies addressed each other affectionately, though Murasaki left a great deal unsaid. She did not want to be one of those who eloquently prepare the world to struggle along without them. She did remark briefly and quietly upon the evanescence of things, and her wistful manner said more than her words.

Genji's royal grandchildren were brought in.

"I spend so much time imagining futures for you, my dears. Do you suppose that I do after all hate to go?"

Still very beautiful, she was in tears. The empress would have liked to change the subject, but could not think how.

"May I ask a favor?" said Murasaki, very casually, as if she hesitated to bring the matter up at all. "There are numbers of people who have been with me for a very long while, and some of them have no home but this. Might I ask you to see that they are taken care of?" And she gave the names.

Having commissioned a reading from the holy writ, the empress returned to her rooms.

Little Niou, the prettiest of them all, seemed to be everywhere at once. Choosing a moment when she was feeling better and there was no one else with her, she seated him before her.

"I may have to go away. Will you remember me?"

"But I don't want you to go away." He gazed up at her, and presently he was rubbing at his eyes, so charming that she was smiling through her tears. "I like my granny,[2] better than Father and Mother. I don't want you to go away."

"This must be your own house when you grow up. I want the rose plum and the cherries over there to be yours. You must take care of them and say nice things about them, and sometimes when you think of it you might put flowers on the altar."

He nodded and gazed up at her, and then abruptly, about to burst into tears, he got up and ran out. It was Niou and the First Princess whom Murasaki most hated to leave. They had been her special charges, and she would not live to see them grow up.

The cool of autumn, so slow to come, was at last here. Though far from well, she felt somewhat better. The winds were still gentle, but it was a time of heavy dews all the same. She would have liked the empress to stay with her just a little while longer but did not want to say so. Messengers had come from the emperor, all of them summoning the empress back to court, and she did not want to put the empress in a difficult position. She was no longer able to leave her room, however much she might want to respect the amenities, and so the empress called on her. Apologetic and at the same time very grateful, for she knew that this might be their last meeting, she had made careful preparations for the visit.

Though very thin, she was more beautiful than ever—one would not have thought it possible. The fresh, vivacious beauty of other years had asked to be likened to the flowers of this earth, but now there was a delicate serenity that seemed to go beyond such present similes. For the empress the slight figure before her, the very serenity bespeaking evanescence, was utter sadness.

---

1. The speaker may be either Murasaki or the empress.
2. *Haha,* the most common word for "mother." Some

commentators argue for *baba,* "old woman" or "grand-mother."

Wishing to look at her flowers in the evening light, Murasaki pulled herself from bed with the aid of an armrest.

Genji came in. "Isn't this splendid? I imagine Her Majesty's visit has done wonders for you."

How pleased he was at what was in fact no improvement at all—and how desolate he must soon be!

> "So briefly rests the dew upon the hagi.
> Even now it scatters in the wind."

It would have been a sad evening in any event, and the plight of the dew even now being shaken from the tossing branches, thought Genji, must seem to the sick lady very much like her own.

> "In the haste we make to leave this world of dew,
> may there be no time between the first and last."

He did not try to hide his tears.

And this was the empress's poem:

> "A world of dew before the autumn winds.
> Not only theirs, these fragile leaves of grass."

Gazing at the two of them, each somehow more beautiful than the other, Genji wished that he might have them a thousand years just as they were; but of course time runs against these wishes. That is the great, sad truth.

"Would you please leave me?" said Murasaki. "I am feeling rather worse. I do not like to know that I am being rude and find myself unable to apologize." She spoke with very great difficulty.

The empress took her hand and gazed into her face. Yes, it was indeed like the dew about to vanish away. Scores of messengers were sent to commission new services. Once before it had seemed that she was dying, and Genji hoped that whatever evil spirit it was might be persuaded to loosen its grip once more. All through the night he did everything that could possibly be done, but in vain. Just as light was coming she faded away. Some kind power above, he thought, had kept the empress with her through the night. He might tell himself, as might all the others who had been with her, that these things have always happened and will continue to happen, but there are times when the natural order of things is unacceptable. The numbing grief made the world itself seem like a twilight dream. The women tried in vain to bring their wandering thoughts together. Fearing for his father, more distraught even than they, Yūgiri had come to him.

"It seems to be the end," said Genji, summoning him to Murasaki's curtains. "To be denied one's last wish is a cruel thing. I suppose that their reverences will have finished their prayers and left us, but someone qualified to administer vows must still be here. We did not do a great deal for her in this life, but perhaps the Great Buddha can be persuaded to turn a little light on the way she must take into the next. Tell them, please, that I want someone to give the tonsure. There is still someone with us who can do it, surely?"

He spoke with studied calm, but his face was drawn and he was weeping.

"But these evil spirits play very cruel tricks," replied Yūgiri, only slightly less benumbed than his father. "Don't you suppose the same thing has happened all over again? Your suggestion is of course quite proper. We are told that even a day and a night of the holy life brings untold blessings. But suppose this really is the end—can we hope that anything we do will throw so very much light on the way she must go? No, let us come to terms with the sorrow we have before us and try not to make it worse."

But he summoned several of the priests who had stayed on, wishing to be of service through the period of mourning, and asked them to do whatever could still be done.

He could congratulate himself on his filial conduct over the years, upon the fact that he had permitted himself no improper thoughts; but he had had one fleeting glimpse of her, and he had gone on hoping that he might one day be permitted another, even as brief, or that he might hear her voice, even faintly. The second hope had come to nothing, and the other—if he did not see her now he never would see her. He was in tears himself, and the room echoed with the laments of the women.

"Do please try to be a little quieter, just for a little while." He lifted the curtains as he spoke, making it seem that Genji had summoned him. In the dim morning twilight Genji had brought a lamp near Murasaki's dead face. He knew that Yūgiri was beside him, but somehow felt that to screen this beauty from his son's gaze would only add to the anguish.

"Exactly as she was," he whispered. "But as you see, it is all over."

He covered his face. Yūgiri too was weeping. He brushed the tears away and struggled to see through them as the sight of the dead face brought them flooding back again. Though her hair had been left untended through her illness, it was smooth and lustrous and not a strand was out of place. In the bright lamplight the skin was a purer, more radiant white than the living lady, seated at her mirror, could have made it. Her beauty, as if in untroubled sleep, emptied words like "peerless" of all content. He almost wished that the spirit which seemed about to desert him might be given custody of the unique loveliness before him.

Since Murasaki's women were none of them up to such practical matters, Genji forced himself to think about the funeral arrangements. He had known many sorrows, but none quite so near at hand, demanding that he and no one else do what must be done. He had known nothing like it, and he was sure that there would be nothing like it in what remained of his life.

from *Chapter 41. The Wizard*

Already at the beginning of the Eighth Month the autumn winds were lonely. Genji was busy with preparations for the memorial services. How swiftly the months had gone by! Everyone went through fasting and penance and the Paradise Mandala was dedicated. Chūjō[1] as usual brought holy water for Genji's vesper devotions. He took up her fan, on which she had written a poem:

> "This day, we are told, announces an end to mourning.
> How can it be, when there is no end to tears?"

He wrote beside it:

> "The days are numbered for him who yet must mourn.
> And are they numbered, the tears that yet remain?"

Early in the Ninth Month came the chrysanthemum festival. As always, the festive bouquets were wrapped in cotton to catch the magic dew.

1. One of Murasaki's women.

> "On other mornings we took the elixir together.
> This morning lonely sleeves are wet with dew."

The Tenth Month was as always a time of gloomy winter showers. Looking up into the evening sky, he whispered to himself: "The rains are as the rains of other years." He envied the wild geese overhead, for they were going home.

> "O wizard flying off through boundless heavens,
> find her whom I see not even in my dreams."[2]

The days and months went by, and he remained inconsolable.

Presently the world was buzzing with preparations for the harvest festival and the Gosechi dances. Yūgiri brought two of his little boys, already in court service, to see their grandfather. They were very nearly the same age, and very pretty indeed. With them were several of their uncles, spruce and elegant in blue Gosechi prints, a very grand escort indeed for two little boys. At the sight of them all, so caught up in the festive gaiety, Genji thought of memorable occurrences on ancient festival days.

> "Our lads go off to have their Day of Light.[3]
> For me it is as if there were no sun."

And so he had made his way through the year, and the time had come to leave the world behind. He gave his attendants, after their several ranks, gifts to remember him by. He tried to avoid grand farewells, but they knew what was happening, and the end of the year was a time of infinite sadness. Among his papers were letters which he had put aside over the years but which he would not wish others to see. Now, as he got his affairs in order, he would come upon them and burn them. There was a bundle of letters from Murasaki among those he had received at Suma from his various ladies. Though a great many years had passed, the ink was as fresh as if it had been set down yesterday. They seemed meant to last a thousand years. But they had been for him, and he was finished with them. He asked two or three women who were among his closest confidantes to see to destroying them. The handwriting of the dead always has the power to move us, and these were not ordinary letters. He was blinded by the tears that fell to mingle with the ink until presently he was unable to make out what was written.

> "I seek to follow the tracks of a lady now gone
> to another world. Alas, I lose my way."

Not wanting to display his weakness, he pushed them aside.

The women were permitted glimpses of this and that letter, and the little they saw was enough to bring the old grief back anew. Murasaki's sorrow at being those few miles from him now seemed to remove all bounds to their own sorrow. Seeking to control a flow of tears that must seem hopelessly exaggerated, Genji glanced at one of the more affectionate notes and wrote in the margin:

> "I gather sea grasses no more, nor look upon them.
> Now they are smoke, to join her in distant heavens."

---

2. In "The Song of Everlasting Sorrow" the emperor sends a wizard in search of the dead Yang Kuei-fei. In Chapter 1, Genji's grieving father is put in mind of the same passage. The word *maboroshi,* "wizard," occurs in the tale only these two times.

3. Toyonoakari, the day following the harvest festival proper.

And so he consigned them to flames.

In the Twelfth Month the clanging of croziers as the holy name was invoked was more moving than in other years, for Genji knew that he would not again be present at the ceremony. These prayers for longevity—he did not think that they would please the Blessed One. There had been a heavy fall of snow, which was now blowing into drifts. The repast in honor of the officiant was elaborate and Genji's gifts were even more lavish than usual. The holy man had often presided over services at court and at Rokujō. Genji was sorry to see that his hair was touched with gray. As always, there were numerous princes and high courtiers in the congregation. The plum trees, just coming into bloom, were lovely in the snow. There should have been music, but Genji feared that this year music would make him weep. Poems were read, in keeping with the time and place.

There was this poem as Genji offered a cup of wine to his guest of honor:

> "Put blossoms in your caps today. Who knows
> that there will still be life when spring comes round?"

This was the reply:

> "I pray that these blossoms may last a thousand springs.
> For me the years are as the deepening snowdrifts."

There were many others, but I neglected to set them down.

It was Genji's first appearance in public. He was handsomer than ever, indeed almost unbelievably handsome. For no very good reason, the holy man was in tears.

Genji was more and more despondent as the New Year approached.

Niou scampered about exorcising devils, that the New Year might begin auspiciously.

"It takes a lot of noise to get rid of them. Do you have any ideas?"

Everything about the scene, and especially the thought that he must say goodbye to the child, made Genji fear that he would soon be weeping again.

> "I have not taken account of the days and months.
> The end of the year—the end of a life as well?"

The festivities must be more joyous than ever, he said, and his gifts to all the princes and officials, high and low—or so one is told—quite shattered precedent.

❦

RESONANCES

Murasaki Shikibu: from *Diary of Murasaki Shikibu*[1]

His Majesty was listening to someone reading the *Tale of Genji* aloud. "She must have read the CHRONICLES OF JAPAN!" he said. "She seems very learned." Saemon no Naishi heard this and apparently jumped to conclusions, spreading it abroad among the senior courtiers that I was flaunting my learning. She gave me the nickname Our Lady of the Chronicles. How utterly ridiculous! Would I, who hesitate to reveal my learning in front of my women at home, ever think of doing so at court?

---

1. Translated by Richard Bowring.

When my brother, Secretary at the Ministry of Ceremonial, was a young boy learning the Chinese classics, I was in the habit of listening to him and I became unusually proficient at understanding those passages which he found too difficult to grasp. Father, a most learned man, was always regretting the fact: "Just my luck!" he would say. "What a pity she was not born a man!" But then gradually I realized that people were saying, "It's bad enough when a man flaunts his learning; she will come to no good," and ever since then I have avoided writing even the simplest character. My handwriting is appalling. And as for those classics, or whatever they are called, that I used to read, I gave them up entirely. Still I kept on hearing these malicious remarks. Worried what people would think if they heard such rumors, I pretended to be unable to read even the inscriptions on the screens. Then Her Majesty asked me to read to her here and there from the COLLECTED WORKS OF PO CHÜ-I, and, because she evinced a desire to know more about such things, we carefully chose a time when other women would not be present and, amateur that I was, I read with her the two books of Po Chü-i's "New Ballads" in secret; we started the summer before last. I hid this fact from the others, as did Her Majesty, but somehow His Excellency and the Emperor got wind of it and they had some beautiful copies made of various Chinese books, which His Excellency then presented to Her Majesty. That gossip Saemon no Naishi could never have found out that Her Majesty had actually asked me to study with her, for, if she had, I would never have heard the last of it. Ah what a prattling, tiresome world it is!

Now I shall be absolutely frank. I care little for what others say. I have decided to put my trust in Amitābha[2] and immerse myself in reading sutras. You might expect me to have no compunction in becoming a nun, for I have lost what little attachment I retained for the trials and pains that life has to offer, and yet still I hesitate; even if I were to commit myself to turning my back on the world, there might still be moments of irresolution before He came for me, trailing clouds of glory. The time too is ripe. If I get much older my eyesight will surely weaken to the point that I shall be unable to read the sutras, and my spirits will fail. It may seem that I am merely going through the motions of being a true believer, but I assure you that I can think of little else at the present moment. But then someone with as much to atone for as myself may not qualify for salvation; there are so many things that serve to remind one of the transgressions of a former existence. Ah the wretchedness of it all!

Daughter of Sugawara no Takasue: from Sarashina Diary[1]

As a person brought up in the back of beyond, even further than the end of the road to the East Country,[2] how rustic and backward I must have been, but, however it was that I first came to know about them, once I knew that such things as tales existed in the world and what they were like, all I could think of over and over was how much I wanted to read them. At leisure times during the day and evening, when I heard my

---

2. The Buddha.

1. Translated by Sonja Arntzen. The author of the *Sarashina Diary* was the daughter of Sugawara no Takasue (a provincial governor) and the niece of the author of *The Kagerō Diary,* another important woman's diary. In the 1060s, while in her fifties, the author wrote *Sarashina Diary,* which looks back on her youth and life from the perspective of a woman of advanced age. The diary is known for its vivid, poetic description of the trip from

Kazusa in the East Country to the capital which occupies the first part of the narrative, and for its depiction of the author as a young girl addicted to vernacular tales or novels. The diary in fact provides important evidence for the degree of popularity of *The Tale of Genji* among readers one generation after the tale's composition.

2. The province of Kazusa occupied most of present-day Chiba peninsula directly east of Tokyo.

elder sister and step-mother tell bits and pieces of this or that tale, or talk about what the Shining Genji[3] was like, my desire to read these tales for myself only increased; (for how could they recite the tales to my satisfaction from memory alone?) I became so impatient that I made an image of the Healing Buddha, in my own size,[4] and, performing purification rituals, when no one else was around, I would secretly enter the room; "Please grant that I should go to the capital as soon as possible where there are so many tales, and please, let me get to read all of them," thus, touching my forehead to the floor, I would pray with abandon. Then, the year I was thirteen, it did come about that we were to go up to the capital. On the third day of the Ninth Month, we made a preliminary start by moving to a place called Imatachi "Departing Now."[5]

At sunset, a heavy unsettling fog drifted in and covered the house in which I was so used to playing for years; it was turned inside out with goods all dismantled and scattered about in preparation for our departure. Looking back, I was so sad to leave behind the Buddha standing there where I used to go when no one else was looking and touch my forehead to the floor, that I burst into tears without letting anyone else know.

* * *

[*They finally arrive in the capital on the second day of the Twelfth Month and take up residence in what is now the eastern ward of the city.*]

It was a large wild place, not inferior in wildness to the mountains we had passed through; there were huge frightening trees like those in the deep moutains; it was a place one could scarcely believe was in the capital. We were not settled yet and extremely busy with one thing or another, but it occurred to me, "If not now, then when?" so I pestered my mother,[6] "Please find me some tales to read, please!" She sent off a letter to a relative of ours known as Lady Emon no Myobu who served at the Third Avenue Palace.[7] She was delighted with our news and sent us some tales "that her highness has deigned to pass down to me." These were particularly splendid scrolls packed in the lid of a ink stone box. I was beside myself with joy, day or night, the first thing I applied myself to was reading these tales. I wanted to read more and more. In this city, where we were not really settled yet, where might there be a person who could seek out more tales for me? * * *

My mother worried about the depression I had sunk into and thought to brighten my spirits by finding some more tales for me to read, and, indeed as a matter of course, this did lighten my spirits. After I had read the part of the *Tale of Genji* about the purple affinity,[8] I had desired even more to see what would happen next, but there

---

3. *The Tale of Genji* was written only about ten years before the time recorded here.

4. If this were a statue, one would assume the author commissioned it rather than made it herself, but since such a costly commission would seemingly be beyond the personal means of a young girl, there is speculation that she made a drawing of the Healing Buddha herself.

5. It was the custom in the Heian period to start journeys on astrologically auspicious days or from auspicious directions, which usually necessitated a pro forma start, removal to a temporary lodging nearby from which the actual trip could begin at the convenience of the travelers rather than the calendar. The place name Imatachi is translated here indicating that from here on, the author plays with place names in her text.

6. This is the first mention of the author's mother, who had not accompanied the father to the provinces but maintained their residence in the capital. Her mother is the daughter of the much younger sister by a different mother, the Mother of Michitsuna, the author of *The Kagerō Diary*.

7. The residence of Princess Shūshi (997–1050), daughter of the late ill-fated Empress Teishi who had been the patron of Sei Shōnagon.

8. Genji's mother, who died when he was only two, was referred to as the Kiritsubo (Paulownia Court) Consort. The paulownia tree has purple flowers. Genji's stepmother, with whom he had a secret affair, was called the Fujitsubo (Wisteria Court) Consort. The wisteria is also a purple flower. Genji falls in love with young Murasaki because of her resemblence to Fujitsubo. The murasaki plant (a millet) has roots which yield a purple dye. The connection between these three characters is called the purple affinity. The author is likely referring to Chapter 4 of *The Tale of Genji,* "Young Murasaki."

was no one I could approach to obtain the rest of the tale, and everyone else in our household was as yet so new to the capital, they were unable to find it for me. Feeling so terribly impatient and eager to read more, I prayed in my heart, "Please grant that I may get to read the *Tale of Genji* from the first chapter the whole way through." Even when I went along with my parents into religious retreat at Uzumasa,[9] this was the only object of my prayers, and, when we departed the temple, I thought for certain I would get to see this tale, but it did not appear and I regretted this sorely. Then my parents had me meet an aunt who had come up from the countryside. "My, what a beautiful girl you have grown into," she said among other things and seemed to take a great liking to me. When she was about to return, she said, "What shall I give you for a present? Certainly it should not be anything practical. I would like to give you something you really want." Then, upon her departure, I received the fifty odd chapters of the *Tale of Genji* in a large box,[1] as well as the tales *Middle Captain*,[2] *Toogimi, Serikawa, Shirara, A Souzu*[3] and others in a bag; the joy I felt was incredible.

With my heart pounding with excitement, I was able to read the *Tale of Genji*, (this tale that had confused me and made me so impatient when I had read only a piece of it) right from chapter one. I did not have anything to do with the rest of the household; I just lay down inside my curtains, and the feeling I had as I unrolled scroll after scroll[4] was such that what would I have cared even had I a chance to become Empress. I read all day long and as long as I could stay awake at night with the lamp pulled close to me. I found it quite amazing that passages I knew by heart would come floating unbidden into my head (since I did nothing but read, I suppose it was only natural). Then, in a dream, I saw a pure looking monk wearing a surplice of yellow cloth who said to me, "Quickly, memorize the Fifth Chapter of the *Lotus Sutra*." But I told no one, nor did I feel particularly inclined to memorize the *Lotus Sutra*. I was just infatuated with tales. I was rather ugly in those days, you know, but I imagined that when I grew up I would be extremely beautiful and my hair too would be splendidly long; I would just be like the Shining Genji's Yūgao or the Uji Captain's Ukifune—now it seems to me that my thoughts were frightfully frivolous.

Around the first of the Fifth Month, gazing at the scattered and ever so white petals of the nearby orange blossom tree, I composed this:

> Gazing at this,
> I might think that snow had fallen
> out of season,
> if it were not for the fragrance
> of this orange blossom tree.

Since our place was as thick with trees as the dark woods on the flanks of the Ashigaru mountains, the crimson leaves of the Tenth Month were even more beautiful than those of the hills on all sides. When they were just like lengths of brocade spread over the forest, some visitors came who said, "There was a place on the way here that was simply beautiful with crimson leaves!" On the spot, it came to me,

---

9. Uzumasa is in the western part of the city. The temple there is Kōryūji.

1. This indicates that the full length of *The Tale of Genji* at this time was "fifty odd" chapters. Genji textual scholars wish the author had been more specific about the number.

2. *The Tales of Ise.*

3. None of these tales survive.

4. Women would often read tales aloud to each other, but this comment is evidence that solitary, silent reading was also practiced.

> This lodging of ours,
> is not inferior to anywhere else
> at autumn's end,
> the scenery just satiates
> those weary of the world.

I thought about tales all day long, and even at night as long as I could stay awake, this was all I had on my mind. Then, I had a dream in which a person said, "For the sake of Her Highness of the First Rank,[5] I constructed a small stream in the Hexagonal Hall."[6] When I asked, "Why is this so?" the response was, "Worship the Great Heaven Shining God."[7] Such was my dream, but I did not tell anyone and let it go without a thought; what a hopeless case I was.

[An interval of about two years has passed before the next entry.]

In this way, life went on and my mind was constantly occupied with nothing in particular. When on the rare occasion I went on a pilgrimage, even then, I could not concentrate my prayers on becoming somebody in the world, (nowadays people read sutras and devote themselves to religious practice even from the age of seventeen or eighteen, but I just could not put my mind to that sort of thing).[8] What finally captivated my thoughts was this scene—I would be a noble and elegant woman, beautiful in appearance and manner whom some hero in a tale, someone like the Shining Genji, would hide away in the mountains like the Lady Ukifune and would visit, even if it were only once a year.[9] There, I would gaze out at the blossoms, the crimson leaves, the moon, the snow; sunk in a melancholy langour, I would wait to read from time to time his letters that would of course be splendid—this was all I dreamed about, and I even felt this was the future I wanted for myself.

Then, my father's life came to a turning point.[1] He had somehow hoped to see me settled in even a distinguished position, but time had just passed by without his intentions taking any direction, and now, finally he was to take up a post far away in the distant East Country. "For years now, I have been expecting to receive a posting in the nearby provinces, and then, with a mind free of worry, the first thing I could attend to would be taking care of you in fine style. I could take you with me on tours of duty, show you the seaside and mountain scenery, and, as a matter of course, see you settled into a higher social position than mine where all your needs would be met. This is what I wanted, but, since it is our fate, both yours and mine, not to be blessed with good fortune, after all this waiting and hoping, now I am to take up a post far away. In your youth, even when I took you with me down to the East Country, I felt a little bad about it. I thought, 'What would happen if I have to abandon her to wander lost in this wild province; if it were just me alone facing the

---

5. Princess Teishi (1013–1094), a granddaughter of Michinaga, not to be confused with the late Empress Teishi mentioned above.
6. A temple in central Kyoto that houses one of the "Seven Kannon of the Capital."
7. This is the Sun Goddess, Amaterasu, patron god of the imperial family. The author's perception of the identity of Amaterasu seems to have been quite vague. It is not at all certain that she conceived of this being as a "Goddess." The mention of Amaterasu in connection with a temple dedicated to Kannon may indicate the widespread belief at the time that Amaterasu was an avatar of Kannon.

8. The remark about "nowadays" indicates the retrospective nature of this entry.
9. Her imagined scene combines two characters in *The Tale of Genji* that are unconnected in the tale itself. Genji is the hero of the first 41 chapters of the work; Ukifune makes her first physical appearance in Chapter 49. It is Kaoru who hides Ukifune at Uji.
1. The year is 1032, the author is 25 years old. Her father is 60 years old and has been expecting to get a governorship in one of the provinces close to the capital, but instead he is appointed to Hitachi, the province next to his former post in Kazusa.

dangers of this alien country, I would be calm, but dragging her and the household with me, I could not even say what I wanted to say, nor do what I want to do. How painful this is,' and my heart was torn to pieces with worry. Now, this time, how much more so am I concerned. I cannot take you off to the provinces as an adult when I cannot be certain about my own life (even though left behind in the capital, it is to be expected you will be living in reduced circumstances). Still that is preferable to imagining you adrift, wandering around as a country rustic in the East Country; that would be too terrible. Yet, even in the capital, there is no relative or intimate friend upon whom I can rely to take you in. Nonetheless, since I am not in a position to refuse this posting I have just barely been given, all I can do is leave you behind in the capital and resign myself to a long separation. Yet, it is not as though even in the capital, I can leave you maintained in the style I should."[2] I felt so sad listening to my father lament like this day and night, I even lost my feeling for the blossoms and crimson leaves; although I bemoaned this situation terribly, what could I do about it?

Father went down to his province on the thirteenth day of the Seventh Month. For five days before his departure, he had been unable to bear seeing me and so had not come into my room. On the day he was to leave, everyone was busy with the departure; how much worse I felt at the very moment when he raised the bamboo blind of my room and looked at me with tears pouring down his face. He left just like that. My eyes were blind with tears and I had just laid down in my room when household servants who were to remain behind had come back from seeing him off and delivered this letter written on folded note paper.

> If I were in a
> position that fulfilled the
> wishes of my heart,
> then would I savour deeply
> the feeling of this autumn parting.[3]

This was all he had written, yet I could hardly read it through. Even at the best of times, I can only think up verses with "broken backs,"[4] but somehow I felt I must say something, so in that state of mind I wrote almost unconsciously,

> Never at all
> did I ever think that
> in this world,
> even for a little while
> I would be parted from you.

Now more than ever, no visitors came, I gazed constantly into space feeling lonely and bereft, imagining day and night how far he might have gone. Since I knew the path he was taking, as the distance grew between us, there was no limit to my yearning, loving thoughts. From dawn until dusk, I would spend my days staring at the rim of the mountains to the East.

* * *

2. The father's rambling, repetitive speech shows the anxiousness of his mind.

3. Parting in autumn, although sad, is celebrated in poetry. If her father had received the post he hoped for, he would have been able to appreciate the poetic feelings of parting in autumn. In his present situation, there is no such pleasure.

4. A fault in poetry composition in which the third line (thought of as the backbone of a poem) does not connect well with the fourth line.

In this way, as I drifted along in life, I wondered why I had not gone on pilgrimages. Of course, my mother was very old fashioned, "A trip to Hase Temple? How frightening the thought! What would I do if you were abducted on the slopes of the Nara hills? Ishiyama Temple? It would be terrifying to cross the Barrier Mountain. As for Kurama, the thought of taking you to that mountain is also frightening. Anyway, until your father gets back, it is out of the question." She seemed to think me troublesome as though I were some kind of outcast. Finally, she took me on a retreat to Kiyomizu temple. But that time too, as was my habit, I simply could not concentrate on my prayers. It was around the time of the equinox rites and the temple was terribly noisy to the point of being frightening. When I finally fell into a fretful slumber, I dreamed that a monk, apparently a kind of steward, dressed in a blue woven robe and wearing a brocade head-piece and brocade shoes came up to the railing where my curtain was and said in a chiding way, "Unaware of the sad future awaiting you, you just waste your time on idle concerns"; then he made as though to enter my curtains. Even having seen such a dream and having woke up with a start, I did not tell people "I have seen such and such," and, not even taking it particularly to heart, I went back home.

Then mother had a mirror one foot in circumference cast, and saying that it would be in place of taking me on a pilgrimage, she sent a monk on a pilgrimage to Hase. She apparently told him, "Go perform devotions for three days. Please divine what future is in store for this person by having a dream." For that same period of time, she also had me maintain a regime of abstinence.

This monk returned and made the following report, "Were I to come back without having at least seen one dream, it would be so disappointing, and what would I have to say for myself, so I made obeisances fervently and when I fell asleep, I saw a wonderfully noble and lovely looking woman emerge from behind curtains of state garbed in lustrous robes; she carried the offering mirror in her hand. 'Was there a letter of vows with this?' she asked. I respectfully replied, 'There was not. This mirror by itself is the offering.' 'How strange.' She said, 'This should be accompanied by a letter of vows.' Then she said, 'Look at what is reflected here in this mirror. When you look, it will be deeply sad!' and she wept and sobbed softly. When I looked in the mirror, there was the reflection of someone collapsed on the floor crying and lamenting. 'When you look at this reflection, it is very sad, is it not? Now, look at this,' and she showed me the reflection on the other side of the mirror.[5] Amid beautiful bamboo blinds and other hangings, various robes poured out from under curtains of state; plum and cherry blossoms were in bloom and from the tips of tree branches, warblers were singing. 'Looking at this makes one very happy, does it not?' she said. That is what I saw in the dream." Such was his report, but I did not really pay attention to what had been seen.

Even though I was of such a frivolous turn of mind, there was someone who was always telling me, "Pray to the Holy Deity Amaterasu." I had no idea of where Amaterasu might be or even whether this friend was speaking of a god or a Buddha,[6] even so, gradually I began to be interested and asked about it. I was told, "It is a god; this god dwells in Ise. In the province of Kii, the one they call the 'Creator of Ki' is also

---

5. A mirror would normally have only one polished side. This is a dream, however, so considerations of realism are not at issue.

6. Amaterasu, literally "Illuminating Heaven," is the Sun Goddess, patron deity of the imperial family. The author claims ignorance of whether Amaterasu is a god or Buddha. Certainly she appears to have no consciousness of this deity as being gendered female.

the same holy god.[7] Moreover, it is also this god who is the Guardian Diety in the Sacred Mirror Room in the Palace.[8] As far as going to the province of Ise to worship, that did not seem to be anything I could consider, and as for the Sacred Mirror Room of the palace, how could I go and worship there? Since it seemed that all there was to do was to pray to the light of the sky, I felt rather in the air.

* * *

In the Tenth Month, we moved into the capital. Mother became a nun; although she stayed in the same house with us, she lived apart in her own quarters. As for father, he just wanted to have me assume the position of mistress of the household, but when I saw that this would mean I would be hidden away and never mix with the world, I felt bereft of support. Around this time, a suggestion came from someone with whom we had a connection and who knew about me that I might serve at court,[9] "Surely it would be better than having her mope around the house with nothing to do." My old fashioned parents found the idea of my becoming a serving woman most distasteful and so I stayed at home. However, there were several people who said, "Nowadays, almost every young woman goes into service like that, and there have been cases of women who have done very well for themselves indeed. Why don't you give a try?" So grudgingly father became willing to send me to court.

On the first occasion, I went into service for just one night.[1] I wore a not so deeply dyed ensemble of only eight layers with a jacket of lustrous silk. For me, who had only concentrated my mind on tales and aside from this had known nothing of the world, and who, just living under the protection of my old fashioned parents, had only visited with relatives, and, who was used only to gazing at the moon and the blossoms—as for my feelings at this moment of stepping out into court service—I could hardly believe it was me or that this was reality. In this state of mind, I returned home at dawn.

When I was a house-bound woman, I used to occasionally feel that rather than being stuck forever at home, to go and serve at court would give me the opportunity to see interesting things and might even brighten my outlook, but now I felt uncertain; it seemed to me that indeed there would be things about this new life that might cause me sorrow. Nonetheless, what could I do about it?

In the Twelfth Month, I went again to serve. I was given my own sleeping quarters and this time I performed duties during the day. Sometimes, I would go up to my mistress's chambers and serve night duty for a few nights. Having to lie down among strangers, I was unable to sleep a wink. I felt so embarrassed and on my guard not to make mistakes that I could not help weeping in secret from the strain. At the first light of dawn while it was still quite dark, I would go back to my own sleeping quarters and spend the whole day distractedly yearning for my family, thinking about my father who now aged and in decline depended especially on me. In fact we depended on

7. This remark actually betrays a confusion between a pre-Nara period official title, "Creator of Ki" and the worship of the sun goddess in the province of Ki.
8. This information is correct.
9. To serve at court means to take a position as lady-in-waiting in the entourage of any of the members of the imperial family.
1. She becomes a lady-in-waiting to Princess Yūshi (1038–1105), an infant of less than two years at the time. Princess Yūshi was the daughter of the reigning Emperor

Go-Suzaku and the late Princess Genshi. Genshi had been adopted by Fujiwara Yorimichi after her mother Empress Teishi had died. Thus Princess Yūshi was being raised in the Takakura Palace of her adoptive grandfather Yorimichi, who was Regent at the time. Service in that household had the potential of putting the author in touch with members of the inner circle of Heian aristrocracy. It appears that she starts as a part-time lady-in-waiting for a trial period.

each other. Then, there were my orphaned nephews and niece[2] who had been with me since they were born and slept on my left and right side at night and got up with me in the morning; how poignantly I now recalled them. So I would end up spending my time lost in homesick reverie. My ears would prick up and sense that someone was peeking in at me, how terribly uneasy I was.

After a period of ten days of service, when I returned home, I found my father and mother waiting for me having kindled a fire in the hearth. At the moment of see-ing me get down from the carriage, they broke into tears and said, "While you were here, we would see people from time to time, but since you have gone into service, days go by without the sound of human voices and we hardly see anyone, how forlorn and lonely we have been. If this goes on, what is going to become of us."

Seeing them made me feel so sad. The next morning, they exclaimed, "Since you are home today, the family members and visitors are many; the house feels really lively." Face to face with them, I was moved; some indefinable joy brought me to the verge of tears.

Even for religious adepts it is very difficult to learn about former lives through dreams, but somehow I felt that going on like this with no sense of direction was not very satisfying, so I had someone try to divine my former life in a dream. I was at the main hall of Kiyomizu Temple. A monk who was a kind of steward came out and re-ported, "You were actually once a monk in this very temple. As a monk artisan, you accumulated merit by making many Buddha statues. And so you were born into this life well above that lowly station. You built the thirty foot Buddha[3] who resides in the east section of this hall. As a matter of fact, you passed away while you were applying the gold foil to this image." "My goodness! This means, does it, that I applied the gold foil to that Buddha over there?" "Since you passed away while you were doing it, it was a different person who applied the gold foil, and a different person who per-formed the offering ceremony when it was done." Having received the report of such a dream, afterwards, had I made fervent pilgrimages to Kiyomizu Temple; on the strength of having worshipped the Buddha at that main hall in a former life, I would as a matter of course have done something good for my salvation. But there is really nothing I can say for myself, this affair ended with me being no more assiduous about making pilgrimages than before.

On the twenty-fifth of the Twelfth Month,[4] I was invited to attend the rite of "Calling the Buddha's Names"[5] at the Princess's palace, I went only expecting to stay that night. There were as many as forty attendants all in layers of white robes with jackets of lustrous silk. I hid myself behind the lady who was my guide at court, and after barely showing myself, returned home at dawn. Snow had begun to flutter down; in the amazingly severe freezing chill of the dawn light, the moon faintly reflected in my lustrous sleeves truly recalled the "face damp with tears" of long ago.[6] On the road back, I composed,

> The year is ending,
> the night begins to dawn,

2. The children of her elder sister. It is now 15 years since her sister had died.
3. From its size, description, and placement, the monk is likely referring to the central image of the Amida Buddha in the Kiyomizu Main Hall.
4. In 1039.
5. The "Calling of the Buddha's Names" was an annual

event at the Imperial palace that involved reciting the three thousand names of the Buddha to expiate the sins of the past year.
6. Allusion to poem 756 in the *Kokinshū:* "Joining me when I brood on things, the moon dwelling in these sleeves of mine also has a face damp with tears."

> both ephemeral
> as the rays of the moon
> reflected on these sleeves of mine.

Well, even if my debut had been like this, somehow, I began to accustom myself to service at court. Although I was somewhat distracted by other things, it was not to the extent that people regarded me as eccentric, and as a matter of course, it seemed as though I had come to be regarded and treated as one of the company, but my parents did not understand, and before long, they ended up shutting me away at home.[7] Even so, it is was not as though my way of life became suddenly bright and lively, rather, although I was used to feeling very much at odds with life, now the situation I found myself in was utterly contrary to all my hopes.

> How many thousand times
> have I plucked the field parsely[8]
> from the water thus,
> without a dew drop falling
> in the direction of my hopes.

With just this solitary complaint, I let matters go.

Meanwhile, I became distracted by this and that, and completely forgot even about the world of the tales. I actually ended up feeling quite down to earth. Over the years and months, as I lay down and got up in meaningless activity, why had I not devoted myself to religious practices or pilgrimages? Ah, but, the things I had hoped for, the things I had wished for, could they ever really happen in this world? After all, was a man like the Shining Genji ever likely to exist in this world? No, this is a world in which being hidden away at Uji by Captain Kaoru could never happen.[9] Oh, how crazy I was and how foolish I came to feel. Such were the thoughts that sunk in, and had I then carried on with my feet on the ground, maybe things would have been all-right, but it did not end up that way.

* * *

On the twenty-fifth day of the Ninth Month, my husband fell ill; on the fifth day of the Tenth Month, he died. I felt as though it was a bad dream; I could not imagine something like this happening. The image that had been seen in the mirror offered to Hase Temple[1] of a figure collapsed on the ground weeping; this was me now. The image of the joyous figure had never happened. Now, there was no hope of its ever happening. On the twenty-third day, the night when the evanescent clouds of smoke were to be kindled, the one whom I had watched go off with his father in such a magnificent costume, now wore mourning white over a black robe and accompanied the funeral carriage crying and sobbing as he walked away. Seeing him off, remembering the other time—I had never felt like this before. I grieved as though lost in a dream; I wondered if my departed one could see me.

If from long ago, rather than being infatuated with all those useless tales and poems, I had only devoted myself to religious practice day and night, I wonder, would I have been spared seeing this nightmarish fate? The time that I went to Hase Temple

---

7. This is a veiled reference to her marriage to Tachibana no Toshimichi (1002–1058). From the comments that follow, it does not appear that it was a match to her taste at first.

8. A proverbial expression for putting all one's heart into some project and having it come to nothing.

9. Recalling her youthful dream to be kept in a rural setting by someone as handsome as Genji.

1. A reference to the mirror her mother had had cast and sent as an offering to Hase Temple in order to try and divine her future as a young woman.

when someone in a dream threw me something saying, "This is a sacred branch bestowed from the Inari Shrine," if I had just gone right then and there on a pilgimage to
Inari, maybe this would not have happened. The dreams that I had had over the years
in which I had been told, "Worship the god Amaterasu" had been divined as meaning
that I should become a nurse to an imperial child, serving within the palace and receiving the protection of the Imperial Consort.[2] But nothing like that had ever come to
be. Only the sad image in the mirror had been fulfilled. Pitifully, I grieved. Since I
had ended up as one without one thing going as I had wished, I drifted along without
doing anything to accumulate merit.

Yet somehow, it seemed that although life was sad, it was going to go on. I worried that perhaps even my hopes for the afterlife might not be granted. There was only
one thing I could put my faith in. It was a dream I had had on the thirteenth day of the
Tenth Month in the third year of Tenki.[3] Amidha Buddha appeared in the front garden
of the house where I lived. He was not clearly visible but appeared through what
seemed like a curtain of mist. When I strained to look through gaps in the mist, I
could see a lotus dais about three to four feet above the ground, the holy Buddha was
about six feet in height. He glowed with a golden light, and as for His hands, one was
spread open, and with the other He was making a mudra.[4] Other people could not see
Him; only I could see Him. Unaccountably, I experienced a great sense of fear and
was unable to move closer to the bamboo blinds to see. The Buddha deigned to speak,
"If this is how it is, I will go back this time, but later I will return to welcome you."
Only my ears could hear His voice, the others could not. Such was the dream I saw,
when I woke up with a start, it was the fourteenth. Only this dream is my hope for the
afterlife.

My nephews, whom I had seen day and night when we lived in the same place,
had gone off to different places after this regrettably sad event had occurred, so it was
rare for me to see anyone. On a very dark night, the sixth youngest nephew[5] came for
a visit; I felt this was rare and precious. This poem came spontaneously,

> Not even the moon
> has come out in the dark of
> Obasuteyama,
> for what reason then might you
> have come visiting tonight.[6]

And to a friend with whom I had corresponded warmly before, but from whom I had
not heard since I had come to this pass,

> Is it that you think
> I am one no longer living
> in this world of ours?

---

2. Here readers are finally given the precise content of the
hopes she had entertained for practical success in the
world.

3. The year 1055, three years before the death of her husband. This is the only time in the diary that the author
gives such a complete date.

4. A sacred hand gesture.

5. This reference has puzzled commentators because the
author had never before mentioned having as many as six
nephews.

6. Obasuteyama, literally "the mountain where old
women are abandoned" is a "pillow-phrase" with complex

associations. Obasuteyama is in the Sarashina district of
Nagano and is famous both for its connection with the
folk belief about an ancient custom of abandoning old
women and for being a beautiful place to view the moon.
Poem 879 in the *Kokinshū* is the touchstone for the place
name's association with the moon—"My heart finds no
consolation. Ah Sarashina! here am I gazing at the moon
shining on Obasuteyama." The place name has a further
personal association for the author because Sarashina and
Obasuteyama are in the province of Shinano, the last
posting for her husband. The traditional title for this diary,
Sarashina nikki, is derived from this poem.

> Sadly I cry and cry,
> yet I do indeed live on.

At the time of the Tenth Month, crying as I gazed out at the exceeding brightness of the full moon,

> Even to a heart
> clouded by tears that fall
> with no respite,
> the light pouring from the moon
> can appear so radiant.

The years and months change and pass by, but when I recall that dream-like time, my mind wanders, and it is as though my eyes grow dark so that I cannot recall clearly the events of that time.

Everyone has moved to live elsewhere; only I am left at the old house. One time when I stayed up all night in gloomy contemplation feeling so bereft and sad, I sent this to someone I had not heard from for a long time.

> The mugwort grows more
> and more rank, the dew on it
> soaks through and through;
> not visited by anyone,
> my voice is only raised in sobs.

She was a nun and so replied,

> Ah, yours is mugwort
> growing at an ordinary
> dwelling in the world,
> imagine the clumps of weeds
> in my garden of renouncement.

The Riverside Counselor's Stories: The Lady Who Preferred Insects[1]

Next door to the lady who was fond of butterflies lived another lady, daughter of the Lord Inspector. She had been reared with uncommon love and attention.

Said she: "It is silly of people to make so much of flowers and butterflies. They do far better to inquire seriously into the nature of things." Indiscriminately she gathered ugly specimens. "We will observe how they grow and change," she said, putting her specimens in cages in which she could observe them. "See how serious and intent the caterpillars seem to be." Her hair tucked out of the way behind her ears all the day long, she would hold them affectionately in her hand and gaze intently at them.

---

1. Translated by Edward Seidensticker. *The Riverside Counselor's Stories* (1055) consists of ten short stories, which are thought to have been written sometime between the 11th and 14th centuries. "The Lady Who Preferred Insects" is the most famous of these. If pathos was the pervading tone for the earlier *Tale of Genji*, that of later vernacular tales, such as those in *The Riverside Counselor's Stories*, was marked by subtle and ironic humor. Significantly, "The Lady Who Preferred Insects" begins with the phrase, "the lady who was fond of butterflies," which embodies the opposite of the protagonist. Fondness for butterflies represented the typical good taste of Heian aristocratic ladies, an attitude that is here inverted to reveal the underside of such a world. In fact, almost all of the protagonist's views are either an implicit critique or a form of resistance toward aristocratic aesthetic and social standards, with the protagonist seeking her own individuality and identity in contradiction to these norms. Like many of the other protagonists of the late Heian and early Kamakura periods, the protagonist appears ill, highly eccentric, or extreme in some way.

Her women being afraid of them, she gathered urchins of the lower orders who were afraid of nothing. She had them take out her insects and tell her their names, and when they had none she would invent names for them. It was her view that people should live the natural way. Against all common sense, she declined to pluck her eyebrows, and said that blackening the teeth was troublesome and unsanitary. Smiling an uncompromisingly white smile, she doted on her insects morning and night. Because her women were constantly fleeing, her room was in great confusion. Life was not easy for them. She was forever berating them and glowering at them through her thick black brows.

"Why can't she be like other girls?" her parents would say. "But she must have her reasons. It is all very strange. When you speak seriously to her the answers are sensible enough. So it is not that she is merely stupid." They were quite at a loss.

"This is all very well. But think what people are saying. They like a girl to be pretty. It does not do to have them say that you are devoted to repulsive caterpillars."

"I don't care in the least. Things make sense only when you observe and watch them develop. People are silly. A caterpillar becomes a butterfly." And she showed them how it was happening. "The silk that we wear is made by worms before they have wings. When they take wing it's all over." They had no answer.

Yet she was a lady. She did not address her parents openly. Devils and women were not to be looked upon. She would raise the blinds of the sitting room slightly and set out a post curtain, and thus discreetly receive them.

Her young women heard it all. "She may love her caterpillars, but they drive us to distraction. How pleasant it must be to work for the lady who likes butterflies."

A woman called Hyōei offered a poem.

> Am I to leave before she sees the light?
> A caterpillar is not that forever.

Laughing, a woman called Kodayū answered:

> Happy they with flowers and butterflies.
> For us it is the stench of caterpillars.

"How sad. Her eyebrows are genuine caterpillars. And her teeth are bare."[2]

Said a woman called Sakon:

> "So many furry creatures all about—
> We will survive the winter without coats.

And so, we may hope, will she."

An irritable old woman overheard. "And what are you children babbling about? I don't think it so fine that the lady next door likes butterflies. Indeed it seems stupid. Who could call a row of caterpillars a row of butterflies? The point is that they shed their skins and become butterflies. Watching it happen is a serious matter. When you take up a butterfly you get that nasty powder all over your hand. And you might get an attack of ague too. Isn't that reason enough to avoid butterflies?"

But this view of the matter only added to the shrillness of the criticism.

The boys meanwhile were kept busy. Knowing that there would be rewards, they brought in all manner of horrid creatures.

---

2. Heian aristocratic women normally blackened their teeth, much as women use lipstick today.

"The fur of the caterpillar is so interesting. Why don't the poets and the story tellers have more to say about it?"

The boys brought her mantises and they brought her snails, and sang loud songs about them, and the lady sang the loudest. "Why do the horns of the snail do battle?" Thinking the names of her boys rather dull, she renamed them after specimens in her collection: Cricket, Toad, Mayfly, Grasshopper, Centipede.

Word of all this spread abroad, and there were extravagant rumors. One young man, son of a high courtier, dashing and gallant and handsome as well, said that he had something to frighten her with. He took a cutting from a fine sash and shaped it into a most life-like snake, even contriving that it would move. He put it in a pouch with a scale pattern and a drawstring and attached a poem to it.

> Crawling, crawling, it will stay beside you,
> telling of a heart forever steadfast.

As if it were nothing, a serving woman brought it to the lady. "There is this pouch. So heavy you can hardly open it."

The lady did open it, and the snake raised its head. Though all her women were hysterical, the lady was calm.

"Praise Amida Buddha,[3] and let it be my guardian through this life. There is nothing to raise such a stir about." Her voice quavered and she looked away. "It is wrong to admire something only while it is beautiful." She brought it to her side, but she did after all seem uneasy about it. She jumped up and she sat down again, like a butterfly over a flower. Her voice was like a cicada's. Beside themselves with mirth, her women left the room. They reported these happenings to her father the Inspector.

"This is inexcusable. You have left her alone with the creature?"

Sword in hand, he rushed to her side. The snake was very realistic. He took it up and examined it.

"He is certainly very clever. He has played this trick on you because you are a scholar and connoisseur of insects and such. You must get off an answer immediately." And he departed.

"What an unpleasant fellow," said the women, learning of the contrivance. "But indeed you must answer."

The answer was on stiff, inelegant paper. Not yet up to the flowing feminine script, she wrote in the angular masculine one.

> "Perhaps we are fated to meet in paradise.
> Uninviting is this form beside me. Until then."

A most unusual letter, thought the man, who was a cavalry officer. "I must see her."

He consulted with a friend, a certain captain of the guards. Disguising themselves as women of the lower orders, they visited the Inspector's house at an hour when he would be away. They looked in through a crack in the partition to the north of the lady's room.

---

3. Amida Buddha is the Buddha who resides in the Western Pure Land. A bodhisattva, the Amida made 48 vows to save all sentient beings before becoming a Buddha. Thus, in 11th-century Japan, it was believed that Amida would take believers who chanted his name to the Pure Land upon their deaths.

A boy stood in the undistinguished plantings. "This tree is crawling with bugs. I never saw anything like it. Come have a look." He raised her blind. "The best swarm of caterpillars you could hope to find."

"How splendid," she answered in a strong, clear voice. "Bring them here."

"There are too many. See. Right here. Come on over."

She emerged with a firm, masculine stride. Pushing the blind before her she gazed wide-eyed at the caterpillar branch. She had a robe pulled over her head. The flow of the hair was good, but, perhaps because it was untended, it had a bushy untidiness. The black eyebrows were rich and cool, though the whiteness of the teeth was disconcerting.

"She would be pretty if she took care of herself. What a shame."

Clearly she neglected herself. Yet she was not at all ugly, and gave an impression of fresh elegance, and a cleanness as of a summer sky. The pity of it all. She was wearing a figured robe of pale yellow, a cloak decorated with grasshoppers, and white trousers.

She leaned forward to examine the caterpillars. "How very nice. But we can't leave them out in the sunlight. Come, men. Herd them inside. Don't let a single one get away."

The boy shook the branch and they fell to the ground.

"Put them on this."

She offered a white fan on which someone had been practicing Chinese characters. He did as ordered.

The two young men looked on in amazement. The master of the house was a learned man, and he had quite a daughter. More, perhaps, than he could manage.

A boy espied the pair. "A couple of handsome young men hiding behind that shutter. An odd-looking couple they are too."

"How awful," said Tayū. "There she is, chasing after those bugs of hers, completely exposed to the world. I must warn her."

Outside the blind as before, the lady was in a great stir getting caterpillars from leaves.

"Come inside." The woman was afraid to go near. "Someone might see you, way out there."

"What difference does it make?" said the lady, sure that this was merely a device to distract her.

"You think I'm lying? I'm told there are two fine young men behind that shutter. See, out there in back."

"Go have a look, Cricket."

"It's true," said the boy, running back.

Putting some caterpillars in her sleeve, the lady hurried inside.

She was neither too tall nor too short. Rich hair fell to the hem of her robe. Because the edges were untrimmed, it did not fall in perfect tresses. Yet it was good after its fashion, and rather charming.

Even someone less favored, thought the cavalry officer, could easily pass muster. She may not seem very approachable, but she is pretty and elegant, and there is a certain distinction even in her eccentricities. If only she did not have that peculiar hobby. It would be a pity to run off and not even let her know he had seen her. Using the juice from a grassy stem for ink, he set down a poem on a fold of paper:

> Having seen the fur of the caterpillar,
> I wish that I could take it for my own.

He tapped with his fan and ordered a boy to deliver it. The boy gave it to Tayū, saying that it was from the gentleman over there, for the lady.

"Frightful." Tayū was loud in her complaints. "I know who it's from. That cavalry man. Because of those stupid bugs you let him see you."

"When you look into the nature of things, there is nothing in the world to be ashamed of. This life of ours is a dream. Who can tell what is good in it and what is bad?"

What was a person to say? The women were in despair.

The young men waited, thinking there would surely be an answer. Presently, to their disappointment, all the boys were called inside.

There seems to have been at least one woman who saw the need for an answer. It would not do to have them wait in vain.

> I am not like the others. Only having heard
> The name of the caterpillar do I wish to answer.

To this the cavalry officer replied:

> Like the fur of the caterpillar, possibly,
> There is no other who matters so much as a hair.

Laughing, he departed.

⇒╪ PERSPECTIVES ╪⇐
Courtly Women

One of the striking characteristics of the emergence of Japanese vernacular literature was the central role played by women writers. What are now known as the central Heian Japanese classics—*The Tale of Genji, The Pillowbook,* the *Sarashina Diary*—were written by women either at or closely associated with the imperial court in the late tenth and early eleventh centuries, and most of the prominent authors of the period—Ono no Komachi, Murasaki Shikibu, Sei Shōnagon, the Mother of Michitsuna, and the Daughter of Sugawara no Takasue—are aristocratic women.

One major reason for the prominent role of aristocratic women at this time is the writing system. Kana, or the vernacular syllabary, emerged in the early tenth century, enabling the Japanese to write more easily in their own language. Until then, writing had been in Chinese or had used thousands of complex Chinese graphs to phonographically transcribe the native Japanese language. Despite the emergence of a native syllabary, men continued to write in Chinese, which remained the most prestigious language and the language of government, scholarship, and religion. By contrast, women were generally relegated to a non-public sphere and used the native syllabary as their first language, and writing diaries, memoirs, poetry, and fiction in the vernacular. One consequence was that women's writing had an internal, psychological dimension that was rarely to be found even in men's kana writing, which, with the exception of Japanese poetry (*waka*), remained secondary to their work in Chinese.

The second major reason for the development of women's writing was the political, social, and cultural importance of women at the imperial court. In the tenth and eleventh centuries, when a regency system came to the fore, the leaders of the Fujiwara clan competed to marry their daughters to the emperor in the hopes of becoming a grandfather of a future emperor and the ruling regent. As a consequence, they poured their resources into the female entourages of their daughters, who, when successful, became imperial consorts and empresses.

The major women writers of the period, including Murasaki Shikibu and Sei Shōnagon, were ladies-in-waiting to high royalty who vied for the attention of the emperor. These ladies-in-waiting, who were immensely cultivated, received the backing necessary to produce major works of literature and wrote for highly educated audiences. All of these women writers were the daughters of provincial governors, the second tier of aristocracy, who produced the male scholars and intelligentsia of the period, thus giving their daughters an educated outsider's perspective (and often a critical one) on the court. This was even more true of the Mother of Michitsuna and the Daughter of Takasue, who either did not become ladies-in-waiting or did not find it to their liking. Taken together, their works give a range of exceptional women's writing unmatched anywhere in the medieval world.

PRONUNCIATIONS:
>*Kokinshū:* ko-kin-sheu
>*Ono no Komachi:* oh-no no ko-ma-chee
>*Michitsuna:* mee-chee-tsoo-na
>*Sei Shōnagon:* say shoh-nah-gon

⊢─ ⇛╪⊒ ─⊣

Ono no Komachi
fl. c. 850

Ono no Komachi was an early Heian period female poet noted for her *waka,* the thirty-one syllable classical form. Not much is known about her actual life, which has become enshrouded in

Japanese court women from *The Tale of Genji Picture Scroll,* late 12th century. A female attendant is tending to Ukifune's hair (left), while another (middle) reads aloud from a text.

legend. She is thought to have been beautiful and a number of legends have sprung up about her intimate relationship with Ariwara no Narihira (825–880), a noted poet who also became a legendary lover, most specifically the amorous protagonist of *The Tales of Ise.* Komachi was a pioneer in the field of Heian women's poetry, and she exchanged poetry with other notable ninth-century *waka* poets, contributing to the renaissance of classical poetry at this time. Of her poems, a large number are love poems, typically marked by vivid passion, a melancholy sense of impermanence and of the uncertainty of life, and a desire to enter into a dream world. Her poems frequently rely on complex puns and word associations. She has eighteen poems in the *Kokinshū,* the first and most prestigious of the imperial *waka* collections. The *Komachi shū* (Komachi Poetry Collection) contains 110 poems, many of which are thought to be apocryphal. All of the poems that follow are from the *Kokinshū,* (Anthology of Poems Old and New, c. 905), which is thought to be the most reliable source for Komachi's poems. They are given here with the numbers they have in the *Kokinshū.* Most are from the love volumes of the *Kokinshū.* The five volumes of love poems in the *Kokinshū* are arranged in narrative order, from the beginnings of love to the aftermath, and are based on the assumption that love can never be satisfactory.

113[1]

Hana no iro wa	While watching
utsuri ni keri na	the long rains falling on this world
itazura ni	my heart, too, fades
waga mi yo ni furu	with the unseen color
nagameseshi ma ni	of the spring flowers.

552

Omoitsutsu	Did he appear
nureba ya hito no	because I fell asleep

1. Translated by Jane Hirschfield with Mariko Aratani. *Kokinshū,* Spring 2, No. 113, is one of Komachi's most famous poems. Some commentators believe that the "color of the flower" (*hana no iro*) is a metaphor for the author's face, but others read this poem literally as a spring poem. *Furu* is a homonym meaning both "(for time) to pass" and "(for rain) to fall." The poet's life passes as the spring rains fall. *Nagame* is a homonym for "long rains," "to gaze in a melancholy state," and "to recite aloud a poem."

mietsuramu   thinking of him?
yume to shiriseba   If only I'd known I was dreaming,
samezaramashi o   I'd never have wakened.[2]

554

Ito semete   When my desire
koishiki toki wa   grows too fierce
nubatama no   I wear my bedclothes
yoru no koromo o   inside out
kaeshite zo kiru   dark as the night's rough husk[3]

623

Mirume naki   The seaweed gatherer's weary feet
waga mi o ura to   keep coming back to my shore.
shiraneba ya   Doesn't he know
karenade ama no   there's no harvest for him
ashi tayuku kuru   in this uncaring bay?[4]

635

Aki no yo mo   The autumn night
na nomi narikeri   is long only in name—
au to ieba   We've done no more
koto zo tomonaku   than gaze at each other
akenuru mono o   and it's already dawn.[5]

656

Utsutsu ni wa   I know it must be this way
sa mo koso arame   in the waking world,
yume ni sae   but how cruel—
hitome o yoku to   even in my dreams
miru ga wabishisa   we hide from other's eyes.[6]

657

Kagiri naki   My longing for you—
omoi no mama ni   Too strong to keep within bounds.
yoru mo komu   At least no one can blame me

2. *Kokinshū*, Love 2, No. 552. This is the first poem in a series of three in the *Kokinshū* (No. 552–554) on meeting a lover in a dream. Her passion is such that she has paradoxically come to rely on dreams, the most ephemeral of things.

3. *Kokinshū*, Love 2, No. 554. This poem is based on a contemporary folk belief that if one slept with one's bedrobes inside out, one's lover would appear in a dream.

4. *Kokinshū*, Love 3, No. 623. Presented in the *Kokinshū* as a woman's reply to a poem by the male poet Ariwara no Narihira, in which the poet speaks of visiting his love but not meeting her. The fisherman keeps coming to this bay, until his feet grow weary, not knowing that there is no seaweed (*mirume*) to harvest. You (the man) similarly keep coming to meet me, until your feet grow weary, not

knowing that there is no chance to meet me (*mirume*). *Mirume* is a homonym meaning both "opportunity to meet" and a type of seaweed.

5. *Kokinshū*, Love 3, No. 635. It was assumed by poetic convention that autumn nights were long, just as summer nights were considered short, but here the autumn night is long only in name.

6. *Kokinshū*, Love 3, No. 656. The appearance of a lover in a dream means that the lover has traveled to see one on the path of dreams. Here the woman poet is expressing resentment that normally she and her lover cannot meet but now her lover does not even visit her in a dream. This poem is the first in a sequence of three poems by Komachi in the *Kokinshū* (No. 656–658).

yumeji o sae ni	When I go to you at night
hito wa togameji	Along the road of dreams.[7]

658

Yumeji ni wa	Though I go to him constantly
ashi mo yasumezu	on the paths of dream,
kayoedomo	never resting my feet,
utsutsu ni hitome	in the real world
mishigoto wa arazu	it doesn't equal a single glance.[8]

797

When Fun'ya no Yasuhide was appointed governor of Mikawa, he wrote to ask if I would like to come visit his district. I replied:

Iro miede	How invisibly
utsurou mono wa	it changes color
yo no naka no	in this world,
hito no kokoro no	the flower
hana ni zo arikeru	of the human heart.[9]

938

Wabinureba	This body
mi o ukigusa no	Grown fragile, floating
ne o taete	A reed cut from its roots . . .
sasou mizu araba	If a stream would ask me
inamu to zo omou	to follow, I'd go, I think.[1]

Michitsuna's Mother
936–995

The Kagerō Diary was written from approximately 971 to 974 by a woman now referred to as Michitsuna's Mother.[1] The diary covers a period of the author's life from 954, when she first encounters her husband-to-be, to 974, when her son enters into a courtship with a woman.

Michitsuna's Mother became a noted *waka* poet, and one of her poems was included in the prestigious *Hundred Poems by a Hundred Poets* edited by Fujiwara Teika. Poetry plays a key

---

7. *Kokinshū,* Love 3, No. 657. If the relationship is forbidden, people will look askance at the visits, but no one can blame her for visiting on the road of dreams—implying that the road of dreams at times seems better than reality.
8. *Kokinshū,* Love 3, No. 658. This poem is a kind of response to the previous poem, No. 657, stating that though the poet can visit her lover on the road of dreams constantly, these visits do not equal even a single glimpse of one's lover in reality—i.e., dreams are no substitute for reality.
9. *Kokinshū,* Love 5, No. 797, also in *Hyakunin isshu,* No. 9. The poem suggests that it is one thing for the body, to be

the physical world (as represented by *iro,* or color), to be impermanent, but it is another—even more surprising and devastating—to find the flower in the heart (implicitly, the feelings of love) changing or fading as quickly.
1. *Kokinshū,* Miscellaneous 2, No. 938. *Uki* is a homonym meaning "floating" and "sorrowful." The poet compares herself to floating grass (a reed cut at the roots), a metaphor for the wandering life of a traveler, and answers that she is ready to go wherever the stream takes her. One of the main themes of this volume of the *Kokinshū* is impermanence (*mujō*), which is reflected in this poem.
1. Introduction by Christina Laffin.

role in *The Kagerō Diary*. The author's father, Fujiwara Tomoyasu, belonged to the provincial governor class. At the age of nineteen, Michitsuna's Mother received a proposal of marriage from Fujiwara Kaneie (929–990), who was twenty-six and captain of the Right Guards at the time. As a son of Fujiwara Morosuke, the Minister of the Right, he was in a strong position to rise in the political hierarchy, and he eventually reached the powerful position of regent. Michitsuna's Mother, however, appears to have enjoyed few of the benefits of Kaneie's political ascension, largely due to the fact that she bore him only one child (Michitsuna).

Before his marriage to Michitsuna's Mother, Kaneie already had one son by his first wife, Tokihime, who was the official principal wife in a polygamous marital arrangement typical of the time. In aristocratic marriage the man and wife lived in separate locations, with the man visiting the woman, who usually remained with her family or lived by herself with her children. The result is that the frequency and duration of the visits reflected the status of the marriage, and the termination of visits was equivalent to divorce. The family system was matrilineal, with the daughter inheriting the house and property and continuing to be supported by her family. Although Tokihime's position as a member of the provincial governor's class was similar to that of Michitsuna's Mother, the key difference was that she provided Kaneie with two daughters, who became imperial consorts, and three sons (one of whom later became regent), thus cementing her status as the principal wife. Though the author laments the nature of her marriage to Kaneie, the fact that it lasted for sixteen years is an indication of how highly he valued her both as a wife and as a poet. The diary reveals that Kaneie had lasting affection for their son, Michitsuna, and must have provided support so that he was eventually able to rise to the status of major counselor.

Kaneie may have asked the author to collect their poetry exchanges, which could have evolved into a family poetry collection and then finally into this literary diary. Although the work contains much of the poetry exchanged between the author and Kaneie, including poems she wrote on his behalf, Michitsuna's Mother refers to her work as a diary, which included a day-to-day recording of actual facts and which, in this case, also had an autobiographical dimension. She may have been influenced by male courtier diaries written in Chinese, or perhaps had even read early *kana* diaries such as the *Tosa Diary* by Ki no Tsurayuki. More importantly, she invented a new form of self-expression and psychological exploration that expanded the potential of *kana* prose writing and that was to have an impact on subsequent women's writing, including *The Tale of Genji*.

The author was apparently strongly influenced by the vernacular tale (*monogatari*). From the condemnation of *monogatari* in a work called the *Illustration of the Three Jewels*, we know that these tales were numerous and well circulated. *The Kagerō Diary* often draws from the style of the *monogatari* and, like the author of the *Sarashina Diary*, Michitsuna's Mother views herself through the lens of the stories she has heard and read. Yet it is these very tales that have deluded her into thinking that courtship and married life would resemble that found in the *monogatari*. As Michitsuna's Mother notes at the beginning of *The Kagerō Diary*, she writes about her life to prove "the odds and ends of the old tales—of which there are so many, they are just so much fantasy."

In Book 1, which covers a fourteen-year span, the author focuses on her courtship and marriage to Kaneie. At each stage, he appears to fall short of the kind of courtship found in *monogatari*. Over the three-year period described in Book 2, the author's resentment builds until it finally climaxes in her decision to retreat to Hannya Temple at Narutaki, on the outskirts of the capital. Having removed herself physically and psychologically from her marriage and from society, Michitsuna's Mother faces the decision of either returning to her life in the capital or leaving this secular life forever to become a nun. The threat of permanently severing her ties to the world are what her servants, friends, her son, her father, and Kaneie himself work against as they try to convince the author to return with them. Taking the tonsure might have seriously jeopardized the position of her son and her father at court and reflected poorly on Kaneie's reputation.

By Book 3, which depicts the final three years, the author has gained a new perspective, distancing herself from Kaneie and taking pleasure in her son's and adopted daughter's relationships, which she supports by writing poetry for them. While we will never know exactly what sort of person Kaneie was, there are glimpses of happiness in their poetry exchanges, in their common concern for their son, and in adopting the daughter of one of his other women. The adoption of a daughter and Michitsuna's courtship are both presented as if in a *monogatari*, with the author now crafting her own tale.

from The Kagerō Diary[1]

Thus the time has passed and there is one in the world who has lived such a vain existence, catching on to neither this nor that. As for her appearance, she can hardly be compared to others, and her intelligence—to say she has some is as good as saying she has none at all—so it is only natural that she has come to such a useless state she thinks again and again; it is just that in the course of living, lying down, getting up, dawn to dusk when she looks at the odds and ends of the old tales—of which there are so many, they are just so much fantasy—that she thinks perhaps if she were to make a record of a life like her own, being really nobody, it might actually be novel, and could even serve to answer, should anyone ask, what is it like, the life of a woman married to a highly placed man, yet the events of the months and years gone by are vague; places where I have just left it at that are indeed many.

Well then, for this ultimately disappointing affair, there was, of course, the exchange of love letters; from about the time that he became "a tall tree among oak trees," it seems that he made his intentions known. An ordinary person would have sent a discreet letter using a serving maid or someone like that as a go-between to make his feelings known, but this man goes right to my father, half-joking, half-serious, hinting at the idea, and even though I told my father that it did not suit me at all, just as if he did not know, one day he sends a retainer riding on a horse to pound on our gate. Who was bringing whose messages, we had not a hint, so there is a big commotion, we were quite perplexed, and accepting the message brings on another commotion. When I look at it, the paper and so on are not what you would expect in such a letter; I had heard from of old that in such a case the hand would be perfect, but the writing in this is so bad that I feel it couldn't be that sort of letter; it is so very strange. The words were:

> Only to listen
> to your sound alone is sad,
> cuckoo bird,
> would that I could speak with you,
> this is what my heart longs for.

and that was all. When we all discuss it, "How about it? Does it require a reply?" my old mother says, "It does." So feeling obliged, I have someone write:

> Toward this village
> where there's no one to speak with,
> cuckoo bird,
> do not flutter a voice that
> would be quite to no avail.

1. Translated by Sonja Arntzen.

With that as a beginning, there were missives one after another, but as I did not reply, there came this:

> So faint, I strain
> to hear this soundless waterfall,
> you are its water,
> though I know not where it goes,
> yet I seek the ford to meet.

* * *

I passed a miserable spring and summer, and then, around the end of the Eighth Month, I somehow gave birth to a child. His care for me at that time was most tender.

Then, around the Ninth Month, just when he had left one day, for no particular reason, I opened a box that happened to be there and saw a letter obviously intended for another woman. Greatly astonished and thinking I would at least let him know that I had seen it, I write on the letter:

> How suspicious,
> I see this letter's tracks lead
> to another's door,
> As for here, am I to think
> your visits will be no more?

As I worried, things went much as I feared, and around the end of the Tenth Month, there comes a time when I do not see him for three nights in a row. With an air of unconcern, he excuses himself by saying, "I just wanted to test your feelings by staying away for a while."

When evening falls, he says, "There is some business at court that I can't get out of," and leaves; I do not believe him and have a man follow him who comes back saying, "It seems that his Lordship went to a certain place on Machi Alley and stayed there." So that is how it was; although I was utterly miserable, I didn't know what to say; it was about two or three days afterward, just before dawn, that there was a knocking on my gate. Thinking that it must be him, I felt wretched, and as I did not have the gate opened, he went off to that other place. The next morning, I felt I couldn't just leave things as they were, so I composed:

> Sorrow, sorrowing
> when one sleeps alone the time
> until night opens
> into day, how long it is
> perhaps you now know it too.

I wrote this with more than usual care and sent it attached to a faded chrysanthemum. His response, "I was going to wait until dawn to see what would happen, but just then a messenger from the court came and called me away. It was just as you say":

> Truly, truly so,
> even though the fine wood gate is
> not a winter's night,
> to be so late to open,
> how miserable it is.

Well, it got very strange; he carried on quite openly as though there was nothing amiss when one might have expected him to try and hide the affair a little and make excuses about having to work at court and such. He became more and more inconsiderate; there was no end to it.

* * *

Just as I thought would happen, I have ended up going to bed and waking up alone. So far as the world at large is concerned, there is nothing unsuitable about us as a couple; it's just that his heart is not as I would have it; it is not only me who is being neglected, I hear he has stopped visiting the place that he has been familiar with for years. As I have exchanged correspondence with that lady before, I send this to her on the third or fourth day of the Fifth Month:

> Even from your pond's depths,
> they say it has been reaped,
> the wild rice,
> in what marsh now does it put
> down its roots and stay to sleep?

Her reply:

> The wild rice,
> whence it is reaped, is of course,
> this Yodo marsh, its home,
> but I thought the marsh where it
> took root and slept was your place.

* * *

At the place that was in such ascendancy these days, it became time for the birth of a child, and choosing an auspicious direction in which to remove her for the lying in, he rode out in a single carriage with her, raising a continuous din that could be heard over the entire capital. It was such a racket, so painful to my ears, and did he really have to pass right by my gate? I scarcely felt like myself at all, unable to say anything, and hearing noisy complaints from the lowliest servants to my closest attendants, who were saying things like, "Such a thing, it tears one apart. And there are so many other streets he could have taken," I thought that all I wanted to do was die, yet things do not go as we want. From now on, I thought wretchedly, if the best is not to be, then it would be better to break off relations entirely so that I wouldn't have to see him. About three or four days after this, there is a letter from him. Thinking over and over to myself as I read it how awfully cold it was, I noticed this, "Someone has not been feeling well here, so I have not been able to come and visit. However, just yesterday, a safe delivery was accomplished. I haven't wanted to trouble you with the ritual pollution." This surpassed all for being bizarre. I merely sent back, "Message received." When I heard that in response to my servant's inquiries, the messenger had responded, "The household was blessed with a boy," I felt as though my chest were blocked. About three or four days later, he showed up himself as though nothing were the matter. With a look on my face of *what are you doing here,* I did not welcome him in, and finding things very uncomfortable, he left. This happened often.

* * *

Things going along in this fashion, it seems that after the birth of her child, that "splendid" personage of Machi Alley lost favor; in the midst of my feelings of hatred, I had wished to see her live long enough to suffer just as I had; now not only had that come to pass, but to top it all off, was not the child that had been the occasion of all that annoying clatter dead? The lady was the "wild oats" of an unrecognized son of a prince.

Needless to say, she was extremely base. Just for a time, she had been able to cause a stir among unknowing people; now suddenly it had come to this—how must she be feeling? When I thought she must be even a little more miserable than I had been, at that moment, I felt as though I could breathe again. Now, I hear they have "swept the pillow" for him at his former place. However, as for here, since he visits as irregularly as before, there are times when I think there is no affection left between us. My little one here has just begun to say a few words. Whenever his father takes leave of us, he always says, "See you soon," and the little one hearing this goes around imitating him.

* * *

In this way, our marriage has continued for ten plus one or two more years, looking like a match others would not find disagreeable. Yet, actually I had spent all this time, dawn until dusk, ceaselessly lamenting that it was not a marriage like others. This is understandable for someone in a position like mine—on the nights when he neglects to visit, I feel forlorn about having so few people in the household. And these days, as for the only man I can really rely on, my father, he has just been marching around the provinces for the last ten years and more. Even on the rare occasions when he is in the capital, since he lives between Fourth and Fifth Avenues and I live alongside the stables for the Guardsmen of the Left, we are so far apart. Thus, my house, with no one to take it in hand, falls into a worse and worse state of disrepair. And that my husband can come and go from this house without noticing a thing makes me feel especially forlorn; when I think that it must indicate a lack of deep regard for me, a thousand weeds of worry grow rank in my mind. He says he is overrun with busy affairs, well, he must be more overrun than my rundown house is overrun with mugwort. With my brooding on such things as these, the Eighth Month arrived.

One day when we were passing a quiet time together, we began to argue over a trifle and ended up, both he and I, saying nasty things to one another; he had a fit of anger and left. He walked out onto the veranda and called our young one to him, and among other things said, "I will no longer be coming here." As soon as he had left, my son came into the room, convulsed with sobbing. "Now, now, what's the matter?" I said, but he didn't answer. Of course, I could imagine how it was for him, but as it seemed foolish to have everybody else hear about it, I stopped questioning him and did what I could to calm him down. Thus, as many as five or six days passed without a word from him. He had never done anything like this before, it seemed crazy, and here I was thinking that it was a kind of joke, but as our relationship was such a fragile thing, it could actually end just like this, I thought. Brooding despondently, I happened to notice the basin of water he had used for dressing his hair the day he had left; there it was, just as it had been. There was dust on it. Has it come to this? Startled I wrote:

> Is this the end?
> I would ask your reflection
> if it were there, but
> on the water left behind as a
> memento, a film has formed.

On the very day I was brooding on such things as these, he appeared. It was difficult between us as usual. At times like this, I felt just as though my chest was being crushed, my heart could not feel at ease, I was wretched.

* * *

Thus, the years and months have piled up. As I lament that this has not been the life I wanted, even the voices of well-wishers mingling with the birds singing anew bring no happiness. All the more I sense how fleeting everything is. The feeling arises—am I, is the world, here or not?—this could be called the diary of a mayfly or the shimmering heat on a summer's day.

* * *

I continued to sink deeper into a depression; all I could think about was if only I could die as my heart desired, but when I think about my only child, I get very sad. If only he would grow up and I could leave him in the care of some dependable wife, then I could die in peace, but failing that, how bereft he would be; thinking about that, it seems very difficult to die. When I said to him one day, "How would it be, if I were to take the tonsure and try separating myself from the suffering of this world," even though he is still not capable of deeply understanding things, he began to sob piteously. "If you were to do that, I would surely become a monk myself. How could I involve myself in the affairs of the world after that?" And as he broke out sobbing again, I too could no longer hold back my tears, but in the midst of our misery, I tried to make a joke out of it. "Well then, if you became a monk, how could you possibly manage without your hawks," at which he got up quietly, ran to his tethered hawks, untied them all, and let them go. Even the attendants looking on couldn't help crying, and I was sad the whole day long. This is just how I felt:

> Quarrel between us
> miserable, I would become
> a nun, yet how sad,
> first to see his hawks soaring
> to the sky, he to shave his head.

At the end of the day, a letter appeared from my husband. As I thought that it was full of nothing but boldfaced lies, I sent back, "I'm not feeling very well at the moment."

* * *

On the first day of the fourth month, I called my son from the other house, "I am to start a long fast. I have been told to have you accompany me." Saying this, I began. From the first, I had not intended to have my devotions be an elaborate thing; I just burned some incense in an earthenware container, placed it on top of an armrest, and, leaning over it, intoned prayers to the Buddha. The sense of my prayers was just this: *I have become a person of no happiness. Thinking how miserable it was that over the years my heart has never known any peace and now it has come to this awful turn in our marriage, please let me quickly perfect my practice and achieve enlightenment.* Performing my devotions in this manner, the tears trickled down. Ah, I remember one time when I heard that at that time there was hardly a woman without a rosary dangling from her wrist and a sutra in her hand, I had said, "What a miserable sight they must be; that sort of woman is bound to lose her husband"; now where had it gone, that desire to criticize. From dawn to dusk, with unsettled heart, not letting up for a minute, even though I had no sense of getting anywhere, I poured myself into the practice. Ah, but the thought came again and again—*how strange I must look to people who had heard me condemn other women in the same situation, "And when she had such a fragile marriage herself, how could she say such things."* There was not a time when that thought came to mind that the tears did not well up. Before the eyes of others, I felt so ashamed to present such a miserable appearance; I passed each day from dawn till dusk constantly repressing tears.

On about the twentieth day of my practice, in a dream, I see myself with my hair cut short and parted at the forehead. I know not whether it bodes well or ill. About seven or eight days later, I dream that there is a snake moving around inside me eating my liver, and to cure this I have to splash water on my face. I have no idea whether this dream too bodes well or ill, but I record them here so that people who might see how I ended up may judge whether these dreams were sent from the Buddha or not.

+—+ ≡◆≡ +—+

Sei Shōnagon
c. 965–c. 1017

Sei Shōnagon came from the same kind of social background as Murasaki Shikibu. She was the daughter of Kiyohara Motosuke, a provincial governor and a famous *waka* poet. (The name Sei is the Sino-Japanese reading for the initial element, Kiyo, in Kiyohara.) Shōnagon, which means minor councilor, was the position she had in the palace. She is thought to have married Tachibana no Norimitsu, a provincial governor, when they were both around eighteen.

In 990 Fujiwara Kaneie, the husband of the author of *The Kagerō Diary,* stepped down from his position as regent and gave it to Fujiwara Michitaka, who was referred to as Middle Regent. Michitaka married his daughter, Teishi, to Emperor Ichijō in 990, and she soon became an imperial consort and then empress. Sei Shōnagon became a lady in waiting to Teishi in 993, the year that Michitaka became Chancellor. In 994, Korechika, Michitaka's eldest son and the apparent heir to the regency, became Minister of the Center, but in 995 Michitaka died in an epidemic, and in the following year Korechika was exiled (in a move engineered by Michitaka's younger brother and rival Michinaga), and Teishi was forced to leave the imperial palace. Until Teishi died from childbirth in 1000, Sei Shōnagon continued to serve her. Meantime, Shōshi, Michinaga's daughter and Murasaki Shikibu's mistress, became an imperial consort to Emperor Ichijō in 999, marking the ascent of Michinaga to the pinnacle of power.

The Pillowbook was finished around 1005, after the demise of Teishi's salon. It focuses on the years 993–994, when the Michitaka family and Teishi had been at the height of their glory and ignores the subsequent tragedy. A number of the noted women writers of this time, such as Murasaki Shikibu, Izumi Shikibu, and Akazome'emon, were ladies-in-waiting in Empress Shōshi's salon. Only Sei Shōnagon's *Pillowbook* represents the rival salon of Empress Teishi. Like many other diaries by court women, *The Pillowbook* can be seen as a memorial to the author's patron, specifically, an homage to the family of the Middle Regent (Michitaka) and a literary prayer to the spirit of the deceased empress Teishi. One of the few indirect references to the sad circumstances that befell Teishi's family is "The Cat Who Lived in the Palace," a story about the cruel punishment, sudden exile, and ignominious return of the dog Okinamaro, who, like the Middle Regent's son Korechika, secretly returned to the capital and was later pardoned.

The three hundred short sections of *The Pillowbook* can be divided into three different types—aesthetic, essay, and diary—which sometimes overlap. The aesthetic sections consist of noun sections, which describe particular categories of things such as "Flowering trees," and which tend to focus on nature or poetic topics, and adjectival sections, which describe a particular state, such as "Depressing things" and "Hateful things," and which include interesting lists; particularly in the case of negative adjectives, these sections are often humorous and witty.

Some manuscripts of *The Pillowbook* treat these three section types by separating them into three large groups. By contrast, these three types are mixed together in the versions known as "the Nōin variant" and "the Sankan variant," which is translated below and which has become the canonical version. The end result is that *The Pillowbook* tends to appear ahistorical; events aren't presented in chronological order but instead move back and forth in time, with no particular development or climax, creating a sense of a world suspended in time, a mode perhaps appropriate for a paean to Teishi's family.

Much of *The Pillowbook* is about aristocratic women's education, especially the need for aesthetic awareness as well as erudition, allusiveness, and extreme refinement in communication. Sei Shōnagon shows a particular concern for delicacy and harmony, for the proper combination of object, sense, and circumstance, usually a fusion of human and natural worlds. Incongruity and disharmony, by contrast, become the butt of Sei Shōnagon's sharp wit. *The Pillowbook* is often read as a personal record of accomplishments, with a number of sections focusing on incidents that display the author's talent. Indeed, much of the interest of *The Pillowbook* has been in the strong character and personality of Sei Shōnagon.

The Pillowbook is noted for its distinctive prose style: its rhythmic, quick-moving, compressed, and varied sentences, often set up in alternating couplets. Japanese syntax usually ends with a verb, but the phrases and sentences in *The Pillowbook* often end with nouns or eliminate the exclamatory and connective particles so characteristic of Heian women's literature. The compact, forceful, bright, witty style stands in contrast to the soft, meandering, often somber style found in *The Tale of Genji* and other works by Heian women. Indeed, the adjectival sections in particular have the quality of comic linked verse, marked by witty, unexpected juxtapositions, with a topic or puzzle given at the beginning and then answered or linked in different, unexpected, and often humorous ways.

The Pillowbook is now considered one of the twin pillars of Heian literature, but in contrast to the *Kokinshū, The Tales of Ise,* and *The Tale of Genji,* which had become the vernacular canon by the end of the twelfth century, *The Pillowbook* was not a required text for *waka* poets (perhaps because it contained almost no poetry) and was relatively neglected in the Heian and medieval periods. *The Pillowbook,* however, became popular among the new commoner audience in the Edo period and was widely read for its style, humor, and interesting lists. By the modern period, it was treated as an exemplar of the genre known as *zuihitsu* (literally, meanderings of the brush), the miscellaneous essay centered on personal observations and musings.

from The Pillowbook[1]

1. In Spring It Is the Dawn

In spring it is the dawn that is most beautiful. As the light creeps over the hills, their outlines are dyed a faint red and wisps of purplish cloud trail over them.

In summer the nights. Not only when the moon shines, but on dark nights too, as the fireflies flit to and fro, and even when it rains, how beautiful it is!

In autumn the evenings, when the glittering sun sinks close to the edge of the hills and the crows fly back to their nests in threes and fours and twos; more charming still is a file of wild geese, like specks in the distant sky. When the sun has set, one's heart is moved by the sound of the wind and the hum of the insects.

In winter the early mornings. It is beautiful indeed when snow has fallen during the night, but splendid too when the ground is white with frost; or even when there is no snow or frost, but it is simply very cold and the attendants hurry from room to room stirring up the fires and bringing charcoal, how well this fits the season's mood! But as noon approaches and the cold wears off, no one bothers to keep the braziers alight, and soon nothing remains but piles of white ashes.

---

1. Translated by Ivan Morris.

8. The Cat Who Lived in the Palace

The cat who lived in the Palace had been awarded the head-dress of nobility and was called Lady Myōbu. She was a very pretty cat, and His Majesty saw to it that she was treated with the greatest care.

One day she wandered on to the veranda, and Lady Uma, the nurse in charge of her, called out, "Oh, you naughty thing! Please come inside at once." But the cat paid no attention and went on basking sleepily in the sun. Intending to give her a scare, the nurse called for the dog, Okinamaro.

"Okinamaro, where are you?" she cried. "Come here and bite Lady Myōbu!" The foolish Okinamaro, believing that the nurse was in earnest, rushed at the cat, who, startled and terrified, ran behind the blind in the Imperial Dining Room, where the Emperor happened to be sitting. Greatly surprised, His Majesty picked up the cat and held her in his arms. He summoned his gentlemen-in-waiting. When Tadataka, the Chamberlain, appeared, His Majesty ordered that Okinamaro be chastised and banished to Dog Island. The attendants all started to chase the dog amid great confusion. His Majesty also reproached Lady Uma. "We shall have to find a new nurse for our cat," he told her. "I no longer feel I can count on you to look after her." Lady Uma bowed; thereafter she no longer appeared in the Emperor's presence.

The Imperial Guards quickly succeeded in catching Okinamaro and drove him out of the Palace grounds. Poor dog! He used to swagger about so happily. Recently, on the third day of the Third Month, when the Controller First Secretary paraded him through the Palace grounds, Okinamaro was adorned with garlands of willow leaves, peach blossoms on his head, and cherry blossoms round his body. How could the dog have imagined that this would be his fate? We all felt sorry for him. "When Her Majesty was having her meals," recalled one of the ladies-in-waiting, "Okinamaro always used to be in attendance and sit opposite us. How I miss him!"

It was about noon, a few days after Okinamaro's banishment, that we heard a dog howling fearfully. How could any dog possibly cry so long? All the other dogs rushed out in excitement to see what was happening. Meanwhile a woman who served as a cleaner in the Palace latrines ran up to us. "It's terrible," she said. "Two of the Chamberlains are flogging a dog. They'll surely kill him. He's being punished for having come back after he was banished. It's Tadataka and Sanefusa who are beating him." Obviously the victim was Okinamaro. I was absolutely wretched and sent a servant to ask the men to stop; but just then the howling finally ceased. "He's dead," one of the servants informed me. "They've thrown his body outside the gate."

That evening, while we were sitting in the Palace bemoaning Okinamaro's fate, a wretched-looking dog walked in; he was trembling all over, and his body was fearfully swollen.

"Oh dear," said one of the ladies-in-waiting. "Can this be Okinamaro? We haven't seen any other dog like him recently, have we?"

We called to him by name, but the dog did not respond. Some of us insisted that it was Okinamaro, others that it was not. "Please send for Lady Ukon," said the Empress, hearing our discussion. "She will certainly be able to tell." We immediately went to Ukon's room and told her she was wanted on an urgent matter.

"Is this Okinamaro?" the Empress asked her, pointing to the dog.

"Well," said Ukon, "it certainly looks like him, but I cannot believe that this loathsome creature is really our Okinamaro. When I called Okinamaro, he always used to come to me, wagging his tail. But this dog does not react at all. No, it cannot be the same one. And besides, wasn't Okinamaro beaten to death and his body thrown away? How could any dog be alive after being flogged by two strong men?" Hearing this, Her Majesty was very unhappy.

When it got dark, we gave the dog something to eat; but he refused it, and we finally decided that this could not be Okinamaro.

On the following morning I went to attend the Empress while her hair was being dressed and she was performing her ablutions. I was holding up the mirror for her when the dog we had seen on the previous evening slunk into the room and crouched next to one of the pillars. "Poor Okinamaro!" I said. "He had such a dreadful beating yesterday. How sad to think he is dead! I wonder what body he has been born into this time. Oh, how he must have suffered!"

At that moment the dog lying by the pillar started to shake and tremble, and shed a flood of tears. It was astounding. So this really was Okinamaro! On the previous night it was to avoid betraying himself that he had refused to answer to his name. We were immensely moved and pleased. "Well, well, Okinamaro!" I said, putting down the mirror. The dog stretched himself flat on the floor and yelped loudly, so that the Empress beamed with delight. All the ladies gathered round, and Her Majesty summoned Lady Ukon. When the Empress explained what had happened, everyone talked and laughed with great excitement.

The news reached His Majesty, and he too came to the Empress's room. "It's amazing," he said with a smile. "To think that even a dog has such deep feelings!" When the Emperor's ladies-in-waiting heard the story, they too came along in a great crowd. "Okinamaro!" we called, and this time the dog rose and limped about the room with his swollen face. "He must have a meal prepared for him," I said. "Yes," said the Empress, laughing happily, "now that Okinamaro has finally told us who he is."

The Chamberlain, Tadataka, was informed, and he hurried along from the Table Room. "Is it really true?" he asked. "Please let me see for myself." I sent a maid to him with the following reply: "Alas, I am afraid that this is not the same dog after all." "Well," answered Tadataka, "whatever you say, I shall sooner or later have occasion to see the animal. You won't be able to hide him from me indefinitely."

Before long, Okinamaro was granted an Imperial pardon and returned to his former happy state. Yet even now, when I remember how he whimpered and trembled in response to our sympathy, it strikes me as a strange and moving scene; when people talk to me about it, I start crying myself.

13. Depressing Things

A dog howling in the daytime. A wickerwork fish-net in spring. A red plum-blossom dress in the Third or Fourth Months. A lying-in room when the baby has died. A cold, empty brazier. An ox-driver who hates his oxen. A scholar whose wife has one girl child after another.

One has gone to a friend's house to avoid an unlucky direction, but nothing is done to entertain one; if this should happen at the time of a Seasonal Change, it is still more depressing.

A letter arrives from the provinces, but no gift accompanies it. It would be bad enough if such a letter reached one in the provinces from someone in the capital; but then at least it would have interesting news about goings-on in society, and that would be a consolation.

One has written a letter, taking pains to make it as attractive as possible, and now one impatiently awaits the reply. "Surely the messenger should be back by now," one thinks. Just then he returns; but in his hand he carries, not a reply, but one's own letter, still twisted or knotted as it was sent, but now so dirty and crumpled that even the ink-mark on the outside has disappeared. "Not at home," announces the messenger, or else, "They said they were observing a day of abstinence and would not accept it." Oh, how depressing!

Again, one has sent one's carriage to fetch someone who had said he would definitely pay one a visit on that day. Finally it returns with a great clatter, and the servants hurry out with cries of "Here they come!" But next one hears the carriage being pulled into the coach-house, and the unfastened shafts clatter to the ground. "What does this mean?" one asks. "The person was not at home," replies the driver, "and will not be coming." So saying, he leads the ox back to its stall, leaving the carriage in the coach-house.

With much bustle and excitement a young man has moved into the house of a certain family as the daughter's husband. One day he fails to come home, and it turns out that some high-ranking Court lady has taken him as her lover. How depressing! "Will he eventually tire of the woman and come back to us?" his wife's family wonder ruefully.

The nurse who is looking after a baby leaves the house, saying that she will be back presently. Soon the child starts crying for her. One tries to comfort it by games and other diversions, and even sends a message to the nurse telling her to return immediately. Then comes her reply: "I am afraid that I cannot be back this evening." This is not only depressing; it is no less than hateful. Yet how much more distressed must be the young man who has sent a messenger to fetch a lady friend and who awaits her arrival in vain!

It is quite late at night and a woman has been expecting a visitor. Hearing finally a stealthy tapping, she sends her maid to open the gate and lies waiting excitedly. But the name announced by the maid is that of someone with whom she has absolutely no connexion. Of all the depressing things this is by far the worst.

With a look of complete self-confidence on his face an exorcist prepares to expel an evil spirit from his patient. Handing his mace, rosary, and other paraphernalia to the medium who is assisting him, he begins to recite his spells in the special shrill tone that he forces from his throat on such occasions. For all the exorcist's efforts, the spirit gives no sign of leaving, and the Guardian Demon fails to take possession of the medium. The relations and friends of the patient, who are gathered in the room praying, find this rather unfortunate. After he has recited his incantations for the length of an entire watch, the exorcist is worn out. "The Guardian Demon is completely inactive," he tells his medium. "You may leave." Then, as he takes back his rosary, he adds, "Well, well, it hasn't worked!" He passes his hand over his forehead, then yawns deeply (he of all people!) and leans back against a pillar for a nap.

Most depressing is the household of some hopeful candidate who fails to receive a post during the period of official appointments. Hearing that the gentleman was bound to be successful, several people have gathered in his house for the occasion; among them are a number of retainers who served him in the past but who since then have either been engaged elsewhere or moved to some remote province. Now they are all eager to accompany their former master on his visit to the shrines and temples, and their carriages pass to and fro in the courtyard. Indoors there is a great commotion as the hangers-on help themselves to food and drink. Yet the dawn of the last day of the appointments arrives and still no one has knocked at the gate. The people in the house are nervous and prick up their ears.

Presently they hear the shouts of fore-runners and realize that the high dignitaries are leaving the Palace. Some of the servants were sent to the Palace on the previous evening to hear the news and have been waiting all night, trembling with cold; now they come trudging back listlessly. The attendants who have remained faithfully in the gentleman's service year after year cannot bring themselves to ask what has happened. His former retainers, however, are not so diffident. "Tell us," they say, "what appointment did His Excellency receive?" "Indeed," murmur the servants, "His Excellency was Governor of such-and-such a province." Everyone was counting on his receiving a new appointment, and is desolated by this failure. On the following day the people who had crowded into the house begin to slink away in twos and threes. The old attendants, however, cannot leave so easily. They walk restlessly about the house, counting on their fingers the provincial appointments that will become available in the following year. Pathetic and depressing in the extreme!

One has sent a friend a verse that turned out fairly well. How depressing when there is no reply-poem! Even in the case of love poems, people should at least answer that they were moved at receiving the message, or something of the sort; otherwise they will cause the keenest disappointment.

Someone who lives in a bustling, fashionable household receives a message from an elderly person who is behind the times and has very little to do; the poem, of course, is old-fashioned and dull. How depressing!

One needs a particularly beautiful fan for some special occasion and instructs an artist, in whose talents one has full confidence, to decorate one with an appropriate painting. When the day comes and the fan is delivered, one is shocked to see how badly it has been painted. Oh, the dreariness of it!

A messenger arrives with a present at a house where a child has been born or where someone is about to leave on a journey. How depressing for him if he gets no reward! People should always reward a messenger, though he may bring only herbal balls or hare-sticks. If he expects nothing, he will be particularly pleased to be rewarded. On the other hand, what a terrible let-down if he arrives with a self-important look on his face, his heart pounding in anticipation of a generous reward, only to have his hopes dashed!

A man has moved in as a son-in-law; yet even now, after some five years of marriage, the lying-in room has remained as quiet as on the day of his arrival.

An elderly couple who have several grown-up children, and who may even have some grandchildren crawling about the house, are taking a nap in the daytime. The children who see them in this state are overcome by a forlorn feeling, and for other people it is all very depressing.

To take a hot bath when one has just woken is not only depressing; it actually puts one in a bad humour.

Persistent rain on the last day of the year.

One has been observing a period of fast, but neglects it for just one day—most depressing.

A white under-robe in the Eighth Month.

A wet-nurse who has run out of milk.

14. Hateful Things

One is in a hurry to leave, but one's visitor keeps chattering away. If it is someone of no importance, one can get rid of him by saying, "You must tell me all about it next time"; but, should it be the sort of visitor whose presence commands one's best behaviour, the situation is hateful indeed.

One finds that a hair has got caught in the stone on which one is rubbing one's inkstick, or again that gravel is lodged in the inkstick, making a nasty, grating sound.

Someone has suddenly fallen ill and one summons the exorcist. Since he is not at home, one has to send messengers to look for him. After one has had a long fretful wait, the exorcist finally arrives, and with a sigh of relief one asks him to start his incantations. But perhaps he has been exorcizing too many evil spirits recently; for hardly has he installed himself and begun praying when his voice becomes drowsy. Oh, how hateful!

A man who has nothing in particular to recommend him discusses all sorts of subjects at random as though he knew everything.

An elderly person warms the palms of his hands over a brazier and stretches out the wrinkles. No young man would dream of behaving in such a fashion; old people can really be quite shameless. I have seen some dreary old creatures actually resting their feet on the brazier and rubbing them against the edge while they speak. These are the kind of people who in visiting someone's house first use their fans to wipe away the dust from the mat and, when they finally sit on it, cannot stay still but are forever spreading out the front of their hunting costume or even tucking it up under their knees. One might suppose that such behaviour was restricted to people of humble station; but I have observed it in quite well-bred people, including a Senior Secretary of the Fifth Rank in the Ministry of Ceremonial and a former Governor of Suruga.

I hate the sight of men in their cups who shout, poke their fingers in their mouths, stroke their beards, and pass on the wine to their neighbours with great cries of "Have some more! Drink up!" They tremble, shake their heads, twist their faces, and gesticulate like children who are singing, "We're off to see the Governor." I have seen really well-bred people behave like this and I find it most distasteful.

To envy others and to complain about one's own lot; to speak badly about people; to be inquisitive about the most trivial matters and to resent and abuse people for not telling one, or, if one does manage to worm out some facts, to inform everyone in the most detailed fashion as if one had known all from the beginning—oh, how hateful!

One is just about to be told some interesting piece of news when a baby starts crying.

A flight of crows circle about with loud caws.

An admirer has come on a clandestine visit, but a dog catches sight of him and starts barking. One feels like killing the beast.

One has been foolish enough to invite a man to spend the night in an unsuitable place—and then he starts snoring.

A gentleman has visited one secretly. Though he is wearing a tall, lacquered hat, he nevertheless wants no one to see him. He is so flurried, in fact, that upon leaving he bangs into something with his hat. Most hateful! It is annoying too when he lifts up the Iyo blind that hangs at the entrance of the room, then lets it fall with a great rattle. If it is a head-blind, things are still worse, for being more solid it makes a terrible noise when it is dropped. There is no excuse for such carelessness. Even a head-blind does not make any noise if one lifts it up gently on entering and leaving the room; the same applies to sliding-doors. If one's movements are rough, even a paper door will bend and resonate when opened; but, if one lifts the door a little while pushing it, there need be no sound.

One has gone to bed and is about to doze off when a mosquito appears, announcing himself in a reedy voice. One can actually feel the wind made by his wings and, slight though it is, one finds it hateful in the extreme.

A carriage passes with a nasty, creaking noise. Annoying to think that the passengers may not even be aware of this! If I am travelling in someone's carriage and I hear it creaking, I dislike not only the noise but also the owner of the carriage.

One is in the middle of a story when someone butts in and tries to show that he is the only clever person in the room. Such a person is hateful, and so, indeed, is anyone, child or adult, who tries to push himself forward.

One is telling a story about old times when someone breaks in with a little detail that he happens to know, implying that one's own version is inaccurate—disgusting behaviour!

Very hateful is a mouse that scurries all over the place.

Some children have called at one's house. One makes a great fuss of them and gives them toys to play with. The children become accustomed to this treatment and start to come regularly, forcing their way into one's inner rooms and scattering one's furnishings and possessions. Hateful!

A certain gentleman whom one does not want to see visits one at home or in the Palace, and one pretends to be asleep. But a maid comes to tell one and shakes one awake, with a look on her face that says, "What a sleepyhead!" Very hateful.

A newcomer pushes ahead of the other members in a group; with a knowing look, this person starts laying down the law and forcing advice upon everyone—most hateful.

A man with whom one is having an affair keeps singing the praises of some woman he used to know. Even if it is a thing of the past, this can be very annoying. How much more so if he is still seeing the woman! (Yet sometimes I find that it is not as unpleasant as all that.)

A person who recites a spell himself after sneezing. In fact I detest anyone who sneezes, except the master of the house.

Fleas, too, are very hateful. When they dance about under someone's clothes, they really seem to be lifting them up.

The sound of dogs when they bark for a long time in chorus is ominous and hateful.

I cannot stand people who leave without closing the panel behind them.

How I detest the husbands of nurse-maids! It is not so bad if the child in the maid's charge is a girl, because then the man will keep his distance. But, if it is a boy, he will behave as though he were the father. Never letting the boy out of his sight, he insists on managing everything. He regards the other attendants in the house as less than human, and, if anyone tries to scold the child, he slanders him to the master. Despite this disgraceful behaviour, no one dare accuse the husband; so he strides about the house with a proud, self-important look, giving all the orders.

I hate people whose letters show that they lack respect for worldly civilities, whether by discourtesy in the phrasing or by extreme politeness to someone who does not deserve it. This sort of thing is, of course, most odious if the letter is for oneself, but it is bad enough even if it is addressed to someone else.

As a matter of fact, most people are too casual, not only in their letters but in their direct conversation. Sometimes I am quite disgusted at noting how little decorum people observe when talking to each other. It is particularly unpleasant to hear some foolish man or woman omit the proper marks of respect when addressing a person of quality; and, when servants fail to use honorific forms of speech in referring to their masters, it is very bad indeed. No less odious, however, are those masters who, in addressing their servants, use such phrases as "When you were good enough to do such-and-such" or "As you so kindly remarked." No doubt there are some masters who, in describing their own actions to a servant, say, "I presumed to do so-and-so!"

Sometimes a person who is utterly devoid of charm will try to create a good impression by using very elegant language; yet he only succeeds in being ridiculous. No doubt he believes this refined language to be just what the occasion demands, but, when it goes so far that everyone bursts out laughing, surely something must be wrong.

It is most improper to address high-ranking courtiers, Imperial Advisers, and the like simply by using their names without any titles or marks of respect; but such mistakes are fortunately rare.

If one refers to the maid who is in attendance on some lady-in-waiting as "Madam" or "that lady," she will be surprised, delighted, and lavish in her praise.

When speaking to young noblemen and courtiers of high rank, one should always (unless Their Majesties are present) refer to them by their official posts. Incidentally, I have been very shocked to hear important people use the word "I" while conversing in Their Majesties' presence. Such a breach of etiquette is really distressing, and I fail to see why people cannot avoid it.

A man who has nothing in particular to recommend him but who speaks in an affected tone and poses as being elegant.

An inkstone with such a hard, smooth surface that the stick glides over it without leaving any deposit of ink.

Ladies-in-waiting who want to know everything that is going on.

Sometimes one greatly dislikes a person for no particular reason—and then that person goes and does something hateful.

A gentleman who travels alone in his carriage to see a procession or some other spectacle. What sort of a man is he? Even though he may not be a person of the greatest quality, surely he should have taken along a few of the many young men who are anxious to see the sights. But no, there he sits by himself (one can see his silhouette through the blinds), with a proud look on his face, keeping all his impressions to himself.

A lover who is leaving at dawn announces that he has to find his fan and his paper. "I know I put them somewhere last night," he says. Since it is pitch dark, he gropes about the room, bumping into the furniture and muttering, "Strange! Where on earth can they be?" Finally he discovers the objects. He thrusts the paper into the breast of his robe with a great rustling sound; then he snaps open his fan and busily fans away with it. Only now is he ready to take his leave. What charmless behaviour! "Hateful" is an understatement.

Equally disagreeable is the man who, when leaving in the middle of the night, takes care to fasten the cord of his head-dress. This is quite unnecessary; he could perfectly well put it gently on his head without tying the cord. And why must he spend time adjusting his cloak or hunting costume? Does he really think someone may see him at this time of night and criticize him for not being impeccably dressed?

A good lover will behave as elegantly at dawn as at any other time. He drags himself out of bed with a look of dismay on his face. The lady urges him on: "Come, my friend, it's getting light. You don't want anyone to find you here." He gives a deep sigh, as if to say that the night has not been nearly long enough and that it is agony to leave. Once up, he does not instantly pull on his trousers. Instead he comes close to the lady and whispers whatever was left unsaid during the night. Even when he is dressed, he still lingers, vaguely pretending to be fastening his sash.

Presently he raises the lattice, and the two lovers stand together by the side door while he tells her how he dreads the coming day, which will keep them apart; then he slips away. The lady watches him go, and this moment of parting will remain among her most charming memories.

Indeed, one's attachment to a man depends largely on the elegance of his leave-taking. When he jumps out of bed, scurries about the room, tightly fastens his trouser-sash, rolls up the sleeves of his Court cloak, over-robe, or hunting costume, stuffs his belongings into the breast of his robe and then briskly secures the outer sash—one really begins to hate him.

47. Rare Things

A son-in-law who is praised by his adoptive father; a young bride who is loved by her mother-in-law.

A silver tweezer that is good at plucking out the hair.

A servant who does not speak badly about his master.

A person who is in no way eccentric or imperfect, who is superior in both mind and body, and who remains flawless all his life.

People who live together and still manage to behave with reserve towards each other. However much these people may try to hide their weaknesses, they usually fail.

To avoid getting ink stains on the notebook into which one is copying stories, poems, or the like. If it is a very fine notebook, one takes the greatest care not to make a blot; yet somehow one never seems to succeed.

When people, whether they be men or women or priests, have promised each other eternal friendship, it is rare for them to stay on good terms until the end.

A servant who is pleasant to his master.

One has given some silk to the fuller and, when he sends it back, it is so beautiful that one cries out in admiration.

63. Embarrassing Things

While entertaining a visitor, one hears some servants chatting without any restraint in one of the back rooms. It is embarrassing to know that one's visitor can overhear. But how to stop them?

A man whom one loves gets drunk and keeps repeating himself.

To have spoken about someone not knowing that he could overhear. This is embarrassing even if it be a servant or some other completely insignificant person.

To hear one's servants making merry. This is equally annoying if one is on a journey and staying in cramped quarters or at home and hears the servants in a neighbouring room.

Parents, convinced that their ugly child is adorable, pet him and repeat the things he has said, imitating his voice.

An ignoramus who in the presence of some learned person puts on a knowing air and converses about men of old.

A man recites his own poems (not especially good ones) and tells one about the praise they have received—most embarrassing.

Lying awake at night, one says something to one's companion, who simply goes on sleeping.

In the presence of a skilled musician, someone plays a zither just for his own pleasure and without tuning it.

A son-in-law who has long since stopped visiting his wife runs into his father-in-law in a public place.

80. Things That Have Lost Their Power

A large boat which is high and dry in a creek at ebb-tide.

A woman who has taken off her false locks to comb the short hair that remains.

A large tree that has been blown down in a gale and lies on its side with its roots in the air.

The retreating figure of a *sumō* wrestler who has been defeated in a match.

A man of no importance reprimanding an attendant.

An old man who removes his hat, uncovering his scanty topknot.

A woman, who is angry with her husband about some trifling matter, leaves home and goes somewhere to hide. She is certain that he will rush about looking for her; but he does nothing of the kind and shows the most infuriating indifference. Since she cannot stay away for ever, she swallows her pride and returns.

99. Adorable Things

The face of a child drawn on a melon.

A baby sparrow that comes hopping up when one imitates the squeak of a mouse; or again, when one has tied it with a thread round its leg and its parents bring insects or worms and pop them in its mouth—delightful!

A baby of two or so is crawling rapidly along the ground. With his sharp eyes he catches sight of a tiny object and, picking it up with his pretty little fingers, takes it to show to a grown-up person.

A child, whose hair has been cut like a nun's, is examining something; the hair falls over his eyes, but instead of brushing it away he holds his head to the side. The pretty white cords of his trouser-skirt are tied round his shoulders, and this too is most adorable.

A young Palace page, who is still quite small, walks by in ceremonial costume.

One picks up a pretty baby and holds him for a while in one's arms; while one is fondling him, he clings to one's neck and then falls asleep.

The objects used during the Display of Dolls.

One picks up a tiny lotus leaf that is floating on a pond and examines it. Not only lotus leaves, but little hollyhock flowers, and indeed all small things, are most adorable.

An extremely plump baby, who is about a year old and has a lovely white skin, comes crawling towards one, dressed in a long gauze robe of violet with the sleeves tucked up.

A little boy of about eight who reads aloud from a book in his childish voice.

Pretty, white chicks who are still not fully fledged and look as if their clothes are too short for them; cheeping loudly, they follow one on their long legs, or walk close to the mother hen.

Duck eggs.

An urn containing the relics of some holy person.

Wild pinks.

157. One Day, When the Snow Lay Thick on the Ground

One day, when the snow lay thick on the ground and it was so cold that the lattices had all been closed, I and the other ladies were sitting with Her Majesty, chatting and poking the embers in the brazier.

"Tell me, Shōnagon," said the Empress, "how is the snow on Hsiang-lu peak?"

I told the maid to raise one of the lattices and then rolled up the blind all the way. Her Majesty smiled. I was not alone in recognizing the Chinese poem she had quoted; in fact all the ladies knew the lines and had even rewritten them in Japanese. Yet no one but me had managed to think of it instantly.

"Yes indeed," people said when they heard the story. "She was born to serve an Empress like ours."

185. It Is Getting So Dark

It is getting so dark that I can scarcely go on writing; and my brush is all worn out. Yet I should like to add a few things before I end.

I wrote these notes at home, when I had a good deal of time to myself and thought no one would notice what I was doing. Everything that I have seen and felt is included. Since much of it might appear malicious and even harmful to other people, I was careful to keep my book hidden. But now it has become public, which is the last thing I expected.

One day Lord Korechika, the Minister of the Centre, brought the Empress a bundle of notebooks. "What shall we do with them?" Her Majesty asked me. "The Emperor has already made arrangements for copying the 'Records of the Historian.'"

"Let me make them into a pillow," I said.

"Very well," said Her Majesty. "You may have them."

I now had a vast quantity of paper at my disposal, and I set about filling the notebooks with odd facts, stories from the past, and all sorts of other things, often including the most trivial material. On the whole I concentrated on things and people that I found charming and splendid; my notes are also full of poems and observations on trees and plants, birds and insects. I was sure that when people saw my book they would say, "It's even worse than I expected. Now one can really tell what she is like." After all, it is written entirely for my own amusement and I put things down exactly as they came to me. How could my casual jottings possibly bear comparison with the many impressive books that exist in our time? Readers have declared, however, that I can be proud of my work. This has surprised me greatly; yet I suppose it is not so strange that people should like it, for, as will be gathered from these notes of mine, I am the sort of person who approves of what others abhor and detests the things they like.

Whatever people may think of my book, I still regret that it ever came to light.

❄ CROSSCURRENTS: COURTLY WOMEN ❄

- Much of the literature written by women during the medieval era emerged from imperial or royal courts. Sei Shōnagon's contemporary Murasaki Shikibu (page 146) was a lady-in-waiting to Empress Shōshi. The section "Women in Early China" (page 22) includes work by a member of the ruling family, an instructor to the empress, and the daughter of a landowning family. Marie de France (page 785) was a prominent member of the Anglo-Norman court of Henry II and Eleanor of Aquitaine. But there were also women writing in non-courtly settings: the Arab poet Al-Khansa (page 335) was official poet of her nomadic tribe, while Héloïse (page 856) was head abbess in a French convent. How do these different social roles manifest themselves in the themes and forms of the poems of these women?

- Anonymous and male-authored poems and tales in the voice of a woman speaker are nearly as common during the medieval era as works we can confidently identify as authored by women. What differences, if any, do you find between women-voiced literature such as the anonymous Chinese poems in "Voices of Women" (page 35), the tales recounted by Shahrazad in *The Thousand and One Nights* (page 408), and the Galician-Portuguese *cantigas de amigo* and the works by the courtly women in this section?

- In what ways can we compare the literature of the imperial court of medieval Japan with literature from courtly contexts in other times and places? What different concerns, themes, and forms emerged from the royal courts of ancient Tamil country in south India (Volume A), or women writers in eighteenth-century Europe ("Court Culture and Female Authorship," Volume D)? What similarities can you find between these disparate contexts?

- Much of the writing by women in the nineteenth and twentieth centuries was primarily concerned with the changing role of women in modern society, and often with changing that role. In what ways can we compare the writing of the writing of these courtly women with the literature of feminist writers such as Charlotte Perkins Gilman (Volume E), Mina Loy (Volume F), Virginia Woolf (Volume F), Ingeborg Bachmann (Volume F), Assia Djebar (Volume F), Zhang Aileen (Volume F), Mahasweta Devi (Volume F), and the writers in the Perspectives section on gendered spaces (Volume F)?

END OF PERSPECTIVES: COURTLY WOMEN

Tales of the Heike

14th century

Tales of the Heike (*Heike monogatari*) concerns the the Genpei War (1180–1185), fought between the Heike (Taira) clan, led by Kiyomori, and the Genji (Minamoto) clan, eventually led by Yoritomo. The initial, rapid ascent to power by the Taira is followed by an extended series of defeats, beginning with the abandonment of the capital by the Taira in 1183 (taking with them Antoku, the child emperor). By 1183 Yoritomo had gained control of the Kanto or eastern region; Yoshinaka, another Minamoto leader, had brought Kyōto under his power, and the Taira had fallen back to the Inland Sea. In an interlude of fighting among the Minamoto, Yoshinaka is defeated and eliminated by Yoritomo and his half brother Yoshitsune in 1184. In a major battle at Ichi-no-tani, in 1184, near the present-day city of Kōbe, Yoshitsune, leading the Minamoto forces, decisively defeats the Taira, driving them into the Inland Sea. Finally, in 1185, the last of the Taira forces is crushed at Dan-no-ura, in a sea battle on the west end of the Inland Sea. In the same year, Rokudai, the last potential heir of the Taira clan, is captured and later executed.

This war between the Taira and the Minamoto, which marks one of the important beginnings of the medieval period, became the basis for *Heike*, which focuses on the lives of different samurai or warriors from both clans. The narrative also includes numerous non-samurai stories drawn from popular or folk literature, many of which deal with women and priests and which are frequently transformed by the composers of *Heike* into religious narratives. So while *Heike* is a military epic, it has strong Buddhist overtones, which is especially evident in the opening passage, which stresses the Buddhist law of impermanence, that all things must pass, and in the many stories of Buddhistic disillusionment and awakening. These then culminate in a final "Death of the Imperial Lady," which leads to the salvation of Kenreimon'in, the daughter of Kiyomori. Of particular importance is the belief in the Pure Land (Jōdo)—a Western Paradise presided over by the Amida Buddha. The Pure Land Buddhist sect believed that if one chanted or invoked the name of the Amida Buddha and placed one's faith in the Amida Buddha, one would be welcomed into the Pure Land at the point of death.

Initial versions of *Heike* were probably written down by writers and priests associated with Buddhist temples, who gave the chronological, historically oriented narrative a Buddhist framework. These texts in turn were recited from memory, sung to lute music by blind minstrels who entertained a largely illiterate audience and who in turn had an impact on subsequent variants of *Heike,* which combines both highly literary texts and orally based material. Of the many variants of *Heike,* the most famous today is the Kakuichi text, a selection of which is translated here. This version was recorded in 1371 by a man named Kakuichi, a lute reciter who created a twelve-volume narrative shaped around the decline of the Heike clan and who gave the long work closure as a Buddhist text.

Due largely to Kakuichi, the oral performance of *Heike* eventually won upper-class acceptance and became a major performing art, reaching its height in the mid-fifteenth century. Such performances declined in popularity after the Ōnin War (1467–1477), but *Heike* continued to serve as a rich source for countless dramas and prose narratives. Most of the sixteen warrior pieces in today's Noh drama repertoire are drawn from *Heike.* In the Edo period, stories from *Heike* became the foundation for a number of important kabuki and jōruri (puppet) plays, thus making it one of the most influential works of premodern Japanese culture.

The first half of *Heike,* Chapters 1–6, is centered on the history of Kiyomori, the head of the Taira (Heike) clan, who comes into conflict with the Retired Emperor Go-Shirakawa and then the various Minamoto (Genji). In the latter half, Chapters 7–12, there are three important Minamoto (Genji) leaders: Yoritomo, the head of the Genji in the east; Yoshinaka (Lord Kiso), who becomes a Genji leader farther to the west; and Yoshitsune, Yoritomo's brother. However, the real focus of the narrative is not on the Genji victors—Yoritomo, the ultimate victor, plays almost a peripheral role—but on a series of defeated Taira clan figures, including Yoshinaka, or Lord Kiso (a Genji who is defeated by Yoritomo during a period of Minamoto infighting). Shigemori, Shigehira, Koremori, Munemori, and Kenreimon'in—all children of Kiyomori— bearing the sins of the father, suffer different fates on the way to death. It is not until "The Six Paths of Existence" that the tragedy of the Taira becomes an opportunity for reconciliation between Kenreimon'in, Kiyomori's daughter, and the Retired Emperor Go-Shirakawa, Kiyomori's former archenemy.

KEY FIGURES

Imperial Family

Go-Shirakawa, Retired Emperor, head of imperial clan, son of Retired Emperor Toba, and the archenemy of Kiyomori.

Kenreimon'in (Taira), Kiyomori's daughter, Emperor Takakura's consort, mother of Emperor Antoku, taken prisoner at Dan-no-ura, dies a nun.

Nun of Second Rank (Niidono), Kiyomori's principal wife and mother of Munemori, Shigehira, and Kenreimon'in, dies at Dan-no-ura.

Taira (Heike)

Atsumori, a young Taira warrior, dies at Ichi-no-tani.

Kiyomori, Taira clan head, Chancellor, lay priest of Rokuhara, dominated the court even after taking holy vows.

Munemori, son of Kiyomori and Nun of Second Rank, follows Kiyomori to become head of Taira clan.

Minamoto (Genji)

Yoritomo, leader of the Minamoto in the east, founder of the Kamakura Shogunate.

Yoshinaka, Lord Kiso, cousin of Yoritomo, leader of northern anti-Taira forces, captures Kyoto, later killed by Yoritomo's forces.

Yoshitsune, Yoritomo's younger half brother, one of Yoritomo's chief commanders, defeats Heike (Taira) at Dan-no-ura.

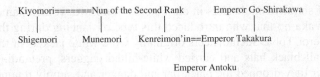

PRONUNCIATIONS:

Heike: hay-key

Minamoto: mee-na-mo-to

Kiyomori: kee-yo-mo-ri

Atsumori: ah-tsoo-mo-ri

Kenreimon'in: ken-ray-mon-in

Tales of the Heike

The Bells of Gion Monastery (1:1)[1]

The bells of the Gion monastery in India echo with the warning that all things are impermanent. The blossoms of the sal trees beneath which the Buddha died teach us through their hues that what flourishes must fade.[2] The proud do not prevail for long, but vanish like a spring night's dream. The mighty too in time succumb—all are dust before the wind.

Long ago in a different land Chao Kao of the Ch'in dynasty in China, Wang Mang of the Han, Chu Yi of the Liang, and An Lu-shan of the T'ang all refused to obey the ways laid down by former sovereigns. Pursuing every pleasure, deaf to warnings, heedless of the chaos overtaking the nation, ignorant of the sufferings of the common people, they all alike before long met downfall.

More recently in our own country there have been men like Masakado, Sumitomo, Gishin, and Nobuyori, each of them proud and fierce in the extreme. But Taira no Kiyomori, the lay priest of Rokuhara[3] and one-time Chancellor, the most recent of such men—the tales told of him are beyond the power of words to describe or the mind to imagine.

* * *

1. Translated by Burton Watson.
2. The blossoms, ordinarily yellow, turned white to express their grief.

3. Rokuhara was located in the eastern section of the capital and was the headquarters of the Taira clan.

Giō (1:6)

As Chancellor, Kiyomori now held the entire realm within the four seas in the palm of his hand. Thus, ignoring the carpings of the age, turning a deaf ear to censure, he indulged in one caprice after another. For example, there was the case of Giō and Ginyo—sisters renowned in the capital at the time for their skillful performance as *shirabyōshi* dancers. They were the daughters of a shirabyōshi dancer named Toji. Giō, the older sister, had succeeded in winning extraordinary favor with Kiyomori. Thus, the younger sister, Ginyo, enjoyed wide repute among the people of the time. Kiyomori built a fine house for the mother, Toji, providing her with a monthly stipend of a hundred piculs of rice and a hundred strings of coins, so that the entire family prospered and lived a life of ease.

The first shirabyōshi dancers in our country were two women named Shima-no-senzai and Waka-no-mai who introduced this type of dancing during the time of the Retired Emperor Toba. Such dancers originally wore white jackets of the kind called *suikan* and tall black hats and carried white-hilted daggers, pretending to be male dancers. Later they dropped the black hat and dagger and simply retained the *suikan* jacket, and at that time they became known as shirabyōshi or "white tempo" dances.[1]

As Giō became renowned among the shirabyōshi of the capital for the extraordinary favor she enjoyed, there were some who envied her and others who spoke of her with spite. Those who envied her said, "What splendid good fortune this Lady Giō enjoys! Any woman entertainer would be delighted to be in her place. Her good fortune doubtless derives from the Gi element that makes up the first part of her name. We should have a try at that too!" Giichi, Gini, Gifuku and Gitoku were some of the names that resulted.

But the scorners took a different view. "How could fortune come from a name alone?" they asked. "It is due solely to good karma acquired in a previous existence!" and they declined for the most part to change their names.

After some three years had passed, another highly skilled shirabyōshi dancer appeared in the capital, a native of the province of Kaga named Hotoke or "Buddha." She was said to be only sixteen. Everyone in the capital, high and low alike, exclaimed over her, declaring that among all the shirabyōshi dancers from times past, none could rival her.

Lady Hotoke thought to herself, "I have won fame throughout the realm, but I have yet to realize my true ambition, to be summoned by this Chancellor of the Taira clan who is now at the height of power. Since it is the practice among entertainers, why should I hold back? I will go present myself!" Accordingly she went and presented herself at Kiyomori's Nishi Shijō mansion.

When Kiyomori was informed that the Lady Hotoke who enjoyed such renown in the capital at that time had come to call, he exclaimed, "What does this mean? Entertainers of that type should wait for a summons—they do not simply take it upon themselves to appear! I don't care whether she's a god or a buddha—I already have Giō in my service! Send her away!"

Refused admission in this summary manner, Hotoke was preparing to take her leave when Giō spoke to the Chancellor. "It is quite usual for entertainers to present themselves in this way. Moreover, the girl is still young and has just happened to hit on this idea—it would be a shame to dismiss her in such a cold fashion. I for one

---

1. Shirabyōshi, literally "white tempo," was a popular dance form that emerged in the late Heian period.

would be greatly distressed. We are devotees of the same art and I cannot help feeling sympathy for her. Even if you do not let her dance or listen to her singing, at least admit her into your presence before you send her away. That would be the kind thing to do. Bend your principles a bit and call her in."

"If you are so insistent," replied Kiyomori, "I will see her," and he sent word to have her admitted.

Lady Hotoke, having been rudely dismissed, was about to mount her carriage and depart, but at the summons she returned and presented herself.

"I had no intention of admitting you," Kiyomori announced when they met. "But Giō for some reason was so adamant that, as you see, I agreed to the meeting. And since you are here, I suppose I should find out what sort of voice you have. Try singing an *imayō*[2] for me."

"As you wish," replied Lady Hotoke, and she obliged with the following song in the imayō style:

> Since I met you, I'm like the little pine
>> destined for a thousand years!
> On turtle-shaped isles of your pond,
>> how many the cranes that flock there![3]

She repeated the song, singing it three times over, while all the persons present listened and looked on in wonder at her skill.

Kiyomori was obviously much impressed. "You are very good at *imayō*," he said, "and I have no doubt that your dancing is of the same order. Let's have a look. Call in the musicians!"

When the musicians appeared, Hotoke performed a dance to their accompaniment. Everything about her was captivating, from her hairdo and costume to her appearance as a whole, and her voice was pleasing and artfully employed, so her dancing could not fail to make an impression. In fact, it far exceeded Kiyomori's expectations, and he was so moved by her performance that he fell in love with her immediately.

"This is somewhat troubling," said Hotoke. "Originally I was not to be admitted but sent away at once. But through the kind offices of Lady Giō, I was allowed to present myself. Having done so, I would be most reluctant to do anything that would run counter to Lady Giō's intentions. I beg to be excused as soon as possible so that I may be on my way."

"There is no reason for that!" replied Kiyomori. "But if you feel uneasy in Giō's presence, I will see that she withdraws."

"But how would that look?" objected Hotoke. "It was uneasy enough to find that the two of us had been summoned here together. If now, after all her kindness, she were dismissed and I were to remain behind, think how dreadful I would feel! If by chance you happen to remember me, perhaps you might summon me again at some future time. But for today I beg to take my leave."

Kiyomori, however, would not hear of this. "Nonsense!" he said. "You will do no such thing. Let Giō withdraw at once!" Three times he repeated these instructions to the attendant.

---

2. A song form consisting of four lines of 7/5 syllables, which became popular from the 11th century onward.

3. Pines, turtles, and cranes are symbols of longevity.

Giō had long been aware that something like this might happen, but she was not expecting it "this very day."[4] Faced with repeated orders to quit the house at once, however, she resigned herself to doing so and set about sweeping and tidying her room and clearing it of anything unsightly.

Even those who have only sought shelter under the same tree for a night, or merely dipped water from the same stream, will feel sorrow on parting. How sorrowful, then, was Giō's departure from the place where she had lived these three years. Her tears, futile as they were, showered down. Since there was nothing to be done, however, she prepared to take her leave. But, thinking perhaps to leave behind some reminder of herself, she inscribed the following poem on the sliding panel of the room, weeping as she did so:

> Those that put out new shoots,
> those that wither are the same
> grasses of the field—
> come autumn,
> is there one that will not fade?

Mounting her carriage, she returned to her home and there, sinking down within the panels of the room, gave herself up to weeping.

"What has happened? What is wrong?" her mother and sister inquired, but she made no reply. It was only when they questioned the maid who had accompanied her that they learned the truth.

Before long the monthly stipend of five hundred bushels of rice and a hundred strings of coins came to an end, while Hotoke's friends and relations learned for the first time the meaning of happiness and prosperity. Among high and low, word spread throughout the capital. "They say that Giō has been dismissed from the Chancellor's service," people said. "We must go call on her and keep her company!" Some sent letters, others dispatched their servants to make inquiries. But Giō, faced with such a situation, could not bring herself to receive visitors. The letters she declined to accept, the messengers she sent off without an interview. Such gestures only served to deepen her mood of melancholy, and she passed all her time in weeping. So the year came to an end.

The following spring Kiyomori dispatched a servant to Giō's house with this message: "How have you been since we parted? Lady Hotoke appears to be so hopelessly bored that I wish you would come and perform one of your imayō songs or your dances to cheer her up."

Giō declined to give any answer.

Kiyomori tried again. "Why no answer from you, Giō? Won't you come for a visit? Say if you are not coming! I have ways of dealing with the matter!"

When Giō's mother Toji learned of the situation, she was greatly distressed and, having no idea what to do, could only plead with her daughter in tears. "Giō, at least send an answer," she begged. "Anything is better than facing these threats!"

But Giō replied, "If I had any intention of going, I would have answered long ago. It is because I have no such intention that I'm at a loss how to reply. He says that if I do not respond, he has ways of dealing with the matter. Does this mean I will be

---

4. An allusion to Ariwara Narihira's death poem: "Though I have heard often of the path each must take in the end, I never thought it would be so soon." The poem appears in both the *Kokinshū* (No. 861) and the final chapter of *The Tales of Ise*.

banished from the capital? Or that I will be put to death? Even if I were expelled from the capital I would have no great regrets. And if he wants to deprive me of my life, what of that? He once sent me away a despised person—I have no heart to face him again." Thus she refused to send an answer.

But the mother continued her entreaties. "So long as you continue to live within the realm, you cannot hope to defy the wishes of the Chancellor! The ties that bind man and woman are decreed from a past existence—they do not originate in this life alone. Those who vow to be faithful for a thousand or ten thousand years often end by parting, while those who think of it merely as an affair of the moment find themselves spending their whole lives together. In this world of ours there's no predicting how things will fare between a man and a woman.

"For three whole years you enjoyed favor with the Chancellor. That was a stroke of fortune hardly to be matched. Now if you refuse to answer his summons, it is scarcely likely you will be put to death. Probably you will merely be banished from the capital. And even if you are banished, you and your sister are young and can manage to live even in the wildest and most out-of-the-way spot. But what of your mother? I am a feeble old woman—suppose I am banished too? Just the thought of living in some strange place in the countryside fills me with despair. Let me live out the rest of my days here in the capital. It could be thought of as being filial in this world as well as the next."

Giō, much as it pained her, did not feel that she could disobey these pleas from her mother and so, weeping all the while, she set out for the Chancellor's mansion. But her heart was filled with foreboding. It would be too trying to make the trip alone, Giō felt, and therefore she took her younger sister Ginyo with her. The group of four, the sisters and two other *shirabyōshi* dancers, proceeded in one carriage to Nishi Shijō.

Upon arrival, Giō was not shown to the seat she had previously been accustomed to occupy, but instead to a far inferior place where makeshift arrangements had been made. "How can this be?" she exclaimed. "Though I was guilty of no fault, I was driven out of the house. And now I find that even the seat I occupy is subject to demotion! This is too heartless! What am I to do?" In an effort to hide her confusion, she covered her face with her sleeve, but the trickle of tears gave her away.

Hotoke, or Lady Buddha, moved to pity by the sight, appealed to Kiyomori. "What is meaning of this?" she asked. "If this were someone who had never been summoned before, it might be different. But surely she should be seated here with us. If not, I beg leave to go where she is."

"There is absolutely no reason for that!" replied Kiyomori, and Hotoke was thus helpless to make a move.

Later, Kiyomori, apparently quite unaware of Giō's feelings, asked how she had been faring since they met last. "Lady Hotoke seems so terribly bored," he remarked. "You must sing us an *imayō*."

Giō, having put in an appearance, did not feel that she could disregard the Chancellor's wishes. And so, holding back her tears, she sang the following song in *imayō* style:

> Buddha was once a common mortal,
> and we too one day will become Buddhas.
> All alike endowed with the Buddha nature,
> how sad this gulf that divides us!

Weeping all the while, she sang the song twice over. The many members of the Taira clan who were seated there—from the ministers of state, lords and high-ranking courtiers down to the housemen—were all moved to tears. Kiyomori himself listened with keen interest. "A song admirably suited to the occasion," he commented. "I wish we could watch you dance, but unfortunately today there are other things to be attended to. In the future you must not wait to be summoned but come any time you like and perform your *imayō* songs and dances for Hotoke's amusement."

Giō made no answer but, suppressing her tears, withdrew.

Reluctant to disobey her mother's command, Giō had made the trip to the Chancellor's mansion, painful as it was, and exposed herself a second time to callous treatment. Saddened by the experience, and mindful that so long as she remained in the world similar sorrows in all likelihood awaited her, Giō spoke of throwing her life away.

"If you do away with yourself," said her sister Ginyo, "I will do likewise!"

The mother, learning of these intentions, in her alarm had no course but to tearfully plead with Giō. "You have every reason to be resentful," she said. "I prevailed on you to go and thereby inflicted this pain, though I could hardly have known what would happen. But now should you do away with yourself, your sister will follow your example. If I am to lose both my daughters then, old and feeble as I am, I would do better to commit suicide myself rather than live on alone. In inducing a parent to carry out such an act before the destined time for death has come, however, you will be committing one of the five deadly sins. We are mere sojourners in this life and must suffer one humiliation after another, but these are nothing compared to the long night of suffering that may await us hereafter. Whatever this life may entail, think how frightful it would be if you should condemn yourself to rebirth in one of the evil paths of existence!"

Faced with these fervent entreaties, Giō, wiping back her tears, replied, "You are right. I would be guilty of one of the five deadly sins. I will abandon any thought of self-destruction. But so long as I remain in the capital I am likely to encounter further grief. My thought now is simply to quit the capital."

Thus at the age of twenty-two Giō became a nun and, erecting a simple thatched retreat in a mountain village in the recesses of the Saga region,[5] she devoted herself to the recitation of the Buddha's name.

"I vowed that if you committed suicide, I would do likewise," said her sister Ginyo. "If your plan is now to withdraw from the world, who would hesitate to follow your example?" At the age of nineteen she accordingly donned clerical apparel and joined Giō in her retreat, devoting all her thoughts to the life to come.

The mother Toji, moved by the sight of them, said, "In a world where my daughters, young as they are, have taken the tonsure, how could I, old woman that I am, cling to these gray hairs of mine?" Thus at the age of forty-five she shaved her head and, in company with her two daughters, gave herself wholly to the recitation of Amida's name, mindful only of the life hereafter.

And so spring passed, and the heat of summer, and as the autumn winds began to blow, the time came for the two star lovers to meet, the Herd Boy poling his boat

5. An area to the immediate west of the capital.

across the River of Heaven, and people gazed up into the sky and wrote pleas to them on the leaves of the paper mulberry.[6]

As the nuns watched the evening sun sinking beyond the hills to the west, they said to each other, "There, where the sun went down, that is where they say the Western Paradise of Amida is. One day we too will be reborn there and will no longer know these cares and sorrows." Giving themselves up to melancholy thoughts of this kind, their tears never ceased to flow.

When the twilight had passed, they closed their door of plaited bamboo, lit the dim lamp, and all three, mother and daughters, began their invocation of the Buddha's name.

But just then they heard someone tap-tapping at the bamboo door. The nuns started up in alarm. "Has some meddling demon come to interrupt our devotions, ineffectual as they are?" they exclaimed. "Even in the daytime no one calls on us in our thatched hut here in the remote hills. Who would come so late at night? Whoever it is can very well batter down the door without waiting for it to be opened, so we may as well open it. And if it should be some heartless creature come to take our lives, we must be firm in our faith in Amida's vow to save us, and call unceasingly on his holy name. He is certain to heed our call and come with his sacred host to greet us. And then surely he will guide us to his Western Paradise. Come, let us take heart and not be tardy in pronouncing his name!"

When they had thus reassured one another and mustered the courage to open the bamboo door, they discovered it was no demon at all, but Lady Hotoke who stood before them.

"What do I see?" said Giō. "Lady Hotoke! Am I dreaming or awake?"

"If I tell you what has happened, I may seem to be merely making excuses," said Lady Hotoke, straining to hold back her tears. "But it would be too unkind to remain silent, and so I will start from the beginning. As you know, I originally went to the Chancellor's house of my own accord and was turned away. It was only through your intervention that I was called back. We women are frail things and cannot do as we wish. I was far from happy when the Chancellor detained me at his mansion. Then, when you were summoned again and sang your *imayō* song, my position became ever more clear to me. I could take no delight in it because I knew that sooner or later my turn would come to fall from favor. I felt it even more when I saw the poem you wrote on the sliding panel with its warning that 'come autumn, all alike must fade!'

"After that I lost track of your whereabouts. But when I heard that you and your mother and sister had all entered religious life, I was overcome with envy. Again and again I asked the Chancellor to release me from service, but he would not hear of it.

"What joy and delight we have in this world is no more than a dream within a dream, I told myself—what could such happiness mean to me? It is a rare thing to be born a human being, and rarer still to encounter the teachings of the Buddha. If because of my actions now I should be reborn in hell or should spend endless eons transmigrating through the other realms of existence, when would I ever find salvation? Youth cannot be counted on. The young may go before the old. Death does not wait for the space of a breath; life is as fleeting as the shimmering heat of summer or a flash of lightning. To revel in a moment's happiness and take no thought for the life to

6. The lovers, two stars known as the Herd Boy and the Weaving Maiden, are permitted to meet only one night a year, when the Herd Boy crosses the River of Heaven or Milky Way in his boat. The occasion, known as Tanabata, takes place on the seventh night of the seventh lunar month, at which time celebrants write their wishes on leaves and dedicate them to the lovers.

come would be a pitiful course of action indeed! So this morning I stole away from the Chancellor's mansion and have come here."

With these words she threw off the cloak that she had around her. She was attired in a nun's habit.

"I have come dressed in this fashion," she said, "because I wish to ask pardon for my past offenses. If you say you can forgive me, I would like to join you in your devotions, and perhaps we may be reborn on a single lotus leaf in the Western Paradise. And if you cannot bring yourself to forgive me, I will make my way elsewhere. Wherever I may sink down, on some bed of moss or by the roots of some pine tree, I will devote what life is left to me reciting the Buddha's name, hoping, as I have so long hoped, for rebirth in his paradise."

Giō, near to tears, replied, "I never dreamed you felt this way. In a world of sadness, we are all no doubt fated to endure such trials. And yet I could not help envying you, and it seemed that such feelings of envy would prevent me from ever achieving the salvation I yearned for. I was in a merely half-resolved frame of mind, one suitable neither for this life nor the life to come.

"But now that I see you dressed in this manner, these past failings of mine fall away like so much dust, and I am certain at last of gaining salvation. All my joy hereafter will be to strive for that long-cherished goal. The whole world wondered when my mother and sister and I became nuns, deeming it an unprecedented step, and we too wondered in a way, and yet we had good reasons for doing what we did. But what we did was nothing compared to the action you have taken! Barely turned seventeen, with neither hatred nor despair to spur you on, you have chosen to cast aside the world of defilement and turn all your thoughts toward the Pure Land. How fortunate we are to meet such a fine guide and teacher! Come, we will work toward our goal together!"

So the four women, sharing the same hut, morning and evening offered flowers and incense before the Buddha, all their thoughts given over to their devotions. And sooner or later, it is said, each of the four nuns attained what she had so long sought, rebirth in the Western Paradise.

Thus, on the curtain that lists the departed in the Eternal Lecture Hall founded by the Retired Emperor Go-Shirakawa are to be found, inscribed in one place, the names of the four, "The honored dead, Giō, Ginyo, Hotoke, Toji."

Theirs was a moving story.

The Death of Kiyomori (6:7)

After this, the warriors of the island of Shikoku all went over to the side of Kono no Michinobu. Reports also came that Tanzo, the Superintendent of the Kumano Shrine, in spite of the manifold kindness shown him by the Heike, had shifted his sympathies to the Genji side. All the provinces in the north and the east were thus in rebellion against the Taira, and in the regions to the west and southwest of the capital the situation was as just described. Report on report of uprisings in the outlying areas came to startle the ears of the Heike, and word repeatedly reached them of further acts of rebellion that were impending. As in China in ancient times, it seemed as though the "barbarian tribes to east and west" had suddenly risen up against them. The members of the Taira clan were not alone in thinking that the end of the world was close at hand. No person of true discernment could fail to lament the ominous turn of events.

On the twenty-third day of the Second Month, a council of the senior Taira nobles was convened. At that time Lord Munemori,[1] the former General of the Right, spoke as follows. "We made an earlier attempt to put down the rebels in the east, but the results were not all that might have been desired. This time I would like to be appointed commander-in-chief to move against them."

"What a splendid idea!" the other nobles exclaimed in obsequious assent. A directive was accordingly handed down from the Retired Emperor appointing Lord Munemori commander-in-chief of an expedition against the traitorous elements in the eastern and northern provinces. All high ministers and courtiers who held military posts or were experienced in the use of arms were ordered to follow him.

Word had already gotten abroad that Lord Munemori would set forth on his mission to put down the Genji forces in the eastern provinces on the twenty-seventh day of the same month, when his departure was cancelled because of reports that the Lay Priest and Chancellor Minister Kiyomori was not in his customary good health.

On the following day, the twenty-eighth, it became known that Kiyomori was seriously ill, and throughout the capital and the Rokuhara district people whispered to one another, "This is just what we were afraid of!"

From the first day that Kiyomori took sick, he was unable to swallow anything, not even water. His body was as hot as though there were a fire burning inside it—those who attended him could scarcely come within twenty-five or thirty feet of him, so great was the heat. All he could do was cry out, "I'm burning! I'm burning!" His affliction seemed quite unlike any ordinary illness.

Water from the Well of the Thousand-Armed Kannon on Mount Hiei was brought to the capital and poured into a stone bathtub, and Kiyomori's body was lowered into it in hopes of cooling him. But the water began to seethe and boil furiously and in a moment had all gone up in steam. In a further attempt to afford him some relief, wooden pipes were rigged in order to pour streams of water down on his body, but the water sizzled and sputtered as though it were landing on fiery rocks or metal and virtually none of it reached his body. The little that did so burst into flames and burned up, filling the room with black smoke and sending flames whirling upward.

Long ago, the eminent Buddhist priest Hozo was said to have been invited by Enma, the king of hell, to visit the infernal regions. At that time he asked if he might see the place where his deceased mother had been reborn. Enma, admiring his filial concern, directed the hell wardens to conduct him to the Hell of Scorching Heat, where Hozo's mother was undergoing punishment. When Hozo entered the iron gates of the hell, he saw flames leaping up like shooting stars, ascending hundreds of yojanas into the air. The sight must have been much like that which those attending Kiyomori in his sickness now witnessed.

Kiyomori's wife, the Nun of the Second Rank, had a most fearful dream. It seemed that a carriage enveloped in raging flames had entered the gate of the mansion. Stationed at the front and rear of the carriage were creatures, some with the head of a horse, others with the head of an ox. To the front of the carriage was fastened an iron plaque inscribed with the single word *mu* or "never."

In her dream the Nun of the Second Rank asked, "Where has this carriage come from?"

---

1. The son of Kiyomori and a future leader of the Taira.

"From the tribunal of King Enma," was the reply. "It has come to fetch His Lordship, the Lay Priest and Chancellor of the Taira clan."

"And what does the plaque mean?" she asked.

"It means that, because of the crime of burning the one-hundred-and-sixty foot gilt-bronze image of the Buddha Vairochana in the realm of human beings, King Enma's tribunal has decreed that the perpetrator shall fall into the depths of the Hell of Never-Ceasing Torment. The 'Never' of Never-Ceasing is written on it; the 'Ceasing' remains to be written."

The Nun of the Second Rank woke from her dream in alarm, her body bathed in perspiration, and when she told others of her dream, their hair stood on end just hearing of it. She made offerings of gold, silver, and the seven precious objects to all the temples and shrines reputed to have power in such matters, even adding such items as horses, saddles, armor, helmets, bows, arrows, long swords, and short swords. But no matter how much she poured forth as accompaniment to her supplications, the latter were wholly without effect. Kiyomori's sons and daughters gathered by his pillow and bedside, inquiring in anguish if there were nothing that could be done, but all their cries were in vain.

On the second day of the second intercalary month, the Nun of the Second Rank, braving the formidable heat, approached her husband's pillow and spoke through her tears. "With each day that passes, it seems to me, there is less hope for your recovery. If you have anything you wish to say before you depart this world, it would be well to speak now while your mind is still clear."

The Chancellor in his former days had always been brusque and forceful in manner, but now, tormented by pain, he had barely breath enough to utter these words. "Ever since the Hōgen and Heiji uprisings, I have on numerous occasions put down those who showed themselves enemies of the throne, and have received rewards and acclaim far surpassing what I deserve. I have had the honor to become grandfather to a reigning Emperor and to hold the office of Chancellor, and the bounties showered upon me extend to my sons and grandsons. There is nothing more whatever that I could wish for in this life. Only one regret remains to me—that I have yet to behold the severed head of that exile to the province of Izu, Minamoto no Yoritomo! When I have ceased to be, erect no temples or pagodas in my honor, conduct no memorial rites for me! But dispatch forces at once to strike at Yoritomo, cut off his head and hang it before my grave—that is all the ceremony that I ask!" Such were the deeply sinful words that he spoke!

On the fourth day of the same month, the illness continuing to torment him, Kiyomori's attendants thought to provide some slight relief by pouring water over a board and laying him on it, but this appeared to do no good whatsoever. Moaning in desperation, he fell to the floor and there suffered his final agonies. The sound of horses and carriages rushing about seemed to echo to the heavens and to make the very earth tremble. Even if the sovereign of the realm himself, the lord of ten thousand chariots, had passed away, there could not have been a greater commotion.

Kiyomori had turned sixty-four this year. He was thus not particularly advanced in age. But the life span decreed him by his actions in previous existences had abruptly come to an end. Hence the large-scale ceremonies and secret ceremonies performed on his behalf by the Buddhist priests failed to have any effect, the gods and the Three Treasures of Buddhism ceased to shed their light on him, and the benevolent deities withdrew their guardianship.

And if even divine help was beyond his reach, how little could mere human beings do! Though tens of thousands of loyal troops stationed themselves within his mansion and in the grounds around it, all eager to sacrifice themselves and to die in his place, they could not, even for an instant, hold at bay the deadly devil of impermanence, whose form is invisible to the eye and whose power is invincible. Kiyomori went all alone to the Shide Mountains of death, from which there is no return; alone he faced the sky on his journey over the River of Three Crossings to the land of the Yellow Springs. And when he arrived there, only the evil deeds he had committed in past days, transformed now into hell wardens, were there to greet him. All in all, it was a pitiful business.

Since further action could not be postponed, on the seventh day of the same month Kiyomori's remains were cremated at Otagi in the capital. The Buddhist priest Enjitsu placed the ashes in a bag hung around his neck and journeyed with them down to the province of Settsu, where he deposited them in a grave on Sutra Island.

Kiyomori's name had been known throughout the land of Japan and his might had set men trembling. But in the end his body was no more than a puff of smoke ascending in the sky above the capital, and his remains, after tarrying a little while, in time mingled with the sands of the shore where they were buried, dwindling at last into empty dust.

The Death of Lord Kiso (9:4)

Lord Kiso[1] had brought with him from the province of Shinano two women attendants, Tomoe and Yamabuki. Yamabuki had remained in the capital because of illness. Of these two, Tomoe, fair complexioned and with long hair, was of exceptional beauty. As a fighter she was a match for a thousand ordinary men, skilled in arms, able to bend the stoutest bow, on horseback or on foot ever ready with her sword to confront any devil or god that came her way. She could manage the most unruly horse and gallop down the steepest slopes. Lord Kiso sent her into battle clad in finely meshed armor and equipped with a sword of unusual size and a powerful bow, depending on her to perform as one of his leading commanders. Again and again she emerged unrivaled in feats of valor. And this time too, though so many of Lord Kiso's other riders had fled from his side or been struck down, Tomoe was among the seven who remained with him.

Certain reports claimed that Yoshinaka was heading toward Tamba by way of the Long Slope, others that he had crossed over Ryūge Pass and was proceeding to the northern provinces. In fact he was fleeing west toward Seta, anxious to discover where Imai Kanehira and his men were. Imai meanwhile had been defending his position at Seta with the eight hundred or more men under him. But when his forces had been reduced by fighting to a mere fifty riders, he furled his banners and started back toward the capital, thinking that his superior in command, Yoshinaka, must be wondering about him. In Ōtsu, at a place on the Lake Biwa shore called Uchida, he met up with Lord Kiso as the latter was proceeding west.

While still some distance apart, the two groups recognized one another and their leaders spurred their horses forward in anticipation of the meeting. Lord Kiso, seizing Imai's hand, said, "I had intended to die in the fighting in the riverbed at Rokujō, but I wanted to find out what had become of you. That's why I dodged my way through all those enemy troops and slipped off so I could come here!"

---

1. Yoshinaka, the cousin of Yoritomo, a leader of the northern anti-Taira forces. After his military success as a Minamoto leader, including the capture of Kyoto, he was, as described here, hunted down by Yoritomo's forces.

"Your words do me great honor," replied Imai. "I too had fully expected to die in the encounter at Seta, but I hastened here in hopes of finding out how you were faring."

"The bonds of karma that link us have not come to an end yet!" said Lord Kiso. "My own forces have been broken up and scattered by the enemy, but they have most likely taken shelter in the hills and woods hereabouts and are still in the vicinity. Unfurl those banners you are carrying and raise them aloft!"

When Imai hoisted the banners, three hundred or more friendly horsemen, having spotted them, gathered around, some having escaped from the capital, others among the troops that had fled from Seta.

Yoshinaka was overjoyed. "With a force this size, there's no reason we can't fight one last battle!" he said. "Whose men are those I see massed there in the distance?"

"I believe they're under the command of Lord Ichijō Tadayori of Kai."

"How many men would you say there are?"

"Some six thousand or more, I would judge."

"They will make an excellent opponent. If we are to die in any event, let's confront a worthy foe and meet death in the midst of a great army!" With these words he spurred his horse forward.

That day Yoshinaka was wearing a red brocade undergarment and a suit of finely laced armor. He had a horned helmet on his head and carried a sword of forbidding size. On his back was a quiver containing what arrows were left from the day's fighting, fledged with eagle tail feathers, their tips projecting above his head, and in his hand he grasped a bow bound with rattan. He rode his famed horse Oniashige or Demon Roan, a powerful beast of brawny build, and was seated in a gold-rimmed saddle.

Raising himself up in the stirrups, he called out his name in a loud voice. "From times past you've heard of him—Kiso no Kanja. Now take a look at him! Minamoto no Yoshinaka, Director of the Imperial Stables of the Left, Governor of Iyo, the Rising Sun Commander! And you, I hear, are Ichijō of Kai. We are well matched. Come attack me and show that man in Kamakura—Yoritomo—what you can do!" Shouting these words, he galloped forward.

Ichijō of Kai addressed his troops. "The one who just spoke is the commander. Man! Don't let him get away! You young fellows! Attack him!" Vastly superior in number, Ichijō's troops surrounded Yoshinaka, each man eager to be the first to get at him.

Encircled by over six thousand enemy horsemen, Yoshinaka's three hundred galloped forward and back, left and right, employing the spider leg formation, the cross formation, in an effort to escape the circle. When they finally broke through to the rear, there were only fifty left.

Free at last, they found their path blocked by two thousand or more horsemen under the command of Toi no Jirō Sanehira. Battling their way through these troops, they confronted four or five hundred of the enemy here, two or three hundred there, a hundred and fifty in another place, a hundred in still another, dashing this way and that until only five riders, Yoshinaka and four of his followers, were left. Tomoe, still uninjured, was among the five.

Lord Kiso turned to her. "Hurry, hurry now! You're a woman—go away, anywhere you like!" he said. "I intend to die fighting. And if it looks as though I'm about to be captured, I'll take my own life. But I wouldn't want it said that Lord Kiso fought his last battle in the company of a woman!"

But Tomoe made no move to go. When Lord Kiso continued to press her, she thought to herself, "What luck! If only I had a worthy opponent so I could show him one last time what I can do in battle!"

While she was hesitating, they came upon thirty horsemen under the command of Onda no Moroshige, a warrior of the province of Musashi who was renowned for his strength. Tomoe charged into the midst of Onda's men, drew her horse up beside his and, abruptly dragging him from his seat, pressed his head against the pommel of her saddle. After holding him motionless for a moment, she wrenched his head off and threw it away. She then doffed her helmet and armor and fled in the direction of the eastern provinces.

Of the other remaining horsemen, Tezuka Tarō was killed in the combat and Tezuka no Bettō fled. Only two men, Lord Kiso and Imai, remained.

"Up to now I never gave a thought to my armor, but today it seems strangely heavy!" said Lord Kiso.

"You can't be tired yet, My Lord," said Imai, "and your horse is in good shape. A few pounds of choice armor could not weigh on you that heavily. It's just that your spirits are flagging because we've so few men left. You still have me, though, and I'm a match for a thousand. I have seven or eight arrows remaining and I'll use them to keep the enemy at bay. Those trees you see there in the distance are the pine groves of Awazu. Go over among those trees and make an end of things!"

As they spurred their horses onward, they spied a new group of some fifty mounted warriors heading toward them. "Hurry over to that grove of pines. I'll hold these men off!" he repeated.

"I ought to have died in the fighting in the capital," said Lord Kiso, "but I've fled this far because I wanted to die with you. Rather than one dying here and the other there, it's better that we should die together!"

When Lord Kiso persisted in galloping at his side, Imai leaped to the ground, seized the bit of Lord Kiso's horse, and said, "No matter how fine a name a warrior may make for himself, if he should slip up at the end, it could mean an everlasting blot on his honor. You are tired and we have no more men to fight with us. Suppose we became separated in combat and you were surrounded and cut down by some mere retainer, a person of no worth at all! How terrible if people were to say, 'Lord Kiso, famous throughout the whole of Japan—done in by so-and-so's retainer!' You must hurry to that grove of pines!"

"If it must be—" said Lord Kiso, and he turned his horse in the direction of the Awazu pines.

Imai, a lone rider, charged into the midst of the fifty enemy horsemen. Rising up in his stirrups, he shouted in a loud voice, "Up to now you've heard reports of me—now get a look with your own eyes! Imai no Shirō Kanehira, foster brother of Lord Kiso, thirty-three years of age. Even the Lord of Kamakura has heard of me. Come cut me down and show him my head!"

Then, fitting his eight remaining arrows to his bow in rapid succession, he sent them flying. With no thought for his own safety, he proceeded to shoot down eight of the enemy riders. Then, drawing his sword, he charged this way and that, felling all who came within reach of his weapon, so that no one could get near him. He took many trophies in the process. His attackers encircled him with cries of "Shoot him! Shoot him!" But although the arrows fell like rain, they could not pierce his stout armor or find an opening to get through, and so he remained uninjured.

Meanwhile, Lord Kiso galloped off alone toward the Awazu pine grove. It was the twenty-first day of the First Month, and evening was drawing on. The winter rice paddies were covered with a thin layer of ice and Lord Kiso, unaware of how deep the water was, allowed his horse to stumble into one of them. In no time the horse had sunk into the mud till its head was hardly visible. He kicked the horse again and again, laid on lash after lash with his whip, but could not get the animal to move.

Wondering what had become of Imai, he turned to look behind him, when one of the enemy riders who had been pursuing him, Ishida Tamehisa of Miura, drew his bow far back and shot an arrow that pierced the area of Lord Kiso's face unprotected by his helmet. Mortally wounded, he slumped forward, the bowl of his helmet resting on the horse's head, whereupon two of Ichida's retainers fell on him and cut off his head. Ishida impaled the head on the tip of his sword and, raising it high in the air, shouted, "Lord Kiso, famed these days throughout all of Japan, has been killed by Ishida no Jirō Tamehisa of Miura!"

Imai had continued to battle the enemy, but when he heard this, he said, "Who is left now to go on fighting for? You lords of the eastern provinces, I'll show you how the bravest man in all Japan takes his life!" Then he thrust the tip of his sword into his mouth and flung himself down from his horse in such a way that the sword passed through his body, and so he died. Thus no final battle occurred at the place called Awazu.

The Death of Atsumori (9:16)

The Heike had lost the battle. "Those Taira lords will be heading for the shore in hopes of making their getaway by boat!" thought Kumagae Naozane[1] to himself. "Fine! I'll go look for one of their generals to grapple with!" and he turned his horse in the direction of the beach.

As he did so, he spotted a lone warrior riding into the sea, making for the boats in the offing. He was wearing an undergarment of finely woven silk embroidered in a crane design, armor of light green lacing, and a horned helmet. He carried a sword with gilt fittings and a quiver whose arrows were fledged with black and white eagle feathers, and held a rattan-wound bow in his hand. He was seated in a gold-rimmed saddle, astride a gray horse with white markings.

The lone warrior's horse had swum out about two hundred feet from the shore when Kumagae, waving with his fan, called out, "Hey there, General! I see you. Don't shame yourself by showing your back to an enemy. Come back!"

The rider, acknowledging the call, turned toward the beach. As he was about to ride up out of the waves, Kumagae drew alongside and grappled with him, dragging him from his horse. Pinning him down so as to cut off his head, Kumagae pushed aside his helmet. The face he saw was that of a young man of sixteen or seventeen, lightly powdered and with blackened teeth.[2]

Gazing at the boy's handsome face, Kumagae realized that he was just the age of his own son Kojirō, and he could not bring himself to use his sword. "Who are you? Tell me your name and I'll let you go!" he said.

"Who are you?" asked the young man.

"No one of great importance—Kumagae Naozane of the province of Musashi."

---

1. A Minamoto (Genji) warrior.   2. A sign of aristocratic upbringing.

"Then there's no need for me to tell you my name," the young man replied. "I'm worthy enough to be your opponent. When you take my head, ask someone who I am—they will know all right!"

"Spoken like a true general!" thought Kumagae. "But simply killing this one man can't change defeat into victory, or victory into defeat. When my son Kojirō has even a slight injury, how greatly I worry about him! Just think how this boy's father will grieve when he hears that he's been killed! If only I could spare him."

But as he glanced quickly behind him, he saw some fifty Genji horsemen under Toi and Kajiwara coming toward him. Fighting back the tears, he said, "I'd like to let you go, but our forces are everywhere in sight—you could never get away. Rather than fall into someone else's hands, it's better that I kill you. I'll see that prayers are said for your salvation in the life to come."

"Just take my head and be quick about it!" the boy said.

Kumagae was so overcome with pity that he did not know where to strike. His eyes seemed to dim, his wits to desert him, and for a moment he hardly knew where he was. But then he realized that, for all his tears, no choice was left him, and he struck off the boy's head.

"We men who bear arms—how wretched is our lot!" he said. "If I had not been born of a warrior family, would I ever have faced a task like this? What a terrible thing I have done!" Again and again he repeated the words as he raised his sleeve to brush the tears from his face.

After some time, aware that he must get on with the business, he removed the boy's armor and undergarment and wrapped the head in them. As he was doing so, he noticed a brocade bag with a flute in it that had been fastened to the boy's waist. "Ah, how pitiful!" he said. "Those people I heard at dawn this morning playing music in the enemy stronghold—he must have been one of them! Among all the ten thousand troops from the eastern provinces fighting on our side, is there anyone who carries a flute with him into battle? These highborn people—how gentle and refined they are!"

Later, when Kumagae's battle trophies were presented to Yoshitsune for inspection, there were none among the company who did not weep at the sight.

It was subsequently learned that the young man slain by Kumagae was Atsumori,[3] the seventeen-year-old son of the master of the Palace Repair Office Taira no Tsunemori. The incident had a great deal to do with Kumagae's later decision to become a Buddhist monk. The flute in question had been presented by the Retired Emperor Toba to Atsumori's grandfather, who was a skilled player. From him it passed down to the son, Tsunemori, and in turn was given to Atsumori because of his marked aptitude for the instrument. It was known by the name Saeda or Little Branch.

It is moving to think that even music and the arts, for all their exaggerated phrases and flowery embellishments, can in the end lead a man to praise of the Buddha way.

The Drowning of the Emperor (11:9)

By this time the Genji warriors had succeeded in boarding the Heike boats, shooting the sailors and helmsmen dead with their arrows or cutting them down with their swords. The bodies lay heaped in the bottom of the boats and there was no longer anyone to keep the boats on course.

3. A Taira warrior and the nephew of Kiyomori.

The New Middle Counselor Tomomori[1] boarded a small craft and made his way to the vessel in which the Emperor[2] was riding. "This is what the world has come to!" he exclaimed. "Have all these unsightly creatures thrown into the sea!" Then he began racing from prow to stern, tossing bodies overboard, wiping, cleaning up, attempting with his own hands to put the boat into proper order.

"What of the battle, Lord Tomomori?" asked the ruler's ladies-in-waiting, pressing him with questions.

"You'll have a chance to see some splendid gentlemen from the eastern region!" he replied with a cackling laugh.

"How can you joke at a time like this!" they protested, their voices joined in a chorus of shrieks and wails.

The Nun of the Second Rank,[3] the Emperor's grandmother, observing the situation and evidently prepared for some time for such an eventuality, slipped a two-layered nun's robe over her head and tied her glossed silk trousers high at the waist. She placed the sacred jewel, one of the three imperial regalia, under her arm, thrust the sacred sword in her sash, and took the child Emperor in her arms.

"I may be a mere woman, but I have no intention of falling into the hands of the enemy! I will accompany my lord. All those of you who are resolved to fulfill your duty by doing likewise, make haste to follow me!" So saying, she strode to the side of the boat.

The Emperor had barely turned eight but had the bearing of one much older than that. The beauty of his face and form seemed to shed a radiance all around him. His black hair fell in waves that rippled the length of his back.

Startled and confused, he said, "Grandma, where are you going to take me?"

The Nun, gazing at his innocent face and struggling to hold back her tears, replied, "Don't you understand? In your previous life you were careful to observe the ten good rules of conduct, and for that reason you were reborn in this life as a ruler of ten thousand chariots. But now evil entanglements have you in their power and your days of good fortune have come to an end.

"First," she told him tearfully, "you must face east and bid farewell to the Goddess of the Grand Shrine at Ise. Then you must turn west and trust in Amida Buddha to come with his hosts to greet you and lead you to his Pure Land. Come now, turn your face to the west and recite the invocation of the Buddha's name. This far-off land of ours is no bigger than a millet seed, a realm of sorrow and adversity. Let us leave it now and go together to a place of rejoicing, the Paradise of the Pure Land!"

Dressed in a dove-gray robe, his hair now done in boyish loops on either side of his head, the child, his face bathed in tears, pressed his small hands together, knelt down and bowed first toward the east, taking his leave of the deity of the Ise Shrine. Then he turned toward the west and began chanting the nembutsu, the invocation of Amida's name. The Nun then took him in her arms. Comforting him, she said, "There's another capital down there beneath the waves!" So they plunged to the bottom of the thousand-fathomed sea.

---

1. A Taira leader and the son of Kiyomori, the former head of the Taira clan. This is a description of the climactic battle in which the Taira (Heike) are decisively defeated.
2. Antoku (r. 1180–1185), the child emperor and the son

of Emperor Takakura, held by the Taira. Antoku is the son of Kenreimon'in, Kiyomori's daughter.
3. Kiyomori's principal wife and the mother of Munemori, Shigehira, and Kenreimon'in.

How pitiful, that the spring winds of impermanence should so abruptly scatter the beauty of the blossoms; how heartless, that the rough waves of reincarnation should engulf this tender body! Long Life is the name they give the imperial palace, signaling that one should reside there for years unending; its gates are dubbed Ageless, a term that tells of a reign forever young. Yet before he had reached the age of ten, this ruler ended as refuse on the ocean floor.

Ten past virtues rewarded with a throne, yet how fleeting was that prize! He who once was a dragon among the clouds, now become a fish in the depths of the sea. Dwelling once on terraces lofty as those of the god Brahma, in palaces like the Joyful Sight Citadel of the god Indra, surrounded by great lords and ministers of state, a throng of kin and clansmen in his following, now in an instant to end his life beneath this boat, under these billows—sad, sad indeed!

The Six Paths of Existence (4)

"A nun must do such things—why should it seem such a hardship?" said Awa-no-naishi.[1] "You must receive His Majesty so that he may begin his journey back." Kenreimon'in[2] accordingly returned to her hut.

"Before the window where I recite a single invocation of the Buddha's name, I look for the rays of light that tell of his advent. By my brushwood door with ten invocations I await the host of holy ones coming to escort me. But how strange and beyond all thought is this visit from Your Majesty!" She wept as she greeted him.

The Retired Emperor[3] surveyed her form and attire. "Even those beings in the abode of No-Thought, though they live for eighty thousand kalpas," he said, "must suffer the sadness of inevitable extinction. Even those in the Sixth Heaven of the realm of form cannot escape the woe of the five marks of decay. The delights of longevity enjoyed by the god Indra in his Joyful Sight Citadel or the soaring pavilions of the god Brahma in the midst of the Meditation Heavens are no more than dreamlike boons, phantom pleasures of the moment. All are bound to the wheel of unending change and transmigration, like cartwheels turning. And the sadness of the five marks of decay suffered by these heavenly beings must be borne, it seems, by us humans as well!" And then he added, "Who comes to visit you here? You must brood much on the happenings of the past."

"I do not receive visits from anyone," Kenreimon'in replied, "though I have some vague tidings now and then from my sisters, the wives of Takafusa and Nobutaka. In past times I would never for a moment have supposed that I would one day look to them for support." She wept as she said this, and the women attending her likewise wet their sleeves with tears.

Restraining her tears, Kenreimon'in spoke once more. "My present mode of existence is no more than a passing tribulation, and when I think that it may lead to wisdom in the world to come, I look on it as joyful. I have made haste to join the latter-day disciples of Shakyamuni[4] and reverently entrust myself to Amida's original vow of salvation, so that I may escape the bitterness of the five obstacles and three submissions

---

1. A nun in attendance upon Kenreimon'in.
2. The daughter of Kiyomori by the Nun of the Second Rank, the former consort of Emperor Takakura, and the mother of Emperor Antoku. She was taken prisoner by the Minamoto at Dan-no-ura and has become a nun. She is referred to here as the Imperial Lady.

3. The former Emperor Go-Shirakawa, the father of Emperor Takakura and the grandfather of Emperor Antoku and, most importantly, the former archenemy of Kiyomori.
4. The historical Buddha.

imposed upon a woman.[5] Three times daily and nightly I labor to purify the six senses, hopeful that I may straightway win rebirth in one of the nine grades of the Pure Land. My sole prayer is that all we members of the Taira clan may gain enlightenment, ever trusting that the three venerable ones will come in greeting. The face of my son, the late Emperor,[6] I will never forget, whatever world may come. I try to forget but I can never do so, I try to endure the pain but it is unendurable. There is no bond more compelling than that between parent and child. Day and night I make it my duty to pray for his salvation. And this endeavor has been like a good friend leading me into the path of the Buddha."

The Retired Emperor spoke in answer. "Though I have been born in these far-off islands no bigger than scattered millet seeds, because in a past existence I reverently observed the ten good acts of conduct, I have been privileged in this one to become a ruler of ten thousand chariots. Everything I could wish for has been granted me, my heart has been denied nothing. And most particularly, because I have been fortunate enough to be born in an age when the Buddhist teachings are propagated, I have set my heart on practice of the Buddha way and do not doubt that in the time to come I will be reborn in a far better place. We should have learned by now, I suppose, not to wonder at the miseries of human existence. And yet, seeing you like this seems too pitiful a sight!"

The Imperial Lady began to speak once more. "I was the daughter of the Taira Chancellor and the mother of the nation's ruler—anything in the entire realm and the four seas surrounding it was mine for the asking. Beginning with the rites that mark the advent of spring, through the seasonal changes of clothing, to the recitation of Buddha names that brings the year to a close, I was waited upon by all the high ministers and courtiers, from the Regent on down. There were none of the hundred officials who did not look up to me with awe, as though I dwelt on the clouds of the Six Heavens of the realm of desire or the four Meditation Heavens, the eighty thousand heavenly beings encircling me. I was housed in the Seiryō or Shinshin palaces, curtained by jeweled hangings, in spring whiling away the day with eyes fixed on the cherries of the Southern Pavilion; enduring the oppressive heat of summer's three months through the comfort of fountain waters; never left without companions to view the cloud-borne autumn moon; on winter nights when the snow lay cold, swathed in layers of bed clothing. I desired to learn the arts of prolonging life and evading old age, even if it meant seeking the herbs of immortality from the isle of P'eng-lai, for my sole wish was to live on and on. Day and night I thought of nothing but pleasure, believing that the happy fortune enjoyed by the heavenly beings could not surpass this life of mine.

"And then, in early autumn of the Juei era (1183), because of threats from Kiso no Yoshinaka or others, all the members of our Taira clan saw the capital that had been our home grow distant as the clouds themselves, looked back as our former dwellings in Fukuhara were reduced to fire-blackened fields. We made our way by water from Suma to Akashi, places that in past times were mere names to us, grieving at our lot. By day we plied the boundless wave tracts, wetting our sleeves with spray; nights we cried till dawn with the plovers on sandy points along the shore. Moving from bay to bay, island to island, we encountered scenes pleasant enough but could

5. According to Buddhist belief, a woman may not become a Brahma, an Indra, a devil king, a wheel-turning king, or a Buddha. She is expected to submit to and obey her father in childhood, her husband in maturity, and her son in old age when she is widowed.
6. Emperor Antoku, who died at Dan-no-ura.

never forget our old home. With no place to take refuge, we knew the misery of the five marks of decay and the prospect of certain extinction.

"Separation from loved ones, meeting with suffering, encounter with all that is hateful—in my life as a human being I have experienced all of these. The four trials, the eight trials—not one of them have I been spared! And then, in a place called Dazaifu in the province of Chikuzen, we were driven away by a person called Koreyoshi who refused us lodging in Kyūshū—a broad land of mountains and plains but with nowhere that we could take shelter. Once more autumn drew to a close, but the moon, that we used to gaze at from the heights of the nine-tiered palace, this year we watched from salt-sea paths eightfold in their remoteness.

"So the days and nights passed until, in the Tenth Month, the Godless Month, the Middle Captain Kiyotsune[7] declared, 'The capital has fallen to the Genji, we have been hounded out of Kyūshū by Koreyoshi—we're like fish caught in a net! Where can we find safety? What hope have I of living out my life?' And with these words he drowned himself in the sea, the beginning of a new round of sorrows.

"We passed our days on the waves, our nights in the boats. No articles of tribute came in as they had in the past, no one received any supplies or provisions. Even on the rare occasion when provisions were to be had, there was no water with which to prepare them. We were afloat on the vast ocean, but its waters, being salt, were undrinkable. Thus I came to know the sufferings of those who inhabit the realm of hungry spirits.

"After that, we won victory in certain encounters such as those at Muroyama and Mizushima, and our people began to be somewhat more cheerful in countenance. But then came Ichi-no-tani,[8] where we lost so many of our clansmen. Thereafter, instead of informal robes and court dress, our men donned helmets, buckled on armor, and morning to night we heard only the din and cry of battle. Then I knew that the assaults of the asura demons, their clashes with the god Indra, must present just such a spectacle as this.

"After the defeat at Ichi-no-tani, young men perished before their fathers, wives were torn from husbands. When we spied a boat in the offing, we trembled lest it be an enemy craft; when we glimpsed herons roosting in distant pine trees our hearts stopped, for we took them for the white banners of the Genji. Then came the naval battle in the straits between the Moji and Akama barriers, and it seemed as though that day must be our last.

"My mother, the Nun of the Second Rank, said to me, 'At such a time as this a man has little more than one chance in ten thousand of surviving. And even though some distant relative might come through the day alive, he would not be the kind who could offer prayers for our wellbeing in the life hereafter. But it has been the custom from times past to spare the women in such a conflict. If you should manage to live out the day, you must pray that your son, the Emperor, may find salvation in the life to come, and aid the rest of us with your prayers as well!' Over and over she urged this on me, and I listened as though in a dream.

"But then the wind began to blow and thick clouds blanketed the sky. Our warriors' hearts failed them, for it seemed that whatever fortune we had enjoyed with Heaven had now run out and human efforts were no longer of any avail.

---

7. A Taira (Heike) warrior whose suicide by drowning became the centerpiece of a later Noh play called *Kiyotsune*.

8. The major battle near present-day Kōbe, where the Taira were decisively defeated.

"When the Nun of the Second Rank saw how things stood, she lifted the Emperor in her arms and hastened to the side of the boat. Startled and confused, the child said, 'Grandma, where are you going to take me?'

"'Don't you understand?' she said, gazing at his innocent face and struggling to hold back her tears. 'In your previous life you were careful to observe the ten good rules of conduct, and for that reason you were reborn in this life as a ruler of ten thousand chariots. But now evil entanglements have you in their power and your days of good fortune have come to an end. First, you must face east and bid farewell to the Goddess of the Grand Shrine at Ise. Then you must turn west and trust in Amida Buddha to come with his hosts to greet you and lead you to his Pure Land. Turn your face to the west now and recite the invocation of the Buddha's name. This far-off land of ours is no bigger than a millet seed, a realm of sorrow and adversity. Let us leave it now and go together to a place of rejoicing, the Paradise of the Pure Land!'

"The child was dressed in a dove-gray robe, his hair done in boyish loops on either side of his head. His face bathed in tears, he pressed his small hands together, knelt down and bowed first toward the east, taking his leave of the deity of the Ise Shrine. Then he turned toward the west and began chanting the invocation of Amida's name. And when I saw the nun, with the boy in her arms, at last sink beneath the sea, my eyes grew dim and my wits seemed to leave me. I try to forget that moment but I can never do so, I try to endure the pain but it is more than I can endure. The wails of the wrongdoers who suffer in the depths of the Hell of Shrieks and the Hell of Great Shrieks could not be more heartrending, I believe, than the screams and cries of those of us who lived to witness these events!

"After that, I was taken prisoner by the Genji warriors and set out on the journey back to the capital. When we had put in at the bar of Akashi in the province of Harima, I happened to doze off, and in my dream found myself in a place far surpassing in beauty the imperial palace I had known in former times. My son, the late Emperor, was there, and all the high ministers and courtiers of the Taira clan, waiting upon him with the most solemn ceremony. Never since leaving the capital had I beheld such magnificent surroundings, and I said to the people, 'What place is this?'

"Someone who appeared to be my mother, the Nun of the Second Rank, replied, 'This is the palace of the dragon king.'

"'What a wonderful place!' I exclaimed. 'And do those who live here undergo no suffering?'

"'Our lot is described in the sutras on dragons and beasts. You must pray in all earnestness for our salvation in the world to come!'

"As soon as she had spoken these words, I woke from my dream. Since then I have been more diligent than ever in reciting sutras and invoking the Buddha's name, hopeful that thereby I may assist them to attain salvation. And so you see, I have in this manner experienced all the six paths of existence."

When she had finished speaking, the Retired Emperor said, "The Tripitaka Master Hsüan-tsang in China is reported to have viewed the six paths of existence before he attained enlightenment, and in our own country the Venerable Nichizō, we are told, was able to see them through the power of the deity Zaō Gongen of Mt. Yoshino. But that you have seen them manifested before your very eyes is miraculous indeed!"

He wept as he spoke these words, and the lords and courtiers attending him all wet their sleeves with tears. Kenreimon'in too broke down in tears, as did her women companions.

The Death of the Imperial Lady (5)

While they were speaking, the bell of the Jakkō-in sounded its note, signalling the close of the day, and the sun sank beyond the western hills. The Retired Emperor, reluctant though he was to leave, wiped back his tears and prepared to begin the journey back.

Kenreimon'in, all her memories of the past brought back to her once more, could scarcely stem the flood of tears with her sleeve. She stood watching as the imperial entourage set out for the capital, watching till it was far in the distance. Then she turned to the image of the Buddha and, speaking through her tears, uttered this prayer: "May the spirit of the late Emperor and the souls of all my clanspeople who perished attain complete and perfect enlightenment, may they quickly gain the wisdom of the Buddhas!"

In times gone by she had faced eastward with this petition: "Great Deity of the Grand Shrine of Ise, Great Bodhisattva Hachiman, may the Son of Heaven be blessed with most wonderful longevity, may he live a thousand autumns, ten thousand years!" But now she had changed direction and, facing west with palms pressed together, in sorrow spoke these words: "May the souls of all those who have perished find their way to Amida's Pure Land!"

On the sliding panel of her sleeping room she had inscribed the following poems:

> When did my heart
> learn such ways?
> Of late I think so longingly
> of palace companions I once knew!

> The past—
> it too has vanished like a dream—
> my days by this brushwood door
> cannot be long in number!

The following poem is reported to have been inscribed on a pillar of Kenreimon'in's retreat by the Minister of the Left Sanesada, one of the officials who accompanied the Retired Emperor on his visit:

> You who in past times were likened to the moon—dwelling now
> deep in these faraway mountains, a light no longer shining—.

Once, when Kenreimon'in was bathed in tears, overwhelmed by memories of the past and thoughts of the future, she heard the cry of a mountain cuckoo and wrote this poem:

> Come then, cuckoo, let us compare tears—I too
> do nothing but cry out in a world of pain.

The Taira warriors who survived the Dan-no-ura hostilities and were taken prisoner were paraded through the main streets of the capital and then either beheaded or sent into exile far from their wives and children. With the exception of Taira no Yorimori, not one escaped execution or was permitted to remain in the capital.

With regard to the forty or more Taira wives, no special punitive measures were taken—they were left to join their relatives or to seek aid from persons they had known in the past. But even those fortunate enough to find themselves seated within sumptuous hangings were not spared the winds of uncertainty, and those who ended in humble brushwood dwellings could not live free of dust and turmoil. Husbands and wives who had slept pillow to pillow now found themselves at the far ends of the sky.

Parents and children who had nourished one another no longer even knew each other's whereabouts. Though loving thoughts never for a moment ceased, lament as they might, they had somehow to endure these things.

And all of this came about because the Lay Priest and Chancellor Minister Taira no Kiyomori, holding the entire realm within the four seas in the palm of his hand, showed no awe for the ruler above, nor the slightest concern for the masses of common people below. He dealt out sentences of death or exile in any fashion that suited him, took no heed of how the world or those in it might view his actions—and this is what happened! There can be no room for doubt—it was the evil deeds of the father, the patriarch, that caused the heirs and offspring to suffer this retribution!

After some time had gone by, Kenreimon'in fell ill. Grasping the five-colored cord attached to the hand of Amida Buddha, the central figure in the sacred triad, she repeatedly invoked his name: "Hail to the Thus Come One Amida, lord of teachings of the Western Paradise—may you guide me there without fail!" The nuns Dainagon-no-suke and Awa-no-naishi attended her on her left and right, their voices raised in unrestrained weeping, for they sensed in their grief that the end was now at hand. As the sound of the dying woman's recitations grew fainter and fainter, a purple cloud appeared from the west, the room became filled with a strange fragrance, and the strains of music could be heard in the sky. Human life has its limits, and that of the Imperial Lady came to an end in the middle days of the second month in the second year of the Kenkyū era.[1]

Her two women attendants, who from the time she became Imperial Consort had never once been parted from her, were beside themselves with grief at her passing, helpless though they were to avert it. The support upon which they had depended from times past had now been snatched from them and they were left destitute, yet even in that pitiable state they managed to hold memorial services each year on the anniversary of her death. And in due time they too, we are told, imitating the example of the dragon king's daughter in her attainment of enlightenment, following in the footsteps of Queen Vaidehī, both fulfilled their long-cherished hopes for rebirth in the Pure Land.

NOH: DRAMA OF GHOSTS, MEMORIES, AND SALVATION

Noh is the oldest form of Japanese drama still being performed.[1] Although a primitive form of Noh first emerged at the beginning of the fourteenth century, it was the innovations introduced by playwrights Kan'ami (1333–1384) and his son Zeami (c. 1363–c. 1443) that shaped the genre as it is performed today.

Noh plays encompass dance, song, and dialogue. The plays are generally categorized into five groups, according to the type of leading character: (1) plays about gods; (2) warrior plays; (3) plays about women; (4) miscellaneous plays, which include all the plays that don't fit into the other four categories; and (5) demon plays, also called ending plays.

Many of the most popular Noh plays today are two-act dream or ghost dramas, a form introduced by Zeami. In the first act, a traveling monk meets a ghost disguised as a local commoner; in the second act, the ghost appears in its true form in the monk's dream and reenacts the event—usually the most momentous incident in its former life—that is responsible for its current attachment to the world, which obstructs its path to Buddhahood. In other words, in a

---

1. In 1191.

1. Introductions to this section and the two Noh plays that follow are by Akiko Takeuchi.

ghost drama the main incident occurs not in present time, the time when the traveler and ghost meet, but in a scene from the past as recalled by the supernatural protagonist, often through the haze of memory. Ghost dramas had a religious function, the pacification of vengeful or unenlightened spirits, and in fact, in many plays, the ghost ultimately attains enlightenment through the monk's prayers. *Atsumori* has been included here as an example of this form.

All of the roles are traditionally performed by male actors and are categorized into four types: the leading role, the companion to the leading role, the supporting role, who is opposite—but not necessarily antagonistic to—the leading role, and the supporting role's companion.

Another component of Noh is the chorus, consisting of six to ten members who sit motionless throughout the play at the right side of the stage. Unlike the chorus in a Greek tragedy, the Noh chorus doesn't assume a specific role in the play. Its members chant in unison, at times chanting the lead actor's or the supporting actor's words, and at other times describing scenes as a narrator. Musicians accompany the dances and some of the chanting, as well as the entrances and exits of characters. The instruments used are the flute, shoulder drum, hip drum, and stick drum.

The Noh stage consists of a square main stage, about nineteen by nineteen feet, and a bridgeway that leads from the far left corner of the main stage toward the dressing room. The audience sits in front of, and also to the left of, the stage. The actors usually enter and exit the stage along the bridgeway, which in some plays serves as a second stage, signifying a separate space, distinct from the setting on the main stage. Although a pine tree is painted on the back wall of the stage, it doesn't function as scenery. The setting is depicted only verbally, and in many plays no stage props are used. In others, only a symbolic prop is used; when placed on the bare stage this prop becomes one of the play's focal points.

Most of the actors wear masks, although child actors and actors portraying living male adult characters generally do not. The supporting actor and his companions, who always portray living male characters, never use masks. Performers not wearing masks must not show any facial expression or use make-up. Most masks express generic character types, and the same mask may be worn by different characters and used in various plays. Masks of human characters (including ghosts) usually display static and rather neutral expressions instead of specific emotions, although the expression appears to change according to the angle at which the mask is worn. When a performer lets his head droop slightly, the mask looks sad; when he subtly tilts his head upward, the same mask may look joyful. Moreover, masks without definite expressions encourage audience members to project onto the mask what they glean from the chanting, and thus are capable of conveying a wide range of emotions.

Noh costumes are noted for their exquisite beauty and splendor. Most of them are made of stiff, heavy materials, which are folded around the performer's body. The physicality of the performer, like his face, is concealed in this manner. The beauty and expressiveness of his performance are thus sought not in his physical or facial features but rather in the grace of his movements.

Movements on the Noh stage are strictly choreographed and, in general, are very slow and highly stylized. Unlike kabuki, in which female roles are played by male actors who have mastered specific gestures connoting femininity, there are no explicitly feminine gestures in Noh. Nor are performers categorized according to the gender of the characters they play. Gender is expressed by subtle variations in the angles of the performer's limbs, especially in his manner of walking. The same is true with respect to differences in age, social status, and mental state. Because such emphasis is placed upon simple movement, Noh is often said to be "the art of walking."

Dance is performed to musical accompaniment, either by the musicians alone, or by musicians and chorus together. It is mostly made up of abstract movements, which in themselves do not carry specific meanings. As with the masks, many of the dances done to instrumental accompaniment are generic; the same dance, for example, is performed by a noble youth in *Atsumori* and by a female salt-maker in *Pining Wind*.

The chanting style of Noh is divided into speech and song, with the speech being intoned. Both the spoken and the sung parts are divided into musical and textual subsections. Each subsection has its own specific pattern of musical structure and/or content, which remains consistent from play to play. In the following translations, the names of the subsections are indicated to the left of the text to inform readers that the frequent shifts of topic and mood in the text are accompanied by changes in chanting style. The subsections can be roughly categorized as follows:

- a measured song style (chanted in a steady rhythm, keeping precise time with the drums): *age-uta, chū-noriji, kuse, noriji, rongi, sage-uta, shidai, uta*
- a more lyrical song style (incorporating prolonged grace notes on key phrases and not chanted in measured time): *go-no-ei, issei, jō-no-ei, kakeai, kudoki, kudoki-guri, kuri, sashi, waka*
- the speech style: *mondō, nanori, tsuki-zerifu*

PRONUNCIATIONS:
Atsumori: ah-tsoo-mo-ri
Zeami: zay-ah-mee

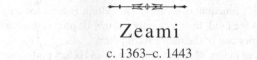

Zeami

c. 1363–c. 1443

ATSUMORI. The protagonists of warrior plays, the second of the five categories of Noh plays, are ghosts of those who have fallen in battle. In earlier versions, they are typically portrayed as denizens of a hellish realm; having died in the frenzy of battle, they are still obsessed with the passion for killing, and they continue to fight one another for eternity. Zeami's contribution to this category was to move away from such demonic representations of fallen warriors. In *The Three Paths,* Zeami recommends selecting famous characters from *Tales of the Heike* as protagonists for warrior plays and depicting them in an elegant manner. In this fashion Zeami transformed warrior plays to suit the tastes of his cultural patrons in the capital, such as court nobles or high-ranking samurai, who favored elegant beauty rather than the mimicry of demonic battles of long dead warriors.

Tales of the Heike is an oral narrative describing the rise and fall of the Heike clan. Chanted by blind reciters, it was enormously popular at the beginning of the medieval period. *Atsumori* is Zeami's adaptation of a famous episode from the *Heike.* The story unfolds as follows: near the end of the battle at Ichi-no-tani on Suma Bay, Naozane, a follower of the rival Genji clan, catches sight of an apparently high-ranking warrior of the Heike alone on the seashore. Wrestling his enemy to the ground and removing his helmet, Naozane realizes that the soldier—Atsumori—is only a boy of about sixteen, nearly the same age as his own son. Although his first impulse is to spare the boy's life, he detects the approach of other Genji followers, and knows they will surely kill the boy. Thus, with tears in his eyes, Naozane is compelled to cut off the boy's head. When he tears off a piece of Atsumori's garment in which to wrap the head, he notices a flute, a symbol of courtly elegance, hidden under the boy's armor. Some time afterward, disillusioned by the calling that has led him to commit such a brutal act, Naozane takes the tonsure.

The Noh play *Atsumori* revisits the encounter at Suma Bay between Naozane, who is now a monk named Renshō, and the ghost of Atsumori, disguised as a grass cutter. In the first act, the ghost of Atsumori shows his love for music by playing the flute. An inquiry into the sound of his flute opens the conversation between the monk and the ghost, which soon leads to a song reciting the names of famous flutes.

The play alludes frequently to the "Suma" chapter of *The Tale of Genji* (page 184). The background scene, the shore at Suma, is depicted not as a bloody battlefield but as a highly poetic landscape with strong associations to aristocratic culture. These associations even suggest an analogy between Atsumori and the Shining Genji, as both characters fled the capital for this remote seashore under adverse circumstances. Moreover, the climax of the second act, unlike in a typical warrior play, is not a description of the warriors' torment in hell, but rather of Atsumori's recollection of a banquet he enjoyed with his family the night before his death. Atsumori's ghost reenacts the singing, flute-playing, and dancing that took place during the banquet.

The play's basic structure is that of a ghost drama in two acts, a structure that Zeami established, although he didn't follow it strictly here. In a standard ghost play, for example, the monk would simply be a passerby having no personal connection with the ghost, while in *Atsumori,* the monk is Naozane, who killed Atsumori. Such an exceptional personal relationship between the ghost and the monk results from the fact that the original episode in the *Heike* is a tragedy not only for Atsumori but also for Naozane himself, who is forced to kill the young boy against his will. Consequently, just as Atsumori needs to be saved from the torment of hell, Naozane, too, is desperate to be delivered from his anguish.

Atsumori, A Tale of Heike Play[1]

Characters in Order of Appearance

MONK RENSHŌ, formerly the Minamoto warrior Kumagai no Jirō Naozane
YOUTH, the ghost of Atsumori appearing as a grass-cutter
Two or three COMPANIONS to the Youth
A VILLAGER
Ghost of the Taira warrior ATSUMORI (*Atsumori, jūroku,* or *chūjō* mask)

Place: Ichinotani, in Settsu

ACT 1

[*To* shidai *music, enter Renshō, carrying a rosary. He stands in base square,*[2] *facing rear of stage.*]

RENSHŌ: (*shidai*) The world is all a dream, and he who wakes
    the world is all a dream, and he who wakes,
    casting it from him, may yet know the real.

[*He turns to the audience.*]

(*nanori*) You have before you one who in his time was Kumagai no Jirō Naozane, a warrior from Musashi province. Now I have renounced the world, and Renshō is my name. It was I, you understand, who struck Atsumori down; and the great sorrow of this deed moved me to become the monk you see. Now I am setting out for Ichinotani, to comfort Atsumori and guide his spirit towards enlightenment.

---

1. Translation by Royall Tyler.   2. Back left corner of the stage.

(*age-uta*) The wandering moon,
    issuing from among the Ninefold Clouds[3]
    issuing from among the Ninefold Clouds,
    swings southward by Yodo and Yamazaki,
    past Koya Pond and the Ikuta River,   [*Mimes walking.*]
    and Suma shore, loud with pounding waves,
    to Ichinotani, where I have arrived
    to Ichinotani, where I have arrived.

(*tsuki-zerifu*) Having come so swiftly, I have reached Ichinotani in the province of Tsu. Ah, the past returns to mind as though it were before me now. But what is this? I hear a flute from that upper field. I will wait for the player to come by and question him about what happened here.

    [*Sits below witness pillar. To* shidai *music, enter the Youth and Companions. Each carries a split bamboo pole with a bunch of mowed grass secured in the cleft. They face each other at front.*]

YOUTH AND COMPANIONS: (*shidai*) The sweet music of the mower's flute
    the sweet music of the mower's flute
    floats, windborne, far across the fields.
YOUTH: (*sashi*) Those who gather grass on yonder hill
    now start for home, for twilight is at hand.
YOUTH AND COMPANIONS: They too head back to Suma, by the sea,
    and their way, like mine, is hardly long.
    Back and forth I ply, from hill to shore,
    heart heavy with the cares of thankless toil.
(*sage-uta*) Yes, should one perchance ask after me,
    my reply would speak of lonely grief.[4]
(*age-uta*) On Suma shore
    the salty drops fall fast, though were I known
    the salty drops fall fast, though were I known,
    I myself might hope to have a friend.[5]
    Yet, having sunk so low, I am forlorn,
    and those whom I once loved are strangers now.

    [*While singing, Youth goes to stand in base square, Companions before Chorus.*]

    But I resign myself to what life brings,
    and accept what griefs are mine to bear
    and accept what griefs are mine to bear.

    [*Renshō rises.*]

RENSHŌ: (*mondō*) Excuse me, mowers, but I have a question for you.
YOUTH: For us, reverend sir? What is it, then?

---

3. The moon suggests the monk Renshō himself. The "Ninefold Clouds" refer to the Capital.
4. These and the following three lines allude to a poem by Ariwara no Yukihira (818–893) that figures so prominently in *Pining Wind* (page 293). Yukihira was exiled to Suma.

5. Yukihira's poem alludes to a friend in the Capital; and the Youth is probably longing for a similar friend, in the Capital now lost to him, who would know his true quality. In fact, his only possible friend, Renshō, is already present.

RENSHŌ: Was it one of you I just heard playing the flute?

YOUTH: Yes, it was one of us.

RENSHŌ: How touching! For people such as you, that is a remarkably elegant thing to do! Oh yes, it is very touching.

YOUTH: It is a remarkably elegant thing, you say, for people like us to do? The proverb puts the matter well: "Envy none above you, despise none below." Besides, the woodman's songs and the mower's flute

YOUTH AND COMPANIONS: are called "sylvan lays" and "pastoral airs":[6]

> they nourish, too, many a poet's work,
> and ring out very bravely through the world.
> You need not wonder, then, to hear me play.

RENSHŌ: (*kakeai*) I do not doubt that what you say is right.
> Then, "sylvan lays" or "pastoral airs"

YOUTH: mean the mower's flute,

RENSHŌ: the woodman's songs:

YOUTH: music to ease all the sad trials of life,

RENSHŌ: singing,

YOUTH: dancing.

RENSHŌ: fluting—

YOUTH: all these pleasures

[*Youth begins to move and gesture in consonance with the text.*]

CHORUS: (*age-uta*) are pastimes not unworthy of those
> who care to seek out beauty: for bamboo,
> who care to seek out beauty: for bamboo,
> washed up by the sea, yields Little Branch,
> Cicada Wing, and other famous flutes;
> while this one, that the mower blows,
> could be Greenleaf, as you will agree.[7]
> Perhaps upon the beach at Sumiyoshi,
> one might expect instead a Koma flute;[8]
> but this is Suma. Imagine, if you will,
> a flute of wood left from saltmakers' fires
> a flute of wood left from saltmakers' fires.

[*Exeunt Companions. Youth, in base square, turns to Renshō.*]

RENSHŌ: (*kakeai*) How strange! While the other mowers have gone home, you have stayed on, alone. Why is this?

YOUTH: You ask why have I stayed behind? A voice called me here, chanting the Name. O be kind and grant me the Ten Invocations![9]

RENSHŌ: Very gladly. I will give you Ten Invocations, as you ask. But then tell me who you are.

---

6. In a line of Chinese verse by a Japanese poet, included in *Wakan rōei shū* (Collection of Japanese and Chinese Poems for Chanting Aloud, 1013).

7. It was felt that bamboo washed up by the sea yielded particularly fine flutes. Atsumori's own was in fact the one named Little Branch. The divine music of Greenleaf was legendary.

8. Because Sumiyoshi was where ships from Koma (Korea) once used to put in. The "Koma flute" is used in ancient court music.

9. The Name is that of Amida, the Buddha of Infinite Light, whose invocation goes *Namu Amida Bu* ("Hail Amida Buddha"). The Ten Invocations (ten callings of the Name for the benefit of another) were often requested of holy persons even by the living. Renshō's teacher, Hōnen, was an outstanding Amida devotee.

YOUTH: In truth, I am someone with a tie to Atsumori.

RENSHŌ: One with a tie to Atsumori?
Ah, the name recalls such memories!

[Presses his palms together in prayer over his rosary.]

"Namu Amida Bu," I chant in prayer:

[Youth goes down on one knee and presses his palms together.]

YOUTH AND RENSHŌ: "If I at last become a Buddha,
then all sentient beings who call my Name
in all the worlds, in the ten directions,
will find welcome in Me, for I abandon none."[1]

CHORUS: (*uta*) Then, O monk, do not abandon me!
One calling of the Name should be enough,
but you have comforted me by night and day—
a most precious gift! As to my name,
no silence I might keep could quite conceal
the one you pray for always, dawn and dusk;   *[Youth rises.]*
that name is my own. And, having spoken,
he fades away and is lost to view
he fades away and is lost to view.   *[Exit Youth.]*

* * *

[Villager passes by and, in response to Renshō's request for information, describes how Atsumori was defeated by Kumagai on this very coast. He expresses deep sympathy for the former and a fierce hatred for the latter. Renshō reveals his identity. Greatly surprised, the villager apologizes for his previous indignation, advises Renshō to pray for the peace of Atsumori's spirit, and exits.]

ACT 2

RENSHŌ: (*age-uta*) Then it is well: to guide and comfort him
then it is well: to guide and comfort him,
I shall do holy rites, and through the night
call aloud the Name for Atsumori,
praying that he reach enlightenment
praying that he reach enlightenment.

[To issei *music, enter Atsumori, in the costume of a warrior. He stops in base square.]*

ATSUMORI: (*jō-no-ei*) Across to Awaji the plovers fly,
while the Suma barrier guard sleeps on;
yet one, I see, keeps nightlong vigil here.
O keeper of the pass, tell me your name.[1]

1. The canonical vow made by Amida, before he became a Buddha, to save all beings by his grace. See Color Plate 3 for a sculpture of a monk chanting the Buddha's name.
1. The barrier on the pass through the hills behind Suma was well known in poetry, as was its nameless guard. In the language of poetry, an older man seen at night at

Suma can only be this guard; so that Atsumori's playful challenge, "O keeper of the pass, tell me your name," seems intended to remind the more rustic Renshō of his place. His words, based on a 12th-century poem, are as elegant as the music of his flute.

(*kakeai*) Behold, Renshō: I am Atsumori.

RENSHŌ: Strange! As I chant aloud the Name,
    beating out the rhythm on this gong,
    and wakeful as ever in broad day,
    I see Atsumori come before me.
    The sight can only be a dream.

ATSUMORI: Why need you take it for a dream?
    For I have come so far to be with you
    in order to clear karma that is real.

RENSHŌ: I do not understand you: for the Name
    has power to clear away all trace of sin.
    Call once upon the name of Amida
    and your countless sins will be no more:
    so the sutra promises. As for me,
    I have always called the Name for you.
    How could sinful karma afflict you still?

ATSUMORI: Deep as the sea it runs. O lift me up,

RENSHŌ: that I too may come to Buddhahood!

ATSUMORI: Let each assure the other's life to come,

RENSHŌ: for we, once enemies,

ATSUMORI: are now become,

RENSHŌ: in very truth,

ATSUMORI: fast friends in the Law.

[*Below, Atsumori moves and gestures in consonance with the text.*]

CHORUS: (*uta*) Now I understand!
    Leave the company of an evil friend,
    cleave to the foe you judge a good man:
    and that good man is you! O I am grateful!
    How can I thank you as you deserve?
    Then I will make confession of my tale.
    and pass the night recounting it to you
    and pass the night recounting it to you.

[*Atsumori sits on a stool at centre, facing audience.*]

(*kuri*)   The flowers of spring rise up and deck the trees
    to urge all upwards to illumination;
    the autumn moon plumbs the waters' depths
    to show grace from on high saving all beings.

ATSUMORI: (*sashi*) Rows of Taira mansions lined the streets:
    we were the leafy branches on the trees.

CHORUS: Like the rose of Sharon, we flowered one day;
    but as the Teaching that enjoins the Good
    is seldom found,[2] birth in the human realm
    quickly ends, like a spark from a flint.

---

2. It is only rarely, and by great good fortune, that a sentient being is able to hear the Buddha's teaching; and it is only as a human being that one can reach enlightenment.

This we never knew, nor understood
that vigor is followed by decline.
ATSUMORI: Lords of the land, we were, but caused much grief;
CHORUS: blinded by wealth, we never knew our pride.

[*Atsumori rises now, and dances through the* kuse *passage below.*]

(*kuse*)   Yes, the house of Taira ruled the world
twenty years and more: a generation
that passed by as swiftly as a dream.
Then came the Juei years, and one sad fall,
when storms stripped the trees of all their leaves
and scattered them to the four directions,
we took to our fragile, leaflike ships,
and tossed in restless sleep upon the waves.
Our very dreams foretold no return.
We were like caged birds that miss the clouds,
or homing geese that have lost their way.
We never lingered long under one sky,
but traveled on for days, and months, and years,
till at last spring came round again,
and we camped here, at Ichinotani.
So we stayed on, hard by Suma shore,
ATSUMORI: while winds swept down upon us off the hills.
CHORUS: The fields were bitterly cold. At the sea's edge
our ships huddled close, while day and night
the plovers cried, and our own poor sleeves
wilted in the spray that drenched the beach.
Together in the seafolk's huts we slept,
till we ourselves joined these villagers,
bent to their life like the wind-bent pines.
The evening smoke rose from our cooking fires
while we sat about on heaps of sticks
piled upon the beach, and thought and thought
of how we were at Suma, in the wilds,
and we ourselves belonged to Suma now,
even as we wept for all our clan.

[*Atsumori stands before drums.*]

ATSUMORI: (*kakeai*) Then came the sixth night of the Second Month.
My father, Tsunemori, summoned us
to play and dance, and sing *imayō*[3]
RENSHŌ: Why, that was the music I remember!
A flute was playing so sweetly in their camp!
We, the attackers, heard it well enough.
ATSUMORI: It was Atsumori's flute, you see:
the one I took with me to my death

---

3. The popular songs (much appreciated at court) of the late 12th century.

RENSHŌ: and that you wished to play this final time,
ATSUMORI: while from every throat
RENSHŌ: rose songs and poems
CHORUS: (*issei*) sung in chorus to a lively beat.

[*Atsumori performs a lively* chū-no-mai *dance, ending in base square. Below, he continues dancing and miming in consonance with the text.*]

ATSUMORI: (*unnamed*) Then, in time, His Majesty's ship sailed,
CHORUS: (*noriji*) with the whole clan behind him in their own.
    Anxious to be aboard, I sought the shore,
    but all the warships and the imperial barge
    stood already far, far out to sea.
ATSUMORI: (*unnamed*) I was stranded. Reining in my horse,
    I halted, at a loss for what to do.
CHORUS: (*chū-noriji*) There came then, galloping behind me,
    Kumagai no Jirō Naozane,
    shouting, "You will not escape my arm!"
    At this Atsumori wheeled his mount
    and swiftly, all undaunted, drew his sword.
    We first exchanged a few rapid blows,
    then, still on horseback, closed to grapple, fell,
    and wrestled on, upon the wave-washed strand.
    But you had bested me, and I was slain.
    Now karma brings us face to face again.
    "You are my foe!" Atsumori shouts,   [*Brandishes sword.*]
    lifting his sword to strike; but Kumagai   [*Drops to one knee.*]
    with kindness has repaid old enmity,   [*Rises, retreats.*]
    calling the Name to give the spirit peace.
    They at last shall be reborn together
    upon one lotus throne in paradise.
    Renshō, you were no enemy of mine.

[*He drops his sword and, in base square, turns to Renshō with palms pressed together.*]

    Pray for me, O pray for my release!
    Pray for me, O pray for my release!

[*Facing side from base square, stamps the final beat.*]

Pining Wind

The Japanese title of *Pining Wind* (*Matsukaze*) is taken from the name of its protagonist, the ghost of a female salt-maker. It means "wind (*kaze*) in the pines (*matsu*)" as well as "the wind that keeps waiting (*matsu*)," since in Japanese *matsu* means both "pine tree" and "to wait" (rather like the English word "pine," conveniently). Poetic puns on this double meaning recur throughout the play. The girl's character befits this double connotation; she is the ghost of a rural girl, lingering at the desolate seashore of Suma—like a lonely wind blowing through pines on the coast—and waiting for the return of her lover, who set off from home for the capital and never returned.

The central plot of the play—an affair between Ariwara no Yukihira (818–893), a grandson of Emperor Heizei, and two local sisters in Suma Bay—cannot be found anywhere else, although Yukihira was in fact once exiled to Suma for some unknown reason. Already in *The Tale of Genji,* the image of Yukihira in Suma, a nobleman lamenting his exile to a desolate seashore, had been linked to the romantic portrayal of seafolk girls. Like Yukihira, Genji, in a self-imposed exile, stays first in Suma and then in Akashi, a nearby coastal province, for three years. There he becomes involved with Lady Akashi, who has grown up amid this remote scenery as a daughter of the ex-governor of the province. Coming from a middle-ranking aristocratic family, she likens her own status, in comparison with Genji's high social standing, to that of rural girls working at the coast.

Pining Wind takes up from *Genji* this relationship between a noble exile and a local girl at the seacoast and rewrites it as a story about Yukihira, who stays in Suma for three years, has affairs with two local girls, and leaves behind his robe and court cap as keepsakes before making the journey back to the capital, just as Genji had left his robe with Lady Akashi on his own return to the capital. The text of the play is also replete with citations from *Genji,* especially in its description of the seashore at Suma. According to one medieval linked-verse manual, the "Suma" chapter of *Genji,* in which Genji visits Suma, should be closely associated with the "Wind in the Pines" chapter, in which Lady Akashi and her daughter finally move to the capital.

Wind in the pines is also connected to autumn rain, since both poetic themes are representative of autumnal imagery. At the same time, wind and rain being both natural and celestial phenomena, the two sisters' names also allude to the goddess of Mount Wu Shan in China, portrayed in a poem called "Ode to Gaotang." The goddess, who appears to Emperor Huai in a dream in which she sleeps with him, promises to manifest herself to him as "clouds in the morning and rain in the evening" on Mount Wu Shan, which, henceforth, remains forever obscured by a mysterious haze. This episode suggests erotic beauty in the hazy clouds and misty rain engulfing distant mountains, and it became a popular example of the concept of *yūgen*—meaning "profound and refined beauty," the dominant aesthetic among the upper circles of society in medieval Japan. Through association with the goddess of Wu Shan, the two sisters' names suggest that they, too, might be amorous incarnations of natural phenomena along the Suma coast.

There is another pair of natural images in the play which are also implicitly erotic: the moon and pails. Both of them appear in the first half of the play, in which the ghosts of the two sisters draw brine under the moon. The moon was traditionally a metaphor for a beautiful young man, and in some popular songs in the medieval period, a young girl is compared to a flower basket; one such song even employs the combination of the moon and a basket as a metaphor for sexual intercourse. Considering such contemporary associations, it seems reasonable to read erotic implications in the scene in which the two sisters rejoice on seeing the moon reflected in their water-filled pails.

Pining Wind is the oldest example among extant Noh plays that depicts love not merely negatively, as a sinful attachment, but also positively, as an illogical yet irresistible passion. In earlier plays, those who were obsessed with the fervent passion of love in their former lives come to be tortured in hell, for such clinging to earthly desire was considered an obstacle to attaining Buddhahood. In *Pining Wind,* too, the sisters' longing for Yukihira is repeatedly referred to as a sinful attachment. However, at the end of the play, both give themselves up entirely to their passion and to the illusion that a pine tree standing on the seashore *is* Yukihira, who has come back to them at last. Instead of representing torturous retribution in hell, the play shows the deranged dance of a girl (Pining Wind) completely enraptured by an illusory reunion with her lover. *Pining Wind* thus marks a significant departure from the purely negative treatment of earthly desires, a remnant of the original religious function of Noh, in a move by Zeami toward the poetic representation of human emotions.

Pining Wind[1]

Characters in Order of Appearance
A MONK
A VILLAGER
PINING WIND (*Waka-onna* mask)
AUTUMN RAIN (*Ko-omote* mask)

[*Stage assistant places a small pine tree, set in a stand, at front of stage; a poem-slip hangs in its branches. To* shidai *music, enter the Monk. He stands in base square.*]

MONK: (*shidai*) Suma! and on down the shore to Akashi
     Suma! and on down the shore to Akashi
     I will go roaming with the moon.

(*nanori*) You have before you a monk who is looking at every province. Since I have not yet seen the lands of the west,[2] I have decided this autumn to make my way there and watch the moon over Suma and Akashi.

(*tsuki-zerifu*) Having come so swiftly, I have already reached Suma shore, as I believe it is called, in the province of Tsu. On the beach, I see a single pine with a sign placed before it and a poem-slip hanging in its branches. There must be a story about this tree. I will ask someone what it is.

(*mondō*) Is any resident of Suma shore nearby?

[*Villager, who has slipped in to sit at villager position, now rises and comes to first pine.*]

VILLAGER: What do you need, reverend sir, from a resident of Suma shore?

MONK: I see this pine has a tablet planted before it, and a poem-slip hanging in its branches. There must be a story about it. Would you kindly tell it to me?

VILLAGER: Why, certainly. Long ago there were two young women—two saltmakers[3]—named Pining Wind and Autumn Rain. This pine stands in their memory. People who wished to honour them put this tablet here and hung in the pine's branches the poem-slip you see. Such people also give them comfort and guidance as they pass. Of course, reverend sir, you yourself have no connection with them,[4] but it would be good of you to do so, too, as you pass by.

MONK: Thank you for your account. Then I will go to the pine and comfort the spirits of those two young women.

VILLAGER: If there is anything else you need, reverend sir, please let me know.

MONK: I promise to do so.

---

1. Translated by Royall Tyler.
2. *Saigoku,* a vague term for the region west of Kyoto and along the Inland Sea.
3. Saltmaking is so important in *Pining Wind* that it deserves a description. Workers cut seaweed offshore or raked it up from the beach, then poured brine over it repeatedly. Next, they burned this salt-saturated seaweed, mixed the ashes with water, let the ashes settle, and skimmed off the salt solution. Only then did they boil down this elaborately prepared brine.
4. If the Monk was a relative of the two sisters, he would have a natural duty to comfort their spirits. Since he isn't, he could choose to pass on without doing so.

VILLAGER: Very well.

[*Exit Villager. Monk comes to center and stands facing pine.*]

MONK: (*unnamed*) So, this pine is the relic of two saltmakers who lived long ago:
Pining Wind, one was called, and the other Autumn Rain.

> A sad, sad story!
> There they lie buried deep in the earth,
> yet their names still linger, and in sign,
> ever constant in hue, a single pine
> leaves a green autumn.[5]
> Ah, very moving!

And now that I have comforted them by chanting the Sutra and by calling for them
upon our Lord Amida, the sun—as it will on these short autumn days—has all too
quickly set. That village below the hills is still a good way off. I will go instead to
this salt-house and see the night through here.

[*Stage assistant places the brine wagon near corner pillar: a small, light evocation of a wagon, with a pail on it and a long brocade rope to pull it by. To* shin-no-issei *music,[6] enter Autumn Rain, who stops at first pine. She is followed by Pining Wind, who stops at third pine. Autumn Rain carries a second pail. Both are dressed in white robes over red trouser-skirts. They stand facing each other.*]

PINING WIND AND AUTUMN RAIN: (*issei*) A brine wagon wheels meagerly
our dreary world round and round:[7]
O sorry life!
RAIN: Waves here at our feet: on Suma shore

[*They face audience.*]

BOTH: the very moon moistens a trailing sleeve.[8]

[*Face each other.*]

[*To* ashirai *music, both come on stage. Autumn Rain stands at center, Pining Wind in base square.*]

(*shidai*) We of Suma, long familiar with fall
we of Suma, long familiar with fall—
come, under the moon, let us draw brine!

[*Face audience.*]

---

5. The pine that stands "in sign" of the sisters' memory "leaves a green autumn" because it alone remains green amid the red autumn foliage.
6. Normally reserved for the entrance of the lead character in a god play. It underscores the exceptional beauty and purity of the two sisters, who are dressed mainly in white.

7. In Japanese, *kuruma* means both "wheel" and "wagon." These two lines evoke not only the drearily repetitious cycle of their daily labor but their sufferings on the wheel of birth and death.
8. The sisters' sleeves are wet with the brine they gather, but even the moon moistens their sleeves because, seeing it, they recall the past and weep.

WIND: (*sashi*) Fall winds were blowing, to call forth sighs,[9]
and although the sea lay some way off,
Yukihira, the Middle Counsellor,

[*Face each other.*]

BOTH: sang of the breeze from Suma shore
blowing through the pass; and every night,
waves sound so near the saltmakers' home,
apart and lonely. On the way to the village,
beside the moon, there is no company.

WIND: The sorry world's labours claim us,
and wholly wretched the seafolk's craft

BOTH: that makes no way through life, a dream
where, bubbles of froth, we barely live,
our wagon affording us no safe haven:
we of the sea, whose grieving hearts
never leave these sleeves dry!

CHORUS: (*sage-uta*) So thoroughly   [*Face audience.*]
this world of ours
appears unlivable,
one only envies
the brilliant moon[1]   [*Pining Wind steps forward,*
rising now, come, draw the rising tide   *as though towards the sea.*]
rising now, come, draw the rising tide!   [*Notices her reflection in a tide pool.*]

(*age-uta*) Image of shame, my reflection
image of shame, my reflection
shrinks away, withdrawing
tides leave behind stranded pools,   [*Gazes at water again.*]
and I, how long will I linger on?
Dew agleam on meadow grasses
soon must vanish in the sun,
yet on this stony shore
where saltmakers rake seaweed in,
trailing fronds they leave behind,
these sleeves, can only wilt away
these sleeves can only wilt away.   [*Retreats to base square.*]

WIND: (*sashi*) How lovely, though so familiar,
Suma as twilight falls!
Fishermen's calls echo faintly;

BOTH: out at sea, their frail craft loom   [*They face each other.*]
dim, the face of the moon:
wild geese in silhouette,
flocks of plovers, cutting gales,

9. The next six and a half lines quote freely from the "Suma" chapter of *The Tale of Genji* (page 184). Genji lived in a house some way back from the sea. Finding the noise of the waves still very loud, he recalled a poem by Yukihira, who had preceded him at Suma and who had lived at the same spot. Since Yukihira had spoken in verse of the breeze from Suma shore blowing through the pass (over the hills along the beach), Genji realized that this breeze must stir up the waves. The two sisters thus would live roughly where Genji, and Yukihira before him, had lived. This is inconsistent with the rest of the play, however, since a salt-house would need to be beside the sea.
1. A poem by Fujiwara no Takamitsu in the imperial anthology *Shūishū* (c. 1006).

salt sea winds—yes, each one
at Suma speaks of autumn alone.[2]
Ah, the nights' long, heart-chilling hours!

WIND: (*kakeai*) But come, let us draw brine!   [*Face audience.*]
At the sea's edge flood and ebb
clothe one in salt robes:

RAIN: tie the sleeves across your shoulders

WIND: to draw brine[3]—or so we wish,

RAIN: yet no, try as we may,

WIND: a woman's wagon

CHORUS: (*age-uta*) rolled in, falls back, weak and weary

[*Autumn Rain goes before drums. Pining Wind advances slightly, gazes after the cranes.*]

rolled in, falls back, weak and weary.[4]
Cranes start from the reeds with cries
while all four storm winds add their roar.[5]
The dark, the cold: how can they be endured?

[*Pining Wind looks at the moon, then glances into the buckets on the brine wagon.*]

As night wears on, the moon shines so bright!
Now we draw the moon's reflections!
Salt-fire smoke—O do take care![6]
This is the way we of the sea
live through the gloom of fall.

[*Kneels by brine wagon.*]

CHORUS: (*sage-uta*) Pine Islands! where Ojima's seafolk,[7]
beneath the moon,

[*With her fan mimes drawing brine, then gazes at the moon's reflection in her pail.*]

draw reflections, ah, with keen delight
draw reflections, ah, with keen delight!

[*To base square.*]

(*rongi*)   Far away they haul their brine[8]
in Michinoku: though the name

---

2. All these sights and sounds of Suma recall what Prince Genji sees in the "Suma" chapter.

3. The long, dangling sleeves had to be tied back in order to allow freedom of movement for work.

4. The two lines beginning with "a woman's wagon" defy translation. This is one possible paraphrase. They also contain the fleeting image of a great "male wave" approaching the shore only to recede, and this wave might conceivably point to Yukihira.

5. Storm winds from the four directions.

6. "Take care lest the smoke of the salt fires should drift across the moon and hide it." The motif is from classical poetry.

7. "Pine Islands" is Matsushima, a celebrated scenic spot on the northeast coast of Honshū, near the Shiogama mentioned below. The name Ojima is associated with Matsushima in poetry.

8. *Tōei*, the play from which Zeami transplanted this passage, is set at Ashiya, and that is why Ashiya and its environs figure in it when Suma does not. Having no continuous grammatical or narrative structure, the passage is almost untranslatable. Only its discontinuous phrases matter—to one who already knows the poetic tradition. In their aesthetic exaltation, Pining Wind and Autumn Rain play with fragments of poems that name, and hence eulogize, places associated with saltmaking.

is "near," Chika, where workers tend
the Shiogama salt-kilns.[9]

WIND: And where the poor folk carried salt-wood:
Akogi beach, that was, and the tide withdrawing

CHORUS: on down the same Ise coast lies Futami shore,
and its Paired Rocks: O I would pair
a past life in the world with one renewed![1]

WIND: When pines stand misty in spring sun,
the sea-lanes seem to stretch away
past the tide-flats of Narumi,
Bay of the Sounding Sea.[2]

CHORUS: Ah, Narumi, that was,
but here at Naruo,[3]
beneath the shadowing pines,
no moon ever shines to touch
the village huts roofed with rushes
at Ashinoya,[4]

WIND: drawing brine from Nada seas
sorely burdens me with care
though none will tell, and I am come,
no boxwood comb in my hair,[5]

CHORUS: while in comb the rolling billows

[*Autumn Rain places her pail on the brine wagon. Pining Wind gazes at it.*]

for us to draw brine, and look:
the moon is in my pail!

WIND: In mine, too, there is a moon!

CHORUS: How lovely! A moon here, too!

[*Pining Wind looks into the other pail, then up to the sky, then again at the two pails. Having received the wagon-rope from Autumn Rain, she pulls the wagon up to drums, then looks back at it one more time.*]

WIND: The moon is one,

CHORUS: reflections two, three the brimming tide,
for tonight we load our wagon with the moon.[6]

---

9. Michinoku is northern Honshū, where Matsushima and Shiogama are to be found. *Shiogama* means "salt-kiln," and the name of Chika, near Shiogama, resembles *chika* [*shi*], "near."

1. Akogi beach is near the Grand Shrine of Ise, on Ise Bay. Just off Futami-ga-ura ("Futami, or 'Twice-See' Shore"), also near the Ise Shrine, two tall rocks rise from the water. They are called the Husband-and-Wife Rocks, and a sacred straw rope encircles them both. The "poor folk" carrying "salt-wood" (wood to fuel the saltmakers' fires) on Akogi beach recall several classical poems.

2. Narumi-gata is a spot on the coast near present Nagoya. Its name means something like "Bay of the Sounding Sea."

3. Naruo, which sounds like Narumi, is along the coast east of Suma.

4. Ashinoya (or Ashiya) is a well-known locality on the coast east of Suma, now between Kobe and Osaka. Its name means "rush houses."

5. The line "at Ashinoya" begins a five-line passage that is a variant of a poem in *Tales of Ise*, episode no. 87. Nada is the name of the shore near Ashinoya. The passage puns elaborately on *tsuge* ("boxwood") and *tsugeji* ("will not tell [of my plight]"); and on *sashi* ("insert" a comb in one's hair) and *sashi-kuru* ("[waves] come surging in"). In the original poem, the girl explains to her lover that she has been so busy gathering brine, she has not been able even to dress her hair with a comb before coming to meet him.

6. To "one [moon]" and "two [reflections]," the original adds the puns *mitsu* ("three" or "brimming") and *yo* ("four" or "night"). "For" is meant to sound like "four."

O no, I do not find them dreary,
the tide-roads of the sea!

[*Stage assistant removes the wagon. Pining Wind sits on a stool before drums, while Autumn Rain sits directly on stage, slightly behind her and to her left. They are in the salt-house.*]

MONK: (*unnamed*) The people of the salt-house have returned. I will ask them to give me shelter for the night.
(*mondō*) I beg your pardon, there in the salt-house! Excuse me, please!
RAIN [*rises*]: What is it?
MONK: I am a traveller, and now the sun has set. May I have shelter for the night?
RAIN: Please wait a moment. I will ask the owner.

[*Turns to Pining Wind, kneels on one knee.*]

I beg your pardon, but a traveller is here. He says he wants shelter for the night.
WIND: We could easily give him shelter, but our house simply is not fit to be seen. No, we cannot let him stay.
RAIN [*rises, turns to Monk*]: I gave your request to the owner. She says that our house is not fit to be seen, and that we cannot offer you lodging for the night.
MONK: I understand, of course, but please realize that I do not mind what condition your house is in. I am a monk, after all. Do pass on again my urgent request for shelter here tonight.
RAIN [*turns to Pining Wind, kneeling on one knee*]: The traveller is a monk and he in- sists on asking again for a night's shelter.
WIND: What? the traveller is a monk, you say? Why yes, the moonlight shows me one who has renounced the world. Well, it will do, this saltmakers' home, with its posts of pine and fence of bamboo.[7] The night is cold, I know. Tell him he may stay and warm himself at our rush fire.
RAIN [*rises, turns to Monk*]: Do please come in.
MONK: Thank you for your kindness.

[*Autumn Rain sits as before. Monk rises, advances a few steps, sits again. He too is now in the salt-house.*]

WIND: From the start I wanted to have you stay, but this house is simply not fit to be seen. That is why I refused.
MONK: It is very good of you to have me. Since I am a monk and have always been one, my travels have no particular goal. On what grounds, then, should I prefer one lodging to another? Besides, here on Suma shore, any sensitive person ought actu- ally to prefer a somewhat melancholy life:

Should one perchance
ask after me,
say that on Suma shore,

---

7. Prince Genji's house at Suma is described in this way in the "Suma" chapter.

salt, sea-tangle drops
are falling as I grieve.[8]

Yes, that was Yukihira's poem. By the way, I noticed that pine tree on the shore.
When I asked a man about it, he told me that it stands in memory of two saltmakers named Pining Wind and Autumn Rain.

[*Pining Wind and Autumn Rain weep.*]

I have no connection of my own with them, of course, but I prayed for them before
going on. Why, how strange! When I mentioned Yukihira, both of you seemed
overcome with sorrow. What is the meaning of your grief?

WIND AND RAIN: Oh, it is true! When love is within, love's colours will show without![9] The way you quoted his poem, "Should one by chance inquire for me,"
brought on such pangs of longing! So tears of attachment to the human world once
more moistened our sleeves.

[*They weep.*]

MONK: Tears of attachment to the human world? You talk as though you were not of
the living. And Yukihira's poem seems to afflict you with feelings of painful longing, I do not understand. Please, both of you, tell me your names!

WIND AND RAIN: (*kudoki-guri*) I am ashamed!
            As the tale rises to my lips,
            I whom none ask after, ever,
            rejoin a world gone long ago,
            where, brine-drenched, I learn no lesson
            but suffer on in bitterness of heart.[1]
(*kudoki*) Yet having spoken,
            perhaps we need dissemble no more.
            Some while ago, as twilight fell,
            you kindly comforted those who lie
            under that pine, beneath the moss:
            two young women,
            Pining Wind and Autumn Rain.
            We before you are their phantoms.
            Yes, Yukihira, those three years,
            lightened his leisure with pleasant boating
            and watched the moon here on Suma shore.
            While seafolk maidens each night drew brine,
            he chose and courted us, two sisters.
            Pleased with names that fit the season,
            he called us Pining Wind and Autumn Rain.
            We Suma seafolk, familiars of the moon,

---

8. According to the imperial anthology *Kokinshū* (905),
Yukihira, in exile at Suma, sent this poem back to someone in the capital. The "salt, sea-tangle drops" are at once
the brine that drips from the seaweed gathered by saltmakers along the beach, and the poet's own tears.
9. A well-known saying, ultimately derived from the Chinese classic *Mencius*.

1. The brine that drenches her in her daily work also represents the memories from which she can never be free.
This passage uses language from the "Suma" chapter. It is
translated in the singular ("I am ashamed") because such
sentiments are too private to make sense in the plural
("we"). The "we" of the *kudoki* that follows is, likewise,
the translator's choice.

WIND: found our saltburner's clothing suddenly changed
BOTH: to silken summer robes censed with sweet fragrance.
WIND: So those three years slipped quickly by.
        Then Yukihira went up to The Capital
RAIN: and, not long after, came the news
BOTH: that he, so young, had passed away.[2]
WIND: O how I love him!
        But perhaps once, in another life

   [*Weeps.*]

        he again will come,
CHORUS: (*uta*) pining, Wind and Autumn Rain
        wet these sleeves, helpless, alas,
        against a love so far beyond us.
        We of Suma are deep in sin:[3]

   [*They appeal to Monk with palms pressed together.*]

        O in your kindness, give us comfort!
(*age-uta*) Upon passion's tangled grasses,
        dew and longing mingle wildly

   [*Below, Autumn Rain goes to sit before Chorus while Monk moves to witness position.*]

        dew and longing mingle wildly,
        till the heart, spellbound, yields to madness.
        The Day of the Serpent brings purification,[4]
        yet sacred streamers to ask the God's help.
        wave on, useless, wave-borne froth,
        we melt into grief and lasting sorrow.

   [*Below, stage assistant gives Pining Wind a man's hat and robe. Carrying them, she dances and mimes in consonance with the text.*]

(*kuse*) Ah, as those old days return to mind,
        I miss him so!
        Yukihira, the Middle Counsellor,
        three years dwelt on Suma shore,
        then went away up to the Capital,
        but left as keepsakes of our love
        his tall court hat, his hunting cloak.
        Each time I see them, ever more
        passion grasses spring,
        the pale dewdrops on each blade
        so swiftly gone—might I so soon

---

2. Zeami invented this death. Yukihira actually died at the age of 75.

3. This "sin" is neither social (as it involves love across class lines) nor moral. It is the sin of "wrongful clinging": the error of desiring intensely what one cannot possibly have. Such clinging leads only to misery.

4. A purification rite was regularly performed on the Day of the Serpent early in the third lunar month. Evil influences were transferred into dolls that were then floated down rivers or out to sea. The same rite appears in the "Suma" chapter of *Genji* (page 184).

forget this agony!
His parting gifts,
O they are enemies:
were they gone from me,
a moment of forgetfulness
might even now be mine:[5]
so someone sang. O it is true!
My love for him only deepens.

[*Lowers hat and cloak, which she had clasped to her, and weeps. Below, she continues miming.*]

WIND: Night after night,
         I remove on lying down
         this, my hunting cloak,[6]
CHORUS: and on and on I only pray
         that he and I might share our life—
         but fruitlessly.
         His keepsakes bring me no joy!
         She throws them down but cannot leave them;
         picks them up, and his own face
         looms before her. Do as she may,
         From the pillow,
         from the foot of the bed,
         love comes pursuing.[7]
         Down she sinks in helpless tears,
         lost in misery.

[*The Donning of the Robe: In base square, Pining Wind collapses to a sitting position and weeps. To* ashirai *music, stage assistant clothes her in the robe and places the hat on her head. She weeps once more.*]

WIND: (*ge-no-ei*) River of Three Crossings:[8]
         the grim ford of ceaseless weeping
         yet conceals a gulf of churning love!

(*kakeai*) O what happiness! Yukihira is standing there, calling my name, Pining Wind! I am going to him!

[*She rises and starts towards the pine. Autumn Rain comes up behind her and catches her right sleeve.*]

RAIN: How awful! This state you are in is exactly what drowns you in the sin of clinging! You have not yet forgotten the mad passion you felt when we still belonged to the world. That is a pine tree. Yukihira is not there.

---

5. An anonymous poem from the *Kokinshū*.
6. The first half of a poem by Ki no Tomonori, from the *Kokinshū*. The speaker of the poem says that just as he removes his hunting cloak each night before lying down and hangs it on a stand, he constantly thinks of his love. The key words in the poem are *kakete,* "hang" (the cloak

on its stand) and "constantly," here rendered "on and on."
7. From an anonymous *Kokinshū* poem, originally light-hearted in meaning.
8. The river that the soul must cross to reach the afterworld. It has three fords (deep, medium, or shallow) depending upon the sins that burden the soul.

WIND: You are too cruel, to talk that way! That pine *is* Yukihira!
         Though for a time we may say goodbye,
         should I hear you pine, I will return:
         so said his poem, did it not?[9]
RAIN: Why, you are right! I had forgotten!
         A while, perhaps, we may say goodbye,
         but should you miss me, I will come:
         those were the words
WIND: I had not forgotten, pining
         wind is rising now:
         he promised he will come—
RAIN: news to start an autumn rain,
         leaving sleeves a moment moistened;
WIND: yes, pining still, he will return:
RAIN: we rightly trusted
WIND: his dear poem:
BOTH: (*waka*) Now I say goodbye,

[*In tears, Pining Wind runs on to bridgeway, while Autumn Rain, also weeping, goes to sit before Chorus. Pining Wind then returns to stage, pauses in base square, and performs a* chū-no-mai *dance.*]

WIND: bound for Inaba's
         far green mountains;
         yet, my love, pine
         and I will come again.[1]
(*noriji*) Yonder, Inaba's far mountain pines;
CHORUS: here, my longing, my beloved lord
         here on Suma shore pines:[2] Yukihira
         back with me once more, while I,
         beside the tree, rise now, draw near:
         so dear, the wind-bent pine—
         I love him still!

[*Dance: Pining Wind ceases weeping, then lifts her head and dances around the pine. As text continues, she continues to dance and mime.*]

CHORUS: In the pine a wind blows wild.
         The Suma breakers rage night-long
         While wrongful clinging brings you this, our dream.
         In your kindness, give us comfort!

---

9. Pining Wind quotes Yukihira's poem inaccurately; so does Autumn Rain, a few lines later. It is a climactic moment when, a little later still, their mounting excitement recalls it to them perfectly.

1. This poem, from the *Kokinshū*, is generally taken as a farewell addressed by Yukihira to a friend or friends in the capital, when he set out for Inaba province in 855 as

the new governor. The translation corresponds to Zeami's use of it, but the original suggests nothing precise about the person or persons to whom it may have been addressed.

2. This "pines" is meant to include the meaning "is a pine."

> Now, farewell:
(*uta*)   receding waves fall silent
> along Suma shore
> a breeze sweeps down from off the hills.
> On the pass, the cocks are crowing.
> The dream is gone, without a shadow
> night opens into dawn.
> It was autumn rain you heard,
> but this morning see:
> pining wind alone lingers on
> pining wind alone lingers on.

[*Facing side from base square, stamps the final beat.*]

꧁

RESONANCE
Kyōgen, Delicious Poison

Kyōgen (comic drama) plays are relatively short and performed as comic relief before or between performances of Noh drama. In contrast to Noh drama, which is marked by chanting and dance, kyōgen is a theater of dialogue. It is performed without masks, a chorus, or music, elements that elevate Noh. Unlike Noh drama, which often focuses on the spirits of the dead, the characters in kyōgen are usually people who live in this world, in everyday reality. We know the playwrights of most Noh plays, but kyōgen plays are anonymous in authorship, reflecting a more popular base. Kyōgen focuses not on courtiers and powerful warriors, as Noh drama does, but on commoners or lesser figures such as servants. In kyōgen, those of lesser position often get the best of their superiors, thus temporally and comically inverting the social hierarchy, as is the case in *Delicious Poison*. Kyōgen emerged in the late medieval period, during an era of great social upheaval, when those of lower status overcame those of higher rank. Kyōgen, reflecting the times, looks up from below with both a critical and humorous eye.

Kyōgen drama draws its material from contemporary life, not from classical texts, as Noh drama does. *Delicious Poison (Busu)* is an exception in that it has a clearly identifiable literary source, the *Shasekishū,* a thirteenth-century collection of religious and secular tales compiled by the Zen priest Mujū (1225–1312). The tales in the collection were meant both to entertain and to teach Buddhist morality to commoners.

Delicious Poison is the most popular play in the kyōgen repertory and the canonical play of the genre. No character better represents kyōgen than Tarō Kaja, the leading character in this play. He is the archetypal clever servant, willing to exhaust every stratagem in order to outwit his master. Despite the fact that Tarō and his fellow servant Jirō destroy two of their master's treasured art objects in this play, the audience's sympathy clearly lies with the servants because of the master's deceitful treatment of the pair. Tarō shows that his trickery is far more clever and effective than anything his master can imagine.

Kyōgen's humor walks the fine path between the psychologically real and the physically and vocally ridiculous, as when the two servants desperately exhort each other and wave their fans as they fearfully approach the poison, hoping to blow its deadly fumes in the other direction. This activity, as silly and energetic as it is, is executed with the elegance and precision that characterize all kyōgen performance, and which have maintained the art form as classical comic theater, impossible to mistake for clowning or buffoonery.

Delicious Poison[1]

Characters
The MASTER, a wealthy man
TARŌ and JIRŌ, his servants

[*The Master, Tarō, and Jirō enter down the bridgeway, or* hashigakari. *The Master goes to the* shite *position, or* jōza, *and his two servants kneel down side by side about eight feet behind him.*]

MASTER: I am a man who lives in this area. Today I must go over the mountains on business. Now I will call my two servants and order them to look after the house while I am away.

[*Walking to the* waki *position, or* waki-za.]

Hey, hey, the both of you, come here!
TARŌ AND JIRŌ: Yeeeees.

[*They rise and go to the* shite *position, standing on either side of it, facing the Master who is at the* waki *position.*]

MASTER: Are you there?
TARŌ AND JIRŌ: We are both at your service.
MASTER: I didn't call you about anything special. I have to go over the mountains on a little business, and I want you to look after the house while I'm away.
TARŌ: Wait. I'll go with you, so have Jirō look after the house.
JIRŌ: No, no, I'll go with you, so have Tarō look after the house.
MASTER: No, today my business is such that I need neither of you to accompany me. Now both of you wait here.
TARŌ AND JIRŌ: Yes, sir.
MASTER [*speaks his next line while going to the stage assistant, picking up a large, lidded, cylindrical lacquer barrel, and carrying it to downstage center, where he places it*]: This is poison, so take special care when you guard the house.

[*He returns to the* waki *position.*]

TARŌ: In that case both of us . . . right?
JIRŌ: Right . . .
TARŌ AND JIRŌ: Will go with you.
MASTER: And why is that?
TARŌ: After all, if that *person* will watch the house while you're gone, no one else . . . right?
JIRŌ: Right . . .
TARŌ AND JIRŌ: Is needed to guard the house.
MASTER: You both have terrible ears. I didn't say "*person,*" I said "*poison.*" Busu is a poison so deadly that if a breeze blows over it and even a whiff of it reaches your noses, you will die instantly. Be aware of this and guard it carefully.
TARŌ: In that case, we'll do as you command.

1. Translated and with introduction by Laurence Kominz.

JIRŌ: I have one small question.

MASTER: And what is that?

JIRŌ: Well, if this Busu is so deadly that even a whiff is fatal, how is it that *you* are able to handle it?

TARŌ: You asked a very good question.

JIRŌ: I sure did.

MASTER: Your uncertainty is most reasonable. This poison is the Master's treasured possession, and as long as *I* touch it, it will do no harm. But if you two come any- where near, it will kill you for sure. So be aware of this while you guard the house.

TARŌ: In that case . . .

TARŌ AND JIRŌ: We will do as you command.

MASTER: Well, I'm going now.

TARŌ AND JIRŌ: Are you going already?

MASTER: I'm counting on you to look after the house.

TARŌ: Don't worry about the house, we'll take good care of everything. Please take your time . . .

TARŌ AND JIRŌ: And enjoy yourself while you are away.

MASTER: I'm depending on you. I'm depending on you.

[*The Master exits down the bridgeway and the two servants turn to watch him leave.*]

TARŌ: My, he sure left in a hurry.

JIRŌ: You're right. He sure left in a hurry.

TARŌ: First of all, let's sit down.

JIRŌ: Right.

TARŌ AND JIRŌ: *Ei ei yattona.*

[*Uttering this expression of physical effort, they sit alongside each other upstage, facing straight out at the barrel and the audience.*]

TARŌ: Actually, what I said to Master about wanting to go with him was a lie. Really, staying at home and guarding the house is a lot easier than working, isn't it?

JIRŌ: You're right. Nothing is easier than what we're doing right now.

TARŌ [*slapping the stage and then running down the bridgeway*]: Quick, run away, run away!

JIRŌ: What happened, what happened?

     [*Following Tarō.*]

TARŌ: Just now there was a cold breeze blowing from the direction of the Busu.

JIRŌ: That's pretty scary.

TARŌ: Let's move a little farther away from it.

JIRŌ: Good idea.

TARŌ: Around here would be good.

JIRŌ: Right.

TARŌ AND JIRŌ: *Ei ei yattona*

[*They sit side by side on a diagonal line in front of the flute position, facing the gazing pillar.*]

JIRŌ: You know, I asked Master about it, but don't you think it's strange that poison so deadly a breeze passing over it can kill you, is harmless when the Master handles it? I wonder why that's so?

TARŌ: You're right. There's something strange about all this.

JIRŌ [*slapping the stage and then running down the bridgeway*]: Quick, run away, run away!

TARŌ: What happened, what happened?

   [*Following Jirō onto the bridgeway.*]

JIRŌ: Just now a warm, damp breeze blew from the direction of the Busu.

TARŌ: This is getting worse and worse. You know what I think? Why don't we take a quick look and see what's inside that Busu?

JIRŌ: What do you mean? How do you expect to get a look at it when even a whiff of it means sudden death?

TARŌ: We'll fan the wind blowing toward us back the other way and that's when we take a peek.

JIRŌ: That's a fine idea!

TARŌ: Okay, help me by fanning with all of your might.

JIRŌ: Right.

TARŌ: Fan hard, fan hard!

JIRŌ: I'm fanning, I'm fanning!

   [*Tarō takes the lead position, advancing toward the Busu while hiding his head behind his raised left arm, and fanning under his left sleeve. Jirō follows, holding his fan in both hands and fanning with an up-and-down motion.*]

TARŌ: Fan hard, fan hard!

JIRŌ: I'm fanning, I'm fanning!

TARŌ: All right. I'm ready to loosen the cord, so fan with all your might.

JIRŌ: Right, right!

TARŌ: Fan hard, fan hard!

JIRŌ: I'm fanning, I'm fanning!

TARŌ: Run away, run away!

   [*He runs back onto the bridgeway, Jirō following him.*]

JIRŌ: What happened, what happened?

TARŌ: I managed to untie the cord. Please, you go and take off the lid.

JIRŌ: No, taking off the cord was just the first step in taking off the lid. You go do it.

TARŌ: No, no. The two of us have to take turns doing the dangerous work. Please, this time you have to go and take off the lid.

JIRŌ: In that case, I'll go take it off, but please fan for me with all your might.

TARŌ: Right.

JIRŌ: Fan hard, fan hard!

TARŌ: I'm fanning, I'm fanning!

   [*This time Jirō takes the lead fanning position, with Tarō in the following position.*]

JIRŌ: Fan hard, fan hard!

TARŌ: I'm fanning, I'm fanning!

JIRŌ: All right, I'm ready to take the lid off, so fan with all your might!

TARŌ: Right.

JIRŌ: Fan hard, fan hard!

TARŌ: I'm fanning, I'm fanning!

JIRŌ: Quick, run away, run away!

TARŌ: What happened, what happened?

JIRŌ: I got the lid off.

TARŌ: That's a relief.

JIRŌ: Why do you say that?

TARŌ: If something alive were inside it would have jumped out. At least we know it's not something alive.

JIRŌ: It might be playing possum you know.

TARŌ: It's scary, but I'm going to go look at what's inside.

JIRŌ: That's a good idea.

TARŌ: You help me fan the breeze the other way with all your might, okay?

JIRŌ: Right.

TARŌ: Fan hard, fan hard!

JIRŌ: I'm fanning, I'm fanning!

[*Tarō takes the lead position with Jirō following.*]

TARŌ: Fan hard, fan hard!

JIRŌ: I'm fanning, I'm fanning!

TARŌ: I'm ready to look in now. Keep fanning with all your might.

JIRŌ: Right.

TARŌ: Fan hard, fan hard!

JIRŌ: I'm fanning, I'm fanning!

TARŌ: Quick, run away, run away!

JIRŌ: What happened, what happened?

TARŌ: You know what? It's brown and sticky, and looks delicious!

JIRŌ: What's that? It looks delicious?

TARŌ: That's right.

JIRŌ: In that case, I'll go take a look too. You help me fan with all your might.

TARŌ: Right.

JIRŌ: Fan hard, fan hard!

TARŌ: I'm fanning, I'm fanning!

[*Jirō takes the lead position, with Tarō following.*]

JIRŌ: Fan hard, fan hard!

TARŌ: I'm fanning, I'm fanning!

JIRŌ: Fan hard, fan hard!

TARŌ: I'm fanning, I'm fanning!

JIRŌ: Quick, run away, run away!

TARŌ: What happened, what happened?

JIRŌ: Just like you said, it looks delicious.

TARŌ: You know what? Suddenly, I want to eat that Busu. I'll go eat it up.

JIRŌ: What's the matter with you? That's a poison so deadly a breeze passing over it will kill you. How do you think you can eat it?

TARŌ: Maybe I've been possessed by the Busu because I have a terrible craving for it. I'll go eat it up!

JIRŌ: Wait! As long as I'm by your side, I won't let you go.

[*He seizes Tarō's sleeve.*]

TARŌ: Let go of me!
JIRŌ: I won't let go!
TARŌ: I'm telling you to let go!
JIRŌ: And I say I won't!

[*Tarō shakes loose from Jirō's grip and sings as he approaches the barrel.*]

TARŌ: *Casting off my darling's sleeves I bid farewell . . .*
               And approach the deadly Busu poison.

JIRŌ: Oh, no, you've gone near the Busu! Now you're doomed!

[*Tarō kneels on one knee behind the bucket. He sticks the bamboo handle of his closed fan into the barrel, stirs, and then says the following as he mimes eating a sticky substance off the handle of his fan.*]

TARŌ: *Ahm ahm ahm ahm.*
JIRŌ: Oh no! You're eating the Busu. Now you are truly doomed!
TARŌ: Ooooh, I'm dying.

[*Tarō strikes his forehead with his left hand and slumps forward.*]

JIRŌ [*running to Tarō's side and supporting him with his left arm*]: Tarō, what happened? Pull yourself together.
TARŌ [*in apparent pain*]: Who is it, who is it?
JIRŌ: It's me, Jirō.
TARŌ [*gleefully*]: Hey, Jirō.
JIRŌ: What happened?
TARŌ: It's so *delicious,* I'm dying.
JIRŌ: What's that? It's delicious?
TARŌ: Yes.
JIRŌ: So what is the poisonous Busu?
TARŌ: Here, take a look, it's *sugar!*
JIRŌ: Let me see it. It really *is* sugar!
TARŌ: So, let's dig in!
JIRŌ: Right you are.
TARŌ AND JIRŌ [*stirring with closed fans, then miming eating the sugar off the handles*]: *Ahm ahm ahm ahm.*
TARŌ: Well, well, isn't it delicious?
JIRŌ: You're right. It *is* delicious.
TARŌ: And because it's so delicious, master tried to stop us from eating it, saying it was "Busu . . ."
JIRŌ: "Poison" . . .
TARŌ AND JIRŌ [*laugh*]: *Ha, ha, ha, ha, ha.*
TARŌ: It sure was nasty of him. *Ahm ahm ahm ahm.*
JIRŌ: Let's keep eating and stuff ourselves. *Ahm ahm ahm ahm.*
TARŌ: It's so delicious I'm afraid my chin will drop off! *Ahm ahm ahm ahm.*

[*Tarō takes the barrel off to stage left, where he continues to eat alone. Jirō notices this and when Tarō isn't looking, he takes it to stage right and proceeds to eat alone.*]

JIRŌ: I can't stop eating it. *Ahm ahm ahm ahm.*

TARŌ [*notices the barrel is gone and confronts Jirō*]: Hey! Aren't you going to let me have any?

JIRŌ: You were hogging it. I've got to eat some too!

TARŌ: No, I've got to eat it. Give it here!

> [*They tussle over the Busu.*]

JIRŌ: Give it here!

TARŌ: Give it here!

JIRŌ: Give it here!

TARŌ: All right, let's place it here, right between us and share it.

JIRŌ: That's fine with me.

TARŌ: Well, well, let's dig in!

JIRŌ: Yes, let's.

TARŌ AND JIRŌ: *Ahm ahm ahm ahm.*

TARŌ: All my life I've never tasted anything this good. *Ahm ahm ahm ahm.*

JIRŌ: It's so delicious I'm afraid my chin will drop off! *Ahm ahm ahm ahm.*

TARŌ: Eat up, eat up. *Ahm ahm ahm ahm.*

JIRŌ: Right you are, right you are. *Ahm ahm ahm ahm.*

> [*Tarō notices the Busu is almost gone and leaves. He goes to the* shite *position where he stands facing forward.*]

JIRŌ [*stirring with a clattering sound as he scrapes the inside of the barrel*]: There's still some left, there's still some left. *Ahm ahm ahm ahm.* Hey, what's this? The Busu is all gone.

> [*He goes to the* waki *position and turns to face Tarō.*]

TARŌ: What?! You've just done something fine.

JIRŌ: What do you mean "something fine"?

TARŌ: Well, Master didn't want you and I to eat the Busu. That's why he told us it was deadly poison. Now you've gone and eaten it all up and I don't think he will be very pleased about it. When the Master comes home, I'm going to tell him right away.

JIRŌ: Hey, wait, wait! It was *you* who first looked at the Busu and first ate the Busu, and when the Master comes home, I'll tell him about it right away.

TARŌ: Now wait, wait! What I just said was a joke.

JIRŌ: You shouldn't be telling bad jokes like that. So, what should we do for an excuse?

TARŌ [*pointing to the right of the* waki *pillar*]: Tear up that hanging scroll.

JIRŌ: What? If I rip it up will it give us an excuse?

TARŌ: Oh, it will, it will!

JIRŌ: In that case, I'll tear it up.

> [*He goes to the right of the* waki *pillar where, to the following vocalization, he mimes pulling down a scroll, ripping it up, and throwing the pieces away.*]

Zarrari, zarrari, bassari! There, I've ripped it to shreds.

TARŌ: What?! You just did something fine again.

JIRŌ: What do you mean?

TARŌ: Now it's true that I was the first to see and the first to eat the Busu. But because the Master treasures that scroll more than any other I don't think he'll be
pleased when he sees it ripped up like that. When he returns I'll tell him right away
just who it was that ripped it up.

JIRŌ: Hey, what do you mean?! It was you who told me to rip it up, and when the
Master returns I'll tell him about it right away.

TARŌ: Now wait, wait! That was another joke.

JIRŌ: How many times do I have to tell you this is no time for bad jokes. Now
what's our excuse?

TARŌ: Smash that huge Chinese vase.

[*He points in the direction of the gazing pillar.*]

JIRŌ: I'm not going to do anything you tell me anymore.

TARŌ: And why is that?

JIRŌ: You'll tell on me, right?

[*Both laugh.*]

TARŌ: So, let's get together, and *both* smash it.

JIRŌ: That's a good idea.

TARŌ: Come over here.

JIRŌ: Right.

[*They walk downstage, to the left of the gazing pillar.*]

TARŌ AND JIRŌ [*they crouch down together and mime lifting a heavy object*]: *Ei ei
yattona.*

TARŌ: For this we need three lifts, and on the third we'll let it go.

JIRŌ: Right.

TARŌ AND JIRŌ: *Iiiiyaaaa. Eiii.*

TARŌ: That was one.

TARŌ AND JIRŌ: *Iiiiyaaaa. Eiii.*

JIRŌ: That was two.

TARŌ: This is the important one. Don't forget to drop it.

JIRŌ: I won't forget to drop it.

TARŌ AND JIRŌ: *Iiiiiyaaaaaa. Eiii!*

TARŌ: *Garari!* (Crash!)

JIRŌ: *Chin!* (Tinkle, tinkle.)

TARŌ: There's a lot more of it now!

JIRŌ: It's in smithereens!

[*Tarō and Jirō laugh together as they return to their respective places at the* shite
and waki *positions.*]

JIRŌ: Well, now what do we do for an excuse?

TARŌ: My, you are a weakling. When the Master comes home, burst into tears!

JIRŌ: What? Will crying be an excuse?

TARŌ: Oh, it will, it will.

[*He looks toward the bridgeway.*]

Oh, look, he'll be back soon. Come over here and sit down.

[*The two sit side by side in front of the left side of the orchestra position,* daishōmae, *facing the audience.*]

MASTER [*at the first pine*]: My business is finally over.

[*Walking toward the main stage.*]

Even though I told Tarō and Jirō to guard the house, I'm worried about them so I'll hurry home.

[*Arriving at the main stage.*]

What do you know, I'm home already.

TARŌ: He's back. Start crying.

TARŌ AND JIRŌ: *Eheh, eheh, heh, heh, heh, heh.*

[*This is the vocalization used for weeping.*]

MASTER: Hey, Tarō, Jirō, I'm home!

[*The two servants continue to weep as the Master takes his place at the* waki *position.*]

Something's wrong. You should be happy to see your Master return. Why are you crying like that?

TARŌ: Jirō, please, you explain it to him.

JIRŌ: No Tarō, please, you do it.

[*They continue to weep.*]

MASTER: Enough! You two are making me very angry. Either one of you tell me what is going on right away.

TARŌ: In that case, I guess I'll tell you. We had important work to do guarding the house, and we knew we shouldn't fall asleep, so I sumo wrestled Jirō to keep awake. He was stronger, and lifted me up higher than his head. I didn't want to be thrown, so I grabbed onto that scroll, and—look—that's what's become of it.

[*The two servants weep.*]

MASTER [*looking at the remains of the scroll on the ground*]: What's this? My precious scroll is torn to shreds!

JIRŌ: Then we had a rematch, and I fell with a crash onto the big china vase, and there—it's in smithereens.

[*The two servants weep.*]

MASTER [*moving to stage right and looking at the shards of the vase on the ground*]: Oh my god! You smashed my precious vase to bits!

[*Returning to the* waki *position.*]

The two of you don't deserve to live!

TARŌ: We knew we had no right to live, and so we hoped to kill ourselves by eating the Busu. Right, Jirō?

JIRŌ: Riiiiiight!

TARŌ AND JIRŌ [*singing*]: We took one mouthful
                           But we did not die.

Two mouthfuls, and still we did not die.
Three mouthfuls, four mouthfuls, five mouthfuls,
Ten mouthfuls and more.

[*They begin dancing.*]

We ate up all the Busu
And still we could not die.
Destined to live, what lucky fellows!
Aren't we sturdy guys?

[*Tarō and Jirō end the dance by striking the head of the standing master with their open fans. They then run off stage, down the bridgeway.*]

MASTER: What do you mean, "sturdy guys"? You rascals! I'll get you, I'll get you.
TARŌ AND JIRŌ [*exiting down the bridgeway*]: Please forgive us, forgive us!
MASTER [*chasing the servants, and exiting down the bridgeway*]: Where are you going? Someone stop them please! I'll get you, I'll get you!

⧜

[END OF NOH: DRAMA OF GHOSTS, MEMORIES, AND SALVATION]

Calligraphy of the name of the Prophet Muhammad, Turkey, 1827. Based on centuries-old calligraphic traditions, this dynamic verbal "image" of the Prophet is surrounded by a description (*hilyah*) of the Prophet by his son-in-law 'Ali, which concludes: "When walking, he leaned forward, as if descending a slope. If he turned to see something, he would turn with his whole body. Between his shoulders he had the Seal of Prophethood. He was the last of the Prophets."

Classical Arabic and
Islamic Literatures

This section introduces the early contribution of Arabic and Islamic culture to the world of literature and thought. Islam is now one of the major world religions, with more than one billion believers, nearly twenty percent of the world's population. Yet to call this section simply "Islamic literature" would be to confuse the works here with the long tradition of theological and religious works denoted as "Islamic." No one identifies the literatures of the many lands that believe in Christianity as "Christian literature," for this term has also its specific theological use. Furthermore, the region's literary traditions date back to the earliest periods of literacy, as can be seen in the section on the Ancient Near East in Volume A. Growing out of these earlier literatures, Arabic literature itself began long before the rise of Islam. Yet Islam plays an essential part in the worldview that informed most of the literature included in this section and is appropriately a major focus in the following pages.

How best to name this region is another question. The common term "Middle East" did not exist at the time studied here, but was coined centuries later by Europeans, for whom the region was nearer home than the "Far" East of China and Japan. Moreover, the geographic area covered in this section is much larger than the present Middle East. "Classical Arabic literature" *How best to name this region is another question.*
is the term most widely used in Arabic culture to refer to the literature of this period, but this section is not solely devoted to Arabic literary works, for it contains a number of works written in other languages such as Persian and Turkish, and closes with an epic from Mali in West Africa. The double title "Arabic and Islamic Literatures" is meant to suggest the richly varied character of this group of literary and cultural traditions.

Three elements are essential for an understanding of this section: the place, the language, and the man who changed their history—in other words, the geography of the region in which Islam emerged; the Arabic language in which the holy book of Islam, the Qur'an, was revealed; and Muhammad, the man who inspired the Arabs to create a new culture and a vast empire and who immortalized their language. These elements played a crucial role in the emergence of Islam, which changed the destiny of the Arabs and the history of the entire region.

THE PLACE

Let us start with the place: the Arabian Peninsula (see map on page 325). The present division of the Peninsula into various political entities was unknown during the rise of Islam. The peninsula lies at the heart of the ancient Near East, yet until the seventh century C.E. it contributed little to the Near East's long history of vibrant civilizations—Babylonian, Assyrian, Egyptian, Phoenician, Hittite, Hebrew, and Persian. The exception to this generalization is the Nabataean civilization, which emerged and flourished in the

315

southwestern corner of the peninsula. The lack of early influential cultures elsewhere in the region is perhaps due to the fact that the peninsula is the product and the victim of harsh natural conditions and is not an integral part of either Asia or Africa, the two continents between which it resides. Although surrounded by five seas, it has hardly any hospitable coasts, and there is scarcely a single river to facilitate transport and communication through these vast sun-scorched deserts and steppes.

Apart from a relatively small mountainous area in the south and southwest, the peninsula is arid desert—vast expanses known for their breathtaking beauty and sand dunes, some spectacularly formed of red sand. In the south, the region is sufficiently elevated to avoid the rigors of tropical heat. However, the lowlands along the Red Sea, the Gulf of Aden, and the Arabian Sea have a semitropical climate. The summer heat is intense, and the scarcity of rainfall makes life difficult. Rains may come as torrential downpours and flash floods that provide enough water to carpet the desert with spectacular wild flowers.

The climatic juxtaposition of torrential rain and drought is one dimension of the geographical extremes in the peninsula. Yet south of the central area known as the Empty Quarter lies fertile and luxuriant land. This region produces an abundance of flora, with the lush frankincense tree contrasting sharply with the date palm of the desert. Life in the south is also different from its counterpart in the desert: unlike the nomadic Bedouin, the southern Arabs are sedentary terrace farmers who are totally in control of their movement and social life. The agricultural abundance in the south constituted the basis of its economic prosperity and the rich culture of *Arabia Odorifera,* Fragrant Arabia, the land of frankincense and myrrh.

In the last millennium B.C.E., the coexistence of these geographical extremes decisively shaped the history of the peninsula and created two distinct groups in the north and the south, with different Semitic languages. (The term "Semitic" derives from Noah's son Shem, legendary founder of the region's peoples, including both Arabs and Jews.) The inhabitants of the southern parts spoke Sabaic, a Semitic language. They were the Phoenicians of the south and early colonizers of the African mainland. But their most remarkable achievement was their commercial success in the ancient world, for they brought together the worlds of the Indian Ocean, the Fertile Crescent, and the Mediterranean, and made each of them aware of the existence of the other. They extended the caravan route via the Indian Ocean as far as India, Somalia, and Zanzibar. They linked the Hellenic civilization of the Mediterranean to the culture of India. Yet the southern Arabs achieved none of their artistic beauty in sculpture or architecture. Their most notable artistic achievement was their calligraphy, Musnad, an elegant and graceful script.

Ironically, it was not these southern Arabs who changed the course of history seven centuries after the advent of Christianity; it was their much poorer brethren in the north.

Ironically, it was not these southern Arabs who changed the course of history seven centuries after the advent of Christianity; it was their much poorer brethren to the north.

The greater part of the Arabian Peninsula was steppe or arid desert, with scattered oases providing barely enough water for regular cultivation. In the oases settled tribes, or sometimes larger communities, cultivated grain or palm trees. Although these oases sustained sedentary life, which helped to consolidate large tribes, they were vulnerable to the depredations of sandstorms and attack by Bedouin nomads ("Bedouin" means "desert dweller"). Their inhabitants were sedentary when the oasis was prosperous, but they reverted to the nomadic life when necessary and to the fighting traditions this required. This is in marked contrast to the people of the south, who were strongly rooted in their environment and settled in cities or transformed the rugged, mountainous terrain with dams and terraces.

Scattered nomads occupied the vast arid desert and sustained themselves by tending camels, sheep, and goats. The camel was their most vital animal, the *sine qua non* of Bedouin life. The Bedouins were constantly moving in search of pasture and water, and the camel, "the ship of the desert," as the Arabs call it, was the essential element of this lifestyle. Bedouins developed a strong tribal and familial ethos, which was essential for their survival in a hostile environment. Dates were their most important staple food and both the date palm and the camel displayed the hardiness and endurance which characterized the Bedouins. The Bedouins' mobility was patterned by climatic conditions. Droughts forced people to migrate in search of water, the most vital of all geographical determinants. The scarcity of water and other vital resources often led to fighting. Unlike the southern Arabians, whose ethos was that of an affluent society built on luxury goods, that of the Bedouins was built on the dictates of a life that demanded endurance, courage, generosity, hospitality, loyalty to the tribe, and pride of ancestry. Over the long history of Arabia, war became an important institution, celebrated in the pre-Islamic poetry with which this section opens, and the battle-hardened Bedouins became an invaluable resource for the spread of Islam.

> *The camel was their most vital animal, the* sine qua non *of Bedouin life . . . "the ship of the desert" . . .*

By the third century C.E. the northern Arabs emerged as a trading force to be reckoned with, with caravan cities such Petra and Palmyra adorning their desert. The Bedouin was no longer only a cameleer but also a horseman with well-honed fighting skills. The domestication of the horse played an important role in the militarization of Arabia. The Bedouins were no longer content with the role of passive trader, but started to interfere in the affairs of the south and pursue independent economic policies and trade alliances, often not to the advantage of their southern counterparts. The southern Arabs were also under tremendous pressure from the Ptolemies of Egypt, who wanted to make the Red Sea their own lake, and the Abyssinians of Axum in Africa were poised to challenge the trade and maritime control of southern Arabia.

With the dwindling power of the south, Mecca became the major trade center in Arabia, and the influence of the Bedouins of the north rose. The fourth and the fifth centuries C.E. witnessed the emergence of Christian Byzantium and Zoroastrian Persia, both with definite religious and economic agendas, and with designs on Arabia. In the fifth century, Judaism gained the upper hand when a number of the southern kings converted to Judaism, while Christianity made large strides in some areas. A century of anarchy and upheaval occurred in the sixth century, as first Ethiopia and later Persia invaded the Arabian Peninsula. The sixth century filled the chaotic religious scene in southern Arabia with proponents and martyrs of every religious denomination available at the time in the wider Middle East. It became an arena for conflicting ideas, while in the north Mecca rose to prominence as a new cultural and trade center. It was from Mecca that the message of Islam emerged, and it was here that Muhammad, its messenger, spent his formative years and early youth as a caravan trader. But before dealing with the message and its messenger, a few words about the language in which this message was conveyed are essential.

THE LANGUAGE

When it comes to the word, the language that played a substantial role in the shaping and development of Arabic culture, Islam shares the emphasis on language and writing that also governed Judaism and Christianity. The emergence of Islam and the codification of the Arabic language in the Qur'an ensured the continuous development of Arabic over two millennia— a sharp contrast to other Semitic languages of Arabia, which waned and in some cases disappeared.

. . . Islam shares the emphasis on language and writing that also governed Judaism and Christianity.

The Arabic language shares many traits with Semitic languages farther south, and with the northwest Semitic branch that includes Hebrew and other Canaanite languages. As a distinct language of this family, Arabic stands between the two branches and has been enriched by its contact with both.

Its standardization as a coherent language with its own literary tradition long preceded the rise of Islam. The oldest record of Arabic appeared in an Assyrian account of fighting from 853–626 B.C.E. The earliest texts recorded in Arabic script are three graffiti on a wall in the temple of Ramm in the Sinai dating from 300 C.E. and an inscription of Imru' al-Qays, a pre-Islamic poet included in this section, dated 328 C.E. Naturally in such a vast area as Arabia there were several dialectical variations, but what is important for the emergence of Arabic culture is the existence of a literary language. Partial translations of the Bible probably circulated in different parts of Arabia before Islam. A fragment of the Psalms in Arabic in Greek characters dates to the pre-Islamic period, and poetry composed in a standardized Arabic language was current in different parts of Arabia long before the emergence of Islam.

The various Bedouin tribes may have used different dialects in their spoken language, but their poets wrote in one standardized language, the language known now as classical Arabic. Mecca, the commercial center of Arabia, acted as a linguistic melting pot and played a significant role in the language's standardization. Meccans adapted it to the needs of an articulate and urbanized culture and widened its expressive potential without disrupting its structure. This common language of Mecca was closely linked to the dialect of the Quraysh, which was the dominant tribe in Mecca and the one that controlled trade. By the sixth century, there was a widely recognized literary language distinct from all forms of the spoken language in common currency in Arabia. The diverse dialects and various approaches to the use of vocabulary were blended into a unique literary language, which developed and evolved over a long period of time. This language is the one whose origins can be glimpsed from what remains of the period's poetry and prose. It had an extremely rich vocabulary because of the many dialectical variations and used vivid imagery based on the Bedouin power of observation and poetic exuberance. The richness of the language and the breadth of its expressive ability reflect a richness of ideas and views and a complex morality.

Pre-Islamic Arabia developed a high morality, emphasizing honor, generosity, valor, integrity, and dignity. The jewel of this literature was poetry, *shi'r* or *qasida*. Pre-Islamic poetry was highly developed and sophisticated. Described as a great "necklace of pearls," with each line considered a pearl in its own right, it was an art that required a long period of apprenticeship before novice-poets gained full acceptance into the world of poetry. Elaborate poetic structures had taken a definitive form by around a hundred and fifty years before the emergence of Islam in the early 600s. Some of the fine *mu'allaqat* (great odes) portray an existential anguish, a contemplation of the fragility and transience of human life. Both the poets and their audience saw the poem in its perfect artistic form as capable of achieving a triumph over the decaying influence of time, preserved for posterity. In addition the *qasida* was seen as the reservoir of collective memory, a form of oral history and a means of protecting poetic forms from oblivion.

Arabic poetry is deeply rooted in oral tradition, and it was a voice long before it was expressed through an alphabet. This oral tradition had a rich poetic language full of synonyms and comparisons, a predilection for allusive expression, and the use of stable, often predictable, poetic hybrids and rhymes. Poetic engagement was derived from the limpidity of the verse and the familiarity of experienced listeners with the wording and themes, for the poets did not create poetry for themselves but for the tribe and on behalf of the whole community.

> *Arabic poetry is deeply rooted in oral tradition, and it was a voice long before it was expressed through an alphabet.*

This poetry was often connected to religious ritual, a dimension that was enhanced by the concept of divine inspiration. Both poets and their audiences believed that the poet was touched by a *jinn* (a demon or Muse), who revealed the poem to him. This belief enhanced the value of the poem as well as the status of the poet who was perceived as an exceptional person divinely inspired and able to utter perfect verbal icons. Because of their oral beauty, such exquisite poems became popular quickly and spread far beyond the domain of the tribe. A eulogy could elevate its subject and preserve the reputation of the person being praised, while a satire could condemn its subject for life. Once a charge was uttered in a poem it had the power of a perpetual curse. As explained in a pre-Islamic line of poetry, "What has been said has been said, be it true or false. How can you be excused against words already spoken?" The poet of this era might be seen as the equivalent of today's pop star in fame and riches. Those with the talent set their hearts on becoming poets. In the Courts of Muhammad's successors the caliphs, the chief poet was seen as occupying the number one position in the charts.

The power of the spoken word in a largely oral culture made the emergence of a poet something to celebrate. His words were as important as deeds. Indeed without singing the tribe's or the caliph's deeds in poetry, no one in Arabia would even know of them. Poetry was the reservoir of knowledge in Arabia at the time, and intellectuals occupied a prominent position in society. Instead of today's presidential speech writers and political, economic, and security advisers, the caliph surrounded himself with literary scholars, theologians, and poets. Poetry played the role of the media in our present time: poets spread the news, elaborated the official line on issues, and attacked the caliph's enemies. Great poets managed to strike a fine balance between the collective and political on the one hand and the individual and personal on the other. The Qur'an too developed poetic oral recitation and used it very effectively; it is no coincidence that the only miracle of Muhammad was a verbal miracle, the Qur'an itself. Poetry continued to maintain its position in the culture for centuries, even though Muhammad had an early aversion to poetry and the Qur'an says of poets that "most of them are liars" who "wander distractedly in every valley" (26:223–25).

Muhammad and the Rise of Islam

Mecca was the commercial and financial center of Arabia in the sixth century, and it gained further importance because of its constitution, which provided for periods of sanctuary during which blood feuds would be suspended. During these sacred months, no blood could be shed in the city. It is highly significant that it was in Mecca that the Prophet Muhammad was born and Islam emerged. The Islamic belief that he is the Messenger of God, *rasūl Allāh*, is second only to the monotheistic belief in the oneness of God. Despite Muhammad's exalted position in the creed, Islam emphasizes that he was fully human, with no supernatural attributes and no miracles to perform. Yet the global impact of the movement he started has been as great as that of Jesus Christ, whom Christians see as God's incarnation on earth. In Islam Muhammad was God's chosen Prophet and Messenger, and God is directly responsible for Muhammad's triumph over polytheism and evil.

> *Despite Muhammad's exalted position in the creed, Islam emphasizes that he was fully human, with no supernatural attributes and no miracles to perform.*

Whether one is seeking to understand his story theologically, emphasizing the role of God acting through the Prophet, or historically, looking at the exceptional role that this one individual played in changing world history, one has to acknowledge the phenomenal accomplishment of this great man. Naturally, the most important source for the story of Muhammad is the Qur'an. There are also many other sources, including biographies of the Prophet as well as collections of the Prophet's sayings or traditions. In terms of literature, his life story is vague enough to accommodate all the legendary elements of the rise of a prophetic personality. He was born around 570 C.E. into a distinguished Meccan family, which was one of the less wealthy clans of Quraysh, the major tribe in Mecca. Muhammad was orphaned in early childhood and was brought up by a grandfather, who died when he was eight. He was then taken into the custody of his uncle, Abu Talib, who became the head of the clan. Abu Talib was a caravan trader, and there are many stories of the young Muhammad accompanying him on his journeys to Christian Syria when he was as young as ten years old.

Muhammad had to fend for himself from an early age. He worked first as a shepherd, then joined the most prestigious Meccan profession at the time, caravan trading. Mecca had several rich women merchants who would compete for the service of an honest and skilled caravan trader from a respectable clan of the Quraysh tribe. Historical sources tell us of Muhammad's caravan journeys in the service of a rich Meccan woman, Khadija, who was so impressed by his honesty and trading skills that she married him in around 595, despite the fact that he was poor and several years her junior. This marriage put him in the affluent echelon of Meccan society and produced four daughters, who later played a significant role in early Islam, as well as several sons who all died in infancy. Little is known of the period between his marriage at the age of twenty-five and the revelation of the message of Islam to him at the age of forty around the year 610. Some sources emphasize the role of Khadija's cousin, Waraqa Ibn Nawfal, and others in acquainting Muhammad with the various monotheistic ideas and movements that existed in Arabia at the time. Other sources accentuate the role of meditation and reflection in changing his beliefs during this extended period. Nothing is certain about this period or what transformed Muhammad's consciousness and provided him with the spiritual strength that changed the course of his life after the age of forty.

One clear explanation is theological: the archangel Gabriel suddenly appeared to him and gave him a prophetic call. Several verses of the Qur'an have been designated as the first revelations. The revelation appeared to him as a cryptic mystery that at first he only divulged to his wife, Khadija. Most of the Qur'an's chapters (*suras*) agree that Muhammad didn't recognize these early revelations as an indication that he was being called to be a prophet. Tradition states that there was a period of three years between the time he received these first revelations and the time he began his public ministry. Perhaps he used the time to absorb and digest the revelations before calling others to Islam, first secretly until he converted a handful of followers, then openly.

Muhammad's public proclamation of Islam in his early Meccan period was not an easy task, despite the fact that he only emphasized in this phase the moral appeal rather than the theological aspects of his call. The early Meccan verses of the Qur'an deal with ideas related to the moral responsibility of humanity, created by God. They enumerated the various manifestations of God in nature that should convince those who have time to reflect and logically deduce that there is sublime power greater than human power—*islam* means "surrender" to God. The early revelations were concerned with the devotional aspects of religion, called for belief in God and appeal to Him for forgiveness of sins through prayers, night vigils, and charitable deeds, particularly helping the needy. Muhammad's early preaching was tolerated because it didn't threaten the gods of Mecca or disturb its social hierarchy. He called for belief in one God, Allah, and Allah happened to be the supreme god of the numerous Meccan deities. Muhammad managed to convince a small number of men, most of them young or relatives and of no distinguished social standing.

Things changed when he openly attacked polytheism and the gods of Mecca, and declared that the Ka'bah, the traditional Meccan sanctuary, belonged only to the one true God, Allah. Islam encountered severe opposition when it revealed radical teachings concerning social justice, opposing slavery and the burying of newly born girls alive (a custom common in Arabia at the time because of the shame of producing girls and the pressures of poverty). The powerful merchant class turned against Muhammad when he called for justice, attacked greed and the oppression of the poor, and asked people to free themselves from love of wealth and from all forms of deceit. Muhammad warned of dire consequences for unbelievers, and emphasized the inevitability of the final judgment on the day of resurrection, the pleasures of paradise for the believers and severe punishment in hell for the damned.

Meccan opposition started by persecuting the early believers, but Muhammad persevered in his call and found fertile ground for his new creed during the times of the fairs and the pilgrimage, when a large number of tribes congregated in Mecca. Some men from Yathrib (later called Medina) who came as pilgrims to Mecca in 620 showed interest in his call, swore allegiance to him, and promised to convert their small town to Islam upon their return. When they succeeded in doing so by 621, Muhammad negotiated with them the possibility of providing him with sanctuary in their city, and

The hijra *marked the beginning of the formative years of Islam itself as a major religion and the emergence of the community of believers as a force to reckon with from that time on.*

they concluded an agreement by which they pledged to protect him as they would their own nearest kinsmen. The acceleration and severity of the opposition of the notables of Mecca to his call, combined with the death of his wife, Khadija, led to his migration to Medina in 622.

The year of this great migration, *hijra,* of the Prophet and seventy followers from Mecca to Medina was with good reason chosen as the first year of the Islamic lunar calendar. The *hijra* marked the beginning of the formative years of Islam itself as a major religion and the emergence of the community of believers as a force to reckon with from that time on. Muhammad's migration with all his followers to Medina was not only a major logistical operation but also a great political and diplomatic challenge. In the ten years that followed, he proved himself to be a political and military genius. At the time of the *hijra,* Medina was not a compact town like Mecca, but a collection of scattered settlements surrounded by groves of date palms and cultivated fields. It was torn by violent conflict between Jews and Arabs, with small clans living in a balance of terror. Once in Medina, Muhammad embarked on the task of social and political organization of the new community of believers, the nucleus of the Islamic *'umma,* community or nation. It started by a process of bonding or brotherhood between the migrants and their hosts in Medina. This was followed by the organization of representation and consultation, outlined in the pact known as the "Constitution of Medina," which stipulated the rights and obligations of the believers as well as other religious groups and clans and the appointment of their representatives. With this constitution Muhammad succeeded in forming a remarkably united community from all these discordant and often warring tribes and embarked on the spreading of his call.

> *Medina . . . was torn by violent conflict between Jews and Arabs, with small clans living in a balance of terror.*

There are early references in the Qur'an to the Jews being favored for their belief in one God, but this soon turned to references to their animosity and treachery when they actively opposed him and allied with his enemies. The change was gradual, for Muhammad continued for several years to nourish the hope that they would accept him or at least maintain a neutral posture in his conflict with the polytheists. Muhammad's first major battle against the polytheists of Mecca and their allies took place at Badr in 624. Muhammad himself led his people, and the Meccan army, which was far superior in number and weapons, was led by their commander, Abu-Jahl. The victory of Muhammad in the Battle of Badr and the slaying of Abu-Jahl resonated throughout Arabia. The victory of a small number of believers over a large army of nonbelievers was seen as portentous and as irrefutable confirmation of Muhammad's prophethood, and this led to the steady increase of his followers.

Gradually Muhammad's forces overcame the polytheists, and many Arab tribes embraced Islam. During these various battles, Muhammad realized that the major Jewish clans of Medina played a significant role in the wars against him. This was a devastating blow to Muhammad, since up to his third year in Medina, he didn't clearly declare that he was establishing a new religion but was restoring the true religion proclaimed by numerous prophets before him. The emphasis was on the revelation to Muhammad of the one book of God that was previously revealed to Moses and Jesus. In these first two years, Muhammad tolerated opposition by Jews and continued to argue with them peacefully, but this situation changed when it became clear the Jews were the fifth column of the Meccans inside Medina. This was coupled with the fact that the Jews refused to recognize the Qur'an as identical to their scripture and accept an Arab as the long-awaited Messiah. Passages discrediting Jewish scripture began to appear in the Qur'an. The early Medinan Suras are full of references to the partial revelation of the Book to Moses and how the Jews were concealing their scripture from Muhammad and even fabricating verses. The return to the true religion of Abraham, who was claimed by Jews and Christians as the progenitor of their faith, opened the door to discrediting the practice of these two religions as distortions of the true Abrahamic tradition. The people of the Book (Scripture) had strayed from the Book and distorted it, and in doing so had brought elements of polytheism to the fully monotheistic creed of Abraham. Hence, the need to reveal it afresh was confirmed, and with it the assertion that Abraham was neither a Jew nor a Christian, but the first Muslim.

In 628 a treaty was negotiated with Mecca, allowing Muhammad and his followers to make their annual pilgrimage there. The treaty allowed Islam to build up the strength of the Islamic community ('umma) and enlarge its basis in Arabia. When the Meccans broke the treaty the following year, Muhammad decided to invade his birthplace, and the conquest of Mecca was achieved in 630 almost without bloodshed. Muhammad became the strongest man in Arabia, and people flocked in large numbers from all corners of Arabia to join his creed or to seek alliance with him. He was powerful enough to offer his valuable alliance to those seeking it, provided that they accepted Islam, and this brought much of Arabia under the *pax Islamica.* In March 632, Muhammad led the largest pilgrimage to Mecca, known as the

> *. . . this brought much of Arabia under the* pax Islamica.

Farewell Pilgrimage of the ninth year of the *hijra,* thus incorporating this complex pre-Islamic ceremony into Islam. This sealed Muhammad's message in terms of its religious, social, and political aspects. Muhammad died a few months later. Although Mecca had been a central city in the life of Arabia before Muhammad's conquest, the rise of Islam and the pilgrimage, or *hajj,* enhanced its role, and it became the most sacred city in Islam.

The early militancy of the Bedouins, formerly dissipated in tribal feuds, acquired a focus and a sense of mission that channeled their chivalry and utilized their skills for the spread of Islam. Muhammad succeeded in uniting the complementary resources of the nomadic and the urban Arabs, and the Arab area within the peninsula was integrated in a manner never before attained. Without Islam, many of these achievements might have perished. The rise of Islam involved a radical transformation of the Arabs from materialism to a newly born Islamic 'umma inspired and animated by the ideals of the new faith and the quest for a universal state. Soon the nation became a vast empire, and developed a civilization religious in spirit and manifestation, and the new 'umma vastly extended the Meccan achievement of a purposeful cohesive community.

THE CALIPHATE AND ITS LITERATURE

The danger of the disintegration of the Muslim community loomed large after Muhammad's death, particularly when others in different parts of Arabia claimed to be prophets too. In the last days of Muhammad's life, when he was too ill to maintain a leadership role, his disciple Abu Bakr was appointed as a deputy for him, but no arrangements were made for the succession. For a brief period it seemed that the Islamic state was on the verge of breaking up, but after a heated debate in Medina Abu

Bakr was accepted as the successor or Caliph of the Messenger of God. Abu Bakr was Muhammad's closest and most pious companion, and the father of his favorite wife, 'A'isha. His selection established the Caliphate, a unique Islamic system of selection and mutual obligations between the ruler and the ruled.

The Muslim domain continued to expand under Abu Bakr and his successors, who consolidated Islam's control over the rest of Iraq and conquered the whole of Persia by 642. In the meantime another campaign advanced through Syria and Palestine, and in 638 the Caliph 'Umar traveled personally to Damascus and assured the Christians of their right to worship freely, if they paid a tax smaller than the one they had been paying to Byzantium. He then proceeded to Jerusalem and ordered the building of a mosque on the site of the present Dome of the Rock Mosque in Jerusalem. By 647 Muslim Arabs had conquered Egypt and North Africa as far as present-day Tunisia.

The ten years of the Caliphate of 'Umar (634–644) transformed Islam into an empire of world-wide importance. It covered areas inhabited by people of different races and varied civilizations and succeeded in incorporating their achievements into the unitary dynamics of this invigorating new creed. The Islamic sphere of influence spread far more rapidly than the ability of its core believers to communicate its tenets to the newly converted. In this stage of the development of the Islamic 'umma community, 'Umar allowed local governors full power, but they remained directly accountable to Medina. Later scholars attribute the whole organization of the Muslim state to his political skills and the maintenance of a vigilant and ever expanding army to defend and extend the empire. 'Umar was fatally wounded at the age of forty-three and died in 644.

He was succeeded by 'Uthman Ibn 'Affan as the third caliph. Islam continued to expand during his reign, northward to central Asia and the Caspian Sea, eastward to eastern Iran and beyond to the edge of the Indian subcontinent, and westward across the rest of North Africa. However, there were turbulent problems at home related to the question of his ascent to the caliphate, the administration of a large empire, the deviation from austere early Islamic practice, and the rise of an affluent class. They ended in his violent death and the selection of 'Ali, the Prophet's cousin and son-in-law, who sided with those who rebelled against 'Uthman, as the fourth Caliph in 656. 'Ali held radical views that threatened the affluent class among the Quraysh, and a civil war began that ended in 661 with his assassination and the beginning of the 'Umayyad Caliphate in Damascus, which ruled the Muslim Empire from 661 to 750. The Umayyads were the descendants of the richest and most powerful clan in Mecca during the rise of Islam and its ardent enemy until the fall of Mecca. Their ascent to power started with their desire to avenge 'Uthman's death, for he was a member of their clan. It was also supported by those who saw the need for an experienced political clan to run the vast empire, and considered this to be more pressing than the need to guard the strict tenets of the faith and spread its word. In this struggle, the Muslims divided into two main groups: the followers of the Umayyads, known as Sunni or orthodox Muslims, and the supporters of 'Ali, known as the Shi'ites ("followers"). This division persists to the present day, creating two different Islamic denominations, despite continuous attempts to heal the rift since the time of the Umayyads. The majority of Muslims declared their allegiance to the Umayyads and they continued to maintain the Muslim Empire and expand it to India and sub-Saharan Africa, and to Andalusia in Spain.

It was the Umayyads, with their flexible approach to wealth and tolerance of other cultures, who encouraged the development of Arabic language and literature. Poetry flourished under their generous patronage. New poetic genres were developed

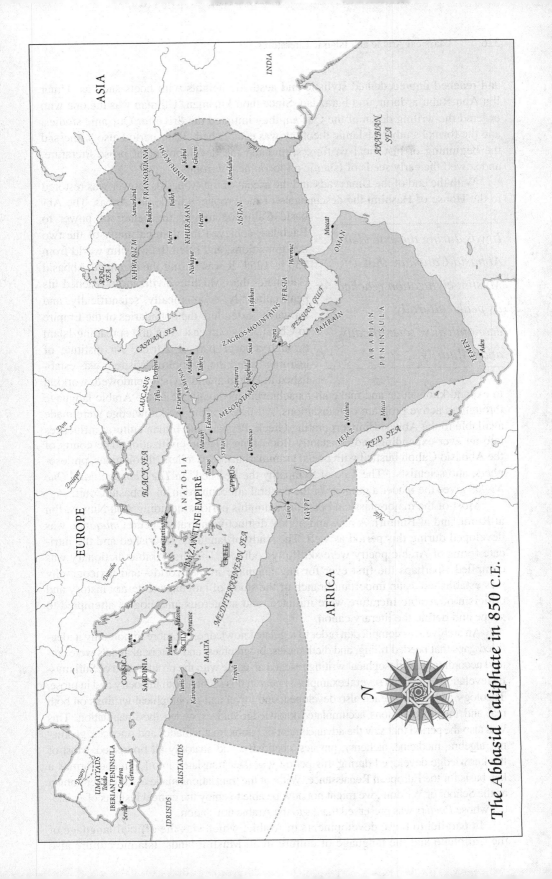

The Abbasid Caliphate in 850 C.E.

and reached unprecedented stylistic and aesthetic heights with poets such as 'Umar Ibn Abu-Rabu'a, Jarur, and Farazdaq. Since their kinsman 'Uthman was the one who ordered the writing down of the Qur'an, they initiated the drive for Qur'anic studies, and the formal study of Islamic theology was established. Their period also witnessed the beginning of historical writing, stimulated the development of prose literature, and sowed the early seeds of Islamic philosophical writings.

With the end of the Umayyads and the ascent of the Abbasids, power was restored to the House of Hashim, the descendants of the Prophet's uncle, al-'Abbas. The Abbasid Caliphate moved the center of power to Baghdad, achieved the nominal unity of the two denominations, and ruled the Muslim world from 750 to 1258. It was during the extended Abbasid Caliphate that Muslim civilization reached its peak culturally, economically, scientifically, and militarily, extending the boundaries of the Empire to China and Southeast Asia and spreading Islam through a large part of Africa. An institute of learning called the School of Wisdom was established in Baghdad and lavishly endowed, working to expand knowledge and make all its achievements available in the Arabic language through an active program of translations. All facets of human knowledge were made available to the Abbasids, incorporating Greek, Persian, and Indian cultural influences into an ever-expanding and constantly flourishing Islamic civilization. The courts of the Abbasid Caliph bustled with poets, grammarians, storytellers, theologians, philosophers, and scientists. "The Tale of Sympathy the Learned" in *The Thousand and One Nights* gives the reader a glimpse of the cultural atmosphere in an Abbasid Court.

> *It was during the extended Abbasid Caliphate that Muslim civilization reached its peak culturally, economically, scientifically, and militarily . . .*

Most of the major classical poets are from this period, including Abu Nuwas, Ibn al-Rumi, and al-Buhturi. A new and highly distinctive narrative genre, *maqama,* was developed during this period as well. The study of language flourished and the intricate forms of Arabic poetry were skillfully codified. The first Arabic dictionary was compiled—perhaps the first ever for any language in the world—and lexicography was established as an important branch of the study of language. Literary history and criticism of Arabic literature were initiated, and numerous anthologies attempted to shape and define the literary canon.

An archive was compiled in order to regulate knowledge, but more importantly it identified gaps that needed filling, and dictionaries, biographies, and historical annals were created accordingly. Philosophical writing reached an acme with the proliferation of Sufi mystic revelations, of which several examples appear in this section both in poetry and in prose. Theology and jurisprudence also developed, and travel and geographical writings on both real and imagined regions accumulated knowledge and expanded the imagination. This was also the period that saw the advancement of Arabic mathematics and sciences: geometry, algebra, medicine, alchemy, physics, chemistry, and anatomy all flourished. Most of the knowledge developed during this period was later translated into Latin and formed a key basis for the European Renaissance. Without the translations made at the center known as the School of Wisdom, we might not now be able to enjoy the critical insights of Aristotle, whose *Poetics* was preserved thanks to the Arabic translation.

In parallel to these developments in Arabic, which was the official language of the Caliphate and the language of culture in all Muslim lands, Islamic culture also

Mosque of Muhammad Ali, Cairo, early 19th century. This exuberant, imposing mosque was built by Egypt's ruler Muhammad Ali after he established effective independence from Ottoman rule and founded his own dynasty in 1805. The mosque testifies to the lasting vitality of Islamic architecture, here blended with elements drawn from French Baroque style; the clock tower in front of the domes was a gift from the French ruler Louis Philippe.

continued to develop in Persian and other languages of the Muslim world. Arabic culture persisted despite the fall of the Abbasid dynasty in 1258 and the rise of numerous centers of power in many parts of the Islamic world. The principal center of power moved first to Egypt and then to Turkey with the rise of the Ottomans (1500–1900), and Arabic culture and literature continued to develop. The most notable developments took place in Andalusia in Spain, in the field of intellectual inquiry and Islamic philosophy, and in Egypt in the field of narrative and popular epics. The work of the most distinguished Islamic philosopher, Ibn Rushd or Averroes of Cordoba, is a product of the Arabic culture in Andalusia. He had immense

Without the translations made at the . . . School of Wisdom, we might not now be able to enjoy the critical insights of Aristotle . . .

influence on the Jewish and Christian worlds of philosophy. In Egypt, a proliferation of popular literature gave rise to exquisite epics such as those of Bani-Hilal and 'Antara, and a large number of the stories of *The Thousand and One Nights* were elaborated.

If pre-Islamic poetry was a crucial factor in shaping a unified Arabic language, enhancing the Arabs' sense of unity, and increasing their awareness of their identity, the Qur'an developed this further. It sanctified the Arabic language, provided it with its greatest stylistic icon, and raised the Arabs' sense of unity to the level of national pride in an *'umma* with a great spiritual mission. It is certain that without the Qur'an, Arabic would have remained an obscure Semitic language like many of its earlier counterparts in Arabia. With the spread of Islam, Arabic was extended into many lands. Egypt, for example, had more developed languages yet embraced Arabic to the detriment of their own languages. Other lands, such as Persia, embraced Islam and Arabic but preserved their own language as well, enriching it by importing a vast number of Arabic words into Persian. With the expansion of Islam and the foundation of the Arab Empire, Arabic became a world language, the language of medieval Islamic civilization, the Latin of the Muslim world. The Qur'an preserved its integrity, stabilized its structures, and protected it from Latin's fate of disintegration into a myriad of languages, despite the fact that Arabic has been continuously used in all the countries of the Arab world. The maintenance of the original structures of Arabic from pre-Islamic Arabia to the present Arab world has far-reaching ramifications in Arab history. It proved to be the single most important and durable factor in the rise of Arab nationalism in the twentieth century and has functioned to sustain the unity of feeling, if not of politics, in the Arab world. It has become seemingly indestructible and synonymous with Islam in the minds of many, who use it in their prayers even if they don't understand its meaning or appreciate its stylistic beauty.

> *The Qur'an preserved its integrity, stabilized its structures, and protected it from Latin's fate of disintegration into a myriad of languages . . .*

The inspirational role of Islam and the invigorating influence of its successes enabled the new community to develop into an imperial race. Islam integrated many of the social and cultural achievements of pre-Islamic Arabia into its spiritual fabric, from the unitary Arabic language to the rituals of the pilgrimage that ensured the central position of Mecca. The poetry of the pre-Islamic period, with its elaborate rhyming schemes, became the model of Islamic poetic composition, which was encouraged during the time of Muhammad and has prospered ever since, making literature the most important constituent of Islamic civilization. With the expansion of the Islamic *'umma* into a multiracial and multicultural civilization, many other cultural influences have been absorbed into Arabic culture and enriched its capacity for expression. New literary genres emerged and different strands of poetry flourished, from the seventh century to the present.

The influence of these cultural developments was not confined to the Arabic language, for the form of the Arabic *qasida* penetrated many other languages and cultures. The marriage between African and Islamic traditions, for example, is symbolized in *The Epic of Son-Jara* or *Sunjata*, at the close of this section. The epic's hero, Son-Jara, is described as inheriting the African *nyama*, the power of the occult, from his mother, descendant of the Buffalo-Woman of Du, and the Islamic *baraka,* spiritual grace, from his father, descendant of an immigrant from Mecca. This powerful combination of African motherland and the Islamic spirit empowers Son-Jara with the best combination of sorcery and wisdom, and the fusion of *baraka* and *nyama* echoes the fusion of the panegyric Arabic *qasida* genre, with its tradition of structured praise, with lyrical African song and music. The epic narrative of *Son-Jara* gives the pilgrimage a central place in its travel narrative and infuses the trip with spirituality and an opportunity to utilize proverbs, a literary form favored by the Arabs since pre-Islamic times.

The interaction between these different literary modes in the epic helps to resolve the aesthetic tension between the singer and the musical accompaniment, between melody and rhythm. At a deeper structural level, the Islamic concepts of preordained destiny and self-sacrifice inform the trajectory of events in the epic and the vicissitudes of its characters. In addition, the poem structures the fundamental relationship between Son-Jara and his great rival Sumamuru not as a simple one of good and evil but as a more profound manifestation of the opposing forces within both good and evil, and within individual people themselves. Furthermore, the epic narrative of Son-Jara and his legendary endeavor to save his land and unite his divided people mirrors, to a large extent, the popular version of the story of Muhammad and his rise to power and adulation. This is but one example of the inspirational creativity of Islam and its robust ability to seed its concepts and tenets in many different cultures and lands down through the centuries.

PRONUNCIATIONS:

> *Abbasids:* AH-bah-sids
> *Abu Bakr:* AH-bou BAH-ker
> *Bedouin:* BED-ou-inn
> *hijra*: HEEJ-rah
> *Khadija:* cah-DEE-jah
> *qasida:* KA-see-dah
> *Qur'an:* COO-RAHN
> *Quraysh:* COO-RAYSH
> *rasūl Allāh:* rah-SOOL ah-LAH
> *Shi'ites:* SHE-ites
> *Sunni:* SOU-nee
> *Umayyad:* ooh-MAY-yad
> *'umma:* ooh-MAH

PRE-ISLAMIC POETRY

Early Arabic, or pre-Islamic, poetry is the earliest body of literature in the Arabic language, and it is still read and studied today with delight and even reverence. It is seen as both a reservoir of knowledge and the expression of the Arabs' very existence. In the words of a ninth-century critic, Ibn Sallam al-Jumahi, "Pre-Islamic poetry was to the Arabs the register of all they knew, and the utmost compass of their wisdom." It expressed their life in a form that was capable of easy dissemination throughout the desert. Its stylistic elegance and profound musicality preserved its integrity, despite problems of oral transmission, and established it as a coveted art form. Each tribe celebrated with joy, festivity, and pride the emergence of a poet among its members, for a poet defended the tribe's honor, perpetuated its glorious deeds, and established its fame forever. Tribes were keen to transmit their poetry and ensure its passage from one reciter to another. This among other factors guaranteed its integrity and authenticity.

The earliest surviving poems go back to the beginning of the sixth century C.E. and the later ones date from the time of the Prophet Muhammad (c. 570–632). But the surviving poems' high degree of consistency, formal coherence, and uniform structure give us reason to believe that the formative works of this poetry have been lost. It is inherent in the dynamics of oral transmission that later and more sophisticated examples replace earlier ones. The surviving poems demonstrate through their artistic maturity and structural homogeneity that the conventions of poetry had been widely established. They all follow a single meter and rhyme throughout the normally lengthy composition.

Pre-Islamic poetry is basically tribal poetry: the poetry of nomadic tribes rather than of settled Arab communities. The hierarchical order of tribes was based more on the excellence of their poetry, lineage, and legends of the tribe's history than on their land, camels, goods, or numbers. Poetry was revered for its power and its ability to transcend tribal boundaries and travel throughout the desert. The poetry of a tribe was what differentiated it from other tribes, preserved its name, articulated its genealogy, and narrated its legends for posterity. It expressed and vaunted its values and virtues. The symbolic capital that poetry and the poet represent was unmatched by wealth, for it was seen as the one thing that lasts when all is seized and destroyed by enemies or decimated by nature. In addition, each poet was perceived as being inspired by his unique *jinn* (muse), and eloquent poetical utterances were believed to have magical force.

Pre-Islamic poetry is the art of nomadic people who lived in the desert, depended on their camels or horses, and had an elaborate code governing social and ethical values both within and between tribes—often leading to tribal wars. As a result, its world and the language in which it was written are alien to the Western reader. Yet the values and emotions it expressed are as universal as any elaborated by great poets in any part of the world. One may find the tribal ethos peculiar and the detailed description of animals excessive, but one is deeply touched by the universality of the poems' treatment of war, peace, love, death, and the struggle to live in a bleak and hostile environment. The portrayal of the desert can be seen as pioneering the contemporary nostalgia for the unspoiled beauty of the desert, and the treatment of animals was centuries ahead of its time. The poets' practice of attributing human feelings to animals and treating them with great fondness and sympathy is unprecedented, something that emerged only more recently in Western literatures. The hunted oryx in early Arabic poems usually escapes, and when it fails to escape, its killing is treated as a tragedy, almost with cosmic ramifications.

Pre-Islamic poetry is characterized by its minimalism. As the contemporary scholar Alan Jones has observed, "What in Shakespeare would be a soliloquy is in Arabic a line or even a hemstich. Seven lines of 'Lamiyyat al 'Arab' (lines 54–60) would have provided the Greek tragedians with the plot for a full play." This minimalism is more than compensated for by the well-defined form and structure and the formal prosody that can be scanned mathematically. Pervasive references from poem to poem help to decipher many seemingly cryptic images. Pre-Islamic poetry is highly formal in its pattern or format with many variations. Apart from the early form of *rajaz* (songs for traveling on camelback) which was perceived as inferior and not proper poetry, poetry (*shi'r*) was divided into the *qit'a* (short occasional piece), no more than twenty lines, and often shorter, and the *qasida* (ode) with its distinctive structure and thematic development. Al-Khansa's elegies are among the good examples of *qit'a*, while Imru' al-Qays's *mu'allaqa* is one of the finest *qasidas*.

PRONUNCIATIONS:

  mu'allaqa: mou-AH-la-KAH

  qasida: KA-see-dah

  qit'a: key-TAH

  shi'r: SHEER

Imru' al-Qays

died c. 550

Imru' al-Qays ibn ("son of") Iujr al-Kindi is the most outstanding of all pre-Islamic poets. His *mu'allaqa* or ode is a remarkable poem that continues to fascinate Arab readers today. It is taught throughout the Arab world and is the most famous, and most frequently quoted, of all pre-Islamic poems. The story of Imru' al-Qays's life is told with several romanticized variants and legendary embellishments. As the son of the King of Kinda, he lived a lavish and licentious life in his youth, but when his father was killed by a rival, he abandoned his libertine life and tried to avenge his death and restore the power of Kinda. Roaming the desert, he gained the support of many tribes and eventually was able to enlist the help of the court of the Byzantine emperor Justinian in Constantinople. While there he succumbed once again to his lascivious nature and seduced the emperor's daughter. In return her father presented him with a poisoned shirt, which caused his death near Ankara in about 550.

The term *mu'allaqa* is widely debated. It is one of several names by which the most famous early Arabic odes are known, others being *mudhahhabat,* "the gilded ones," and *aumt,* "the strings of a necklace"; but the term *mu'allaqa* (pl. *mu'allaqat*) is the most common and it comes from the verb "to hang," as odes were being hung on the walls of the *Ka'ba* Shrine at Mecca. There are said to be seven or nine early odes, one by Imru' al-Qays, the rest by one or another combination of other classic poets. But in all accounts there is no dispute that Imru' al-Qays's ode is always included and often as the first one. It is the first in more than one sense. It is towering in its poetic power and unique in its formal structure. It contains over seventy descriptive topics, a vivid portrayal of a series of erotic adventures, a hunting theme, a flashback to boyhood, and one of the most memorable descriptions of horses in Arabic poetry.

PRONUNCIATION:
   Imru' al-Qays: IM-rou all-CASE

Mu'allaqa[1]

Stop, let us weep at the memory of a loved one and her dwelling at the place
     where the sands twist to an end between al-Dakhūl and Ḥawmal,
And Tūḍiḥ and al-Miqrāt. Her traces have not been effaced, with all the
     weaving of the wind from south and north.[2]
In their hollows and broad spaces you can now see the dung of gazelles
     looking like peppercorns.
On the morning of departure, on the day they packed their baggage at the
     tribe's thorn-trees it was as though I were splitting colocynths,[3]
5   When my companions halted their camels for me, saying "Don't perish
     from grief. Have some patience."
My cure lies in our poured tears. Is there anything to give me support when
     I halt at traces almost completely effaced?
Such tears were your custom before her, caused by Umm al-Ḥawārith and
     her neighbour Umm al-Rabāb at Ma'sal;[4]

---

1. Translated by Alan Jones.
2. The place where the desert sands twist to an end is located between the four places mentioned in the opening two verses.

3. A sour, lemonlike fruit.
4. The two women named here are from the Kalb tribe.

When they stood up, the scent of musk wafted from them like breath of the east wind bearing the fragrance of cloves.

Through yearning for them my tears poured down on to my throat until they wet my sword-strap.

10 Ah, many is the excellent day I've had because of such women. I specially remember a day at Dāra Juljul—

A day when I hamstrung my camel for the young unmarried women, and what wonder there was in the baggage it had carried;

The women kept on throwing on to the fire its flesh and fat that looked like the twisted frills of silk cloth—

A day when I entered the litter, the litter of 'Unayza, and she said, "Woe to you, you will make me have to travel on foot."

When her camel-saddle slipped with the two of us on it together,[5] she said, "You've brought my camel to its knees, Imru' al-Qays. Get down."

15 I said to her, "Ride on, but slacken the reins. Do not put me at a distance from the fruit that can be plucked time and time again from you."

Many is the woman like you, both pregnant and suckling, whom I have visited by night and whose attention I have distracted from her one-year old child with its amulets,

When the child cried behind her, she turned to it with half her body—her other half not able to move under me.

And I remember one who drew back from me one day on the ridge of a sand-hill and swore an oath such as is not annulled.

O Fāṭima, gently, less of this disdain. Even if you are resolved on breaking your link with me, do it gently.

20 And if there is some trait of mine that has vexed you, draw my garments from yours and they will slip away.

You are filled with boldness towards me by the fact that my love for you is killing me and that whatever you order my heart to do it will do.

Your eyes have shed their tears only that you may smite me with the two arrows of your eyes that strike into the fragments of a slaughtered heart.

Often, too, I think of a secluded maid, who was not to be hoped for, dalliance with whom I enjoyed with no undue haste.

To reach her I bypassed guards and tribesmen eager to deal with me, avid to be able to announce that they had killed me;

25 At the time that the Pleiades showed themselves like the strands of a belt adorned with jewels, white standing out from black.

I arrived when she had slipped off her clothes for sleep behind a screen, all but the covering of a *mifḍal*.

She said, "God's oath, you have no way of evading them. I see that your ways of error have not left you."

I took her out and walked with her and she drew the skirts of an embroidered gown[6] behind us over our tracks.

When we crossed the enclosure of the tribe and we were taken out of sight by the bottom of a piece of low ground with high sides, a place of twists and turns,

---

5. An expression of joyous, even amorous, activities.

6. The lovers fear being followed and erase any trace that would enable the men of her tribe to find them.

30   I drew the two sides of her head to me, and she leaned towards me, slender
        of waist and supple of ankle,
     Slim, fair-skinned, not flabby, her breast-bones polished like a burnished
        mirror,
     She turns away and reveals a soft cheek and wards me off with the glance of
        a wild gazelle of Wajra with its fawn,
     And with a throat like that of an antelope, not ugly when she shows it nor
        unadorned,
     And with dark hair that adorns her back, jet black, abundant, the stalks of a
        date palm, with many clusters of fruit,
35   The locks of which are twisted up to the top of her head, the plaiting threads
        lost in hair folded up and then let down,
     And with a delicate waist, slender as a camel's nose-rein, and a leg like a
        stalk of well-watered papyrus, overshadowed by palm-trees.
     In the morning crumbled musk lies on her bed, as she sleeps into the later
        morning,[7] not wearing a belt nor having put on her *mifḍal*
     She raises hands that have delicate skin, not rough; her fingers are like the
        sand-worms of Ẓaby or tooth-picks of *isḥil* wood.
     In the evening she lights up the darkness as though she were the light in the
        place where the hermit does his eventide devotions.
40   On the like of her a man of self-control will gaze with passion, when she re-
        veals her fine proportions mid-way between that of a matron and a young
        girl,
     She is like the first egg of an ostrich, its white shell mixed with yellow,
        nourished by pure water, that has not been trodden in by animals.
     The follies of other men leave them to be distracted from passion for such
        as her, but my heart will never be distracted from love of her.
     Many, many is the stubborn rival for you that I have rebutted, sincere de-
        spite his censuring of me, not falling short in the advice he gives.
     Many, too, the night like the waves of the sea that has let down on me its
        curtains containing all kinds of cares so that it might test me.
45   I said to it when it stretched its loins and then raised its buttocks behind and
        then removed its chest,
     "Come, long night, come, give way to morning, though the arrival of morn-
        ing is no better if it comes wrapped in you.
     O what a night you are! It is as though all your stars were anchored to
        Mount Yadhbul by tightly-twisted ropes.
     It is as though up in their place in the sky the Pleiades were fixed by ropes
        of flax to slabs of stone."
     Many is the time that I have had a water-skin from people and slung its
        strap on the back of my neck and shoulders, humble and loaded with
        baggage.
50   And many a valley I have crossed that was as bare as the belly of a wild-ass,
        where the wolf howls as it seeks food like a *ṣu'lūk*.[8]
     And I have said to the wolf when he howled, "If you haven't acquired any-
        thing to eat our state is one of little substance,

---

7. A sign of a higher class, for the poor have to wake up
early and work.   8. Brigand.

When either of us gets something, it slips away from him. Whoever tills
   your tilth or mine will find lean pickings."

From time to time I used to journey in the morning, whilst the birds were still
   in their nests, on a well-built short-haired horse, able to rein in wild game,

Ready to charge, ready to flee, advancing, retreating equally well; its speed
   is like a massive rock brought down from on high by a raging torrent,[9]

55   A dark bay, who causes the saddle-felt to slip from the middle of his back,
   just as smooth stones cause anything that tries to settle on them to slip off.

Full of mettle despite his leanness—when his ardour boils up in him, his
   neighing is like the boiling of a cauldron,

Still moving swiftly when the mares have begun to kick up the dust because
   of their tiredness on hard-trodden, rugged ground.

The light-weight boy slips from the middle of his back; and he throws off
   the body of the rough and heavy-handed,

Swift, like a child's top which is made to travel by the constant movement
   of its hands with a piece of joined-up thread.

60   It has the flanks of a gazelle and the legs of an ostrich. It can travel at a
   wolf's fast speed or at the trot of a young fox.

With a perfect frame—when you see the back of it, the gap between its legs
   is blocked by a bushy tail coming to a little above the ground, not with a
   short spine.[1]

As it stands beside the tent, his back looks as smooth as the pounding stone
   of a bride or a stone for splitting colocynth.

The blood of the leading vein on his neck is like the juice pressed out of a
   henna plant on combed grey hair.

A flock of oryx appeared before us, the females like the maidens of Duwār
   in garments with long trailing skirts.

65   They turned aside looking like pieces of light onyx with dark pieces in between on the neck of a boy with respected paternal and maternal uncles
   in the tribe.

The horse enabled me to overtake the leading game, in reaching which we had
   passed those lagging behind them in a small herd that had not scattered.

He made a run between a bull and a cow, moving without interruption, neither sprinkled with nor bathed in sweat.

Those cooking the meat had to stay long, some cooking strips of meat
   placed on the coals for grilling, others minding the meat cooked quickly
   in a pot.

We would come to camp in the evening, and the gaze of those who saw him
   was scarcely able to take him in; whenever the eye rose over him, it
   came down again.

70   He passed the night wearing saddle and bridle, standing where my eye
   could see him, not let out to pasture.

My friend, can you see lightning? Let me point out to you its flashes in the
   distance gleaming like the flash of hands as it moves swiftly in a mass of
   cloud piled up like a crown.

Its light giving illumination, or like the lamps of a hermit who has been generous with oil on the twisted wicks.

---

9. The sound of the line in Arabic imitates the sound of   1. A description of a rare Arab horse.
the movement of the horse.

I sat watching it with my companions between Ḍārij and al-'Udhayb, and
    how far did I have to gaze.

As far as we could tell the right hand of its downpour rose over Quaṭan and
    its left over al-Sitār and Yadhbul.

75 It began shedding its load of rain around Kutayfa, flattening the *kanahbul*
    trees to the ground.

Then some of its spray passed over al-Qanān and drove down from there the
    white-footed ibex from every place where they were resting.

At Taymā' it did not leave standing the trunk of a single palm nor any large
    building except one built of stone.

In the onslaught of its deluge Thabīr was like an elder of the people
    wrapped up in a striped cloak.

In the morning the top of the peaks of al-Mujaymir was like the whirl of a
    spindle from the torrent and the debris swirling round them.

80 It had cast the water it contained on to the expanse of al-Ghabīt as a Yemeni
    merchant bringing bags of cloth for sale dumps them on the ground.

In the morning the finches of the valleys had been given drink of the finest
    wine—wine fiery as pepper—so noisy were they,

In the evening the beasts of prey were lying there drowned in its furthest
    reaches like bulbous plants uprooted and twisted into unreal shapes.

Al-Khansa'
c. 575–646

Al-Khansa' is probably the most famous Arab woman poet of pre-Islamic times; her poetry was praised by her contemporaries and is still much admired. Born Tuma'ir bint 'Amr and later nicknamed al-Khansa' (snub-nosed or gazelle), she was a member of the Sulaym tribe and lived through the time of 'Umar's Caliphate (634–644) and beyond. Her early fame led the outstanding poet-warrior Durayd ibn al-Simma to ask for her hand in marriage, but she rejected his suit, married one of her kinsmen, and had six children, two of whom were famous warriors. She clearly wanted to maintain her position as the poet of her tribe. As such she is an early example of a woman subverting patriarchal/tribal order by ostensibly accepting its dictates. Although the theme of her elegies is the grandeur of fallen men, they focus on women. In other words, the men in her poems are dead, the women are very much alive and noble. They are the subject of the act of lamentation and men are their object.

    Her fame rests on her poetic work and above all on her elegiac poems for her two brothers Mu'awiya and Sakhr, killed in defense of the tribe's honor. The elegy over a dead person, particularly one killed in battle, was a well-established poetic genre long before al-Khansa' appeared on the scene. Her work provided the genre with unrivaled intensity and poetic power, and developed it from a fairly rudimentary *qit'a* into deeply moving elegies that make the sorrow and grief of the bereaved palpable. Lamenting the dead was traditionally a female speciality, but al-Khansa' raised it by her accomplished elegies, new style, and metrical embellishments to the status of poetry. Her elegies are marked by their intensity, themes of violence, and tenderness of feeling that made them the model for this genre for many years to come. As a talented poet from a well-known tribe, she made the woman's role in the symbolic order potent

and visible. The two poems included here are from her elegiac work and are marked by fine
construction and powerful imagery as well as a sensitive rendering and delicate diction.

PRONUNCIATION:

   al-Khansa': all-CAHN-sah

A mote in your eye, dust blown on the wind?[1]

1

A mote in your eye, dust blown on the wind?
Or a place deserted, its people gone?
This weeping, this welling of tears, is for one
now hidden, curtained by recent earth.
5 None can escape the odds of death
in the ever-changing deals of chance.
To the pool that all men shun in awe
you have gone, my brother, free of blame,
as the panther goes to his fight, his last,[2]
10 bare fangs and claws his only defence.
No mother, endlessly circling her foal,
calling it softly, calling aloud,
grazing where grass was, remembering then,
going unendingly back and forth,
15 fretting for ever where grass grows new,
unceasingly crying, pining away,
was closer than I to despair when he left—
a stay too brief, a way too long.
For to him we looked for protection and strength,
20 who in winter's blast would see none want
nor keep to his tent to husband stores
but set his board at the bite of the cold,
ready his welcome, with open hand,
a heart so quick to command in need.

2

25 How many a marksman of Ṭayy[3]
sliding his hands from his sleeves,
lifting his strong-made bow
with a twang in its idle string,
has drawn and taken aim
30 as the quarry came to drink,
shot it straight in the breast
as it stood at the water's brink,
with a shaft from the quiver drawn,
flashing like sparks from the blaze,
35 feathered with eagle plumes,
sharp from the whetting stone.

1. Translated by Charles Greville Tuetey.   3. The tribe of al-Khansa'.
2. The panther signifies her brother's valor, and his death
for the tribe.

His quarry never moves:
Unusual, strange, that man,
who for ever lives by the hunt
40 and nought else knows in his age . . .
Friends whose roads led apart:
I've refused to weep in their tracks.
Cousins who sullied my drink:
I've given the best in return.
45 And cousins, light of the moon
in splendour, departed, gone . . .
A story told on the march;
a story, brief, remains.[4]

Elegy for Rithâ' Ṣakhr[1]

In the evening remembrance keeps me awake, and in the morning I am
    worn out by the overwhelming disaster that has befallen us,
In the case of Ṣakhr, and what youth is there like Ṣakhr to deal with a day of
    warring and skillful spear-thrust?
And to deal with tenacious opponents when they transgress, so that he can
    assert the right of someone on whom oppression has fallen?
I have not seen his like in the extent of the disaster caused by his death,
    either among *jinn* or among men,[2]
5   Truly strong against the vicissitudes of fortune and decisive in affairs,
    showing no confusion,
At times when people were suffering hardship most generous in his endeav-
    ours towards those who sought help or towards neighbours or to his wife.
Many was the guest who arrived by night or the man who was seeking pro-
    tection, people whose hearts were alarmed at every sound.
He treated them kindly and made them safe, so that their state was free from
    every pressing need.
Ah, O Ṣakhr, I shall never forget you until I part from my soul and my
    grave is cut.
10 The rising of the sun reminds me of Ṣakhr, and I remember him every time
    the sun sets.
But for the multitude of people around me weeping for their kin I would
    have killed myself.
All the time I can see the woman grieving for her dead child and the woman
    wailing over the death of her husband on a day of misfortune.
Both of them weep for their lost ones in the evening of the day disaster
    befell them or after that.
Yet they are not weeping for the like of my brother; but I console myself
    with the example of those who bear grief patiently.
15 On the day that I parted from Abū Ḥassān Ṣakhr I said farewell to my plea-
    sures and my cheer.
Alas for my sorrow for him; alas for the sorrow of my mother! Does he
    really spend the morning in the grave and spend the evening in it?

---

4. The brief story that remains is the poem itself.
1. Translated by Alan Jones.

2. The Arabs believed that there are two parallel worlds:
one of supernatural beings, and another of humans.

The Brigand Poets—Al-Sa'alik

c. 6th century

The term *sa'alik,* "outlaws" or "outcasts," refers to a group of pre-Islamic poets who were repudi-ated by their tribes, mostly for dishonorable deeds, or who in rare cases rejected the tribe them-selves for a life of solitude and rebellion. The strong bond between the individual and the tribe was vital for the survival and harmonious life of both in the harsh desert environment. It was based on a set of moral codes founded on manliness and virtue. The tribal code was so austere and strict that when this bond was broken it was irrevocable. The *sa'alik* are the early embodiment of the spirit of individualistic rejection of the sway of the collective. They led the life of outlaws, raided tribal en-campments, resided in mountain caves, and were men of valor and insight. They had the knowl-edge and the understanding of insiders and the freedom and rebellious spirit of outsiders, a combi-nation that enriched their poetry and sharpened their vision. Their poetry is unique in its imagery, structure, and diction and falls into three categories: the apologetic, the lyric, and the therapeutic.

'Urwa ibn al-Ward from the 'Abs clan is the most prolific of all *sa'alik* poets. He didn't completely sever his links with the tribe, and his name, *'urwa* (bond), may indicate that he was the link between the tribe and the outlaws. His poetry is rich in imagery and variety of human experience. Its subjects range from lyrical romance and rash conduct under the influence of drink to tragic love and solitude. He was excessively generous, with a tumultuous spirit and sensitive and compassionate temperament that led him to join in raiding rich tribes to give to the poor, an early prototype of Robin Hood.

The nickname of the poet Thabit ibn Jabir ibn Sufyan was Ta'abbata Sharrā, "one who carries an evil under his arm," indicating his inborn tendency to cause nuisance, his unconquer-able determination, and relentless intransigence. He was one of the most fearless *sa'alik* poets and is considered, with his alleged nephew al-Shanfara', as the best of the brigand poets. There is much controversy concerning his nickname and his relationship to his tribe, but there is no doubt about his towering talent and his mastery of the poetic form. He virtually banished the pronoun "we" from his poetry, championing the individual "I" over the collective "we." On the rare occasions when "we" appears it describes his enemies and those he attacks and pillages. Goethe translated his "Lamiyya" into verse in 1819, using Freytag's Latin translation, and praised its bare style, profound order, and harmony.

PRONUNCIATIONS:

al-sa'alik: all-SAH-ah-leek
Ta'abbata Sharrā: tah-ah-BAH-tah shah-RAH
'Urwa: OOR-wah

'Urwa ibn al-Ward: Do not be so free with your blame of me[1]

Do not be so free with your blame of me, O daughter of Mundhir.[2] Go to
    sleep—or, if you do not desire sleep, then pass the night awake.
Leave me alone with my self, Umm Ḥussān, for I will purchase with it
    before I can no longer make such a purchase
Enduring fame, for man is not eternal since he becomes a spectre hovering
    over a tomb,
Which causes the stones of al-Kinās[3] to echo and makes complaint to every
    person he sees, both known and unknown.

1. Translated by Alan Jones.
2. A famous tribe.

3. A fictitious desert location.

5   Let me roam freely in the land, so that I may make you free or make you
          independent of the evil of having to be present at a place to seek sustenance.
     If an arrow belonging to death is successful, I shall not grieve, for is anyone
          given deferment from that?
     But if my arrow is the one that wins, it will prevent you from ever having to
          sit behind the backs of the tents and wait.
     Umm Ḥussān says, "Woe upon you! Won't you give up lying in ambush,
          whether it be with a party of men on foot or a party of horsemen?
     And will you not stay quiet in your wealth this year? I see you on the saddle
          of a camel that has little milk and bears only male offspring,[4]
10   One disastrous to honest folk, and a snare: it is to be feared that the death
          which she can bring will strike you down, so be on your guard."
     [My reply is:] the people who resort to you [Umm Ḥussān]—I mean those
          related by blood, and all those women, black of wrist, who come to you,
          prevent my staying at rest.
     And those who ask for help, whose father is Zayd—I see no way of turning
          them away. So hold fast to your respect and endure the situation.
     May God cover with shame a ṣu'lūk who, when night falls for him, is one
          who rummages about for odd pieces of bone, while he frequents every
          place where a camel has been slaughtered.
     He reckons as good fortune from his fate every night in which he meets
          with hospitality from a friend who has resources.
15   He sleeps in the evening, then wakes in the morning drowsy, scraping the
          grit from his dusty side.
     He takes little thought for seeking sustenance except for himself, since by
          midday he is like a tumble-down old shack.
     He helps the women of the tribe when they ask him to assist them, but then
          in the evening he is tired, like an over-ridden camel.
     But a real ṣu'lūk—the surface of his face is like the gleam of the flame of
          one who kindles a fire to give himself light,
     Being one who overtops his enemies—they cry out at him in their encamp-
          ment, as one cries out at the ill-famed losing arrow.
20   And even if they are far away they are not secure against his coming close,
          peering out with the anxiety of the household of an absent man who is
          eagerly awaited.
     That man, if he meets with death, meets it gloriously; or if some day he
          becomes a wealthy man, how worthy he is of that!
     Shall Mu'tamm and Zayd perish when I have not diced with death at any
          time on their behalf, in spite of the fact that I have the spirit of a venture-
          some man.
     The mares kicking the hind quarters of the last of the stampeding flocks will
          terrify anyone who was not previously scared of us, after he has given up
          the expectation of seeing us;
     While we defend the stolen animals against the vanguard of the opposing
          horsemen, by means of spears and light swords, the blows from which
          are famed.
25   One day we are on raids on Najd and its folk, another day we are in a land
          covered with shathth and juniper.

---

4. This is the worst type of camel in the desert, since camels are sought for their milk and female offspring.

The mares pick their way with care carrying riders who are grizzled, noble and sagacious along passages traversed through the mountain passes of the Ḥijāz.

Night brings home to me guests of a generous and noble man, and my flocks, when they go out in the morning, are the flocks of a poor man.

Taʿabbata Sharrā: Come, who will convey to the young men[1]

Come, who will convey to the young men of Fahm the news of what I encountered face to face at Raḥā Biṭān?[2]

Truth to tell, I met a *ghūl* darting along on a waterless stretch of desert, flat and featureless like a sheet of writing material.

I said to her, "Both of us are worn out by fatigue and are ever travelling, so leave my place free for me."

She rushed to attack me, and I stretched out to her my hand that was holding a polished Yemeni sword.

5   I was not confounded, and I struck her, and she fell, mortally stricken, on to her hands and her neck.

She said to me, "Strike again." I answered her, "Just stay where you are. I am firm in my resolve."

And I remained lying on top of her, so that I might see in the morning what had come and attacked me:

Two eyes in an ugly head, like the head of a tom-cat, with a cleft tongue,

And two legs with cloven hooves and the scalp of a dog and clothing of a striped woollen cloak or of old water-skins.[3]

Taʿabbata Sharrā: A piece of news has come to us[1]

A piece of news has come to us, terrible, so serious that the most serious matter becomes dwarfed in it.

There, in a ravine that is on this side of Sal', lies a dead man, whose blood is not avenged.

He has left a burden on me[2] and turned his back; I will make little of taking up the burden for him.

Ready for revenge stand I, his nephew, warlike—things that I tie are not untied.

5   A man who attacks by night, exuding poison, just as a viper attacks by night, spitting venom, a fearsome serpent.

Fortune has been unjust and has taken from me a man who was unyielding and whose neighbour was never humiliated;

a man who gave warmth in the cold of winter, and then when Sirius was hot, he was cold and shade;

lean-sided though not suffering hardship, with generous hands, enduring and acting with boldness.

A man who journeyed with prudence, and then when he halted prudence halted where he halted,

1. Translated by Alan Jones.
2. Not a known place, yet this is the only point in the poem where reality surfaces.
3. Lines 8–9 demonstrate the nature of the beast.

1. Translated by Alan Jones. In the 19th century this poem was translated by Goethe.
2. The burden of avenging his blood.

10   the abundant rain of a rain-cloud, overflowing when he made his gifts, but
        when he attacked he was a violent lion.

When at peace in the tribe he used to let his black hair grow and let his *izār*[3]
down, but when raiding he was a sleek wild cat.

He had two flavours: honey and colocynth;[4] and everyone tasted one of the two.

He rode Terror alone, accompanied only by a notched Yemeni sword.

Many is the band of young warriors that has started its journey in the middle of the day and then travelled through the night and then halted when
dawn came,

15   Each of them sharp, girt with a sharp blade, which flashes like the flash of
        lightning whenever it is unsheathed.

And we have attained vengeance from them, and only a very few out of the
two clans escaped.

On their way they sipped some draughts of sleep, but when they nodded
their heads you terrified them and they dispersed.

If Hudhayl have broken his sharpness, it was in return for the same treatment he gave to Hudhayl.[5]

And it was in return for his attacks on them in the early morning when they
were behind their shelter; from that, after the killing, there was plundering and driving off of camels.

20   And it was in return for the times when he made them kneel at a rough
        kneeling-place on which the soles are soon worn away.

Hudhayl has been burned by me, a swift warrior who will not tire of Evil
before they tire of it,

Who causes his spear to drink once, and then when it has drunk for the first
time he provides it with a second drink.

Wine, once forbidden, is now lawful again; with some difficulty it approached as something lawful;[6]

So give me a drink of it O Sawād ibn 'Amr; my body is drained from
avenging my uncle.

25   The hyena laughs over the dead men of Hudhayl, and you can see the wolf
        smiling because of them.

The vultures become gorged on them, treading all over them, and they do
not have to be satisfied with little.

[END OF PRE-ISLAMIC POETRY]

The Qur'an
610–632

The Qur'an, also known as *al-kitab* (the Book) or *Kitab Allah* (the Book of God) is the name
of the Muslim scripture. It contains the divine text that was revealed in its fixed and finite form
to the Prophet Muhammad through the archangel Gabriel, a celestial messenger serving as

3. Cloak.
4. A bitter fruit.
5. Lines 18–20 return to the events that led to the man's
killing.

6. Wine was not usually forbidden in pre-Islamic times,
but once there was blood to be avenged, all pleasures of
life had to be suspended.

intermediary between God and Muhammad. It is the word of Allah revealed to his Prophet, Muhammad, over some twenty years (between 610–632), to transmit to the whole of humanity. Moses parted the Red Sea, Jesus had the ability to walk on water and resurrect the dead; the Qur'an was Muhammad's sole miracle. It has been approached as a linguistic miracle by Muslim scholars for centuries.

The earliest attested use of the word *qur'an* is in the Qur'an itself, where it occurs about seventy times; *al-kitab* ("the book") occurs 255 times, establishing self-reference as one of the book's textual strategies. The word *qur'an* comes from the Arabic root *qara'a*, "read," which is the first word of the first verse that was revealed to Muhammad. In the Qur'an itself, the most frequently used synonym for the Qur'an is *al-kitab*, which is also used to refer to the books revealed to Moses and to Jesus' disciples, thus establishing the genealogy of the Qur'an as the final version of previous divine revelations that were, according to the Qur'an, subjected to human interference. Thus the preservation of the accurate text of the Qur'an was of paramount importance if it was not to suffer the fate of previous revelations.

The Qur'an was preserved orally and in written form during the life of Muhammad. Upon revelation, each verse was committed to memory by several of his followers and written down by others known as the scribes of the revelation, the most famous of them being Zayd ibn Thabit, the Prophet's secretary. Before his death, Muhammad read the final version of the Qur'an in its entirety to his followers and secretaries. This was later preserved in written form during the time of his successor, Abu Bakr (r. 632–634) under the auspices of Thabit. Thus within two years of Muhammad's death a definitive text was written down, kept by Abu Bakr, then passed to his successor 'Umar (634–644). In the time of the third caliph, 'Uthman (644–656), several manuscripts were made on the basis of the first one ordered by Abu Bakr and distributed to conquered lands outside Arabia.

The verses of the Qur'an vary in length from a few letters to 128 words, and these are grouped in sections or chapters (suras), which vary in length from 3 to 286 verses. They are roughly arranged in decreasing order of length. The first sura, "The Opening," is liturgical in nature, as are the final short suras, a number of which have the form of incantations. The other suras are in many different forms and genres, which vary from the short oath to a lengthy narrative of several biblical and nonbiblical stories.

The Qur'an consists of 114 suras, eighty-five revealed in Mecca, and twenty-nine revealed in Medina. The early Meccan suras call for belief in one God and in social justice, transcendent truths, and the practice of personal and altruistic virtues. They are mainly short and their language is full of poetic imagery and eloquent appeals to the hearer to worship and embrace Islam as the final creed. The suras of the middle Meccan period are longer and more prosaic, though they still retain some poetic qualities, referring mainly to the manifestations of God in nature and his divine attributes, while the late Meccan suras are full of narrative stories and sermons. The Medinan suras tend to be more prescriptive and legislative, and they contain more narrative concerning the organization of the community and the lessons it should learn from the mistakes of the past. They were revealed after the creation of the first Islamic community in Medina and aimed to provide it with guidance and consolidate its identity and cohesion.

As will be seen in the selections included here, the Qur'an embraces many literary and linguistic forms, from the oath and prophetic utterance, to the imperative and didactic "say-passages," to dramatic and narrative forms. Many of the Qur'anic narratives retell traditional stories found in Near and Middle Eastern cultures, such as the story of creation. Others are derived from biblical or apocryphal Christian texts and oral tradition. The Qur'an relates the stories of the prophets or messengers of God from Noah to Jesus, including Abraham, Ishmael, David, Elijah, Jonah, Jacob, Joseph, Job, Moses, and Solomon. The stories of these biblical characters are retold with some variations and often major alterations. The story of Joseph (Sura 12) follows the biblical account rather closely, while that of Jesus differs in some essential details. It accepts the biblical story but denies an essential aspect of the Christian account, the resurrection of Jesus. In addition to all these biblical characters, the Qur'an has many nonbiblical ones, including several from Greek sources.

Narrative stories comprise a substantial part of the Qur'an, and many of them were augmented and elaborated in several commentaries and exegeses. As a text, the Qur'an relies on cross-referencing and it often relates a story in more than one chapter. It relates segments or kernels of a specific story in one sura, picks it up again in another to complement or enforce certain aspects of its narrative, then gives its final parts in a third sura. This serves many different functions—to sustain our attention and interest in the story, or to test our comprehension of its implications, or even enforce its significance in the text. The story of creation is a good example. In order to get the complete story and to understand its relations with other biblical variants, we have to gather its scattered segments from four or five suras, as in the opening selections given here. We find a segment on the creation of earth in one sura, the nature of its oval shape in another, and the time of this creation and how to calculate it in our modern manner in a third sura.

This narrative strategy was elaborated and developed into a fine art centuries later in *The Thousand and One Nights,* in which we find fascinating and artistic renderings of many Qur'anic stories, notably those of Solomon, of the Kings of ancient Persia, and of Alexander the Great, to mention but a few. The Qur'anic concern with mythic and fantastic narrative may have provided a further source of inspiration for *The Thousand and One Nights.* The most important link between the Qur'an and *The Thousand and One Nights* is the cultural one. The Qur'anic worldview and its whole system of values and beliefs inform the world of *The Thousand and One Nights* and structure its ethos. In addition the Qur'anic concept of destiny and preordained fate is essential to the understanding of narrative progression in Scheherazade's text. Without a clear understanding of the philosophical assumptions underlying this concept, we cannot fathom the constant interplay between the frame tale and the enframed stories of *The Thousand and One Nights.* What appears in this wonderful narrative text as mere chance should be understood as the vicissitudes of destiny that conceal a deeper wisdom. Such wisdom is often beyond the comprehension of mere mortals, and this is the source of its never-ending fascination.

The Qur'an has had an immense influence on later Arabic literature, and it is treasured for its own language as well. The beauty of its language is majestic, not seductively entrancing; it amazes rather than excites, and arouses pleasure through repose not movement. Its dialogic nature implies respect for the reader and emphasizes the text's rational dimension as well as its spiritual nature. It was and still remains the pinnacle of the Arabic word, the reservoir of its rhetorical, poetic, and stylistic devices.

PRONUNCIATIONS:

Iblīs: ee-BLEES
Qur'an: coo-RAHN
sura: SUE-rah

from THE QUR'AN[1]

from Sura 41. Revelations Well Expounded
In the Name of God, the Compassionate, the Merciful

Revealed by the Compassionate, the Merciful: a Book of revelations well expounded, an Arabic Qur'an for men of knowledge.

1. Translated by N. J. Dawood. The first five selections (from Suras 41, 79, 15, 2, and 7) bring together some of the Qur'an's major passages on creation.

It proclaims good news and a warning: yet most men turn their backs and pay no heed. They say: "Our hearts are proof against the faith to which you call us. Our ears are stopped, and a thick veil stands between us. Do as you think fit, and so will we."

Say: "I am but a mortal like yourselves. It is revealed to me that your God is one God. Therefore take the straight path to Him and implore His forgiveness. Woe betide those who serve other gods besides Him; who give no alms and disbelieve in the life to come. As for those who have faith and do good works, an endless recompense awaits them."

Say: "Do you indeed disbelieve in Him who created the earth in two days? And do you make other gods His equals? The Lord of the Universe is He."

He set upon the earth mountains towering high above it. He pronounced His blessing upon it, and in four days provided it with sustenance for all alike. Then, turning to the sky, which was but a cloud of vapour, He said to it and to the earth: "Come forward both, willingly or perforce."

"We will come willingly," they answered. In two days He formed the sky into seven heavens, and to each heaven He assigned its task. We decked the lowest heaven with brilliant stars and guardian comets. Such is the design of the Mighty One, the All-knowing.

from Sura 79. The Soul-Snatchers

Are you harder to create than the heaven which He has built? He raised it high and fashioned it, giving darkness to its night and brightness to its day.

After that He spread the earth, and, drawing water from its depth, brought forth its pastures. He set down the mountains, for you and for your cattle to delight in.

from Sura 15. The Rocky Tract

It was We that revealed the Admonition, and shall Ourself preserve it. We have sent forth apostles before you to the older nations: but they scoffed at each apostle We sent them. Thus do We put doubt into the hearts of the guilty: they deny him, despite the example of the ancients.

If we opened for the unbelievers a gate in heaven and they ascended through it higher and higher, still they would say: "Our eyes were dazzled: truly, we must have been bewitched."

We have decked the heavens with constellations and made them lovely to behold. We have guarded them from every cursèd devil. Eavesdroppers are pursued by fiery comets.

We have spread out the earth and set upon it immovable mountains. We have planted it with every seasonable fruit, providing sustenance for yourselves and for those whom you do not provide for. We hold the store of every blessing and send it down in appropriate measure. We let loose the fertilizing winds and bring down water from the sky for you to drink; its stores are beyond your reach.

It is surely We who ordain life and death. We are the Heir of all things.

We know those who have gone before you, and know those who will come hereafter. It is your Lord who will gather them all before Him. He is wise and all-knowing.

We created man from dry clay, from black moulded loam, and before him Satan from smokeless fire. Your Lord said to the angels: "I am creating man from dry clay, from black moulded loam. When I have fashioned him and breathed of My spirit into him, kneel down and prostrate yourselves before him."

The angels, one and all, prostrated themselves, except Satan. He refused to prostrate himself as the others did.

"Satan," said God, "why do you not prostrate yourself?"

He replied: "I will not bow to a mortal whom You created of dry clay, of black moulded loam."

"Get you hence," said God, "you are accursed. The curse shall be on you till Judgement-day."

"Lord," said Satan, "reprieve me till the Day of Resurrection."

He answered: "You are reprieved till the Appointed Day."

"Lord," said Satan, "since You have thus seduced me, I will tempt mankind on earth: I will seduce them all, except those of them who are your faithful servants."

He replied: "This is My straight path. You shall have no power over My servants, only the sinners who follow you. They are all destined for Hell. It has seven gates, and through each gate they shall come in separate bands. But the righteous shall dwell among gardens and fountains; in peace and safety they shall enter them."

from Sura 2. The Cow

He created for you all that the earth contains; then, ascending to the sky, He fashioned it into seven heavens. He has knowledge of all things.

When your Lord said to the angels: "I am placing on the earth one that shall rule as My deputy," they replied: "Will You put there one that will do evil and shed blood, when we have for so long sung Your praises and sanctified Your name?"

He said: "I know what you know not."

He taught Adam the names of all things and then set them before the angels, saying: "Tell Me the names of these, if what you say be true."

"Glory be to You," they replied, "we have no knowledge except that which You have given us. You alone are all-knowing and wise."

Then said He: "Adam, tell them their names." And when Adam had named them, He said: "Did I not tell you that I know the secrets of the heavens and the earth, and know all that you reveal and all that you conceal?"

And when We said to the angels: "Prostrate yourselves before Adam," they all prostrated themselves except Satan, who in his pride refused and became an unbeliever.

We said: "Adam, dwell with your wife in Paradise and eat of its fruits to your hearts' content wherever you will. But never approach this tree or you shall both become transgressors."

But Satan lured them thence and brought about their banishment. "Get you down," We said, "and be enemies to each other. The earth will for a while provide your dwelling and your sustenance."

Then Adam received commandments from his Lord, and his Lord relented towards him. He is the Relenting One, the Merciful.

"Get you down hence, all," We said. "When My guidance is revealed to you, those that follow My guidance shall have nothing to fear or to regret; but those that deny and reject Our revelations shall be the inmates of the Fire, and there shall they abide for ever."

* * *

God: there is no god but Him, the Living, the Eternal One.[2] Neither slumber nor sleep overtakes Him. His is what the heavens and the earth contain. Who can intercede with Him except by His permission? He knows what is before and behind men. They can grasp only that part of His knowledge which He wills. His throne is as vast as the heavens and the earth, and the preservation of both does not weary Him. He is the Exalted, the Immense One.

from Sura 7. The Heights
In the Name of God, the Compassionate, the Merciful

Alif lām mīm sād.[3] This Book has been revealed to you—let not your heart be troubled about it—so that you may thereby give warning and admonish the faithful.

Observe that which is brought down to you from your Lord and follow no other masters besides Him. But you seldom take warning.

How many cities have We destroyed! In the night Our scourge fell upon them, or at midday, when they were drowsing.

And when Our scourge fell upon them, their only cry was: "We have indeed been wicked men."

We will surely question those to whom the messengers were sent, and We will question the messengers themselves. With knowledge We will recount to them what they have done, for We were never away from them.

On that day all shall be weighed with justice. Those whose good deeds weigh heavy in the scales shall triumph, but those whose deeds are light shall lose their souls, because they have denied Our revelations.

We have given you power in the land and provided you with a livelihood: yet you are seldom thankful.

We created you and gave you form. Then We said to the angels: "Prostrate yourselves before Adam." They all prostrated themselves except Satan, who refused to prostrate himself.

"Why did you not prostrate yourself when I commanded you?" He asked.

"I am nobler than he," he replied. "You created me from fire, but You created him from clay."

He said: "Get you down hence! This is no place for your contemptuous pride. Away with you! Humble shall you henceforth be."

He replied: "Reprieve me till the Day of Resurrection."

"You are reprieved," said He.

"Because You have led me into sin," he declared, "I will waylay Your servants as they walk on Your straight path, then spring upon them from the front and from the rear, from their right and from their left. Then You will find the greater part of them ungrateful."

"Begone!" He said. "A despicable outcast you shall henceforth be. As for those that follow you, I shall fill Hell with you all."

To Adam He said: "Dwell with your wife in Paradise, and eat of any fruit you please; but never approach this tree or you shall both become transgressors."

But Satan tempted them, so that he might reveal to them their shameful parts, which they had never seen before. He said: "Your Lord has forbidden you to

2. This paragraph is a prayer that is believed to have a magic, incantatory power.

3. Several suras begin with a set of Arabic letters, whose meaning is uncertain.

approach this tree only to prevent you from becoming angels or immortals." Then he swore to them that he would give them friendly counsel.

Thus did he cunningly seduce them. And when they had eaten of the tree, their shame became visible to them, and they both covered themselves with the leaves of the garden.

Their Lord called out to them, saying: "Did I not forbid you to approach that tree, and did I not say to you that Satan was your inveterate foe?"

They replied: "Lord, we have wronged our souls. Pardon us and have mercy on us, or we shall surely be among the lost."

He said: "Get you down hence, and may your descendants be enemies to each other. The earth will for a while provide your dwelling and your comforts. There you shall live and there shall you die, and thence shall you be raised to life."

Children of Adam! We have given you clothes to cover your shameful parts, and garments pleasing to the eye; but the finest of all these is the robe of piety.

That is one of God's revelations. Perchance they will take heed.

Children of Adam! Let not Satan tempt you, as he seduced your parents out of Paradise. He stripped them of their garments to reveal to them their shameful parts. He and his minions see you whence you cannot see them. We have made the devils guardians over the unbelievers.

Sura 1. The Opening[4]

IN THE NAME OF GOD THE COMPASSIONATE THE MERCIFUL

Praise be to God, Lord of the Universe,
The Compassionate, the Merciful,
Sovereign of the Day of Judgement!
You alone we worship, and to You alone we turn for help.
Guide us to the straight path,
The path of those whom You have favoured,
Not of those who have incurred Your wrath,
Nor of those who have gone astray.

from Sura 4. Women[5]
In the Name of God, the Compassionate, the Merciful

You people! Have fear of your Lord, who created you from a single soul. From that soul He created its spouse, and through them He bestrewed the earth with countless men and women.

Fear God, in whose name you plead with one another, and honour the mothers who bore you. God is ever watching you.

Give orphans the property which belongs to them. Do not exchange their valuables for worthless things or cheat them of their possessions; for this would surely be a grievous sin. If you fear that you cannot treat orphans[6] with fairness, then you may

---

4. This sura is read in every prayer, and often several times during each of the five prayers of the day.
5. This sura pays detailed attention to women and to

family issues. It is exceptional for its era in giving women a definite share in their family's inheritance.
6. Orphan girls.

marry other women who seem good to you: two, three, or four of them. But if you fear that you cannot maintain equality among them, marry one only or any slave-girls you may own. This will make it easier for you to avoid injustice.

Give women their dowry as a free gift; but if they choose to make over to you a part of it, you may regard it as lawfully yours.

Do not give the feeble-minded the property with which God has entrusted you for their support; but maintain and clothe them with its proceeds, and speak kind words to them.

Put orphans to the test until they reach a marriageable age. If you find them capable of sound judgement, hand over to them their property, and do not deprive them of it by squandering it before they come of age.

Let not the rich guardian touch the property of his orphan ward; and let him who is poor use no more than a fair portion of it for his own advantage.

When you hand over to them their property, call in some witnesses; sufficient is God's accounting of your actions.

Men shall have a share in what their parents and kinsmen leave; and women shall have a share in what their parents and kinsmen leave: whether it be little or much, they shall be legally entitled to a share.

If relatives, orphans, or needy men are present at the division of an inheritance, give them, too, a share of it, and speak kind words to them.

Let those who are solicitous about the welfare of their young children after their own death take care not to wrong orphans. Let them fear God and speak for justice.

Those that devour the property of orphans unjustly, swallow fire into their bellies; they shall burn in a mighty conflagration.

God has thus enjoined you concerning your children:

A male shall inherit twice as much as a female. If there be more than two girls, they shall have two-thirds of the inheritance; but if there be one only, she shall inherit the half. Parents shall inherit a sixth each, if the deceased have a child; but if he leave no child and his parents be his heirs, his mother shall have a third. If he have brothers, his mother shall have a sixth after payment of any legacy he may have bequeathed or any debt he may have owed.

You may wonder whether your parents or your children are more beneficial to you. But this is the law of God; surely God is all-knowing and wise.

You shall inherit the half of your wives' estate if they die childless. If they leave children, a quarter of their estate shall be yours after payment of any legacy they may have bequeathed or any debt they may have owed.

Your wives shall inherit one quarter of your estate if you die childless. If you leave children, they shall inherit one-eighth, after payment of any legacy you may have bequeathed or any debt you may have owed.

If a man or a woman leave neither children nor parents and have a brother or a sister, they shall each inherit one-sixth. If there be more, they shall equally share the third of the estate, after payment of any legacy he may have bequeathed or any debt he may have owed, without prejudice to the rights of the heirs. That is a commandment from God. God is all-knowing, and gracious.

Such are the bounds set by God. He that obeys God and His apostle shall dwell for ever in gardens watered by running streams. That is the supreme triumph. But he that defies God and His apostle and transgresses His bounds, shall be cast into a Fire wherein he will abide for ever. Shameful punishment awaits him.

If any of your women commit a lewd act, call in four witnesses from among yourselves against them; if they testify to their guilt confine them to their houses till death overtakes them or till God finds another way for them.

If two men among you commit a lewd act, punish them both. If they repent and mend their ways, let them be. God is forgiving and merciful.

God forgives those who commit evil in ignorance and then quickly turn to Him in penitence. God will pardon them. God is all-knowing and wise. But He will not forgive those who do evil and, when death comes to them, say: "Now we repent!" Nor those who die unbelievers: for them We have prepared a woeful scourge.

Believers, it is unlawful for you to inherit the women of your deceased kinsmen against their will, or to bar them from re-marrying, in order that you may force them to give up a part of what you have given them, unless they be guilty of a proven lewd act. Treat them with kindness; for even if you dislike them, it may well be that you dislike a thing which God has meant for your own abundant good.

If you wish to replace one wife with another, do not take from her the dowry you have given her even if it be a talent of gold. That would be improper and grossly unjust; for how can you take it back when you have lain with each other and entered into a firm contract?

You shall not marry the women whom your fathers married: all previous such marriages excepted. That was an evil practice, indecent and abominable.

Forbidden to you are your mothers, your daughters, your sisters, your paternal and maternal aunts, the daughters of your brothers and sisters, your foster-mothers, your foster-sisters, the mothers of your wives, your step-daughters who are in your charge, born of the wives with whom you have lain (it is no offence for you to marry your step-daughters if you have not consummated your marriage with their mothers), and the wives of your own begotten sons. You are also forbidden to take in marriage two sisters at one and the same time: all previous such marriages excepted. Surely God is forgiving and merciful. Also married women, except those whom you own as slaves. Such is the decree of God. All women other than these are lawful for you, provided you court them with your wealth in modest conduct, not in fornication. Give them their dowry for the enjoyment you have had of them as a duty; but it shall be no offence for you to make any other agreement among yourselves after you have fulfilled your duty. Surely God is all-knowing and wise.

If any one of you cannot afford to marry a free believing woman, let him marry a slave-girl who is a believer (God best knows your faith: you are born one of another). Marry them with the permission of their masters and give them their dowry in all justice, provided they are honourable and chaste and have not entertained other men. If after marriage they commit adultery, they shall suffer half the penalty inflicted upon free adulteresses. Such is the law for those of you who fear to commit sin: but if you abstain, it will be better for you. God is forgiving and merciful.

* * *

The People of the Book ask you to bring down for them a book from heaven. Of Moses they demanded a harder thing than that. They said to him: "Show us God distinctly." And for their wickedness the thunderbolt smote them. They worshipped the calf after clear signs had been revealed to them; yet We forgave them that, and bestowed on Moses clear authority.

When We made a covenant with them We raised the Mount above them and said: "Enter the gates in adoration. Do not break the Sabbath." We took from them a solemn covenant. But they broke their covenant, denied the revelations of God, and killed the prophets unjustly. They said: "Our hearts are sealed."

It is God who has sealed their hearts, on account of their unbelief. They have no faith, except a few of them.

They denied the truth and uttered a monstrous falsehood against Mary.[7] They declared: "We have put to death the Messiah, Jesus son of Mary, the apostle of God." They did not kill him, nor did they crucify him, but they thought they did.

Those that disagreed about him were in doubt concerning him; they knew nothing about him that was not sheer conjecture; they did not slay him for certain. God lifted him up to Him; God is mighty and wise. There is none among the People of the Book but will believe in him before his death; and on the Day of Resurrection he will bear witness against them.

Because of their iniquity, We forbade the Jews wholesome things which were formerly allowed them; because time after time they have debarred others from the path of God; because they practise usury—although they were forbidden it—and cheat others of their possessions. Woeful punishment have We prepared for those that disbelieve. But those of them that have deep learning, and those that truly believe in what has been revealed to you and what was revealed before you; who attend to their prayers and render the alms levy and have faith in God and the Last Day—these shall be richly recompensed.

We have revealed Our will to you as We revealed it to Noah and to the prophets who came after him; as We revealed it to Abraham, Ishmael, Isaac, Jacob, and the tribes; to Jesus, Job, Jonah, Aaron, Solomon and David, to whom We gave the Psalms. Of some apostles We have already told you, but there are others of whom We have not yet spoken (God spoke directly to Moses): apostles who brought good news to mankind and admonished them, so that they might have no plea against God after their coming. God is mighty and wise.

God bears witness, by that which He has revealed to you, that He revealed it with His knowledge; and so do the angels. There is no better witness than God.

Those that disbelieve and debar others from the path of God have strayed far into error. God will not forgive those who disbelieve and act unjustly; nor will He guide them to any path other than the path of Hell, wherein they shall abide for ever. Surely that is easy enough for God.

from Sura 5. The Table[8]

Believers, when death approaches you, let two just men from among you act as witnesses when you make your testament; or two men from another tribe if the calamity of death overtakes you while you are travelling the land. Detain them after prayers, and if you doubt their honesty, let them swear by God: "We will not sell our testimony for any price even to a kinsman. We will not hide the testimony of God; for we should then be evil-doers." If both prove dishonest, replace them by another pair from among those immediately concerned, and let them both swear by God, saying: "Our testimony is truer than theirs. We have told no lies, for we should then be wrongdoers." Thus will they be more likely to bear true witness or to fear that the oaths of

---

7. Understanding Jesus as a human prophet rather than divine, the Qur'an criticizes the Christian treatment of Mary as the Mother of God.
8. A further discussion of Jesus and his mission.

others may contradict theirs. Have fear of God and be obedient. God does not guide the evil-doers.

One day God will gather all the apostles and ask them: How were you received?" They will reply: "We have no knowledge. You alone know what is hidden." God will say: "Jesus son of Mary, remember the favour I bestowed on you and on your mother: how I strengthened you with the Holy Spirit, so that you preached to men in your cradle and in the prime of manhood; how I instructed you in the Book and in wisdom, in the Torah and in the Gospel; how by My leave you fashioned from clay the likeness of a bird and breathed into it so that, by My leave, it became a living bird; how, by My leave, you healed the blind man and the leper, and by My leave restored the dead to life; how I protected you from the Israelites when you had come to them with clear signs: when those of them who disbelieved declared: 'This is but plain sorcery'; how, when I enjoined the disciples to believe in Me and in My apostle, they replied: 'We believe; bear witness that we submit.'"

"Jesus son of Mary," said the disciples, "can your Lord send down to us from heaven a table spread with food?"

He replied: "Have fear of God, if you are true believers."

"We wish to eat of it," they said, "so that we may reassure our hearts and know that what you said to us is true, and that we may be witnesses of it."

"Lord," said Jesus son of Mary, "send down to us from heaven a table spread with food, that it may mark a feast for the first of us and the last of us: a sign from You. Give us our sustenance; You are the best provider."

God replied: "I am sending one to you. But whoever of you disbelieves hereafter shall be punished as no man will ever be punished."

Then God will say: "Jesus son of Mary, did you ever say to mankind: 'Worship me and my mother as gods besides God?'"

"Glory be to You," he will answer, "I could never have claimed what I have no right to. If I had ever said so, You would have surely known it. You know what is in my mind, but I know not what is in Yours. You alone know what is hidden. I told them only what You bade me. I said: 'Serve God, my Lord and your Lord.' I watched over them while living in their midst, and ever since You took me to Yourself, You have been watching them. You are the witness of all things. If You punish them, they surely are Your servants; and if You forgive them, surely You are mighty and wise."

God will say: "This is the day when their truthfulness will benefit the truthful. They shall for ever dwell in gardens watered by running streams. God is pleased with them, and they are pleased with Him. That is the supreme triumph."

God has sovereignty over the heavens and the earth and all that they contain. He has power over all things.

from Sura 8. The Spoils[9]

Believers, when you encounter the infidels on the march, do not turn your backs to them in flight. If anyone on that day turns his back to them, except for tactical reasons, or to join another band, he shall incur the wrath of God and Hell shall be his home: an evil fate.

It was not you, but God, who slew them. * * *

---

9. A discussion of a major battle at Badr in 624, in which Muhammad's forces routed a much larger army of Meccans.

You were encamped on this side of the valley and the unbelievers on the farther side, with the caravan below. Had they offered battle, you would have surely declined; but God sought to accomplish what He had ordained, so that, by a clear sign, he that was destined to perish might die, and he that was destined to live might survive. God hears all and knows all.

God made them appear to you in a dream as a small band. Had He showed them to you as a great army, your courage would have failed you and discord would have triumphed in your ranks. But this God spared you. He knows your innermost thoughts.

And when you met them, He made each appear to the other few in number, that God might accomplish what He had ordained. To God shall all things return.

Believers, when you meet their army stand firm and pray fervently to God, so that you may triumph. Obey God and His apostle and do not dispute with one another, lest you lose courage and your resolve weaken. Have patience: God is with those that are patient.

Do not be like those who left their homes elated with insolence and vainglory. They debar others from the path of God: but God has knowledge of all their actions.

Satan made their foul deeds seem fair to them. He said: "No man shall conquer you this day. I shall be at hand to help you." But when the two armies came within sight of each other, he took to his heels, saying: "I am done with you, for I can see what you cannot. I fear God. God's punishment is stern."

The hypocrites, and those whose hearts were tainted, said: "Their religion has deceived them." But he that puts his trust in God shall find God mighty and wise.

If you could see the angels when they carry off the souls of the unbelievers! They shall strike them on their faces and their backs, saying: "Taste the torment of the Conflagration! This is the punishment for what your hands committed." God is not unjust to His servants.

Like Pharaoh's people and those before them, they disbelieved God's revelations. Therefore God will smite them for their sins. Mighty is God and stern His retribution.

God does not change the blessings He has bestowed upon a people until they change what is in their hearts. God hears all and knows all.

Like Pharaoh's people and those before them, they disbelieved their Lord's revelations. Therefore We will destroy them for their sins even as We drowned Pharaoh's people. They were wicked men all.

The basest creatures in the sight of God are the faithless who will not believe; those who time after time violate their treaties with you and have no fear of God. If you capture them in battle discriminate between them and those that follow them, so that their followers may take warning.

If you fear treachery from any of your allies, you may fairly retaliate by breaking off your treaty with them. God does not love the treacherous.

Let not the unbelievers think that they will ever get away. They have not the power so to do. Muster against them all the men and cavalry at your command, so that you may strike terror into the enemy of God and your enemy, and others besides them who are unknown to you but known to God. All that you give in the cause of God shall be repaid to you. You shall not be wronged.

If they incline to peace, make peace with them, and put your trust in God.[1] It is surely He who hears all and knows all. Should they seek to deceive you, God is

---

[1] Although the previous verses ask for preparation for war, this one emphasizes the obligation for peace when the enemy seeks it.

all-sufficient for you. He has made you strong with His help and rallied the faithful round you, making their hearts one. If you had given away all the riches of the earth, you could not have so united them: but God has united them. He is mighty and wise.

Prophet, God is your strength, and the faithful who follow you.

Prophet, rouse the faithful to arms. If there are twenty steadfast men among you, they shall vanquish two hundred; and if there are a hundred, they shall rout a thousand unbelievers, for they are devoid of understanding.

God has now lightened your burden, for He knows that you are weak. If there are a hundred steadfast men among you, they shall vanquish two hundred; and if there are a thousand, they shall, by God's will, defeat two thousand. God is with those that are steadfast.

A prophet may not take captives until he has fought and triumphed in the land. You seek the chance gain of this world, but God desires for you the world to come. God is mighty and wise. Had there not been a previous writ from God, you would have been sternly punished for what you took. Enjoy therefore the good and lawful things which you have gained in war, and fear God. God is forgiving and merciful.

Prophet, say to those you have taken captive: "If God finds goodness in your hearts, He will give you that which is better than what has been taken from you, and He will forgive you. God is forgiving and merciful."

But if they seek to betray you, know they have already betrayed God. Therefore He has made you triumph over them. God is all-knowing and wise.

Those that have embraced the Faith and fled their homes, and fought for the cause of God with their wealth and with their persons; and those that have sheltered them and helped them, shall be as friends to each other.

Those that have embraced the Faith, but have not left their homes, shall in no way become your friends until they have done so. But if they seek your help in the cause of the true Faith, it is your duty to assist them, except against a people with whom you have a treaty. God is cognizant of all your actions.

from Sura 12. Joseph[2]
In the Name of God, the Compassionate, the Merciful

Alif lām rā'. These are the verses of the Glorious Book. We have revealed the Qur'an in the Arabic tongue so that you may grow in understanding.

In revealing this Qur'an We will recount to you the best of narratives, though before it you were heedless.

Joseph said to his father: "Father, I dreamt of eleven stars and the sun and the moon; I saw them prostrate themselves before me."

"My son," he replied, "say nothing of this dream to your brothers, lest they plot evil against you: Satan is the sworn enemy of man. Even thus shall you be chosen by your Lord. He will teach you to interpret visions, and will perfect His favour to you and to the house of Jacob, as He perfected it to your forefathers Abraham and Isaac before you. Your Lord is all-knowing and wise."

Surely in Joseph and his brothers there are signs for doubting men.

They said to each other: "Surely Joseph and his brother are dearer to our father than ourselves, though we are many. Truly, our father is much mistaken. Let us slay

---

2. The Qur'an's account of the story of Joseph is remarkably similar to the biblical one (see "The Joseph Story," Volume A); the sura closes by emphasizing its fidelity to received sacred history.

Joseph, or cast him away in some far-off land, so that we may have no rivals in our father's love, and after that be honourable men."

One of the brothers said: "Do not slay Joseph; but, if you must, rather cast him into a dark pit. Some caravan will take him up."

They said to their father: "Why do you not trust us with Joseph? Surely we wish him well. Send him with us tomorrow, that he may play and enjoy himself. We will take good care of him."

He replied: "It would much grieve me to let him go with you; for I fear lest the wolf should eat him when you are off your guard."

They said: "If the wolf could eat him despite our number, then we should surely be lost!"

And when they took him with them, they resolved to cast him into a dark pit. We revealed to him Our will, saying: "You shall tell them of all this when they will not know you."

At nightfall they returned weeping to their father. They said: "We went off to compete together, and left Joseph with our packs. The wolf devoured him. But you will not believe us, though we speak the truth." And they showed him their brother's shirt, stained with false blood.

"No!" he cried. "Your souls have tempted you to evil. Sweet patience! God alone can help me bear the loss you speak of."

And a caravan passed by, who sent their water-bearer to the pit. And when he had let down his pail, he cried: "Rejoice! A boy!"

They concealed him as part of their merchandise. But God knew what they did. They sold him for a trifling price, for a few pieces of silver. They cared nothing for him.

The Egyptian who bought him said to his wife: "Be kind to him. He may prove useful to us, or we may adopt him as our son."

Thus We established Joseph in the land, and taught him to interpret dreams. God has power over all things, though most men may not know it. And when he reached maturity We bestowed on him wisdom and knowledge. Thus do We reward the righteous.

His master's wife attempted to seduce him. She bolted the doors and said: "Come!"

"God forbid!" he replied. "My lord has treated me with kindness. Wrongdoers shall never prosper."

She made for him, and he himself would have succumbed to her had he not seen a sign from his Lord. Thus did We shield him from wantonness, for he was one of Our faithful servants.

They both rushed to the door. She tore his shirt from behind. And at the door they met her husband.

She cried: "Shall not the man who wished to violate your wife be thrown into prison or sternly punished?"

Joseph said: "It was she who attempted to seduce me."

"If his shirt is torn from the front," said one of her people, "she is speaking the truth and he is lying. If it is torn from behind, then he is speaking the truth, and she is lying."

And when her husband saw that Joseph's shirt was rent from behind, he said to her: "This is but one of your tricks. Your cunning is great indeed! Joseph, say no more about this. Woman, ask pardon for your sin. You have assuredly done wrong."

In the city, women were saying: "The Prince's wife has sought to seduce her servant. She has conceived a passion for him. We can see that she has clearly gone astray."

When she heard of their intrigues, she invited them to a banquet prepared at her house. To each she gave a knife, and ordered Joseph to present himself before them. When they saw him, they were amazed at him and cut their hands, exclaiming: "God preserve us! This is no mortal, but a gracious angel."

"This is he," she said, "on whose account you blamed me. I attempted to seduce him, but he was unyielding. If he declines to do my bidding, he shall be thrown into prison and shall be held in scorn."

"Lord," said Joseph, "sooner would I go to prison than give in to their advances. Shield me from their cunning, or I shall yield to them and lapse into folly."

His Lord answered his prayer and warded off their wiles from him. He hears all and knows all.

Yet, for all the evidence they had seen, they thought it right to jail him for a time.

Two young men entered the prison with him. One said: "I dreamt that I was pressing grapes." And the other: "I dreamt I was carrying a loaf upon my head, and the birds came and ate of it. Tell us the meaning of these dreams, for we can see you are a man of virtue."

Joseph replied: "Whatever food you are provided with, I can divine for you its meaning, even before it reaches you. This knowledge my Lord has given me, for I have left the faith of those that disbelieve in God and deny the life to come. I follow the faith of my forefathers, Abraham, Isaac and Jacob. We will serve no idols besides God. Such is the grace which God has bestowed on us and on all mankind. Yet most men do not give thanks.

"Fellow prisoners! Are sundry gods better than God, the One who conquers all? Those you serve besides Him are nothing but names which you and your fathers have devised and for which God has revealed no sanction. Judgement rests only with God. He has commanded you to worship none but Him. That is the true faith: yet most men do not know it.

"Fellow prisoners, one of you will serve his lord with wine. The other will be crucified, and the birds will peck at his head. That is the answer to your question."

And Joseph said to the prisoner who he knew would survive: "Remember me in the presence of your lord."

But Satan made him forget to mention Joseph to his lord, so that he stayed in prison for several years.

The king said: "I saw seven fatted cows which seven lean ones devoured; also seven green ears of corn and seven others dry. Tell me the meaning of this vision, my nobles, if you can interpret visions."

They replied: "They are but a medley of dreams; nor are we skilled in the interpretation of dreams."

Thereupon the man who had been freed remembered after all that time. He said: "I shall tell you what it means. Give me leave to go."

"Joseph," he said, "man of truth, tell us of the seven fatted cows which seven lean ones devoured; also of the seven green ears of corn and the other seven which were dry: so that I may go back to my masters and inform them."

He replied: "You shall sow for seven consecutive years. Leave in the ear the corn you reap, except a little which you may eat. There shall follow seven hungry years which will consume all but a little of what you stored. Then will come a year of abundant rain, in which the people will press the grape."

The king said: "Bring this man before me."

But when the envoy came to him, Joseph said: "Go back to your master and ask him about the women who cut their hands. My master knows their cunning."

The king questioned the women, saying: "What made you attempt to seduce Joseph?"

"God forbid!" they replied. "We know no evil of him."

"Now the truth must come to light," said the Prince's wife. "It was I who attempted to seduce him. He has told the truth."

"From this," said Joseph, "my lord will know that I did not betray him in his absence, and that God does not guide the mischief of the treacherous. Not that I claim to be free from sin: man's soul is prone to evil, except his to whom my Lord has shown mercy. My Lord is forgiving and merciful."

The king said: "Bring him before me. I will choose him for my own."

And when he had spoken with him, the king said: "You shall henceforth dwell with us, honoured and trusted."

Joseph said: "Give me charge of the granaries of the land. I shall husband them wisely."

Thus did We establish Joseph in the land, and he dwelt there as he pleased. We bestow Our mercy on whom We will, and shall never deny the righteous their reward. Surely better is the recompense of the life to come for those who believe in God and keep from evil.

Joseph's brothers arrived and presented themselves before him. He recognized them, but they knew him not. And when he had given them their provisions, he said: "Bring me your other brother from your father. Do you not see that I give just measure and am the best of hosts? If you refuse to bring him, you shall have no measure, nor shall you come near me again."

They replied: "We will endeavour to fetch him from his father. This we will surely do."

He said to his servants: "Put their silver into their packs, so that they may discover it when they return to their people. Perchance they will come back."

When they returned to their father, they said: "Father, corn is henceforth denied us. Send our brother with us and we shall have our measure. We will take good care of him."

He replied: "Am I to trust you with him as I once trusted you with his brother? But God is the best of guardians: and of all those that show mercy He is the most merciful."

When they opened their packs, they discovered that their money had been returned to them. "Father," they said, "what more can we desire? Here is our money paid back to us. We will buy provisions for our people, and take good care of our brother. We should receive an extra camel-load; a camel-load should be easy enough."

He replied: "I will not send him with you until you promise in God's name to bring him back to me, unless the worst befall you."

And when they had given him their pledge, he said: "God is the witness of what we say. My sons, do not enter from one gate; enter from different gates. In no way can I shield you from the might of God; judgement is His alone. In Him I have put my trust. In Him let the faithful put their trust."

And when they entered as their father bade them, he could in no way shield them from the might of God. It was but a wish in Jacob's soul which he had thus fulfilled. He was possessed of knowledge which We had given him. But most men have no knowledge.

When they went in to Joseph, he embraced his brother, and said: "I am your brother. Do not grieve at what they did."

And when he had given them their provisions, he hid a drinking-cup in his brother's pack.

Then a crier called out after them: "Travellers, you are surely thieves!"

They turned back, and asked: "What have you lost?"

"We miss the king's drinking-cup," they replied. "He that brings it shall have a camel-load of corn. I pledge my word for it."

"In God's name," they cried, "you know we did not come to do evil in the land. We are no thieves."

The Egyptians said: "What punishment shall be his who stole it, if you prove to be lying?"

They replied: "He in whose pack the cup is found shall render himself your bondsman. Thus do we punish the wrongdoers."

Joseph searched their bags before his brother's, and then took out the cup from his brother's bag.

Thus We directed Joseph. By the king's law he had no right to seize his brother: but God willed otherwise. We exalt whom We will to a lofty station: and above those that have knowledge there is One who is all-knowing.

They said: "If he has stolen—know then that a brother of his stole before him."

But Joseph kept his secret and revealed nothing to them. He said: "Your deed was worse. God best knows the things you speak of."

They said: "Noble prince, this boy has an aged father. Take one of us, instead of him. We can see you are a generous man."

He replied: "God forbid that we should take any but the man with whom our property was found: for then we should surely be unjust."

When they despaired of him, they went aside to confer in private. The eldest said: "Do you not know that your father took from you a pledge in God's name, and that long ago you did your worst with Joseph? I will not stir from the land until my father gives me leave or God makes known to me His judgement: He is the best of judges. Return to your father and say to him: 'Father, your son has stolen. We testify only to what we know. How could we guard against the unforeseen? Inquire at the city where we lodged, and from the caravan with which we travelled. We surely speak the truth.'"

"No!" cried their father. "Your souls have tempted you to evil. But I will have sweet patience. God may bring them all to me. He alone is all-knowing and wise." And he turned away from them, crying: "Alas for Joseph!" His eyes went white with grief, and he was oppressed with silent sorrow.

His sons exclaimed: "In God's name, will you not cease to think of Joseph until you ruin your health and die?"

He replied: "I complain to God of my sorrow and sadness. God has made known to me things that you know not. Go, my sons, and seek news of Joseph and his brother. Do not despair of God's spirit; none but unbelievers despair of God's spirit."

And when they went in to him, they said: "Noble prince, we and our people are scourged with famine. We have brought but little money. Give us our full measure, and be charitable to us: God rewards the charitable."

"Do you know," he replied, "what you did to Joseph and his brother? You are surely unaware."

They cried: "Can you indeed be Joseph?"

"I am Joseph," he answered, "and this is my brother. God has been gracious to us. Those that keep from evil and endure with fortitude, God will not deny them their reward."

"By the Lord," they said, "God has exalted you above us all. We have indeed done wrong."

He replied: "None shall reproach you this day. May God forgive you: of all those that show mercy He is the most merciful. Take this shirt of mine and throw it over my father's face: he will recover his sight. Then return to me with all your people."

When the caravan departed their father said: "I feel the breath of Joseph, though you will not believe me."

"In God's name," said those who heard him, "it is but your old illusion."

And when the bearer of good news arrived, he threw Joseph's shirt over the old man's face, and he regained his sight. He said: "Did I not tell you, God has made known to me what you know not?"

His sons said: "Father, implore forgiveness for our sins. We have indeed done wrong."

He replied: "I shall implore my Lord to forgive you. He is forgiving and merciful."

And when they went in to Joseph, he embraced his parents and said: "Welcome to Egypt, safe, if God wills!"

He helped his parents to a couch, and they all fell on their knees and prostrated themselves before him.

"This," said Joseph to his father, "is the meaning of my old vision: my Lord has fulfilled it. He has been gracious to me. He has released me from prison, and brought you out of the desert after Satan had stirred up strife between me and my brothers. My Lord is gracious to whom He will. He alone is all-knowing and wise.

"Lord, You have given me authority and taught me to interpret dreams. Creator of the heavens and the earth, my Guardian in this world and in the world to come! Allow me to die in submission, and admit me among the righteous."

That which We have now revealed to you[3] is a tale of the unknown. You were not present when Joseph's brothers conceived their plans and schemed against him. Yet strive as you may, most men will not believe.

You shall demand of them no recompense for this. It[4] is but an admonition to all mankind.

Many are the marvels of the heavens and the earth; yet they pass them by and pay no heed to them. The greater part of them believe in God only if they can worship other gods besides Him.

Are they confident that God's scourge will not fall upon them, or that the Hour of Doom will not overtake them unawares, without warning?

from Sura 16. The Bee

By the Lord, We have sent apostles before you to other nations. But Satan made their foul deeds seem fair to them, and to this day he is their patron. A woeful scourge awaits them.

We have revealed to you the Book so that you may resolve their differences for them: a guide and a blessing to true believers.

---

3. The Prophet Muhammad.   4. The Qur'an.

God sends down water from the sky with which He quickens the earth after its death. Surely in this there is a sign for prudent men.

In cattle too you have a worthy lesson. We give you to drink of that which is in their bellies, between the bowels and the blood-streams: pure milk, pleasant for those who drink it.

And the fruits of the palm and the vine, from which you derive intoxicants and wholesome food. Surely in this there is a sign for men of understanding.

Your Lord inspired the bee, saying: "Make your homes in the mountains, in the trees, and in the hives which men shall build for you. Feed on every kind of fruit, and follow the trodden paths of your Lord."

From its belly comes forth a syrup of different hues, a cure for men. Surely in this there is a sign for those who would take thought.

God created you, and He will then reclaim you. Some shall have their lives prolonged to abject old age, when all that they once knew they shall know no more. All-knowing is God, and mighty.

In what He has provided, God has favoured some among you above others. Those who are so favoured will not allow their slaves an equal share in what they have. Would they deny God's goodness?

God has given you wives from among yourselves and, through your wives, sons and grandchildren. He has provided you with good things: will they then believe in falsehood and deny God's favours?

They worship helpless idols which can confer on them no benefits from heaven or earth. Compare God with none: God has knowledge, but you have not.

God makes this comparison. On the one hand there is a helpless slave, the property of his master. On the other, a man on whom We have bestowed Our bounty, so that he gives of it both in private and in public. Are the two equal? God forbid! Most men have no knowledge.

God also makes this comparison. Take a dumb and helpless man, a burden on his master: wherever he sends him he returns with empty hands. Is he as good as he that enjoins justice and follows a straight path?

To God belong the secrets of the heavens and the earth. The business of the Final Hour shall be accomplished in the twinkling of an eye, or in a shorter time. God has power over all things.

God brought you out of your mothers' wombs devoid of all knowledge, and gave you ears and eyes and hearts, so that you may give thanks.

Do they not see the birds that wing their way in heaven's vault? None but God sustains them. Surely in this there are signs for true believers.

God has given you houses to dwell in, and animals' skins for tents, so that you may find them light when you travel and easy to pitch when you halt for shelter; while from their wool, fur, and hair, He has for a space of time provided you with comforts and domestic goods.

By means of that which He created, God has given you shelter from the sun. He has given you refuge in the mountains. He has furnished you with garments to protect you from the heat, and with coats of armour to shield you in your wars. Thus He perfects His favours to you, so that you may submit to Him.

But if they[5] pay no heed, your mission is only to give clear warning.

They recognize God's favours, yet they deny them. Most of them are ungrateful.

---

5. The Meccans, who were resisting Muhammad's message.

from Sura 18. The Cave[6]

Moses said to his servant: "I will journey on until I reach the land where the two seas meet, though I may march for ages."

But when at last they came to the land where the two seas met, they forgot their fish, which made its way into the water, swimming at will.

And when they had journeyed farther on, Moses said to his servant: "Bring us some food; we are worn out with travelling."

"Know," he replied, "that I forgot the fish when we were resting on the rock. It was Satan who made me forget to mention this. The fish made its way miraculously into the sea."

"This is what we have been seeking," said Moses. They went back the way they came, and found one of Our servants to whom We had vouchsafed Our mercy and whom We had endowed with knowledge of Our own. Moses said to him: "May I follow you, so that you may guide me by that which you have been taught?"

"You will not bear with me," replied the other. "For how can you bear with that which is beyond your knowledge?"

Moses said: "If God wills, you shall find me patient: I shall in no way cross you."

He said: "If you are bent on following me, you must not question me about any-thing until I mention it to you myself."

The two set forth, but as soon as they embarked, Moses' companion bored a hole in the bottom of the ship.

"Is it to drown her passengers that you have bored a hole in her?" Moses asked. "A strange thing you have done."

"Did I not tell you," he replied, "that you would not bear with me?"

"Pardon my forgetfulness," said Moses. "Do not be angry with me on account of this."

They journeyed on until they fell in with a certain youth. Moses' companion slew him, and Moses said: "You have killed an innocent man who has slain no one. Surely you have done a wicked thing."

"Did I not tell you," he replied, "that you would not bear with me?"

Moses said: "If ever I question you again, abandon me; for then I should deserve it."

They travelled on until they came to a city. They asked its people for some food, but they declined to receive them as their guests. There they found a wall on the point of falling down. His companion restored it, and Moses said: "Had you wished, you could have demanded payment for your labours."

"Now has the time arrived when we must part," said the other. "But first I will explain to you those acts of mine which you could not bear to watch with patience.

"Know that the ship belonged to some poor fishermen. I damaged it because at their rear there was a king who was taking every ship by force.

"As for the youth, his parents both are true believers, and we feared lest he should plague them with wickedness and unbelief. It was our wish that their Lord should grant them another in his place, a son more righteous and more filial.

"As for the wall, it belonged to two orphan boys in the city whose father was an honest man. Beneath it their treasure is buried. Your Lord decreed, as a mercy from

---

6. This is one of several fascinating stories in the Qur'an of the testing of Moses.

your Lord, that they should dig up their treasure when they grew to manhood. What I did was not done by my will.

"That is the meaning of what you could not bear to watch with patience."

from Sura 19. Mary[7]

And you shall recount in the Book the story of Mary: how she left her people and betook herself to a solitary place to the east.

We sent to her Our spirit in the semblance of a full-grown man. And when she saw him she said: "May the Merciful defend me from you! If you fear the Lord, [leave me and go your way]."

"I am but your Lord's emissary," he replied, "and have come to give you a holy son."

"How shall I bear a child," she answered, "when I have neither been touched by any man nor ever been unchaste?"

"Thus did your Lord speak," he replied. "'That is easy enough for Me. He shall be a sign to mankind and a blessing from Ourself. Our decree shall come to pass.'"

Thereupon she conceived him, and retired to a far-off place. And when she felt the throes of childbirth she lay down by the trunk of a palm-tree, crying: "Oh, would that I had died before this and passed into oblivion!"

But a voice from below cried out to her: "Do not despair. Your Lord has provided a brook that runs at your feet, and if you shake the trunk of the palm-tree it will drop fresh ripe dates in your lap. Therefore eat and drink and rejoice; and should you meet any mortal say to him: 'I have vowed a fast to the Merciful and will not speak with any man today.'"

Carrying the child, she came to her people, who said to her: "Mary, this is indeed a strange thing! Sister of Aaron, your father was never a whore-monger, nor was your mother a harlot."

She made a sign to them, pointing to the child. But they replied: "How can we speak with a babe in the cradle?"

Whereupon he spoke and said: "I am the servant of God. He has given me the Book and ordained me a prophet. His blessing is upon me wherever I go, and He has exhorted me to be steadfast in prayer and to give alms as long as I shall live. He has exhorted me to honour my mother and has purged me of vanity and wickedness. Blessed was I on the day I was born, and blessed I shall be on the day of my death and on the day I shall be raised to life."

Such was Jesus son of Mary. That is the whole truth, which they still doubt. God forbid that He Himself should beget a son! When He decrees a thing He need only say: "Be," and it is.

God is my Lord and your Lord: therefore serve Him. That is a straight path.

---

7. The Qur'an accepts and narrates here the virgin birth of Christ, and gives a story of the miraculous child speaking eloquently in his infancy.

from Sura 21. The Prophets[8]

To Solomon We subjected the raging wind: it sped at his bidding to the land which We had blessed. We had knowledge of all things.

We assigned him devils who dived for him into the sea and who performed other tasks besides. Over them We kept a watchful eye.

And tell of Job: how he called on his Lord, saying: "I am sorely afflicted: but of all those that show mercy You are the most merciful."

We answered his prayer and relieved his affliction. We restored to him his family and as many more with them: a blessing from Ourself and an admonition to the devout.

And you shall also tell of Ishmael, Idrīs,[9] and Dhūl-Kifl,[1] who all endured with patience. To Our mercy We admitted them, for they were upright men.

And of Dhūl-Nūn:[2] how he went away in anger, thinking We had no power over him. But in the darkness he cried: "There is no god but You. Glory be to You! I have done wrong."

We answered his prayer and delivered him from distress. Thus shall We save the true believers.

And of Zacharias, who invoked his Lord, saying: "Lord, let me not remain childless, though of all heirs You are the best."

We answered his prayer and gave him John, curing his wife of sterility. They vied with each other in good works and called on Us with piety, fear, and submission.

And of the woman who kept her chastity. We breathed into her of Our spirit, and made her and her son a sign to all mankind.

Your community is but one community, and I am Your only Lord. Therefore serve Me. Men have divided themselves into factions, but to Us shall they all return. He that does good works in the fullness of his faith, his endeavours shall not be lost: We record them all.

It is ordained that no community We have destroyed shall ever rise again. But when Gog and Magog are let loose and rush headlong down every hill; when the true promise nears its fulfilment; the unbelievers shall stare in amazement, crying: "Woe betide us! Of this we have been heedless. We have assuredly done wrong."

You and your idols shall be the fuel of Hell; therein shall you all go down. Were they true gods, your idols would not go there: but there shall they abide for ever. They shall groan with anguish and be bereft of hearing.

But those to whom We have long since shown Our favour shall be far removed from Hell. They shall not hear its roar, but shall delight for ever in what their souls desire.

The Supreme Terror shall not grieve them, and the angels will receive them, saying: "This is the day you have been promised."

On that day We shall roll up the heaven like a scroll of parchment. Just as We brought the First Creation into being, so will We restore it. This is a promise We shall assuredly fulfil.

We wrote in the Psalms after the Torah was revealed:

"The righteous among My servants shall inherit the earth."[3] That is an admonition to those who serve Us.

---

8. In this sura the Qur'an relates the stories of many biblical prophets.
9. Enoch.

1. Probably Ezekiel.
2. Jonah.
3. Quoting Psalm 37:29.

We have sent you forth but as a blessing to mankind. Say: "It is revealed to me that your God is one God. Will you submit to Him?"

If they pay no heed, say: "I have warned you all alike, though I cannot tell whether the scourge you are promised is imminent or far off. He knows your spoken words and hidden thoughts. For all I know, this may be a test for you and a short reprieve."

Say: "Lord, judge with fairness. Our Lord is the Merciful, whose help We seek against your blasphemies."

from Sura 24. Light

God is the light of the heavens and the earth. His light may be compared to a niche that enshrines a lamp, the lamp within a crystal of star-like brilliance. It is lit from a blessed olive tree neither eastern nor western. Its very oil would almost shine forth, though no fire touched it. Light upon light; God guides to His light whom He will.

God speaks in parables to mankind. God has knowledge of all things.

His light is found in temples which God has sanctioned to be built for the remembrance of His name. In them, morning and evening, His praise is sung by men whom neither trade nor profit can divert from remembering God, from offering prayers, or from giving alms; who dread the day when men's hearts and eyes shall writhe with anguish; who hope that God will requite them for their noblest deeds and lavish His grace upon them. God gives without reckoning to whom He will.

from Sura 28. The Story
In the Name of God, the Compassionate, the Merciful

Tā' sīn mīm. These are the verses of the Glorious Book. In all truth We shall recount to you the tale of Moses and Pharaoh for the instruction of the faithful.

Now Pharaoh made himself a tyrant in the land. He divided his people into castes, one group of which he persecuted, putting their sons to death and sparing only their daughters. Truly, he was an evil-doer.

But it was Our will to favour those who were oppressed in the land and to make them leaders among men, to bestow on them a noble heritage and to give them power in the land; and to inflict on Pharaoh, Haman, and their warriors the very scourge they dreaded.

We revealed Our will to Moses' mother, saying: "Give him suck, but if you are concerned about his safety, then put him down onto the river. Have no fear, nor be dismayed; for We shall restore him to you and shall invest him with a mission."

Pharaoh's household picked him up, though he was to become their adversary and their scourge. For Pharaoh, Haman, and their warriors were sinners all.

His wife said to Pharaoh: "This child may bring joy to us both. Do not slay him. He may show promise, and we may adopt him as our son." But they little knew what they were doing.

Moses' mother's heart was sorely troubled. She would have revealed who he was, had We not given her strength so that she might become a true believer. She said to his sister: "Go, and follow him."

She watched him from a distance, unseen by others. Now We had caused him to refuse his nurses' breasts. His sister said to them: "Shall I direct you to a family who will bring him up for you and take good care of him?"

Thus did We restore him to his mother, so that she might rejoice in him and grieve no more, and that she might learn that God's promise was true. Yet most men are not aware of this.

And when he had reached maturity and grown to manhood We bestowed on him wisdom and knowledge. Thus do We reward the righteous.

He entered the town unnoticed by its people, and found two men at each other's throats, the one of his own race, the other an enemy. The Israelite appealed for Moses' help against his enemy, so that Moses struck him with his fist and slew him. "This is the work of Satan," said Moses. "He is the sworn enemy of man and seeks to lead him astray. Forgive me, Lord," he said, "for I have sinned against my soul."

And God forgave him; for He is the Forgiving One, the Merciful. He said: "By the favour You have shown me, Lord, I vow that I will never lend a helping hand to wrongdoers."

Next morning, as he was walking in the town in fear and caution, the man who sought his help the day before cried out to him again for help. "Clearly," said Moses, "you are a quarrelsome man."

And when Moses was about to lay his hands on their enemy, the Egyptian said: "Moses, would you slay me as you slew that man yesterday? You are surely seeking to be a tyrant in the land, not an upright man."

A man came running from the farthest quarter of the city. "Moses," he cried, "the elders are plotting to kill you. Fly for your life, if you will heed my counsel!"

He went away in fear and caution, saying: "Lord, deliver me from the wicked people." And as he made his way towards Midian, he said: "May the Lord guide me to the even path."

When he came to the well of Midian he found around it a multitude of men watering their flocks, and beside them two women who were keeping back their sheep. "What is it that troubles you?" he asked.

They replied: "We cannot water them until the shepherds have driven away their flocks. Our father is an aged man."

Moses watered their sheep for them and then retired to the shade, saying: "Lord, I surely stand in need of the blessing which You have sent me."

One of the two girls came bashfully towards him and said: "My father calls you. He wishes to reward you for watering our flock."

And when Moses went and recounted to him his story, the old man said: "Fear nothing. You are now safe from the wicked people."

One of the girls said: "Father, take this man into your service. A man who is strong and honest is the best that you can hire."

The old man said: "I will give you one of these two daughters of mine in marriage if you stay eight years in my service; but if you wish it, you may stay ten. I shall not deal harshly with you; God willing, you shall find me an upright man."

"So be it between us," said Moses. "Whichever term I shall fulfil, I trust I shall not be wronged. God is the witness of what we say."

And when he had fulfilled his term and was journeying with his folk, Moses descried a fire on the mountain-side. He said to his people: "Stay here, for I can see a fire. Perhaps I can bring you news, or a lighted torch to warm yourselves with."

When he came near, a voice called out to him from a bush in a blessed spot on the right side of the valley, saying: "Moses, I am God, Lord of the Universe. Throw down your staff."

And when he saw it slithering like a serpent, he turned and fled, without a backward glance.

"Moses," said the voice, "approach and have no fear. You are safe. Put your hand in your pocket: it will come out white, although unharmed. Now draw back your arm, and do not stretch it out in terror. These are two signs from your Lord for Pharaoh and his people. Surely, they are sinful men."

"Lord," said Moses, "I have killed one of their number and fear that they will slay me. Aaron my brother is more fluent of tongue than I; send him with me that he may help me and confirm my words, for I fear they will reject me."

He replied: "We will strengthen your arm with your brother, and will bestow such power on you both, that none shall harm you. Set forth, with Our signs. You, and those who follow you, shall surely triumph."

And when Moses came to them with Our undoubted signs, they said: "This is nothing but baseless sorcery; nor have we heard of the like among our forefathers."

Moses replied: "My Lord knows best the man who brings guidance from His presence and gains the recompense of the life to come. The wrongdoers shall never prosper."

"Nobles," said Pharaoh, "you have no other god that I know of except myself. Make me, Haman, bricks of clay, and build for me a tower that I may climb to the god of Moses. I am convinced that he is lying."

Pharaoh and his warriors conducted themselves with arrogance and injustice in the land, thinking they would never be recalled to Us. But We took him and his warriors, and We cast them into the sea. Consider the fate of the evildoers.

We made them leaders who called men to the Fire, but on the Day of Resurrection none shall help them. In this world We laid a curse on them, and on the Day of Resurrection they shall be among the damned.

After We had destroyed the first generations We gave the Book to Moses as a clear sign, a guide and a blessing for mankind, so that they might take thought.

You[4] were not present on the western side of the Mountain when We charged Moses with his commission, nor did you witness the event. We raised many generations after him whose lives were prolonged. You did not dwell among the people of Midian, nor did you recite to them Our revelations; but it was We who sent you forth.

You were not present on the mountain-side when We called out. Yet have We sent you forth, as a blessing from your Lord, to forewarn a nation to whom no one has been sent before, so that they may take heed and may not say, when evil befalls them on account of their misdeeds: "Lord, had You sent us an apostle, we should have obeyed Your revelations and believed in them."

And now that they have received the truth from Us, they ask: "Why is he not given the like of what was given to Moses?" But do they not deny what was formerly given to Moses? They say: "Two works of sorcery complementing one another!" And they declare: "We will believe in neither of them."

Say: "Bring down from God a scripture that is a better guide than these and I will follow it, if what you say be true!"

If they make you no answer, know that they are led by their desires. And who is in greater error than the man who is led by his desire, without guidance from God? God does not guide the evil-doers.

4. Muhammad.

from **Sura 36. Ya Sin**[5]

We have taught him no poetry, nor does it become him to be a poet. This is but an admonition: an eloquent Qur'an to exhort the living and to pass judgement on the unbelievers.

Do they not see how, among the things Our hands have made, We have created for them the beasts of which they are masters? We have subjected these to them, that they may ride on some and eat the flesh of others; they drink their milk and put them to other uses. Will they not give thanks?

They have set up other gods besides God, hoping that they may help them. They cannot help them: yet their worshippers stand like warriors ready to defend them.

Let not their words grieve you. We have knowledge of all that they conceal and all that they reveal.

Is man not aware that We created him from a little germ? Yet is he flagrantly contentious. He answers back with arguments, and forgets his own creation. He asks: "Who will give life to rotten bones?"

Say: "He who first brought them into being will give them life again: He has knowledge of every creature; He who gives you from the green tree a flame, and lo! you light a fire."

Has He who created the heavens and the earth no power to create others like them? That He surely has. He is the all-knowing Creator. When He decrees a thing He need only say: "Be," and it is.

Glory be to Him who has control of all things. To Him shall you all be recalled.

from **Sura 48. Victory**
In the Name of God, the Compassionate, the Merciful

We have given you a glorious victory,[6] so that God may forgive you your past and future sins, and perfect His goodness to you; that He may guide you to a straight path and bestow on you His mighty help.

It was He who sent down tranquillity into the hearts of the faithful, so that their faith might grow stronger (God's are the legions of the heavens and the earth: God is all-knowing and wise); that He may bring the believers, both men and women, into gardens watered by running streams, there to abide for ever; that He may forgive them their sins (this, in God's sight, is a glorious triumph); and that He may punish the hypocrites and the idolaters, men and women, who think evil thoughts about God. A turn of evil shall befall them, for God is angry with them. He has laid on them His curse and prepared for them the fire of Hell: an evil fate.

God's are the legions of the heavens and the earth. God is mighty and wise.

We have sent you[7] forth as a witness and as a bearer of good news and warnings, so that you may have faith in God and His apostle and that you may assist Him, honour Him, and praise Him morning and evening.

Those that swear fealty to you, swear fealty to God Himself. The Hand of God is above their hands. He that breaks his oath breaks it at his own peril, but he that keeps his pledge to God shall be richly recompensed by Him.

5. On Muhammad's mission as prophet, not poet.   7. The Meccans.
6. Probably the taking of Mecca in 630.

The desert Arabs who stayed behind[8] will say to you: "We were occupied with our goods and families. Implore God to pardon us." They will say with their tongues what they do not mean in their hearts.

Say: "Who can intervene on your behalf with God if it be His will to do you harm or good? Indeed, God is cognizant of all your actions."

No. You[9] thought the Apostle and the believers would never return to their people; and with this fancy your hearts were delighted. You harboured evil thoughts and thus incurred damnation.

As for those that disbelieve in God and His apostle, We have prepared a blazing Fire for the unbelievers. God has sovereignty over the heavens and the earth. He pardons whom He will and punishes whom He pleases. God is forgiving and merciful.

Sura 71. Noah
In the Name of God, the Compassionate, the Merciful

We sent forth Noah to his people, saying: "Give warning to your people before a woeful scourge overtakes them."

He said: "My people, I come to warn you plainly. Serve God and fear Him, and obey me. He will forgive you your sins and give you respite for an appointed term. When God's time arrives, none shall put it back. Would that you understood this!"

"Lord," said Noah, "night and day I have pleaded with my people, but my pleas have only aggravated their aversion. Each time I call on them to seek Your pardon, they thrust their fingers into their ears and draw their cloaks over their heads, persisting in sin and bearing themselves with insolent pride. I called out loud to them, and appealed to them in public and in private. 'Seek forgiveness of your Lord,' I said. 'He is ever ready to forgive. He sends down abundant water from the sky for you and bestows upon you wealth and children. He has provided you with gardens and with running brooks. Why do you deny the greatness of God when He created you in gradual stages? Can you not see how God created the seven heavens one above the other, placing in them the moon for a light and the sun for a lantern? God has brought you forth from the earth like a plant, and to the earth He will restore you. Then He will bring you back afresh. God has made the earth a vast expanse for you, so that you may roam its spacious paths.'"

And Noah said: "Lord, my people disobey me, and follow those whose wealth and offspring will only hasten their perdition. They have devised an outrageous plot, and said to each other: 'Do not renounce your gods. Do not forsake Wadd or Suwāʿ or Yaghūth or Yaʿūq or Naṣr.'[1] They have led numerous men astray. You surely drive the wrongdoers to further error."

And because of their sins they were overwhelmed by the Flood and cast into the Fire. They found none besides God to help them.

And Noah said: "Lord, do not leave a single unbeliever on the earth. If You spare them, they will mislead Your servants and beget none but sinners and unbelievers. Forgive me, Lord, and forgive my parents and every true believer who seeks refuge in my house. Forgive all the faithful, men and women, and hasten the destruction of the wrongdoers."

---

8. Away from battle.   1. Different idols.
9. The desert Arabs.

Sura 87. The Most High
In the Name of God, the Compassionate, the Merciful

Praise the Name of your Lord, the Most High, who has created all things and gave them due proportions; who has ordained their destinies and guided them; who brings forth the green pasture, then turns it to withered grass.

We shall make you recite Our revelations, so that you shall forget none of them except as God pleases. He has knowledge of all that is manifest, and all that is hidden.

We shall guide you to the smoothest path. Therefore give warning, if warning will avail. He that fears God will heed it, but the wicked sinner will flout it. He shall burn in the gigantic Fire, where he shall neither die nor live. Happy shall be the man who keeps himself pure, who remembers the name of his Lord and prays.

Yet you[2] prefer this life, although the life to come is better and more lasting.

All this is written in earlier scriptures; the scriptures of Abraham and Moses.

Sura 93. Daylight
In the Name of God, the Compassionate, the Merciful

By the light of day, and by the dark of night, your Lord has not forsaken you,[3] nor does He abhor you.

The life to come holds a richer prize for you than this present life. You shall be gratified with what your Lord will give you.

Did He not find you an orphan and give you shelter?

Did He not find you in error and guide you?

Did He not find you poor and enrich you?

Therefore do not wrong the orphan, nor chide away the beggar. But proclaim the goodness of your Lord.

Sura 96. Clots of Blood[4]
In the Name of God, the Compassionate, the Merciful

Recite in the name of your Lord who created—created man from clots of blood.

Recite! Your Lord is the Most Bountiful One, who by the pen taught man what he did not know.

Indeed, man transgresses in thinking himself his own master: for to your Lord all things return.

Observe the man who rebukes Our servant when he prays. Think: does he follow the right guidance or enjoin true piety?

Think: if he denies the Truth and pays no heed, does he not realize that God observes all?

No. Let him desist, or We will drag him by the forelock, his lying, sinful forelock.

Then let him call his helpmates. We will call the guards of Hell.

No, never obey him! Prostrate yourself and come nearer.

---

2. Unbelievers.
3. Muhammad.

4. These are the first lines ever revealed to Muhammad.

Sura 110. Help
In the Name of God, the Compassionate, the Merciful

When God's help and victory come, and you see men embrace God's faith in multitudes, give glory to your Lord and seek His pardon. He is ever disposed to mercy.

❦

RESONANCE

A knowledge of the life of the Prophet Muhammad is essential for a true understanding of the Qur'an, Islam, and Muslim cultures. Although both Muhammad himself and the Qur'an repeatedly emphasize that he is a mere human with no supernatural power, the belief that he is the "Messenger of God" is one of the tenets of Islam. It is repeated twice in every call for prayer five times a day and several times during each prayer. In addition, a substantial amount of his biography is incorporated in the Qur'an itself. A great many verses of the Qur'an cannot be fully understood without the context in which they were revealed to him on the one hand, and a full knowledge of his life and his mission on the other. His life, sayings, and deeds, passed down as *hadith* or tradition, form with the Qur'an the most vital sources for Islam's theological and legislative doctrines, giving insight into his life and the nature of the early community that he established, which is still seen as prototype for any Islamic society.

Ibn Sa'ad: from *The Prophet and His Disciples*[1]

ACCOUNT OF THE DEPARTURE OF THE APOSTLE OF ALLĀH, MAY ALLĀH BLESS HIM, AND ABŪ BAKR, ON *HIJRAH* TO AL-MADĪNAH.

Muḥammad Ibn 'Umar informed us; he said: Ma'mar related to me on the authority of al-Zuhrī, he on the authority of 'Urwah he on the authority of 'Āyishah; (second chain) Ibn Sa'ad said: Ibn Abī Ḥabībah related to me on the authority of Dāwūd Ibn al-Ḥuṣayn Ibn Abī Ghaṭfān, he on the authority of Ibn 'Abbās; (third chain) Ibn Sa'ad said: Qudāmah Ibn Mūss related to me on the authority of 'Āyishah Bint Qudāmah; (fourth chain) Ibn Sa'ad said: 'Abd Allāh Ibn Muḥammad Ibn 'Uma Ibn 'Alī Ibn Abī Ṭālib related to me on the authority of his father, he on the authority of 'Ubayd Allāh Ibn Abi Rāfi', he on the authority of 'Alī; (fifth chain) Ibn Sa'ad said: Ma'mar related to me on the authority of al-Zuhrī, he on the authority of 'Abdal-Raḥmān Ibn Mālik Ibn Ju'shum, he on the authority of Surāqa Ibn Ju'shum; their narrations are mixed up; they said: When the infidels found that the Companions of the Apostle of Allāh may Allāh bless him, had sent their children and descendants to al-Aws and al-Khazraj, they realised that they were

---

1. Translated by S. Moinul Haq and H. K. Ghazanfar. Ibn Sa'ad (Abu 'Abdullah Muhammad ibn Mani' al-Basri) was one of the most outstanding scholars of his time. He was born in Basra c. 784 and died in Baghdad in 845. He studied theology, tradition, and genealogy under the most prominent scholars of his time, traveled widely in search of knowledge, and worked as secretary (to be understood in present terms as research assistant) to another great scholar, al-Waqidi (d. 822). The student surpassed his master in knowledge and rigor of scholarship. His encyclopedic compilation, *The Book of Classes,* is the most reliable "Who's Who" of the early period of Islam, containing biographies of 4,250 persons, including about 600 women. The book starts with a biography of the Prophet Muhammad and follows with his companions and all those persons down to Ibn Sa'ad's time, who played a role in narrating the *hadith* or tradition concerning the Prophet's sayings and doings. *The Book of Classes* is not only the first biographical dictionary, but it is also methodically developed and ordered in a manner that was long ahead of its time.

resourceful people possessing martial spirit, so they began to entertain fears of the departure of the Apostle of Allāh, may Allāh bless him. They assembled in the Dār al-Nadwah and none of them who had prudence and sagacity abstained from attending the meeting and expressing his opinion about this matter. Iblīs [Satan] attended the meeting in the guise of an old man of Najd and his sword was hanging by his side. They discussed the affair of the Apostle of Allāh, may Allāh bless him, and every one gave his opinion; Iblīs rejected each in turn, not approving any of them.

At length Abū Jahl said: Let us select a dexterous and sturdy person from every tribe of the Quraysh and supply him with a sharp sword, and all of them should strike him simultaneously. The blood feud will thus be shared by all of them, and Banū 'Abd Manāf will not be in a position to decide what to do. Ibn Sa'ad said: The Najdī said: The excellent opinion of this youth is from Allāh! this is the real opinion, and there is no other better than this! They agreed on this and dispersed. Gabriel came to the Apostle of Allāh, may Allāh bless him, and revealed this information and asked him not to sleep in his bed that night. The Apostle of Allāh, may Allāh bless him, went to Abū Bakr and said: Allāh has permitted me to set out. Thereupon Abū Bakr said: (What about my) accompanying you, O Apostle of Allāh! The Apostle of Allāh, may Allāh bless him, said: Yes. Abū Bakr said: My father and mother be sacrificed for you! take one of these two beasts of burden. The Apostle of Allāh said: (I shall take it after paying) the price. Abū Bakr had purchased them from the flock of Banū Qushayr for eight hundred *dirhams*. The Apostle of Allāh, may Allāh bless him, took one of them; it was (named) al-Qaṣwā.

The Prophet asked 'Alī to sleep in his bed that night. 'Alī passed the night there, having covered (himself) with the red Ḥaḍramī sheet in which the Apostle of Allāh, may Allāh bless him, used to sleep. A group of the Quraysh assembled there and began peeping through the crevices in the door, and sat in ambush with the intention of (seizing him by) his clothes. They were consulting as to which of them was to attack the person sleeping in the bed. (In the meantime) the Apostle of Allāh, may Allāh bless him, came out, and they were sitting at the door; he took a handful of dust and sprinkled at their heads and recited:

"Yāsīn. By the wise Qur'an. Lo! thou art of those sent. On a straight path. A revelation of the Mighty, the Merciful, That thou mayst warn a folk whose fathers were not warned, so they are heedless. Already hath the word proved true of most of them, for they believe not. Lo! We have put on their necks carcans reaching unto the chins, so that they are made stiff necked. And We have set a bar before them and a bar behind them, and (thus) have covered them so that they see not. Whether thou warn them or thou warn them not, it is alike for them, for they believe not."

The Apostle of Allāh, may Allāh bless him, passed by them. Then a person said: What are you waiting for? They said: For Muḥammad. He said: You are disappointed and have suffered a loss. By Allāh, he passed by you and sprinkled dust at your heads. They said: By Allāh! we did not notice him. They stood up, removing dust from their heads; they were Abū Jahl al-Ḥakam Ibn Abī al-'Āṣ, 'Uqbah Ibn Abī Mu'ayṭ, al-Naḍr Ibn al-Ḥārith, Umayyah Ibn Khalaf, Ibn al-Ghayṭalah, Zam'ah Ibn al-'Aswad, Ṭu'aymah Ibn 'Adī, Abu Lahab, Ubayyi Ibn Khalaf and Nubayh and Munabbih, sons of al-Ḥajjāj. When it was morning, 'Alī got up from his bed. They enquired from him about the Apostle of Allāh, may Allāh bless him. He said: I have no information. The Apostle of Allāh, may Allāh bless him, went to the house of Abū Bakr and stayed there in the night. At last they set out, went to the cave of Thawr and entered it [through a] spider span cobweb, some parts of which covered others. The Quraysh made a frantic search for the Apostle of Allāh, may Allāh bless him. They even came to the entrance of the cave, but some one among them said: Verily, spiders haunt this place from before the birth of Muḥammad; and they returned.

Muslim Ibn Ibrāhīm informed us: 'Awn Ibn 'Amr al-Qaysī brother of Riyāḥ al-Qaysī informed us: Abū Muṣ'ab al-Makk informed us; he said: I went to Zayd Ibn Ar-qam, Anas Ibn Mālik and al-Mughīrah Ibn Shu'bah and heard them talking among themselves: The Prophet, may Allāh bless him, passed the night in the cave. Allāh commanded a tree to grow in front of the Prophet, may Allāh bless him, which con-cealed him. (Similarly) Allāh commanded the spider which span its cobweb and thus concealed him. (In the same way) Allāh commanded two wild pigeons, and they be-gan to live at the mouth of the cave. The youth of the Quraysh—one person from each tribe—with their sword, clubs and sticks approached (the cave), and they were only (at a distance of) forty cubits from the Prophet, may Allāh bless him; the first among them noticed the two pigeons, and so he withdrew. His companions said to him: Why did you not look into the cave? He said: I noticed two wild pigeons at the mouth of the cave, from which I concluded that there was none inside it. Ibn Sa'ad said: The Prophet, may Allāh bless him, had heard his voice and realized that Allāh had kept them away. Then the Prophet, may Allāh bless him, wished good for the pigeons and in reward they were shifted to the sanctuary of Allāh (the Ka'bah). * * *

* * * The Apostle of Allāh, may Allāh bless him, migrated from Makkah to al-Madīnah along with Abū Bakr, 'Āmir Ibn Fuhayrah, the *mawlā* of Abū Bakr and their guide 'Abd Allāh Ibn Urayqiṭ al-Laythī; they passed by the tents of Umm Ma'bad al-Khuzā'ī, who was stout and sturdy and kept herself covered. She sat in front of her tent providing food and water (to the people). They asked her to sell some dates and meat to them. But there was nothing with her because the people were suffering from famine and drought. She said: If we had something with us, you would not have gone without hospitality. Thereupon the Apostle of Allāh, may Allāh bless him, noticed a goat tied in a corner of the tent. He said: O Umm Ma'bad! what about this goat? She said: It has remained behind the flock because it is weak. He said: Does it give milk? She replied: It is too weak (to give any milk). He said: Will you permit me to milk it? She said: My father and mother be sacrificed for you, I do permit, if you find any milk with it.

The Apostle of Allāh, may Allāh bless him, asked the goat to be brought before him and touched its udder and recited in the name of Allāh, O Allāh! Bless her through this goat. Ibn Sa'ad said: It stretched its legs, its udder became saturated (with milk), which it yielded. Then the Prophet asked for a large utensil which could con-tain milk sufficient for all of them. He milked the goat and there were foams in it. He, then, made her drink till she drank to satisfaction and then he made his Companions drink till they too were satisfied; and he, may Allāh bless him, drank the milk in the end. Ibn Sa'ad said: the Prophet remarked that the person who provides the drink (*sāqi*) should take in the end. Then they drank a second time and were satisfied. Then he milked it again and gave it to her. Then they set out.

After a short time her husband Abū Ma'bad came in leading his goats which were feeble, lean and thin without fat. When he saw the milk he was surprised. He said: Where from did you get this milk, in spite of the fact that there was no goat in the house capable of yielding it? She said: By Allāh, this is due to a blessed man of this description who passed by us. He said: I believe he is the same person of the

Quraysh tribe who is being pursued, so give his detailed description, O Umm Ma'bad. She said: I noticed a man whose cleanliness was manifest, whose face was bright and lustrous, whose habits were nice, who was not a glutton, who was free from the blemish of a short neck and small skull, who was handsome, having black eyes and thick eye-lashes, whose voice was distinct, whose eyes were large with black pupils, very black, and white area very white, whose eyebrows were thick and whose neck was high and whose beard was profuse. When he was quiet, he commanded respect and when spoke, the beauty of his speech became evident. His speech was like a string of pearls, and very sweet. The last words uttered by him were neither brief, suppressing the sense, nor superfluous and unnecessary. From a distance his voice was very clear and he appeared handsome, and when he was close, he became sweet and more handsome. His stature was not too tall nor too short, it was middle sized. He was the loveliest of all the three to look at, and most honoured of them. His Companions surrounded him. When he spoke, they lent their ears to his words, and when he commanded, every one obeyed it. He was neither frowning nor loquacious. Abū Ma'bad said: By Allāh, he was the Qurayshite whose affair has been mentioned to us. O Umm Ma'bad! If I had witnessed him, I would have asked to accompany him and I shall do it if I get an opportunity. * * *

'Abd al-Malik said: It has been conveyed to us that Umm Ma'bad migrated and went to the Prophet, may Allāh bless him, and embraced Islām.

The Apostle of Allāh, may Allāh bless him, came out from the cave on the night of Monday, when four nights of the month of First Rabī' had passed. Then he had a *siesta* at Qudayd on Tuesday. When they set out from there, Surāqah Ibn Mālik Ibn Ju'shum confronted them. He was riding a horse when the Apostle of Allāh, may Allāh bless him, cursed him, and the legs of his horse sank (under the ground). He said: O Muḥammad! pray to Allāh to set my horse free and I shall return from here and I shall make those also return who are behind me. The Prophet did (pray) and the legs of the horse were freed. Surāqah returned and found the people coming in search of the Apostle of Allāh, may Allāh bless him, to whom he said: Go back, I have searched for him on behalf of you. He is not there and you know well my skill in recognising the footprints. Therefore they returned.

'Uthmān Ibn 'Umar informed us on the authority of Ibn 'Awn, he on the authority of 'Umayr Ibn Isḥāq; he said: The Apostle of Allāh, may Allāh bless him, set out, and Abū Bakr was with him. Surāqah Ibn (Mālik Ibn) Ju'shum confronted them but the legs of his horse sank (in the ground). Thereupon he said: O you two! pray to Allāh for me and I (promise) not to repeat this. They prayed for him, but he repeated and again his horse sank. He again said: Pray for me and I shall not repeat it. Ibn Sa'ad said: He offered them provisions and a ride. They said; yourself is sufficient for us. He said: I shall do that. * * *

'Affān Ibn Muslim informed us: Hammād Ibn Salamah informed us on the authority of Thābit, he on the authority of Anas: Verily, Abū Bakr was co-rider with the Prophet, may Allāh bless him, between Makkah and al-Madīnah. As Abū Bakr used to visit Syria, he was known, but the Prophet was not known there. Therefore they said: O Abū Bakr! who is this youth before you? He said: He is the one who leads me. When they came close to al-Madīnah, they got down at al-Ḥarrah and sent for al-Anṣār. They came and said: Stay (here), you are safe and secure. He (Anas) said: I saw him on the day he entered al-Madīnah, and I never saw a day brighter and more shining than the day on which he entered al-Madīnah; and I saw him on the day he breathed his last, and no day was darker and more terrible than the day on which he expired.

Hāshim Ibn al-Qāsim al-Kinānī informed us: Abū Ma'shar informed us on the authority of Abū Wahb the *mawlā* of Abū Hurayrah; he said: The Apostle of Allāh, may Allāh bless him, rode behind Abū Bakr on his she-camel. Abū Wahb said: Whenever a person met him (on the way) and asked him as to who he was, he replied: I am a searcher in search. Then he asked: Who is behind you? He replied: He is the leader who leads me.

Muslim Ibn Ibrāhim Informed us: Ja'far Ibn Sulaymān informed us; he said: Thābit al-Bunānī informed us on the authority of Anas Ibn Mālik; he said: The day when the Apostle of Allāh, may Allāh bless him, entered al-Madīnah, every thing looked very bright.

Wahb Ibn Jarīr Ibn Ḥāzim informed us: Shu'bah informed us on the authority of Abū Isḥāq, he on the authority of al-Barā; he said: The Prophet, may Allāh bless him, came to al-Madinah. I did not see a day of more happy than that of the arrival of the Prophet, may Allāh bless him, so much so that I heard the women, the children and slave-girls saying: This is the Apostle of Allāh, and he has come, he has come! * * *

Yaḥyā Ibn 'Abbād and 'Affān Ibn Muslim informed us; they said: Shu'bah informed us; he said: Abū Isḥāq informed us: He said: I heard al-Barā saying: The first from among the Companions of the Apostle of Allāh who came to us were Muṣ'ab, Ibn 'Umayr and Ibn Umm Maktūm. They began to teach the Qur'an to the people. Then came in Ammār, Bilāl and Sa'd. Al-Barā said: Then 'Umar Ibn al-Khaṭṭāb came with a party of twenty persons. Then came the Apostle of Allāh, may Allāh bless him. Al-Barā said: I never saw the people expressing more joy than on that occassion. I noticed babies and children saying: "This is the Apostle of Allāh, who has come to us."

Hafiz

c. 1317–1389

Hafiz is the pen name of the great Persian poet Shams al-Din Muhammad Shirazi. The name Hafiz denotes one who had memorized the Qur'an in his early youth, and he no doubt earned this name early in his literary career. The information on his life is scarce and most of it is deduced from his texts. Though he was of humble origins, he is reputed to have acquired in his youth a solid education and knowledge of Arabic, Islamic sciences, and Persian literature. His father was said to have migrated from Isfahan to Shiraz, but he died while Hafiz was an infant, and the family was reduced to penury. At the time Shiraz was a flourishing city and buzzing center of Islamic civilization, so poverty did not impede the desire of a bright young boy for an education. He worked as a baker's apprentice and manuscript copyist during his adolescence. It was copying manuscripts that satisfied his insatiable appetite for reading and acquisition of knowledge that opened his eyes to the vast world of literature.

He read avidly and joined a mystical order, whose regular meetings were similar to the life of Europe's most learned literary salons of the nineteenth century. This provided his poetry with spiritual richness, profound insight, and a sense of verbal perfection unequaled in Persian poetry. He is also reputed to have led a libertine life and to have enjoyed the patronage and friendship of very powerful people. He dedicated some of his poems to Qiwam al-Din Hasan (d. 754), the vizier of Shah Abu-Ishaq, and nostalgic references to Shiraz notables in other poems indicate that by the age of thirty he must have gained access to the upper circles of power as panegyric poet—a writer of verses in praise of a patron. At the peak of his poetic productivity, the city of Shiraz suffered a protracted struggle between warring Sunni forces, which affected him as a Shi'ite. By then his poetry and fame had spread throughout Persia, westward to the Arab lands and eastward to India. When Shiraz fell into the hands of the Mongol conqueror Timur in 1387, he allegedly showed the poet sporadic favor until the end of his life.

Despite references to poverty and suffering throughout his poetry, Hafiz seems to have led a full and rich life. He enjoyed wine and women and immortalized both in his *ghazals* (love poetry). He is widely regarded as the exalted master of the *ghazal* in Persian. One can glean from his poetry some aspects of a life rich in emotions and hedonistic pleasures as well as knowledge, wisdom and spirituality. His poetry shows also his preoccupation with universal and philosophical issues, such as mortality and mystical love. Hafiz was the master of interweaving the erotic with the mystic, and expressed this unique blend in superb linguistic craftsmanship and intuitive insight. He developed the genre of *ghazal* beyond the traditional domain of the *qasida* and created a new concept of artistic unity that is neither thematic nor dramatic in the Western sense. It is a classically Persian unity that results from weaving imagery and allusions round one or more central concepts, among which the concept of divine/carnal love occupies the center stage.

PRONUNCIATIONS:
  ghazal: GHA-zul
  Hafiz: HA-feez

The House of Hope[1]

The house of hope is built on sand,
And life's foundations rest on air;
Then come, give wine into my hand,
That we may make an end of care.

5   Let me be slave to that man's will
Who 'neath high heaven's turquoise bowl
Hath won and winneth freedom still
From all entanglement of soul;

Save that the mind entangled be
10   With her whose radiant loveliness
Provoking love and loyalty
Relieves the mind of all distress.

Last night as toping° I had been   *drinking*
In tavern, shall I tell to thee
15   What message from the world unseen
A heavenly angel brought to me?

"Falcon of sovereign renown,
High-nesting bird of lofty gaze,

---

1. Translated by A. J. Arberry.

20

This corner of affliction town
Befits thee ill, to pass thy days.

"Hearest thou not the whistle's call
From heaven's rampart shrills for thee?
What chanced I cannot guess at all
This snare should now thy prison be."

25

Heed now the counsel that I give,
And be it to thy acts applied;
For these are words I did receive
From him that was my ancient guide.

30

"Be pleased with what the fates bestow,
Nor let thy brow be furrowed thus;
The gate to freedom here below
Stands not ajar to such as us."

Look not to find fidelity
Within a world so weakly stayed;

35

This ancient crone, ere flouting thee,
A thousand bridegrooms had betrayed.

Take not for sign of true intent
Nor think the rose's smile sincere;
Sweet, loving nightingale, lament:

40

There is much cause for weeping here.

What envying of Hafiz' ease,
Poor poetaster, dost thou moan?
To make sweet music, and to please,
That is a gift of God alone.

Zephyr[1]

Zephyr, should'st thou chance to rove
By the mansion of my love,
From her locks ambrosial bring
Choicest odours on thy wing.

5

Could'st thou waft me from her breast
Tender sighs to say I'm blest,
As she lives! my soul would be
Sprinkl'd o'er with ecstasy.

But if Heav'n the boon deny,

10

Round her stately footsteps fly,
With the dust that thence may rise,
Stop the tears which bathe these eyes.

---

1. Translated by J. H. Hindley. "Zephyr" means a light breeze.

Lost, poor mendicant! I roam
Begging, craving she would come:
15   Where shall I thy phantom see,
Where, dear nymph, a glimpse of thee?

Like the wind-tost reed my breast
Fann'd with hope is ne'er at rest,
Throbbing, longing to excess
20   Her fair figure to caress.

Yes, my charmer, tho' I see
Thy heart courts no love with me,
Not for worlds, could they be mine,
Would I give a hair of thine.

25   Why, O care! shall I in vain
Strive to shun thy galling chain,
When these strains still fail to save,
And make Hafiz more a slave.

A Mad Heart[1]

1

Long years my heart had made request
Of me, a stranger, hopefully
(Not knowing that itself possessed
The treasure that it sought of me),
5   That Jamshid's chalice I should win
And it would see the world therein.

That is a pearl by far too rare
To be contained within the shell
Of time and space; lost vagrants there
10   Upon the ocean's margin, well
We know it is a vain surmise
That we should hold so great a prize.

2

There was a man that loved God well;
In every motion of his mind
15   God dwelt; and yet he could not tell
That God was in him, being blind:
Wherefore as if afar he stood
And cried, "Have mercy, O my God!"

3

This problem that had vexed me long
20   Last night unto the taverner

1. Translated by A. J. Arberry.

I carried; for my hope was strong,
His judgement sure, that could not err,
Might swiftly solve infallibly
The riddle that had baffled me.

25   I saw him standing in his place,
A goblet in his grasp, a smile
Of right good cheer upon his face,
As in the glass he gazed awhile
And seemed to view in vision clear
30   A hundred truths reflected there.

4

"That friend who, being raised sublime
Upon the gallows, glorified
The tree that slew him for his crime,
This was the sin for which he died,
35   That, having secrets in his charge,
He told them to the world at large."

So spake he; adding, "But the heart
That has the truth within its hold
And, practising the rosebud's art,
40   Conceals a mystery in each fold,
That heart hath well this comment lined
Upon the margin of the mind.

"When Moses unto Pharaoh stood,
The men of magic strove in vain
45   Against his miracle of wood;
So every subtlety of brain
Must surely fail and feeble be
Before the soul's supremacy.

"And if the Holy Ghost descend
50   In grace and power infinite
His comfort in these days to lend
To them that humbly wait on it,
Theirs too the wondrous works can be
That Jesus wrought in Galilee."

5

55   "What season did the Spirit wise
This all-revealing cup assign
Within thy keeping?" "When the skies
Were painted by the Hand Divine
And heaven's mighty void was spanned,
60   Then gave He this into my hand."

"Yon twisted coil, yon chain of hair
Why doth the lovely Idol spread
To keep me fast and fettered there?"

"Ah, Hafiz!", so the wise man said,
65 "'Tis a mad heart, and needs restraint
That speaks within thee this complaint."

Cup in Hand[1]

When my Beloved the cup in hand taketh
The market of lovely ones slack demand taketh.

I, like a fish, in the ocean am fallen,
Till me with the hook yonder Friend to land taketh.

5 Every one saith, who her tipsy eye seëth,
"Where is a shrieve,° that this fair firebrand taketh?"   *sheriff*

Lo, at her feet in lament am I fallen,
Till the Beloved me by the hand taketh.

Happy his heart who, like Hafiz, a goblet
10 Of wine of the Prime Fore-eternal's brand taketh.

Last Night I Dreamed[1]

Last night I dreamed that angels stood without
The tavern door, and knocked in vain, and wept;
They took the clay of Adam, and, methought,
Moulded a cup therewith while all men slept.
5 Oh dwellers in the halls of Chastity!
You brought Love's passionate red wine to me,
Down to the dust I am, your bright feet stept.

For Heaven's self was all too weak to bear
The burden of His love God laid on it,
10 He turned to seek a messenger elsewhere,
And in the Book of Fate my name was writ.
Between my Lord and me such concord lies
As makes the Huris° glad in Paradise,   *heavenly maidens*
With songs of praise through the green glades they flit.

15 A hundred dreams of Fancy's garnered store
Assail me—Father Adam went astray
Tempted by one poor grain of corn! Wherefore
Absolve and pardon him that turns away
Though the soft breath of Truth reaches his ears,
20 For two-and-seventy jangling creeds he hears,
And loud-voiced Fable calls him ceaselessly.

That, that is not the flame of Love's true fire
Which makes the torchlight shadows dance in rings,

---

1. Translated by J. Payne.   1. Translated by Gertrude Bell.

But where the radiance draws the moth's desire
25   And sends him forth with scorched and drooping wings.
The heart of one who dwells retired shall break,
Rememb'ring a black mole and a red cheek,
And his life ebb, sapped at its secret springs.

Yet since the earliest time that man has sought
30   To comb the locks of Speech, his goodly bride,
Not one, like Hafiz, from the face of Thought
Has torn the veil of Ignorance aside.

Harvest[1]

In the green sky I saw the new moon reaping,
    And minded was I of my own life's field:
    What harvest wilt thou to the sickle yield
When through thy fields the moon-shaped knife goes sweeping?

5   In other fields the sunlit blade is growing,
    But still thou sleepest on and takest no heed;
    The sun is up, yet idle is thy seed:
Thou sowest not, though all the world is sowing.

Back laughed I at myself: All this thou'rt telling
10   Of seed-time! The whole harvest of the sky
    Love for a single barley-corn can buy,
The Pleiads at two barley-corns are selling.

Thieves of the starry night with plunder shining,
    I trust you not, for who was it but you
15   Stole Kawou's crown, and robbed great Kaikhosru
Of his king's girdle—thieves, for all your shining!

Once on the starry chess-board stretched out yonder
    The sun and moon played chess with her I love,
    And, when it came round to her turn to move,
20   She played her mole—and won—and can you wonder?

Ear-rings suit better thy small ears than reason,
    Yet in their pink shells wear these words to-day:
    "HAFIZ has warned me all must pass away—
Even my beauty is but for a season."

All My Pleasure[1]

All my pleasure is to sip
Wine from my beloved's lip;
I have gained the utmost bliss—
God alone be praised for this.

---

1. Translated by Richard le Gallienne.   1. Translated by A. J. Arberry.

5 Fate, my old and stubborn foe,
 Never let my darling go:
 Give my mouth the golden wine
 And her lips incarnadine.

 (Clerics bigoted for God,
10 Elders who have lost the road—
 These have made a tale of us
 "Drunken sots and bibulous."

 Let the ascetic's life be dim,
 I will nothing have of him;
15 If the monk will pious be,
 God forgive his piety!)

 Darling, what have I to say
 Of my grief, with thee away,
 Save with tears and scalding eyes
20 And a hundred burning sighs?

 Let no infidel behold
 All the bitterness untold
 Cypress knows to see thy grace,
 Jealous moon to view thy face.

25 It is yearning for thy kiss
 That hath wrought in Hafiz this,
 That no more he hath in care
 Nightly lecture, matin prayer.

Wild Deer[1]

1

 Whither fled, wild deer?
I knew thee well in days gone by,
When we were fast friends, thou and I;
Two solitary travellers now,
5 Bewildered, friendless, I and thou,
We go our separate ways, where fear
  Lurks ambushed, front and rear.

  Come, let us now enquire
How each is faring; let us gain
10 (If gain we may, upon this plain
Of trouble vast, where pastures pure
   From fear secure
Are not to find) the spirit's far desire.

---

1. Translated by A. J. Arberry.

2

Beloved friends, declare:
What manner of man is there
That shall the lonely heart befriend,
That shall the desolate attend?
Khizer, the heavenly guide,
He of the footfall sanctified,
Perchance he cometh, and shall bring
In purpose deep and mercy wide
An end of all my wayfaring.

3

'Twas little courtesy
That ancient comrade shewed to me.
Moslems, in Allah's name I cry!
The pitiless blow he struck me by,
So pitiless, to strike apart
The cords that bound us heart to heart,
To strike as if it were
No love was ever there.

He went; and I that was so gay
To grief convert; was such the way
Brother should act with brother? Yea,
Khizer, the heavenly guide,
He of the footfall sanctified,
Haply the shadow of his gracious wing
Lone soul to lonely soul shall bring.

4

But surely this the season is
When of the bounty that is His
Allah dispenses; for I took
Lately this omen from the Book:
"Leave me not issueless!" the Prophet cried.

It happened on a day one sat beside
The road, a rare bold fellow; when there went
Upon that way a traveller intent
To gain the goal. Gently the other spake:
"What in thy scrip, Sir traveller, dost thou take?
If it be truly grain, come, set thy snare."
The traveller answered, "Grain indeed I bear;
But, mark this well, the quarry I would win
Shall be the Phoenix." "Certes, then how begin
The quest?" the other asked. "What sign has thou
To lead thee to his eyrie? Not till now
Have we discovered any mark to guide
Upon that quest. By what weight fortified

Shall our dire need those scales essay to hold
Wherein the sun hath cast his purse of gold?"

5

    Since that cypress tall and straight
    Joined the parting camel-train,
60   By the cypress sit, and wait
    Watchful till he come again.
    Here, beside the bubbling spring
    Where the limpid river runs,
    Softly weep, remembering
65   Those beloved departed ones.
    As each pallid ghost appears,
    Speak the epic of thy pain,
    While the shower of thy tears
    Mingles with the summer rain.
70   And the river at thy feet
    Sadly slow, and full of sighs,
    Tributaries new shall meet
    From the fountains of thine eyes.

6

    Give never the wine-bowl from thy hand,
75   Nor loose thy grasp on the rose's stem;
    'Tis a mad, bad world that the Fates have planned—
    Match wit with their every stratagem!

      Comrades, know each other's worth;
    And when ye have this comment lined
80   Upon the margin of the mind,
      Recite the text by heart:
    So say the moralists of this earth;
    For lo, the archer ambushed waits,
    Th' unerring archer of the Fates,
85   To strike old friends apart.

7

    When I take pen in hand to write
    And thus my marshalled thoughts indite,
      By the Eternal Pen,
      What magic numbers then
90   Flow from my fingers, what divine
      And holy words are mine!
    For I have mingled Soul with Mind,
Whereof the issuing seed I have consigned
      To music's fruitful earth;
95   Which compound brings to birth
(As having for its quintessential part

Of poesy the purest art)
　　Most gladsome mirth.

Then come, I bid thee; let this fragrant scent
100　　Of fairest hope, and soft content,
　　Bear to thy soul delight eternal:
For verily the musk's sweet blandishment
Was sprinkled from the robe of sprites supernal;
　　It was not wafted here
105　　From that wild, man-forsaking deer!

❧

RESONANCE

Johann Wolfgang Goethe: Blissful Yearning[1]

Tell it no one, but to sages,
Since the crowd at once will blame it:
To the life I vow my praises
That desires to die enflamèd.

5　In the cool of lovers' evenings,
Procreated, procreating,
You fall prey to foreign feeling,
While the candle's calmly shining.

You remain embraced no longer
10　In the darkness-deepened shading,
And new yearning ever stronger
Sweeps you on to higher mating.

Distance could not slow your passage,
Wingèd and enthralled you came,
15　And at last, athirst for brightness,
Moth, you are consumed in flame.

And until you have the rest,
Namely: Die and grow!
You are but a darkling guest
20　On the earth below.

❧

---

1. Translated by Jane K. Brown. Johann Wolfgang Goethe, who coined the term "world literature," was fascinated by Asian and Middle Eastern poetry. He felt a special affinity for Hafiz's sensual mysticism, and based many of the poems in his 1819 collection *Divan of West and East* on Hafiz's works.

⇒ PERSPECTIVES ⇐
Poetry, Wine, and Love

Poetry was seen from pre-Islamic days as the prime literary genre in the Arabic language, and it preserved this status throughout the Islamic period. It was regarded as the *diwan* of the Arabs, the register of their deeds and gallantry, battles and genealogy, as well as the repository of their values, tradition and wisdom. After the pre-Islamic period, the Abbasid period (750–1258) is widely considered as the second epoch in which poetry reached a pinnacle of exquisite artistic heights. All the poets in this section are from this period of great prosperity and cultural confidence generated by the spread of Islam—throughout the rest of the Middle East, and across north Africa to Spain, and eastward from Persia to China. This vast expansion and the development of a number of central Arab cities—Damascus, Baghdad, Basra, and Kufa—as prosperous urban centers, brought a multitude of cultural influences and practices to bear on poetic composition. This was also a period of augmentation of knowledge, which normally follows expanding geography and assimilation of different cultures. Tolerance and open-mindedness became prevalent modes of operation and interaction, and new genres emerged to express this, notably the *ghazal* and *khamriyya*.

The *ghazal* is a genre concerned with love and its associated pleasures, mostly written by a man addressing his beloved. It is full of flirtation and adulation, as well as agitation, and frustration at the beloved's coldness or inaccessibility. There are many types of *ghazal,* from the ideal and courtly to the sensual and explicitly erotic, expressed in tones varying from exalted passion to languid, melancholy reflection. The genre received a tremendous boost with increased wealth and the proliferation of palaces on the banks of the Tigris River in Baghdad, where poetry and music were combined to entertain an indolent society with a morally lax attitude to pleasure. The *ghazal* soon extended its range, particularly at the hands of Abu-Nuwas, to homosexual love. It also acquired a dialogic nature and enriched the variation of Arabic poetry by introducing new meters. The language of poetry was purged of archaic diction and excessive wordplay, as the era breathed a fresh air of delicacy, naturalness, and simplicity into its language.

The genre started as light, lyrical, and pleasurable poetry, concerned more with the celebration of beauty and the pleasures of life than with the torment and suffering often associated with love. It soon acquired depth and philosophical dimensions, with love seen as an endeavor to ward off the inevitability of death. The *ghazal* also acquired a mystical dimension obliterating the fine line between erotic love, sublime love, and Sufi yearning for unity with God. Since poetry in Arabic was cultivated in all the intellectual centers of the Muslim world, the form of the *ghazal* was adopted by other languages, in Persian as seen in the poetry of Hafiz, and in Turkish, Urdu, and other African and Asian languages.

The *khamriyya* is a Bacchic or wine poem. Different types of alcoholic drinks were widely known in Arabia long before Islam, and Bacchic sections were common in many early Arabic *qasidas*. In the Abbasid period with the expanding Islamic Empire and a growing idle aristocracy, the Bacchic poem as a genre flourished and gained currency. The genre owes its emergence to a number of eminent poets such as the caliph and poet al-Walid ibn Yazid, and more significantly the poet who devoted all his energy to the genre, Abu'l-Hindi al-Riyahi. The great poet Abu-Nuwas, who is often mistakenly accredited with the creation of the *khamriyya,* identified Abu'l-Hindi as its creator, and admitted that he had learned a lot from him. He created poems of exquisite craftsmanship, harmonious language, and lively spirit that became the hallmark of the genre. His love for wine inspired him to create poems as translucent as the finest wine and as delicate and ethereal as its impact on refined souls.

Another important figure was the Abbasid poet Ahmad ibn Ishaq, who made the public practice of debauchery a fitting topic for poetry. Abu-Nuwas added to these pleasures that of pederasty, the love of boys and young men. There is a clear interaction between amorous and Bacchic poems, for they shared certain structures and thematic concerns, but the Bacchic poems remained an independent genre. Later they acquired a Sufi dimension when drunkenness was seen as synonymous

Medieval portrait of four musicians, accompanying an evening of feasting and poetry recitations.

with forgetfulness of all that is not God. In a span of two centuries, the genre developed a well-defined form and structure, a more spontaneous and sensitive language, a uniquely subversive tone, and a symbolic code based on frequent recourse to amorous or floral themes. In addition, in most elegant examples, it transcended the pleasurable and mundane to reach the existential and mystic. The poets in this section express the various aspects of this rich and lively poetic tradition.

Abu-Nuwas
755–c. 815

Abu-Nuwas al-Hasan ibn Hani' al-Hakami is perhaps the most beloved of Arab poets of any period. He spent his boyhood in Basra in southern Iraq, studying there and then in Kufa, which was one of the major intellectual centers of the Islamic Empire. He studied with the leading poets and grammarians of his time. It is claimed that his first poetry teacher, the poet Walid ibn al-Hubab, was in love with him, so that poetry and homosexual love joined together for Abu-Nuwas from a young age. His education included a period of time among the Bedouin to perfect his linguistic skills. He then went to Baghdad to seek the favor of the caliph, Haroun al-Rashid. This he failed to achieve, but the powerful family of the Barmakids warmly received him in their salon, which was frequented by the leading lights of the age. However, when the caliph turned against the Barmakids (see the Resonance that accompanies *The Thousand and One Nights*, page 408), he had to flee to Egypt, where the notables and the leading intellectuals of the country welcomed him. After the death of the caliph in 809, he returned to his beloved city of Baghdad. This time the new caliph, al-Amin, bestowed his favors on him, and Abu-Nuwas became his boon companion. These final six years (809–815) were the most brilliant years of his life, for the security and protection that al-Amin provided enabled him to devote his energy to living and writing. For Abu-Nuwas, living and writing were two sides of the same coin, for he lived his poetry and inscribed his life's experience into his poems. There are different reports concerning his tragic death. One version speaks of his death in prison where he was incarcerated for writing blasphemous verse. Another claims that he died in the house of a woman of ill-repute or a tavern-keeper, a third maintains that he was murdered for lampooning an influential person, and a fourth version affirms that his death was in the house of a learned Shi'ite family.

Abu-Nuwas is a great poet by any standard. He combined an innovative drive, a remarkable talent, a wide range of poetic genres, a rich reservoir of imagery, a fine poetic technique, and an original style. He wrote panegyric poetry as well as heterosexual and homosexual *ghazals* and handled Bacchic poems with incomparable skill. In fact, he was the poet who gave the Bacchic poem its existential significance and endowed it with depth and immortality in a culture that forbids drinking. He summed up everything that it had been possible for anyone to write before him, and took poetry into fresh territory; hence he is considered as the innovative force behind the vitality and vigor of Abbasid poetry. His innovations swept through the whole structure of poetry, for in his hands, the poetic language shimmers with energy and sparkles with light and joy. He combines sensibility, elegance, and intelligence in a unique aesthetic blend. His towering talent was recognized during his time and has continued to be appreciated to this day, to the extent that when scholars of classical Arabic poetry come across a sparkling poem that shines with talent and beauty, they ascribe it to him.

Although he is at his best in his poems on wine and pederasty, he wrote memorable panegyrics (poems in praise of the caliph) and wonderful *ghazals*. His *ghazals* acquired an existential edge, and became endowed with exuberance and an Epicureanism that embraces every kind of pleasure and satisfaction. Pleasure became an aim in itself, an insatiable hedonistic quest, and the poet's eyes are no longer fixed on beautiful ladies alone but on loose women and young men. He provides the genre with fresh accent and wit and depicts his bold adventures in a realistic manner and with a fine sense of humor. He does not spare himself in his humorous and ironic treatment of his themes, and this provides his poems with humanity and universal significance. This is what makes him relevant to contemporary Arab reality, as is attested by constant references to his work in modern Arabic poetry. The Resonance that follows, by the contemporary Iraqi poet Hasab al-Shaikh Ja'far, is but one example of this.

PRONUNCIATIONS:
   Abu-Nuwas: AH-bou nou-WASS
   Hasab al-Shaikh Ja'far: ha-SAHB all-SHAKE jah-FAR

Splendid young blades, like lamps in the darkness[1]

Splendid young blades, like lamps in the darkness,[2] proud-nosed,
  stiff-necked, keen—
Who assaulted Fate with dalliance to which they clung assiduously, so that
  their attachment to it could not be severed,
For whom Time brought round its felicitous spheres and halted, bending its
  tender neck over them—
I drank with them sharp Isfant wine, imported from Takrīt, clear and chilled;

5   One of those whose hand we asked for in haste, when we roused the owners
  of the wine-shops
In a host of the night, turbulent and swollen, like the sea which dazes the
  sailor with fear.
Suddenly at that moment there appeared an infidel[3] crone, like a solemn
  anchoress,
Tracing her lineage back through infidel stock, monastic idol-worshippers,
Who said, "Who are you?" We replied, "People you know, every one open-
  handed, noted for his prodigality,

10   Who, along the way, have stopped at your house: so seize the liberality of
  the generous and name your price,
For you have won a life of ease, provided you seize from us what David
  seized from Goliath.
Be lively in making a profit from them, doing—at the same time—a noble
  deed until they have left your house. Then you can sleep like the dead!"
She said, "I have what you want. Wait until the morning." We replied, "No,
  bring it now!
It is itself the morning; its clear radiance dispels the night when it shoots out
  sparks like rubies

15   As the patrolling angels do, when, at night, they stone with the stars the rebellious Afrits."
It advanced in the cup as bright as the sun at day-break, poured from an amphora upturned, bleeding at the waist.
We said to her, "How long has it been in the amphora, since it was hidden
  away?" She replied, "It was made in the time of Saul.
It was concealed in the amphora and has grown to be an old spinster buried
  inside a coffin in the earth.
It has been brought to you from the depths of its resting-place, so be careful
  not to take it in the cup with food."[4]

20   The odour that wafts from it to the drinkers is like the scent of crushed
  musk from a newly slit vesicle;
When mixed with clear rain-water it is like a network of pearls on ruby brocade
Carried round by a youth like the moon with large black eyes from which
  the magic of Hārūt could have sprung,
With a lutenist in our midst who moves us as he sings "Abode of Hind in
  Dhāt al-Jizˁ, Hail!"

---

1. Translated by Arthur Wormhoudt.
2. A reference to Imru' al-Qays's famous line about his
beloved who "lights up the darkness" with her beauty; see
page 333.
3. Or "grey-haired," an adjective that is sometimes used

for well-aged wine.
4. In Abu-Nuwas's time, wine drinking was too important
an activity to be adulterated with other activities like eating food.

Our gazes are constrained to turn towards him—you should see us looking
    at him, as if bedazzled.

25   He is from Hītī,[5] swaying gracefully, refined, and I say to him in fun, "Hit
    it, Hītī!"

So he begins with accurate diction to sing polished and well-articulated
    songs, keeping the time,

Until when the sphere of the strings, together with the drums, spins us
    round, we are left as if in a trance.

We glory in it in gardens thick with myrtle, acacia, pomegranate and mulberry,

Where the birds distract you from every other pleasure when they warble in
    antiphonal strains.

30   Blessings upon that time which slipped away too quickly—a lovely time
    which was not hateful to me then.

Dalliance did not turn me from coming to drink it and I did not fail to an-
    swer its urges

Until, lo! grey hair surprised me by its appearance—How hateful is the ap-
    pearance of cursed grey hair

In the eyes of beautiful women; when they see its appearance they announce
    severance and separation from love.

Now I regret the mistakes I have made and the misuse of the times pre-
    scribed for prayer.

35   I pray to you, God, praised be Your name!, to forgive me just as You,
    Almighty One, forgave Him of the Fish![6]

My body is racked with sickness, worn out by exhaustion[1]

My body is racked with sickness, worn out by exhaustion: my heart smarts
    with a pain searing like a blazing fire!

For I have fallen in love with a darling whom I cannot mention without the
    water of my eyes bursting forth in streams.

The full moon is his face and the sun his brow. To the gazelle belong his
    eyes and his breast.

Wearing the *zunnār,* he walks to his church; his god is the Son, so he said,
    and the Cross.

5   O I wish I were the priest or the metropolitan of his Church! No, I wish that
    I were the Gospel and the Scriptures for him!

No, I wish that I were a Eucharist which he is given or the chalice from
    which he drinks the wine! No, I wish I were the very bubbles!

So that I might obtain the benefit of being close to him and my sickness,
    grief and cares be dispelled!

Praise wine in its sweetness[1]

Praise wine in its sweetness and
    Name it with the best of its names
Do not make the water overpower it, do

---

5. A place on the Euphrates, noted for its wine.
6. Jonah, swallowed by a great fish when he tried to shirk
his duty as a prophet.

1. Here Abu-Nuwas uses the courtly *ghazal* for a homosexual love.
1. Wine is a generic term here for alcoholic drinks.

Not make it too strong for its water
5   Made in Karkh it has aged a long time
       Until most of its addition has gone
Its froth does not keep it from attaining
       Itself except for the last of its aroma
It circles and revives without blame souls
10   In their weariness and love sickness
Wine, the world has drunk of and they
       Never have enough of it if they return.

O censor, I satisfied the Imam, he was content

O censor, I satisfied the Imam, he was content
       I said what was in my mind and it was plain
I said to our saqi:° Remove it, shall the Emir   *wine-server*
       Al Muminun forbid and one be drunk?
5   So let pass by me a wine that seemed to have
       From its topmost point rays stretched out
When a hard drinker gulped it you thought him
       Kissing a star in the dark of night
The east of the house seems to be where it is
10   There is no west for it in the house
A nasal saqi brings it round and you see on
       The curve of his ear the frizzled locks
He poured for them and winked at me with eyes
       And that was for my heart sweeter and nicer.

Bringing the cup of oblivion for sadness

Bringing the cup of oblivion for sadness
       Both of them wonderful in wonder's sight
She[1] rose to show me, night's order was full,
       A dawn born between water and the grape
5   As if the small and the great of her bubbles
       Were pebbles of pearl in a land of gold
As if Turks in rank at her sides shot
       At intervals arrows from nearby
From a female hand, what a brave cupbearer
10   With fine shape both in grace and culture
She had conquered the master of singers
       With a skilled group, a profitable group
She saw and understood them and branched off
       Between them and those who loved books
15   Until youth's water boiled in her and
       Swelled in full body and branch
She was hugged by a light glance and hugged
       As she set a vow twixt true and false

---

1. Abu-Nuwas personifies the wine as a beloved woman.

She ended and men saw not her like of those
20   Allah created from foreign and Arab
One who if her shape was absent from an eye
    My need for her would not end nor my love.

What's between me and the censurers

What's between me and the censurers
    That adorned me with gossip
They ran through every hill pass
    Slandering my mistress
5   They commanded that I dismiss
    From my life my peace of mind
And that is what I will not see
    Happening until my death
By Allah who revealed surah Taha[1]
10   Mount Sinai and Scatterers
And Ra and Sad and Qaf and
    The Resurrection and One Sent
And the Lord of Hud and Nun
    And Light and Soul Snatchers
15 I did not want your flight my love
    Until or if you came not to me
O alas for you both, what a thing
    Between the heart and throat
Two fires wanting to burn
20   They inclined to my ribs
I am the weary one and who will
    Lament me in my long complaint
The expresser of tears
    The restrainer of sighs
25 I am tested in my purposes
    In each of my evil affairs
O inquirer into my trouble
    Behold my glances
Love appeared in the silence
30   And sounds of the beloved
I swore by the running camel
    On the seas of the wasteland
Returning for the sacrifice
    To be slashed in the throat
35 And those gathering to assembly
    And standing at 'Arafat
If you called me to take my soul
    I could wish my faith true
Alas for him in passion's fire
40   Climbing to the pleasures
It pays the eye with tears

---

1. A chapter of the Qur'an; Abu-Nuwas lists several more suras dealing with salvation.

Flowing in the Forat's torrent
Many a friend has for me in my
Love been suspicious
45   My affairs do not seem to be
Any but my suspect griefs
And while we were at evening
We traveled on the ways
When one said: The day's sun
50   Is on the perfumed meadows
I said: The sun, by my lord
Has revealed the darkness
It exhausted my eyes' water
And brought up my sighs
55   And love in it was calamity
Linked to a misfortune
At times it results in happiness
At times in grief intense.

His friend called him Sammaja for his beauty[1]

His friend called him Sammaja for his beauty
And he was very proud if named and merry
A fawn, as if the Thurayya were on his forehead
And Mushtara in the rising house and lamps
5   An artful eye, a sword bloodied its glance
When aimed at a heart he said: No harm!
He ceased not to point it at men and draw it
Until heart's blood flowed from its abode
May Allah not relieve me if I stretch my hand
10   To him asking him for relief from your love
Nor desire consolation from you O my hope and
Settle in my heart your love that goes not.

One possessed with a rosy cheek

One possessed with a rosy cheek
The white skin like a touchstone
Men have contemplated in her
Beauties that are not exhausted
5   Beauty is in every part of her
A place often returned to
Some of it is attained and
Some of it is being born
And each time you return to it
10   It is praised in the return
So drink to the face of the moon
Copiously without bad temper.

---

1. Uncomfortable with this poem's content, one early commentator wrote that "He spoke these verses about a girl named Sammaja, but he refers to her as if she were a boy."

❦

RESONANCE

Hasab al-Shaikh Ja'far: from Descent of Abu Nuwas[1]

Jinan[2] means eternal waiting.
Jinan means defeat.
Jinan means death by your own hand.

Be what you choose, Ibn Hani.[3] Be a stone. Be the drinking companion whose black laugh coughs up his old defeats. Be the road to the tavern where the parrot is every-one's favorite friend.

    Your banner remains the muddy coat you dragged, tossed
    in the tavern and forgot there.

                At end of night

You bend under pearl clouds to hold up the walls and pull out the illusory thread from wine bottles as you sit among drunken friends until the dawn brightens your face.

                  * * *

    And so Ibn Hani, be what you like,
    a wave, or a sail
    to the Hakaman[4] of sorrow.
    Be our Magi huddled in a tavern.
    Be the confidant of gilded dolls,
    or the beggar at the door
    of her gruff master.

Songs are the horses tamed at the gathering of deaf men. Be a stone or an echo. Be space or dew waiting for Jinan's caravan. Be a face or its shadow on the jug. The night is a drum. And though you are slapped and whipped, the Babylonian star fades in its dome, longing for your face and your songs. Surrounded by your drunken friends the light of the dawn turns into a lavender in your hands. The wine skin is empty, your coat frayed, and your face the object of snickers. Be the flame or the ashes.

    Jinan means eternal waiting.
    Jinan is defeat.
    Jinan is suicide.

❦

1. Translated by Diana Der Hovanessian, with Salma Khadra Jayyusi. Born in southern Iraq in 1939, Hasab al-Shaikh Ja'far graduated from Baghdad University in 1960. Thus he was brought up near the area where Abu-Nuwas lived in his formative years and, like Abu-Nuwas, lived most of his adult life in his favorite city, Baghdad. In 1960, he went to Moscow to further his literary educa-tion at the Gorky Institute for Literature and spent the fol-lowing six years there, which introduced him to the world of Russian literature and poetry. He returned to Baghdad in 1966 and soon established himself as the leading poetic talent of his generation. His poetry makes a significant contribution to contemporary Arabic poetry and provides a vital intertextual link with classical genres. He still lives in Baghdad and has published numerous collections of poetry.

2. A beautiful slave girl with whom Abu-Nuwas fell in love. Though Abu-Nuwas wrote many *ghazals* about beautiful young men, he wrote equally wonderful love poems about Jinan.

3. Another name for Abu-Nuwas.

4. The palace of Jinan's master.

+—+ ⯊◆⯊ +—+

Ibn al-Rumi
836–889

Abu al-Hasan 'Ali ibn al-'Abbas ibn Jurayju ibn al-Rumi was born in Baghdad to a father of Byzantine Christian origin, but the family had converted to Islam. His mother, Hasana, was of Persian descent, and he was sent to a school attended by upper-class children. In his early youth he was in contact with numerous outstanding intellectuals who provided him with an in-depth knowledge of Arabic language and literature. He also acquired an extensive knowledge of Shi'ite doctrines and those of a related sect, the Mutazalites, and their emphasis on rationality and social justice struck a chord in his rebellious nature. This is clearly demonstrated in the philosophical dimensions of his poetry and in his interest in individual concerns and abstract issues. His erudition and scholarly reputation have led him at times to be described as primarily a philosopher. Yet his poetic talent demonstrated itself from an early age, and by the time he was twenty he was an accomplished poet with an outstanding reputation. His strong sense of individualism manifested itself in his excessive confidence and pride in his talent and in the right of the talented poet, by virtue of his divine gift, to occupy a prominent position in society.

Ibn al-Rumi excelled both in long poems and in short epigrams. His sense of integrity and pride set him apart from his predecessors. In stark contrast to al-Buhturi, Ibn al-Rumi broke with the tradition of the poet as a docile follower in the court of the caliph and started the era of the poet as a dissident intellectual. In 865 he openly supported a revolt in Kufa against the central caliphate, and his elegy to the leader of that revolt, Yahya ibn 'Umar, was read as a Shi'ite revolutionary manifesto and a condemnation of the ruling establishment. The poet's reconciliation with the court was achieved only when the Court changed its policies toward the Shi'ites. His poetry made the transitional shift from the formal neoclassical work of Abu-Tammam to the powerful poetry of al-Mutanabbi and al-Ma'arri, for it was stylistically elegant, rich in imagery, and profound in thought and philosophical ideas.

PRONUNCIATION:
Ibn al-Rumi: ibb'n all-ROO-me

Say to whoever finds fault with the poem of his panegyrist[1]

Say to whoever finds fault with the poem of his panegyrist: Can you not see
    what a tree is made of?
It is made of bark, dry wood and thorns and in between is the fruit.
But it should, after all, be so, that what the Lord of Lords, not Man, creates
    is finely made.
But it was not so but otherwise, for a reason Divine Wisdom ordained,
5   And God knows better than we what he brings about and in everything he
    resolves there is always good.
Therefore let people forgive whoever does badly or falls short of his aim in
    poetry; he is (after all only) a human being.
Let them remember that his mind is heavily taxed and his thoughts are
    exhausted in writing his verse.
His task is like pearl-fishing at the bottom of the sea: there before the pearls
    lies danger.[2]

---

1. Translated by Peter Blum, after Gregor Schoeler. This is a poem about poetry.

2. This line equates the writing of poetry with the highly dangerous but rewarding pursuit of diving for pearls.

In pearl-fishing, there is the expensive, the precious that the choice accepts,
   but also what it leaves behind,
10   And it is inevitable that the diver bring with him what is selected and what
   is scorned.

I have been deprived of all the comforts of life[1]

I have been deprived of all the comforts of life, deprived even of the gentle
   pleasure of dreams.
So I feel, as soon as in my sleep I see myself eating or turning to food,
Unfortunately, as if I were drawn away from it and restrained by a bridle.
And I see my beloved—when his vision approaches and the desire to kiss
   him is the strongest desire—
5   Only in his struggle of love with me that causes a major ritual impurity and
   kindles within me—what a blaze!
Then I set off, since ablution has become a duty and I have received only
   yearning and love-sickness from the one I love.
He has driven away my sound sleep and cheated me out of my desire—and
   he has imposed on me the money for the baths.
Praised be the Lord, who has unceasingly destined him to make my debts
   and infatuation grow.

I thought of you the day my journeys[1]

I thought of you the day my journeys landed me at Abū al-Khaṣīb Canal,
When at sundown great ships with hoisted sails had cast their anchors by its
   banks with us aboard,
Having travelled by day and night heavily laden with hearts and souls heavy
   with worries,
Traversing the seas after setting forth, the north wind carrying us south,
5   Torn by longing for family and friends, tossed far from our wide, welcoming land in the belly of a ship,
Forcibly torn from pleasures, from the embrace of pretty girls, thrown into
   lands of war,
Into an abode, now desolate, where the Fates refuse any reunion of lover
   and beloved.
And I said, holding back my tears, out of bashfulness before my friends:
"Maybe one day the lone Possessor of sovereignty will decree the return of
   the lone stranger."
10   Our ships had scarcely left the confluence of the two rivers[2] behind when
   they were turned up towards al-Ubullah.
Heavily laden they glided at evening time, swaying to and fro, up to the
   deserted abode of Abū al-Ḥasan,
A place to alight where strewn all about were men prostrated, flung on the
   ground, cheeks in the dust.
We tarried long there, so long that the hands of death very nearly got hold
   of our souls.

---

1. Translated by Peter Blum, after Gregor Schoeler.   Canal is near Basra in southern Iraq.
1. Translated by Robert McKinney. The Abu al-Khasib   2. Where the Tigris and Euphrates meet in southern Iraq.

We had no means by which we might seek our salvation but humble supplication to Him that answers.

15 And when the hour for our return was at hand and our hearts' resolve was
quickened with the thought of setting forth,

We boarded great big black daughters of the sea[3] that heaved with their load
of men both young and old.

Swift [camels] in a vast flood plain plunging their bows into the fearful
unknown,

Their sterns tightly harnessed, plowing ahead as if quickly slithering on
their bellies and loins.

When the winds bandy them about, urging them on each in its turn, they
very nearly outstrip even the winds at the gale's stiff blowing.

20 Ordained for the purpose they traverse the dark of night, like a fine mare
with tufted tail, black as the night itself,

Their hind quarters refusing all but compliance to the south wind, and their
fore parts too,

Dispensing with all need for heads and necks to lead, or for saddling them
up for the journey.

After seven nights they alighted with their loads in Wāsiṭ, when the sun was
inclining towards setting.

And breezes reached us, bearing our way the fragrance of strong wine that
befuddles the party of drinkers.

25 Faint they came, like a traveller emaciated by the hand of Fate, his body
gaunt from fatigue long endured,

The midday heat of waterless deserts crossed having given him, for the
bright freshness of his face, a garment of pale languor.

Then we could no longer hold back those firstlings from our lids, ulcerated
and sore, soon followed by copious tears.

And when they came within sight of Baghdad bearing us on, when the night
was tightly buttoned up,

And great sails had been hoisted high that their bows not be turned aside,

30 Patient enduring of your absence, and desire, became too great for me to
bear and my guarded sighs gave way to loud wailing.

I passed that night keeping watch over the night stars, waiting for the
Pleiades that herald the dawn, the fretful, stealthy vigil of one watching
out for his warden.

And my lids did not taste sleep till I had alighted in the courtyards of my
beloved's people.

There in Quṭrubbul are the traces of an abode, the playground now of
domesticated gazelles.

How many a time I've turned their way, sighs rising in my breast like burning flames.

35 And how many glances they've sent my way that left scars on my very soul
when they turned away.

We betook ourselves to you that evening with haste born of eager desire,
like a sick man repairing to his doctor,

To quench our thirsting souls with your close presence that waters the
thirsty with its rains.

3. A specific type of sailing boat.

We passed by the outlying villages of Baghdad till voices calling the faithful to the sunset prayer showed us our way to you.

And the gentle East wind, when it blew, roused and inflamed the despondent heart with the fragrance it bore from you,

40   And there in the place of pride in Sāmarrā we again faced faces that gave
the lie to those who said we would never return,

Faces that restored vitality to my face after long pining, and the blackness to
my locks after they had turned hoary.

Great is He Who unites those separated, Who brings home the one long distant,

And Who has not let Dāwūd maliciously delight in my absence from court
that he so foolishly desired.

Sweet sleep has been barred from my eyes[1]

Sweet sleep has been barred from my eyes by their preoccupation with copious tears.

What sleep is possible after the great misfortunes that have befallen Basra?

What sleep is possible after the Zanj have violated openly the sacred places
of Islam?

This indeed is such an affair as could scarcely have arisen in the
imagination.

5   Wide awake we have witnessed matters which it would have sufficed us
were they visions seen in a dream.

The accursed traitor ventured how recklessly against her[2] and against God

And named himself without right an Imam—may God not guide aright his
labours as Imam!

My soul cries alas for thee, O Basra, with a sigh like the blaze of a
conflagration;

My soul cries alas for thee, O mine of excellences, with a sigh that makes
me to bite my thumb;

10   My soul cries alas for thee, O tabernacle of Islam, with a sigh whence my
anguish is prolonged;

My soul cries alas for thee, O anchorage of the lands, with a sigh that shall
continue for long years;

My soul cries alas for thy concourse that has perished; my soul cries alas for
thy grievously injured glory.

Even whilst her inhabitants were enjoying the fairest circumstances, their
slaves assailed them with sudden destruction.

They entered her as though they were portions of night when it has become
shrouded in darkness.

15   What terror the inhabitants beheld by reason of them! What terror, fit to turn
hoary the head of youth!

When they assailed them with their fire from right and left, from behind
them and before,

How many a toper they choked with an unexpected draught! How many a
feaster they choked with an unpalatable dish!

---

1. Translated by A. J. Arberry.   2. Basra.

How many a man niggardly with his soul sought a way of escape, and they
   met his brow with the sword!
How many a brother beheld his brother felled to the ground, dusty of cheek,
   amongst many nobles so fallen!
20 How many a father beheld the dearest of his sons hoisted aloft on a tren-
   chant blade!
How many a one most precious to his kinsmen they betrayed, since there
   was not one there to protect him!
How many a suckling child they weaned with the edge of the sword before
   the time of weaning!
How many a young virgin with the seal of God upon her they violated
   openly without any concealment!
How many a chaste maiden they carried into captivity, her face displayed
   without a veil!
25 They came upon them in the morning, and the people endured their cruelty
   through the length of a day that was as if a thousand years.
Who beheld the women captives driven like beasts, bleeding from head to
   foot?
Who beheld them in the partitioning between the Zanj, being divided
   amongst them by lots?
Who beheld them being taken as bondswomen, after themselves possessing
   bondswomen and servants?
I never recall what was perpetrated by the Zanj without it kindles what a
   conflagration in my heart;
30 I never recall what was perpetrated by the Zanj without I am anguished by
   the bitterness of humiliation.
Many a purchase they there cheapened that had long been very dear to the
   hagglers.
Many a house they there destroyed that was a shelter for the infirm and for
   orphans;
Many a palace they there broke into that had hitherto been difficult indeed
   of access.
Many a one there possessed of wealth and plenty they left in league with
   utter deprivation.
35 Many a people who passed the night in closest unity, they left their unity
   utterly disordered.
Turn aside, my two comrades, at Basra the brilliant, as one wasted with
   sickness turns aside,
And enquire of her—but answer is not to be found in her to any question,
   and who is there to speak for her?—
"Where is the clamour of them that dwelt in her? Where are her jostling
   markets?
Where is any ship sailing from her or sailing to her—ships raised up in the
   sea like landmarks?
40 Where are those palaces and mansions that were in her? Where is that well-
   secured edifice?"
Those palaces have been changed into rubbish-mounds of ashes and heaped
   dust;

Flood and fire have been given authority over them, and their columns have
    crumbled down in utter destruction,
They have become empty of those that dwelt in them, and they are desolate;
    the eye descries nothing amongst those mounds
But severed hands and feet, flung aside amidst them skulls split
    asunder
45   And faces smeared with blood—may my father be a ransom for those
    bloody faces!—
Trampled down perforce in contempt and humiliation, after they were so
    long magnified and revered.
So you may see them, the winds blowing upon them, scattering over them
    as they pass dark dust,
Lowly and humbled, as if they were weeping, displaying their teeth—but
    not in a smile!
Rather, my comrades, repair to the congregational mosque, if you be men
    apt to tarry,
50   And enquire of it—but answer is not to be found in it—"Where are its wor-
    shippers, who stood long in prayer?
Where are its throngers who used to throng it, passing all their time in
    recitation and fasting?
Where are its young men with their handsome faces? Where are its old men
    prudent and wise?"
What a calamity, what a mighty disaster has overtaken us, in the loss of
    those kinsmen!
How many we forsook—earnest ascetic, erudite scholar learned in his
    religion.
55   Ah, how I regret that I deserted them; but little avails my regret for their loss.
Ah, how I shall be shamed before them, when we meet together before the
    Judge of Judges!
What excuse shall we have to offer, what response to give, when we are
    summoned over the heads of mankind?
"O My servants, were you not angry on My behalf, on behalf of Me, the
    Majestic, the Splendid?
Did you forsake your brethren and desert them—out upon you!—as ignoble
    men desert their fellows?
60   How did you not have compassion for your sisters tied in the ropes of slaves
    of the sons of Ham!
You were not jealous on account of My jealousy, so you abandoned My
    inviolable ones to those who defiled My sanctuary.
Surely he who was not jealous for My inviolable ones is no fit mate for
    chaste dwellers in the heavenly tents;
How should houri approve of a man's action, when he did not stand de-
    fender over the inviolable?"
Ah, how I shall be shamed before the Prophet, when he reproaches me con-
    cerning them with severest rebuke,
65   And I am all alone, when they rise up to accuse me, and the Prophet himself
    takes charge of the case against me on their behalf.
Picture how he will say to you, O men, when he reproaches you along with
    the reproachers,

"My community! Where were you, when there called upon you a free
    woman, of the noble women of the people?
'O Muhammad!' she shrieked, and why did there not rise up on her behalf
    the guardians of my right in my stead?
I did not answer her, for I was dead; but why was there not one man living
    to answer on behalf of my bones?"

70   May my father be a ransom for those bones, great men that they were! And
    may heaven water them with flood-charged clouds!
And upon them be blessing from the Sovereign God and peace fortified
    with peace!
Go forth, you nobles, light and heavy, against the vile slaves;
They managed well their enterprise whilst you were sleeping—shame,
    shame upon the sleep of the sleepers!
Make true the belief of your brothers who had high expectations of you, and
    put their hopes in you in all vicissitudes.

75   Exact vengeance for them, for that will be to them like the restoring of their
    spirits to their bodies.
You did not comfort them by coming to their assistance, so do you now
    comfort them by taking revenge.
Deliver them that are captives: little enough is that by way of protection and
    observance of obligations.
The shame they suffered attaches to you, O men, because the ties of religion
    are as the ties of kinship.
If now you neglect to punish the accursed one, you will all be partners of
    the accursed one in his crimes.

80   Hasten against him with resolution before deliberation, and with bridling
    before saddling;
He who has put his saddle on the back of a generous steed, prohibited to
    him thereafter is the binding of the girth.
Do not tarry long away from eternal Paradise, for you are not in an abode of
    tarrying;
So purchase the abiding things with the price of the meanest mundane
    goods, and sell detachment from them for eternal life.

Al-Mutanabbi
915–955

Abu'l-'Ayyib Ahmad ibn al-Husain al-Ju'fi, usually known as al-Mutanabbi, is the most admired of all neoclassical Arab poets. He was born in Kufa, Iraq, to a family of noble southern
Arabian descent, or at least he was convinced of the superiority of his family background. He
received his early education in a school with Shi'ite leanings and distinguished himself from an
early age with his sharp intelligence, prodigious memory, and poetic talent. He lived for three
years among the Bedouins, which enhanced his command of Arabic, then returned in 927 to
Kufa and established himself as a major poet, believing that poetry would be a sure way to
achieve wealth and power. He soon left for Baghdad, and then moved to Damascus, Aleppo,
and later Cairo, impressing in each of these cities with his poetic talent and powerful intellect.
During his sojourns in these urban cultural centers, he enjoyed the patronage of the rich and

powerful and wrote some of the most admired poems in Arabic literature. It is important to note that he spent his youth and early adulthood in a turbulent time, when any deviation from the orthodox path led to imprisonment. As a rebellious intellectual, he was imprisoned twice for his subversive ideas, once for proclaiming himself a prophet and again for involvement with the Bedouins in revolts and brigandage. In 955 while traveling from Shiraz to Baghdad, he was killed. There are many different theories about his murder, ranging from robbery and revenge to professional jealousy and political intrigue.

If the towering talent of Abu-Nuwas revolutionized the *qasida* form with its innovative force, and if Abu-Tammam and his student al-Buhturi returned to the classical mold, then al-Mutanabbi consecrated their neoclassicism and provided it with its zenith. He is widely considered to be the best neoclassical poet, both for the quality of his composition and for the depth of his insights—the name by which he is known, al-Mutanabbi, means "the one who claims to be a prophet." His fame spread to many Muslim lands, and he is recognized as an important influence on the development of new Persian poetry. Al-Mutanabbi was essentially a lone intellectual with a visionary idea, a tremendous sense of his own worth, and a rebellious nature in turbulent times. He wrote some of the best panegyrics of Arabic poetry and provided the neoclassical *qasida* with vigor and philosophical resonance. His bitter and sometimes scurrilous epigrams earned him the rancor of many influential people and perhaps led to his murder. The poems selected here demonstrate the range of his themes, the depth of his vision, and the power of his composition.

PRONUNCIATION:
> *al-Mutanabbi:* all-mou-tah-NAH-bee

On hearing in Egypt that his death had been reported to Saif al-Daula in Aleppo[1]

With what shall I console myself, being without my people and home,
    having neither boon-fellow, nor cup, nor any to comfort me?
I desire of this my time to bring me to what time of itself cannot obtain.
Do not meet your destiny save with indifference, so long as your body
    keeps your spirit company,
for the joy whereby you are rejoiced does not remain, neither does sorrow
    restore to you what is gone.
5   Among what has hurt the people of passion is that they yearned, and did not
    know or understand the world.
Their eyes wear away with tears, and their souls are in the track of every
    hideous one whose face is handsome.
Depart—may every fleet she-camel transport you—for every separation is
    secure from hurt for me today.
What you have in your litters[2] is no substitute or price for my soul if I
    should die of yearning.
You in whose court my death was announced at a distance, what the announcers asserted is bound to happen to every man.
10   How many times I have been killed and have died, as you have had it, then I
    shook myself, and tomb and shroud passed from me.
A whole crowd witnessed my burial, before these men spoke, then died
    before the man they buried.

---

1. Translated by A. J. Arberry.

2. A reference to the traditional appearance of beautiful women.

A man does not attain everything that he desires; the winds convey whither the ships do not list.

I have seen that your neighbour guards not his honour intact, and milk does not flow over your pasture.

The reward of whoever is close to you is weariness, and the portion of every lover from you is hatred;

15 you are angry with him who obtains your gift, so that annoyance and reproaches requite him following.

Flight has left between me and you a pathless wilderness in which eye and ear play false;

the fleet camels, after being speedy, crawl along in it, and their callosities ask the earth about their soles.[3]

I keep my self-restraint company so long as it is a sign of nobility in me, but I do not keep my self-restraint company when it is cowardice in me.

I do not stand holding on to wealth by which I am humiliated, neither do I take delight in what defiles my honour.

20 I was sleepless after my departure, feeling desolate without you, then my rope became firm, and slumber repented.

If I were afflicted by a love like your love, then I would be apt for a parting like it.

My rule has worn out its trappings in the society of other than you, and its check-straps and halter have been changed in al-Fusṭāṭ[4]

in the society of the noble father of musk, in whose bounty red Muḍar[5] and Yemen are drowned.

Even if some of his promise is slow in coming to me, yet my hopes do not languish or weaken.

25 He is faithful to his word, only I have mentioned to him my love, and he is testing and trying it.

Satire on Kāfūr composed on 9 Dhu'l-Hijja 350,[1] one day before the poet's departure from Egypt

Festival day—with what circumstance have you returned, day of festival? With what has happened in the past, or with some matter quite new that is to occur in you?

As for my dear ones, the desert stretches between me and them; would that there stretched between me and you a desert, beyond which were a desert.

But for my questing the heights, lean, powerful she-camel had never travelled with me where I have ridden her, neither long-bodied, short-haired mare,

and more agreeable as bed-fellow than my sword would have been the slender, delicate maidens matching its lustre.

5 Time has left not of my heart nor of my liver anything to be enslaved by eye or neck.

---

3. Lines 12–16 satirize the poet's previous patron, Saif al-Daula, who has failed to get him killed.
4. A place south of Cairo, or more generally a large encampment.

5. A northern Arabian tribe.
1. Equivalent to 19 January 962; this festival commemorates Muhammad's migration from Mecca.

My two wine-bearers, is this wine in your cups, or is there in your cups anxiety and sleeplessness?

Am I a rock? What is it with me, that I am not stirred by this liquor and these songs?

When I desired pure red wine, I found it when the beloved of my soul was missing.

What have I encountered of the world? and the most astonishing part of it is that I am envied[2] for that over which I weep.

10   I am become the most ample of the wealthy as to treasurer and hand; I am the rich one, and my properties are promises.[3]

Indeed I have alighted amongst liars whose guest is denied alike hospitality and departure;

men's generosity is with their hands, and their generosity is with their tongues—would that neither they existed nor their generosity!

Death seizes not a soul of their souls, without death has in his hand a stick because of its stench,

every one of them flaccid as to the leather strap of his belly, swollen in the flanks, not to be counted amongst either men or women.

15   Whenever a wicked slave assassinates his master or betrays him, has he to get his training in Egypt?

There, the eunuch has become the chieftain of the runaway slaves, the free man is enslaved, and the slave is obeyed.

The gardeners of Egypt are asleep to the tricks of its foxes which have gotten indigestion, and yet the grape-clusters are not at an end.[4]

The slave is no brother to the godly free man, even though he be born in the clothes of the free.

Do not buy a slave without buying a stick with him, for slaves are filthy and of scant good.[5]

20   I never thought I should live to see the day when a dog would do me evil and be praised into the bargain,

nor did I imagine that true men would have ceased to exist, and that the like of the father of bounty would still be here

and that that negro with his pierced camel's lip would be obeyed by those cowardly hirelings.

Hungry, he eats of my provisions, and detains me, that he may be called, "Mighty of worth, much sought after."

A man who is controlled by a pregnant slave-woman[6] is indeed oppressed, hot-eyed, faint-hearted.

25   What a predicament! alas for one accepting it—for the like of it were created the long-necked Mahrī camels;

in such a situation, he who drinks of death enjoys its taste; doom is honey-sweet when one is humiliated.

Who ever taught the eunuch negro nobility? His "white" people, or his royal ancestors?

---

2. By other poets after Kafur took him as his court poet.
3. A clear reference to the unfulfilled promises of Kafur to reward the poet.
4. This line has become proverbial for its insight into the

dynamic of life and corrupt government in Egypt.
5. A reference to Kafur's origin as a slave.
6. A metaphor for the fat-bellied Kafur.

or his ear bleeding in the hand of the slave-broker? or his worth, seeing that
for two farthings he would be rejected?

Wretched Kāfūr is the most deserving of the base to be excused in regard to
every baseness—and sometimes excusing is a reproach—

30   and that is because white stallions[7] are incapable of gentility, so how about
black eunuchs?

Panegyric to 'Aḍud al-Daula and his sons Abu'l-Fawāris and Abū Dulaf

The abodes of the Valley[1] in respect of delightfulness are, in relation to all
other abodes, as spring among all other times,

but the Arab lad amidst them is a stranger in face, hand and tongue.

They are places of jinns to play in—if Solomon had journeyed in them, he
would have journeyed with an interpreter;[2]

they invited our horsemen and steeds, until I feared, for all their nobility,
that they would be refractory.

5   We set out in the morning, the branches scattering over their manes the like
of pearls,

and I proceeded, the branches veiling the sun from me and yet bringing me
sufficient radiance,

and the orient sun cast from them upon my garments dinars that fled from
my fingers.

On the branches were fruits, pointing to you sweet potions standing without
vessels;

and there were waters in which the pebbles chinked like the chink of ornaments on the hands of young girls.

10   If they had been Damascus, my reins would have been turned back by a
man skilled in respect of his *tharīd*,[3] having Chinese bowls,

aloes-wood being heaped up on his fires of hospitality, its smoke fragrant as
nadd;[4]

you alight with him with a heroic heart, and depart from him out of a cowardly heart—

dwelling-places, the phantom of which has not ceased to accompany me to
al-Naubandhajān;[5]

when the grey doves chanted therein, the songs of the minstrel-girls responded to them;

15   and the dwellers in the Valley have greater need of clear expression than a
dove when it sings and laments,

the two descriptions being very close to each other, whilst the two described
by them are remote from each other.

My steed says at the Valley of Bauwān, "Must we proceed from this place
to thrusting at the foe?

7. The other princes who have already failed the poet.

1. The Bauwan Valley in Persia, a famous lush and scenic
spot.

2. The Qur'an describes Solomon as a master of the birds
and the jinn.

3. A popular Bedouin meal consisting of meat and bread
soaked in its gravy.

4. An aromatic herb.

5. A small town near the valley of Bauwan close to the
city of Shiraz.

Your father Adam laid down for you disobedience and taught you to depart
from Paradise."

I replied, "When I saw Abū Shujā'[6] I forgot the rest of mankind, and this
place;

20   for men, and this world, are a road leading to him who has no second
amongst men."

I had taught myself to speak concerning them as jousting is learned without
spear-points.

Through 'Adud al-Daula the State is impregnable and mighty, and none has
hands who lacks a fore-arm

nor any grip on the cutting swords, nor any enjoyment of the supple
lances.

The State calls him the refuge of its members on a day of war, whether virgin or oft repeated,

25   and none names any like Fannākhusru,[7] and none nicknames any like
Fannākhustu.

His virtues are not comprehended by supposition, or report, or
eyewitnessing.

The earths of other men are of dust and fear, but the earth of Abū Shujā' is
of security

protecting against robbers every merchant, and guaranteeing to the swords
every wrongdoer.

When their deposits demand trustees, they are committed to the valley
windings and the mountaintops

30   and thereon pass the night uncompanioned, calling to all who passes by,
"Do you not see me?"

His magic charm is every Mashrafī blade[8] against every deaf basilisk and
viper,

yet his bounties are not charmed against his munificence, neither his noble
wealth against contempt.

A man of vigour protects the boundaries of Fārs, inciting to survival by
means of annihilation

with a blow that arouses the emotions of the fates, not the striking of the
lutes' second and third strings.

35   It is as though the blood of the crania among the scattered locks had dotted
the lands with the feathers of francolins;

so that if the hearts of lovers were flung down there, they would not fear the
eyeballs of lovely women.

I had not seen, before him, two lion-cubs the like of his cubs, nor two racing
colts

more vigorously contesting nobility of stock, or more like in appearance to
a pure-blooded sire,

or listening in his assemblies more eagerly to "So-and-so shattered a spear
in So-and-so."

40   The first object they beheld was the heights, and they were passionate for
them before the due season;

---

6. 'Adud al-Daula's title, meaning "father of the brave."   8. The best type of sword, highly valued by real warriors.
7. 'Adud al-Daula's name before his rise to power.

and the first utterance they understood, or spoke, was to succour the suppliant, or to free the captive.

You were the sun dazzling every eye; so how now, seeing that two others
have appeared along with it.

May they live the life of the sun and moon, giving life by their light, not envious of each other,

and may they not rule save the kingdom of their enemies, neither inherit
save from those they kill,

45   and may the two sons of any foe with whom they vie in numbers be to him
as the two *yās* in the letters of the word *unaisiyān*.

This prayer is as praise without hypocrisy, conveyed from heart to
heart;

You have become in respect of it arrayed in the water of a blade, and it has
become in respect of you upon a Yemeni sword.

But for your being amongst mankind, mankind would have a babble, like
words without meanings.

❀ CROSSCURRENTS: POETRY, WINE, AND LOVE ❀

- The selections from *The Thousand and One Nights* (page 408) present the poetic
  themes of poetry, wine, and love within the context of stories and storytelling.
  Indeed, in several instances they present the recitation of poems, including those
  by Abu-Nuwas, a memorable character as well as a great poet. How does the narrative presentation of these poems and their themes compare with your reading of
  them as isolated lyrics?

- Compare the depiction of and attitudes toward poetry, love, and (less frequently) wine in the medieval love lyrics and diary entries in the Perspectives
  sections on "Courtly Women" (page 237) and the lyrics in "Iberia, the Meeting of Three Worlds" (page 756). What is similar and what is different in
  their depiction of love? How does the absence of alcohol affect the activity of
  lovemaking?

- The love lyric has been a major literary genre since ancient times. What continuity and what variation do you see between the lyrics of the ancient Greek poets
  Arkhilokhos, Sappho, and Alkaios (Volume A), Catullus in ancient Rome (Volume A), Francis Petrarch and the early modern European poets in the Perspectives section, "Lyric Sequences and Self-Definition" (Volume C), the poets of
  the Ottoman Empire (Volume D), the *ghazals* of Ghalib (Volume E), and the
  Parisian lyrics of Charles Baudelaire (Volume E)?

- The lyrics in "Poetry, Wine, and Love" are frank in their depiction of the
  pleasures and pains of physical love. Compare these poems with other
  traditions concerned with the sexual dimensions of love, such as the lyrics
  of early South Asia in "Love in a Courtly Language" (Volume A), the tales
  of Geoffrey Chaucer (Volume B) and Giovanni Boccaccio (Volume C), or
  the libertine writing in the Perspectives section "Liberty and Libertines"
  (Volume D).

‹— ☵✦☲ —›

The Thousand and One Nights
9th–14th centuries

Apart from the Qur'an, *Alf Layla wa-Layla* (*The Thousand and One Nights* or *The Arabian Nights*) is perhaps the most influential, well-known and widely read work of Arabic and Islamic culture. The earliest evidence that a work or a compilation of this nature existed goes back to the ninth century, and certainly by the twelfth century there are many manuscripts of *The Thousand and One Nights* in Egypt, Syria, and Iraq. The present title of the work is a twelfth-century coinage, for earlier mentions of the work refer to it simply as *Alf Layla* ("The Thousand Nights"). Earlier manuscripts are incomplete and led to speculation that the title *The Thousand Nights* was only meant to denote a large number of stories rather than a formal organization of the work. Recent scholarship and application of modern critical approaches have challenged this assumption and established the structural cohesion of the work. Similarly there is much speculation concerning the origin of the work, its genealogy, and development. It has been suggested that a Persian collection of tales, *Hazar Afsana* ("Thousand Tales"), is the source of *The Thousand and One Nights.* Others claim that its source text is an Indian narrative of different stories similar to the frame story of *The Thousand and One Nights,* yet neither of these accounts for the richness of the work and its infinite variety of narratives.

The text's unity is grounded in a constant interplay between the frame story and the enframed stories. In the famous frame tale, the vizier's daughter Scheherazade or Shahrazad offers her stories as ransom for her life to avert the violence of a tyrant king, but the ransom only works through the suspension of time by using storytelling to stop its flow. Narrative manipulates time, and the suspension of time enhances the power of narrative, hence the circular nature of *The Thousand and One Nights.* Because of this circularity, the structural unity of the work develops through variations, echoes, and references forward and back, rather than through cause-and-effect progressions. This linking can be seen in the first set of stories, when the threat of violence is averted or postponed by the telling of stories. But in certain tales the link with the frame story is different. In "The Tale of Sympathy the Learned" one sees the whole work mirrored in one of its stories of how a learned woman is able to tame the powerful men around her. This tale may be studied as the first ever "feminist" literary text, which enhances the position of the woman, subverting the patriarchal order and exposing its weaknesses. In other stories on the other hand, the link to the frame tale seems weak, yet they often involve themes—the evanescence of worldly pleasures, ascetic piety, and the need for humble acceptance of God—that are basic Islamic tenets also implied in the main frame.

The tales are further connected by the fact that tales often generate other tales or kernels of tales within themselves. The narrative of *The Thousand and One Nights* is similar in form to nested Russian dolls, one hidden inside another. Unlike the Russian doll, the tales aren't identical or symmetrical and are varied in location, characters, and action. Yet there is a deep structure that makes them a whole within every tale, and at the same time part of the organic whole that is *The Thousand and One Nights.* The nested tales often replicate in their flow the very structure of the whole work—that is, a basic frame story and a number of enframed stories within its overreaching thematic unity. This confirms both the circularity and the self-reference of the work.

Another dimension of the work enhances its coherence. The set of philosophical and religious assumptions underpinning the deep structure of *The Thousand and One Nights* is essentially Islamic in its tenets and uniquely Arabic in its orientation. As a result, the book has often been known as *The Arabian Nights.* Early European translators noted its cultural difference. Richard Burton, for example, noted the parallels between the cultural ethos of *The Thousand*

and One Nights and the Muslim customs in the Arab and Indian worlds, which he himself witnessed in his travels. These philosophical and religious aspects of the work are an essential part of the motivation of its narrative, whose ultimate aim is to re-educate the tyrant king, to acclimate him to a tolerant and humane civilization. The various strata or cycles of stories correspond to the different Arabic/Islamic virtues and concepts that are necessary for a comprehensive re-education of a tyrant. *The Thousand and One Nights* reflects the culmination of Arabic and Islamic civilization at the peak of its assimilation of many elements of the older cultures that embraced Islam, such as Persian, Egyptian, Iraqi, Indian, and even Chinese.

Yet the work is primarily the product of the Arabic imagination and the Islamic worldview embodied in the Qur'an, for it carries the distinct mark of Arabic culture in two of its major centers: Iraq and Egypt. Although the majority of characters in *The Thousand and One Nights* are of Arabic origin and carry Arabic names, there are characters with Indian, Persian, Turkish, Hebrew, and other foreign names. This makes *The Thousand and One Nights* a mirror of the Islamic world with people from a myriad of cultures and nations, and of the Islamic civilization's ability to assimilate various strands of other cultures. Another aspect of this is that one finds Christians, Zoroastrians, and pagans converting to Islam but not Muslims being converted to Christianity or any other religion in these tales, for *The Thousand and One Nights* is a reflection of the triumph of Islamic culture.

The Thousand and One Nights is generally considered as a work of collective imagination rather than of one author, but it is an imagination that puts the woman, Scheherazade, in the center of the creative assembly. It is usually divided into two parts. In the Baghdad part, characters, action, and space are dominated by this Islamic metropolis during the peak of the Abbasid period in the days of Haroun al-Rashid. In the Egyptian part, the location and characters reflect the specificity of Egyptian culture as demonstrated in the use of Egyptian names and places, the Coptic names of months, and the manipulation of *jinn* or *genies* through a talisman or magic object, rather than directly as in the Baghdad section. The tales in which jinn act independently are seen to be inspired by Persian or Indian stories. Another group of tales reflects influences of ancient Babylonian and Mesopotamian narratives and of some historic events and characters, particularly those related to Alexander the Great. *The Thousand and One Nights* is also brimming with characters, motifs, and stories that come to it from the Qur'an, or via the Qur'an, such as those of the Hebrew king Solomon.

Most of the stories in our selection are from the Baghdad part, with the partial exception of "The Tale of Sympathy the Learned," which originated in Baghdad and was reshaped in Egypt, demonstrating the convergence of the two parts. Since Baghdad was the metropolis of a large empire, its stories reflect the life of an affluent capital and the myriad of cultural influences on it. The tales of the Caliph and that of the poet Abu-Nuwas demonstrate this. The Egyptian stories provided *The Thousand and One Nights* with different narrative genres, such as tales of thieves, tricksters, and rogues, tales in which people use talismans to control genies and demons, and stories that might be called "bourgeois romances" of love and adultery. Between them, the two parts of *The Thousand and One Nights* embrace an impressive number of narrative genres, from travel narratives and romances to fairy tales, legends, humorous or fantasy tales, didactic stories, anecdotes, and short stories. One can identify every conceivable narrative configuration in *The Thousand and One Nights,* from early narrative kernels to the most developed fiction, from realistic rendering to the fantastic and the absurd. In addition there are 1,420 poems or fragments of poetry; this interweaving of poetry and prose can be compared to that found in *The Tale of Genji* (page 148).

The Thousand and One Nights is often considered the archetypal narrative text, or the mother of all narrative, and this may explain its universal appeal and enduring influence through the ages. There is ample evidence to suggest that medieval Europeans knew it, and the comic tales of Boccaccio and Marguerite de Navarre (Volume C) can well be compared to those of the *Nights*. Like any long collectively composed oral text, it went through many stages of development. The text in the form that we know now in the West owes its existence to the first European translation by a French orientalist, Jean Antoine Galland (1646–1715), who used a manuscript that dates from 1536. The first volume of his *Les Mille et Une Nuits: Contes Arabes Traduits en Français* appeared in 1704, with eleven more volumes thereafter. The work was a great success, thus inspiring its translation into other European languages, including into English in 1792 and German in 1823.

Since its first appearance in Europe, *The Thousand and One Nights* fascinated writers and poets from Coleridge to Robert Louis Stevenson (who wrote a *New Thousand and One Nights* in 1882), to the father of modern magic realism, Jorge Luis Borges. The contemporary American writer John Barth resurrected Scheherazade's sister Dunyazad to deal with the modern dilemmas of passion and of writing in his story "Dunyazadiad" (see Volume F). In the Arab world the impact of this archetypal text is ubiquitous, and no study of modern Arabic narrative is possible without a clear knowledge of its rubrics. The Egyptian Nobel laureate Naguib Mahfouz has endeavored to rewrite certain tales in his *Arabian Nights and Days* (1982), selections of which are included in Volume F. Perspectives: *The Thousand and One Nights* in the Twentieth Century, also in Volume F, gives a range of examples of the enduring fascination of this treasury of stories.

PRONUNCIATIONS:
Dunyazad: DOON-yah-zadh
Shahrazad: SHAH-rah-zahd
Shahrayar: SHAH-ree-yar
Shahzaman: SHAH zah-MANN

from THE THOUSAND AND ONE NIGHTS

Prologue[1]

[THE STORY OF KING SHAHRAYAR AND SHAHRAZAD, HIS VIZIER'S DAUGHTER]

It is related—but God knows and sees best what lies hidden in the old accounts of bygone peoples and times—that long ago, during the time of the Sasanid dynasty,[2] in the peninsulas of India and Indochina, there lived two kings who were brothers. The older brother was named Shahrayar, the younger Shahzaman. The older, Shahrayar, was a towering knight and a daring champion, invincible, energetic, and implacable. His power reached the remotest corners of the land and its people, so that the country was loyal to him, and his subjects obeyed him. Shahrayar himself lived and ruled in India and Indochina, while to his brother he gave the land of Samarkand to rule as king.[3]

Ten years went by, when one day Shahrayar felt a longing for his brother the king, summoned his vizier[4] (who had two daughters, one called Shahrazad, the other Dinarzad) and bade him go to his brother. Having made preparations, the vizier journeyed day and night until he reached Samarkand. When Shahzaman heard of the vizier's arrival, he went out with his retainers to meet him. He dismounted, embraced him, and asked him for news from his older brother, Shahrayar. The vizier replied that he was well, and that he had sent him to request his brother to visit him. Shahzaman complied with his brother's request and proceeded to make preparations for the journey. In the meantime, he had the vizier camp on the outskirts of the city, and took care

---

1. The Prologue is translated by Husain Haddawy, in a lively oral-flavored style, using an Egyptian manuscript that gives the heroine's name as Shahrazad, her sister (usually called Dunyazad) as Dinarzad, and the king as Shahrayar rather than the more usual Shahryar.

2. A dynasty of Persian kings who ruled from c. 226–641 C.E.
3. Samarkand is in central Asia.
4. A caliph's or king's chief administrator.

of his needs. He sent him what he required of food and fodder, slaughtered many sheep in his honor, and provided him with money and supplies, as well as many horses and camels.

For ten full days he prepared himself for the journey; then he appointed a chamberlain in his place, and left the city to spend the night in his tent, near the vizier. At midnight he returned to his palace in the city, to bid his wife good-bye. But when he entered the palace, he found his wife lying in the arms of one of the kitchen boys. When he saw them, the world turned dark before his eyes and, shaking his head, he said to himself, "I am still here, and this is what she has done when I was barely outside the city. How will it be and what will happen behind my back when I go to visit my brother in India? No. Women are not to be trusted." He got exceedingly angry, adding, "By God, I am king and sovereign in Samarkand, yet my wife has betrayed me and has inflicted this on me." As his anger boiled, he drew his sword and struck both his wife and the cook. Then he dragged them by the heels and threw them from the top of the palace to the trench below. He then left the city and going to the vizier ordered that they depart that very hour. The drum was struck, and they set out on their journey, while Shahzaman's heart was on fire because of what his wife had done to him and how she had betrayed him with some cook, some kitchen boy. They journeyed hurriedly, day and night, through deserts and wilds, until they reached the land of King Shahrayar, who had gone out to receive them.

When Shahrayar met them, he embraced his brother, showed him favors, and treated him generously. He offered him quarters in a palace adjoining his own, for King Shahrayar had built two beautiful towering palaces in his garden, one for the guests, the other for the women and members of his household. He gave the guest house to his brother, Shahzaman, after the attendants had gone to scrub it, dry it, furnish it, and open its windows, which overlooked the garden. Thereafter, Shahzaman would spend the whole day at his brother's, return at night to sleep at the palace, then go back to his brother the next morning. But whenever he found himself alone and thought of his ordeal with his wife, he would sigh deeply, then stifle his grief, and say, "Alas, that this great misfortune should have happened to one in my position!" Then he would fret with anxiety, his spirit would sag, and he would say, "None has seen what I have seen." In his depression, he ate less and less, grew pale, and his health deteriorated. He neglected everything, wasted away, and looked ill.

When King Shahrayar looked at his brother and saw how day after day he lost weight and grew thin, pale, ashen, and sickly, he thought that this was because of his expatriation and homesickness for his country and his family, and he said to himself, "My brother is not happy here. I should prepare a goodly gift for him and send him home." For a month he gathered gifts for his brother; then he invited him to see him and said, "Brother, I would like you to know that I intend to go hunting and pursue the roaming deer, for ten days. Then I shall return to prepare you for your journey home. Would you like to go hunting with me?" Shahzaman replied, "Brother, I feel distracted and depressed. Leave me here and go with God's blessing and help." When Shahrayar heard his brother, he thought that his dejection was because of his homesickness for his country. Not wishing to coerce him, he left him behind, and set out with his retainers and men. When they entered the wilderness, he deployed his men in a circle to begin trapping and hunting.

After his brother's departure, Shahzaman stayed in the palace and, from the window overlooking the garden, watched the birds and trees as he thought of his wife and what she had done to him, and sighed in sorrow. While he agonized over his misfortune, gazing at the heavens and turning a distracted eye on the garden, the private gate of his brother's palace opened, and there emerged, strutting like a dark-eyed deer, the lady, his brother's wife, with twenty slave-girls, ten white and ten black. While Shahzaman looked at them, without being seen, they continued to walk until they stopped below his window, without looking in his direction, thinking that he had gone to the hunt with his brother. Then they sat down, took off their clothes, and suddenly there were ten slave-girls and ten black slaves dressed in the same clothes as the girls. Then the ten black slaves mounted the ten girls, while the lady called, "Mas'ud, Mas'ud!" and a black slave jumped from the tree to the ground, rushed to her, and, raising her legs, went between her thighs and made love to her. Mas'ud topped the lady, while the ten slaves topped the ten girls, and they carried on till noon. When they were done with their business, they got up and washed themselves. Then the ten slaves put on the same clothes again, mingled with the girls, and once more there appeared to be twenty slave-girls. Mas'ud himself jumped over the garden wall and disappeared, while the slave-girls and the lady sauntered to the private gate, went in and, locking the gate behind them, went their way.

All of this happened under King Shahzaman's eyes. When he saw this spectacle of the wife and the women of his brother the great king—how ten slaves put on women's clothes and slept with his brother's paramours and concubines and what Mas'ud did with his brother's wife, in his very palace—and pondered over this calamity and great misfortune, his care and sorrow left him and he said to himself, "This is our common lot. Even though my brother is king and master of the whole world, he cannot protect what is his, his wife and his concubines, and suffers misfortune in his very home. What happened to me is little by comparison. I used to think that I was the only one who has suffered, but from what I have seen, everyone suffers. By God, my misfortune is lighter than that of my brother." He kept marveling and blaming life, whose trials none can escape, and he began to find consolation in his own affliction and forget his grief. When supper came, he ate and drank with relish and zest and, feeling better, kept eating and drinking, enjoying himself and feeling happy. He thought to himself, "I am no longer alone in my misery; I am well."

For ten days, he continued to enjoy his food and drink, and when his brother, King Shahrayar came back from the hunt, he met him happily, treated him attentively, and greeted him cheerfully. His brother, King Shahrayar, who had missed him, said, "By God, brother, I missed you on this trip and wished you were with me." Shahzaman thanked him and sat down to carouse with him, and when night fell, and food was brought before them, the two ate and drank, and again Shahzaman ate and drank with zest. As time went by, he continued to eat and drink with appetite, and became lighthearted and carefree. His face regained color and became ruddy, and his body gained weight, as his blood circulated and he regained his energy; he was himself again, or even better. King Shahrayar noticed his brother's condition, how he used to be and how he had improved, but kept it to himself until he took him aside one day and said, "My brother Shahzaman, I would like you to do something for me, to satisfy a wish, to answer a question truthfully." Shahzaman asked, "What is it, brother?" He replied, "When you first came to stay with me, I noticed that you kept losing weight, day after day, until your looks changed, your health deteriorated, and your energy sagged. As you continued like this, I thought that what ailed you was your homesickness for your family and your country, but even though I kept noticing that you were wasting away and looking ill, I refrained from questioning you and hid my feelings from you. Then I went hunting, and when I came back, I found that you had recovered and had regained your health. Now I want you to tell me everything and to explain the cause of your deterioration and the cause of your subsequent recovery, without hiding anything from me." When Shahzaman heard what King Shahrayar said, he bowed his head, then said, "As for the cause of my recovery, that I cannot tell you, and I wish that you would excuse me from telling you." The king was greatly astonished at his brother's reply and, burning with curiosity, said, "You must tell me. For now, at least, explain the first cause."

Then Shahzaman related to his brother what happened to him with his own wife, on the night of his departure, from beginning to end, and concluded, "Thus all the while I was with you, great King, whenever I thought of the event and the misfortune that had befallen me, I felt troubled, careworn, and unhappy, and my health deteriorated. This then is the cause." Then he grew silent. When King Shahrayar heard his brother's explanation, he shook his head, greatly amazed at the deceit of women, and prayed to God to protect him from their wickedness, saying, "Brother, you were fortunate in killing your wife and her lover, who gave you good reason to feel troubled, careworn, and ill. In my opinion, what happened to you has never happened to anyone else. By God, had I been in your place, I would have killed at least a hundred or even a thousand women. I would have been furious; I would have gone mad. Now praise be to God who has delivered you from sorrow and distress. But tell me what has caused you to forget your sorrow and regain your health?" Shahzaman replied, "King, I wish that for God's sake you would excuse me from telling you." Shahrayar said, "You must." Shahzaman replied, "I fear that you will feel even more troubled and careworn than I." Shahrayar asked, "How could that be, brother? I insist on hearing your explanation."

Shahzaman then told him about what he had seen from the palace window and the calamity in his very home—how ten slaves, dressed like women, were sleeping with his women and concubines, day and night. He told him everything from beginning to end (but there is no point in repeating that). Then he concluded, "When I saw your own misfortune, I felt better—and said to myself, 'My brother is king of the world, yet such a misfortune has happened to him, and in his very home.' As a result I forgot my care and sorrow, relaxed, and began to eat and drink. This is the cause of my cheer and good spirits."

When King Shahrayar heard what his brother said and found out what had happened to him, he was furious and his blood boiled. He said, "Brother, I can't believe what you say unless I see it with my own eyes." When Shahzaman saw that his brother was in a rage, he said to him, "If you do not believe me, unless you see your misfortune with your own eyes, announce that you plan to go hunting. Then you and I shall set out with your troops, and when we get outside the city, we shall leave our tents and camp with the men behind, enter the city secretly, and go together to your palace. Then the next morning you can see with your own eyes."

King Shahrayar realized that his brother had a good plan and ordered his army to prepare for the trip. He spent the night with his brother, and when God's morning broke, the two rode out of the city with their army, preceded by the camp attendants, who had gone to drive the poles and pitch the tents where the king and his army were to camp. At nightfall King Shahrayar summoned his chief chamberlain and bade him take his place. He entrusted him with the army and ordered that for three days no one was to enter the city. Then he and his brother disguised themselves and entered the city in the dark. They went directly to the palace where Shahzaman resided and slept there till the morning. When they awoke, they sat at the palace window, watching the garden and chatting, until the light broke, the day dawned, and the sun rose. As they watched, the private gate opened, and there emerged as usual the wife of King Shahrayar, walking among twenty slave-girls. They made their way under the trees until they stood below the palace window where the two kings sat. Then they took off their women's clothes, and suddenly there were ten slaves, who mounted the ten girls and made love to them. As for the lady, she called, "Mas'ud, Mas'ud," and a black slave jumped from the tree to the ground, came to her, and said, "What do you want, you slut? Here is Sa'ad al-Din Mas'ud." She laughed and fell on her back, while the slave mounted her and like the others did his business with her. Then the black slaves got up, washed themselves, and, putting on the same clothes, mingled with the girls. Then they walked away, entered the palace, and locked the gate behind them. As for Mas'ud, he jumped over the fence to the road and went on his way.

When King Shahrayar saw the spectacle of his wife and the slave-girls, he went out of his mind, and when he and his brother came down from upstairs, he said, "No one is safe in this world. Such doings are going on in my kingdom, and in my very palace. Perish the world and perish life! This is a great calamity, indeed." Then he turned to his brother and asked, "Would you like to follow me in what I shall do?" Shahzaman answered, "Yes. I will." Shahrayar said, "Let us leave our royal state and roam the world for the love of the Supreme Lord. If we should find one whose misfortune is greater than ours, we shall return. Otherwise, we shall continue to journey through the land, without need for the trappings of royalty." Shahzaman replied, "This is an excellent idea. I shall follow you."

Then they left by the private gate, took a side road, and departed, journeying till nightfall. They slept over their sorrows, and in the morning resumed their day journey until they came to a meadow by the seashore. While they sat in the meadow amid the thick plants and trees, discussing their misfortunes and the recent events, they suddenly heard a shout and a great cry coming from the middle of the sea. They trembled with fear, thinking that the sky had fallen on the earth. Then the sea parted, and there emerged a black pillar that, as it swayed forward, got taller and taller, until it touched the clouds. Shahrayar and Shahzaman were petrified; then they ran in terror and, climbing a very tall tree, sat hiding in its foliage. When they looked again, they saw that the black pillar was cleaving the sea, wading in the water toward the green meadow, until it touched the shore. When they looked again, they saw that it was a black demon, carrying on his head a large glass chest with four steel locks. He came out, walked into the meadow, and where should he stop but under the very tree where the two kings were hiding. The demon sat down and placed the glass chest on the ground. He took out four keys and, opening the locks of the chest, pulled out a full-grown woman. She had a beautiful figure, and a face like the full moon, and a lovely smile. He took her out, laid her under the tree, and looked at her, saying, "Mistress of all noble women, you whom I carried away on your wedding night, I would like to sleep a little." Then he placed his head on the young woman's lap, stretched his legs to the sea, sank into sleep, and began to snore.

Meanwhile, the woman looked up at the tree and, turning her head by chance, saw King Shahrayar and King Shahzaman. She lifted the demon's head from her lap and placed it on the ground. Then she came and stood under the tree and motioned to them with her hand, as if to say, "Come down slowly to me." When they realized that she had seen them, they were frightened, and they begged her and implored her, in the name of the Creator of the heavens, to excuse them from climbing down. She replied, "You must come down to me." They motioned to her, saying, "This sleeping demon is the enemy of mankind. For God's sake, leave us alone." She replied, "You must come down, and if you don't, I shall wake the demon and have him kill you." She kept gesturing and pressing, until they climbed down very slowly and stood before her. Then she lay on her back, raised her legs, and said, "Make love to me and satisfy my need, or else I shall wake the demon, and he will kill you." They replied, "For God's sake, mistress, don't do this to us, for at this moment we feel nothing but dismay and fear of this demon. Please, excuse us." She replied, "You must," and insisted, swearing, "By God who created the heavens, if you don't do it, I shall wake my husband the demon and ask him to kill you and throw you into the sea." As she persisted, they could no longer resist and they made love to her, first the older brother, then the younger. When they were done and withdrew from her, she said to them, "Give me your rings," and, pulling out from the folds of her dress a small purse, opened it, and shook out ninety-eight rings of different fashions and colors. Then she asked them, "Do you know what these rings are?" They answered, "No." She said, "All the owners of these rings slept with me, for whenever one of them made love to me, I took a ring from him. Since you two have slept with me, give me your rings, so that I may add them to the rest, and make a full hundred. A hundred men have known me under the very horns of this filthy, monstrous cuckold, who has imprisoned me in this chest, locked it with four locks, and kept me in the middle of this raging, roaring sea. He has guarded me and tried to keep me pure and chaste, not realizing that nothing can prevent or alter what is predestined and that when a woman desires something, no one can stop her." When Shahrayar and Shahzaman heard what the young woman said, they were greatly amazed, danced with joy, and said, "O God, O God! There is no power and no strength, save in God the Almighty, the Magnificent. Great is women's cunning." Then each of them took off his ring and handed it to her. She took them and put them with the rest in the purse. Then sitting again by the demon, she lifted his head, placed it back on her lap, and motioned to them, "Go on your way, or else I shall wake him."

They turned their backs and took to the road. Then Shahrayar turned to his brother and said, "My brother Shahzaman, look at this sorry plight. By God, it is worse than ours. This is no less than a demon who has carried a young woman away on her wedding night, imprisoned her in a glass chest, locked her up with four locks, and kept her in the middle of the sea, thinking that he could guard her from what God had foreordained, and you saw how she has managed to sleep with ninety-eight men, and added the two of us to make a hundred. Brother, let us go back to our kingdoms and our cities, never to marry a woman again. As for myself, I shall show you what I will do."

Then the two brothers headed home and journeyed till nightfall. On the morning of the third day, they reached their camp and men, entered their tent, and sat on their thrones. The chamberlains, deputies, princes, and viziers came to attend King Shahrayar, while he gave orders and bestowed robes of honor, as well as other gifts. Then at his command everyone returned to the city, and he went to his own palace and ordered his chief vizier, the father of the two girls Shahrazad and Dinarzad, who will be mentioned below, and said to him, "Take that wife of mine and put her to death." Then Shahrayar went to her himself, bound her, and handed her over to the vizier, who took her out and put her to death. Then King Shahrayar grabbed his sword, brandished it, and, entering the palace chambers, killed every one of his slave-girls and replaced them with others. He then swore to marry for one night only and kill the woman the next morning, in order to save himself from the wickedness and cunning of women, saying, "There is not a single chaste woman anywhere on the entire face of the earth." Shortly thereafter he provided his brother Shahzaman with supplies for his journey and sent him back to his own country with gifts, rarities, and money. The brother bade him good-bye and set out for home.

Shahrayar sat on his throne and ordered his vizier, the father of the two girls, to find him a wife from among the princes' daughters. The vizier found him one, and he slept with her and was done with her, and the next morning he ordered the vizier to put her to death. That very night he took one of his army officers' daughters, slept with her, and the next morning ordered the vizier to put her to death. The vizier, who could not disobey him, put her to death. The third night he took one of the merchants' daughters, slept with her till the morning, then ordered his vizier to put her to death, and the vizier did so. It became King Shahrayar's custom to take every night the daughter of a merchant or a commoner, spend the night with her, then have her put to death the next morning. He continued to do this until all the girls perished, their mothers mourned, and there arose a clamor among the fathers and mothers, who called the plague upon his head, complained to the Creator of the heavens, and called for help on Him who hears and answers prayers.

Now, as mentioned earlier, the vizier, who put the girls to death, had an older daughter called Shahrazad and a younger one called Dinarzad. The older daughter, Shahrazad, had read the books of literature, philosophy, and medicine. She knew poetry by heart, had studied historical reports, and was acquainted with the sayings of men and the maxims of sages and kings. She was intelligent, knowledgeable, wise, and refined. She had read and learned. One day she said to her father, "Father, I will tell you what is in my mind." He asked, "What is it?" She answered, "I would like you to marry me to King Shahrayar, so that I may either succeed in saving the people or perish and die like the rest." When the vizier heard what his daughter Shahrazad said, he got angry and said to her, "Foolish one, don't you know that King Shahrayar has sworn to spend but one night with a girl and have her put to death the next morning? If I give you to him, he will sleep with you for one night and will ask me to put you to death the next morning, and I shall have to do it, since I cannot disobey him." She said, "Father, you must give me to him, even if he kills me." He asked, "What has possessed you that you wish to imperil yourself?" She replied, "Father, you must give me to him. This is absolute and final." Her father the vizier became furious and said to her, "Daughter, 'He who misbehaves, ends up in trouble,' and 'He who considers not the end, the world is not his friend.' As the popular saying goes, 'I would be sitting pretty, but for my curiosity.' I am afraid that what happened to the donkey and the ox with the merchant will happen to you." She asked, "Father, what happened to the donkey, the ox, and the merchant?" He said:

[THE TALE OF THE OX AND THE DONKEY]

There was a prosperous and wealthy merchant who lived in the countryside and labored on a farm. He owned many camels and herds of cattle and employed many men, and he had a wife and many grown-up as well as little children. This merchant was taught the language of the beasts,[5] on condition that if he revealed his secret to anyone, he would die; therefore, even though he knew the language of every kind of animal, he did not let anyone know, for fear of death. One day, as he sat, with his wife beside him and his children playing before him, he glanced at an ox and a donkey he

---

5. This ability has precedence in the Qur'an, which records that God taught Solomon the language of the beasts.

kept at the farmhouse, tied to adjacent troughs, and heard the ox say to the donkey, "Watchful one, I hope that you are enjoying the comfort and the service you are getting. Your ground is swept and watered, and they serve you, feed you sifted barley, and offer you clear, cool water to drink. I, on the contrary, am taken out to plow in the middle of the night. They clamp on my neck something they call yoke and plow, push me all day under the whip to plow the field, and drive me beyond my endurance until my sides are lacerated, and my neck is flayed. They work me from nighttime to nighttime, take me back in the dark, offer me beans soiled with mud and hay mixed with chaff, and let me spend the night lying in urine and dung. Meanwhile you rest on well-swept, watered, and smoothed ground, with a clean trough full of hay. You stand in comfort, save for the rare occasion when our master the merchant rides you to do a brief errand and returns. You are comfortable, while I am weary; you sleep, while I keep awake."

When the ox finished, the donkey turned to him and said, "Green-horn, they were right in calling you ox, for you ox harbor no deceit, malice, or meanness. Being sincere, you exert and exhaust yourself to comfort others. Have you not heard the saying 'Out of bad luck, they hastened on the road'? You go into the field from early morning to endure your torture at the plow to the point of exhaustion. When the plowman takes you back and ties you to the trough, you go on butting and beating with your horns, kicking with your hoofs, and bellowing for the beans, until they toss them to you; then you begin to eat. Next time, when they bring them to you, don't eat or even touch them, but smell them, then draw back and lie down on the hay and straw. If you do this, life will be better and kinder to you, and you will find relief."

As the ox listened, he was sure that the donkey had given him good advice. He thanked him, commended him to God, and invoked His blessing on him, and said, "May you stay safe from harm, watchful one." All of this conversation took place, daughter, while the merchant listened and understood. On the following day, the plowman came to the merchant's house and, taking the ox, placed the yoke upon his neck and worked him at the plow, but the ox lagged behind. The plowman hit him, but following the donkey's advice, the ox, dissembling, fell on his belly, and the plowman hit him again. Thus the ox kept getting up and falling until nightfall, when the plowman took him home and tied him to the trough. But this time the ox did not bellow or kick the ground with his hoofs. Instead, he withdrew, away from the trough. Astonished, the plowman brought him his beans and fodder, but the ox only smelled the fodder and pulled back and lay down at a distance with the hay and straw, complaining till the morning. When the plowman arrived, he found the trough as he had left it, full of beans and fodder, and saw the ox lying on his back, hardly breathing, his belly puffed, and his legs raised in the air. The plowman felt sorry for him and said to himself, "By God, he did seem weak and unable to work." Then he went to the merchant and said, "Master, last night, the ox refused to eat or touch his fodder."

The merchant, who knew what was going on, said to the plowman, "Go to the wily donkey, put him to the plow, and work him hard until he finishes the ox's task." The plowman left, took the donkey, and placed the yoke upon his neck. Then he took him out to the field and drove him with blows until he finished the ox's work, all the while driving him with blows and beating him until his sides were lacerated and his neck was flayed. At nightfall he took him home, barely able to drag his legs under his tired body and his drooping ears. Meanwhile the ox spent his day resting. He ate all his food, drank his water, and lay quietly, chewing his cud in comfort. All day long he kept praising the donkey's advice and invoking God's blessing on him. When the donkey came back at night, the ox stood up to greet him, saying, "Good evening, watchful one! You have done me a favor beyond description, for I have been sitting in comfort. God bless you for my sake." Seething with anger, the donkey did not reply, but said to himself, "All this happened to me because of my miscalculation. 'I would be sitting pretty, but for my curiosity.' If I don't find a way to return this ox to his former situation, I will perish." Then he went to his trough and lay down, while the ox continued to chew his cud and invoke God's blessing on him.

"You, my daughter, will likewise perish because of your miscalculation. Desist, sit quietly, and don't expose yourself to peril. I advise you out of compassion for you." She replied, "Father, I must go to the king, and you must give me to him." He said, "Don't do it." She insisted, "I must." He replied, "If you don't desist, I will do to you what the merchant did to his wife." She asked, "Father, what did the merchant do to his wife?" He said:

[THE TALE OF THE MERCHANT AND HIS WIFE]

After what had happened to the donkey and the ox, the merchant and his wife went out in the moonlight to the stable, and he heard the donkey ask the ox in his own language, "Listen, ox, what are you going to do tomorrow morning, and what will you do when the plowman brings you your fodder?" The ox replied, "What shall I do but follow your advice and stick to it? If he brings me my fodder, I will pretend to be ill, lie down, and puff my belly." The donkey shook his head, and said, "Don't do it. Do you know what I heard our master the merchant say to the plowman?" The ox asked, "What?" The donkey replied, "He said that if the ox failed to get up and eat his fodder, he would call the butcher to slaughter him and skin him and would distribute the meat for alms and use the skin for a mat. I am afraid for you, but good advice is a matter of faith; therefore, if he brings you your fodder, eat it and look alert lest they cut your throat and skin you." The ox farted and bellowed.

The merchant got up and laughed loudly at the conversation between the donkey and the ox, and his wife asked him, "What are you laughing at? Are you making fun of me?" He said, "No." She said, "Tell me what made you laugh." He replied, "I cannot tell you. I am afraid to disclose the secret conversation of the animals." She asked, "And what prevents you from telling me?" He answered, "The fear of death." His wife said, "By God, you are lying. This is nothing but an excuse. I swear by God, the Lord of heaven, that if you don't tell me and explain the cause of your laughter, I will leave you. You must tell me." Then she went back to the house crying, and she continued to cry till the morning. The merchant said, "Damn it! Tell me why you are crying. Ask for God's forgiveness, and stop questioning and leave me in peace." She said, "I insist and will not desist." Amazed at her, he replied, "You insist! If I tell you what the donkey said to the ox, which made me laugh, I shall die." She said, "Yes, I insist, even if you have to die." He replied, "Then call your family," and she called their two daughters, her parents and relatives, and some neighbors. The merchant told them that he was about to die, and everyone, young and old, his children, the farmhands, and the servants began to cry until the house became a place of mourning. Then he summoned legal witnesses, wrote a will, leaving his wife and children their due portions, freed his slave-girls, and bid his family good-bye, while everybody, even the witnesses, wept. Then the wife's parents approached her and said, "Desist, for if your husband had not known for certain that he would die if he revealed his secret, he wouldn't have gone through all this." She replied, "I will not change my mind," and everybody cried and prepared to mourn his death.

Well, my daughter Shahrazad, it happened that the farmer kept fifty hens and a rooster at home, and while he felt sad to depart this world and leave his children and relatives behind, pondering and about to reveal and utter his secret, he overheard a dog of his say something in dog language to the rooster, who, beating and clapping his wings, had jumped on a hen and, finishing with her, jumped down and jumped on another. The merchant heard and understood what the dog said in his own language to the rooster, "Shameless, no-good rooster. Aren't you ashamed to do such a thing on a day like this?" The rooster asked, "What is special about this day?" The dog replied, "Don't you know that our master and friend is in mourning today? His wife is demanding that he disclose his secret, and when he discloses it, he will surely die. He is in this predicament, about to interpret to her the language of the animals, and all of us are mourning for him, while you clap your wings and get off one hen and jump on another. Aren't you ashamed?" The merchant heard the rooster reply, "You fool, you lunatic! Our master and friend claims to be wise, but he is foolish, for he has only one wife, yet he does not know how to manage her." The dog asked, "What should he do with her?"

The rooster replied, "He should take an oak branch, push her into a room, lock the door, and fall on her with the stick, beating her mercilessly until he breaks her arms and legs and she cries out, 'I no longer want you to tell me or explain anything.' He should go on beating her until he cures her for life, and she will never oppose him in anything. If he does this, he will live, and live in peace, and there will be no more grief, but he does not know how to manage." Well, my daughter Shahrazad, when the merchant heard the conversation between the dog and the rooster, he jumped up and, taking an oak branch, pushed his wife into a room, got in with her, and locked the door. Then he began to beat her mercilessly on her chest and shoulders and kept beating her until she cried for mercy, screaming, "No, no, I don't want to know anything. Leave me alone, leave me alone. I don't want to know anything," until he got tired of hitting her and opened the door. The wife emerged penitent, the husband learned good management, and everybody was happy, and the mourning turned into a celebration.

"If you don't relent, I shall do to you what the merchant did to his wife." She said, "Such tales don't deter me from my request. If you wish, I can tell you many such tales. In the end, if you don't take me to King Shahrayar, I shall go to him by myself behind your back and tell him that you have refused to give me to one like him and that you have begrudged your master one like me." The vizier asked, "Must you really do this?" She replied, "Yes, I must."

Tired and exhausted, the vizier went to King Shahrayar and, kissing the ground before him, told him about his daughter, adding that he would give her to him that very night. The king was astonished and said to him, "Vizier, how is it that you have found it possible to give me your daughter, knowing that I will, by God, the Creator of heaven, ask you to put her to death the next morning and that if you refuse, I will have you put to death too?" He replied, "My King and Lord, I have told her everything and explained all this to her, but she refuses and insists on being with you tonight." The king was delighted and said, "Go to her, prepare her, and bring her to me early in the evening."

The vizier went down, repeated the king's message to his daughter, and said, "May God not deprive me of you." She was very happy and, after preparing herself and packing what she needed, went to her younger sister, Dinarzad, and said, "Sister, listen well to what I am telling you. When I go to the king, I will send for you, and when you come and see that the king has finished with me, say, 'Sister, if you are not sleepy, tell us a story.' Then I will begin to tell a story, and it will cause the king to stop his practice, save myself, and deliver the people." Dinarzad replied, "Very well."

At nightfall the vizier took Shahrazad and went with her to the great King Shahrayar. But when Shahrayar took her to bed and began to fondle her, she wept, and when he asked her, "Why are you crying?" she replied, "I have a sister, and I wish to bid her goodbye before daybreak." Then the king sent for the sister, who came and went to sleep under the bed. When the night wore on, she woke up and waited until the king had satisfied himself with her sister Shahrazad and they were by now all fully awake. Then Dinarzad cleared her throat and said, "Sister, if you are not sleepy, tell us one of your lovely little tales to while away the night, before I bid you goodbye at daybreak, for I don't know what will happen to you tomorrow." Shahrazad turned to King Shahrayar and said, "May I have your permission to tell a story?" He replied, "Yes," and Shahrazad was very happy and said, "Listen."

from The Tale of the Porter and the Young Girls[1]

There was once a young man in the city of Baghdad, who was by faith a bachelor and by trade a porter.

One day, as he was leaning idly against his basket in the market-place, a woman, wearing a full veil of Mosul silk, tasselled with gold and turned with rare brocade, stopped before him and raised the veil a little from her face. Above it there showed dark eyes with long lashes of silk and lids to set a man dreaming. Her body was slight, her feet were very small, and clear perfection shone about her. She said, and oh, but her voice was sweet: "Take up your basket, porter, and follow me." Hardly believing that so exquisite words could have been said to him, the porter took up his basket and followed the girl, who stopped eventually before the door of a house. She knocked at the door and immediately a Christian opened to her, who gave her, in exchange for a dīnār, a great measure of olive-clear wine which she put into the basket,[2] saying to the porter: "Lift and follow me." "By Allah, this is a day of days!" exclaimed the porter, as he lifted his basket and followed the girl. Arrived at the stall of a fruiterer, she bought Syrian apples, Osmāni quinces, peaches from Uman, jasmine of Aleppo, Damascene nenuphars, cucumbers from the Nile, limes from Egypt, Sultāni citrons, myrtle berries, flowers of henna, blood-red anemones, violets, pomegranate bloom, and the narcissus. All these she put into the porter's basket, and said: "Lift!"; so he lifted and followed her until she came to a butcher's stall. Here she said: "Cut me ten pounds of mutton." So they cut her ten pounds which she wrapped in banana leaves and put into the basket, and said: "Lift!" He lifted and followed her to an almond seller, from whom she bought every kind of almond that there is. Then the porter followed her to a sweetmeat seller from whom she bought a great platter which she covered with things from the stall: open-work sugar tarts with butter, velvet pastries perfumed with musk and stuffed deliciously, sābūnīyah biscuits, small cakes, lime tarts,

---

1. This tale and the remaining selections are translated by Powys Mathers from the classic French translation by J. C. Mardrus. Whereas Haddawy's translation of the Prologue is based on a lean early manuscript, the Mardrus/Mathers version reflects the ongoing, expansive tradition, which added in poetry and many tales not found in the earlier manuscripts. From this point onward, Shahrazad's sister's name is found in its best-known form, Dunyazad. Shahrazad tells the story of the Porter beginning on the ninth night, after a series of shorter stories (always leading onward at daybreak) has fascinated the king and enticed him to postpone her murder night by night.

2. Since wine is forbidden in Islam, only Christians are licensed to trade in it.

honey-tasting jam, those sweets called mushabbak, little souffléd patties called lukaimāt al-Kādī,[3] and those others named combs of Zainab which are made with butter and mingled with milk and honey. All these pleasant things she put upon the platter and then placed the platter in the basket. "If you had told me, I would have brought a mule," said the porter. Smiling at his jest, she stopped at the stall of a distiller of perfumes and bought ten sorts of waters, rose water, water of orange flowers, willow flower, violet and other kinds; she bought also a spray of rose-musk-scented water, grains of male incense, aloe wood, ambergris and musk; finally she selected candles of Alexandrian wax and put all in the basket, saying: "Lift and follow!" Obediently the porter took up his basket and followed the young lady until she came to a splendid palace, having a great court set in an inner garden; it was tall, magnificent and four-square, and the door had two leaves of ebony, plated with plates of red gold.

The young girl rapped gently upon the door and it flew wide open. Then the porter looked at her who had opened the door and saw that she was a child having a slim and gracious body, the very model of all a young girl should be, not only for her round and prominent breasts, not only for her beauty and her air of breeding, but also for the perfection of her waist and of her carriage. Her brow was as white as the first ray fallen from the new moon, her eyes were the eyes of a gazelle, and the brows above them were as the crescent moons of Ramadān.[4] Her cheeks were anemones, her mouth the scarlet seal of Sulaimān, her face pale as the full moon when she first rises above the grasses, her breasts twin passion-fruit. As for her young white pliant belly, it lay hid beneath her robe like some precious love letter in a silken case. Seeing her, the porter felt that he was losing his wits and nearly let the basket slip from his shoulders. "As Allah lives, this is the most blessed day of all my life!" he said. Standing within, the young portress said to her sister the cateress and also to the porter: "Enter, and be your welcome as great as it is good!"

They went in and came at last to an ample hall giving on the central court, hung over with silk brocade and gold brocade, and full of fair gold-crusted furniture. There were vases and carved seats, curtains and close-shut presses all about it, and in the middle a marble couch, inlaid with pearl and diamond, covered with a red satin quilt. On the bed lay a third girl who exceeded all the marvel that a girl can be. Her eyes were Babylonian, for all witchcraft has its seat in Babylon. Her body was slim as the letter alif,[5] her face so fair as to confuse the bright sun. She was as a star among the shining of the stars, a true Arabian woman, as the poet says:

> Who sings your slender body is a reed
> His simile a little misses,
> Reeds must be naked to be fair indeed
> While your sweet garments are but added blisses.

> Who sings your body is a slender bough
> Also commits a kindred folly,
> Boughs to be fair must have green leaves enow
> And you, my white one, must be naked wholly.

The young girl got up from the bed, moved a few paces into the middle of the hall until she was near her two sisters and then said to them: "Why are you standing still like

---

3. Mushabbak and lukaimāt al-Kādī are two types of doughnut-like sweets soaked in honey.
4. The new moons that mark the beginning and end of the

holy month of Ramadan, a time of fasting and atonement.
5. The first letter of the Arabic alphabet, which looks like the English letter *l*.

this? Take the basket from the porter's head." Then the cateress came in front of the
porter, the portress came behind him and, helped by their third sister, they relieved
him of his burden. When they had taken everything out of the basket, they arranged
all neatly and gave two dīnārs to the porter, saying: "Turn and be gone, O porter!" But
he looked at the young girls, admiring the perfection of their beauty, and thought that
he had never seen the like. He noticed that there was no man with them and, marvelling at all the drinks, fruits, perfumed flowers, and other good things, had no desire to
go away.

The eldest of the girls said: "Why do you not go? Do you find your payment too
little?" and then, turning to her sister the cateress: "Give him a third dīnār." But the
porter said: "As Allah lives, fair ladies, my ordinary pay is but two half dīnārs; you
have paid me well enough and yet all my heart and the inner parts of my soul are troubled about you. I cannot help asking myself what this life of yours is, that you live
alone and have no man here to bear you human company. Do you not know that a
minaret is of no value unless it be one of the four minarets of a mosque? You are but
three, my ladies, you need a fourth. Women cannot be truly happy without men. The
poet has said: 'There can be no harmony save with four joined instruments: the lute,
the harp, the cithern and flagiolet.' Now you are only three, my ladies; you need a flagiolet, a fourth instrument, a man of discretion, full both of sentiment and intellect, a
gifted artist with sealed lips!"

"But, porter," said the young girls, "do you not know that we are virgins and so
are fearful of confiding ourselves to the indiscretion of a man? We also have read the
poets, and they say: 'Confide in none; a secret told is a secret spoiled.'"

Hearing this, the porter cried: "I swear on your dear lives, my ladies, that I am a
man sure, faithful and discreet, one who has studied the annals and read books. I
speak of only pleasing things and am carefully silent about all the rest. I act always
according to the saying of the poet:

> I know the duties of high courtesy,
> Your dearest secrets shall be safe with me;
> I'll shut them in a little inner room
> And seal the lock and throw away the key.

Their hearts were much moved towards the porter when they heard his verses and all
the rhymes and rhythms he recited, and in jest they said: "You must know that we
have spent a great sum of money on this place. Have you the silver to pay us back?
For we would not ask you to sit with us unless you paid the reckoning. We take it you
desire to stay here, to become our companion in the wine and, above all, to keep us
waking all the night until the shadow of the dawn fall on our faces." "Love without
gold is a poor make-weight in the scales," added the eldest of the girls, the mistress of
the house; and the portress said: "If you have nothing, get you gone with nothing!"
But here the cateress interrupted, saying: "Let us leave this joke, my sisters. As Allah
lives, this boy has not spoiled our day and another might not have been so patient. I
myself will undertake to pay for him."

At this the porter rejoiced with all his heart and said to the cateress: "By Allah, I
owe this wonderful bargain all to you!" "Stay with us, then, brave porter," she replied,
"and rest assured that you shall be the darling of our eyes." So saying, she rose and,
after clasping his waist, began to arrange the flasks, to clarify and pour the wine, and
to set places for the feast near a pool of water in the center of the hall. She brought
in everything of which they might have need, handed the wine, and saw that all

were seated. The porter with these girls on every hand thought that he was dreaming in his sleep.

Soon the cateress took the wine flagon and filled a cup from which each drank three times. Then she filled it afresh and passed it to her sisters and then to the porter, who drank and said these lines:

> In this red wine is liveliness
> And strength and well-being,
> In this red wine is all caress
> And every wanton thing;
> Drink deep and you will find, I trust,
> In this red wine is very lust.

On this he kissed the hands of the three girls and drained the cup. Then he went up to the mistress of the house, saying: "Mistress, I am your slave, your thing, your chattel!" and he recited, in her honour, this stanza of a certain poet:

> I stand most like a slave
> Outside your door,
> Must I an entrance crave
> In vain for ever more?
> There is one gift I have—
> I stand most like a slave.

Then, "Drink, my friend," said she, "and may the wine be sweet and wholesome in its going down: may it give you strength to set out upon that road where lies all bodily well-being." The porter took the cup, kissed the girl's hand and, in a sweetly-modulated voice, sang very low these verses of the poet:

> I gave my love a wine
> Splendidly red as are her cheeks, I said.
> Then she: "I cannot drink these cheeks of mine."
> "Ah, let me speak," I said,
> "Thou can'st not drink those cheeks of thine;
> Then drink these tears and blood of mine!"

Again the young girl took the cup to the porter and, after holding it to his lips, sat down beside her sister. Soon they began to dance and sing and to play with the wonderful petals, the porter all the time taking them in his arms and kissing them, while one said saucy things to him, another drew him to her, and the third beat him with flowers. They went on drinking until the grape sat throned above their reason, and, when her reign was fully established, the portress rose and stripped off all her clothes until she was naked. Jumping into the water of the fountain, she began to play with it, taking it in her mouth and blowing it noisily at the porter, washing all her body, and letting it run between her childish thighs. At length she got out of the fountain, threw herself on the porter's lap, stretched out on her back and, pointing to the thing which was between her thighs, said:

"My darling, do you know the name of that?" "Aha," answered the porter, "usually that is called the house of compassion." Then she cried: "Yū, yū! Are you not ashamed?" and taking him by the neck she began to slap him. "No, no!" he cried. "It is called the thing." But she shook her head, and "Then it is your behind piece," said the porter. Again she shook her head, and "It is your hornet," said he. At these words she began to slap him so hard that she abraded his skin. "You tell me its name!" he shouted, and she told him: "Basil of the bridges." "At last," cried the porter. "Praise be to Allah for your safety, O my basil of the bridges!"

After that, they let the cup go round and round; and the second girl, taking off her clothes, jumped into the basin. There she did as her sister had done and then, getting out, threw herself on to the porter's lap. Pointing to her thighs and the thing between them, she said: "Light of my life, what is the name of that?" "Your crack," he answered. "O listen to his naughty word!" she cried, and slapped him so hard that the hall echoed with the sound. "Then it is basil of the bridges," he hazarded, but she again cried that it was not and went on slapping his neck. "Well, what is its name?" he yelled, and she answered: "The husked sesame."

Now the third girl, in her turn, got up, undressed, and went down into the basin, where she did as her sisters had done. Afterwards she put on some of her clothes and stretched herself over the thighs of the porter. "Guess the name of that," she said, pointing to her delicate parts. The porter tried this name and that and ended by asking her to tell him and cease her slapping. "The khān of Abu-Mansūr," she replied.

Then, in reprisal, the porter rose, undressed and went down into the water, and lo! his blade swam level with the surface. He washed as the girls had done, came out of the basin, and, throwing himself into the lap of the portress, rested his feet in that of the cateress. Pointing to his organ, he asked the mistress of the house: "What is his name, my queen?" At this all the girls laughed till they fell over on their backs, and cried together: "Your zabb!" "No," he said, and took a little bite at each by way of forfeit. Then they cried: "Your tool, then!" But he said: "No," and pinched their breasts. "But it is your tool," they cried in astonishment, "for it is hot. It is your zabb, because it moves." Each time the porter shook his head and kissed and bit and pinched and hugged them until they laughed again. In the end they had to ask him to tell them; and the porter reflected a moment, looked between his thighs, and winking, said: "Ladies, this child, my zabb, says for himself:

'My name is the Mighty Ungelt Mule who feeds on the basil of bridges, feasts on husked sesame, and stays the night in father Mansūr's khān.'"

At these words, the girls laughed so much that they fell over on their bottoms; and afterwards all four went on drinking from the same cup until the approach of evening. When night fell, they said to the porter: "Be gone, now, turn your face and let us see the width of your shoulders." But the porter cried: "By Allah, it is easier for my soul to quit my body than for me to quit your house, my ladies! Let us make the night continue the sweet day, and tomorrow all can part and follow their destiny upon the road of Allah." The young cateress then spoke up saying: "By my life, sisters, let us ask him to pass the night with us; we will have many good laughs at the naughty fellow who is so shameless and yet so gentle." The others agreed, and said to the porter: "Very well, you can stay with us this night on condition that you obey implicitly and ask no reason or explanation of anything you see." "I agree to that, ladies," he said. "Get up, then, and read what is over the door," they commanded; so he rose, and found over the door these words lettered in gold:

"Speak not of that which concerns you not or you will hear that which shall please you not."

Reading this, the porter said: "Ladies, I call you to witness that I will never speak of that which concerns me not."

At this point Shahrazād saw the approach of morning and discreetly fell silent.

But when the tenth night had come

Dunyazād said: "Finish your tale, dear sister."

So Shahrazād answered: "Gladly and as in duty bound," and thus continued:

It is related, O auspicious King, that when the porter had made his promise to the girls, the cateress rose and set meat before them all, which they ate with good appetite. After the meal, candles were lighted, perfumed wood and incense burned, and all began to drink again and to eat the various delicacies from the market; especially the porter who also recited well-formed verses all the time, shutting his eyes and shaking his head. Suddenly they heard a knocking on the door, which, though it did not interrupt their pleasure, caused the portress to rise. She came back, saying: "Indeed, tonight's pleasure is to be perfect, for there are three strangers at the door with shaved beards and each blind of the left eye, which is a strange coincidence. It is easy to see that they come from the lands of Rūm, each has different features and yet their faces all match in their fittingness for being laughed at. If we let them in, we can have much fun at their expense." She persuaded her companions, who said: "Tell them that they may come in, but be sure they understand the condition: 'Speak not of that which concerns you not or you will hear that which shall please you not.'" So the young girl ran joyously to the door and came back leading the three one-eyed men, who indeed had shaved beards, moustaches twisted back, and all the signs of that brotherhood of beggars called kalandars. As soon as they came in, they wished peace to the company, backing one by one as they did so; on which the girls stood up and invited them to be seated. The three men, after they had sat down, looked at the porter, who was very drunk, and supposing him to belong to their brotherhood, said among themselves: "Here is another kalandar; he is sure to bear us friendly company." But the porter, who had heard what they said, jumped to his feet and, eyeing them sternly and a little squintingly, said: "All right, all right, my friends, make yourselves at home; and begin by digesting those words written above the door." The girls burst out laughing at his words and said to each other: "We are going to have fun with these kalandars and the porter." They set food before the kalandars—who ate like kalandars!—then wine— and the kalandars drank turn and turn about, reaching out again and again for the cup. When the drink was passing round at a rare pace, the porter said: "Come, brothers, have you not some good tale of marvellous adventure in your scrips to amuse us?" Cheered by this suggestion, the kalandars asked for musical instruments and, when the portress had fetched out a Mosul drum fitted with crotals, a lute of Irāq, and a Persian flagiolet, they stood up and began to play while the girls sang with them. The porter became frenzied with pleasure and kept on shouting: "Ha! yā Allah!", so struck was he by the harmonious voices of the singers.

In the middle of all this, knocking was again heard upon the door and the portress rose to see who was there.

Now this was the reason for the second knocking on the door:

That night the Khalīfah, Hārūn al-Rashīd, had gone down to wander about his city to see and hear for himself what might be going on there. He was accompanied by his wazīr, Jafar al-Barmaki,[6] and by Masrūr, his sword-bearer, the instrument of his justice. You must know that it was a habit of his to disguise himself as a merchant and make such expeditions.

---

6. The trusted vizier and companion of Harun (or Haroun) al-Rashid (r. 786–809), the most famous of all the Abbasid caliphs.

While he was walking through the streets of the city, he passed that palace and heard the sounds of music and gaiety which issued from it. Then said the Khalīfah to Jafar: "I wish to enter that place to see those singers." Jafar answered: "They must be a crowd of drunkards. If we go in some hurt may come to you." But the Khalīfah said: "Certainly we must go in. I wish to find a way in which we can enter and take them by surprise." "I hear and I obey," said Jafar at this command and, going up to the door, he knocked.

When the young portress opened the door, the wazīr said to her: "My mistress, we are merchants from Tiberias. Ten days ago we came to Baghdad with our goods and took lodging in the khān of the merchants. One of the other traders at the khān asked us to his house tonight to eat with him. After the meal, which lasted an hour in which we ate and drank excellently, he gave us leave to depart. We came out but, the night being dark and we strangers, lost our way to the khān where we lodge. So now we beg you of your great goodness to let us come in and pass the night at your house. Allah will reward your kindness." The portress looked at them closely and, seeing that they had the appearance of most respectable merchants, went in to ask the advice of her two companions. The other two said: "Let them come in!" So she returned to the door, crying: "Enter!" On this invitation the Khalīfah and Jafar and Masrūr came in and the girls rose, putting themselves at their service and saying: "Be very welcome. Take your ease here, dear companions; but accept, we pray, this one condition: 'Speak not of that which concerns you not or you will hear that which shall please you not.'" The newcomers answered: "Be it so," and sat down with the others. While they were being invited to drink and to send round the cup, the Khalīfah looked at the three kalandars and was astonished to see that each was blind of the left eye; then at the girls and was overcome with surprise at all their beauty and grace. When the girls, in their ministrations to the guests, offered the Khalīfah a cup of the rarest wine, he refused, saying: "I am vowed to pilgrimage." So the portress got up and placed a little table of finest inlay before him on which she set a cup of Chinese porcelain into which she poured spring water refreshed with snow, mingling sugar and rose-water within it. The Khalīfah accepted this, thanking her cordially and saying to himself: "Tomorrow I shall reward her for her kindness."

The girls continued to act the hostess and pass about the wine till the wits of the companions were dancing dizzily. Then she who was the mistress of the house rose up and, having asked if any wanted more, took the cateress by the hand saying: "Rise, my sister, that we may do that which we have to do." "Be it as you say," the other answered. On this the portress also rose and, telling the kalandars to get up from the center of the hall and seat themselves by the door, herself cleared and tidied the central space. The other two called to the porter: "By Allah, your friendship is of but little use! You are no stranger here but belong to the house." On this the porter stood up, lifted the skirts of his robe and tightened his belt, saying: "Tell me what to do and I shall do it." "Follow me," said the portress. So he followed her out of the hall and saw two black bitches with chains round their necks, which, as he was bid, he led back into the middle of the hall. Then the eldest pulled up her sleeves, took a whip, and told the porter to lead forward one of the bitches. When he had done so, dragging her by the chain, the animal began to weep, raising its head piteously towards the girl; but the latter, without seeming to notice, fell upon it, beating it over the head with her whip till the bitch yelled and wept and she herself could strike no more. Then she threw down the whip and, taking the bitch in her arms, clasped it to her breast, wiped away its tears, and kissed its head which she held between her hands. After a little, she said to the porter: "Bring me the other, and take this one back." So the porter brought the other bitch forward and the girl treated it as she had the first.

The Khalīfah felt his heart filled with pity at this sight; his breast shook with grief and he signed with his eye to Jafar to question the young woman. But Jafar signed to him that it were better to keep silent. Soon the mistress of the house turned to her sisters saying: "Come, let us do as is our custom." They answered: "Yes"; so she got up on to the marble bed which was plated with gold and silver and said to the other two: "Let it be done!" Then the portress also got up on to the bed; but the cateress went into her own room and brought back a satin bag fringed with green silk. Halting before the other two, she opened the bag and drew a lute from it. First tuning this and then playing upon it, she sang these lines of love and all the sadness of love:

> Love at my door
> Knocked and I gave him bed.
> When sleep saw this
> He took offence and fled.
> "Give me back sleep;
> Where has he gone?" I said.
>
> * * *
>
> It's not that time
> Has passed, but that so has she,
> It's not that love
> Won't last, but that nor will she,
> Not that life's gone,
> But that she's gone from me.
>
> My soul is bound
> By the scents of her body,
> Jasmine and musk
> And rose of her body,
> Amber and nard,
> The scents of her body.

"Allah comfort you, my sister," cried out the portress, when the song was finished; then, tearing all her clothes in an ecstasy of grief, she fell in a faint upon the floor.

Her body being in some sort bared, the Khalīfah was able to see upon it the prints of whips and rods, a circumstance which astonished and appalled him. But the cateress came and cast water in her sister's face until she recovered consciousness; then she brought her a new robe and helped her into it.

The Khalīfah whispered to Jafar: "You do not seem moved by this. Do you not see the marks of the scourge on the woman? I can hardly keep silent and I will know no rest until I have found out the truth of all this and of the matter of the two bitches." "Lord and Master," answered Jafar, "remember the condition: 'Speak not of that which concerns you not or you will hear that which shall please you not.'"

While they were talking thus, the cateress again took up the lute and, pressing it against her rounded breast, sounded the chords and sang:

> If one came to us plaining of love,
> What would we answer?
> Seeing that we also are drowned in love,
> What would we do?

> If we charged a speaker to speak for us,
> What would he know of it?

* * *

Again the portress fell fainting and again her naked body showed the marks of whips and rods.

The three kalandars began whispering together when they saw this: "It had been better for us if we had never come into this house, even though we had to sleep on the naked ground; for what we have just seen is enough to melt the marrow in our spines." The Khalīfah turned to them and said: "Why is that?" "We are afraid of what has happened," they answered. "Is that so?" said the Khalīfah, "then you are not of this house?" "We are not," they answered, "we imagined it belonged to that man beside you." "By Allah, it does not!" cried the porter. "This is the very first time that I have entered here. Also, God knows, it would have been better for me to have slept on the rubbish heaps among the ruins."

So they concerted with each other and said: "We are seven men to three women, let us demand an explanation of these things and, if they will not answer willingly, we can use force." They all agreed to this except Jafar, who said: "Do you think that right and equitable? Remember, we are their guests and that they laid down certain conditions which we swore to keep. The night is nearly over; it would be better for each of us to go forth and seek his destiny upon the road of Allah." Then, winking at the Khalīfah and drawing him aside, he continued: "We have but one more hour to stay here. Tomorrow I promise that I will bring them up before you, and then we can compel them to tell their story." But the Khalīfah said: "I have not the patience to wait till tomorrow." The others continued their planning, some saying this and some saying that, but it all came back to the question: "Who is to ask them?" At last it was decided that the porter should do so.

So, when the girls said: "Good folk, what are you talking about?", the porter rose to his feet and, standing up straight before the lady of the house, addressed her courteously: "My queen, I ask and pray you in the name of Allah, on behalf of all us jolly fellows, to tell us the tale of those two bitches and why you so beat them and then weep over them and kiss them. Tell us, too, for we wait to hear it, the cause of the marks of whips and rods on the body of your sister. This we ask of you; that is all, my queen." Then the lady of the house questioned them: "Is this that the porter has said asked in the name of all?" And each, with the exception of Jafar, answered: "Yes." Jafar said nothing.

The eldest girl, hearing this answer of theirs, exclaimed: "As Allah lives, you who are our guests have done us here the most grievous of wrongs. We bound you to this condition: 'Speak not of that which concerns you not or you will hear that which shall please you not.' Was it not enough for you to come into our house and eat our good food? Perhaps, though, it was less your fault than the fault of our sister who let you in."

So saying, she pulled the sleeves of her robe away from her wrist and beat the floor with her foot three times, calling: "Come quick, come quick!" The door of one of the great curtained presses opened and out glided seven strong negroes carrying sharpened swords. To these she said: "Bind the arms of these prattling guests and fasten them one to the other." This the negroes did, saying: "O mistress, O hidden flower beyond the sight of men, may we cut off their heads?" "Have patience for an hour," she answered. "I wish to know what sort of men they are before they die."

On this the porter cried: "By Allah, mistress queen, do not kill me for the crime of others. All these have sinned, committing a notable crime against you, but not I. As God lives, how happy, how paradisal would our night have been if we had never set eyes on these ill-omened kalandars.[7] I have always said that kalandars could lay waste the loveliest of cities just by coming into it." And he added these lines:

> The fairest gift of strength is clemency
> If the weak offend;
> So do not, for our love's sake, punish me
> For the fault of a friend.

The eldest girl burst out laughing when the porter had finished speaking.

At this point Shahrazād saw the approach of day and discreetly fell silent.

But when the eleventh night had come

She said:

It is related, O auspicious King, that when the eldest girl burst out laughing after having been angry, she came down to the company and said: "Tell me all that there is to tell, for you have but one hour to live. I give you this indulgence because you are poor folk. If you were among the most noble, great ones of your tribes or even governors, it is true that I would hurry on your punishment."

"Jafar, we are in sorry case," said the Khalīfah, "tell her who we are or she may kill us." "Which is exactly what we deserve," said Jafar. Then said the Khalīfah: "There is a time for being witty and a time for being serious, there is a time for everything."

Now first of all the eldest girl approached the kalandars and asked them: "Are you brothers?" To this they answered: "No, by Allah, we are only poor men of the poorest who live by cupping and scarifying."[8] Then she turned to one of them and said: "Were you born without one eye?" "As God lives, I was not," he answered, "but the tale of the way I lost my eye is so extraordinary that, if it were written with a needle in the corner of another eye, yet would it be a lesson to the circumspect." The second and the third made the same kind of answer; then all three said: "Each of us was born in a different country; the stories of our lives are strange and our adventures pass the marvellous." "Well, then," said the girl, "each of you must tell his story and the reason of his coming to our house. Should the tale seem good to us, each then may make his bow and go his way."

The first who came forward was the porter; and he said: "My queen, I am a porter, nothing more. Your cateress here gave me things to carry and led me to you. You know well what happened to me after I got here and, if I refuse to be more particular, you know why. That is all my tale. I will not add another word to it, and Allah bless you." Then said the eldest girl: "Get you gone, make your bow and let us see the last of you." "But," said the porter, "no, by God, I will not stir until I have heard the tales of these friends of mine."

* * *

7. There was a superstitious belief that one-eyed people bring bad luck.

8. Performing simple medical treatments.

When she had heard the tale of the first kalandar, the mistress of the house said to him: "That is well, make your bow and depart with all speed."

The first kalandar answered: "Indeed, mistress, I shall not stir from here until I have heard the tales of all the other companions."

So, while all were marvelling at the story and the Khalīfah was even whispering to Jafar: "Never in all my life have I heard a like adventure," the first kalandar sat down cross-legged on the floor and the second kalandar, advancing, kissed the earth between the hands of the young mistress of the house and said:

[TALE OF THE SECOND KALANDAR]

Indeed, mistress, neither was I born with one eye only; and the story which I am going to tell you is so marvellous that, if it were written with a needle on the inner corner of any eye, yet it would serve as a lesson to the circumspect.

Though you see me thus, I am a king and the son of a king, a man of education beyond the ordinary. I have read the Koran with all its seven narratives,[9] I have read all essential books and the writings of the masters of science, I have studied the lore of the stars and the starlike lore of the poets. So rapidly did I learn that I surpassed in knowledge all the men of my time.

Especially did my fame spread abroad as a calligrapher; I became renowned in all countries and my worth was known among kings. So it happened that the King of Hind heard tell of me and sent begging my father to let me visit him. This invitation he accompanied with sumptuous gifts and presents meet for us; so my father consented and fitted out six ships for me with all manner of luxuries, and I departed.

After a month's voyage, we came to land and, unshipping the horses and camels we had with us, loaded them with presents for the King of Hind and set out on our journey. But hardly had we started than a great dust storm rose, filling all the sky and the earth with sand for the space of an hour. When it died down, we found close upon us a troop of sixty armed men, raging like lions, desert Arabs, cutpurses of the highway. We turned and fled, but, when they saw our ten camels loaded with gifts for the King of Hind, they pursued us at a gallop. So we signed to them with our finger that we were envoys to the mighty King and should not be molested. But they answered: "We know nothing of kings," and forthwith killed some of my slaves. The rest of us took to flight in all directions, I with a great and terrible wound, while the Arabs contented themselves with pillaging our rich belongings.

I fled and I fled, despairing bitterly at my change of fortune, till I came to the top of a mountain, where I found a cave in which I passed the night.

Next morning I left the cave and journeyed on until I came to a great and beautiful city, whose air was of such potent balm that Winter might not lay hand upon her but the Spring covered her with his roses all the year. I wept with joy when I reached this city, being fatigued and broken by my journey, worn and pale from my wound and utterly changed from my former state.

I was wandering ignorantly about the streets when I passed a tailor sewing in his shop, whom I greeted and who greeted me. He cordially invited me to seat myself, embraced me, and asked me generous questions about my wanderings. I told him all that had befallen me from beginning to end and he was much moved at my recital, saying to me: "My sweet young man, you must on no account tell this story to any

---

9. A reference to the seven accepted ways in which the Qur'an can be recited.

other person here; for the king of this city is a deadly enemy of your father, having an old grudge against him, and I fear for your safety."

He gave me food and drink, and we ate and drank together. After a long conversation, he brought out a mattress and a quilt for me, and let me sleep that night in a corner of his shop. I stayed with him for three days, and at the end of that time he asked if I knew any trade by which I could earn a livelihood. "Certainly I do," I answered, "I am deeply read in the law, I am a past-master of all sciences, literature and computation are thoroughly well known to me." "My friend," he answered "all that is not a trade, or rather, if you wish, it is a trade" (for he saw that I was annoyed), "but it is not of very much account in the markets of our city. No one here knows anything of study or of writing or of reading, they simply know how to make money." I could only answer that I knew nothing beside these things. Said he: "Come, my son, pull yourself together, take an axe and a cord, go out and cut wood in the countryside till Allah show you a better occupation. Above all, tell your story to no one or they will kill you." With this the good man bought me an axe and a rope, and sent me out in charge of a gang of woodcutters, under whose special care he placed me.

I went out with the woodcutters and, when I had chopped sufficient faggots, loaded them on my head and sold them in the streets of the city for half a dīnār. With a little of this money I bought food, and the rest I carefully put aside. I laboured in this way for a full year, visiting my friend the tailor in his shop every day and resting there in my corner without having to pay him anything.

One day, straying away from the others, I came to a thickly-wooded glade where there were many faggots to be had. I chose a dead tree and was beginning to loosen the earth about her roots when the head of my axe was caught in a copper ring. I removed the earth all about this ring and, coming to a wooden cover in which it was fastened, lifted it and found an underground staircase. In my curiosity I went down the stairs to the bottom and, opening a door, entered the mighty hall of a most marvellous palace. In this hall there was a young girl, more beautiful than all the pearls of history; I had endured much and yet at the sight of her all my troubles were left behind and I knelt down in adoration before Allah who had moulded so perfect a beauty out of the centuries.

She looked at me and said: "Are you a man or a Jinnī?" "A man," I answered, and she asked: "Who then has led you to this hall where for full twenty years I have not seen a human face?" I found her words and herself so sweet that I answered: "Lady, it was Allah who led me to your home that all my troubles and my sorrows might be forgotten." I told her my story from beginning to end; she wept for me and told me her story likewise:

"I am the daughter of King Ifītāmūs, latest of the Kings of Hind and master of the Isle of Ebony. I was to be married to my cousin, but on my wedding night, even before my virginity had been taken, the Ifrīt Jurjīs, son of Rajmūs, son of the Foul Fiend himself, carried me off and put me in this place, which he had provisioned with all I could desire of sweet things and of jams, of robes and precious stuffs, of furniture and meat and drink. Since then he has come to see me every ten days and lies one night with me, going away in the morning. Also he has told me that if I have need of him during the ten days that he is away I have nothing to do but to touch with my hand two lines which are written under the cupola of that little room. If I but touch them he will appear at once. It is four days since he has been here, so that there will be six more before he comes again. Therefore you can stay with me for five days and go away on the day before he comes."

"Most certainly I can," I answered, and she was filled with joy. She got up from where she was lying and, taking me by the hand, led me through many arched apartments to a warm agreeable hammām[1] where all the air was scented. Here we both undressed naked and bathed together. After our bath, we sat side by side on the hammām couch and she regaled me with musk-sweetened sherbert and delicious cakes. We talked for a long time and ate unsparingly of the provisions of the Ifrīt who had ravished her.

At last she said: "For this evening you had better sleep and rest after all your toil; you will be the more ready for me then."

I was indeed weary, so I thanked her and lay down to sleep, forgetting all my cares. When I woke I found her by my side, pleasantly massaging my limbs and my feet. So I called down all the blessings of Allah upon her, and we sat together for an hour saying sweet things to each other. "As God lives," she sighed at last, "before you came I was all alone in this underground palace for twenty years, no one to speak to, with no companion save sorrow and a bosom filled by sobs, but now glory be to Allah that He has brought you to me!"

Then in a sweet voice she sang this song:

> For your feet,
> If we had known of your coming,
> We would have been weaving
> Our heart's blood,
> The velvet of our eyes
> To a red and black carpet.
>
> For your couch,
> If we had known of your coming,
> We would have been spreading
> Our cool cheeks,
> The young silk of our thighs,
> Dear stranger in the night.

Hand on heart I thanked her for her song, my love for her increased in me and all my sorrows fell away. We drank together from the same cup till nightfall, and all night I lay with her in a heaven of bliss. Never was such a night; and, when morning came, we rose in love with each other and with happiness.

I was still all passion and, thinking to prolong my rapture, I said: "Shall I not take you from this underground place and free you from the Jinnī?" "Be quiet," she answered, laughing, "and be content with what you have. The poor Ifrīt has only one night in ten; I promise you all the other nine." But I, lifted by passion and by wine, spoke thus extravagantly: "Not so! I am going to destroy that alcove with its magic inscription, and then the Ifrīt will come and I shall kill him. For a long time it has been my custom to amuse myself by killing Ifrīt."

To calm my frenzy she recited these lines:

> You who would bind love
> Thinking to make us
> Yours by the binding
> Soon shall discover

---

1. Bath.

> Ever a lover
> Finishes finding
> Love will forsake us,
> The bound and unkind love;
> But if you unbind love
> He'll wrap us and take us
> In nets of his winding
> And never be over.

But, paying no attention to the lines, I gave a violent kick with my foot at the wall of the alcove.

At this point Shahrazād saw the approach of morning and discreetly fell silent.

And when the thirteenth night had come

She said:

It is related, O auspicious King, that the second kalandar continued telling his story to the young mistress of the house in these words:

Mistress, when I kicked down the alcove, the woman cried: "The Ifrīt is upon us! Did I not warn you? As Allah lives, you have destroyed me! Flee by the way you came and save yourself!"

I rushed to the staircase, forgetting my sandals and my axe in the hurry of my terror. When I had climbed a few steps, I remembered them and went back to look for them; but the earth opened and an Ifrīt of terrible size and ugliness sprang from it, crying to the woman: "What does all this violence mean? It frightened me. What harm has befallen you?" "No harm," she answered, "save that, just now, I felt my heart heavy with solitude and, rising to get some drink to lighten it, I fell against the alcove." But the Ifrīt, who had looked about the hall and seen my sandals and my axe, cried: "Oh, and what are these things, you lying whore? Tell me, what man do they belong to?" "I never saw them before you showed them to me," she answered, "probably they were hanging to the back of your clothes and you brought them here yourself." "Weak and tortuous and foolish words!" exclaimed the furious Jinnī. "They will not take me in, you wanton."

On this, he stripped her naked, crucified her between four pegs fastened in the earth, and, putting her to the torture, began to question her. I could not bear to see this or to hear her sobs, so I ran trembling up the stairs and, reaching the outer air, put back the cover and removed all traces of the entrance. I repented bitterly of the foolish thing I had done, thinking of the girl's beauty and of all the torture which the wretch who had kept her there for twenty years had inflicted on her for my sake. From this I fell to lamenting my father, my own lost kingdom, and the miserable descent I had made to be a woodcutter. So I wept and recited a suitable verse. Making my way to the city, I found that my friend the tailor had been, as the saying is, on coals of fire at my absence. In his anxiety, he called to me: "When you did not come yesterday, my heart lay awake all night because of you. I feared that a savage beast or other mischance had destroyed you in the forest. Praise be to Allah that you are safe!" Thanking him and sitting down in my accustomed corner, I began to brood on what had happened and to curse myself for the unlucky kick that I had given the alcove. All of a sudden my good friend the tailor came to me, saying: "There is a man at the shop door, a Persian, who has your axe and your sandals and is asking for you. He has been going round all the woodcutters in the street, saying that he found them in the road when he went out to pray at dawn at the call of the muezzin. Some of the woodcutters recognised them and directed the Persian to come here. He is outside the door; go and thank him for his trouble, and take your sandals and your axe again." I paled and nearly fainted at his words and, while I stayed prostrate where I was, the ground in front of my corner opened and the Persian leapt from it, showing himself to be the Ifrīt.

You must know that he had put the young woman to terrible tortures without getting her to admit anything, and so, taking up my axe and sandals, had said: "I will show you that I am indeed Jurjīs of the true seed of the Evil One. You shall see whether or no I can find the owner of these things." And, as I have told you, he tracked me among the woodcutters by a trick.

Swiftly he came to me, swiftly lifted me, and flew with me high into the air. When I had lost consciousness, he plunged with me down through the earth to the palace where I had tasted so much lustful bliss. When I saw the girl, naked and with blood flowing from her flanks, I wept bitterly. But the Ifrīt, going to her and seizing her arm, said: "Here is your lover, you licentious bitch." The girl looked me straight in the face, saying: "I do not know him; I have never seen him before." "What," shrieked the Ifrīt, "here is the very body that you sinned with and you deny it!" But she continued, saying: "I do not know him. I have never seen him in my life, nor would it be right for me to lie in the face of God." "If that is so," said the Ifrīt, "take this sword and cut off his head." She took the sword and stopped before me. Yellow with fear and weeping copiously, I signed to her with my eyebrows to spare me. She winked at me, saying at the same time in a loud voice: "You are the cause of all our troubles." I signed to her again with my eyebrows, at the same time reciting these ordinary lines, whose inner significance the Ifrīt could not understand:

> I could not say I had a secret for your ears,
> But my eyes said so.
> I could not say that you had caused my tears,
> But my eyes said so.
> I could not say my fingers mean I love you,
> I could not say my brows are meant to move you,
> I could not say my heart is here to prove you,
> But my eyes said so.

The poor girl understood my signs and my verses, and therefore threw the sword at the feet of the Ifrīt, who picked it up and handed it to me. "Cut off her head," he said, "and you shall depart free and unharmed." "Certainly," I answered, grasping the sword, stepping forward and raising my arm; but she said with her brows: "Did I betray you?" So I wept and threw away the sword, saying to the Ifrīt: "Great Jinnī, robust unconquerable hero, if she, who being a woman has neither faith nor reason, found it unlawful to cut off my head and threw away the sword, how can I, who am a man, find it lawful to cut off her head, especially as I have never seen her before? Even if you make me drink the bitterest cup of death I shall not do so." "Ah, now I know that there is love between you," said the Ifrīt.

Then, mistress, that devil cut off both the hands and both the feet of the poor girl with four strokes of the sword, so that I thought I should die of grief at the sight.

But even so she looked at me sideways and winked at me and, alas, the Ifrīt saw the wink. "O harlot's daughter," he cried, "would you commit adultery with your eyes?" So saying, he cut off her head with the sword and, turning to me, addressed me in these words: "Learn, O human, that among us Jinn it is allowed, and even praiseworthy, to kill an adulteress. I bore away this girl on her wedding night, when she was but twelve years old and still unknown of man. I brought her here and visited her every tenth day, coupling with her in the form of a Persian. Finding her unfaithful, I have killed her. For she was unfaithful, even if it was only with her eye. As for you, since I am not sure that you have fornicated with her, I will not kill you. But, so that you may not laugh at me behind my back, I shall inflict some evil upon you to bring down your pride. Now choose what evil you would prefer."

Naturally, good lady, I rejoiced to the utmost when I saw that I should escape with my life, and this encouraged me to take advantage of the Ifrīt's clemency. Therefore I said: "I find it very hard to choose one out of all the evils that there are. I think I would prefer none."

The Ifrīt stamped in vexation and said: "I told you to choose; choose quickly, then, into what form I shall change you. What, an ass, a dog, a mule, a crow, an ape?" I answered still facetiously, hoping for pardon: "As Allah lives, master Jurjīs of the great tribe of the Evil One, if you spare me Allah will spare you. Well He knows how to reward one who pardons a good Muslim that has done no harm." I went on praying and humbling myself in vain, until he cut me short, saying: "No more words, or I shall kill you. Do not try to take advantage of my goodness, for I am fully determined to bewitch you in some way."

Straightway he caught me up, broke all the palace and the earth about us, and flew so high with me up into the air that the earth appeared below me in the likeness of a little dish of water. At last he set me down on the top of a high mountain, and, taking a handful of earth, mumbled some words over it; then he muttered: "Hum, hum, hum," and threw it over me, crying: "Come out of that shape and be an ape!" On the instant I became an ape, at least a hundred years old and as foul-faced as hell itself. Seeing myself in this form, I jumped about in grief and found myself capable of prodigious leaps. But these did me no good, so I sat down and wept; whereat the Ifrīt laughed in a terrible fashion and disappeared.

After I had remained there for some time, thinking on the injustice of fate and how it regards not any man, I leapt and gambolled from the top of the mountain to its base; then I set out, walking by day and sleeping by night in the trees, until after a month I came to the beach of the salt sea. I had rested there for an hour when I saw a ship coming up with a favourable breeze out of the sea. I hid behind a rock and waited. After there had been much coming and going among the men, I screwed up my courage and leapt into the ship. "Chase the ill-omened beast out of that!" cried one of the men. "No, kill it!" cried another. "Yes, kill it with a sword!" cried out a third. At this I caught the sword with my paw and burst into bitter tears.

Because of my tears the captain had pity on me and said to those about him: "This ape has asked for my protection and I give it him. Let no one take hold of him or chase him or interfere with him." Then he called me to him and spoke kind words to me, all of which I understood; finally he made me his servant on the boat, and in this duty I did everything correctly for him throughout the voyage.

Favouring winds carried us, after fifty days, to a city so great and so populous that Allah alone could count the people of it. As we cast anchor, certain officers of the King of that place came and welcomed the merchants we had aboard and gave them, with the kind greetings of the King, a roll of parchment on which each man was commanded to inscribe a line in his fairest writing. For the King's wazīr, a great calligraphist, had died and the King had sworn to appoint no one in his place who could not write as well as he.

Ape that I was, I snatched the parchment from their hands and fled away with it, so that they were afraid that I would tear it and throw it into the water. Some were trying to coax me and some to kill me, when I made a sign that I wished to write. Then said the captain: "Let him write. If he only scribbles and messes we can stop him, but if he writes with a fair writing I shall adopt him as my son, for never in my life have I seen an ape so learned."

I took the reed pen and, pressing it upon the pad of the inkpot, carefully spread ink on both its faces, and began to write.

I improvised four stanzas, each in a different character and style: the first in rikāī.

> The Giver has been sung since time was new
> But Givers with a hand like yours are few,
> So first and foremost we will look to God
> And when He fails us we will look to You.

The second in raihānī:

> I'll tell you of this Pen. It is of those
> Pens that are mightier than cedar bows,
> He holds it in five fingers of his hand
> And from it pour five rivers of pure Prose.

The third in thuluthī:

> I'll tell you of his Immortality.
> He is so certain of eternity,
> It is his aim to write such things of Him
> As that last Critic shall not blush to see.

And the fourth in muhakkak:[2]

> Ink is the strongest drug that God has made,
> If you can write of beauty unafraid
> You will be praising Him who gave the ink
> More than all prayers unlearned men have prayed.

When I had finished writing, I handed back the parchment and each of the others, marvelling at what I had done, also wrote a line in the fairest script that he could compass.

Slaves bore the parchment back to the King and of all the writings he was only satisfied with mine, inscribed as they were in four different styles for which, when I had been a prince, I had been famed throughout the whole world.

So the King said to his friends and to his slaves: "Go all of you to this master of fair writing, give him this robe of honour to put on, mount him on the most magnificent of my mules, and bring him to me in a triumph of musical instruments."

They all smiled when he said this, so the King became angry and cried: "How is this? I give you an order and you laugh at me?" "King of all time," they answered, "we would never dare to laugh at any word you said, but we must tell you that the writer of these splendid characters is no man at all but an ape belonging to a ship's captain." The King was first astonished at their words and then convulsed with spacious laughter. "I shall buy that ape," he said, and he ordered all the people of his

---

2. Rikai, raihani, thuluthi and muhakkak are well-known types of Arabic calligraphy.

court to go down to the boat and fetch the ape ashore, taking with them both the mule and the robe of honour. "Yes, yes," he added, "certainly you must clothe him in this robe and bring him to me mounted on the mule."

All of them came down straightway to the boat and bought me at a great price from the captain, who found it hard to let me go. Then they dressed me in the robe of honour, after I had signed to the captain all my grief at leaving him, set me upon the mule, and conducted me through the city to the noise of harmonious instruments. You may imagine that every soul in those streets was stricken with wonder and admiration at such an unusual sight.

When I was brought before the King, I kissed the earth between his hands three times and stood still in front of him. He invited me to sit down and I did so with such grace that all who were there, but especially the King, marvelled at my fine education and the politeness of my behaviour. When I was seated, the King sent all away except his chief eunuch, a certain young favourite slave, and myself.

Then, to my delight, he ordered food, and slaves brought a cloth laid with all such meats and delicacies as the soul could possibly desire. The King signed to me to eat. So, after rising and kissing the earth between his hands according to seven different schools of politeness, I sat down again in my best manner and began to eat, diligently recalling the education of my youth at every point.

Finally, when the cloth was drawn, I rose, washed my hands and, returning to the King, took up an inkpot, a reed and a sheet of parchment. On the last I inscribed these few lines, celebrating the excellence of Arabian pastries:

> Sweet fine pastries
> Rolled between white fingers,
> Fried things whose fat scent lingers
> On him who in his haste tries
> To eat enough!
> Pastries, my love!
>
> Kunāfah swimming in butter,
> Bearded with right vermicelli,
> God has not given my belly
> Half of the words it would utter
> Of kunāfah's sweetness
> And syrup'd completeness.
>
> Kunāfah lies on the table
> Isled in a sweet brown oil,
> Would I not wander and toil
> Seventy years to be able
> To eat in Paradise
> Kunāfah's subtleties?

Finishing, I put down the reed and the sheet and, while the King looked in astonishment at what I had written, sat respectfully at a distance. "But how can an ape compass such a thing?" asked the King. "As Allah lives, it surpasses all the marvels of history."

Just then they brought the King his chess board, and, when he had asked me by signs if I played and I had nodded my head to show him that I did, I arranged the pieces and we settled down to play. Twice I beat him, and he did not know what to think of it, saying: "If this was a man, he would be the wisest man of all our time." And to his eunuch he continued: "Go to our daughter and tell her to come quickly to us, for I wish your mistress to enjoy the sight of this remarkable ape."

The eunuch went out and soon returned with the princess, his young mistress, who as soon as she set eyes on me covered her face with her veil, saying: "Father, what has possessed you to send for me into the presence and sight of a strange man?" "Daughter," answered the King, "here are only my young slave who is still a little boy, the eunuch who brought you up, this ape, and your father. Why do you cover your face?" Then she said: "Know, my father, that this ape is a prince, his father is the King Ifitamarus, ruler of a land far in the interior. The ape is bewitched by the Ifrīt Jurjīs, of the line of Iblīs,[3] who has also killed his own wife, daughter of King Ifitāmūs, master of the Isle of Ebony. This which you think an ape is not only a man, but a learned, wise, and educated man as well."

"Is it true, what my daughter says of you?" asked the King, looking at me fixedly in his astonishment. I nodded and began to weep; so the king, turning to his daughter, asked her how she knew that I was bewitched. "Father," she answered, "when I was little there was an old woman in my mother's house, a sorceress knowing all the shifts and formulas of witchcraft, who taught me magic. Since then I have studied even more deeply and now know nearly a hundred and seventy codes of necromancy, by the least of which I could remove your palace, with all its stones, even the whole city itself, to the other side of Mount Kāf[4] and turn your country to a sheet of water in which the people should swim in the form of fishes."

"Then by the truth of the name of Allah," cried the King, "take off the witchcraft from this poor young man and I will make him my wazīr. It is strange indeed that you should have such art and I did not know it. Take off the witchcraft quickly, for he is both polite and wise."

"With all my heart and as in duty bound," answered the princess.

At this point Shahrazād saw the approach of morning and discreetly fell silent.

But when the fourteenth night had come

She said:

It is related, O auspicious King, that the second kalandar thus continued his story to the mistress of the house:

The princess took in her hands a knife on which were graved words in the Hebrew tongue and with it traced a circle in the middle of the palace which she filled with names of power and talismanic lines. This preparation completed, she stood in the middle of the circle murmuring words of magic import and reading from a book so old that none might understand it. After a few minutes of this, the palace became dark with shadows, so thick that we thought to be buried alive under the ruins of the world. Suddenly the Ifrīt Jurjīs stood before us in his most frightful and repellent guise, with hands like hayforks, legs like masts, and eyes like crucibles of fire. We were all driven to the confines of terror except the princess, who said: "I have no welcome for you, I have no greeting." Then said the Ifrīt: "How can you break your word, O traitress? Did we not swear together that neither would use power against

---

3. The grand Satan in the Qur'an.

4. A major mountain in the imaginary geography of *The Thousand and One Nights.*

the other, nor interfere with the other's doings? Perfidious one, well have you deserved the fate which is about to overtake you—thus!" On the instant he turned into a savage lion which opened wide its throat and hurled itself upon the princess. But as quick as light she plucked a hair from her head and whispered magic words to it, so that it became a sharp sword, with which she cut the lion in two. Then we saw the lion's head become a scorpion which scuttled towards the young girl's heel to bite it, but in the nick of time she changed to a mighty serpent which threw itself upon the naughty scorpion and battled with it for a long while. The scorpion, escaping, turned into a vulture, and the snake became an eagle, which flew at the vulture and put it to flight. The pursuit lasted for an hour, until the vulture became a black cat and the girl turned suddenly to a wolf. Long and long in the middle of the palace the cat and the wolf were locked in deadly strife, till the cat, seeing that it was being vanquished, turned into a very large red pomegranate, which leapt into the basin of the fountain in the courtyard. The wolf jumped in after it and was about to seize it when the pomegranate rose up into the air. But it was too heavy to be sustained there, and so fell with a thump on to the marble and broke in pieces, the seeds of it escaping one by one and covering the whole floor of the courtyard. On this the wolf changed to a cock who pecked at the seeds and swallowed them one by one, till only a single seed remained. Just as the cock was about to swallow this last one, it fell from his beak—in this you may perceive the hand of Destiny and the will of Fate—and lodged in a crack of the marble near the basin, so that the cock could not find it. Thereupon the cock crowed, beat his wings, and signed to us with his beak; but we did not understand what he would say to us. At last he gave so terrible a cry that we, who could not understand what he wished, thought that the palace was falling about us. Round and round, in the middle of the courtyard, trotted the cock until it found the last seed in the crack near the basin. But, when the cock had fetched it out and was about to eat it, the seed fell into the water and became a fish which swam to the bottom. So the cock turned to a whale of prodigious size which leapt into the water and sank in pursuit of the fish, so that we did not see it again for a whole hour. At the end of this time we heard agonised cries coming from the water and trembled for fear. Out of the basin appeared the Ifrīt in his own form, but all on fire, as if he were a burning coal, with smoke leaping from his eyes and mouth and nose. Behind him appeared the princess in her own form, but she also was all on fire as if she were made of molten metal; and she ran after the Ifrīt who was now bearing down on us. We were all terrified of being burnt alive and were on the point of throwing ourselves into the water, when the Ifrīt halted us with a terrible cry and leaping upon us, in the midst of the hall which gave upon the courtyard, blew fire in our faces. But the princess caught up with him and blew fire in his face, so that flames fell on us from both of them. Those coming from her were harmless to us, but a spark, shooting off from him, destroyed my left eye for ever, another burnt all the lower part of the King's face, his beard and his mouth, making his lower teeth fall out, while a third, falling upon the eunuch's breast, burnt him to death upon the instant.

All this time the young girl was pursuing the Ifrīt and blowing fire at him. Suddenly we heard a voice calling: "Only Allah is great! Only Allah is strong! He breaks and destroys the renegade who denies Muhammad, master of the world!" It was the princess who spoke, pointing at the same time to the Ifrīt who had been reduced to a mass of cinders. Coming to us, the princess said: "Quick, fetch me a glass of water!" When this was brought, she chanted certain incomprehensible words over it, and sprinkled me with water, saying: "Be freed, in the name and by the truth of the only Truth! Yea, by the truth of the name of Almighty Allah, return to your first shape!"

On this I became a man as I had been before, except that I was still blind in one eye. "Poor youth," said the princess by way of consolation, "fire will be fire." She said the same also to her father on account of his burnt beard and lost teeth, and finally she said: "Father, I must die; for it is written. Had the Ifrīt been but a man I could have killed him at the first attempt. It was the spilling of the pomegranate seed that was my undoing, for the grain I could not eat was that which held the whole soul of the Jinnī. If only I could have found it he would have been dead upon the instant, but, alas, I could not. It was written. So I was obliged to fight terrible battles below the earth and in the air and under the water, and each time he opened a door of safety I opened a door of danger, until at last he opened the terrible door of fire. When that door is opened there is death ahead. Fate allowed me to burn him before I was burnt myself. Before I killed him I tried to make him embrace our Faith, the blessed Law of Islām; but he would not and I burnt him. Now I die. May Allah fill my place for you."

After this she wrestled with the fire till black sparks sprang up and mounted to her breast and to her face. When they reached her face, she cried out weeping: "I bear witness that there is no God but Allah! I bear witness that Muhammad is His messenger!" and fell, a heap of cinders, by the side of the Ifrīt.

We mourned for her, and I wished that I could have died in her place rather than see her radiant form go down in ashes, this little princess who had freed me; but the word of Allah may not be gainsaid.

When the King saw his daughter fall down in cinders, he tore away the little remnant of his beard, beat his cheeks, and rent his garments. I did the same and we both wept over her, until the chamberlains and the chief men of the court came and found their Sultān fainting and weeping beside two piles of ashes. For an hour, in great stupefaction, they walked round and round the King not daring to speak, until at last he recovered himself a little and told them all that had happened to his daughter. Then they cried: "Allah, Allah, the great grief! The great calamity!"

Lastly came the women and the women slaves, who mourned for seven days and lamented over her in due form.

When the week was past, the King ordered a mighty tomb to be built over the ashes of his child, and this was done by forced labour at the same hour, and candles and lanterns were lighted by it both day and night. But the ashes of the Ifrīt were committed to the air, under the curse of Allah.

Worn out by these griefs and duties, the Sultān fell into a sickness which looked to be mortal and lasted for a whole month. When his strength had come back to him a little, he called me to him and said: "Young man, before you came we lived here in eternal happiness, safe harboured from the assaults of fortune, but with your coming came also the bitterest of all afflictions. Would we had never seen your ill-omened face, your face which brought down desolation on us. First, you have caused the death of my daughter whose life was worth the lives of a hundred men; second, you were the reason of my being burnt and of the loss and spoiling of my teeth; third, through you my poor eunuch, that faithful servant who had reared my daughter, was killed outright. And yet it is not your fault, nor is the remedy yours; what came to us and to you, came from Allah. Praise be to Him, then, who allowed my daughter to free you even at the price of her own life. Yes, it is Destiny, it is Destiny. Leave our country, my child, for we have suffered enough because of you. Yet it was all written before by Allah, so go your way in peace."

Mistress, I went out from before the King, hardly believing that I was still alive and not knowing at all where to go. In my heart I pondered all that had happened to me from beginning to end: how I had escaped safe from the desert robbers, how I had entered as a stranger into a city and met the tailor there, my sweet amour with the young girl below the earth, my deliverance from the hands of the Ifrīt, my life as an ape, servant to a ship's captain, my purchase at a great price by the King because of my excellent handwriting, my freeing from the spell, and, last and most piteous, the adventure that had lost me my eye. Nevertheless I thanked Allah, saying: "Better an eye than a life," and went down to the hammām to bathe before leaving the city. It was there, my lady, that I shaved my beard so that I might travel in safety in the guise of a kalandar. Each day since then I have not ceased to weep and think of my wrongs, especially the loss of my left eye, and so thinking I have felt my right eye blinded by tears so that I could not see, and have not been able to resist saying over the following stanzas of the poet:

> It was only after the blow
> I knew my sorrow could hurt me so,
> How then could Allah know?

> I will abide those whips of His
> That the world may know iniquities
> More bitter than patience is.

> Patience has beauty, I've understood,
> When it is practised by one of the Good;
> But Fate is a thing more rude.

> For Fate was probably setting a snare
> When you were born, wherever you were,
> To take your old feet there.

> She knew the secrets of my bed
> And more than so, but she lay dead,
> The Jinnī cut off her head.

> To him who prates of joy down here
> Say: soon you'll taste a day bitter
> As the quick sap of the myrrh.

I left that city and journeyed through many lands, aiming ever for Baghdad, the city of Peace, where I hoped to tell all my tale to the Prince of Believers. Tonight I reached Baghdad after many long and weary days. By chance I met this other kalandar, and while we were talking together we were joined by our third companion, also a kalandar. Recognising each other as strangers, we wended our way in the darkness together till the kind hand of Destiny led us to your house, my mistress.

That is the story of my shaved beard and lost eye.

When she had heard the tale of the second kalandar, the mistress of the house said to him: "Your tale is truly strange; make your bow and depart with all speed."

But he answered: "Indeed, I shall not stir from here until I have heard the tale of my third companion."[5]

---

5. The third kalandar tells an equally astonishing tale, after which it is Harun al-Rashid's turn to tell his story.

* * *

The young girl then turned to the Khalīfah, Jafar and Masrur, asking for their stories. So Jafar went up and told her the fable that he had already told the portress at the door. After she had heard him, the girl said: "I will pardon you all. Depart quickly and in peace."

When they were safely out in the road, the Khalīfah asked the kalandars whither they were going and, when they answered that they did not know, instructed Jafar to take them to his home and bring them before him in the morning, so that he might see what could be done for them.

After Jafar had done his bidding, the Khalīfah returned to his palace, where he tried in vain to sleep. Early in the morning he rose and, mounting his throne, held audience of all the chief men of his empire. When these had departed, he turned to Jafar, saying: "Bring to me the three young girls and the two bitches and the three kalandars." Jafar brought them all forthwith and, when they stood before the Khalīfah, the girls being heavily veiled, addressed these words to them: "We hold you free of any unkindness; you knew not who we were and yet you pardoned us and treated us well. Now learn that you have come into the hands of the fifth of the line of Abbās, Hārūn al-Rashīd, the Khalīfah. It is unwise to tell him aught but the truth."

When Jafar had thus spoken for the Prince of Believers, the eldest girl came forward, saying: "Prince of Believers, my story is so strange that if it were written with a needle on the corner of an eye yet would it serve as a lesson to the circumspect!"

At this point Shahrazād saw the approach of morning and discreetly fell silent.

But when the sixteenth night had come

She said:

It is related, O auspicious King, that the eldest of the young girls stood up before the Prince of Believers and told this story:

[THE TALE OF ZUBAIDAH, THE FIRST OF THE GIRLS]

Prince of Believers; my name is Zubaidah, my sister who opened the door for you is Amīnah, and our youngest is called Fahīmah. We were all three born of the same father but not of the same mother; these two bitches, on the other hand, are full sisters to me, being born of the same father and the same mother. When our father died, leaving five thousand dīnārs to be divided equally among us, Amīnah and Fahīmah left us to live with their mother, while I and my two sisters lived together. I was the youngest of the three, though I am older than Amīnah and Fahīmah.

Soon after our father's death, my two elder sisters married and, in a little while, their husbands fitted out commercial ventures with their wives' inheritances and set sail, each taking his wife with him and leaving me alone.

My sisters were away for four years, and during that time their husbands, becoming bankrupt, lost all their goods and made off, abandoning them among strangers in strange lands. After bitter sufferings they managed to make their ways back to me, but they looked so like beggars that at first I did not recognise them. Yet when they spoke to me I knew who they were and questioned them tenderly as to what had happened. "Sister, words cannot help us now," they answered. "Allah took the reed pen and wrote that it was to be." I pitied them from the bottom of my heart, sent them to the bath, and put fair new garments upon them, saying: "Sisters, you are the elder, while I am the younger; you stand to me in the place of both father and mother. My inheritance, by Allah's grace, has prospered and increased. Come, use the profit of it as your own and live with me in honour and in peace."

I loaded them with benefits and they stayed with me for a year, sharing my substance. But one day they said: "Marriage would be better for us, we cannot do without it any longer, we have no more patience with living alone." "I fear that you will get little good from marriage," I said, "for an honest man is hard to come by in these days. You tried marriage once; have you forgotten how you found it?"

But they would not listen to me, being set on marrying without my consent; so I married them to husbands, giving them money and the necessary clothes. And the new husbands took them away as before.

It was not long, however, before the new husbands deceived them and decamped with all the dowry which I had provided. Naked and full of excuses, they returned to me, saying: "Do not blame us, we are older than you but you are wiser than we. We promise never to say a word again on the subject of marriage." "Sweet welcome to you, my sisters," I answered, "there are none dearer to me in the world than you." So I kissed them and behaved bountifully towards them as before.

After they had lived with me for another year, it came into my head to fit out a ship with merchandise and to voyage in it to do business at Basrah. So I got ready a vessel, filling it with merchandise and goods of all kinds as well as necessaries for the voyage. I asked my sisters whether they would rather stay at home while I was away or come with me. They decided to accompany me, so I took them with me and we set sail. But first I divided my money into two halves, one of which I took with me and one of which I hid at home in case some misfortune befell the ship and we escaped with our lives.

We sailed on night and day, but by ill-luck the captain lost his course, so that we were driven to the outer ocean and into a sea quite other than the one we had designed to reach. Driving before the wind for ten days, we saw at last a city far off and asked the captain what its name might be. "As Allah lives, I do not know," he answered. "I have never seen it in my life, nor the sea in which we are. But the important thing is that we are now out of danger. It only remains for you to enter that city and offer your merchandise. I suggest that you should sell it there if you can."

An hour later he came to us again, saying: "Disembark now and go into the city to see the marvels of Allah there. Call on His name and you shall go in safety."

We entered the city and saw to our stupefaction that all the inhabitants had been turned into black rocks, but that, while they had been petrified, everything else in the markets and the streets was as it had been, goods of every kind and appointments of gold and silver all about the place. We were delighted with what we saw and, saying to each other: "Surely there must be some extraordinary reason for all this," separated, each going in different directions about the streets, to collect as much as might be conveniently carried of gold, silver and precious fabrics.

It was towards the citadel that I made my way. There I found the King's palace and, entering by a great door of solid gold and lifting a velvet curtain, I saw that all the furniture and everything else there was of fine gold or silver. In the courtyard and in all the rooms soldiers and chamberlains stood or sat, all turned to stone; and in the central hall, filled with chamberlains, lieutenants and wazīrs, I saw the King sitting on his throne, petrified also but arrayed in such noble and costly garments as took my breath away. Fifty silk-clad mamelūks[6] holding naked swords stood there in stone about the King. His throne was encrusted with great pearls lying among other jewels. And each pearl shone so like a star that I thought I should lose my wits in gazing on them.

Going on, I reached the harīm, which I found to be more wonderful than all the rest, built even to the window-bars of solid gold and with silken hangings on the walls and with velvet and satin curtains hanging before the doors and windows. In the midst of a group of women, all turned to stone, I saw the Queen herself dressed in a robe sewn with noble pearls, crowned with a mass of great jewels, with collars and necklaces about her throat of pleasantly carved gold; but herself changed to black stone.

Wandering further, I came to an open door made with two leaves of virgin silver, and beyond it I saw a porphyry staircase of seven steps. Mounting this, I came to a white marble hall, covered with a carpet of gold thread, in the middle of which there rose, between great golden torches, a dais also of solid gold picked out with emeralds and turquoises. An alabaster bed, studded with pearls and upholstered with precious embroidery, stood on the dais with a great light shining by it. I came near and found that the light proceeded from a diamond, as large as an ostrich's egg, lying on a stool by the bedside and shining from all its facets so that the whole hall was filled with radiance.

Although the diamond outshone them utterly, the torches were lighted; therefore I deduced that some human hand was near and went on searching among the other halls, marvelling at all I saw and hunting everywhere for a human being. I was so entranced that I forgot all about my voyage, my ship, and my sisters. Night fell suddenly while I was still in a dream at all that beauty, and when I tried to leave the palace I could not find my way. In my search I came again to the hall with the alabaster bed, the diamond, and the lighted torches. Lying down, I half covered myself with a blue satin quilt wrought with silver and pearl, and took up a copy of our Koran, that sacred book. It was written out in stately gold characters with red devices and illuminations in all colours. From it I read a few verses to the glory of Allah and to reprove myself that my sleep might be holy. I meditated on the words of the Prophet, whom may Allah bless, and tried to sleep.

When the middle of the night had come and I was still awake, I heard a sweet and learned voice reciting the Koran. I rose in haste and, going in the direction of the voice, came to a little room with an open door. I entered softly, leaving the torch which I had caught up outside, and saw that the place was a kind of sanctuary. It was lighted by little green glass lamps and on its floor, facing the East, lay a prayer-rug upon which a very beautiful young man was reading the Koran aloud with grave attention and perfect eloquence. In my astonishment I asked myself how this young man alone could have escaped the fate of all the city. I came towards him and wished him peace. When he turned his eyes upon me and wished me peace, I said: "I conjure you by the truth of the sacred words which you are reading from the book of Allah to answer my question truly."

Calmly and sweetly he smiled at me, saying: "First, O woman, tell me how it is that you have come into this place where I pray, and then I will answer any question you like to put to me." When he had listened in astonishment to my story, I questioned him concerning the extraordinary appearance of the city. He shut the sacred book and, placing it in a satin bag, bade me sit at his side. I did so and, gazing attentively at

---

6. Warrior slaves.

him, found in him that full perfection which is in the moon: sympathy, beauty of face, proportioned elegance of body. His cheeks were as clear as crystal, his face had the delicate tint of the fresh date, as if it had been he of whom the poet was thinking when he wrote these lines:

> A watcher of the stars at night
> Looked up and saw to rose and white
> A boy, with such delicious grace,
> Such brilliant tint of breast and face,
> So curved and delicate of limb,
> That he exclaimed on seeing him:
> "Sure it was Saturn gave that hair,
> A black star falling in the air;
> Those roses were a gift from Mars;
> The Archer of the seven stars
> Gave all his arrows to that eye;
> While great sagacious Mercury
> Did sweet intelligence impart;
> Queen Venus forged his golden heart
> And . . . and . . ." But here the sage's art
> Stopped short; and his old wits went wild
> When the new star drew near and smiled.

Red flames were lighted in my heart when I looked at him and, in the violent trouble of my senses, I regretted that I had not met him long before. "Master and sovereign," I said, "I pray you answer me." "I hear and I obey," he replied, and told me the following remarkable story:

Honourable lady, this was my father's city, filled with his subjects and the people of his kin. He it was whom you saw petrified upon his throne, the Queen you saw was my mother. Both were magicians, worshippers of terrible Nardūn, who swore by fire and light, by shade and heat, and all the turning stars.

For a long time my father had no children. I was the child of his age and he reared me carefully throughout my boyhood, that I might be bred up to the true happiness of kingship.

Now in the palace there was a very old woman who in secret was a Believer in Allah and his Messenger, though in public she pretended to fall in with the creed of my parents. My father had great confidence in her as a faithful and chaste woman, he heaped benefits upon her and firmly believed that she was of his own faith. When I began to grow up, he put me in her charge, commanding her to give me a good education and a grounding in the laws of Nardūn.

The old woman took me into her charge and at once declared to me the religion of Islām, from its rites of purification and ablution to the sacred forms of its prayers. She taught and expounded the Koran to me in the Prophet's own tongue[7] and, when she had taught me all that she knew, warned me to keep my knowledge sedulously from my father lest he should kill me. I did so and, when a short time afterwards that saintly old woman died breathing her last words into my ear, I continued a secret believer in Allah and His Prophet. Far different were the inhabitants of this city who hardened their hearts and dwelt in darkness. But one day, while they continued their idolatry, a

---

7. Arabic.

voice like thunder spoke from an invisible muezzin to far and near, saying: "O people of the city, leave the worship of fire and Nardūn, and turn to the one Almighty King."

Terrified by this voice the inhabitants of the city sought the King, my father, and asked the meaning of these awful words. But my father told them not to be frightened or amazed, and bade them stand firm in their old beliefs.

So for another year they blindly worshipped fire, until the day came round again on which the voice had been heard. Then the voice boomed out once more, and this it did on the same day for the next three years. But the people continued to worship their false god until one morning, out of the clear sky of dawn, wrath and sorrow fell upon them and they were suddenly turned to black stone, they and their horses, their mules and their camels, and all their beasts. I alone, who was the sole Believer in the city, escaped the doom.

Since then I have remained here, praying, fasting, and reciting from the Book, but I have been very lonely, lovely lady, with no one to bear me human company.

On this I said to him: "Youth of every perfection, will you not come with me to the city of Baghdad, where are sages and venerable old men steeped in the teachings of our Religion? There your learning and your faith will be increased together, and I, though I am a woman of some account, will be your slave there. In Baghdad I am mistress among my people, with a following of men, servants and young boys; also I have a ship here full of all necessary goods. Fate threw me upon your coast and Destiny has seen fit to bring us together." I did not cease from fanning his desire to go with me until he consented to do so.

At this point Shahrazād saw the approach of morning and discreetly fell silent as was her custom.

But when the seventeenth night had come

She said:

It is related, O auspicious King, that the girl Zubaidah did not cease from fanning the desire of the young man to go with her until he consented to do so.

They talked long together until sleep overcame them, and Zubaidah slept that night at the feet of the young man. I leave you to imagine whether she was happy or no.

Zubaidah continued her story to the Khalīfah Hārūn al-Rashīd, in the hearing of Jafar and the three kalandars in these words:

When morning broke, we chose out from all the treasures of the palace the best we could carry, and went down towards the city, where we met my slaves and the captain who had been looking for me a long time. They were delighted to see me again and more than a little astonished when I gave them the outline of my story and of the young man's tale concerning the doom which had fallen upon the city. But hardly had my sisters seen the handsome young man than they were filled with violent jealousy and began in their hatred secretly to plot my hurt.

We all went aboard, I in great joy because I loved the youth, and, taking advantage of a favourable wind, sailed away. My sisters never left us alone, and one day they asked me directly what I intended to do with the youth. I told them that I meant to marry him and, turning towards him, I said: "Master, I desire to become your slave. Do not refuse me this." "Indeed, I do not refuse," he answered and, our troth being thus plighted, I said to my sisters: "This young man is enough property for me. All else I have I give to you." "Your wish is law," they answered, but at the same time they schemed against me in their hearts.

We came with favouring winds from the Dread Sea to the Sea of Safety, across which we sailed for several days till we saw the buildings of Basrah rising from the water. That night we cast anchor and all slept.

While we slept, my sisters rose and, lifting the youth and myself, cast us, mattresses and all, into the sea. The poor young man, who could not swim, was drowned. It was written by Allah that he should become one of the martyrs, just as it was written that I should be saved. For, when I fell into the water, Allah sent me a spar of wood to which I clung and supported by which I was carried by the waves to the shore of a nearby island. There I dried my clothes and slept, rising in the morning to look for some track which should lead me to safety. Soon I found a road worn by human feet which I followed into the interior of the island, until I had gone right across it and came out on the other side, opposite the city of Basrah. Suddenly I saw a little snake hurrying towards me, hotly pursued by a much larger snake who was trying to kill it. I felt pity for the little snake which was so weary that its tongue hung out. So I lifted a great stone and smashed in the head of the large snake, killing it on the spot. Immediately to my surprise the little snake spread two wings and, flying up into the air, disappeared from my sight.

Being broken by fatigue, I lay down where I was and slept for about an hour. When I woke, I found a beautiful young negress seated at my feet, rubbing and kissing them. I snatched them away in considerable shame, not knowing whether her intentions towards me were honourable or not, and asked her sharply who she was and what she wanted. "I hastened to come to you," she said, "because of the great service you have done me in killing my enemy. I am a Jinnīyah and was in the likeness of that little snake. The big snake was my enemy, a Jinnī who wished to rape me and to kill me. You saved me, so I flew at once to the ship from which your two sisters threw you. I changed them into black bitches and have brought them to you." Sure enough, there were two black bitches tied to the tree behind me. "Lastly," went on the Jinnīyah, "I transported all your riches to your house in Baghdad and then sank the ship. As for your young man, he is drowned. I can do nothing against death. Allah alone is Almighty."

With these words she took me in her arms together with my sisters, the bitches, and, flying with us through the air, set us down safely on the terrace of my house here in Baghdad.

Looking about me I found all the treasures and the goods that had been in my ship ranged in careful order round the rooms, not one having been lost or spoiled. Before she left, the Jinnīyah said to me: "I command you by the sacred symbol on the Seal of Sulaimān to give each of these bitches three hundred strokes of the whip every day. If you forget even once I shall be obliged to come back and change you also into the same shape."

What could I answer save: "I hear and I obey"?

Ever since then, O Prince of Believers, I have beaten them and then pitifully caressed them as you have seen. That is my story.

* * *

But when the eighteenth night had come

Shahrazād continued in this wise:

It is related, O auspicious King, that, on hearing the stories of the girls Zubaidah and Amīnah, who with their little sister Fahīmah, the two black bitches, and the three kalandars, had been brought before him, the Khalīfah Hārūn al-Rashīd rejoiced at the marvel of the two tales and ordered them to be written out in fair calligraphy by his scribes. * * *

Then al-Amīn was remarried to the young Amīnah, Zubaidah to the first kalandar who was a king's son, the other two sisters to the other two kalandars, princes both, and the Khalīfah himself wedded the youngest of the five sisters, the maiden Fahīmah, the witty and agreeable cateress.

Hārūn al-Rashīd had a palace built for each couple and endowed them with riches that they might live happily. Also, hardly had night fallen when he himself hastened to bed with the young Fahīmah, and they passed the sweetest of nights together.

from The Tale of Sympathy the Learned

But when the two-hundred-and-seventieth night had come

Little Dunyazād waited until Shahrazād had finished her act with the King, and then raised her head, crying: "O sister, why do you not start at once the anecdotes which you promised us concerning that delightful poet Abū Nuwās,[1] the Khalīfah's friend, the sweetest singer of Irāq and Arabia?" Shahrazād smiled at her sister, saying: "I only wait the King's permission before telling you some of the adventures of Abū Nuwās, who was not only an exquisite poet but a notorious evil-liver."

Dunyazād ran to her sister and embraced her, saying: "What did he do? Tell us at once, if you please."

But King Shahryār turned to Shahrazād and said: "O Shahrazād, it would give me great pleasure to hear one or two of these adventures, for I am sure that they are most entertaining; but tonight my mind is more inclined to higher things and would rather hear words of wisdom from you. If you know some tale which can fortify our souls with moral precepts and help us to profit by the experience of the wise, do not scruple to begin at once. Afterwards, if my patience be not exhausted, you may recount the adventures of Abū Nuwās."

Shahrazād hastened to reply: "By chance I have been thinking all day, O auspicious King, of a story which concerns a girl who was called Sympathy, a slave unequalled both in beauty and learning; I am ready to tell you all that I have heard of what she did and what she knew."

"As Allah lives," cried King Shahryār, "you may begin at once; for nothing pleases me more than to learn wisdom from the lips of beauty. I hope that the tale will satisfy and profit me with an example of that learning which becomes a faithful Muslim woman."

Shahrazād reflected for a short time and then raised her finger, saying:

It is related—but Allah is all-wise and all-knowing—that there was once a very rich merchant in Baghdad, who had honour and privilege of every kind, but whom Allah had deprived of one happiness. He had no child, not even a daughter. He grew old in sorrow, seeing his bones becoming more and more transparent, his back more and more arched, without being able to obtain any consoling result from his numerous wives. One day, however, after he had distributed a great alms, visited saints, fasted and prayed fervently, he lay with his youngest wife and, by Allah's grace, got her with child.

---

1. One of the major poets of the Abbasid period; see page 385.

At the end of nine months to a day she bore him a man-child as fair as a fragment of the moon; therefore the merchant in gratitude to Allah entertained the poor, the widow, and the orphan for seven whole days, and then named his son Abū al-Husn.[2]

The child was carried in the arms of nurses and beautiful slaves, cared for like some jewel of price by all the women, until he reached the age when he might begin to learn. Then wise masters were given to him, who taught him the wonderful words of the Koran, beautiful writing, poetry, arithmetic, and especially the science of shooting with the bow.

Not only was his education finer than that of any other child then living, but his beauty was almost a magic thing. His boyish graces, the fresh colour of his cheeks, the flowers of his lips, and the young down of his face were thus celebrated by a poet:

> Though spring has passed already over the rose trees,
> Here are some buds not fully opened yet,
> In this sweet garden ignorant of weather:
> See, the down feather
> Of the violet
> Under those trees!

Young Abū al-Husn was his father's joy and the light of his eyes, during the old man's remaining term upon this earth. When he felt that his debt was about to be paid to Allah, he called his son to him, saying: "My child, quittance nears and I have nothing left to do but prepare myself to stand before the Master. I leave you great riches, money and goods, rich fields and farms, which should last your lifetime and the lifetime of your children's children. Enjoy your property without excess, thanking the Giver and being mindful of Him all your days." With that the old merchant died, and his son shut himself in with grief, after superintending his father's funeral.

Soon, however, his friends led him away from his sorrow and persuaded him to go to the hammām and change his garments, saying: "He who is born again in a son like yourself does not die. Have done with tears; make the most of your riches and your youth."

So Abū al-Husn little by little forgot the counsels of his father and learnt to look upon happiness and gold as inexhaustible. He satisfied every caprice of his nature, frequenting singers and musicians, eating enormous quantities of chicken every day (for he was very fond of chicken), unsealing old jars of strong wine, and hearing ever about him the noise of chinking goblets. He exhausted all that he could exhaust and spent all that he could spend, until he woke one morning to find that there remained of all his possessions only a single slave girl.

But here you must pause to admire the workings of Fate, who had decreed that this one remaining slave should be the supreme marvel of Western and Eastern women. She was called Sympathy; and never had a name been better given. She was as upright as the letter alif, and her figure was so slim that she might defy the sun to cast a shadow by her; the colouring of her young face was wonderful, and its expression was both fortunate and filled with blessing. Her mouth seemed to have been sealed with the seal of Sulaimān to guard the pearls within; the two pomegranates of her breasts were separated by a valley of shadows and delights; and her navel was

2. "The handsome one."

carved so deep that it would have held an ounce of nutmeg butter. Her reed-like waist ended in so heavy a croup that she left deep prints of it in every sofa and mattress which she used. A certain poet had her in mind when he wrote:

> If you can call the sun and the moon and the rose tree
> Sad-coloured,
> Call her sad-coloured also.
>
> Hearts beat the advance as she advances,
> And the retreat when she retreats.
> The river of life flows through the meadows of Eden,
> And the meadows of Eden are below her garment,
> The moon is beneath her mantle.
>
> Her body is a song of colours:
> Carnation of roses answers to silver,
> Black ripe berries
> And new-cut sandal-wood
> Are one note.
>
> The man who takes her is more blessed
> Than the God who gives her;
> And He is continually called blessed.

Such was the slave Sympathy, the last possession of the prodigal Abū al-Husn of Baghdad.

At this point Shahrazād saw the approach of morning and discreetly fell silent.

But when the two-hundred-and-seventy-first night had come

She said:

Seeing that he was ruined for ever, Abū al-Husn fell into a desolation which robbed him of both hunger and sleep; for three days and three nights he refused food and drink and sleep, so that the slave Sympathy thought he was on the point of dying and determined to save him at any cost to herself.

She put on the rest of her jewels and those robes which remained most fit to be seen; then she went to her master and said with an encouraging smile: "Allah will put an end to your misfortunes by my help. You have only to take me with you to the Commander of the Faithful, Hārūn al-Rashīd, fifth of the line of Abbās, and offer me to him for ten thousand dīnārs. If he objects that the price is too high, you must say: 'Prince of Believers, this girl is worth more; as you will discover if you put her to the proof. You will find that she is without equal or near equal, and worthy to serve the Khalīfah.'" She finished by recommending that he should not bate his price on any consideration.

Abū al-Husn had neglected, in his careless way, to notice the supreme gifts of his beautiful slave; therefore he merely thought that the idea was not a bad one and held some chances of success. He led Sympathy into the presence of the Khalīfah without delay, and repeated the offer which she had recommended to him.

The Khalīfah turned towards her, asking: "What is your name?" "I am called Sympathy," she answered, and he continued: "O Sympathy, are you indeed learned, and can you tell me the various branches of knowledge in which you excel?" "My master," she answered, "I have studied syntax, poetry, civil and canon law, music, astronomy, geometry, arithmetic, the law concerning inheritance, the art of elucidating books of spells and reading ancient inscriptions. I know the Sublime Book by heart and can read it in seven different ways;[3] I know the exact number of its chapters, verses, divisions, parts, and combinations; how many lines, words, consonants, and vowels there are in it; I know which are the inspired chapters written at Mecca and those which were dictated at Madinah. I know both laws and dogmas, and can determine the degrees of authenticity among them from the point of tradition; I am acquainted with architecture, logic, and philosophy; with eloquence, language, rhetoric, and the rules of versification. I know every artifice by which words can be ordered into musical lines. I am equally at home in the construction of simply flowing verses and very complicated examples suited for subtle palates alone; if I introduce an occasional obscurity into my compositions, it is to hold the attention and to delight such minds as can disentangle a fragile thread. I have learnt many things and remembered all I have learnt. I can sing perfectly, dance like a bird, play the lute and the flute, and perform in fifty different ways on every stringed instrument. When I dance and sing, those who see and hear me are damned by my beauty; when I walk in my perfumed clothing, balanced upon my feet, I kill; when I move my bottom, I overthrow; when I wink, I pierce; when I shake my bracelets, I make blind; I give life with a touch, and death by going away; I am skilful in all the arts and have carried my education so far that only those who have worn out their life in study may see it, as it were, upon the far horizon."

Hārūn al-Rashīd was delighted and astonished to find so much eloquence and beauty in the child who stood before him with lowered eyes. He turned to Abū al-Husn, saying: "I shall send at once for all the masters of art and science in my kingdom, to put the knowledge of your slave to public proof. If she comes victorious from the trial, I will not give you ten thousand dīnārs but cover you with honours for having brought so great a marvel to me. If she fails in her examination, she shall remain your property."

The Khalīfah straightway sent for the most learned man of that time, Ibrāhīm ibn Siyyār,[4] a sage who had gone to the depths of all human knowledge; and he also commanded the presence of the chief poets, grammarians, theologians, doctors, philosophers, astronomers and lawyers of his kingdom. They hastened to the palace and assembled in the great hall, without knowing why they had been summoned. They seated themselves in a circle upon carpets about the Khalīfah's golden chair, while Sympathy stood meekly in their presence, smiling upon them through her light veil.

At this point Shahrazād saw the approach of morning and discreetly fell silent.

But when the two-hundred-and-seventy-second night had come

She said:

When a silence had fallen upon this assembly so deep that the far-off fall of a needle upon the ground might have been heard, Sympathy made a graceful and dignified bow to those present and said to the Khalīfah in a melodious voice:

---

3. The seven ways of reciting the Qur'an.

4. One of the most erudite intellectuals of the era of Harun Al-Rashid.

"Prince of Believers, it is for you to order and for me to obey; I stand ready to answer any question posed to me by these venerable sages, these readers of the Koran, lawyers, doctors, architects, astronomers, geometrists, grammarians, philosophers and poets."

Hārūn al-Rashīd turned to those who were about him, saying: "I have called you hither that you may examine the learning of this girl in all directions and to any depth; it is for you to spare no pains in exhibiting your own scholarship and erudition." All the sages bowed to the earth, carrying their hands to their eyes and foreheads, and answering: "Obedience and obeisance to Allah and to you, O Prince of Believers!"

The slave Sympathy stood for some moments in thought with lowered head; then she looked up, saying: "Tell me, my masters, which of you is the most learned in the Koran and the traditions of our Prophet (upon whom be prayer and peace!)." All fingers were pointed to one of the doctors, who rose, saying: "I am that man." Then said Sympathy: "Ask me what you will of your own subject." So the learned reader of the Koran said:

"O young girl, since you have studied the sacred Book of Allah, you must know the number of the chapters, words, and letters in it; and also the precepts of our faith. Tell me first who is your Lord, who is your Prophet, who is your Imām, what is your orientation, what is your rule of life, what is your guide, and who are your brothers?"

She answered: "Allah is my Lord, Muhammad (upon whom be prayer and peace!) is my Prophet; the Koran is my law and therefore my Imām; the Kaabah, the house of Allah builded by Abraham at Mecca, is my orientation; the example of our holy Prophet is my rule of life; the Sunnah,[5] the collection of traditions, is my guide; and all Believers are my brothers."

While the Khalīfah marvelled to hear such precise answers from such lovely lips, the sage said:

"Tell me, how do you know that there is a God?"

She answered: "By reason."

"What is reason?"

"Reason is a double gift: it is both innate and acquired. Innate wisdom is that which Allah has placed in the hearts of His chosen servants that they may walk in the way of truth. Acquired wisdom is the fruit of education and labour in an intelligent man."

"That is an excellent answer. But can you tell me, where is the seat of reason?"

"In the heart, whence inspirations rise to the brain."

"That is so. How have you learnt to know the Prophet (upon whom be prayer and peace!)?"

"By reading the Book of Allah, by the phrases contained therein, by the proofs and witnessings of His divine mission."

"What are the indispensable duties of our religion?"

"The indispensable duties of our religion are five: the profession of Faith: 'There is no God but Allah and Muhammad is the messenger of Allah!', prayer, alms, fasting during the month of Ramadān, and pilgrimage to Mecca when that is possible."

"What are the most praiseworthy acts of piety?"

"They are six in number: prayer, alms, fasting, pilgrimage, fighting bad instincts and forbidden things, to take part in a holy war."

---

5. The set of rules derived from the conduct and sayings of the Prophet Muhammad. The Kaabah is the central shrine in Mecca; an imam is a prayer leader.

"What is the aim of prayer?"

"To offer the homage of my virtue to the Lord, to celebrate His praises, and to lift my soul towards the calm places."

"Yā Allah! That is an excellent reply. Does not prayer necessitate certain indispensable preparations?"

"Certainly it does. It is necessary to purify the whole body by ritual ablutions, to put on garments which have no stain of dirt, to choose a clean place in which to pray, to protect that part of the body which lies between the navel and the knees, to have pure intent, and to turn towards the Kaabah, in the direction of holy Mecca."

"What is the value of prayer?"

"It sustains faith, of which it is the foundation."

"What is the fruit or utility of prayer?"

"True prayer has no terrestrial use; it should be regarded only as a spiritual tie between the creature and his Lord. It can produce ten immaterial results: it lights the heart, it brightens the face, it pleases the Compassionate, it infuriates the devil, it attracts pity, it repels evil, it preserves from ill, it protects against enemies, it fortifies the wavering spirit, and brings the slave nearer to his Master."

"What is the key of prayer? And what is the key of that key?"

"The key of prayer is ablution and the key of ablution is the preparatory formula: 'In the name of Allah, the Merciful, the Compassionate.'" * * *

When the learned commentator of the Book heard Sympathy's answers, he could not but admit to himself that she knew as much as he did; but, being unwilling to confess his inability to catch her out, he asked her the following subtle question: "What is the linguistic meaning of the word *ablution?*"

"To get rid of all internal or external impurity by washing."

"What is the meaning of the word to *fast?*"

"To abstain."

"What is the meaning of the word to *give?*"

"To enrich oneself."

"To go on a *pilgrimage?*"

"To attain the end."

"To make *war?*"

"To defend oneself."

The sage rose up, crying: "In truth I am short of questions and arguments. This slave astonishes me with her knowledge and the clearness of her exposition, O Commander of the Faithful!"

Sympathy smiled slightly, saying: "I would like, in my turn, to ask you one question: can you tell me what are the foundations of Islām?"

He reflected for a moment, and then replied: "They are four in number: faith illuminated by sane reason; righteousness; knowledge of duty and equity, together with discretion; and the fulfilment of all promises."

Sympathy said again: "Allow me to ask you a further question. If you cannot answer it, it will be my right to take away the distinctive garment which you wear as a learned reader of the Book."

"I accept," he answered, "put your question, O slave."

"What are the branches of Islām?" she asked.

After a long time spent in reflection, the wise man could not answer, so the Khalīfah said to Sympathy: "If you can give us the answer yourself, the gown belongs to you."

Sympathy bowed and answered: "The branches of Islām are twenty: strict observance of the Book's teaching, conformation with the traditions and oral instructions of the Prophet, the avoidance of injustice, eating permitted food, never to eat unpermitted food, to punish evil doers that vice may not increase owing to the exaggerated clemency of the virtuous, repentance, profound study of religion, to do good to enemies, to be modest, to succour the servants of Allah, to avoid all innovation and change, to show courage in adversity and strength in time of trial, to pardon when one is strong, to be patient in misfortune, to know Allah, to know His Prophet (upon whom be prayer and peace!), to resist the suggestions of the Evil One, to fight against the passions and wicked instincts of the soul, to be wholly vowed in confidence and submission to the service of Allah."

When the Khalīfah Hārūn al-Rashīd heard this answer, he ordered the sage's gown to be stripped from him and given to Sympathy; this was immediately done, and the learned man left the hall in confusion, with his head bowed.

Then a second theologian, famous for his subtlety, to whom all eyes voted the honour of next questioning the girl, rose and turned towards Sympathy, saying: "I will only ask you a few short questions, O slave. What duties are to be observed while eating?"

"In eating a man must first wash his hands and invoke the name of Allah. He must sit upon the left haunch, and use only the thumb and two first fingers in conveying the food to his mouth. He must take small mouthfuls, masticate each piece of food thoroughly, and not look at his neighbour for fear of embarrassing him and spoiling his appetite."

"Can you tell me what is something, what is half something, and what is less than something?"

"A Believer is something, a hypocrite is half something, and an infidel is less than something."

"That is correct. Now can you tell me where faith is found?"

"Faith abides in four places: in the heart, in the head, in the tongue, and in the members. The strength of the heart consists in joy, the strength of the head in knowledge of the truth, the strength of the tongue in sincerity, and the strength of the members in submission."

"How many hearts are there?"

"There are several: the heart of the Believer is a pure and healthy heart, the heart of an Infidel is exactly the opposite." * * *

At this point Shahrazād saw the approach of morning and discreetly fell silent.

But when the two-hundred-and-seventy-sixth night had come

She said:

"There is a heart attached to the things of this world, and a heart attached to spiritual joys; there is a heart mastered by the passions, by hate or avarice; there is a slack heart, a heart burning with love, a heart puffed with pride; there is a lighted heart like that of the companions of our holy Prophet; and there is the heart of the Prophet himself, which is the heart of the Chosen."

When the learned theologian heard this answer, he cried: "You have won my approbation, O slave!"

Sympathy looked at the Khalīfah, saying: "O Commander of the Faithful, allow me to ask one question of my examiner and to take his gown if he cannot answer." Hārūn al-Rashīd gave his permission, and she asked:

"Can you tell me what duty must be fulfilled before all other duties, however important those may be?"

The wise man did not know what to say, so the girl took his gown from him and herself answered the question:

"The duty of ablution; for we are bidden to purify ourselves before fulfilling the least of religious duties or any of those acts prescribed by the Book or the Sunnah."

Sympathy cast a glance round the assembly, and this was answered by one of the most celebrated men of the century, supposed without equal in a knowledge of the Koran. He rose and said:

"Since you know the Book of Allah, O girl full of the sweet perfume of the spirit, can you give me a sample of your study?"

"The Koran is composed of a hundred and fourteen chapters, seventy of which were dictated at Mecca and forty-four at Madinah. It is divided into six hundred and twenty-one divisions, called decades, and into six thousand two hundred and thirty-six verses. It contains seventy-nine thousand, four hundred and thirty-nine words, and three hundred and twenty-three thousand, six hundred and seventy letters, to each of which attach ten special virtues. The names of twenty-five prophets are mentioned: Adam, Noah, Ishmael, Isaac, Jacob, Joseph, Elisha, Jonah, Lot, Sālih, Hūd, Shuaib, David, Solomon, Dhūl-kafl, Idrīs, Elias, Yahyā, Zacharias, Job, Moses, Aaron, Jesus, and Muhammad (upon all these be prayer and peace!). Nine birds or winged beasts are mentioned: the gnat, the bee, the fly, the hoopoe, the crow, the grasshopper, the ant, the bulbul, and the bird of Jesus (upon whom be prayer and peace!), which is none other than the bat."

"You are marvellously exact. Now can you tell me in what verse our holy Prophet judges the Unbelievers?"

"In this verse: 'The Jews say that the Christians are wrong and the Christians say that the Jews are wrong; to this extent both are right!'" * * *

The learned questioner could contain himself no longer, but cried out: "I bear witness, O Prince of Believers, that this young girl is unequalled in knowledge!"

Sympathy demanded leave to ask a question in her turn, and said:

"Can you tell me which verse of the Koran contains the letter kāf twenty-three times, which contains the letter mīm sixteen times, and which contains the letter ain forty times?"

The sage stayed with his mouth open, unable to make the least attempt at an answer; so Sympathy first took away his gown and then herself indicated the required verses to the general stupefaction of all.

Next, a learned doctor of medicine rose in the assembly, one famous for the studies he had made and the books he had written, and said:

"You have spoken excellently of the things of the spirit; now it is time that we turn our attention to the body. I require you, O beautiful slave, to give us some information about the body of man, its composition, its nerves, its bones, its vertebrae, and why Adam was called Adam."

"The name of Adam comes from the Arabic word adīm, which signifies the surface of the earth; it was given to the first man because he was created from earth taken from different parts of the world. His head was made from the soil of the East, his breast from the soil of the Kaabah, and his feet from the soil of the West. Allah made seven entrances and two exits for the body: the two eyes, the two ears, the two nostrils, and the mouth for entrances, and for exits, one before and one behind. Then the Creator united in Adam four elements to give him a nature: water, earth, fire and air;

so that a bilious temperament is of the nature of fire, which is hot and dry; a nervous temperament is of the nature of earth, which is dry; a lymphatic temperament is of the nature of water, which is cold and moist; and a sanguine temperament is of the nature of air, which is warm and dry. After this Allah assembled the human body. He placed within it three hundred and sixty ducts and two hundred and forty bones. He gave it three instincts: of life, reproduction, and appetite. He gave it a heart, a spleen, lungs, six intestines, a liver, two kidneys, a brain, two eggs, a member, and a skin. He dowered it with five senses, guided by seven vital spirits. As for the position of the organs, he placed the heart upon the left of the breast, and the stomach below it, the lungs to act as fans for the heart, the liver on the right to guard the heart, and, for the same purpose, he placed the interlacing intestines and the articulation of the ribs. The head is composed of forty-eight bones, the chest of twenty-four ribs and twenty-five in a woman; this extra rib is on the right, and is useful to fasten the child in the belly of its mother and to support it, as it were, by an arm." * * *

"So far there has been nothing lacking in your answers. Now I wish to ask you a question of capital importance, which will show if you have a true knowledge of the facts of life. Can you give us a clear account of copulation?"

On hearing this question the young girl blushed and lowered her head, so that the Khalīfah thought that she was unable to answer: but she turned towards him, saying: "As Allah lives, O Commander of the Faithful, my silence is not due to ignorance; for the answer is upon the tip of my tongue, but refuses to leave my lips because of my respect for the Khalīfah." Hārūn al-Rashīd answered: "It would give me very great pleasure to hear such an answer from your mouth. Speak freely, explicitly, and without fear." So the learned Sympathy spoke as follows:

"Copulation is that act which unites the sexes of man and woman. It is an excellent thing, having many virtues and conferring many benefits: it lightens the body and relieves the soul, it cures melancholy, tempers the heat of passion, attracts love, contents the heart, consoles in absence, and cures insomnia. These are its effects when a man couples with a young woman: it is far otherwise when he has to do with an old one. Connection with an old woman exposes a man to many maladies, among others disease of the eyes, disease of the kidneys, disease of the thighs, and disease of the back. In a word, it is a terrible thing, to be avoided as one would avoid a deadly poison. Best of all is to choose a woman expert in the art, one who understands a wink, who can speak with her feet and hands, and spare her owner the necessity of keeping a garden and flower beds.

All complete copulation is followed by moisture. In the woman this moisture is produced by the emotion felt in her honourable parts; in the man, by the running of that sap which is secreted by the two eggs. This sap follows a complicated road; man possesses one large vein which gives birth to all the other veins; the blood which fortifies these three hundred and sixty smaller veins runs at last into a tube which debouches in the left egg; in this egg the blood turns about, clarifies, and changes into a white liquid which thickens because of the heat of the egg, and smells like palm milk."

At this point Shahrazād saw the approach of morning and discreetly fell silent.

But when the two-hundred-and-eighty-second night had come

She said:

"You have answered wisely!" cried the sage. "I have only two more questions to ask. Can you tell me what thing lives always in prison and dies when it breathes the free air? Also, what are the best fruits?"

"The first is a fish; and the second, citrons and pomegranates."

When the doctor heard the wonderful replies of Sympathy, he confessed himself incapable of making her stumble and would have returned to his place, but Sympathy signed to him to remain, saying: "I will now ask you a question. Can you tell me what is round like the earth, and lives in an eye, sometimes going through that eye, and sometimes separated from it, copulating without an organ, leaving its companion for the night, and embracing her again during the day, choosing its habitation upon the edge of things?"

The learned man cudgelled his brains for an answer but could find none, so Sympathy took away his gown and gave the answer herself: "The button and the button-loop." * * *

Hārūn al-Rashīd was edified in the extreme by so much knowledge and wisdom, and ordered the learned Ibrāhīm ibn Siyyār to give his own gown to the girl. The sage did so and then, lifting his right hand, witnessed publicly that the slave had surpassed him in scholarship and was the marvel of the age.

"Can you play upon instruments of music and accompany yourself while you sing?" asked the Khalīfah, and, when Sympathy replied that she could, had a lute brought to her, which was contained in a red satin case with a tassel of saffron coloured silk and a gold clasp. Sympathy drew the lute from its covering and found carved about it, in interlaced and flowering character, the following verses:

> I was the green branch of a tree
> Birds loved and taught their songs to.
> Haply the teaching lingers,
> For, when I lie on beauty's knee,
> Remember under beauty's fingers,
> The woodland song I sing belongs to
> The birds who sang to me.

She leaned over the lute as a mother over her nursling and, drawing twelve different harmonies from the strings, sang in a voice that echoed long after in all hearts and brought tears of emotion to every eye.

When she had finished, the Khalīfah rose up, crying: "May Allah increase your gifts within you, O Sympathy, and have in His benign keeping those who taught you and those who gave you birth!" So saying, he had ten thousand golden dīnārs, in a hundred sacks, given to Abū al-Husn and then turned to Sympathy, saying: "Tell me, O child of marvel, would you rather enter my harīm and have a palace and retinue for yourself, or return home with this young man?"

At this point Shahrazād saw the approach of morning and discreetly fell silent.

But when the two-hundred-and-eighty-seventh night had come

She said:

Sympathy kissed the earth between the Khalīfah's hands and answered: "May Allah continue to shower His blessings upon our master! Your slave would prefer to return to the house of him who brought her here."

Instead of being offended by this answer, the Khalīfah immediately gave Sympathy a further five thousand dīnārs, saying: "May you be found as expert in love as you are in answering questions!" After this he put the crown upon his generosity by raising Abū al-Husn to high employment and numbering him among his intimate favourites.

The two young people left the hall, one staggering under all the gowns of the sages, and the other under all the sacks of gold. As they went, they were followed by the whole marvelling assembly, who lifted their arms, crying: "Was ever in the world a liberality like that of the descendants of Abbās?"

Such, O auspicious King, continued Shahrazād, were the answers given by Sympathy before the assembly of sages and handed down in the royal annals to be an instruction to every woman of the Faith.

Then Shahrazād, seeing that King Shahryār was still frowning and racking his brains, began at once upon the Adventures of the Poet Abū Nuwās.

Little Dunyazād, who had been half asleep, woke up suddenly on hearing the name of Abū Nuwās and, large-eyed with attention, made ready to listen with all her ears.

from An Adventure of the Poet Abū Nuwās

It is related—but Allah is all-wise and all-knowing—that the Khalīfah Hārūn al-Rashīd was afflicted one night with lack of sleep and a preoccupation of spirit, so he went out alone from his palace and walked in the gardens to distract his weariness. He came at last to a pavilion the door of which was open, but guarded by a black eunuch who slept across the sill. The Khalīfah stepped over the body of the slave and, entering the single hall of the pavilion, saw a bed with lowered curtains, which was lighted on the right and left by tall torches. Beside the bed stood a little table holding a jar of wine topped by an inverted cup.

Hārūn al-Rashīd was astonished to find these things of which no one had informed him, so he lifted the curtains of the bed and stood stock-still with amazement at the sleeping beauty of a slave who lay there, as fair as the full moon, covered for sole garment with her fallen hair. He took the cup and filled it; then he drank slowly, saying beneath his breath: "To the roses in your cheeks, O child!" Setting down the cup, he leaned over the youthful face and dropped a kiss upon a little black mole which smiled to the left of the parted lips. Though this kiss was light as air, it woke the girl, who recognised the Prince of Believers and jumped up in the bed. The Khalīfah calmed her fright, saying: "O young slave, there is a lute beside you which I am sure you can play charmingly. Give me a taste of your skill, for I am determined to pass the night with you although I do not know you, and wish, as a preliminary, to hear your voice."

The girl took the lute and played upon it in twenty-one different modes, so that the Khalīfah was exalted with delight. Seeing the good impression that she had made, the young woman determined to profit by it, and said: "O Prince of Believers, I suffer from the assaults of Destiny." "How is that?" asked the Khalīfah, and she continued: "Your son al-Amīn bought me a few days ago for ten thousand dīnārs, intending to give me as a present to your majesty; but your wife, the lady Zubaidah, heard of his intention and, paying him back the money he had spent, gave me to a black eunuch with instructions to keep me a prisoner in this isolated pavilion."

The Khalīfah was annoyed when he heard this; therefore, after promising to give the girl a palace and a train worthy of her beauty on the morrow, he hastened to waken the sleeping eunuch and ordered him to go at once to command the poet Abū Nuwās to present himself at the palace. For you must know that Hārūn al-Rashīd was always wont to send for the poet when he was in an evil humour, in order to distract himself with the improvised poems and rhymed adventures of that remarkable man.

The eunuch went to Abū's house and, not discovering him there, searched throughout all the public places in Baghdad until he found him in a disreputable tavern at the lower end of the quarter of the Green Gate. He went up to him, saying: "O Abū Nuwās, our master the Khalīfah sends for you." The poet laughed as he answered: "O father of whiteness, how am I going to leave this place when I am in pawn for a young boy?"[1] "Where is he and who is he?" asked the eunuch, and Abū Nuwās replied: "He is slender, beardless and pretty. I promised him a thousand dirhams; as I have not the money about me, I can hardly go away."

"In Allah's name," cried the eunuch, "show me this boy and, if he is as delightful as you say, you shall be excused and more than excused."

As they were talking in this way, the pretty pet put his head round the door, and Abū Nuwās exclaimed: "If the branch wavers so pleasantly, will not the song of the birds be beautiful?"

At this point Shahrazād saw the approach of morning and discreetly fell silent.

But when the two-hundred-and-eighty-eighth night had come

She said:
On this the boy came right into the room of the tavern; and indeed his beauty was wonderful; also he was dressed in three tunics, one on top of the other, white and red and black.

Seeing him all in white, Abū Nuwās felt the fire of inspiration sparkle in his soul and he improvised these verses:

> His robe was white like milk,
> His eyes love-heavy underneath blue lids,
> His cheeks the shadow of wine-coloured silk
> Thrown upon snow.
> "What modesty forbids?
> Why do you pass me so?
> I am as patient for your hand
> As a white lamb is patient for the priest."
> "You sing three whites and I have four at least:
> A destiny which would be white without you,
> A body white and bland,
> A face of white,
> A garment blanched and exquisite.
> You did not count my white aright
> And so I flout you."

Hearing these lines the boy smiled and, taking off his white tunic, appeared all in brilliant red; so that Abū Nuwās was again inspired and sang without a pause:

> His tunic was as red as cruelties.
> "O child, you boasted white;
> What is the meaning of this sight,
> Two cheeks dyed in our broken hearts,
> A garment stolen from anemones?"

---

1. Abu-Nuwas was a well-known bisexual.

> "The dawn has lent me her attire,
> The evening sun has put his clouds apart
> And given me his fire,
> Red are my cheeks' embroideries,
> And red the veils which cling about my thighs,
> Red is the wine which painted
> Red lips where souls have fainted.
> So you have missed the addition of my red,"
> He said.

Delighted with this song, the minion threw aside his red garment and appeared in a black tunic, which clung to his skin and outlined a charming waist girt in by a silken belt. Seeing him, Abū Nuwās was exalted beyond reason, and sang again:

> He would not look at me.
> His tunic was as black as night
> By no intrusive moon beguiled;
> Therefore I said:
> "Now I will get it right;
> After the white and red,
> After the red and white,
> Black is the garden of your hair,
> Black is your tunic everywhere,
> Black are your eyes and black my destiny.
> My computation shows no lack;
> There's black and black and black on black."
> He smiled.

When the eunuch had considered the beauty of these poems and of the boy who inspired them, he forgave Abū Nuwās in his mind and returned straightway to the palace, where he informed the Khalīfah that Abū was held in pawn at a tavern because he could not pay what he had promised to a delightful youth. The Khalīfah, who was both amused and annoyed, sent back the eunuch with the sum of money required, bidding him bring the poet without delay.

The man hastened to the tavern and brought away the poet, who staggered a little from drink. When Abū Nuwās had been supported into the presence of the Khalīfah, Hārūn al-Rashīd lectured him in a voice which he strove to make furious; but, seeing that the poet burst out laughing, he took him by the hand and led him to the pavilion which the young girl occupied. * * *

The young woman gave wine to the Khalīfah, who invited the poet to empty the great cup himself. Abū Nuwās took it off at a single draught and soon felt the effects of the heavy vintage. As he reeled where he stood, the Khalīfah rose in jest and fell upon him sword in hand, making as if to cut off his head. The poet ran hither and thither about the hall with great cries of terror, and Hārūn al-Rashīd pursued him into all the corners, pricking him with the blade. At last the Khalīfah cried: "Enough! return and drink another cup." At the same time he signed to the girl to hide the vessel. She immediately concealed it beneath her robe, but Abū Nuwās saw the movement in spite of his drunkenness and sang:

> Even as I desire the cup
> The cup desires
> Lips secret and more pleasant,

> And has gone up
> Within her garments hollow,
> Whither the cup aspires
> Nuwās would follow,
> If only Hārūn were not present.

The Khalīfah laughed consumedly and, as a further jest, said to the poet: "As Allah lives, I must raise you to some high employment. From this time forth, I appoint you accredited chief of all the pimps in Baghdad." "In that case, O Commander of the Faithful," retorted Abū Nuwās with a grin, "what may I have the pleasure of doing for you tonight?"

Hārūn al-Rashīd flew into a rage and commanded the eunuch to call for Masrūr the sword-bearer, his executioner of justice.

At this point Shahrazād saw the approach of morning and discreetly fell silent.

But when the two hundred-and-ninetieth night had come

She said:

The Khalīfah ordered Masrūr to strip Abū Nuwās of all his clothes, to saddle him with an ass's pack-saddle, to pass an ass's halter round his neck, and to thrust a spur up his fundament. When this had been done, the unfortunate poet was led up and down before all the pavilions of the King's favourites, that they might laugh at him; and Masrūr had instructions, when this exhibition had been completed, to take Abū Nuwās to the gate of the city, to cut off his head in the presence of the people, and to bring it back upon a dish.

The despairing poet was paraded before each of the three hundred and sixty-five palaces, and, when their inhabitants heard of the death he was about to die, they grieved for him because they loved his wit, and as a sign of their sympathy threw gold and jewels before his path. Then they came out of their dwellings and followed him with words of encouragement, so that the wazīr Jafar al-Barmakī, who was passing on his way to the palace, halted before the weeping man and said: "Is that you, O Abū Nuwās? What crime have you committed to have earned so grave a punishment?" "As Allah lives," answered Abū Nuwās, "I have not committed even the suspicion of a crime. On the contrary I recited some of my most exquisite poems before the Khalīfah, and he has rewarded me by giving me his own robe of honour."

The Khalīfah, who was hiding behind a curtain of the nearest pavilion, heard this answer and burst into a hearty laugh. He not only pardoned Abū Nuwās, but gave him a real robe of honour and a large sum of money; also he continued to make him the inseparable companion of his black hours, as heretofore.

When Shahrazād had finished this tale of the poet Abū Nuwās, little Dunyazād, who had been endeavouring to stifle her silent laughter in the carpet, ran to her sister, crying: "As Allah lives, dear Shahrazād, that is a funny tale!"

from The Flowering Terrace of Wit and the Garden of Gallantry[1]

[THE YOUTH AND HIS MASTER]

It is related that the wazīr Badr al-Dīn, governor of Yaman, had a young brother, whose beauty was so incomparable that both men and women would stop and turn

---

1. A heading for a loose collection of anecdotes, three of which are included here.

when he passed them and stand bathing their eyes in the charm of his appearance. The wazīr, who feared that some untimely adventure might come to so fair a being, kept him far from the regard of men and prevented him from companionship with lads of his own age. Not wishing to send him to school, where he might not be sufficiently watched, he had a venerable and pious old man, whose manners were notoriously chaste, come to the house as tutor. This old man visited every day and was shut up for many hours together with the pupil in a room which the wazīr had set aside for the lessons.

It was not long before the beauty and seduction of the boy had their usual effect; after a few days the old man was so violently in love with his young charge that he heard all the birds singing again in his soul and, at their singing, something woke which had long slept.

Knowing no other way to master this feeling, he opened his heart to the boy and assured him that he could no longer live without him. "Alas," said the youth, who was deeply touched by the emotion of his teacher, "my hands are tied, and every minute of my time is watched over by my brother." The old man sighed and said: "How I long to pass an evening alone with you!" "You may well say so," retorted the other. "If my days are so well guarded, what do you think is done about my nights?" "I know, I know," said the old man, "but the terrace of my house joins the terrace of this; it should be easy, when your brother is asleep, to climb up noiselessly on to your terrace. There I will meet you and lead you over the little barrier wall on to my terrace. No one can spy on us there."

At this point Shahrazād saw the approach of morning and discreetly fell silent.

Said King Shahryār to himself: "I will not kill her until I know what passed between the youth and his master!"

So when the three-hundred-and-seventy-fifth night had come

Shahrazād said:

The youth accepted the invitation. He pretended to go to sleep that night, but, as soon as his brother the wazīr had retired, climbed on to the terrace, where the old man was waiting for him. The sage led him by the hand over the boundary wall on to his own terrace, where fruits and filled wine cups were arranged for his entertainment. They sat down on a white mat in the moonlight and began to drink and sing together, the clear night aiding and inspiring them and the stars' soft rays lighting them on to ecstasy.

As the time was thus passing pleasantly, the wazīr Badr al-Dīn took it into his head to visit his young brother, before lying down himself to sleep, and was mightily astonished not to find him. After searching the whole house, he went up on to the terrace and, approaching the boundary wall, saw his brother and the old man sitting side by side with wine cups in their hands. As good luck would have it, the old man had, on his side, noticed the approach of the wazīr and, being possessed of a ready tact, he broke off the song on which he was engaged and improvised a stanza so adroitly that it appeared to belong to the original:

> His mouth graced the cup with his spittle
> Before it met mine,
> And the shame of his cheek dimmed a little
> The red of the wine. . . .
>
> His excellent brother, the Full Moon of Duty,
> Can hardly object

If I call this sweet other the Full Moon of Beauty
Serene and unflecked.

When the wazīr Badr al-Dīn heard this delicate allusion, being a discreet and very gallant man, and also seeing nothing improper between the two, he retired, saying to himself: "As Allah lives, I will not trouble their festivity." So the couple continued their evening in perfect happiness.

Having told this anecdote, Shahrazād paused for a moment, and then said:

[THE WONDERFUL BAG]

It is related that one night, when the Khalīfah Hārūn al-Rashīd was plagued with sleeplessness, he called to him Jafar his wazīr, saying: "O Jafar, tonight my breast is heavy for lack of sleep. I charge you with the lightening of it." "Commander of the Faithful," answered Jafar, "I have a friend called Alī the Persian, who has in his scrip many delicious tales which are sovereign remedies for the blackest humours and annoyances." "Bring him to me at once," said al-Rashīd, and when Jafar had obeyed and the man was seated in the presence, he continued: "Listen, Alī, I am told that you know stories which can dissipate weariness and bring sleep to the sleepless. I require one of them now." "I hear and I obey, O Prince of Believers," answered Alī the Persian. "I pray you tell me whether you wish a story of things heard or a tale of things seen with my own eyes?" "One in which you have taken part yourself," said Hārūn al-Rashīd. So Alī the Persian began:

I was sitting one day in my shop when a Kurd came up and began bargaining with me for certain of my goods; suddenly he took up a little bag and, without attempting to hide it, tried most openly to walk off with it, as if it had belonged to him ever since he was born. I jumped out into the street and, stopping him by the skirts of his robe, told him to give me back my bag. He only shrugged his shoulders, saying: "That bag, and all that is in it, belongs to me." In rising anger, I cried out: "O Muslims, save my goods from this wretched unbeliever!" At once all who were in the market crowded round us, and my fellow merchants advised me to lay a complaint before the kādī[2] without further delay. I agreed to this, and immediately willing hands helped me to drag the Kurd who had stolen my bag into the presence of the kādī. As we all stood respectfully before him, he asked: "Which of you is the plaintiff and which the defendant?" Without giving me time to open my mouth, the Kurd stepped forward, crying: "Allah increase the power of our master the kādī! This bag is my bag, and all that it contains belongs to me! I lost it and then found it again on this man's counter." "When did you lose it?" asked the kādī. "I lost it yesterday," answered the impudent fellow, "and I could not sleep all night for thinking of it." "In that case," said the judge, "give me a list of its contents." Without a moment's hesitation, the Kurd answered: "O kādī, there are in my bag two crystal flasks filled with kohl, two silver sticks for putting on kohl, a handkerchief, two lemonade glasses with gilded rims, two torches, two ladles, a cushion, two carpets for gaming tables, two water-pots, two basins, one dish, one cook-pot, one earthen water-jar, one kitchen dipper, one large knitting-needle, two provision sacks, a pregnant cat, two bitches, a rice-jar, two donkeys, two bedroom sets for women, a linen garment, two pelisses, a cow, two calves, a sheep with two lambs, a camel with two little camels, two racing

2. Judge.

dromedaries with their females, a buffalo and two oxen, a lioness and two lions, a female bear, two foxes, one couch, two beds, a palace with two reception halls, two
green tents, two canopies, a kitchen with two doors, and an assembly of Kurds of my
own kind all ready to swear that the bag is my bag."

At this point Shahrazād saw the approach of morning and discreetly fell silent.

But when the three-hundred-and-seventy-sixth night had come

She said:
Then the kādī turned to me, saying: "What answer have you to this?"
I was so astonished by what the Kurd had said, O Commander of the Faithful,
that it was a little time before I was able to advance and answer: "May Allah lift up
and honour our master the kādī! I know that, in my sack, there are only a ruined pavilion, a house without a kitchen, a large dog-kennel, a boys' school, some jolly young
fellows playing dice, a brigand's lair, an army with captains, the city of Basrah and
the city of Baghdad, the ancient palace of the amīr Shaddād son of Ād, a smith's furnace, a fishing net, a shepherd's crook, five pretty boys, twelve untouched girls, and a
thousand leaders of caravans all ready to bear witness that this bag is my bag."

When the Kurd had heard my answer, he burst into tears and cried between his
sobs: "O our master the kādī, my bag is known and well known; it is universally acknowledged to be my property. Beside those things which I mentioned before, it contains two fortified cities and ten towns, two alchemical alembics, four chess players, a
mare and two foals, a stallion and two geldings, two long lances, two hares, a bug-
gered boy and two pimps, a blind man and two far-seeing men, a lame man and two
paralytics, a sea captain, a ship with sailors, a Christian priest and two deacons, a patriarch and two monks, and a kādī and two witnesses ready to swear that this bag is my
bag." Then the kādī turned to me again, and said: "What answer have you to all that?"

Being filled with hot rage, even to my nose, O Commander of the Faithful, I advanced and replied as calmly as I could: "Allah lighten and make strong the judgment of
our master the kādī! I ought to add that there are in the bag, beside the things which I
have already mentioned, headache cures, filtres and enchantments, coats of mail and ar-
mouries filled with arms, a thousand rams trained for fighting, a deer park, men who love
women, boy fanciers, gardens filled with trees and flowers, vines loaded with grapes, apples and figs, shades and phantoms, flasks and cups, new married couples with all their
marriage fresh about them, cries and jokes, twelve disgraceful farts and as many odour-
less funks, friends sitting in a meadow, banners and flags, a bride coming out of the bath,
twenty singers, five fair Abyssinian slaves, three Indian women, four Greek women, fifty
Turkish women, seventy Persian women, forty women from Kashmir, eighty Kurdish
women, as many Chinese women, ninety women from Georgia, the land of Irāq, the
Earthly Paradise, two stables, a mosque, many hammāms, a hundred merchants, a plank,
a nail, a black man playing on the clarinet, a thousand dīnārs, twenty chests full of stuffs,
twenty dancers, fifty storehouses, the city of Kūfah, the city of Gaza, Damietta, al-
Sawan, the palace of Khusran Ānūshīrwān, the palace of Sulaimān, all the lands between
Balkh and Isfahān, the Indies and Sūdān, Baghdad and Khurāsān, and—may Allah preserve the days of our master the kādī—a shroud, a coffin, and a razor for the beard of the
kādī if the kādī does not recognise my rights and say that this bag is my bag!"

When he had heard all this, the kādī looked at us and said: "As Allah lives, either
you are two rascals mocking at the law and its representatives, or else this bag is a
bottomless abyss or the Valley of the Day of Judgment itself."

Finally, to see which of us had spoken the truth, the kādī opened the bag before his witnesses and found in it a little orange peel and some olive stones.

At once I told the flabbergasted kādī that the bag must belong to the Kurd and that mine had disappeared. Then I went my way.

When the Khalīfah Hārūn al-Rashīd heard this tale, he was knocked over on his backside by the explosive force of his laughter. He gave a magnificent present to Alī the Persian, and that night slept soundly until the morning.

But do not believe, O auspicious King, added Shahrazād, that this little tale is more delicious than one in which al-Rashīd finds himself in an embarrassing predicament because of love. "I do not know that tale. What is it?" cried King Shahryār, so Shahrazād said:

[AL-RASHĪD JUDGES OF LOVE]

It is related that one night Hārūn al-Rashīd, lying between two fair girls whom he loved equally and of whom one was from Madinah and the other from Kūfah,[3] did not wish to decide with whom he should finish, especially since if one gained the other would have to lose.

Therefore he decided that the prize should go to her who should win it. At once the slave from Madinah clasped his hands and began to caress them gently, while the one from Kūfah, lying lower, rubbed his feet and took advantage of her position to slip up her hand from time to time and dandle the principal merchandise. Under the influence of these delicate touches the merchandise suddenly began to increase considerably in weight; then the girl from Kūfah laid open hold of it and, pulling it towards her, shut it all up in the hollow of her hand. On this the Madinah woman exclaimed: "You are keeping the capital for yourself and you will not even let me have any of the interest." Then with a quick movement she pushed her rival away and, taking hold of the capital herself, shut it carefully in her hands. The cheated slave, who was deeply learned in the traditions of the Prophet, said to the other: "I have a right to the capital, according to these words of the Prophet (upon whom be prayer and peace!): He who makes the dead earth live again shall own it for himself!" But the slave from Madinah, who was no less versed in the Book than her rival, kept hold of the merchandise and answered: "The capital belongs to me, according to these words of the Prophet (on whom be prayer and peace!): Game shall belong, not to him who starts it, but to him who kills it."

When the Khalīfah heard these quotations, he considered them so much to the point that he satisfied both the girls on that one night.

from The End of Jafar and the Barmakids[1]

When she had made an end of this admirable series of tales, Shahrazād fell silent, and King Shahryār cried: "O Shahrazād, you have instructed me in many things, but I think that you have forgotten to speak of the wazīr Jafar. I have long desired to hear all that you know concerning him, for I find that he strangely resembles in his quality

---

3. Medina is a large city in the Arabian Peninsula and the second sacred city in Islam. Kufa is a large city in southern Iraq and has been the seat of Islamic learning for many centuries.
1. As can be seen from the Resonance that follows, this

story dramatizes the actual historical record of the waning of Haroun al-Rashid's reign. Placed near the end of *The Thousand and One Nights*, it serves as a kind of leavetaking to the world of the stories themselves.

my own grand wazīr, your excellent father. It is that likeness which urges me to hear the whole of his surely admirable story." But Shahrazād hung her head, as she replied: "Allah keep us from calamity, O King of time, and have compassion upon Jafar the Barmakid and all his people! I beg you to excuse me from telling that story, for it is full of tears. Alas, who would not weep to hear of the end of Jafar, and of his father Yahya, and of his brother al-Fadl, and of all the Barmakids! So lamentable was their taking off that stone itself would become tender at the telling of it." "Yet tell me all the same, O Shahrazād," said King Shahryār, "and may Allah keep us from all calamity!"

So Shahrazād said: Here then, O auspicious King, is that sorry tale which mars the reign of the Khalīfah Hārūn al-Rashīd with a bloodstain which not even the four rivers[2] shall wash away.

As is already known, O king of time, Jafar was one of the four sons of Yahya ibn Khālid ibn Barmak. His eldest brother, al-Fadl, was in some sort al-Rashīd's foster-brother, for, because of the great friendship which existed between the family of Yahya and that of the Abbāsids, and because of the tender affection which bound the two women themselves, al-Rashīd's mother, the Princess Khayzarān, and al-Fadl's mother, the noble Itabah, exchanged nurslings and each gave to her friend's son that milk which Allah had destined for her own. That is why al-Rashīd always spoke of Yahya as: "My father," and al-Fadl as: "My brother."

At this point Shahrazād saw the approach of morning and discreetly fell silent.

But when the nine-hundred-and-ninety-fifth night had come

She said:

The most reliable chroniclers place the origin of the Barmakids in the city of Balkh in Khurāsān, where they occupied a position of great distinction. It was not until a little more than a hundred years after the Hijrah of our Prophet (upon whom be prayer and peace!) that the family moved to Damascus and took root there under the dynasty of Umar. In the reign of Hishām, the head of the house was converted from the Magian cult and became ennobled in Islām.

But it was not until the accession of the Abbāsids that the family was admitted into the counsels of the court, and began to brighten the earth with its glory. Khālid ibn Barmak was made grand-wazīr by Abū al-Abbās al-Saffah, the first of the Abbāsids; and, during the reign of al-Mahdī, the third in the line of Abbās, Yahya ibn Khālid was charged with the education of Hārūn al-Rashīd, the Khalīfah's favourite son, who was born only seven days after al-Fadl, Yahya's son.

When al-Rashīd was invested with the supreme power, after the unexpected death of his brother al-Hādi, he had no need to go back to the memories of his earliest youth, spent with the Barmakid children, before calling Yahya and his two sons to share in his aggrandizement; it was only necessary for him to recall his education by Yahya and the devotion which that good man had shown in braving the menaces of al-Hādi in order to assure his pupil's inheritance. On the very night of al-Hādi's death the tyrant had given order that Yahya and his children should be beheaded.

When Yahya went in the middle of the night with Masrūr to tell Hārūn that he was now master of the empire and Khalīfah of Allah upon earth, al-Rashīd immediately

2. Of Paradise.

named him grand-wazīr and raised his two sons, al-Fadl and Jafar, to be wazīrs under him. This action augured most happily for the new reign.

After that the Barmakids were an ornament for the brow of their century, and a crown upon its head. Destiny showered her most favourable gifts upon them, so that Yahya and his sons became bright stars, vast oceans of generosity, impetuous torrents of kindness, beneficent rains. The world lived at their breath, and under their hands the empire reached the pinnacle of its splendour. They were the refuge of the afflicted, the final resort of the comfortless. The poet Abū Nuwās said of them:

> Since earth has put you away, O sons of Barmak,
> The roads of morning twilight and evening twilight
> Are empty. My heart is empty, O sons of Barmak.

They were admirable wazīrs, wise administrators, they filled the public treasure. They were strong, eloquent, and of a good counsel; they surpassed in learning; their generosity equalled the generosity of Hātim Taiy. They were rivers of happiness, they were good winds bringing up the fruitful clouds; it was through them that the name and glory of Hārūn al-Rashīd clanged from the flats of Central Asia to the northern forests, from Morocco and Andalusia to the farthest bounds of China and Tartary.

And suddenly the sons of Barmak were cast from the greatest height which men have reached to the lowest depths of horror; they drank the most bitter cup which calamity can pour. Alas, for the unfaith of time, they had not only ruled a vast empire, they had been the dear friends, the inseparable companions of their King. Jafar was the life of al-Rashīd's eyes; his place was so great in the Khalīfah's mind and heart that, one day, Hārūn even had a double mantle made, so that they both could wear it and be, as it were, one man. Such were the terms on which they lived together until the final tragedy.

O pain of my soul, listen to the coming of that black cloud which veiled the sky of Islam and cast dismay upon every heart!

One day—be such days far from us!—al-Rashīd, returning from Mecca, went by water from Hīrah to the city of Anbār. He halted at the monastery of al-Umr, on the banks of the Euphrates, and night found him in feasts and pleasures, as so many other nights had found him.

But this time his dear companion Jafar was not with him; he had gone for a few days of hunting in the plains of the river. Gifts and messages from the Khalīfah followed him everywhere in his sport. No hour passed without the arrival at his tent of some messenger, bearing a precious reminder of al-Rashīd's love.

Now that night—be such nights far from us!—Jafar sat in his tent with the doctor Jibrīl Bakhtiyāshū, al-Rashīd's personal physician, and with the Khalīfah's favourite poet, blind Abū Zakār. Hārūn had deprived himself of the company of both these men, in order that the one might watch over Jafar's health and the other entertain him with his improvisations.

It was the time of the evening meal, and Abū Zakār, the blind poet, was playing upon the mandoline and singing verses of fickle chance.

At this point Shahrazād saw the approach of morning and discreetly fell silent.

But when the nine-hundred-and-ninety-sixth night had come

She said:
Suddenly Masrūr, the Khalīfah's sword-bearer, the instrument of his anger, strode unceremoniously into the tent. When Jafar saw him thus enter, in defiance of

all etiquette, without demanding an audience or even announcing his proposed visit, he turned yellow in the face, and said: "You are welcome, Masrūr, your presence is ever a fresh delight. But I must confess, my brother, that I am astonished to see you come to me, for the first time in your life, without sending some servant to give news of your arrival." "The matter is too grave for ceremony," replied Masrūr, without deigning the least salute to his old friend. "Rise up now, Jafar, and testify to your Faith for the last time. The Commander of the Faithful demands your head from me."

Jafar rose to his feet, and said: "There is no God but Allah, and Muhammad is the Prophet of Allah! From His hands we come and, soon or late, to His hands we return again!" Then he faced his old friend of so many years and moments, and cried out: "O Masrūr, it is impossible. Our master must have given you the order in a moment of drunkenness. I conjure you, by our walks together and our community of life by day and night, to return to the Khalīfah; for I believe that you will find he has forgotten what he said." But Masrūr answered: "It is my head or yours. I cannot return with my duty unfulfilled. Write your last wishes, for that is the only privilege I can accord you in memory of our ancient friendship." Then said Jafar: "We belong to Allah! I have no last wishes to write. May Allah prolong the span of the Commander of the Faithful by those days which are shorn from mine."

He left the tent, knelt upon the leather of blood which Masrūr had already spread, and bandaged his eyes with his own hands. Then his head was struck off. Allah have him in His mercy!

After this, Masrūr returned to the Khalīfah, and entered the royal presence bearing Jafar's head upon a shield. Al-Rashīd looked at the head of his old friend and, leaning forward suddenly, spat upon it.

But his resentment was stronger than death. He ordered the body to be crucified at one end of the bridge of Baghdad, and the head to be exposed at the other. This punishment was more degrading than any which had ever been inflicted upon even the worst of malefactors. At the end of six months he ordered that his wazīr's remains should be burnt on cattle dung and scattered among the privies.

O pitiful misery, that the scribe Imrānī should have been able to write on the same page of the register of treasury accounts: "For a robe of state, given by the Commander of the Faithful to his wazīr Jafar, son of Yahya al-Barmakī, four hundred thousand dīnārs of gold," and a little further down: "Naphtha, reeds, and dung to burn the body of Jafar ibn Yahya, ten silver dirhams."

Such was the end of Jafar. Yahya his father, the guide of al-Rashīd's infancy, and al-Fadl his brother, al-Rashīd's foster-brother, were arrested on the morning following the execution, and with them were taken all the rest of the Barmakids, to the number of about a thousand, who had any public charge or employment. They were thrown into foul dungeons, their great riches were confiscated, their wives and children were left without shelter, shunned by the regard of man. Some died of starvation, and others were strangled; but Yahya, his son al-Fadl and his brother Muhammad died under the torture. Allah have them all in His mercy! Their fall was great!

And now, O King of Time, if you wish to hear me speak of the cause of this disgrace and lamentable death:

One day, some years after the end of the Barmakids, Alīyah, al-Rashīd's young sister, plucked up heart to say to him: "My lord, I have not known you pass one tranquil day since the death of Jafar and the disappearance of his family. How did he come to merit such disgrace?" Al-Rashīd's face grew dark, and he pushed her away, saying: "My child, my life, my sole remaining happiness, how would it advantage you to know the reason? If I thought that my shirt knew, I would tear my shirt in pieces."

The historians and annalists are far from being agreed as to the cause of this catastrophe. Here are some of the differing versions which they give of the events which may be supposed to have led up to it.

According to some, al-Rashīd became offended at last by the extravagant liberalities of Jafar and the Barmakids, the tale of which became a weariness even in the ears of those who benefited, and which called forth rather envy and dislike than grateful friendship. * * *

According to other historians, the growing jealousy of al-Rashīd was fanned by the many enemies which the power of the Barmakids raised up against them, and by anonymous detractors, who allowed unsigned bitter verses and perfidious prose to come to the ears of the Khalīfah. These same annalists aver that it was a grave indiscretion on the part of Jafar which placed the final stone on the tower of his master's resentment. Once, when al-Rashīd had commanded him secretly to destroy a descendant of Alī and Fātimah, the daughter of the Prophet, a man named al-Saiyid Yahya ibn Abdallāh al-Husainī, Jafar had pity upon this Alid and allowed him to escape, although the Khalīfah had marked him as a danger to the dynasty of Abbās. This generous action was reported to al-Rashīd, with exaggeration and distortion; and it became that drop of gall which overflowed the angry cup. When he was questioned, Jafar frankly confessed what he had done, and said: "I acted for the glory and good name of my master." "You acted well," answered al-Rashīd, turning very pale, but he was heard to mutter to himself: "Allah do so to me and more also, if I do not destroy you, Jafar!"

Other historians would trace the fall of the Barmakids to their heretical opinions in the face of Islamic orthodoxy. It must not be forgotten that, when they lived in Balkh before their conversion to the Faith, they practised the Magian cult. During the expedition into Khurāsān, the birthplace of the Barmakids, al-Rashād noticed that Yahya and his sons exerted all their power to prevent the destruction of the temples and monuments of the Magi. His suspicion of their religious integrity grew greater afterwards, for he found that they always showed clemency to every kind of heretic, and especially to his personal enemies among the Jabarīyah and Zandakah. Those who hold this theory cite in proof of it the fact that serious religious troubles broke out in Baghdad immediately after the death of al-Rashīd, and almost proved the death-blow to orthodoxy.

But the most probable reason for the destruction of the Barmakids is adduced both by Ibn Khillikān, and by Ibn al-Athīr. They say:

"At the time when Jafar lay so near the heart of the Khalīfah that al-Rashīd had that double mantle made for the two of them, the Khalīfah could not abide to be separated from his favourite, and desired to look upon his face at all hours of the day and night. But al-Rashīd also loved, with a strange and deep tenderness, his own sister Abbāsah, perhaps the most beautiful and cultivated woman of her time. No other of her sex influenced al-Rashīd so greatly, and he was as incapable of living without her as if she had been a woman Jafar. These two loves made up his happiness; yet, for his joy's perfection, they had to be indulged at the same time. Thus it was necessary that the two favourites should be present together. But the law of our Faith forbids a man to look upon a woman, or for a woman to be looked upon by a man, unless he be her husband or near relation. To transgress this law is to lose honour, and therefore al-Rashīd, who was a strict observer of the law which it was his high privilege to administer, could not enjoy the simultaneous presence of Jafar and Abbāsah without the constraint of veils and the irksomeness of silence.

"That is why he one day said to Jafar: 'My friend, I have no true pleasure save when I sit with you and my dear sister Abbāsah. I wish you to wed the girl; but I forbid you to come together save in my presence, and I insist that there shall be no consummation of the marriage, lest the noble sons of Abbās be cheated out of their inheritance.' Jafar bowed before the desire of his master and had, perforce, to accept this marriage with all its unnatural conditions.

"The young husband and wife met only in the presence of the Khalīfah, and even then their glances hardly crossed. Al-Rashīd rejoiced at the new arrangement and seemed not to know that he was torturing his two best friends. How can love be controlled by a third person? How can such restraint between two young and handsome beings not break out into the flame of love?"

At this point Shahrazād saw the approach of morning and discreetly fell silent.

But when the nine-hundred-and-ninety-seventh night had come

She said:

"These two married lovers, who had every right to come together and yet could not, sighed more deeply every day, and felt that drunkenness which, when it is hidden, becomes a fever about the heart. Abbāsah, in her deprivation, became madly desirous of her husband. At length she told her love, coming upon Jafar in secret as often as she was able and soliciting him to grant her right; but the wazīr was too loyal and too prudent to give way to her. He was bound by his oath to al-Rashīd, and he also knew how hasty the Khalīfah could be in his anger.

"When Princess Abbāsah saw that her entreaties were in vain, she took the part of all women and sought out a devious way. She sent a message to the noble Itabah, the mother of Jafar, saying: 'O our mother, I require you to introduce me into Jafar's household, as if I were one of those slaves which you procure for him every day.' It was a fact that Itabah would send her dear son a fresh and chosen virgin slave each Thursday, and that the wazīr would not touch this child until he had eaten richly and partaken of generous wines. * * *

"Abbāsah decked herself for her part, and then went to the house of Jafar's mother, who, at nightfall, introduced her into the apartment of her son. Jafar, whose senses were a little dulled by the fermentation of the wines, did not recognise his wife in the virgin slave who stood before him. It must be remembered that neither had looked often or directly on the other's face, for fear of the Khalīfah's resentment, and that modesty had ever caused Abbāsah to turn away from Jafar's furtive glances.

"The marriage became a marriage in fact, and, after a night of mutual transport, Abbāsah rose, saying: 'How do you like King's daughters, my master? Are they different from slaves who are bought and sold?' 'King's daughters?' asked the astonished Jafar. 'Are you one yourself? Are you some captive of our victorious arms?' 'O Jafar,' she answered, 'I am both a captive and a slave. I am Abbāsah, sister of al-Rashīd, daughter of al-Mahdī. I am of the blood of Abbās, uncle of the Prophet (upon whom be prayer and peace!).'

"These words cleared off the last clouds of Jafar's drunkenness, and he cried: 'You have destroyed yourself, you have destroyed me, O daughter of my masters!'

"He hastened to Itabah, and said to her: 'O mother, mother, you have sold me cheap!' For answer Yahya's trembling wife told her son how she had been forced to forward this stratagem, in order to save her household from a worse misfortune.

"In fulness of time Abbāsah bore a son whom she confided to Riyāsh, a man faithful in her service, and to the nursing of a woman called Barrah. Then, fearing lest a rumour of this birth should escape in spite of all her precautions, she sent her child to Mecca with his two guardians.

"Now Yahya, Jafar's father, was responsible for order in the palace and harem of al-Rashīd. After a certain hour of night he would shut all the communicating doors and take away the keys, a severity of discipline which soon caused discontent among the women and especially in the Lady Zubaidah. When she complained to al-Rashīd and cursed the old man's misplaced zeal, he called Yahya to him, and asked: 'My father, what grievance has Zubaidah against you?' 'Does she complain that I am lax in my supervision of the harem?' demanded Yahya. 'Not so, my father,' answered al-Rashīd with a smile. 'In that case,' cried the Barmakid, 'take no notice of what she says, O Commander of the Faithful!' And, after that, he redoubled his severity in door locking.

"Zubaidah came to her lord a second time, crying out in bitter resentment against Yahya; so al-Rashīd tried to pacify her, saying: 'O daughter of my uncle, my guide and father Yahya is only obeying orders and doing his duty, when he schools my harem in this way.' 'If he is so deeply concerned with his duty,' retorted Zubaidah with some feeling, 'why does he not begin by schooling the imprudence of his son?' 'What imprudence?' demanded al-Rashīd. Zubaidah at once told him the whole story of Abbāsah, though not as a matter of great importance. 'Are there proofs of this?' asked the Khalīfah in a sombre voice. 'What better proof could there be than the child himself?' demanded Zubaidah. 'Where is he?' asked the Khalīfah, and she replied: 'In the Holy City, the cradle of our race.' 'Does any beside you know of these things?' he asked, and she replied: 'There is not a woman in the whole palace, not a slave who does not know.'

"Al-Rashī said no further word, but soon afterwards he departed on pilgrimage for Mecca and took Jafar with him.

"At once Abbāsah sent a letter to Riyāsh and the nurse, ordering them to leave the city and pass into Yemen with the child.

"As soon as the Khalīfah arrived at Mecca he bade certain of his trusted spies make enquiry concerning the infant, and these soon returned with the news that they had found proof of his existence, and that he was in perfect health. In a few days the child was seized in Yemen and sent secretly to Baghdad.

"It was on his return from that pilgrimage, when lying at the monastery of al-Umr near Anbār on the Euphrates, that al-Rashīd gave his fateful command to Masrūr.

"Abbāsah was buried alive with her son in a ditch dug in the floor of her own apartment.

"Allah have them both in His compassion!"

It remains for me to say, O auspicious King, that other and quite worthy historians contend that Jafar and the Barmakids had done nothing to deserve their fate, and that it would not have come upon them if it had not been written in their Destiny.

But Allah knows all!

* * *

As for the Khalīfah Hārūn al-Rashīd: after his cruel vengeance for some wrong known only to himself and Allah, he returned to Baghdad, but passed it by. He found that he could not live any longer in that city which it had been his delight through so many years to embellish. He established himself at Rākah and never returned to the Place of Peace. This sudden abandonment of his capital by al-Rashīd inspired the poet Abbās ibn al-Ahnaf, who was of his train, to write the following lines:

> Scarce had we made the camels kneel
> Before we had to ride again,
> The friends who watched our coming
> Saw us turn the camels round.
>
> They cried us welcome, but it was
> "Farewell," that we replied again,
> "Farewell, O city of Baghdad,
> O consecrated ground."

Since the disappearance of his friends, al-Rashīd got no good of his sleep; his regrets burned him day and night, and he would have given his kingdom to bring back Jafar. If any courtiers had the misfortune to speak even a little slightingly of the Barmakids, the Khalīfah would angrily cry out on them: "Allah damn your fathers! Either cease from blaming them, or try to fill the place which they left empty."

Though he remained all-powerful until his death, al-Rashīd imagined that he was surrounded by traitors. He feared to be poisoned by his sons, who were indeed no cause for pride. At the beginning of a punitive expedition into Khurāsān, from which he was not destined to return alive, he sadly admitted his doubts to al-Tabarī, the annalist, who was one of the courtiers most in his confidence. When al-Tabarī tried to reassure him as to certain presages of death which he had received, he drew the chronicler into the shadow of a great tree, where they might be rid of prying glances, and opened his robe to show him a silk bandage wrapped about his belly. "I have a deep and incurable disease," he said. "No one knows of it save you. And I have spies round me, sent by al-Amīn and al-Mamūn to filch away the little remainder of my life. They feel that I have lived too long. They have corrupted my most faithful servants. Masrūr is the spy of my favourite son al-Mamūn, my doctor Jibrīl Bakhtiyāshū is al-Amīn's spy. And there are many more. Would you have proof of their plots? I have ordered a riding horse to be sent to me, and instead of choosing one with a strong and easy action, you will see them bring to me a worn beast, having a broken pace to aggravate my suffering."

This prophecy was fulfilled; al-Rashīd was given such a horse as he described, and he accepted it with a look of sad understanding to al-Tabarī.

A few weeks after this incident, Hārūn saw in his dreams a hand stretched out above his head, holding a little red earth. A voice cried: "This shall be his sepulchre." "Where?" asked another voice, and the first replied: "In Tūs."[3]

Some days later the course of his malady obliged al-Rashīd to halt at Tūs. At once he showed signs of grave disquiet, and sent Masrūr to bring him a little earth from the outskirts of the city. The eunuch returned in an hour, bearing a handful of red soil, and al-Rashīd cried: "There is no God but Allah, and Muhammad is the Prophet of Allah! My vision is accomplished, my death is very near!"

He did not see Irāq again. The next day he was weaker, and said to those about him: "The moment is at hand. I was envied by all the world, but now the world might pity me."

---

3. A city in the Khurasan region of northern Iran.

He died at Tūs on the third day of Jumāda, second month in the one hundred-and-ninety-third year of the Hijrah. According to Abulfidā, he was forty-seven years, five months, and five days old at the time of his death. Allah pardon his mistakes and have him in pity! He was an orthodox Khalīfah.

Conclusion

Then she fell silent, and King Shahryār cried: "O Shahrazād, that was a noble and admirable story! O wise and subtle one, you have taught me many lessons, letting me see that every man is at the call of Fate; you have made me consider the words of kings and peoples passed away; you have told me some things which were strange, and many that were worthy of reflection. I have listened to you for a thousand nights and one night, and now my soul is changed and joyful, it beats with an appetite for life. I give thanks to Him Who has perfumed your mouth with so much eloquence and has set wisdom to be a seal upon your brow!"

Little Dunyazād rose quite up from her carpet, and ran to throw her arms about her sister, crying: "O Shahrazād, how soft and delicate are your words, how moving and delightful! With what a savour they have filled our hearts! Oh, how beautiful are your words, my sister!"

Shahrazād leaned over the child and, as she embraced her, whispered some words which caused her to glide from the room, as camphor melts before the sun.

Shahrazād stayed alone with Shahryār, but, as he was preparing to take this marvellous bride between his joyful arms, the curtains opened and Dunyazād reappeared, followed by a nurse with twin children hanging at her breasts. A third child hurried after them on all fours.

Shahrazād embraced the three little ones and then ranged them before Shahryār; her eyes filled with tears, as she said: "O King of time, behold these three whom Allah has granted to us in three years."

While Shahryār kissed the children and was moved with joy through all his body to touch them, Shahrazād said again: "Your eldest son is more than two years old, and these twins will soon be one. Allah protect them from the evil-eye! You remember, O King of time, that I was absent through sickness for twenty days between the six hundred and seventy-ninth night of my telling and the seven hundredth. It was during that absence that I gave birth to the twins. They pained and wearied me a great deal more than their elder brother in the previous year. With him I was so little disturbed that I had no need to interrupt the tale of Sympathy the Learned, even for one night."

She fell silent, and King Shahryār, looking from her to his sons and from his sons to her, could say no word.

Then little Dunyazād turned from kissing the infants a twentieth time, and said to Shahryār: "Will you cut off my sister's head, O King? Will you destroy the mother of your sons, and leave three little kings to miss her love?"

"Be quiet and have no fear, young girl," answered King Shahryār, between two fits of sobbing. It was not for a long time that he could master his emotion, and say: "O Shahrazād, I swear by the Lord of Pity that you were already in my heart before the coming of these children. He had given you gifts with which to win me; I loved you in my soul because I had found you pure, holy, chaste, tender, straightforward, unassailable, ingenious, subtle, eloquent, discreet, smiling, and wise. May Allah bless you, my dear, your father and mother, your root and race! O Shahrazād, this thousand

and first night is whiter for us than the day!" When he had said these things, he rose and embraced the woman's head.

Shahrazād took her King's hand and carried it to her lips, her heart, and her brow, saying: "O lord of time, I beg you to call your old wazīr, that he may rejoice at my salvation and partake in the benediction of this night."

So the King sent for his wazīr, and the old man entered carrying Shahrazād's winding-sheet over his arm, for he was sure that her hour had come at last. Shahryār rose in his honour and kissed him between the eyes, saying: "O father of Shahrazād, O begetter of benediction, Allah has raised up your daughter to be the salvation of my people. Repentance has come to me through her!" Joy penetrated the old man's heart so suddenly that he fell into a swoon. When rose-water had brought him to himself, Shahrazād and Dunyazād kissed his hand, and he blessed them. The rest of that night passed for them all in a daze of happiness.

Shahryār sent for his brother Shahzamān, King of Samarkand al-Ajam, and went out to meet his coming with a glorious retinue. The city was gay with flags, and in the streets and markets the people burnt incense, sublimated camphor, aloes, Indian musk, nard and ambergris. They put fresh henna upon their fingers and saffron upon their faces. Drums, flutes, clarinets, fifes, cymbals and dulcimers filled every ear with a rejoicing sound.

While great feasts were being given at the royal expense, King Shahryār took his brother aside and spoke of the life which he had led with Shahrazād for the last three years. He recounted for Shahzamān's benefit some of the maxims, phrases, tales, proverbs, jests, anecdotes, characteristics, marvels, poems, and recitations which he had heard during that time. He praised the wazīr's daughter for her eloquence, wisdom, purity, piety, sweetness, honesty and discretion. "She is my wife," he said, "the mother of my children."

When King Shahzamān had a little recovered from his astonishment, he said: "Since you have been so fortunate, I too will marry. I will marry Shahrazād's sister, the little one, I do not know her name. We shall be two brothers married to two sure and honest sisters; we will forget our old misfortune. That calamity touched me first, and then through me it reached to you. If I had not discovered mine, you would never have known of yours. Alas, my brother, I have been mournful and loveless during these years. Each night I have followed your example by taking a virgin to my bed, and every morning I have avenged our ills upon her life. Now I will follow you in a better deed, and marry your wazīr's second daughter."

Shahryār went joyfully to Shahrazād and told her that his brother had, of his own accord, elected Dunyazād for his bride. "We consent, O King of time," she said, "on condition that your brother stays henceforth with us. I could not bear to be separated from my little sister, even for one hour. I brought her up and educated her; she could not part from me. If Shahzamān will give this undertaking, Dunyazād shall be his slave. If not, we will keep her."

When Shahzamān heard Shahrazād's answer, he said: "As Allah lives, my brother, I had intended no less than to remain with you always. I feel now that I can never abide to be parted from you again. As for the throne of Samarkand, Allah will send to fill it." "I have longed for this," answered King Shahryār. "Join with me in thanks to Allah, my brother, that He has brought our hearts together again after so many months!"

The kādī and witnesses were summoned, and a marriage contract was written out for King Shahzamān and Dunyazād. Rejoicing and illuminations with coloured fire followed upon the news of this; and all the city ate and drank at the King's expense for forty days and forty nights. The two brothers and two sisters entered the hammām and bathed there in rose-water, flower-water, scented willow-water, and perfumed water of musk, while eagle wood and aloes were burned about them.

Shahrazād combed and tressed her little sister's hair, and sprinkled it with pearls. Then she dressed her in a robe of antique Persian stuff, stitched with red gold and enhanced by drunken animals and swooning birds embroidered in the very colours of life. She put a fairy collar about her neck, and Dunyazād became below her fingers fairer than Alexander's wife.

When the two Kings had left the hammām and seated themselves upon their thrones, the bridal company, the wives of the amīrs and notables, stood in two motionless lines to right and left. Time came, and the sisters entered between these living walls, each sustaining the other, and having the appearance of two moons in one night sky.

Then the noblest ladies there took Dunyazād by the hand and, after removing her robes, dressed her in a garment of blue satin, a sea tint to make reason fail upon her throne. A poet said of her:

> Her veil is torn from the bright blue
> Which all the stars are hasting to,
> Her lips control a hive of bees,
> And roses are about her knees,
> The white flakes of the jasmine twine
> Round her twin sweetness carnaline,
> Her waist is a slight reed which stands
> Swayed on a hill of moving sands.

Shahzamān came down to be the first to look upon her. When he had admired her in this dress, he sat upon his throne again, and this was a signal for the second change. So Shahrazād and the women clad their bride in a robe of apricot silk. As she passed before her husband's throne, she justified the words of the poet:

> You are more fair than a summer moon
> On a winter night, you are more fair.
> I said when I saw your falling hair:
> "Night's black wing is hiding day."
> "A cloud, but lo! the moon is there,"
> You, rose child, found to say.

When Shahzamān had come down and admired her in this dress, Shahrazād put a tunic of grenade velvet upon her sister. * * * Shahrazād slipped her hand to her sister's waist, and they walked before the Kings and between the guests toward the inner chambers. Then the Queen undressed little Dunyazād and laid her upon the bed with such recommendations as were suitable. They kissed and wept in each other's arms for a little, as it was the first night for which they had been separated.

That was a white and joyful night for the two brothers and the two sisters, it was a fair continuation of the thousand and one which had gone before, a love tale better than them all, the dawn of a new era for the subjects of King Shahryār.

When the brothers had come from the hammām in the morning and joined their wives, the wazīr sought permission to enter. They rose in his honour and the two women kissed his hand; but, when he asked for the day's orders, the four said with one voice: "O father, we wish that you should give commands in the future and not receive them. That is why we make you King of Samarkand al-Ajam." "I yield my throne to you," said Shahzamān; and Shahryār cried: "I will only give you leave to do so, my brother, if you will consent to share my royalty and reign with me day and day about." "I hear and I obey," said Shahzamān.

The wazīr kissed his daughters in farewell, embraced the three little sons, and departed for Samarkand al-Ajam at the head of a magnificent escort. Allah had written him security in his journey, and the inhabitants of his new kingdom hailed his coming with delight. He reigned over them in all justice and became a King among great Kings. So much for him.

After these things, King Shahryār called together the most renowned annalists and proficient scribes from all the quarters of Islām, and ordered them to write out the tales of Shahrazād from beginning to end, without the omission of a single detail. So they sat down and wrote thirty volumes in gold letters, and called this sequence of marvels and astonishments: THE BOOK OF THE THOUSAND NIGHTS AND ONE NIGHT. Many faithful copies were made, and King Shahryār sent them to the four corners of his empire, to be an instruction to the people and their children's children. But he shut the original manuscript in the gold cupboard of his reign and made his wazīr of treasure responsible for its safe keeping.

King Shahryār and Queen Shahrazād, King Shahzamān and Queen Dunyazād, and Shahrazād's three small sons, lived year after year in all delight, knowing days each more admirable than the last and nights whiter than days, until they were visited by the Separator of friends, the Destroyer, the Builder of tombs, the Inexorable, the Inevitable.

Such are the excellent tales called THE THOUSAND NIGHTS AND ONE NIGHT, together with all that is in them of wonder and instruction, prodigy and marvel, astonishment and beauty.

But Allah knows all! He alone can distinguish between the true and the false. He knows all!

⟨∾⟩

RESONANCE

Muhammad al-Tabari: from *History of the Prophets and Kings*[1]

THE REASON FOR AL-RASHĪD'S KILLING OF JA'FAR AL-BARMAKĪ, THE MANNER OF HIS KILLING, AND WHAT AL-RASHĪD DID TO HIM AND THE MEMBERS OF HIS FAMILY

Among the events taking place during this year was al-Rashīd's killing of Ja'far ibn Yaḥyā ibn Khālid and his swooping down on the Barmakīs.

Concerning the reason for al-Rashīd's anger against him, occasioning the Caliph's killing of him, there are varying accounts. One of them is what is mentioned from Bukhtīshū ibn Jibrīl, who had it from his father, that the latter related: I

---

1. Translated by C. E. Bosworth. Muhammad ibn Jarir al-Tabari (c. 839–923) was a preeminent historian, jurist, and commentator on the Qur'an. His monumental *History of the Prophets and Kings,* from which this reading is extracted, is a voluminous chronicle of history from creation to the year 915. His account of the Abbasid period, in which he lived, is the most authoritative work on this period. He is cited in *The Thousand and One Nights* as a confidant of Haroun al-Rashid (see page 470), and the storyteller has drawn on his dramatic account, which gives a range of contemporary explanations and speculations concerning the shocking downfall of the caliph's closest adviser and friend.

was sitting in al-Rashīd's court circle when Yaḥyā ibn Khālid appeared. It had always been the practice previously that he should enter without seeking formal permission. Now, when he entered, drew near to al-Rashīd and greeted him, the latter returned only a perfunctory salutation. Yaḥyā then realized that their relationship had changed.

He related: Then al-Rashīd came up to me and said, "O Jibrīl, does anyone enter upon your presence, without your permission, when you are in your house?" I replied, "No, and no one would presume to do that." He commented, "Why, then, should we have to put up with intrusions upon us without permission?" Yaḥyā rose and explained, "O Commander of the Faithful, may God bring my term of life to an end before yours! By God, I haven't inaugurated this practice at this very moment, and it is no more than an honor with which the Commander of the Faithful has favored me and has thereby increased my prestige, to the extent that I used to come into his presence when he was in his bed, at times garmentless, or at other times just dressed in one of his loincloths. I did not realize that the Commander of the Faithful now disliked what he used to approve. But now that I have realized it, in future I will take my place in the second or third rank of those seeking permission to enter, if my master so commands." He related: Al-Rashīd was thereupon ashamed—among all the Caliphs, he related, al-Rashīd had one of the mildest countenances—and he remained with his eyes to the ground, not looking upwards at Yaḥyā. Then he said, "I didn't intend anything to discomfit you, but people are talking." He related, I had the impression that al-Rashīd had not been able to think of a satisfactory reply on the spur of the moment, and hence had answered him thus. Al-Rashīd refrained from saying any more to Yaḥyā, and Yaḥyā departed. * * *

Abū Muḥammad al-Yazīdī—and according to what is said, he was one of the persons most knowledgeable about the story of the Barmakīs—has mentioned, saying: "If anyone says that al-Rashīd killed Ja'far ibn Yaḥyā for any other reason but over Yaḥyā ibn 'Abdallāh ibn Ḥasan, don't believe him!" The story here is that al-Rashīd handed over Yaḥyā to Ja'far, who thereupon imprisoned him. Then, one night, Ja'far summoned Yaḥyā and interrogated him about some aspects of his affairs and position, and Yaḥyā gave him suitable answers, until he said, "Show piety towards God in my regard, and don't lay yourself open to the possibility that [the Prophet] Muḥammad may speak unfavorably against you on the Last Day, for by God, I have not introduced any heretical innovations nor have I given shelter to any perpetrator of such misdeeds!" So Ja'far relented towards him and told him, "Go forth into wherever you like of God's lands!" But Yaḥyā replied, "How can I go forth, when I have no assurance that I shall not be arrested after a short while and sent back to you or someone else?" Hence, Ja'far sent along with Yaḥyā someone who could conduct him to a secure place for him. The news of this reached al-Faḍl ibn al-Rabī' through a spy of his within the inner circle of Ja'far's servants whom he had over Ja'far.

Al-Faḍl made a full investigation into the matter; he found it to be perfectly true, and it was fully revealed to him. So he went into al-Rashīd's presence and informed him. The latter indicated to al-Faḍl ostensibly that he was uninterested in his information, and said, "What's the matter got to do with you, may you be deprived of your mother? For all you know, this may be at my express command!" At this, al-Faḍl was crushed. Ja'far now came to al-Rashīd. The latter called for food; the two of them ate together, and the Caliph began to put tasty morsels of food into Ja'far's mouth and to converse with him, until finally, at the end of their session together, al-Rashīd asked,

"What has Yahyā ibn 'Abdallāh been up to?" Ja'far replied, "He is just as he was before, O Commander of the Faithful, in a cramped prison cell, loaded with fetters." Al-Rashīd commented, "By my life!" At this, Ja'far—who had one of the acutest intelligences and soundest perceptions among all mankind—drew back, and realized within himself that the Caliph in fact knew something about the affair. So he then said, "Nay, by your life, my lord, in reality I set him free, having learnt that there was nothing to be gained by holding him and that he was completely harmless." The Caliph replied, "You did well! You have done exactly what was in my own mind!" But when Ja'far went out, al-Rashīd followed him with his gaze until Ja'far became almost hidden from his sight, and then he burst out, "May God slay me with the sword of right guidance for having committed an erroneous act if I don't kill you!" What subsequently happened regarding him is well-known. * * *

The Barmakīs' Wealth and Ostentation as a Reason for Their Fall

Ya'qūb ibn Ishāq (al-Isfahānī) has mentioned that Ibrāhīm ibn al-Mahdī transmitted the information to him, saying: I visited Ja'far ibn Yahyā in that palace of his which he had built. He said to me, "Aren't you astonished at Mansūr ibn Ziyād?" He said: I replied, "In what connection?" He said, "I asked him whether he discerned any defect at all in my palace, and he replied, 'Yes, it doesn't contain any sun-dried brick or pine trunk (in its construction).'" Ibrāhīm related: I said, however, "What renders it faulty, in my view, is that you have expended on it around twenty million dirhams, and this is a thing concerning which I would not guarantee your personal security, at some future date, in the Caliph's eyes." He retorted, "He knows well that he has given me in presents more than that, and as much as that again, in addition to what he has left open for me to acquire." He related: I remarked, "An enemy has only to go to the Caliph over this with the intention of saying to him, 'O Commander of the Faithful, since he has been able to expend twenty million dirhams on a single palace, what about his ordinary expenditure? And all the gifts he bestows? And provision against all the eventualities and misfortunes which may assail him? Moreover, O Commander of the Faithful, what do you think about expenditure beyond all that? This is a sum which can speedily be disbursed, but getting oneself into a position to acquire it is difficult.'" Ja'far replied, "If he hears anything about me, I shall respond, 'The Commander of the Faithful has bestowed many favors on people who have displayed ingratitude for these favors by concealing them or by outwardly displaying only a small part from a great number of these favors. I, on the other hand, am a man who has considered the Caliph's bounty to me; as a result, I have placed it on a mountain top and then instructed the people, "Come forth and gaze on it!"'"

The Alleged Misconduct Between Ja'far and the Caliph's Sister 'Abbāsah

Ahmad ibn Zuhayr—I think from his paternal uncle Zāhir ibn Harb—transmitted the information to me that the reason behind the destruction of Ja'far and the Barmakīs was that al-Rashīd could not bear to be away from the company of Ja'far and of his own sister 'Abbāsah bint al-Mahdī. He used to invite them both to be present when he had one of his drinking sessions, this being after he had told Ja'far how little able he was to endure Ja'far's and 'Abbāsah's absence from him. He said to Ja'far, "I will give her to you in marriage so that it will be licit for you to look on her when I invite her to my court sessions," and he ordered him not to touch her or do anything at all of what a man usually does with his wife. So al-Rashīd gave her to him in marriage on these conditions. He used to invite them both to his circle when he held a drinking

RESONANCE: Muhammad al-Tabari   477

session, then he would get up from the circle and leave the two of them together. They would then become intoxicated with the wine, and both of them being in the vigor of youth, Ja'far would make for her and copulate with her. Subsequently, she became pregnant by him and gave birth to a boy. She was afraid of her own safety from al-Rashīd, if he should get to know about that, so she sent the newly born child, accompanied by nurses for him from among her own slaves, to Mecca. The matter remained concealed from Hārūn until some bad blood arose between 'Abbāsah and a certain slave girl of hers, and this latter thereupon communicated the story of her affair and the matter of the child to al-Rashīd, informing him at the same time of the child's whereabouts, of the slave girls of 'Abbāsah who were looking after him, and of the ornaments with which his mother had adorned him. So when Hārūn performed this particular Pilgrimage, he sent to the place where the slave girl had told him the child was someone who would bring back to him the child and the nurses looking after him. When they were brought before him, he questioned the women who were caring for the child, and they told him substantially the same story which 'Abbāsah's detractor had told him. It is alleged that he wanted to kill the child but then restrained himself from that.

Now whenever al-Rashīd made the Pilgrimage, Ja'far used to organize a feast for him at 'Usfān, in order to show him hospitality when he returned from Mecca and set off in the direction of Iraq. When the time came round in this year, Ja'far prepared the feast there, as was his wont, and then requested al-Rashīd to visit him. But the latter adduced an excuse to him, and did not attend the feast. Ja'far nevertheless remained with him until he halted at his encampment at al-Anbār, and then there took place the events involving him and his father which I am about to relate, if God Most High wills.

THE KILLING OF JA'FAR

Al-Fadl ibn Sulaymān ibn 'Alī has mentioned that al-Rashīd performed the Pilgrimage in the year 186 (802), and that he returned homewards from Mecca and reached al-Ḥīrah in al-Muḥarram, 187 (December, 802-January, 803) on his return journey from the Pilgrimage. He stayed for a few days at the palace of 'Awn al-'Ibādī and then set out by boat until he stopped at al-'Umr in the vicinity of al-Anbār. When it was the night of Saturday, the thirtieth of al-Muḥarram, he sent the eunuch Masrūr, together with Abū 'Iṣmah Ḥammād ibn Sālim and a detachment of troops. They encircled Ja'far ibn Yaḥyā's lodging by night, and Masrūr burst in on him. Ja'far had with him Ibn Bukhtīshū' the physician and Abū Zakkār al-Kalwādhānī the blind singer, and was engaged in a convivial session. Masrūr dragged him out roughly and hustled him along until he brought him to the lodging where al-Rashīd was. He imprisoned him, bound him up with a rope used for hobbling asses, and informed al-Rashīd that he had arrested Ja'far and had brought him back. Al-Rashīd then ordered Ja'far to be beheaded, and Masrūr did that.

It is mentioned from 'Alī ibn Abū Sa'īd that Masrūr the eunuch communicated the information to him, saying: Al-Rashīd sent me to bring back to him Ja'far ibn Yaḥyā when he had decided to kill him. I came to Ja'far, and he had with him Abū Zakkār the blind singer, who was at that moment singing the verse

> Go not far away, for death will come upon
> every brave youth, whether by night or in the morning!

He related: I said to him, "O Abū al-Fadl, what I have come for is indeed something of that kind, by God, it has come to you by night! Give an account of yourself to the

Commander of the Faithful!" He related: He raised his arms and fell at my feet, kissing them, and said, "Give me until I can go back into my lodging and make my last testament." I replied, "There's no possibility of your going back inside, but make your last dispositions here and now with whatever arrangements you wish." So he gave the appropriate orders in his testament for the effecting of his wishes, and freed his slaves. At that point, messengers came to me from the Commander of the Faithful urging me to deal with him speedily. He related: So I took Ja'far along with me to his lodging and informed him about this. The Caliph said to me—being himself at that moment in his bed—"Bring me his head!" I went back to Ja'far and told him that. He exclaimed, "O Abū Hāshim, O God, O God! By God, he wouldn't order you to do that if he were not drunk! Put off killing me till the morning, or else go and consult with him about me a second time!" So I went back to consult al-Rashīd. But when he heard my whispered words of intercession, he burst out, "O you who suck your mother's clitoris! Bring me Ja'far's head!" So I returned to Ja'far and told him. He thereupon said, "Go back to him on my behalf a third time!" I went back to al-Rashīd, but he struck me with a staff and exclaimed, "May I be excluded from the offspring of al-Mahdī! If you come back to me and don't bring Ja'far's head, I shall certainly send to you someone who will first of all bring back to me your head and, secondly, Ja'far's!" He related: So I went forth and brought back to him Ja'far's head.

He related: That same night, al-Rashīd ordered men to be sent who would seize Yahyā ibn Khālid and all his children, and everyone in any way connected with them; not one of those who were present there escaped. Al-Faḍl ibn Yahyā was removed by night and then imprisoned in a wing of one of al-Rashīd's residences. Yahyā ibn Khālid was imprisoned in his own house. He confiscated all the wealth, estates, possessions, and so forth, which they were found to have, and the soldiers did not allow a single one of them to go forth to the City of Peace or anywhere else. That same night, he despatched the eunuch Rajā' to al-Raqqah with orders to seize their wealth and possessions there and to arrest all their slaves and retainers. He gave Rajā' complete charge in dealing with them. That same night, he sent out letters to all the governors and chief officials in the various regions and administrative divisions of the provinces ordering them to seize the Barmakīs' wealth and arrest their agents.

Muhammad ibn Isḥāq (al-Hāshimī) has mentioned that Ja'far ibn Muhammad ibn Hakīm al-Kūfī communicated the information to him, saying that al-Sindī ibn Shāhik had given him the information, saying: One day, I was sitting, when suddenly at my side there appeared a servant, who had arrived by the *barīd* service, and he handed me a slim letter. I broke open the seal, and lo, it was a letter from al-Rashīd, in his own handwriting, running as follows: "In the name of God, the Merciful, the Compassionate. O Sindī, when you examine this letter of mine, if you happen to be sitting, then arise, and if you are already standing, then don't sit down again until you come to me."

Al-Sindī related: I accordingly called for my riding-beasts and got on my way. Al-Rashīd was at that moment at al-'Umr. Al-'Abbās ibn al-Faḍl ibn al-Rabī' (later) told me, "Al-Rashīd sat in his gondola on the Euphrates awaiting you. A cloud of dust became visible, and he said to me, 'O 'Abbās, that must be al-Sindī and his attendants!' I replied, 'O Commander of the Faithful, it is very likely he!'" He related, "Then you came in sight." Al-Sindī continued the story: I dismounted from my steed and stood there. Al-Rashīd sent a messenger for me, and I therefore went to him. I remained standing before him for a while. He told his servants who were with him to arise and go, which they did, so there only remained al-ʿAbbās ibn al-Faḍl and myself. After an interval he said to al-ʿAbbās, "Go forth, and order the seatboards arranged in the boat to be lifted out," and he did that. Then he said to me, "Come near to me," so I drew near to him. He said to me, "You know why I sent the message to you?" I replied, "No, by God, O Commander of the Faithful." He said, "I have sent for you concerning an affair which, if the buttons of my own shirt knew about it, I would throw the shirt into the Euphrates! O Sindī, who is the most trustworthy of my commanders here within my entourage?" I replied, "Harthamah." He said, "You have spoken truly. Who, then, is the most trustworthy of my servants here within my entourage?" I replied, "Masrūr the Elder." He said, "You have spoken truly! Get on your way immediately and ride flat out until you reach the City of Peace. Gather together your trusty retainers and watchmen and order them and their aides to get themselves ready. Then when the groups are ready, go off to the houses of the Barmakīs, station at every one of their gates one of the watchmen appointed to keep public order. Order him not to let anyone enter or leave—with the exception of the gate of Muḥammad ibn Khālid—until my further orders reach you." Muḥammad ibn Isḥāq related: At this point of time, he had not yet moved against the Barmakīs. Al-Sindī continued the story: I began to ride off furiously until I reached the City of Peace, and there I gathered my retainers together and did what he had commanded me. He related: Very soon Harthamah ibn Aʿyan came up to me, accompanied by the body of Jaʿfar ibn Yaḥyā on the back of a mule, without a pack-saddle, and with its head severed, and lo, there was the Commander of the Faithful's letter ordering me to chop Jaʿfar's body into halves and gibbet him on three bridges, with the head for the third bridge. He related: I did what he commanded me.

Muḥammad ibn Isḥāq related: Jaʿfar's corpse remained gibbeted until al-Rashīd decided to set out for Khurāsān. I went along and looked at it. When al-Rashīd went to the eastern side of Baghdad, by the Gate of Khuzaymah ibn Khāzim, he sent for al-Walīd ibn Jusham al-Shārī from prison, and gave orders to his executioner Aḥmad ibn al-Junayd al-Khuttalī, and the latter beheaded al-Walīd. Then al-Rashīd turned to al-Sindī and said, "This"—meaning Jaʿfar's corpse—"must be burnt." When he had gone on his way, al-Sindī gathered together thorny brushwood and firewood for this purpose and burnt the corpse.

Jaʿfar ibn Yaḥyā was killed on the night of Saturday, the first of Ṣafar, 187, when he was thirty-seven years old, their vizierate having lasted seventeen years.

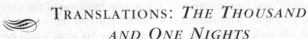

TRANSLATIONS: *THE THOUSAND AND ONE NIGHTS*

The Thousand and One Nights has attracted many translators over the past three centuries, but it has always posed many challenges for them. Translators have always had to begin by asking themselves which text to use: one or another of the varied medieval manuscripts or one of the modern editions, which have many newly added stories not found in the older manuscripts. And what of the ten thousand lines of poetry scattered through the tales?

Should the poems be translated at all, and if so, how should their unfamiliar forms be rendered? How much cultural information should be given to help European readers make sense of the tales? Should such information be quietly inserted into the text or should extensive footnotes be used? And what of the various vulgarisms and erotic episodes in the *Nights*—should they be translated directly, discreetly toned down, or eliminated altogether? A look at three different translations can suggest some of the strategies that have been adopted over the years.

In 1839 an Arabist named Edward William Lane published what became the standard Victorian translation. Using as his base text an Arabic version containing only two hundred tales, Lane left out nearly half of them, seeking to avoid anything "objectionable" or "approaching to licentiousness." He kept in some of the poetry but translated it as prose, and he rendered the often musical prose of the Arabic original in rather plain, decorous English. His approach can be seen in the following passage, in which Shazaman first discovers his sister-in-law's infidelity to his brother Shahyrar:

> A door of the palace was opened, and there came forth from it twenty females and twenty male black slaves; and the King's wife, who was distinguished by extraordinary beauty and elegance, accompanied them to a fountain, where they all disrobed themselves, and sat down together. The king's wife then called out, O Mes'ud! and immediately a black slave came to her, and embraced her; she doing the like. So also did the other slaves and the women; and all of them continued revelling together until the close of day.

This passage reads very differently in Sir Richard Burton's 1885 version, privately printed so as to avoid prosecution for obscenity:

> So King Shah Zaman . . . abode thinking with saddest thought over his wife's betrayal and burning sighs issued from his tortured breast. And as he continued in this case lo! a pastern of the palace, which was carefully kept private, swung open and out of it came twenty slave girls surrounding his brother's wife who was wondrous fair, a model of beauty and comeliness and symmetry and perfect loveliness and who paced with the grace of a gazelle which panteth for the cooling stream. Thereupon Shah Zaman drew back from the window, but he kept the bevy in sight espying them from a place whence he could not be espied. They walked under the very lattice and advanced a little way into the garden till they came to a jetting fountain amiddlemost a great basin of water; then they stripped off their clothes and behold, ten of them were women, concubines of the King, and the other ten were white slaves. Then they all paired off, each with each: but the Queen, who was left alone, presently cried out in a loud voice, "Here to me, O my lord Saeed!" and then sprang with a drop-leap from one of the trees a big slobbering blackamoor with rolling eyes which showed the whites, a truly hideous sight. He walked boldly up to her and threw his arms round her neck while she embraced him as warmly; then he bussed her and winding his legs round hers, as a button-loop clasps a button, he threw her and enjoyed her. On like wise did the other slaves with the girls till all had satisfied their passions, and they ceased not from kissing and clipping, coupling and carousing till day began to wane.

Burton gives us details that Lane has suppressed, and then some; he added in the slave's minstrellike rolling eyes, and he seems to have come up with the button-loop metaphor on his own. Excessive though his version is, Burton does try to render the lively oral style of the Arabic original, whose prose often uses alliteration and even rhyme. He also uses phrases loosely drawn from Middle English, so as to reflect the medieval period of the *Nights'* composition. Compare Hussein Haddawy's 1990 translation:

> While he agonized over his misfortune, gazing at the heavens and turning a distracted eye on the garden, the private gate of his brother's palace opened, and there emerged, strutting like a dark-eyed deer, the lady, his brother's wife, with twenty slave girls, ten white and ten black. While Shahzaman looked at them, without being seen, they continued to walk until they stopped below his window, without looking in his direction, thinking that he had gone to the hunt with his brother. Then they sat down, took off their clothes, and suddenly there were ten slave girls and ten black slaves dressed in the same clothes as the girls. Then the ten black slaves mounted the ten girls, while the lady called, "Mas'ud, Mas'ud!" and a black slave jumped from the tree to the ground, rushed to her, and, raising her legs, went between her thighs and made love to her. Mas'ud topped the lady, while the ten slaves topped the ten girls, and they carried on till noon.

Haddawy uses a different Arabic text than Burton used, and it differs notably from the one Lane used as well. How do the versions differ in what they present? How does Haddawy's modern style compare with Burton's Arthurian flavor? Do you prefer one over another? Should children—or even teenagers—still be given Lane's version, or would Haddawy or Burton now be acceptable for them? Asking such questions as these can help in assessing the differences in approach between the two translations used in this volume, Haddawy's for the opening stories and J. C. Mardrus for the rest; and while few texts have ever been as variable as *The Thousand and One Nights,* comparable questions will be useful to pursue with many other translations as well.

⊢⊣ ⊠◆⊠ ⊢⊣

Jalal al-Din Rumi
1207–1273

Jalal al-Din Rumi ibn Baha' al-Din Sultan al-'Ulama' Khatibi, known by the sobriquet Mawlana, was a great Muslim mystic poet, and the founder of the Mawlawiyya (Mevlevi) Sufi order of dervishes (men living in religious poverty). He was born in Afghanistan, but his family emigrated to Quniya in Rum, Anatolia, hence his name Rumi. His father was an established Muslim preacher, and this provided Jalal al-Din with a solid education. After his father's death in 1231, he followed a Sufi mystic, Sayyid Burhan al-Din Muhaqqiq, to Aleppo and Damascus to further his education and expand his knowledge of Sufism, a major religious and philosophical movement stressing self-denial and the intimate direct union of the soul with God. Sayyid made him aware that the public knowledge he had obtained from his father was only one facet, and that he still required an esoteric and more fundamental knowledge that could not be gained through study, but only through inner experience. He acquired this knowledge, went back to Quniya, and rose to the rank of professor of religious sciences. When a famous wandering dervish, Shams al-Din Tabrizi, visited Quniya, Jalal al-Din met him and fell under his influence.

Persuading him to abandon his teaching career and devote himself entirely to the mystic path, Tabrizi taught him Sufi devotion and enabled him to relearn everything. From that time until his death in 1273, Rumi received divine illumination, and the love of God became the whole basis of his endeavour, a love seen as one that disregards rites and formulas and concentrates on inner feeling.

Shams Tabrizi turned Jalal al-Din into a poet who devoted his work to the love of his master, and contrary to Muslim practice Rumi gave music and dance a central place in his religious expression. He instituted the circular dance, still often practiced by Sufis, based on harmonious movement that replicates the movement of the universe and is an expression of cosmic love. It is a representation of all creatures dancing in joy around the center (God), and expressing their love for Him. Rumi devoted his poetry to the explication of his order, and the elaboration of its tenets with poetry, music, and dervish dancing at its center. He saw humans as virtually the extension of God through a union of love. Even the ugly were a manifestation of the glory of God. His beloved teacher Tabrizi was murdered in 1247—possibly by one of Rumi's own sons acting in conjunction with some of Rumi's students, who felt that Rumi's devotion for Tabrizi had eclipsed them entirely. Rumi responded to Tabrizi's death by seeking to embody his master's spirit and poetic voice, and this became the subject of Rumi's monumental work *Spiritual Couplets* (*Mathnawi*). His *diwan* (collected poems) and *ghazals* show strength of emotion and merriness of heart intended to work off excitement in the dance. His odes have been chanted by crowds on pilgrimages for centuries and are sung with the greatest reverence even today. He used the language of romance, but was often outrageous, for many of his poems are songs of sexual love and drunkenness and often reveal a sense of ambiguity and the excitement of the forbidden, common to much Sufi poetry.

PRONUNCIATIONS:
   Jalal al-Din Rumi: ja-LALL all-DEEN ROO-mee
   Sufi: SOU-fee

What excuses have you to offer, my heart, for so many shortcomings?[1]

What excuses have you to offer, my heart, for so many shortcomings? Such constancy on the part of the Beloved, such unfaithfulness on your own!

So much generosity on his side, on yours such niggling contrariness! So many graces from him, so many faults committed by you!

Such envy, such evil imaginings and dark thoughts in your heart, such drawing, such tasting, such munificence by him!

Why all this tasting? That your bitter soul may become sweet. Why all this drawing? That you may join the company of the saints.

5   You are repentant of your sins, you have the name of God on your lips; in that moment he draws you on, so that he may deliver you alive.

You are fearful at last of your wrongdoings, you seek desperately a way to salvation; in that instant why do you not see by your side him who is putting such fear into your heart?

1. Translated by A. J. Arberry.

If he has bound up your eyes, you are like a pebble in his hand; now he rolls you along like this, now he tosses you in the air.

Now he implants in your nature a passion for silver and gold and women; now he implants in your soul the light of the form of Muṣṭafā.[2]

On this side drawing you towards the lovely ones, on that side drawing you to the unlovely; amid these whirlpools the ship can only pass through or founder.

10   Offer up so many prayers, weep so sorely in the night season, that the echo may reach your ears from the sphere of the seven heavens.

When Shu'aib's[3] groaning and lamentation and tears like hailstones passed beyond all bounds, in the morning a proclamation came to him from heaven:

"If you are a sinner, I have forgiven you and granted you pardon for your sins. Is it paradise you seek? Lo, I have given it to you; be silent, cease these petitions!"

Shu'aib retorted, "I seek neither this nor that. What I desire is to see God face to face; though the seven seas all turn to fire, I will plunge therein if only I may encounter Him.

But if I am banished from that spectacle, if my tear-stained eyes are shut against that vision, I am more fit to dwell in hellfire; paradise becomes me not.

15   Without His countenance, paradise for me is hateful hell. I am consumed by this hue and scent of mortality; where is the splendour of the lights of immortality?"

They said, "At least moderate your weeping, lest your sight be diminished, for the eye becomes blind when weeping passes beyond bounds."

He said, "If my two eyes in the end should be seeing after that fashion, every part of me will become an eye: why then should I grieve over blindness?

But if in the end this eye of mine should be deprived forever, let that sight indeed become blind which is unworthy to behold the Beloved!"

In this world, every man would become a ransom for his beloved; one man's beloved is a bag of blood, another's the sun in splendour.

20   Since every man has chosen a beloved, good or bad, as suits his own nature, it would be a pity if we should annihilate ourselves for the sake of nothing!

One day a traveller was accompanying Bā Yazīd[4] on a certain road. Presently Bā Yazīd said to him, "What trade have you chosen, you rogue?"

The man replied, "I am an ass-driver." Bā Yazīd exclaimed, "Be gone from me!—Lord, grant that his ass may die, that he may become the slave of God!"

---

2. One of the many names of the Prophet Muhammad.
3. A well-known Arab character who went through many trials and tribulations. He can be compared to the biblical figure of Job (see Volume A).
4. An Ottoman Sultan.

The king has come, the king has come, adorn the palace-hall

The king has come, the king has come; adorn the palace-hall; cut your fore-
   arms in honour of the fair one of Canaan.

Since the Soul of the soul of the soul has come, it is not meet to mention the
   soul; in his presence of what use is the soul, save as a sacrifice?

Without love I was one who had lost the way; of a sudden love entered. I
   was a mountain; I became a straw for the horse of the king.

Whether he be Turk or Tajik, this slave is near to him even as soul to body;
   only the body does not behold the soul.

5   Ho, my friends, good luck has arrived; the time has come for offering up the
   load; a Solomon has come to the throne, to depose Satan.

Leap from your place; why do you tarry? Why are you so helpless?
   If you know it not, seek from the hoopoe the way to Solomon's
   palace.

There make your litanies, there utter your secrets and your needs; Solomon
   indeed knows the speech of all the birds.[1]

Speech is a wind, O slave, and distracts the heart; but he commands it,
   "Gather together the scattered ones!"

Have you ever seen any lover who was satiated with this passion?

Have you ever seen any lover who was satiated with this passion? Have you
   ever seen any fish that had become satiated with this sea?

Have you ever seen any image that was fleeing from the engraver? Have
   you ever seen any Vāmiq asking pardon of 'Adhrā?[1]

In separation, the lover is like a name empty of meaning; but a meaning
   such as belovedness has no need of names.

You are the sea, I am a fish—hold me as you desire; show compassion, exercise kingly power—without you, I remain alone.

5   Puissant emperor, what dearth of compassion is this then? The moment you
   are not present, the fire rages so high.

If the fire beholds you, it withdraws to a corner; for whoever plucks a rose
   from the fire, the fire bestows a lovely rose.

Without you, the world is a torment; may it not be without you for a single
   instant; by your life I implore this, for life without you is a torture and an
   agony to me.

Your image like a sultan was parading within my heart, even as a Solomon
   entering the Temple of Jerusalem;

Thousands of lanterns sprang into flame, all the temple was illumined;
   paradise and the Pool of Kauthar thronged with Riḍwān and houris.[2]

10   Exalted be God, exalted be God! Within heaven so many moons! This
   tabernacle is full of houris, only they are hidden from the eyes of the
   blind.

---

1. According to the Qur'an, God gave Solomon the ability
to understand the language of birds and animals. A
hoopoe is a colourful, crested bird often associated with
Solomon.

1. A virgin; "Vamiq" is an ex-lover.
2. Houris are heavenly women; Riḍwān is the Angel who
acts as the gatekeeper of Paradise. The Pool of Kauthar is
a pool of the river of Paradise.

Splendid, happy bird that has found a dwelling in love! How should any but
the 'Anqā[3] find place and lodging in Mount Qāf?
Splendid, lordly 'Anqā, Emperor Shams-i Tabrīz! For he is the Sun neither
of the east nor of the west, nor of any place.

Three days it is now since my fair one has become changed

Three days it is now since my fair one has become changed; sugar is never
bitter—how is it that that sugar is sour?
I dipped my pitcher into the fountain that contained the Water of Life, and I
saw that the fountain was full of blood.
In the garden where two hundred thousand roses grew, in place of fruit and
blossom there are thorns and stones and desert.
I chant a spell and whisper it over the face of that peri[1]—for incantation is
always the business of the exorcist—
5   Yet for all my incantations my peri came not back into the bottle, since his
activities transcend chants and spells.
Between his brows there are ancient angers; the frown on the brow of Lailā
is destruction to Majnūn.[2]
Come, come, for without you I have no life; see, see, for without you my
eyes are a veritable flood.
By the light of your moonlike countenance, brighten my eye, though my
sins are greater than the whole of mankind's.
My heart turns about itself, saying, "What is my sin? For every cause is
conjoined with a consequence."
10   A proclamation comes to me from the Marshal of eternal judgment: "Seek
not about your own self, for this cause belongs not to now."
God gives and seizes, brings and carries away; His business is not to be
measured by reason's scales.
Come, come, for even now by the grace of *Be and it is* paradise opens its
gate which is ungrudging.
Of the essence of the thorn you behold marvellous flowers; of the essence
of the stone you see the treasure of Korah.
Divine grace is eternal, and thereof a thousand keys lie hidden between the
kāf and the ship of the *nūn*.[3]

The month of December has departed, and January too

The month of December has departed, and January too; come, for the
spring has come, the earth is green and joyous, the time of the tulips
has come.
See how the trees stagger and shake their hands as if drunk! The zephyr has
recited a spell, so that the rosebower cannot rest.

---

3. A phoenix. Mount Qāf is a mythical magic mountain.
1. A seductive sprite.
2. "Lailā and Majnūn" is a well-known Arab story of the

beautiful Lailā and her impassioned lover.
3. Kāf and nun are two letters of the Arabic alphabet.

The nenuphar[1] said to the jasmine, "See how twisted together I am!"
The blossoms said to the meadow, "The grace of the Omnipotent has
descended."
The violet genuflected when the hyacinth bowed humbly, when the narcissus gave a wink, saying, "A time for taking note has come."

5   What did the tossing willow say, that it became light-headed with drunkenness? What did that fair-statured cypress behold, that it departed and returned firm of foot?
The painters have taken the brush, with whose hands my soul is intoxicated,
for their lovely imageries have lent beauty to the grove.
Thousands of sweet-feathered birds seated on their pulpits are praising and
reciting lauds, that the time of divulging has come.
When the soul's bird says "Yā Hū!"[2] the ringdove replies "Where, where?"
The former says, "Since you have not caught the scent, your portion is
waiting."
The roses are bidden to show their hearts; it is not seemly to hide the heart,
when the unveiling of the friend of the cave has come.

10   The rose said to the nightingale, "Look at the green lily—though it has a
hundred tongues, it is steadfast and keeps its secret."
The nightingale replied, "Go forth, be busy disclosing my secret, for this
love which I possess is reckless like you."
The plane-tree lowered its face to the vine—"Prostrate one, stand up!" The
vine answered, "This prostrating of mine is not voluntary.
I am pregnant with that draught which smites at the drunkards; my inward is
as fire, your outward is mere plane."
The saffron came forth gay, the mark of lovers on its cheek; the rose pitied
it and said, "Ah, this poor creature, how abject it is!"

15   This encounter reached the ears of the laughing-faced, ruby apple, which
said to the rose, "It knows not that the Beloved is longsuffering."
When the apple advanced this claim, that "I think well of the Lord," to put it
to the proof stones rained from every side.
Someone stoned him; if he was a true lover, he laughs; why should not
Shīrīn laugh when pelted by Khusrau?[3]
The throwing of clods by the fair ones is meant for calling the lover; the
cruelty of lovers to one another is not a sign of aversion.
If Zulaikhā that moment tore Joseph's shirt and collar, know that it was in
sport and play that she unveiled his secret.[4]

20   The apple absorbs the blow and comes not down, saying, "I am happy hanging here, for this honour of being hung on high has come upon me, like
Mansūr.[5]
I am Mansūr hanging from the branch of the gallows of the All-Merciful;
such kissing and embracing has come upon me far from the lips of the
vile ones."
Ho, kissing is done with; hide your heart like a turnover; within the breast
utter secretly the words innumerable.

---

1. Waterlily.
2. "It is He!"
3. Lovers in the most famous of Persian love stories.

4. According to the Qur'an, Zulaikhā is the name of the
woman who tried to seduce Joseph.
5. A reference to the poet al-Hallaj (see page 491).

We have become drunk and our heart has departed

We have become drunk and our heart has departed, it has fled from us—
   whither has it gone?
When it saw that the chain of reason was broken, immediately my heart
   took to flight.
It will not have gone to any other place, it has departed to the seclusion of
   God.
Seek it not in the house, for it is of the air; it is a bird of the air, and has
   gone into the air.
5   It is the white falcon of the Emperor; it has taken flight, and departed to the
   Emperor.

We are foes to ourselves, and friends to him who slays us

We are foes to ourselves, and friends to him who slays us; we are drowned
   in the sea, and the waves of the sea are slaying us.
For this reason, laughing and gay, we are yielding up sweet life, because
   that king is slaying us with honey and sugar and sweetmeat.
We make ourselves out fat for the sacrifice of the feast, because that butcher
   of lovers slays the very fine and handsome.
That Iblis[1] without light begs for a respite from Him; He gave him respite,
   because He is slaying him after tomorrow.
5   Like Ishmael, cheerfully lay your neck before the knife;[2] do not steal your
   throat away from Him, if He is slaying, until He slays.
Azrael[3] has no power or way to overcome lovers; love itself and passion
   slays the lovers of love.
The slain ones shout, "Would that my people knew"; secretly the Beloved
   bestows a hundred lives, and openly slays.
Put forth a head out of the earth of the body, and then see that He is either
   drawing you to heaven, or slaying you.
The spirit of breath He takes away, the comfort spiritual He bestows; He releases the falcon of the soul, and slays the owl of sorrow.
10   That idea the Christian carries abroad, the Moslem has not that idea, that He
   is slaying this Messiah upon the cross.
Every true lover is like Manṣūr, they slay themselves; show any beside the
   lover who deliberately slays himself!
Death daily makes a hundred requisitions on mankind; the lover of God
   without requisition slays himself.
I make this enough, else I will myself utter the lovers' secret, though the unbeliever slays himself of anger and fury.
Shams-i Tabrīzī has climbed over the horizon like the sun; unceremoniously
   he is extinguishing the candles of the stars.

---

1. The Persian name for Satan.   3. A demon.
2. When God commanded his father Abraham to slay him.

Not for one single moment do I let hold of you

Not for one single moment do I let hold of you, for you are my whole concern, you are my whole affair.

I eat and enjoy your candy, I labour at your counselling; I am a heart-
wounded quarry, you are my heart-devouring lion.

You might say that my soul and your soul are one; I swear by this one soul
that I care not for other than you.

I am a bunch of herbs from the garden of your beauty, I am a strand of your
union's robe of honour.

5   Around you this world is thorn on the top of a wall; in the hope of culling
the rose of union it is a thorn that I scratch.

Since the thorn is like this, how must be your rosebower! O you whose
secrets have swallowed and borne away my secrets.

My soul, in the sky the sun is the moon's companion; I know that you will
not leave me in this assembly of strangers.

I went to a dervish and said, "May God befriend you!" You might say that
through his blessing a king such as you became my friend.

I beheld the whole world to be a painting on the gates of a bath; you who
have taken my turban away, likewise towards you I stretch my hand.

10   Every congener bursts his chain to come to his congener;[1] whose congener
am I, who am held fast in this snare here?

Like a thief, my soul, you ever steal around me; I know what you are seeking, crafty sweetheart of mine.

My soul, you are hiding a candle under the cloak, you desire to set fire to
my stook and rick.

O my rosebower and rosegarden, O cure of my sickness, O Joseph of my
vision and luster of my market,

You are circling round my heart, I am circling round your door; circling am
I giddily in your hand like compasses.

15   In the gladness of your face if I tell the tale of woe, if then sorrow drinks my
blood, by Allah, I deserve it.

To the beat of the tambourine of your decree all these creatures are dancing;
without your melody does a single lute-string dance? I do not think so.

The voice of your tambourine is hidden, and this dance of the world is visible; hidden is that itch, wherever I scratch.

I will be silent out of jealousy, because from your sugarcane I am a cloud
scattering sugar; it is only your candy that I rain.

I am in water, in earth, in fire, in air; these four are all around me, but I am
not of these four.[2]

20   Now I am Turk, now Hindu, now Rumi,[3] now Zangi;[4] it is of your engraving, my soul, that I believe or disbelieve.

Tabriz, my heart and soul are with Shams-i Haqq here, even though in body
I vex him no more.

---

1. One of the same kind or race.
2. The four elements from which everything was thought
to be made.
3. Both the name of the poet, but also a general word for

someone from the western Islamic world.
4. A group who rebelled against central authority during
the Abbasid period.

Who'll take us home, now we've drunk ourselves blind?[1]

Who'll take us home, now we've drunk ourselves blind?
How many times must I say, You've had too much wine!

Not a sober person in this whole town do I see:
One's worse than the other, stoned out of his mind

5   Let's to the tavern, dear friend, to see the soul's delight
When my loved one's not with me life's joyless, I find

A souse in every corner, hands waving at the sky
To each of them He carries a cup of the royal kind

The tavern's your legacy, and wine is its cash flow
10   For sober folk not one drop of the fruit of the vine

O gypsy lutenist, who is drunker, you or I?
Ah, matched with your madness, my magic cannot bind

As I left home, a tippler weaved his way towards me
A hundred blossomy bowers in his glances were enshrined

15   He listed and lurched like an unmoored ship
And a hundred sobersides enviously whined

When I asked him, Where are you from? he grinned:
Half of me is Turkistan, half to Ferghana inclined

Half water and clay, and half heart and soul
20   Half made of pearl, half like the seashore's line

Then be my friend, I said, for I must be related to you
Stranger and kin, he replied, are to me all one kind

I am drunk and disheveled in the winemaster's house
Shall I speak? My heart has so many knots to unwind

25   Since you alone have caused a hundred riotous ecstasies
Divine Sun of Tabriz, why do you hide from mankind?

---

1. Translated by Amin Banani.

⇥ PERSPECTIVES ⇤
Asceticism, Sufism, and Wisdom

Although Islam started in the austere environment of the Arabian desert, it soon spread into countries that had known flourishing cultures and great luxuries, from Egypt, Persia, Mesopotamia, and Syria to various parts of the Byzantine dominion. By the second century of the Hijra (eighth century C.E.), the mode of life of these older cultures and the wealth they brought to the central Islamic caliphate started to transform the Muslim community. Strict observance of the religious code of conduct was relaxed and libertine practices began to proliferate. By the ninth century, the Muslim community was polarized into rich and poor, and the ideas of equality, fraternity, and justice that dominated the early community of the faithful disappeared. Social discontent vented itself in many different forms, including religious turmoil. In reaction to the evanescence of worldly pleasures and the widening gulf between

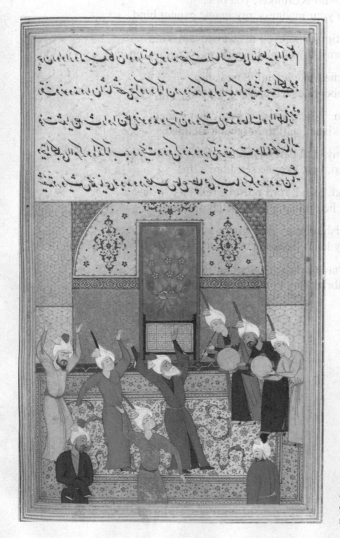

Page from Husayn Bayqara's *Majalis al-Ushshaq* ("Sessions of the Lovers"), 16th century, showing Sufi dervishes dancing.

rich and poor, some learned religious figures called for the renunciation of worldly comforts and the rejection of the prevailing social order on the grounds that it was corrupt, unjust, and distorted.

Some of these thinkers practiced what they preached, and since silk was the symbol of luxury, they spun rough wool (*suf*) from which they made their garments, something akin to present-day environmentalists returning to nature. Naturally, they were seen as antisocial, lawless, and antigovernment, but their response was to remove themselves further from corrupt society and strive to become closer to God. The movement acquired mystical and spiritual elements, and it was responsible for the emergence of Islamic philosophy. Renouncing of the world and adopting an ascetic conduct enabled these seekers to develop their spiritual insights and to emphasize the importance of religious knowledge, which was synonymous with God. God was in turn synonymous with love and was seen as both lover and beloved, according to the Qur'anic verse "God loves them, and they love Him" (5.54).

At first and for want of a more appropriate term, they were called *sufi*, probably after their rough woolen garments, though it has also been suggested that their name is derived from the Arabic root *saffa,* to purify. They were also called "seekers of knowledge" of God. But the term Sufi became the most common and accepted one. Sufism embraces all the concepts implied in these terms: asceticism, knowledge, wisdom, and the rejection of ephemeral worldly comforts. But the essence of Sufism is spiritual and godly love, with ascetic conduct being but a means to attain that love. Other means were also pursued, such as the acquisition of both exterior knowledge of the perceptible and discernible world and the esoteric knowledge of the inner self and the invisible, often through the celebration of the beloved through poetry.

The Sufi poets developed the *ghazal* genre and brought it to unprecedented levels. The beloved who was celebrated in their poems was God, and the love relation described was their relation to him. The Sufi has to exercise self-discipline and become free of all the impulses of the will in order to achieve complete submission to God, the true meaning of "Islam" as "surrender" to God's will. The renunciation of self enables the Sufi to ascend to become worthy of the Beloved, hence the philosophical paradox at the heart of Sufism, that complete surrender leads to ultimate elevation. This is seen as a drawn-out process, as an arduous path; the lengthy journey along it has several stations and requires constant vigilance, all of which lead to various stages of identification with God.

━┤ ⊞◆⊠ ├━

Al-Hallaj
857–922

Al-Hallaj ("the wool-carder") is the common name for the great early Sufi mystic and theologian Abu al-Mughith al-Husain ibn Mansur al-Baydawi. His legacy exerts an influence to the present day, for his life, teaching, and tragic death shed light on a crucial period in the history of Islamic culture. He was born in 857 at Tur, in the region of Fars in present-day Iran. But unlike the rest of Fars, where Persian was spoken, Tur was an Arabised village. Al-Hallaj's father was a cotton-wool carder, who moved to Wasit, the center of the textile trade in Iraq, when al-Hallaj was a little boy. Early in his life his inquisitive mind led him to search for the inner meaning of the Qur'an, which he learned by heart before he reached the age of twelve. He became a Sufi and traveled first to Basra and then to Baghdad in search of instruction, beginning a period of thirty years of wandering. This was a time of turbulent philosophical debates in Islamic culture and even political and social rebellions in the south of Iraq and the Gulf region. Unconvinced by any of the warring views of the period, al-Hallaj went to Mecca to perform his first pilgrimage. There he stayed in the sanctuary for a whole year in a state of perpetual fasting, meditation, contemplation, and silence.

This spiritual experience enabled al-Hallaj to achieve a personal union with God, and, against the principle of secrecy that was the rule of Sufi circles, he began to proclaim it and attract disciples. He then traveled widely and preached more freely, proclaiming a mission to enable his disciples to find God within their own hearts. This earned him the name of Hallaj al-Asrar ("the carder of consciences"), exposed him to suspicion, and led many establishment figures to accuse him of deception and to incite the public against him. But this neither stopped him nor diminished his appeal for his disciples, who soon numbered in the hundreds. In 902 he returned to Mecca for his third and last pilgrimage, after which he made his way to Baghdad, where he started preaching in the streets and marketplaces. The following ten years witnessed the writing of his most important work and the refining of his philosophical and mystic ideas. He wrote highly cryptic works that were widely debated, attracted large followings, aroused far-reaching popular emotions, sparked a movement for moral and political reform, and caused anxiety among the educated and influential classes, some of whom (including the caliph and his mother) inclined toward his teachings, while others saw him as a fomenter of popular discontent in a time of rampant corruption. His preaching was unique and unusual, proclaiming an ultimate union with God and the belief that his disciples could become one with Him.

Al-Hallaj's enemies accused him of blasphemy, and his unmeasured utterances did away with the usual Sufi observance of secrecy. The corrupt religious establishment finally succeeded in bringing him to court, but his condemnation wasn't easy, for it turned into a lengthy theological wrangle. The last eight years of his life were spent as prisoner in Baghdad, and in 922 he was tortured, half-killed, and exhibited still alive on a scaffold. The caliph's warrant for his decapitation finally arrived at nightfall, and his execution took place on the following day. His body was burned and his ashes cast into the Tigris River. After his tragic death, his disciples went into hiding, but they formed a Sufi community that spread his thought and today still sustains the influence of his writing and (often apocryphal) ecstatic utterances, advocating complete union with God through love and suffering.

PRONUNCIATION:
al-Hallaj: all hall-AJH

I have a dear friend whom I visit in the solitary places[1]

I have a dear friend whom I visit in the solitary places;
He is at the same time present and absent to one's glances.
You do not see me attentive to him with the ear,
Listening to hear the words which he says.
5   His words are without vowels or utterance
Or the inflection of voices.
It is as though I were the speaker,
Speaking to my essence by the idea which springs from my essence.
He is present and absent, he is near and far.
10   The description by divine attributes cannot contain Him.
He is closer than is the imagination to the innermost mind,
More hidden than the flash of a hidden thought.

I continued to float on the sea of love[1]

I continued to float on the sea of love,
One surging wave lifting me up, another pulling me down;
And so I went on, now rising, now falling,
Till I found myself in the middle of the deep sea,
5   Brought by love to a point where there was no shore.

1. Translated by D. P. Brewster.   1. Translated by M. M. Badawi.

In alarm I called out to Him whose name I would not reveal,
One to whose love I have never been untrue:
"Your rule is indeed just," I said, "Your fair dealings I am ready to defend
    with my very life;
But *this* is not in the terms of our covenant."

Painful enough it is that I am ever calling out to You[1]

Painful enough it is that I am ever calling out to You,
As if I were far away from You or You were absent from me,
And that I constantly ask for Your grace, yet unaware of the need.
Never before have I seen such an ascetic so full of desire.

Your place in my heart is the whole of my heart[1]

Your place in my heart is the whole of my heart,
For your place cannot be taken by anyone else.
My soul has lodged You between my skin and my bones,
So what would I do were I ever to lose You?

You who blame me for my love for Him[1]

You who blame me for my love for Him,
If only you knew Him of whom I sing, you would cease your blame.
Other men go away for their pilgrimage, but my own pilgrimage is towards
    the place where I am.
Other men offer sacrifices, but my sacrifice is my own heart and blood.
5   They physically circumambulate the temple,
But were they to proceed reverently around God Himself,
They would not need to go round a sacred building.

I swear to God, the sun has never risen or set[1]

I swear to God, the sun has never risen or set without Your love being the
    twin of my breath;
Neither have I confided in anyone except to talk about You.
Never have I mentioned Your name in gladness or in sorrow,
Unless You were in my heart, wedged in my obsessive thoughts.
5   Nor have I touched water to quench my thirst without seeing Your image in
    the glass.
Were it possible for me to reach You I would come to you at once, crawling
    on my face or walking on my head.
I say to our minstrel that if he is to sing he should choose for this theme my
    grief at the hardness of Your heart.
What cause have foolish people to blame me? They have their own faith
    and I have mine.

Ah! I or You? These are two Gods[1]

Ah! I or You? These are two Gods.
Far be it for You, far be it for You to assert that there are two.

1. Translated by M. M. Badawi.   1. Translated by M. M. Badawi.
1. Translated by M. M. Badawi.   1. Translated by Samah Salim.
1. Translated by M. M. Badawi.

There is only Your One Ipseity° in my nothingness, forever.   *self-identity*
This is my all before All, deceptive; two-faced.
5   Where then is Your essence, apart from me, that I may see clearly. . . .
But already my essence is made manifest to the point that there is
    no more space.
And where is Your Face, object of my doubled gaze
In the depths of the heart or in the depths of the eye?
Between me and You (there lingers) an "it is I" which torments me. . . .
10   So lift with Your I this I from between us both.

Here am I, here am I, O my secret, O my trust![1]

Here am I, here am I, O my secret, O my trust!
Here am I, here am I, O my hope, O my meaning!
I call to You . . . no, it is You who calls me to Yourself.
How could I say "it is You!"—if You had not whispered to me "it is I"?
5   O essence of the essence of my existence,—O aim of my intent,
O You who make me speak; O You, my utterances,—You, my winks!
O All of my all,—O my hearing and my sight,
O my assembling, my composition and my parts!
O All of my all,—the all of all things, equivocal enigma,
10   It is the all of Your all that I obscure in wanting to express You!

I am not I and I am not He[1]

I am not I and I am not He; then who am I and who is He?
Not "and I" for He is not I and not "not I" for He is not He
If it is He at whom and by whom we gaze
There is nothing in existence but us, I and He and He and He
5   Thus whoever is for us, with us, of us is as he who is for Him, with Him,
    of Him
I am the One I desire and the One I desire is me
There is nothing in the mirror except us two
Distracted is the singer who sings "we are two souls infused in one body"
And he who makes distinctions between us only proves his *shirk*.[2]
10   I do not call upon *Him* and I do not remember *Him* for my calling and my
    remembrance are directed towards Myself.

━━━ ❈ ━━━

Ibn 'Arabi
1165–1240

Muhyi al-Din Abu 'Abdullah Muhammad ibn 'Ali, known as Ibn 'Arabi, is one of the greatest
Sufis and the exponent of metaphysical Sufism. He left an extensive body of work, some of
which is still in manuscript form and has yet to be published. He was born at Murcia in Arab
Spain to a distinguished family of pure Arab descent with wide contacts in the educated classes
and many Sufis among its members; his father was a friend of the distinguished philosopher

---

1. Translated by Samah Salim.   2. I.e., declares that there is more than One God.
1. Translated by Samah Salim.

Ibn Rushd (Averroës) (page 766). His family moved to Seville when he was eight. As a bright and ambitious young man, he worked as a secretary to various governors. But during a period of illness he enjoyed a vision that changed the course of his life. He abandoned his previous habits and sought the company of the learned of his time. He spent his twenties in a quest for knowledge, traveling between the cultural centers of Spain and North Africa.

From the age of thirty his career was a mixture of travel in a quest for knowledge, and prolific writing. In 1202 he traveled to Mecca via Cairo and Jerusalem to perform the Pilgrimage, and was deeply moved by the sight of the Kaabah shrine, which was for him the point of contact between the worlds of the invisible and the visible. He stayed for two years at Mecca reading, meditating, enjoying many visions and dreams, and writing some of his major work, particularly *Meccan Visions,* a massive work covering many topics and primarily explicating his Sufi metaphysics. He traveled next to Asia Minor, where he spent twenty years teaching and writing, before settling in Damascus at the end of his life.

Ibn 'Arabi was certainly the most prolific of all Sufi writers, producing no fewer than 239 works, mostly in prose with interspersed poetry. His metaphysical magnum opus was called *Bezels of Wisdom* (a bezel is the sparkling, cut surface of a jewel). This book is considered his most difficult work and has engendered a large body of commentary. It encodes his metaphysical Sufism, sometimes in highly cryptic and poetic language inspired by both experimental and symbolic religiosity. Ibn 'Arabi used a new vocabulary designed to elaborate his ideas and his subtle system of ambiguous metaphysics, which transformed Islam's personal God into the principle of absolute being, where all is God and God is all with humankind, occupying a central role as revealed divine being. At the same time Ibn 'Arabi was a major poet, casting his highly philosophical reflections into lyrical form. The poems included here and in "Iberia, the Meeting of Three Words" (page 756) engagingly dramatize his spiritual and philosophical quest.

O domicile without rival, neither abandoned[1]

O domicile without rival, neither abandoned,
    we still inhabit you in our hearts!
Ah, but my heart is broken, thus, in proportion, as it were,
    with the lay-out of your chambers and my missing of you.
5   The happy one for whom you art his place of sweet refuge
    will never cease enjoying most perfect felicity
In the delight and order of domestic contentment
    within your walls unto the end of ages!

I am "The Reviver"—I speak not allusively

I am "the Reviver"—I speak not allusively
    nor foolishly. I am "the Ḥātimite Arab," *Muḥammad!*
To every age is one who is its Essence,
    and I alone am now that Individual.
5   For people come only one after another—
    there cannot be two "Individuals" in one age. . . .

Of knowers, am I not most avaricious

Of Knowers, am I not most avaricious
    with my Creed and my Heart—most ungenerous?
No! This is not niggardliness, but, rather,

1. Translated by Gerald Elmore.

it is the most *generous* form of Favor.
5   I will accommodate [my Lord] whenever
        my knowing Heart realizes [His presence].
    I am the Sun, disclosed by my own Essence,
        if I will. And the waning Moons reveal me
    When I will *that*—all of this in accordance
10   with my Station. And the Stars will reveal me
    When the night becomes most dark from my absence,
        and the world benighted loses [sight of] me.
    When my Mantle clothes the [world's] essence,
        all will be bewildered [by its brilliance]!

Truly, my two Friends, I am a keeper of the Holy Law

Truly, my two Friends, I am a keeper of the Holy Law,
    but it has a Secret hidden from the [mere] keeper's gaze:
He who perseveres in worship and puts into practice
    what God has enjoined, never walks in darkness all his days,
5   And the Secret of Being, as the Caliphate of Man,
    will be his—being without time and being without space!

Time is passing by my youth and my vigor

Time is passing by my youth and my vigor,
    intending to admit me to the House of Perdition.
Indeed, underneath the dust and broken stones
    my make-up shall be undone, my form lost to corruption.
5   —Amazing how a distance which has nearness part of it
    can bar the way between me and those of my affection!
Truly, I am caught in an abode of desolation,
    in endless longing for my dear beloved. . . .

Bouts of dryness came upon me constantly from every side

Bouts of dryness came upon me constantly from every side;
    pensiveness and sleepless nights filled me with apprehension.
The summons of Death to decrepitude disquiets me
    and distracts me from all that is exalted and disdainful.
5   Though my firm trust in my Creator fortifies my heart,
    my powers of hearing and sight are debilitated.
In truth, my heart's fondest Desire was removed from my reach
    by my being reduced to the most abject form of life:
My spirit to the ideal-world called forth, Death it must be
10   that will summon my body to the pit of the graveyard,
As the body is the captive of the tomb in its decay,
    while the Spirit has been resurrected in the world of Forms.
For were I not one of the Real, I would be bound to Death;
    and were I not of Creation, I would be in peril:
15   My "Truth" endows me with the Virtues that are within me;
    my "Creation" adorns me with all that is most human.
How sweet the experience of that which I have savored
    of belief in my Fair Lord, most-beauteous to behold!

And how sharp the taste of that which I have had to taste
20   of the knowledge which desires only God—and *pungent!*
Thus it was as though I fed on fresh dates, on the one hand,
    whereas, regarding knowledge, what I ate was bitter herbs.
I have been given to the fullest that which God imposed
    upon me in my fate and by His preordained Decree—
25 The Providence of One Chosen, All-Knowing—and I came
    as Moses had come, "in compliance with His preordained Decree."

Law and Soundness make of him a heretic

Law and Soundness make of him a heretic,
    whoever seeks Religion with loquation.
So turn to the Law; do not be prolix° therein,   *wordy*
    for, truly, that is all abomination.
5 The "science" of theology is *nescience,*°   *unknowing*
    as can be seen in every situation.
There is no religion but the Word of my God
    or else the Lord-Imām's true declaration,
—the Way of the Elect, Expected Apostle
10   (upon whom be Divine felicitation!).

The time of my release, which I had always calculated

The time of my release which I had always calculated
    has come to pass already, with all I have attained therein.
I have endured with patience because [my Time] resisted me,
    and that which I have had to suffer meanwhile is well known:
5 From loss of all the things which I had sought of Him
    in order that He might conclude a time-frame He had set up.
And now the time of the Approach comes asking thanks of me,
    for He Who dwells there has blessed me with Union with Him.
Therefore, I say: "O my Time, I am *in Him* a certain time,
10   while you, by God, you do *not* know me, but I *do* know Him!"

To that which they don't understand all people do oppose

To that which they don't understand all people do oppose
    contrary doctrines—versus those of Ashʿari,[1] for instance:
While Ashʿarites have what *they* say as to their restrictions,
    others than they offer opposite tenets to theirs,
5 And that only is "true" which *they* choose and depend upon!
    Consider, then, their type of contract, then consider *mine.*

The abode from which you are absent is sad

The abode from which you are absent is sad,
    while abodes in which you are, are thus made glad.
But praise your Lord in every condition,
    and take Him as your Prop and Protection.

1. A well-known Sufi.

Farid al-Din al-'Attar
c. 1119–c. 1190

Farid al-Din Muhammad ibn Ibrahim al-'Attar is a great Persian mystic whose dates of birth and death cannot be fixed with any degree of certainty. 'Attar—the name means "herbalist"—was a pharmacist and doctor, but from early youth he was fascinated by holy men, beguiled by their miraculous tales, and keen to watch the Sufi rituals. Though he himself didn't attempt to become a Sufi, 'Attar developed a deep and creative understanding of the concepts of Sufism. A distinguished classical poet, Jami, remarked that the light of al-Hallaj had manifested itself after 150 years in 'Attar. It does seem that al-Hallaj strongly influenced 'Attar's work and contributed to his profound understanding of the role of love and suffering in humanity's union with God.

'Attar is best known for three epic works marked by clear and well-constructed main stories interspersed with numerous shorter subsidiary tales. The charm and strength of 'Attar's verse epics lies in the fecund variety of these shorter tales; told with masterly skill, they demonstrate a wealth of religious and secular life. The most influential and beloved of these works is *The Conference of the Birds,* a grandiose poetic work based on an earlier *Treatise of the Birds* by a poet named Ahmad Ghazzali. The birds, led by the hoopoe, set out to seek a fabulous bird called the Simurgh (or Simorgh, the variation given in our translation), whom they wish to have as their king. All but thirty of the birds perish during an arduous journey which leads them through seven dangerous valleys, and at the end the survivors recognize themselves as the very Simurgh they have been seeking. They merge into one and by doing so they also perish in the divine, in an ultimate Sufi act of fulfillment and realization.

PRONUNCIATIONS:
Farid al-Din al-'Attar: fur-EED al-DEEN al-ah-TAR
Simurgh: sea-MURG

from THE CONFERENCE OF THE BIRDS[1]
THE BIRDS ASSEMBLE AND THE HOOPOE TELLS THEM OF THE SIMORGH

The world's birds gathered for their conference and said: "Our constitution makes no sense. All nations in the world require a king; how is it we alone have no such thing? Only a kingdom can be justly run; we need a king and must inquire for one."

They argued how to set about their quest. The hoopoe fluttered forward; on his breast there shone the symbol of the Spirit's Way and on his head Truth's crown, a feathered spray. Discerning, righteous and intelligent, he spoke: "My purposes are heaven-sent; I keep God's secrets, mundane and divine, in proof of which behold the holy sign *Bismillah*[2] etched for ever on my beak.

"No one can share the grief with which I seek our longed-for Lord, and quickened by my haste my wits find water in the trackless waste. I come as Solomon's close friend[3] and claim the matchless wisdom of that mighty name (he never asked for those who quit his court, but when I left him once alone he sought with anxious vigilance for my return—measure my worth by this great king's concern!). I bore his letters—back again I flew—whatever secrets he divined I knew; a prophet loved me;

---

1. Translated by Afkham Darbandi and Dick Davis.
2. "In the name of God the merciful, the compassionate," the religious formula used before reciting any verse of the Qur'an, and as a brief prayer to bring God's blessing to an action.

3. The biblical Solomon who is famed, in the Qur'anic version, for his ability to speak to the birds.

God has trusted me; what other bird has won such dignity? For years I travelled over many lands, past oceans, mountains, valleys, desert sands, and when the Deluge rose I flew around the world itself and never glimpsed dry ground; with Solomon I set out to explore the limits of the earth from shore to shore. I know our king—but how can I alone endure the journey to His distant throne? Join me, and when at last we end our quest our king will greet you as His honoured guest. How long will you persist in blasphemy? Escape your self-hood's vicious tyranny—whoever can evade the Self transcends this world and as a lover he ascends. Set free your soul; impatient of delay, step out along our sovereign's royal Way: we have a king; beyond Kaf's mountain peak the Simorgh lives, the sovereign whom you seek, and He is always near to us, though we live far from His transcendent majesty.[4] A hundred thousand veils of dark and light withdraw His presence from our mortal sight, and in both worlds no being shares the throne that marks the Simorgh's power and His alone—He reigns in undisturbed omnipotence, bathed in the light of His magnificence—no mind, no intellect can penetrate the mystery of His unending state. How many countless hundred thousands pray for patience and true knowledge of the Way that leads to Him whom reason cannot claim, nor mortal purity describe or name; there soul and mind bewildered miss the mark and, faced by Him, like dazzled eyes, are dark—no sage could understand His perfect grace, nor seer discern the beauty of His face. His creatures strive to find a path to Him, deluded by each new, deceitful whim, but fancy cannot work as she would wish; you cannot weigh the moon like so much fish! How many search for Him whose heads are sent like polo-balls in some great tournament from side to giddy side—how many cries, how many countless groans assail the skies! Do not imagine that the Way is short; vast seas and deserts lie before His court. Consider carefully before you start; the journey asks of you a lion's heart. The road is long, the sea is deep—one flies first buffeted by joy and then by sighs; if you desire this quest, give up your soul and make our sovereign's court your only goal. First wash your hands of life if you would say: "I am a pilgrim of our sovereign's Way"; renounce your soul for love; He you pursue will sacrifice His inmost soul for you.

"It was in China, late one moonless night, the Simorgh first appeared to mortal sight—He let a feather float down through the air, and rumours of its fame spread everywhere; throughout the world men separately conceived an image of its shape, and all believed their private fantasies uniquely true! (In China still this feather is on view, whence comes the saying you have heard, no doubt, "Seek knowledge, unto China seek it out."[5]) If this same feather had not floated down, the world would not be filled with His renown—it is a sign of Him, and in each heart there lies this feather's hidden counterpart. But since no words suffice, what use are mine to represent or to describe this sign? Whoever wishes to explore the Way, let him set out—what more is there to say?"

The hoopoe finished, and at once the birds effusively responded to his words. All praised the splendour of their distant king; all rose impatient to be on the wing; each would renounce the Self and be the friend of his companions till the journey's end. But when they pondered on the journey's length, they hesitated; their ambitious strength dissolved: each bird, according to his kind, felt flattered but reluctantly declined.

---

4. The word Simorgh involves a pun, for it means "magnificent king," but if divided into *si* (thirty) and *morgh* (bird) it means thirty birds, the hidden meaning which is revealed at the end of the story.

5. A well-known saying of the Prophet Muhammad, which puts the acquisition of knowledge at the heart of the tenets of Islam.

THE NIGHTINGALE'S EXCUSE

The nightingale made his excuses first. His pleading notes described the lover's thirst, and through the crowd hushed silence spread as he descanted on love's scope and mystery. "The secrets of all love are known to me," he crooned. "Throughout the darkest night my song resounds, and to my retinue belong the sweet notes of the melancholy lute, the plaintive wailing of the love-sick flute; when love speaks in the soul my voice replies in accents plangent as the ocean's sighs. The man who hears this song spurns reason's rule; grey wisdom is content to be love's fool. My love is for the rose; I bow to her; from her dear presence I could never stir. If she should disappear the nightingale would lose his reason and his song would fail, and though my grief is one that no bird knows, one being understands my heart—the rose. I am so drowned in love that I can find no thought of my existence in my mind. Her worship is sufficient life for me; the quest for her is my reality (and nightingales are not robust or strong; the path to find the Simorgh is too long). My love is here; the journey you propose cannot beguile me from my life—the rose. It is for me she flowers; what greater bliss could life provide me—anywhere—than this? Her buds are mine; she blossoms in my sight—how could I leave her for a single night?"

THE HOOPOE ANSWERS HIM

The hoopoe answered him: "Dear nightingale, this superficial love which makes you quail is only for the outward show of things. Renounce delusion and prepare your wings for our great quest; sharp thorns defend the rose and beauty such as hers too quickly goes. True love will see such empty transience for what it is—a fleeting turbulence that fills your sleepless nights with grief and blame—forget the rose's blush and blush for shame! Each spring she laughs, not *for* you, as you say, but *at* you—and has faded in a day.

THE STORY OF A DERVISH AND A PRINCESS

"There was a king whose comely daughter's grace was such that any man who glimpsed her face declared himself in love. Like starless dusk her dark hair hung, soft-scented like fine musk; the charm of her slow, humid eyes awoke the depths of sleeping love, and when she spoke, no sugar was as sweet as her lips' sweet; no rubies with their colour could compete. A dervish saw her, by the will of fate. From his arrested hand the crust he ate dropped unregarded, and the princess smiled. This glance lived in his heart—the man grew wild with ardent love, with restless misery; for seven years he wept continually and was content to live alone and wait, abject, among stray dogs, outside her gate. At last, affronted by this fool and tired of his despair, her serving-men conspired to murder him. The princess heard their plan, which she divulged to him. 'O wretched man,' she said, 'how could you hope for love between a dervish and the daughter of a queen? You cannot live outside my palace door; be off with you and haunt these streets no more. If you are here tomorrow you will die!' The dervish answered her: 'That day when I first saw your beauty I despaired of life; why should I fear the hired assassin's knife? A hundred thousand men adore your face; no power on earth could make me leave this place. But since your servants want to murder me, explain the meaning of this mystery: Why did you smile at me that day?' 'Poor fool, I smiled from pity, almost ridicule—your ignorance provoked that smile.' She spoke, and vanished like a wisp of strengthless smoke."

THE PARROT'S EXCUSE

The pretty parrot was the next to speak, clothed all in green, with sugar in her beak, and round her neck a circle of pure gold. Even the falcon cannot boast so bold a loveliness—earth's variegated green is but the image of her feathers' sheen, and when she talks the fascinating sound seems sweet as costly sugar finely ground; she trilled: "I have been caged by heartless men, but my desire is to be free again; if I could reassert my liberty I'd find the stream of immortality guarded by Khezr[6]—his cloak is green like mine, and this shared colour is an open sign I am his equal or equivalent. Only the stream Khezr watches could content my thirsting soul—I have no wish to seek this Simorgh's throne of which you love to speak."

THE HOOPOE ANSWERS HER

The hoopoe said: "You are a cringing slave—this is not noble, generous or brave, to think your being has no other end than finding water and a loyal friend. Think well—what is it that you hope to gain? Your coat is beautiful, but where's your brain? Act as a lover and renounce your soul; with love's defiance seek the lover's goal.

A STORY ABOUT KHEZR

"Khezr sought companionship with one whose mind was set on God alone. The man declined and said to Khezr: 'We two could not be friends, for our existences have different ends. The waters of immortal life are yours, and you must always live; life is your cause as death is mine—you wish to live, whilst I impatiently prepare myself to die; I leave you as quick birds avoid a snare, to soar up in the free, untrammelled air."

* * *

GABRIEL AND THE UNBELIEVER

"One night in paradise good Gabriel heard the Lord say: 'I am here,' and at His word there came another voice which wept and prayed—'Who knows whose voice this is?' the angel said. 'It comes from one, of this at least I'm sure, who has subdued the Self, whose heart is pure.' But no one in the heavens knew the man, and Gabriel swooped toward the earth to scan the deserts, seas and mountains—far and wide he searched, without success, until he cried for God to lead his steps. 'Seek him in Rome,' God said. 'A pagan temple is his home.' There Gabriel went and saw the man in tears—a worthless idol ruled his hopes and fears. Astonished, Gabriel turned and said: 'Tell me, dear Lord, the meaning of this mystery; you answer with your kindness one who prays before a senseless idol all his days!' And God replied: 'He does not know our Way; mere ignorance has led this man astray—I understand the cause of his disgrace and will not coldly turn aside My face; I shall admit him to My sanctuary where kindness will convert his blasphemy.'"[7]

---

6. An enigmatic prophet mentioned in the Qur'an.   7. This is the Islamic version of Jesus's parable of the Prodigal Son.

The hoopoe paused and raised his voice in prayer, then said: "This man for whom God showed such care was one like you—and if you cannot bring great virtues to the presence of our king, do not alarm yourself; the Lord will bless the saint's devotions and your nothingness.

A SUFI WHO WANTED TO BUY SOMETHING FOR NOTHING

"A voice rang out one morning in Baghdad: 'My honey's sweet, the best that can be had—the price is cheap; now who will come and buy?' A sufi passing in a street nearby asked: 'Will you sell for nothing?' But he laughed: 'Who gives his goods for nothing? Don't be daft!' A voice came then: 'My sufi, turn aside—a few steps higher—and be satisfied. For nothing We shall give you everything; if you want more, that "more" We'll also bring. Know that Our mercy is a glittering sun; no particle escapes its brilliance, none—did We not send to sin and blasphemy Our Prophet as a sign of clemency?'"

A BIRD ASKS HOW LONG THE JOURNEY IS, AND THE HOOPOE DESCRIBES THE SEVEN VALLEYS OF THE WAY

Another bird said: "Hoopoe, you can find the way from here, but we are almost blind—the path seems full of terrors and despair. Dear hoopoe, how much further till we're there?"

"Before we reach our goal," the hoopoe said, "the journey's seven valleys lie ahead; how far this is the world has never learned, for no one who has gone there has returned—impatient bird, who would retrace this trail? There is no messenger to tell the tale, and they are lost to our concerns below—how can men tell you what they do not know? The first stage is the Valley of the Quest; then Love's wide valley is our second test; the third is Insight into Mystery, the fourth Detachment and Serenity—the fifth is Unity; the sixth is Awe, a deep Bewilderment unknown before, the seventh Poverty and Nothingness—and there you are suspended, motionless, till you are drawn—the impulse is not yours—a drop absorbed in seas that have no shores.

THE VALLEY OF THE QUEST

"When you begin the Valley of the Quest misfortunes will deprive you of all rest, each moment some new trouble terrifies, and parrots there are panic-stricken flies. There years must vanish while you strive and grieve; there is the heart of all you will achieve—renounce the world, your power and all you own, and in your heart's blood journey on alone. When once your hands are empty, then your heart must purify itself and move apart from everything that is—when this is done, the Lord's light blazes brighter than the sun, your heart is bathed in splendour and the quest expands a thousandfold within your breast. Though fire flares up across his path, and though a hundred monsters peer out from its glow, the pilgrim driven on by his desire will like a moth rush gladly on the fire. When love inspires his heart he begs for wine, one drop to be vouchsafed him as a sign—and when he drinks this drop both worlds are gone; dry-lipped he founders in oblivion. His zeal to know faith's mysteries will make him fight with dragons for salvation's sake—though blasphemy and curses crowd the gate, until it opens he will calmly wait, and then where is this faith? this blasphemy? Both vanish into strengthless vacancy.

EBLIS AND GOD'S CURSE

"God breathed the pure soul into Adam's dust, and as He did so said the angels must, in sight of Adam, bow down to the ground (God did not wish this secret to be found). All bowed, and not one saw what God had done, except Eblis,[8] who bowed himself to none. He said: 'Who notices if I don't bow? I don't care if they cut my head off now; I know this Adam's more than dust—I'll see why God has ordered all this secrecy.' He hid himself and kept watch like a spy. God said: 'Come out—I see you peer and pry; you know my treasure's home and you must die. The kings who hide a treasure execute their secret's witnesses to keep them mute—you saw the place, and shall the fact be spread through all the world? Prepare to lose your head!' Eblis replied: 'Lord, pity me; I crave for mercy, Lord; have mercy on your slave.' God answered him: 'Well, I will mitigate the rigour and the justice of your fate; but round your neck will shine a ring to show your treachery to all the world below—for fraudulence and guile you will be known until the world ends and the last trump's blown.' Eblis replied: 'And what is that to me? I saw the treasure and I now go free! To curse belongs to You and to forgive, all creatures of the world and how they live; curse on! This poison's part of Your great scheme and life is more than just an opium-dream. All creatures seek throughout the universe what will be mine for ever now—Your curse!' Search for Him endlessly by day and night, till victory rewards your stubborn fight; and if He seems elusive He is there—your search is incomplete; do not despair.

THE DEATH OF SHEBLI[9]

"As Shebli's death approached his eyes grew dim; wild torments of impatience troubled him—but strangest was that round his waist he tied a heathen's belt, and weeping sat beside heaped ash, with which he smeared his hair and head. 'Why wait for death like this?' a stranger said, and Shebli cried: 'What will become of me? I melt, I burn with fevered jealousy, and though I have renounced the universe I covet what Eblis procured—God's curse.' So Shebli mourned, uncaring if his Lord gave other mortals this or that reward; bright jewels and stones are equal from His hand, and if His gems are all that you demand, ours is a Way you cannot understand—think of the stones and jewels he gives as one; they are not yours to hope for or to shun. The stone your angry lover flings may hurt, but others' jewels compared with it are dirt. Each moment of this quest a man must feel his soul is spilt, and unremitting zeal should force him onward at whatever cost—the man who pauses on our path is lost."

* * *

THE JOURNEY

The hoopoe paused, and when the group had heard his discourse, trembling fear filled every bird. They saw the bow of this great enterprise could not be drawn by weakness, sloth or lies, and some were so cast down that then and there they turned aside and perished in despair. With fear and apprehension in each heart, the remnant rose up ready to depart. They travelled on for years; a lifetime passed before the longed-for goal was reached at last. What happened as they flew I cannot say, but if you journey on that narrow Way, then you will act as they once did and know the miseries they

---

8. Satan (called Iblis in Arabic).   9. A well-known Islamic Sufi master.

had to undergo. Of all the army that set out, how few survived the Way; of that great retinue a handful lived until the voyage was done—of every thousand there remained but one. Of many who set out no trace was found. Some deep within the ocean's depths were drowned; some died on mountain-tops; some died of heat; some flew too near the sun in their conceit, their hearts on fire with love—too late they learned their folly when their wings and feathers burned; some met their death between the lion's claws, and some were ripped to death by monsters' jaws; some died of thirst; some hunger sent insane, till suicide released them from their pain; some became weak and could no longer fly (they faltered, fainted, and were left to die); some paused bewildered and then turned aside to gaze at marvels as if stupefied; some looked for pleasure's path and soon confessed they saw no purpose in the pilgrims' quest; not one in every thousand souls arrived—in every hundred thousand one survived.

THE BIRDS ARRIVE AND ARE GREETED BY A HERALD

A world of birds set out, and there remained but thirty when the promised goal was gained, thirty exhausted, wretched, broken things, with hopeless hearts and tattered, trailing wings, who saw that nameless Glory which the mind acknowledges as ever-undefined, whose solitary flame each moment turns a hundred worlds to nothingness and burns with power a hundred thousand times more bright than sun and stars and every natural light. The awe-struck group, bewildered and amazed, like insubstantial, trembling atoms, gazed and chirped: "How can we live or prosper here, where if the sun came it would disappear? Our hearts were torn from all we loved; we bore the perils of a path unknown before; and all for this? It was not this reward that we expected from our longed-for Lord." It seemed their throats were cut, as if they bled and weakly whimpered until left for dead, waiting for splendour to annihilate their insubstantial, transitory state. Time passed; then from the highest court there flew a herald of the starry retinue, who saw the thirty birds, trembling, afraid, their bodies broken and their feathers frayed, and said: "What city are you from? What race? What business brings you to this distant place? What are your names? You seem destroyed by fear; what made you leave your homes and travel here? What were you in the world? What use are you? What can such weak and clumsy creatures do?" The group replied: "We flew here for one thing, to claim the Simorgh as our rightful king; we come as suppliants and we have sought through grievous paths the threshold of His court—how long the Way was to complete our vow; of thousands we are only thirty now! Was that hope false which led us to this place, or shall we now behold our sovereign's face?"

THE HERALD TELLS THE BIRDS TO TURN BACK

The herald said: "This king for whom you grieve governs in glory you cannot conceive—a hundred thousand armies are to Him an ant that clambers up His threshold's rim, and what are you? Grief is your fate—go back; retrace your steps along the pilgrims' track!" And when they heard the herald's fearsome words, a deathly hopelessness assailed the birds; but they replied: "Our king will not repay with sorrow all the hazards of the Way; grief cannot come to us from majesty; grief cannot live beside such dignity. Think of Majnoun,[1] who said: 'If all the earth should every passing moment praise my worth, I would prefer abuse from Leili's heart to all creation's

---

1. A reference to the famous love story of Laila and Majnoun.

eulogizing art—the world's praise cannot equal Leili's blame; both worlds are less to me than Leili's name.' We told you our desire—if grief must come, then we are ready and shall not succumb."

The herald said: "The blaze of Majesty reduces souls to unreality, and if your souls are burnt, then all the pain that you have suffered will have been in vain." They answered him: "How can a moth flee fire when fire contains its ultimate desire? And if we do not join Him, yet we'll burn, and it is this for which our spirits yearn—it is not union for which we hope; we know that goal remains beyond our scope."

The birds narrated then the moth's brief tale: "They told the moth: 'You are too slight, too frail to bear the vivid candle-flame you seek—this game is for the noble, not the weak; why die from ignorance?' The moth replied: 'Within that fire I cannot hope to hide—I know I could not penetrate the flame; simply to reach it is my humble aim.'"

Though grief engulfed the ragged group, love made the birds impetuous and unafraid; the herald's self-possession was unmoved, but their resilience was not reproved—now, gently, he unlocked the guarded door; a hundred veils drew back, and there before the birds' incredulous, bewildered sight shone the unveiled, the inmost Light of Light. He led them to a noble throne, a place of intimacy, dignity and grace, then gave them all a written page and said that when its contents had been duly read the meaning that their journey had concealed, and of the stage they'd reached, would be revealed.

JOSEPH'S BROTHERS READ OF THEIR TREACHERY

When Malek Dar bought Joseph as a slave, the price agreed (and which he gladly gave) seemed far too low—to be quite sure he made the brothers sign a note for what he'd paid; and when the wicked purchase was complete he left with Joseph and the sealed receipt. At last when Joseph ruled in Egypt's court his brothers came to beg and little thought to whom it was each bowed his humbled head and as a suppliant appealed for bread. Then Joseph held a scroll up in his hand and said: "No courtier here can understand these Hebrew characters—if you can read this note I'll give you all the bread you need." The brothers could read Hebrew easily and cried: "Give us the note, your majesty!" (If any of my readers cannot find himself in this account, the fool is blind.) When Joseph gave them that short document they looked—and trembled with astonishment. They did not read a line but in dismay debated inwardly what they should say. Their past sins silenced them; they were too weak to offer an excuse or even speak. Then Joseph said: "Why don't you read? You seem distracted, haunted by some dreadful dream." And they replied: "Better to hold our breath than read and in so doing merit death."

THE BIRDS DISCOVER THE SIMORGH

The thirty birds read through the fateful page and there discovered, stage by detailed stage, their lives, their actions, set out one by one—all that their souls had ever been or done: and this was bad enough, but as they read they understood that it was they who'd led the lovely Joseph into slavery—who had deprived him of his liberty deep in a well, then ignorantly sold their captive to a passing chief for gold. (Can you not see that at each breath you sell the Joseph you imprisoned in that well, that he will be the king to whom you must naked and hungry bow down in the dust?) The chastened spirits of these birds became like crumbled powder, and they shrank with shame. Then, as by shame their spirits were refined of all the world's weight, they began to find a new life flow towards them from that bright celestial and ever-living Light—their souls rose free of all they'd been before; the past and all its actions were no more. Their life came from that close, insistent sun and in its vivid rays they shone as one. There in the Simorgh's radiant face they saw themselves, the Simorgh of the world—with awe they gazed, and dared at last to comprehend they were the Simorgh and the journey's end. They see the Simorgh—at themselves they stare, and see a second Simorgh standing there; they look at both and see the two are one, that this is that, that this, the goal is won. They ask (but inwardly; they make no sound) the meaning of these mysteries that confound their puzzled ignorance—how is it true that "we" is not distinguished here from "you"? And silently their shining Lord replies: "I am a mirror set before your eyes, and all who come before my splendour see themselves, their own unique reality; you came as thirty birds and therefore saw these selfsame thirty birds, not less nor more; if you had come as forty, fifty—here an answering forty, fifty, would appear; though you have struggled, wandered, travelled far, it is yourselves you see and what you are." (Who sees the Lord? It is himself each sees; what ant's sight could discern the Pleiades? What anvil could be lifted by an ant? Or could a fly subdue an elephant?) "How much you thought you knew and saw; but you now know that all you trusted was untrue. Though you traversed the valleys' depths and fought with all the dangers that the journey brought, the journey was in Me, the deeds were Mine—you slept secure in Being's inmost shrine. And since you came as thirty birds, you see these thirty birds when you discover Me, the Simorgh, truth's last flawless jewel, the light in which you will be lost to mortal sight, dispersed to nothingness until once more you find in Me the selves you were before." Then, as they listened to the Simorgh's words, a trembling dissolution filled the birds—the substance of their being was undone, and they were lost like shade before the sun; neither the pilgrims nor their guide remained. The Simorgh ceased to speak, and silence reigned.

THE ASHES OF HALLAJ[2]

Hallaj's corpse was burnt and when the flame subsided, to the pyre a sufi came who stirred the ashes with his staff and said: "Where has that cry 'I am the Truth' now fled?[3] while in a state of religious exaltation. All that you cried, all that you saw and knew, was but the prelude to what now is true. The essence lives; rise now and have no fear, rise up from ruin, rise and disappear—all shadows are made nothing in the one unchanging light of Truth's eternal sun."

A hundred thousand centuries went by, and then those birds, who were content to die, to vanish in annihilation, saw their Selves had been restored to them once more, that after Nothingness they had attained Eternal Life, and self-hood was regained. This Nothingness, this Life, are states no tongue at any time has adequately sung—those who can speak still wander far away from that dark truth they struggle to convey, and by analogies they try to show the forms men's partial knowledge cannot know. (But these are not the subject for my rhyme; they need another book, another time—and those who merit them will one day see this Nothingness and this Eternity; while you still travel in your worldly state, you cannot pass beyond this glorious gate.) Why do you waste your life in slothful sleep? Rise up, for there is nothing you

---

2. The Sufi poet al-Hallaj: see above, page 491.
3. "I am the Truth" was al-Hallaj's cry while in a state of
Sufi exaltation, leading to the accusation of blasphemy against him.

can keep; what will it profit you to comprehend the present world when it must have an end? Know He has made man's seed and nourished it so that it grows in wisdom until fit to understand His mysteries, to see the hidden secrets of Eternity. But in that glorious state it cannot rest—in dust it will be humbled, dispossessed, brought back to Nothingness, cast down, destroyed, absorbed once more within the primal void— there, lost in non-existence, it will hear the truths that make this darkness disappear, and, as He brings man to blank vacancy, He gives man life to all eternity. You have no knowledge of what lies ahead; think deeply, ponder, do not be misled—until our king excludes you from His grace, you cannot hope to see Him face to face; you cannot hope for Life till you progress through some small shadow of this Nothingness. First He will humble you in dust and mire, and then bestow the glory you desire.

CROSSCURRENTS: ASCETICISM, SUFISM, AND WISDOM

- As a philosophical movement, Sufism has often involved paradoxically reversing the usual terms of thought and expression. How do the writings in this section compare with the paradox-filled Daoist texts of early China such as the *Dao De Jing* and the *Zhuangzi*, included in Volume A, or the mystical poetry of Han-shan in medieval China (page 78)? How do the problems of law and freedom, engagement and ascetic withdrawal seen in this section compare with their development in the *Bhagavad-Gita* (Volume A) and in Kalidasa's *Shakuntala* (Volume A)?

- Mystical poetry such as Sufi-inspired *ghazals* often describes God in terms adapted from love poetry, while love poets can in turn come to describe the beloved in theological terms. How does the mystical longing expressed by Al-Hallaj and Ibn 'Arabi compare to the overlaying of human and divine love in the biblical Song of Songs (Volume A), in the poetry of Petrarch (Volume C), and in the *ghazals* of Ghalib (Volume E) and the enigmatic verse of Emily Dickinson (Volume E)?

- Mystical texts in many cultures describe journeys in search of enlightenment. How does the allegorical quest of *The Conference of the Birds* (page 498) compare with Dante's otherworldly journey (page 893), Chaucer's comparably comic but far more earthly pilgrimage (page 1061), and Matsuo Bashō's meditative *Narrow Road to the Deep North* (Volume D)?

END OF PERSPECTIVES: ASCETICISM, SUFISM, AND WISDOM

Firdawsi

c. 940–1020

Abu al-Qasim Mansur ibn Hasan, known as Firdawsi, is the greatest Persian epic poet and the author of the celebrated *Shah-nama* (The Book or Epic of Kings). Little is known about his life other than that he was born in an eastern Persian village to a family of educated landowners. He studied Arabic and Persian in his early education and used his family resources to begin writing poetry and to advance his knowledge of the history and literature of his country.

This interest proved to have a broader resonance at the Persian court. Persia or Iran (both names have been used at various times over the centuries) had been under Arab rule in the seventh and eighth centuries, and those rulers had taken little interest in Iran's pre-Islamic past, but in the ninth century an Iranian dynasty, the Samanids, came to power. Muslims themselves, they nevertheless wanted to recall and celebrate the country's ancient heritage. Having had prose records of earlier centuries assembled, the court commissioned a prominent poet, Daqiqi, to compose an epic account of Persia's early history. Daqiqi, however, was murdered by one of his own slaves while still in the early stages of this work, and the commission passed to Firdawsi.

Firdawsi completed a first version by around 981, but he continued to polish and revise it for thirty more years until he produced the final version in 1010, at which point the poem had become a vast and powerful epic, 60,000 lines in length. Like many major Islamic works, the *Shah-nama* begins with the creation of the universe; then a few thousand lines later, it moves to the kings of Iran, focusing on the ancient Parthian and Sassanid dynasties (third century B.C.E. through the mid-seventh century C.E.). In classic epic style, the poem shows the kings as benefactors of humanity struggling against the demons that infest the world. A Muslim recounting episodes of Persia's Zoroastrian past, Firdawsi gives few details of the older religion, but incorporates in his poem a basic conflict between good, personified in "the Wise God," Ahura Mazdah, and evil, personified in the increasingly powerful demon Ahriman. For more than a thousand years these forces of good and evil confront each other in a ceaseless duel full of dramatic episodes. At last one of the ancient kings establishes meaningful peace for half a century, but then the world relapses into its normal chaos when his three sons start to struggle with each other again. The one who rules Persia is treacherously assassinated by his brothers, and this initiates an endless cycle of revenge, during which wars are waged for centuries.

Wars allow for the display of valor and bravery, and the poet excels in the poetic construction of battle scenes. Firdawsi never belittles the enemy's valor and understands that his narrative benefits when the adversaries are worthy of each other. Among the greatest of his heroes is Rostám, whose story is given here, centering on his tragic conflict with his own unrecognized son, Sohráb. One of the most interesting aspects of the *Shah-nama* is its ability to establish plausible representations of social life, conveyed both in vivid descriptive passages and in lively dialogue. The epic at once revived Persia's pre-Islamic history and the Persian language, and provided the country with a unique sense of national identity. The importance of Firdawsi's work is that its gripping adventures articulated the desired imagined community at a decisive historical juncture. Persia needed to imagine itself as a unique Islamic community with a distinct history and a particular strand of heroism to enable it both to accept its Islamic character and to forget its defeat at the hands of the Arabs three centuries earlier. The narrative in the *Shah-nama* stands in the tradition of epic poetry in which the poet maintains a colorful description and a strong sense of ardent patriotism, and it has had a lasting influence and has inspired many subsequent poets. It was, however, a much longer and more ambitious work than Persia's rulers had expected—or wished to pay for. Legend has it that Firdawsi was insulted by the modest payment offered when he presented his completed masterpiece, and he refused it. He died in 1020, still completely confident of the lasting contribution of his work to the literature of his country and bitter for not receiving the recognition he deserved.

PRONUNCIATIONS:
Firdawsi: fare-DAU-see
Rostám: ross-TAHM
Shah-nama: SHAH-nah-MAH
Sohráb: soh-RAHB
Tahminé: tah-me-NAY

Shah-nama: The Book of Kings[1]

from *The Tragedy of Sohráb and Rostám*

PROLOGUE

A vagrant wind springs up quite suddenly,
And casts a green unripened fruit to earth.
Shall we call this a tyrant's act, or just?
Shall we consider it as right, or wrong?
5   If death is just, how can this not be so?
Why then lament and wail at what is just?
Your soul knows nothing of this mystery;
You cannot see what lies beyond this veil.
Though all descend to face that greedy door,
10   For none has it revealed its secrets twice.
Perhaps he'll like the place he goes to better,
And in that other house he may find peace.
Death's breath is like a fiercely raging fire
That has no fear of either young or old.
15   Here in this place of passing, not delay,
Should death cinch tight the saddle on its steed,
Know this, that it is just, and not unjust.
There's no disputing justice when it comes.
Destruction knows both youth and age as one,
20   For nothing that exists will long endure.
If you can fill your heart with faith's pure light,
Silence befits you best, since you're His slave.
You do not understand God's mysteries,
Unless your soul is partners with some demon.
25   Strive here within the world as you pass through,
And in the end bear virtue in your heart.
Now I'll relate the battle of Sohráb—
First how his father's enmity began.

[*The hero Rostám goes hunting. As he is cooking his prey, his beloved horse wanders off, and is captured by a roving band of Turkish horsemen. Rostám ventures into Turkish territory in search of his horse, and is hospitably received by the Shah of Semengán.*]

The ruler then gave him a place within
His castle keep, and waited by his side.
He summoned all the city's great, those who
Were worthy to be seated at the feast.
5   The bearer of the wine, the harper too,
And dark-eyed, rose-cheeked idols of Taráz,[2]
All joined with the musicians gathered there,
To see that great Rostám should not be sad.
When he grew drunk, and sleep came to his eyes,

1. Translated by Jerome W. Clinton.   2. A central Asian city.

10   He wished to leave the feast and seek his rest.
         They led him to a place fit for a prince,
         A quiet chamber sweet with scent and musk.

TAHMINÉ

         And when one watch had passed on that dark night,
         And Sirius rose on the heaven's wheel.
         The sound of secret voices could be heard.
         The chamber door was opened quietly.
5   A single slave, a scented candle in
         Her hand, came to the pillow of Rostám.
         Behind the slave, a moon-faced maid appeared,
         Adorned and scented like the shining sun.
         Her eyebrows bows, her tresses lassos coiled,
10   In stature like a slender cypress tree.
         Her soul was wisdom and her body seemed
         Of spirit pure, as though not made of earth.
         Amazed, Rostám the fearless lion-heart,
         Cried out unto the Maker of the World.
15   He questioned her, and asked, "What is your name?
         Here in the dead of night, what do you seek?"
         She answered him, "My name is Tahminé.
         It seems my heart's been rent in two by grief.
         The daughter of the shah of Semengán,
20   From lions and from tigers comes my seed.
         In all the world no beauty is my match.
         Few are my like beneath the azure wheel.°   *the sky*
         Outside these walls, there's none who's looked on me.
         Nor has my voice been heard by any ear.
25   From everyone have I heard tales of you—
         So wonderful they seemed to me like myths.
         You they say fear no leopard and no demon.
         No crocodile nor lion is so fierce.
         At night alone, you journey to Turán,
30   And wander freely there, and even sleep.
         You spit an onager° with just one hand,   *wild donkey*
         And with your sword you cause the air to weep.
         When you approach them with your mace in hand,
         The leopard rends his claws, the lion his heart.
35   The eagle when he sees your naked blade,
         Dares not take wing and fly off to the hunt.
         The tiger's skin is branded by your rope.
         The clouds weep blood in fear of your sharp lance.
         As I would listen to these tales of you,
40   I'd bite my lip in wonder, and yearn
         To look upon those shoulders and that chest.
         And then Izád° sent you to Semengán.   *God*
         I'm yours now should you want me, and, if not,

None but the fish and birds will see my face.
45 It's first because I do so long for you,
    That I've slain reason for my passion's sake.
    And next, perhaps the Maker of the World
    Will place a son from you within my womb.
    Perhaps he'll be like you in manliness
50 And strength, a child of Saturn and the Sun.
    And third, that I may bring your horse to you,
    I'll search throughout the whole of Semengán."

        Rostám, when he looked on her angel face,
    And saw in her a share of every art,
55 And that she'd given him some news of Rakhsh,°   *Rostám's horse*
    He saw no end to this that was not good.
    As she had wished, and with goodwill and joy,
    Rostám sealed firm his bond with her that night.
    And when in secret she'd become his mate,
60 The night that followed lasted late and long.
    But then at last, from high above the world,
    The radiant sun cast down his shining rope.
    Upon his arm Rostám had placed a jewel,
    A seal that was well known throughout the world.
65 He gave it to her as he said, "Keep this.
    And if the times should bring a girl to you,
    Then take this gem and plait it in her hair—
    A world-illumining omen of good luck.
    But if the star of fate should send a son,
70 Then bind this father's token to his arm.
    He'll be as tall as Sam or Narimán,[3]
    In strength and manliness a noble youth,
    He'll bring the eagle from the clouds above.
    The sun will not look harshly on this boy."
75 Rostám conversed the night with his new moon,
    And spoke with her of all he'd known and seen.

        The radiant sun at last rose to the heights
    And shed his glorious light upon the earth.
    The worthy shah approached the chamber of
80 Rostám, to ask if he had rested well.
    And this once said, he gave him news of Rakhsh.
    The Giver of the Crown rejoiced at this.
    He went and stroked his steed and saddled him,
    Then thanked the shah, well pleased at his return.

THE BIRTH OF SOHRÁB

    When nine months passed for Tahminé, she bore
    A healthy boy whose face shone like the moon.

---

3. Two of Rostám's heroic ancestors.

It seemed he was the pahlaván° Rostám,   *hero*
Or that he was the lion Sam, or Narimán.
5   Because he laughed and had a cheerful face,
His mother called him by the name Sohráb.°   *rose-colored*
In but a single month he'd grown a year.
His chest was like Rostám's, the son of Zal.
At three he learned the game of polo, and
10   At five he mastered bow and javelin.
When he was ten, in all of Semengán
Not one would dare to meet him in the field.
Sohráb went to his mother, Tahminé,
To question her, "Tell me the truth," he said.
15   "I'm taller than the boys who nursed with me.
It seems my head can touch the very sky.
Whose seed am I, and of what family?
When asked, 'Who is your sire?' What shall I say?
If you should keep this answer from me now,
20   I will not leave you in this world alive."
His mother answered him, "Be not so harsh,
But hear my words and be rejoiced by them.
Your father is the pahlaván Rostám,
Your ancestors are Sam and Narimán.
25   And thus it is your head can touch the sky.
You are descended from that famous line.
Since first the World Creator made the earth,
There's been no other horseman like Rostám.
Nor one like Sam the son of Narimán.
30   The turning sphere does not dare brush his head."
And then she brought a letter from his sire,
Rostám, and showed it secretly to him.
Enclosed with it Rostám had sent as well,
Three shining emeralds in three golden seals.
35   "Afrasiyáb⁴ must never know of this,"
She said, "he must not hear a single word.
And if your father learns that you've become
A brave and noble warrior like this,
He'll call you to his side, I know.
40   And then your mother's heart will break."

[*Still only twelve years old, Sohráb becomes the greatest Turkish warrior, and leads the Turks into battle against Iran, quickly defeating several Iranian heroes. Desperate, the shah entreats the aid of Rostám, who comes to the battlefield and prepares to face his unknown opponent—concealing his own identity as well, perhaps because enemies usually flee rather than face him.*]

Within his tent, Rostám could hear the fight.
"This is the work of Ahrimán,"° he thought,   *the evil god*
"This turmoil's not the work of just one man."

4. The king of Turán.

He quickly seized his tiger-skin cuirass,
5   And tied the royal belt around his waist,
Then mounted Rakhsh and rode to war. The host
He left his brother, Zavaré, to guard.
They bore his banner at his side, and as
He rode along, rage mounted in his heart.
10 When he could see Sohráb, his neck and arms,
His chest as broad as that of warlike Sam,
He called to him, "Let's move a little way
Apart, and face each other on the field."
Sohráb just rubbed his hands together and
15 Moved off to wait before the battle lines.
He told Rostám, "I've shown my readiness
For war. It's you who now must choose to fight.
Don't look to any in Irán for help.
It is enough when you and I are here.
20 You don't belong upon the battlefield.
You can't withstand a single blow of mine.
Although you're tall in stature and you have
A mighty chest, your wings now droop with age."
Rostám looked on that noble mien, that fist
25 And neck, that massive leg, and said with warmth,
"Oh, savage youth. Your speech is full of heat.
Alas, the earth is dry and cold. In my
Long years I've looked on many battlefields,
And many foes I've stretched upon the ground.
30 Not few the demons I've slain with my two hands,
And nowhere have I ever known defeat.
Look on me now. When you have fought with me,
And lived, you need not fear the crocodile.
The mountains and the sea know what I've done
35 To all the bravest heroes of Turán.
The stars bear witness too. In manliness
And bravery the world is at my feet."
Sohráb replied, "I have a single question,
But you must answer it with truth. I think
40 That you must be Rostám, or that you are
The seed of Narimán. Is this not so?"
Rostám thus answered him, "I am not he,
Nor descended from great Sam or Narimán.
Rostám's a pahlaván, I'm less than he.
45 I have no throne, no palace, and no crown."
From hope Sohráb was cast into despair.
The day's bright face turned to the darkest night.

THE FIRST BATTLE

He rode onto the battlefield, armed with
His lance and wondering at his mother's words.
Upon the field of war they chose a narrow

5   Space to meet and fought with shortened lance.
     When neither points nor bindings held,
     They reined their horses in and turned aside,
     And then with Indian swords renewed their fight,
     Sparks pouring from their iron blades like rain.
     With blows they shattered both their polished swords.
10   Such blows as these will fall on Judgment Day.
     And then each hero seized his heavy mace.
     The battle had now wearied both their arms.
     Although their mounts were panting and both heroes
     Were in pain, they bent them with their might.
15   The armor flew from their two steeds; the links
     That held their coats of mail burst wide apart.
     Both mounts stood still; nor could their masters move.
     Not one could lift a hand or arm to fight.
     Their bodies ran with sweat, dirt filled their mouths,
20   And heat and thirst had split their tongues. Once more
     They faced each other on that plain—the son
     Exhausted and the father weak with pain.
     Oh, world! How strange your workings are! From you
     Comes both what's broken and what's whole as well.
25   Of these two men, not one was stirred by love.
     Wisdom was far off, the face of love not seen.
     The fishes in the sea, the mustangs on
     The plain, all beasts can recognize their young.
     But man who's blinded by his wretched pride,
30   Alas, cannot distinguish son from foe.

[*They fight at length, and Sohráb almost kills Rostám, who manages to escape. Later, they meet again on the battlefield.*]

     Again they firmly hitched their steeds, as ill-
     Intentioned fate revolved above their heads.
     Once more they grappled hand to hand. Each seized
     The other's belt and sought to throw him down.
5   Whenever evil fortune shows its wrath,
     It makes a block of granite soft as wax.
     Sohráb had mighty arms, and yet it seemed
     The skies above had bound them fast. He paused
     In fear; Rostám stretched out his hands and seized
10   That warlike leopard by his chest and arms.
     He bent that strong and youthful back, and with
     A lion's speed, he threw him to the ground.
     Sohráb had not the strength; his time had come.
     Rostám knew well he'd not stay down for long.
15   He swiftly drew a dagger from his belt
     And tore the breast of that stout-hearted youth.
     He writhed upon the ground; groaned once aloud,
     Then thought no more of good and ill. He told
     Rostám, "This was the fate allotted me.

20   The heavens gave my key into your hand.
     It's not your fault. It was this hunchback fate,
     Who raised me up then quickly cast me down.
     While boys my age still spent their time in games,
     My neck and shoulders stretched up to the clouds.
25   My mother told me who my father was.
     My love for him has ended in my death.
     Whenever you should thirst for someone's blood,
     And stain your silver dagger with his gore,
     Then Fate may thirst for yours as well, and make
30   Each hair upon your trunk a sharpened blade.
     Now should you, fishlike, plunge into the sea,
     Or cloak yourself in darkness like the night,
     Or like a star take refuge in the sky,
     And sever from the earth your shining light,
35   Still when he learns that earth's my pillow now,
     My father will avenge my death on you.
     A hero from among this noble band
     Will take this seal and show it to Rostám.
     'Sohráb's been slain, and humbled to the earth,'
40   He'll say, 'This happened while he searched for you.'"
     When he heard this, Rostám was near to faint.
     The world around grew dark before his eyes.
     And when Rostám regained his wits once more,
     He asked Sohráb with sighs of grief and pain,
45   "What sign have you from him—Rostám? Oh, may
     His name be lost to proud and noble men!"
     "If you're Rostám," he said, "you slew me while
     Some evil humor had confused your mind.
     I tried in every way to draw you forth,
50   But not an atom of your love was stirred.
     When first they beat the war drums at my door,
     My mother came to me with bloody cheeks.
     Her soul was racked by grief to see me go.
     She bound a seal upon my arm, and said,
55   'This is your father's gift, preserve it well.
     A day will come when it will be of use.'
     Alas, its day has come when mine has passed.
     The son's abased before his father's eyes.
     My mother with great wisdom thought to send
60   With me a worthy pahlaván as guide.
     The noble warrior's name was Zhende Razm,
     A man both wise in action and in speech.
     He was to point my father out to me,
     And ask for him among all groups of men.
65   But Zhende Razm, that worthy man, was slain.
     And at his death my star declined as well.
     Now loose the binding of my coat of mail,
     And look upon my naked, shining flesh."

When he unloosed his armor's ties and saw
70   That seal, he tore his clothes and wept.
"Oh, brave and noble youth, and praised among
All men, whom I have slain with my own hand!"
He wept a bloody stream and tore his hair;
His brow was dark with dust, tears filled his eyes.
75   Sohráb then said, "But this is even worse.
You must not fill your eyes with tears. For now
It does no good to slay yourself with grief.
What's happened here is what was meant to be."

* * *

115   Rostám then mounted Rakhsh, as swift as dust.
His eyes bled tears, his lips were chilled with sighs.
He wept as he approached the army's camp,
His heart was filled with pain at what he'd done.
When they first spied his face, the army of Irán
120   Fell prostrate to the earth in gratitude,
And loudly praised the Maker of the World,
That he'd returned alive and well from war.
But when they saw him thus, his chest and clothes
All torn, his body heavy and his face
125   Begrimed by dust, they asked him all at once,
"What does this mean? Why are you sad at heart?"
He told them of his strange and baffling deed,
Of how he'd slain the one he held most dear.
They all began to weep and mourn with him,
130   And filled the earth and sky with cries of grief.

[ROSTÁM'S GRIEF]

Then all the pahlaváns and Shah Kavús
Sat with him in the dust beside the road.
They spoke to him with counsel and advice—
In grief Rostám was like one driven mad—
5   "This is the way of fortune's wheel. It holds
A lasso in this hand, a crown in that.
As one sits happily upon his throne,
A loop of rope will snatch him from his place.
Why is it we should hold the world so dear?
10   We and our fellows must depart this road.
The longer we have thought about our wealth,
The sooner we must face that earthy door.
If heaven's wheel knows anything of this,
Or if its mind is empty of our fate,
15   The turning of the wheel it cannot know,
Nor can it understand the reason why.
One must lament that he should leave this world,
Yet what this means at last, I do not know."
Then Kay Kavús spoke to Rostám at length,
20   "From Mount Alborz to the frailest reed,

The turning heavens carry all away.
You must not fix your heart upon this world.
One sets off quickly on the road, and one
Will take more time, but all pass on to death.
25   Content your heart with his departure and
Give careful heed to what I tell you now.
If you should bring the heavens down to earth,
Or set the world aflame from end to end,
You won't recall from death the one who's gone.
30   His soul's grown ancient in that other mansion.
Once from afar I saw his arms and neck,
His lofty stature and his massive chest.
The times impelled him and his martial host
To come here now and perish by your hand.
35   What can you do? What remedy is there
For death? How long can you bewail his loss?"

* * *

All in Sistán went forth to meet Rostám;
They came to him prostrate with pain and grief.
When first he looked upon that wooden bier,
Dastán dismounted from his golden seat.
5   Rostám came forward then, on foot, his clothes
Were torn to shreds, his heart was pierced by grief.
The heroes one and all let fall their arms,
And bowed down to the earth before his bier.
Zal spoke, "This was a strange event indeed.
10   Sohráb could lift the heavy mace; of this
The greatest in the land would speak with awe.
No mother in the world will bear his like."
And Zal spoke on; his eyes were filled with tears
His tongue with words of praise for bold Sohráb.
15   When Tahamtán[5] had reached his palace gate,
He cried aloud and set the coffin down.
He wrenched the nails out, threw the lid aside,
And drew the shroud off as his father watched.
He showed his body to those noble men.
20   It was as if the heavens burned with grief.
Those famous heroes tore their clothes and wept;
Like dust their cries ascended to the clouds.
From end to end the palace seemed a tomb,
In which a lion had been laid to rest.
25   It seemed as though great Sam were lying there.
The battle'd wearied him, and now he slept.
He covered him again with gold brocade,
And firmly closed the coffin's narrow lid.
"If now I build Sohráb a golden tomb

5. "The giant one," Rostám.

30   And strew it round with fragrant sable musk,
      When I am gone, it won't remain for long.
      If that's not so, yet so it seems to me."
      With horses' hooves they built a warrior's tomb;
      And all the world went blind with weeping there.
35   Thus spoke Bahrám the wise and eloquent,
      "Don't bind yourself too closely to the dead,
      For you yourself will not remain here long.
      Prepare yourself to leave, and don't be slow.
      One day your sire gave you a turn at life.
40   The turn is now your son's, that's only right.
      That's how it is, the secret why's unknown.
      The door is locked; nor will the key be found.
      You won't discover it, why even try?
      And if you should, you'll spend your life in vain."
45   It is a tale that's filled with tears and grief.
      The tender heart will rage against Rostám.

Muhammad Visiting Paradise, Persian miniature, 15th century. Reflecting a history of contact and conversion, this illustration also portrays a fanciful episode of religious exploration. The Qur'an often speaks of the heavenly paradise awaiting faithful believers, and in medieval times a legend arose that the Prophet Muhammad had actually been carried up to heaven to receive a direct vision of paradise. Carried aloft by his human-headed deer Buraq, Muhammad observes the serving girls of paradise gathering flowers and fruits. This miniature was made for the *Miraj Namah,* a lavishly illustrated Persian book describing Muhammad's otherworld journey. Though Paradise is depicted as described in the Qur'an, its rendering here is in Persian style, both by directly portraying the Prophet (never shown in strict Arab Islamic circles) and in the specifics of the figures' costume: the heavenly maidens are dressed for life at the Persian court, and even Buraq wears an elaborate Persian headdress.

Ibn Battuta
1304–1369

No one we know of in history had ever traveled as far as the Moroccan legal scholar Mohammed Ibn Abdallah Ibn Battuta. In a quarter century of travels starting in 1325, Ibn Battuta covered a total of some seventy-five thousand miles, visiting what are now forty-four different countries from Mali in West Africa, to southern Europe, Asia Minor, Russia, Persia, Afghanistan, central Asia, China, India, Ceylon, and Sumatra. He also left an extraordinary record of his travels, like Marco Polo dictating it late in life. He was first moved to leave home at age twenty-one in order to perform the hajj, or pilgrimage, to Mecca and the holy sites associated with the birth of Islam. This major journey through northern Africa and the Arabian Peninsula only whetted his appetite, however, and fate had much more travel in store for him. So, in fact, a prophetic wise man tells him as he is first going toward Mecca, predicting that he'll eventually meet several of the wise man's relatives in distant India and China. He instructs Ibn Battuta to give his greetings to each of them.

This prophecy comes true, and Ibn Battuta does deliver the greetings, though not through any special divine intervention. Rather, his travels were made possible by the ongoing spread of Islam. Islamic empires formed a connected chain from Asia Minor through Mesopotamia, Persia, Afghanistan, and northern India, and an extensive network of Muslim traders operated in these regions and beyond them into China and down to Indonesia. Prominent traders and officials in key locations along this network kept in steady contact. Ibn Battuta himself first went to India on hearing that the sultan of Delhi was hiring scholars trained in Islamic law. Ibn Battuta took his time reaching India, visiting many places on the way, particularly holy sites and renowned Muslim sages. Once in Delhi, he worked there as a judge for eight years, narrowly escaping death on two occasions that he recounts in selections given here—once, when an associate fell from royal favor, once when he was sent with an embassy abroad, only to have his party attacked by bandits. Eventually, Ibn Battuta left India and went south to Ceylon and then to the Maldive Islands, where he served as a judge for the new Islamic sultanate there. Ibn Battuta's skill in law and in Qur'anic interpretation gave him employment and made him friends, while his deep piety allowed him to appreciate as God's gifts the wives, concubines, slaves, and lavish presents he received along the way.

Eventually Ibn Battuta returned to North Africa and settled at Fez in Morocco, whose sultan ordered one of his principal secretaries, Mohammed Ibn Juzayy, to record Ibn Battuta's travels. As with Rustichello's expansive treatment of Marco Polo's account, Ibn Juzayy's composition elaborated freely on Ibn Battuta's reminiscences, at times borrowing directly from earlier travel writing to flesh out the story. The work then circulated in manuscript in various forms; the one used here was revised by a scribe named El Bailuni, who gives a clear and highly readable version that effectively conveys Ibn Battuta's dramatic adventures and his fascination with a wider world than any of his contemporaries had ever seen.

PRONUNCIATIONS:
Abu'l Barakat: ah-BOUL bar-ah-KAHT
El Murshidi: ell moor-SHE-dee
Ibn Battuta: IB'n bah-TOO-tah
imam: EE-mamm

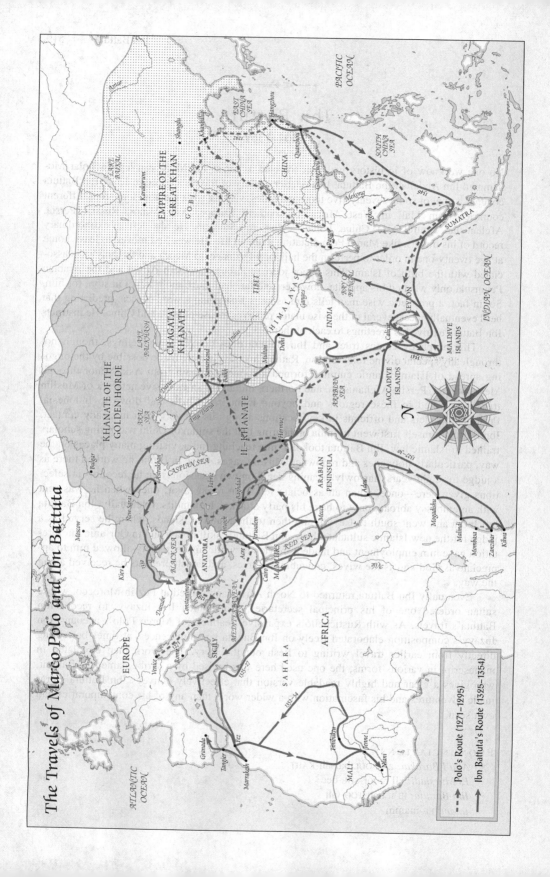

The Travels of Marco Polo and Ibn Battuta

from The Travels of Ibn Battuta[1]

In the name of the compassionate and merciful God. Praise be ascribed to God the lord of worlds; and the blessing of God be upon our Lord Mohammed, and upon all his posterity and companions. So to proceed: Mohammed Ibn Fatah Allah El Bailuni, poor and needy of the forgiveness of his bountiful lord, states that the following is what he extracted from the account of the scribe Mohammed Ibn Juzayy (upon whom be the mercy of God), from the travels of the theologian Mohammed Ibn Abdallah El Lawati of Tangier, known by the surname of Ibn Battuta. He only included what he himself considered as true, because of the traveler's veracity, and because he had written what he believed to be credible from histories of various nations and countries; and also because what has been reported by faithful witnesses generally receives credit. Some of his statements, indeed, are opposed to the statements of others; as, for instance, his accounts of what he saw of the aromatic plants of Hindustan, which differ from those given by the physicians, and yet his accounts are probably the true ones.

[IBN BATTUTA SETS OUT]

I left my native Tangier on the second of Rajab, 725;[2] I was twenty-two years old. I intended to make the pilgrimage to Mecca and the Tomb of the Prophet. I had no one to accompany me and lighten the journey with friendly discourse, and no traveling group to join. Yet moved by a powerful impulse within me and the long-held desire to visit those great holy places, I left friends and home behind. My parents were then still alive, and my going weighed heavily on both them and me.

[TRAVELS IN EGYPT]

One of the greatest saints in Alexandria at this time was the learned and pious imam[3] Borha ad-Din El Aaraj, a man who had the power of working miracles. One day when I went in to him he said, "I perceive that you are fond of traveling into various countries." I said yes, although I had at the time no intention of traveling into very distant parts. He replied, "You must visit my brother Farid ad-Din in India, and my brother Rokn ad-Din Ibn Zakarya in Sind, and also my brother Borhan ad-Din in China; and when you see them, give them my greetings." I was astonished at what he said and determined with myself to visit those countries, and I did not give up my purpose until I had met all three that he mentioned and gave his greetings to them.

*** In Alexandria, I heard of the character of Abu Abdallah El Murshidi, and that he was one of the great interpreting saints secluded in the country, where he had a cell but was without either servants or companions. Here he was daily visited by emirs, viziers, and crowds of other people whose principal object it was to eat with him. So he gave them whatever food they wished to have, whether meat, fruit or sweets, whether in season or not—a circumstance which has seldom taken place in any day but his. The learned also came to him for appointments to office or dismissal. These were his constant and well-known practices. Even the Sultan of Egypt, El Malik El Nasir, often visited him in his cell.

I then left Alexandria with the intention of visiting this sheikh (may God bless him) and got to the village of Taruja, then to the city of Damanhur, the metropolis of the Delta, and then to Fawwah, not far from which is the sheikh's cell. I went to the cell and entered, whereupon the sheikh arose and embraced me. He then brought out

---

1. Translated by Samuel Lee (revised by the editor).
2. Muslims date events from the founding of Islam in 622 C.E. In this manuscript, the dates are an even 600
years off from the common European reckoning, so the date 725 corresponds to 1325 C.E.
3. Muslim religious leader.

food and ate with me. After this I slept upon the roof of his cell. That night, in a dream I saw myself placed on the wings of a great bird who flew away with me towards the temple at Mecca. He then verged towards Yemen, then towards the East, and then took his course to the South. After this, he went far away into the East, and alighted with me safely in the northern regions of darkness, where he left me.

I was astonished at this vision, and I said to myself, "No doubt the sheikh will interpret it for me, for he is said to do things of this sort." When the morning had arrived, and I was about to perform my devotions, the sheikh made me officiate; after this, his usual visitors—emirs, viziers, and others—made their calls upon him and took their leave after they each had received a small cake from him.

When the prayer at noon was over, he called me. I then told him my dream, and he interpreted it for me. He said, "You will perform the pilgrimage and visit the tomb of the Prophet; you will then traverse the countries of Yemen, Iraq, Turkey, and India, and you will remain in these some time. In India you will meet with my brother, Dilshad, who will save you from a calamity that will have befallen you." He then provided me with some dried cakes and some money, and I bade him farewell. Since I left him, I experienced nothing but good fortune in my travels, but I never met with a person like him, except my Lord El Wali Mohammed El Mowwalla in India.

[TRAVELS IN INDIA]

At length I left the town of Abuhar and proceeded for one day through a desert that is enclosed on both sides by mountains inhabited by infidel and rebel Hindus. In general, the inhabitants of India are infidels; some of them live under the protection of the Muslims and reside either in the villages or cities; others, however, infest the mountains and rob along the highways. I happened to be of a party of twenty-two men, when a number of these Hindus, consisting of two horsemen and eighty men on foot, made an attack upon us. But we engaged them and, by God's help, put them to flight, having killed one horseman and twelve of the men on foot.

After this we arrived at a fortress, and proceeding on from it came at length to the city of Ajudahan, which is small. Here I met the holy Sheikh Farid ad-Din El Bodhawondi, of whom the Sheikh El Wali Borhan ad-Din El Aaraj had spoken to me in the port of Alexandria, telling me that I should meet him. So I met him and presented him with the Sheikh's greetings, which surprised him. He said, "I am unworthy of this." This Sheikh was very much broken by the temptations of the Devil. He allowed no one to touch his hand or approach him. And whenever anyone's clothes happened to touch his, he washed them immediately.

In this region, I also saw those women who burn themselves when their husbands die. The woman adorns herself, and is accompanied by a cavalcade of the infidel Hindus and Brahmans with drums, trumpets, and men; following her for mere pastime are both Muslims and infidels. The fire had been already kindled, and into it they threw the dead husband. The wife then threw herself upon him, and both were entirely burnt. A woman's burning herself with her husband, however, is not considered as absolutely necessary among them, but it is encouraged; and when a woman burns herself with her husband, her family is considered as being ennobled and supposedly worthy of trust. But when she does not burn herself, she is ever after clothed coarsely and remains in constraint among her relations, on account of her lack of fidelity to her husband.

The woman who burns herself with her husband is generally surrounded by women who bid her farewell and commission her with salutations for their deceased friends, while she laughs, plays or dances until the very time in which she is to be burnt.

Some of the Hindus, moreover, drown themselves in the river Ganges, to which they perform pilgrimages, and into which they pour the ashes of those who have been burnt. When any one intends to drown himself, he reveals his intentions to one of his companions and says, "You are not to suppose that I do this for the sake of anything worldly; my only motive is to draw near to Kisai"—which is a name of God with them. And when he is drowned, they draw him out of the water, burn the body, and pour the ashes into the Ganges.

After four days' journey, I arrived at the city of Sarsati. It is large and abounds with rice, which they carry to Delhi, and after this I came to Hansi, which is a very beautiful and closely built city with extensive fortifications. I next came to Masud Abad, after two days traveling, and remained there three days. The Sultan Mohammed, whom it was our object to see, had at this time left his residence in Delhi and had gone to Kinnoje, which is ten days distant from that place. He sent his vizier, however, Khaja Jahan Ahmed Ibn Ayas, a native of Rum, with a number of emirs, learned men, and nobles, to receive the travelers. The vizier then so arranged the procession that each one had a place according to his rank.

We then proceeded on from Masud Abad till we came to Delhi, the capital of the empire. It was a magnificent city, combining at once both beauty and strength. Its walls are such as to have no equal in the whole world. This is the greatest city of Hindustan, and indeed of all Islam in the East. It now consists of four cities, which have grown together and become one. This city was conquered in the year of the Hejira 584. Its walls are eleven cubits thick. They keep grain in this city for a very long time without it undergoing any change whatsoever. I myself saw rice brought out of the storehouse that was quite black, but nevertheless it had lost none of the goodness of its taste. Flowers too are in continual blossom in this place. Its mosque is very large, and in the beauty and extent of its building, it has no equal. Before the taking of Delhi, it had been a Hindu temple, which the Hindus call El Bur Khana; but, after that event, it was used as a mosque. In its courtyard is a building to which there is no equal in the cities of the Muslims: its height is such that men appear from the top of it like little children. In its courtyard, too, there is an immense pillar, which they say is composed of stones from seven different quarries. Its height is thirty cubits; its circumference is eight, which is truly miraculous.[4] Outside the city is a reservoir for rainwater, and out of this the inhabitants have their water for drinking. It is two miles in length and one in width. About it are pleasure-gardens, to which the people resort. There are some forty pavilions there, and musicians live nearby.

[IBN BATTUTA'S JUDGESHIP IN DELHI]

On the third day after our arrival, each of the travelers presented himself at the palace. The Sultan inquired whether there were any among us who wished to take office either as clerk, judge or magistrate, saying that he would give such appointments. No one replied at first, for their desire was to acquire riches and return home to their own countries, but then some of them made appropriate answers. Then the vizier asked me in Arabic, "And what do you say?" I answered, "I have no desire either for rule or clerkship, but the office of both judge and magistrate my fathers and I myself have filled." These replies were carried to the Sultan, who commanded each person to be brought before him, and he then gave him a suitable appointment, bestowing on him at the same time a robe of honor and a horse furnished with an ornamented saddle. He also gave him money, appointing likewise the amount of his salary,

---

4. It was an engineering feat to build a stone tower 48 feet high but only 12 feet around.

which was to be drawn from the treasury. He also appointed a portion of the produce of the villages, which each was to receive annually, according to his rank.

When I was called, I went in and did homage. The vizier said, "The Lord of the World appoints you to the office of judge in Delhi. He also gives you a robe of honor, with a saddled horse as well as twelve thousand dinars for your immediate support. He has also appointed you a yearly salary of twelve thousand dinars and a portion of lands in the villages, which will produce annually an equal sum." I then did homage according to their custom, and withdrew.

* * * On this occasion, the Sultan said to me, "Do not suppose that the office of Judge of Delhi will cost you little trouble; on the contrary, it will require the greatest attention." I understood what he said, but I did not return him a good answer. He understood the Arabic and was not pleased with my reply. "I am," I said, "of the sect of Ibn Malik, but the people of Delhi follow the rite of Hanafi; besides, I am ignorant of their language." He replied, "I have appointed two learned men to be your deputies and they will advise you. It will be your business to sign the legal instruments." He then added, "If what I have appointed prove not an income sufficient to meet your numerous expenses, I have likewise given you a household, the bequests appropriated to which you may expend, taking this in addition to what is already appointed." I thanked him for this and returned to my house.

A few days after this, he made me a present of twelve thousand dinars. It often happens, however, that there is a long delay in the payment of the Sultan's gifts—though they are always paid eventually—and for six months I received nothing. By then, I found myself involved in great debts, amounting to about fifty-five thousand dinars, according to the computation of India, which with them amounts to five thousand five hundred tankas, but which according to the computation of the West would amount to thirteen thousand dinars. I had incurred this debt by borrowing money from the merchants with whom I had traveled to India, for the expenses of the journey and my present to the Sultan and my living expenses in Delhi. Now the merchants wished to return home, and they begged me to pay my debts. So I composed a long poem in praise of the Sultan, which I wrote in Arabic and read to him. He translated it for himself, and was wonderfully pleased with it, for the Indians are fond of Arabic poetry, and are very desirous of appearing in it. I then informed him of the debt I had incurred, which he ordered to be discharged from his own treasury, and he said, "Take care in the future not to exceed the extent of your income." May God reward him.

Some time after the Sultan's return from the Ma'abar districts and his arranging my residence in Delhi, his mind happened to change respecting a sheikh in whom he had placed great confidence and even visited, and who then resided in a cave outside the city. He took him accordingly and imprisoned him, and then interrogated his children as to who had associated with him. They named the persons who had done so, and myself among the rest, for it happened that I had visited him in the cave. I was consequently ordered to attend at the gate of the palace for a council that was to meet inside. I attended in this way for four days, and few were those who did so who escaped death. I devoted myself, however, to continual fasting, and tasted nothing but water. On the first day, I repeated the sentence "God is our support, and the most excellent patron" thirty-three thousand times. After the fourth day, by God's goodness, I was delivered, but the sheikh and all those who had visited him, except myself, were put to death.

Upon this I gave up the office of judge, and bidding farewell to the world, attached myself to the holy and pious imam, the saint and phoenix of his age, Kamal ad-Din Abdullah El Gazi, who had wrought many open miracles. All I had, I gave to the Fakirs,[5] and putting on one of their tunics, I attached myself to this imam until I had kept a fast of five continued days; I then breakfasted on a little rice.

[EMBASSY TO CHINA]

The Sultan heard of my retreat from the world and summoned me to him. I went to him in my tunic, and he received me more graciously than ever. He said, "It is my wish to send you as ambassador to the Emperor of China, for I know you love traveling in various countries." I consented, and he sent me robes of honor, horses, money, and everything necessary for the journey.

The Emperor of China had at this time sent presents to the Sultan, consisting of a hundred male slaves, fifty slave girls, five hundred bolts of velvet and silk cloth, five hundred measures of musk, five dresses wrought with jewels, five quivers wrought with gold, and five swords set with jewels. His request with the Emperor was that he should be permitted to rebuild an idol-temple in the country about the mountain range of Kora, on which infidel Hindus resided, on top of which was a plain of three months' journey, and to which there was no approach. Here, too, resided many infidel Hindu kings. The extremities of these parts extend to the confines of Tibet where the musk gazelles are found. There are also mines of gold on these mountains, and poisonous grass growing, such that when the rains fall upon it and run in torrents to the neighboring rivers, no one dares drink the water during the time of their rising; and, should anyone do so, he dies immediately. This idol-temple they usually call the Bur Khana. It stood at the foot of the mountains and was destroyed by the Muslim army when they became masters of these parts. The inhabitants of the mountains were in no condition to fight the Muslims on the plain, but the plain was necessary to them for farming. And so they had requested the Emperor of China to send presents to the King of India and to ask this favor for them. Besides, the people of China also made pilgrimages to this temple. It was situated in a place called Samhal. The reply of the Emperor was that this could not be permitted among a people who were Muslims, nor could there exist any temple whatsoever in countries subject to them except where tribute was paid; but if they chose to do this, their request would be complied with, for the place in which this idol-temple was situated had been conquered and so had become a Muslim district.

The Sultan also sent presents much more valuable than those he had received, which were the following: one hundred horses of the best breed saddled and bridled; one hundred male slaves; one hundred Hindu singing slave girls; one hundred Bairami dresses, each worth a hundred dinars; one hundred silken dresses; five hundred saffron colored dresses; one hundred pieces of the best cotton cloth; one hundred dresses of the various styles of India; numerous instruments of gold and silver; swords and quivers set with jewels; ten robes of honor wrought with gold of the Sultan's own supplies; and various other articles.

The Sultan appointed as my companions the Emir Zahir ad-Din of Zanjani, one of the eminent men of learning, together with the eunuch Kafur, his cup-bearer, with whom the present was entrusted. These were favorite officers of the Emperor. He also sent with us a thousand cavalry who were to conduct us to the place at which we were to board ship. The servants of the Emperor of China, who amounted to about a hundred, including a great Emir, also returned with us. We left the Sultan's presence on the seventeenth day of the month Safar in the year 743, and after a few days we arrived at the large city of Biana. We next arrived at Kul, which is a beautiful city, most

5. Hindu or Muslim holy men supported by charity.

of whose trees are vines. When we had arrived here, we were informed that the infidel Hindus had besieged the city of El Jalali, which is seven days from Kul.

The intention of these infidels was to destroy the inhabitants, and this they nearly succeeded in doing. We made such a vigorous attack upon them, however, that not one of them was left alive. But many of our companions suffered martyrdom at the onset, and among them was the eunuch Kafur, the person to whom the presents had been confided. We immediately sent an account of this affair to the Sultan and waited for his answer. In the meantime, whenever any of the infidel Hindus made an attack on the places in the neighborhood of El Jalali, either some or all of us gave assistance to the Muslims. One day, however, I stepped into a garden just outside the city of Kul when the heat of the sun was excessive; while we were in the garden, someone cried out that the Hindus were making an attack upon one of the villages. So I ran off with some of my companions to their assistance. When the infidels saw this, they fled, but the Muslims were so scattered in pursuing them that only five others and I were left. Some of their people saw this, and a considerable number of cavalry then attacked us. Seeing their strength, we retreated while they pursued us. I saw three of them coming after me when I was left quite alone. It happened just then that the forefeet of my horse had stuck fast between two stones, so that I was obliged to dismount and free him. I was now on a path that led into a valley between two hills, and here I lost sight of the infidels. Yet my situation was that I knew neither the country nor the roads. I then gave my horse free rein to take us where he would.

While I was in a valley closely interwoven with trees, suddenly a party of about forty cavalry rushed upon me and took me prisoner before I was even aware of their being there. I was much afraid they would shoot me with their arrows, and so I alighted from my horse and gave myself up as their prisoner. They then stripped me of all I had, bound me, and took me with them for two days, intending to kill me. There were two Muslims among them who spoke to me in Persian; I told them part of my story, but hid the fact that I had come from the Sultan.

I was put in the charge of three men, who I understood had orders to kill me: an old man, his son, and a wicked black man. They talked together and motioned for me to go with them to a water tank nearby, and I could see they were intending to kill me, so I pleaded with the old man, and he took pity on me. About noon some other men came along and asked my guards to come with them, but they declined. The three of them sat in front of me, with a rope on the ground in front of them. As I watched them, I said, "They will tie me up with this rope when they are ready to kill me." Nothing happened for some time, and then three of the others spoke to them, and I understood he was asking why they had not killed me. The old man pointed to the black, on whom God had sent a fever, as if to excuse himself because of the man's illness. One of the three men asked me if I wanted to be set free. I said yes, and gave him my tunic, and he showed me a way to escape. I went off but I was much afraid they would change their minds and pursue me, so I hid myself in a forest so thickly interwoven with trees and thorns that a person wishing to hide himself could not be discovered.

Whenever I ventured upon the roads, I found they always led either to one of the villages of the infidels or to some ruined village. So I always had to return to my hiding place, and thus passed seven whole days during which I experienced the greatest horrors. My food was the fruit and leaves of the mountain trees. At the end of the seventh day, however, I got sight of a black man, who had with him a walking staff shod with iron and a small water vessel. He saluted me, and I returned the salute. He then said, "What is your name?" I answered, "Mohammed." I then asked him his name: he replied, "Joyful Heart." He then gave me some food that he had with him, and some water to drink. He asked me whether I would accompany him. I did so, but I soon found myself unable to move, and I sank to the ground. He then carried me on his shoulders, and as he walked on with me, I fell asleep. I awoke, however, around dawn and found myself at a village of Hindu peasants, with a Muslim governor, who gave me clothing and a horse. Then I thought of what the saint Abu Abdallah El Murshidi had told me long before, that I would enter the land of India and there meet his brother Dilshad, who would deliver me from a calamity that would have befallen me. And I remembered that when I asked my rescuer his name he told me "Joyful Heart," which translated into Persian would be "Dilshad." So I realized that he was the one whom the saint had foretold.

News had been sent to the Sultan of what had happened, and he now appointed one of his Emirs, the eunuch Sumbul, to continue the journey with me.

[Hindu Magicians]

We traveled on to Galyur or Guyalyur, which is a large town with a great fortress atop a high hill. The governor there is an honest man, and he treated me with respect. While we were there, he told me of the magicians called yogis, who could change themselves into the form of a tiger. I refused to believe him, but other people told me the same things, and so I will say something more about these magicians. The Sultan thinks highly of them and has them visit him. Some of them eat only vegetables, and most eat no meat; they have become so disciplined in ascetic practices that they have no need for worldly things. Some of them can kill a man simply by looking at him. The common people say that if one cuts open the chest of a man who has been killed in this manner, it is found that his heart is gone, and they say it has been eaten.

This is most often done by women, and such women are called *goftars*. Once during a time of famine in Delhi, a number of the people came to me, bringing a woman with them who they said was a goftar, and had killed a child that happened to be near her. I sent her to the vizier, who ordered four large water jars to be filled with water and tied to her. She was then thrown into the great river. She did not sink in the water, but remained unhurt, so they knew she was a goftar. The vizier then ordered her to be burnt, which was done. The people distributed her ashes among themselves, believing that if anyone would fumigate himself with them, he would be secure from the fascinations of a goftar for that year. But if she had sunk, they would have taken her out of the water, for then they would have known that she was not a goftar.

I was once in the presence of the Sultan of Hindustan when two yogis came in, wrapped up in cloaks with their heads covered (for they remove all their hair, both of their heads and armpits, with powder). The Sultan welcomed them and said, pointing to me, "This is a stranger; show him something he has never yet seen." They said that they would. One of them then took the form of a cube and rose off the ground, and in this cubic shape he occupied a place in the air over our heads. I was so much astonished and terrified at this that I fainted and fell to the earth. The Sultan then ordered some medicine for me, and upon taking this I recovered and sat up, and this cubic figure was still in the air just as it had been. His companion then took a sandal belonging to one of those who had come out with him, and struck it upon the ground as if he had been angry. The sandal then ascended until it was next to the cube. It then struck it upon the neck, and the cube descended gradually to the earth, and at last rested where it had been. The Sultan then told me, "The man who took the form of a cube was a disciple of the owner of the sandal." He continued, "Had I not entertained fears for the safety of your intellect, I should have ordered them to show you greater things than these." From this, however, I had palpitations of the heart until the Sultan ordered me a medicine which restored me.

[TRAVELS IN SOUTHERN INDIA; A MAGICAL TREE]

We next arrived at the city of Jurkannan, whose king is one of the greatest on these coasts. We next came to Dadkannan, which is a large city abounding with gardens and situated upon a mouth of the sea. In this are found the betel leaf and nut, and the coconut. Outside the city is a large pond for retaining water, with gardens around it. The king is an infidel. His grandfather, who had become Muslim, built its mosque and made the pond. The cause of the grandfather's conversion was a tree, over which he had built the mosque. This tree was a very great wonder; its leaves are green and like those of the fig, except that they are soft. The tree is called the Tree of Testimony. I was told in these parts that this tree does not generally drop its leaves; but, in autumn each year, one of them changes color, first to yellow, then to red, and that upon this is written, with the pen of divine power, "There is no God but God; Mohammed is the Prophet of God," and that this leaf alone falls. Many trustworthy Muslims told me this, and said that they had witnessed its fall and had read the writing. They further said that every year at the time of the leaf's fall, credible persons among the Muslims, as well as some of the infidels, sat beneath the tree waiting for the fall of the leaf. When this took place, one half was taken by the Muslims as a blessing and for curing their diseases; and the other was taken by the king of the infidel city and laid up in his treasury as a blessing. Now the grandfather of the present king could read Arabic; he witnessed, therefore, the fall of the leaf, read the inscription, and understanding its meaning, he became a Muslim accordingly. At the time of his death he appointed his son, who was a violent infidel, to succeed him. This man adhered to this own religion, cut down the tree, tore up its roots, and effaced every vestige of it. After two years, the tree grew and regained its original state, in which it is now. This king died suddenly, and none of his infidel descendants since his time has done anything to the tree.

[THE MALDIVE ISLANDS][6]

These islands constitute one of the wonders of the world, for their number is about two thousand, nearly a hundred of which are so close to each other as to form a sort of ring, each of which is nevertheless surrounded by the sea. When ships approach any one of them, they are obliged to show who they have on board; if not, a passage is not permitted between them, for such is their proximity to each other that the people of one are recognized by those of another.

The greatest trees on these islands are the coconut, whose fruit they eat with fish. The coconut palm will produce fruit twelve times a year, each month supplying a fresh crop, so that you will see fruit that on some trees is large, on others small, on others dry, and on others green. And this is always the case. From these they make palm-wine and oil, and from its honey they make sweets, which they eat with the coconuts. These foods greatly enhance sexual performance, and the people there have remarkable powers. I myself had several slave girls and four wives during my residence here. I used to see each of them every day, and to spend the night with each wife in turn, and I did so the entire eighteen months I was there. The people are religious, chaste, and peaceable. They eat what is lawful, and their prayers are answered. Their bodies are weak. They make no war, and their weapons are prayers. * * *

The women of the islands of India cover their faces, and also their bodies from the naval downwards. They all do this, even the wives of the kings. When I held the office of judge among them, I was quite unable to get them covered entirely. In these

6. A group of tropical islands in the Indian Ocean, southwest of India.

islands, the women never eat with the men but only among themselves. While I was judge, I tried to get my wives to eat with me, but I could never prevail. Their conversation is very pleasing, and they are exceedingly beautiful.

The cause of these islands becoming Muslim was as follows, as it is generally received among them and as some learned and respectable persons informed me. When they were still in a state of infidelity, a specter from among the genii appeared to them every month. It came from the sea, and its appearance was that of a ship filled with candles. When they saw it, it was their custom to take a young virgin, dress her up, and place her in the idol-temple which stood on the seashore and had windows looking towards the specter. Here they would leave her for the night. When they came in the morning, they would find her violated and dead. They continued doing this month after month, casting lots among themselves, each one to whom the lot fell giving up his daughter and dressing her for the specter. After this had been going on for some time, a western Arab named Abu'l Barakat the Berber came to them. This was a holy man and one who had committed the Koran to memory. He happened to lodge in the house of an old woman on the island of Mohl. One day when he entered the house, he saw her with the company of her female companions weeping and lamenting, and he asked them what was the matter. A person who acted as interpreter between them said that the lot had fallen upon this old woman, who was now adorning her daughter for the specter. So she was crying, and this, moreover, was her only child.

The Mahgrebi,[7] who was a beardless man, said to her, "I will go to the specter tonight instead of your daughter. If he takes me, then I will redeem her, but if I come off safe, then that will be to the glory of God." They therefore took him to the idol-house that night, as if he had been the daughter of the old woman. The magistrate knew nothing of the matter. The Mahgrebi went in, and sitting down at the window, he began to read the Koran. By and by the specter came, with eyes flaming like fire, but when he got near the Koran, he plunged into the sea. In this manner, the Mahgrebi remained until morning reading his Koran, whereupon the old woman came with her household and the great personages of the district in order to fetch out the young woman and burn her, as was their custom. But when they saw the old man reading the Koran, just as they had left him, they were greatly astonished. The old woman then told them what she had done and why she had desired him to do this. They then carried the Mahgrebi to their king, whose name was Shanwan, and told him the whole affair, and he too was much astonished at the Arab.

Upon this, the Mahgrebi presented the doctrine of Islam to the King and pressed him to receive it. The King replied, "Stay with us another month, and then, if you can do as you have now done and escape the specter with safety, I will become a Muslim." So before the completion of the month, God opened the heart of the King for the reception of Islam—for himself, his household, his children, and his nobles. And when the second month came, they went with the Mahgrebi to the idol-house according to former custom, but with the King himself also present. When the following morning had arrived, they found the Mahgrebi sitting and reading his Koran, having had the same encounter with the specter that he had on the former occasion. They then broke the images, razed the idol-house to the ground, and all became Muslims.

[TRAVELS IN CHINA]

We then left the countries of Tialisi, and after a voyage of seven days with a favorable wind, we arrived at the first of the Chinese provinces. This is a most extensive country and abounds in good things of every description—fruits, agriculture, gold, and

7. North African Arab.

silver—and these are without parallel. It is divided by a river called the Water of Life. It is also called the River of Sibar, like the name of a river in India. It has its source in the mountains in the neighborhood of the city Khan Balik,[8] called the Mountain of the Apes. It then proceeds through the middle of China for a distance of six months, until it passes by Sin El Sin, both of whose banks are covered with villages and farms just like the Nile of Egypt, except that this is much more populous. In China, sugarcane grows, and it is much better than that of Egypt. All the fruits of our countries are found in China, but they are much more plentiful and cheap in China.

The Chinese are all infidels; they worship images and burn their dead just like the Hindus. The King of China is a Tartar, and one of the descendants of Gengiz Khan who entered the Muslim countries and desolated many. In all the Chinese provinces, there is a town for the Muslims to reside in. They also have homes, schools, and mosques, which are made much of by the Kings of China. Most of the Chinese eat the flesh of dogs and swine, both of which are sold in their markets. They are much addicted to the comforts and pleasures of life but not much in their luxuries of dress, for you may see one of their immensely wealthy merchants clothed in the coarsest cotton. *** The people of China are, in other respects, the most skillful artificers. In painting, none come near to them. One thing I myself witnessed was the following. I once briefly visited one of their cities but then some time afterward I had occasion to visit again. What should I see upon its walls, and upon the papers stuck up in the streets, but pictures of myself and my companions! This is constantly done with all who pass through their towns. Should any stranger do anything to make flight necessary, they would then send out his picture to the other provinces, and wherever he might happen to be, he would be captured. ***

The care they take of travelers among them is truly surprising, and hence their country is the best and the safest for travelers, for here a man may travel alone for nine months together with a great quantity of wealth without the least fear. The reason for this is that in every district there is an inn, over which the magistrate of the place has control. Every evening the magistrate comes with his secretary to the inn and registers in a book the names of all the guests there. He then locks them up. In the morning he comes again with his secretary and compares the names written down with everyone in the inn. The register so made out is sent to the presiding magistrate of the next way station by a messenger; he also brings back vouchers that such and such persons have safely arrived with their property. This is done at every way station. When it is discovered that any person happens to be lost or anything is stolen, the magistrate who has control over the inn in which the loss is sustained is taken into custody on that account. In all the inns, anything that a traveler can want is provided. * * *

In Kanjura I resided fifteen days. I then proceeded by the river, and after four days arrived at the city of Bairam Katlu, which is a small place with very hospitable inhabitants. In this place there were not more than four Muslims, with one of whom I resided for three days, then proceeded by the river for ten days, and arrived at the city of El Khansa.[9] The name of this place is similar to that of the poetess, El Khansa, but I do not know whether the word is Arabic or not, or whether Arabic has any agreement or not with their language.

This is the largest city I have ever seen on the face of the earth; its length is a journey of three days, in which a traveler may proceed and find lodgings. It is, as I have already said of the manner of building among the Chinese, so constructed that each inhabitant has his house in the middle of his land and gardens. This city is

8. In northern China.
9. Arabic version of Marco Polo's "Kin-sai" (see pages   1078–1079 for Polo's description). Both names are approximations of a Chinese name meaning "Temporary Capital."

divided into six cities, all of which are surrounded by a wall, and of which we shall presently say more. * * *

The fourth city is the most beautiful of all the six. It is intersected by three rivers. I was entertained by the Emir Karti, in his own house, most splendidly. He had brought together to this feast the great men of both the Muslims and the Chinese. We also had musicians and singers. I stayed with him one night. At the banquet, the Khan's jugglers were present. The chief of them was ordered to show some of his wonders. He took a wooden sphere with holes, and threaded through the holes was a long strap. He threw the sphere up into the air until it went out of sight, while the strap remained in his hand. He then commanded one of his disciples to take hold of this strap and climb up it, which he did until he too went out of sight. His master then called him three times, but no answer came. He then took a knife in his hand, apparently in anger, and set it against the strap, then he too ascended until he went out of sight; he then threw the hand of the boy down to the ground, then his foot, his other hand, his other foot, his body, and finally his head. He then came down panting for breath, his clothes stained with blood. The man then kissed the ground before the General, who addressed him in Chinese and gave him some other order. The juggler then took the limbs of the boy and applied them to one another. He stamped upon them, and it stood up complete and erect. I was astonished and was seized by a palpitation of the heart, but they gave me some drink and I recovered. The judge of the Muslims who was sitting by my side swore that there had not been any ascent or descent or cutting away of limbs, but the whole was mere trickery.

[RETURN TO MOROCCO]

I then returned by the river, descending from El Khansa to Kanjanfur, and thence to the city of El Zaitun. When I got there, I found some junks bound for India and got into one belonging to the eunuch El Zahir, King of Sumatra, whose servants are Muslims. In this we sailed with a good wind for ten days. The sky then became obscure and dark, a storm arose, and the vessel got blown into a sea unknown to the sailors. The people in the junk were all terribly afraid and wished to go back, but it was impossible. After this, we saw one morning at daybreak a mountain in the sea, at the distance of about twenty miles. Towards this the wind was carrying us. The sailors wondered at this because we were far from land, and because no mountain had been observed in that part of the sea. It was certain that if the wind should force us to it, we should be lost. We then betook ourselves to repentance and prayer to Almighty God with all our hearts; and, in addition to this, the merchants made many vows. The wind then calmed down to some degree. Then after sunrise, we perceived that the mountain we had seen was in the air, and there was light between it and the sea. I was much astonished at this, but seeing the sailors in the utmost perturbation and bidding farewell to one another, I said, "Tell me, what is the matter?" They said, "What we supposed to be a mountain is really a Rokh,[1] and if he sees us, we shall assuredly perish, for it is only ten miles away." But God in his goodness gave us a good wind, and we steered our course away so that we saw no more of him, nor could I learn the particulars of his shape.

Two months later, we got to Java and shortly after landed at Sumatra. * * *

I then hired a passage back to Cairo but a desire of seeing my native country now came upon me, and I prepared to take my journey to the West. I traveled accordingly to

1. A legendary bird of vast proportions. Marco Polo's version is smaller than this, but still able to carry an elephant (page 1082).

Alexandria, and in the month Safar, 750, I set sail and arrived at the island of Jarba. From this place I sailed in another vessel to Safakus, then to Milyana, then to the city of Tunis, then to Tilimsan, then to Fez, where I arrived at the palace in the later part of the month Shaaban in the year 750. The reigning king at this time was the Commander of the Faithful, Abu Anan. I presented myself to him and was honored to see him. The awe that surrounded him made me forget that of the King of Iraq, his elegance that of the Sultan of India, his politeness that of the King of Yemen, his bravery that of the King of the Turks, his mildness that of the Emperor of Constantinople, his religious bearing that of the King of Sumatra, for he so overwhelmed me with his favors that I found myself quite unequal to express my gratitude. In Fez I terminated my travels, having assured myself that it is the most beautiful of countries. The poet has truly said of it:

> Ask me my proof: Why in the west
> Countries you find the sweetest, best?
> 'Tis this: Hence rides the full-orbed moon,
> And hither hastes the sun at noon.

The Epic of Son-Jara
13th–20th centuries

Son-Jara was the legendary founder of the empire of Old Mali, or Manden, in central West Africa, in around 1250 C.E. Since then, his exploits have been preserved and elaborated in oral poetic tradition by village bards. Differing versions have circulated around West Africa, and the hero's name itself takes different forms; it is often found pronounced as "Sunjata" or "Sundiata." Like other epic heroes such as Homer's Achilles and Virgil's Aeneas, Son-Jara came to be seen as a great cultural hero, effective founder of the entire Mande people. The epic accounts invest him with the powers of a warrior and a sorcerer, at once ruthless and magnificent, who overcomes crippling disadvantages at birth—he is literally born lame, a younger son of uncertain status—to rise to prominence, repel a foreign invader, and found an empire. In keeping with his expansive role, Son-Jara is invoked in the epic by many names of praise, some clear in meaning ("Sorcerer-Seizing-Sorcerer"), some of unknown origin ("Biribiriba").

The epic shows a deep interweaving of native West African traditions with Islamic theology and history. The story begins by tracing Son-Jara's lineage back to Adam and then to the circles around the prophet Muhammad. Son-Jara's great rival, the foreign king Sumamuru, is an enemy of Islam as well as an oppressor of Son-Jara's people, and his defeat is a religious triumph as well as a political victory. At the same time, Son-Jara and his Mande compatriots blend ancient local traditions and rituals with their Muslim beliefs—employing the magical properties of local trees and plants, consulting fetishes (sacred objects associated with ancestors or divine forces), even at one point sacrificing an infant in order to gain spiritual power. Son-Jara receives his double heritage at birth: his father is descended from immigrants from Mecca, and from him Son-Jara receives "grace," *barakah,* from the Arabic term for "blessing." His mother, on the other hand, is descended from a West African sorceress known as the Buffalo-Woman of Du, and from her Son-Jara inherits *nyama,* the Mali term for a sorcerer's power.

The version given here was tape-recorded in 1968 by an American folklorist, Charles S. Bird, then transcribed and translated by John William Johnson and several African collaborators, to produce a rendering faithful to the scene of performance. The performer was a professional bard named Fa-Digi Sisòkò, who mixed all kinds of materials into his overall recitation, particularly chanted praise-poems (indented in this text), and actual songs (italicized) that comment

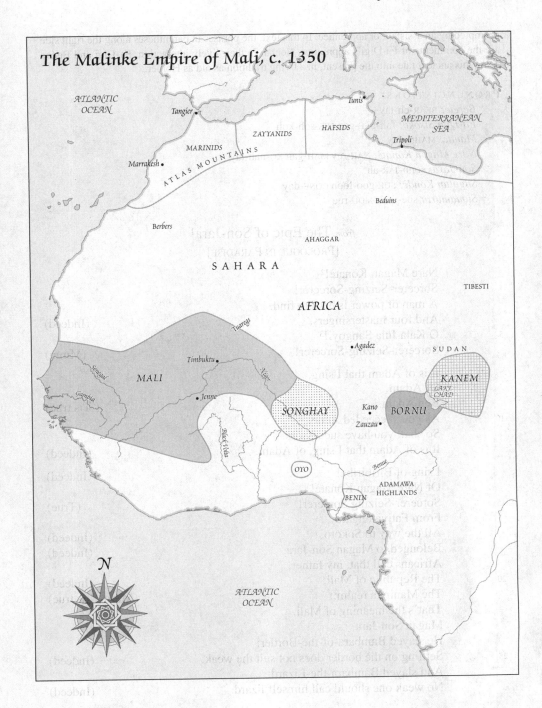

The Malinke Empire of Mali, c. 1350

generally on the action. Bards have a prominent role in Mali society, at once serving as historians and as mediators between the human and divine realms, their songs charged with sacred power. They can read divinations and administer blessings and curses, and they can serve as mediators between parties in social conflicts. As important as their role is socially, the bards are also skilled entertainers, telling their tales in close cooperation with their responsive audience, who are often prompted by an assistant or apprentice. In this text, the phrases in parentheses along the right side are the comments of Fa-Digi's apprentice, Benba. In their lively interaction, Fa-Digi and Benba bring this ancient tale into the present, in a living tradition as old as Homer.

PRONUNCIATIONS:

Berete: BEAR-eh-tay
Fa-Digi Sisòkò: fah-DEE-gee SEE-soh-koh
Mande: MAHN-day
Nare Magan Kònatè: NAH-ray MAH-gan KO-nah-tay
Son-Jara: sonn-JAR-ah
Sugulun Kòndé: SUE-goo-loon CONE-day
Sumamuru: sue-mah-MOU-rue

from The Epic of Son-Jara[1]
[PROLOGUE IN PARADISE]

    Nare Magan Kònatè![2]
    Sorcerer-Seizing-Sorcerer!
    A man of power is hard to find.
    And four mastersingers.   (Indeed)
5   O Kala Jula Sangoyi![3]
    Sorcerer-Seizing-Sorcerer!   (Mmm)

    It is of Adam that I sing.
    Of Adam,
    Ben Adam.[4]   ('Tis true)
10   As you succeeded some,
    So shall you have successors!
    It is of Adam that I sing, of Adam.   (Indeed)

    I sing of Biribiriba!   (Indeed)
    Of Nare Magan Kònatè!
15 Sorcerer-Seizing Sorcerer!   (True)
    From Fatiyataligara
    All the way to Sokoto,   (Indeed)
    Belonged to Magan Son-Jara.   (Indeed)
    Africans call that, my father,
20 The Republic of Mali,   (Indeed)
    The Maninka realm: (Mmm, 'tis true)
    That's the meaning of Mali.
    Magan Son-Jara,
    He slayed Bambara-of-the-Border;
25 Settling on the border does not suit the weak.   (Indeed)
    And slayed Bambara-the-Lizard;
    No weak one should call himself lizard.   (Indeed)

---

1. Translated by John William Johnson, from whom the following notes are adapted.
2. One of many praise-names for Son-Jara; "Nara" is likely his home village, "Magan" is a given name that may mean

"master," Kònatè is the clan name of his father's family.
3. A legendary bard of Old Mali.
4. First man on earth; from Arabic *bani Adama,* "the sons of Adam," a common term in the Qur'an for humanity.

And slayed Bambara-of-the-Backwoods;

Settling the backwoods does not suit the weak.   (Indeed)

30   All this by the hand of Nare Magan Kònatè.

Sorcerer-Seizing-Sorcerer!

Simbon,[5] Lion-Born-of-the-Cat.   ('Tis true)

I sing of Biribiriba.   (Indeed)

Stump-in-the-Dark-of-Night!

35   Should bump against it,

It will bump against you.

Granary-Guard-Dog.   (Indeed)

The thing discerning not the stranger,   (Indeed)

Nor the familiar.

40   Should it come upon any person,

He will be bitten!   (Indeed)

Kirikara Watita![6]   (Indeed)

Adversity's-True-Place!   (Indeed)

Man's reason and a woman's are not the same.   (Indeed)

45   Pretty words and truth are not the same.   (Indeed)

Almighty God created Adam,   (Indeed)

Nine Adams.   (Indeed)

The tenth one was Ben Adam.   (True)

Ah, Bèmba!   (Indeed)

50   Almighty God created Adam, the forefather,   (Indeed)

And caused him to stand upon the earth,

And said that all creation's beings should submit to him.

And all the beings of creation did submit to him,   (Indeed)

Save Iblis alone.[7]

55   May God deliver us from Satan!   (Amen, O my Lord)

Almighty God declared, "Iblis!   (Indeed)

"If you do not submit to Adam,   (Indeed)

"I will make you wretched.   (Mmm)

"He is the last of all the Adams."   (True)

60   Iblis replied, "My Lord,   (Indeed)

"I'll not submit to Adam.   (Indeed)

"For eighty years,

"I've taught the angels.   (Indeed)

"Not one hand span, have I traveled o'er the earth,   (Indeed)

65   "Where I did not submit to you.   (Indeed)

"O God, reward me for all this."   (Indeed)

"So be it," the reply.   (Indeed)

"I will reward you.   (Indeed)

"Ne'er will you catch disease.   (Indeed)

70   "Ne'er your memory will fail.   (Indeed)

---

5. "Hunter."

6. Term for a fierce warrior, accompanied by a haughty
shrug of the shoulders.

7. In the Qur'an, God's favorite but rebellious angel (see
pages 345–346).

"Ne'er will you need to sleep,
"Until the day the trumpet blows for man.
"Whosoe'er you lead astray,
"Among the next world's chosen will not be."   (Ah, Fa-Digi,
                                                      That's the truth)

75   And Iblis replied, "My Lord,
      "Reward me still!"   (Indeed)
      "I will reward you," the reply.   (Indeed)
      "I will create a thing for your reward.
      "I will create something just for you,
80   "And call it 'wealth.'"
      "But the name of wealth should not be 'Wealth.'
      "Call it the Voice of Transgression."   (Indeed)
      The Voice of Transgression: (Indeed)
      Should man obtain it,   (Indeed)
85   All his kin will he mistake.   (Indeed)
      And should man want of it,
      'Tis he mistaken by his kin.
      Its name is thus, the Voice of Transgression.   (That's the truth)
      These six lines it addresses to its keeper: (Indeed)
90   "O My Keeper!   (Indeed)
      "Should I not be finished before you,
      "You will be finished before me, my Keeper.
      "If with this world I do not meld you,   (Indeed)
      "From this world I will divorce you.   (Indeed)
95   "And if I get you not to Heaven,   (Indeed)
      "Then I'll send you down to Hell."   (Indeed)
      May God preserve us from these people!   (Amen, my Lord)
      Almighty God then spoke,   (Indeed)
      "Adam! what may I offer you in life?"   (True)
100   "O Lord," the reply,   (Indeed)
      "Give me beauty, O God."   (Indeed)
      "Adam, you are not the first to ask.   (Indeed)
      "It's to the jinns[8] that I've given beauty, Adam."   (Indeed)

      Almighty God then asked, "Now what may I offer to you?"   (Indeed)
105   "O Lord," the reply,   (Mmm)
      "Give me morality, O God."   (Indeed)
      "Adam, you are not the first to ask.   (Indeed)
      "It's to the angels I've given morality, Adam."   (Indeed)

      Then Adam, our forefather, said, "O God,   (Indeed)
110   "Whatever man may offer man, such will have an end.   (Indeed)
      "Whatever God may offer man, no gift need follow that.
      "Whatever you will give to me,
      "That is what I wish."   ('Tis the truth)

8. Spirits invisible to humans. In Manden folklore, jinns are thought to live in fetishes and are consulted for advice.

"Adam," the reply,   (Indeed)
115 "I will grant you dignity.
"And how will you come to know
"That I did grant you dignity?
"Not as angel will Muhammad the Prophet be,   (Indeed)
"Nor will I create him as a jinn.
120 "I will make him of Adam's seed."   (Indeed)
Filardi Samawaati.[9]
Paradise and Earth were made according to His Love.   (Indeed)
Where we have passed the day in Grace,
There may we also pass the night, Amen.   (Amen, O my Lord)

125 Ah! Bèmba!   (Indeed)
Almighty God, after all of this, my father, took Adam   (Indeed)

And brought him forth from Paradise.   (Indeed)
He set him down in a land,   (Indeed)
The name of which was India.   (Indeed)
130 Ask the ones who know of this!
Adam was placed in the land of India.   (Mmm)
The land from whence the sun arises.
The land from whence the moon arises.   (Indeed)
'Twas God who created the sun,   (Indeed)
135 With its three hundred paths and thirty paths
And three paths,   (Indeed)
And created the moon,   (Indeed)
Three hundred paths and thirty paths and three paths.   (Indeed)
When the sun leaves its path   (Indeed)
140 To sit in the path of the moon,   (Indeed)
When its light falls behind the moon,   (Indeed)
The people cry out saying,
"The cat has seized the moon!"
The cat has not caught the moon.   (Indeed)
145 The light of the sun is but behind it.   (Indeed)
Our grandparent Eve and our ancestor Adam,   (Indeed)
They sought each other out,   (Indeed)
For forty days,   (Indeed)
They were seeking for each other.   (Indeed)
150 The mount whereon they met,
Its name was Arafan.[1]   (True)
Ask the ones who know of this!   (True. That's true, Fa-Digi.)

Our grandparent Eve and our ancestor Adam,   (Indeed)
Conceived some forty times,   (Mmm)
155 And begat eighty children!
Ben Adam,   (Indeed)
His first grandchild was Noah,   (Indeed)
And he had three sons.

---

9. On earth, in heaven (Arabic).   1. A mountain in Mecca, goal of Muslim pilgrimages.

	Ah! Bèmba!	(Indeed)
160	Noah begat three sons:	(Indeed)
	Ham, Shem, and Japheth.	(Indeed)
	Japheth went forth and crossed the sea.	(Indeed)
	His descendants became the Masusu and the Masasa.[2]	(Indeed)
	Ham, black people descended from him, my father.	(Indeed)
165	Shem, the twelve white clans	(Indeed)
	Descended from him.	(Indeed)

	I sing of Biribiriba!	(Indeed)
	Kirikisa, Spear-of-Access, Spear-of-Service!	(Indeed)

	The Messenger of God, Muhammad, was born,	(Indeed)
170	On the twelfth day of the month of Dònba.	(Indeed)
	On the thirteenth day,	
	Tuesday, Bilal was born in Samuda.[3]	(Indeed)
	Ask the ones who know of this!	(Mmm)
	That Bilal,	(Indeed)
175	His child was Mamadu Kanu.	
	That Mamadu Kanu,	(Mmm)
	He had three sons:	(Indeed)
	Kanu Simbon,	(Indeed)
	Kanu Nyògòn Simbon,	
180	Lawali Simbon.	(Indeed)
	Ah! Bèmba!	(Indeed)
	The races of man were ninety in number.	(Indeed)
	There were twelve clans of Marakas	(Indeed)
	Which came from Wagadugu.[4]	(Indeed)
185	The Sises came from Wagadugu.	(Mmm)
	The Janes came from Wagadugu.	(Mmm)
	The Tures came from Wagadugu.	(Indeed)
	The Beretes came from Wagadugu.	(Indeed)
	The Sakòs came from Wagadugu.	
190	The Fulani came from Wagadugu.	(Indeed)
	The Jawaras came from Wagadugu.	(Indeed)
	The Nyarès came from Wagadugu.	(Indeed)
	The Tunkaras came from Wagadugu.	(Mmm)

	The peoples of Wagadugu thus scattered.	(Indeed)
195	O Bèmba!	(Indeed)

* * *

[SON-JARA'S BIRTH AND CHILDHOOD]

[*Families have multiplied and spread across the earth. Gradually thirty-three clans settle the Manden region in West Africa. Two heroes of the Tarawere clan, the brothers Dan Mansa Wulandin and Dan Mansa Wulanba, make a journey and slay a great*

2. Probably Asians, in keeping with biblical and Qur'anic traditions that credit Noah's three sons as the ancestors of the three races of humanity.
3. Or Thamuda, an Arabian city. Bilal was Muhammad's steward.
4. An early West African empire, at its height in the 9th and 10th centuries.

buffalo, then are rewarded with a bride, Sugulun Kòndè. It is prophesied that her son will rule the Manden. The brothers take the reluctant Sugulun Kòndè and head home.]

	And thus they rose and journeyed forth	(Mmm)
	From the time the sun rose	(Indeed)
	Until the sun fell.	(Indeed)
950	As they reached a certain village,	(Indeed)
	Dan Mansa Wulandin said, "My elder,	(Indeed)
	"Should the elder and the younger venture forth,	
	"To seek their fortune together,	(Indeed)
	"Should it be wealth they find,	(Indeed)
955	"They should use it to marry a wife,	
	"Giving her to the elder.	(Indeed)
	"Whatever may be found after that,	(Indeed)
	"Should be given to the younger.	(Indeed)
	"This woman then should stay with you.	
960	"Whatever may be found next time,	
	"Let that maiden be mine!"	(Mmm)
	They entered the town.	(Indeed)
	Dan Mansa Wulanba	(Indeed)
	With the maiden entered a hut.	(True)
965	The night had passed its prime, lelelele!	(Mmm)
	Dan Mansa Wulandin lay down outside.	(Indeed)
	Dan Mansa Wulanba rose up,	(True)
	To seek pleasure and duty with his wife.	(Indeed)
	He laid his hand on the Kòndè maid.	(Indeed)
970	Now, all women were taller than Sugulun Kòndè.	
	All of them larger than Sugulun Kòndè.	
	But she stretched out: bilililili,	
	Putting her feet against the back wall,	(Mmm)
	And laying her head at the door,	
975	And projected two spikes from her breasts.	(Indeed)
	"O Tarawere! Lie back down!	(Indeed)
	"My husband's in the Manden.	
	"And your wife will be there, too!"	(True)
	Dan Mansa Wulanba came running outside:	
980	"Ha! Hey!"	
	Dan Mansa Wulandin said:	
	"My brother, what has happened?"	
	"Ah, little brother!	
	"All women are taller than Sugulun Kòndè;	
985	"All of them larger than Sugulun Kòndè;	
	"Yet when I put my hand on her,	(Indeed)
	"Saying I sought pleasure and duty with my wife,	
	"She stretched herself: bilililili,	
	"Putting her feet against the back wall,	(Mmm)
990	"And laying her head at the door,	
	"And projecting two spikes from her breasts,	

"And told me to lie back down,   (Mmm)
"Saying that her husband's in the Manden,
"And that my wife would be there, too."
995   They both lay back down   (Indeed)
Until the break of day.   (Mmm)
At that they rose up.   (Indeed)
Now, Fata Magan, the Handsome was about to leave that town.
He was leaving to trade in a far market.   (Mmm)
1000 But a jinn came and laid a hand on him: (Mmm)
"Stay right here!   (Indeed)
"Two youths have come amongst us,   (Mmm)
"Two youths with an ugly young maid.   (Mmm)
"Should you come by that ugly maid,   (Mmm)
1005 "She will bear you a son.   (Indeed)
"The Manden will belong to him."   (Indeed)

O! Bèmba!   (Indeed)
   I sing of the Sorcerer's future;   (Mmm, that's true)
   Of the life ahead of Son-Jara!
1010 There were two ways to greet in the Manden of Old.   (Mmm)
Brave young men said, "Ilu tuntun!"   (That's true)
To which the reply, "Tuntun bèrè!"[5]
The women said, "Ilu kònkòn!"
To which the reply, "Kònkòn lògòsò!"   (Indeed)
1015 The Taraweres came forward: (True)
"I tuntun!"
He answered them, "Tuntun bèrè!   (Mmm)
"Where do you come from?
"Where are you going?"
1020 "We have come from the land of Du.
"We go to Bintanya Kamalen."
"Whose people are you?"   (Mmm)
"We are Taraweres."   (Mmm)
"O Taraweres,
1025 "Were this young prince to find the right wife,   (Mmm)
"She would be the reward of a Tarawere struggle."   (True)

"My flesh-and-blood sister is here,   (Indeed)
"Nakana Tiliba.   (Indeed)
"I will give her to you.
1030 "You must give me your ugly maid.   (Mmm)
"My forefather Bilal,   (Indeed)
"When he departed from the Messenger of God,   (True)
"He designed a certain token,[6]   (Mmm)
"Saying that his ninth descendant,   (Indeed)
1035 "Having taken his first wife,   (True)
"When he takes his second wife,   (Indeed)

---

5. Old greetings, meaning unknown today.   6. A talisman or amulet with magic powers.

"Must add that token to that marriage.   (Mmm)
"I am adding that token
"Together with Nakana Tiliba,   (Mmm)
1040 "And giving them to you,
"You must give me your ugly little maid."
That token was added to Nakana Tiliba,
Exchanging her for Sugulun Kòndè.   (Indeed)
It is said that Fata Magan, the Handsome
1045 Took the Kòndè maiden to bed.   (Mmm)
His Berete wife became pregnant.   (Indeed)
His Kòndè wife became pregnant.   (Indeed)

One day as dawn was breaking,   (Indeed)
The Berete woman gave birth to a son.   (Indeed)
1050 She cried out, "Ha! Old Women!   (Indeed)
"That which causes co-wife conflict
"Is nothing but the co-wife's child.   (True)
"Go forth and tell my husband   (Indeed)
"His first wife has borne him a son."   (Indeed)

1055 The old women came up running.   (Indeed)
"Alu kònkòn!"   (Mmm)
They replied to them, "Kònkòn dògòsò!
"Come let us eat."   (Mmm)
They fixed their eyes on one another:
1060 "Ah! Man must swallow his saliva!"   (True)
They sat down around the food.   (Indeed)
The Kòndè woman then bore a son.   (Indeed)
They sent the Kuyatè matriarch, Tumu Maniya: (Indeed)
"Tumu Maniya, go tell it,   (True)
1065 "Tell Fata Magan, the Handsome,
"Say, 'the Tarawere trip to Du was good.'   (True)
"Say, 'the ugly maid they brought with them,'
"Say, 'that woman has just borne a son.'"   (True)

The Kuyatè matriarch came forward: (True)
1070 "Alu kònkòn!"   (Mmm)
They replied to her, "Kònkòn dògòsò!   (Indeed)
"Come and let us eat."[7]

[*The female bard Tumu Maniya goes to find the king and, like the old women who
preceded her, is also invited to eat, but she rejects the food until her message is delivered. The announcing of the birth of Son-Jara first, though he was actually born second, causes the father to designate him as first-born. The old women then burst out
their message of the Berete woman's child, but alas, they are too late. The reversal of
announcements is viewed as theft of birthright, and the Berete woman is understand-
ably furious at the old women, who flop their hands about nervously.*]

7. The bard took a break at this point; when he resumed, he continued the story at a later point than he'd left it. The following paragraph summarizes what would have taken place in the story.

Some just flopped their hands about:
"I will not hear of this from anyone!
1075 "I spent a sleepless night.
"The lids of my eyes are dried out, bèrè-bèrè-bèrè.   (That's true)
"But I will not hear of this from anyone!"
Some just clasped their hands together.
What travail it had become!
1080 Ha! The old woman had forgotten her message
And abandoned it for a meal.
Those-Caught-by-their-Craws!
That was the first day of battle in the Manden.
Pandemonium broke loose! bòkòlen!

1085 I sing of Biribiriba.
Ah! He who would cultivate,
Let him cultivate.   (Mmm)
He who would deal in commerce,
Let him deal in commerce!   (That's true)

1090 Ah! Bèmba!   (Mmm)
War may give to some, my father,
Although it be not theirs.
War may take from some,
Although it be their own.
1095 If there be no war,
Men of power would not be known.   (Indeed)

Both women were confined in one hut.
Pandemonium broke loose! bòkòlen!   (Indeed)
Saman Berete,
1100 The daughter of Tall Magan Berete-of-the-Ruins,
Saman Berete,   (Indeed)
Still bloodstained, she came out.   (Indeed)
"What happened then?
"O Messengers, what happened?   (Indeed)
1105 "O Messengers, what became of the message?"   (Indeed)

The Kuyatè matriarch spoke out:
"Nothing happened at all.   (Indeed)
"I was the first to pronounce myself.   (Indeed)
"Your husband said the first name heard,
1110 "Said, he would be the elder,   (Indeed)
"And thus yours became the younger."   (Indeed)
She cried out, "Old women,   (Indeed)
"Now you have really reached the limit!   (True)
"I was the first to marry my husband,
1115 "And the first to bear him a son.   (Indeed)
"Now you have made him the younger.   (Indeed)
"You have really reached your limit!"
She spoke then to her younger co-wife,   (Indeed)

	"Oh Lucky Karunga,	(Indeed)
1120	"For you marriage has turned sweet.	(Indeed)
	"A first son birth is the work of old,	(Indeed)
	"And yours has become the elder."	(That's the truth)

	The infants were bathed.	(Indeed)
	Both were laid beneath a cloth.	(Indeed)
1125	The grandmother had gone to fetch firewood.	(Indeed)
	The old mother had gone to fe . . . , to fetch firewood.	(Indeed)
	She then quit the firewood-fetching place,	
	And came and left her load of wood.	(Indeed)
	She came into the hut.	(Indeed)
1130	She cast her eye on the Berete woman,	(Indeed)
	And cast her eye on the Kòndè woman,	(Indeed)
	And looked the Berete woman over,	
	And looked the Kòndè woman over.	(Indeed)

	She lifted the edge of the cloth.	
1135	And examined the child of the Berete woman,	
	And lifted again the edge of the cloth,	
	And examined the child of the Kòndè woman.	(Indeed)
	From the very top of Son-Jara's head,	(Indeed)
	To the very tip of his toes, all hair!	(Indeed)

1140	The old mother went outside.	(Indeed)
	She laughed out: "Ha! Birth-givers! Hurrah!	
	"The little mother has borne a lion thief."	(That's true)
	Thus gave the old mother Son-Jara his name.[8]	(Indeed)
	"Givers of birth, Hurrah!	
1145	"The little mother has borne a lion thief.	(That's true)
	"Hurrah! The mother has given birth to a lion thief."	
	Biribiriba!	(Indeed)
	And thus they say of him,	
	Son-Jara, Nare Magan Kònatè.	(Indeed)
1150	Simbon, Lion-Born-of-the-Cat.	(Indeed)
	The Berete woman,	
	She summoned to her a holy-man,	
	Charging him to pray to God,	(Indeed)
	So Son-Jara would not walk.	(Indeed)
1155	And summoned to her an Omen Master,	(Indeed)
	For him to read the signs in sand,	(Indeed)
	So Son-Jara would not walk.	(Indeed)

	For nine years, Son-Jara crawled upon the ground.	(Indeed)
	Magan Kònatè could not rise.	(Indeed)
1160	The benefactor of the Kòndè woman's child,	
	It was a jinn Magan Son-Jara had.	(Indeed)

8. "Jara" means "lion."

His name was Tanimunari.
Tanimunari,   (Indeed)
He took the lame Son-Jara   (Indeed)
1165   And made the hājj[9]   (Indeed)
To the gates of the Kaabah.   (Indeed)
Have you never heard this warrant of his hājj?   (Indeed)
"Ah! God!   (Indeed)
"I am the man for the morrow.   (Indeed)
1170   "I am the man for the day to follow.   (Indeed)
"I will rule over the bards,   (Indeed)
"And the three and thirty warrior clans.
"I will rule over all these people.   (Indeed)
"The Manden shall be mine!"   (Indeed)
1175   That is how he made the hājj.
He took him up still lame,
And brought him back to Bintanya Kamalen.   (Indeed)
In the month before Dònba,   (Indeed)
On the twenty-fifth day,
1180   The Berete woman's Omen Master emerged from retreat: (Indeed)
"Damn! My fingers are worn out!   (Indeed)
"My buttocks are worn out!   (Indeed)
"A tragic thing will come to pass in the Manden.   (Indeed)
"There is no remedy to stop it.
1185   "There is no sacrifice to halt it.
"Its cause cannot be ascertained,   (Indeed)
"Until two rams be sacrificed.   (Indeed)

"The one for Son-Jara, a black-headed ram.   (True)
"Dankaran Tuma,[1] an all white ram.   (Indeed)
1190   "Have them do battle this very day."   (Indeed)
By the time of the midday meal,
Son-Jara's ram had won.   (Indeed)
They slaughtered both the rams,   (Indeed)
And cast them down a well,
1195   So the deed would not be known.   (Indeed)
But known it did become.   (Indeed)
Knowing never fails its time,
Except its day not come.   (That's true, eh, Fa-Digi, that's true)

* * *

1275   O Sorcerer-Seizing-Sorcerer!
A man of power is hard to find.   (Mmm)
All people with their empty words,
They all seek to be men of power.   (That's true)
Ministers, deputies and presidents,   (Indeed)
1280   All of them seek after power,
But there is no easy way to power.   (That's true)

---

9. The Muslim pilgrimage to Mecca, whose central shrine   1. Son-Jara's older brother, the Berete woman's son.
is called the Kaabah.

Here in our Mali,
We have found our freedom.   (Indeed)
Though a person find no gold,
1285   Though he find no silver,   (Indeed)
Should he find his freedom,
Then noble will he be.   (That's the truth)
A man of power is hard to find.   (Mmm)
Ah! Bèmba!

1290   On the tenth day of Dòmba,   (Indeed)
The Wizard's mother cooked some couscous,   (Indeed)
Sacrificial couscous for Son-Jara.
Whatever woman's door she went to,   (Indeed)
The Wizard's mother would cry: (Indeed)
1295   "Give me some sauce of baobab leaf."   (Indeed)
The woman would retort,
"I have some sauce of baobab leaf,
"But it is not to give to you.
"Go tell that cripple child of yours
1300   "That he should harvest some for you.   (Mmm)
"'Twas my son harvested these for me."   (True)

And bitterly did she weep: bilika bilika.
She went to another woman's door;   (Mmm)
That one too did say: (Mmm)
1305   "I have some sauce of baobab leaf,
"But it is not to give to you.
"Go tell that cripple child of yours
"That he should harvest some for you.
"'Twas my son harvested these for me."   (True)

1310   With bitter tears, the Kòndè woman came back, bilika bilika.
"King of Nyani, King of Nyani,[2]
"Will you never rise?   (Mmm)
"King of Nyani, King of Nyani,
"Will you never rise?   (Mmm)
1315   "King of Nyani with helm of mail,
"He says he fears no man.
"Will you never rise?
"Rise up, O King of Nyani!   (That's true)

                              * * *

1370   On that, his mother left,
And went to the east of Bintanya,   (Indeed)
To seek a custard apple tree.[3]   (Indeed)

Ah! Bèmba!   (Indeed)
And found some custard apple trees,   (Indeed)
1375   And cut one down,   (Indeed)

2. A town on the Mali border, perhaps used here because   3. A tree believed to have magical and healing powers.
it means "Misery."

And trimmed it level to her breast,   (Indeed)
And stood as if in prayer: (Indeed)
  "O God!
  "For Son-Jara I have made this staff.   (Indeed)
1380 "If he be the man for the morrow,   (Indeed)
  "If he be the man for the day to follow,   (Indeed)
  "If he is to rule the bards,   (Indeed)
  "If he is to rule the smiths,   (Indeed)
  "The three and thirty warrior clans,   (Indeed)
1385 "If he is to rule all those,   (Indeed)
  "When this staff I give to Nare Magan Kònatè,   (Indeed)
  "Let Magan Kònatè arise.   (True)
  "If he be not the man for the morrow,   (Indeed)
  "If he be not the man for the day to follow,   (Indeed)
1390 "If he is not to rule the bards,   (Indeed)
  "If he is not to rule the smiths,   (Indeed)
  "When this staff I give to the King of Nyani,
  "Let Son-Jara not arise,
  "O God, from the day of my creation,   (Indeed)
1395 "If I have known another man,
  "Save Fata Magan, the Handsome alone,
  "When this staff I give to the King of Nyani,
  "Let Son-Jara arise.   (Indeed)
  "From the day of my creation,   (True)
1400 "If I have known a second man,
  "And not just Fata Magan, the Handsome,   (Indeed)
  "Let Magan Kònatè not arise!"   (True)
She cut down that staff,
Going to give it to Nare Magan Kònatè,
1405 To the Kòndè woman's child, the Answerer-of-Needs!   (True)
The Wizard took the staff,   (Mmm)
And put his right hand o'er his left,   (Indeed)
And upwards drew himself,   (Indeed)
And upwards drew himself.
1410 Magan Kònatè rose up!   (Mmm)
Running, his mother came forward,
And clasped his legs
And squeezed them,   (Indeed)
And squeezed them: (True)
1415   *"This home of ours,*
  "The home of happiness.   (Indeed)
  "Happiness did not pass us by.
  "Magan Kònatè has risen!"   (Indeed)
  "Oh! Today!   (Indeed)
1420   *"Today is sweet!*   (Indeed)
  "God the King ne'er made today's equal!   (Indeed)
  "Magan Kònatè has risen!"   (Indeed)
  "There is no way of standing without worth.

> *"Behold his way of standing: danka!*
1425   *"O Kapok Tree and Flame Tree!"*   (Fa-Digi, that's true)

* * *

As Biribiriba walked forth one day,   (That's true)
A jinn came upon him,
1565   And laid his hand on Son-Jara's shoulder:
"O Son-Jara!   (Mmm)
"In the Manden, there's a plot against you.   (Mmm)
"That spotted dog you see before you,   (Indeed)
"Is an offering made against you,   (Indeed)
1570   "So that you not rule the bards,   (Indeed)
"So that you not rule the smiths,
"So, the three and thirty warrior clans,
"That you rule over none of them.   (Mmm)
"When you go forth today,   (Mmm)
1575   "Make an offering of a safo-dog,   (Indeed)
"Should God will it,
"The Manden will be yours!"   (Indeed)

Ah! Bèmba!
On that, Biribiriba went forth, my father,
1580   And made an offering of a safo-dog,
And hung a weight around its neck,
And fastened an iron chain about it.   (Indeed)
Even tomorrow morning,
The Europeans will imitate him.
1585   Whenever the Europeans leave a dog,   (Mmm)
Its neck weight,
They fasten that dog with an iron chain, Manden!   (Indeed)

O! Bèmba!
He hung a weight around the dog's neck,
1590   And fastened it with a chain.   (Mmm)
That done, whatever home he passed before,   (Indeed)
The people stood gaping at him:
"Causer-of-Loss!   (Indeed)
"A cow with its neckweight,
1595   "But a dog with a neckweight?"   (Indeed)
To which the Wizard did retort:
"Leave me be!   (True)
"Cast your eyes on the dog of the prince.
"There's not a tooth in that dog's mouth!
1600   "But there are teeth in my dog's mouth,
"My commoner's dog. Leave me be!   (Indeed)
"My dog's name is Tomorrow's Affair."[4]

* * *

---

4. The name reflects Son-Jara's patience in biding his time until his rise to power.

[Son-Jara in Exile][5]

1725 He went to seek refuge
With the patriarch of the Magasubaas in Sigiri.   (That's true)
The Jane patriarch, Bukari Jane, the Pure, made his ḥājj.   (Indeed)
He entrusted his pregnant wife
To the patriarch of the Magasubaa, Tulunbèn, King of Kòlè.

1730 And went forth upon his ḥājj.   (Indeed)
He went forth to make the ḥājj.   (Mmm)
Now, Magan Son-Jara had this fetish,   (Mmm)
A fetish accepting no offering,
Unless, if a woman grow great with child,   (Indeed)

1735 The unborn babe be that offering.   (Eh, Fa-Digi)
And Bukari Jane, the Pure, was making his ḥājj.   (That's true)
He had entrusted his pregnant wife,   (That's true)
To the patriarch of the Sigiri Magasubaa, Tulunbèn, King of Kòlè.
Bukari Jane, the Pure,   (Indeed)

1740 They slew his wife,   (Mmm)
And offered the babe to the fetish,
And then gave it to Son-Jara,
So he could go seek refuge
With the nine Queens-of-Darkness,

1745 Saying, the Manden would thus be his.   (That's true)

Three days after this,
The holy-man returned from his ḥājj.
When night had reached its midpoint,   (Indeed)
Having said his pair of litanies:

1750 "Ah! God!
"What have I done to Thee?   (Indeed)
"Alas, for pagans to slay my wife,
"And to make an offering of her babe,
"And to give it to some person,

1755 "In his search for power,
"What have I done to Thee?"
And God carried on from there,   (Indeed)
And cast a chain round the neck   (Indeed)
Of that Tulunbèn, King of Kòlè,   (Indeed)

1760 And cast a chain round his right arm,   (Indeed)
And cast one round his left,   (Indeed)
And raised Tulunbèn, King of Kòlè,   (Indeed)
Up between heaven and earth.   (Mmm)
The lake in which he was sent splashing down,

1765 Fikiri!   (Mmm)
This is what is meant by Lowering-by-Chain.

---

5. Son-Jara's stepmother the Berete woman forces his father to send him into exile, still pursued by his brother's anger. He seeks refuge with a neighboring king, Tulunbèn.

That is what happened to the Sigiri Magasubaa patriarch.   (Mmm)
Biribiriba went on to seek refuge
With the nine Queens-of-Darkness.
1770   "What brought you here?" they asked of him.   (Mmm)
"Have you not heard that none come here?"   (Indeed)
"What brought you here?"   (Indeed)
The Sorcerer spoke out,
"Ah! Those who are feared by all,
1775   "If you join them, you are spared.
"It is that which made me come here."
He sat down.   (Indeed)
His flesh-and-blood-elder, King Dankaran Tuman,   (Indeed)
He took his first-born daughter,   (Indeed)
1780   Caress-of-Hot-Fire,   (Indeed)
And gave her to the Kuyatè patriarch, Dòka the Cat,   (Indeed)
Saying, "Give her to Susu Mountain Sumamuru,"[6]   (Indeed)
Saying, "Should he not slay the King of Nyani,"
Saying, "He's gone to seek refuge with the nine Queens-of-Darkness,"
1785   Saying, "The folk have lost their faith in him."   (True)

* * *

[SON-JARA COMES TO POWER]

[While Son-Jara is in exile, the evil king Sumamuru conquers the Manden and makes its heroes captive. Sought out in a distant village, Son-Jara agrees to return and liberate his country. Before recounting these climactic events, the bard Fa-Digi pauses to recall his own moment of fame as he is asked to record this epic.]

God is the King!
2395   A man of power . . .   (That's the truth)
Mansa Magan[7] came for me,   (Indeed)
A letter was given to me,
Saying I should speak on Radio Mali,
To sing the praise of Fa-Koli.   (Indeed, that happened!
That really happened!)

2400   I was there at my farming village,   (Indeed)
In brotherhood and affection.   (Indeed)
Mansa Magan came to get me, my father,
Saying I should sing for the whiteman.[8]   (Indeed)
God is the King!   (That's the truth)

2405   O Garan!   (Indeed)
O Great-Host-Slaying-Stranger and the Twisted Well.   (Indeed)
And the Devourers-of-the-Knowing!   (Indeed)
The explanations were made to the Wizard,   (Indeed)
To Nare Magan Kònatè.   (Indeed)

6. Sorcerer king of the country of Susu, an enemy of Islam and archenemy of Son-Jara.
7. Massa Makan Diabaté, a Mali folklorist.

8. Charles Bird, a professor of linguistics at Indiana University, who recorded this text.

2410	Son-Jara had a certain fetish,	(Indeed)
	Accepting no sacrifice save shea butter.[9]	(Indeed)
	There were no shea trees there in Mèma.	(Indeed)
	O Mansa Magan!	(Indeed)
	Wherever you sacrifice to the shea tree,	(Indeed)
2415	That town must be in Mandenland.	(Indeed)
	All of them are in the Manden.	(Indeed)
	No shea trees were there in Mèma,	(Indeed)
	Save one old dry Shea tree in Mèma.	(Indeed)
	Son-Jara's mother came forward:	(Indeed)
2420	"Ah! God!	(Indeed)
	"Let Son-Jara go to the Manden.	(Indeed)
	"He is the man for the morrow.	(Indeed)
	"He is the man for the day to follow.	(Indeed)
	"He is to rule o'er the bards,	(Indeed)
2425	"He is to rule o'er the smiths,	(Indeed)
	"And the three and thirty warrior clans.	(Indeed)
	"He will rule o'er all those people.	(Indeed)
	"Ah, God!	(Indeed)
	"Before the break of day,	(Indeed)
2430	"That dried up shea tree here,	(Indeed)
	"Let it bear leaf and fruit.	(Indeed)
	"Let the fruit fall down to earth,	(Indeed)
	"So that Son-Jara may gather the fruit,	
	"From it to make shea butter,	(Indeed)
2435	"To offer his fetish.	(Indeed, yes, Fa-Digi)
	"Ah, God!	(Indeed)
	"Let Son-Jara go to the Manden.	(Indeed)
	"He is the man for the morrow.	
	"He is the man for the day to follow.	(Indeed)
2440	"He will rule the bards and smiths.	(Indeed)
	"The Manden belongs to the Wizard.	(Indeed)
	"Before the break of day,	(Indeed)
	"Let me change my dwelling,	(Indeed)
	"Old am I and cannot travel.	(Indeed)
2445	"Let Nare Magan Kònatè go home."	(Indeed)
	When the day was dawning,	(Indeed)
	The dried up shea tree did bear leaf.	(Indeed)
	Its fruit did fall to earth.	(Indeed)
	Son-Jara looked in on the Kòndè woman,	(Indeed)
2450	But the Kòndè woman had abandoned the world.	(Indeed)
	He washed his mother's body,	(Indeed)
	And then he dug her grave,	(Indeed)
	And wrapped her in a shroud,	(Indeed)

9. Mali kings would often inaugurate their reign with rituals involving fruit from the shea tree, whose name resembles the word *se*, "power."

	And laid his mother in the earth,	(Indeed)
2455	And then chopped down a kapok tree,	(Indeed)
	And wrapped it in a shroud,	(Indeed)
	And laid it in the house,	(Indeed)
	And laid a blanket over it,	(Indeed)
	And sent a messenger to Prince Birama,	
2460	Asking of him a grant of land,	(Indeed)
	In order to bury his mother in Mèma,	
	So that he could return to the Manden.	(Indeed)
	This answer they did give to him	
	That no land could he have,	
2465	Unless he were to pay its price.	(Indeed)

	Prince Birama[1] decreed,	(Indeed)
	Saying he could have no land,	(Indeed)
	Unless he were to pay its price.	(Indeed)
	He took feathers of Guinea fowl and partridge,	(Indeed)
2470	And took some leaves of arrow-shaft plant,	(Indeed)
	And took some leaves of wild grass reed,	(Indeed)
	And took some red fanda-vines,	(Indeed)
	And took one measure of shot,	(Indeed)
	And took a haftless knife,	(Indeed)
2475	And added a cornerstone fetish to that,	(Indeed)
	And put it all in a leather pouch,	(Indeed)
	Saying go give it to Prince Birama,	(Indeed)
	Saying it was the price of his land.	(Indeed, ha, Fa-Digi)

	That person gave it to Prince Birama.	(Indeed)
2480	Prince Birama summoned his three sages,	(Indeed)
	All-Knowing-Sage,	(Indeed)
	All-Seeing-Sage,	(Indeed)
	All-Saying-Sage.	(Indeed)
	The three sages counseled Prince Birama.	(Indeed)
2485	He said, "O Sages!	(Indeed)
	"The forest by the river is never empty.	(Indeed)
	"You also should take this.	(Indeed)
	"That which came first,	(Indeed)
	"I will not take it.	(Indeed)
2490	"Tis yours."	(Indeed)
	O Garan!	(Indeed)
	All-Seeing-Sage,	
	All-Saying-Sage,	
	All-Knowing-Sage,	(Indeed)
2495	They untied the mouth of the pouch,	
	And shook its contents out.	(Indeed)
	The All-Seeing-Sage exclaimed,	(Indeed)
	"Anyone can see that!	(Indeed)

1. The local prince controlling the area.

	"I am going home!"	(Indeed)
2500	The All-Knowing-Sage exclaimed,	(Indeed)
	"Everybody knows that!	(Indeed)
	"I am going home."	(Indeed)
	All-Saying-Sage exclaimed,	(Indeed)
	"Everyone knows that?	(Indeed)
2505	"That is a lie!	(Indeed)
	"Everyone sees that?	(Indeed)
	"That is a lie!	(Indeed)
	"There may be something one may see,	
	"Be it ne'er explained to him,	
2510	"He will never know it.	(Indeed)
	"Prince Birama,	(Indeed)
	"Did you not see feathers of Guinea fowl and partridge?	
	"They are the things of ruins.	(Indeed)
	"Did you not see the leaf of arrow-shaft plant?	
2515	"That is a thing of ruins.	(Indeed)
	"Was not your eye on the wild grass reed?	(Indeed)
	"That is a thing of ruins.	(Indeed)
	"Did you not see those broken shards?	(Indeed)
	"They are the things of ruins.	(Indeed)
2520	"Did you not see that measure of shot?	(Indeed)
	"The annihilator of Mèma!	(Indeed)
	"Did you not see that haftless knife?	(Indeed)
	"The warrior-head-severing blade!	(Indeed)
	"Was not your eye on the red fanda-vine?	(Indeed)
2525	"The warrior-head-severing blood!	
	"If you do not give the land to him,	(Indeed)
	"That cornerstone fetish your eye beheld,	
	"It is the warrior's thunder shot!	(Indeed)
	"If you do not give the land to him,	
2530	"To Nare Magan Kònatè,	
	"The Wizard will reduce the town to ruin.	(Indeed)
	"Son-Jara is to return to the Manden!"	(That's the truth)
	They gave the land to the Sorcerer,	(Indeed)
	He buried his mother in Mèma's earth.	
2535	He rose up.	
	That which sitting will not solve,	
	Travel will resolve.	(Indeed)

[Son-Jara's War Against Sumamuru]

	The Kuyatè matriarch took the iron rasp,	
	And sang a hunter's song behind him:	(Indeed)
2540	*"Took up the bow,*	(Indeed)
	"Simbon, Master-of-the-Bush	
	"Took up the bow!	
	"Took up the bow!	(Indeed)
	"Simbon, Master-of-the-Beasts	(Indeed)

2545	*"Took up the bow!*	(Indeed)
	"Took up the bow!	(Indeed)
	"Ruler of the bards and smiths,	
	"Took up the bow!	
	"The Kòndè woman's child,	
2550	*"Answerer-of-Needs*	(Indeed)
	"Took up the bow!	(Indeed)
	"Sugulun's Magan took up the bow!	(Indeed)
	"You seized him, O Lion!	(Indeed)
	"The sorcerer slew him.	
2555	*"Simbon, 'tis the sound of your chords!"*	(Indeed)

	Biribiriba rose up,	
	And went to find the Dabò patriarch.[2]	
	He was sitting at the crossroads boiling a potion.	(Indeed)
	It was the voice of the Dabò patriarch:	(Indeed)
2560	"Sorcerer, let us play awhile the warrior game!"	(Indeed)
	He made Son-Jara fall to his right.	(Indeed)
	Said the Tarawere patriarch, Tura-Magan-and-Kanke-jan:	
	"Let us abandon Son-Jara.	(Indeed)
	"This person that Dabò has thrown,	(Indeed)
2565	"Given that, if we not abandon him,	(Indeed)
	"Were we to go to the Manden,	
	"Sumamuru would destroy our folk!"	(Indeed)
	Son-Jara was enraged at that,	(Indeed)
	And jamming his foot on Dabò's instep,	
2570	He stretched him out by the neck,	(Indeed)
	Ripping off his head.	(Indeed)
	The clamor, "A d'a bò! He ripped it off!	(Indeed)
	Thus, that became the Dabò surname.	(Indeed, that's the truth)
	He fled because of suffering!	(Indeed)
2575	O Biribiriba!	(Indeed)
	When he and his mother were going to Mèma,	(Indeed)
	She took her silver bracelet off,	
	And gave it to the Boatman patriarch,	
	To Sasagalò, the Tall.	(Indeed)
2580	The ancestor of the boatman was Sasagalò, the Tall.	
	She took her silver bracelet off:	(Indeed)
	"When one digs a distant-day well,	
	"Should a distant-day thirst descend, then drink!"	(Indeed)
	A partridge was sent to deliver the message	(Indeed)
2585	To Susu Mountain Sumamuru:	(Indeed)
	"Manda and Sama Kantè!	(Indeed)
	"Susu Bala Kantè!	
	"Kukuba and Bantanba!	
	"Nyani-nyani and Kamasiga!	(Indeed)
2590	*"Brave child of the warrior!*	

2. Son-Jara seeks allies but instead finds opposition.

> *"And Deliverer-of-the-Benign!*
> *"Sumamuru came among us*
> *"With pants of human skin!*   (Indeed)
> *"Sumamuru came among us*
2595 *"With coat of human skin.*   (Indeed)
> *"Applaud him!*   (Indeed)
> *"Susu Mountain Sumamuru!*
> "The Sorcerer with his army has left Mèma.   (Indeed)
> "He has entered the Manden!"   (Indeed)

2600 Susu Mountain Sumamuru,   (Indeed)
He took four measures of gold,   (Indeed)
To the Boatman patriarch,
Sasagalò, the Tall, did give them,   (Indeed)
Saying, "That army coming from Mèma,   (Indeed)
2605 "That army must not cross!"   (Indeed)

For one entire month,   (Indeed)
Son-Jara and his army by the riverbank sat.   (Indeed)
He wandered up and down.   (Indeed)
One day Son-Jara rose up
2610 And followed up the river: (Indeed)
"Being good, a bane.   (Indeed)
"Not being good, a bane.   (Indeed)
"When my mother and I were going to Mèma,   (Indeed)
"She took her silver bracelet off,   (Indeed)
2615 "And gave it to a person here,   (Indeed)
"Saying when you dig a distant-day well,
"When a distant-day thirst descends, then drink.   (Indeed)
"Thus have I come with my army,   (Indeed)
"And we have not yet made a crossing."   (Indeed)
2620 The Boatman patriarch responded: (Indeed)
"Ah! Is it you who are Son-Jara?"   (Indeed)
The reply, "It is I who am Son-Jara."   (Indeed)
"You are Son-Jara?"   (Indeed)
"Indeed I am Son-Jara!"   (Indeed)
2625 "It is you who are Nare Magan Kònatè?   (Indeed)
"If God wills,
"With the break of day,
"Tomorrow will the army cross."   (Indeed)

At the break of day,   (Indeed)
2630 The Boatman patriarch, Sasagalò the Tall,   (Indeed)
He brought Son-Jara across.   (Indeed)
The Wizard advanced with his army.   (Indeed)
They fell upon Sumamuru at Dark Forest.   (Indeed)
But he drove them off.   (Indeed)
2635 Susu Mountain Sumamuru drove Son-Jara off.   (Indeed)
He went and founded a town called Anguish,   (Indeed)
Of which the bards did sing:

"We will not move to Anguish.   (Indeed)
"Should one go to Anguish,
2640   "Should not anguish he endure,   (Indeed)
"Then nothing would he reap.   (Indeed)
"We will not move to Anguish."   (Indeed)

That Anguish,   (Indeed)
The Maninka sing this of it, my father:
2645   "There is no joy in you."   (Indeed)
Our name for that town is Anguish (Nyani).   (Indeed)

The Wizard advanced with his army.   (Indeed)
They went to fall on Susu Mountain Sumamuru.   (Indeed)
He drove Son-Jara off again.   (Indeed)
2650   He went to found the town called Resolve.   (Indeed)
The bards thus sing of it:
        "We will not move to Resolve.
        "Should one move to Resolve,
        "Should not resolve he entertain,
2655   "Then nothing would he reap.   (Indeed)
        "We will not move to Resolve."   (Indeed)
The Wizard advanced again.   (Indeed)
He with his bards advanced.   (Indeed)
They went to fall on Susu Mountain Sumamuru.   (Indeed)
2660   Sumamuru drove him off with his bards.   (Indeed)
They went to found the town called Sharing.   (Indeed)
And they sang:
        "Let us move to the Wizard's town, my father.
        "To Sharing,   (Indeed)
2665   "The town where sharing is not done,
        "Founding that town is not easy."   (Indeed)
They went to found the town called Sharing.   (Indeed)

Son-Jara's flesh-and-blood-sister, Sugulun Kulunkan,   (Indeed)
She said, "O Magan Son-Jara,   (Indeed)
2670   "One person cannot fight this war.   (Indeed)
"Let me go seek Sumamuru.   (Indeed)
"Were I then to reach him,
"To you I will deliver him,   (Indeed)
"So that the folk of the Manden be yours,   (Indeed)
2675   "And all the Mandenland you shield."   (Indeed)
Sugulun Kulunkan arose,   (Indeed)
And went up to the gates of Sumamuru's fortress: (Indeed)
        "Manda and Sama Kantè!   (Indeed)
        "Kukuba and Bantamba
2680   "Nyani-nyani and Kamasiga!   (Indeed)
        "Brave child of the Warrior,
        "And Deliverer-of-the-Benign.   (Indeed)
        "Sumamuru came amongst us
        "With pants of human skin.   (Indeed)

2685   *"Sumamuru came amongst us*
     "With shirt of human skin.   (Indeed)
     "Sumamuru came amongst us
     "With helm of human skin.   (Indeed)
     "Come open the gates, Susu Mountain Sumamuru!   (Indeed)

2690   "Come make me your bed companion!"   (Indeed)
     Sumamuru came to the gates: (Indeed)
     "What manner of person are you?"   (Indeed)
     "It is I Sugulun Kulunkan!"   (Indeed)
     "Well, now, Sugulun Kulunkan,   (Indeed)
2695   "If you have come to trap me,   (Indeed)
     "To turn me over to some person,   (Indeed)
     "Know that none can ever vanquish me.   (Indeed)
     "I have found the Manden secret,   (Indeed)
     "And made the Manden sacrifice,   (Indeed)
2700   "And in five score millet stalks placed it,   (Indeed)
     "And buried them here in the earth.   (Indeed)
     "'Tis I who found the Manden secret,   (Indeed)
     "And made the Manden sacrifice,   (Indeed)
     "And in a red piebald bull did place it,   (Indeed)
2705   "And buried it here in the earth.   (Indeed)
     "Know that none can vanquish me.   (Indeed)
     "'Tis I who found the Manden secret   (Indeed)
     "And made a sacrifice to it,   (Indeed)
     "And in a pure white cock did place it.   (Indeed)
2710   "Were you to kill it,   (Indeed)
     "And uproot some barren groundnut plants,   (Indeed)
     "And strip them of their leaves,
     "And spread them round the fortress,   (Indeed)
     "And uproot more barren peanut plants,   (Indeed)
2715   "And fling them into the fortress,   (Indeed)
     "Only then can I be vanquished."   (Indeed)
     His mother sprang forward at that: (Indeed)
     "Heh! Susu Mountain Sumamuru!   (Indeed)
     "Never tell all to a woman,
2720   "To a one-night woman!   (Indeed)
     "The woman is not safe, Sumamuru."   (Indeed)
     Sumamuru sprang towards his mother,   (Indeed)
     And came and seized his mother,   (Indeed)
     And slashed off her breast with a knife, magasi!   (Indeed)
2725   She went and got the old menstrual cloth.   (Indeed)
     "Ah! Sumamuru!" she swore.   (Indeed)
     "If your birth was ever a fact,
     "I have cut your old menstrual cloth!"[3]

     O Kalajula Sangoyi Mamunaka!   (Indeed)
2730   He lay Sugulun Kulunkan down on the bed.   (Indeed)

---

3. She disowns him, weakening his occult power.

After one week had gone by,
Sugulun Kulunkan spoke up: (Indeed)
"Ah, my husband,   (Indeed)
"Will you not let me go to the Manden,   (Indeed)
2735   "That I may get my bowls and spoons,
"For me to build my household here?"   (Indeed)
From that day to this,
Should you marry a woman in Mandenland,   (Indeed)
When the first week has passed,
2740   She will take a backward glance,   (Indeed)
And this is what that custom means.   (Yes, Fa-Digi, that's the truth)

Sugulun returned to reveal those secrets
To her flesh-and-blood-brother, Son-Jara.   (Indeed)
The sacrifices did Son-Jara thus discover.   (Indeed)
2745   The sacrifices did he thus discover.   (Indeed)
Now five score wives had Susu Mountain Sumamuru,   (Indeed)
One hundred wives had he.   (Indeed)
His nephew, Fa-Koli, had but one,   (Indeed)

. . . . .   (Mmm)
2750   And Sumamuru, five score!   (Indeed)
When a hundred bowls they would cook
To make the warriors' meal,   (Indeed)
Fa-Koli's wife alone would one hundred cook
To make the warriors' meal,   (That's the truth, eh, Fa-Digi,
                                               indeed, indeed)
2755   "Let the fonio increase!   (Indeed)
"Let the rice increase!   (Indeed)
"Let the groundnuts increase!   (Indeed)
"Let the groundpeas increase!   (Indeed)
"Let the beans increase!"   (Indeed)
2760   She took them all one by one,   (Indeed)
And put them all in one pot,   (Indeed)
And in that pot they all were cooked,   (Indeed)
And served it all in her calabash,   (Indeed)
And all of this for Fa-Koli.   (Indeed)
2765   . . . . .

[*Sumamuru takes Fa-Koli's wife from him.*][4]

. . . . .
Ah! Garan!   (Indeed)

[*Fa-Koli leaves Sumamuru and comes to Son-Jara's camp.*]

. . . . .
. . . . .
2770   Hero-of-the-Original-Clans and Magan Sukudana!   (Indeed)
Son-Jara called out,   (Indeed)

4. Lines obscure on the tape recording.

"Who in the Manden will make this sacrifice?"   (Indeed)

"I shall!" Fa-Koli's reply.   (Indeed)

"The thing that drove me away,   (Indeed)

2775   "And took my only wife from me,

"So that not even a weak wife have I now,

"I shall make the whole sacrifice!"   (Indeed)

Fa-Koli thus made the whole sacrifice.   (Indeed)

He came and reported to the Wizard.   (Indeed)

2780   Son-Jara then called out: (Indeed)

"Who will bring us face to face,

"That we may join in battle?"   (Indeed)

"I shall," Fa-Koli's reply.   (Indeed)

On that Fa-Koli rose up.   (Indeed)

2785   He arrived in Dark Forest.   (Indeed)

As he espied the rooftops of Sumamuru's city, Dark Forest,   (Indeed)

With every single step he took,   (Indeed)

He thrust a dart into the earth,   (Indeed)

And in a tree fork laid another.   (Indeed, yes, Fa-Digi)

2790   With every single step he took,   (Indeed)

He thrust a dart into the earth,   (Indeed)

And in a tree fork laid another,   (That's the truth)

Until he entered the very gates,

Until he entered the city.   (Indeed)

2795   O, Garan!   (Indeed)

The daughter given by King Dankaran Tuman,   (Indeed)

Given to Susu Mountain Sumamuru,   (Indeed)

That he should go and kill Son-Jara,   (Indeed)

Fa-Koli went and seized that maiden,   (Indeed)

2800   "Come! Your uncle has left Mèma!   (Indeed)

"Your uncle has summoned you.   (Indeed)

"Your uncle has now come. He has left Mèma!"   (Indeed)

The people of Susu pursued them: biri biri biri.   (Indeed)

They came attacking after them: yrrrrrrr!   (Indeed)

2805   With every single step he took,   (Indeed)

He drew a war dart from the earth,

And hurled it at the Susu,   (Indeed)

And from a tree fork grabbed another,   (Indeed)

And hurled it at the Susu,   (Indeed)

2810   "Heh! Come to my aid!   (Indeed)

"Heaven and Earth, come aid me!

"Susu Mountain Sumamuru is after me!"   (Indeed, yes, father)

He retreated on and on.

He drew a war dart from the earth,

2815   And hurled it at the Susu,   (Indeed)

And from a tree fork grabbed another,   (Indeed)

And fired it at the Susu.   (Indeed)

"Heh! Come to my aid!   (Indeed)

"Heaven and Earth, come to my aid!

2820   "Susu Mountain Sumamuru is after me!"   (That's the truth)

	At that, the Susu said, my father,	(Indeed)
	"If we do not fall back from Fa-Koli,	(Indeed)
	"Fa-Koli will bring all our folk to an end!	(Indeed)
	"Let us fall back from Fa-Koli!	(Indeed)
2825	Hero-of-the-Original-Clans and Magan Sukudana,	
	. . . . .	(That's the truth)
	And thus they fell back from Fa-Koli.	(Indeed)
	They readied themselves for battle.	(Indeed)
	Susu Mountain Sumamuru came forward,	(Indeed)
2830	And taking his favorite wife,	
	On the saddle's cantle[5] sat her,	(Indeed)
	With golden ladle and silver ladle.	(Indeed)
	Son-Jara attacked and encircled the walls.	(Indeed)
	He had split the enemy army,	(Indeed)
2835	And taken the fortress gates.	(Indeed)
	Susu Mountain Sumamuru charged out at a gallop.	(Indeed)
	Fa-Koli,	(Indeed)
	With Tura-Magan-and-Kanke-jan,	(Indeed)
	And Bee-King-of-the-Wilderness,	(Indeed)
2840	And Fa-Kanda Tunandi,	(Indeed)
	And Sura, the Jawara patriarch,	(Indeed)
	And Son-Jara,	(Indeed)
	They all chased after Sumamuru.	(True)
	They arrived at Kukuba.	(Indeed)
2845	He told them, "I am not ready!"	(Indeed)
	They let him go:	(Indeed)
	"Prepare yourself!"	(Indeed)
	They arrived at Kamasiga,	(Indeed)
	"I am not ready."	(Indeed)
2850	They let him go:	(Indeed)
	"Prepare yourself!"	(Indeed)
	They arrived at Nyani-Nyani.	(Indeed)
	Said, "I am not ready."	(Indeed)
	They let him go again:	
2855	"Prepare yourself!"	(Indeed)
	They arrived at Bantanba,	(Indeed)
	"I am not ready."	(Indeed)
	And again they let him go:	
	"Prepare yourself!"	(Indeed)
2860	And still they attacked him from behind,	
	Behind Susu Mountain Sumamuru.	(That's the truth, yes, Fa-Digi)
	Sumamuru crossed the river at Kulu-Kòrò,	(Indeed)
	And had his favored wife dismount,	(Indeed)
	And gave her the ladle of gold,	
2865	Saying that he would drink,	(Indeed)
	Saying else the thirst would kill him.	(That's the truth)

5. Back edge.

The favored wife took the ladle of gold,   (Indeed)
And filled it up with water,   (Indeed)
And to Sumamuru stretched her hand,
2870   And passed the water to him.   (Indeed)
Fa-Koli with his darts charged up:
        "O Colossus,   (Indeed)
        "We have taken you!   (That's the truth)
        "We have taken you, Colossus!
2875   "We have taken you, Colossus!
        "We have taken you!"   (Indeed)
Tura Magan held him at bladepoint.   (Indeed)
Sura, the Jawara patriarch held him at bladepoint.   (Indeed)
Fa-Koli came up and held him at bladepoint.
2880   Son-Jara held him at bladepoint: (Indeed)
        "We have taken you, Colossus!   (That's the truth)
        "We have taken you!"   (Indeed)
Sumamuru dried up on the spot: nyònyòwu!   (Indeed)
He has become the sacred fetish of Kulu-Kòrò.[6]   (Indeed)
2885   The Bambara worship that now, my father.
Susu Mountain Sumamuru,
He became that sacred fetish.   (That's the truth, indeed,
                                         father, yes, yes, yes, yes)

[FINAL CONQUESTS ESTABLISH THE KINGDOM]

Biribiriba turned back, Son-Jara!   (Indeed)
    Stranger-in-the-Morning, Chief-in-the-Afternoon!   (Indeed)
2890   Great-Host-Slaying-Stranger!
Stump-in-the-Dark-of-Night!   (Indeed)
Should you bump against it,
It will bump against you!   (That's the truth)
The Granary Guard Dog.   (Indeed)
2895   The thing discerning not the stranger,
Nor the familiar.
Should it come upon any person,
He will be bitten.   (That's the truth)
Kirikara Watita!   (Indeed)
2900   Adversity's true place!
Man's reason and woman's are not the same.
Pretty words and truth are not the same.   (That's the truth)
No matter how long the roád,
It always comes out at someone's home.   (Indeed)
2905   The Nyani king with his army came forward,   (Indeed)
Saying the Manden belonged to him,   (That's the truth)
Saying no more was he rival to any,   (That's the truth)
Saying the Manden belonged to him.   (That's the truth)

---

6. This fetish still exists; it is a globe-shaped stone carved with interlaced diamond patterns. It is thought to be served by Sumamuru's spirit and is consulted for many concerns, including infertility.

	He found the Kuyatè patriarch with tendons cut,	(Indeed)
2910	And beckoned him to rise, "Let us go!	(Indeed)
	"Bala Faseke Kuyatè, arise. Let us go!"	(Indeed)
	He lurched forward,	(Indeed)
	Saying he would rise.	
	He fell back to the ground again,	(Indeed)
2915	His two Achilles tendons cut:	(Indeed)
	"O Nare Magan Kònatè!"	(Indeed)
	"Arise and let us go!	(Indeed)
	"I have no rival in Mandenland now!	(That's the truth)
	"The Manden is mine alone."	(Indeed)
2920	He lurched forward,	(Indeed)
	Saying that he would rise.	(Indeed)
	He fell back to the ground again.	(Indeed)
	"Had Sumamuru no child?" they queried.	(Indeed)
	"Here is his first born son," the reply.	(Indeed)
2925	"What is his name?"	(Indeed)
	"His name is Mansa Saman."	(Indeed)
	They summoned Mansa Saman	(Indeed)
	And brought forth Dòka the Cat,	
	And placed him on Mansa Saman's shoulders,	(Indeed)
2930	Laying the balaphone[7] on his head, serew!	(Indeed)
	He followed after the Wizard:	(Indeed)
	"Biribiriba!	(Indeed)
	"O Nare Magan Kònatè!	(Indeed)
	"Entered Kaya,	
2935	*"Son-Jara entered Kaya.*	(That's the truth)
	"Entered Kaya,	
	"Sugulun's Magan entered Kaya.	(Yes, Fa-Digi)
	"If they took no gold,	(Indeed)
	"If they took no measure of gold for the Wizard,	(Indeed)
2940	"The reason for Son-Jara's coming to the Manden,	
	"To stabilize the Manden,	
	"To improve the people's lot: jon jon!	(That's the truth)
	"O Sorcerer, you have come for the Manden people!	(Indeed)
	"O Nare Magan Kònatè,	(Indeed)
2945	"O Khalif Magan Kònatè!"	(That's the truth)
	They arrived back in the Manden.	(Indeed)
	The Sorcerer ruled over everyone.	(Indeed)
	He continued on at that.	(Indeed)
	Bulanbulan Sulemani,	(Indeed)
2950	Along with Yari Sise,	(Indeed)
	He sent them forth,	(Indeed)
	That they should go after horses,	(Indeed)
	Saying the Manden belonged to him.	(Indeed)
	Bulanbulan Sulemani,	(Indeed)

7. A kind of xylophone.

2955	Along with Yari Sise,	(Indeed)
	They went on after the horses,	(Indeed)
	In the land of Dark Jòlòf.[8]	(Indeed)
	The Dark Jòlòf king fell on the messengers,	(Indeed)
	And seizing the nine and ninety stallions,	(Indeed)
2960	Selected hound dogs one score and ten,	(Indeed)
	Saying to the Nyani King give them,	(Indeed)
	Saying he knew Son-Jara for naught	(Indeed)
	Save a runner of dogs,	
	Saying he had no reason to doubt that.	(That's the truth)

2965 O Garan!   (Indeed)
      Biribiriba in his hut with his wife,   (Indeed)
      The bards came up to him singing:
          "Khalif Magan Kònatè!   (Yes, Fa-Digi)
          "Succeeded, the King succeeded!   (Indeed)
2970   *"The Sorcerer and Sovereignty!*   (Indeed)
          "Who has seen the goat bite a dog?
          "O Nare Magan Kònatè!
          "Will you not arise?"   (Indeed)
      Son-Jara transformed himself on the spot,
2975 And turned into a lion,   (Indeed)
      Saying he was going out after those bards.   (Indeed)
      His wife grabbed hold and soothed him,   (Indeed)
      And had him lay back down,   (Indeed)
      . . . . .   (That's the truth)
2980 . . . . .   (Indeed)
      Ah! Kala Jula Sangoyi!   (Indeed)
      Those are the words the bards said that day: (True)
      "O Wizard,   (Indeed)
      "'Twas you who sent Bulanbulan Sulemani
2985 "Along with Yari Sise   (Indeed)
      "That they should go . . .   (Indeed)
      "After nine and ninety stallions.   (Indeed)
      "To thirty.   (Indeed)
      "It was he who plundered the horses,   (Indeed)
2990 "And thirty . . . ,   (Indeed)
      "And gave the hound dogs, score and ten,   (Indeed)
      "Saying we should give you them,   (Indeed)
      "Since you are but a runner of dogs,
      "Saying you have not yet mastered war.   (That's the truth)
2995 "O Wizard, a goat bites not a dog!"   (That's the truth)

      In turn, the warriors swore their fealty: (Indeed)
      "Let me the battle-master be!"   (Indeed)
      Fa-Koli and Tura Magan swore their fealty.[9]   (Indeed)

---

8. Neighboring Wolof kingdom, known as a place of sorcery.

9. Fa-Koli, Sumamuru's nephew, is now loyal to Son-Jara,

as is Tura Magan—the greatest Tarawere warrior, a descendant of Son-Jara's mother's would-be husband Dan Manse Wulandin.

"Let me lead the army!" Fa-Koli adjured.   (That's the truth)

3000   "Let me lead the army!" Tura Magan adjured.   (Indeed)
        Son-Jara finally spoke,   (Indeed)
        "'Tis I who will lead the army,   (Indeed)
        "And go to Dark Jòlòf land."   (Indeed)
        O Nare Magan Kònatè!   (Indeed)
3005   Tura Magan plunged into grief,   (Indeed)
        And went to the graveyard to dig his grave,   (Indeed)
        And laid himself down in his grave.   (Indeed)
        The bards came forth: "O Nare Magan Kònatè,   (Indeed)
        "If you don't go see Tura Magan,   (Indeed)
3010   "Your army will not succeed!"   (Indeed)
        He sent the bards forth
        That they should summon Tura Magan.
        And so the bards went forth,   (Indeed)
        But Tura Magan they could not find.   (That's the truth)
3015   Son-Jara came and stood in the graveyard: (Indeed)
            "Bugu Turu and Bugu Bò!   (Indeed)
            "Muke Musa and Muke Dantuman!   (Indeed)
            "Juru Kèta and Juru Moriba!   (Indeed)
            "Tunbila the Manden Slave!   (Indeed)
3020   "Kalabila, the Manden Slave!   (Indeed)
            "Sana Fa-Buren, Danka Fa-Buren!   (Indeed)
            "Dark-Pilgrim and Light-Pilgrim!   (Indeed)
        "Ah! Bards,   (Indeed)
        "Let us give the army to Tura Magan,   (Indeed)
3025   "To the Slave-of-the-Tomb, Tura Magan,   (Indeed)
        "O Tura Magan-and-Kanke-jan!"   (That's the truth)

        Tura Magan spoke out,   (Indeed)
        "That is the best of all things to my ear!"   (Indeed)
        To Tura Magan they gave quiver and bow.   (Indeed)
3030   Tura Magan advanced to cross the river here,   (Indeed)
        At the Passage-of-Tura-Magan.   (Indeed)
        A member of the troop cried out,   (Indeed)
        "Hey! The war to which we go,   (Indeed)
        "That war will not be easy!   (Indeed)
3035   "Ninety iron drums has the Dark Jòlòf King.   (Indeed)
        "No drum like this has the Manden,   (Indeed)
        "Nor balaphone has the Manden.   (Indeed)
        "There is no such thing in the Manden,   (Indeed)
        "Save the Jawara patriarch, Sita Fata,   (Indeed)
3040   "Save when he puffs out his cheeks,   (Indeed)
        "Making with them like drum and balaphone,
        "To go awaken the Nyani King.   (Indeed)
        "This battle will not be easy!"   (Indeed)
        But they drove this agitator off,   (Indeed)
3045   Saying better in the bush a frightened brave
        Then a loudmouthed agitator.   (That's the truth)

	He went back across the river,	(Indeed)
	At the place they call Salakan,	(Indeed)
	And Ford-of-the-Frightened.	(Indeed)
3050	The Ford-of-the-Frightened-Braves.	(Indeed)
	Tura Magan with battle met.	(Indeed)
	He slayed that dog-giving king,	(Indeed)
	Saying he was but running the dogs.	(That's the truth)
	Tura Magan with army marched on,	(Indeed)
3055	He went to slay Nyani Mansa,	
	Saying he was but running the dogs.	(That's the truth)
	Tura Magan with the army marched on,	(Indeed)
	He slayed the Sanumu King,	
	Saying that he was but running the dogs,	(Indeed)
3060	He slayed Ba-dugu King	(Indeed)
	Saying he was but running the dogs,	(Indeed)
	And marched on thus through Jòlòf land.	(Indeed)
	Their name for stone is Jòlòf.	(Indeed)
	Once there was this king . . . ,	(Indeed)
3065	The stone there that is red,	(Indeed)
	The Wòlòf call it Jòlòf.	(Indeed)
	There once was a king in that country, my father,	
	Called King of Dark Jòlòfland.	(Indeed)
	And that is the meaning of this.	(That's the truth)
3070	He slayed that Dark Jòlòf King,	(Indeed)
	Severing his great head at his shoulders,	(Indeed)
	From whence comes the Wòlòf name, Njòp![1]	(Indeed)
	They are Taraweres.	(Indeed)
	Sane and Mane,	(Indeed)
3075	They are Taraweres.	(Indeed)
	Mayga, they are Taraweres.	(Indeed)
	Magaraga, they are Taraweres.	(Indeed)
	Tura Magan-and-Kanke-jan,	(Indeed)
	He with the army marched on,	
3080	To destroy the golden sword and the tall throne.	(That's the truth)
	This by the hand of Tura Magan-and-Kanke-jan.	
	Kirikisa, Spear-of-Access, Spear-of Service!	(Indeed)
	Ah! Garan!	(Indeed)
	Let us leave the words right here.	(That's the truth, indeed, it's over now!)

---

1. Comically taking this clan name as coming from the sound of a chopping axe.

Cathedral of Notre Dame, Paris, 13th century

Cathedral of Notre Dame, Paris, 12th century.

Medieval Europe

Encompassing a thousand years of history from the fall of the Roman Empire in the fifth century to the beginning of the modern era in the sixteenth, a terrain extending from Iceland to Jerusalem, and more languages, ethnicities, religions, and cultures than are easily counted, there is very little that can be generalized about medieval Europe; there is also very little that would not hold true for at least some small corner of it. Indeed, we are far closer today to the end of the Middle Ages than its inhabitants were to the beginning of them. The idea of Europe itself as a cohesive geographical, political, or cultural entity was only a faint glimmer even during Charlemagne's rule in the late eighth century. Although later rulers would hold the title of Holy Roman Emperor, their control seldom exceeded the bounds of Germany and northern Italy. Medieval leaders—and there were many of them—were far more conscious of their insuperable distance from the wealth, culture, and power of classical Rome than of being able to restore them. "Medieval Europe" was coined as a term and as a historical period only at the end of these thousand years, to stand for everything that Renaissance writers considered themselves not to be: ignorant, superstitious, uncivilized, and above all unclassical. To be "medieval" (from the Latin term *medium aevum* or "middle age") meant to be part of a long, dark nightmare of history between the glories of classical Rome and the bright new day the Renaissance saw itself to be.

There is no doubt that the Middle Ages were a difficult time in which to live. Waves of raids, invasions, and tribal migrations rolled through and destabilized the former Empire: Germanic tribes in the fifth and sixth centuries, followed by Vikings from the north, Muslims from the south, and Magyar and other Central Asian tribes from the east. While borders solidified around the turn of the millennium and living conditions gradually improved, war remained a way of life both in territorial skirmishes and in the many Crusades into Iberia, the Middle East, and North Africa through the thirteenth century. Overpopulation had already caused an economic depression before the Black Plague killed off a third of Europe's population in the mid-fourteenth century. Nevertheless, for all of its terrors the Middle Ages bequeathed to later European culture much of its identity and heritage: the geographic, social, and political conceptions of Europe and most of the European nations; the cathedrals, castles, and cities; the institutions of government and religion; the codes of honor and chivalry, the languages; the poetry of love; and the stories of adventure. A good argument can be made that the Renaissance was itself a medieval invention.

> *. . . for all of its terrors the Middle Ages bequeathed to later European culture much of its identity and heritage. . .*

While this legacy is easy enough to recognize in the modern West, its sources are less immediately familiar, as they took shape amid the ruins of the Roman Empire and the expansive organization of the Catholic Christian church. Imperial rule had spread the Latin language across the continent, and it continued to play a key role in ecclesiastical and monastic life as well as in government, administration, and law.

Imperial forces had built cities and towns as administrative and political centers in every province. Partially preserved by their role as bishoprics, these towns were pretty much the only urban centers in much of early medieval Europe. The Empire had officially adopted Christianity during the fourth century, and the imperial religion dominated the entire Mediterranean region until the rise of Islam three centuries later began to check its expansion. During the Middle Ages, the institutions of the church promoted an internationalist rather than a local approach to society. Monastic communities, mendicant orders (whose members took a vow of poverty and subsisted on alms), and the later schools and universities were seldom associated with any local governing body, and the papacy was generally considered to possess an authority exceeding that of any single temporal ruler. Moreover, members of the nobility all over the continent upheld at least to some degree a code of honor and chivalry inherited from the warrior culture of the Germanic tribes who had taken the continent from the Romans.

These elements of unity were strongest during the first centuries after the collapse of Rome, when medieval Europe was at its most fragmented and chaotic. As economic expansion brought relative social and political stability in the twelfth and thirteenth centuries, the vernacular languages as we know them today began to predominate—English, French, Spanish, German, and Italian among others—and many of the national borders (and border disputes) began to solidify. (See "The Rise of the Vernacular in Europe," in Volume C.) In this period, usually known as the High Middle Ages, internationalism came to mean not so much a shared culture and authority as a broad knowledge of many different cultures and authorities. The English poet Geoffrey Chaucer was a professional diplomat equally at ease in the local dialects around Britain, in French in Paris, and in Tuscan Italian in Florence; the Florentine poet Dante Alighieri wrote a treatise on the Romance languages and incorporated the vocabulary of Latin, Occitan (also known as Provençal), French, and many Italian dialects into his *Divine Comedy*. England was ruled for several centuries by Normans, descendants of the original "Northmen," ninth-century Danish invaders who had settled in Normandy in northwest France; the court language was Anglo-Norman, a version of Old French. At a strategic crossroads of the Mediterranean, the kingdom of southern Italy and Sicily was first controlled by Muslims, then by Normans, Hohenstaufens, and the kings of Aragon. The mix of Byzantine, Muslim, Jewish, Lombard, Norman, and later peoples made long-established cities such as Palermo new centers of cultural interchange and innovation. Muslim rulers long controlled southern Iberia, known then as al-Andalus: their administrations were full of Jewish courtiers, their cities crowded with Mozarabs, or arabized Christians, and their armies strengthened by complex alliances with neighboring Christian rulers. While a dominant theme of the Middle Ages was the search to reclaim the lost unity of Roman Europe, either through the church, through learning, or through a new empire, the extraordinary wealth of art and literature that emerged from that search came into being under the influence of the myriad cultures and traditions to which that unity eventually, and permanently, gave way.

> *... internationalism came to mean not so much a shared culture and authority as a broad knowledge of many different cultures and authorities.*

Medieval Europe, c. 1100 C.E.

NORWAY

SWEDEN

SCOTLAND

NORTH SEA

IRELAND

DENMARK

BALTIC SEA

ENGLAND

WALES

Oxford • Cambridge

London • Canterbury

Elbe

POLAND

RUSSIAN PRINCIPALITIES

ATLANTIC OCEAN

Rheims

Cologne

HOLY ROMAN EMPIRE

Prague

Rhine

Worms

Bec • Paris

Chartres

Angers • Orleans

Tours Meung

Danube

HUNGARY

FRANCE

ALPS

Grenoble

Milan

Vicenza

Padua Venice

VENETIAN REPUBLIC

Montpellier

Piacenza Bologna

Genoa

SERBIA

BULGARIA

NAVARRE

Toulouse

Béziers

Avignon

Pisa Arezzo

Siena Perugia

León

Pamplona

Marseille

Assisi

Rome

CORSICA

BYZANTINE EMPIRE

LEÓN

CASTILE

Salamanca

• Tarazona

ARAGON

Segovia

Barcelona

PAPAL STATES

Naples • Salerno

Coimbra

PORTUGAL

Toledo

SARDINIA

KINGDOM OF SICILY

Lisbon

Cordova

Seville

ALMOHAD EMPIRE

BALEARIC ISLANDS

Palermo

SICILY

CRETE

MEDITERRANEAN SEA

N

England

Holy Roman Empire

Byzantine Empire

France

Poland

Almohad Empire

LANGUAGE AND CULTURE

Rome was sacked by the Germanic tribe of Visigoths, or Western Goths, in 410. Traditionally, this date marks the end of the Roman Empire and the onset of the "Dark Ages," a barbaric period from which few records remain and about which the most that is usually said is that by the eleventh century the High Middle Ages were gradually emerging out of it. The symbolic shock reverberated around the world, but in fact the Empire had been unsettled for a couple of centuries, and the main imperial capital had already been moved east to Constantinople. In the late first century the Roman historian Tacitus had unfavorably compared his corrupt and degenerate countrymen to the simple and upright barbarians to the north. Possessing no written culture, the Germanic tribes had none of the sophisticated and abstract bodies of laws and customs that had governed the Empire, but neither were they simply uncivilized. For the most part, they preferred sharing in Roman wealth to destroying it. They grouped together in frequently changing warrior bands, or *comitati,* as Tacitus termed them, bound by loyalty to a king or chief, and governed by specific values such as valor and fidelity rather than the patriotism and Roman virtue (not to mention the steady pay) of the traditional legionary. Indeed, worse damage was done to Rome by later, Christian adversaries than by the Visigoths or the Asiatic Huns who followed on their heels.

While the Huns vanished from the scene after the death of their leader Attila, the Visigoths were converted to Christianity, intermarried with the already mixed inhabitants of the Empire, and moved on through Gaul to establish a kingdom in Iberia. In the course of subsequent waves of migration, Germanic tribes out of northern and southeastern Europe took over and settled different regions of the now-dissolved empire: Franks in Gaul, Angles and Saxons in Britain, Ostrogoths in Italy, Lombards in northern Italy (still known as Lombardy today), and Vandals in North Africa, where they captured the city of Hippo in the year of Augustine's death there. Many episcopal towns survived under the control of the local bishop, especially where there were important shrines or relics to attract pilgrims; isolated monasteries created other enclaves, but most of Europe for the next few centuries was agrarian. Latin remained the lingua franca, but the written High Latin of antiquity quickly gave way to a Low Latin closer to what was actually spoken, a second language alongside local dialects and whatever mixtures were arrived at to allow locals to converse with various occupiers and traders, travelers and pilgrims. Through the Middle Ages and beyond, proper Latin remained the mark of literacy and high culture. Monastic communities and ambitious churchmen and rulers invested much time, money and artistry in copying ancient manuscripts and attempting to preserve a Latin heritage in danger of vanishing forever.

Through the Middle Ages and beyond, proper Latin remained the mark of literacy and high culture.

Most of the literature that has come down to us from before the eleventh century is in medieval Latin, as is just about all of the scholarly writing, which consists primarily of vast compendia of classical lore, Bible commentary and popular myth, as well as similarly encyclopaedic histories. It is handwritten in ink on sheets of parchment (made from the skin of cattle, sheep, or goats) bound together down one edge into what is known as a codex. Its authors sometimes apologize for the poverty of their grammar and style, but notwithstanding its all-inclusiveness their writing possesses a directness and connection with everyday life not always evident in the rarified refinement of High Latin literature. So the ninth-century Irish poet Sedulius Scotus writes with great intimacy of the natural splendors of spring and the pleasures of nature that he, as a monk, has supposedly renounced:

> Now the grain is green, now field-grass is in flower;
> Now the vines are heavy; now's the best of the year;
> Now colored birds soothe the heavens with their songs;
> Now sea, now earth, now stars in the sky are laughing.
>
> But not one drop disturbs me with sad-making swill,
> Since Mead and Beer and the gifts of Bacchus I lack.
> Alas! how I miss the multiple substance of flesh
> Which is born on the tender earth, in the dew-filled air.

In addition to such lyrics of nature and of love, hymns and other forms of religious poetry were dominant genres, often similarly emotional and direct in their language and imagery.

Alongside these bodies of poetry, there were local oral traditions such as the Celtic tales or *lais*, the Anglo-Saxon epic about the great chieftain Beowulf, and popular songs all over the continent. It is difficult to know exactly what forms this oral tradition took, as it has come down to us mediated by what later literate writers chose to record. Such translations were important documents in the foundation of what would later be called national traditions, as when Ferdinand and Isabella celebrated the union of their two kingdoms in the late fifteenth century to form the modern state of Spain by collecting its popular lyrics into *Cancioneros,* or songbooks. A collection of oral material could also serve as novel subject matter for a jaded court audience, as when the Anglo-Norman writer Marie de France worries in the prologue to her *Lais* that too many people have already retold Latin stories:

It is difficult to know exactly what forms this oral tradition took, as it has come down to us mediated by what later literate writers chose to record.

> That's why I began to think
> about composing some good stories
> and translating from Latin to Romance;
> but that was not to bring me fame:
> too many others have done it.
> Then I thought of the *lais* I'd heard. . . .
> I have heard many told;
> and I don't want to neglect or forget them.
> To put them into word and rhyme
> I've often stayed awake.

Like many other writers in the vernacular, Marie was being defensive about her decision. With a few notable exceptions, Latin was considered the only language of serious thought and significant literature until well into the Renaissance.

Most educated Romans had been fluent in both Latin and Greek, but once the empire was divided between East and West in the fourth century, this gradually ceased to be the case. Byzantine culture remained Greek, and by the time the Eastern Orthodox Church was officially established in 680, it had lost its familiarity with Latin. The situation was only exacerbated by the culmination of the conflict between the two Churches in the schism of 1054, which resulted in the rivalry between two centers of Christianity: Latin-based Roman Christianity in the West and Greek-derived eastern Christianity based in Constantinople. Greek was thus a lost language in Western Europe. Homer was known only by reputation, and the philosophy of Plato and Aristotle only through Roman commentaries of a few minor works. Medieval scholars were acutely aware of their inability to access much of the exalted heritage of the classical age. Manuscripts even of Roman literature and philosophy were scarce and often corrupt from generations of copiers' errors, as Peter Abelard established in great detail in his polemical work, *Yes and No* (page 870). The Islamic Empire contained most early medieval centers of learning, where scholars made important innovations on Greek philosophy, medicine, astronomy, and mathematics. Greek thought eventually made its way back into Christian Europe across the boundary between Islam and Christianity and by means of Arabic translations, accompanied by learned glosses by contemporary philosophers such as the Jewish scholar Moses Maimonides and Ibn Rushd, also known as Averroës the Commentator. In important frontier cities such as Toledo (recaptured from al-Andalus in 1058) and Palermo (known as the city of the threefold tongue, taken by the Normans in 1072), Jewish, Muslim, and Christian scholars debated while they translated the wisdom of the ancients into Latin. Translators at work in the thirteenth-century Galician-Portuguese court of Alfonso X, for instance, included five Jews, four Spanish Christians, four Italians, a Muslim converted to Christianity, technical editors to deal with difficult terms, and secretaries to write everything down.

A record left by the Andalusian poet Ibn 'Arabi of his meeting with Ibn Rushd gives a sense of the heady mood of these days, and of the mystical bent shared by many Iberian Muslims, Christians, and Jews:

> When I entered, the master arose from his place, received me with signal marks of friendship and consideration, and finally embraced me. Then he said "Yes." His joy was great at noting that I had understood. But then taking cognizance of what had called forth his joy, I added: "No." Immediately Averroës winced, the color went out of his cheeks, he seemed to doubt his own thought. He asked me this question: "What manner of solution have you found through divine illumination and inspiration? Is it identical with that which we obtain from speculative reflection?" I replied: "Yes and no. Between the yes and the no, spirits take their flight from their matter, and heads are separated from their bodies . . ."

This meeting of "divine illumination and inspiration" with "speculative reflection" should remind us that Iberia and Sicily were also two of the great centers of lyric poetry, building on a long tradition of Arabic verse, notably the stanzas known as *kharjas,* the earliest known vernacular love poetry in Europe.

In a culture insecure about its own foundations, translation was not only a source of novelty, inspiration, and knowledge, but also a way of enhancing authority and reputation. In a rhetorical flourish known as the *translatio imperii* (literally, the "translation of empire"), monarchs were accustomed to trace their lineage fancifully back to heroes of antiquity, primarily to the royal family of Troy, scattered after its defeat by the Greeks in the legendary past. Virgil's *Aeneid* had shown its hero escaping the city's fall to become the founder of Rome; similar bloodlines were invented for rulers all over medieval Europe, including the mythical Briton King Arthur. When the Carolingian ruler Charlemagne was crowned Emperor by the pope on Christmas Day of the year

Shrine of the Book of Dimma. Ireland, 12th century. This elaborate silver case for a gospel manuscript combines pre-Christian Celtic interlacings with Christian crosses.

800, the underlying message was that he had restored the Roman Empire, carrying on its legacy in an act of political translation. New epics were made on the classical model to commemorate (or invent) great figures in contemporary empire building, such as Roland and El Cid. At the same time, the epic matter of antiquity was translated into verse and prose "romances" that recounted the events of the Trojan War, the Theban War, the *Aeneid*, and the tales of Ovid in a form that was partly classical and partly adapted to local tastes and interests. Italian poets were especially keen to revive the glories of their lost empire and counter the growing cultural prestige and political power of France. In fourteenth-century Florence, Dante, Boccaccio, and Petrarch immersed themselves in the classical world to lend authority to a new humanism that would come to appear in retrospect as a break with the church-centered Middle Ages (Boccaccio and Petrarch, consequently, will be found in "Early Modern Europe," Volume C).

RELIGION AND THE CHURCH

Catholic Christianity was simultaneously the strongest link between the Middle Ages and the classical world and the strongest impediment to that link. The great Church Fathers of the fourth and early fifth centuries—Ambrose, Augustine, and Jerome—had made a tremendous effort to specify the proper relationship between a dangerously pagan body of classical literature and philosophy and a scriptural tradition often regarded as inferior in style and lacking in sophistication. All three remained extremely influential throughout the Middle Ages, especially Augustine's interpretation of Platonic and Neoplatonic thought and Roman history in the light of scripture, and Jerome's Vulgate, the canonical Latin translation of the Bible's original Hebrew, Aramaic, and Greek. Their concerns over the misuse of pagan antiquity were not so much of a problem during the early Middle Ages, when sources were scarce and Christian scholars were more concerned with preservation and error-free copying than with innovation. Until the twelfth century, scholarship was conducted almost entirely under

Until the twelfth century, scholarship was conducted almost entirely under the auspices of the church . . .

the auspices of the church, first in the monasteries and later in the courts of rulers such as Charlemagne and in cathedral towns. Following their conversion by Saint Patrick in the fifth century, the Irish had developed a rich monastery-based church organization in isolation from the town-based bishops on the continent, and they were the first to devote themselves to an austere life of rigorous scholarship and simple sanctity. As opposed to the courtier's life that characterized the southern frontier cities and Islamic capitals, monastic scholarship prided itself on detachment from worldly concerns.

By contrast, the papacy, increasingly embroiled in the temporal demands of politics and governance and generally suspicious of new ideas, more closely resembled the southern courts than the monasteries. This is hardly surprising, given that its hierarchical structure and broad network of influence made it at times the sole source of stability in the medieval world. The papal states accumulated vast wealth and power through being a principal player or influence in nearly every one of the countless negotiations, treaties, wars, and betrayals that raged throughout the period. Not all were as corrupt as the eleventh-century pope Benedict IX, who caused a schism when he tried to retrieve the pontificate after he had sold it off for profit, or the fifteenth-century Borgia pope Alexander VI, who murdered and schemed while accumulating scores of bastard children. Nevertheless, the worldly preeminence of the papacy was seen by many reformers to be at odds with the Gospel message of Jesus that salvation was to be found in discarding wealth and earthly ties: "Anyone who has forsaken home, brothers, sisters, father, mother, wife, children, or lands for my name's sake will be repaid a hundred times over and inherit everlasting life" (Matthew 19:29). Great damage was done to papal prestige when in 1378 the Great Schism led to thirty-seven years of competing French and Italian popes in Avignon and in Rome. The stage was set for the Protestant Reformation to challenge the papacy's thousand-year supremacy as the spiritual voice of the Christian church.

Reform took many shapes before Martin Luther's definitive rebellion in 1518, from powerful figures within the ecclesiastical inner circles to abbots, abbesses, monks, and nuns to laymen and -women whom divine inspiration led to take up preaching or writing. One of the earliest was Saint Benedict (c. 480–c. 550), whose celebrated "Rule" guided the rituals of daily monastic life for centuries to come,

Saint Benedict writing his rule. Seated in his cloister, Benedict is framed by Old and New Testament visions. On the left, the Hebrew patriarch Jacob dreams of angels ascending and descending on a ladder to heaven; on the right, the satanic dragon of the Book of Revelation—held on a leash by God—swallows the damned while above the sword-wielding angel the blessed ascend to God.

covering even details of eating, drinking, and sleeping: "Therefore let two cooked dishes suffice for all the brothers: and, if it is possible to obtain apples or growing vegetables, a third may be added. One full pound of bread shall suffice for a day, whether there be one refection, or a breakfast and a supper." Benedict instituted a daily routine of prayer, reading, and work (indoors, outdoors, or in copying) that gave structure and a modicum of variety to the basic asceticism that had characterized monasticism since the early days of the church.

In addition to finding a proper outlet for the ascetic piety and desire for structure of so many medieval men and women, Benedictines and later orders were also invested in expanding the frontiers of Christianity through conversion. Monasteries were a major reason for the spread of Christianity northward from its Mediterranean stronghold. The conversion of England began at the end of the sixth century; even distant Iceland had been Christianized by around the year 1000. The conversion of the Norsemen and the Magyars (who settled in what is now Hungary) was an important element in abating their damaging raids; the same was true in Russia, although in this instance it was the Eastern Church that took the prize.

Conversion to Christianity no more eliminated local beliefs and customs than conquest by the Roman Empire had made Europeans speak Latin exclusively. Christian theology promulgated several complex and counterintuitive beliefs as the cornerstones of its doctrine, and these were often replaced by simplified versions. Most Christians had no access to the labyrinthine treatises that had theoretically resolved such fundamental paradoxes as an all-powerful and benevolent deity who allowed evil to exist, a messiah who was simultaneously human and divine, a deity who was three different beings at once and who foreknew the fate of each individual but nevertheless managed to grant each person the free will to determine his or her own damnation or salvation. Nor for that matter did many parish priests have a much better idea, and Christian doctrine was often assimilated and adapted to local customs and traditions.

To be sure, the church hierarchy did attempt to control the situation as much as possible. Popular piety was directed into construction of the chapels, churches, cathedrals, and monasteries that represent one of the great wonders of world culture (see Color Plate 8). Translating (and mistranslating) the stories and lessons of scripture into narratives in stone and, later, stained glass, the cathedrals' very walls and windows constituted the primary religious education received by most Christians. And since they were produced by local masons and artists (albeit with a fair amount of input from church authorities), all manner of unorthodox subjects and beliefs found their way into the final product. Architects and artists were especially intrigued by the figure of the Devil and the sufferings of Hell, images closer at the time to popular beliefs and legends than to official theology.

> *. . . the cathedrals' very walls and windows constituted the primary religious education received by most Christians.*

When they found expression in less sanctioned directions, popular piety and the desire for a better life led to splinter movements quickly labeled as heretical and violently repressed. To be heretical meant to be preaching without having been trained and ordained in proper doctrine, or to be teaching or disseminating particular ideas that had been ruled to be contrary to official doctrine. The Lyon merchant who became known as Peter Waldo fell under the first category when the Church refused his request to preach a life of apostolic poverty. His movement, called the Waldensians after him, was also suspect because it included women, who had been barred by eleventh-century reforms from performing many ecclesiastical duties. When the Waldensians defied the ban on their preaching, their movement was condemned and suppressed. Perhaps the most widespread and enduring heresy was that of the Cathars, or Albigensians, who combined a protest against ecclesiastical wealth and privilege with an esoteric theology derived from Persia. As one peasant described them:

> They are men like the others! Their flesh, their bones, their shape, their faces are all exactly like those of other men! But they are the only ones to walk in the ways of justice and truth which the Apostle followed. They do not lie. They do not take what belongs to others. Even if they found gold or silver lying in their path, they would not "lift" it unless someone made them a present of it. Salvation is better achieved in the faith of these men called heretics than in any other faith.

Although it was ascetic in the extreme, requiring abstinence from all material things, including in the end a fasting unto death, in practice the intricate theology of Catharism just as often led to extremes of licentiousness, or so its accusers claimed. Catharism was strongest in the independent region of Languedoc, or Occitania, in what is now the southwest of France. The combined interests of the Church and the king of France in the north could not tolerate such dissent, and in 1208 Pope Innocent III proclaimed the Albigensian Crusade. Following a brutal twenty years of war that decimated the region, a papal Inquisition was instituted for the first time to root out any surviving heretics.

Crusading was an important way of uniting the Christians of Europe and channeling outward their military energy and thirst for plunder. Quixotic enthusiasts such as the founder of the Franciscan order of mendicant (or begging) friars saw it as their duty to convert the heathens across the Mediterranean (Saint Francis of Assisi was martyred in Egypt in 1226), but the customary ecclesiastical response to heathens was to kill them. The first Crusade was proclaimed by Pope Urban II in 1095 following the Byzantine emperor's request for aid against the Muslims. Urban took the opportunity to proclaim peace throughout the Latin west, prohibiting (with some success) the endemic local quarreling of Christian against Christian. Unfortunately, the inflamed piety of the Crusaders marching eastward took its toll on non-Christians along the way, especially the Jews, who were slaughtered indiscriminately. The Crusaders made it all the way to Jerusalem, which they took on 15 July 1099. The events were recorded by several eyewitnesses, including this anonymous Christian historian:

> *Crusading was an important way of uniting the Christians of Europe and channeling outward their military energy and thirst for plunder.*

> The pilgrims entered the city, pursuing and killing the Saracens up to the Temple of Solomon, where the enemy gathered in force. The battle raged throughout the day, so that the Temple was covered with their blood. When the pagans had been overcome, our men seized great numbers, both men and women, either killing them or keeping them captive, as they wished. . . . . Afterward, the army scattered throughout the city and took possession of the gold and silver, the horses and mules, and the houses filled with goods of all kinds. Rejoicing and weeping for joy, our people came to the Sepulchre of Jesus our Saviour to worship and pay their debt.

Following this initial triumph, Crusades were undertaken through the end of the thirteenth century in the Middle East, North Africa, and Spain, ending for the most part in calamitous defeat for the Christian armies. There were seven named Crusades, many other related expeditions, and even a disastrous Children's Crusade in 1212.

FEUDALISM

The Crusaders considered themselves pious warriors of the Lord and the booty they amassed during their crusading to be the just deserts of their piety. Their piety thus had a firm economic underpinning, for warfare was a way of life for an entire estate of the medieval population, the *chevalier,* or knight. Charlemagne had united most of Europe under what would later be called the Holy Roman Empire. After his death, the

C.TRANSIERVNT:FLVMEN:COSNONIS:ETVENERVNT   AD

hIC:hAROLD:DVX:TRAhEBAT:EOS:

DEARENA

Scenes from the Bayeux Tapestry, France, late 11th century. Attributed to Queen Matilda (wife of William the Conqueror) and her attendants, this great scroll of embroidered linen (230 feet long by 20 inches high) depicts the Norman Conquest of England in exuberant detail.

empire crumbled into pieces of various sizes and influence, each one occupied by a lord with a certain amount of land under his control, himself often beholden to other lords, dukes, or kings with broader jurisdictions. It was customary for holdings to be divided among all descendants upon the death of a lord, so there was no stable pattern of inheritance from first-born to first-born (the practice known as primogeniture). Lands were constantly being brought together and split apart in an endless, many-sided tug-of-war. As families intermarried and allegiances overlapped and inter-twined, the form of social and political organization known as feudalism emerged as a way of giving some sort of structure to this chaos.

Feudalism varied across Europe, but there were some fundamental features. The primary relation was between lord and vassal, formalized by an oath of fealty, swear-ing aid, mutual defense if attacked, and vengeance if one party were killed. Often, the knight would receive a fief, or holding of land, sometimes in perpetuity, but often for a shorter period of time, or for his lifetime only. Lord and vassal were thus bound by a set of laws and a broader set of customs and traditions of which many elements survive to this day in the abstract concepts of honor and chivalry, a phenomenon explored at uproarious length many centuries later in Cervantes's novel, *Don Quixote* (Volume C). In practice, of course, things were not as simple as Don Quixote would regard them: vassals were often obligated to several lords simultaneously, allegiances were bartered and sold, and a bond could dissolve in an instant if something better (for one party) came along. The following legal agreement from France offers one permutation of these variables:

I, Thiebault, count palatine of Troyes, make known to those present and to come that I have given in fee to Jocelyn d'Avalon and his heirs the manor which is called Gillencourt, which is of the castellanerie of La Ferte sur Aube; and whatever the same Jocelyn shall be able to acquire in the same manor I have granted to him and his heirs in augmentation of that fief. I have granted, moreover, that in no free manor of mine will I retain men who are of this gift. The same Jocelyn, moreover, on account of this has become my liege man, saving however, his allegiance to Gerard d'Arcy, and to the lord duke of Burgundy, and to Peter, count of Auxerre. Done at Chouaude, by my own witness, in the year of the Incarnation of our Lord 1200 in the month of January.

The Occitan poet Bertran de Born (page 1003) was less fortunate than Jocelyn: he spent much of his life fighting with his brother for sole possession of the family castle.

Epic and chivalric literature tended to codify this complexity into variations on the tension-laden situation of the heroic vassal and his weak and sometimes treacherous lord, often with a noble lady of whom her lord is insanely jealous. As the townspeople exclaim of the Castilian general, Rodrigo Díaz de Vivar (El Cid), "What a good vassal. If only he had a good lord!" (page 662). The main role of the vassal was to fight in battle by the side or in the name of his lord. With territorial boundaries shifting constantly, there were always grievances, whether local feuds or large-scale civil wars between heirs or pretenders to thrones.

> *With territorial boundaries shifting constantly, there were always grievances, whether local feuds or large-scale civil wars between heirs or pretenders to thrones.*

Moreover, the plunder and ransom that ensued from war were a fundamental ingredient of the medieval economy, especially in the later Middle Ages as trade with the wealthy East increased, luxury goods became more accessible, and greater debts were accumulated.

The other principal component of the feudal hierarchy was the worker. The traditional use of slaves for field labor was less customary by this time. There were some peasants of free status who owed only rent, but most were serfs, bound to both lord and land. In the commonest scenario, a serf would be allowed to cultivate a plot of land for himself in return for cultivating other plots belonging to the lord. In theory at least, the serf would also receive a place to live in the village appended to the local manor, with protection in the event of attack from outside. Still, hunger was the immediate concern, for survival was heavily dependent on the vagaries of nature. As the peasant hero of William Langland's fourteenth-century poem *Piers Plowman* laments:

> "I have no penny," quoth Piers, "Pullets° for to buy   *young hens*
> Nor neither geese nor piglets, but two green° cheeses,   *new*
> A few curds and cream and an oaten cake
> And two loaves of bread and beans to bake for my little ones.
> And besides I say by my soul I have no salt bacon,
> Nor no little eggs, by Christ, collops° for to make.   *bacon and eggs*
> But I have parsley and leeks and many cabbages,
> And besides a cow and a calf and a cart mare
> To draw afield my dung the while the drought lasteth.
> And by this livelihood we must live till lammas time.°   *August*
> And by that I hope to have harvest in my croft."°   *field*
>   (tr. Donaldson)

The clergy was equally embroiled in the feudal web, for local parish appointments and bishoprics were often controlled by local lords. A successful churchman had to be skilled in balancing the demands of the various local authorities with the needs of his parish and the orders that came from the papacy in Rome. Monasteries were also subject to such authority, as we see in the case of the abbess Hildegard von Bingen, who parlayed her fame as a visionary author into a charter for her own monastery at Bingen on the Rhine. Unsurprisingly, in a milieu rife with alliances and intrigues, the culture of feudalism excelled in the portrayal of situational ethics, using tales of knight errantry and epic heroism to explore the costs and benefits of the different choices of action and different types of behavior possible (or impossible) within the constraints of its world.

LYRIC AND SONG

The cultural milieu of the feudal world was the court. The love lyric was elaborated in the worldly Andalusian cities of Córdoba, Granada, and Seville, and it flourished in the isolated castles of Occitania, the Anglo-Norman courts of England, the northern French seats such as Troyes in Champagne, and the courts of the German monarchs. When they were not off fighting in battle, the knights and their lords required entertainment. This was the role of the *jongleur,* who would perform the songs produced by the troubadours and other songwriters around Europe. The lyrics reflect the interests of the audience: there is some singing of battle, a little of God, and much of the highly codified courtly pastimes of hunting, falconing, and, above all, lovemaking. For several centuries during the High Middle Ages, there was not a court without its resident poets, and the love lyrics they perfected remain with us to this day.

When they were not off fighting in battle, the knights and their lords required entertainment.

A four-line stanza by the German poet known as "The One from Kürenberg" succinctly combines the leisure-time pursuits of the court:

> I nurtured a falcon for more than a year.
> When I had him tamed exactly as I wished
> and had gracefully decked his feathers with gold
> he raised himself so high and flew to other lands.
>
> (tr. Dronke)

Medieval lyric is a celebration of skill: skill at wordplay, versification, and spinning new variations on familiar themes; skill at composition and performance; skill in the manly arts of hunting, falconry, and war; and skill at the dangerous game of love. As in these four lines, the celebration of skill usually is presented as a sensation of loss. The speaker is most likely a lady who has lost her lover, but the situation also resonates with those of the poet-lover and the feudal lord. The first two lines express the joy of taming a fiercely independent creature, which is also implicitly the joy of winning one's love, and also the essence of the feudal bond between lord and vassal. In an equally concise manner, the concluding lines vividly capture the dissolution of all three bonds, leaving the speaker with nothing to do but sing in sorrow.

Like the other activities of court, songwriting was considered a mark of high accomplishment for a ruler. And although many of the best songwriters were not of noble blood, many of noble blood were accomplished songwriters, including the first known troubadour, duke Guillem de Peiteus, and the Plantagenet ruler of England, Richard the Lion-Heart. Noblewomen, too, composed love-lyrics, some quite similar in tone to those of the men, others giving a different perspective on the theme of unrequited love between aspiring poet and unattainable lady, as in these unusually direct verses by the Comtessa de Dia:

> I have been in great distress
> for a knight for whom I longed;
> I want all future times to know
> how I loved him to excess.
>   Now I see I am betrayed—
> he claims I did not give him love—
> Such was the mistake I made,
> naked in bed, and dressed.
>   (tr. Dronke)

It is unlikely that these are literally confessional words; the emotions expressed in this manner were part of a highly developed vocabulary of courtly love. At the same time, the immediacy and power of the emotions could certainly have been based on experience. We will probably never know to what degree the medieval culture of courtly love was based in actual behavior. What we do know is that it was a great source of pleasure and an important means of making sense of the complex relations of power, desire, and envy endemic to feudal society.

Song was not restricted to the feudal courts. Hymns and chants were integral to the experience of mass, and to the everyday life of many monks and nuns. Many working songs survive as well, songs for spinning, songs of injustice and rebellion, songs mimicking the sounds of different occupations. The *jongleurs* and other performers who traveled from court to court were well versed in many genres besides the love lyric. At court, they might also perform traditional epics, such as the *Song of Roland,* the legendary tale of Charlemagne's worthy vassal, or folktales, such as those Marie de France translated in her *Lais,* or satirical and parodic songs. Perhaps not at court, but at inns and on the road, they might also perform from a broad repertory of popular songs for less cultivated audiences. There was an entire clerical caste known as the Goliards, or vagabond scholars, who specialized in Latin drinking songs, usually clever parodies of courtly love and religious lyric. Music and song were another medieval lingua franca, exalting commonalities of emotion, of sensation, and of life and death. Traveling performers and pilgrims carried both sacred and profane tunes and lyrics back and forth across the continent, adapting and transforming them to suit different audiences, different musical instruments, and different expectations.

Music and song were another medieval lingua franca, exalting commonalities of emotion, of sensation, and of life and death.

The Rise of the Cities

The irreverent songs of the vagabond scholars had little in common with the isolated refinement of the courts. The Goliard phenomenon was directly linked to the rise of cities and the universities within them in the twelfth and thirteenth centuries. A medieval culture developed in this milieu that was dependent neither on the feudal structure of the countryside nor the church-based hierarchy that had dominated the monasteries and what remained of northern towns in the earlier Middle Ages. The technology and social and political organization that would allow Europe to dominate the modern world emerged primarily from these cities: the printing press, the cannon, the expansive trading networks that would lead to global colonization and free market capitalism. There was no sudden leap from medieval to modern; rather, there was an urban culture in which many elements of what is now modern society were wholly intermingled with much that is now unfamiliar.

There was no sudden leap from medieval to modern . . .

The East had always been more densely populated and more highly civilized than the West, and through the first part of the Middle Ages, the only large Western cities were in the south of Europe, in Muslim Iberia and in Sicily, which was by turns Byzantine, Muslim, and Norman. Better crop rotation, a healthier diet, and new technology—the heavy plow, pulled by teams of horse or oxen, the water mill, and later the windmill—helped the population of Europe to double between the eleventh and the fourteenth centuries, from about 35 or 40 million to around 70 or 80 million. Increased political stability and long-distance trade contributed to the growth, as did a marked warming trend in the weather. The new population migrated to the growing cities, first in Italy, center of trade with the East and with North Africa, and later in northern Europe. Plying the rivers of Europe, commercial networks developed to link north and south further.

A new class emerged along with the traditional three estates of those who worked, those who prayed, and those who fought: those who produced, bought, and sold, the manufacturers and traders, or burghers of the towns. Early signs of their impact were to be found in the Lombard city-states, or communes, of northern Italy, where, according to the far-from-egalitarian historian Otto Freising in the twelfth century,

> There is hardly to be found any noble or great man with so great an influence, as not to owe obedience to the rule of his own city. And they are all accustomed to call these various territories their own *Comitatus,* from this privilege of living together. And in order that the means of restraining their neighbours may not fail, they do not disdain to raise to the badge of knighthood, and to all grades of authority, young men of low condition, and even workmen of contemptible mechanical arts, such as other people drive away like the plague from the more honourable and liberal pursuits.

In order to protect themselves from aristocratic tolls, merchants and manufacturers all over Europe began forming themselves into trade guilds, gaining charters from the local lords that guaranteed a certain amount of freedom and autonomy in their affairs and those of their towns.

The ability to congregate freely in towns and cities and imbibe new ideas of liberty and equality did not necessarily improve the everyday life of peasants and other laborers, but it certainly made them more likely to rebel. Violent reactions against injustice manifested the decline of the feudal system in the fourteenth century; during previous centuries similar feelings were more likely to have been expressed in the equally intense but less economically destructive modes of heresy and other forms of popular piety. Peasant revolts and uprisings occurred in the twelfth and thirteenth centuries, but they were particularly prevalent in the unsettled days of the fourteenth century, where figures such as the chaplain John Ball advised ridding the lands of "all the lords, and of the archbishops and bishops, and abbots, and priors, and most of the monks and canons," and where the peasants of Navarre could be so incensed at their lords as to rampage through the countryside burning every castle and house they found and slaughtering the inhabitants.

During these same centuries, European society was transformed from an oral to a literate culture. By 1300 commerce and government were dependent on written records and financial recordkeeping, introduced by Jewish merchants familiar with the practice from the wealthier and more sophisticated cultures of Islam and Byzantium. One reason for the rise of the universities was the need to train a body of clerks in these newly required skills. They gradually superseded the monastic schools, whose primary purpose had been the conservation of knowledge. The universities began as guilds of students and teachers, and only gradually became rooted in particular cities, buildings, and residential colleges. Many, such as those in Bologna, Paris, Oxford, Cambridge, Heidelberg, and Salamanca, survive to this day (see map, page 569). The standard curriculum was based on the foundation of classical education, the seven liberal arts. The first part was called the *trivium* of grammar and rhetoric (Latin language and literature) and logic, or dialectic; the second, the *quadrivium,* the sciences of geometry, arithmetic, astronomy, and music. Having completed these, the intrepid student might continue to the higher realms of theology (which included philosophy), canon law, and medicine. Students and teachers were frequently planning to be or already were members of the secular clergy, unattached to a monastery or particular church. This "clerkly" culture was instrumental in the philosophical and literary movement known as the twelfth-century renaissance: a renewed interest in classical philosophy and literature paired with an increased investment in rational argumentation and the study of the physical world. It also gave rise to a body of writings that used women as the target for an attack against marriage and sensuality steeped in the ascetic tradition of ancient Roman *virtus* while reveling in the worldliness it detailed. The ambivalence of clerkly misogyny was captured well in Chaucer's "Wife of Bath's Prologue."

It is hard to know whether the medieval city was a more corrupt place than the courts or the monasteries; what is certain is that its vices were more public and more freely documented. Students were notoriously rowdy, frequenting the brothels and gaming houses that sprang up around the universities. As the thirteenth-century teacher and philosopher John of Garland advised, "Even though you be a Socrates, if you have rude manners, you are a ditch-digger. . . . Regard as models of comportment the graven images of the churches, which you should carry in your mind as living and indelible pictures. . . . Be not a fornicator, O student, a robber, a murderer, a deceitful merchant, a champion at dice. In the choirstalls a cleric should chant without noise and commotion." Although his experience was by no means typical, the wild career of the fifteenth-century Parisian student and poet François Villon can stand as a notable extreme of the medieval student's life: his extracurricular activities included every one of those warned against by John of Garland. But even Villon was by no means lacking in pious sentiments and a firm belief in the concept of sin.

Villon treated life as matter-of-factly as he found it, an attitude that, at least as a consciously intellectual stance, dates to the twelfth century as well. Translations of Arabic sources had made more and more of classical philosophy and science available, accompanied by often heretical commentaries. The relationship between classical learning and faith-based doctrine became a more pressing issue than it had been since the days of Ambrose, Jerome, and Augustine. The intellectual focus on rationality and experience was seen by many religious figures to come at the expense of the basic tenets of the Christian faith. One of the great disputes of the twelfth century matched the Cistercian abbot and mystic Bernard of Clairvaux against the Parisian philosopher and teacher Peter Abelard, a reformed Goliard and veteran of a scandalous love affair with his then-student Heloïse. There were political differences involved, but Bernard's primary accusation was that Abelard was using the tools of logic to analyze those parts of doctrine—the trinity, the dual nature of Christ—which a devout Christian must take on faith. Abelard's questioning of received authority is well expressed by the title of one of his books, *Sic et Non*–Yes and No. Abelard lost: he was branded a heretic, forbidden to teach, and his books were burned.

Translations of Arabic sources had made more and more of classical philosophy and science available, accompanied by often heretical commentaries.

It was nothing so simple as a debate between religion and irreligion, however; Abelard was as devout in his way as Bernard. Nevertheless, the seeds of rational inquiry planted by him have been seen by many to spread through the Renaissance and into the Reformation, privileging the autonomy of the rational thinking mind from the mediation of the Roman Catholic church. In a similar way, the new burghers were for the most part also pious, although their piety didn't always manifest itself in ways pleasing to the ecclesiastical authorities. A common ground was found in the magnificent cathedrals erected during these centuries and funded in large part by the new urban wealth. Cathedrals such as Chartres or Notre Dame de Paris (see page 566), by far the tallest buildings in the land and visible for many miles, were holy places, but they were also the skyscrapers of their day, a brand-new architectural form symbolizing the new wealth and power of secular cities. The stained-glass windows (a twelfth-century innovation) are wonders of biblical storytelling; they also epitomize the art and invention of the urban artisans and manufacturers and the resources of the benefactors able to fund their artistry (see Color Plate 8). Cathedrals weren't simply houses of worship: they were guardians of relics and places of pilgrimage, the center of the social calendar, site of baptisms, marriages, and funerals. Since they often had at their feet the largest open spaces in the densely packed medieval city, they were the focal point of nearly every aspect of urban life.

ALLEGORY AND ADVENTURE

One of the reasons that so many different uses and contradictions could coexist in the same place and in a single person is that the medieval mind preferred analogy to symbolism. Post-medieval symbolic thinking typically attaches a unique and unchanging meaning to a specific word or object (the cathedral as a sacred place of worship), and an individual to a single, fixed identity from cradle to grave. By contrast, medieval modes of thinking tended to conceptualize the world in terms of a complex network of parallel relations. This habit of mind was grounded on doctrine: God was widely considered to have created two books, Scripture and the world. Consequently, each book could be assumed to possess a perfect structure capable of generating endless significance and meaning. Each object and every person in the world was capable at any time of assuming any number of roles in the greater narrative of a book that unrolled not only in space but in time. Viewed in this way, the cathedrals were urban Christendom's attempt to create another version of God's book, as complex and multifarious as the world, but also as cohesively full of significance. The visual programs of medieval cathedrals, the sculptures on the different porches and facades, the rose windows, the niches of the saints, the countless side details all fit into a grand narrative, a particular way of journeying through the stories and lessons of scripture. There are secular details as well—figures of benefactors scattered among the saints, corners of obscenity, and lovingly rendered pictures of sin—but these could be rationalized in the same way as Saint Augustine had rationalized evil: necessary in order for the sheer beauty of creation to stand out even more, an integral part of the divine plan.

In the endeavor to mimic the complexity of divine creation, many cathedrals included statuary and details hidden in the shadows of their highest and remotest corners, visible only to the eyes of God. When Dante Alighieri wrote the *Commedia,* his account of the three realms of the afterlife, he incorporated numerical sequences so recondite and complex that some of them have

> *In the endeavor to mimic the complexity of divine creation, many cathedrals included statuary and details . . .*
>
> *visible only to the eyes of God.*

come to light only with the help of computer technology. A critical device in this analogical way of thinking about the world was allegory, a mode of writing that marks nearly every aspect of medieval culture, most memorably perhaps in the realm of literature. To approach the world allegorically is to regard it as simultaneously possessing a multitude of meanings. When the pilgrim at the start of the *Inferno* encounters a wolf that blocks his way, Dante expected his reader to see more than just a wild beast encountered in a dark wood. He did not expect, however, that his reader would simply answer, "aha, a symbol of avarice" (a traditional meaning of a wolf in the Middle Ages). The wolf does carry the meaning of avarice, but it also carries an autobiographical significance related to Dante's misfortunes in his native city of Florence, as well as a probable reference to the ravagings of at least one specific political figure of the time. Just as medieval people were accustomed to juggling several languages and several different cultures, so were they accustomed to keeping multiple meanings in mind simultaneously, or to singing sacriligious songs in the tavern while piously praying in church, without feeling obligated to choose irrevocably between any of the several apparently contradictory possibilities.

Allegory began as a way of making sense of a passage in a sacred text that appeared on the surface to urge a behavior contrary to expectation. For early Christians, for example, this meant explaining how the patriarch Abraham could have had children by both his wife Sarah and his servant Hagar without simply saying that God had gotten the facts wrong or condoned a sin that was barely considered such in many parts of medieval Europe. Readers found it quite plausible that Abraham's sinless adultery could be historically true but also contain several hidden meanings more applicable to the current day. Such readings became especially popular in the High Middle Ages as a way of including obviously impious classical writers such as Ovid or philosophers such as Aristotle and Plato in the university curriculum. A similar process occurred earlier with non-Christian legends. We find, for example, moments of allegory in most Arthurian romances, especially when the knights leave the everyday world of the court for the shadowy Other World of adventure.

One of the effects of allegorical thinking is to splinter the linear development of plot and to make characters appear as something other than what we think of as psychologically unified. The epic hero El Cid is simultaneously the historical Rodrigo Díaz, a personification of the perfect vassal, a figure of the ideal Christian, a loosely tied-together conglomeration of several different legends about El Cid, and an argument for the legitimacy of the new Castilian nation; little wonder that he doesn't resemble the unified profile of a contemporary drama. The mysterious behavior of the Green Knight in the fourteenth-century romance *Sir Gawain and the Green Knight* is neither psychologically consistent nor immediately comprehensible; nevertheless, it compels the reader's attention, demanding that his riddle be solved even as the complexities of the characters and events belie any simple answer. Significance inheres not in how characters change and evolve over the course of a narrative, but in the analogy between different situations in which they find themselves, the actions they take, the interplay between the different possible meanings of characters and events, and the similarities with and the differences from other works in the same genre.

This is true as well in narratives that are not obviously allegorical. In the *Lais* of Marie de France, for example, we find a series of stories that repeat specific situations of feudal life almost as if the author is running through all of the different permutations of knight, lady, and lord. What happens if the knight has a secret he must keep from his lady, and the lady is not worthy of it? What happens if the court is not worthy of the knight who belongs to it? Medieval narratives in general expect their readers not to identify with the characters so much as to analogize with them. In Marie's *Lais*, the reader soon realizes that a major concern is the place of individual needs and desires in a social milieu that doesn't officially recognize them. But this important theme is nowhere spelled out explicitly, nor is it developed with reference to a single character. It appears by reading and translating back and forth between analogous situations, actions and characters with slight variations in set-up and outcome.

The medieval world, like the literature that has survived from it, is a fascinating combination of familiarity and alienness. We recognize many of the myths, many of the stories, characters, and genres as those of our own time. We see institutions, languages, and monuments that are still with us today. We acknowledge many of the same injustices and prejudices. But if we make the mistake of seeing all of these familiar features as identical with those of our own time, we risk seeing only that period that used to be called the Middle Ages, a middling apprenticeship to the modern world. In order to come to terms with the legacy of this thousand years of history, and to enjoy it, we should remind ourselves how alien so much of it is, not so much in substance as in attitude. Much that seems to us traditional, even timeless, was in fact brand new in the Middle Ages, from chivalry and love poetry to the cathedrals and cities to the Catholic Christian church and the very idea of Europe. And much of what the Renaissance chose to exclude from its idea of the Middle Ages, especially the legacy of the classical world, was for the medieval person a fact of everyday life. To think medievally is to think several ways at once; that was their great accomplishment and the great challenge and joy their literature poses to a modern reader, accustomed to think in one language, one culture, and one identity at a time.

> *Much that seems to us traditional, even timeless, was in fact brand new in the Middle Ages . . .*

PRONUNCIATIONS:
Boccaccio: boh-KAH-chee-oh
Cancioneros: kahn-see-oh-NEHR-ohz
Charlemagne: SHAHR-le-mahn
Chaucer: CHAHW-sehr
Dante: DAHN-teh
Lais: lay
Occitan: OH-ki-tahn
Petrarch: PEH-trahrk
Trobairitz: troh-bah-REETS
Troubadours: TROO-bah-dorz

Beowulf
c. 750–950

"I had always thought of English literature as the richest in the world," wrote the Argentine poet Jorge Luis Borges of his experience of first reading Old English poetry; "the discovery now of a secret chamber at the very threshold of that literature came to me as an additional gift." It is easy to fall under the spell of *Beowulf*'s strangeness and antiquity, of a poetry that makes its characters feel both alien and intensely present, as if freshly arisen from centuries of oblivion beneath the earthen mounds where the Geats and other Germanic tribes would bury their fallen leaders. *Beowulf* is replete with the pagan customs of the *comitati,* the warrior-bands that in the fifth century had swept across Europe from their strongholds in the north: Angles, Saxons, and Jutes across the North Sea to England, Ostrogoths and other tribes southward to topple the Roman Empire. Their heroic code, steeped in values such as revenge, honor, and the gift-giving recalled by Borges above, imbues the poem with the sense of an epoch already lost to time, just as the narrative mirrors its account of the youthful exploits of the hero Beowulf with the story of the end of his long life, battling against a marauding dragon. Composed several centuries later, in a world since converted to Christianity, and set in a land across the North Sea, *Beowulf* is intensely engaged with the ways in which change occurs—from old customs to new, kings to heirs, heathen to Christian, oral culture to the written word—and the deeply conflicted feelings such changes never fail to elicit.

Much of the history of the poem's reception resembles the "secret chamber" of which Borges wrote. We don't know when or where it was composed—hypotheses range from seventh-century East Anglia or Northumbria to tenth-century England—nor do we know who wrote it, layperson or cleric, or whether it was originally written at all—some scholars believe it was dictated by a *scop,* a bard or singer of tales at an Anglo-Saxon court. It survives, by chance, in a single manuscript known as the Nowell Codex, which was copied by two scribes around the year 1000. Nothing is known of its history before the sixteenth century; it was scorched in a fire and nearly destroyed in 1731, and no one realized its value until the early nineteenth century, when it was transcribed and edited by a Danish scholar. Although the author assumed his audience had prior knowledge of the underlying history, there are few known sources for the events described, nor did the poem leave a discernible trace on the literature that came after it—until, that is, the nineteenth century. Like its hero, it seems to stand alone.

THE SOCIAL WORLD

Also like its hero, however, *Beowulf* is immersed in a highly developed and sophisticated social world. Its first two parts, some 2,000 lines, are set in the land of the Danes, the Scyldings, or descendants of Scyld, a people blessed by fate, prosperous and secure. When they construct a glorious mead-hall, a gathering place for drinking and feasting, their harp-songs disturb a neighbor, the man-monster Grendel, who plagues their land for a dozen years. The young retainer Beowulf hears of their plight, journeys across the sea from his home in Geatland (in what is now southwestern Sweden), and purges the land of its monsters. In the second part, some thousand lines, more than fifty years have passed, and Beowulf himself now rules the Geats, who find themselves threatened by a monster of their own, a treasure-hoarding dragon awakened from its slumber by a clumsy thief. Beowulf slays the dragon but loses his life, and the poem concludes as the Geats bury their leader and lament their fate, exposed to the might of the neighboring peoples—the Swedes, the Frisians, the Franks—who will lose no time in seizing their land and goods, and probably their lives. *Lif is læne,* the poem tells us, "life is transitory."

The main action revolves around three fights with three superbly imagined monsters: Beowulf pitted against Grendel in the mead-hall, against Grendel's vengeful mother in her underwater lair, and against the dragon in its buried barrow-mound. And while the poem gives ample space to the battle descriptions that were essential to any heroic narrative, the poet was equally engrossed by the intricate web of events and associations touched upon during these duels or arising out of them. Rather than using the linear narration familiar from classical Greek and Latin literature, the *Beowulf* poet structured his story in what scholars of oral poetry call "ring composition"—interlinked rings radiating out from the central events. Viewed this way, the fight with Grendel's mother would occupy the poem's center, while the prior battle with her son and the subsequent combat with the dragon would "ring" the center, developing related themes in parallel and in contrast. Similarly, paired episodes with queens both introduce (Hildeburh and Wealhtheow) and follow (Hygd and Modthryth) the encounter with Grendel's mother, raising other questions of succession and conflict between generations, and probing the place of women in the warrior-code of the Germanic tribes.

The poet—and we can assume his audience as well—delighted in interpolating episodes from other times and places, sometimes flashbacks to prior conflicts—such as the tale of Sigemund the dragon-slayer—sometimes glimpses of events to come in the future, and sometimes barely connected tales of past blood-feuds. He (or perhaps she, as a few critics have conjectured) expected the audience or readers not only to fill in the context behind the often brief hints of famous or infamous deeds, but also to read laterally, moving sideways through the text from connection to connection, comparing and contrasting different characters, different situations, different outcomes. As in the *Lais* of Marie de France, the *Poem of the Cid,* and many other medieval narratives, an entire social milieu and a complex ethic emerge not so much from individual psychology or particular events, as from a broader mirroring. As in the Mali *Epic of Son-Jara* (page 534), the narrative's multiple detours and asides take a call-and-response form, filled with repetitions of situations and events, even ones we have already seen, as when Beowulf, returned to his lord Hygelac, recounts the fights we have already heard about, but gives them a new meaning for a new context.

THE POEM'S DOUBLE VISION

In addition to this horizontal structure of parallels and contrasts, there is also a vertical structure to the poem that derives from the gap in time between the date of the events and the date of composition. Although most of the characters (with the exception of Beowulf, who seems to have been a fictional creation) appear elsewhere in Scandinavian legend and genealogies, only Hygelac's death in battle with the Frisians (in what is now the northern Netherlands) can actually be documented (somewhere between 515 and 530 C.E.). Between this period and the composition of the poem, Christianity had spread through the region, and the poet depicted the lives of the heathen Germans from the point of view of a pious Christian. Rather than simply dismiss their pre-Christian practices or transform these ancestors into practicing Christians, the poet struck a fragile balance, leaving much unsaid. The pagan characters voice pious sentiments—"put aside pride," counsels the wise old Danish king Hrothgar—somewhere between the harsh realities of the heroic code and the metaphysical dictates of the Christian virtues. When depicting certain practices incompatible with the rituals of the newer religion—burial rites, for example, or the Danes' panicked prayer to "war-idols" (lines 155–161)—the narrator will sometimes note the distinction. For the most part, however, the peoples of the poem exist in a threshold world neither wholly pagan nor wholly Christian, where God is known but the mysteries of Christ and the sacraments are not, and where a heathen delight in booty and pride in fighting prowess do not preclude a deep-seated religiosity—a situation perhaps not so different from that of the recently converted Angles and Saxons of early-medieval England. The poem's audience could read the poem in either direction, finding the descendants of Cain in Grendel and Satan in the serpentine Dragon, and an allegory of the ideal Christian ruler in Beowulf, or recalling the blood-feuds, gift-giving, and pleasures of the mead-hall in the old customs, or merging them together in their imagination.

Names were a key component of the ability to view the world doubly, for Christianity entered the language through already existing words. It is impossible to know to what degree the poem's original audience would have heard a Norse god or the Christian God in words such as *metod* (which originally meant "fate") or *dryhten* ("ruler," "king"), that could now refer to either figure. Similarly, a phrase such as "the Lord lent them aid in their anguish, weaving their war-luck" (page 605, lines 623–624) combines a Christian sentiment of a grace-bestowing God with a pagan image of a God weaving a web of fate. A term like *wyrd,* another word for fate, which appears throughout the poem to describe the destined moment of a warrior's death, could be accepted either as a natural force ruling the world or as a synonym for divine Providence, inscrutable to mortals but part of God's plan. Word-weaving was fundamental to the composition of Old English poetry, and just as new concepts could be grafted onto preexistent names and terms, so the *scop*'s skill was demonstrated by the ability to make new and unforeseen combinations out of the "word-hoard" of the oral tradition.

Characters' names are themselves compounds. Scyld Scefing ("shield of the sheaf") is the founder of the Danish royal house; the name Beowulf means "bear," literally a "bee-wolf," a plunderer of bees for their honey. The fundamental facts of the warriors' world are likewise not granted simple names, but "kennings," combinations evoking their attributes, their uses, their greater meaning—the poem contains more than 1,500 compounds. The sea can be a "whale-road" or a "swan's road"; a king a "ring-giver" or a "treasure-giver"; weapons, ships, and sails receive similar treatment. Words have power in this world—to define and to enhance a character, to provoke, as when the *scop*'s song arouses Grendel to carnage, or to send to defeat, as when Beowulf humbles the envious Unferth in a *flyting,* or verbal duel. Part of this variation is due to the requirements of oral composition: different epithets, names of different metrical lengths can be used as needed to fill out the lines of the heroic song, but this variety equally bespeaks a way of thinking about the world as an interconnected web of relationships, just as genealogies defined people in terms of their heritage, and alliances and blood-feuds alternated in a give-and-take of gifts and blows.

THE POETRY AND LANGUAGE

Repetition and variation are at the heart of Old English poetry, for its unrhymed meter is based in alliteration, a repeated consonant in different words. The lines of *Beowulf* consist of two half-verses separated by a caesura, or pause, with two beats or stressed syllables in each half. The first beat of the first half always alliterates with the first beat of the second half; the second beat of the first half may also alliterate, but not the final beat of the line. Thus the dragon's revenge on the Geats for the theft of its treasure:

> . . . Hord-weard onbād
> earfoðlīce, oððæt æfen cwōm;
> wæs ðā gebolgen beorges hyrde
> wolde [s]e lāða līge forgyldan
> drinc-fæt dȳre. þā wæs dæg sceacen
> wyrme on willan; nō on wealle læ[n]g
> bīdan wolde, ac mid bæle fōr,
> fȳre gefȳsed.

A literal translation by Howard J. Chickering gives a good sense of the word-choice and rhythm of the passage:

> . . . The hoard-keeper waited,
> miserable, impatient, till evening came.
> By then the barrow-snake was swollen with rage,
> wanted revenge for that precious cup,
> a payment by fire. The day was over
> and the dragon rejoiced, could no longer lie
> coiled within walls but flew out in fire,
> with shooting flames.[1]

---

1. This rendering makes a useful comparison to the fluidity and compactness of Sullivan and Murphy's version used in this anthology (page 636, lines 2030–2035).

Standard formulae—*oððæt æfen cwōm, þā wæs dæg sceacen*—punctuate the passage of time as the dragon waits for its nighttime revenge. The repetition of its names stresses its waiting and its power, while the variation in kennings—*Hord-weard, beorges hyrde*—and the earthy metaphor of its proper name, *wyrme*, allies the dragon's character both with man—hoard-keeper, miserable, vengeful, enraged, rejoicing—and beast—coiled, fire-breathing, monstrous. Through it all, the lines keep the forward beat as the alliteration also looks back to the beginning of the line, undulating like the dragon as it awaits its burst into freedom, *fȳre gefȳsed.*

As the scholar of Old English, J. R. R. Tolkien, wrote in an influential essay on a poem he would incorporate in significant ways into his novels of epic fantasy, the poet "esteemed dragons, as rare as they are dire. . . . He liked them—as a poet, not as a sober zoologist; and he had good reason." The poet's gift was to make a dragon that was simultaneously real and marvelous, symbolic and deadly, human and bestial. In just the same way he blended Christian borrowings with Scandinavian legend, the incompatible opposites of which the medieval world would be wrought, refusing to yield either to one or to the other, holding past and future counterbalanced together.

PRONUNCIATIONS:
Beowulf: BAY-oh-woolf
Jorge Luis Borges: HOR-hay loo-WEES BOR-hayz
Geats: KHAY-ahts
Hrothgar: HRAWTH-gahr
Hygd: heegd
Hygelac: HEE-ah-lack
Wealhtheow: WAYL-thay-oh
Weohstan: WAY-oh-stan

Beowulf[1]
1. Grendel

So! The Spear-Danes   in days of old
were led by lords   famed for their forays.
We learned of those princes'   power and prowess.
Often Scyld Scefing[2]   ambushed enemies,
5 took their mead-benches,   mastered their troops,
though first he was found   forlorn and alone.[3]
His early sorrows   were swiftly consoled:
he grew under heaven,   grew to a greatness
renowned among men   of neighboring lands,
10 his rule recognized   over the whale-road,
tribute granted him.   That was a good king!

Afterward God   gave him an heir,
a lad in the hall   to lighten all hearts.
The Lord had seen   how long and sorely

---

1. The modern English translation is by Alan Sullivan and Timothy Murphy (2002, revised 2003).
2. The traditional founder of the Danish royal house. His name means "shield" or protection of the "sheaf," suggesting an earlier association in Norse mythology with the god of vegetation. The Danes are known afterward as "Scyldings," descendants of Scyld.

3. Scyld Scefing arrives among the Danes as a foundling, a dangerous position in both Norse and Anglo-Saxon cultures. Solitaries and outcasts were generally regarded with suspicion; it is a tribute to Scyld Scefing that he surmounted these obstacles to become the leader and organizer of the Danish people.

15   the people had languished   for lack of a leader.
        Beow[4] was blessed   with boldness and honor;
        throughout the North   his name became known.
        A soldierly son   should strive in his youth
        to do great deeds,   give generous gifts
20   and defend his father.   Then in old age,
        when strife besets him,   his comrades will stand
        and his folk follow.   Through fair dealing
        a prince shall prosper   in any kingdom.

        Still hale on the day   ordained for his journey,
25   Scyld went to dwell   with the World's Warder.
        His liegemen bore   his bier to the beach:
        so he had willed   while wielding his words
        as lord of the land,   beloved by all.
        With frost on its fittings,   a lordly longboat
30   rode in the harbor,   ring-bowed and ready.
        They placed their prince,   the gold-giver,
        the famous man   at the foot of the mast,
        in the hollow hull   heaped with treasures
        from far-off lands.   I have not heard another
35   ship ever sailed   more splendidly stocked
        with war-weapons,   arms and armor.
        About his breast   the booty was strewn,
        keepsakes soon to be   claimed by the sea.
        So he'd been sent   as a child chosen
40   to drift on the deep.   The Danes now returned
        treasures no less   than those they had taken,
        and last they hoisted   high overhead
        a golden banner   as they gave the great one
        back to the Baltic   with heavy hearts
45   and mournful minds.   Though clever in council
        or strong under sky,   men cannot say
        or know for certain   who landed that shipload.

        But the son of Scyld   was hailed in the strongholds
        after the father   had fared far away,
50   and he long ruled   the lordly Scyldings.
        A son was born   unto Beow also:
        proud Healfdene,   who held his high seat,
        battle-hardened   and bold in old age.
        Four offspring   descended from Healfdene,
55   awake in the world: Heorogar, Hrothgar,
        kindly Halga;   I have heard that the fourth
        was Onela's queen[5]   and slept with the sovereign
        of warlike Swedes.

---

4. The manuscript reads "Beowulf" here, the copyist's mind having skipped ahead to the story's protagonist.
5. The daughters of Germanic royal families were married to the heads of opposing tribes in an attempt to cement military alliances. Often, as here, they are not named in the poem.

Hrothgar was granted

swiftness for battle   and staunchness in strife,[6]

60 so friends and kinfolk   followed him freely.
His band of young soldiers   swelled to a swarm.
In his mind he mulled   commanding a meadhall
higher than humankind   ever had heard of,
and offering everyone,   young and old,

65 all he could give   that God had granted,
save common land   and commoners' lives.
Then, I am told,   he tackled that task,
raising the rafters   with craftsmen summoned
from many kingdoms   across Middle-Earth.

70 They covered it quickly   as men count the time,
and he whose word   held the land whole
named it Heorot,[7]   highest of houses.
The prince did not fail   to fulfill his pledge:
feasts were given,   favor and fortune.

75 The roof reared up;   the gables were great,
awaiting the flames   which would flare fiercely
when oaths were broken,   anger awakened;
but Heorot's ruin   was not yet at hand.[8]

Each day, one evil   dweller in darkness

80 spitefully suffered   the din from that hall
where Hrothgar's men   made merry with mead.
Harp-strings would sound,   and the song of the scop
would recount the tales   told of time past:
whence mankind had come,   and how the Almighty

85 had fashioned flat land,   fair to behold,
surrounded with water.   The worker of wonders
lifted and lit   the sun and moon
for Earth's dwellers;   He filled the forests
with branches and blooms;   He breathed life

90 into all kinds of creatures.
So the king's thanes
gathered in gladness;   then crime came calling,
a horror from hell,   hideous Grendel,
wrathful rover   of borders and moors,
holder of hollows,   haunter of fens.

95 He had lived long   in the homeland of horrors,
born to the band   whom God had banished
as kindred of Cain,   thereby requiting
the slayer of Abel.[9]   Many such sprang

---

6. Significantly, Hrothgar is not the first-born of his generation. Leadership of the tribe was customarily conferred by acclamation upon the royal candidate who showed the greatest promise and ability.

7. The name of Hrothgar's hall in Anglo-Saxon literally means "hart" or "stag," a male deer. The epithet "adorned with horns," which is applied to Heorot later, may further suggest its function as a hunting lodge.

8. The peace concluded between the Danes and the Heathobards through intermarriage is already doomed before it has taken place. The events foreshadowed here will occur long after the time of the poem.

9. See Genesis 4:3–16.

from the first murderer: monsters and misfits,
100   elves and ill-spirits,   also those giants
whose wars with the Lord   earned them exile.

After nightfall   he nosed around Heorot,
saw how swordsmen   slept in the hall,
unwary and weary   with wine and feasting,
105   numb to the sorrows   suffered by men.
The cursed creature,   cruel and remorseless,
swiftly slipped in.   He seized thirty thanes
asleep after supper,   shouldered away
what trophies he would,   and took to his lair
110   pleased with the plunder,   proud of his murders.

When daylight dawned   on the spoils of slaughter,
the strength of the fiend   was readily seen.
The feast was followed   by fits of weeping,
and cries of outrage   rose in the morning.
115   Hrothgar the strong   sank on his throne,
helpless and hopeless   beholding the carnage,
the trail of the terror,   a trouble too wrathful,
a foe too ferocious,   too steadfast in rage,
ancient and evil.   The evening after
120   he murdered again   with no more remorse,
so fixed was his will   on that wicked feud.
Henceforth the fearful   were easily found
elsewhere, anywhere   far from the fiend,
bedding in barns,   for the brutal hall-thane
125   was truly betokened   by terrible signs,
and those who escaped   stayed safer afar.

So wrath fought alone   against rule and right;
one routed many;   the mead-hall stood empty.
Strongest of Spear-Danes,   Hrothgar suffered
130   this fell affliction   for twelve winters' time.
As his woes became known   widely and well,
sad songs were sung   by the sons of men:
how season on season,   with ceaseless strife,
Grendel assailed   the Scylding's sovereign.
135   The monster craved   no kinship with any,
no end to the evil   with wergeld[1] owed;
nor might a king's   council have reckoned
on quittance come   from the killer's hand.
The dark death-shadow   daunted them all,
140   lying in ambush   for old and young,
secretly slinking   and stalking by night.

---

1. A cash payment for someone's death. *Wergeld* was regarded as an improvement over violent revenge, and Grendel is marked as uncivilized because he refuses to acknowledge this practice.

No man knows where   on the misty moor
the heathen keepers   of hell-runes[2] wander.

So over and over   the loathsome ogre
145   mortally menaced   mankind with his crimes.
Raiding by night,   he reigned in the hall,
and Heorot's high   adornments were his,
but God would not grant   throne-gifts to gladden
a scourge who spurned   the Sovereign of Heaven.

150   Stricken in spirit,   Hrothgar would often
closet his council   to ponder what plan
might be deemed best   by strong-minded men.
Sometimes the elders   swore before altars
of old war-idols,   offering prayers
155   for the soul-slayer   to succor their people.[3]
Such was their habit,   the hope of heathens:
with hell in their hearts,   they were lost to the Lord.
Their inmost minds   knew not the Almighty;
they never would worship   the world's true protector.

160   Sorry is he   who sears his soul,
afflicted by flames   he freely embraced.
No cheer for the chastened!   No change in his fate!
But happy is he   whom heaven welcomes,
and after his death-day   he dwells with the Father.

165   So in his sorrow   the son of Healfdene[4]
endlessly weighed   how a wise warrior
might fend off harm.   The hardship this foe
of his folk inflicted   was fierce and long-lasting,
most ruinous wrath   and wracking night-evil.

170   A thane[5] of Hygelac   heard in his homeland
of Grendel's deeds.   Great among Geats,[6]
this man was more mighty   than any then living.
He summoned and stocked   a swift wave-courser,
and swore to sail   over the swan-road
175   as one warrior should   for another in need.
His elders could find   no fault with his offer,
and awed by the omens,   they urged him on.
He gathered the bravest   of Geatish guardsmen.
One of fifteen,   the skilled sailor
180   strode to his ship   at the ocean's edge.

2. By rendering the Old English *helrunan*, which means "those adept in the mysteries of hell," as "heathen keepers of hell-runes," the translators are taking the liberty of suggesting that "demons" such as Grendel are familiar with runes—the letters of the early Germanic alphabet.
3. In their fear, the Danes resume heathen practices. In Christian belief, the pagan gods were transformed into devils.
4. Hrothgar. He is referred to by his patronymic, his father's name, as is frequent with male characters in the poem.
5. One of the king's principal retainers, chief among these being the earls.
6. A Germanic tribe who lived along the southwestern coast of what is now Sweden.

He was keen to embark: his keel was beached
under the cliff   where sea-currents curled
surf against sand;   his soldiers were ready.
Over the bow   they boarded in armor,
185   bearing their burnished   weapons below,
their gilded war-gear   to the boat's bosom.
Other men shoved   the ship from the shore,
and off went the band,   their wood-braced vessel
bound for the venture   with wind on the waves
190   and foam under bow,   like a fulmar in flight.[7]

On the second day   their upswept prow
slid into sight   of steep hillsides,
bright cliffs, wide capes   at the close of their crossing,
the goal of their voyage   gained in good time.
195   Swiftly the sailors   steered for the shore,
moored their boat   and debarked on the berm.
Clad in corselets   of clattering mail,
they saluted the Lord   for their smooth sailing.

From the post he held   high on the headland,
200   a Scylding had spied   the strangers bearing
bright bucklers   and battle-armor
over their gangplank.   Avid for answers
and minded to know   what men had come hence,
Hrothgar's thane   hastened on horseback
205   down to the beach   where he brusquely brandished
spear-haft in hand   while speaking stern words:

"What warriors are you,   wearers of armor,
bearers of weapons,   daring to bring
your lofty longboat   over the sea-lane?
210   Long have I looked   out on the ocean
so foreign foes   might never float hither
and harry our homeland   with hostile fleets.
No men have ever   more brazenly borne
shields to our shores,   nor have you sought
215   leave from our lords   to land in this place,
nor could you have known   my kin would consent.
I have never beheld   an earl on this earth
more mighty in arms   than one among you.
This is no hall-warmer,   handsome in harness,
220   showy with shield,   but the noblest of knights
unless looks belie him.   Now let me know
who are your fathers   before you fare further
or spy on the Danes.   I say to you, sailors
far from your homes: hear me and hasten
225   to answer me well.   Whence have you wandered?"

7. Gull-like sea bird of the far north Atlantic.

Why have you come?"
                              Wisest with words,
the eldest offered   an answer for all:
"From Geat-land we come;   we are Geatish men,
sharers of Hygelac's   hearth and hall.
230 My father was famous   among our folk
as a lordly leader   who lived many winters
before, full of years,   he departed our fastness.
His name was Ecgtheow.   All over Earth
every wise man   remembers him well.
235 We have landed in friendship   to look for your lord,
the son of Healfdene,   sovereign of Scyldings.
Give us good guidance: a great errand
has driven us hence   to the holder of Danes.
Our purpose is open;   this I promise;
240 but you could attest   if tales tell the truth.
They speak of some scourge,   none can say what,
secretly stalking   by night among Scyldings,
a shadowy shape   whose malice to men
is shown by a shameful   shower of corpses.
245 I offer Hrothgar,   with honest heart,
the means to make   an end to this menace.
Wise and good,   he will win his reward,
the scalding surges   of care will be cooled
if ever such awful   evil is vanquished.
250 So his sorrows   shall swiftly be soothed
or else his anguish   haunt him, unaltered,
as long as his house   holds on the hilltop."

Astride his steed,   the guard spoke again:
"A sharp-witted warrior   often must weigh
255 words against works   when judging their worth.
This I have learned: you honor our lord.
Thus you may come,   though clad in corselets
and weaponed for war.   I shall show you the way.
Meanwhile those thanes   who are mine to command
260 shall stand by the ship   you steered to our shore.
No thief will trouble   your newly-tarred craft
before you return   and take to the tide.
A swan-necked bow   will bear you back
to your windward coast.   Most welcome of men,
265 may you be granted   good fortune in battle,
enduring unharmed   the deed you would do."

So they set out   while the ship sat at rest,
the broad-beamed vessel   bound to the beach,
lashed by its lines.   Lustrous boar-icons
270 glinted on cheek-guards.   Adorned with gold,
the flame-hardened helms   defended their lives.
Glad of their mettle   while marching together,

the troop hastened   until they beheld
the highest of halls   raised under heaven,
275 most famed among folk   in foreign lands.
Sheathed with gold   and grandly gabled,
the roof of the ruler   lit up his realm.
The foremost warrior   waved them forward
and bade the band go   straight to that building,
280 court of the king   and his brave kinsmen.
Reining his steed,   he spoke a last word:
"It is time I returned.   May All-Ruling Father
favor your errand.   I fare to the ocean,
to watch and ward off   wrathful marauders."

285 The street was stone-paved;   a straight path
guided the band.   Byrnies glittered,
jackets of chain-mail   whose jingling rings,
hard and hand-linked,   sang on harnesses.
Marshaled for battle,   they marched to the building.
290 Still sea-weary,   they set their broad-shields
of well-hardened wood   against Heorot's wall.
Their corselets clinked   as they bent to a bench
and stood their sturdy   spears in a row,
gray from the ash grove,   ground to sharp points.
295 This was a war party   worthy of weapons.

Then a proud prince   questioned their purpose:
"Where are you bringing   these burnished bosses,
these gray mail-shirts,   grimly-masked helms
and serried spears?   I am Hrothgar's
300 herald and door-ward.   I have never beheld
a band of wanderers   with bearings so brave.
I believe that boldness   has brought you to Hrothgar,
not banishment's shame."
                                    The eldest answered,
hard and hardy   under his helmet,
305 a warlike prince   of the Weder[8] people:
"We are Hygelac's   hearth-companions.
My name is Beowulf;   my purpose, to bear
unto Healfdene's son,   your lordly leader,
a message meant   for that noblest of men,
310 if he will allow us   leave to approach."

Wise Wulfgar,   man of the Wendels,
known to many   for boldness in battle,
stoutly spoke out: "I shall ask our sovereign,
well-wisher of Danes   and awarder of wealth,
315 about this boon   you have come to request

---

8. An alternate name for Geat.

and bear you back,   as soon as may be,
whatever answer   the great man offers."

He went straightaway   where Hrothgar waited,
old and gray-haired,   with thanes gathered round.

320 Squarely he stood   for his king to assess him.
Such was the Scylding   custom at court,
and so Wulfgar spoke   to his sovereign and friend:
"Far-sailing Geats   have come to our kingdom
across the wide water.   These warriors call

325 their leader *Beowulf*   and bid me bring
their plea to our prince,   if it pleases him
to allow them entrance   and offer them audience.
I implore you to hear them,   princely Hrothgar,
for I deem them worthy   of wearing their armor

330 and treating with earls.   Truly the elder
who led them hither   is a lord of some stature."

Helm of the Scyldings,   Hrothgar held forth:
"I knew him once.   He was only a lad.
His honored father,   old Ecgtheow,

335 received the sole   daughter of Hrethel.
The son now seeks us   solely from friendship.
Seamen have said,   after sailing hence
with gifts for the Geats,   that his hand-grip would match
the might and main   of thirty strong men.

340 The West-Danes[9] have long   awaited God's grace.
Here is our hope   against Grendel's dread,
if I reckon rightly   the cause of his coming.
I shall give this brave man   boons for boldness.
Bring him in quickly.   The band of my kinsmen

345 is gathered together.   Welcome our guest
to the dwelling of Danes."
                         Then Wulfgar went
through the hall's entry   with word from within:
"I am ordered to answer   that the lord of East-Danes
honors your father   and offers you welcome,

350 sailors who sought us   over the sea-waves,
bravely bent   on embarking hither.
Now you may march   in your mail and masks
to behold Hrothgar.   Here you must leave
war-shields and spears   sharpened for strife.

355 Your weapons can wait   for words to be spoken."

The mighty one rose   with many a man
marshaled about him,   though some were bidden
to stay with the weapons   and stand on watch.

---

9. Hrothgar is, in fact, king of all the Danes: North, South, East, and West. The different terms merely conform to the Anglo-Saxon alliterative pattern established in each line.

Under Heorot's roof   the rest hastened
360   when Beowulf brought them   boldly before
the hearth of Hrothgar.   Helmed and hardy,
the war-chief shone   as he stood in skillfully
smithied chain-mail   and spoke to his host:

"Hail to you, Hrothgar!   I am Hygelac's
365   kinsman and comrade,   esteemed by the king
for deeds I have done   in the years of youth.
I heard in my homeland   how Grendel grieves you.
Seafarers say   that your splendid hall
stands idle and useless   after the sun
370   sinks each evening   from Heaven's height.
The most honored among us,   earls and elders,
have urged me to seek you,   certain my strength
would serve in your struggle.   They have seen me return
bloody from binding   brutish giants,
375   a family of five   destroyed in our strife;
by night in the sea   I have slain monsters.
Hardship I had,   but our harms were avenged,
our enemies mastered.   Now I shall match
my grip against Grendel's   and get you an end
380   to this feud with the fiend.   Therefore one favor
I ask from you, Hrothgar,   sovereign of Spear-Danes,
shelter of shield-bearers,   friend to your folk:
that I and my officers,   we and no others,
be offered the honor   of purging your hall.
385   I have also heard   that the rash thing reckons
the thrust of a weapon   no threat to his thews,[1]
so I shall grab   and grapple with Grendel.
Let my lord Hygelac   hear and be glad
I foreswore   my sword and strong shield
390   when I fought for life   with that fearsome foe.
Whomever death takes,   his doom is doubtless
decreed by the Lord.   If I let the creature
best me when battle   begins in this building,
he will freely feast   as he often has fed
395   on men of much mettle.   My corpse will require
no covering cloth.   He will carry away
a crushed carcass   clotted with gore,
the fiend's fodder   gleefully eaten,
smearing his lonesome   lair on the moor.
400   No need to worry   who buries my body
if battle takes me.   Send back to my sovereign
this best of shirts   which has shielded my breast,
this choice chain-mail,   Hrethel's heirloom
and Weland's work.[2]   Fate goes as it will."

---

1. Well-developed sinew or muscle.   2. Legendary blacksmith of the Norse gods.

405 Helm of the Scyldings,   Hrothgar answered:
"It is fair that you seek   to defend us, my friend,
in return for the favor   offered your father
when a killing fanned   the fiercest of feuds
after he felled   the Wylfing, Heatholaf.
410 Wary of war,   the Weder-Geats wanted
Ecgtheow elsewhere,   so over the sea-swells
he sought the South-Danes,   strong Scyldings.
I had lately become   king of my kinsmen,
a youth ruling   this jewel of a realm,
415 this store-house of heroes,   with Heorogar gone,
my brother and better,   born of Healfdene.
I calmed your father's   quarrel with wergeld
sent over sea   straight to the Wylfings,
an ancient heirloom;   and Ecgtheow's oath
420 I took in return.
                          "It pains me to tell
what grief Grendel   has given me since,
what harm in Heorot,   hatred and shame
at his sudden onset.   My circle is shrunken;
my guardsmen are gone,   gathered by fate
425 into Grendel's grip.   How simply the Sovereign
of Heaven could hinder   deeds of this hell-fiend!
Beer-swollen boasters,   brave in their ale-cups,
often have sworn   to stay with their swords
drawn in the dark,   to strike down the demon.
430 Then in the morning   the mead-hall was drenched,
blood on the bench-boards,   blood on the floor,
the highest of houses   a horror at dawn.
Fewer were left   to keep faith with their lord
since those dear retainers   were taken by death.
435 But sit now to sup   and afterward speak
of soldierly pride,   if the spirit prompts you."

A bench was then cleared   there in the beer-hall
so all of the Geats   could sit together,
sturdy soldiers,   proud and stout-hearted.
440 A dutiful Dane   brought them bright ale-cups
and poured sweet mead   while the scop was singing
high-voiced in Heorot.   That host of warriors,
Weders and Scyldings,   shared in the wassails.

But envious Unferth,[3]   Ecglaf's son,
445 spat out his spite   from the seat he took
at his sovereign's feet.   The seafarer's quest
grieved him greatly,   for he would not grant

---

3. Hrothgar's spokesman or court jester; his rude behavior toward Beowulf is consistent with other figures in epics and romances who taunt the hero before he undertakes his exploits. "Unferth" may mean "strife."

any man ever,   in all middle-earth,
more fame under heaven   than he himself had.

450   "Are you that Beowulf   Breca bested
when both of you bet   on swimming the straits,
daring the deep   in a dire struggle,
risking your lives   after rash boasting?
Though friend or foe,   no man could deflect
455   your foolhardy foray.   Arms flailing,
you each embraced   the billowing stream,
spanned the sea-lane   with swift-dipping hands
and wended over   the warring ocean.
Winter-like waves   were roiling the waters
460   as the two of you toiled   in the tumult of combers.
For seven nights   you strove to outswim him,
but he was the stronger   and saw at sunrise
the sea had swept him   to Heathoraem[4] shores.
Breca went back   to his own homeland,
465   his burg on the bluff,   stronghold of Brondings,
a fair realm and wealthy.   The wager was won;
Beanstan's son   had brought off his boast.
However you fared   in onslaughts elsewhere,
I doubt you will live   the length of a night
470   if you dare to linger   so near Grendel."

Then Beowulf spoke,   son of Ecgtheow:
"Listen, Unferth,   my fuddled friend
brimful of beer,   you blabber too much
about Breca's venture.   I tell you the truth:
475   my force in the flood   is more than a match
for any man   who wrestles the waves.
Boys that we were,   brash in our youth
and reckless of risk,   both of us boasted
that each one could swim   the open ocean.
480   So we set forth,   stroking together
sturdily seaward   with swords drawn
hard in our hands   to ward off whale-fish.
No swifter was he   in those heaving seas;
each of us kept   close to the other,
485   floating together   those first five nights.
Then the storm-surges   swept us apart:
winter-cold weather   and warring winds
drove from the north   in deepening darkness.
Rough waves rose   and sea-beasts raged,
490   but my breast was bound   in a woven mail-shirt.
Hard and hand-linked,   hemmed with gold,
it kept those creatures   from causing me harm.

---

4. Coastal tribe of central Sweden near the Norwegian border.

I was drawn to the depths,   held fast by the foe,
grim in his grasp;   yet granted a stab,
495 I stuck in my sword-point,   struck down the horror.
The mighty sea-monster   met death by my hand.

"Often afterward   snatchers of swimmers
snapped at my heels.   With my strong sword
I served them fitly.   I would fatten no foes,
500 feed no man-banes   munching their morsels
when setting to feast   on the floor of the sea.
Instead at sunrise   the sword-stricken
washed up in windrows   to lie lifelessly,
lodged by the tide-line,   and nevermore trouble
505 sailors crossing   the steep-cliffed straits.
As God's beacon   brightened the East,
I spied a cape   across calming seas,
a windward wall.   So I was spared,
for fate often favors   an unmarked man
510 if he keeps his courage.   My sword was the slayer
of nine monsters.   I've not heard of many
who fended off   a more fearsome assault
while hurled by the waves   under heaven's vault.
Yet I broke the beasts' grip   and got off alive,
515 weary of warfare.   Swiftly surging
after the storm,   the sea-current swept me
to Finland's coast.
                    "Such close combat
or stark sword-strokes   you have not seen,
you or Breca.   No tale has told
520 how either of you two   ever attempted
so bold a deed   done with bright sword,
though I would not claim   a brother's bane
if the killing of kin   were all I'd accomplished.
For that you are certain   to suffer in Hell,
525 doomed with the damned   despite your swift wit.
I say straight out,   son of Ecglaf,
that ghastly Grendel,   however gruesome,
would never have done   such dreadful deeds,
harming your lord   here in his hall,
530 if your spirit were stern,   your will, warlike,
as you have affirmed.   The foe has found
that he need not reckon   with wrathful swords
or look with alarm   on the likes of you,
Scylding victor.   He takes his tribute,
535 sparing no man,   snatching and supping
whenever he wishes   with wicked delight,
expecting no strife   with spear-bearing Danes.
But soon, very soon,   I shall show him the strength
and boldness of Geats   giving him battle.

540
When morning comes   to light up the land,
you may go again   and gladly get mead
as the bright sun   beams in the South
and starts a new day   for the sons of men."

Gray-haired Hrothgar,   giver of hoard-wealth,
545
was happy to hear   Beowulf bolster
hope for his folk   with forthright avowal.
About the Bright-Danes'   battle-leader
rang warriors' laughter   and winsome words.
The queen, Wealtheow,[5]   by custom courteous,
550
greeted the party   aglitter with gold
and bore the full cup   first to her lord,
the keeper of East-Danes,   dear to his people,
bidding him drink   and be glad of his beer.
That soldierly sovereign   quaffed and supped
555
while his Helming princess   passed through the hall
offering everyone,   young man and old,
the dole he was due.   Adorned with rings,
she bore the burnished   mead-bowl to Beowulf,
last of them all,   and honored the Geat
560
with gracious words,   firm in her wisdom
and grateful to God   for granting her wish.
Here was the prayed-for   prince who would help
to end the ill deeds.   He emptied the cup
Wealtheow offered;   then the willing warrior,
565
Ecgtheow's son,   spoke as one ready
for strife and slaughter:
                    "When I set my ship
to sail on the sea   and steered her hence
with my squadron of swords,   I swore to fulfill
the will of the Scyldings   or die in the deed,
570
fall with the slain,   held fast by the foe,
my last day lived out   here in your hall."

The wife was well-pleased   with Beowulf's words,
this oath from the Geat;   and glinting with gold
the queen, Wealtheow,   went to her king.
575
Boasts were bandied   once more in the beer-hall,
the hearty speech   of a hopeful household,
forceful fighters.   But soon the sovereign,
son of Healfdene,   hankered for sleep.
He knew his enemy   brooded on battle
580
all day from dawn   until deepening dusk.
Covered by darkness,   the creature would come,

---

5. "Weal theow" means "foreign slave," and she may be British or Celtic in origin. Even after her marriage to Hrothgar, she continues to maintain her identity as the "lady of the Helmings," an epithet recalling her father Helm.

a shade under shadows.   The company stood.
One man to another,   Hrothgar hailed
brave Beowulf,   wishing him well
585   and granting him leave   to guard the wine-hall.

"So long as my hand   has hefted a shield,
I never have yielded   the Danes' mansion
to any man else,   whatever his mettle.
Now you shall hold   this highest of houses.
590   Be mindful of fame;   make your might known;
but beware of the brute.   You will want no boon
if you tackle this task   and live to request it."

Hrothgar and his princes   departed the hall;
the warder of Danes   went to his woman,
595   couched with his queen.   The King of Glory
had granted a guard   against Grendel's wrath,
as all had now learned.   One man had offered
to take on this task   and watch for the terror.
The leader of Geats   would gladly trust
600   the force of God's favor.   He flung off his mail-shirt,
then handed his helmet   and inlaid sword
to the steward assigned   safe-keeping of iron
and gilded war-gear.   Again the bold
Beowulf boasted   while bound for his bed:

605   "I am no weaker   in works of war,
no less a grappler   than Grendel himself.
Soon I shall sink him   into his death-sleep,
not with my sword   but solely by strength.
He is unschooled in skills   to strike against me,
610   to shatter my shield,   though feared for his fierceness.
So I shall bear   no blade in the night
if he sees fit   to fight without weapons.
May God in His wisdom   grant whom He wills
blessing in battle."
               The brave soldier
615   stretched out for sleep,   and a bolster pillowed
his proud cheekbone.   About him were sprawled
the strong sea-warriors,   each one wondering
whether he ever   would walk once again
his beloved land,   or find his own folk
620   from childhood's time   in an untroubled town.
All had been told   how often before
dreadful death   had swept up the Danes
who lay in this hall.   But the Lord lent them
aid in their anguish,   weaving their war-luck,
625   for one man alone   had the might and main
to fight off the fiend,   crush him in combat,

proving who ruled   the races of men,
then and forever: God, the Almighty.[6]

Cunningly creeping,   a spectral stalker
630   slunk through the gloom.   The bowmen were sleeping
who ought to have held   the high-horned house,
all except one,   for the Lord's will
now became known: no more would the murderer
drag under darkness   whomever he wished.
635   Anger was wakeful,   watching the enemy;
hot-hearted Beowulf   was bent upon battle.

Then from the moor   under misty hillsides,
Grendel came gliding   girt with God's anger.
The man-scather sought   someone to snatch
640   from the high hall.   He crept under clouds
until he caught sight   of the king's court
whose gilded gables   he knew at a glance.
He often had haunted   Hrothgar's house;
but he never found,   before or after,
645   hardier hall-thanes   or harder luck.
The joyless giant   drew near the door,
which swiftly swung back   at the touch of his hand
though bound and fastened   with forge-bent bars.
The building's mouth   had been broken open,
650   and Grendel entered   with ill intent.
Swollen with fury,   he stalked over flagstones
and looked round the manse   where many men lay.
An unlovely light   most like a flame
flashed from his eyes,   flared through the hall
655   at young soldiers dozing   shoulder to shoulder,
comradely kindred.   The cruel creature laughed
in his murderous mind,   thinking how many
now living would die   before the day dawned,
how glutted with gore   he would guzzle his fill.
660   It was not his fate   to finish the feast
he foresaw that night.
                  Soon the Stalwart,
Hygelac's kinsman,   beheld how the horror,
not one to be idle,   went about evil.
For his first feat   he suddenly seized
665   a sleeping soldier,   slashed at the flesh,
bit through bones   and lapped up the blood
that gushed from veins   as he gorged on gobbets.
Swiftly he swallowed   those lifeless limbs,
hands and feet whole;   then he headed forward

6. This interpolation of Christian belief into what is essentially a pagan tradition has been taken as evidence of a conscious rewriting of much earlier material. The narrative assures its reader that Christian beliefs were still valid, regardless of what the characters in the story may have believed.

670   with open palm   to plunder the prone.
         One man angled   up on his elbow:
         the fiend soon found   he was facing a foe
         whose hand-grip was harder   than any other
         he ever had met   in all Middle-Earth.
675   Cravenly cringing,   coward at heart,
         he longed for a swift   escape to his lair,
         his bevy of devils.   He never had known
         from his earliest days   such awful anguish.

         The captain, recalling   his speech to the king,
680   straightaway stood   and hardened his hold.
         Fingers fractured.   The fiend spun round;
         the soldier stepped closer.   Grendel sought
         somehow to slip   that grasp and escape,
         flee to the fens;   but his fingers were caught
685   in too fierce a grip.   His foray had failed;
         the harm-wreaker rued   his raid on Heorot.
         From the hall of the Danes   a hellish din
         beset every soldier   outside the stronghold,
         louder than laughter   of ale-sodden earls.
690   A wonder it was   the wine-hall withstood
         this forceful affray   without falling to earth.
         That beautiful building   was firmly bonded
         by iron bands   forged with forethought
         inside and out.   As some have told it,
695   the struggle swept on   and slammed to the floor
         many mead-benches   massive with gold.
         No Scylding elders   ever imagined
         that any would harm   their elk-horned hall,
         raze what they wrought,   unless flames arose
700   to enfold and consume it.   Frightful new sounds
         burst from the building,   unnerved the North-Danes,
         each one and all   who heard those outcries
         outside the walls.   Wailing in anguish,
         the hellish horror,   hateful to God,
705   sang his dispair,   seized by the grip
         of a man more mighty   than any then living.

         That shielder of men   meant by no means
         to let the death-dealer   leave with his life,
         a life worthless   to anyone elsewhere.
710   Then the young soldiers   swung their old swords
         again and again   to save their guardian,
         their kingly comrade,   however they could.
         Engaging with Grendel   and hoping to hew him
         from every side,   they scarcely suspected
715   that blades wielded   by worthy warriors
         never would cut   to the criminal's quick.
         The spell was spun   so strongly about him

that the finest iron   of any on earth,
the sharpest sword-edge   left him unscathed.
720   Still he was soon   to be stripped of his life
and sent on a sore   sojourn to Hell.
The strength of his sinews   would serve him no more;
no more would he menace   mankind with his crimes,
his grudge against God,   for the high-hearted kinsman
725   of King Hygelac   had hold of his hand.
Each found the other   loathsome in life;
but the murderous man-bane   got a great wound
as tendons were torn,   shoulder shorn open,
and bone-locks broken.   Beowulf gained
730   glory in war;   and Grendel went off
bloody and bent   to the boggy hills,
sorrowfully seeking   his dreary dwelling.
Surely he sensed   his life-span was spent,
his days upon days;   but the Danes were grateful:
735   their wish was fulfilled   after fearsome warfare.

Wise and strong-willed,   the one from afar
had cleansed Heorot,   hall of Hrothgar.
Great among Geats,   he was glad of his night-work
ending the evil,   his fame-winning feat,
740   fulfilling his oath   to aid the East Danes,
easing their anguish,   healing the horror
they suffered so long,   no small distress.
As token of triumph,   the troop-leader hung
the shorn-off shoulder   and arm by its hand:
745   the grip of Grendel   swung from the gable!

Many a warrior   met in the morning
around Hrothgar's hall,   so I have heard.
Folk-leaders fared   from near and far
over wide lands   to look on the wonder,
750   the track of the terror,   glad he had taken
leave of his life   when they looked on footprints
wending away   to the mere of monsters.
Weary and weak,   defeated in war,
he dripped his blood-trail   down to dark water,
755   tinting the terrible   tide where he sank,
spilling his lifeblood   to swirl in the surge.
There the doomed one   dropped into death
where he long had lurked   in his joyless lair,
and Hell received   his heathen soul.

760   Many went hence: young men and old
mounted white mares   and rode to the mere,
a joyous journey   on brave battle-steeds.
There Beowulf's   prowess was praised
and approved by all.   Everyone said

765   that over the Earth   and under bright sky,
       from north to south   between sea and sea,
       no other man   was more worthy of wearing
       corselet or crown,   though no one denied
       the grace of Hrothgar: that was a good king.

770   Sometimes they galloped   great-hearted bays;
       races were run   where roads were smooth
       on open upland.   Meanwhile a man
       skilled as a singer,   versed in old stories,
       wove a new lay   of truly-linked words.

775   So the scop started   his song of Beowulf's
       wisdom and strength,   setting his spell
       with subtle staves.   Of Sigemund[7] also
       he said what he knew: many marvels,
       deeds of daring   and distant journeys,

780   the wars of Waels' son,   his wildness, his sins,
       unsung among men   save by Fitela,
       Sigemund's nephew,   who knew his secrets
       and aided his uncle   in every conflict
       as comrade-at-need.   A whole clan of ogres

785   was slain by the Waelsing   wielding his sword.
       No small esteem   sprang up for Sigemund
       after his death-day.   Dauntless in war,
       he struck down a serpent   under gray stone
       where it held its hoard.   He fared alone

790   on this fearsome foray,   not with Fitela;
       but fate allowed him   to lunge with his blade,
       spitting the scaly   worm to the wall.
       His pluck repaid,   Sigemund was pleased
       to take his pick   of the piled-up treasure

795   and load bright arms   in his longboat's breast
       while the molten worm   melted away.

       Thus that wayfarer   famed far and wide
       among nations of men,   that mighty war-maker,
       shelter of shield-bearers,   outshone another:

800   unhappy Heremod,[8]   king of the Danes,
       whose strength, spirit,   and courage were spent.
       He fell among foes,   was taken by traitors
       and swiftly dispatched.   So his sorrows
       ended at last.   Too long had lords

805   and commoners suffered,   scourged by their king,
       who ought to have honored   his father's office,

---

7. The story of Sigemund is also told in the Old Norse *Volsunga Saga* and with major variations in the Middle High German *Niebelungenlied*. The scop's comparison of Sigemund with Beowulf is ironic in that the order and the outcome of Beowulf's later encounter with a dragon will be reversed.

8. Heremod, an earlier Danish king, was the stock illustration of the unjust and unwise ruler. After bringing bloodshed upon his own house, Heremod took refuge among the Jutes, who eventually put him to death.

defending his homeland,   his hoard and stronghold.
Evil had entered him.   Dearer to Danes
and all humankind   was Hygelac's kinsman.

810 Still running heats,   the horses hurtled
on sandy lanes.   The light of morning
had swung to the south,   and many men sped,
keen to behold   the hall of the king,
the strange sights inside.   Hrothgar himself,
815 keeper of treasures   and leader of troops,
came from the queen's   quarters to march
with measured tread   the track to his mead-hall;
the queen and her maidens   also came forth.
He stopped on the stairs   and gazed at the gable,
820 glinting with gold   behind Grendel's hand.

"My thanks for this sight   go straight to Heaven!
Grendel has given me   grief and grievance;
but God often works   wonders on wonders.
Not long ago   I had no hope at all
825 of living to see   relief from my sorrows
while slaughter stained   the highest of houses,
wide-spilling woes   the wisest advisors
despaired of stanching.   None of them knew
how to fend off our foes: the ghosts and ghasts
830 afflicting our folk   here in our fastness.
Now, praise Heaven,   a prince has proven
this deed could be done   that daunted us all.
Indeed the mother   who bore this young man
among mankind   may certainly say,
835 if she still is living,   that the Lord of Old
blessed her child-bearing.   Henceforth, Beowulf,
best of the brave,   I shall hold you in heart
as close as a son.   Keep our new kinship,
and I shall award you   whatever you wish
840 that is mine to command.   Many a time
I have lavished wealth   on lesser warriors,
slighter in strife.   You have earned your esteem.
May the All-Wielder   reward you always,
just as He gives you   these goods today."

845 Beowulf spoke,   son of Ecgtheow:
"We gladly engaged   in this work of war
and freely faced   the unknowable foe,
but I greatly regret   that you were not granted
the sight of him broken,   slathered with blood.
850 I sought to grip him   swiftly and strongly,
wrestle him down   to writhe on his death-bed
as life left him,   unless he broke loose.
It was not my fate   to fasten the man-bane

firmly enough.   The fiend was so fierce
855   he secured his escape   by leaving this limb
to ransom his life,   though little the wretch
has gained for his hurt,   held in the grip
of a dire wound,   awaiting death
as a savage man,   besmirched by his sins,
860   might wait to learn   what the Lord wills."

Unferth was silent.   He spoke no more boasts
about works of war   when warriors gazed
at the hand hanging   from Heorot's roof,
the fiend's fingers   jutting in front,
865   each nail intact,   those terrible talons
like spikes of steel.   Everyone said
that the strongest sword   from smithies of old,
the hardest iron   edge ever forged,
would never have harmed   that monstrous mauler,
870   those bloody claws   crooked for combat.

2. Grendel's Mother

Inside Heorot   many hands hastened
at Hrothgar's command: men and women
washed out the wine-hall,   unfurled on the walls
gold-woven hangings   to gladden their guests,
875   each of whom gazed   wide-eyed in wonder.
Though bound with iron,   the bright building
was badly battered,   its hinges broken.
Only the roof   had escaped unscathed
before the fell creature   cringed and fled,
880   stained by his sin   and despairing of life.
Flee it who will,   a well-earned fate
is not often altered,   for every earth-dweller
and soul-bearing son   must seek out a spot
to lay down his body,   lie on his death-bed,
885   sleep after feasting.
              So came the season
for Healfdene's son   to stride through his hall:
the king himself   would sup with his kin.
I have never heard   in any nation
of such a great host   so graciously gathered,
890   arrayed on benches   around their ruler,
glad of his fame   and glad for the feast.
Many a mead-cup   those masterful kinsmen
Hrothgar and Hrothulf   raised in the hall.
All were then friends   who filled Heorot,
895   treason and treachery   not yet contrived.[1]

---

1. Possibly an allusion to the later usurpation of the Danish throne by Hrothgar's nephew Hrothulf.

Crowning his conquest,   the King of the Danes
bestowed on the soldier   a battle-standard
embroidered with gold,   a helmet, mail-shirt,
and unblemished blade   borne out while ranks
900   of warriors watched.   Then Beowulf drank
a flagon before them: he would feel no shame
facing bold spearmen   with boons such as these.
Not many men   on mead benches
have given another   four golden gifts
905   in friendlier fashion.   The head-guard was flanged
with windings of wire.   Facing forward,
it warded off harm   when the wearer in war
was obliged to bear shield   against enemy blades
that were hammer-hardened   and honed by files.
910   The sovereign ordered   eight swift steeds
brought to the court   on braided bridles.
One bore a saddle   studded with gems
and glinting gold-work: there the great king,
son of Healfdene,   would sit during sword-strife,
915   never faltering,   fierce at the front,
working his will   while the wounded fell.
Then Hrothgar awarded   horses and weapons
both to Beowulf,   bade that he keep them
and wield them well.   So from his hoard
920   he paid the hero   a princely reward
of heirlooms and arms   for braving the battle;
no man could fairly   or truthfully fault them.

That lord also lavished   gifts on the Geats
whom Beowulf brought   over broad seas,
925   and wergeld he gave   for the one Grendel
had wickedly killed,   though the creature would surely
have murdered more   had God in his wisdom,
man in his strength   failed to forestall it.
So the Almighty   has always moved men;
930   yet man must consistently   strive to discern
good from evil,   evil from good
while drunk with days   he dwells in this world.

Music and story   now sounded together
as Hrothgar's scop   sang for the hall-fest
935   a tale often told   when harp was held:[2]
how Finn's followers,   faithless Jutes,

---

2. The following episode is one of the most obscure in *Beowulf*. It seems that Hnaef and Hildeburh are both children of an earlier Danish king named Hoc and that Hildeburh has been sent to marry Finn, the son of Folcwalda and king of the Jutes and Frisians, in order to conclude a marriage alliance and thus settle a prior blood feud between the two tribes. Upon going to visit his sister and her husband, Hnaef is treacherously ambushed and killed by Finn's men; Hildeburh's son by Finn is also killed. In her role as peace-weaver, Hildeburh is torn by conflicting allegiances, foreshadowing the fate of Hrothgar's own daughter Freawaru in her marriage to Ingeld.

fell to fighting   friends in his fortress;
how Hnaef the Half-Dane,   hero of Scyldings,
was fated to fall   in Frisian warfare;
940 how by shield-swagger   harmless Hildeburh,
faithful to Finn   though daughter of Danes,
lost her beloved   brother and son
who were both born   to be struck by spears.
Not without cause   did Hoc's daughter
945 bewail the Lord's will   when morning awoke:
she who had known   nothing but happiness
beheld under heaven   the horror of kin-strife.

War had taken   its toll of attackers;
few men remained   for Finn to muster,
950 too few to force   the fight against Hengest,
a dutiful thane   who had rallied the Danes.
As tokens of truce   Finn offered these terms:
a haven wholly   emptied of foes,
hall and high seat,   with an equal share
955 in gifts given   his own gathered kin.
Each time he treated   his sons to treasures
plated with gold,   a portion would go
to sweeten Hengest's   stay in his hall.
The two sides swore   a strict treaty;
960 and Finn freely   affirmed to Hengest
that all would honor   this oath to the Danes,
as his council decreed,   and further declared
no Frisian would ever,   by word or work,
challenge the peace   or mention with malice
965 the plight of survivors   deprived of their prince
and wintered-in   at the slayer's stronghold.
Should any Frisian   enter in anger,
the sword's edge   would settle the quarrel.

That oath offered,   the hoard was opened
970 for gold to array   the greatest of War-Danes.
Iron-hard guardians   gilded with gold,
bloody mail-shirts   and boar-tusked helms
were heaped on his bier,   awaiting the balefire.
Many a warrior,   weakened by wounds,
975 had faltered and fallen   with foes he had slain.
Hildeburh ordered   her own dear son
be placed on the pyre,   the prince and his uncle
shoulder to shoulder.   Their bodies were burned
while the stricken lady   sang out her sorrow.
980 Streamers of smoke   burst from the bier
as corpses kindled   with cruelest of flames.
Faces withered,   wounded flesh yawned,
and blood boiled out   as the blaze swallowed
with hateful hunger   those whom warfare

985   had borne away,   the best of both houses.
       Their glory was gone.
                         The Frisians were fewer
       heading for home;   their high stronghold
       was empty of allies.   For Hengest also
       that winter was woeful,   walled up in Frisia,
990   brooding on bloodshed   and longing to leave,
       though knowing his vessel   never could breast
       the wind-darkened swells   of a wide ocean
       seething with storms,   or break the ice-bindings
       that barred his bow   from the bitter waters.
995   Constrained to wait   for kindlier weather,
       he watched until spring,   season of sunlight,
       dawned on men's dwellings   as ever it did
       and still does today.   Winter withdrew
       and Earth blossomed.
                         Though the exile was eager
1000   to end his visit,   he ached for vengeance
       before sailing home.   Loathe to foreswear
       the way of this world,   he schemed to assail
       the sons of slayers.   So Hengest heeded
       Hunlaf's son,   who laid on his lap
1005   the sword War-Flame,   feared by all foes,
       asking its edge   be offered the Jutes.
       His heart was hot;   he could hold back no more;
       gladly he answered   Guthlaf and Oslaf,
       who wrathfully spoke   of the wrong they suffered,
1010   the shame of Scyldings   sharing their plight.
       Then fierce-hearted Finn   fell in his turn,
       stricken by swords   in his own stronghold.
       The building was bloody   with bodies of foemen:
       the king lay slain,   likewise his kin;
1015   and the queen was captured.   Scyldings carried
       off in their ship   all of the chattels
       found in Finn's fortress,   gemstones and jewels.
       The lady was borne   to the land of her birth.

       So that story   was sung to its end,
1020   then mirth mounted   once more in Heorot.
       Revelry rang   as wine-bearers brought
       finely-wrought flagons   filled to the brim.
       Wearing her circlet,   Wealtheow walked
       where uncle and nephew,   Hrothgar and Hrothulf,
1025   were sitting in peace,   two soldiers together,
       each still believing   the other was loyal.
       Likewise the officer,   Unferth, was honored
       to sit at the feet   of the Scylding sovereign.
       Everyone thought him   honest and trustworthy,
1030   blameless and brave,   though his blade had unjustly

stricken a kinsman.
　　　　　　So the queen spoke:
"Receive this cup,　sovereign of Scyldings,
giver of gold;　drink and be glad;
greet the Geats mildly　as well a man might,
1035　mindful of gifts　graciously given
from near and far,　now in your keeping.
They say you would name　that knight as a son
for purging the ring-hall.　Employ as you please
wealth and rewards,　but bequeath to your kin
1040　rule of this realm　when the Ruler of All
holds that you must.　I know that Hrothulf
will honor our trust　and treat these youths well
if you have to leave　this life before him.
I am counting on him　to recall our kindness
1045　when he was a child　and repay our children
for presents we gave　and pleasures we granted."

She turned to the bench　where her sons were seated,
Hrethric and Hrothmund.　Between the two brothers
Beowulf sat;　and the cup-bearer brought him
1050　words of welcome,　willingly gave him
as tokens of favor　two braided arm-bands,
jerkin, corselet,　and jeweled collar
grander than any　other on Earth.[3]
I have heard under heaven　of no higher treasure
1055　hoarded by heroes　since Hama stole off
to his fair fortress　with Freya's necklace,
shining with stones　set by the Fire-Dwarves.
So Hama earned　Eormanric's anger,
and fame for himself.　Foolhardy Hygelac,
1060　grandson of Swerting　and sovereign of Geats,
would wear it one day　on his final foray.
He fell in the fray　defending his treasure,
the spoils he bore　with his battle-standard.
Recklessly raiding　the realm of Frisia,
1065　the prince in his pride　had prompted misfortune
by crossing the sea　while clad in that collar.
He fell under shield,　fell to the Franks,
weaker warriors　stripping the slain
of armor and spoil　after the slaughter.
1070　Hygelac held　the graveyard of Geats.

The hall approved　the princely prize
bestowed by the queen,　and Wealtheow spoke

---

3. The narrative jumps ahead beyond Beowulf's return home to the Geats. His uncle, Hygelac, the king, will not only receive the collar from Beowulf but will die with it in battle among the Frisians. The collar thus connects different events at different times.

for the host to hear: "Keep this collar,
beloved Beowulf.   Bear this armor,
1075   wealth of our realm.   May it ward you well.
Swear that your strength   and kindly counsel
will aid these youngsters,   and I shall reward you.
Now your renown   will range near and far;
your fame will wax wide,   as wide as the water
1080   hemming our hills,   homes of the wind.
Be blessed, Beowulf,   with abundant treasures
as long as you live;   and be mild to my sons,
a model admired.   Here men are courtly,
honest and true,   each to the other,
1085   all to their ruler;   and after the revels,
bolstered with beer,   they do as I bid."

The lady left him   and sat on her seat.
The feast went on;   fine wine was flowing.
Men could not know   what fate would befall them,
1090   what evil of old   was decreed to come
for the earls that evening.   As always, Hrothgar
headed for home,   where the ruler rested.
A great many others   remained in the hall,
bearing bright benches   and rolling out beds
1095   while one drunkard,   doomed and death-ripened,
sprawled into sleep.   They set at their heads
round war-shields,   well-adorned wood.
Above them on boards,   their battle-helms rested,
ringed mail-shirts   and mighty spear-shafts
1100   waiting for strife.   Such was their wont
at home or afield,   wherever they fared,
in case their king   should call them to arms.
Those were stern people.

                     They sank into slumber,
but one paid sorely   for sleep that evening,
1105   as often had happened   when grim Grendel
held the gold-hall,   wreaking his wrongs
straight to the end: death after sins.
It would soon be perceived   plainly by all
that one ill-wisher   still was alive,
1110   maddened by grief: Grendel's mother,
a fearsome female   bitterly brooding
alone in her lair   deep in dread waters
and cold currents   since Cain had killed
the only brother   born of his father.
1115   Marked by murder,   he fled from mankind
and went to the wastes.   Doomed evil-doers
issued from him.   Grendel was one,
but the hateful Hell-walker   found a warrior
wakefully watching   for combat in Heorot.

1120   The monster met there   a man who remembered
        strength would serve him,   the great gift of God,
        faith in the All-Wielder's   favor and aid.
        By that he mastered   the ghastly ghoul;
        routed, wretched,   the hell-fiend fled,
1125   forlornly drew near   his dreary death-place.
        Enraged and ravenous,   Grendel's mother
        swiftly set out   on a sorrowful journey
        to settle the score   for her son's demise.

        She slipped into Heorot,   hall of the Ring-Danes,
1130   where sleeping soldiers   soon would endure
        an awful reversal.   Her onslaught was less
        by as much as a woman's   mettle in war
        is less than a man's   wielding his weapon:
        the banded blade   hammered to hardness,
1135   a blood-stained sword   whose bitter stroke
        slashes a boar-helm   borne into battle.
        In the hall, sword-edge   sprang from scabbard;
        broadshield was swung   swiftly off bench,
        held firmly in hand.   None thought of helmet
1140   or sturdy mail-shirt   when terror assailed him.

        Out she hastened ,   out and away,
        keen to keep living   when caught in the act.
        She fastened on one,   then fled to her fen.
        He was Hrothgar's   highest counselor,
1145   boon companion   and brave shield-bearer
        slain in his bed.   Beowulf slept
        elsewhere that evening,   for after the feast
        the Geat had been given   a different dwelling.
        A din of dismay   mounted in Heorot:
1150   the gory hand   was gone from the gable.
        Dread had retaken   the Danes' dwelling.
        That bargain was bad   for both barterers,
        costing each one   a close comrade.

        It was grim for the sovereign,   the grizzled soldier,
1155   to learn his old thane   was no longer living,
        to know such a dear one   was suddenly dead.
        Swiftly he sent   servants to fetch
        battle-blessed Beowulf   early from bed,
        together with all   the great-hearted Geats.
1160   He marched in their midst,   went where the wise one
        was wondering whether   the All-Wielder
        ever would alter   this spell of ill-fortune.
        That much-honored man   marched up the floor,
        and timbers dinned   with the tread of his troop.
1165   He spoke soberly   after the summons,
        asking how soundly   the sovereign had slept.

Hrothgar answered,   head of his house:
"Ask not about ease!   Anguish has wakened
again for the Danes.   Aeschere is dead.
1170 He was Yrmenlaf's   elder brother,
my rune-reader   and keeper of counsel,
my shoulder's shielder,   warder in war
when swordsmen struck   at boar-headed helms.
Whatever an honored   earl ought to be,
1175 such was Aeschere.   A sleepless evil
has slipped into Heorot,   seized and strangled.
No one knows where   she will wander now,
glad of the gory   trophy she takes,
her fine fodder.   So she requites
1180 her kinsman's killer   for yesterday's deed,
when you grabbed Grendel   hard in your hand-grip.
He plagued and plundered   my people too long.
His life forfeit,   he fell in the fray;
but now a second   mighty man-scather
1185 comes to carry   the feud further,
as many a thane   must mournfully think,
seeing his sovereign   stricken with grief
at the slaying of one   who served so well.

"I have heard spokesmen   speak in my hall,
1190 country-folk saying   they sometimes spotted
a pair of prodigies   prowling the moors,
evil outcasts,   walkers of wastelands.
One, they descried,   had the semblance of woman;
the other, ill-shapen,   an aspect of man
1195 trudging his track,   ever an exile,
though superhuman   in stature and strength.
In bygone days   the border-dwellers
called him *Grendel*.   What creature begot him,
what nameless spirit,   no one could say.
1200 The two of them trekked   untraveled country:
wolf-haunted heights   and windy headlands,
the frightening fen-path   where falling torrents
dive into darkness,   stream beneath stone
amid folded mountains.   That mere[4] is not far,
1205 as miles are measured.   About it there broods
a forest of fir trees   frosted with mist.
Hedges of wood-roots   hem in the water
where each evening   fire-glow flickers
forth on the flood,   a sinister sight.
1210 That pool is unplumbed   by wits of the wise;
but the heath-striding hart   hunted by hounds,
the strong-antlered stag   seeking a thicket,

4. A small lake.

running for cover,   would rather be killed
at bay on the bank   before hiding its head
1215   under that welter.   It is no peaceful place
where water-struck waves   whipped into clouds,
surge and storm,   swept by the winds,
so the heights are hidden   and heaven weeps.
Now you alone   can relieve our anguish:
1220   look, if you will,   at the lay of the land;
and seek, if you dare,   that dreadful dale
where the she-demon dwells.   Finish this feud,
and I shall reward you   with age-old wealth,
twisted-gold treasures,   if you return."

1225   Beowulf spoke,   son of Ecgtheow:
"Grieve not, good man.   It is better to go
and avenge your friend   than mourn overmuch.
We all must abide   an end on this earth,
but a warrior's works   may win him renown
1230   as long as he lives   and after life leaves him.
Rise now, ruler;   let us ride together
and seek out the signs   of Grendel's mother.
I swear to you this: she shall not escape
in chasm or cave,   in cliff-climbing thicket
1235   or bog's bottom,   wherever she bides.
Suffer your sorrow   this one day only;
I wish you to wait,   wait and be patient."

The elder leapt up   and offered his thanks
to God Almighty,   Master of all,
1240   for such hopeful speech.   Then Hrothgar's horse,
a steed with mane braided,   was brought on its bridle.
The sage sovereign   set out in splendor
with shield-bearing soldiers   striding beside him.
Tracks on the trail   were easy to trace:
1245   they went from woodland   out to the open,
heading through heather   and murky moors
where the best of thanes   was borne off unbreathing.
He would live no longer   in Hrothgar's house.
Crossing the moorland,   the king mounted
1250   a stony path   up steepening slopes.
With a squad of scouts   in single file,
he rode through regions   none of them knew,
mountains and hollows   that hid many monsters.
The sovereign himself,   son of great forebears,
1255   suddenly spotted   a forest of fir-trees
rooted on rock,   their trunks tipping
over a tarn   of turbulent eddies.
Danes were downcast,   and Geats, grim;
every soldier   was stricken at heart
1260   to behold on that height   Aeschere's head.

As they looked on the lake,   blood still lingered,
welled to the surface.   A war-horn sounded
its bold battle-cry,   and the band halted.
Strange sea-dragons   swam in the depths;
1265   sinuous serpents   slid to and fro.
At the base of the bluff   water-beasts lay,
much like monsters   that rise in the morning
when seafarers sail   on strenuous journeys.
Hearing the horn's   high-pitched challenge,
1270   they puffed up with rage   and plunged in the pool.
One Geatish lad   lifted his bow
and loosing an arrow,   ended the life
of a wondrous wave-piercer.   War-shaft jutting
hard in its heart,   the swimmer slowed
1275   as death seized it.   With startling speed
the waters were torn   by terrible tuskers.
They heaved the hideous   hulk to the shore
with spear-hooked heads   as warriors watched.

Undaunted, Beowulf   donned battle armor.
1280   His woven war-corselet,   wide and ornate,
would safeguard his heart   as he searched underwater.
It knew how to armor   the breast of its bearer
if an angry grappler   grasped him in battle.
The bright war-helm   would hold his head
1285   when he sought the seafloor   in swirling flood.
A weapon-smith   had skillfully worked
its gilding of gold   in bygone days
and royally ringed it.   He added afterward
figures of boars   so blades of foemen
1290   would fail to bite.   One further aid
Beowulf borrowed: Unferth offered
the hilt of Hrunting,   his princely sword,
a poisoned war-fang   with iron-edged blade,
blood-hardened   in battles of old.
1295   It never had failed   in any man's grasp
if he dared to fare   on a dreadful foray
to fields of foes.   This was not the first time
it was forced to perform   a desperate deed.

Though strong and sly,   the son of Ecglaf
1300   had somehow forgotten   the slander he spoke,
bleary with beer.   He loaned his blade
to a better bearer,   a doer of deeds
that he would not dare.   His head never dipped
under wild waves,   and his fame waned
1305   when bravery failed him   as battle beckoned.
Not so, the other,   armed and eager.

Beowulf spoke,   son of Ecgtheow:
"Remember, wise master,   mover of men

and giver of gold,   since now I begin
1310 this foray full-willing,   how once before
you pledged to fill   the place of a father
if I should be killed   acquitting your cause.
Guard these young aides,   my partners in arms,
if death takes me.   The treasures you dealt,
1315 Hrothgar, my lord,   I leave to Hygelac.
Let the king of Geats   gaze on the gold
and see that I found   a fair bestower,
a generous host   to help while I could.
Let Unferth have back   his heirloom, Hrunting,
1320 this wonderful weapon,   wavy-skinned sword
renowned among men.   Now I shall conquer
or die in the deed."
                     So saying, he dived,
high-hearted and hasty,   awaiting no answer.
The waters swallowed   that stout soldier.
1325 He swam a half-day   before seeing sea-floor.
Straightaway someone   spied him as well:
she that had hidden   a hundred half-years
in the void's vastness.   Grim and greedy,
she glimpsed a creature   come from above
1330 and crept up to catch him,   clutch him, crush him.
Quickly she learned   his life was secure;
he was hale and whole,   held in the ring-mail.
Linked and locked,   his life-shielding shirt
was wrapped around him,   and wrathful fingers
1335 failed to rip open   the armor he wore.
The wolf of the waters   dragged him away
to her den in the deep,   where weapons of war,
though bravely wielded,   were worthless against her.
Many a mere-beast   banded about him,
1340 brandishing tusks   to tear at his shirt.

The soldier now saw   a high-roofed hall:
unharmed, he beheld   the foe's fastness
beyond the reach   of the roiling flood.
Fire-light flared;   a blaze shone brightly.
1345 The lordly one looked   on the hellish hag,
the mighty mere-wife.   He swung his sword
for a swift stroke,   not staying his hand;
and the whorled blade   whistled its war-song.
But the battle-flame   failed to bite her;
1350 its edge was unable   to end her life,
though Hrunting had often   hacked through helmets
and slashed mail-shirts   in hand-to-hand strife.
For the first time   the famous blade faltered.

Resolve unshaken,   courage rekindled,
1355 Hygelac's kinsman   was keen for conquest.

In a fit of fury,   he flung down the sword.
Steely and strong,   the ring-banded blade
rang on the stones.   He would trust in the strength
of his mighty hand-grip.   Thus should a man,
1360   unmindful of life,   win lasting renown.
Grabbing the tresses   of Grendel's mother,
the Geats' battle-chief,   bursting with wrath,
wrestled her down: no deed to regret
but a favor repaid   as fast as she fell.
1365   With her grim grasp   she grappled him still.
Weary, the warrior   stumbled and slipped;
the strongest foot-soldier   fell to the foe.
Astraddle the hall-guest,   she drew her dagger,
broad and bright-bladed,   bent on avenging
1370   her only offspring.   His mail-shirt shielded
shoulder and breast.   Barring the entry
of edge or point,   the woven war-shirt
saved him from harm.   Ecgtheow's son,
the leader of Geats,   would have lost his life
1375   under Earth's arch   but for his armor
and Heaven's favor   furnishing help.
The Ruler of All   readily aided
the righteous man   when he rose once more.

He beheld in a hoard   of ancient arms
1380   a battle-blessed sword   with strong-edged blade,
a marvelous weapon   men might admire
though over-heavy   for any to heft
when finely forged   by giants of old.
The Scyldings' shielder   took hold of the hilt
1385   and swung up the sword,   though despairing of life.
He struck savagely,   hit her hard neck
and broke the bone-rings,   cleaving clean through
her fated flesh.   She fell to the floor;
the sword sweated;   the soldier rejoiced.

1390   The blaze brightened,   shining through shadows
as clearly as Heaven's   candle on high.
Grim and angry,   Hygelac's guardsman
glanced round the room   and went toward the wall
with his weapon raised,   holding it hard
1395   by the inlaid hilt.   Its edge was ideal
for quickly requiting   the killings of Grendel.
Too many times   he had warred on the West-Danes.
He had slain Hrothgar's   hearth-mates in sleep,
eagerly eaten   fifteen of those folk
1400   and as many more borne   for his monstrous booty.
He paid their price   to the fierce prince,
who looked on the ground   where Grendel lay limp,
wound-weary,   defeated in war.

The lifeless one lurched   at the stroke of the sword
1405 that cleaved his corpse   and cut off his head.

At once the wise men   waiting with Hrothgar
and watching the waters   saw the waves seethe
with streaks of gore.   Gray-haired and glum,
age around honor,   they offered their counsel,
1410 convinced that no victor   would ever emerge
and seek out the sovereign.   All were certain
the mere-wolf had mauled him.   It was mid-afternoon,
and the proud Danes   departed the dale;
generous Hrothgar   headed for home.
1415 The Geats lingered   and looked on the lake
with sorrowful souls,   wistfully wishing
they still might see   their beloved leader.

The sword shrank   from battle-shed blood;
its blade began melting,   a marvel to watch,
1420 that war-icicle   waning away
like a rope of water   unwound by the Ruler
when Father releases   fetters of frost,
the true Sovereign   of seasons and times.
The Weders' warlord   took only two treasures
1425 from all he beheld: the head and the hilt,
studded with gems.   The sword had melted.
Its banded blade   was burnt by the blood,
so hot was the horror,   so acid the evil
that ended thereon.   Soon he was swimming:
1430 the strife-survivor   drove up from the deep
when his foe had fallen.   The foaming waves,
the wide waters   were everywhere cleansed;
that alien evil   had ended her life-days,
left the loaned world.
                              Landward he swam;
1435 the strong-minded savior   of sea-faring men
was glad of his burden,   the booty he brought.
Grateful to God,   the band of brave thanes
hastened gladly   to greet their chieftain,
astonished to see him   whole and unharmed.
1440 His helm and chain-mail   were swiftly unstrapped.
Calm under clouds,   the lake lay quietly,
stained by the slain.   They found the foot-path
and marched manfully,   making their way
back through the barrens.   Proud as princes,
1445 they hauled the head   far from the highland,
an effort for each   of the four who ferried it
slung from spear-shafts.   They bore their booty
straight to the gold-hall.   Battle-hardened,
all fourteen strode   from the field outside,
1450 a bold band of Geats   gathered about

their leader and lord,   the war-worthy man,
peerless in prowess   and daring in deeds.
He hailed Hrothgar   as Grendel's head
was dragged by the hair,   drawn through the hall
1455   where earls were drinking.   All were awe-stricken:
women and warriors   watched in wonder.

Beowulf spoke,   son of Ecgtheow:
"Hail, Hrothgar,   Healfdene's son.
Look on this token   we took from the lake,
1460   this glorious booty   we bring you gladly.
The struggle was stark;   the danger, dreadful.
My foe would have won   our war underwater
had the Lord not looked   after my life.
Hrunting failed me,   though finely fashioned;
1465   but God vouchsafed me   a glimpse of a great-sword,
ancient and huge,   hung from the wall.
All-Father often   fosters the friendless.
Wielding this weapon,   I struck down and slew
the cavern's keeper   as soon as I could.
1470   My banded war-blade   was burned away
when blood burst forth   in the heat of battle.
I bore the hilt here,   wrested from raiders.
Thus I avenged   the deaths among Danes
as it was fitting,   and this I assure you:
1475   henceforth in Heorot   heroes shall sleep
untroubled by terror.   Your warrior troop,
all of your thanes,   young men and old,
need fear no further   evil befalling,
not from that quarter,   king of the Scyldings."

1480   He gave the gold hilt   to the good old man;
the hoary war-chief   held in his hand
an ancient artifact   forged by giants.
At the devils' downfall,   this wondrous work
went to the Danes.   The dark-hearted demon,
1485   hater of humans,   Heaven's enemy,
committer of murders,   and likewise his mother,
departed this Earth.   Their power passed
to the wisest world-king   who ever awarded
treasure in Denmark   between the two seas.

1490   Hrothgar spoke   as he studied the hilt,
that aged heirloom   inscribed long ago
with a story of strife: how the Flood swallowed
the race of giants   with onrushing ocean.
Defiant kindred,   they fared cruelly,
1495   condemned for their deeds   to death by water.
Such were the staves   graven in gold-plate,
runes rightly set,   saying for whom

the serpent-ribbed sword   and raddled hilt[5]
were once fashioned   of finest iron.
1500   When the wise one spoke,   all were silent.

"Truth may be told   by the homeland's holder
and keeper of kinfolk,   who rightly recalls
the past for his people: this prince was born
bravest of fighters.   My friend, Beowulf,
1505   your fame shall flourish   in far countries,
everywhere honored.   Your strength is sustained
by patience and judgement.   Just as I promised,
our friendship is firmed,   a lasting alliance.
So you shall be   a boon to your brethren,
1510   unlike Heremod   who ought to have helped
Ecgwela's sons,   the Honor-Scyldings.
He grew up to grief   and grim slaughter,
doling out death   to the Danish nation.
Hot-tempered at table,   he cut down comrades,
1515   slew his own soldiers   and spurned humankind,
alone and unloved,   an infamous prince,
though mighty God   had given him greatness
and raised him in rank   over all other men.
Hidden wrath   took root in his heart,
1520   bloodthirsty thoughts.   He would give no gifts
to honor others.   Loveless, he lived,
a lasting affliction   endured by the Danes
in sorrow and strife.   Consider him well,
his life and lesson.
                         "Wise with winters,
1525   I tell you this tale   as I mull and marvel
how the Almighty   metes to mankind
the blessings of reason,   rule and realm.
He arranges it all.   For a time He allows
the mind of a man   to linger in love
1530   with earthly honors.   He offers him homeland
to hold and enjoy,   a fort full of fighters,
men to command   and might in the world,
wide kingdoms   won to his will.
In his folly, the fool   imagines no ending.
1535   He dwells in delight   without thought of his lot.
Illness, old age,   anguish or envy:
none of these gnaw   by night at his mind.
Nowhere are swords   brandished in anger;
for him the whole world   wends as he wishes.
1540   He knows nothing worse   till his portion of pride
waxes within him.   His soul is asleep;
his gate, unguarded.   He slumbers too soundly,

---

5. On the sword hilt is the story of the flood, written in runes (letters of the early Germanic alphabet), and a decorative pattern of twisted serpent shapes.

sunk in small cares.   The slayer creeps close
and shoots a shaft   from the baneful bow.

1545   The bitter arrow   bites through his armor,
piercing the heart   he neglected to guard
from crooked counsel   and evil impulse.
Too little seems all   he has long possessed.
Suspicious and stingy,   withholding his hoard

1550   of gold-plated gifts,   he forgets or ignores
what fate awaits him,   for the world's Wielder
surely has granted   his share of glory.
But the end-rune   is already written:
the loaned life-home   collapses in ruin;

1555   some other usurps   and openly offers
the hoarded wealth,   heedless of worry.

"Beloved Beowulf,   best of defenders,
guard against anger   and gain for yourself
perpetual profit.   Put aside pride,

1560   worthiest warrior.   Now for awhile
your force flowers,   yet soon it shall fail.
Sickness or age   will strip you of strength,
or the fangs of flame,   or flood-surges,
the sword's bite   or the spear's flight,

1565   or fearful frailty   as bright eyes fade,
dimming to darkness.   Afterward death
will sweep you away,   strongest of war-chiefs.

"I ruled the Ring-Danes   a hundred half-years,
stern under clouds   with sword and spear

1570   that I wielded in war   against many nations
across Middle-Earth,   until none remained
beneath spacious skies   to reckon as rivals.
Recompense happened   here in my homeland,
grief after gladness   when Grendel came,

1575   when the ancient enemy   cunningly entered.
Thereafter I suffered   constant sorrows
and cruelest cares.   But God has given me
long enough life   to look at this head
with my own eyes,   as enmity ends

1580   spattered with gore.   Sit and be glad,
war-worthy one: the feast is forthcoming,
and many gifts   will be granted tomorrow."

Gladly the Geat   sought out his seat
as the old man asked.   Hall-guests were given

1585   a second feast   as fine as the first.
The helm of Heaven   darkened with dusk,
and the elders arose.   The oldest of Scyldings
was ready to rest   his hoary-haired head
at peace on his pillow.   Peerless with shield,

1590   the leader of Geats   was equally eager

to lie down at last.   A thane was appointed
to serve as his esquire.   Such was the courtesy
shown in those days   to weary wayfarers,
soldiers sojourning   over the ocean.

1595 Beneath golden gables   the great-hearted guest
dozed until dawn   in the high-roofed hall,
when the black raven   blithely foretold
joy under Heaven.   Daybreak hastened,
sun after shadow.   The soldiers were ardent,
1600 the earls eager   to hurry homeward;
the stern minded man   would make for his ship,
fare back to his folk.   But first he bade
that Hrunting be sent   to the son of Ecglaf,
a treasure returned   with thanks for the loan
1605 of precious iron.   He ordered the owner
be told he considered   the sword a fine friend,
blameless in battle.   That man was gallant!
Keen for the crossing,   his weapons secure,
the warrior went   to the worthy Dane;
1610 the thane sought the throne   where a sovereign sat,
that steadfast hero,   Hrothgar the Great.

Beowulf spoke,   son of Ecgtheow:
"Now we must say   as far-sailing seamen,
we wish to make way   homeward to Hygelac.
1615 Here we were well   and warmly received.
If anything further   would earn your favor,
some deed of war   that remains to be done
for the master of men,   I shall always be ready.
Should word ever wend   over wide ocean
1620 that nearby nations   menace your marches,
as those who detest you   sometimes have tried,
I shall summon a thousand   thanes to your aid.
I know Hygelac,   though newly-anointed
the nation's shepherd,   will surely consent
1625 to honor my offer   in word and action.
If you ever need men,   I shall muster at once
a thicket of spears   and support you in strength.
Should Hrethric, your son,   sail overseas,
he shall find friends   in the fort of the Geats.
1630 It is well for the worthy   to fare in far countries."

Hrothgar offered   these answering words:
"Heaven's Sovereign   has set in your heart
this vow you have voiced.   I never have known
someone so young   to speak more wisely.
1635 You are peerless in strength,   princely in spirit,
straightforward in speech.   If a spear fells
Hrethel's son,   if a hostile sword-stroke
kills him in combat   or after, with illness,

slays your leader   while you still live,
1640   the Sea-Geats surely   could name no better
to serve as their king   and keeper of treasure,
should you wish to wield   rule in your realm.
I sensed your spirit   the instant I saw you,
precious Beowulf,   bringer of peace
1645   for both our peoples: War-Danes and Weders,
so often sundered   by strife in the past.
While I wield the rule   of this wide realm,
men will exchange   many more greetings
and riches will ride   in ring-bowed ships
1650   bearing their gifts   where the gannets bathe.
I know your countrymen   keep to old ways,
fast in friendship,   and war as well."

Then the hall's holder,   Healfdene's son,
gave his protector   twelve more treasures,
1655   bidding he bear   these tokens safely
home to his kin,   and quickly return.
That hoary-haired king   held and kissed him,
clasping his neck.   The noble Scylding
was too well aware   with the wisdom of age
1660   that he never might meet   the young man again
coming to council.   So close had they grown,
so strong in esteem,   he could scarcely endure
the surfeit of sorrow   that surged in his heart;
the flame of affection   burned in his blood.
1665   But Beowulf walked   away with his wealth;
proud of his prizes,   he trod on the turf.
Standing at anchor,   his sea-courser
chafed for its captain.   All the way home
Hrothgar's gifts   were often honored.
1670   That was a king   accorded respect
until age unmanned him,   like many another.

High-hearted,   the troop of young soldiers
strode to the sea,   wrapped in their ring-mesh,
linked and locked shirts.   The land-watcher spied
1675   the fighters faring,   just as before.
He called no taunts   from the top of the cliff
but galloped to greet them   and tell them the Geats
would always be welcome,   armored warriors
borne on their ship.   The broad-beamed boat
1680   lay by the beach,   laden with chain-mail,
chargers and treasures   behind its tall prow.
The mast soared high   over Hrothgar's hoard.

The boat-guard was given   a gold-bound sword;
thereafter that man   had honor enhanced,
1685   bearing an heirloom   to Heorot's mead-bench.

They boarded their vessel,   breasted the deep,
left Denmark behind.   A halyard hoisted
the sea-wind's shroud;   the sail was sheeted,
bound to the mast,   and the beams moaned
1690   as a fair wind wafted   the wave-rider forward.
Foamy-throated,   the longboat bounded,
swept on the swells   of the swift sea-stream
until welcoming capes   were sighted ahead,
the cliffs of Geat-land.   The keel grounded
1695   as wind-lift thrust it   straight onto sand.

The harbor-guard hastened   hence from his post.
He had looked long   on an empty ocean
and waited to meet   the much-missed men.
He moored the broad-beamed   bow to the beach
1700   with woven lines   lest the backwash of waves
bear off the boat.   Then Beowulf ordered
treasures unloaded,   the lordly trappings,
gold that was going   to Hygelac's hall,
close to the cliff-edge,   where the ring-giver kept
1705   his comrades about him.
                            That building was bold
at the hill's crown;   and queenly Hygd,
Haereth's daughter,   dwelt there as well.
Wise and refined,   though her winters were few,
she housed in the stronghold.   Open-handed,
1710   she granted generous   gifts to the Geats,
most unlike Modthryth,[6]   a maiden so fierce
that none but her father   dared venture near.
The brave man who gazed   at Modthryth by day
might reckon a death-rope   already twisted,
1715   might count himself quickly   captured and killed,
the stroke of a sword   prescribed for his trespass.
Such is no style   for a queen to proclaim:
though peerless, a woman   ought to weave peace,
not snatch away life   for illusory slights.

1720   Modthryth's temper   was tamed by marriage.
Ale-drinkers say   her ill-deeds ended
once she was given   in garlands of gold
to Hemming's kinsman.   She came to his hall
over pale seas,   accepted that prince,
1725   a fine young heir,   at her father's behest.
Thenceforth on the throne,   she was famed for fairness,
making the most   of her lot in life,
sustained by loving   her lordly sovereign.
That king, Offa,   was called by all men

---

6. "Modthryth" may mean "arrogant in temper"; it may be a reference to an arrogant woman rather than a proper name.

1730   the ablest of any   ruling a realm
        between two seas,   so I am told.
        Gifted in war,   a wise gift-giver
        everywhere honored,   the spear-bold soldier
        held his homeland   and also fathered
1735   help for the heroes   of Hemming's kindred:
        war-worthy Eomer,   grandson of Garmund.

        Brave Beowulf   marched with his band,
        strode up the sands   of the broad beach
        while the sun in the south   beamed like a beacon.
1740   The earls went eagerly   up to the keep
        where the strong sovereign,   Ongentheow's slayer,
        the young war-king   doled out gold rings.
        Beowulf's coming   was quickly proclaimed.
        Hygelac heard   that his shoulder-shielder
1745   had entered the hall,   whole and unharmed
        by bouts of battle.   The ruler made room
        for the foot-guests crossing   the floor before him.

        Saluting his lord   with a loyal speech
        earnestly worded,   the winner in war
1750   sat facing the king,   kinsman with kinsman.
        A mead-vessel moved   from table to table
        as Haereth's daughter,   heedful of heroes,
        bore the wine-beaker   from hand to hand.
        Keen to elicit   his comrade's account
1755   in the high-roofed hall,   Hygelac graciously
        asked how the Sea-Geats   fared on their foray:

        "Say what befell   from your sudden resolve
        to seek out strife   over salt waters,
        to struggle in Heorot.   Have you helped Hrothgar
1760   ward off the well-known   cares of his kingdom?
        You have cost me disquiet,   angst and anguish.
        Doubting the outcome,   dearest of men,
        for anyone meeting   that murderous demon,
        I sought to dissuade you   from starting the venture.
1765   The South-Danes themselves   should have settled their feud
        with ghastly Grendel.   Now I thank God
        that I see you again,   safe and sound."

        Beowulf spoke,   son of Ecgtheow:
        "For a great many men   our meeting's issue
1770   is hardly hidden,   my lord Hygelac.
        What a fine fracas   passed in that place
        when both of us battled   where Grendel had brought
        sore sorrow   on scores of War-Scyldings!
        I avenged every one,   so that none of his kin
1775   anywhere need   exult at our night-bout,
        however long   the loathsome race lives,

covered with crime.   When Hrothgar came
and heard what had happened   there in the ring-hall,
he sat me at once   with his own two sons.

1780 "The whole of his host   gathered in gladness;
all my life long   I never have known
such joy in a hall   beneath heaven's vault.
The acclaimed queen,   her kindred's peace-pledge,
would sometimes circle   the seated youths,
1785 lavishing rings   on delighted young lords.
Hrothgar's daughter   handed the elders
ale-cups aplenty,   pouring for each
old trooper in turn.   I heard the hall-sitters
call her Freawaru   after she proffered
1790 the studded flagon.   To Froda's fair son
that maiden is sworn.   This match seems meet
to the lord of Scyldings,   who looks to settle
his Heatho-Bard feud.   Yet the best of brides
seldom has stilled   the spears of slaughter
1795 so swiftly after   a sovereign was stricken.

"Ingeld and all   his earls will be rankled,
watching that woman   walk in their hall
with high-born Danes   doing her bidding.
Her escorts will wear   ancient heirlooms:
1800 Heatho-Bard swords   with braided steel blades,
weapons once wielded   and lost in war
along with the lives   of friends in the fray.
Eyeing the ring-hilts,   an old ash-warrior
will brood in his beer   and bitterly pine
1805 for the stark reminders   of men slain in strife.
He will grimly begin   to goad a young soldier,
testing and tempting   a troubled heart,
his whispered words   waking war-evil:

"'My friend, have you spotted   the battle-sword
1810 that your father bore   on his final foray?
Wearing his war-mask,   Withergyld fell
when foemen seized   the field of slaughter.
His priceless blade   became battle-plunder.
Today a son   of the Scylding who slew him
1815 struts on our floor,   flaunting his trophy,
an heirloom that you   should rightfully own.'

"He will prick and pique   with pointed words
time after time   till the challenge is taken,
the maiden's attendant   is murdered in turn,
1820 blade-bitten   to sleep in his blood,
forfeit his life   for his father's feat.
Another will run,   knowing the road.
So on both sides   oaths will be broken;

and afterward Ingeld's   anger will grow
1825   hotter, unchecked,   as he chills toward his wife.
Hence I would hold   the Heatho-Bards likely
to prove unpeaceable   partners for Danes."

"Now I shall speak   of my strife with Grendel,
further acquainting   the kingdom's keeper
1830   with all that befell   when our fight began.
Heaven's gem   had gone overhead;
in darkness the dire   demon stalked us
while we stood guard   unharmed in Heorot.
Hondscioh was doomed   to die with the onslaught,
1835   first to succumb,   though clad for combat
when grabbed by Grendel,   who gobbled him whole.
That beloved young thane   was eaten alive.
Not one to leave   the hall empty-handed,
the bloody-toothed terror   intended to try
1840   his might upon me.   A curious creel
hung from his hand,   cunningly clasped
and strangely sewn   with devilish skill
from skin of a dragon.   The demon would stuff me,
sinless, inside   like so many others;
1845   but rising in wrath,   I stood upright.
It is too long a tale,   how the people's plaguer
paid for his crimes   with proper requital;
but the feat reflected   finely, my lord,
on the land you lead.   Though the foe fled
1850   to live awhile longer,   he left behind him
as sign of the strife   a hand in Heorot.
Humbled, he fell   to the floor of the mere.

"The warder of Scyldings   rewarded my warfare
with much treasure   when morning arrived,
1855   and we sat for a feast   with songs and sagas.
He told many tales   he learned in his lifetime.
Sometimes a soldier   struck the glad harp,
the sounding wood;   sometimes strange stories
were spoken like spells,   tragic and true,
1860   rightly related.   The large-hearted lord
sometimes would start   to speak of his youth,
his might in war.   His memories welled;
ancient in winters,   he weighed them all.

"So we delighted   the livelong day
1865   until darkness drew   once more upon men.
Then Grendel's mother,   mourning her son,
swiftly set out   in search of revenge
against warlike Geats.   The grisly woman
wantonly slew   a Scylding warrior:
1870   aged Aeschere,   the king's counselor,

relinquished his life.   Nor in the morning
might death-weary Danes   bear off his body
to burn on a bier,   for the creature clutching him
fled to her fastness   under a waterfall.

1875   This was the sorest   of sorrows that Hrothgar
suffered as king.   Distraught, he beseeched me
to do in your name   a notable deed.
If I dived in the deep,   heedless of danger,
to war underwater,   he would reward me.

1880   "Under I went,   as now is well-known;
and I found the hideous   haunter of fens.
For a time we two   contested our hand-strength;
then I struck off her head   with a huge sword
that her battle-hall held,   and her hot blood

1885   boiled in the lake.   Leaving that place
was no easy feat,   but fate let me live.
Again I was granted   gifts that the guardian,
Healfdene's son,   had sworn to bestow.
The king of that people   kept his promise,

1890   allotting me all   he had earlier offered:
meed for my might,   with more treasures,
my choice from the hoard   of Healfdene's son.
These, my lord,   I deliver to you,
as proof of fealty.   My future depends

1895   wholly on you.   I have in this world
few close kin   but my king, Hygelac."

He bade the boar-banner   now be brought in,
the high helmet,   hard mail-shirt,
and splendid sword,   describing them thus:

1900   "When Hrothgar gave me   this hoarded gear,
the sage sovereign   entreated I tell
the tale of his gift: this treasure was held
by Heorogar, king,   who long was the lord
of Scylding people.   It should have passed

1905   to armor the breast   of bold Heoroweard,
the father's favorite,   faithful and brave;
but he willed it elsewhere,   so use it well."

I have heard how horses   followed that hoard,
four dappled mounts,   matching and fleet.

1910   He gave up his gifts,   gold and horses.
Kinsmen should always   act with honor,
not spin one another   in snares of spite
or secretly scheme   to kill close comrades.
Always the nephew   had aided his uncle;

1915   each held the other's   welfare at heart.
He gave to Queen Hygd   the golden collar,
wondrously wrought,   Wealtheow's token,

and also three steeds,   sleek and bright-saddled.
Thereafter her breast   was graced by the gift.

1920   So Ecgtheow's son   won his repute
as a man of mettle,   acting with honor,
yet mild-hearted   toward hearth-companions,
harming no one   when muddled with mead.
Bold in battle,   he guarded the guerdon
1925   that God had granted,   the greatest strength
of all humankind,   though once he was thought
weak and unworthy,   a sluggardly sloucher,
mocked for meekness   by men on the mead-bench,
and given no gifts   by the lord of the Geats.
1930   Every trouble   untwined in time
for the glory-blessed man.

                    A blade was brought
at the king's request,   Hrethel's heirloom
glinting with gold.   No greater treasure,
no nobler sword   was held in his hoard.
1935   He lay that brand   on Beowulf's lap
and also bestowed   a spacious estate,
hall and high seat.   When land and lordship
were left to them both,   by birthright and law,
he who ranked higher   ruled the wide realm.

3. The Dragon

1940   It happened long after,   with Hygelac dead,
that war-swords slew   Heardred, his son,
when Battle-Scylfings   broke his shield-wall
and hurtled headlong   at Hereric's nephew.
So Beowulf came   to rule the broad realm.
1945   For fifty winters   he fostered it well;
then the old king,   keeper of kinfolk,
heard of a dragon   drawn from the darkness.
He had long lain   in his lofty fastness,
the steep stone-barrow,   guarding his gold;
1950   but a path pierced it,   known to no person
save him who found it   and followed it forward.
That stranger seized   a singular treasure.
He bore it in hand   from the heathen hoard:
a finely-worked flagon   he filched from the lair
1955   where the dragon dozed.   Enraged at the robber,
the sneaking thief   who struck while he slept,
the guardian woke   glowing with wrath,
as his nearest neighbors   were soon to discern.

It was not by choice   that the wretch raided
1960   the wondrous worm-hoard.   The one who offended
was stricken himself,   sorely mistreated,

the son of a warrior   sold as a slave.
Escaped and seeking   a safe refuge,
he guiltily groped   his way below ground.
1965   There the intruder,   trembling with terror,
sensed an ancient   evil asleep.
His fate was to find   as fear unmanned him
his fingers feeling   a filigreed cup.

Many such goblets   had gone to the earth-house,
1970   legacies left   by a lordly people.
In an earlier age   someone unknown
had cleverly covered   those costly treasures.
That thane held the hoard   for the lifetime allowed him,
but gold could not gladden   a man in mourning.
1975   Newly-built   near the breaking waves,
a barrow stood   at the base of a bluff,
its entrance sculpted   by secret arts.
Earthward the warrior   bore the hoard-worthy
portion of plate,   the golden craftwork.
1980   The ringkeeper spoke   these words as he went:

"Hold now, Earth,   what men may not,
the hoard of the heroes,   earth-gotten wealth
when it first was won.   War-death has felled them,
an evil befalling   each of my people.
1985   The household is mirthless   when men are lifeless.
I have none to wear sword,   none to bear wine
or polish the precious   vessels and plates.
Gone are the brethren   who braved many battles.
From the hard helmet   the hand-wrought gilding
1990   drops in the dust.   Asleep are the smiths
who knew how to burnish   the war-chief's mask
or mend the mail-shirts   mangled in battle.
Shields and mail-shirts   molder with warriors
and follow no foes   to faraway fields.
1995   No harp rejoices   to herald the heroes,
no hand-fed hawk   swoops through the hall,
no stallion stamps   in the stronghold's courtyard.
Death has undone   many kindreds of men."

Stricken in spirit,   he spoke of his sorrow
2000   as last of his line,   drearily drifting
through day and dark   until death's flood-tide
stilled his heart.   The old night-scather
was happy to glimpse   the unguarded hoard.
Balefully burning,   he seeks out barrows.
2005   Naked and hateful   in a raiment of flame,
the dragon dreaded   by outland dwellers
must gather and guard   the heathen gold,
no better for wealth   but wise with his winters.

For three hundred winters   the waster of nations
2010   held that mighty   hoard in his earth-hall
till one man wronged him,   arousing his wrath.
The wretched robber   ransomed his life
with the prize he pilfered,   the plated flagon.
Beholding that marvel   men of old made,
2015   his fief-lord forgave   the skulker's offense.
One treasure taken   had tainted the rest.
Waking in wrath,   the worm reared up
and slid over stones.   Stark-hearted,
he spotted the footprints   where someone had stepped,
2020   stealthily creeping   close to his head.
The fortunate man   slips swiftly and safely
through the worst dangers   if the World's Warder
grants him that grace.
                        Eager and angry,
the hoard-guard hunted   the thief who had haunted
2025   his hall while he slept.   He circled the stone-house,
but out in that wasteland   the one man he wanted
was not to be found.   How fearsome he felt,
how fit for battle!   Back in his barrow
he tracked the intruder   who dared to tamper
2030   with glorious gold.   Fierce and fretful,
the dragon waited   for dusk and darkness.
The rage-swollen holder   of headland and hoard
was plotting reprisal: flames for his flagon.
Then day withdrew,   and the dragon, delighted,
2035   would linger no longer   but flare up and fly.
His onset was awful   for all on the land,
and a cruel ending   soon came for their king.

When the ghastly specter   scattered his sparks
and set their buildings   brightly burning,
2040   flowing with flames   as householders fled,
he meant to leave   not one man alive.
That wreaker of havoc   hated and harried
the Geatish folk   fleeing his flames.
Far and wide   his warfare was watched
2045   until night waned   and the worm went winging
back to the hall   where his hoard lay hidden,
sure of his stronghold,   his walls and his war,
sure of himself,   deceived by his pride.

Then terrible tidings   were taken to Beowulf:
2050   how swiftly his own   stronghold was stricken,
that best of buildings   bursting with flames
and his throne melting.   The hero was heart-sore;
the wise man wondered   what wrong he had wrought
and how he trangressed   against old law,

2055   the Lord Everlasting,   Ruler of All.
His grief was great,   and grim thoughts
boiled in his breast   as never before.
The fiery foe   had flown to his coastlands,
had sacked and seared   his keep by the sea.

2060   For that the war-king   required requital.
He ordered a broad-shield   fashioned of iron,
better for breasting   baleful blazes
than the linden-wood   that warded his warriors.
Little was left   of the time lent him

2065   for life in the world;   and the worm as well,
who had haughtily held   his hoard for so long.
Scorning to follow   the far-flying foe
with his whole host,   the ring-giver reckoned
the wrath of a dragon   unworthy of dread.

2070   Fearless and forceful,   he often had faced
the straits of struggle   blessed with success.
Beowulf braved   many a battle
after ridding Hrothgar's   hall of its horrors
and grappling with Grendel's   gruesome kin.

2075   Not least of his clashes   had come when the king
Hygelac fell   while fighting the Frisians
in hand-to-hand combat.   His friend and fief-lord,
the son of Hrethel,   was slain in the onslaught,
stricken to death   by a blood-drinking blade.

2080   Beowulf battled   back to the beach
where he proved his strength   with skillful swimming,
for he took to the tide   bearing the trophies
of thirty warriors   won on the field.
None of the Hetware   needed to boast

2085   how they fared on foot,   flaunting their shields
against that fierce fighter,   for few remained
after the battle   to bear the tale home.

Over wide waters   the lone swimmer went,
the son of Ecgtheow   swept on the sea-waves

2090   back to his homeland,   forlorn with his loss,
and hence to Hygd   who offered her hoard:
rings and a realm,   a throne for the thane.
With Hygelac dead   she doubted her son
could guard the Geats   from foreigners' forays.

2095   Refusing her boon,   Beowulf bade
the leaderless lords   to hail the lad
as their rightful ruler.   He chose not to reign
by thwarting his cousin   but to counsel the king
and guide with good will   until Heardred grew older.

2100   It was Heardred who held   the Weder-Geats' hall
when outcast Scylfings   came seeking its safety:

Eanmund and Eadgils,   nephews of Onela.
That strong sea-king   and spender of treasures
sailed from Sweden   pursuing the rebels
2105   who challenged his right   to rule their realm.
For lending them haven,   Hygelac's son
suffered the sword-stroke   that spilled out his life.
The Swede headed home   when Heardred lay dead,
leaving Beowulf   lordship of Geats.
2110   That was a good king,   keeping the gift-seat;
yet Heardred's death   dwelled in his thoughts.
A long time later   he offered his aid
to end the exile   of destitute Eadgils.
He summoned an army,   and Ohthere's son,
2115   cold in his cares,   went over wide waters
with weapons and warriors   to kill off a king.

Such were the struggles   and tests of strength
the son of Ecgtheow   saw and survived.
His pluck was proven   in perilous onslaughts
2120   till that fateful day   when he fought the dragon.
As leader of twelve   trailing that terror,
the greatest of Geats   glowered with rage
when he looked on the lair   where the worm lurked.
By now he had found   how the feud flared,
2125   this fell affliction   befalling his kingdom,
for the kingly cup   had come to his hand
from the hand of him   who raided the hoard.
That sorry slave   had started the strife,
and against his will   he went with the warriors,
2130   a thirteenth man   bringing the band
to the barrow's brink   which he alone knew.
Hard by the surge   of the seething sea
gaped a cavern   glutted with golden
medallions and chains.   The murderous man-bane,
2135   hidden within,   hungered for warfare.
No taker would touch   his treasures cheaply:
the hoard's holder   would drive a hard bargain.

The proud war-king   paused on the sea-point
to lighten the hearts   of his hearth-companions,
2140   though his heart was heavy   and hankered for death.
It was nearing him now.   That taker of treasure
would sunder the soul   from his old bones and flesh.
So Beowulf spoke,   the son of Ecgtheow,
recalling the life   he was loathe to lose:

2145   "From boyhood I bore   battles and bloodshed,
struggles and strife: I still see them all.
I was given at seven   to house with King Hrethel,
my mother's father   and friend of our folk.

He kept me fairly   with feasts and fine gifts.

2150   I fared no worse   than one of his sons:
Herebeald, Hathcyn,   or princely Hygelac
who was later my lord.   The eldest, Herebeald,
unwittingly went   to a wrongful death
when Hathcyn's horn-bow   hurled an arrow.

2155   Missing the mark,   it murdered the kinsman;
a brother was shot   by the blood-stained shaft.
This blow to the heart   was brutal and baffling.
A prince had fallen.   The felon went free.[1]

"So it is sore   for an old man to suffer

2160   his son swinging   young on the gallows,
gladdening ravens.   He groans in his grief
and loudly laments   the lad he has lost.
No help is at hand   from hard-won wisdom
or the march of years.   Each morning reminds him

2165   his heir is elsewhere,   and he has no heart
to wait for a second   son in his stronghold
when death has finished   the deeds of the first.
He ceaselessly sees   his son's dwelling,
the desolate wine-hall,   the windswept grave-sward

2170   where swift riders   and swordsmen slumber.
No harp-string sounds,   no song in the courtyard.
He goes to his bed   sighing with sorrow,
one soul for another.   His home is hollow;
his field, fallow.
                          "So Hrethel suffered,

2175   hopeless and heart-sore   with Herebeald gone.
He would do no deed   to wound the death-dealer
or harrow his household   with hatred and anger;
but bitter bloodshed   had stolen his bliss,
and he quit his life   for the light of the Lord.

2180   Like a luckier man,   he could leave his land
in the hands of a son,   though he loved him no longer.

"Then strife and struggle   of Geats and Swedes
crossed the wide water.   Warfare wounded
both sides in battle   when Hrethel lay buried.

2185   Ongentheow's sons,   fierce and unfriendly,
suddenly struck   at Hreosna-Beorh
and bloodied the bluff   with baneful slaughter.
Our foes in this feud   soon felt the wrath
of my kinsman the king   claiming our due,

2190   though the counterblow   cost his own life.
Hathcyn was killed,   his kingship cut short.

---

1. Even in cases of involuntary manslaughter, punishment was required to avenge the dead. In this instance, it seems that a ritual, sacrificial hanging was performed to spare Hathcyn for murdering his brother Herebeald.

The slayer himself   was slain in the morning.
I have heard how Eofor   struck the old Scyfing.
Sword-ashen,   Ongentheow sank

2195 with his helm split: heedful of harm,
to kinsman and king,   the hand would not halt
the death-blow it dealt.
                              "My own sword-arm
repaid my prince   for the gifts he granted.
He gave me a fiefdom,   the land I have loved.

2200 He never had need   to seek among Spear-Danes,
Gifthas or Swedes   and get with his gifts
a worse warrior.   I wielded my sword
at the head of our host;   so shall I hold
this blade that I bear   boldly in battle

2205 as long as life lasts.   It has worn well
since the day when Daeghrefn   died by my hand,
the Frankish foe   who fought for the Frisians,
bearing their banner.   He broke in my grip,
never to barter   the necklace he robbed

2210 from Hygelac's corpse.   I crushed that killer;
his bones snapped,   and his life-blood spilled.
I slew him by strength,   not by the sword.
Now I shall bear   his brand into battle:
hand and hard sword   will fight for the hoard."

2215 Now Beowulf spoke   his last battle-boast:
"In boyhood I braved   bitter clashes;
still in old age   I would seek out strife
and gain glory   guarding my people
if the man-bane comes   from his cave to meet me."

2220 Then he turned to his troop   for the final time,
bidding farewell   to bold helmet-bearers,
fast in friendship: "I would wear no sword,
no weapon at all   to ward off the worm
if I knew how to fight   this fiendish foe

2225 as I grappled with Grendel   one bygone night.
But here I shall find   fierce battle-fire
and breath envenomed;   therefore I bear
this mail-coat and shield.   I shall not shy
from standing my ground   when I greet the guardian,

2230 follow what will   at the foot of his wall.
I shall face the fiend   with a firm heart.
Let the Ruler of men   reckon my fate:
words are worthless   against the war-flyer.
Bide by the barrow,   safe in your byrnies,

2235 and watch, my warriors,   which of us two
will better bear   the brunt of our clash.
This war is not yours;   it is meted to me,
matching my strength,   man against monster.

2240 I shall do this deed   undaunted by death
and get you gold   or else get my ending,
borne off in battle,   the bane of your lord."

The hero arose,   helmed and hardy,
a war-king clad   in shield and corselet.
He strode strongly   under the stone-cliff:
2245 no faint-hearted man,   to face it unflinching!
Stalwart soldier   of so many marches,
unshaken when shields   were crushed in the clash,
he saw between stiles   an archway where steam
burst like a boiling   tide from the barrow,
2250 woeful for one   close to the worm-hoard.
He would not linger long   unburned by the lurker
or safely slip   through the searing lair.
Then a battle-cry broke   from Beowulf's breast
as his rightful wrath   was roused for the reckoning.
2255 His challenge sounded   under stark stone
where the hateful hoard-guard   heard in his hollow
the clear-voiced call   of a man coming.

No quarter was claimed;   no quarter given.
First the beast's breath   blew hot from the barrow
2260 as battle-bellows   boomed underground.
The stone-house stormer   swung up his shield
at the ghastly guardian.   Then the dragon's grim heart
kindled for conflict.   Uncoiling, he came
seeking the swordsman   who'd already drawn
2265 the keen-edged blade   bequeathed him for combat.
Each foe confronted   the other with fear.
His will unbroken,   the warlord waited
behind his tall shield,   helm and armor.
With fitful twistings   the fire-drake hastened
2270 fatefully forward.   His defense held high,
Beowulf felt   the blaze blister through
hotter and sooner   than he had foreseen.
So for the first time   fortune was failing
the mighty man   in the midst of a struggle.
2275 Wielding his sword,   he struck at the worm
and his fabled blade   bit to the bone
through blazoned hide: bit and bounced back,
no match for the foe   in this moment of need.

The peerless prince   was hard-pressed in response,
2280 for his bootless blow   had maddened the monster
and fatal flames   shot further than ever,
lighting the land.   The blade he bared
failed in the fray,   though forged from iron.
No easy end   for the son of Ecgtheow:
2285 against his will   he would leave this world

to dwell elsewhere,   as every man must
when his days are done.   Swiftly the death-dealer
moved to meet him.   From the murderous breast
bellows of breath   belched fresh flames.
2290   Enfolded in fire,   he who formerly
ruled a whole realm   had no one to help him
hold off the heat,   for his hand-picked band
of princelings had fled,   fearing to face
the foe with their lord.   Loving honor
2295   less than their lives,   they hid in the holt.
But one among them   grieved for the Geats
and balked at the thought   of quitting a kinsman.

This one was Wiglaf,   son of Weohstan,
kinsman of Aelfhere,   earl among Scylfings.
2300   Seeing his liege-lord   suffering sorely
with war-mask scorched   by the searing onslaught,
the thankful thane   thought of the boons
his sovereign bestowed: the splendid homestead
and folk-rights his father   formerly held.
2305   No shirker could stop him   from seizing his shield
of yellow linden   and lifting the blade
Weohstan won   when he slew Eanmund,
son of Ohthere.   Spoils of that struggle,
sword and scabbard,   smithwork of giants,
2310   a byrnie of ring-mail   and bright burnished helm
were granted as gifts,   a thane's war-garb,
for Onela never   acknowledged his nephews
but struck against both   of his brother's sons.
When Eadgils avenged   Eanmund's death,
2315   Weohstan fled.   Woeful and friendless,
he saved that gear   for seasons of strife,
foreseeing his son   someday might crave
sword and corselet.   He came to his kinsman,
the prince of the Geats,   and passed on his heirlooms,
2320   hoping Wiglaf   would wear them with honor.
Old then, and wise,   he went from the world.

This war was the first   young Wiglaf would fight
helping the king.   His heart would not quail
nor weapon fail   as the foe would find
2325   going against him;   but he made his grim mood
known to the men: "I remember the time
when taking our mead   in the mighty hall,
all of us offered   oaths to our leige-lord.
We promised to pay   for princely trappings
2330   by staunchly wielding   sword-blades in war
if need should arise.   Now we are needed
by him who chose,   from the whole of his host,
twelve for this trial,   trusting our claims

as warriors worthy   of wearing our blades,
2335   bearing keen spears.   Our king has come here
bent on battling   the man-bane alone,
because among warriors   one keeper of kinfolk
has done, undaunted,   the most deeds of daring.
But this day our lord   needs dauntless defenders
2340   so long as the frightful   fires keep flaring.
God knows I would gladly   give my own body
for flames to enfold   with the gold-giver.
Shameful, to shoulder   our shields homeward!
First we must fell   this fearsome foe
2345   and protect the life   of our people's lord.
It is wrong that one man   be wrathfully racked
for his former feats   and fall in this fight,
guarding the Geats.   We shall share our war-gear:
shield and battle-shirt,   helm and hard sword."

2350   So speaking, he stormed   through the reek of smoke,
with helmet on head,   to help his lord.
"Beloved Beowulf,   bear up your blade.
You pledged in your youth,   powerful prince,
never to let   your luster lessen
2355   while life was left you.   Now summon your strength.
Stand steadfast.   I shall stand with you."

After these words   the worm was enraged.
For a second time   the spiteful specter
flew at his foe,   and he wreathed in flames
2360   the hated human   he hungered to harm.
His dreadful fire-wind   drove in a wave,
charring young Wiglaf's   shield to the boss,
nor might a mail-shirt   bar that breath
from burning the brave   spear-bearer's breast.
2365   Wiglaf took cover   close to his kinsman,
shielded by iron   when linden was cinder.
Then the war-king,   recalling past conquests,
struck with full strength   straight at the head.
His battle-sword, Naegling,   stuck there and split,
2370   shattered in combat,   so sharp was the shock
to Beowulf's great   gray-banded blade.
He never was granted   the gift of a sword
as hard and strong   as the hand that held it.
I have heard that he broke   blood-hardened brands,
2375   so the weapon-bearer   was none the better.

The fearful fire-drake,   scather of strongholds,
flung himself forward   a final time,
wild with wounds   yet wily and sly.
In the heat of the fray,   he hurtled headlong
2380   to fasten his fangs   in the foe's throat.

Beowulf's life-blood   came bursting forth
on those terrible tusks.   Just then, I am told,
the second warrior   sprang from his side,
a man born for battle   proving his mettle,
2385   keen to strengthen   his kinsman in combat.
He took no heed   of the hideous head
scorching his hand   as he hit lower down.
The sword sank in,   patterned and plated;
the flames of the foe   faltered, faded.
2390   Quick-witted still,   the king unsheathed
the keen killing-blade   he kept in his corselet.
Then the Geats' guardian   gutted the dragon,
felling that fiend   with the help of his friend,
two kinsmen together   besting the terror.
2395   So should a thane   succor his sovereign.

That deed was the king's   crowning conquest;
Beowulf's work   in the world was done.
He soon felt his wound   swelling and stinging
where fell fangs   had fastened upon him,
2400   and evil venom   enveloped his heart.
Wisely he sought   a seat by the stone-wall,
and his gaze dwelled   on the dark doorway
delved in the dolmen,   the straight stiles
and sturdy archway   sculpted by giants.
2405   With wonderful kindness   Wiglaf washed
the clotting blood   from his king and kinsman;
his hands loosened   the lord's high helm.
Though banefully bitten,   Beowulf spoke,
for he knew his lifetime   would last no longer.
2410   The count of his days   had come to a close.
His joys were done.   Death drew near him.

"Now I would wish   to will my son
these weapons of war,   had I been awarded
an heir of my own,   holder of heirlooms.
2415   I fathered the Weders   for fifty winters.
No warlike lord   of neighboring lands
dared to assail us   or daunt us with dread.
A watchful warden,   I waited on fate
while keeping our people   clear of quarrels.
2420   I swore many oaths;   not one was wrongful.
So I rejoice,   though sick with my death-wound,
that God may not blame me   for baseless bloodshed
or killing of kin   when breath quits my body.
Hurry below   and look on the hoard,
2425   beloved Wiglaf.   The worm lies sleeping
under gray stone,   sorely stricken
and stripped of his gold.   Go swiftly and seize it.

Get me giltwork   and glittering gems:
I would set my sight   on that store of wealth.
2430 Loath would I be   to leave for less
the life and lordship   I held for so long."

I have heard how swiftly   the son of Weohstan
hastened to heed   his wounded and weakening
war-lord's behest.   In his woven mail-shirt,
2435 his bright byrnie,   he entered the barrow;
and passing its threshold,   proud and princely,
he glimpsed all the gold   piled on the ground,
the walled-in wealth   won by the worm,
that fierce night-flyer.   Flagons were standing,
2440 embossed wine-beakers   lying unburnished,
their inlays loosened.   There were lofty helmets
and twisted arm-rings   rotting and rusting.
Gold below ground   may betray into grief
any who hold it: heed me who will!

2445 Wiglaf saw also   a gold-woven standard,
a wonder of handiwork,   skillfully filigreed,
high above ground.   It gave off a glow
that let him behold   the whole of the hoard.
I am told he took   from that trove of giants
2450 goblets and platters   pressed to his breastplate,
and the golden banner   glinting brightly.
He spotted no sign   of the stricken dragon.
The iron-edged brand   old Beowulf bore
had mortally wounded   the warder of wealth
2455 and fiery foe   whose flames in the night
welled so fiercely   before he was felled.

Bent with his burden,   the messenger hastened
back to his master,   burning to know
whether the brave   but wound-weakened
2460 lord of the Weders   was lost to the living.
Setting his spoils   by the storied prince
whose lifeblood blackened   the ground with gore,
Wiglaf wakened   the war-lord with water,
and these words thrust   like spears through his breast
2465 as the ancient one grimly   gazed on the gold:

"I offer my thanks   to the Almighty Master,
the King of Glory,   for granting my kindred
these precious things   I look upon last.
Losing my life,   I have bought this boon
2470 to lighten my leave-day.   Look to our people,
for you shall be leader;   I lead no longer.
Gather my guard   and raise me a grave-mound
housing my ashes   at Hronesnaesse,

reminding my kin   to recall their king
2475 after his pyre   has flared on the point.
Seafarers passing   shall say when they see it
'Beowulf's Barrow'   as bright longboats
drive over darkness,   daring the flood."

So the stern prince   bestowed on his sword-thane
2480 and keen spear-wielder   the kingly collar,
his gold-plated helm   and hammered armor.
He told him to bear them   bravely in battle:
"Farewell, Wiglaf,   last Waegmunding.
I follow our fathers,   foredestined to die,
2485 swept off by fate,   though strong and steadfast."
These heartfelt words   were the warrior's last
before his body   burned in the bale-fire
and his soul sought   the doom of the truthful.

Smitten with sorrow,   the young man saw
2490 the old lord he loved   lying in pain
as life left him.   Slain and slayer
died there together: the dread earth-dragon,
deprived of his life,   no longer would lurk
coiled on the hoard.   Hard-hammered swords
2495 had felled the far-flyer   in front of his lair.
No more would he sport   on the midnight sky,
proud of his wealth,   his power and pomp.
He sprawled on stone   where the war-chief slew him.
Though deeds of daring   were done in that land,
2500 I have heard of no man   whose might would suffice
to face the fire-drake's   fuming breath
or help him escape   if he handled the hoard
once he had woken   its warder from sleep.
Beowulf paid   for that lode with his life;
2505 his loan of days   was lost to the dragon.

Before long the laggards   limped from the woods,
ten cowards together,   the troth-breakers
who had failed to bare   their blades in battle
at the moment their master   needed them most.
2510 In shame they shouldered   their shields and spears.
Armored for war,   they went to Wiglaf
who sorrowfully sat   at their sovereign's shoulder.
Laving his leader,   the foot-soldier failed
to waken the fallen   fighter one whit,
2515 nor could he will   his lord back to life.
The World's Warden   decided what deeds
men might achieve   in those days and these.

A hard answer   was easily offered
by young Wiglaf,   Weohstan's son.

2520 With little love   he looked on the shirkers:
"I tell you in truth,   takers of treasure,
bench-sitting boasters   brave in the hall:
Beowulf gave you   the gear that you wear,
the most finely fashioned   found near or far
2525 for a prince to proffer   his thankless thanes;
but he wasted his wealth   on a worthless troop
who cast off their king   at the coming of war.
Our lord had no need   to laud his liege-men;
yet God, giver   of glory and vengeance,
2530 granted him strength   to stand with his sword.
I could do little   to lengthen his life
facing that foe,   but I fought nonetheless:
beyond my power   I propped up my prince.
The fire-drake faltered   after I struck him,
2535 and his fuming jaws   flamed less fiercely,
but too few friends   flew to our king
when evil beset him.   Now sword-bestowing
and gold-getting   shall cease for the Geats.
You shall have no joy   in the homeland you love.
2540 Your farms shall be forfeit,   and each man fare
alone and landless   when foreign lords
learn of your flight,   your failure of faith.
Better to die   than dwell in disgrace."

Then Wiglaf bade   that the battle-tidings
2545 be sent to the camp   over the sea-cliff
where warriors waited   with shields unslung,
sadly sitting   from dawn until noon
to learn if their lord   and beloved leader
had seen his last sunrise   or soon would return.
2550 The herald would leave them   little to doubt;
he sped up the headland   and spoke to them all:

"Now the wish-granter,   warlord of Weders,
lies on his death-bed.   The leader of Geats
stays in the slaughter-place,   slain by the worm
2555 sprawled at his side.   Dagger-stricken,
the slayer was felled,   though a sword had failed
to wound the serpent.   Weohstan's son,
Wiglaf is waiting   by Beowulf's body;
a living warrior   watches the lifeless,
2560 sad-heartedly   sitting to guard
the loved and the loathed.   Look now for war
as Franks and Frisians   learn how the king
has fallen in combat.   Few foreigners love us,
for Hygelac angered   the harsh Hugas
2565 when his fleet forayed   to far-off Frisia.
Fierce Hetware   met him with forces

bigger than his.   They broke him in battle;
that mail-clad chieftain   fell with his men.
Hygelac took   no trophies to thanes;
2570   no king of the Meroving   wishes us well.

"I also foresee   strife with the Swedes,
feud without end,   for all know Ongentheow
slew Hrethel's son   when Hathcyn first forayed
near Ravenswood   with hot-headed Geats
2575   and raided the realm   of Scylf-land's ruler.
That fearsome old foe,   father of Ohthere,
quickly struck back.   He cut down our king
to rescue the queen   Hathcyn had captured.
Her captors had shorn   the crone of her gold,
2580   dishonored the aged   mother of Onela.
Ongentheow followed   hard on their heels.
Wounded, weary   and fiercely-harried,
those left unslain   by Swedish swords
limped off leaderless,   hid in the holt.
2585   A huge army   beleaguered them there.
All night long   Ongentheow taunted
the wretched raiders.   At daybreak, he swore,
he would slice them to slivers.   Some would swing
slung on his gallows,   sport for the ravens.
2590   But gladness came   again to grim Geats
hearing Hygelac's   horns in the morning,
the trumpet calls   of the troop that tracked them.
Hathcyn's brother,   bold with his band,
had rallied for battle.

                    "A bloody swath
2595   Scylfings and Geats   left on the landscape,
everywhere smeared   with gore from the stricken.
So the two folks   stirred further feuds.
Wise in warfare,   old Ongentheow
grimly stood off,   seeking the safety
2600   of higher ground.   He had heard of Hygelac's
strength in struggles,   his pride and prowess.
Mistrusting his force   to fend off the foray,
he feared for his family   and fell back to guard
the hoard hidden   behind his earthworks.
2605   Then Hrethel's people   pressed the pursuit:
the standards of Hygelac   stormed the stronghold.
There the Swede   was snared between swords.
Eofor humbled   that hoary-haired leader,
though Wulf struck first,   fierce with his weapon,
2610   and a cut vein colored   the king's white head.
Undaunted, Ongentheow   warded him off;
Wulf was wounded   the worse in return:
Ongentheow's blow   broke open his helm,

hurled him headlong,   helpless and bleeding
2615   though not destined   to die on that day.
Then Eofor faced   the folk-lord alone.
Sternly he stood   when his brother slumped:
Hygelac's soldier   with sword in his hand
and helmet on head,   hoarded smithwork
2620   shaped by old crafts,   shattered the shield-wall.
The king crumpled,   struck to the quick.

"Now the Geats gathered   after the slaughter.
Some bound the wound   of Eofor's brother
and bundled him off   the field of battle.
2625   Meanwhile one warrior   plundered the other:
Eofor stripped   the hard-hilted sword,
helm and corselet   from Ongentheow's corpse.
He handed that heap   of armor to Hygelac.
Pleased with his prizes,   the king pledged in turn
2630   to reward war-strokes   as lord of the Weders.
He gave great riches   to Wulf and Eofor.
Once they were home,   he honored each one
with a hundred thousand   in land and linked rings.
No man in middle-earth   ever begrudged them
2635   favor and fortune   bestowed for their feat.
Yet a further honor   was offered Eofor:
the king's only daughter   adorned his house,
awarded in wedlock   to Wonred's son.

"Full of this feud,   this festering hatred,
2640   the Swedes, I am certain,   will swiftly beset us,
as soon as they learn   our lord lies lifeless
who held his hoard,   his hall and his realm
against all foes   when heroes had fallen,
who fostered his folk   with fair kingship.
2645   Now must we hasten,   behold our sovereign,
and bear him for burial.   The brave one shall not
be beggared of booty   to melt on his bier.
Let funeral flames   greedily fasten
on gold beyond measure,   grimly gotten,
2650   lucre our leader   bought with his life.
No thane shall take   tokens to treasure
nor maiden be made   fairer with finery
strung at her throat.   Stripped of their wealth,
they shall wander woefully   all their lives long,
2655   lordless and landless   now that their king
has laid aside laughter,   sport and song.
Their hands shall heft   many a spear-haft,
cold in the morning.   No call of the harp
shall waken warriors   after their battles;
2660   but the black raven   shall boast to the eagle,

crowing how finely   he fed on the fated
when, with the wolf,   he went rending the slain."

Thus the terrible   tidings were told,
and the teller had not   mistaken the truth.
2665 The warriors all rose   and woefully went
to look on the wonder   with welling tears.
They found on the sand   under Earnanaess
their lifeless lord   laid there to rest,
beloved giver   of gifts and gold rings,
2670 the war-king come   at the close of his days
to a marvelous death.   At first the monster
commanded their gaze: grim on the ground
across from the king,   the creature had crumpled,
scaly and scorched,   a fearsome fire-drake
2675 fifty feet long.   He would fly no more,
free in the darkness,   nor drop to his den
at the break of dawn.   Death held the dragon;
he never would coil   in his cavern again.
Beyond the serpent   stood flagons and jars,
2680 plated flatware   and priceless swords
rotting in ruin,   etched out with rust.
These riches had rested   in Earth's embrace
for a thousand winters,   the heritage held
by warders of old,   spell-enwoven
2685 and toilfully tombed   that none might touch them,
unless God Himself,   granter of grace,
true Lord of glory,   allotted release
to one of His choosing   and opened the hoard.

It little profited   him who had wrongfully
2690 hidden the hand-wrought   wealth within walls.
He payment was scant   for slaying the one
with courage to claim it: the kill was quickly
and harshly requited.   So the kingly
may come to strange ends   when their strength is spent
2695 and time meted out.   They may not remain
as men among kin,   mirthful with mead.
Beowulf goaded   the gold's guardian,
raised up the wrath,   not reckoning whether
his death-day had dawned,   not knowing the doom
2700 solemnly sworn   by princes who placed
their hoard in that hollow: the thief who held it
would fall before idols,   forge himself hell-bonds,
waste in torment   for touching the treasure.
He failed to consider   more fully and sooner
2705 who rightfully owned   such awesome riches.

So spoke Wiglaf,   son of Weohstan:
"By the whim of one man,   many warriors

sometimes may suffer,   as here has happened.
No means were at hand   to move my master;

2710 no counsel could sway   the kingdom's keeper
never to trouble   the treasure's taker,
but leave him lying   where long he had hidden,
walled with his wealth   until the world's ending.
He kept to his course,   uncovered the hoard.

2715 Fate was too strongly   forcing him hither.
I have entered that hall,   beheld everything
golden within,   though none too glad
for the opening offered   under its archway.
In haste I heaved   much from the hoard;

2720 a mighty burden   I bore from the barrow
straight to my sovereign.   He still was alive.
His wits were clear;   his words came quickly.
In anguish, the Ancient   asked that I say
he bade you to build   a barrow for him

2725 befitting the deeds   of a fallen friend.
You shall heap it high   over his ashes,
since he was the world's   worthiest warrior,
famed far and wide   for the wealth of his fortress.

"Now let us hurry   hence to the hoard.

2730 For a second time   I shall see that splendor
under the cliff-wall,   those wonders of craftwork.
Come, I shall take you   close to the trove,
where you may behold   heaps of broad gold.
Then let a bier   be readied to bear

2735 our beloved lord   to his long dwelling
under the watch   of the World's Warden."

Then Weohstan's heir   ordered the earls,
heads of houses   and fief holders,
to fetch firewood   fit for the folk-leader's

2740 funeral pyre.   "Flames shall now flare,
feed on the flesh   and fade into darkness,
an ending for him   who often endured
the iron showers   shot over shield-walls
when string-driven storms   of arrows arose

2745 with feathered fins   to steer them in flight
and barbed arrowheads   eager to bite."

Wisely Wiglaf,   son of Weohstan,
summoned the seven   most steadfast thanes.
They went in together,   eight earls entering

2750 under the evil   arch of the earth-house
with one man bearing   a blazing torch.
No lot was cast   to learn which liege-man
would plunder the loot   lying unguarded,
as each searcher   could see for himself;

2755   yet none was unhappy   to hurry that hoard
         out into daylight.   They heaved the dragon
         over the sea-cliff   where surges seized him:
         the treasure's keeper   was caught by the tide.
         Then they filled a wain   with filigreed gold
2760   and untold treasures;   and they carried the king,
         their hoary-haired warlord,   to Hronesnaess.

         There the king's kinsmen   piled him a pyre,
         wide and well-made   just as he willed it.
         They hung it with helmets,   shields and mail-shirts,
2765   then laid in its midst   their beloved lord,
         renowned among men.   Lamenting their loss,
         his warriors woke   the most woeful fire
         to flare on the bluff.   Fierce was the burning,
         woven with weeping,   and wood-smoke rose
2770   black over the blaze,   blown with a roar.
         The fire-wind faltered   and flames dwindled,
         hot at their heart   the broken bone-house.
         Sunken in spirit   at Beowulf's slaying,
         the Geats gathered   grieving together.
2775   Her hair wound up,   a woebegone woman
         sang and resang   her dirge of dread,
         foretelling a future   fraught with warfare,
         kinfolk sundered,   slaughter and slavery
         even as Heaven   swallowed the smoke.

2780   High on the headland   they heaped his grave-mound
         which seafaring sailors   would spy from afar.
         Ten days they toiled   on the scorched hilltop,
         the cleverest men   skillfully crafting
         a long-home built   for the bold in battle.
2785   They walled with timbers   the trove they had taken,
         sealing in stone   the circlets and gems,
         wealth of the worm-hoard   gotten with grief,
         gold from the ground   gone back to Earth
         as worthless to men   as when it was won.
2790   Then sorrowing swordsmen   circled the barrow,
         twelve of his earls   telling their tales,
         the sons of nobles   sadly saluting
         deeds of the dead.   So dutiful thanes
         in liege to their lord   mourn him with lays
2795   praising his peerless   prowess in battle
         as it is fitting   when life leaves the flesh.
         Heavy-hearted   his hearth-companions
         grieved for Beowulf,   great among kings,
         mild in his mien,   most gentle of men,
2800   kindest to kinfolk   and keenest for fame.

RESONANCES

from *The Saga of King Hrolf Kraki*[1]

[KING HRING OF NORWAY MARRIES HVIT]

It is said that to the north in Norway a king named Hring ruled over Uppdales. He had a son named Bjorn. It is told that the queen died, and the king and many others found this a great loss. Hring's countrymen and counsellors asked him to remarry, and so he sent men to the south seeking a wife. But strong headwinds and powerful storms forced them to turn their prows around, letting the ships run before the wind. So it happened that driven by the wind, they were forced north to Finnmark, where they remained for the winter.

One day they went onshore. They walked inland and came to a house. Inside sat two beautiful women, who received them well. The women asked them where they had come from, and the king's men gave an account of their journey and explained their errand. They asked the women about themselves, inquiring why women so beautiful and refined were there alone, so far from other people.

The older woman answered, "For everything, friends, there is a reason. We are here because a powerful king asked for my daughter's hand. Because she did not want to marry him, he threatened her with rough treatment. So I am keeping her here in this secret hiding place while her father is away at war."

They asked who her father might be.

"She is the daughter of the King of the Lapps," said the woman.

The men asked for their names.

The older woman replied, "I am called Ingebjorg and my daughter is named Hvit. I am the Lapp king's mistress."

A girl was there to serve them. The king's men, much taken with these women, decided to ask whether Hvit would go back with them and marry King Hring. The man in charge of the king's mission brought up the question. Hvit did not respond quickly; instead, she deferred the issue to her mother's consideration.

"As the old saying goes," said her mother, "out of every trouble comes some gain. But it displeases me that we are making this arrangement without first asking her father's consent. Nevertheless, it must be ventured, if Hvit is to get ahead."

Hvit then prepared herself to go with them, and they started on the journey to King Hring. The messengers at once inquired whether the king wanted to marry the woman or if she should be sent back. The king, well pleased with the woman, married her at once. He was not concerned that she was neither rich nor powerful. At this

---

1. Translated by Jesse L. Byock. A prose saga or tale written anonymously in Iceland in the 14th century, *The Saga of King Hrolf Kraki* shares many elements with *Beowulf;* Hrolf himself appears in *Beowulf* as Hrothulf, who shares the kingdom with Hrothgar. Both texts draw on a common fund of legends about the Danes in the 5th and 6th centuries, mixing historical events with tales of magic and monstrous transformations. Given here are episodes concerning two bearlike men, Bjorn—whose name means "bear"—and his son Bodvar Bkjarki ("warlike bear-cub"). Beowulf's name similarly means "Bear" (literally "Bee-wolf," a compound term for "bear"). Like Beowulf, Bodvar slays a dragon, which is ravaging the king's court much as Grendel does in *Beowulf.*

The saga gives these magical events a sharply realistic slant. Bodvar visits King Hrolf's court, and befriends a hapless scapegoat named Hott, in comic scenes that give a lively picture of what life was like in the old mead-halls, particularly for those at the bottom of the pecking order. Like Beowulf, and like his father Bjorn, Bodvar is an uncanny hero, not easily fit into the life of the court, an outsider who is the only one able to counter the monstrous threat that comes from outside the mead-hall's walls.

time, the king was getting on in years, and the effects of his age were soon apparent in the queen's behaviour.

[THE LOVE OF BERA AND BJORN]

A freeman's farm lay a short distance from the king's estate. The farmer had a wife and one daughter, who was named Bera. She was young and lovely to look at. Bjorn, the king's son, and Bera, the freeman's daughter, had played together as children, and the two were very close. The freeman was wealthy; he had long been out raiding and in his youth had been a great champion. Bera and Bjorn loved each other deeply and they often met.

Time passed and nothing noteworthy took place. Bjorn, the king's son, matured to manhood. He grew large and strong; he was well bred and was accomplished in all skills. When King Hring was away at war for long periods, which frequently happened, Hvit stayed at home and governed the land. She was not well liked by the people; toward Bjorn, however, she was gentle and tender, though he paid no heed.

One time when the king was about to set out from home, the queen suggested that Bjorn should stay home to help her govern the land. The king thought that her proposal was advisable. The queen was now becoming overbearing and arrogant. The king told his son Bjorn to stay at home and watch over the kingdom with the queen. Bjorn replied that he had little liking for this idea and that he liked the queen even less. The king then told Bjorn to remain behind, and he then set out with a large force.

[BJORN REJECTS QUEEN HVIT'S ADVANCES: THE CURSE]

Bjorn went back to his quarters after arguing with his father, each thinking the other to be wrong. Bjorn, downcast and angry, his face as red as blood, then took to his bed. The queen, wanting to lift his spirits, spoke tenderly to him. He asked her to go away, which she did for a time.

The queen often spoke with Bjorn, telling him that, while the king was away, they had an opportunity to share one bed. She said that their living together would be much better than her experience with a man as old as King Hring.

Bjorn, taking this proposal badly, gave the queen a hard slap. He told her to leave him alone and then threw her out. She said that she was unaccustomed to being rejected or beaten. "And it seems that you, Bjorn, think it preferable to embrace a commoner's daughter. You deserve a punishment, something far more disgraceful than enjoyment of my love and my tenderness. It would not come as a surprise if something should happen to make you suffer for your stubbornness and your stupidity."

She then struck him with her wolfskin gloves, telling him to become a cave bear, grim and savage: "You will eat no food other than your own father's livestock and, in feeding yourself, you will kill more than has ever been observed before. You will never be released from the spell, and your awareness of this disgrace will be more dreadful to you than no remembrance at all."

[BJORN'S TRANSFORMATION INTO A BEAR AND THE BIRTH OF BODVAR]

Then Bjorn disappeared, and no one knew what had become of him. When people realized that Bjorn was missing, they searched for him. As might have been expected, he was not to be found.

Next to be told is that the king's cattle were being killed in large numbers by a grey bear, large and fierce. One evening it happened that Bera, the freeman's daughter, saw the savage bear. It approached her unthreateningly. She thought she recognized in the bear the eyes of Bjorn, the king's son, and so she did not try to run away. The beast then moved away from her, but she followed it all the way until it came to a cave.

When she entered the cave, a man was standing there. He greeted Bera, the freeman's daughter, and she recognized that he was Bjorn, Hring's son. Theirs was a joyful reunion. For a time they stayed together in the cave, because she did not want to part from him while she still had a choice. He told her it was not right for her to be there with him, because he was a beast by day, even if he again became a man at night.

King Hring, when he returned home from the wars, was told everything that had happened while he was away. He learned about the disappearance of his son Bjorn. He was also told about the huge creature that had arrived in the land, attacking mostly the king's own livestock. The queen strongly urged killing the animal, but this was delayed for a time. The king expressed no opinion, even though he thought the events most unusual.

One night, while Bera and the prince lay in their bed, Bjorn began to speak, "I suspect that tomorrow will be my death's day, for they will hunt and trap me. In truth, I find no pleasure in living because of the curse that lies upon me. You are my only delight, but that too will now cease. I want to give you the ring that is under my left arm. Tomorrow you will see the men stalking me. When I am dead, go to the king and ask him to give you whatever is under the beast's left shoulder; he will grant you this request.

"The queen," Bjorn continued, "will be suspicious of you when you want to leave. She will try to make you eat some of the bear's meat, but you must not eat it, because, as you well know, you are pregnant and will give birth to three boys. They are ours, and it will be obvious from their appearance if you have eaten any of the bear's meat. This queen is a great troll.[2] Then go home to your father, where you will give birth to the boys, one of whom will seem best to you. If you are not able to raise them at home, because of their strange and uncontrollable natures, bring them here to the cave. You will find here a chest with three bottoms. Runes are carved on it, and they will tell what each of the boys should receive as his inheritance. Three weapons are imbedded in the rock, and each of our sons shall have the one intended for him. Our firstborn will be called Elk-Frodi, the second son, Thorir, and the third, Bodvar. It seems to me most likely that they will not be weaklings and that their names will long be remembered."

Bjorn foretold many things to her, and afterwards the bear-shape came over him. Then the bear went out, and she followed him.

When she looked around, she saw a great company of men circling the side of the mountain. A large pack of hounds raced in front of the men, and now the bear began to run. Turning away from the cave, he ran along the slope of the mountain. The hounds and the king's men gave chase, but the bear proved difficult for them to catch. Before he was overtaken he maimed many men and killed all the dogs.

At last the men formed a ring around him. The bear ranged about inside the ring, but understood the situation and knew that he would not be able to escape. Then he attacked in the direction of the king. Grabbing the man who stood next to the king, he ripped the man apart while still alive. By then the bear was so exhausted that he threw himself down on the ground. The men seized the opportunity and quickly killed him.

---

2. The Norse term "troll" included witches, ghosts, and giants.

The freeman's daughter saw these events. She went up to the king and said, "Sire, will you give me what is under the beast's left shoulder?"

The king granted her request, saying that nothing there could be unsuitable to give to her. By then, the king's men were well along in flaying the bear. Bera went to the carcass and took the ring, hiding it carefully. The men did not see what she took, but then no one was paying much attention.

The king asked who Bera was, because he did not recognize her. She gave whatever answer she thought best, although it was not the truth.

The king then returned home and Bera found herself swept along among his followers. The queen, now very cheerful, made Bera welcome, inquiring who she was. As before, Bera concealed the truth.

The queen prepared a great feast and had the bear meat readied for the men's enjoyment. The freeman's daughter was in the queen's chamber, unable to get away because the queen was suspicious about her identity. Sooner than expected, the queen entered the room with a plate of bear meat. She told Bera to eat, but Bera did not want to eat.

"How uncommonly rude," said the queen, "that you reject the hospitality that the queen herself has chosen to offer you. Eat it quickly, otherwise something worse will be prepared for you."

The queen cut a small piece of the meat for Bera, and in the end Bera ate it. The queen then cut another piece and put it into Bera's mouth. Bera swallowed a small morsel of it, then spat the rest out of her mouth. She declared that she would not eat any more, even if she were to be tortured or killed. "It may be," said the queen, "that this bit will be enough," and she burst out laughing.

Bera then escaped and went home to her father. She had a very difficult pregnancy. She told her father the whole story relating to her condition and the reasons for what had happened. A little while later she fell ill and gave birth to a boy, though of an extraordinary kind. He was a man above the navel, but an elk below that. He was named Elk-Frodi. She bore another son, who was named Thorir. He had dog's feet from his insteps down. Because of this, he was called Thorir Hound's Foot; otherwise, he was the most handsome of men. A third boy was born, and this one was the most promising. He was named Bodvar, and there was no blemish on him. Bera loved Bodvar the most. * * * [3]

[BODVAR'S VENGEANCE]

Bodvar remained at home with his mother, who loved him dearly. Of all men, he was the most accomplished and handsome, but as yet he had not met very many people. Once he asked his mother who his father was. She told him about his father's killing, giving her son all the information. She explained how Bjorn had fallen under the spell of his stepmother.

Bodvar said, "We have wrongs to repay this witch."

Then Bera told him how the queen had forced her to eat the bear's flesh, "and the result can be seen in your brothers, Thorir Hound's Foot and Elk-Frodi."

Bodvar said, "I think Frodi ought to have felt more bound to take vengeance on this cowardly witch for our father than to kill innocent men for their money and carry out other vile acts. Likewise, I think it is odd that Thorir went away without giving this ogress something to remember. So it seems to me that I should punish her on our behalf."

Bera replied, "Arrange it so that she is not able to use her black arts to injure you."

---

3. Frodi and Thorir grow up as wild, unruly youths, and soon leave home.

He said that it would be so arranged.

Bera and Bodvar now went to see the king. Following Bodvar's advice, Bera explained to the king how everything had come about. She showed him the ring, which she had taken from under the shoulder of the beast, explaining that Bjorn, his son, had owned it.

The king agreed that without a doubt he recognized the ring; "I suspected that the queen was behind the strange events that have happened here, but for the sake of my love for her I have let matters remain quiet."

Bodvar said, "Send her away now or else we will take vengeance on her."

The king said that he wished to compensate Bodvar for his loss with as much treasure as he might want, but that matters were to remain quiet, as they had been before. He would give Bodvar a position of command, the title of jarl straightaway and, after his days were over, the kingdom, if only no harm were done to her.

Bodvar replied that he did not want to be king; rather he said that he wanted to be with the king and to serve him. "You are so trapped by this monster that you hardly have the wits to run your rightful kingdom, and from now on she will never thrive in this place."

Bodvar became so filled with fury that the king dared not stand in his way. Carrying a pouch in his hand, Bodvar went to the queen's chamber; the king and Bodvar's mother followed after him. Bodvar entered the chamber and turned to Queen Hvit. He placed the rough leather bag over her head. Then he pulled it down and tied it around her throat. He knocked her off her feet and with beatings and torments sent her to Hel,[4] dragging her through every street.

Many or most of those who were within the hall thought this punishment was only half of what she deserved. The king, however, took it very badly, but there was nothing he could do about it. In this way Queen Hvit lost her miserable life.

Bodvar was eighteen years old when this happened. A little later King Hring took sick and died. Bodvar became the ruler of the kingdom, but he was content with this position for only a short while. Then he called an assembly of the men of the land. At that meeting he announced that he wanted to leave and that he was marrying his mother to the man named Valsleyt, a jarl already in the land. Bodvar took part in the wedding feast before riding away.

[BODVAR AT THE COURT OF KING HROLF]

Nothing is said of Bodvar's travels until he arrived in Denmark and was only a short distance from Hleidargard.

One day a heavy rainstorm soaked Bodvar thoroughly. His horse, which he had ridden hard, was exhausted under him. The going was heavy since the ground had turned to mud. That night it grew very dark and the downpour continued steadily. Bodvar took no notice until his horse stumbled on a large obstacle. He dismounted and looked around, soon realizing that he had come upon some sort of house. He found the door, knocked on it and a man came out of the house. Bodvar asked for shelter for the night. The farmer answered that he would not send him away in the dead of night, especially as he was a stranger. From what the farmer could see, the stranger seemed to be very imposing. Bodvar stayed there overnight and was treated hospitably. He asked many questions about the exploits of King Hrolf and his champions, inquiring also about the distance to Hleidargard.

---

4. Goddess of the underworld.

"It is now a very short distance," said the farmer. "Do you intend to go there?"
"Yes," replied Bodvar, "that is my intention."

The farmer declared that it would be fitting for him to do so, "because I see you are a large, powerful man, and they think themselves great champions." And the old woman living there sobbed aloud, as she did whenever they mentioned King Hrolf and his champions at Hleidargard.

Bodvar asked, "Why are you crying, you simple old woman?"

The old woman said, "My husband and I have one son, who is named Hott. One day he went to the stronghold to amuse himself, but the king's men taunted him. He could not stand up to such conduct, so the men took hold of him and stuck him into a pile of bones. It is their habit at mealtimes, when they are finished gnawing the meat from a bone, to throw it at him. Sometimes, if the bone hits him, he is badly injured. Whether he is alive or dead I do not know. But I ask this reward from you, in return for my hospitality, that you throw smaller bones at him rather than larger ones; that is, if he is not already dead."[5]

Bodvar answered, "I will do as you request, but I do not think it is warriorlike to strike people with bones or to harm children or men of small account."

"Then you will do well," said the old woman, "because your hand seems to be strong, and I know for certain that, if you chose not to hold back, an opponent would have no refuge from your blows."

Bodvar continued on his way to Hleidargard. After arriving at the king's royal residence, he immediately stabled his horse in the stall with the king's best mounts without asking anyone's permission. Then he entered the hall, where there were only a few men. He sat down near the entrance, and after he had been there for a short time, he heard a noise coming from somewhere in the corner. Bodvar looked in that direction and saw a man's hand emerging from a huge pile of bones lying there. The hand was very black.

Bodvar walked over to the corner and asked who was in the bone pile. He was answered, though timidly, "My name is Hott, kind sir."

"Why are you here?" asked Bodvar. "Or what are you doing?"

Hott's reply was, "I am making myself a shield wall, kind sir."

"You and your shield wall are pathetic," said Bodvar. He grabbed hold of the man and yanked him out of the bone pile.

Hott screamed loudly and then said, "You are acting as though you want me dead, since I had prepared my defences so well. Now you have broken my shield wall into pieces even though I had built it so high around me that it protected me against all your blows. No blow has reached me now for some time, yet the wall was not as complete as I had intended it to be."

Bodvar said, "You will no longer build your shield wall."

Hott replied, "Are you going to kill me now, kind sir?"

Bodvar, telling Hott to be quiet, picked him up and carried him from the hall to a nearby lake. Few paid attention to this. Bodvar washed Hott completely and then returned to the same place on the bench where he had sat previously. He led Hott there and sat him down beside himself. Hott was so scared that all his limbs and joints trembled, although he seemed to understand that this man wanted to help him.

Later in the evening men crowded into the hall. Hrolf's champions saw that Hott had been seated on one of the benches, and it seemed to them that the man who had

---

5. Bone-throwing was popular at Scandinavian feasts, and several medieval legal codes list killing by bone-throwing as a serious offense.

undertaken to do that was indeed brave. Hott cast a fearful glance in the direction of his old acquaintances, for he had received only harm from them. Afraid for his life, he tried to get back to his bone pile, but Bodvar held on to Hott and he was unable to get away. Hott thought that, if he could manage to get to the heap of bones, he would not be so exposed to the men's blows.

The king's men now took up their old habits. At first they threw small bones across the floor at Bodvar and Hott. Bodvar acted as if he saw nothing. Hott was so frightened that he took neither food nor drink, expecting to be struck at any moment.

Then Hott said to Bodvar, "Kind sir, here comes a large knuckle bone, which is intended to do us much harm."

Bodvar told Hott to be quiet. He cupped his hand and caught the knuckle bone, which included the attached leg bone. Bodvar threw the knuckle back, and it smashed with such force into the man who had thrown it that he was killed. The king's men were struck with fear.

King Hrolf and his champions up in the fortress were now told that an imposing man had arrived in the hall and had killed one of the king's retainers. The other retainers wanted to have the man put to death.

The king asked whether his follower had been killed without cause.

"Almost," they said.

Then the full truth came out. King Hrolf said that by no means should this man be killed: "It is a bad habit that you have adopted, throwing bones at innocent men. It brings dishonour to me and shame to you. I have repeatedly spoken to you about this matter, but you have paid no attention. I suspect that this man, whom you have now attacked, is no weakling. Summon him to me, so that I can find out who he is."

Bodvar went before the king and greeted him artfully. The king asked for his name.

"Your retainers call me Hott's protector, but my name is Bodvar."

The king said, "What compensation are you prepared to offer me for my man?"

Bodvar replied, "He got what he deserved."

The king said, "Do you want to be my man and occupy his place?"

Bodvar answered, "I will not refuse to become your man, but Hott and I will not, as matters stand, be separated. We will both sit closer to you on the benches than that man did, or else we both leave."

The king said, "I see no honour in him, but I will not begrudge him food."

Bodvar now chose a seat that pleased him, not bothering to sit in the place the other man had occupied. At one point he pulled three men up out of their seats, and then he and Hott sat down in their places. They had now moved much farther into the hall than earlier. Men thought Bodvar difficult to deal with, and there was strong resentment against him.

As Yuletime drew near, gloom settled over the men.[6] Bodvar asked Hott what caused their dejection. Hott told him that a huge, monstrous beast had come there the past two winters. "The creature has wings on its back and it usually flies. For two autumns now it has come here, causing much damage. No weapon can bite into it, and the king's champions, even the greatest among them, do not return home."

Bodvar said, "The hall is not so well manned as I had thought, if one animal alone could destroy the king's lands and his livestock."

Hott said, "It is not an animal, rather it is the greatest of trolls."

---

6. The pre-Christian winter feast of Yule was often a time of supernatural occurrences.

Then came Yule eve, and the king said, "It is my wish that tonight men remain calm, making no noise, and I forbid any of my men to put themselves in danger with the beast. The livestock will be left to their fate, because I do not want to lose any of my men." Everyone faithfully promised the king to do as he asked.

Bodvar stole away in the night and took Hott with him. Hott went only after being forced to do so, declaring that he was being steered straight toward death. Bodvar said, "Things will turn out for the better."

They now left the hall behind them, with Bodvar carrying Hott because he was so frightened. They saw the creature, and immediately Hott started to scream as loudly as he could, crying that the beast would swallow him. Bodvar told the dog to be quiet and threw him down on the moor. There he lay, not a little scared, at the same time not daring to go home.

Bodvar now went against the beast. He was hampered by his sword, which, as he tried to draw it, stuck fast in its scabbard. Determined, Bodvar urged the sword out until the scabbard squeaked. Then he grasped the scabbard and the sword came out of the sheath. Immediately he thrust it up under the beast's shoulder, striking so hard that the blade reached quickly into the heart. Then the beast fell dead to the ground.

After this encounter Bodvar went to the place where Hott was lying. He picked up Hott and carried him to where the beast lay dead. Hott was trembling violently.

Bodvar said, "Now you will drink the beast's blood." For a while Hott was unwilling, although certainly he dared do nothing else. Bodvar made him drink two large mouthfuls as well as eat some of the beast's heart. After that Bodvar seized Hott, and they fought each other for a long time.

Bodvar said, "You have now become remarkably strong, and I expect that from this day forward you will have no fear of King Hrolf's retainers."

Hott replied, "From now on, I will fear neither them nor you."

"Then, Hott, my friend," said Bodvar, "things have turned out well. Let us now go back to the beast, raising him up in such a way that men will think the creature must be alive."

They did just that and afterward went home. They kept these events to themselves, and so no one knew what they had done.

In the morning, the king asked what was known about the beast, whether it had visited them in the night. He was told that all the livestock were safe in the pens, unharmed. The king ordered men to inquire if there were any indications that the beast had visited them. The guards went out but quickly returned. They told the king that the beast was coming toward them, furiously advancing on the stronghold. The king ordered his retainers to be valiant. Each was to do his best according to his courage, so that they might overcome this monster. Obeying the king's command, the men prepared themselves.

The king looked toward the beast, saying finally, "I see no movement in it, but which one of you will now seize the opportunity to go against it?"

Bodvar said, "That would likely satisfy the curiosity of the bravest man. Hott, my friend, throw off the slander that men have laid on you, claiming that you have neither spirit nor courage. Go and kill the beast. You can see that no one else is too eager to do so."

"Right," said Hott, "I will set myself to that task."

The king said, "I do not know where your courage has come from, Hott, but much has changed about you in a short time."

Hott said, "For this task, give me the sword Golden Hilt, the one that you are holding, and then I will either kill the beast or find my own death."

King Hrolf said, "That sword is not to be carried except by a man who is both strong in body and noble in spirit."

Hott replied, "Assume, Sire, that I am made from such a mould."

The king retorted, "How can one tell? Perhaps more has changed about you than is evident. Few would think that you are the same person. Take the sword, for it will serve you well if my instincts about you turn out to be correct."

Then Hott went boldly against the beast, thrusting at it as soon as he was within striking distance. The beast fell down dead.

Bodvar said, "See, Sire, what he has now accomplished."

The king answered, "Certainly he has changed greatly, but Hott alone did not kill the beast; rather you did it."

Bodvar said, "That may be."

The king said, "I knew when you came here that few would be your equal, but it seems to me that your finest achievement is that you have made Hott into another champion. He was previously thought to be a man in whom there was little probability of much luck. I do not want him called Hott any longer; instead, from now on he will be called Hjalti.[7] You will now be called after the sword Golden Hilt."

And here ends this tale of Bodvar and his brothers.

Jorge Luis Borges: Poem Written in a Copy of Beowulf [1]

> At various times I have asked myself what reasons
> moved me to study while my night came down,
> without particular hope of satisfaction,
> the language of the blunt-tongue Anglo-Saxons.[2]
> Used up by the years my memory
> loses its grip on words that I have vainly
> repeated and repeated. My life in the same way
> weaves and unweaves its weary history.[3]
> Then I tell myself: it must be that the soul
> has some secret sufficient way of knowing
> that it is immortal, that its vast encompassing
> circle can take in all, accomplish all.
> Beyond my anxiety and beyond this writing
> the universe waits, inexhaustible, inviting.

---

7. "Hilt."

1. Translated by Alastair Reid. Jorge Luis Borges (1899–1986) was born in Buenos Aires, Argentina. His paternal grandmother came from Northumbria, a connection that, in what he called "a romantic superstition," linked him with the "Saxon and perhaps Danish past" of Old English poetry, and the legends of Beowulf. A celebrated poet, short-story writer, essayist, and polymath, Borges in all of his writing treated books and the life of the imagination as if they were interchangeable (if not superior) to the world of "real" people and events. Wide-ranging and eccentric in his influences and the connections he made between writings from every epoch and every corner of the globe, Borges first took up the serious study of Old English in the 1950s, when his sight failed him, and he returned to the mnemonic forms of poetry, more amenable to composition in the head. "Anglo-Saxon," he wrote, "was as intimate an experience to me as looking at a sunset or falling in love." For more on Borges, see his principal listing in Volume F.

2. "While my night came down" is reminiscent of the twilight mood of the second part of Beowulf, while also referring both to the poet's advancing years and the increasing severity of his blindness. Rather than for mastery, he wrote, he had undertaken the study of Old English for the pleasure of the doing.

3. Both the theme of repetition and that of the weaving of a life are central motifs in Beowulf.

⊷ ⊰◈⊱ ⊶

The Poem of the Cid
late 12th–early 13th centuries

The Poem of the Cid is unique among medieval epics in being based on the life of a near-contemporary historical figure rather than a distant legend. Rodrigo Díaz de Vivar lived in the eleventh century. He was nicknamed the Cid (from the Arabic *sayyid,* or "leader") by his Muslim allies, and was renowned by both friends and enemies as the greatest general of his time. As Ibn Bassan, a Muslim historian of the period, put it: "This man, who was the scourge of his age, was, by his unflagging and clearsighted energy, his virile character, and his heroism, a miracle among the great miracles of the Almighty." Like most epic heroes, the Cid is exemplary in his behavior, yet *The Poem of the Cid* is unusual in being dedicated to the mature years of its hero rather than to the making of his reputation. What further sets him apart is his essential humanity: in his reaction to being exiled, in his behavior toward his wife and daughters, in his desire to improve his lot in life, in his stubborn refusal to accept his king's unjust treatment of him, he certainly remains heroic, but he also becomes credible as an individual.

The kingdom of Castile reflected in the background of the *Cid* was the shifting, embattled center of an unsettled Iberian peninsula. In the early eleventh century, civil war in al-Andalus, the Moorish territories primarily in the south, had left the Muslim empire broken into weak *taifas,* or splinter-states. By 1039, Ferdinand I had united Castile and León, carving them partially out of al-Andalus. When Ferdinand died in 1065, he left his kingdoms partitioned between Sancho, his eldest son, who received Castile, Alfonso, who was given León, and García, the youngest, who was granted Galicia and Portugal. Sancho refused to accept the partition, and, with the help of his young knight, Rodrigo Díaz, captured Alfonso in battle, reunited the kingdoms, and began extracting tribute from the *taifas.* Sancho was assassinated in 1072, presumedly at the behest of Alfonso and his allies, the Beni-Gómez clan. When Alfonso was crowned king of León-Castile, he took on the Cid as his vassal, arranging his marriage to his niece, Jimena, to assure his loyalty.

The Cid's first exile, in 1081, was the result of exercising too much freedom during his trips south to collect tribute. On one such journey, the Cid had skirmished with Count García Ordóñez of the Beni-Gómez clan, routing him in battle and humiliating him by plucking his beard. He was later accused by Alfonso of skimming off what he had collected. Choosing not to take up arms against his lord, as a knight was entitled to do if unjustly banished, the Cid offered his services to the north. It was at this time that the Cid cultivated the alliance of the Muslim emir of Saragossa and the enmity of the Christian count Berenguer Ramón II of Barcelona. Meanwhile, Alfonso was constrained to recall his banished general in 1086 when the Almoravids, a highly organized orthodox Muslim sect, swept up through Iberia out of North Africa. Given a free hand by his lord, the Cid managed to subdue most of eastern al-Andalus, including the important port city of Valencia. But only three years later, apparently fearful of the Cid's growing power, Alfonso banished him again. This time, he also imprisoned the Cid's wife Jimena and their three children, stripped him of his estates and riches, and destroyed his houses. The Cid returned to the lands he had subjected in the east, winning a famous victory at the pine grove of Tévar against the combined forces of his old enemy Berenguer and his former lord, Mostain of Saragossa. When Alfonso pardoned him a second time, the Cid chose to remain where he was, holding Valencia against Almoravid forces until his death in 1099, at the age of about fifty-six.

The Poem of the Cid compresses the thirteen years of the Cid's two exiles (1081–1094) into five years of events. It imparts some of the complex flavor of the political alliances and multiple factions, but also conclusively resolves the conflict between Alfonso and Rodrigo in a way it never was historically. And while the real Cid was evidently as magnanimous and loyal as his poetic counterpart, his character is idealized in many ways, taking on the attributes of a Christ-like martyr. Fictional events are introduced to underline key aspects of his exemplary character: an episode with Jewish moneylenders who are tricked into bankrolling the Cid's first expedition into Moorish territory; disastrous first marriages of his two daughters, against his will; a tragicomic encounter with a lion; and a famous court scene at Toledo in which he brilliantly orchestrates his revenge.

Modern readers are sometimes surprised over the poem's fascination with the nitty-gritty economics of war and exile. We are told in detail how the Cid financed his expedition, what manner of booty he won at every turn, and how he apportioned it. Such marauding as the Cid and his men perpetrate in eastern al-Andalus was considered a legitimate response to the need to support oneself in exile, and it also became a primary indication of one's prowess as a warrior. The booty that the Cid is able to accumulate corresponds directly to the magnitude of his fame. Moreover, the plunder he takes from Muslim Spain was thought of in Christian circles as equivalent to the spoils of a Crusade. Alfonso's push southward has traditionally been termed the beginning of the *reconquista,* the recapturing of Spain by Christian forces that culminated in the Muslim surrender of Granada in 1492, followed by the expulsion of the Jews later the same year. The Cid's indomitable Christian faith is in evidence from the moment in the opening stanza when he thanks God, Job-like, for the evil his enemies have plotted against him. This crusading faith is not mitigated by the fact that at times he holds Muslims as his allies and friends and at others he battles against fellow Christians; the poem is unusually realistic in its combination of the complexity of everyday human interactions with the powerful simplicity of ideological certainties.

Because *The Poem of the Cid* has traditionally been considered the foundational epic of Castilian culture, there has been intense debate over the date of composition of this anonymous poem, preserved in a single, early fourteenth-century manuscript. To what degree is it an accurate historical record of eleventh-century Spain, and to what degree does it slant events to please a particular court? Although the debate is unlikely ever to be resolved, it is generally accepted today that the manuscript was transcribed from a poem originally composed orally in sung performances in a court setting. Evidence of oral composition remains in the use of stock phrases (such as "born in a fortunate hour") metrically fitted to half or full lines of verse, the same sort of filling out of lines found in Homer. The poem is made up of 152 epic stanzas, ranging in length from three to more than a hundred lines. The lines themselves are also of irregular length, usually around fourteen syllables broken into two half-lines. The lines of any stanza, or *laisse,* all terminate in the same final vowel, allowing for complex effects of rhythm and rhyme. Consider, for example, the five lines of *laisse* 2, a simple transition to take the Cid from his ancestral home to the town of Burgos from which he will set off into exile:

> Allí piensan de aguijar,   allí sueltan las rriendas;
> a la exida de Bivar   ovieron la corneja diestra
> e entrando a Burgos   oviéronla siniestra.
> Meció Mio Cid los ombros   e engrameó la tiesta:
> '¡Albricia, Álbar Fáñez,   ca echados somos de tierra!'

> There they set spur   there they released the reins.
> At the gate of Bivar   on their right hand the crow flew;
> As they rode into Burgos   it flew on their left.
> My Cid raised his head   and shrugged his shoulders:
> "Rejoice Alvar Fáñez,   though this exile is ours!" (page 666)

The endings play variations on "r" and "a." The central action of the pair of crows is set off from the others and unified by a rich rhyme (*-estra*), the alliteration and parallelism between *exida* and *entrando* and *Bivar* and *Burgos,* and the repetition of *ovieron* to begin the second half-line in each of the two verses. The alliteration of *tiesta* and *tierra* unifies the last two lines, setting up the climactic close of the *laisse,* a characteristic example of the Cid's gallows humor (softened in the translation: literally, "Rejoice, Alvar Fáñez, for we are chased from the land").

The poem's larger structure duplicates the focus of individual episodes on acquisition and its counterpart, loss and separation. Although the opening stanzas have not survived (they are supplemented here with prose from later chronicles) the poem now begins powerfully by introducing the Cid at the moment of his greatest trial. Medieval narrative, especially when stemming from oral performance, tends to establish character through action and comparison rather than reflection or analysis, and the way in which the Cid reacts to this extreme test of his mettle reflects his behavior throughout the poem. Although divided into three *cantares,* or sung parts, the poem structurally falls into two interlocking halves: the story of the Cid's acquisition of booty and fame following his exile, and the story of his daughters' marriages and his eventual acquisition of social status, following his survival of a second, equally traumatic test.

Perhaps the key quality the Cid exhibits is that of *mesura,* a nearly untranslatable but essential trait of feudal character. Moderation is its central component, but its meaning extends far beyond that. For example, we never witness the ruthless violence to which a general of the Cid's stature would have had to resort. Battles are neatly and cleanly resolved so that attention can be devoted to their aftermath; ruthless violence is left to the villains of the epic, the Infantes of Carrión. Their lack of moderation stands in strict contrast to the Cid's self-control, just as his beard recurs as the physical sign of his maturity, faith, and loyalty. Indeed, even King Alfonso shows need of improvement when compared to the Cid. The poet reserves the epithet "the good king Don Alfonso" for the second half of the poem; we begin, by contrast, with the townspeople's lament, "*¡Dios, que buen vassallo, si oviesse buen senor!*" ("What a good vassal. If only he had a good lord!") The uneasy situation of the worthy knight bound as vassal to an unworthy lord is a constant theme in epic and courtly narrative, already found with Achilles and Agamemnon in the ancient Greek *Iliad.* Perhaps the most noteworthy of the Cid's many exemplary qualities is not his individual heroism but his ability to improve the character of his lord. The Cid's humanity makes him perhaps the most accessible of all epic heroes; the idealized perfection through which that humanity is expressed makes his epic a window into the aspirations and obsessions of medieval Castile.

PRONUNCIATIONS:
    cantar: cahn-TAHR
    Corpes: KOHR-pess
    El Cid: el SEED
    Féliz Muñoz: FAY-lease MOON-yohs
    Jimena: hee-MEN-ah
    Rodrigo Díaz de Vivar: rod-REE-go DEE-ahs day vee-VAHR

The Poem of the Cid[1]

The First Cantar

King Alfonso sent Ruy Díaz, My Cid, to collect the annual tribute from the Kings of Córdova and Seville. Almutamiz, King of Seville, and Almudafar, King of Granada,

---

1. Translated by W. S. Merwin. The first folio (about 50 verses) is evidently missing from the manuscript of the poem. The opening prose account is translated from the *Chronicle of Castile* (early 14th century) and several others which recount the same events of 1079.

at that time were bitter enemies and wished each other's death.[2] And there were then with Almudafar, King of Granada, these noblemen who supported him: the Count Don García Ordóñez, and Fortún Sánchez, the son-in-law of King García of Navarre, and Lope Sánchez; and each of these noblemen with all his power supported Almudafar, and went against Almutamiz, King of Seville.[3]

Ruy Díaz Cid, when he heard that they were coming against the King of Seville, who was a vassal and tributary of his lord King Alfonso, took it ill and was much grieved; and he sent letters to all of them begging them not to come against the King of Seville nor destroy his land, because of the allegiance they owed to King Alfonso; for they might know if they continued to do so, King Alfonso could not do otherwise than to come to the aid of his vassal, who was his tributary. The King of Granada and the noblemen took no note of the Cid's letters, but using violence they destroyed all the land of the King of Seville as far as the castle of Cabra.[4]

When Ruy Díaz Cid saw this, he took all the force of Christians and Moors that he could muster, and went against the King of Granada to expel him from the land of the King of Seville. And the King of Granada and the noblemen who were with him, when they knew that he was coming thus, sent to tell him that they would not leave the land on his account. Ruy Díaz Cid, when he heard this, could not rest until he had set upon them, and he went against them and fought with them in the field, and the battle lasted from nine o'clock until midday, and the Moors and Christians on the side of the King of Granada suffered great slaughter, and the Cid overcame them and forced them to flee from the field. And in this battle the Cid took prisoner the Count Don García Ordóñez and pulled out part of his beard,[5] and took prisoner many other gentlemen and so many of the ordinaries that they lost count; and the Cid held them three days and then released them all. While he held them prisoner he sent his men to gather together the belongings and things of value which remained on the field; afterwards the Cid with all his company and all his gains returned to Almutamiz, King of Seville, and gave to him and to all his Moors whatever they knew to be theirs, and whatever they wished to take besides.[6] And always after that, both Moors and Christians called this same Ruy Díaz of Bivar the Cid Campeador, which is to say, the warrior, the winner of battles.[7]

Then Almutamiz gave him many fine presents and the tribute for which he had come, and the Cid with all the tribute went back to King Alfonso, his lord. The King received him very well and was highly pleased with him and most satisfied with all he had done there. Because of this, many were envious and sought to do him evil, and spoke against him to the King.

2. The Caliphate of Córdoba or Córdova, which ruled al-Andalus during the 10th century, declined during the tumultuous first decades of the 11th, which led to the rise of numerous *taifas,* or independent kingdoms, on which the Christian rulers to the north were able to impose tribute. Seville, ruled at this time by the Muslim poet-prince Almutamiz, controlled most of southern al-Andalus, with one notable exception being Granada, ruled by Almudafar.

3. The historical figure Count Don García Ordóñez was a favorite of Alfonso VI. He was married to Urraca, daughter of King García of Navarre and Alfonso's niece. He had been guarantor of the Cid's own marriage. The following incident marks the end of their friendship. Fortún Sánchez de Yárnoz was married to another of García's daughters.

4. Now a town in the province of Córdoba, the castle of Cabra was between Seville and Granada, quite a bit closer to Granada.

5. In medieval Spain, a man's beard was the symbol of his virility and honor. The Cid's action is one of nearly unequalled humiliation for Don García.

6. The collection of booty was legal and customary at the time, and a prime motive for the constant warmongering of the Spanish lords. The Cid's sharing and redistribution of the booty is a sign of his correct behavior as a lord and of his particular generosity.

7. The chronicle chooses this episode as the origin of the appellation "Cid Campeador," "the warrior, winner of battles," for Rodrigo Díaz of Bivar. The family estate (now called Vivar del Cid) was in the valley of the river Ubierna, six miles north of the old Castilian capital of Burgos.

The King, who already nursed an ancient rancor against him, came to believe them, and sent letters to the Cid telling him that he must leave the kingdom. The Cid, when he had read the letters, was much grieved, and yet he did not wish to disobey, although he was allowed only nine days' grace in which to leave the kingdom.

1

[HERE PER ABBAT'S MANUSCRIPT BEGINS]

"and those who come with me   God's good mercy sustain,[8]
and those who remain here   I shall be content with them."
Then spoke Alvar Fáñez,   his first cousin:
"We shall go with you, Cid,   through deserts, through towns,
5   *and never fail you   while we are whole in limb;*
with you we shall wear out   horses and beasts of burden
and our goods—and our garments
and serve you always   as faithful liege men."
Then to what Don Alvaro had said   all gave their consent;
10   *My Cid thanked them deeply   for all they had there spoken.*
     My Cid went out from Bivar,   toward Burgos riding,[9]
and left his palaces   disinherited and barren.

His eyes,   grievously weeping,
he turned his head   and looked back upon them.[1]
15   He saw doors standing open   and gates without fastenings,
the porches empty   without cloaks or coverings
and without falcons   and without molted° hawks.   new-feathered
He sighed, My Cid,   for he felt great affliction.
He spoke, My Cid,   well, and with great moderation.
20   "Thanks be to Thee, our Father   Who art in Heaven!
My evil enemies   have wrought this upon me."

2

     There they set spur   there they released the reins.
At the gate of Bivar   on their right hand the crow flew;
as they rode into Burgos   it flew on their left.[2]
25   My Cid raised his head   and shrugged his shoulders:
"Rejoice, Alvar Fáñez,   though this exile is ours!"

3

     My Cid Ruy Díaz   rode into Burgos,
in his company   sixty pennons.[3]
They crowded to see him,   women and men;
30   townsmen and their wives   sat at the windows
weeping from their eyes,   so great was their sorrow.

8. The italicized verses are a fragment of the poem not in the manuscript but preserved in the *Chronicle of the Kings of Castile.*

9. Burgos was the capital of the kingdom of Castile, and held to be the place where Díaz had compelled Alfonso to swear himself innocent of his brother's death.

1. The beginning of the poem as it stands in Per Abbat's manuscript, highly effective in its blunt beginning right in the middle of the action.

2. The crow on the right of their path is a good omen; that on the left is an evil one.

3. A long streamer attached to the head of a lance (or a helmet), here standing for the 60 knights riding with him.

And one sentence only   was on every tongue:
"Were his lord but worthy,   God, how fine a vassal!"

4

    They would have asked him in gladly,   but did not dare,
35   for King Alfonso   cherished such anger.
His letter had come   to Burgos the night before
with all formality   and sealed with a great seal:
that to My Cid Ruy Díaz   no one must give shelter,
that who should do so,   let him learn the truth of the matter,
40   he would lose all that he had   and the eyes out of his face
and, what is more, they would lose   their bodies and their souls.
Those Christian people,   great sorrow they had
hiding from My Cid,   for none dared say a word.

    The Campeador   rode up to the inn;
45   when he reached the portal   he found it closed against him.
For fear of King Alfonso   they had concluded thus:
unless he break the door   on no account admit him.
Those with My Cid   shouted out for them to open,
those within   would not answer them.
50   My Cid spurred forward,   to the door he came,
drew his foot from the stirrup,   kicked a gash in the wood;
the door was well secured   and did not open.

    A little girl of nine   appeared in sight:
"Ah, Campeador, in a good hour   you first girded on sword!
55   The King forbids us this;   last night his letter came here,
with all formality   and sealed with a great seal.
We dare not let you in   nor lodge you for any reason,
or we shall lose   our goods and our houses,
and besides these   the eyes out of our faces.
60   Cid, you will gain nothing   by our miseries;
but the Creator bless you   with all his holy virtues."[4]
The child spoke this   and then turned back to her house.
Now the Cid can see that he finds   no grace in the King's eyes.
He went from the doorway   and spurred through Burgos;
65   at the Church of Santa María,   there he stepped from his horse;
there he knelt down,   from his heart he prayed.
The prayer ended,   once more he mounted,
rode out of the gate,   passed over the Arlanzón.[5]
Outside the town of Burgos   at the river bed he stayed,
70   set his tent   and there dismounted.
My Cid Ruy Díaz,   who in good hour girded on sword,
when no house would have him   pitched camp on the shingle,
and a goodly company   encamped around him.
There he camped, My Cid   as in a wilderness.
75   In the town of Burgos   the law forbade

---

4. Both the oft-repeated epithet, "in a good hour you first   are signs of the poem's oral composition.
girded on sword," and the repetition of the king's order   5. Burgos was located on the banks of the river Arlanzón.

that he should so much as buy   anything that was food;
no one dared sell him   a pennyworth of bread.

5

Martín Antolínez,   the accomplished man of Burgos,[6]
to My Cid and his men   brought bread and wine
80   which was not bought   because it was his own;
of all manner of food   they had ample provision.
He was pleased, My Cid   the accomplished Campeador,
and all the others   who were in his train.
Martín Antolínez spoke,   you will hear what he said:
85   "Ah, Campeador,   in a good hour you were born!
We stay here tonight,   we must be gone by morning,
for I shall be accused   of this service I have done;
in King Alfonso's anger   I shall be included.
If I escape with you   alive and sound of limb,
90   sooner or later the King   will love me as a friend;
if not, all that I leave,   I value at nothing."

6

My Cid spoke,   who in good hour girded on sword:
"Martín Antolínez,   you are a hardy lance!
If I live,   I will double your pay.
95   Gone is my gold   and all my silver;
you can see plainly   that I carry nothing
and I need money   for all my followers;
I am forced to this   since freely I can have nothing.
With your aid   I will build two coffers;
100   we shall stuff them with sand   to make them heavier,
stud them with nails   and cover them with worked leather,
the leather crimson   and the nails well gilded.[7]

7

Go in haste and find me   Raquel and Vidas,[8] and say:
'Since in Burgos I may not buy,   and the King's disfavor pursues me,
105   I cannot carry this wealth   for it is too heavy.
I must put it in pawn   for whatever is reasonable.
So that no Christians may see it,   come and fetch it in by night.'
Let the Creator see it   and all His saints besides;
I cannot do otherwise   and for this have little heart."

8

110   Martín Antolínez   without delay
went into Burgos,   into the castle.
For Raquel and Vidas   he asked immediately.

9

Raquel and Vidas   were both in the same place
counting over the goods   that they had gained.

---

6. Martín Antolínez, a fictional character, is a vassal of the Cid and one of his principal knights.
7. The deceit practiced by the Cid and Martín Antolínez to take advantage of the moneylenders' own greed is evidently fictitious and a medieval commonplace, including its apparent anti-Semitism. His vassal's principal role in the actual deed also keeps the Cid from directly sullying his hands, while still demonstrating his resourcefulness.
8. The moneylenders are both men, and probably Jewish, as usury was prohibited under Church law.

115 Martín Antolínez approached with all shrewdness.
 "Are you there, Raquel and Vidas, my dear friends?
 I would speak with you both in secret confidence."
 They did not keep him waiting; all three withdrew together.
 "Raquel and Vidas, give me your hands,
120 swear you will not betray me to Moors or Christians;
 I shall make you rich forever, you will lack for nothing.
 The Campeador was sent for the tribute;
 he seized much wealth and great possessions.
 He kept for himself a considerable portion,
125 whence he has come to this, for he was accused.[9]
 He has two coffers full of pure gold.
 You know full well the King's disfavor pursues him.
 He has left houses and palaces, all his inheritance.
 He cannot take these for they would be discovered.
130 The Campeador will leave the coffers in your hands;
 lend him, in money, whatever is reasonable.
 Take the coffers into your safekeeping,
 but you must both pledge your faiths, with a great oath,
 for the rest of this year not to look inside them."
135 Raquel and Vidas conferred together:
 "In any business we must gain something.
 Of course we know that he gained something;
 in the lands of the Moors he seized much booty.
 His sleep is uneasy who has money with him.
140 As for the coffers, let us take both of them
 and put them in a place where no one will sniff them.
 But tell us, concerning the Cid, what sum will content him,
 what interest will he give us for the whole of this year?"
 Martín Antolínez answered with all shrewdness:
145 "My Cid desires whatever is reasonable;
 he asks little of you for leaving his wealth in safety.
 Needy men from all sides are gathering around him;
 he requires six hundred marks."[1]
 Raquel and Vidas said, "We will gladly give that many."
150 "You see, night is falling the Cid has no time,
 we have need that you give us the marks."
 Raquel and Vidas said, "Business is not done that way,
 but by first taking and giving afterwards."
 Martín Antolínez said, "I am content with that.
155 Come, both of you, to the famous Campeador,
 and we will help you, as is only just,
 to carry away the coffers to where you can keep them safely
 so that neither Moors nor Christians may know where they lie."
 Raquel and Vidas said, "That will content us.

---

9. The key to the deceit is the moneylenders' belief in the false accusation that led to the Cid's exile—that he had kept most of the tribute for himself.

1. A considerable sum. The mark was a Castilian coin equivalent to eleven ounces either of silver or of gold.

160 When the coffers are here,   you may take the six hundred marks."
        Martín Antolínez   rode off at once
with Raquel and Vidas   willingly and gladly.
He did not go by the bridge,   but through the water,
so that no man in Burgos   should get wind of it.
165   They have come to the tent   of the famous Campeador;
they kiss the hands of the Cid   when they enter.
My Cid smiled   and spoke with them:
"Greetings, Don Raquel and Vidas,   had you forgotten me?
I must depart into exile   for the King's disfavor pursues me.
170 From the look of things   you will have something of mine;
as long as you live   you will not be paupers."
Raquel and Vidas   kissed My Cid's hands.
Martín Antolínez   sealed the bargain.
Six hundred marks   they would give for those coffers
175 and would guard them well   till the end of the year,
and to this they vowed their consent   and to this swore:
that should they break their promise   and open them before,
the Cid should not give so much   as one wretched farthing for their profit.
Martín Antolínez said,   "Carry them off at once.
180 Take them, Raquel and Vidas,   put them in your safe place;
I shall go with you   to bring back the money,
for My Cid must depart   before the cock sings."
When they went to load the coffers   you could see how great was their
        pleasure.
They could not lift them   although they were strong.
185 They rejoiced, Raquel and Vidas,   to have so much treasure;
they should be rich   as long as they lived.

10

    Raquel has kissed   the hand of My Cid:
"Ah, Campeador,   in good hour you girded on sword!
You go from Castile   forth among strangers.
190 Such is your fortune   and great are your gains;
I kiss your hand   begging you to bring me
a skin of crimson leather,   Moorish and highly prized."
My Cid said, "Gladly,   from this moment it is ordered.
I will send it to you from there.   If not, count it against the coffers."
195   Raquel and Vidas   took up the coffers.
With Martín Antolínez   they went back to Burgos;
with all caution   they came to their house.
In the middle of the dwelling   a carpet was spread,
a sheet over it   pure white, of fine cloth.
200 At the first fling there fell   three hundred marks of silver.
Don Martino counted   and without weighing took them;
the other three hundred   in gold they paid him.
Don Martino has five squires.   He loaded them all.
You will hear what he said   when this was done:
205 "Raquel and Vidas,   in your hands are the coffers;
I who gained them for you   have well deserved my commission."

11

Raquel and Vidas   walked to one side:
"Let us make him a fine gift   since he found this for us.
Martín Antolínez,   renowned man of Burgos,
210   we will make you a fine gift.   You have deserved your commission;
we will give you enough to make trousers,   a good cloak and rich tunic.
We will make you a present   of thirty marks,
as is only proper   and what you have deserved,
since you shall testify   to this that we have agreed."
215   Don Martino thanked them   and took the money;
he was glad to go from the house   and leave them both.

He has gone out of Burgos,   passed over the Arlanzón
and come to the tent of him   who in good hour was born.
The Cid received him   with his arms open:
220   "Welcome, Martín Antolínez,   my faithful vassal!
May I see the day   when you will receive something from me!"
"I come, Campeador,   with all care and prudence;
you have gained six hundred   and I thirty.
Bid them strike the tent   and let us leave at once;
225   in San Pedro of Cardeña   let the cock sing to us.[2]
We shall see your wife   of gentle birth and good report,
rest for a little   then quit the kingdom,
as we must, for the term   of the sentence draws near."

12

These words said,   the tent is struck.
230   My Cid and his followers   mount at once.
He turned his horse   toward Santa María,
raised his right hand,   crossed himself:
"Praise be to Thee, O God,   Who guide earth and sky;
thy grace be with me,   glorious Santa María!
235   Now I depart Castile   since the King's wrath pursues me,
and know not if I shall return   in all my days.
Thy favor be with me,   thou Glorious, on my going;
aid and sustain me   by night and by day;
Grant thou as I beg,   and if fortune bear with me,
240   fine gifts on thy altar,   rich offerings I shall lay,
and a thousand Masses   have sung in thy chantry."°   *chapel*

13

He the excellent one   bade hearty farewell.
They release the reins   and set spur to their horses.
Martín Antolínez,   the loyal man of Burgos,
245   said, "I shall see my wife,   who is all my solace,
and leave instructions   as to what must be done.
I care not if the King   should seize my possessions.
I shall be with you   before the sun shines."

---

2. That is, best to arrive there before daybreak. San Pedro of Cardeña is a Benedictine monastery five miles southeast of Burgos. Rodrigo Díaz was buried there in 1102, and the monastery played a primary role in the dissemination of his legend.

14

Don Martino turned toward Burgos,   and My Cid spurred on
250   with all speed   toward San Pedro of Cardeña
with those knights   who do his pleasure.
        The cocks quicken their song   and dawn is breaking
when the good Campeador   rode up to San Pedro;
the abbot Don Sancho,   a servant of the Lord,
255   was saying his matins   in the gray morning.
And there Doña Jimena[3]   with five gentlewomen
was praying to Saint Peter   and to the Creator praying:
"Thou Who guidest all creatures,   bless My Cid the Campeador."

15

They called at the door,   the message was taken;
260   the abbot Don Sancho,   God, how great was his rejoicing!
There was running in the courtyard   with candles and torches
to receive with gladness   him who in good hour was born.
"Thanks be to God, My Cid,"   said the abbot Don Sancho,
"that I see you before me   to share my dwelling."
265   My Cid answered,   who in good hour was born:
"My thanks, abbot,   I am well pleased with you;
I would have a meal made ready   for myself and my followers,
and since I must leave this land   I give you fifty marks;
if I live,   you shall have two for each of these.
270   I would not occasion this abbey   a farthing of loss;
take these hundred marks   for Doña Jimena,
wait on her this full year   and on her daughters and ladies.
My two small daughters,   clasp them safe in your arms;
they and my wife,   care for them closely.
275   I commend them to you,   to you, abbot Don Sancho.
If this money runs out   or you need anything,
yet provide for them well;   I shall pay accordingly,
for each mark you spend,   four to the abbey."
The abbot agreed   to all of this gladly.
280   Behold where Doña Jimena   is coming with her daughters,
each carried and brought   in the arms of a nurse.
And Doña Jimena knelt down   on both knees before him.
She kissed his hands,   weeping from her eyes:
"Grace, Campeador,   who in good hour was born!
285   Because of evil meddlers   you are sent into exile."

16

"Grace, Campeador   of the excellent beard!
Here before you   are your daughters and I,
and they in their infancy,   and their days are tender,
with these my ladies   who wait upon me.
290   I know well   that you pause here merely,

---

3. Daughter of Diego Rodríguez, count of Oviedo, and niece of Alfonso. She married Rodrigo Díaz in 1074. After his death in Valencia, she organized a retreat from that city in 1102, died in Castile, and was buried with her husband at San Pedro (Saint Peter) of Cardeña.

and in this life   must part from us.
In the name of Santa María,   give us counsel!"

He stretched out his hands,   he of the splendid beard;
his two daughters   in his arms he took,
295   drew them to his heart   for he loved them dearly.
He weeps from his eyes   and sighs deeply:
"Ah, Doña Jimena,   my perfect wife,
I love you   as I do my own soul.
You know well   we must part in this life;
300   I shall go from here   and you will stay behind.
May it please God   and Santa María
one day with my own hands   I may give my daughters in marriage,
and may good fortune attend me   and few days be left me
that you, my honored wife,   may receive once more my homage."

                    17
305   They laid a great banquet   for the good Campeador.
They clanged and pealed   the bells of San Pedro.
Through all Castile   the cry goes:
"He is leaving the land,   My Cid the Campeador."
Some leave houses   and others honors.[4]
310   On that day   at the bridge on the Arlanzón
a hundred fifteen horsemen   are come together,
all of them asking   for My Cid the Campeador.
Martín Antolínez   rode up where they were.
They set off for San Pedro   to him who was born in good hour.

                    18
315   When My Cid of Bivar   heard the news
that his band was growing,   that his strength was increasing,
he mounted in haste   and rode out to receive them;
he broke into smiles   as soon as he saw them.
Each of them came up   and kissed his hand.
320   My Cid spoke   with all his heart:
"I pray to God   our Father in heaven
that you who for me have left   home and possessions,
before I die,   may receive from me some gain;
that all you lose now   twofold may be returned."
325   My Cid rejoiced   that his company had grown.
All rejoiced   who were there with him.

    Six days of the sentence   already have run;
three remain   and afterwards none.
The King has sent   to keep watch on My Cid,
330   so that if when the time was up   they could take him in the land,
not for silver nor gold   might he escape.
The day went   and night came in.
He called together   all his horsemen:
"Hear me, my knights,   let no heart be heavy.

---

4. Lands or posts bestowed by the king; by following the Cid, they will forfeit both their homes and anything their feudal ties had granted them. In contrast, the Cid's own vassals were protected by law from such confiscations.

335　　I own little;　I would give you your portion.
　　　　Listen and learn　what must be done:
　　　　In the morning　when the cocks sing,
　　　　have the horses saddled　without delay;
　　　　in San Pedro　the good abbot will ring matins
340　　and sing us the Mass　of the Holy Trinity.[5]
　　　　We shall set out　when Mass has been sung,
　　　　for time runs out　and we have far to go."
　　　　All will do　as the Cid has commanded.
　　　　The night passes　and morning comes;
345　　at the second cock　they saddle their horses.
　　　　　　With all dispatch　the matins are rung;
　　　　My Cid and his wife　into the church have gone.
　　　　On the steps before the altar　Doña Jimena knelt down
　　　　praying to the Creator　with all her heart
350　　that God might keep from harm　My Cid the Campeador:
　　　　"Glorious Lord, Father　Who art in heaven,
　　　　Who made heaven and earth　and the sea the third day,
　　　　Who made stars and moon　and the sun to warm us,
　　　　Who became incarnate　in Santa María Thy mother,
355　　Who, as was Thy will,　appeared in Bethlehem;
　　　　shepherds praised Thee　and glorified Thee.
　　　　Three kings of Arabia　came to adore Thee,
　　　　Melchior　and Gaspar and Balthasar,
　　　　gold and frankincense and myrrh　with glad hearts they offered Thee;
360　　Thou didst save Jonas°　when he fell into the sea,　　　　　　　*Jonah*
　　　　Thou savedst Daniel　from the evil den of lions,
　　　　Thou in Rome savedst　lord Saint Sebastian,
　　　　Thou didst save Saint Susannah　from the lying criminal;[6]
　　　　Father in heaven, Thou didst walk　thirty-two years on earth
365　　showing miracles　of which we must tell:
　　　　Thou didst from water make wine　and bread from stones,
　　　　Thou didst raise Lazarus　as was Thy intention,
　　　　Thou didst let the Jews take Thee;　on Mount Calvary
　　　　where it is called Golgotha　on a cross they hanged Thee
370　　and, one on each side,　two thieves with Thee.
　　　　One is in paradise,　the other did not go there.
　　　　Much grace didst Thou work　on the cross hanging:
　　　　Longinus[7] was blind　and had never seen anything;
　　　　he thrust his spear in Thy side,　from which blood came,
375　　which down the shaft ran　and anointed his hands,
　　　　which covered his arm　and to his face came;

he opened his eyes   and looked in all directions
and believed in Thee then,   from whence came his salvation.
Thou from the sepulchre   didst rise again,
380 descended into hell,   as was Thy will,
burst open the doors   and saved the holy fathers.[8]
Thou art King of Kings   and of the whole world Father.
I adore Thee and believe   with all my will,
and I pray to Saint Peter   that he may aid my prayer
385 that God may keep from harm   My Cid the Campeador.
Though we part now,   in this life may we come together."
        When the prayer was ended,   Mass was said.
They went out from the church   and made ready to ride.
My Cid went   and embraced Doña Jimena;
390 Doña Jimena   kissed My Cid's hand,
weeping;   she could not hold back the tears.
He turned and looked   upon his daughters.
"To God I commend you   and to the heavenly Father;
now we part. God knows   when we shall come together."
395 Weeping from his eyes,   you have never seen such grief,
thus parted the one from the others   as the nail from the flesh.
        My Cid and his vassals   set off riding,
he looking behind him   delaying them all.
Minaya[9] Alvar Fáñez   spoke with great wisdom:
400 "Cid, who in good hour were born   of mother, where is your strength?
We must be on our way;   this is idleness.
All these sorrows   will yet turn to joy:
God who gave us souls   will give us guidance."
        They turned and bade   the abbot Don Sancho
405 to serve Doña Jimena   and her two daughters
and all the ladies   who were with them there;
the abbot knew well   that he would be recompensed.
Don Sancho has turned   and Alvar Fáñez spoke:
"Abbot, if you meet with any   who would come with us,
410 tell them to take up our trail   and ride after us,
so that in wasteland or town   they may overtake us."
        They slackened the reins   and rode forward;
the time draws near   when they must quit the kingdom.
The Cid pitched camp   by Espinazo de Can;
415 that night from all hands   men flocked to go with him.
Next day in the morning   they rode on again.
He is leaving the land,   the loyal Campeador.
By the left of San Esteban,   a goodly city;
he passed through Alcubilla   on the edge of Castile;
420 to the path of Quinea   they came, and passed over;
at Navapalos   crossed over the Duero;

8. The apocryphal story of the Harrowing of Hell told that between his crucifixion and resurrection, Jesus descended into Hell and saved from it all of the worthies of Old Tes-   tament days who had believed in advance in his coming. 9. "My brother," a form of title or address often used in the poem as a nickname for Alvar Fáñez.

at the Figueruela   My Cid paused for the night.[1]
Still from all hands   men gathered to go with him.

19

There lay down, My Cid,   after night had come;
425   he slept so deeply   a dream seized him sweetly.
The angel Gabriel   came to him in a vision:[2]
"Ride forward, Cid,   good Campeador,
for no man ever rode forth   at so propitious a moment;
as long as you live   that which is yours will prosper."
430   He crossed himself, My Cid,   when he awoke.

20

He made the sign of the cross,   and commended himself to God.
He was deeply glad   because of the dream he had dreamed.
Next day in the morning   they ride onward;
the last day of their time has come.   Know, after that there is no more.
435   By the mountains of Miedes   they were going to halt,
on the right the towers of Atienza,   which the Moors hold.[3]

21

It was still day,   the sun not down,
When My Cid the Campeador   assembled his men.
Not counting the foot soldiers,   and brave men they were,
440   he counted three hundred lances,   each with its pennon.

22

"Let the horses be fed early   and may the Creator keep you!
Let those who desire to, eat,   and those who do not, ride on.
We shall cross over that range,   high and forbidding;
this same night   we shall leave Alfonso's kingdom.
445   He who comes looking for us   may find us then."
They crossed the range in the night,   and morning came,
and on the downward ridge   they began riding.
Halfway down a mountain   which was marvelous and high,
My Cid halted   and fed the horses their barley.
450   He told them all that he wished   to ride on all that night;
all were stout hearted   and good liege men
who for their lord   would do anything.
Before night fell   they set off again;
My Cid pressed on   so that none might discover them.
455   They rode forward by night   without resting.
Where it is called Castejón,   on the bank of the Henares,[4]
My Cid lay in ambush   with those who were with him.

23

All that night   My Cid lies in ambush.

---

1. A similar route will be taken by Félix Muñoz and the Cid's two daughters after the incident at Corpes (page 733).
2. Prophetic visions or dreams are common in medieval literature; the Archangel appears at the crucial moment of the crossing of the frontier of Castile and in apparent response to Doña Jimena's prayer.
3. At the time of the Cid's first exile in 1081, the mountains of Miedes formed the frontier between Moorish and Christian territories; following the fall of Toledo in 1085, the frontier had moved further south.
4. Sixty miles south-southeast of Miedes de Atienza, Castejón de Henares was a strategically important site defended by two castles, although the poem represents it as less well protected.

Alvar Fáñez Minaya   thus advised them:

460 "Ah, Cid, in good hour   you girded on sword!
With one hundred   of our company,
after we have surprised   and taken Castejón,
do you remain there   and be our fixed base.
Give me two hundred   to go on a raid;

465 with God and good fortune   we shall take rich spoils."
The Campeador said,   "You speak well, Minaya.
You with two hundred   ride out raiding;
take Alvar Alvarez   and Alvar Salvadórez
and Galindo García,   who is a hardy lance,

470 all of them brave knights;   let them go with Minaya.
Ride forward boldly,   let no fear detain you.
Ride down along the Fita   and along the Guadalajara,
take your raiders   as far as Alcalá⁵
and let them carry off   all that is of value,

475 leaving nothing behind   out of fear of the Moors.
I with the hundred   shall stay here behind
and hold Castejón,   where we will be secure.
If on your raiding foray   any trouble befalls you,
send word at once   to me here behind;

480 all Spain° will talk   of the aid I shall bring."   *Muslim Spain*
They have been named   who will ride out on the raid,
and they who will remain   with My Cid in the fixed base.
The dawn goes gray   and the morning comes,
the sun came forth.   God, how fair was the dawn!

485 All began to stir   in Castejón;
they opened the gates   and went out of the town
to see to their tasks   and all their property.
All have gone out   and left the gates open,
few there are   who remain in Castejón;

490 all who have gone out   are scattered abroad.
The Campeador   came out of hiding;
he rode around Castejón   all the way.
He has seized   the Moors and their women
and those cattle   that were about there.

495 My Cid Don Rodrigo   rode up to the gate;
those there to defend it,   when they saw the attack,
were taken with fear,   and the gate was unguarded.
My Cid Ruy Díaz   rode in at the gate;
in his hand he carried   a naked sword.

500 Fifteen Moors he killed   who came in his way,
took Castejón   and its gold and its silver.
His knights arrive   with the spoils;
they give it to My Cid;   all this, to them, is nothing.

5. This entire region southwest of Castejón was until 1085 a Moorish kingdom tributary to Alfonso VI, and, under Castilian law, fair game for the exiled Cid's livelihood.

Behold now the two hundred and three   in the raiding party;
505   they ride on without pausing   and plunder all the land.
As far as Alcalá,   went the banner of Minaya,
and from there with the spoils   they return again,
up along the Henares   and along the Guadalajara.
Such great spoils   they bring back with them:
510   many flocks   of sheep and of cattle,
and clothing   and great quantities of other riches.
Forward comes   the banner of Minaya;
no one dares   attack the band of raiders.
That company returns   with its plunder;
515   see, they are in Castejón,   where the Campeador was.
Leaving the castle secure,   the Campeador rode out,
rode out to receive them   with his company.
He greeted Minaya   with his arms open:
"Have you returned, Alvar Fáñez,   hardy lance!
520   Wherever I send you   I may well be hopeful.
Your booty and mine together,   of all we have gained
a fifth is yours   if you will take it, Minaya."[6]

24

"I thank you from my heart,   famous Campeador,
for this fifth part   which you offer me;
525   it would please   Alfonso the Castilian.
I give it up   and return it to you.
I make a vow   to God Who is in heaven:
Until I have satisfied myself   on my good horse
with joining battle   in the field with the Moors,
530   with handling the lance   and taking up the sword,
with the blood running   to above my elbow,
before Ruy Díaz   the famous warrior,
I shall not take from you   a wretched farthing.
Until by my hand you have won   something truly of value,
535   behold, I leave everything   in your hands."

25

All they had taken   was gathered together.
My Cid, who girded on sword   in a good hour, considered
that King Alfonso   would send forces to follow him
and would seek to work him evil   with all his armies.
540   He bade them divide   all they had taken;
he bade his partitioners   parcel it out.[7]
There good fortune   befell his knights:
a hundred marks of silver   went to each of them,
and to the foot soldiers   half as much without stint;
545   all the fifth part   remained to My Cid.
He could not sell it there   nor give it as a present,

---

6. According to the law, a fifth of any booty belonged to the king, but because the Cid is no longer the king's dependent but an independent leader, it falls to him instead.

7. The careful division and written record of the booty was customarily undertaken by official "partitioners" in order to avoid disputes.

nor did he wish to have men or women   as slaves in his train.
He spoke with those of Castejón,   he sent to Hita and Guadalajara,
to learn how much   they would give him for his fifth;
550 even with what they gave   their gain would be great.
The Moors offered   three thousand marks of silver.[8]
My Cid was content   with this offering.
On the third day   they paid it all.
   My Cid was of the opinion,   with all his company,
555 that in the castle   there would not be room for them
and that it might be held,   but there would be no water.
"Let us leave these Moors in peace   for their treaty is written;
King Alfonso will seek us out   with all his host.[9]
Hear me, my men and Minaya,   I would quit Castejón!"

26

560   "Let no one take amiss   what I have to say:
We cannot remain   in Castejón;
King Alfonso is near   and will come seeking us.
But as for the castle,   I would not lay it waste;
I wish to set free   a hundred Moors and a hundred Moorish women,
565 that they may speak no evil of me   since I took it from them.
You have full share, every one,   and no one is still unrewarded.
Tomorrow in the morning   we must ride on;
I do not wish to fight   with Alfonso my lord."
All are contented   with what My Cid spoke.
570 All went away rich   from the castle they had taken;
the Moors and their women   are giving them their blessings.
   They go up the Henares   as far as they can,
passed through Alcarria   and went on from there;
by the Caves of Anguita   they are going,
575 crossed over the waters   into the Plain of Taranz
and through those lands below there   as far as they extend.
Between Ariza and Cetina   My Cid pitched his tent.[1]
Great spoils he takes   in the lands through which he goes;
the Moors do not know   what their intention is.
580 My Cid of Bivar   the next day moved on;
beyond Alhama,   beyond La Hoz he rode on,
beyond Bubierca   to Ateca farther on.
Close to Alcocer   My Cid came to camp
on a round hill   that stood high and strong.
585 The stream Jalón around them,   none could cut off their water.
My Cid Don Rodrigo   thinks to take Alcocer.

27

He mans the hill strongly,   makes strong the encampments,
some along the hillside,   some near the water.

---

8. Goods and slaves are difficult to transport, so the Cid converts his share into cash.
9. These Moors have a treaty with Alfonso; this is a protectorate rather than conquered territory. If the Cid's men seek to occupy the town, Alfonso might come lay siege to them, and there is no water within to let them withstand a siege.
1. The Cid and his men have traveled a (not quite credible) distance of 45 miles northeast to the valley of the river Jalón.

The good Campeador,   who in good hour girded on sword,
590 set all his men   to digging a moat
on all sides of the hill   down near the water,
so that by day or night   they might not be surprised
and that the Moors might know that My Cid   meant to remain there.

28

Through all those lands   the news had gone
595 that My Cid the Campeador   had built an encampment there.
He has gone out from the Christians   and come among the Moors;
all about their encampment   none dares work the land.
My Cid and all his vassals   begin to rejoice:
the castle of Alcocer   is beginning to pay tribute.

29

600 Those of Alcocer   now send tribute to My Cid,
and those of Ateca   and of the village of Terrer
and of Calatayud,   you may know, though it weighed heavy on them.
Fully fifteen weeks   My Cid remained there.
When My Cid saw that Alcocer   would not yield to him,
605 he thought of a stratagem   and wasted no time:
He left one tent standing,   he carried off the rest;
he went down the Jalón   with his banner raised,
his men in their armor   with their swords girded,
shrewdly   to take them by ambush.
610 God, how those of Alcocer   rejoiced to see it!
"My Cid has no more provisions   of bread and barley.
He can hardly bear off the tents,   he has left one standing.
He makes off, My Cid,   like one fleeing from a rout.
Let us fall upon him   and we shall seize great gains
615 before he is taken   by those of the town of Terrer,
for if those of Terrer take him   they will give us nothing.
He shall return twofold   the tribute we sent him."
They went out from Alcocer,   their haste was unseemly.
When My Cid saw them   he rode on as from a rout.
620 He went down the stream Jalón   with his men.
Those of Alcocer said,   "Our plunder is escaping!"
They ran out of the town,   all, big and little,
thirsting to take him;   beyond that, not thinking.
They left the gates open   with none to guard them.
625 The Campeador   turned his face round;
he judged the distance   between the Moors and their castle,
bade them turn with the banner.   With all speed they rode forward.
"Charge them, knights,   let none lag behind.
With the Creator's blessing   ours is the gain!"
630 Halfway across the meadow   they came together.
God, their hearts were glad   upon that morning!
My Cid and Alvar Fáñez   rode on ahead;
they had good horses,   you may know, that went at their pleasure;
they rode clear between   the Moors and the castle.
635 My Cid's vassals   attacked without mercy;

they kill three hundred Moors   in a short time.
Those who are in the ambush,   giving great shouts,
leaving those who are in the van,°   charged upon the castle,   *vanguard*
halted at the door   bare swords in their hands.
640   Then their own men rode up,   for they had routed them.
Know, in this manner   My Cid took Alcocer.

30

    Pedro Bermúdez[2] came   with the banner in his hand;
he flew it from the peak,   from the highest point of all.
My Cid spoke, Ruy Díaz,   who in good hour was born:
645   "Thanks be to God in heaven   and to all His saints,
both horses and riders   now shall have better lodging."

31

    "Hear me, Alvar Fáñez   and all my men!
In this castle   we have taken great gains;
the Moors lie dead,   I see few living.
650   We cannot sell   the Moors and their women;
it would gain us nothing   to cut off their heads.
Let us take them in   for we are the lords here;
we shall live in their houses   and they shall wait upon us."

32

    My Cid is in Alcocer   with all he has taken;
655   he has sent back for the tent   which he left standing.
They are grieved in Ateca,   and those of Terrer are not merry,
and those of Calatayud,   you may know, are heavy hearted.
They have sent a message   to the King of Valencia,
telling how one who is called   My Cid Ruy Díaz of Bivar,
660   "whom King Alfonso   has banished from his kingdom,
came to camp near Alcocer   in a strong place,
drew us out into ambush   and has taken the castle.
If you send us no help   you will lose Ateca, lose Terrer,
lose Calatayud,   which cannot escape;
665   all will go ill   here on the bank of the Jalón
as well as in Jiloca   on the other side."
    When King Tamín heard this   his heart was heavy.[3]
"Three Kings° of the Moors   are here with me;   *generals; leaders*
let two without delay   proceed to the place,
670   take three thousand Moors   armed for battle.
Muster from the frontier   all who will come to your aid,
take him alive   and fetch him before me;
since he entered my lands   I will mete him his due."
    Three thousand Moors   mount and ride off;
675   they came at night   to camp in Segorbe.
Next day in the morning   they ride on again;

---

2. The third of the Cid's four most loyal and able followers, Pedro Bermúdez may have been a historical personage, but he has not been identified conclusively; in the
poem he is the Campeador's nephew and standard-bearer.

3. As with nearly all of the Moorish characters in the
poem, King Tamín of Valencia is fictitious. The king at
the time of the first exile was Abu Bakr ibn 'Abd al-Aziz,
who died in 1085 and was succeeded by his son, 'Utman.

they came at night   to camp at Celfa.
From there to the frontier   they send letters ahead;
none lag behind,   from all sides they gather.
680   They went out from Celfa,   which is called the Canal.[4]
All that day   without rest they went forward
and came that night   to camp in Calatayud.
Through all those lands   the cry goes
and many have come;   great crowds have assembled
685   with those two Kings   called Fáriz and Galve
to surround My good Cid   in Alcocer.

                              33

        They set up their tents   and built an encampment;
their host is great already   and still it grows stronger.
The sentinels   whom the Moors post
690   go armed   by day and by night;
many are the sentinels   and great is the host.
They cut off the water   from My Cid's men.
Those who were with My Cid   wished to give battle;
he who was born in good hour   strictly forbade it.
695   Fully three weeks   the Moors lay camped around them.

                              34

        At the end of three weeks,   as the fourth was beginning,
My Cid called   his men to council.
"They have cut off our water,   our bread will soon be gone;
if we tried to leave by night   they would not let us;
700   if we should give battle   their strength is great;
tell me, my knights,   what you think were best done."
Minaya spoke first,   that worthy knight:
"From sweet Castile   we have come to this place;
unless we fight with the Moors   they will give us no bread.
705   We are six hundred   and something over;
in the name of the Creator   we can do no other
than attack them   when this next day dawns."
The Campeador said,   "You speak to my liking;
your speech does you honor, Minaya,   as will your action."
710   All the Moors and their women   he sent from the castle,
so that no one might know   what was planned in secret.
That day and that night   they made themselves ready.
Next day in the morning   as the sun rose
My Cid was armed,   and all his men.
715   He spoke, My Cid,   you will hear what he said:
"Let us all go out,   let no one remain behind
except two foot soldiers   who will guard the gate.
If we die in the field   they will possess the castle;
if we beat them in battle   we may add to our wealth.
720   And you, Pedro Bermúdez,   take my banner;

4. "Canal" refers to an ancient Roman aqueduct, dug out of the rock and partly subterranean, origin of several local legends.

you are a good vassal,   you will bear it faithfully;
but do not charge with it   until I send you word."
He kisses My Cid's hand   and goes to take the banner.
      They open the gates   and ride out onto the field;
725   the Moors' sentinels see them   and turn back to their army.
What haste among the Moors!   They set to arm;
it seemed the earth would split   with the noise of drums.
You could see the Moors arm   and rush into ranks.
On the side of the Moors   there were two kingly banners,
730   and as for the colored pennons,   who could number them?
The files of the Moors   are moving forward
to meet, hand to hand,   My Cid and his men.
      "Stay, knights, where you are,   here in this place;
let no one break ranks   till I give the word."
735   That same Pedro Bermúdez   could not abide it,
took the banner in hand   and spurred forward.
"The Creator bless you,   loyal Cid Campeador!
I shall set your standard   in the main rank there;
those who owe it allegiance,   let us see how they aid it."
740   The Campeador said,   "No, in charity's name!"⁵
Pedro Bermúdez answered,   "Nothing can keep it here!"
He spurred his horse   into their main rank;
Moors rush upon him   to gain the banner,
give him great blows   but can break no armor.
745   The Campeador said,   "To his aid, for charity's sake!"

                              35

      They clasp their shields   over their hearts,
they lower the lances   swathed in their pennons,
they bowed their faces   over their saddletrees,°   *saddle frames*
with strong hearts   they charged to attack them.
750   He who in good hour was born   cried with a great voice:
"Attack them, knights,   for the love of the Creator!
I am Ruy Díaz, the Cid,   the Campeador of Bivar!"
      All rushed at the rank   where Pedro Bermúdez was.
They were three hundred spears,   each with its pennon;
755   all struck blows   and killed as many Moors;
on the second charge   they killed three hundred more.

                              36

      You would have seen so many lances   rise and go under,
so many bucklers°   pierced and split asunder,   *small shields*
so many coats of mail   break and darken,
760   so many white pennons   drawn out red with blood,
so many good horses   run without their riders.
The Moors call on Mohammed   and the Christians on Saint James.⁶

---

5. "Charity," that is *caritas* or Godly love, the most important of the three theological virtues of Christianity.
6. St. James was the customary saint to invoke as a specifically military protector; the exchange of religious invocations stresses the religious differences between the Cid's knights and some of the opposing forces, but seldom if ever takes on the explicitly crusading tone of the Reconquest or the Crusades proper.

A thousand three hundred   of the Moors fell dead
upon the field   in a little space.

37

765   How well they fight   above their gilded saddletrees:[7]
My Cid Ruy Díaz,   the good warrior,
Minaya Alvar Fáñez,   who commanded at Zorita,
Martín Antolínez,   the excellent man of Burgos,
Muño Gustioz,   who was his vassal,
770   Martín Muñoz,   from Monte Mayor,[8]
Alvar Alvarez   and Alvar Salvadórez,
Galindo García,   excellent knight from Aragón,
Félix Muñoz,   the nephew of the Campeador!
These and the rest,   as many as are there,
775   support the banner   and My Cid the Campeador.

38

They have killed the horse from under   Minaya Alvar Fáñez;
hosts of Christians   charge to his aid.
His lance is broken,   his sword in his hand;
even afoot   he deals great blows.
780   Ruy Díaz the Castilian,   My Cid, saw him,
rode up to a Moorish lord   who had a good horse,
struck so with his sword,   with his right arm,
he cut him through at the belt;   half the body fell to the field.
He took the horse   to Minaya Alvar Fáñez.
785   "Mount, Minaya,   you who are my right arm!
This very day   I shall have need of you;
the Moors stand firm,   they have not yet fled the field.
We must fall upon them   relentlessly."
Minaya mounted,   his sword in his hand,
790   fighting bravely   through all that host,
delivering of their souls   all who came near him.
My Cid Ruy Díaz,   who in good hour was born,
has aimed three blows   at King Fáriz;
two of them missed   and the third struck home;
795   the blood ran down   over the tunic of chain mail;
he turned his horse   to flee from the field.
With that blow   the army was beaten.

39

Martín Antolínez   struck Galve a blow.
He broke in pieces   the rubies of his helmet;
800   he split the helmet,   cut into the flesh;
the other dared not wait,   you may know, for another.
King Fáriz and King Galve   and their armies are routed.
It is a great day   for Christendom,
for the Moors flee   on either hand.

---

7. The catalogue of forces was a standard component of classical epic as well as of its medieval descendants.
8. Martín Muñoz was governor of Monte Mayor in Portugal, named Count of Coimbra by Alfonso VI in 1091. He could not have accompanied the Cid in his exile, but it is possible that he was an ally later on, after 1094.

805   My Cid's vassals   ride in pursuit.

King Fáriz   has gone into Terrer;

as for Galve,   they would not receive him.

Toward Calatayud   he rode on at full speed.

The Campeador   rode in pursuit;

810   they continued the chase   as far as Calatayud.

40

    The horse ran well   under Minaya Alvar Fáñez;

he killed thirty-four   of those Moors.

His sword cut deep,   his arm was crimson,

the blood ran   above his elbow.

815   Minaya said,   "My vow is fulfilled,

the news will travel   into Castile

that My Cid Ruy Díaz   has won in pitched battle."

    So many Moors lie dead,   few are left living.

Pursuing without pause,   they struck them down.

820   Already his men turn back,   his who in good hour was born.

He rode, My Cid,   on his fine horse,

his skullcap pushed back[9]—   God, how splendid his beard!—

his mailed hood on his shoulders,   his sword in his hand.

    He saw his men   as they were returning:

825   "Thanks be to God   Who is in heaven

that we have triumphed   in such a battle."

    My Cid's men   have sacked the Moors' encampment,

seized shields and arms   and much else of value;

when they had brought them in,   they found they had taken

830   five hundred and ten   Moorish horses.

There was great joy   among those Christians;

not more than fifteen   of their men were missing.

They took so much gold and silver,   none knew where to put it down;

all those Christians   were made rich

835   with the spoils   that had fallen to them.

They have called back the Moors   who lived in the castle;

My Cid ordered   that even they should be given something.

My Cid rejoiced greatly,   and all his men.

He bade them divide the money   and those great spoils;

840   in the Cid's fifth   there were a hundred horses.

God, they were well content,   all his vassals,

both the foot soldiers   and they who rode horses!

He who in good hour was born   deals with them justly;

all who came with him   are well content.

845   "Hear me, Minaya,   who are my right arm!

Take from this treasure,   which the Creator has given,

as much as may please you;   take it with your own hand.

I wish to send you   to Castile with the news

of this battle   which we have won.

---

9. The Cid has removed his helmet and the hood of his mail; now he removes the close-fitting cloth cap protecting his scalp from the abrasive metal armor.

850   I would send   a gift of thirty horses
to King Alfonso,   whose anger is turned against me,
each with its saddle   and lavishly bridled,
each with a sword   slung from the saddletree."[1]
Minaya Alvar Fáñez   said, "I will do that gladly."

41

855   "Here I have   gold and fine silver,
a bootful,   and the boot brimming over.
In Santa María of Burgos   pay for a thousand Masses;
give what is left over   to my wife and daughters,
ask them to pray for me   by night and by day;
860   they will command riches   if I live."

42

Minaya Alvar Fáñez   is well pleased with this;
the men are named   who will go with him.
Now they give the beasts barley,   already the night has come;
My Cid Ruy Díaz   confers with his men.

43

865   "Are you off, Minaya,   for Castile the noble?
When you meet our friends   you may say to them:
'God gave us aid   and we won the battle.'
When you come back,   if we are not here,
when you learn where we are   follow us there.
870   Lances and swords   must be our shelter
or else on this meager earth   we cannot live,
and for that same reason   I think we must move on."

44

All is made ready;   Minaya will depart in the morning
and the Campeador   stayed there with his men.
875   The land is poor,   gaunt and barren.
Every day   Moors from the frontier
and some from beyond   kept watch on My Cid;
they plotted with King Fáriz,   whose wounds have healed.
Among those of Ateca   and those of the town of Terrer
880   and those of Calatayud,   which is a place of more note,
as the bargain was driven   and set down on paper,
My Cid sold them Alcocer   for three thousand marks of silver.

45

My Cid Ruy Díaz   has sold Alcocer;
how well he rewarded   each of his vassals!
885   He has made his knights rich   and his foot soldiers;
in all his company   you would not find a needy man.
Who serves a good lord   lives always in luxury.

46

When My Cid came   to leave the castle,
the Moors and their women   fell to lamenting.

---

1. The Campeador takes up the hint made by Álvar Fáñez in line 525, and for the first of three times sends to Alfonso the fifth part of the spoils as if he were still the king's vassal.

890   "Are you leaving us, My Cid?   Our prayers go before you,
We are well content, sire,   with what you have done."
When My Cid of Bivar   left Alcocer,
the Moors and their women   fell to weeping.
He raised the banner,   the Campeador departed,
895   rode down the Jalón,   spurred forward.
As they left the Jalón   there were many birds of good omen.
The departure pleased those of Terrer   and still more those of Calatayud;
it grieved those of Alcocer,   for he had done much for them.
My Cid spurred his horse   and rode on
900   and halted on a stone ledge   at El Poyo near Monreal;[2]
high is that ledge   great and wonderful;
it fears no attack,   you may know, from any side.
From Daroca onwards   he forced them to pay tribute
as far as Molina,   on the other side,
905   and a third town, Teruel,   which is farther on;
he brought under his hand   Celfa of the Canal.

47

    My Cid Ruy Díaz,   God give him grace!
Alvar Fáñez Minaya   has gone to Castile.
Thirty horses   he gave to the King;
910   the King smiled with pleasure   when he saw them.
"Who gave you these,   as God may save you, Minaya?"
"My Cid Ruy Díaz,   who in good hour girded on sword.
When you had banished him,   he took Alcocer by a ruse;
the King of Valencia   sent a message
915   bidding them surround him,   and they cut off his water.
My Cid went out of the castle   and fought in the field
and overcame two Kings of the Moors   in that battle.
Enormous, sire,   are the spoils he has taken.
He sends this gift   to you, honored King;
920   he kisses your feet   and both your hands
and begs mercy of you   in the name of the Creator."
The King said,   "It is early in the day
to receive into one's favor   at the end of three weeks[3]
one who was banished   having lost his lord's love.
925   But I shall take this gift   since it comes from the Moors;
I am pleased that the Cid   has taken such spoils.
Above all,   I forgive you, Minaya.
I return to you freely   your lands and honors.[4]
Come and go   henceforth in my favor;
930   but of the Cid Campeador   I will say nothing.

48

    "And furthermore, Alvar Fáñez,   concerning this,
in all my kingdom   those good and valiant

---

2. Now begins the third of the Cid's campaigns in the poem, aimed at the Moorish towns on the river Jiloca in lower Aragón, historically protectorates of the emir of Zaragoza.

3. A symbolic number (many months at least have passed), meaning simply, "too short a time."
4. Restoring everything that had been confiscated from Minaya in consequence of his following the Cid.

who wish to go   to aid My Cid,
I shall not forbid them   nor seize their possessions."

935   Minaya Alvar Fáñez   kissed his hands.
"Thanks, thanks, my King   and natural lord;[5]
you concede this now,   later you will grant more;
with God's aid we shall do   such things as will persuade you."
The King said, "Minaya,   enough has been said.

940   Go through Castile   unmolested,
return at your liberty   to My Cid."

49

I would tell you of him   who in good hour girded on sword:
By the stone ledge of El Poyo   he set up his camp;
as long as there are Moors   and Christian people

945   it will be called: The Chair of My Cid.[6]
While he was there   he pillaged much of the country.
All the Martín valley   he forced to pay tribute.
The news of him went   to Zaragoza[7]
and did not please the Moors   but weighed heavy on them.

950   Fully fifteen weeks   My Cid stayed there.
When it was clear to My Cid   that Minaya delayed,
he took all his men   and marched by night;
he left El Poyo,   abandoned the place.
Beyond Teruel   Don Rodrigo passed;

955   in the pine grove of Tévar   Ruy Díaz pitched his camp.[8]
He overran all   the country around there
and made them pay tribute   as far as Zaragoza.

At the end of three weeks   when this was done,
Minaya came   out of Castile

960   and two hundred with him,   all with swords girded,
and of foot soldiers, you may know,   there were great numbers.
When My Cid   sets eyes on Minaya
he spurs his horse,   rides forward to embrace him;
he kissed his mouth   and the eyes in his face.

965   All was told to him,   nothing left hidden.
The Campeador   smiled with pleasure.
"Thanks be to God   and His holy virtues,
as long as you live   I shall prosper, Minaya!"

50

God, how they rejoiced,   all that company,

970   that Minaya Alvar Fáñez   had returned thus,
bringing them greetings   from cousins and brothers
and from the families   they had left behind!

---

5. "Natural lord" because Minaya resides within the territory of Castile.
6. Until recently, the place was in fact referred to as "El Poyo," the stone seat.
7. Capital of the *taifa* of Zaragoza, 60 miles northeast of El Poyo. During his first exile, between 1081 and 1086,

the historical Rodrigo Díaz had taken refuge there as a vassal of its emir, Moktadir, one of the most powerful Moorish rulers in Iberia.
8. To the northeast of Teruel, which was capital of the province of the same name, and a Muslim stronghold until 1171.

51

God, how he rejoices,   he, bearded handsomely,
because Alvar Fáñez   had paid the thousand Masses
975   and had given greetings   to his wife and his daughters!
God, the Cid was pleased   and rejoiced!
"Ah, Alvar Fáñez,   may you live many days!
You are worth more than us all,   you have done your mission so well!"

52

He who in good hour was born   did not delay;
980   he took two hundred knights,   chose them with his own hand;
he went on a raid,   riding all night.
He leaves black behind him   the lands of Alcañiz;[9]
he goes pillaging   the lands round about.
On the third day   he has come back again.

53

985   The news has gone   through all the country around there;
it grieves the people of Monzón   and of Huesca;
it pleases those of Zaragoza   to give tribute
that they may fear no affront   from My Cid Ruy Díaz.

54

With what he had taken   he came back to the encampment.
990   All rejoice,   they bear with them great spoils;
My Cid was pleased,   and Alvar Fáñez also.
My Cid, the perfect one,   could not help smiling.
"Ah, knights,   I must tell you the truth:
One would grow poor   staying in one place always;
995   tomorrow in the morning   let us move on,
let us leave the encampment   and go forward."
My Cid moved next   to the Pass of Olocau;
from there he overran   as far as Huesa and Montalbán;[1]
he was away ten days   on that foray.
1000   The news went out   in all directions
that the exile from Castile   was using them ill.

55

The tidings have gone out   in all directions;
the news has come   to the Count of Barcelona[2]
that My Cid Ruy Díaz   overruns all his land!
1005   It weighed on him heavily,   he took it as an affront.

56

The Count is a great braggart   and spoke foolishly:
"My Cid of Bivar   inflicts great losses on me.

9. An important town in Teruel on the banks of the Guadalope, southeast of Zaragoza.
1. About 15 miles apart, midway between Tévar and El Poyo.
2. The historical count of Barcelona (here called Ramón Berenguer) was Berenguer Ramón II the Fratricide, with whom Rodrigo Díaz twice fought: in Almenara in the *taifa* of Lérida in 1082 and in the pine grove of Tévar in 1090, during both of which battles he took Berenguer prisoner. His nephew Ramón Berenguer III married María, one of Díaz's daughters. Between 1076 and 1082, Berenguer had governed jointly with his brother, Ramón Berenguer II, whom he would later murder. During his first exile, Díaz had offered the pair his services and been refused before becoming the vassal of Moktadir of Zaragoza.

He offended me once   in my own court:
he struck my nephew   and gave no reparation;
1010   now he sacks the lands   under my protection.
I have never affronted him   nor withdrawn my friendship,
but since he seeks me out   I shall force him to a reckoning."
    Great are his armies,   they assemble with speed.
Moors and Christians   all gather about him
1015   and ride forward   toward My good Cid of Bivar;[3]
three days and two nights,   still they rode on
and came to My Cid   in the pine grove of Tévar;
they come in such numbers   they think to take him in their hands.
    My Cid Don Rodrigo,   bringing great spoils,
1020   came down from a mountain   into a valley.
The message arrives   from Count Ramón;
when My Cid heard it   he sent back an answer:
"Tell the Count   not to take it amiss.
I have nothing of his.   Tell him to let me alone."
1025   The Count answered,   "That is not true!
Now he shall pay me all   from now and from before;
he shall learn, this outcast,   whom he has dishonored."
The messenger returned   at full speed.
Thereupon My Cid   of Bivar understood
1030   that he could not leave that place   without a battle.

57

    "Now, knights,   set the spoils to one side.
Arm yourselves quickly,   put on your armor;
Count Ramón   seeks a great battle;
he has with him multitudes   of Moors and Christians,
1035   Without a battle,   on no account will he let us go.
If we go on, they will follow us;   let the battle be here.
Cinch tight the saddles   and arm yourselves.
They are coming downhill,   all of them in breeches;
their saddles are flat   and the girths loose.
1040   We shall ride with Galician saddles,   with boots over our hose;
with a hundred knights   we should overcome their host.[4]
Before they reach the plain   let us greet them with lances;
for every one that you strike,   three saddles will be emptied.
Ramón Berenguer will see   whom he has come seeking
1045   in the pine grove of Tévar,   to take back the spoils from me."

58

    When My Cid had spoken,   all made ready;
they have taken up their arms   and mounted their horses.

---

3. The battle of Almenar had pitted the Cid and the forces of Moktadir's son Mutamin against a coalition of Berenguer of Barcelona, King Sancho Ramírez of Aragón and Navarre, and Al-Hajib, another son of Moktadir. At Tévar eight years later, Berenguer and Al-Hajib were joined by Mutamin's son, Mostain, now ruler of Zaragoza; their vastly superior forces were defeated by the Campeador in a famous victory.

4. The Cid's forces number 500, but he says that 100 would be enough to defeat the Count's ill-equipped courtiers.

They saw the Catalans[5]   descending the slope;
when they came near the foot of the hill,   where it joins the plain,
1050   My Cid, who in good hour was born,   called to his men to attack.
His knights charged forward   with a will,
skillfully handling   their pennons and lances,
wounding some   and unhorsing the rest.
He who was born in good hour   has won the battle.
1055   He has taken prisoner   the Count Ramón;
he has taken the sword Colada,   worth more than a thousand marks.

59

Thus he won the battle,   honor to his beard,
took the Count prisoner   and brought him to his tent
and ordered his servants   to mount guard upon him.
1060   He went at once   out of the tent again;
from all sides   his men came together.
My Cid was pleased   with the great spoils they had taken.
For My Cid Don Rodrigo   they prepared a great banquet.
The Count Don Ramón   takes no interest in this;
1065   they bear him food,   they bring it before him.
He will not eat it.   He rebuffed them all:
"I will not eat a mouthful   for all the wealth in Spain;
I will abandon my body first   and give up the ghost,
since such ill-shod outcasts   have beaten me in battle."[6]

60

1070   As for My Cid Ruy Díaz,   you will hear what he said:
"Count, eat this bread   and drink this wine.
If you do as I say,   I shall set you free;
if not, for the rest of your days   you will never see Christendom."

61

"Eat if you please, Don Rodrigo,   and lie down and rest.
1075   I would rather die;   I will eat nothing."
They could not persuade him   until the third day.
They continued to make division   of the great spoils they had taken,
but they could not make him eat   a morsel of bread.

62

My Cid said,   "Count, eat something,
1080   for unless you eat   you will see no Christian soul;
if you eat   to satisfy me,
I shall set free,   out of my hand,
You, Count,   and two of your knights."
When the Count heard this   he felt more joyful.
1085   "Cid, if you do   as you have promised,
as long as I live   I will marvel at it."

---

5. Literally "francos," because the territory of Catalonia had originally been a dependency of the Carolingian empire, although it was independent by the 9th century; the word draws a further distinction with the Castilians.

6. With this scene, the episode takes on a comic tone that concludes the first cantar. Ramón's hunger strike has no particular goal beyond showing his aristocratic disdain for the Cid and his Castilian knights.

"Then eat, Count,   and when you have eaten
I shall set you at liberty,   and the two knights besides.
But of all that which you lost   and I won on the field,
1090   you may know, I will not give you   so much as one wretched farthing.
I need it for my men,   who share my pauperdom.
We keep alive   by taking from you and from others.
And while it pleases our heavenly Father,   we shall continue thus,
as one must who is out of favor   and exiled from his country."
1095   The Count was joyful;   he asked for water for his hands
and they brought it before him   at once, and gave it to him.
And with the two knights   whom the Cid had promised him,
the Count began to eat.   God, he ate with a will!
He who was born in good hour   sat beside him.
1100   "Unless you eat well, Count,   and to my full satisfaction,
you will remain here;   we shall not part from each other."
The Count said, "I will eat,   I will eat with a will."
With those two knights   he eats quickly.
My Cid, sitting there watching,   is well pleased
1105   because the Count Don Ramón   moved his hands so expertly.
   "If it please you, My Cid,   we are ready to go;
tell them to give us our beasts   and we shall ride at once.
I have not eaten so heartily   since I was made a Count;
the pleasure of that meal   will not be forgotten."
1110   They were given three palfreys,°   all with fine saddles,   *saddle-horses*
and rich garments,   fur tunics and cloaks.
The Count Don Ramón   entered between his two knights;
the Castilian rode with them   to the end of the encampment.
"Now depart from us, Count,   a free Catalan.[7]
1115   I extend you my thanks   for what you have left me.
If it should occur to you   to wish vengeance
and come seeking me,   let me know beforehand,
and either you will leave something of yours   or bear off something of mine."
"Be at peace, My Cid,   on that account.
1120   I have paid you tribute   for all this year;[8]
I have no intention   of coming to seek you."

63

   The Count spurred his horse   and rode forward,
turning his head   and looking behind him
for fear that the Cid   might change his mind,
1125   which that perfect one would not have done   for the world's wealth,
for in all his life   he had done no treachery.
   The Count is gone;   he of Bivar turned back,
returned to his vassals.   God, how great was their rejoicing,
for great and wonderful   was the booty they had won.
1130   His men are so rich   they cannot count all they have.

---

7. The Cid puns on the double meaning of "franco": "free" and "Catalan."

8. That is, from the booty the Cid has taken from him.

The Second Cantar

64

Here begins the story   of My Cid of Bivar.[1]
My Cid has made his camp   by the Pass of Olocau;
he has left Zaragoza   and the country there;
he has left Huesa   and the lands of Montalbán.

5   He has carried his war   toward the salt sea;
the sun comes from the east,   he turned to that direction.
My Cid took Jérica   and Onda and Almenara,
and he has overrun   all the lands of Burriana.

65

The Creator aided him,   the Lord in heaven,
10 and by that means,   he took Murviedro;[2]
My Cid knew well   that God was his strength.
There was great fear   in the city of Valencia.

66

It grieves those of Valencia.   Know, they are not pleased.
They took counsel   and came to besiege him.
15 They rode all night;   next day at dawn
around Murviedro   they set up their tents.
My Cid saw them   and exclaimed:
"Thanks be to Thee,   Father Who art in heaven!
We ride through their lands   and do them mischief,
20 we drink their wine   and eat their bread;
if they come to besiege us   they are within their rights.[3]
We shall not leave here   without a battle;
send out the messages   to those who should aid us,
some in Jérica   and others in Olocau,
25 from there to Onda   and to Almenara,
and to those of Burriana,   bid them come here.
We shall begin   this pitched battle;
I trust in God   Who will favor us."
On the third day   all have come together.
30 He who was born in good hour   began to address them:
"Hear me, my vassals,   as the Creator may save you!
Ever since we came   out of clean Christendom—
not at our own choice,   for we could not do otherwise—
God be thanked,   we have met no reverses.
35 Now those of Valencia   have encircled us;
if we are to remain   in these lands,
we must defeat them   most severely.

67

"When the night has passed   and morning has come,

---

1. With the second cantar begins the Cid's major campaign against the kingdom of Valencia in the Levant, or east.
2. Murviedro, which the Campeador makes his base for this campaign, is six miles south-southeast of Almenara

and 17 miles north-northeast of Valencia.
3. A good example of the poem's basis in the complex power struggles and social dynamics of Iberia rather than the black-and-white ideology of the Crusades, notwithstanding the piety of its Christian protagonist.

I would have the horses saddled   and the arms ready;
40   we shall go and see   that army of theirs.
We are exiles from   a foreign country;
there we shall see   who is worth his wages."

                        68
       Hear Minaya Alvar Fáñez,   what he had to say:
"Campeador,   let us do as you will.
45   Give me a hundred knights,   I ask for no more.
You with the rest   ride to the attack.
You will strike them hard,   I have no doubt.
I with the hundred   will charge from another side.
As I trust in God,   the field will be ours."
50   The Campeador was much pleased   with what he had said.
It was morning   and they set to arm;
each of them knows well   what he must do.
       When the dawn came,   My Cid rode to attack them.
"In the name of the Creator   and of Saint James the apostle,
55   attack them, knights,   heartily, with a will.
I am Ruy Díaz,   My Cid of Bivar!"
       You would have seen   so many tent cords snapped,
the poles wrenched out,   the canvas collapsing.
The Moors are many   and begin to recover.
60   Alvar Fáñez   rode in from another side;
hard against their wills   they were forced to flee
on foot or on horse,   those who could escape.
In that chase they killed   two Kings of the Moors;
they continued the pursuit   as far as Valencia.
65   My Cid   has taken great spoils;
they despoil the camp   and start to return;
they enter Murviedro   with those spoils they bear;
great is the rejoicing   in that town.
"They have taken Cebolla   and all that lies beyond it;[4]
70   they are frightened in Valencia,   they do not know what to do.
Know, the fame of My Cid   has gone everywhere."

                        69
       His fame goes re-echoing   even beyond the sea;[5]
My Cid rejoiced,   and all his company,
because God had given him aid   and he had routed them there.
75   He sent out raiders,   all night they rode;
they came to Cullera   and to Játiva
and below there   to the town of Denia.
They destroyed the lands of the Moors   as far as the seashore.
They took Benicadell,   its exits and entrances.[6]

                        70
80   When the Cid Campeador   had taken Benicadell,

---

4. Between Valencia and Murviedro.
5. That is, into North Africa, whence the king of Morocco will eventually come in reply.

6. Towns to the south and southwest of Valencia. Benicadell was a fortress that dominated the road between Valencia and Alicante; it was rebuilt by Rodrigo Díaz in 1092.

they are grieved in Játiva,   and in Cullera.
As for Valencia,   its dismay is boundless.

71

Seizing and despoiling,   riding at night,
sleeping in the daytime,   taking those towns,
My Cid spent three years   in the lands of the Moors.[7]

85

72

And he has chastised severely   those of Valencia.
They do not dare leave the city   or meet him in battle;
he has laid waste their farmlands   and brought havoc among them;
every year of those three,   My Cid deprived them of bread.
They grieve in Valencia,   not knowing what to do.
They cannot obtain   bread from anywhere;
the father cannot help his son   nor the son his father,
friend and friend   cannot console each other.
Great hardship it is, sirs,   to be without bread,
to see children and women   dying of hunger.
And they see their affliction growing,   that there is no remedy,
and they have sent word   to the King of Morocco;
he was so deep in war   with the King of the Atlas,
that he neither sent to advise them   nor came to their rescue.[8]

90

95

My Cid learned of this;   it gladdened his heart.
He went out from Murviedro   one night, and rode all night;
he appeared at daybreak   in the lands of Monreal.[9]
He sent forth a herald   to Aragón and Navarre;
he sent his messages   to the lands of Castile:[1]
"Whoever would leave   his toil and grow rich,
let him come to My Cid,   whose taste is for battle.
He would now lay siege to Valencia   to give it to the Christians."

100

105

73

"Whoever will come with me   to besiege Valencia—
let all come freely   and no one against his will—
I shall wait three days for him   by the Canal of Celfa."

110

74

This he spoke, My Cid,   the loyal Campeador.
He returned to Murviedro,   which he had already taken.
The cries went out,   you may know, in all directions;
at the odor of riches   they do not wish to delay;
great numbers gather to him   from good Christendom.
The fame of him resounds   in every direction;
more flock to My Cid,   you may know, than go from him
and his wealth increases,   My Cid's of Bivar.
When he saw so many assembled   he rejoiced.

115

---

7. As often in the poem, "three" is a number of convention rather than fact; it actually took Ruy Díaz six years to subjugate the Levant.
8. Most likely refers to Yusuf ibn Tesufin, the first Almoravid caliph of Morocco (1059–1106); the Almohads, who conquered the Atlas around 1122, waged war against Yusuf's grandson, Tesufin. Yusuf terrorized Christian Spain from the time of his landing at Algeciras in June 1086 at the invitation of the Sevillian ruler Almutamiz, inflicting a severe defeat on Alfonso's army at Sagrajas and proceeding to subjugate the *taifas*.
9. An impossible journey of around 100 miles.
1. The Cid sends his message to all of the Christian kingdoms of Iberia.

120   My Cid Don Rodrigo   did not wish to delay;
he set out for Valencia   and will attack them.
My Cid besieges it closely;   there was no escape.
He permits no one   to enter or depart.
He gave them a term of grace   if any would come and save them.[2]

125   Nine full months   his tents surrounded them;
when the tenth began   they were forced to surrender.
Great is the rejoicing   in that place
when My Cid took Valencia   and entered the city.
Those who had gone on foot   became knights on horses,[3]

130   and who could count   the gold and the silver?
All were rich,   as many as were there.
My Cid Don Rodrigo   sent for his fifth of the spoils;
in coined money alone   thirty thousand marks fell to him;
and the other riches,   who could count them?

135   My Cid rejoiced,   and all who were with him,
when his flag flew from the top   of the Moorish palace.

75

      Then my Cid rested,   and all his men.
The news came   to the King of Seville[4]
that Valencia was taken,   there had been no help for it;

140   he set out to attack it   with thirty thousand armed men.
Beyond the farmlands   they joined battle.
My Cid of the long beard   routed them there;
as far as Játiva   the pursuit went on.
Crossing the Júcar,   you would have seen them struck down;

145   Moors caught in the current,   forced to drink water.
That King of Seville   escaped with three wounds.
My Cid returned   with all his gains.
Great were the spoils of Valencia   when they took that city;
those from this victory,   you may know, were still richer;

150   to the least among them   fell a hundred marks of silver.
You can see how the fame   of this warrior has grown.

76

      There is great rejoicing   among all those Christians
with My Cid Ruy Díaz,   who in good hour was born.
His beard grows on him,   it grows longer upon him;

155   these words My Cid   spoke of it with his mouth:
"For love of King Alfonso,   who sent me into exile."
No scissors would touch it   nor one hair be cut,
and let Moors and Christians   all tell of this.[5]

---

2. The Cid allowed the Moors of Valencia a respite of 15 days to send for aid from the emirs of Zaragoza and Murcía on condition that they would surrender if they had not succeeded in breaking the siege by the end of that time.
3. More specifically, those who had been peasant farmers were enriched to the extent that they became *caballeros pardos,* not noble but able to keep their own horse and arms and enjoying many of the privileges of full-fledged knights.

4. The poem may recall the Almoravid governor Sir ibn Abu Bekr, who had taken the city in 1091, although there is no record of any attack he made on Valencia.
5. Since biblical and Roman days, leaving the beard untrimmed had been a token of mourning. It also serves here as a sign of the Cid's confidence in his prowess, for the longer his beard grew, the more vulnerable it would make him in battle or to a challenge.

My Cid Don Rodrigo   is resting in Valencia;
160   Minaya Alvar Fáñez   does not leave his side.
Those who came with him into exile   have all grown rich.
The renowned Campeador   gave them all, in Valencia,
houses and fiefs   with which they are satisfied;
they all have tasted   of the Cid's generosity.
165   Those who joined him later   are content also;
My Cid knows   that with the gains they have taken,
if they might depart now,   they would go gladly.[6]
My Cid commanded,   as Minaya had advised him,
that no man among them   who with him had gained anything
170   should leave without bidding farewell   and kissing his hand,
or else he would seize him again   wherever he might be hidden
and take from him everything   and hand him on a gallows.[7]
Behold, all this   was put in good order;
he is talking things over   with Minaya Alvar Fáñez:
175   "If you please, Minaya,   I should like to know
how many are with me here   and have received of the spoils.
I would have them all counted   and set down in writing
so that if anyone hide,   or anyone is missing,
his possessions may be returned to me   by those vassals of mine
180   who guard Valencia,   keeping watch around it."[8]
Then Minaya said,   "That is well advised."

77

He bade them all come to the court   and gather together.
When they had come   he numbered them all:
three thousand six hundred   were under My Cid of Bivar;
185   his heart was pleased   and he began to smile.
"God be praised, Minaya,   and Santa María His mother!
With less than these we rode out   from the gate at Bivar,
and now riches are ours   and more shall be ours hereafter.
"If you please, Minaya,   and it would not burden you,
190   I would send you to Castile,   where our lands are,
to King Alfonso,   my natural lord.
Out of these my gains   which we have taken here
I would give him a hundred horses,   I would have you take them,
kiss his hand for me   and urgently beg him
195   that he, of his grace, may allow me   to bring from there
Doña Jimena, my wife,   and my daughters.
I shall send for them;   know, this is the message:
'My Cid's wife   and his daughters
in such wise will be sent for   that with great honor they will come
200   to these foreign lands°   which we have taken.'"   *Moorish territory*
Then Minaya said,   "I will do it gladly."

---

6. The Cid must find a way to guarantee that enough men remain to allow him to hold the territory he has captured.
7. The kiss of the hand was the traditional seal of vassalage; before anyone is permitted to depart, the Cid must agree to dissolve the feudal tie between them.

8. Another sign of the business side of feudal warfare; in order to be successful it was necessary not only to be a valiant warrior and leader, but to be (or to employ) a good accountant and record keeper.

When they had spoken this   they began to make ready.
My Cid gave a hundred men   to Alvar Fáñez
to serve him on his way   and do his will,
205   and he sent a thousand marks   of silver to San Pedro,
five hundred of them to be given   to the abbot Don Sancho.

78

While they were rejoicing   at this news,
out of the east   came a cleric,
the Bishop Don Jerome   is his name.[9]
210   Learned in letters   and with much wisdom
and a ready warrior   on foot or on horse,
he came inquiring   of the Cid's brave deeds,
sighing to see himself   with the Moors in the field,
saying if he should weary   of fighting them with his hands,
215   let no Christian mourn him   all the days of this world.
When My Cid heard this   he was well pleased.
"Hear, Minaya Alvar Fáñez,   by Him Who is in heaven,
when God would give us aid   let us heartily thank Him for it:
I would ordain a bishopric   in the lands of Valencia;[1]
220   I would give it   to this good Christian.
Take the good news   when you go to Castile."

79

Alvar Fáñez was pleased   with what Don Rodrigo said.
That same Don Jerome   they ordained Bishop;
they arranged that he might live   richly in Valencia.[2]
225   God, how great was the rejoicing   of all those Christians
for in the lands of Valencia   there was a lord Bishop!
Minaya was joyful   and bade farewell and set out.

80

Leaving the lands of Valencia   lying in peace,
Minaya Alvar Fáñez   rode toward Castile.
230   I do not wish to recount   all the places where he paused.
He asked for King Alfonso,   asked where he might find him.
The King had gone to Sahagún   only shortly before
and thence to Carrión,   and there he might find him.[3]
Minaya Alvar Fáñez   was pleased to hear this;
235   he rode toward that place   with the gifts he had brought.

81

Just as King Alfonso   had come out from Mass,
behold where Minaya Alvar Fáñez   arrives most opportunely.

9. The fourth of the Cid's most loyal followers is the historical Jérôme of Périgord, in southern France, a cleric who came to Spain in the retinue of Bernard of Sédirac, the first archbishop of Toledo. Jérôme was consecrated as bishop of Valencia in 1098.
1. The creation of a bishopric was a royal prerogative and required the confirmation of the Holy See in Rome: the Cid is thus acting here as an independent ruler.
2. That is, they donated richly to the episcopal see, something Rodrigo Díaz did when the main mosque of Valencia was consecrated as its cathedral and dedicated to the Virgin Mary in 1098.
3. Sahagún was an important medieval abbey much favored by Alfonso VI, who had taken refuge in it in 1072 when his brother Sancho had conquered the kingdom. It was in the kingdom of León, the part of the territory of his father Ferdinand I inherited by Alfonso when the kingdom was divided. About 20 miles to the east, Carrión was the seat of the powerful Beni-Gómez family, who had never ceased to resent the humiliation they had undergone at the hands of Sancho.

He knelt down on his knees   before all the people;
he fell down in great sorrow   at the feet of King Alfonso;
240   he kissed the King's hands   and spoke with all eloquence.

                              82

   "Grace, lord Alfonso,   for the love of the Creator!
My Cid the warrior   kisses your hands,
kisses your feet and your hands   as his duty to so good a lord,
and may you grant him grace   as the Creator may bless you!
245   You sent him from your lands,   he is without your favor;
nevertheless, in foreign lands   he manages well:
he has taken Jérica   and the place called Onda
and seized Almenara,   and Murviedro, which is larger;
likewise he took Cebolla   and Castejón farther on,
250   and Benicadell,   which is a strong hill,
and besides all these   he is lord of Valencia.
The good Campeador   a Bishop has ordained with his own hands,
fought five pitched battles   and triumphed in them all.
Great are the gains   the Creator has given him.
255   Here are the proofs   that it is the truth I tell you:
a hundred horses,   strong-limbed and swift,
each one provided   with saddle and bridle.
He kisses your hands   and begs you to accept them;
he calls himself your vassal   and regards you as his lord."
260   The King raised his right hand   and crossed himself.
"Saint Isidore bless me,[4]   my heart is pleased
with the vast spoils   the Cid has taken!
And I am pleased with the deeds   the Campeador has done;
I accept these horses   which he sends as a gift."
265   Though it pleased the King,   it grieved García Ordóñez:[5]
"It seems that in the lands of the Moors   there is no man living
since the Cid Campeador   thus does as he pleases."
The King said to the Count,   "Leave off such talk;
in whatever he does   he serves me better than you do."[6]
270   Then manfully   Minaya spoke:
"The Cid begs of your grace,   if it meet your pleasure,
that his wife Doña Jimena   and both his daughters
may leave the monastery   where he left them
and go to Valencia   to the good Campeador."
275   Then the King said,   "It pleases my heart;
I shall provide them with escort   while they go through my lands
and keep them from harm and grievance   and from dishonor,
and when these ladies have come   to the end of my lands,
then you and the Campeador   take care to guard them.
280   Hear me, my vassals   and all my court!

---

4. A customary oath of Alfonso, who was said to have
been especially devoted to this saint, an early bishop of
Seville.
5. The villains of the poem will now be introduced, their

bitterness hearkening back to events of the Cid's youth,
when he had humiliated García Ordóñez in the south.
6. In reality, Alfonso VI and the count García remained
closely allied through political as well as familial ties.

I would not have the Campeador   lose anything,
and as for all those vassals   who call him lord,
whom I disinherited,   I return to them all that they had;
let them keep their inheritances   while they serve the Campeador,
285   and I free their bodies   from threat of injury;
all this I do   that they may serve their lord."
Minaya Alvar Fáñez   kissed him on the hands.
The King smiled   and spoke thus sweetly:
"Those who wish to go   to serve the Campeador
290   have my leave,   and may the Creator bless them.
We shall gain more by this   than by disaffection."[7]

    Then the Heirs of Carrión[8]   spoke between themselves:
"Great grows the fame   of My Cid the Campeador;
it would serve our advantage   to marry his daughters.
295   Yet we would not dare   propose such a plan.
My Cid is from Bivar   and we, of the Counts of Carrión."[9]
They spoke of it to no one   and there the scheme rested.

    Minaya Alvar Fáñez   bade the good King farewell.
"Are you leaving us now, Minaya?   May the Creator bless you.
300   Take with you a royal herald,   who will serve your needs;
if you go with the ladies,   care for their comfort
as far as Medinaceli;[1]   in my name demand all they require.
From that point forward   they concern the Campeador."
Minaya bade farewell   and went from the court.

83

305   The Heirs of Carrión   have made their decision;
they went out a little way   with Minaya Alvar Fáñez.
"We have been your friends in all things,   now be friend to us:
give our greetings   to My Cid of Bivar,
we shall serve him in all things   as well as we may;
310   we wish the Cid to lose nothing   by the friendship he bears us."
Minaya answered, "Your message   will not overburden me."

    Minaya has ridden on   and the Heirs turn back.
He rode toward San Pedro,   where the ladies are;
great was their joy   when he appeared.
315   Minaya has dismounted   and prays to San Pedro.
When the prayer ended   he turned to the ladies.
"I humble myself before you,   Doña Jimena;
may God keep you   and both your daughters from evil.
My Cid sends you greetings   from where he is;
320   I left him in health   and with great riches.

---

7. The King reiterates his past concessions and grants a further rapprochement with the Cid, but doesn't yet revoke the order of exile.

8. Diego and Fernando González, grandsons of the Beni-Gómez, counts of Carrión, a noble clan of great political importance in both León and Castile. Although called the "Infantes" or heirs of the family, they have no actual claim to the title.

9. The Cid is a member of the lower nobility, while the Infantes are related to the highest aristocracy of the land. The marriage, they argue, would bring them fame (and fortune), but its inequality could lead to a loss of standing at court.

1. Referred to here as the frontier of Castile, an anachronism, since it was not taken by Alfonso until 1104.

The King, in his grace,   has set you free
so that you may come to Valencia   which is ours for inheritance.[2]
If the Cid might see you   well and without harm,
all would be joy   and he would grieve no longer."

325 Doña Jimena said,   "May the Creator will it so!"
Minaya Alvar Fáñez   chose three knights
and sent them to My Cid   in Valencia where he was:
"Say to the Campeador   —whom may God keep from harm—
that the King has set free   his wife and daughters;

330 while we are in his lands   he will provide us with escort.
Within fifteen days   if God keep us from harm
we shall be with him,   I and his wife and his daughters
and all their good ladies with them,   as many as are here."
The knights have set out   and will take care to do this.

335 Minaya Alvar Fáñez   remained in San Pedro.
    You would have seen knights   ride in from all directions
wishing to go to Valencia   to My Cid of Bivar,
asking Alvar Fáñez   to aid them in this,
Minaya saying,   "I shall do so gladly."

340 Sixty-five warriors   have assembled with him there
besides the hundred   whom he had brought with him;
they made a fine escort   to go with those ladies.
    Minaya gave the abbot   the five hundred marks;
I must tell what he did   with the other five hundred.

345 The good Minaya   took thought to provide
Doña Jimena   and her daughters there,
and the other ladies   who served them and went before them,
with the finest garments   to be found in Burgos
and with palfreys and mules,   that their appearance might be seemly.

350 When he had thus   decked out these ladies
the good Minaya   made ready to ride,
when behold Raquel and Vidas   fall at his feet.[3]
"Grace, Minaya,   worthy knight!
The Cid has undone us,   you may know, if he will not aid us;

355 we shall ignore the interest   if he give back the capital."[4]
"I shall speak of it with the Cid   if God will take me there.
You will be well rewarded   for all you have done."
Raquel and Vidas said,   "May the Creator will it so!
If not, we shall leave Burgos   and go to seek him in Valencia."[5]

360   Minaya Alvar Fáñez   has gone to San Pedro;
many gathered about him,   he made ready to ride.
Their sorrow is great   at the parting from the abbot.

2. That is, that they will live in Valencia and retain it as their personal and hereditary property.

3. The reappearance of the moneylenders briefly underlines the Cid's change in fortune and provides a comic parallel to the equally greedy but far more harmful duo of the Infantes.

4. According to standard practice, the goods left behind could be confiscated if the loan had not been repaid by the set time; the moneylenders are now fully aware of the deceit practiced against them.

5. A patently empty threat that matches the presumedly empty promise of Álvar Fáñez, and concludes the interlude.

"The Creator keep you,   Minaya Alvar Fáñez!
In my name kiss the hands   of the Campeador,
365   let him not forget   this monastery;
all the days of the world   as he may give it aid,
the Cid Campeador   will increase in honor."
Minaya answered,   "I shall tell him gladly."
    They bid farewell   and ride forward,
370   the King's herald with them   to be at their service;
through the lands of the King   they were well escorted.
They go in five days   from San Pedro to Medinaceli;[6]
behold them in Medinaceli,   the ladies and Alvar Fáñez.
    I shall tell you of the knights   who took the message.
375   When My Cid of Bivar   heard the news
it pleased his heart   and he rejoiced,
and in these words   he began to speak:
"He who sends a good messenger   may expect good news.
    You, Muño Gustioz   and Pedro Bermúdez
380   and Martín Antolínez,   loyal man of Burgos,
and you, Bishop Don Jerome,   honored cleric,
ride with a hundred   armed as though for battle,
ride forward   through Santa María
to Molina,   which is farther on;
385   Abengalbón is lord there,   my friend, at peace with me.[7]
He is certain to join you   with another hundred knights;
ride toward Medinaceli   at your best speed;
my wife and my daughters   with Minaya Alvar Fáñez
you will find there,   as I have been told;
390   conduct them here before me   with great honor.
And I shall stay in Valencia,   whose conquest was costly.
It would be great folly   to abandon it now;
I shall stay in Valencia,   which is my inheritance."
    When this was said   they make ready to ride,
395   and as far as they can   they ride on without resting.
They passed Santa María   and lodged at Bonchales,
then another day's riding   and they slept in Molina.
When the Moor Abengalbón   knew of the message
he rode out to receive them   with great rejoicing:
400   "Have you come, vassals   of my dear friend?
It does not sadden me,   believe me, it fills me with joy!"
Muño Gustioz spoke,   he waited for no one:
"My Cid sent you greetings   and asked you to provide us
with a hundred knights   to ride with us at once;
405   his wife and his daughters   are in Medinaceli;
he would have you go   and escort them here
and not go from them   as far as Valencia."

6. About 100 miles, traveled at about half the pace at which the Cid has been accustomed to travel.
7. There may or may not have been an Abengalbón, or Ibn Galbun, governor at the time of Molina; what is significant is that he is a Moorish ally and friend of the Cid in the poem.

Abengalbón said,   "I will do it gladly."
That night he served them   a great banquet.
410   In the morning   they made ready to ride.
They had asked for a hundred,   but he came with two hundred.
They ride into the mountains   which are wild there and high,
and they pass   the Plain of Taranz
riding in such manner   that none feels fear;
415   by the Valley of Arbujuelo   they begin to descend.
      Close guard is mounted   in Medinaceli;
Minaya Alvar Fáñez,   seeing them come armed,
was alarmed, and sent two knights   to find out the truth;
at this they did not take long   for they were eager to know;
420   the one stayed and the other   turned back to Alvar Fáñez:
"Forces of the Campeador   have come to find us;
behold, there at their head   is Pedro Bermúdez,
and Muño Gustioz,   your unfailing friend,
and Martín Antolínez,   who was born in Burgos,
425   and the Bishop Don Jerome,   the loyal cleric,
and the chief Abengalbón,   and his warriors with him;
for the love of My Cid   and to do him honor
they are all riding together;   now they are about to arrive."
Then Minaya said,   "Let us mount and ride."
430   They did so at once   without delay.
All the hundred rode out;   the sight of them was splendid,
mounted on good horses   caparisoned with sendal,[8]
bells on their breast leathers,   shields from their necks hanging,
the knights bearing lances,   from each its pennon hanging,
435   that all might know   with what prudence came Alvar Fáñez
and how he would leave Castile   with these ladies he was bringing.
      Those who rode as scouts   and arrived first
grasped their weapons   and jousted for the sport;
not far from Jalón   there was great rejoicing.
440   When the others came up   they made obeisance to Minaya.
When Abengalbón came up   and set eyes on him,
smiling with his mouth   he went to embrace him;
he kisses him on the shoulder   as is the Moors' custom.
"It is a glad day in which I meet you,   Minaya Alvar Fáñez!
445   You bring with you these ladies   whose presence does us honor,
the wife and the daughters   of the Cid, the warrior;
we must all do them honor   for such is his fortune
that though we should wish him evil   we could not perform it;
in peace or in war   he will have what is ours;
450   who does not know the truth   I hold stupid."

                              84

      Alvar Fáñez Minaya   smiles at these words.
"Greetings, Abengalbón,   unfailing friend!

---

8. Richly covered in silk or linen.

If God allow me to reach the Cid   and this soul may see him,
you will lose nothing   for this that you have done.
455   Come rest for the night with us   for a banquet is spread."
Abengalbón said,   "This courtesy delights me;
before three days have passed   I shall return it to you twofold."
They entered Medinaceli;   Minaya saw to their comfort.
All were well pleased   with the care that was shown them.
460   The King's herald   bade farewell and left them;
far off in Valencia   the Cid was honored
by such pomp and celebration   as were seen in Medinaceli;
the King paid for it all   and Minaya owed no one.
        The night has passed   and morning come
465   and Mass heard,   and then they mounted.
They rode out of Medinaceli   and passed Jalón;
up the river by Arbujuelo   they spurred without pausing,
then they passed by   the Plain of Taranz;
they came to Molina   where Abengalbón was lord.
470   The Bishop Don Jerome,   a good Christian without fault,
guarded the ladies   day and night
with a good war horse on his right   which rode ahead of his weapons.
He and Alvar Fáñez   rode together.
They have entered Molina,   a rich and goodly town.
475   The Moor Abengalbón   without fail serves them well;
there was no lack   of all they might desire.
Even their horses   he shod newly.
And Minaya and the ladies,   God, how he honored them!
Another day in the morning   they mounted again;
480   as far as Valencia   without fail he served them.
The Moor spent his own   and would take nothing from them.
Amid such rejoicings   and tidings of honor
they came within three leagues   of Valencia.
The news came   into Valencia
485   to My Cid,   who in good hour girded sword.

                    85
        Never greater joy,   nor as great, as My Cid's then,
for the news had come   from that which he most loved.
He sent two hundred knights   to ride with all speed
to receive Minaya   and the noble ladies;
490   he himself remained in Valencia   keeping watch and guard
for he trusts Alvar Fáñez   to take every care.

                    86
        Behold, how all these   receive Minaya
and the ladies and the girls   and the rest of their companions.
My Cid ordered   those who were with him
495   to guard the castle   and the other high towers
and all the gates   and the exits and entrances,
and to lead him his horse Babieca,   which he had taken lately
from that King of Seville   when he had defeated him.

My Cid, who in good hour girded sword,   had not yet ridden him
500   nor learned whether he were swift   and answered the reins well;
at the gate of Valencia,   where it was safe,
he wished to bear arms   before his wife and daughters.[9]

The ladies were received   with great honor;
the Bishop Don Jerome   entered ahead of them
505   and dismounted   and went to the chapel;
with as many as he might muster   who were ready in time,
dressed in surplices   and with crosses of silver,
he went out to receive the ladies   and the good Minaya.

He who was born in good hour   did not delay:
510   he put on his silk tunic,   his long beard hung down;
they saddled for him Babieca   and fastened the caparisons.
My Cid rode out upon him   bearing wooden arms.[1]
On the horse they called   Babieca he rode,
rode at a gallop;   it was a wonder to watch.
515   When he had ridden one round   everyone marveled;
from that day Babieca   was famous through all Spain.
When he had ridden,   My Cid dismounted.
He went up to his wife   and his two daughters;
when Doña Jimena saw him   she fell at his feet:
520   "Grace, Campeador,   who in good hour girded sword!
You have delivered me   from much vile shame.
Here am I, sire,   I and both your daughters;
with God's help and yours   they are good and well brought up."
He took his wife in his arms   and then his daughters;
525   such was his joy   the tears flowed from his eyes.
All his vassals   were filled with jubilation;
they jousted with arms   and rode at targets.
Hear what he said,   who in good hour girded sword:
"You, Doña Jimena,   my honored and dear wife,
530   and both my daughters,   my heart and my soul,
enter with me   the town of Valencia,
the inheritance   which I have won for you."
Mother and daughters   kissed his hands.
They entered Valencia   with great celebration.

87

535   My Cid and they   went to the castle;
there he led them up   to the highest place.
Then fair eyes   gaze out on every side;
They see Valencia,   the city, as it lies,
and turning the other way   their eyes behold the sea.
540   They look on the farmlands,   wide and thick with green,
and all the other things   which gave delight;
they raised their hands   to give thanks to God

---

9. As a form of pageantry to celebrate their arrival and his   1. Proper for jousts and tournaments rather than combat.
various triumphs since they have last seen each other.

for all that bounty   so vast and so splendid.

My Cid and his vassals   lived in great content.

545   The winter has gone   and March begun.

I would tell you news   from across the sea,

from that King Yusuf,   who is in Morocco.[2]

88

The King of Morocco was troubled   because of My Cid Don Rodrigo:

"For in lands that are mine   he has trespassed gravely

550   and gives thanks for it to no one   save Jesus Christ."

That King of Morocco   assembled his nobles.

Fifty times a thousand armed men   gathered under him;

they have embarked on the sea,   they have entered into the ships,

they leave for Valencia   to find My Cid Don Rodrigo.

555   The ships have entered harbor,   the men have come forth on land.

89

They arrived at Valencia,   which My Cid conquered.

The unbelievers have made camp,   they have pitched their tents.

The news of this   has come to My Cid.

90

"Thanks be to the Creator   and to the heavenly Father!

560   All that I own   is here before me;

with toil I took Valencia   for my inheritance;

as long as I live   I will not leave it.

Thanks be to the Creator   and Santa María Mother,

that I have here with me   my wife and my daughters.

565   Delight has come to me   from the lands beyond the sea;

I shall arm myself,   I cannot evade it;

my wife and my daughters   will see me in battle,

in these foreign lands they will see   how houses are made,

they will see clearly   how we earn our bread."

570   He led his wife and daughters   up into the castle;

they raised their eyes   and saw the tents pitched.

"What is this, Cid,   in the name of the Creator?"

"My honored wife,   let it not trouble you!

This is great and marvelous wealth   to be added unto us;

575   you have barely arrived here   and they send you gifts,

they bring the marriage portion   for the wedding of your daughters."[3]

"I give thanks to you, Cid,   and to our heavenly Father."

"Wife, stay here in the palace,   here in the castle;

have no fear   when you see me fighting;

580   by the grace of God   and Santa María Mother,

my heart grows within me   because you will be watching;

with God's help I shall triumph   in this battle."

---

2. The Almoravid caliph Yusuf ibn Tasufin sent his forces in 1094 to attempt to recapture Valencia, although he didn't himself lead them. His nephew Muhammad ibn Ayisa was defeated there by Ruy Díaz in 1095.

3. Evidence of the Cid's understated humor as well as his high spirits.

91

The tents are pitched   and the dawn comes;
with a quickening stroke   the Moors beat on the drums.[4]
585   My Cid rejoiced and said,   "A day of delight is this!"
His wife is frightened,   thinks her heart must shatter;
the ladies are frightened also   and both the daughters;
they had not known such terror   since the day they were born.
        He stroked his beard,   the good Cid Campeador.
590   "Have no fear, for all this   is to your favor;
before these two weeks have gone,   if it please the Creator,
we will have wrenched from them   those same drums;
they shall be fetched before you   and you shall see what they are,
then they shall be given   to the Bishop Don Jerome
595   and hung in the Church   of Santa María, mother of God."
This is the vow   the Cid Campeador made.
        The ladies are reassured   and their fear goes from them.
The Moors of Morocco   ride out boldly;
without fear   they have entered the farmlands.

92

600   The sentinel saw them   and rang the bell;
the vassals are ready,   the men of Ruy Díaz;
they arm themselves with a will   and ride from the city.
Where they met the Moors   they charged them at once,
drove them from the farmlands   with much harsh treatment.
605   They killed five hundred of them   on that day.

93

        As far as the tents   they pursued them;
they have accomplished much   and they turn back.
Alvar Salvadórez   remained captive there.
Those who eat the Cid's bread   have returned to his side;
610   he saw it with his own eyes   yet they retell it;
My Cid is pleased   with what they have done.
"Hear me, knights, it must be   thus, and not otherwise;
today has been a good day,   tomorrow will be better.
Be armed all of you   by the time day breaks;
615   the Bishop Don Jerome   will give us absolution;
he will sing us Mass   and then we shall ride.
In the name of the Creator   and of Saint James the apostle
we shall attack them;   thus it must be.
It is better that we should beat them   than that they should take our
        bread."
620   Then all said, "Willingly   and with all our hearts."
Minaya spoke,   he waited no longer:
"Since you wish it so, Cid,   send me another way;
give me for the battle   a hundred and thirty knights;
when you fall upon them.   I shall attack from the other side.

---

4. The key to Yusuf's success in wresting control of al-Andalus from Alfonso was the disciplined coordination of the individual soldiers acting to the deafening beat of drums. The Christian forces, by contrast, were accustomed to single combat.

625   On both sides, or one only,   God will aid us."
       Then the Cid answered,   "I will do it gladly."

94

       The day has gone   and the night come.
       That Christian host   was not slow in making ready.
       By the second cock crow,   before morning came,
630   the Bishop Don Jerome   sang them the Mass.
       When the Mass was said   he gave them full absolution:
       "He who may die here   fighting face to face
       I absolve of his sins,   and God will receive his soul.
       "Cid Don Rodrigo,   who in good hour girded sword,
635   I sang Mass   for you this morning;
       I crave a boon of you,   I beg you to grant it:
       I would have you let me strike   the first blows in the fight."
       The Campeador said,   "From this moment it is granted."

95

       All have ridden out armed   from the towers of Cuarto,
640   My Cid giving full instructions   to his vassals.
       They leave at the gates   men they can count on.
       My Cid sprang   onto his horse, Babieca,
       that is splendidly caparisoned   with all manner of ornaments.
       They ride out with the banner,   they ride out from Valencia;
645   four thousand less thirty   ride with My Cid;
       gladly they go   to attack the fifty thousand.[5]
       Alvar Alvarez and Minaya   rode in from the other side.
       As pleased the Creator,   they overcame them.
       My Cid used his lance   and then drew his sword;
650   he killed so many Moors   that the count was lost;
       above his elbow   the blood ran.
       He has struck King Yusuf   three blows;
       Yusuf escaped from his sword   for hard he rode his horse
       and sheltered in Cullera,   a noble castle;
655   My Cid of Bivar   arrived there in pursuit
       with those of his good vassals   who stay by his side.
       And there he turned back,   he who in good hour was born.
       Great was his joy   at what they had taken,
       and there he knew the worth of Babieca   from head to tail.
660   All those spoils   remain in his hands.
       A count was made: of the fifty thousand Moors,
       only a hundred and four   had escaped.
       My Cid's vassals   have despoiled the field;
       they found three thousand marks   of mixed gold and silver;
665   the other spoils   were beyond numbering.
       My Cid was joyful,   and all his vassals,
       because God of His grace   had given them triumph.
       When they had thus routed   the King of Morocco
       My Cid left Alvar Fáñez   to attend to the rest;

5. Doubtless the disparity of numbers is exaggerated.

670   with a hundred knights   he returned to Valencia.
    He had his helmet off   and his hood drawn back;
    thus he rode in on Babieca,   his sword in his hand.
      There he received the ladies,   who were waiting for him;
    My Cid reined in his horse   and stopped before them.
675   "I bow before you, ladies,   great spoils I have won for you;
    you kept Valencia for me   and I have won in the field;
    this was the will of God   and of all His saints;
    upon your arrival   they have sent us great treasure.
    You see the sword bloody   and the horse sweating:
680   thus it is   that one conquers Moors in the field.
    Pray to the Creator   to grant me a few years' life;
    you will grow in honor   and vassals will kiss your hands."
    This My Cid spoke,   dismounting from his horse.
    When they saw him on foot   when he had dismounted,
685   the ladies and the daughters   and the noble wife
    all kneeled   before the Campeador.
    "By your grace we are all that we are;   may you live long!"
      Then with him   they entered the palace
    and sat with him   on the elaborate benches.
690   "My wife, Doña Jimena,   have you not begged this of me?
    These ladies you bring with you   who so well serve you,
    I wish to marry them   with those vassals of mine;
    to each of them   I give two hundred marks.
    Let it be known in Castile   who it is they have served so well.
695   For your daughters, we shall come   to decide that more slowly."
    All rose   and kissed his hands;
    great was the rejoicing   in the palace.
    And the Cid had spoken,   so it was done.
      Minaya Alvar Fáñez   was abroad in the field
700   with all those men   counting and writing down;
    as for tents and arms   and garments of value,
    it passed belief   what they found.
    I will tell you   what was most important:
    there was no counting   all the horses
705   who went without riders   and none to take them.
    Even the Moors in the farmlands   captured some,
    and despite this there fell   to the famous Campeador
    a thousand horses   of the best and best broken,
    and when My Cid   received so many,
710   surely the others   were well requited.
    So many precious tents   and jeweled tent poles
    My Cid has taken   with all his vassals!
    The tent of the King of Morocco,   which surpassed all the others,
    hangs on two tent poles   wrought with gold;
715   My Cid commanded,   the famous Campeador,
    that no Christian touch it,   that it be left standing.
    "Such a tent as this,   which has come from Morocco,
    I wish to send   to Alfonso the Castilian

that he may believe the news   that My Cid has possessions."
720   With all these riches   they have returned to Valencia.
The Bishop Don Jerome,   the mitered man of great merit,
when he has finished fighting   with both his hands
has lost count   of the Moors he has killed.
The spoils that fell to him   also were enormous;
725   My Cid Don Rodrigo,   who was born in good hour,
has sent him a tithe   out of his own fifth.[6]

96

These Christian people   in Valencia rejoice
at their great wealth,   at so many horses and weapons;
Doña Jimena is pleased,   and her daughters,
730   and all the other ladies,   who count themselves already married.
My good Cid   delayed for nothing.
"Where are you, worthy knight?   Come here, Minaya.
For that which has fallen to you   you owe me no thanks;
I mean what I say;   out of this fifth that is mine
735   take what you wish   and leave the rest for me.
And when tomorrow dawns   you must go without fail
with horses from this fifth   which I have taken,
with saddles and bridles   and each with its sword;
for my wife's sake   and that of my daughters,
740   since he sent them here   where they are content,
these two hundred horses   will go to him as a gift,
that King Alfonso may speak no ill   of him who rules in Valencia."
He commanded Pedro Bermúdez   to go with Minaya.
The next day in the morning   they rode off early
745   to kiss the King's hands   with the Cid's greetings,
and two hundred men   rode as their retinue.
My Cid sent as a gift   two hundred horses
from this battle   in which he had triumphed.
"And I shall serve him always   while my soul is with me."

97

750   They have left Valencia   and begin their journey;
they bear such riches with them   they must guard them closely.
They ride two days and nights   without pausing to rest,
and they have passed the mountains   that cut off the other country.
They begin to inquire   for King Alfonso.[7]

98

755   They have passed the ranges,   the mountains and the waters;
they arrive in Valladolid   where King Alfonso is.[8]
Pedro Bermúdez and Minaya   sent a message
requesting him to prepare   to receive this company,
for My Cid of Valencia   was sending him a gift.

---

6. A tithe, or tenth, of total income or goods was the customary tax exacted by the Church of its members, though its existence in Iberia has not been documented before the 12th century.

7. Courts were itinerant in the High Middle Ages, so Minaya must first find out where the king is at the present moment.
8. On the border between León and Castile, Valladolid was within the sphere of influence of the Beni-Gómez.

99

760   The King rejoiced;   you have not seen him so pleased.
He commanded all his nobles   to mount at once,
and the King rode out   among the first
to see those messengers   from him who was born in good hour.
The Heirs of Carrión,   you may know, murmured at this,
765 and the Count Don García,   the Cid's sworn enemy.
What pleases some   weighs heavy upon others.
Those sent by My Cid   came into sight;
one would have thought them an army,   not mere messengers;
King Alfonso   crosses himself.
770 Minaya and Pedro Bermúdez   have arrived before him;
they set foot on the earth,   they get down from their horses,
they kneel down   before King Alfonso,
they kiss the ground   and both his feet.
"Grace, King Alfonso,   greatly honored!
775 We kiss your feet   for My Cid the Campeador;
he calls you his lord   and remains your vassal
and prizes greatly   the honor you have given him.
A few days since, King,   he triumphed in a battle
over that King of Morocco   whose name is Yusuf
780 and fifty thousand besides;   he beat them from the field.
The spoils that he took   are very great;
all of his vassals   have become rich men,
and he sends you two hundred horses   and kisses your hands."
King Alfonso said,   "I receive them with pleasure.
785 I send thanks to My Cid   for this gift he has sent me;
he will yet see the hour   I shall do as much for him."
This pleased many   and they kissed his hands.
      It weighed heavy on Count Don García;   it enraged him deeply.
With ten of his kinsmen   he rode to one side.
790 "What a marvel, this Cid,   how his honor grows.
And in his honor   we are dishonored.
For killing Kings in the field   as casually
as though he had found them dead   and seized their horses,
for his deeds of this sort   we shall suffer."

100

795   King Alfonso spoke,   hear what he said:
"I thank the Creator   and lord Saint Isidore
for these two hundred horses   which My Cid has sent me.
In the coming days of my kingdom   I shall expect still greater things.
You, Minaya Alvar Fáñez,   and Pedro Bermúdez there,
800 I command   that you be given rich garments,
and choose arms for yourselves   at your pleasure
so that you may appear well   before Ruy Díaz, My Cid.
I give you three horses;   take them now.
Thus it seems to me,   and I am convinced
805 that from these new things   good must follow."

101

They kissed his hands   and went in to rest;
he commanded that they should be served   with whatever they needed.
    I would tell you   of the Heirs of Carrión
taking counsel together,   plotting in secret:
810   "The Cid's affairs   prosper greatly;
let us ask   for his daughters in marriage;
our honor will grow   and we shall prosper."
They come to King Alfonso   with this secret.

102

    "We beg your grace   as our King and lord,
815   by your leave   we would have you ask for us
for the hands of the daughters   of the Campeador;
we would marry them,   to his honor and our advantage."
A long while   the King thought and meditated:[9]
"I sent the good Campeador   into exile
820   and wrought him harm,   and he has returned me much good.
I cannot tell   if he will favor this marriage,
but since you wish it   I shall discuss it with him."
    Then King Alfonso   called to himself
Minaya Alvar Fáñez   and Pedro Bermúdez
825   and took them aside   into another room.
"Hear me, Minaya,   and you, Pedro Bermúdez.
Ruy Díaz, Campeador,   My Cid, serves me well.
He shall receive my pardon   as he deserves;
let him come and appear before me   if it meet his pleasure.[1]
830   There are further tidings   from here in my court:
Diego and Fernando,   the Heirs of Carrión,
wish to marry   his two daughters.
Be good messengers,   I beg of you,
and tell all this   to the good Campeador:
835   his name will be ennobled   and his honor increase
by thus contracting marriage   with the Heirs of Carrión."
Minaya spoke,   in agreement with Pedro Bermúdez:
"We shall ask him   as you have told it to us,
then the Cid may do   what meets his pleasure."[2]
840   "Say to Ruy Díaz,   who in good hour was born.
that I shall come to meet him   wherever he prefers;
wherever he says,   let us meet each other.
I wish to help My Cid   however I may."
They said farewell to the King   and turned away;
845   they depart for Valencia   with all who are with them.
    When the good Campeador   heard they were coming
he mounted in haste   and rode out to receive them.

---

9. This formula will be used several times to denote the receipt of bad news.
1. The language is the same as that ordering a solemn convocation of the court, as for a judicial function, although here it may only imply a high degree of formality.
2. As in his first conversation with the Infantes (page 700, line 311), Álvar Fáñez studiously refuses to divulge his own opinion.

He smiled, My Cid,   and warmly embraced them;
"Have you come, Minaya,   and you, Pedro Bermúdez!
850   In few lands   are there two such knights.
What greeting   from Alfonso my lord?
Is he satisfied?   Did he receive the gift?"
Minaya said,   "With heart and soul
he is satisfied   and returns you to his favor."
855   My Cid replied,   "The Creator be thanked!"
And when this was said   they began to tell
what Alfonso of León   had asked of them,
of giving the Cid's daughters   to the Heirs of Carrión
that his name might be ennobled   and he increase in honor,
860   that the King approved this   with heart and soul.
When he heard this, My Cid,   the good Campeador,
a long while   he thought and meditated:
"I give thanks   to Christ, to my lord.
I was sent into exile   my honors were taken away;
865   with toil and pain I have taken   what is now mine.
I give thanks to God   that I have regained the King's love
and that he asks for my daughters   for the Heirs of Carrión.
Tell me, Minaya,   and you, Pedro Bermúdez,
what do you think   of this marriage?"
870   "Whatever would please you   seems best to us."
    The Cid spoke: "They have a great name,   these Heirs of Carrión;
they are swollen with pride   and have a place in the court,
and this marriage   would not be to my liking.
But since he wishes it   who is worth more than we,
875   let us talk of the matter   but do it in secret,
and may God in heaven   turn it to the best."
    "And besides this,   Alfonso sends to tell you
that he will meet you   wherever you please;
he wishes to see you   and make manifest his favor,
880   after which you may decide   what you think best."
Then the Cid said,   "It pleases my heart."
    And Minaya said,   "As for this meeting,
you are to decide   where it is to be."
    "It would be no marvel   if King Alfonso had bid me
885   come where he was,   and we should have gone
to do him honor   as befits a King and lord.
But what he wishes   we must wish also.
By the Tagus,   the great river,[3]
let us meet   when my lord pleases."
890   They wrote letters   and sealed them straitly,[4]
and they sent them   in the hands of two horsemen;
the Campeador will do   what the King desires.

3. The longest river in Iberia.
4. The letters would have been written by scribes, but the sender would write the heading, sign the document, and seal it personally.

103

The letters have come   to the honored King;
he rejoiced   when he saw them.

895   "My greetings to My Cid,   who in good hour girded on sword,
let the meeting be   three weeks from now;
if I live   I shall be there without fail."
They returned to My Cid   without delay.

On this side and that   they made ready for the meeting;
900   who had ever seen   so many fine mules in Castile,
and so many palfreys   of graceful gait,
heavy chargers   and swift horses,
so many fair pennons   flown from good lances,
shields braced at the center   with gold and with silver,
905   cloaks and furs,   fine cloth from Alexandria?
The King has them send   ample provisions
to the banks of the Tagus   where the meeting will be.
A splendid company   goes with the King.
In high spirits   go the Heirs of Carrión;
910   here they make new debts   and there pay the old,
as though their fortunes   had so much increased already
and they had gold and silver   as much as they could wish for.[5]
The King Don Alfonso   mounts without delay;
counts and nobles ride with him   and a host of vassals.
915   And a goodly company goes   with the Heirs of Carrión.
With the King go men of León   and of Galicia,
and Castilians,[6]   you may know, without number;
they release the reins,   they ride to the meeting.

104

In Valencia   My Cid the Campeador
920   does not delay,   but makes ready for the meeting.
So many fat mules   and fine palfreys,
so many splendid weapons   and so many swift horses,
so many fine capes   and cloaks and furs;
everyone, young and old,   all dressed in colors.
925   Minaya Alvar Fáñez   and that same Pedro Bermúdez,
Martín Muñoz,   lord of Monte Mayor,
and Martín Antolínez,   the loyal citizen of Burgos,
the Bishop Don Jerome,   the worthy cleric,
Alvar Alvarez   and Alvar Salvadórez,
930   Muño Gustioz,   that excellent knight,
Galindo García,   who came from Aragón,
these make ready   to go with the Campeador,
and all the others,   as many as there were.
Alvar Salvadórez   and Galindo García of Aragón,

---

5. A clear indication of the Infantes' motive for marrying; like many land-holding aristocrats, their family wielded much power but lacked liquid assets.

6. Representatives of the three regions of the kingdom, and a reminder of the three parts into which Ferdinand I had divided his kingdom between his sons, the root of the simmering resentment and conflict here.

935   the Campeador   commanded these two
   to guard Valencia   with heart and soul,
   and he commanded all who should remain there   to obey these two.
   My Cid ordered   that they should not open
   the gates of the palace   by day or by night;
940   his wife and both his daughters   are within,
   in whom his heart is   and his soul,
   and there also are the other ladies   who wait upon their pleasure.[7]
   My Cid in his prudence   has commanded
   that none may come forth   out of the castle
945   until he himself returns   who in good hour was born.
    They went out from Valencia   and spurred forward,
   so many fine horses,   sleek, and swift runners;
   My Cid had won them,   they had not been given as gifts.
   And they rode on toward the meeting   arranged with the King.
950   The King arrived   one day before him,
   and when he saw   the Campeador coming
   he rode out to meet him   to do him honor.
   When he who was born in good hour   saw the King coming
   he commanded those who were with him   to come to a halt,
955   all except a few knights   nearest to his heart.
   Then as he had thought to do   who in good hour was born,
   he and fifteen knights   got down from their horses
   and on his knees and hands   he knelt down on the ground;
   he took the grass of the field   between his teeth[8]
960   and wept from his eyes   so great was his joy,
   and thus he rendered homage   to Alfonso his lord
   and in this manner   fell at his feet.
   The King Don Alfonso   was grieved at this sight:
   "Rise, rise,   Cid Campeador,
965   kiss my hands   but not my feet;
   if you humble yourself further   you will lose my love."
   The Campeador   remained on his knees:
   "I beg grace of you,   my natural lord,
   thus on my knees I beg you   to extend to me your favor
970   so that all may hear it,   as many as are here."
   The King said, "I will do it   with all my heart and soul;
   I hereby pardon you   and grant you my favor;
   be welcome from this hour   in all my kingdom."
    My Cid spoke,   here is what he said:
975   "My thanks. I accept the pardon,   Alfonso, my lord;
   I thank God in heaven   and afterwards you
   and these vassals   here about us."
   Still on his knees   he kissed the King's hand
   then rose to his feet   and kissed him on the mouth.[9]

---

7. The city gates remain open, but those of the fortified palace are to be shut.

8. An ancient act of submission and request for mercy.

9. The climax of this highly formal encounter: the Cid kisses the King's hands in the customary Spanish gesture of vassalage, and then gives him the kiss of fidelity.

980 And all who were there   rejoiced to see it,
but it grieved Alvar Díaz[1]   and García Ordóñez.
    My Cid spoke,   here is what he said:
"I give thanks   to our Father the Creator
for this grace I have received   from Alfonso my lord;
985 now God will be with me   by day and by night.
If it please you, my lord,   be my guest."
The King said,   "That would not be right.
You arrive only now   and we came here last night;
you must be my guest,   Cid Campeador,
990 and tomorrow we shall do   what meets your pleasure."
My Cid kissed his hand   and agreed to this.[2]
Then the Heirs of Carrión   came and made him obeisance.
"We bow before you,   Cid, who in good hour were born!
We shall serve your fortune   as far as we are able."
995 The Cid answered,   "God grant that it may be so."
My Cid Ruy Díaz,   who in good hour was born,
on that same day   was the guest of the King,
who so loved him   he could not have enough of his company
and looked a long while at his beard,   which had grown so long.
1000 All who beheld the Cid   marveled at the sight of him.
    The day has passed   and the night has come.
Next day in the morning   the sun rose bright;
the Campeador   called together his men,
bade them prepare a meal   for all who were there.
1005 My Cid the Campeador   so well contented them,
all were merry   and of one mind;
they had not eaten better,   not for three years.
    The next day in the morning   as the sun was rising
the Bishop Don Jerome   sang Mass for them.
1010 When they came from Mass,   all assembled together;
the King did not delay,   but began to speak.
"Hear me, my vassals,   counts and barons:
I would express a wish   to My Cid the Campeador,
and may Christ grant   that it be for the best,
1015 I ask you for your daughters,   Doña Elvira and Doña Sol;
I ask you to give them as wives   to the Heirs of Carrión.
The marriage, to my eyes,   is honorable and to your advantage;
the Heirs request it   and I commend it to you.[3]
And on this and on that side   as many as are here,
1020 your vassals and mine,   may they second what I ask for;
give us your daughters, My Cid,   and may the Creator bless you."
"I have no daughters ready for marriage,"   the Campeador answered,

---

1. Lord of Oca and brother-in-law of García Ordóñez.
2. This kiss signifies the acceptance of the honor of the king's invitation.
3. Rodrigo Díaz did in fact have two daughters, actually named Cristina and María, as well as a son, Diego, to whom the poem never alludes. This statement essentially orders the Cid to accept the double marriage, but it also binds the king to guarantee its success.

"for their age is slight   and their days are few.[4]

I fathered them both   and you brought them up;

1025 they and I   wait upon your mercy.

The fame is great   of the Heirs of Carrión,

enough for my daughters   and for others of higher station.

Doña Elvira and Doña Sol   I give into your charge;

give them to whom you think best   and I shall be content."

1030 "My thanks," said the King,   "to you and to all this court."

The Heirs of Carrión   then got to their feet,

went and kissed the hands   of him who was born in good hour,

and they exchanged swords   before Alfonso the King.[5]

        The King Don Alfonso spoke   as a worthy lord:

1035 "My thanks, Cid, for your goodness,   you, favored of the Creator,

who have given me your daughters   for the Heirs of Carrión.

Here I take into my charge   Doña Elvira and Doña Sol

and give them as wives   to the Heirs of Carrión.

By your leave   I marry your daughters;

1040 may it please the Creator   that good may come of it.

Here I give into your hands   the Heirs of Carrión;

they will go with you now   for I must return.

Three hundred marks of silver   I give to help them,

to be spent on the wedding   or whatever you please;

1045 let them remain under you   in Valencia, that great city.

Sons-in-law and daughters,   all four are your children:

do with them   as seems best to you, Campeador."

My Cid kissed his hands   and received the Heirs.

"My deep thanks,   my King and lord.

1050 It is you, not I,   who have married my daughters."[6]

        The words are said,   the promises given.

The next day in the morning   when the sun rose

each one would return   to the place from which he had come.

Then My Cid the Campeador   did a thing they would tell about:

1055 So many fat mules   and so many fine palfreys,

so many precious garments   of great value

My Cid gave   to whomever would receive gifts,

and he denied no one   whatever he asked for.

My Cid gave as gifts   sixty of his horses.

1060 All went from the meeting contented,   as many as there were;

it was time to part   for the night had come.

        The King took   the Heirs' hands

and put them in the hands   of My Cid the Campeador.

"These now are your sons,   since they are your sons-in-law.

1065 Know, from today forward   they are yours, Campeador;

let them serve you as their father   and honor you as their lord."

---

4. Since the Cid has already mentioned his desire to marry off his daughters, this appears a final attempt to evade the event at hand.

5. The Cid and the Infantes exchange swords (although not the famous Colada) as a token of their alliance.

6. Indicating the king's responsibility for anything that may happen as a result of this marriage.

"My thanks, King,   and I accept your gift.
May God Who is in heaven   give you reward."

105

    "I beg grace of you,   my natural King:

1070 Since you marry my daughters   as suits your will,
name someone to give them in marriage   in your name.
I will not give them with my hand;   none shall boast of that."
The King answered,   "Here is Alvar Fáñez;
let him take them by the hand   and give them to the Heirs.

1075 Let him act at the wedding   as though he were myself;
at the ceremony   let him be as the godfather
and let him tell me of it   when next we come together."
Alvar Fáñez said,   "With all my heart, sire."

106

    You may know, all this was done   with great care.

1080 "Ah, King Alfonso,   my honored lord,
take something of mine   to commemorate our meeting;
I have brought you thirty palfreys   with all their trappings
and thirty swift horses   with their saddles;
take these   and I kiss your hands."

1085 King Alfonso said,   "You fill me with confusion.
I accept this gift   which you have brought me;
may it please the Creator   and all His saints besides
that this pleasure you give me   may be well rewarded.
My Cid Ruy Díaz,   you have done me great honor;

1090 you have served me well   and I am contented;
if I live   I shall reward you somehow.
I commend you to God;   now I must leave.
May God Who is in heaven   turn all to the best."

107

    My Cid mounted   his horse Babieca.

1095 "Here I say   before Alfonso my lord:
Whoever will come to the wedding   and receive gifts from me,
let him come with me   and he shall not regret it."
    The Cid has said good-bye   to Alfonso his lord;
he would not have the King escort him   on his way, but parted there.

1100 You would have seen knights   of excellent bearing
saying farewell to King Alfonso,   kissing his hands:
"Grant us your grace   and give us your pardon;
we go as the Cid's vassals   to Valencia, that great city;
we shall be at the wedding   of the Heirs of Carrión

1105 and the daughters of My Cid,   Doña Elvira and Doña Sol."
This pleased the King,   he gave them all his consent;
the Cid's company grows   and that of the King dwindles.
There are many   who go with the Campeador.
    They ride for Valencia,   which in a blessed hour he had taken.

1110 He sent Pedro Bermúdez   and Muño Gustioz—
there were not two better knights   among all the Cid's vassals—
to ride as companions   with Fernando and Diego

that they might learn the ways   of the Heirs of Carrión.
And with them went Asur González,[7]   who was a noisy person,
1115   more ready of tongue   than of other things.
They paid much honor   to the Heirs of Carrión.
They have arrived in Valencia,   which My Cid had taken;
the closer they come   the greater is their rejoicing.
My Cid said to Don Pedro   and to Muño Gustioz:
1120   "See to the lodging   of the Heirs of Carrión
and stay with them   for I command it.
When the morning comes   and the sun rises
they will see their wives,   Doña Elvira and Doña Sol."

108

That night everyone   went to his lodging.
1125   My Cid the Campeador   entered the palace;
Doña Jimena received him   and both his daughters.
"Have you returned, Campeador,   who girded sword in good hour?
Many days may we look upon you   with these eyes of ours."
"The Creator be thanked,   honored wife, that I have returned;
1130   I bring you two sons-in-law   in whom we have much honor;
give me thanks, my daughters,   for I have married you well."

109

His wife and his daughters   kissed his hand,
as did all the ladies   who wait upon them.
"The Creator be thanked,   and you, Cid of the splendid beard.
1135   All you have done   has been done well.
They will lack for nothing   as long as you live."
"When you give us in marriage,   father, we shall be rich."

110

"Doña Jimena, my wife,   I give thanks to the Creator.
And I say to you, my daughters,   Doña Elvira and Doña Sol,
1140   that by your marriage   we shall increase in honor.
But you may know   that none of this was my doing:
my lord Alfonso   asked me for your hands,
and that so urgently   with all his heart,
that I in no way   could have denied him.
1145   I gave you into his hands,   both of you, my daughters;
believe this that I say: he will marry you, not I."

111

Then they began   to get the palace ready:
they covered the floor   and the walls with carpets,
with bolts of silk and purple   and many precious fabrics.
1150   You would have been well pleased   to sit and eat in the palace.
All the Cid's knights   have gathered together.
Then they sent   for the Heirs of Carrión,
and the Heirs took horse   and rode to the palace
covered in finery   and splendid garments;

7. Elder (and equally unsavory) brother of the Infantes.

1155   on foot and in seemly fashion   God, how meekly they entered!
My Cid received them   with all his vassals;
they humbled themselves   before him and his wife
then went and sat down   on a bench of precious work.
All My Cid's vassals,   quiet and prudent,
1160   sit watching his face   who in good hour was born.
    The Campeador   rose to his feet:
"Since it must be done,   why should we delay?
Come here, Alvar Fáñez,   beloved knight,
Both my daughters   I hereby give into your hands;
1165   you know that the King   has commanded that it be so
and I would in every way   satisfy the agreement.
With your hand give them   to the Heirs of Carrión,
let them receive the benediction   and let it be properly done."
Then Minaya said,   "I will do it gladly."
1170   The girls stood up   and he took them by the hands.
Minaya speaks   to the Heirs of Carrión:
"Now both you brothers   stand before Minaya.
By the hand of King Alfonso,   who has commanded me thus,
I give you these ladies,   both of gentle birth;
1175   take them for wives   for the honor and good of all."
Both received them   with love and joy
and went to kiss the hands   of My Cid and his wife.
    When they had done this   they went out from the palace
and without delay   rode to Santa María;[8]
1180   the Bishop Don Jerome   put on his vestments;
at the door of the church   he waited for them,
gave them his benedictions   and sang them Mass.
    When they came from the church   all mounted in haste
and rode out   to the arena of Valencia.
1185   God, how well they jousted,   My Cid and his vassals!
Three times he changed horses,[9]   he who was born in good hour.
My Cid was well content   with what he saw there:
the Heirs of Carrión   proved themselves good horsemen.
They returned to the ladies   and re-entered Valencia;
1190   there were rich wedding feasts   in the gorgeous palace,
and the next day   My Cid set up seven tablets:
all must be ridden at and broken   before they went in to eat.
    Two full weeks   the wedding feasts went on;
at the end of that time   the noble guests went home.
1195   My Cid Don Rodrigo,   who in good hour was born,
gave at least a hundred   of all sorts of beasts,
palfreys and mules   and swift running horses,
besides cloaks and furs   and many other garments,
and there was no counting   the gifts of money.
1200   My Cid's vassals   also gave presents;

---

8. The cathedral of Valencia, endowed by Rodrigo Diaz.   9. He jousted for so long, he wore out three horses.

each one gave something   to the guests who were there.
Whatever the guests might wish for   their hands were filled;
all who had come to the wedding   returned rich to Castile.
Then those guests   made ready to leave,
1205   took leave of Ruy Díaz,   who in good hour was born,
and of all those ladies   and the knights who were there;
they parted contented   from My Cid and his vassals.
They spoke well   of the way they had been treated.
And Diego and Fernando   were highly pleased,
1210   they, the sons   of the Count Don Gonzalo.
    The guests have departed   for Castile;
My Cid and his sons-in-law   remain in Valencia.
And there the Heirs dwell   nearly two years,
and all in Valencia   showered them with their favor.
1215   My Cid was joyful,   and all his vassals.
May it please Santa María   and the heavenly Father
to bless My Cid   and him who proposed this marriage.
    Herewith are ended   the verses of this cantar.
The Creator be with you   and all His saints besides.

The Third Cantar

112

    My Cid is in Valencia   with all his vassals,
and with him his sons-in-law,   the Heirs of Carrión.
The Campeador was asleep,   lying on a bench,
when, you may know, there occurred   an unlooked-for misfortune:
5   the lion broke from his cage   and stalked abroad.[1]
Great terror ran   through the court;
the Campeador's men   seize their cloaks
and stand over the bench   to protect their lord.
Fernando González,   Heir of Carrión,
10   could find nowhere to hide,   no room nor tower was open;
he hid under the bench,   so great was his terror.
Diego González   went out the door
crying, "I shall never   see Carrión again."
Behind a beam of the wine press   he hid in his fear;
15   there his cloak and his tunic   were covered with filth.
    At this point he wakened   who in good hour was born;
he saw the bench surrounded   by his brave vassals.
"What is this, knights,   what do you wish?"
"Ah, honored lord,   we are frightened of the lion."
20   My Cid rose to his elbow,   got to his feet,
with his cloak on his shoulders   walked toward the lion;
the lion, when he saw him,   was so filled with shame,
before My Cid he bowed his head   and put his face down.[2]

---

1. Medieval rulers often kept fierce beasts caged in their castles as signs of their social standing and prowess.

2. The ability to dominate wild beasts was a traditional attribute of the hero.

My Cid Don Rodrigo   took him by the neck,
25 led him as with a halter   and put him in his cage.
And all marveled,   as many as were there,
and the knights returned   from the palace to the court.
    My Cid asked for his sons-in-law   and could not find them;
though he calls out   no one answers.
30 When at last they were found,   their faces were without color;
you have not seen such mockery   as rippled through the court;
My Cid the Campeador   commanded silence.
And the Heirs of Carrión   were covered with shame
and bitterly mortified   at this occurrence.[3]

113

35   While they were still sore   with the smart of this,
hosts from Morocco   came to surround Valencia;
they pitched their camp   in the field of Cuarto;
they set up their tents,   fifty thousand of the largest:
this was King Búcar,[4]   of whom you have heard tell.

114

40   The Cid rejoiced,   and all his knights;
they thanked the Creator,   for the spoils would enrich them.
But, you may know, it grieved   the Heirs of Carrión;
so many Moorish tents   were not to their taste.
Both brothers   walked to one side:
45 "We thought only of the wealth   and not of the dangers;
for we have no choice   but to go into this battle.
This could keep us from ever again   seeing Carrión,
and the daughters of the Campeador   will be left widows."
Muño Gustioz   overheard them talking in secret
50 and brought what he had heard   to My Cid the Campeador.
"These sons-in-law of yours   are so filled with daring
that now at the hour of battle   they yearn for Carrión.
Go and console them,   as God is your grace,
let them sit in peace   and not enter the battle;
55 with you we shall conquer   and the Creator will give us aid."
My Cid Don Rodrigo   went up to them smiling:
"God save you, sons-in-law,   Heirs of Carrión,
you have in your arms my daughters   white as the sun.
I look forward to battle   and you to Carrión;
60 remain in Valencia   at your pleasure,
for I am seasoned   at managing the Moors
and shall make bold to rout them   with the help of the Creator."

115

[There is a gap of about fifty lines in the manuscript at this point, here filled by a passage from the prose "Chronicle of Twenty Kings."]

3. There are three comic episodes in the poem: the chests of sand, the Count of Barcelona, and now the escaped lion. Opening the third cantar, this wholly invented incident, unlike most of the poem, has the flavor of a myth. It also serves both to deflate the tension created by the expectation of catastrophe to come and initiates that catastrophe by making the Infantes a public laughingstock and revealing their true colors.
4. Abu Bakr, Almoravid prince.

As they were speaking of this, King Búcar sent to tell the Cid to leave Valencia, and he, Búcar, would let him go in peace; but if he would not go, then Búcar would make the Cid pay for everything he had done. The Cid said to the messenger: "Go and tell Búcar, that son of my enemies, that within three days I shall give him what he asks for." The next day My Cid bade them all arm, and they rode out against the Moors. The Heirs of Carrión then begged of him the honor of striking the first blows; and when the Cid had formed his ranks, Don Fernando, one of the Heirs, rode forward to attack a Moor named Aladraf. When the Moor saw him he spurred toward him, and the Heir, overcome with terror, turned his horse and fled, not daring to wait.

Pedro Bermúdez, who was near him, when he saw this, attacked the Moor and fought with him and killed him. Then he took the Moor's horse and went after the Heir, where he was still fleeing, and said: "Don Fernando, take this horse and tell everyone that you killed the Moor who was its master, and I will affirm it."

The Heir said to him: "Don Pedro Bermúdez, I thank you deeply,

> and may the hour come   when I can doubly repay you."
> Then they returned   riding together.

65 And Don Pedro affirmed the deed   of which Don Fernando boasted.
It pleased My Cid   and all his vassals.
"If it please God,   our Father Who is in heaven,
both my sons-in-law   will prove brave in the battle."
    As they speak thus,   the armies draw together.

70 The drums are sounding   through the ranks of the Moors,
and many of these Christians   marveled much at the sound,
for they had come lately to the war   and never heard drums.
Don Diego and Don Fernando   marveled more than any;
they would not have been there   if the choice had been theirs.

75 Hear what he said,   he who was born in good hour:
"Ho, Pedro Bermúdez,   my dear nephew,
watch over Don Diego   and watch over Don Fernando,
my sons-in-law,   for whom I have much love,
and with God's help   the Moors will not keep the field."

116

80 "I say to you, Cid,   in the name of charity,
that today the Heirs   will not have me for protector;
let who likes watch over them   for I care little for them.
I wish to attack in the van   with my men,
and you with yours   might guard the rear;

85 and if I have need,   you can come to my aid."
    Minaya Alvar Fáñez   then rode up.
"Hear me, Cid,   loyal Campeador.
This battle   the Creator will decide
and you, of so great worth,   who have His favor.

90 Send us to attack   where you think best,
let each one of us   look to his obligation.
With God and your good fortune   we shall attack them."
My Cid said,   "Let us proceed calmly."
    Then came Don Jerome   the Bishop, heavily armed.

95 He stopped before the Campeador   of unfailing fortune.

"Today I have said you the Mass   of the Holy Trinity;
I left my own country   and came to find you
because of the hunger I had   for killing Moors;
I wish to gain honor   for my hands and for my order,

100   and I wish to go in the van°   and strike the first blows.   *vanguard*
I bear pennon and arms   blazoned with crosiers;°   *bishops' staffs*
if it please God   I wish to display them,
and thus my heart   will be at peace,
and you, My Cid,   will be further pleased with me.

105   Unless you do me this favor   I shall leave you."
Then My Cid answered,   "I am pleased with your request.
Now the Moors are in sight;   go try yourself against them.
Now we shall see   how the monk does battle."

117

The Bishop Don Jerome   began

110   and charged against them   at the end of the camp.
By his good fortune   and the grace of God Who loved him,
with the first blows   he killed two Moors.
His lance splintered   and he drew his sword.
God, how hard he fought,   the Bishop, how well he did battle!

115   He killed two with his lance   and five with the sword.
And many Moors came   and surrounded him
and dealt him great blows   but could not break through his armor.
    He who was born in good hour   kept his eyes upon him,
clasped his shield   and lowered his lance,

120   set spur to Babieca,   his swift horse,
and rode to attack them   with heart and soul.
In the first ranks   which he entered, the Campeador
unhorsed seven   and killed four.
There the rout began,   as it pleased God.

125   My Cid and his knights   rode in pursuit;
you would have seen so many tent cords   snapped, and the poles down,
and so many embroidered tents   lying on the ground;
My Cid's vassals   drove Búcar's men from their camp.

118

They drove them from the camp   and pursued them closely;

130   you would have seen fall   so many arms with their bucklers,
and so many heads in their helmets   fall in the field,
and horses without riders   running in all directions.
Seven full miles   the pursuit went on.
    My Cid overtook   Búcar the King:

135   "Turn, Búcar,   who have come from beyond the sea!
Now you must face the Cid,   he of the long beard;
we must greet each other   and swear friendship."[5]
Búcar answered the Cid,   "God confound such friendship:
you have a sword in your hand,   you ride at full speed,

5. A wordplay: *tajaremos amistad* can mean either "to seal a friendship" or "to cut a friendship" (or anything else) as with a sword.

140 and it would seem that you wish   to prove your sword upon me.
But if my horse does not stumble   or fall under me,
you will not overtake me   though you follow me into the sea."
Then My Cid answered,   "That cannot be true."
Búcar had a good horse,   he rode in great bounds,
145 but the Cid's Babieca   gained steadily on him.
The Cid overtook Búcar   three fathoms° from the sea,   *several yards*
raised Colada   and struck him a great blow,
and there he cut away   the jewels of his helmet,
split the helmet   and, driving through all below,
150 as far as the waist   his sword sank.
He killed Búcar,   the King from beyond the sea,
and captured the sword Tizón,   worth a thousand marks of gold.
My Cid has won   that marvelous great battle;
here all who are with him   have gained honor.

119

155   They turned back from the chase   with the spoils they had taken;
you may know, before they went   they stripped the field.
They have come to the tents   with him who was born in good hour,
My Cid Ruy Díaz,   the famous Campeador;
he came with two swords   which were worth much to him,[6]
160 at full speed came riding   over the field of slaughter,
his face bare,   hood and helmet off,
and the cowl loose   over his hair.
From all directions   his knights regather;
My Cid saw a thing   which pleased him greatly;
165 he lifted his eyes   and looked before him
and saw approaching him   Diego and Fernando,
both the sons   of the Count Don Gonzalo.
My Cid rejoiced,   fair was his smiling:
"Greetings, my sons-in-law,   both of you are my sons!
170 I know you are well contented   with the fighting you have done;
the good news of your deeds   will go to Carrión,
and the tidings of our conquest   of Búcar the King.
I trust in God   and in all His saints
that we shall be satisfied   with the results of this victory."
175 Minaya Alvar Fáñez   rode up at this moment,
his shield at his neck   marked with sword dents
and with blows of lances   beyond number;
and those who had aimed them   had not profited by it.
Down from his elbow   the blood is dripping;
180 he had killed more than twenty   of the Moors.
"Thanks be to God   and to our heavenly Father
and to you, Cid,   who in good hour were born!
You have killed Búcar   and we have won the field.
All these spoils   are for you and your vassals.

---

6. The two swords he has won in battle—Colada from Ramón Berenguer and now Tizón—henceforth appear as a pair.

185 And your sons-in-law   here have proved themselves
and sated themselves with fighting   with Moors in the field."
My Cid said,   "I am pleased with this;
they have been brave today   and in time to come they will be braver."
My Cid intended it kindly   but they took it as a jeer.

190   All the spoils   have been brought to Valencia;
My Cid rejoices,   and all his vassals;
to each one there falls   six hundred marks of silver.
My Cid's sons-in-law,   when they had taken this portion
which was theirs from the victory   and had put it safely away,

195 were sure that in all their days   they should not lack for money.
Those in Valencia   were lavishly provided
with excellent food,   fine furs and rich cloaks.
And My Cid and his vassals   all rejoiced.

                    120
It was a great day   in the court of the Campeador

200 after they had won that battle   and King Búcar had been killed;
the Cid raised his hand   and grasped his beard.
"I give thanks to Christ   Who is lord of the world,
that now I have seen   what I have wished to see:
both my sons-in-law   have fought beside me in the field;

205 good news concerning them   will go to Carrión;
they have been much help to us   and won themselves honor."

                    121
All have received   enormous spoils;
much was theirs already,   now these new gains are stored away.
My Cid, who was born   in a good hour, commanded

210 that from this battle   which they had won
each one should take   what fell by rights to him,
and the fifth which went to My Cid   was not forgotten.
This they all do   without disagreements.
In the fifth which fell to My Cid   were six hundred horses,

215 and other beasts of burden   and large camels;[7]
there were so many   they could not be counted.

                    122
All these spoils   the Campeador has taken.
"Thanks be to God   Who is lord of the world!
In the old days I was poor,   now I am rich,

220 for I have wealth and domains   and gold and honor,
and my sons-in-law   are the Heirs of Carrión;
I win battles,   as pleases the Creator;
Moors and Christians   go in fear of me.
There in Morocco,   where the mosques are,

225 they tremble   lest perhaps some night
I should take them by surprise,   but I plan no such thing.
I shall not go seeking them,   but stay in Valencia,

---

7. Camels had been introduced to Iberia by the Almoravids.

and they will send me tribute,   as the Creator aids me;
they will send money to me   or to whomever I please."

230   Great were the rejoicings   in Valencia, that great city,
among all the company   of My Cid the Campeador
at this rout   in which heartily they had fought;
and great was the joy   of both the sons-in-law;
five thousand marks   was the portion which fell to them.

235   These Heirs of Carrión   considered themselves rich.
     They with the others   came to the court;
there with My Cid   was the Bishop Don Jerome,
the good Alvar Fáñez,   knight and warrior,
and many others   whom the Campeador had reared.

240   When the Heirs of Carrión   entered there
Minaya received them   for My Cid the Campeador:
"Come here, my kinsmen,   we profit by your company."
As they approached,   the Campeador grew more pleased:
"Here, my sons-in-law,   are my excellent wife

245   and both my daughters,   Doña Elvira and Doña Sol,
to embrace you closely   and serve you with all their hearts.
I thank Santa María,   mother of the lord our God,
that from this marriage   you shall have gained honor.
Good news will go to   the lands of Carrión."

                    123

250   At these words   the Heir Fernando spoke:
"I thank the Creator   and you, honored Cid,
that so much wealth,   that riches beyond measure are ours.
From you we receive our honor   and for you we fought;
we conquered the Moors   in the field and killed

255   that King Búcar,   a proved traitor.
Think of other things,   for our affairs are in good order."
     The vassals of My Cid   smiled to hear this;
some had battled bravely   and some ridden in pursuit,
but they had not seen   Diego nor Fernando there.

260   Because the mockeries   made at their expense,
day and night, always,   so tormented them,
both the Heirs   conceived of an evil plan.
They walked aside.   Indeed, they were brothers;
let us have no part   in what they said:[8]

265   "Let us go to Carrión;   we have stayed here too long.
The wealth we have   is great and immeasurable;
we could not spend it all   in the rest of our lives.

                    124

Let us ask for our wives   from the Cid Campeador;
let us say we will take them   to the lands of Carrión,

270   for we must show them   the lands that are theirs.
We shall take them from Valencia,   from the power of the Campeador;

---

8. The narrator himself chooses to maintain a distance from the Infantes' plan.

afterwards, on the journey,   we shall do as we please with them
before they reproach us   with the story of the lion.
For we are descended   from the Counts of Carrión!

275   We shall take much wealth with us,   riches of great value;
we shall work our punishment   on the daughters of the Campeador."
"With the wealth we have now,   we shall be rich forever;
we can marry the daughters   of kings or emperors,[9]
for we are descended   from the Counts of Carrión.

280   Therefore we shall punish   the daughters of the Campeador
before they throw in our faces   what happened with the lion."
        When they had made up their minds   they turned back again.
Fernando González spoke,   requesting silence in the court:
"As the Creator may bless you,   Cid Campeador,

285   may it please Doña Jimena   and before all others, you,
and Minaya Alvar Fáñez   and as many as are here,
to give us our wives,   who have been blessed to us;
we would take them with us   to our lands of Carrión
so that they may possess the lands   we have given them for their honor;

290   your daughters will see   what belongs to us,
in which our children   will have a share."
        My Cid the Campeador   suspected no harm:
"I will give you my daughters   and more things that are mine;
you have given them as wedding gifts   villages in Carrión;

295   I would give them for their betrothal   three thousand marks,
and I give you mules and palfreys   sleek and fine limbed,
and war horses   strong, and swift runners,
and many garments of cloth   and of cloth-of-gold,
and I will give you two swords,   Colada and Tizón;

300   you know well that I gained them   as befits a man.
Both of you are my sons   since I give you my daughters;
you bear away with you   the threads of my heart.
Let them know in Galicia   and in Castile and in León
how richly I send from me   my two sons-in-law.

305   Cherish my daughters,   who are your wives;
if you treat them well   I shall reward you handsomely."
The Heirs of Carrión   have agreed to everything.
They receive the daughters   of the Campeador,
and now they take   the Cid's gifts.

310   When they are sated   with receiving presents
the Heirs of Carrión bade them   load up the beasts of burden.
There is much bustle   in Valencia, that great city;
all seize their arms   and mount in haste;
they are sending off the Cid's daughters   to the lands of Carrión.

315   They are ready to ride,   they are saying good-bye.
Both the sisters,   Doña Elvira and Doña Sol,
knelt down   before the Cid Campeador:

---

9. Because their actions will signal the renunciation of their wives, they will be free to remarry.

"We beg your blessing, father,   and may the Creator be with you;
you sired us,   our mother brought us forth;
320   here we are before you both,   our lady and our lord.
Now you send us   to the lands of Carrión;
we owe it to you to obey you   in whatever you demand.
And thus we beg   your blessing on us both.
Send messages to us   in the lands of Carrión."
325   My Cid embraced them   and kissed them both.

125

Their mother embraces them   twice over:
"Now go hence, daughters,   and the Creator bless you,
and take with you   your father's blessing and mine.
Go to Carrión,   where you are heirs;
330   in my eyes it seems   that you were well married."
They kissed the hands   of their father and mother,
who both blessed them   and gave them their grace.

My Cid and the others   began to ride;
there were great provisions   and horses and arms.
335   The Heirs have ridden out   from Valencia the Shining;
they have said good-bye to the ladies   and all their companions.
Through the farmlands of Valencia   they ride, playing at arms;
My Cid goes merrily   among all his companions.

But he who in good hour was born   looked upon the omens
340   and saw that this marriage   will not be without stain.
But now he may not repent   for both of them are wedded.

126

"Oh, where are you, my nephew,   you, Félix Muñoz:
you are cousin to my daughters   and love them with heart and soul.
I command you to go with them   all the way to Carrión;
345   you will see the inheritances   which have been given to my daughters
and with news of these things   return to the Campeador."
Félix Muñoz said,   "It pleases my heart and soul."

Minaya Alvar Fáñez   stopped before My Cid:
"Let us go back, Cid,   to Valencia, the great city,
350   and if it please God   and our Father the Creator,
one day we shall go to see them   in the lands of Carrión."
"To God I commend you,   Doña Elvira and Doña Sol;
behave in such manner   as shall give us cause for pleasure."
The sons-in-law answered,   "May God send that it be so."
355   Great were their sorrows   when they came to part.
The father and the daughters   wept from their hearts,
as did also the knights   of the Campeador.

"Hear me, my nephew,   you, Félix Muñoz;
go to Molina   and spend the night there;
360   in my name greet my friend,   the Moor Abengalbón;
let him receive my sons-in-law   with his fairest welcome;
tell him I am sending my daughters   to the lands of Carrión;
let him serve their pleasure   in whatever they need
and, for love of me, bid him escort them   as far as Medinaceli.

365   For all he does for them   I shall reward him well."
They parted, one from the other,   as nail from flesh.
        He has turned back to Valencia   who in good hour was born.
The Heirs of Carrión   ride forward;
at Santa María of Albarracín   the camp was made;
370   from there the Heirs of Carrión   spur forward at all speed;
they have come to Molina   and the Moor Abengalbón.
When the Moor knew they were there   it pleased his heart;
with great rejoicing   he rode out to receive them.
God, how well he served them   in whatever they pleased!
375   The next day in the morning   he rode on with them
with two hundred knights   whom he sent to escort them;
they have passed the mountains   called the range of Luzón,
crossed the valley of Arbujuelo   and come to Jalón;
where it is called Ansarera   they made their camp.[1]
380   The Moor gave presents   to the Cid's daughters
and fine horses for each   of the Heirs of Carrión;
all this the Moor did for love   of the Cid Campeador.
        When they saw the riches   which the Moor had brought
both brothers   began to plot to betray him:
385   "Now that we plan to desert   the Campeador's daughters,
if we could murder   the Moor Abengalbón
all his wealth   would be ours.
We could keep it as safely   as what is ours in Carrión,
and the Cid Campeador   could enforce no claim against us."
390   While they of Carrión   were speaking of this deceit,
a Moor who knew Castilian   heard what they said
and did not keep it secret   but told Abengalbón:
"My lord, my master,   have a care of these,
for I have heard them plotting your death,   these Heirs of Carrión."

                        127
395   The Moor Abengalbón   was tough and stouthearted;
with the two hundred who were with him   he came riding;
all of them were armed;   they halted before the Heirs.
What the Moor said to the Heirs   gave them no pleasure:
"If it were not for respect   for My Cid of Bivar
400   I would wreak such deeds on you   as the whole world would hear of
and I would return his daughters   to the loyal Campeador;
and as for Carrión,   you would never see it again.

                        128
        "Tell me what harm have I done you,   Heirs of Carrión!
I serve you without malice   and you plot my death.
405   Here I leave you,   vile men and traitors.
By your leave I go,   Doña Elvira and Doña Sol;
I scorn the fame   of the Heirs of Carrión.
May God Who is lord of the world   will and command

---

1. On the north side of the river Jalón, not far from Medinaceli.

that the Campeador may remain   contented with this marriage."

410 When he had said this   the Moor turned away
and they went with their arms at ready   till they had crossed the stream Jalón.
As a man of prudence   he went back to Molina.

The Heirs of Carrión   have left Ansarera.
They march without rest   all day and all night;
415 on their left they leave Atienza,[2]   that is a strong hill;
the mountains of Miedes   fall behind them;
upon Montes Claros   they spur forward,
and on their left leave Griza,   which Alamos peopled,
and there are the caves   where he encircled Elpha;
420 further on, on their right   was San Esteban de Gormaz.
The Heirs have entered   the oak wood of Corpes;[3]
the mountains are high,   the branches touch the clouds
and there are savage beasts   which walk about there.
They found a glade   with a clear spring.
425 The Heirs of Carrión   bade their men set up the tent;
there they spend the night   with as many as are with them,
with their wives in their arms,   showing them love;
yet they meant to do them evil   when the sun rose!

They had the beasts of burden   loaded with their riches,
430 and they have taken down the tent   where they spent the night,
and those who waited on them   have all ridden ahead
as they were orderd to do   by the Heirs of Carrión,
so that none remained behind,   neither man nor woman,
except both their wives,   Doña Elvira and Doña Sol.
435 They wished to amuse themselves with these   to the height of their pleasure.

All had gone ahead,   only these four remained;
the Heirs of Carrión   had conceived great villainy:
"Know this for a certainty,   Doña Elvira and Doña Sol,
you will be tormented here   in these savage mountains.
440 Today we shall desert you   and go on from this place;
you will have no share   in the lands of Carrión.
The news of this will go   to the Cid Campeador,
and we shall be avenged   for the story of the lion."

Then they stripped them   of their cloaks and furs;
445 they left nothing on their bodies   but their shirts and silk undergarments.
The wicked traitors   have spurs on their boots;
they take in their hands   the strong hard saddle girths.
When the ladies saw this,   Doña Sol said:
"You have two swords,   strong and keen edged,
450 one that is called Colada   and the other Tizón.
For God's sake, we beg you,   Don Diego and Don Fernando,
cut off our heads   and we shall be martyrs.
Moors and Christians   will speak harshly of this,
for such treatment   we have not deserved.

2. An impregnable castle in the Sierra de Miedes, west of   3. There has been much dispute over the location of this
Medinaceli in rugged terrain.   forest.

455   Do not visit upon us   so vile an ensample;
    if you whip us   the shame will be yours;
    you will be called to account   at assemblies or courts."[4]
        The ladies' pleadings   availed them nothing.
    Then the Heirs of Carrión   began to lash them;
460   they beat them without mercy   with the flying cinches,
    gored them with the sharp spurs,   dealing them great pain.
    They tore their shirts   and the flesh of both of them,
    and over the silken cloth   the clean blood ran,
    and they felt the pain   in their very hearts.
465   Oh, it would be such good fortune   if it should please the Creator
    that the Cid Campeador   might appear now!
        They beat them so cruelly,   they left them senseless;
    the shirts and the silk skirts   were covered with blood.
    They beat them   until their arms were tired,
470   each of them trying   to strike harder than the other.
    Doña Elvira and Doña Sol   could no longer speak;
    they left them for dead   in the oak grove of Corpes.

                129

        They took away their cloaks   and their furs of ermine,
    and left them fainting   in their shifts and silk tunics,
475   left them to the birds of the mountain   and to the wild beasts.
    They left them for dead,   you may know, with no life left in them.
    What good fortune it would be   if the Cid Ruy Díaz should appear now!

                130

        The Heirs of Carrión   left them there for dead,
    so that neither   might give aid to the other.
480   Through the mountains where they went   they praised themselves:
    "Now we have avenged ourselves   for our marriage.
    We would not have them for concubines   even if they begged us.
    As legitimate wives   they were unworthy of us;
    the dishonor of the lion   thus will be avenged."

                131

485   The Heirs of Carrión   rode on, praising themselves.
    But I shall tell you   of that same Félix Muñoz—
    he was a nephew   of the Cid Campeador—
    they had bidden him ride forward   but this was not to his liking.
    On the road as he went   his heart was heavy;
490   he slipped to one side   apart from the others;
    he hid himself   in a thick wood,
    waiting for his cousins   to come by
    or to see what they had done,   those Heirs of Carrión.
    He saw them come   and heard something of their talk;
495   they did not see him there   nor suspect that he heard them;
    he knew well that if they saw him   they would not leave him alive.
        The Heirs set spur   and ride on.

---

4. Doña Sol reminds the Infantes that revenge for the story of the lion is no legitimate defense for what they are about to do, which will only dishonor them further and expose them to legal action.

Félix Muñoz   turned back the way they had come;
he found his cousins   both lying senseless.
500 He called, "Cousins, cousins!"   Then he dismounted,
tied his horse   and went up to them.
"Cousins, my cousins,   Doña Elvira and Doña Sol,
they have vilely proved themselves,   the Heirs of Carrión!
May it please God   that their punishment find them!"
505 He stayed there   endeavoring to revive them.
Their senses had gone far from them;   they could not speak at all.
The fabrics of his heart   tear as he calls:
"Cousins, my cousins,   Doña Elvira and Doña Sol,
come awake, cousins,   for the love of the Creator!
510 Wake now while the day lasts   before the night comes
and the wild beasts   devour us on this mountain!"
Doña Elvira and Doña Sol   come back to themselves;
they opened their eyes   and saw Félix Muñoz.
"Quickly, cousins,   for the love of the Creator!
515 the Heirs of Carrión   when they miss me
will come looking for me   at full speed;
if God does not aid us   we shall die here."
Then with great pain   Doña Sol spoke:
"If our father the Campeador   deserves it of you, my cousin,
520 give us a little water,   for the love of the Creator."
Then with his hat,   which was new, with its sheen still on it,
which he had brought from Valencia,   Féliz Muñoz
took up water   and gave it to his cousins;
they were gravely hurt   and both had need of it.
525   He urged them a long while   till they sat upright.
He gave them comfort   and made them take heart again
till they recovered somewhat,   and he took them both up
and with all haste   put them on his horse;
he covered them both   with his own mantle,
530 took his horse by the reins   and went off with them both.
They three alone   through the forest of Corpes
between night and day   went out from among the mountains;
they have arrived   at the waters of the Duero;
at the tower of Doña Urraca   he left those two.[5]
535 Félix Muñoz came   to San Esteban
and found Diego Téllez,   who was Alvar Fáñez's vassal;
he was grieved in his heart   when he heard the story,
and he took beasts   and fine garments
and went to receive   Doña Elvira and Doña Sol;
540 he brought them   into San Esteban;
he did them honor   as well as he could.
Those of San Esteban   are always sensible folk;
when they knew of this deed   it grieved their hearts;

5. La Torre de Doña Urraca was above the river Duero, some five miles west of San Esteban.

they brought tribute from their farms   to the Cid's daughters.
545   There the girls remained   until they were healed.
        And the Heirs of Carrión   continued to praise themselves.
Through all those lands   the tidings are made known;
the good King Alfonso   was grieved deeply.
Word of it goes   to Valencia, the great city;
550   when they tell it   to My Cid the Campeador,
for more than an hour   he thought and pondered;
he raised his hand   and grasped his beard:
"I give thanks to Christ   Who is lord of the world;
this is the honor they have done me,   these Heirs of Carrión;
555   I swear by this beard,   which no one ever has torn,
these Heirs of Carrión   shall not go free with this;
as for my daughters   I shall yet marry them well!"
My Cid was grieved   with all his heart and soul,
as were Alvar Fáñez   and all the court.
560   Minaya mounted   with Pedro Bermúdez
and Martín Antolínez,   the worthy man of Burgos,
with two hundred knights   whom My Cid sent;
he commanded them strictly   to ride day and night
and bring his daughters   to Valencia, the great city.
565   They do not delay   to fulfill their lord's command;
they ride with all speed,   they travel day and night;
they came to Gormaz,   a strong castle,
and there in truth   they paused for one night.
The news has arrived   at San Esteban
570   that Minaya is coming   for his two cousins.
The men of San Esteban,   like the worthy folk that they are,
receive Minaya   and all his men;
that night they presented   Minaya with great tribute;
he did not wish to take it   but thanked them deeply:
575   "Thanks, people of San Esteban,   you conduct yourselves well.
For this honor you do us   in this misfortune
My Cid the Campeador   thanks you from where he is,
and here where I am   I do the same.
By God Who is in heaven   you will be well rewarded!"
580   All thank him for what he said   and are content;
they go each to his place   for the night's rest.
Minaya goes to see   his cousins where they are.
Doña Elvira and Doña Sol,   fix their eyes upon him:
"We are as glad to behold you   as though you were the Creator,
585   and give thanks to Him   that we are still alive.
When there is more leisure   in Valencia, the great city,
we shall be able to recount   all our grievance."
                                    132
        Alvar Fáñez and the ladies   could not keep back the tears,
and Pedro Bermúdez   spoke to them thus:
590   "Doña Elvira and Doña Sol,   forget your cares now,
since now you are healed   and alive, and without other harm.

You have lost a good marriage,   you may yet have a better.
And we shall yet see the day   when you will be avenged!"
They spent that night there   amid great rejoicings.

595   The next day in the morning   they mounted their horses.
The people of San Esteban   went with them on their way
as far as the River Amor,   keeping them company;
there they said good-bye   and turned back again,
and Minaya and the ladies   rode on ahead.

600   They crossed over Alcoceba;   on their right they left Gormaz;
where it is called Vadorrey   they came and went by;
in the village of Berlanga   they paused to rest.[6]
Next day in the morning   they rode on again
as far as the place called Medinaceli   where they took shelter,

605   and from Medinaceli to Molina   they came in one day.
The Moor Abengalbón   was pleased in his heart;
he rode out to receive them   with good will;
he gave them a rich dinner   for the love of My Cid.
Then straightway they rode on   toward Valencia.

610   The message came   to him who in good hour was born;
he mounts in haste   and rides out to receive them;
he went brandishing his weapons   and showing great joy.
My Cid rode up   to embrace his daughters;
he kissed them both   and began to smile:

615   "You are here, my daughters!   God heal you from harm!
I permitted your marriage   for I could not refuse it.
May it please the Creator   Who is in heaven
that I shall see you   better married hereafter.
God give me vengeance   on my sons-in-law of Carrión!"

620   Then the daughters   kissed their father's hands.
All rode into the city   brandishing their weapons;
Doña Jimena, their mother,   rejoiced at the sight of them.

He who was born in good hour   wished no delay;
he spoke in secret   with his own men.

625   He prepared to send a message   to King Alfonso in Castile.

133

"Oh, stand before me, Muño Gustioz,   my loyal vassal.
In a good hour I brought you up   and placed you in my court!
Carry my message   to Castile, to King Alfonso;
kiss his hand for me   with all my heart and soul,

630   since I am his vassal   and he is my lord;
this dishonor they have done me,   these Heirs of Carrión,
I would have it grieve the King   in his heart and soul.
He married my daughters;   it was not I who gave them.
Since they have been deserted   and gravely dishonored,

635   whatever in this   may redound to our dishonor,
in small things or in great,   redounds to my lord's.

6. They have only traveled about 20 miles through rough terrain. They go faster the next two days.

They have taken away wealth   beyond measure;
this should be reckoned in   with the other dishonor.
Let them be called to a meeting,   to a court or assembly,[7]

640   and give me my due,   these Heirs of Carrión,
for I bear much rancor   within my heart."
Muño Gustioz   mounted quickly,
and two knights with him   to wait upon his will,
and with him squires   of the Cid's household.

645   They rode out of Valencia   and with all speed go forward;
they take no rest   by day or night.
In Sahagún   they found King Alfonso.
He is King of Castile   and King of León
and of Asturias   and the city of Oviedo;

650   as far as Santiago   he is the lord,
and the Counts of Galicia   serve him as their lord.[8]
There Muño Gustioz,   as soon as he dismounts,
knelt to the saints   and prayed to the Creator;
he went up to the palace   where the court was,

655   and two knights with him   who serve him as their lord.
         When they entered   into the midst of the court
the King saw them   and knew Muño Gustioz;
the King rose   and received them well.
Before King Alfonso   Muño Gustioz

660   went down on his knees   and kissed the King's feet.
"Grace, King of great kingdoms   that call you lord!
The Campeador   kisses your hands and feet;
he is your vassal   and you are his lord.
You married his daughters   with the Heirs of Carrión;

665   the match was exalted   because you wished it so.
You know already what honor   that marriage has brought us:
how the Heirs of Carrión   have affronted us,
how they beat and abused the daughters   of the Cid Campeador,
stripped them naked, lashed them with whips   and deeply dishonored them

670   and abandoned them   in the oak forest of Corpes,
left them to the wild beasts   and the birds of the mountain.
Behold, now his daughters   are once more in Valencia.
For this the Cid kisses your hands   as a vassal to his lord;
he asks you to call these Heirs   to a court or assembly;

675   the Cid has been dishonored   but you still more deeply;
he asks you to share his grief, King,   as you are wise,
and to help My Cid to receive reparation   from these Heirs of Carrión."
For more than an hour the King   thought, and said nothing.
"I tell you, in truth   this grieves my heart,

680   and in this I speak truth   to you, Muño Gustioz.

7. Having reminded the king of his primary responsibility
in this affair, the Cid enumerates the three types of courtly
judicial gatherings, leaving the choice to the king.
8. The first time in the poem the king's territories have
been listed, enhancing his majesty at the moment in
which he will finally begin to show himself worthy of his
vassal. Asturias and Galicia were the most northern and
westerly parts of the kingdom.

I married the daughters   to the Heirs of Carrión;
I did it for the best,   for his advantage.
Oh, that such marriage   never had been made!
As for myself and the Cid,   our hearts are heavy.
685   I must see he receives justice,   so may the Creator keep me!
I never expected   such a thing as this.
My heralds shall go   through all my kingdom
and call my court   to assemble in Toledo;[9]
let all gather there,   counts and nobles;
690   and the Heirs of Carrión,   I shall bid them come there
and give just reparation   to My Cid the Campeador;
he shall not be left with a grievance   if I can prevent it.

134

"Say to the Campeador,   he who was born in good hour,
to be ready with his vassals   seven weeks from now
695   and come to Toledo;   that is the term I set for him.[1]
Out of love for My Cid   I call this court together.
Give my greetings to all   and bid them take comfort;
this which has befallen them   shall yet redound to their honor."
Muño Gustioz took his leave   and returned to My Cid.

700   Alfonso the Castilian,   as he had promised,
took it upon himself.   He brooks no delays,
he sends his letters   to León and Santiago,
to the Portuguese   and the Galicians
and to those of Carrión   and the nobles of Castile,
705   proclaiming that their honored King   called court in Toledo,
that they should gather there   at the end of seven weeks;
and whoever should not come to the court,   he would hold no longer his
     vassal.
Through all his lands   thus the message ran,
and none thought of refusing   what the King had commanded.

135

710   And the Heirs of Carrión   are gravely concerned
because the King holds court   in Toledo;
they are afraid of meeting   My Cid the Campeador.
They ask aid and advice   of their relatives;
they beg the King   to excuse them from this court.
715   The King replied, "In God's name,   I shall not grant you this!
For My Cid the Campeador   will come there
and receive reparation,   for he has a grievance against you.
Whoever does not wish to obey   and come to my court,
let him quit my kingdom,   for he has incurred my displeasure."
720   The Heirs of Carrión   see that it must be done;
they ask aid and advice   from their relatives.

---

9. In order to honor the Cid and to show his own involvement in the affair, Alfonso proclaims *cortes,* the most
solemn and important type of judicial gathering, in
Toledo, the strategically and politically central city taken
by him in 1085 from the Moors.
1. The customary legal period was 30 days; the perfect
number seven is probably symbolic.

The Count Don García   took part in all this;
he was an enemy of My Cid   and sought always to do him harm,
and he gave counsel   to the Heirs of Carrión.
725   The appointed time came;   they must go to the court.
The good King Don Alfonso   arrived there first,
the Count Don Enrique   and the Count Don Ramón—
he was the father   of the good emperor—
the Count Don Fruela   and the Count Don Birbón.[2]
730   And many others learned in law   came from all parts of the kingdom,
and the best came   from all Castile.
The Count Don García,   Twisted-Mouth of Grañón,
and Alvar Díaz,   who governed Oca,
and Asur González   and Gonzalo Ansúrez
735   and Pedro Ansúrez,[3]   you may know, arrived there,
and Diego and Fernando,   both of them came,
and a great crowd with them   came to the court
hoping to abuse   My Cid the Campeador.
        From all sides   they have gathered there.
740   He who in good hour was born   has not yet arrived,
and the King is not pleased,   for he is late.
On the fifth day   My Cid the Campeador came;
Alvar Fáñez   he sent on before him
to kiss the hands   of the King his lord
745   and tell him that the Cid   would arrive that evening.
When the King heard this   his heart was pleased;
with many knights   the King mounted
and went to receive   him who in good hour was born.
Well prepared,   the Cid comes with his men,
750   an imposing company   worthy of such a lord.
When he set eyes   on the good King Alfonso
My Cid the Campeador   flung himself to the ground,
wishing to humble himself   and do honor to his lord.
When the King saw this   in all haste he went forward:
755   "By Saint Isidore,   this shall not be so today!
Remain mounted, Cid,   or I shall be displeased;
we must greet each other   with heart and soul.
That which has befallen you   grieves my heart;
God grant you will honor the court   today with your presence!"
760   "Amen," said My Cid,   the good Campeador;
he kissed the King's hand   and then embraced him.

---

2. Enrique or Henry (d. 1114) was grandson of Robert I, Duke of Burgundy, and nephew of Alfonso's wife, Queen Constanza; by 1095 he was married to Alfonso's natural daughter Teresa and had been made governor of Portugal and of Coimbra. Ramón or Raymond was Count of Amous in Burgundy, and Henry's cousin and rival. He had married Alfonso's daughter and heir Urraca by 1087 and been made governor of Galicia; their son was Alfonso VII, King of Castile and León (1127–1157), who adopted the title "Emperor of all Spain." Froila ("Fruela") Díaz was Count of León, Astorga, and Aguilar, steward of Raymond, and brother of Jimena. For the other Count, the manuscripts read Beltrán, who became Count of Carrión at the death of Pedro Ansúrez, but only in 1117, 18 years after the death of the Cid, a clear anachronism, but the name does not rhyme, so other scholars have suggested Birbón.

3. Asur González was the Infantes' brother and Gonzalo Ansúrez their father, brother of the powerful Pedro Ansúrez, leader of the Beni-Gómez.

"I give thanks to God   for the sight of you, my lord.
I humble myself before you   and before the Count Ramón
and the Count Don Enrique   and all who are here with you;
765   God save your friends   and above all, you, my lord!
My wife, Doña Jimena,   that worthy lady,[4]
kisses your hands,   as do my daughters,
and beg you to partake   of our grief in this, my lord."
The King answered,   "I do so, in God's name!"

136

770   The King has turned   and started toward Toledo;
My Cid did not wish   to cross the Tagus that night:
"Grace, my King,   may the Creator bless you!
Return as you will, my lord,   into the city,
and I with my men   shall lodge in San Serván;
775   the rest of my vassals   will arrive tonight.[5]
I shall hold vigil   in that holy place;
tomorrow in the morning   I shall enter the city
and come to the court   before I have broken my fast."
The King said,   "I am pleased it should be so."
780   The King Don Alfonso   returns to Toledo;
My Cid Ruy Díaz   goes to stay in San Serván.
He sent for candles   to set on the altar;
he wishes to keep vigil   in this holy place,
praying to the Creator,   speaking with Him in secret.
785   Minaya and the other   good vassals who were there
were ready and waiting   when the morning came.

137

As dawn drew near   they said matins and primes,
and Mass was finished   before the sun rose.
All My Cid's men   made precious offerings.
790   "You, Minaya Alvar Fáñez,   my sword arm,
come with me   and you, Bishop Don Jerome
and Pedro Bermúdez   and Muño Gustioz
and Martín Antolínez,   the worthy man of Burgos,
and Alvar Alvarez   and Alvar Salvadórez
795   and Martín Muñoz,   born under a good star,
and my cousin,   Félix Muñoz,
and let Mal Anda come with me,   who is learned in law,
and Galindo García,   the good warrior from Aragón;
and others to make up a hundred   from among my good vassals.
800   Put on your armor   over padded tunics;
put on your breastplates,   white as the sun,
furs and ermines   over your breastplates,
and draw the strings tight   that your weapons be not seen;

---

4. Subtly reminding the king of his close familial tie to Jimena.
5. The king has left the walled city to receive the Cid, who

prefers for reasons of both piety and security to lodge in the castle of San Serván, outside of the walls of Toledo on the other side of the Tagus; at this time it was a monastery.

under your cloaks   gird the sweet keen swords.
805   In this manner   I would go to the court.
to demand justice   and say what I must say.
If the Heirs of Carrión   come seeking a quarrel,
if such a hundred are with me   it will not concern me."
All answered,   "Let it be so, lord."
810   All made ready   as he had commanded.
    He who in good hour was born   made no delay:
he covered his legs   in stockings of fine cloth
and over them he put shoes   of elaborate work.
He put on a woven shirt   as white as the sun,
815   and all the fastenings   were of silver and gold;
the cuffs fitted neatly   for he had ordered it thus.
Over this he put a tunic   of fine brocade
worked with gold   shining in every place.
Over these a crimson skin   with buckles of gold,
820   which My Cid the Campeador   wears on all occasions.
Over the furs he put   a hood of fine cloth
worked with gold   and set there
so that none might tear the hair   of My Cid the Campeador;
his beard was long   and tied with a cord,
825   for he wished to guard all his person   against insult.
On top of it all he wore   a cloak of great value;
all admired it,   as many as were there to see.
    With that hundred   whom he had bidden make ready
he mounted in haste   and rode out of San Serván;
830   thus prepared,   My Cid went to the court.
    At the outer door   they dismounted;
My Cid and his men   entered with due circumspection:
he goes in the middle   with his hundred around him.
When they saw enter   him who in good hour was born,
835   the good King Alfonso   rose to his feet,
and the Count Don Enrique   and the Count Don Ramón,
and all the others,   you may know, who were in the court.
With great honor they receive him   who in good hour was born.
Twisted-Mouth of Grañón   did not wish to stand,
840   nor all the rest of the band   of the Heirs of Carrión.
    The King took   My Cid by the hands:
"Come, sit down here   with me, Campeador,
on this bench   which was a gift from you;
though it annoy some,   you are of more worth than we."
845   Then he who had taken Valencia   thanked him much:
"Sit on your bench   as King and lord;
here I shall stay   among my men."
What the Cid said   pleased the King's heart.
Then My Cid sat down   on a bench of lathwork,
850   and the hundred who guard him   stand around him.
All who are in the court   are watching My Cid
and his long beard   tied with a cord;

his appearance   was in every way manly.
The Heirs of Carrión   can not look up for shame.
855   Then the good King Alfonso   rose to his feet.
"Hear me, my vassals,   and the Creator bless you!
Since I have been King   I have not held more than two courts:
one was in Burgos   and the other in Carrión,[6]
and this third   I open today in Toledo
860   for the love of My Cid,   who in good hour was born,
so that he may receive reparation   from the Heirs of Carrión.
They have done him great wrong,   as all of us know;
now let Counts Don Enrique and Don Ramón   be the judges,
and these other counts   who are not of the Heirs' company.
865   You who are learned in law,   fix well your attentions
and find out what is just,   for I would command no injustice.
Let us have peace today   on one side and the other.
I swear by Saint Isidore   that whoever disturbs my court
will be banished from my kingdom   and lose my favor.
870   I am of that side   on which justice is.
Now let My Cid the Campeador   make his demand,
and let us hear what they answer,   these Heirs of Carrión."
        My Cid kissed the King's hand   and rose to his feet.
"I thank you deeply,   as my King and lord,
875   for having held this court   for my sake.
Here is what I demand   of the Heirs of Carrión:
I am not dishonored   because they abandoned my daughters,
for since you, King, married them,   you will know what to do now;
but when they took my daughters   from Valencia, the great city,
880   from my heart and soul   I showed them much love.
I gave them two swords,   Colada and Tizón—
these I had taken   fighting like a man in the field—
that with them they might do themselves honor,   and you service;
when they abandoned my daughters   in the oak grove of Corpes
885   they wanted nothing more of me   and they lost my love;
let them give me my swords,   since they are no longer my sons-in-law."
        The judges granted,   "He is right in this."
The Count Don García said,   "We must speak of this."
Then the Heirs of Carrión   walked to one side
890   with all their kinsmen   and the company who were with them;
they discuss it quickly   and decide what to say:
"The Cid Campeador   does us a great favor
in not calling to account today   the dishonor of his daughters;
we can easily come to an arrangement   with King Alfonso.
895   Let us give him the swords,   since that will end his demand,
and when he has them   the court will adjourn;
and the Cid Campeador   will have no more claims upon us."

---

6. The poem doesn't specify the prior two occasions; the one in Burgos may have been when the Cid forced Alfonso to swear his innocence of Sancho's death.

Having decided this,   they returned to the court.
"Grace, King Alfonso,   you who are our lord!
900   We cannot deny   he gave us two swords;
now that he claims them   and wants them back again,
we wish to return them   here before you."
     They took out the swords,   Colada and Tizón;
they put them in the hands   of the King their lord.
905   The swords are drawn   and shine through all the court;
the hilts and guards   were all of gold.
All in the court   marveled to see them.
The King called My Cid   and gave him the swords;
he received the swords   and kissed the King's hands;
910   he returned to the bench   from which he had risen.
He held them in his hands   and looked on them both;
they could not have been false ones,   for he knew them well.
All his body was glad   and he smiled from his heart,
he raised his hand   and stroked his beard.
915   "By this beard,   which none has ever torn,
thus proceeds the avenging   of Doña Elvira and Doña Sol."
He summoned his nephew, Don Pedro,°   called him by name.   *Bermúdez*
He stretched out his arm   and gave him the sword Tizón:
"Take it, nephew,   it has found a better master."
920   To Martín Antolínez,   worthy man of Burgos,
he stretched out his arm   and gave him Colada:
"Martín Antolínez,   my worthy vassal,
take Colada;   I won it from a good lord,
from Ramón Berenguer   of Barcelona, the great city.
925   Therefore I give it to you   that you may care for it well.
I know that if the time   or the occasion should find you,
with it you will gain   honor and glory."
Martín Antolínez kissed his hand   and took the sword.
     Then My Cid the Campeador   got to his feet.
930   "I give thanks to the Creator   and to you, King and lord!
I am satisfied as to my swords,   Colada and Tizón.
I bear another grievance   toward the Heirs of Carrión:
When they took my daughters   from Valencia
I gave them three thousand marks   in gold and silver;
935   thus I did,   and they carried out their own business;
let them return me my riches,   since they are not my sons-in-law."
     God, they groaned then,   those Heirs of Carrión!
The Count Don Ramón said,   "Answer him, yes or no."
Then the Heirs of Carrión   answered thus:
940   "For this reason we gave his swords   to the Cid Campeador,
so that he should ask us no more   and end his demands."
Then the Count Don Ramón   answered them thus:
"If it please the King,   the court speaks thus:
You must render to the Cid   what he demands."
945   The good King said,   "I wish it to be so."
My Cid the Campeador   rose again to his feet.

"As for all the riches   which I gave you,
either return them to me   or give me an account."
    Then the Heirs of Carrión   walked to one side
950   but could reach no agreement,   for the riches were great
and the Heirs of Carrión   had spent them.
They returned to the court   and spoke their wish:
"He who took Valencia   presses us close;
since he sets such store   by what is ours
955   we shall pay him in lands   from the country of Carrión."
When they had made this plea   the judges said:
"If such pleases the Cid   we shall not refuse,
but to our judgment   it would appear better
that the money itself be repaid   here in the court."
960   At these words   the King Don Alfonso spoke:
"This affair is plain   for us all to see,
and My Cid the Campeador   has a just claim.
I have two hundred   of those three thousand marks;
they were given me   by the Heirs of Carrión.
965   I wish to return them,   since the Heirs are ruined,
so that they may give them to My Cid,   who in good hour was born;
since they must pay them   I do not wish to keep them."
Fernando González spoke,   hear what he said:
"We do not have   any wealth in coin."
970   Then the Count Don Ramón   answered him:
"You have spent   the gold and the silver;
here is the judgment we give   before the King Don Alfonso:
You must pay in kind   and the Campeador accept it."
    The Heirs of Carrión   know what they must do.
975   You would have seen them lead in   so many swift horses,
so many fat mules,   so many palfreys of good breed,
so many good swords   with all their trappings,
and My Cid took them   at the court's evaluation.
All but the two hundred marks   which were King Alfonso's
980   the Heirs paid   to him who was born in good hour;
they had to borrow from elsewhere,   their own goods were not enough.
You may know, this time   they are sorely mocked.
                138
    These valued goods   My Cid has taken;
his men receive them   and take them in charge.
985   But when this was done   there was something still to do.
    "Grace, King and lord,   for the love of charity!
The greatest grievance   I cannot forget.
Let all the court hear me   and share in my injury;
the Heirs of Carrión   have so gravely dishonored me,
990   I cannot leave this case   without challenging them.[7]

---

7. The challenge was a procedure to resolve actions involving honor between nobles before public tribunals; it is thus distinct from the duel, which was a private affair. The usage is anachronistic, for the procedure did not exist at this time.

139

"Tell me, what did I deserve of you,   Heirs of Carrión,
in jest or in truth   or in any fashion?
Here before the court's judgment   this must be repaired.
Why have you torn   the webs of my heart?

995 When you went from Valencia   I gave you my daughters
with much honor   and countless riches;
if you did not want them,   treacherous dogs,
why did you take them   and their honors from Valencia?
Why did you wound them   with whips and spurs?

1000 You left them alone   in the oak grove of Corpes
to the wild beasts   and the birds of the mountain.
For all you have done   you are infamous.
Let the court judge   if you must not give satisfaction."

140

The Count Don García   rose to his feet.

1005 "Grace, King,   the best in all Spain!
My Cid has rehearsed himself   for this solemn court;
he has let his beard grow   and wears it long;
he strikes fear into some   and dread into others.
The Heirs of Carrión   are of such high birth

1010 they should not want his daughters   even as concubines,
and who would command them to take them   as their lawful wives?
They did what was just   in leaving them.
All that the Cid says   we value at nothing."

Then the Campeador   laid his hand on his beard:

1015 "Thanks be to God   Who rules heaven and earth,
my beard is long   because it grew at its own pleasure.

"What have you, Count,   to throw in my beard?
It has grown at its own pleasure   since it began;
no son of woman   ever dared touch it,

1020 no son of Moor or Christian   ever has torn it
as I tore yours, Count,   at the castle of Cabra.
When I seized Cabra   and you by your beard,
there was not a boy there   who did not tear out his wisp;
that which I tore out   has not yet grown again,

1025 and I carry it here   in this closed pouch."

141

Fernando González   rose to his feet.
Hear what he said   in a loud voice:
"Cid, let your claim   here have an end;
all your goods   have been returned to you.

1030 Let this suit   go no further between us.
We are by birth descended   from the Counts of Carrión:
we should marry the daughters   of kings or emperors;
we are worthy of more than the daughters   of petty squires.
We did what was just   when we abandoned your daughters;

1035 our honor is greater than before,   you may know, and not less."

142

My Cid Ruy Díaz   looked at Pedro Bermúdez.
"Speak, Mute Pedro,[8]   knight who are so much silent!
They are my daughters,   but they are your first cousins;
when they say this to me   they pull your ears also.
1040   If I answer,   you will have no chance to fight."

143

Then Pedro Bermúdez   started to speak,
but his tongue stumbles   and he cannot begin;
yet once he has begun,   know, he does not hesitate:
"I will tell you, Cid,   that is a custom of yours:
1045   always in the courts   you call me Pedro the Mute!
But you know well   that I can do no better,
yet of what I can do   there shall be no lack.
    "You lie, Fernando,   in all you have said,
you gained great honor   through the Campeador.
1050   Now I shall tell   of your ways:
Remember when we fought   near Valencia the great?
You begged the Campeador   to grant you the first blows.
You saw a Moor   and you went toward him,
but before he came upon you   you fled from there.
1055   Had I not been there   the Moor would have used you roughly;
I passed you by   and encountered the Moor;
with the first blows   I overcame him.
I gave you his horse   and have kept all this secret
and told it to no one   until today.
1060   Before My Cid and before all   you were heard to boast
that you killed the Moor   and had done a knightly deed,
and all believed you,   not knowing the truth.
Oh, you are pretty   and a vile coward!
Tongue without hands,   how do you dare to speak?

144

1065   "Speak, Fernando,   admit to this:
Do you not recall   the lion in Valencia,
the time when My Cid slept   and the lion got loose?
And you, Fernando,   what did you do in your terror?
You hid behind the bench   of My Cid the Campeador!
1070   You hid there, Fernando,   and for that I now defame you.
We all stood around the bench   to shield our lord,
until My Cid woke,   who had taken Valencia;
he rose from the bench   and went toward the lion;
the lion bowed his head   and waited for My Cid,
1075   let himself be taken by the neck   and went back into his cage.
And when the good Campeador   returned again
he saw his vassals   all around him;
he asked for his sons-in-law.   No one could find them!

8. The Cid puns on the name of his nephew Pedro Bermúdez, calling him "Pedro Mudo."

I defy your body,   villain and traitor.
1080   I will fight it out here   before King Alfonso
for the daughters of the Cid,   Doña Elvira and Doña Sol;
because you abandoned them   I now defame you.
They are women   and you are men;
in every way   they are worth more than you.
1085   When the fight takes place,   if it please the Creator,
I will make you admit   that you are a traitor,
and all I have said here   I will prove true."
And between those two   the dispute thus ended.

145

As for Diego González,   hear what he said:
1090   "We are by birth   of the purest lineage of counts.
Oh, that this marriage   had never been made
that made us kin   of My Cid Don Rodrigo!
We still do not repent   that we abandoned his daughters;
let them sigh   as long as they live,
1095   and what we have done to them   will be thrown in their face always.
This I will maintain   against the bravest,
for in abandoning them   we have gained in honor."

146

Martín Antolínez   rose to his feet.
"Be silent, traitor,   mouth without truth!
1100   You should not have forgotten   the episode of the lion;
you went out the door   into the courtyard
and hid yourself   behind the beam of the winepress;
since then you have not worn   that cloak and silk shirt again.
I shall maintain this by combat,   it shall not be otherwise,
1105   because you abandoned   the Cid's daughters.
You may know, their honor   in every way exceeds yours.
When the fight is over,   with your own mouth you will admit
that you are a traitor   and have lied in all you have said."

147

The talk was ended   between these two.
1110   Asur González   entered the palace
with an ermine cloak   and his tunic trailing;
his face was red   for he had just eaten.
There was little prudence   in what he said:

148

"Ah, knights,   whoever has seen such evil?
1115   Since when might we receive honor   from My Cid of Bivar!
Let him go now to the river Ubierna   and look after his mills
and be paid in corn   as he used to do!9
Who ever suggested he marry   with those of Carrión?"

---

9. It was common for *infanzones,* members of the lowest nobility, to own mills, although they themselves would not have worked them. (There was a legend that the Cid was his father's illegitimate son by a mill girl.) In the event, Asur had no larger inheritance than the Cid, and one of his principal sources of income would have been the fees collected at his mill.

149

Then Muño Gustioz   rose to his feet.

1120   "Be silent, traitor,   evil and full of deceit!
First you have breakfast   and then you say your prayers
and all whom you kiss   in greeting smell your belches.
You speak no truth   to friend or lord;
you are false to all   and still more false to the Creator.

1125   I want no portion   in your friendship,
and I shall make you confess   that you are all that I say."
King Alfonso said,   "Let this case rest now.
Those who have made challenges   shall fight, as God may save me!"
    Thus they bring   this case to an end,

1130   and behold, two knights   came into the court:
one was called Ojarra   and the other Iñigo Jiménez;
one is the herald   of the Prince of Navarre
and the other the herald   of the Prince of Aragón.[1]
They kiss the hands   of King Alfonso

1135   and ask for the daughters   of My Cid the Campeador
to make them Queens   of Navarre and Aragón
as honored wives   blessed in marriage.[2]
At this all the court   was hushed and listened.
My Cid the Campeador   rose to his feet.

1140   "Grace, King Alfonso,   you are my lord!
I give thanks   to the Creator
for what Navarre and Aragón   have asked of me.
You married my daughters before   and not I;
here once again I say   my daughters are in your hands:

1145   without your bidding   I shall do nothing."
The King rose   and bade the court be silent.
"Cid, perfect Campeador,   I ask that it meet your pleasure
that I should consent   to this marriage.
Let it be arranged   here and now in this court,

1150   and thus may you increase   in fiefs, in estates and honor."
My Cid rose   and kissed the King's hands:
"As it pleases you,   I grant it, lord."
Then the King said,   "God reward you well!
And you, Ojarra,   and you, Iñigo Jiménez,

1155   I consent   to this marriage
of the daughters of My Cid,   Doña Elvira and Doña Sol,
with the Princes   of Navarre and Aragón,
that the girls may be given to them   as their honored wives."
Ojarra and Iñigo Jiménez   rose to their feet;

1160   they kissed the hands   of King Alfonso
and afterwards those   of My Cid the Campeador;

---

1. Historical personages, but from the early 12th century, "infantes," or heirs of the northeastern kingdoms of Spain.
2. Marriage into royalty ratifies the high position achieved by the Cid, and bestows upon his daughters the status claimed by the Infantes of Carrión as their own desserts.

they gave pledges   and swore the oaths,
that all might be   as had been said, or better.
This pleases many   there in the court

1165   but gives no pleasure   to the Heirs of Carrión.
     Minaya Alvar Fáñez   rose to his feet.
"I beg grace of you,   as my King and lord,
and hope it may not displease   the Cid Campeador:
I have heard all speak their minds   here in the court,

1170   and now I would say   something of my own."
The King said,   "Granted gladly.
Speak, Minaya,   say what you wish."
"I beg all the court   to hear what I say,
for I have great grievance against   the Heirs of Carrión.

1175   I gave them my cousins   by the hand of King Alfonso;
they took them in the honor   and blessing of marriage;
My Cid the Campeador   gave them much wealth,
and then they left them   to our sorrow.
I challenge their bodies   as villains and traitors.

1180   You are of the family   of the Beni-Gómez,[3]
in which there have been counts   of worth and courage,
but now we know well   what your ways are.
I give thanks   to the Creator
that the Princes   of Navarre and Aragón

1185   have asked for my cousins,   Doña Elvira and Doña Sol;
before, you had them for wives,   both, between your arms;
now you will kiss their hands   and call them 'My Lady,'
and do them service,   however it pains you.
I give thanks to God in heaven   and to this King Alfonso

1190   that thus grows the honor   of My Cid the Campeador!
In every way   you are as I described you;
if there is any among you   to deny it and say no,
I am Alvar Fáñez,   a better man than any of you."
     Gómez Peláez   rose to his feet.[4]

1195   "To what end, Minaya,   is all this talk?
There are many in this court   as brave as you,
and whoever should wish to deny this,   it would be to his harm.
If God wills   that we should come well out of this
you will have cause   to look to what you have said."

1200   The King said,   "Let this talk end;
let no one add a further claim   to this dispute.
Let the fight be tomorrow   when the sun rises,
the three against three   who challenged here in the court."
     The Heirs of Carrión   answered then:

1205   "Give us more time, King   for we cannot do it tomorrow.

---

3. The name Beni-Gómez is composed of the Andalusi-
Arabic word for "son" and the Christian name, Gómez,
and referred to the descendants of Gómez Díaz (who died
c. 1060), Count of Saldaña, Liébana, and Carrión, and

great-uncle of the Infantes. The principal family at the
end of the 11th century was the Ansúrez.
4. A nobleman of León, perhaps a grandson of Gómez
Díaz.

We have given our arms and horses   to the Campeador;
first we must go   to the lands of Carrión."
The King said   to the Campeador:
"This battle shall take place   wherever you wish."
1210   Then My Cid said,   "I will not do as they say.
I would rather return to Valencia   than go to Carrión."
Then the King said,   "It is well, Campeador.
Give me your knights   all well armed;
let them come with me,   I shall stand surety for them
1215   and see to their safety   as a lord does for his good vassal,
and they will come to no harm   from count or noble.
Here in my court   I set the term:
Three weeks from now   in the plain of Carrión
let this battle take place,   and I there to see;
1220   whoever is not there   forfeits the fight
and will be declared beaten   and called traitor."
The Heirs of Carrión   accepted the decision.
My Cid kissed   the King's hands:
"My three knights   are in your hands;
1225   here I commend them to you   as my King and lord.
They are well prepared   to fulfill what they go for;
send them with honor to Valencia,   for the love of the Creator!"
Then the King answered,   "May God grant it be so."
   Then the Cid Campeador   drew back his hood,
1230   his coif of fine cloth,   white as the sun,
and freed his beard   and undid the cord.
All who are in the court   cannot keep from staring at him.
He went to the Count Don Enrique   and the Count Don Ramón;
he embraced them closely   and asked them from his heart
1235   to take of what he owned   whatever they wished.
These and the others   who had sided with him,
he begged them all   to take what they wished;
and some of them take   and others not.
He bade the King keep   the two hundred marks
1240   and to take from him besides   as much as he wished.
   "I beg grace of you, King,   for the love of the Creator!
Now that all these things   have been provided for,
I kiss your hands   and with your grace, my lord,
would return to Valencia,   for painfully I took it."

[*There is a gap here of some fifty lines filled in from the prose* "Chronicle of Twenty Kings."]

   Then My Cid commanded that mounts and whatever they needed should be given to the messengers from the Princes of Navarre and Aragón, and he sent them on their way.
   Then King Alfonso mounted, with all the nobles of his court, to ride out with My Cid as he left the town. And when they came to Zocodover,[5] the King said to My Cid,

5. The principal plaza of Toledo.

who was riding on his horse, which was called Babieca, "Don Rodrigo, I should like
to see you urge your horse to his full speed, for I have heard much of him." The Cid
began to smile, and said, "Lord, here in your court are many nobles and men who
would be most pleased to do this; ask them to race their horses." The King said to
him, "Cid, I am contented with what you say, but nevertheless I wish you to race your
horse, to please me."

150

1245   Then the Cid set spur to his horse,   who ran so swiftly
          that all who were there   marveled at his speed.
          The King raised his hand   and crossed himself:
          "I swear by Saint Isidore   of León
          that in all our lands   there is not such another knight."
1250   My Cid has ridden forward   on his horse
          and come to kiss the hand   of his lord Alfonso:
          "You have bidden me race   Babieca, my swift horse;
          neither among Moors nor among Christians   is there such another;
          I offer him to you as a gift.   Take him, my lord."
1255   Then the King said,   "I do not wish it so;
          if I take your horse from you   he will not have so fine a master.
          Such a horse as this   needs such a rider as you
          for routing Moors in the field   and pursuing them after the battle.
          May the Creator not bless   whoever would take your horse from you,
1260   since by means of your horse and you   we have all received honor."
               Then they parted   and the court rode on.
          The Campeador gave counsel   to those who were to fight:
          "Martín Antolínez,   and you, Pedro Bermúdez
          and Muño Gustioz,   my worthy vassal,
1265   maintain the field   like brave men;
          send me good news   to Valencia."
          Martín Antolínez said,   "Why do you say this, lord?
          We have accepted the charge,   it is for us to carry it out;
          you may hear of dead men   but not of vanquished."
1270   He who in good hour was born   was pleased at this;
          he said good-bye to them all   for they were his friends.
          My Cid rode toward Valencia   and the King toward Carrión.
               The three weeks of the delay   have all run out.
          Behold, the Campeador's men   have come on the appointed day;
1275   they wish to accomplish   what their lord had required of them.
          They are protected   by Alfonso of León;
          two days they waited   for the Heirs of Carrión.
          The Heirs come well provided   with horses and arms,
          and all their kin with them   and they had plotted
1280   that if they might draw   the Campeador's men to one side
          they should kill them in the field   for the dishonor of their lord.
          They were bent on evil   had they not been prevented,
          for great is their fear   of Alfonso of León.
               My Cid's men held vigil by their arms   and prayed to the Creator.
1285   The night has passed   and the dawn breaks;
          many of the nobles   have gathered together

to see this battle,   which will give them pleasure,
and above them all   is the King Don Alfonso,
to see that justice is done   and prevent any wrong.
1290   The Campeador's men   have armed themselves;
all are of one mind,   since they serve the same lord.
In another place   the Heirs of Carrión arm,
the Count García Ordoñez   giving them advice.
They raised a complaint   and begged King Alfonso
1295   that Colada and Tizón   should be banned from the combat
and that the Campeador's men   should not use them in the fight;
the Heirs deeply regretted   having given them back.
They begged this of the King,   but he would not consent:
"There in the court   you objected to none.
1300   If you have good swords   they will serve you,
and the Campeador's men will be served   by theirs in the same way.
Rise and ride out on the field,   Heirs of Carrión;
you have no choice,   you must fight like men,
for the Campeador's men   will not lack for anything.
1305   If you win on the field   you will have great honor,
and if you are beaten   put no blame on us,
for everyone knows   you have brought this on yourselves."
The Heirs of Carrión   now repent
of what they had done,   they regret it deeply;
1310   they would have given all Carrión   not to have done it.
     The Campeador's men,   all three, are armed;
they have gone to see   the King Don Alfonso.
Then the Campeador's men   said to him:
"We kiss your hands,   as our King and lord;
1315   be a faithful judge   today, between them and us;
aid us with justice   and allow no wrong.
The Heirs of Carrión   have all their kin with them;
we cannot tell   what they may or may not have plotted.
Our lord commended us   into your hands;
1320   see that justice is done us,   for the love of the Creator!"
Then the King said,   "with my heart and soul."
     They bring out   their fine swift horses;
they blessed the saddles   and mounted briskly;
the shields with gilded bucklers   are at their necks;
1325   they take up the lances   tipped with sharp steel,
each of the lances   with its pennon,
and all around them   many worthy men.
They rode out on the field,   where the markers were set.
The Campeador's men   are all in agreement
1330   how each of them   would attack his man.
On the other side   are the Heirs of Carrión,
well accompanied,   for they have many kinsmen.
The King appointed judges   to decide what was just and what not,
and commanded that none should dispute   their yes or their no.
1335   When they were in the field   King Alfonso spoke:

"Hear what I have to tell you,   Heirs of Carrión.
This fight should have been in Toledo   but you did not wish it so.
These three knights   of My Cid the Campeador
I have brought in my safekeeping   to the lands of Carrión.

1340   Now fight justly   and try no trickery,
for if anyone attempts treachery   I am here to prevent it,
and he who tries it shall not be welcome   in all my kingdom."
The Heirs of Carrión   were much cast down at this.
    The judges and the King   pointed out the markers,

1345   then all the spectators went from the field   and stood around it.
They explained carefully   to all six of them
that he will be judged conquered   who leaves the field's borders.
All who stood about there   then drew back
the length of three lances   beyond the markers.

1350   They drew lots for the ends of the field   —the sunlight in each half was the
        same[6]—
and the judges went from the center   and they stood face to face,
the Cid's men facing   the Heirs of Carrión
and the Heirs of Carrión   facing the Campeador's men;
each of them   faced his own opponent;

1355   they hugged their shields   over their hearts,
lowered the lances   wrapped in their pennons,
bent their faces   over their saddletrees,
dug their spurs   into their horses,
and the earth shook   as they leapt forward.

1360   Each of them is bent   on his own opponent;
three against three   they have come together.
All who stand about   fear they will fall dead.
    Pedro Bermúdez,   who had made the first challenge,
came face to face   with Fernando González,

1365   and fearlessly   they struck each other's shields.
Fernando González   pierced Don Pedro's shield
but drove through upon nothing   and touched no flesh,
and in two places   the shaft of his spear snapped.
Pedro Bermúdez remained firm,   he was not shaken by this;

1370   he received one blow,   he struck another,
burst the shield's buckler   and broke it apart,
cut through it all,   nothing withstood him,
drove his lance through to the breast   close to the heart.
Fernando was wearing three suits of chain mail   and this saved him;

1375   two folds were pierced   and the third held firm,
but the mail and the tunic   with its binding
were driven a hand's breadth   into the flesh,
so that the blood ran   from Fernando's mouth,
and the girth° broke,   nothing held it;   *of his saddle*

1380   Fernando was flung to the ground   over the horse's crupper.°   *rump*

6. So that neither side will have an advantage from its position.

It seemed to those who stood there   that he must be dead.
With that Pedro Bermúdez left his lance   and laid hand on his sword.
When Fernando González saw him   and knew Tizón,
he said, "I am beaten"   without waiting for the blow.[7]

1385   The judges agreed   and Pedro Bermúdez left him.

151

Don Martín and Diego González   struck with their spears;
such were the blows   that both were broken.
Martín Antolínez   set hand on his sword;
it is so bright and clean   that it shines over all the field.

1390   It struck a blow   which caught him from the side;
it split apart   the top of the helmet
and it broke all   the helmet buckles;
it sheared the head mail   and to the coif came;
head mail and coif   it cut through them,

1395   razed the hair of the head   and came to the flesh;
part fell to the field,   the rest remained.
      When the precious Colada   had struck this blow
Diego González saw   that he should not escape with his soul;
he drew on the reins of his horse   to turn away;

1400   he had a sword in his hand   but did not use it.
Then Martín Antolínez   struck him with his sword,
a blow with the flat of his sword,   not with the edge.
Then the Heir   shouted aloud:
"Bless me, glorious God,   lord, save me from this sword!"

1405   Reining his horse,   keeping his distance from the sword,
he went beyond the marker;   Don Martín stayed on the field.
      Then the King said,   "Come to my side;
with what you have done   you have won the fight."
The judges agree   that what he says is true.

152

1410   Two have been defeated;   I shall tell you of Muño Gustioz
and how his fight went   with Asur González.
They struck great blows   on each other's shields.
Asur González   was vigorous and brave;
he struck Muño Gustioz   on the shield,

1415   drove through the shield   and to the armor,
then his lance cut through on nothing,   touching no flesh.
When this blow was struck,   Muño Gustioz returned another:
he split his shield   at the middle of the buckler,
nothing withstood his stroke,   he broke the armor;

1420   he sheared it apart   and, though not close to the heart,
drove the lance and pennon   into the flesh
so it came out an arm's length   on the other side,
then he pulled on the lance   and twisted González from his saddle.
When he pulled out the lance   González fell to the ground,

---

7. This pronouncement is equivalent to a formal retraction of the matter of the challenge.

1425   and the spear shaft was red,   and the lance and the pennon.
        All fear that González   is mortally wounded.
        Muño Gustioz again seized his spear   and stood over him.
        Gonzalo Ansúrez said,   "For the love of God, do not strike him!
        The field is won   and the combat is finished!"
1430   The judges said,   "We agree to this."
             The good King Don Alfonso   sent to despoil the field;
        he took for himself   the arms that remained there.
        The Campeador's men   departed in great honor;
        with the aid of the Creator   they had won this fight.
1435   Hearts were heavy   in the lands of Carrión.
             The King warned My Cid's men   to leave at night
        so that none might attack them   and they have no cause for fear.
        They, prudently,   ride night and day.
        Behold, they have come to Valencia,   to My Cid the Campeador.
1440   They had left in shame   the Heirs of Carrión
        and fulfilled the duty   they owed to their lord;
        My Cid the Campeador   was pleased at this.
        The Heirs of Carrión   are in deep disgrace.
        May whoever injures a good woman   and abandons her afterwards
1445   suffer as great harm as this   and worse, besides.
             Let us leave this matter   of the Heirs of Carrión;
        they take no pleasure   in what has befallen them.
        Let us speak of him   who in good hour was born.
        Great are the celebrations   in Valencia the great
1450   because the Campeador's men   have won great honor.
        Ruy Díaz their lord   stroked his beard:
        "Praised be the King of Heaven,   my daughters are avenged!
        Now freed of all debts   is their heritage in Carrión!
        I shall marry them now without shame,   let it weigh on whom it will."
1455   The Princes of Navarre and Aragón   continued their suits,
        and all met together   with Alfonso of León;
        The wedding is performed   of Doña Elvira and Doña Sol;
        the first marriage was noble   but this much more so;
        to greater honor he weds them   than was theirs before.
1460   See how he grows in honor   who in good hour was born;
        his daughters are wives of the Kings   of Navarre and Aragón.[8]
        Now the Kings of Spain   are his kinsmen,
        and all advance in honor   through My Cid the Campeador.
             My Cid, the lord of Valencia,   passed from this world
1465   on the Day of Pentecost,[9]   may Christ give him pardon!
        And may He pardon us all,   both the just and the sinners!
             These were the deeds   of My Cid the Campeador,
        and in this place   the song is ended.

---

8. In fact, Aragón and Navarre formed a single kingdom at the time. Ruy Díaz's daughter Cristina did marry Ramiro, a member of the royal house of Navarre, and their son García Ramírez became king. María married Ramón Berenguer III of Barcelona.
9. There is no record of the month and day of the death of Rodrigo Díaz in 1099.

[The manuscript of the poem bears a conclusion by the copyist, followed by a concluding note by the singer:]

May God grant paradise to the writer of this book, amen!
Per Abbat wrote it in the month of May
In the year of Our Lord 1245 [1207].

And the romance has been read out,
Give us some wine;
If you have no coins,
Throw down a few pledges there,
For you'll get a good return on them.

Iberia, The Meeting of Three Worlds

There are two common names for the period of eight hundred years during which Islamic forces controlled some portion of the Iberian Peninsula: the *Convivencia,* or coexistence, and the *Reconquista,* or reconquest. As these very different terms suggest, medieval Spain can be seen as an extraordinary confluence of the three dominant cultures of the modern West (Arabic, Christian, and Jewish) or as an embattled cohabitation. In either case, there is no denying the unique and multifaceted art and literature that emerged from it. Southern Spain was the portal through which the rich and ancient erudition of North Africa, the Middle East, and Greece made its way back into Europe after the fall of the Roman Empire.

Muslim armies first arrived in the Iberian peninsula in 711, sweeping northward into France, where they were eventually turned back by Charles Martel at Poitiers. The first dynasty of emirs in al-Andalus (Arabic for "the land of the Vandals," earlier rulers of the region; "Andalucía" in Spanish) was the Umayyads, who controlled the entire peninsula outside of the northern quarter—the Christian kingdoms of Asturias, León, Navarre, Aragon, and Catalonia. Most of the cities of al-Andalus remained relatively independent. The great political and cultural centers were Córdoba, Granada, and, later, Seville; here were built the magnificent mosques and palaces still visible today, and here poets were drawn from all over the declining eastern empire. The long-established and highly regular forms of classical, courtly Arabic poetry were renewed through contact with the indigenous forms of Spain.

Poetry was the most prestigious literary mode and the chief cultural institution of the Arabic-speaking world, practiced by rulers, courtiers, philosophers, and religious leaders as well as professional poets (see the introduction to "Classical Arabic and Islamic Literatures," page 315). The incorporation of Greek philosophy from the tenth century on provided a common language and set of problems to Muslims, Christians, and Jews alike. The so-called "courtier rabbis" were especially important to this cultural mélange, benefiting from the Arab principle of toleration for those they called the *dhimmi,* or "people of the book." Wealthy and powerful, fluent in Arabic, pious and learned in Jewish tradition, the community of the Sephardim (as the Jews of Iberia called themselves) saw to the everyday workings of the kingdoms of al-Andalus. They also created an unprecedented corpus of secular Hebrew poetry out of Arabic forms, as if the poetic clash of sensuality, nature, and physical love with divinity were a way of mitigating the contradiction between their public and private lives.

Exile was a great theme, not only for the Hebrew poets adapting a classical Jewish motif to Arabic poetic forms, but to the Arab mystics describing their separation from paradise in the material world. Celebrations of wine, love, and song went hand in hand with an underlying conviction of the transience of physical experience. Even under the fairly stable government of the tenth and eleventh centuries, warfare was constant. Two movements during the eleventh century had far-reaching consequences. In 1035, the Almoravids, a strictly orthodox sect, arose in North Africa; at the same time, the Christian rulers of Castile and León began the centuries-long push southward that became known as the *Reconquista,* which is recorded in part in *The Poem of the Cid.* Invited into al-Andalus to counter the Castilian forces, Almoravid rule initiated a decline in Jewish participation in society. A pogrom in Granada in 1066 resulted in the massacre of 3,000 Jews. When Almoravid power dissipated in the mid-twelfth century, their role was taken over by the Almohads, a new reform movement that preached austere simplicity, rejected the doctrine of *dhimmi,* and caused a further exodus from al-Andalus of Jews and Mozarabs (Christians who had adopted Arabic language and culture without converting to Islam).

Medieval Iberia was a society both enraptured and disturbed by anything hybrid. Jews and Christians held high posts in al-Andalus; their poets and philosophers later found refuge and patronage in the courts of northern Spain, collaborating, for example, in the creation by

The Iberian Peninsula, c. 1180

FRANCE

Toulouse

Carcassonne

BÉARN

NAVARRE

PYRENEES

ANDORRA

Oviedo

Santiago de Compostela

León

Pamplona

Burgos

Huesca

Gerona

LEÓN

ARAGON

Lérida

Valladolid

Saragossa

Barcelona

Oporto

Tarragona

Salamanca

Tortosa

Coimbra

Ávila

CASTILE

Teruel

PORTUGAL

Toledo

MALLORCA

Alcántara

Palma

Santarém

Valencia

IBIZA

Lisbon

Badajoz

BALEARIC

Évora

Calatrava

ISLANDS

Alcácer

ALMOHAD EMPIRE

Alicante

MEDITERRANEAN
SEA

Guadalquivir

Córdoba

Jaén

Murcia

ALGARVE

Seville

Lorca

Silves

ANDALUCIA

Faro

Antequera

Granada

Jerez

Almería

Cádiz

Málaga

Tarifa

Ceuta

ZAYYANIDS

Tangier

N

WATTASIDS

Alfonso X of the thirteenth-century *cantigas de Santa Maria,* a huge collection of over 400 songs celebrating the Virgin Mary. Miniatures in the opulent manuscript depict Arab, Jewish, and Christian performers side by side, singing, dancing, and playing a wide variety of musical instruments. A Castilian general such as Rodrigo Díaz battled other Christians as well as Muslims, and, although a loyal vassal to King Alfonso VI, maintained close friendships and ties of allegiance to Muslim rulers. Poetry and philosophy reflected the same paradoxes. Two hybrid

Christian and Muslim playing chess, illuminated manuscript page from King Alfonso X's *Book of Games,* Castile, mid-thirteenth century.

forms of poetry were invented in al-Andalus: the *muwashshaḥ,* which rendered classical courtly Arabic themes in the syllabic meter of indigenous Iberian dance refrains, attaching the original Mozarabic refrain as the final stanza (the "*kharja*" or "exit"); and the *zajal,* an entirely colloquial form based on the strophic structure of the *muwashshaḥ.* Philosophers too combined and confronted religious worldviews, as can be seen in the selections below from Ramón Llull and Yehuda ha-Levi.

War, too, provided a central metaphor for the mixture of cultures. A traditional Castilian ballad such as "Three Moorish Girls" subtly evokes the simultaneously beautiful and hostile nature of a landscape in which an enemy was never far distant. The bittersweet suggestion of the loss of innocence gains added pathos from its setting in the border city of Jaén, site of an Arab defeat in 1246. The female speakers of the Galician-Portuguese *cantigas de amigo* are haunted by the long absence of a lover, whether crusading in the distant East or the nearby South. As in *The Poem of the Cid,* slogans of religious fervor often go hand in hand with episodes of intimate cooperation. But when Ferdinand and Isabella married to unite conclusively the kingdoms of Castile and Aragon, a sea change was imminent. The last Arab stronghold, Granada, surrendered in 1492, the same year in which the Jews were expelled from Spain, and in which Columbus reached the Americas. The "people of the book" would come together again in other countries under conditions of war, but never again would that hostile proximity also result in a cultural flowering of such local beauty and far-reaching influence.

PRONUNCIATIONS:

Al-Andalus: ahl-AHN-dah-loos
Averroës: ah-ve-RRO-es
Cordoba: KOR-do-bah
Dom Dinis: dohm-DEE-nees
Ibn 'Arabi: ib'n ah-RAH-bee
Solomon Ibn Gabirol: SOHL-oh-mon ib'n GAH-bee-roll
Ibn Ḥazm: ib'n HAZ'm
Kharjas: KHAR-zhas
Ramon Llull: rah-MON LULL
Yehuda ha-Levi: ya-WHO-dah ha-LAY-vee

Castilian Ballads and Traditional Songs
c. 11th–14th centuries

During the late fifteenth century, as the final battles of the *Reconquista* were being decided, Ferdinand and Isabella began forging a national identity for Spain exclusive of Jews and Muslims. One aspect of this process was to collect the oral tradition of Castilian song into written form, a process initiated by Dom Dinis in the late thirteenth century. The result was a series of *Cancioneros,* or songbooks, and *Romanceros,* or books of ballads, including the *Cancionero de Palacio* (1438), *Cancionero de la Colombina* (1493), the *Cancionero musical del palacio* (1500), the *Cancionero general* (1511), the *Cancionero de romances* (1550), and the *Romancero general* (1600). The songs dated from the previous several centuries; many are probably of far earlier origin. In addition to universal motifs of love and celebration, these collections document the complex relationship of Castile over the past centuries with its southern neighbors in al-Andalus.

Ballad of Juliana[1]

"Get on, you hounds, get on,
      And may the furies take you.
Thursday you kill the boar
      And eat the meat on Friday.[2]

5   "Today makes seven years
      I've wandered in these hills.
Now both my feet are bare,
      Blood spurts from my toenails.

"Now I drink fresh gore,
10   The meat I eat is raw,
And sadly seek Juliana,
      Who was the emperor's daughter.

---

1. From the *Cancionero de romances*. Translated by Edwin Honig.

2. It was long the custom in the Catholic Church to abstain from eating meat on Fridays in memory of the crucifixion of Jesus on that day.

        "Early St. John's morning,[3]
           While she gathered flowers,
15   The Moors took her away
           From her father's bowers."

        Juliana hears this said
           Wrapt in the Moor's embrace;
        Twin tears her two eyes shed
20   Fall on that Moor's face.

Abenámar[1]

        "Abenámar, Abenámar
        Moor of Moor's delight
        The hour of your birth
        Comets filled the night.[2]
5   The sea was calm as glass
        The moon was waxing full
        A Moor with stars like yours
        Must never break the spell."
        "I tell the truth, my lord,
10   Though it be death to tell."
        "I thank you, Abenámar,
        Your birth bespeaks you well.
        What castles are those shining
        High on yonder hill?"
15   "The Alhambra there, my lord,
        The mosque tower further still,
        And there, the Alixares,
        Built so wondrous well.[3]
        A Moor was paid to build them
20   A hundred crowns a day
        And lost, for each day idle,
        As much as he was paid.
        When all was built and ready
        The architect was slain
25   So he could build no others
        For Andalusia's reign.
        There lies Crimson Towers
        A castle of renown
        And there, the Generalife,

---

3. June 24, the midsummer festival of St. John's Day, marked the end of the festival season and the beginning of the work of harvesting. Its rituals included gathering grass for auguring and flowers for girls to wear in wreaths, dancing around a bonfire, eating, drinking, and of course lovemaking.

1. Translated by William M. Davis. Abenámar refers to Yusuf IV, or Ibn al-Ahmar, who gained the throne of Granada with the help of Juan II of Castilia in 1431. The poem relates their meeting against the spectacular backdrop of the city, which has the last word in the ballad.

2. Comets were traditionally taken as omens, either for good or for ill.

3. Perched on a hilltop in the Sierra Nevada, the Alhambra was a vast fortified town complex centered around the palace itself. The Alixares was a further palace with gardens.

30 Of matchless garden fame,"[4]
Then spoke King don Juan,
Mark what he will say:
"With your consent, Granada,
I'd marry you today;
35 With Córdoba for dowry,
Sevilla for display."[5]
"I am a wife, King John,
No widow, but a wife,
The Moor who is my husband
40 Loves me more than life."

Those mountains, mother[1]

Those mountains, mother
are steep to climb,
where streams rush down
to fields of thyme.[2]

5 Those mountains, mother
have flowers above:
up where they are,
I have my love.

I will not pick verbena[1]

I will not pick verbena
on the morrow of St. John,[2]
for my lover has gone.

I will not pick sunflowers,
5 honeysuckle or carnations.
Only sorrows will I pluck
and cruel frustrations,
for my lover has gone.

Three Moorish Girls[1]

I am in love with three Moorish lasses in Jaén,[2]
Axa, Fátima and Marién.

---

4. The Torres Bermejas, or Crimson Towers, are a group of fortified towers near the entrance to the Alhambra. The Generalife ("Garden of the Builder") is an extensive series of gardens and pavilions leading eastward from the Alhambra to the summer palace.
5. The other two major cities of al-Andalus. Córdoba had fallen to Ferdinand III of Castilia in 1236, and Seville to the same ruler 12 years later. Granada was the last stronghold to fall, holding out until 1492.
1. Translated by James Duffy. From Diego Pisador, *Libro de Música de Vihuela* (1552), a collection of settings of traditional songs for the *vihuela,* a guitar-shaped instrument whose strings were plucked like a lute.

2. Literally, *toronjil,* lemon balm, a fragrant and medicinal herb of the mint family.
1. Translated by James Duffy. Verbena is a flower and a medicinal herb.
2. The midsummer festival of St. John's Day came on June 24; it was the traditional end of the season of festivals.
1. From the *Cancionero del Palacio.* Translated by Angela Buxton.
2. Lying north of Granada in Andalucía, Jaén was for a long time the frontier between Christians and Moors in medieval Spain, and the region was the scene of many battles before it was captured by Ferdinand III in 1246.

Three pretty Moorish lasses
went to pick olives,
5   and they found them already picked in Jaén.[3]
Axa, Fátima and Marién.

And they found them picked,
and they came back dismayed,
and their colour was gone in Jaén.
10   Axa, Fátima and Marién.

Three such lively Moorish lasses
went to pick apples
and they found them already picked in Jaén.
Axa, Fátima and Marién.

↤ ⟞◆⟠ ↦

Mozarabic Kharjas
10th–early 11th centuries

The *kharja* epitomizes the melting pot that was medieval Iberia. Written in Mozarabic, a Romance vernacular that was the common spoken language of al-Andalus, these brief verses originated in the refrains of popular dance. Hispano-Arabic (and, later, Hebrew) poets adapted these refrains as the final stanza (*kharja* means "exit") of a poetic form they invented in the tenth century, called the *muwashshah*. The body of the poem is a courtly love song with traditional Arabic images but a syllabic meter based on the melody of the concluding vernacular stanza. The *kharja* responds to the refined and idealized male voice of the poem's body with the frank, colloquial voice of a flesh-and-blood woman. Sixty-one *kharjas* survive, representing the earliest known body of Romance lyric.

As if you were a stranger[1]

Como si filyol' alyenu,	As if you were a stranger,
non mas adormis a meu senu.	you no longer fall asleep on my breast.

Ah tell me, little sisters[2]

Garid vos, ay yermanellas,	Ah tell me, little sisters,
com contenir a meu male!	how to hold my pain!
Sin al-habib non vivireyu—	I'll not live without my beloved—
advolarey demandare.	I shall fly to seek him again.

My lord Ibrahim[3]

Meu sidi Ibrahim,	My lord Ibrahim,
ya tu omne dolǧe,	oh my sweet love,
vent' a mib	come to me
de nohte!	at night!

3. The ambiguity over whether it is the girls or the olives that were "plucked" is heightened by the fact that *morilla* (Moorish girl) can also mean a small berry, or *mora*.
1. Translated by Peter Dronke. From two *muwashshahat:* Yehuda ha-Levi, "Panegyric [poem of praise] for Abu l-Hasan ben Qamniel" and an anonymous love poem.

2. Translated by Peter Dronke. From the *muwashshah* by Yehuda ha-Levi, "Panegyric for Ishaq ibn Qrispin."
3. Translated by Peter Dronke. From a *muwashshah* by Muhammad ibn Ubada, the Silk Merchant of Málaga (11th century).

5 In non, si non queris,   If not, if you don't want to,
   yireym' a tib.   I shall come to you.
   Gar me a ob   Tell me where
   legarte!   to see you!

I'll give you such love![4]

Tan t'amaray, illa con al-šarti   I'll give you such love!—but only if
                                            you'll bend

an taḡma' halhali ma' qurti!   my anklets right over to my earrings!

Take me out of this plight[5]

Alsa-me de min hali—   Take me out of this plight—
mon hali qad bare!   my state is desperate!
Que faray, ya 'ummi?—   Mother, what shall I do?—
Faneq bad lebare!   The falcon is about to snatch![6]

Mother, I shall not sleep[7]

Non dormireyo, mamma,   Mother, I shall not sleep
a rayo de manyana: When morning rises
í Bon Abū-l-Qāsim,   But dream of Abū-l-Qāsim,
la fage de matrama!   His features dawning.

Ibn Ḥazm
c. 994–1063

Born into a rich and influential family in Córdoba, Ibn Ḥazm published his masterpiece—and 400 other works in a wide range of fields—amid a life deeply embroiled in the intrigues of the disintegrating caliphate. In *The Dove's Neckring* (*Tawq al-hamama* c. 1024), a treatise on love combining verse and prose, Ibn Ḥazm took the nature imagery of the Islamic love poem—the dove, the garden—and used it to explore the mystical extremes of Greek philosophy. Much of this material was also personal in origin, containing memories of the estate of Ibn Ḥazm's childhood that had been destroyed in 1013. Exiled from Córdoba, he served as vizier to several short-lived caliphs and was several times imprisoned, then chose to withdraw from public life in 1024 or 1027 and write without any patron or court. Controversial to the last, he attached himself to several different schools of theology and law, and ended his life a recluse, prohibited from teaching.

from The Dove's Neckring[1]
A

I love you with a love that knows no waning, whereas some of men's loves
are midday mirages.[2]

---

4. Translated by Peter Dronke. From an anonymous *muwashshaḥ*.
5. Translated by Peter Dronke. From a *muwashshah* by Muhammad ibn Ubada.
6. The comparison of a lover to a falcon was a common image in love lyrics.

7. Translated by William M. Davis. From a *muwashshah* by Ibn Harun al-Asbahi of Lérida (12th century).
1. Translated by James T. Monroe.
2. A mirage is a deceptive apparition of objects in a distance due to the heat of intense sunshine. In midday mirages, objects appear flattened out.

I bear for you a pure, sincere love, and in [my] heart there is a clear picture
and an inscription [declaring] my love for you.
Moreover, if my soul were filled by anything but you, I would pluck it out,
while any membrane [covering it] would be torn away from it by [my]
hands.
I desire from you nothing but love, and that is all I request from you.

5   If I should come to possess it, then all the earth will [seem like] a senile
camel and mankind like motes[3] of dust, while the land's inhabitants will
[seem like] insects.

B

My love for you, which is eternal by reason of its very nature, has reached its
maximum proportions, hence it can neither decrease at all, nor increase.
Its only cause is the will, and no one knows any cause other than that!
When we discover that a thing is its own cause, then it is an existence that is
unperishing,
But when we find that [its cause] is in something other than itself, its destruction will come about when we lack that which gave it existence.

C

Are you from the world of the angels, or are you a mortal? Explain this to me,
for inability [to reach the truth] has made a mockery of my understanding.
I see a human shape, yet if I use my mind, then the body is [in reality] a celestial one.[4]
Blessed be He who arranged the manner of being of His creation in such a
way that you should be the [only] beautiful, natural light [in it].
I have no doubt but that you are that spirit which a resemblance joining one
soul to another in close relationship has directed toward us.

5   We lacked any proof that would bear witness to your creation, which we
could use in comparison, save only that you are visible.
Were it not that our eye contemplates [your] essence we could only declare
that you are the Sublime, True Reason.

D

I enjoy conversation when, in it, he is mentioned to me and exhales a [scent]
of sweet ambergris[5] for me.
If he should speak, among those who sit in my company, I listen only to the
words of that marvelous charmer.
Even if the Prince of the Faithful[6] should be with me, I would not turn aside
from [my love] for the former.
If I am compelled to leave him, I look back [at him] constantly and walk
like [an animal] wounded in the hoof.

---

3. Specks.
4. In the tradition of Neoplatonism, Ibn Ḥazm distinguishes
between a body perceived through the senses, and a celestial one, visible only to the mind. On the literal level, the
subject of the poem is the love object; on an allegorical

level, that love object is the intellect or soul itself.
5. Ambergris is a strongly scented waxy substance used in
perfumes. It is found in the bellies of sperm whales and
floating in warm seas.
6. The Prophet Muhammad.

5 My eyes remain fixed firmly upon him though my body has departed, as the
      drowning man looks at the shore from the fathomless sea.
   If I recall my distance from him, I choke as though with water, like the man
      who yawns in the midst of a dust storm and the sun's noonday heat.
   And if you say: "It is possible to reach the sky," I reply: "Yes, and I know
      where the stairs may be found."

E

   He who claims to love two lyingly commits perjury, just as Mānī is belied
      by his principles.[7]
   In the heart there is no room for two beloveds, nor is the most recent of
      things always the second.
   Just as reason is one, not recognizing any creator other than the One, the
      Clement,[8]
   Likewise the heart is one and loves only one, though he should put you off
      or draw you to him.
5 [He who claims to love two] is a suspect in the law of love; [he is] far from
      the true faith.
   Likewise, religion is one and straight, while he who has two religions is a
      profound disbeliever.

F

   Men have observed that I am a youth driven desperate by love; that I am
      brokenhearted, profoundly disturbed. And yet, by whom?
   When they look at my condition they become certain [of it], yet if they in-
      quire into the matter they are left in doubt.
   [I am] like a handwriting whose trace is clear, but which, if they seek to in-
      terpret it, cannot be explained;
   [I am] like the sound of a dove over a woody copse, cooing with its voice in
      every way,
5 Our ears delight in its melody, while its meaning remains obscure and
      unexplained.
   They say: "By God, name the one whose love has driven sweet sleep
      from you!"
   Yet I will never [name him]! Before they obtain what they seek, I will lose
      all my wits and face all misfortunes.
   Thus will they ever remain prey to doubts, entertaining suspicion like certi-
      tude and certitude like suspicion.

G

   Having seen the hoariness° on my temples and sideburns,   *graying*
      someone asked me how old I was.
   I answered him: "I consider all my life to have been but a short moment and
      nothing else, when I think reasonably and exactly."

---

7. Mānī was the 3rd-century C.E. Persian founder of the dualistic religion of Manichaeism, which maintained that existence was radically divided between Spirit and Matter, Good and Evil, and Light and Darkness, rather than unified under God as in orthodox monotheism.
8. Merciful.

He replied to me: "How was that? Explain it to me, for you have given me
the most grievous news and information."
So I said: "To the [girl] possessed of my heart I once gave one single kiss
by surprise.
5   Hence, no matter how many years I live, I will not really consider any but
that brief moment to have been my life."

H

They said: "He is far away." I replied: "It is enough for me that he is with
me in the same age without being able to escape.
The sun passes over me just as it does over him every day that shines anew.
Furthermore, is one between whom and me there lies only the distance of a
day's journey really far away,
When the wisdom of the God of creation joined us together? This mutual
proximity is enough [for me]; I want nothing further."

Ibn Rushd (Averroës)
1126–1198

Ibn Rushd was a crucial figure in Muslim Aristotelianism and in the rise of Scholasticism in
Christian Europe, where he was known as Averroës the Commentator. Born in Córdoba to a
family of jurists, he held the office of judge both there and in Seville, where he wrote the first
of his many commentaries on Aristotle in 1169. Following a brief period of disgrace and exile,
he was restored to grace before his death in Marrakesh. He wrote a total of thirty-eight commentaries, which restored Aristotle's philosophy to the rest of Europe through translations by
Andalusian Jews. Ibn Rushd was equally influential for his *Decisive Treatise,* which dealt with
the thorny issue of whether the study of philosophy was inimical to the strict observance of religious law.

from The Decisive Treatise Determining the Nature of the Connection Between Religion and Philosophy

from Chapter 1. The Law Makes Philosophic Studies Obligatory[1]

The Law,[2] then, has urged us to have demonstrative knowledge of God the Exalted
and all the beings of His creation. But it is preferable and even necessary for anyone,
who wants to understand God the Exalted and the other beings demonstratively, to
have first understood the kinds of demonstration and their conditions [of validity],
and in what respects demonstrative reasoning differs from dialectical, rhetorical and
fallacious reasoning.[3] But this is not possible unless he has previously learned what
reasoning as such is, and how many kinds it has, and which of them are valid and
which invalid. This in turn is not possible unless he has previously learned the parts of

---

1. Translated by G. F. Hourani.
2. The Qur'an.
3. According to Aristotle, there were three types of acceptable reasoning: demonstrative (based on true and primary

premises), dialectical (based upon generally accepted
opinions), rhetorical or persuasive (also based upon generally accepted opinions); there was also fallacious or faulty
reasoning.

reasoning, of which it is composed, i.e., the premises and their kinds. Therefore he who believes in the Law, and obeys its command to study beings, ought prior to his study to gain a knowledge of these things, which have the same place in theoretical studies as instruments have in practical activities.[4]

For just as the lawyer infers from the Divine command to him to acquire knowledge of the legal categories that he is under obligation to know the various kinds of legal syllogisms, and which are valid and which invalid, in the same way he who would know [God] ought to infer from the command to study beings that he is under obligation to acquire a knowledge of intellectual reasoning and its kinds. Indeed it is more fitting for him to do so, for if the lawyer infers from the saying of the Exalted,[5] "Reflect, you who have vision," the obligation to acquire a knowledge of legal reasoning, how much more fitting and proper that he who would know God should infer from it the obligation to acquire a knowledge of intellectual reasoning![6]

And again it is clear that in the study of beings this aim can be fulfilled by us perfectly only through successive examinations of them by one man after another, the later ones seeking the help of the earlier in that task, on the model of what has happened in the mathematical sciences. For if we suppose that the art of geometry did not exist in this age of ours, and likewise the art of astronomy, and a single person wanted to ascertain by himself the sizes of the heavenly bodies, their shapes, and their distances from each other, that would not be possible for him—e.g., to know the proportion of the sun to the earth or other facts about the sizes of the stars—even though he were the most intelligent of men by nature, unless by a revelation or something resembling revelation.[7] Indeed if he were told that the sun is about 150 or 160 times as great as the earth, he would think this statement madness on the part of the speaker, although this is a fact which has been demonstrated in astronomy so surely that no one who has mastered that science doubts it.

But what calls even more strongly for comparison with the art of mathematics in this respect is the art of the principles of law; and the study of law itself was completed only over a long period of time. And if someone today wanted to find out by himself all the arguments which have been discovered by the theorists of the legal schools on controversial questions, about which debate has taken place between them in most countries of Islam (except the West), he would deserve to be ridiculed, because such a task is impossible for him, apart from the fact that the work has been done already. Moreover, this is a situation that is self-evident not in the scientific arts alone but also in the practical arts; for there is not one of them which a single man can construct by himself. Then how can he do it with the art of arts, philosophy?[8] If this is so, then whenever we find in the works of our predecessors of former nations a theory about beings and a reflection on them conforming to what the conditions of demonstration require, we ought to study what they said about the matter and what they affirmed in their books.[9] And we should accept from them gladly and gratefully

---

4. Ibn Rushd has previously argued that the Law, or Qur'an, urges "reflections on beings," and that this is precisely the activity of philosophy. Here, he refines the relationship between the two: philosophy provides the tools (rational inquiry and syllogistic reasoning) to conduct the task commanded by the Qur'an.

5. God.

6. The phrase is from the Qur'an 59:2, which exhorts disbelievers to believe the power of God to banish them, as it will be demonstrated physically before their eyes.

7. In this argument, there are two means to acquire scientific knowledge: either by the accumulation of centuries of inquiry by many different people, or through divine revelation.

8. Philosophy is here called the "art of arts" because it examines the premises of all other arts and seeks to know first causes, the fundamental principles behind all phenomena.

9. Ibn Rushd is referring in particular to the ancient Greeks.

whatever in these books accords with the truth, and draw attention to and warn against what does not accord with the truth, at the same time excusing them.

From this it is evident that the study of the books of the ancients is obligatory by Law, since their aim and purpose in their books is just the purpose to which the Law has urged us, and that whoever forbids the study of them to anyone who is fit to study them, i.e., anyone who unites two qualities, (1) natural intelligence and (2) religious integrity and moral virtue, is blocking people from the door by which the Law summons them to knowledge of God, the door of theoretical study which leads to the truest knowledge of Him; and such an act is the extreme of ignorance and estrangement from God the Exalted.

And if someone errs or stumbles in the study of these books owing to a deficiency in his natural capacity, or bad organization of his study of them, or being dominated by his passions, or not finding a teacher to guide him to an understanding of their contents, or a combination of all or more than one of these causes, it does not follow that one should forbid them to anyone who is qualified to study them.[1] For this manner of harm which arises owing to them is something that is attached to them by accident, not by essence; and when a thing is beneficial by its nature and essence, it ought not to be shunned because of something harmful contained in it by accident.[2] This was the thought of the Prophet, peace on him, on the occasion when he ordered a man to give his brother honey to drink for his diarrhoea, and the diarrhoea increased after he had given him the honey: when the man complained to him about it, he said, "God spoke the truth; it was your brother's stomach that lied."[3] We can even say that a man who prevents a qualified person from studying books of philosophy, because some of the most vicious people may be thought to have gone astray through their study of them, is like a man who prevents a thirsty person from drinking cool, fresh water until he dies of thirst, because some people have choked to death on it. For death from water by choking is an accidental matter, but death by thirst is essential and necessary.

Ibn Arabi
1165–1240

Raised in Seville, the capital of the Almohad state, Ibn al-'Arabi converted to Sufism while still a teenager, following a warning vision. He traveled across Iberia seeking wisdom and guidance, including several meetings with the philosopher Ibn Rushd (page 766), then journeyed to North Africa and eastward on a pilgrimage to Mecca. He spent the last years of his life in Damascus. He produced numerous, often controversial esoteric works throughout his life; his poetry transposes those concerns through the lyric themes of nature, nostalgia, and love. Steeped in esoteric lore, a poem such as "Gentle now, doves" strives to render that lore immediately present through the experience of verse. (A further selection of his poems can be found in "Asceticism, Sufism, and Wisdom," page 480.)

---

1. This was a key point of contention in the debate over the use of pagan texts in theological study. Ibn Rushd argues that it is the contemporary philosopher rather than the ancient philosophy that is responsible for any error, or divergence from doctrine.
2. In Aristotelian philosophy an essence is a property or quality essential to the conception of a substance; an accident is a property or quality attributed but not essential to it. For example mortality can be considered essential to the definition of "human," while burial is not.
3. The story comes from the *Hadith,* the record of the traditions, or sayings of the Prophet Muhammad, second in authority only to the Qur'an.

Gentle now, doves[1]

Gentle now, doves of the thornberry
and moringa thicket,[2]
don't add to my heartache
your sighs.

5   Gentle now,
or your sad cooing
will reveal the love I hide,
the sorrow I hide away.

I echo back, in the evening,
10   in the morning, echo,
the longing of a love-sick lover,
the moaning of the lost.

In a grove of Gháda[3]
spirits wrestled,
15   bending the limbs down over me,
passing me away.

They brought yearning,
breaking of the heart,
and other new twists of pain,
20   putting me through it.

Who is there for me in Jám',
and the Stoning-Ground at Mína,[4]
who for me at Tamarisk Grove,
or at the way-station of Na'mán?

25   Hour by hour
they circle my heart
in rapture, in love-ache,
and touch my pillars with a kiss.

As the best of creation
30   circled the Ká'ba,[5]
which reason with its proofs
called unworthy,

He kissed the stones there—
and he was entrusted with the word!
35   And what is the house of stone
compared to a man or a woman?

1. Translated by Michael Sells.
2. The thornberry or arak tree grows in Arabia, parts of Africa, and eastern India; its roots and twigs are used as toothpicks. The moringa, or ben-nut tree, is native to India; its berries produce an aromatic oil.
3. The tamarisk is an evergreen-like shrub or small tree that grows in sandy terrain. Its leaves have been used in medicine; ghada wood produces a dense charcoal.
4. These are stations on the pilgrimage to Mecca. Pilgrims camp in Jam' or al-Muzdalifa on the ninth night; on the tenth, they travel to Mina, where they cast stones at a pillar representing the temptation of Shaitan, or Satan.
5. A small shrine near the center of the Great Mosque in Mecca, the Ká'ba is the most holy structure in Islam, held to be the center of the world, the direction in which Muslims perform their prayers. "The best of creation" is the Prophet Muhammad.

They swore, and how often!
they'd never change—piling up vows.
She who dyes herself red with henna
40 is faithless.

A white-blazed gazelle[6]
is an amazing sight,
red-dye signaling,
eyelids hinting,

45 Pasture between breastbones
and innards.
Marvel,
a garden among the flames!

My heart can take on
50 any form:
a meadow for gazelles,
a cloister for monks,

For the idols, sacred ground,
Ká'ba for the circling pilgrim,
55 the tables of the Toráh,
the scrolls of the Qur'án.

I profess the religion of love;
wherever its caravan turns along the way,
that is the belief,
60 the faith I keep.

Like Bishr,
Hind and her sister,
love-mad Qays and his lost Láyla,
Máyya and her lover Ghaylán.[7]

Solomon Ibn Gabirol
c. 1021–c. 1057

Born in Málaga in southern Spain, Ibn Gabirol was orphaned at an early age. Physically weak, temperamental and ill-at-ease with the courtier life, he spent his formative years in Saragossa, an important center of Jewish culture, where he immersed himself in a career of letters. He wrote some twenty volumes on philosophy and religion, most of which haven't survived. His influential secular treatise, *The Source of Life*, was translated from the Arabic into Latin in the twelfth century. Only during the nineteenth century was it discovered that its author, Avice-bron, was identical with the Andalusian Jew celebrated for his hymns and for his lyric poetry.

---

6. The gazelle is a conventional metaphor in Arabic love poetry for the beloved. As with Ibn al-'Arabi's other natural images, it also possesses a mystical meaning.

7. Names of celebrated Arab poets and lovers of previous centuries.

Poems such as "She looked at me and her eyelids burned" demonstrate Ibn Gabirol's skill in forging philosophical and religious preoccupations into powerfully unified visual images.

She looked at me and her eyelids burned[1]

She looked at me and her eyelids burned,
While her goblet brimmed with tears;
The words overflowed her mouth, like strings of pearls,
And the smile on her lips defied compare with gold.
5 But the rebuke she sent my soul
Wounded me like the words of the creditor to the poor debtor.
Meanwhile, the cup passed from hand to hand like the sun amid the
    heavens,
And day receded, fleeting, like waves along the shore,
But my blood, receding at unison of day,
10 Tinged my cheeks bright red: she will not return.

Behold the sun at evening[1]

Behold the sun at evening, red
    As if she wore vermillion robes.
Slipping the wraps from north and south
    She covers in purple the western side.
5 The earth—she leaves it cold and bare
    To huddle in shadows all night long.
At once the sky is dark; you'd think
    Sackcloth it wore for Yequtiel.[2]

The mind is flawed, the way to wisdom blocked[1]

The mind is flawed, the way to wisdom blocked;
    The body alone is seen, the soul is hid,
And those who seek the world find only ill;
    A man can get no pleasure here on earth.[2]
5 The servant rises up and kills his lord,
    And serving girls attack their mistresses.
Sons are raising hands against their parents,
    Daughters too oppose their parents' will.
My friend, from what I've seen of life I'd say
10   The best that one can hope is to go mad.
However long you live you suffer toil,
    And in the end you suffer rot and worms.
Then finally the clay goes back to clay;
    At last the soul ascends to join the Soul.[3]

1. Translated by William M. Davis.
1. Translated by Raymond P. Scheindlin.
2. This elegy was written on the occasion of the death of his patron, Yequtiel Ibn Hassan, in 1039. Sackcloth was a coarse fabric traditionally worn in mourning.
1. Translated by Raymond P. Scheindlin.

2. In the philosophical tradition of Neoplatonism, the soul is regarded as imprisoned in the body, its spiritual nature blocked by bodily needs and desire.
3. The soul is released by death to return to the great World Soul from which it had been torn to descend to its body on earth.

Winter wrote with the ink of its rains and showers[1]

Winter wrote with the ink of its rains and showers,
   The pen of its flashing lightning, and the hand of its clouds
A letter upon the garden in blue and purple,
   Of which no craftsman with all his skill could make the like,
5   Therefore, when the earth longed to see the sky,
   She embroidered on the twigs of her flowerbeds something like the stars.

Yehuda ha-Levi
before 1075–1141

Yehuda (or Judah) ha-Levi is the legendary figurehead of Sephardic Jewry, his life an emblem of the height and decline of its "Golden Age" in al-Andalus. A successful court physician, ha-Levi traveled throughout al-Andalus, frequently crossing into the Christian north, on whose border he had been born. Revered for his poetic gifts during his lifetime (over 800 of his poems survive), he became disenchanted with his success and the gilded life he led. In 1140 he left his home, setting sail for Jerusalem by way of Egypt, where he was seduced by the good life once again, tarrying as a court poet in Cairo and Alexandria for almost a year. He appears never to have reached the Promised Land, but in popular legend his pilgrimage led directly from Spain to the Western Wall of Jerusalem, where he died a violent death just before arriving. Only a few years after Yehuda ha-Levi's departure, Jewish power was fully dispersed by the Almohad dynasty; for the courtier rabbis, the Golden Age was over.

Poems like "My heart is in the East," "Your breeze, Western shore," and "From time's beginning" illustrate the ambivalence of Yehuda ha-Levi's attitude toward al-Andalus, his home from birth but also a place of exile where he was a man of influence yet also subject to Almoravid rule. He skillfully renewed the Arabic theme of the poet's longing for his lost homeland by merging individual longing with the national theme of the Exile of Israel. In addition to such poems of exile, he composed in a wide variety of forms from panegyric to religious meditations; included below are three poems of love and wine, another traditional genre.

Yehuda ha-Levi was equally celebrated for *The Book of the Khazars (Kitab al-khazari),* a prose meditation on Jewish history in the context of Greek philosophy, Islam, and Christianity. Composed in Arabic prose in the 1130s, it was based on the popular story of Bulan, an eighth- or ninth-century king of Khazaria near the Caspian Sea. Inspired by a dream vision, Bulan listens to the arguments of each religion before choosing Judaism and conducting a series of dialogues with a rabbi. He is persuaded by a principle analogous to the one that animates Yehuda ha-Levi's lyrics: not argument derived from abstract principles and beliefs, but on the basis of concrete experience, what had actually been done and prescribed by "the God of Abraham, Isaac, and Israel," whom he considered an active force in history and in his own life.

Cups without wine are lowly[1]

Cups without wine are lowly
As a pot thrown on the ground
But, full of juice, they shine
Like the body with a soul.

---

1. Translated by Raymond P. Scheindlin. Garden poetry was an important genre for both Arab and Jewish poets in Andalusia.

1. Translated by William M. Davis.

Ofra does her laundry with my tears[1]

Ofra does her laundry with my tears
   And spreads it out before her beauty's rays.
With my two eyes she needs no flowing well;
   Nor sun needs she: Her face provides the blaze.

Once when I fondled him upon my thighs[1]

Once when I fondled him upon my thighs
   He caught his own reflection in my eyes
And kissed my eyes, deceitful imp; I knew
   It was his image he kissed, and not my eyes!

From time's beginning, You were love's abode[1]

From time's beginning, You were love's abode:
   My love encamped wherever it was You tented.
The taunts of foes for Your name's sake are sweet,
   So let them torture one whom You tormented.

5   I love my foes; for they learned wrath from You,
   For they pursue a body You have slain.
The day You hated me I loathed myself,
   For I will honor none whom You disdain.

Until Your anger pass, and You restore
10   This people whom You rescued once before.

Your breeze, Western shore, is perfumed[1]

Your breeze, Western shore, is perfumed.
The scent of nard° is in its wings, and the apple.   *an aromatic plant*
Your origin is in the merchants' treasuries,
Surely not from the store-house of the wind.[2]
5   You flutter the wings of the bird, giving him freedom;
You are like flowing myrrh[3] straight from the phial.
How much do people long for you, since, with your help,
They are carried by wooden beams on the backs of the waves.
Do not let your hand slacken its hold on the ship,
10   Whether the day is encamped, or blows fresh at the dawn.
Smooth out the deep, split the heart of the seas,
Come to the holy mountains. There you can rest.
Rebuke the East wind which enrages the sea,
Turning the waves into a boiling cauldron.

---

1. Translated by Raymond P. Scheindlin. *Ofra* in Hebrew means a female fawn and is often a term for the poet's beloved.

1. Adapted by Yehuda ha-Levi from an Arabic original by al-Mutanabbi; English translation by Raymond P. Scheindlin. Homosexuality was common in al-Andalus, and the male beloved was a stock figure in the Arabic love poetry adapted by the Jewish poets.

1. Translated by Raymond P. Scheindlin—Yehuda ha-Levi adapts the Arabic situation of the lover who embraces abasement and rejection by her beloved, using it for Israel's attitude in exile from God.

1. Translated by David Goldstein.

2. Alluding to Psalm 135:7: "He bringeth forth the wind out of his treasuries."

3. Myrrh is a gum resin used for perfume. Like nard, it appears frequently in the Bible.

15 What shall a man do, chained to his Rock,
At one time confined, at another set free.
The essence of my request is in the hand of the Highest,
Who formed the mountains, who created the wind.

My heart is in the East[1]

My heart is in the East, and I in the depths of the West.
My food has no taste. How can it be sweet?
How can I fulfil my pledges and my vows,
When Zion is in the power of Edom, and I in the fetters of Arabia?[2]
5 It will be nothing to me to leave all the goodness of Spain.
So rich will it be to see the dust of the ruined sanctuary.[3]

from The Book of the Khazars[1]

I was asked to state what arguments and replies I could bring to bear against the attacks of philosophers and followers of other religions, and also against [Jewish] sectarians who attacked the rest of Israel. This reminded me of something I had once heard concerning the arguments of a Rabbi who sojourned with the King of the Khazars.[2] The latter, as we know from historical records, became a convert to Judaism about four hundred years ago. To him came a dream, and it appeared as if an angel addressed him, saying: "Thy way of thinking is indeed pleasing to the Creator, but not thy way of acting." Yet he was so zealous in the performance of the Khazar religion, that he devoted himself with a perfect heart to the service of the temple and sacrifices. Notwithstanding this devotion, the angel came again at night and repeated: "Thy way of thinking is pleasing to God, but not thy way of acting." This caused him to ponder over the different beliefs and religions, and finally become a convert to Judaism together with many other Khazars. As I found among the arguments of the Rabbi, many which appealed to me, and were in harmony with my own opinions, I resolved to write them down exactly as they had been spoken.

When the King of Khazar (as is related) dreamt that his way of thinking was agreeable to God, but not his way of acting, and was commanded in the same dream to seek the God-pleasing work, he inquired of a philosopher concerning his religious persuasion. The philosopher replied: There is no favour or dislike in [the nature of] God, because He is above desire and intention. A desire intimates a want in the person who feels it, and not till it is satisfied does he become (so to speak) complete. If it remains unfulfilled, he lacks completion. In a similar way He is, in the opinion of philosophers, above the knowledge of individuals, because the latter change with the

---

1. Translated by David Goldstein.
2. The poet asks how he can travel to the Holy Land ("Zion") when he is a tolerated minority in Arab Iberia, and Palestine has been conquered by the Christians in the First Crusade. (After the conquest of Jerusalem in 1099, the Crusaders had slaughtered not only Muslims but Jews within the city.) The Edomites were enemies of the ancient Israelites; "Edom" became a code word for Rome when Israel was part of the Roman empire, and here means the Christian occupiers of Palestine.
3. The sanctuary, the Temple of Jerusalem, was destroyed by the Romans in 70 C.E. as a consequence of the Jewish rebellion of 66. The ruins that remain are part of the

Western Wall, also known as the Wailing Wall.
1. Translated by Hartwig Hirschfeld. The Khazars were a Turkic people who flourished in southern Russia from around the mid-6th to the 13th centuries. At the height of its power, Khazaria controlled the Caucasus between the Black and the Caspian seas, and far north into what is now Russia.
2. King Bulan was converted in the 8th or 9th century, establishing Khazaria, long a refuge for persecuted Jews, as an independent Jewish kingdom. Khazaria included important trade routes between West and East, and was tolerant of the Christians, Muslims, and pagans living among them.

times, whilst there is no change in God's knowledge. He, therefore, does not know thee, much less thy thoughts and actions, nor does He listen to thy prayers, or see thy movements. If philosophers say that He created thee, they only use a metaphor, because He is the Cause of causes in the creation of all creatures, but not because this was His intention from the beginning. He never created man. For the world is without beginning, and there never arose a man otherwise than through one who came into existence before him, in whom were united forms, gifts, and characteristics inherited from father, mother, and other relations, besides the influences of climate, countries, foods and water, spheres, stars and constellations. Everything is reduced to a Prime Cause; not to a Will proceeding from this, but an Emanation from which emanated a second, a third, and fourth cause.[3] * * * Seek purity of heart in which way thou art able, provided thou hast acquired the sum total of knowledge in its real essence; then thou wilt reach thy goal, viz. the union with this Spiritual, or rather Active Intellect. Maybe he will communicate with thee or teach thee the knowledge of what is hidden through true dreams and positive visions.

Said to him the Khazari: Thy words are convincing, yet they do not correspond to what I wish to find. I know already that my soul is pure and that my actions are calculated to gain the favour of God. To all this I received the answer that this way of action does *not* find favour, though the intention does. There must no doubt be a way of acting, pleasing by its very nature, but not through the medium of intentions. If this be not so, why, then, do Christian and Moslim, who divide the inhabited world between them, fight with one another, each of them serving his God with pure intention, living either as monks or hermits, fasting and praying? For all that they vie with each other in committing murders, believing that this is a most pious work and brings them nearer to God. They fight in the belief that paradise and eternal bliss will be their reward. It is, however, impossible to agree with both.

The Philosopher replied: The philosophers' creed knows no manslaughter, as they only cultivate the intellect.

Al Khazari: What could be more erroneous, in the opinion of the philosophers, than the belief that the world was created in six days, or that the Prime Cause spoke with mortals, not to mention the philosophic doctrine, which declares the former to be above knowing details.[4] In addition to this one might expect the gift of prophecy quite common among philosophers, considering their deeds, their knowledge, their researches after truth, their exertions, and their close connexion with all things spiritual, also that wonders, miracles, and extraordinary things would be reported of them.[5] Yet we find that true visions are granted to persons who do not devote themselves to study or to the purification of their souls, whereas the opposite is the case with those who strive after these things. This proves that the divine influence as well as the souls have a secret which is not identical with what thou sayest, O Philosopher.

After this the Khazari said to himself: I will ask the Christians and Moslims, since one of these persuasions is, no doubt, the God-pleasing one. As regards the Jews, I am satisfied that they are of low station, few in number, and generally despised.[6]

---

3. The philosopher is a neo-Platonist, with a conception of God as the Prime Cause, the unknowable origin necessary to explain the observable natural phenomena to which it gave rise.

4. The king refers to the philosopher's assertion that the creation story of Genesis is only a metaphor for an impersonal emanation of the prime cause.

5. Like the "people of the book," the Jews, Christians and Moslims, Bulan seeks signs of the active working of God in the physical world rather than simply abstract knowledge.

6. The ironic reference to the lowly Jews serves a dramatic purpose in the dialogue and suggests the precarious situation of the Andalusian Jews in the time of the Crusades.

He then invited a Christian scholastic,[7] and put questions to him concerning the theory and practice of his faith.

The Scholastic replied: I believe that all things are created, whilst the Creator is eternal; that He created the whole world in six days; that all mankind sprang from Adam, and after him from Noah, to whom they trace themselves back; that God takes care of the created beings, and keeps in touch with man; that He shows wrath, pleasure, and compassion; that He speaks, appears, and reveals Himself to His prophets and favoured ones; that He dwells among those who please him. In short [I believe] in all that is written in the Tōrāh and the records of the Children of Israel, which are undisputed, because they are generally known as lasting, and have been revealed before a vast multitude. Subsequently the divine essence became embodied in an embryo in the womb of a virgin taken from the noblest ranks of Israelitish women.[8] She bore Him with the semblance of a human being, but covering a divinity, seemingly a prophet, but in reality a God sent forth. He is the Messiah, whom we call the Son of God, and He, is the Father, and the Son and the Holy Spirit. We condense His nature into one thing, although the Trinity appears on our tongues. We believe in Him and in His abode among the Children of Israel, granted to them as a distinction, because the divine influence never ceased to be attached to them, until the masses rebelled against this Messiah, and they crucified Him. Then divine wrath burdened them everlastingly, whilst the favour was confined to a few who followed the Messiah, and to those nations which followed these few. We belong to their number.

∗ ∗ ∗ Then said the Khazari: I see here no logical conclusion; nay, logic rejects most of what thou sayest. If both appearance and experience are so palpable that they take hold of the whole heart, compelling belief in a thing of which one is not convinced they render the matter more feasible by a semblance of logic. This is how natural philosophers deal with strange phenomena which come upon them unawares, and which they would not believe if they only heard of them without seeing them. When they have examined them, they discuss them, and ascribe them to the influence of stars or spirits without disproving ocular evidence. As for me, I cannot accept these things, because they come upon me suddenly, not having grown up in them. My duty is to investigate further.

He then invited one of the Doctors of Islām, and questioned him regarding his doctrine and observance.

The Doctor said: We acknowledge the unity and eternity of God, and that all men are derived from Adam-Noah. We absolutely reject embodiment, and if any element of this appears in the Writ, we explain it as a metaphor and allegory.[9] At the same time we maintain that our Book is the Speech of God, being a miracle which we are bound to accept for its own sake, since no one is able to bring anything similar to it, or to one of its verses. Our prophet is the Seal of the prophets, who abrogated every previous law, and invited all nations to embrace Islām.[1] The reward of the pious consists

---

7. Scholasticism arose in the 11th and 12th centuries out of a desire to reconcile Church dogma with the logical rigor of rational philosophical inquiry. Anselm of Canterbury and Peter Abelard (page 856) were important innovators; so was the engagement of the Andalusian Arabs Ibn Sina (Avicenna) and Ibn Rushd (Averroës) with the works of Aristotle, and of St. Thomas Aquinas after them.
8. From the matter of the Hebrew Bible, the Scholastic passes to that of the New Testament: the incarnation, life,

passion, and resurrection of Jesus Christ. It is implied in Luke's Gospel that Mary, mother of Jesus, was of priestly lineage.
9. According to Islam, Allah does not take human form, nor is it permissible in art to represent him as such.
1. The prophet Muhammad is considered the last and authoritative of the series of prophets ranging from Adam and Noah to Jesus.

in the return of his spirit to his body in paradise and bliss, where he never ceases to enjoy eating, drinking, woman's love, and anything he may desire. The requital of the disobedient consists in being condemned to the fire of hell, and his punishment knows no end.

Said to him the Khazari: If any one is to be guided in matters divine, and to be convinced that God speaks to man, whilst he considers it improbable, he must be convinced of it by means of generally known facts, which allow no refutation, and particularly imbue him with the belief that God has spoken to man. Although your book may be a miracle, as long as it is written in Arabic, a non-Arab, as I am, cannot perceive its miraculous character; and even if it were read to me, I could not distinguish between it and any other book written in the Arabic language.[2]

The Doctor replied: Yet miracles were performed by him, but they were not used as evidence for the acceptance of his law.

Al Khazari: Exactly so; but the human mind cannot believe that God has intercourse with man, except by a miracle which changes the nature of things. He then recognizes that to do so He alone is capable who created them from nought. It must also have taken place in the presence of great multitudes, who saw it distinctly, and did not learn it from reports and traditions. Even then they must examine the matter carefully and repeatedly, so that no suspicion of imagination or magic can enter their minds. Then it is possible that the mind may grasp this extraordinary matter, viz. that the Creator of this world and the next, of the heavens and lights, should hold intercourse with this contemptible piece of clay, I mean man, speak to him, and fulfil his wishes and desires.

The Doctor: Is not our Book full of the stories of Moses and the Children of Israel? No one can deny what He did to Pharaoh, how He divided the sea, saved those who enjoyed His favour, but drowned those who had aroused His wrath. Then came the manna and the quails during forty years, His speaking to Moses on the mount, making the sun stand still for Joshua, and assisting him against the mighty. [Add to this] what happened previously, viz. the Flood, the destruction of the people of Lot; is this not so well known that no suspicion of deceit and imagination is possible?

Al Khazari: Indeed, I see myself compelled to ask the Jews, because they are the relic of the Children of Israel. For I see that they constitute in themselves the evidence for the divine law on earth.[3]

He then invited a Jewish Rabbi, and asked him about his belief.

The Rabbi replied: I believe in the God of Abraham, Isaac and Israel, who led the children of Israel out of Egypt with signs and miracles; who fed them in the desert and gave them the land, after having made them traverse the sea and the Jordan in a miraculous way; who sent Moses with His law, and subsequently thousands of prophets, who confirmed His law by promises to the observant, and threats to the disobedient. Our belief is comprised in the Tōrāh—a very large domain.

I had not intended to ask any Jew, because I am aware of their reduced condition and narrow-minded views, as their misery left them nothing commendable. Now shouldst thou, O Jew, not have said that thou believest in the Creator of the world, its Governor and Guide, and in Him who created and keeps thee, and such attributes

---

2. For Bulan, the phenomenon of the Qur'an is no more provable than the miracles attested to by Christianity.

3. That is, as direct descendants of the tribes who witnessed the events of the Hebrew Bible, the Jews can be said to provide evidence of those events.

which serve as evidence for every believer, and for the sake of which He pursues justice in order to resemble the Creator in His wisdom and justice?[4]

The Rabbi: That which thou dost express is religion based on speculation and system, the research of thought, but open to many doubts. Now ask the philosophers, and thou wilt find that they do not agree on one action or one principle, since some doctrines can be established by arguments, which are only partially satisfactory, and still much less capable of being proved.[5]

Al Khazari: That which thou sayest now, O Jew, seems to be more to the point than the beginning, and I should like to hear more.

The Rabbi: Surely the beginning of my speech was just the proof, and so evident that it requires no other argument.

* * *

After this the Khazari, as is related in the history of the Khazars, was anxious to reveal to his Vizier in the mountains of Warsān[6] the secret of his dream and its repetition, in which he was urged to seek the God-pleasing deed. The king and his Vizier travelled to the deserted mountains on the sea shore, and arrived one night at the cave in which some Jews used to celebrate the Sabbath. They disclosed their identity to them, embraced their religion, were circumcised in the cave, and then returned to their country, eager to learn the Jewish law. They kept their conversion secret, however, until they found an opportunity of disclosing the fact gradually to a few of their special friends. When the number had increased, they made the affair public, and induced the rest of the Khazars to embrace the Jewish faith. They sent to various countries for scholars and books, and studied the Tōrāh. Their chronicles also tell of their prosperity, how they beat their foes, conquered their lands, secured great treasures; how their army swelled to hundreds of thousands, how they loved their faith, and fostered such love for the Holy House that they erected a Tabernacle in the shape of that built by Moses. They also honoured and cherished those born Israelites who lived among them. While the king studied the Tōrāh and the books of the prophets, he employed the Rabbi as his teacher, and put many questions to him on Hebrew matters.

Ramón Llull
1232–1315

A prolific polymath mystic, Ramón Llull wrote over 250 works, in Catalan and in Arabic, on nearly every subject there was. Born on the island of Majorca, during his youth he was a courtier and seneschal, or steward, before a mystical vision led him to retreat for nine years of hermitlike study in order to persuade the Jews and Muslims of the error of their faiths. Immersed in all three cultures of Iberia, his esoteric Christianity is well evident in the 366 allusive and lyrical aphorisms that make up the *Book of the Lover and the Beloved* (*Llibre d'amic et amat*), which forms chapter 99 of *Blanquerna* (1283), the first prose novel written in a romance language.

---

4. Rather than the general principles espoused by the previous three speakers, the Rabbi has based his belief only on those events recorded in Hebrew scripture and those laws recorded in the Torah, the first five books of the Bible.

5. While there is no agreement about the principles that caused the events, all three religions agree on the historical truth of the events themselves.
6. Mountains near the Khazar capital.

from Blanquerna: The Book of the Lover and the Beloved[1]

14. The Lover sought for one who should tell his Beloved how great trials he was enduring for love of Him, and how he was like to die. And he found his Beloved, who was reading in a book wherein were written all the griefs which love made him to suffer for his Beloved, and the joy which he had of his love.

16. "Say, thou bird that singest! Hast thou placed thyself in the care of my Beloved, that He may guard thee from indifference,[2] and increase in thee thy love?" The bird replied: "And who makes me to sing but the Lord of love, Who holds indifference to be sin?"

18. There was a contention between the eyes and the memory of the Lover, for the eyes said that it was better to behold the Beloved than to remember Him. But Memory said that remembrance brings tears to the eyes, and makes the heart to burn with love.

54. As one that was a fool went the Lover through a city, singing of his Beloved; and men asked him if he had lost his wits. "My Beloved," he answered, "has taken my will, and I myself have yielded up to Him my understanding; so that there is left in me naught but memory, wherewith I remember my Beloved."

69. The Lover extended and prolonged his thoughts of the greatness and everlastingness of his Beloved, and he found in Him neither beginning, nor mean,[3] nor end. And the Beloved said: "What measurest thou, O Fool?" The Lover answered: "I measure the lesser with the greater, defect with fulness, and beginning with infinity and eternity, to the end that humility, patience, charity and hope may be planted the more firmly in my remembrance."

70. The paths of love are both long and short. For love is clear, bright and pure, subtle yet simple, strong, diligent, brilliant, and abounding both in fresh thoughts and in old memories.

89. Love went apart with the Lover, and they had great joy of the Beloved; and the Beloved revealed himself to them. The Lover wept, and afterwards was in rapture, and Love swooned thereat.[4] But the Beloved brought life to His Lover by bringing to his memory His virtues.

98. The Beloved left the Lover, and the Lover sought Him in his thoughts, and enquired for Him of men in the language of love.

118. The Lover and the Beloved strove, and their love made peace between them. Which of them, think you, bore the stronger love toward the other?

---

1. Translated by E. Allison Peers. In the context of the novel, *The Book of the Lover and the Beloved* is written by the protagonist Blanquerna as an allegory of the faithful Christian and God, his Beloved, echoing the characters in the biblical Song of Songs (Volume A). Like other mystical writings using the language of love, the numbered aphoristic sentences are equally applicable to the

amorous situations they use to evoke a mystical state.
2. The translator uses "indifference" to translate the frequently occurring Catalan word *desamor,* which literally means "unlove," or "absence of love."
3. Middle.
4. Because of that.

130. With the pen of love, with the water of his tears, and on a paper of suffering, the Lover wrote letters to his Beloved. And in these he told how devotion tarried, how love was dying, and how sin and error were increasing the number of His enemies.

131. The Lover and the Beloved were bound in love with the bonds of memory, understanding, and will, that they might never be parted; and the cord wherewith these two loves were bound was woven of thoughts and griefs, sighs and tears.

132. The Lover lay in the bed of love: his sheets were of joys, his coverlet was of griefs, his pillow of tears. And none knew if the fabric of the pillow was that of the sheets or of the coverlet.

133. The Beloved clothed His Lover in vest, coat and mantle,[5] and gave him a helmet of love. His body He clothed with thoughts, his feet with tribulations, and his head with a garland of tears.

182. The Lover made complaint of his Beloved, because He caused Love so grievously to torment him. And the Beloved made reply by increasing his trials and perils, thoughts and tears.

194. One day the Lover ceased to remember his Beloved, and on the next day he remembered that he had forgotten Him. On the day when it came to the Lover that he had forgotten his Beloved, he was in sorrow and pain, and yet in glory and bliss—the one for his forgetfulness, and the other for his remembrance.

217. The Beloved chastened the heart of His Lover with rods of love, to make him love the tree whence He plucks the rods wherewith He chastens His lovers. And this is that tree whereon He suffered grief and dishonour and death, that He might bring back to love of Him those lovers whom He had lost.[6]

Dom Dinis, King of Portugal
1261–1325

An accomplished poet and patron of the arts, Dom Dinis opened his court to displaced poets from abroad: Provençal troubadours fleeing the Albigensian crusade in southwest France, Jews and Muslims fleeing the unrest in the southern half of the Iberian Peninsula. The coastal town of Santiago de Compostela was an important destination for medieval pilgrims and the performers who accompanied them. The Portuguese court was nourished by these influences, and Dom Dinis put this rich blend of talent to work copying and compiling luxurious illuminated manuscripts of songs.

Over a hundred texts of Dom Dinis's own songs have come down to us, along with the musical notation of seven compositions—all that we have, with seven of Martin Codax's, to indicate how the songs of the Galician-Portuguese tradition were actually performed. Most Occitanian and Northern French songs, with their more elusive melodies and extended, highly expressive lyrics, were rendered by voice alone, or with the spare accompaniment of the medieval fiddle. The Galician-Portuguese songs, although influenced by the French lyrics, also derived from a strong local tradition of refrain-based folk song. With catchier melodies and highly repetitive lyrics, these songs lent themselves to the greater instrumentation and dance beat of a

---

5. Sleeveless cloak.
6. This aphorism makes the Christian allegory more ex-

plicit than many of the others, with its recasting of the Passion of Christ in terms of the Lover and the Beloved.

small orchestra, which included the harp and the *pandeiro,* a square-frame drum, as well as the symphonie, a stringed instrument resembling a hurdy-gurdy.

Dom Dinis's version of the *canso* or love song is generally short with a refrain; he composed seventy-three of them. He also excelled in the *cantiga de amigo,* brief lyrics of love and longing written in the voice of a woman, usually waiting for or going to meet her lover. Nowhere else in medieval Europe were more women's songs composed, often superior in quality to the otherwise more common *cantiga de amor,* written in the voice of the male lover.

Provençals right well may versify[1]

Provençals right well may versify
And say they do with love
But those with verse in flowertime
And never else, I'd vow,
5   Their heart is not in torment
As mine is for my lady.

Although they're bound to versify
And praise as best they can,
Nonetheless, I'd vow
10   That those with verse in spring
And never else, will bring
No grief as deep as mine.

For those who versify with joy
About the verdant° time,   *greening*
15   The flowers do their bidding,
In spring, but soon decline,
Nor is their life perdition
Nor death in life, like mine.

Of what are you dying, daughter[1]

Of what are you dying, daughter, of body so fair?
Mother, I'm dying for the love my friend bestowed.
It's dawn, and quickly he goes.

Of what are you dying, daughter, of body so lithe?
5   Mother, I'm dying for the love my lover bestowed.
It's dawn, and quickly he goes.

Mother, I'm dying for the love my friend bestowed
whenever I look at this sash I tie for his love.
It's dawn, and quickly he goes.

10   Mother, I'm dying for the love my lover bestowed
whenever I look at this sash that I wear for his love.
It's dawn, and quickly he goes.

---

1. Translated by William M. Davis. The verb *trobar* ("versify," literally "to find") is a key word in the vocabulary of Occitan poetry referred to here by Dom Dinis, for it is also the source of the names, *troubadours* and *trobairitz.*

1. This and the following poems are translated by Barbara Hughes Fowler.

Whenever I look at this sash that I tie for his love
and remember, pretty me, how he spoke with me.
15   It's dawn, and quickly he goes.

Whenever I look at this sash that I wear for his love
and remember, pretty me, how both of us spoke.
It's dawn, and quickly he goes.

O blossoms of the verdant pine

O blossoms of the verdant pine,
if you have news of my friend?
    O God, where is he?

O blossoms of the verdant bough,
5   if you have news of my beloved?
    O God, where is he?

If you have news of my friend,
who lied about what he promised to me?
    O God, where is he?

10   If you have news of my beloved,
who lied about what he swore to me?
    O God, where is he?

You ask me about that friend of yours,
and I tell you that he is well and alive.
15   O God, where is he?

You ask me about that friend of yours,
and I tell you that he is alive and well.
    O God, where is he?

And I tell you that he is well and alive,
20   and will be with you before very long.
    O God, where is he?

And I tell you that he is alive and well
and will be with you now very soon.
    O God, where is he?

The lovely girl arose at earliest dawn

The lovely girl
arose at earliest dawn,
and goes to wash her camisoles
    at the river swirl.
5   She goes to wash them at earliest dawn.

The elegant girl
arose at earliest dawn,
and goes to wash her petticoats
    at the river swirl.
10   She goes to wash them at earliest dawn.

She goes to wash her camisoles.
She rose at earliest dawn.
The wind is scattering them
    at the river swirl.
15   She goes to wash them at earliest dawn.

She goes to wash her petticoats.
She rose at earliest dawn.
The wind has born them off
    at the river swirl.
20   She goes to wash them at earliest dawn.

The wind is scattering them.
She rose at earliest dawn.
At dawn she was enraged
    at the river swirl.
25   She goes to wash them at earliest dawn.

Martin Codax
fl. mid-13th century

In 1914, a parchment leaf was found inside the binding of a book in Madrid. It contained the words and music to seven *cantigas de amigo,* or "songs for a friend," composed by Martin Codax in Galician-Portuguese at the court of Ferdinand III of Castile in the mid-thirteenth century. We know nothing about him except the name, but the poems provide rare firsthand evidence of how lyric was performed on the Iberian Peninsula. The high degree of parallelism from stanza to stanza in both words and melody mirrors the dominant image of the sea in the delicate form known as the *marinha,* or sea-song. End-rhyme intensifies the parallelism; in "O waves that I've come to see," for example, rhymes of words ending in *-er* and *-ar* play off each other like the waves of the sea that is serving the speaker as her mirror and confidante. The musical settings stretch out the key words, particularly *amigo* (friend, lover), stressing the mood they create, before finishing on the plaintive and brief monosyllables, *sin min,* "without me."

Ah God, if only my love could know[1]

Ah God, if only my love could know
how much I am alone in Vigo,[2]
    and go about in love.

Ah God, if he knew, my dearest one,
5   how I am in Vigo, all alone!
    and go about in love.

How in Vigo, alone, I stay—
and near me not a single spy,
    and go about in love.

1. Translated by Peter Dronke.
2. The area around Vigo, in Galicia on the northwest coast of the Iberian Peninsula south of Santiago de Compostela,
has been inhabited since prehistory. During the middle ages, it was a port town dependent on the Cistercian monastery of Melón.

10   How in Vigo I stay alone,
with no spies around me, none,
    and go about in love.

And I have no spies with me,
only my eyes, that weep with me,
15   and go about in love.

And near me now I have no spies
—only my pair of weeping eyes—
    and go about in love.

My beautiful sister, come hurry with me[1]

My beautiful sister, come hurry with me
to the church of Vigo beside the turbulent sea,
    and we shall marvel at the waves.

My beautiful sister, come hurry, please,
5   to the church of Vigo beside the tumultuous sea,
    and we shall marvel at the waves.

To the church of Vigo beside the turbulent sea,
and there will come here, mother, my friend,
    and we shall marvel at the waves.

10   To the church of Vigo beside the tumultuous sea,
and there will come here, my mother, my love,
    and we shall marvel at the waves.

O waves that I've come to see[1]

O waves that I've come to see,
if you know, tell to me
    why my love lingers
    without me.

5   O waves that I've come to view,
if you know, reveal to me
    why my love lingers
    without me.

CROSSCURRENTS: IBERIA, THE MEETING OF THREE WORLDS

- Arabic poetry was a dominant genre in the early middle ages from Iberia east-
ward throughout the Islamic empire. For a further selection, see the texts in pre-
Islamic poetry (page 329), and the Perspectives sections "Poetry, Wine, and
Love" (page 384) and "Asceticism, Sufism, and Wisdom" (page 490). The epic

1. Translated by Barbara Hughes Fowler.   1. Translated by Barbara Hughes Fowler.

Poem of the Cid (page 664) provides an equally complex depiction of the relations between Christians and Muslims in medieval Iberia. *Sir Gawain and the Green Knight* (page 801), the *Lais* of Marie de France (page 787), and Dante's *Divine Comedy* (page 903) provide a different perspective on pagan and Christian encounters and influences within medieval Europe.

- The meeting of different worlds has been an important theme since the earliest days of literature. The selections in the section on The Ancient Near East (Volume A) are replete with examples of cross-cultural encounters, especially "Perspectives: Strangers in a Strange Land." Like those selections, Euripides' *Medea* depicts the phenomenon of being an exile in a new land. How do these depictions of exile and immigration differ in emphasis from the depiction of the *Convivencia* in medieval Iberia?

- The description of foreign countries and cultures has long been a staple of literature, frequently employed to comment indirectly on the writer's own culture. How do writers such as Marco Polo (page 1069), Ibn Battuta (page 519), Montaigne ("On Cannibals," Volume C), Lady Wortley Montagu (Volume D), and those in "Perspectives: Journeys in Search of Self" (Volume D) and "Perspectives: Occidentalism—Europe Through Foreign Eyes" (Volume E) use travel writing to comment on both their own world and those to which they travel?

- Although the Muslim rule of medieval Iberia saw its fair share of warfare, it was neither as bloody nor as one-sided as the colonial expansion of Europe. Vivid examples are provided in the selections in "Perspectives: The Conquest and Its Aftermath" (Volume C), Joseph Conrad's *Heart of Darkness* (Volume F), Chinua Achebe's *Things Fall Apart* (Volume F), and the texts in "Perspectives: Postcolonial Conditions" (Volume F). How does the depiction of the encounter between Europeans and the indigenous peoples of the Americas, Africa, and Asia compare with the depiction of medieval Iberia?

⇌ END OF PERSPECTIVES: IBERIA, THE MEETING OF THREE WORLDS ⇌

Marie de France

mid-12th–early 13th centuries

What we know for certain about the author of the *Lais* is neither more nor less than the name she gives herself: *Sui Marie e sui de France* ("I am Marie and am from France"). She wrote in the French dialect called Anglo-Norman, probably for the French-speaking Norman audience in England around the court of Henry II and Eleanor of Aquitaine. It has been conjectured from her familiarity with court life that she may have been an illegitimate half-sister to Henry; she was in all likelihood of noble blood. The *Lais* are her best and best-known work; a collection of animal fables and a translation of a Latin otherworld journey, *St. Patrick's Purgatory*, have also been attributed to her. The *Lais* is a group of short narratives in verse, tales of courtly love and adventure based on the oral traditions of Brittany. The Norman conquest of 1066 had opened up a vogue for the *matière de Bretagne*, the Celtic legends that included those of King Arthur and the lovers Tristan and Yseult.

Marie was writing at a time of enormous change in French society and culture. The tradition of tracing familial descent through the maternal side of the family had recently been supplanted by paternal ancestry. The orally based couplets of the traditional *chanson de geste,* or epic, had given way to the more musical and psychologically flexible eight-syllable couplets of the romance. As Marie translated her Celtic sources into French verse, she changed their focus as well, creating a series of ethical tests for her characters, male and female, in which she could explore the conflicts between social constraints and individual desire, and between real life and the world of fantasy. While rooted in the world of legend, the *Lais* are also concerned with the complex politics of the feudal court. The knight Lanval, for example, suffers first from his lack of status at Arthur's court, and then, like the later Gawain in *Sir Gawain and the Green Knight,* from his lack of poise in fending off the unwanted advances of a powerful ruler, Queen Guinevere.

Legendary motifs are strongly in evidence. The plot of *Bisclavret,* for example, turns on the protagonist's monthly transformation into a wolf. In other tales, we find self-guiding boats, magical women, a man who can transform himself into a bird, a woman who can appear invisibly to her lover, and a potion bestowing superhuman strength. Marie wields these motifs strategically to demarcate places where the cold reality of the feudal structure is incompatible with the more fanciful demands of the individual. In the conventional tale of chivalry, the knight would ride out, seeking to test himself through adventures. But in Marie's world, adventure tends to seek out the knights and ladies, and their response to an unforeseen event or encounter will determine their failure or success in the world. In *Bisclavret,* the wife, the werewolf, and the king are presented in turn with crucial ethical decisions that have no obvious cultural precedent. The scenario of the brief tale *Chevrefoil,* based on the famous legend of Tristan and Yseult, is more limited. Here Marie ignores the best-known parts—the love potion accidentally drunken by Tristan and the bride he is bringing to King Mark or the efforts of the king and his courtiers' to catch the adulterous couple in the act. Instead, Marie selects a little-known episode following the knight's banishment. The adventure that befalls the lovers is a chance meeting; their proper response to this opportunity determines the possibility of a brief, perfect moment of union.

Marie's characters do not reveal themselves through their thoughts, as modern protagonists tend to do. They discover themselves, and we are asked to analyze them, through their actions, and through comparison from one *lai* to the next. The *Lais* are structured like a series of permutations of a fixed set of variables in a laboratory experiment. We find the positive counterpart of Bisclavret's wife in *Eliduc,* for example, and his tragic counterpart in the bird-man of *Yonec.* It is evident that the *Lais* had a didactic component along with their role as court entertainment. The feudal system was based on the exchange of loyalty for land and protection, guided by a complex code of behavior, and resulting in a constantly shifting set of allegiances. The role of women in this society was especially contradictory. An apparently powerful queen and patron such as Eleanor of Aquitaine could just as easily be locked in a tower for fifteen years, as she was by Henry II between 1174 and 1189. Rulers such as Eleanor and Marie, countess of Champagne, could patronize the arts, and women such as Marie could be prominent poets and authors while possessing little or no actual power, being regarded primarily as items of barter, providers of land and heirs. These women were celebrated as goddesses of love while deprived of any agency to act on that love. Marie's female characters both embody this double bind and find ways of negotiating what modicum of freedom and happiness might be possible within it.

PRONUNCIATIONS:
Bisclavret: bees-KLAH-vray
Chevrefoil: CHEV-r'foy

from LAIS

Prologue[1]

Whoever has received knowledge
and eloquence in speech from God
should not be silent or secretive
but demonstrate it willingly.

5 When a great good is widely heard of,
then, and only then, does it bloom,
and when that good is praised by many,
it has spread its blossoms.
The custom among the ancients—

10 as Priscian testifies—
was to speak quite obscurely
in the books they wrote,
so that those who were to come after
and study them

15 might gloss° the letter   *explain*
and supply its significance from their own wisdom.[2]
Philosophers knew this,
they understood among themselves
that the more time they spent,

20 the more subtle their minds would become
and the better they would know how to keep themselves
from whatever was to be avoided.
He who would guard himself from vice
should study and understand

25 and begin a weighty work
by which he might keep vice at a distance,
and free himself from great sorrow.[3]
That's why I began to think
about composing some good stories

30 and translating from Latin to Romance;
but that was not to bring me fame:
too many others have done it.
Then I thought of the *lais* I'd heard.
I did not doubt, indeed I knew well,

35 that those who first began them
and sent them forth
composed them in order to preserve

---

1. Translated by Joan M. Ferrante and Robert W. Hanning. Like many medieval prologues, this one takes a series of commonplaces and gives them a particular spin. The first theme derives from Jesus's parable of the talents (Matthew 25:14–32). Marie justifies her writing the *lais* as the laudable exercise of a God-given talent.
2. Priscian (fl. c. 500 C.E.) wrote what became the standard textbook of Latin grammar in the Middle Ages, the *Institutiones grammaticae* ("Grammatical Foundations").

"Glossing" a text meant not only explaining its grammatical constructions, but also revealing allegorical meaning hidden beneath the "letter" or literal meaning of the words.
3. Here, studying and glossing provide an occupation that both removes temptation toward more vicious activities and distracts the mind from sorrow. This could either mean the tribulations of Fortune (in a philosophical context) or the sufferings of love (in a courtly context, as below).

adventures they had heard.[4]
I have heard many told;
40   and I don't want to neglect or forget them.
To put them into word and rhyme
I've often stayed awake.

In your honor, noble King,[5]
who are so brave and courteous,
45   repository of all joys
in whose heart all goodness takes root,
I undertook to assemble these *lais*
to compose and recount them in rhyme.
In my heart I thought and determined,
50   sire, that I would present them to you.
If it pleases you to receive them,
you will give me great joy;
I shall be happy forever.
Do not think me presumptuous
55   if I dare present them to you.
Now hear how they begin.

Bisclavret (The Werewolf)

Since I am undertaking to compose *lais,*
I don't want to forget Bisclavret;
In Breton, the *lai*'s name is *Bisclavret*—
the Normans call it *The Werewolf.*[1]
5   In the old days, people used to say—
and it often actually happened—
that some men turned into werewolves
and lived in the woods.
A werewolf is a savage beast;
10   while his fury is on him
he eats men, does much harm,
goes deep in the forest to live.
But that's enough of this for now:
I want to tell you about the Bisclavret.

15   In Brittany there lived a nobleman
whom I've heard marvelously praised;
a fine, handsome knight
who behaved nobly.
He was close to his lord,
20   and loved by all his neighbors.
He had an estimable wife,
one of lovely appearance;

---

4. Rather than the classical themes she has been enumerating, Marie proposes the novelty of the *lais*, oral folktales rather than written manuscripts.
5. It was customary for the prologue to conclude with a dedication to the poet's patron, here most likely Henry II.
1. "*Garwaf*." As in the Prologue, Marie emphasizes the task of translation, explaining the meaning of key words in both languages.

he loved her and she him,
but one thing was very vexing to her:
25   during the week he would be missing
for three whole days, and she didn't know
what happened to him or where he went.
Nor did any of his men know anything about it.
One day he returned home
30   happy and delighted;
she asked him about it.
"My lord," she said, "and dear love,
I'd very much like to ask you one thing—
if I dared;
35   but I'm so afraid of your anger
that nothing frightens me more."
When he heard that, he embraced her,
drew her to him and kissed her.
"My lady," he said, "go ahead and ask!
40   There's nothing you could want to know,
that, if I knew the answer, I wouldn't tell you."
"By God," she replied, "now I'm cured!
My lord, on the days when you go away from me
I'm in such a state—
45   so sad at heart,
so afraid I'll lose you—
that if I don't get quick relief
I could die of this very soon.
Please, tell me where you go,
50   where you have been staying.
I think you must have a lover,
and if that's so, you're doing wrong."
"My dear," he said, "have mercy on me, for God's sake!
Harm will come to me if I tell you about this,
55   because I'd lose your love
and even my very self."
When the lady heard this
she didn't take it lightly;
she kept asking him,
60   coaxed and flattered him so much,
that he finally told her what happened to him—
he hid nothing from her.
"My dear, I become a werewolf:
I go off into the great forest,
65   in the thickest part of the woods,
and I live on the prey I hunt down."
When he had told her everything,
she asked further
whether he undressed or kept his clothes on.°   *as a werewolf*
70   "Wife," he replied, "I go stark naked."
"Tell me, then, for God's sake, where your clothes are."

"That I won't tell you;
for if I were to lose them,
and then be discovered,
75   I'd stay a werewolf forever.
I'd be helpless
until I got them back.
That's why I don't want their hiding place to be known."
"My lord," the lady answered,
80   "I love you more than all the world;
you mustn't hide anything from me
or fear me in any way:
that doesn't seem like love to me.
What wrong have I done? For what sin of mine
85   do you mistrust me about anything?
Do the right thing and tell me!"
She harassed and bedeviled him so,
that he had no choice but to tell her.
"Lady," he said, "near the woods,
90   beside the road that I use to get there,
there's an old chapel
that has often done me good service;
under a bush there is a big stone,
hollowed out inside;
95   I hide my clothes right there
until I'm ready to come home."
The lady heard this wonder
and turned scarlet from fear;
she was terrified of the whole adventure.
100   Over and over she considered
how she might get rid of him;
she never wanted to sleep with him again.
There was a knight of that region
who had loved her for a long time,
105   who begged for her love,
and dedicated himself to serving her.
She'd never loved him at all,
nor pledged her love to him,
but now she sent a messenger for him,
110   and told him her intention.
"My dear," she said, "cheer up!
I shall now grant you without delay
what you have suffered for;
you'll meet with no more refusals—
115   I offer you my love and my body;
make me your mistress!"
He thanked her graciously
and accepted her promise,
and she bound him to her by an oath.
120   Then she told him

how her husband went away and what happened to him;
she also taught him the precise path
her husband took into the forest,
and then she sent the knight to get her husband's clothes.
125   So Bisclavret was betrayed,
ruined by his own wife.
Since people knew he was often away from home
they all thought
this time he'd gone away forever.
130   They searched for him and made inquiries
but could never find him,
so they had to let matters stand.
The wife later married the other knight,
who had loved her for so long.
135   A whole year passed
until one day the king went hunting;
he headed right for the forest
where Bisclavret was.
When the hounds were unleashed,
140   they ran across Bisclavret;
the hunters and the dogs
chased him all day,
until they were just about to take him
and tear him apart,
145   at which point he saw the king
and ran to him, pleading for mercy.
He took hold of the king's stirrup,
kissed his leg and his foot.
The king saw this and was terrified;
150   he called his companions.
"My lords," he said, "come quickly!
Look at this marvel—
this beast is humbling itself to me.
It has the mind of a man, and it's begging me for mercy!
155   Chase the dogs away,
and make sure no one strikes it.
This beast is rational—he has a mind.
Hurry up: let's get out of here.
I'll extend my peace to the creature;
160   indeed, I'll hunt no more today!"
Thereupon the king turned away.
Bisclavret followed him;
he stayed close to the king, and wouldn't go away;
he'd no intention of leaving him.
165   The king led him to his castle;
he was delighted with this turn of events,
for he'd never seen anything like it.
He considered the beast a great wonder
and held him very dear.

170   He commanded all his followers,
       for the sake of their love for him, to guard Bisclavret well,
       and under no circumstances to do him harm;
       none of them should strike him;
       rather, he should be well fed and watered.
175   They willingly guarded the creature;
       every day he went to sleep
       among the knights, near the king.
       Everyone was fond of him;
       he was so noble and well behaved
180   that he never wished to do anything wrong.
       Regardless of where the king might go,
       Bisclavret never wanted to be separated from him;
       he always accompanied the king.
       The king became very much aware that the creature loved him.
185   Now listen to what happened next.
       The king held a court;
       to help him celebrate his feast
       and to serve him as handsomely as possible,
       he summoned all the barons
190   who held fiefs from him.[2]
       Among the knights who went,
       and all dressed up in his best attire,
       was the one who had married Bisclavret's wife.
       He neither knew nor suspected
195   that he would find Bisclavret so close by.
       As soon as he came to the palace
       Bisclavret saw him,
       ran toward him at full speed,
       sank his teeth into him, and started to drag him down.
200   He would have done him great damage
       if the king hadn't called him off,
       and threatened him with a stick.
       Twice that day he tried to bite the knight.
       Everyone was extremely surprised,
205   since the beast had never acted that way
       toward any other man he had seen.
       All over the palace people said
       that he wouldn't act that way without a reason:
       that somehow or other, the knight had mistreated Bisclavret,
210   and now he wanted his revenge.
       And so the matter rested
       until the feast was over
       and until the barons took their leave of the king
       and started home.
215   The very first to leave,

---

2. Who were bound to him in oaths of fealty.

to the best of my knowledge,
was the knight whom Bisclavret had attacked.
It's no wonder the creature hated him.
Not long afterward,
220 as the story leads me to believe,
the king, who was so wise and noble,
went back to the forest
where he had found Bisclavret,
and the creature went with him.
225 That night, when he finished hunting,
he sought lodging out in the countryside.
The wife of Bisclavret heard about it,
dressed herself elegantly,
and went the next day to speak with the king,
230 bringing rich presents for him.
When Bisclavret saw her coming,
no one could hold him back;
he ran toward her in a rage.
Now listen to how well he avenged himself!
235 He tore the nose off her face.
What worse thing could he have done to her?
Now men closed in on him from all sides;
they were about to tear him apart,
when a wise man said to the king,
240 "My lord, listen to me!
This beast has stayed with you,
and there's not one of us
who hasn't watched him closely,
hasn't traveled with him often.
245 He's never touched anyone,
or shown any wickedness,
except to this woman.
By the faith that I owe you,
he has some grudge against her,
250 and against her husband as well.
This is the wife of the knight
whom you used to like so much,
and who's been missing for so long—
we don't know what became of him.
255 Why not put this woman to torture
and see if she'll tell you
why the beast hates her?[3]
Make her tell what she knows!
We've seen many strange things
260 happen in Brittany!"
The king took his advice;

3. Torture was a common means of interrogation, especially for gaining confessions. The king's advisor takes the beast's attack as evidence of the lady's guilt.

he detained the knight.
At the same time he took the wife
and subjected her to torture;
265   out of fear and pain
she told all about her husband:
how she had betrayed him
and taken away his clothes;
the story he had told her
270   about what happened to him and where he went;
and how after she had taken his clothes
he'd never been seen in his land again.
She was quite certain
that this beast was Bisclavret.
275   The king demanded the clothes;
whether she wanted to or not
she sent home for them,
and had them brought to Bisclavret.
When they were put down in front of him
280   he didn't even seem to notice them;
the king's wise man—
the one who had advised him earlier—
said to him, "My lord, you're not doing it right.
This beast wouldn't, under any circumstances,
285   in order to get rid of his animal form,
put on his clothes in front of you;
you don't understand what this means:
he's just too ashamed to do it here.
Have him led to your chambers
290   and bring the clothes with him;
then we'll leave him alone for a while.
If he turns into a man, we'll know about it."
The king himself led the way
and closed all the doors on him.
295   After a while he went back,
taking two barons with him;
all three entered the king's chamber.
On the king's royal bed
they found the knight asleep.
300   The king ran to embrace him.
He hugged and kissed him again and again.
As soon as he had the chance,
the king gave him back all his lands;
he gave him more than I can tell.
305   He banished the wife,
chased her out of the country.
She went into exile with the knight
with whom she had betrayed her lord.
She had several children
310   who were widely known

for their appearance:
several women of the family
were actually born without noses,
and lived out their lives noseless.[4]

315   The adventure that you have heard
really happened, no doubt about it.
The *lai* of Bisclavret was made
so it would be remembered forever.

Chevrefoil (The Honeysuckle)

I should like very much
to tell you the truth
about the *lai* men call *Chevrefoil*—
why it was composed and where it came from.

5   Many have told and recited it to me
and I have found it in writing,
about Tristan and the queen
and their love that was so true,
that brought them much suffering

10   and caused them to die the same day.[1]
King Mark was annoyed,
angry at his nephew Tristan;
he exiled Tristan from his land
because of the queen whom he loved.[2]

15   Tristan returned to his own country,
South Wales, where he was born,
he stayed a whole year;
he couldn't come back.
Afterward he began to expose himself

20   to death and destruction.
Don't be surprised at this:
for one who loves very faithfully
is sad and troubled
when he cannot satisfy his desires.

25   Tristan was sad and worried,
so he set out from his land.
He traveled straight to Cornwall,
where the queen lived,
and entered the forest all alone—

4. The *lai* includes a folktale-style explanation of the origin of a physical defect in the family. It also suggests that punishment for misbehavior will be passed through the generations.

1. The tragic love affair of Tristan and Yseult was based on a Celtic legend. There were various written sources Marie could have known, including the Anglo-Norman version of Thomas (c. 1170), composed at the court of Henry II, which was also the source for Gottfried von

Strassburg's celebrated medieval German version. The episode she recounts, however, doesn't exist in other versions, although she assumes her audience was familiar with them, not even naming Yseult ("the queen").

2. Mark, king of Cornwall, had sent Tristan to Ireland to win Yseult as his queen. A love potion caused the pair to fall in love, and when Mark discovered their affair, he banished his nephew.

30 he didn't want anyone to see him;
    he came out only in the evening
    when it was time to find shelter.
    He took lodging that night,
    with peasants, poor people.
35 He asked them for news
    of the king—what he was doing.
    They told him they had heard
    that the barons had been summoned by ban.
    They were to come to Tintagel
40 where the king wanted to hold his court;[3]
    at Pentecost they would all be there,[4]
    there'd be much joy and pleasure,
    and the queen would be there too.
    Tristan heard and was very happy;
45 she would not be able to go there
    without his seeing her pass.
    The day the king set out,
    Tristan also came to the woods
    by the road he knew
50 their assembly must take.
    He cut a hazel tree in half,
    then he squared it.
    When he had prepared the wood,
    he wrote his name on it with his knife.
55 If the queen noticed it—
    and she should be on the watch for it,
    for it had happened before
    and she had noticed it then—
    she'd know when she saw it,
60 that the piece of wood had come from her love.
    This was the message of the writing
    that he had sent to her:
    he had been there a long time,
    had waited and remained
65 to find out and to discover
    how he could see her,
    for he could not live without her.
    With the two of them it was just
    as it is with the honeysuckle
70 that attaches itself to the hazel tree:
    when it has wound and attached
    and worked itself around the trunk,
    the two can survive together;
    but if someone tries to separate them,

3. The Norman castle of Tintagel, on the northwestern coast of Cornwall, was built on the site of a Celtic monastery held to be the birthplace of King Arthur.
4. Pentecost, or Whitsunday, commemorates the descent of the Holy Spirit upon the disciples, seven Sundays after the resurrection of Christ. It was a major spring festival in the Christian year, and, along with Christmas and Easter, a traditional time for a king to hold full court.

75   the hazel dies quickly
and the honeysuckle with it.
"Sweet love, so it is with us:
You cannot live without me, nor I without you."
The queen rode along;
80   she looked at the hillside
and saw the piece of wood; she knew what it was,
she recognized all the letters.
The knights who were accompanying her,
who were riding with her,
85   she ordered to stop:
she wanted to dismount and rest.
They obeyed her command.
She went far away from her people
and called her girl
90   Brenguein,[5] who was loyal to her.
She went a short distance from the road;
and in the woods she found him
whom she loved more than any living thing.
They took great joy in each other.
95   He spoke to her as much as he desired,
she told him whatever she liked.
Then she assured him
that he would be reconciled with the king—
for it weighed on him
100   that he had sent Tristan away;
he'd done it because of the accusation.[6]
Then she departed, she left her love,
but when it came to the separation,
they began to weep.
105   Tristan went to Wales,
to wait until his uncle sent for him.
For the joy that he'd felt
from his love when he saw her,
by means of the stick he inscribed
110   as the queen had instructed,
and in order to remember the words,
Tristan, who played the harp well,
composed a new *lai* about it.
I shall name it briefly:
115   in English they call it *Goat's Leaf*
the French call it *Chevrefoil*.[7]
I have given you the truth
about the *lai* that I have told here.

---

5. Yseult's companion and waiting-woman; Brenguein plays an important role in the Tristan romances.
6. Like most courtly lovers, Tristan and Yseult were harassed by ill-wishing courtiers or *losengiers*, who try to trap them. King Mark, meanwhile, would prefer to believe

that the affair does not exist.
7. As in *Bisclavret*, Marie emphasizes her title word (and the meaning embodied in it) through a focus on its translation.

⊷ ⊠⧫⊠ ⊶

Sir Gawain and the Green Knight
late 14th century

Like the verdant half-giant whose intrusion initiates and concludes its action, *Sir Gawain and the Green Knight* is a dominant and inescapable but also a mysterious and inexplicable presence in medieval English poetry. Like *Beowulf* before it, it survives in a single manuscript. Its importance was not appreciated until the nineteenth century, it is written in a now obscure dialect of Middle English, and its author is destined to remain anonymous. But the intrigue of its history is nothing to the spell of the poem itself. While his contemporary Chaucer set the language and poetic conventions of French and Italian within a narrative frame of everyday realism, the *Gawain*-poet (as scholars refer to the poem's author) made everyday reality fit the adventures and wonders of the Arthurian romance, the (primarily French) tales of King Arthur and his knights that were the most popular reading material of the English aristocracy of the day.

LANGUAGE AND TRADITION
The poem is divided into four "fits," or sections—the right length for an evening's performance to entertain a noble patron and his courtiers. Like the other three poems contained in the manuscript—also most likely by the *Gawain*-poet—it is written in the Middle English dialect of the northwest Midlands, perhaps Cheshire near the border with Wales. Like Chaucer, the *Gawain*-poet was quite familiar with the Anglo-Norman dialect of Old French that had been used at the court since the Norman Conquest, as well as the Latin that had been used by clerics throughout the Middle Ages, but his vocabulary also bears many traces of the Scandinavian rulers the Normans had superseded. Danish and other Viking invaders had held northern England from the mid-ninth until the mid-eleventh century, and their language—not to mention the alliterative poetry bequeathed by earlier Anglo-Saxon colonizers—filters into the poem, just as its wildness bespeaks a northern attitude toward nature and the world quite different from the southward-gazing culture of London. Literate Englanders were conversant with both traditions, however; Chaucer several times parodied the alliterating verse incomprehensible to the "Southren" man, who preferred his lines to rhyme. Having disappeared (at least from written sources) following the Norman Conquest, the alliterative tradition of stressed, unrhymed lines had been revived during the second half of the fourteenth century; still, the new wave for which Chaucer implicitly argued, the rhyming couplets and London dialect that would dominate English poetry for centuries, had won the day by the early fifteenth century.

As one would expect from a poem composed in a self-consciously local language and poetic form, *Gawain* is all about traditions, customs, and conventions. It begins by recounting the legend of *translatio imperii,* tracing Arthur's lineage back to the fall of Troy. Set during the midwinter festival of Christmas, the action is then introduced by one of Arthur's rules for feasting: "he wolde never ete / Upon such a dere day er hym devised were / Of sum aventurus thing an uncouthe tale, / Of sum mayn mervayle, that he might trawe"—he will not sit at table until some marvel or adventure occurs beforehand that he can "trawe," trust or believe. A marvel appears to order: a hulking knight, dressed in green from head to toe, and green of skin besides, who proposes a shocking Beheading Game. These marvelous motifs have their origin in French romance as well as in the nature cults of pre-Christian Britain. The knight Gawain's acceptance of the game will require him to seek out the Green Knight the following winter, in order to receive the blow his adversary has miraculously survived. This quest frames the story, but in the middle, the poet introduces an apparently unconnected episode of temptation and testing in the remote castle of a noble lord and his seductive lady. Only at the very end does the poet reveal the significance of these two stories, and the way they are related to one another as tests of Gawain's faith and mettle.

COURT AND CASTLE

Rather than reconcile his different sources and different traditions, the *Gawain*-poet strikes a fine if precarious balance between them, asking the reader to consider the ramifications of Gawain's choices and predicament, both for himself and for those around him. Nor is the *Gawain*-poet concerned to spell out for his readers how seriously he expects this tale to be taken, and whether we are meant to sympathize with Gawain or to smile at his predicament. It seems that the life of a knight hangs in the balance, and even more so his honor and that of the court to which he belongs, and the Christian virtues associated with that court in the High Middle Ages. But high spirits reign throughout, at Arthur's court, in the manners of the Green Knight, and at the castle of Sir Bertilak de Hautdesert and his queen. In a tale of chivalry such as Marie de France's *Bisclavret* (page 788), there is nothing outside the court for the werewolf beside the alienated inhumanity of the beast; his sufferings show us how essential civility and trust are to society. By contrast, although the Green Knight probably derives from Celtic traditions of the wild man of the woods, he poses a legitimate challenge to the Christian court. He knows its customs, but flaunts them; he conducts himself in the exuberance of arrogant confidence, even as he exposes his neck for the blow of Gawain's axe; he follows some unknown code of conduct, and this makes his appearance all the more uncanny in the familiar world of Camelot.

The poet has other ways of keeping our expectations agreeably off-balance. Just as the Green Knight's challenge recalls but also mutates the pattern of Arthurian adventures, so Gawain's journey to find the unknown site where he must keep his appointment with death gives a surprising twist to the knight errant's customary questing. His goal is fantastic, as is the castle that appears in answer to his Christmas Eve prayers, but the landscape is described in the palpably realistic terms of a northern winter, and the path he takes would have been recognized by readers of the time as the principal route from the south of England through Wales to the region of Cheshire. In a similar fashion, activities at the castle are carefully balanced: for three consecutive days, the lord of the castle rides out hunting, while his lady remains at home, engaging Gawain in amorous games and testing his ability to juggle the rules of courtly love with those of hospitality and honor. Each evening, the two knights "exchange" the "trophies" they have "won" during the day, the wild game of the one for the kisses of the other.

FORM AND RHYTHM

The form of the poem is also a balance of meters, and of control and disorder. Each of its 101 stanzas contains a varying number of long lines: syllables range in number from seven to fourteen, and stressed alliterating consonants vary as well, although three is most normal. Each stanza concludes with what is called a "bob and wheel"—a two-syllable line plus four slightly longer lines, rhymed in an *ababa* scheme, as if in a gesture to the rhyming verse of the Continental romance. Take, for example, the extraordinary scene of the 23-line twentieth stanza, as the headless torso of the Green Knight has just picked up his bleeding head from where it had skipped about the banquet-room floor:

> For the hede in his honde he haldez up even,
> Toward the derrest on the dece he dressez the face,
> And hit lyfte up the yghe-lyddez and loked ful brode,
> And meled thus much with his muthe, as ye may now here:
> "Loke, Gawan, thou be graythe to go as thou hettez,
> And layte as lelly til thou me, lude, fynde,
> As thou hatz hette in this halle, herande thise knyghtes;
> To the grene chapel thou chose, I charge the, to fotte
> Such a dunt as thou hatz dalt, disserved thou habbez
> To be yederly yolden on Nw Yeres morn.
> The knyght of the grene chapel men knowen me mony,
> Forthi me for to fynde if thou fraystez, faylez thou never.

Therfore com, other recreaunt be calde thou behoves."
With a runisch rout the raynez he tornez,
Halled out at the hal dor, his hed in his hande,
That the fyr of the flynt flaghe fro fole hoves.
To quat kyth he becom knwe non there,
Never more than thay wyste from quethen he watz wonnen.
        What thenne?
    The kyng and Gawan thare
    At that grene thay laghe and grenne;
    Yet breved watz hit ful bare
    A mervayl among tho menne.

                   (Tolkien, Gordon, and Davis edition)

For the head in his hand he held it up straight,
towards the fairest at the table he twisted the face,
and it lifted up its eyelids and looked at them broadly,
and made such words with its mouth as may be recounted.
"See thou get ready, Gawain, to go as thou vowedst,
and as faithfully seek till thou find me, good sir,
as thou hast promised in this place in the presence of these knights.
To the Green Chapel go thou, and get thee, I charge thee,
such a dint as thou hast dealt—indeed thou hast earned
a nimble knock in return on New Year's morning!
The Knight of the Green Chapel I am known to many,
so if to find me thou endeavor, thou'lt fail not to do so.
Therefore come! Or to be called a craven thou deservest."
With a rude roar and rush his reins he turned then,
and hastened out through the hall-door with his head in his hand,
and fire of the flint flew from the feet of his charger.
To what country he came in that court no man knew,
no more than they had learned from what land he had journeyed.
        Meanwhile,
    the king and Sir Gawain
    at the Green Man laugh and smile;
    yet to men had appeared, 'twas plain,
    a marvel beyond denial.

The unhurried rhythm of the alliterative lines emphasizes the uncanny lack of hurry in the headless knight's actions, his half-mocking, half-somber mood seemingly unaffected by Gawain's blow. The brevity of the bob-and-wheel perfectly captures the dumbfounded reaction of the king and Gawain to the baffling event they have seen. We don't know whether they are grimacing out of horror, laughing out of defiance, or chuckling in disbelief, and the near-identity of *grene* and *grenne* ("green" and "grin") combines with the alliteration to increase the difficulty of interpreting what has happened. Moreover, the final two lines balance the prior pair, redefining the Old French romance term *mervayl* to capture precisely this combination of laughter, horror, and incomprehension.

And yet, this melodious Continental label cannot erase the lingering dread of the harsh Anglo-Saxon syllables of the Green Man's insistence on what Gawain had *hette,* or pledged, *to fotte / such a dunt as thou hatz dalt,* literally, "to fetch such a dint as thou hast dealt." The *Gawain*-poet knew Dante's *Commedia* well, but what a world of difference there is between this talking head and the dripping "lantern" held up by the dead poet Bertran de Born in the eighth circle of Hell (page 1003)! The head of Dante's poet damns his body in a tragic image of abuse of the gift of language and eloquence, elaborating the Christian law whereby, through his sins, Bertran has equally severed himself from the blessed body of the saved in Heaven. The *Gawain*-poet shares with Dante the use of vivid realism to bring alive an impossible image, but the Green Knight escapes the constraints of the familiar Christian setting of the Christmas Eve feast in the Arthurian court, just as his actions exceed the bounds of decorum, and his body mocks the laws of nature. Like Gawain's ambiguous adversary, this poem delights in its inscrutable power over its audience, and revels in its own refusal to be controlled.

Sir Gawain and the Green Knight[1]
Part 1

When the siege and the assault had ceased at Troy,
and the fortress fell in flame to firebrands and ashes,
the traitor who the contrivance of treason there fashioned
was tried for his treachery, the most true upon earth—
5   it was Aeneas[2] the noble and his renowned kindred
who then laid under them lands, and lords became
of well-nigh all the wealth in the Western Isles.[3]
When royal Romulus to Rome his road had taken,
in great pomp and pride he peopled it first,
10   and named it with his own name that yet now it bears;
Tirius[4] went to Tuscany and towns founded,
Langaberde[5] in Lombardy uplifted halls,
and far over the French flood Felix Brutus
on many a broad bank and brae[6] Britain established
15   full fair,
     where strange things, strife and sadness,
     at whiles in the land did fare,
     and each other grief and gladness
     oft fast have followed there.

20   And when fair Britain was founded by this famous lord,[7]
bold men were bred there who in battle rejoiced,
and many a time that betid they troubles aroused.
In this domain more marvels have by men been seen
than in any other that I know of since that olden time;
25   but of all that here abode in Britain as kings
ever was Arthur most honoured, as I have heard men tell.
Wherefore a marvel among men I mean to recall,
a sight strange to see some men have held it,
one of the wildest adventures of the wonders of Arthur.

1. This translation, remarkably faithful to the original alliterative meter and stanza form, is by J. R. R. Tolkien.
2. Aeneas led the survivors of Troy to Italy, after a series of ambiguous omens and misadventures. In medieval tradition, he was also said to have plotted to betray his own city. "The traitor" in line 3, though, may refer to the Trojan Antenor, also said to have betrayed Troy.
3. Perhaps Europe, or just the British Isles. Many royal houses traced their ancestry to Rome and Troy.
4. Possibly Titus Tatius, ancient king of the Sabines.
5. Ancestor of the Lombards, and a nephew of Brutus.
6. The steep bank bounding a river valley.
7. According to Geoffrey of Monmouth and others, a great-grandson of Aeneas, exiled after accidentally killing his father and later the founder of Britain.

30   If you will listen to this lay but a little while now,
    I will tell it at once as in town I have heard
        it told,
        as it is fixed and fettered
        in story brave and bold,
35   thus linked and truly lettered,
        as was loved in this land of old.

    This king lay at Camelot[8] at Christmas-tide
    with many a lovely lord, lieges most noble,
    indeed of the Table Round[9] all those tried brethren,
40   amid merriment unmatched and mirth without care.
    There tourneyed many a time the trusty knights,
    and jousted full joyously these gentle lords;
    then to the court they came at carols to play.
    For there the feast was unfailing full fifteen days,
45   with all meats and all mirth that men could devise,
    such gladness and gaiety as was glorious to hear,
    din of voices by day, and dancing by night;
    all happiness at the highest in halls and in bowers
    had the lords and the ladies, such as they loved most dearly.
50   With all the bliss of this world they abode together,
    the knights most renowned after the name of Christ,
    and the ladies most lovely that ever life enjoyed,
    and he, king most courteous, who that court possessed.
    For all that folk so fair did in their first estate[1]
55   abide,
        Under heaven the first in fame,
        their king most high in pride;
        it would now be hard to name
        a troop in war so tried.

60   While New Year was yet young that yestereve had arrived,
    that day double dainties on the dais were served,
    when the king was there come with his courtiers to the hall,
    and the chanting of the choir in the chapel had ended.
    With loud clamour and cries both clerks and laymen
65   Noel announced anew, and named it full often;
    then nobles ran anon with New Year gifts,
    Handsels,° handsels they shouted, and handed them out,   *gifts*
    Competed for those presents in playful debate;
    ladies laughed loudly, though they lost the game,
70   and he that won was not woeful, as may well be believed.[2]

8. Arthur's capital, probably in Wales, perhaps at Caerleon-on-Usk where Arthur had been crowned. Knights were expected to gather at his court, in celebration and homage, on the five liturgical holidays on which Arthur wore his crown: Easter, Ascension, Pentecost, All Saints' Day, and Christmas.
9. Its shape symbolized the unity of Arthur's knights but also avoided disputes over precedence.

1. Arthur is emphatically a young king here, even "boyish." The phrase may also recall the Golden Age, an era of uncorrupted happiness.
2. The distribution of New Year's gifts displayed the king's wealth and power; it was also the occasion here of some courtly game of exchange, in which the loser perhaps gave up a kiss.

All this merriment they made, till their meat was served;
then they washed, and mannerly went to their seats,
ever the highest for the worthiest, as well held to be best.
Queen Guinevere the gay was with grace in the midst

75 of the adorned dais[3] set. Dearly was it arrayed:
finest sendal° at her sides, a ceiling above her   *thin silk*
of true tissue of Toulouse, and tapestries of Tharsia
that were embroidered and bound with the brightest gems
one might prove and appraise to purchase for coin

80   any day.
          That loveliest lady there
          on them glanced with eyes of grey;
          that he found ever one more fair
          in sooth might no man say.

85 But Arthur would not eat until all were served;
his youth made him so merry with the moods of a boy,
he liked lighthearted life, so loved he the less
either long to be lying or long to be seated:
so worked on him his young blood and wayward brain.

90 And another rule moreover was his reason besides
that in pride he had appointed: it pleased him not to eat
upon festival so fair, ere he first were apprised
of some strange story or stirring adventure,
or some moving marvel that he might believe in

95 of noble men, knighthood, or new adventures;
or a challenger should come a champion seeking
to join with him in jousting, in jeopardy to set
his life against life, each allowing the other
the favour of fortune, were she fairer to him.

100 This was the king's custom, wherever his court was holden,
at each famous feast among his fair company
          in hall.
          So his face doth proud appear,
          and he stands up stout and tall,

105   all young in the New Year;
          much mirth he makes with all.

Thus there stands up straight the stern king himself,
talking before the high table of trifles courtly.
There good Gawain was set at Guinevere's side,

110 with Agravain a la Dure Main on the other side seated,
both their lord's sister-sons, loyal-hearted knights.
Bishop Baldwin had the honour of the board's service,
and Iwain Urien's[4] son ate beside him.
These dined on the dais and daintily fared,

---

3. A medieval nobleman's hall typically had a raised platform at one end, on which the "high table" stood.
4. Another nephew of Arthur. The relationship of uncle
and nephew is close in many Arthurian romances, and noble youths were often sent to be raised by an uncle on the
mother's side.

115   and many a loyal lord below at the long tables.
       Then forth came the first course with fanfare of trumpets,
       on which many bright banners bravely were hanging;
       noise of drums then anew and the noble pipes,[5]
       warbling wild and keen, wakened their music,
120   so that many hearts rose high hearing their playing.
       Then forth was brought a feast, fare of the noblest,
       multitude of fresh meats on so many dishes
       that free places were few in front of the people
       to set the silver things full of soups on cloth
125   so white.
            Each lord of his liking there
            without lack took with delight:
            twelve plates to every pair,
            good beer and wine all bright.

130   Now of their service I will say nothing more,
       for you are all well aware that no want would there be.
       Another noise that was new drew near on a sudden,
       so that their lord might have leave at least to take food.
       For hardly had the music but a moment ended,
135   and the first course in the court as was custom been served,
       when there passed through the portals a perilous horseman,
       the mightiest on middle-earth in measure of height,
       from his gorge to his girdle so great and so square,
       and his loins and his limbs so long and so huge,
140   that half a troll upon earth I trow° that he was,   *trust; believe*
       but the largest man alive at least I declare him;
       and yet the seemliest for his size that could sit on a horse,
       for though in back and in breast his body was grim,
       both his paunch and his waist were properly slight,
145   and all his features followed his fashion so gay
                in mode;
            for at the hue men gaped aghast
            in his face and form that showed;
            as a fay-man fell he passed,
150   and green all over glowed.

       All of green were they made, both garments and man:
       a coat tight and close that clung to his sides;
       a rich robe above it all arrayed within
       with fur finely trimmed, shewing fair fringes
155   of handsome ermine gay, as his hood was also,
       that was lifted from his locks and laid on his shoulders;
       and trim hose tight-drawn of tincture alike
       that clung to his calves; and clear spurs below
       of bright gold on silk broideries banded most richly,
160   though unshod were his shanks, for shoeless he rode.

5. Holiday banquets were formalized, almost theatrical.

And verily all this vesture was of verdure clear,
both the bars on his belt, and bright stones besides
that were richly arranged in his array so fair,
set on himself and on his saddle upon silk fabrics:

165   it would be too hard to rehearse one half of the trifles
that were embroidered upon them, what with birds and with flies
in a gay glory of green, and ever gold in the midst.
The pendants of his poitrel,° his proud crupper,   *breast-plate*
his molains,° and all the metal to say more, were enamelled,   *mouthpiece*

170   even the stirrups that he stood in were stained of the same;
and his saddlebows in suit, and their sumptuous skirts,
which ever glimmered and glinted all with green jewels;
even the horse that upheld him in hue was the same,
     I tell:

175   a green horse great and thick,
     a stallion stiff to quell,
     in broidered bridle quick:
     he matched his master well.

Very gay was this great man guised all in green,

180   and the hair of his head with his horse's accorded:
fair flapping locks enfolding his shoulders,
a big beard like a bush over his breast hanging
that with the handsome hair from his head falling
was sharp shorn to an edge just short of his elbows,

185   so that half his arms under it were hid, as it were
in a king's capadoce[6] that encloses his neck.
The mane of that mighty horse was of much the same sort,
well curled and all combed, with many curious knots
woven in with gold wire about the wondrous green,

190   ever a strand of the hair and a string of the gold;
the tail and the top-lock were twined all to match
and both bound with a band of a brilliant green:
with dear jewels bedight° to the dock's ending,   *fastened*
and twisted then on top was a tight-knitted knot

195   on which many burnished bells of bright gold jingled.
Such a mount on middle-earth, or man to ride him,
was never beheld in that hall with eyes ere that time;
     for there
     his glance was as lightning bright,

200   so did all that saw him swear;
     no man would have the might,
     they thought, his blows to bear.

And yet he had not a helm, nor a hauberk[7] either,
not a pisane,[8] not a plate that was proper to arms;

205   not a shield, not a shaft, for shock or for blow,

---

6. Probably a hooded cape, fastened under the chin.
7. A tunic of chain mail.

8. A piece of armor to protect the upper part of the chest and neck.

but in his one hand he held a holly-bundle,
that is greatest in greenery when groves are leafless,
and an axe in the other, ugly and monstrous,
a ruthless weapon aright for one in rhyme to describe:

210   the head was as large and as long as an ellwand,°   *yardstick*
a branch of green steel and of beaten gold;
the bit, burnished bright and broad at the edge,
as well shaped for shearing as sharp razors;
the stem was a stout staff, by which sternly he gripped it,

215   all bound with iron about to the base of the handle,
and engraven in green in graceful patterns,
lapped round with a lanyard that was lashed to the head
and down the length of the haft was looped many times;
and tassels of price were tied there in plenty

220   to bosses of the bright green, braided most richly.
Such was he that now hastened in, the hall entering,
pressing forward to the dais—no peril he feared.
To none gave he greeting, gazing above them,
and the first word that he winged: "Now where is," he said,

225   "the governor of this gathering? For gladly I would
on the same set my sight, and with himself now talk
        in town."
        On the courtiers he cast his eye,
        and rolled it up and down;

230   he stopped, and stared to espy
        who there had most renown.

Then they looked for a long while, on that lord gazing;
for every man marvelled what it could mean indeed
that horseman and horse such a hue should come by

235   as to grow green as the grass, and greener it seemed,
than green enamel on gold glowing far brighter.
All stared that stood there and stole up nearer,
watching him and wondering what in the world he would do.
For many marvels they had seen, but to match this nothing;

240   wherefore a phantom and fay-magic folk there thought it,
and so to answer little eager was any of those knights,
and astounded at his stern voice stone-still they sat there
in a swooning silence through that solemn chamber,
as if all had dropped into a dream, so died their voices

245   away.
        Not only, I deem, for dread;
        but of some 'twas their courtly way
        to allow their lord and head
        to the guest his word to say.

250   Then Arthur before the high dais beheld this wonder,
and freely with fair words, for fearless was he ever,
saluted him, saying: "Lord, to this lodging thou'rt welcome!
The head of this household Arthur my name is.

Alight, as thou lovest me, and linger, I pray thee;
255 and what may thy wish be in a while we shall learn."
"Nay, so help me," quoth the horseman, "He that on high is throned,
to pass any time in this place was no part of my errand.
But since thy praises, prince, so proud are uplifted,
and thy castle and courtiers are accounted the best,
260 the stoutest in steel-gear that on steeds may ride,
most eager and honourable of the earth's people,
valiant to vie with in other virtuous sports,
and here is knighthood renowned, as is noised in my ears:
'tis that has fetched me hither, by my faith, at this time.
265 You may believe by this branch that I am bearing here
that I pass as one in peace,[9] no peril seeking.
For had I set forth to fight in fashion of war,
I have a hauberk at home, and a helm also,
a shield, and a sharp spear shining brightly,
270 and other weapons to wield too, as well I believe;
but since I crave for no combat, my clothes are softer.
Yet if thou be so bold, as abroad is published,
thou wilt grant of thy goodness the game that I ask for
    by right."
275   Then Arthur answered there,
    and said: "Sir, noble knight,
    if battle thou seek thus bare,
    thou'lt fail not here to fight."

"Nay, I wish for no warfare, on my word I tell thee!
280 Here about on these benches are but beardless children.
Were I hasped in armour on a high charger,
there is no man here to match me—their might is so feeble.
And so I crave in this court only a Christmas pastime,
since it is Yule and New Year, and you are young here and merry.
285 If any so hardy in this house here holds that he is,
if so bold be his blood or his brain be so wild,
that he stoutly dare strike one stroke for another,
then I will give him as my gift this guisarm[1] costly,
this axe—'tis heavy enough—to handle as he pleases;
290 and I will abide the first brunt, here bare as I sit.
If any fellow be so fierce as my faith to test,
hither let him haste to me and lay hold of this weapon—
I hand it over for ever, he can have it as his own—
and I will stand a stroke from him, stock-still on this floor,
295 provided thou'lt lay down this law: that I may deliver him another.
    Claim I!
    And yet a respite I'll allow,
    till a year and a day go by.

9. A holly branch could symbolize peace and was used in games of the Christmas season.

1. A long-handled ax with a spike at the end.

  Come quick, and let's see now
300   if any here dare reply!"

If he astounded them at first, yet stiller were then
all the household in the hall, both high men and low.
The man on his mount moved in his saddle,
and rudely his red eyes he rolled then about,
305 bent his bristling brows all brilliantly green,
and swept round his beard to see who would rise.
When none in converse would accost him, he coughed then loudly,
stretched himself haughtily and straightway exclaimed:
"What! Is this Arthur's house," said he thereupon,
310 "the rumour of which runs through realms unnumbered?
Where now is your haughtiness, and your high conquests,
your fierceness and fell mood, and your fine boasting?
Now are the revels and the royalty of the Round Table
overwhelmed by a word by one man spoken,
315 for all blench now abashed ere a blow is offered!"
With that he laughed so loud that their lord was angered,
the blood shot for shame into his shining cheeks
   and face;
  as wroth as wind he grew,
320 so all did in that place.
  Then near to the stout man drew
  the king of fearless race,

And said: "Marry! Good man, 'tis madness thou askest,
and since folly thou hast sought, thou deservest to find it.
325 I know no lord that is alarmed by thy loud words here.
Give me now thy guisarm, in God's name, sir,
and I will bring thee the blessing thou hast begged to receive."
Quick then he came to him and caught it from his hand.
Then the lordly man loftily alighted on foot.
330 Now Arthur holds his axe, and the haft grasping
sternly he stirs it about, his stroke considering.
The stout man before him there stood his full height,
higher than any in that house by a head and yet more.
With stern face as he stood he stroked at his beard,
335 and with expression impassive he pulled down his coat,
no more disturbed or distressed at the strength of his blows
than if someone as he sat had served him a drink
   of wine.
  From beside the queen Gawain
340 to the king did then incline:
  "I implore with prayer plain
  that this match should now be mine."

"Would you, my worthy lord," said Gawain to the king,
"bid me abandon this bench and stand by you there,
345 so that I without discourtesy might be excused from the table,
and my liege lady were not loth to permit me,

I would come to your counsel before your courtiers fair.
For I find it unfitting, as in fact it is held,
when a challenge in your chamber makes choices so exalted,
350 though you yourself be desirous to accept it in person,
while many bold men about you on bench are seated:
on earth there are, I hold, none more honest of purpose,
no figures fairer on field where fighting is waged.
I am the weakest, I am aware, and in wit feeblest,
355 and the least loss, if I live not, if one would learn the truth.
Only because you are my uncle is honour given me:
save your blood in my body I boast of no virtue;
and since this affair is so foolish that it nowise befits you,
and I have requested it first, accord it then to me!
360 If my claim is uncalled-for without cavil shall judge
        this court."
        To consult the knights draw near,
        and this plan they all support;
        the king with crown to clear,
365   and give Gawain the sport.

The king then commanded that he quickly should rise,
and he readily uprose and directly approached,
kneeling humbly before his highness, and laying hand on the weapon;
and he lovingly relinquished it, and lifting his hand
370 gave him God's blessing, and graciously enjoined him
that his hand and his heart should be hardy alike.
"Take care, cousin," quoth the king, "one cut to address,
and if thou learnest him his lesson, I believe very well
that thou wilt bear any blow that he gives back later."
375 Gawain goes to the great man with guisarm in hand,
and he boldly abides there—he blenched not at all.
Then next said to Gawain the knight all in green:
"Let's tell again our agreement, ere we go any further.
I'd know first, sir knight, thy name; I entreat thee
380 to tell it me truly, that I may trust in thy word."
"In good faith," quoth the good knight, "I Gawain am called
who bring thee this buffet, let be what may follow;
and at this time a twelvemonth in thy turn have another
with whatever weapon thou wilt, and in the world with none else
385   but me."
        The other man answered again:
        "I am passing pleased," said he,
        "upon my life, Sir Gawain,
        that this stroke should be struck by thee.

390 "Begad," said the green knight, "Sir Gawain, I am pleased
to find from thy fist the favour I asked for!
And thou hast promptly repeated and plainly hast stated
without abatement the bargain I begged of the king here;
save that thou must assure me, sir, on thy honour

395   that thou'lt seek me thyself, search where thou thinkest
    I may be found near or far, and fetch thee such payment
    as thou deliverest me today before these lordly people,"
    "Where should I light on thee," quoth Gawain, "where look for thy place?
    I have never learned where thou livest, by the Lord that made me,
400   and I know thee not, knight, thy name nor thy court.
    But teach me the true way, and tell what men call thee,
    and I will apply all my purpose the path to discover:
    and that I swear thee for certain and solemnly promise."
    "That is enough in New Year, there is need of no more!"
405   said the great man in green to Gawain the courtly.
    "If I tell thee the truth of it, when I have taken the knock,
    and thou handily hast hit me, if in haste I announce then
    my house and my home and mine own title,
    then thou canst call and enquire and keep the agreement;
410   and if I waste not a word, thou'lt win better fortune,
    for thou mayst linger in thy land and look no further—
        but stay!
      To thy grim tool now take heed, sir!
      Let us try thy knocks today!"
415   "Gladly," said he, "indeed, sir!"
      and his axe he stroked in play.

    The Green Knight on the ground now gets himself ready,
    leaning a little with the head he lays bare the flesh,
    and his locks long and lovely he lifts over his crown,
420   letting the naked neck as was needed appear.
    His left foot on the floor before him placing,
    Gawain gripped on his axe, gathered and raised it,
    from aloft let it swiftly land where 'twas naked,
    so that the sharp of his blade shivered the bones,
425   and sank clean through the clear fat and clove it asunder,
    and the blade of the bright steel then bit into the ground.
    The fair head to the floor fell from the shoulders,
    and folk fended it with their feet as forth it went rolling;
    the blood burst from the body, bright on the greenness,
430   and yet neither faltered nor fell the fierce man at all,
    but stoutly he strode forth, still strong on his shanks,
    and roughly he reached out among the rows that stood there,
    caught up his comely head and quickly upraised it,
    and then hastened to his horse, laid hold of the bridle,
435   stepped into stirrup-iron, and strode up aloft,
    his head by the hair in his hand holding;
    and he settled himself then in the saddle as firmly
    as if unharmed by mishap, though in the hall he might wear
        no head.
440   His trunk he twisted round,
      that gruesome body that bled,
      and many fear then found,
      as soon as his speech was sped.

For the head in his hand he held it up straight,
445   towards the fairest at the table he twisted the face,
and it lifted up its eyelids and looked at them broadly,
and made such words with its mouth as may be recounted.
"See thou get ready, Gawain, to go as thou vowedst,
and as faithfully seek till thou find me, good sir,
450   as thou hast promised in this place in the presence of these knights.
To the Green Chapel go thou, and get thee, I charge thee,
such a dint as thou hast dealt—indeed thou hast earned
a nimble knock in return on New Year's morning!
The Knight of the Green Chapel I am known to many,
455   so if to find me thou endeavour, thou'lt fail not to do so.
Therefore come! Or to be called a craven thou deservest."
With a rude roar and rush his reins he turned then,
and hastened out through the hall-door with his head in his hand,
and fire of the flint flew from the feet of his charger.
460   To what country he came in that court no man knew,
no more than they had learned from what land he had journeyed.
      Meanwhile,
       the king and Sir Gawain
       at the Green Man laugh and smile;
465   yet to men had appeared, 'twas plain,
       a marvel beyond denial.

Though Arthur the high king in his heart marvelled,
he let no sign of it be seen, but said then aloud
to the queen so comely with courteous words:
470   "Dear Lady, today be not downcast at all!
Such cunning play well becomes the Christmas tide,
interludes,[2] and the like, and laughter and singing,
amid these noble dances of knights and of dames.
Nonetheless to my food I may fairly betake me,
475   for a marvel I have met, and I may not deny it."
He glanced at Sir Gawain and with good point he said:
"Come, hang up thine axe, sir![3] It has hewn now enough."
And over the table they hung it on the tapestry behind,
where all men might remark it, a marvel to see,
480   and by its true token might tell of that adventure.
Then to a table they turned, those two lords together,
the king and his good kinsman, and courtly men served them
with all dainties double, the dearest there might be,
with all manner of meats and with minstrelsy too.
485   With delight that day they led, till to the land came the night
      again.
       Sir Gawain, now take heed
       lest fear make thee refrain
       from daring the dangerous deed
490   that thou in hand hast ta'en!

---

2. Brief performances between the courses of the banquet.   3. A literal suggestion, but also an invitation to put the matter aside.

Part 2

With this earnest of high deeds thus Arthur began
the young year, for brave vows he yearned to hear made.
Though such words were wanting when they went to table,
now of fell work to full grasp filled with their hands.
495   Gawain was gay as he began those games in the hall,
but if the end be unhappy, hold it no wonder!
For though men be merry of mood when they have mightily drunk,
a year slips by swiftly, never the same returning;
the outset to the ending is equal but seldom.
500   And so this Yule passed over and the year after,
and severally the seasons ensued in their turn:[1]
after Christmas there came the crabbed Lenten
that with fish tries the flesh and with food more meagre;
but then the weather in the world makes war on the winter,
505   cold creeps into the earth, clouds are uplifted,
shining rain is shed in showers that all warm
fall on the fair turf, flowers there open,
of grounds and of groves green is the raiment,
birds are busy a-building and bravely are singing
510   for sweetness of the soft summer that will soon be on
        the way;
        and blossoms burgeon and blow
        in hedgerows bright and gay;
        then glorious musics go
515   through the woods in proud array.

After the season of summer with its soft breezes,
when Zephyr goes sighing through seeds and herbs,
right glad is the grass that grows in the open,
when the damp dewdrops are dripping from the leaves,
520   to greet a gay glance of the glistening sun.
But then Harvest hurries in, and hardens it quickly,
warns it before winter to wax to ripeness.
He drives with his drought the dust, till it rises
from the face of the land and flies up aloft;
525   wild wind in the welkin° makes war on the sun,   *the sky*
the leaves loosed from the linden alight on the ground,
and all grey is the grass that green was before:
all things ripen and rot that rose up at first,
and so the year runs away in yesterdays many,
530   and here winter wends again, as by the way of the world
        it ought,
        until the Michaelmas moon[2]
        has winter's boding brought;
        Sir Gawain then full soon
535   of his grievous journey thought.

---

1. This famous passage on the cycle of seasons draws
both on Germanic conventions of the battle of Winter and

Summer, and on Romance springtime lyrics, the *reverdies*.
2. The harvest moon at Michaelmas, on September 29.

And yet till All Hallows[3] with Arthur he lingered,
who furnished on that festival a feast for the knight
with much royal revelry of the Round Table.
The knights of renown and noble ladies
540 all for the love of that lord had longing at heart,
but nevertheless the more lightly of laughter they spoke:
many were joyless who jested for his gentle sake.
For after their meal mournfully he reminded his uncle
that his departure was near, and plainly he said:
545 "Now liege-lord of my life, for leave I beg you.
You know the quest and the compact; I care not further
to trouble you with tale of it, save a trifling point:
I must set forth to my fate without fail in the morning,
as God will me guide, the Green Man to seek."
550 Those most accounted in the castle came then together,[4]
Iwain and Eric and others not a few,
Sir Doddinel le Sauvage, the Duke of Clarence,
Lancelot, and Lionel, and Lucan the Good,
Sir Bors and Sir Bedivere that were both men of might,
555 and many others of mark with Mador de la Porte.
All this company of the court the king now approached
to comfort the knight with care in their hearts.
Much mournful lament was made in the hall
that one so worthy as Gawain should wend on that errand,
560 to endure a deadly dint and deal no more
         with blade.
     The knight ever made good cheer,
     saying, "Why should I be dismayed?
     Of doom the fair or drear
565   by a man must be assayed."

He remained there that day, and in the morning got ready,
asked early for his arms, and they all were brought him.
First a carpet of red silk was arrayed on the floor,
and the gilded gear in plenty there glittered upon it.
570 The stern man stepped thereon and the steel things handled,
dressed in a doublet of damask of Tharsia,
and over it a cunning capadoce that was closed at the throat
and with fair ermine was furred all within.
Then sabatons[5] first they set on his feet,
575 his legs lapped in steel in his lordly greaves,
on which the polains° they placed, polished and shining   knee-guards
and knit upon his knees with knots all of gold;
then the comely cuisses that cunningly clasped

---

3. All Saints' Day, on November 1, another holiday on which Arthur presided, crowned, over his court.
4. The list that follows would have recalled, especially to readers of French romances, other great quests and challenges encountered by Arthur's knights. The list's order
may also suggest later and more tragic episodes in the Arthurian narrative, ending with Bedivere who throws Excalibur into a lake after Arthur is mortally wounded.
5. A foot-covering worn by warriors in armor.

the thick thews of his thighs they with thongs on him tied;
580   and next the byrnie,° woven of bright steel rings   *coat of mail*
upon costly quilting, enclosed him about;
and armlets well burnished upon both of his arms,
with gay elbow-pieces and gloves of plate,
and all the goodly gear to guard him whatever
585   betide;
      coat-armour richly made,
      gold spurs on heel in pride;
      girt with a trusty blade,
      silk belt about his side.

590   When he was hasped in his armour his harness was splendid:
the least latchet or loop was all lit with gold.
Thus harnessed as he was he heard now his Mass,
that was offered and honoured at the high altar;
and then he came to the king and his court-companions,
595   and with love he took leave of lords and of ladies;
and they kissed him and escorted him, and to Christ him commended.
And now Gringolet stood groomed, and girt with a saddle
gleaming right gaily with many gold fringes,
and all newly for the nonce nailed at all points;
600   adorned with bars was the bridle, with bright gold banded;
that apparelling proud of poitrel° and of skirts,   *breast-plate*
and the crupper and caparison[6] accorded with the saddlebows:
all was arrayed in red with rich gold studded,
so that it glittered and glinted as a gleam of the sun.
605   Then he in hand took the helm and in haste kissed it:
strongly was it stapled and stuffed within;
it sat high upon his head and was hasped at the back,
and a light kerchief was laid o'er the beaver,°   *visor*
all braided and bound[7] with the brightest gems
610   upon broad silken broidery, with birds on the seams
like popinjays depainted, here preening and there,
turtles and true-loves, entwined as thickly
as if many sempstresses had the sewing full seven winters
      in hand.
615   A circlet of greater price
      his crown about did band;
      The diamonds point-device
      there blazing bright did stand.

Then they brought him his blazon° that was of brilliant gules°   *shield / red*
620   with the pentangle[8] depicted in pure hue of gold.
By the baldric° he caught it and about his neck cast it: *strap*

---

6. A cloth or covering spread over the saddle or harness of a horse, often gaily ornamented.
7. The technical language of armor is now joined by an equally technical description of needlework, for which English women were famous.

8. A five-pointed star and symbol of perfection and eternity, since it can be drawn with an uninterrupted line ending at the point of the star where it begins. Inscribed within a circle, it was called Solomon's seal.

right well and worthily it went with the knight.
And why the pentangle is proper to that prince so noble
I intend now to tell you, though it may tarry my story.

625 It is a sign that Solomon once set on a time
to betoken Troth, as it is entitled to do;
for it is a figure that in it five points holdeth,
and each line overlaps and is linked with another,
and every way it is endless; and the English, I hear,
630 everywhere name it the Endless Knot.
So it suits well this knight and his unsullied arms;
for ever faithful in five points, and five times under each,
Gawain as good was acknowledged and as gold refinéd,
devoid of every vice and with virtues adorned.
635   So there
the pentangle painted new
he on shield and coat did wear,
as one of word most true
and knight of bearing fair.

640 First faultless was he found in his five senses,
and next in his five fingers he failed at no time,
and firmly on the Five Wounds all his faith was set
that Christ received on the cross, as the Creed tells us;
and wherever the brave man into battle was come,
645 on this beyond all things was his earnest thought:
that ever from the Five Joys all his valour he gained
that to Heaven's courteous Queen once came from her Child.[9]
For which cause the knight had in comely wise
on the inner side of his shield her image depainted,
650 that when he cast his eyes thither his courage never failed.
The fifth five that was used, as I find, by this knight
was free-giving and friendliness first before all,
and chastity and chivalry ever changeless and straight,
and piety surpassing all points: these perfect five
655 were hasped upon him harder than on any man else.
Now these five series, in sooth, were fastened on this knight,
and each was knit with another and had no ending,
but were fixed at five points that failed not at all,
coincided in no line nor sundered either,
660 not ending in any angle anywhere, as I discover,
wherever the process was put in play or passed to an end.
Therefore on his shining shield was shaped now this knot,
royally with red gules upon red gold set:
this is the pure pentangle as people of learning
665   have taught.
Now Gawain in brave array
his lance at last hath caught.

9. Poems and meditations on the Virgin's joys and sorrows were widespread. Her five joys were the Annunciation, Nativity, Resurrection, Ascension, and Assumption.

He gave them all good day,
        for evermore as he thought.

670   He spurned his steed with the spurs and sprang on his way
        so fiercely that the flint-sparks flashed out behind him.
        All who beheld him so honourable in their hearts were sighing,
        and assenting in sooth one said to another,
        grieving for that good man: "Before God, 'tis a shame
675   that thou, lord, must be lost, who art in life so noble!
        To meet his match among men, Marry, 'tis not easy!
        To behave with more heed would have behoved one of sense,
        and that dear lord duly a duke to have made,
        illustrious leader of liegemen in this land as befits him;
680   and that would better have been than to be butchered to death,
        beheaded by an elvish man for an arrogant vaunt.
        Who can recall any king that such a course ever took
        as knights quibbling at court at their Christmas games!"
        Many warm tears outwelling there watered their eyes,
685   when that lord so beloved left the castle
                that day.
            No longer he abode,
            but swiftly went his way;
            bewildering ways he rode,
690   as the book I heard doth say.

        Now he rides thus arrayed through the realm of Logres,[1]
        Sir Gawain in God's care, though no game now he found it.
        Oft forlorn and alone he lodged of a night
        where he found not afforded him such fare as pleased him.
695   He had no friend but his horse in the forests and hills,
        no man on his march to commune with but God,
        till anon he drew near unto Northern Wales.
        All the isles of Anglesey he held on his left,
        and over the fords he fared by the flats near the sea,
700   and then over by the Holy Head to high land again
        in the wilderness of Wirral: there wandered but few
        who with good will regarded either God or mortal.
        And ever he asked as he went on of all whom he met
        if they had heard any news of a knight that was green
705   in any ground thereabouts, or of the Green Chapel.
        And all denied it, saying nay, and that never in their lives
        a single man had they seen that of such a colour
                could be.
            The knight took pathways strange
710   by many a lonesome lea,
            and oft his view did change
            that chapel ere he could see.

---

1. Identified with England in Geoffrey of Monmouth, elsewhere a vaguer term for Arthur's kingdom. Here, Gawain is heading northward through Wales, then along the coast of the Irish Sea and into the forest of Wirral in Cheshire—a wild area and resort of outlaws in the 14th century.

Many a cliff he climbed o'er in countries unknown,
far fled from his friends without fellowship he rode.
715 At every wading or water on the way that he passed
he found a foe before him, save at few for a wonder;
and so foul were they and fell that fight he must needs.
So many a marvel in the mountains he met in those lands
that 'twould be tedious the tenth part to tell you thereof.
720 At whiles with worms he wars, and with wolves also,
at whiles with wood-trolls that wandered in the crags,
and with bulls and with bears and boars, too, at times;
and with ogres that hounded him from the heights of the fells.
Had he not been stalwart and staunch and steadfast in God,
725 he doubtless would have died and death had met often;
for though war wearied him much, the winter was worse,
when the cold clear water from the clouds spilling
froze ere it had fallen upon the faded earth.
Wellnigh slain by the sleet he slept ironclad
730 more nights than enow in the naked rocks,
where clattering from the crest the cold brook tumbled,
and hung high o'er his head in hard icicles.
Thus in peril and pain and in passes grievous
till Christmas-eve that country he crossed all alone
735   in need.
    The knight did at that tide
    his plaint to Mary plead,
    her rider's road to guide
    and to some lodging lead.

740 By a mount in the morning merrily he was riding
into a forest that was deep and fearsomely wild,
with high hills at each hand, and hoar woods beneath
of huge aged oaks by the hundred together;
the hazel and the hawthorn were huddled and tangled
745 with rough ragged moss around them trailing,
with many birds bleakly on the bare twigs sitting
that piteously piped there for pain of the cold.
The good man on Gringolet goes now beneath them
through many marshes and mires, a man all alone,
750 troubled lest a truant at that time he should prove
from the service of the sweet Lord, who on that selfsame night
of a maid became man our mourning to conquer.
And therefore sighing he said: "I beseech thee, O Lord,
and Mary, who is the mildest mother most dear,
755 for some harbour where with honour I might hear the Mass
and thy Matins[2] tomorrow. This meekly I ask,
and thereto promptly I pray with Pater and Ave
    and Creed."[3]

---

2. First of the canonical hours of prayer and praise in monastic tradition, observed between midnight and dawn.

3. The Paternoster ("Our Father . . ."), Ave Maria ("Hail Mary . . ."), and Creed (the articles of the Christian faith).

In prayer he now did ride,
760   lamenting his misdeed;
he blessed him oft and cried,
"The Cross of Christ me speed!"

The sign on himself he had set but thrice,
ere a mansion he marked within a moat in the forest,
765   on a low mound above a lawn, laced under the branches
of many a burly bole° round about by the ditches: tree trunk
the castle most comely that ever a king possessed
placed amid a pleasaunce with a park all about it,
within a palisade of pointed pales° set closely   stakes
770   that took its turn round the trees for two miles or more.
Gawain from the one side gazed on the stronghold
as it shimmered and shone through the shining oaks,
and then humbly he doffed his helm, and with honour he thanked
Jesus and Saint Julian,[4] who generous are both,
775   who had courtesy accorded him and to his cry harkened.
"Now bon hostel," quoth the knight, "I beg of you still!"
Then he goaded Gringolet with his gilded heels,
and he chose by good chance the chief pathway
and brought his master bravely to the bridge's end
780   at last.
That brave bridge was up-hauled,
the gates were bolted fast;
the castle was strongly walled,
it feared no wind or blast.

785   Then he stayed his steed that on the steep bank halted
above the deep double ditch that was drawn round the place.
The wall waded in the water wondrous deeply,
and up again to a huge height in the air it mounted,
all of hard hewn stone to the high cornice,
790   fortified under the battlement in the best fashion
and topped with fair turrets set by turns about
that had many graceful loopholes with a good outlook:
that knight a better barbican had never seen built.[5]
And inwards he beheld the hall uprising,
795   tall towers set in turns, and as tines° clustering   pinnacles
the fair finials, joined featly, so fine and so long,
their capstones all carven with cunning and skill.
Many chalk-white chimneys he chanced to espy
upon the roofs of towers all radiant white;
800   so many a painted pinnacle was peppered about,
among the crenelles of the castle clustered so thickly
that all pared out of paper it appeared to have been.[6]

---

4. Patron saint of hospitality.
5. The poet again revels in technical vocabulary, here architectural; this is a fashionable (if exaggerated) building
of the 14th century.
6. Models in cut paper sometimes decorated elaborate
feasts such as that at the beginning of the poem.

The gallant knight on his great horse good enough thought it,
if he could come by any course that enclosure to enter,
805   to harbour in that hostel while the holy day lasted
           with delight.
        He called, and there came with speed
        a porter blithe and bright;
        on the wall he learned his need,
810   and hailed the errant knight.

"Good sir," quoth Gawain, "will you go with my message
to the high lord of this house for harbour to pray?"
"Yes, by Peter!"[7] quoth the porter, "and I promise indeed
that you will, sir, be welcome while you wish to stay here."
815   Then quickly the man went and came again soon,
servants bringing civilly to receive there the knight.
They drew down the great drawbridge, and duly came forth,
and on the cold earth on their knees in courtesy knelt
to welcome this wayfarer with such worship as they knew.
820   They delivered him the broad gates and laid them wide open,
and he readily bade them rise and rode o'er the bridge.
Several servants then seized the saddle as he alighted,
and many stout men his steed to a stable then led,
while knights and esquires anon descended
825   to guide there in gladness this guest to the hall.
When he raised up his helm many ran there in haste
to have it from his hand, his highness to serve;
his blade and his blazon both they took charge of.
Then he greeted graciously those good men all,
830   and many were proud to approach him, that prince to honour.
All hasped in his harness to hall they brought him,
where a fair blaze in the fireplace fiercely was burning.
Then the lord of that land leaving his chamber
Came mannerly to meet the man on the floor.
835   He said: "You are welcome at your wish to dwell here.
What is here, all is your own, to have in your rule
           and sway."
        "Gramercy!" quoth Gawain,
        "May Christ you this repay!"
840   As men that to meet were fain
        they both embraced that day.

Gawain gazed at the good man who had greeted him kindly,
and he thought bold and big was the baron of the castle,
very large and long, and his life at the prime:
845   broad and bright was his beard, and all beaver-hued,
stern, strong in his stance upon stalwart legs,
his face fell as fire, and frank in his speech;

---

7. Swearing by St. Peter, keeper of the keys to heaven.

and well it suited him, in sooth, as it seemed to the knight,
a lordship to lead untroubled over lieges trusty.
850 To a chamber the lord drew him, and charged men at once
to assign him an esquire to serve and obey him;
and there to wait on his word many worthy men were,
who brought him to a bright bower where the bedding was splendid:
there were curtains of costly silk with clear-golden hems,
855 and coverlets cunning-wrought with quilts most lovely
of bright ermine above, embroidered at the sides,
hangings running on ropes with red-gold rings,
carpets of costly damask that covered the walls
and the floor under foot fairly to match them.
860 There they despoiled him, speaking to him gaily,
his byrnie doing off and his bright armour.
Rich robes then readily men ran to bring him,
for him to change, and to clothe him, having chosen the best.
As soon as he had donned one and dressed was therein,
865 as it sat on him seemly with its sailing skirts,
then verily in his visage a vision of Spring
to each man there appeared, and in marvellous hues
bright and beautiful was all his body beneath.
That knight more noble was never made by Christ
870   they thought.
He came none knew from where,
but it seemed to them he ought
to be a prince beyond compare
in the field where fell men fought.

875 A chair before the chimney where charcoal was burning
was made ready in his room, all arrayed and covered
with cushions upon quilted cloths that were cunningly made.
Then a comely cloak was cast about him
of bright silk brocade, embroidered most richly
880 and furred fairly within with fells of the choicest
and all edged with ermine, and its hood was to match;
and he sat in that seat seemly and noble
and warmed himself with a will, and then his woes were amended.
Soon up on good trestles a table was raised[8]
885 and clad with a clean cloth clear white to look on;
there was surnape, salt-cellar, and silvern spoons.
He then washed as he would and went to his food,
and many worthy men with worship waited upon him;
soups they served of many sorts, seasoned most choicely,
890 in double helpings, as was due, and divers sorts of fish;
some baked in bread, some broiled on the coals,
some seethed, some in gravy savoured with spices,
and all with condiments so cunning that it caused him delight.

8. A castle's great hall had many uses; tables were set up for dining and then put aside or hung.

A fair feast he called it frankly and often,
895   graciously, when all the good men together there pressed him:
     "Now pray,
     this penance deign to take;
     'twill improve another day!"[9]
     The man much mirth did make,
900   for wine to his head made way.

Then inquiry and question were carefully put
touching personal points to that prince himself,
till he courteously declared that to the court he belonged
that high Arthur in honour held in his sway,
905   who was the right royal King of the Round Table,
and 'twas Gawain himself that as their guest now sat
and had come for that Christmas, as the case had turned out.
When the lord had learned whom luck had brought him,
loud laughed he thereat, so delighted he was,
910   and they made very merry, all the men in that castle,
and to appear in the presence were pressing and eager
of one who all profit and prowess and perfect manners
comprised in his person, and praise ever gained;
of all men on middle-earth he most was admired.
915   Softly each said then in secret to his friend:
"Now fairly shall we mark the fine points of manners,
and the perfect expressions of polished converse.
How speech is well spent will be expounded unasked,
since we have found here this fine father of breeding.
920   God has given us His goodness, His grace now indeed,
Who such a guest as Gawain has granted us to have!
When blissful men at board for His birth sing blithe
     at heart,
     what manners high may mean
925   this knight will now impart.
     Who hears him will, I ween,
     of love-speech learn some art."[1]

When his dinner was done and he duly had risen,
it now to the night-time very near had drawn.
930   The chaplains then took to the chapel their way
and rang the bells richly, as rightly they should,
for the solemn evensong of the high season.
The lord leads the way, and his lady with him;
into a goodly oratory gracefully she enters.
935   Gawain follows gladly, and goes there at once
and the lord seizes him by the sleeve and to a seat leads him,

---

9. An exchange of courtesies. Gawain has politely praised the many fish dishes; his hosts demur, remind him that Christmas Eve is a fast day, and promise him better meals later.

1. Though Gawain is engaged on a serious quest, his reputation as a graceful courtier and master in the arts of love has preceded him.

kindly acknowledges him and calls him by his name,
saying that most welcome he was of all guests in the world.
And he grateful thanks gave him, and each greeted the other,
940   and they sat together soberly while the service lasted.
Then the lady longed to look at this knight;
and from her closet she came with many comely maidens.
She was fairer in face, in her flesh and her skin,
her proportions, her complexion, and her port than all others,
945   and more lovely than Guinevere to Gawain she looked.
He came through the chancel to pay court to her grace;
leading her by the left hand another lady was there
who was older than she, indeed ancient she seemed,
and held in high honour by all men about her.
950   But unlike in their looks those ladies appeared,
for if the younger was youthful, yellow was the elder;
with rose-hue the one face was richly mantled,
rough wrinkled cheeks rolled on the other;
on the kerchiefs of the one many clear pearls were,
955   her breast and bright throat were bare displayed,
fairer than white snow that falls on the hills;
the other was clad with a cloth that enclosed all her neck,
enveloped was her black chin with chalk-white veils,
her forehead folded in silk, and so fumbled all up,
960   so topped up and trinketed and with trifles bedecked
that naught was bare of that beldame but her brows all black,
her two eyes and her nose and her naked lips,
and those were hideous to behold and horribly bleared;
that a worthy dame she was may well, fore God,
965   be said!
    Short body and thick waist,
    with bulging buttocks spread;
    more delicious to the taste
    was the one she by her led.

970   When Gawain glimpsed that gay lady that so gracious looked,
with leave sought of the lord towards the ladies he went;
the elder he saluted, low to her bowing,
about the lovelier he laid then lightly his arms
and kissed her in courtly wise with courtesy speaking.
975   His acquaintance they requested, and quickly he begged
to be their servant in sooth, if so they desired.
They took him between them, and talking they led him
to a fireside in a fair room, and first of all called
for spices, which men sped without sparing to bring them,
980   and ever wine therewith well to their liking.
The lord for their delight leaped up full often,
many times merry games being minded to make;
his hood he doffed, and on high he hung it on a spear,
and offered it as an honour for any to win

985 who the most fun could devise at that Christmas feast—
 "And I shall try, by my troth, to contend with the best
 ere I forfeit this hood, with the help of my friends!"
 Thus with laughter and jollity the lord made his jests
 to gladden Sir Gawain with games that night
990   in hall,
  until the time was due
  that the lord for lights should call;
  Sir Gawain with leave withdrew
  and went to bed withal.

995 On the morn when every man remembers the time
 that our dear Lord for our doom to die was born,
 in every home wakes happiness on earth for His sake.
 So did it there on that day with the dearest delights:
 at each meal and at dinner marvellous dishes
1000 men set on the dais, the daintiest meats.
 The old ancient woman was highest at table,
 meetly to her side the master he took him;
 Gawain and the gay lady together were seated
 in the center, where as was seemly the service began,
1005 and so on through the hall as honour directed.
 When each good man in his degree without grudge had been served,
 there was food, there was festival, there was fullness of joy;
 and to tell all the tale of it I should tedious find,
 though pains I might take every point to detail.
1010 Yet I ween that Gawain and that woman so fair
 in companionship took such pleasure together
 in sweet society soft words speaking,
 their courteous converse clean and clear of all evil,
 that with their pleasant pastime no prince's sport
1015   compares.
  Drums beat, and trumps men wind,
  many pipers play their airs;
  each man his needs did mind,
  and they two minded theirs.

1020 With much feasting they fared the first and the next day,
 and as heartily the third came hastening after:
 the gaiety of Saint John's day[2] was glorious to hear;
 [with cheer of the choicest Childermas followed,]
 and that finished their revels, as folk there intended,
1025 for there were guests who must go in the grey morning.
 So a wondrous wake they held, and the wine they drank,
 and they danced and danced on, and dearly they carolled.[3]
 At last when it was late their leave then they sought
 to wend on their ways, each worthy stranger.

2. December 27, traditionally given over to drinking and   3. Danced in a ring.
celebration.

1030 Good-day then said Gawain, but the good man stayed him,
and led him to his own chamber to the chimney-corner,
and there he delayed him, and lovingly thanked him,
for the pride and pleasure his presence had brought,
for so honouring his house at that high season
1035 and deigning his dwelling to adorn with his favour.
"Believe me, sir, while I live my luck I shall bless
that Gawain was my guest at God's own feast."
"Gramercy, sir," said Gawain, "but the goodness is yours,
all the honour is your own—may the High King repay you!
1040 And I am under your orders what you ask to perform,
as I am bound now to be, for better or worse,
        by right."
        Him longer to retain
        the lord then pressed the knight;
1045   to him replied Gawain
        that he by no means might.

Then with courteous question he enquired of Gawain
what dire need had driven him on that festal date
with such keenness from the king's court, to come forth alone
1050 ere wholly the holidays from men's homes had departed.
"In sooth, sir," he said, "you say but the truth:
a high errand and a hasty from that house brought me;
for I am summoned myself to seek for a place,
though I wonder where in the world I must wander to find it.
1055 I would not miss coming nigh it on New Year's morning
for all the land in Logres, so our Lord help me!
And so, sir, this question I enquire of you here:
can you tell me in truth if you tale ever heard
of the Green Chapel, on what ground it may stand,
1060 and of the great knight that guards it, all green in his colour?
For the terms of a tryst were between us established
to meet that man at that mark, if I remained alive,
and the named New Year is now nearly upon me,
and I would look on that lord, if God will allow me,
1065 more gladly, by God's son, than gain any treasure.
So indeed, if you please, depart now I must.
For my business I have now but barely three days,
and I would fainer fall dead than fail in my errand."
Then laughing said the lord: "Now linger you must;
1070 for when 'tis time to that tryst I will teach you the road.
On what ground is the Green Chapel—let it grieve you no more!
In your bed you shall be, sir, till broad is the day,
without fret, and then fare on the first of the year,
and come to the mark at midmorn, there to make what play
1075   you know.
        Remain till New Year's day,
        then rise and riding go!

We'll set you on your way,
'tis but two miles or so."

1080 Then was Gawain delighted, and in gladness he laughed:
"Now I thank you a thousand times for this beyond all!
Now my quest is accomplished, as you crave it, I will
dwell a few days here, and else do what you order."
The lord then seized him and set him in a seat beside him,

1085 and let the ladies be sent for to delight them the more,
for their sweet pleasure there in peace by themselves.
For love of him that lord was as loud in his mirth
as one near out of his mind who scarce knew what he meant.
Then he called to the knight, crying out loudly:

1090 "You have promised to do whatever deed I propose.
Will you hold this behest here, at this moment?"
"Yes, certainly, sir," then said the true knight,
"while I remain in your mansion, your command I'll obey."
"Well," returned he, "you have travelled and toiled from afar,

1095 and then I've kept you awake: you're not well yet, not cured;
both sustenance and sleep 'tis certain you need.
Upstairs you shall stay, sir, and stop there in comfort
tomorrow till Mass-time, and to a meal then go
when you wish with my wife, who with you shall sit

1100 and comfort you with her company, till to court I return.
        You stay,
    and I shall early rouse,
    and a-hunting wend my way."
    Gawain gracefully bows:

1105   "Your wishes I will obey."

"One thing more," said the master, "we'll make an agreement:
whatever I win in the wood at once shall be yours,
and whatever gain you may get you shall give in exchange.
Shall we swap thus, sweet man—come, say what you think!—

1110 whether one's luck be light, or one's lot be better?"
"By God," quoth good Gawain, "I agree to it all,
and whatever play you propose seems pleasant to me."
"Done! 'Tis a bargain! Who'll bring us the drink?"
So said the lord of that land. They laughed one and all;

1115 they drank and they dallied, and they did as they pleased,
these lords and ladies, as long as they wished,
and then with customs of France and many courtly phrases
they stood in sweet debate and soft words bandied,
and lovingly they kissed, their leave taking.

1120 With trusty attendants and torches gleaming
they were brought at the last to their beds so soft,
        one and all.
    Yet ere to bed they came,
    he the bargain did oft recall;

1125   he knew how to play a game
    the old governor of that hall.

Part 3

Before the first daylight the folk uprose:
the guests that were to go for their grooms they called;
and they hurried up in haste horses to saddle,
1130   to stow all their stuff and strap up their bags.
The men of rank arrayed them, for riding got ready,
to saddle leaped swiftly, seized then their bridles,
and went off on their ways where their wish was to go.
The liege-lord of the land was not last of them all
1135   to be ready to ride with a rout of his men;
he ate a hurried mouthful after the hearing of Mass,
and with horn to the hunting-field he hastened at once.[1]
When daylight was opened yet dimly on earth
he and his huntsman were up on their high horses.
1140   Then the leaders of the hounds leashed them in couples,
unclosed the kennel-door and cried to them "out!",
and blew boldly on bugles three blasts full long.
Beagles bayed thereat, a brave noise making;
and they whipped and wheeled in those that wandered on a scent;
1145   a hundred hunting-dogs, I have heard, of the best
        were they.
      To their stations keepers passed;
      the leashes were cast away,
      and many a rousing blast
1150   woke din in the woods that day.

At the first burst of the baying all beasts trembled;
deer dashed through the dale by dread bewildered,
and hastened to the heights, but they hotly were greeted,
and turned back by the beaters, who boldly shouted.
1155   They let the harts go past with their high antlers,
and the brave bucks also with their branching palms;
for the lord of the castle had decreed in the close season
that no man should molest the male of the deer.
The hinds were held back with hey! and ware!,
1160   the does driven with great din to the deep valleys:
there could be seen let slip a sleet of arrows;
at each turn under the trees went a twanging shaft
that into brown hides bit hard with barbéd head.
Lo! they brayed, and they bled, and on the banks they died;
1165   and ever the hounds in haste hotly pursued them,
and hunters with high horns hurried behind them
with such a clamour and cry as if cliffs had been riven.
If any beast broke away from bowmen there shooting,
it was snatched down and slain at the receiving-station;

---

1. The hunts that follow, for all their violent energy, are as ritualized in their procedure as the earlier feasts and games. The poet delights in describing still another area of knightly lore. A number of contemporary treatises on hunting survive.

1170   when they had been harried from the height and hustled to the waters,
the men were so wise in their craft at the watches below,
and their greyhounds were so great that they got them at once,
and flung them down in a flash, as fast as men could see
with sight.
1175   The lord then wild for joy
did oft spur and oft alight,
and thus in bliss employ
that day till dark of night.

Thus in his game the lord goes under greenwood eaves,
1180   and Gawain the bold lies in goodly bed,
lazing, till the walls are lit by the light of day,
under costly coverlet with curtains about him.
And as in slumber he strayed, he heard stealthily come
a soft sound at his door as it secretly opened;
1185   and from under the clothes he craned then his head,
a corner of the curtain he caught up a little,
and looked that way warily to learn what it was.
It was the lady herself, most lovely to see,
that cautiously closed the door quietly behind her,
1190   and drew near to his bed. Then abashed was the knight,
and lay down swiftly to look as if he slept;
and she stepped silently and stole to his bed,
cast back the curtain, and crept then within,
and sat her down softly on the side of the bed,
1195   and there lingered very long to look for his waking.
He lay there lurking a long while and wondered,
and mused in his mind how the matter would go,
to what point it might pass—to some surprise, he fancied.
Yet he said to himself: "More seemly 'twould be
1200   in due course with question to enquire what she wishes."
Then rousing he rolled over, and round to her turning
he lifted his eyelids with a look as of wonder,
and signed him with the cross, thus safer to be kept
aright.
1205   With chin and cheeks so sweet
of blended red and white,
with grace them him did greet
small lips with laughter bright.

"Good morning, Sir Gawain!" said that gracious lady.
1210   "You are a careless sleeper, if one can creep on you so!
Now quickly you are caught! If we come not to terms,
I shall bind you in your bed, you may be assured."
With laughter the lady thus lightly jested.
"Good morning to your grace!" said Gawain gaily.
1215   "You shall work on me your will, and well I am pleased;
for I submit immediately, and for mercy I cry,
and that is best, as I deem, for I am obliged to do so."

Thus he jested in return with much gentle laughter:
"But if you would, lady gracious, then leave grant me,
1220   and release your prisoner and pray him to rise,
I would abandon this bed and better array me;
the more pleasant would it prove then to parley with you."
"Nay, for sooth, fair sir," said the sweet lady,
"you shall not go from your bed! I will govern you better:
1225   here fast shall I enfold you, on the far side also,
and then talk with my true knight that I have taken so.
For I wot° well indeed that Sir Gawain you are,   *know*
to whom all men pay homage wherever you ride;
your honour, your courtesy, by the courteous is praised,
1230   by lords, by ladies, by all living people.
And right here you now are, and we all by ourselves;
my husband and his huntsmen far hence have ridden,
other men are abed, and my maids also,
the door closed and caught with a clasp that is strong;
1235   and since I have in this house one that all delight in,
my time to account I will turn, while for talk I chance
        have still.
        To my body will you welcome be
        of delight to take your fill;
1240   for need constraineth me
        to serve you, and I will."

"Upon my word," said Gawain, "that is well, I guess;
though I am not now he of whom you are speaking—
to attain to such honour as here you tell of
1245   I am a knight unworthy, as well indeed I know—
by God, I would be glad, if good to you seemed
whatever I could say, or in service could offer
to the pleasure of your excellence—it would be pure delight."
"In good faith, Sir Gawain," said the gracious lady,
1250   "the prowess and the excellence that all others approve,
if I scorned or decried them, it were scant courtesy.
But there are ladies in number who liever would now
have thee in their hold, sir, as I have thee here,
pleasantly to play with in polished converse,
1255   their solace to seek and their sorrows to soothe,
than great part of the goods or gold that they own.
But I thank Him who on high of Heaven is Lord
that I have here wholly in my hand what all desire,
        by grace."
1260   She was an urgent wooer,
        that lady fair of face;
        the knight with speeches pure
        replied in every case.

"Madam," said he merrily, "Mary reward you!
1265   For I have enjoyed, in good faith, your generous favour,

and much honour have had else from others' kind deeds;
but as for the courtesy they accord me, since my claim is not equal,
the honour is your own, who are ever well-meaning."
"Nay, Mary!" the lady demurred, "as for me, I deny it.

1270 For were I worth all the legion of women alive,
and all the wealth in the world at my will possessed,
if I should exchange at my choice and choose me a husband,
for the noble nature I know, Sir Knight, in thee here,
in beauty and bounty and bearing so gay—

1275 of which earlier I have heard, and hold it now true—
then no lord alive would I elect before you."
"In truth, lady," he returned, "you took one far better.
But I am proud of the praise you are pleased to give me,
and as your servant in earnest my sovereign I hold you,

1280 and your knight I become, and may Christ reward you."
Thus of many matters they spoke till midmorn was passed,
and ever the lady demeaned her as one that loved him much,
and he fenced with her featly, ever flawless in manner.
"Though I were lady most lovely," thought the lady to herself,

1285 "the less love would he bring here," since he looked for his bane,
            that blow
        that him so soon should grieve,
        and needs it must be so.
        Then the lady asked for leave

1290   and at once he let her go.

Then she gave him "good day," and with a glance she laughed,
and as she stood she astonished him with the strength of her words:
"Now He that prospers all speed for this disport repay you!
But that you should be Gawain, it gives me much thought."

1295 "Why so?", then eagerly the knight asked her,
afraid that he had failed in the form of his converse.
But "God bless you! For this reason," blithely she answered,
"that one so good as Gawain the gracious is held,
who all the compass of courtesy includes in his person,

1300 so long with a lady could hardly have lingered
without craving a kiss, as a courteous knight,
by some tactful turn that their talk led to."
Then said Gawain, "Very well, as you wish be it done.
I will kiss at your command, as becometh a knight,

1305 and more, lest he displease you, so plead it no longer."
She came near thereupon and caught him in her arms,
and down daintily bending dearly she kissed him.
They courteously commended each other to Christ.
Without more ado through the door she withdrew and departed,

1310 and he to rise up in haste made ready at once.
He calls to his chamberlain, and chooses his clothes,
and goes forth when garbed all gladly to Mass.
Then he went to a meal that meetly awaited him,

and made merry all day, till the moon arose
1315   o'er earth.
          Ne'er was knight so gaily engaged
          between two dames of worth,
          the youthful and the aged:
          together they made much mirth.

1320   And ever the lord of the land in his delight was abroad,
       hunting by holt and heath after hinds that were barren.
       When the sun began to slope he had slain such a number
       of does and other deer one might doubt it were true.
       Then the fell folk at last came flocking all in,
1325   and quickly of the kill they a quarry assembled.
       Thither the master hastened with a host of his men,
       gathered together those greatest in fat
       and had them riven open rightly, as the rules require.
       At the assay they were searched by some that were there,
1330   and two fingers' breadth of fat they found in the leanest.
       Next they slit the eslot,° seized on the arber,°   *throat / gullet*
       shaved it with a sharp knife and shore away the grease;
       next ripped the four limbs and rent off the hide.
       Then they broke open the belly, the bowels they removed
1335   (flinging them nimbly afar) and the flesh of the knot;
       they grasped then the gorge, disengaging with skill
       the weasand° from the windpipe, and did away with the guts.   *esophagus*
       Then they shore out the shoulders with their sharpened knives
       (drawing the sinews through a small cut) the sides to keep whole;
1340   next they burst open the breast, and broke it apart,
       and again at the gorge one begins thereupon,
       cuts all up quickly till he comes to the fork,
       and fetches forth the fore-numbles;[2] and following after
       all the tissues along the ribs they tear away quickly.
1345   Thus by the bones of the back they broke off with skill,
       down even to the haunch, all that hung there together,
       and hoisted it up all whole and hewed it off there:
       and that they took for the numbles, as I trow is their name
              in kind.
1350   Along the fork of every thigh
          the flaps they fold behind;
          to hew it in two they hie,
          down the back all to unbind.

       Both the head and the neck they hew off after,
1355   and next swiftly they sunder the sides from the chine,°   *backbone*
       and the bone for the crow they cast in the boughs.[3]
       Then they thrust through both thick sides with a thong by the rib,

---

2. Internal organs such as heart, liver, lungs.   3. The gristle at the end of the breastbone was left for the
                                                     crows, still another of the prescribed rituals of the hunt.

and then by the hocks of the legs they hang them both up:
all the folk earn the fees that fall to their lot.
1360   Upon the fell of the fair beast they fed their hounds then
on the liver and the lights° and the leather of the paunches   *lungs*
with bread bathed in blood blended amongst them.
Boldly they blew the prise,[4] amid the barking of dogs,
and then bearing up their venison bent their way homeward,
1365   striking up strongly many a stout horn-call.
When daylight was done they all duly were come
into the noble castle, where quietly the knight
        abode
    in bliss by bright fire set.
1370   Thither the lord now strode;
    when Gawain with him met,
    then free all pleasure flowed.

Then the master commanded his men to meet in that hall,
and both dames to come down with their damsels also;
1375   before all the folk on that floor fair men he ordered
to fetch there forthwith his venison before him,
and all gracious in game to Gawain he called,
announced the number by tally of the nimble beasts,
and showed him the shining fat all shorn on the ribs.
1380   "How does this play please you? Have I praise deserved?
Have I earned by mine art the heartiest thanks?"
"Yea verily," the other averred, "here is venison the fairest
that I've seen in seven years in the season of winter!"
"And I give it you all, Gawain," said the good man at once,
1385   "for as our covenant accorded you may claim it as your own."
"That is true," he returned, "and I tell you the same:
what of worth within these walls I have won also
with as good will, I warrant, 'tis awarded to you."
His fair neck he enfolded then fast in his arms,
1390   and kissed him with all the kindness that his courtesy knew.
"There take you my gains, sir! I got nothing more.
I would give it up gladly even if greater it were."
"That is a good one!" quoth the good man. "Greatly I thank you.
'Tis such, maybe, that you had better briefly now tell me
1395   where you won this same wealth by the wits you possess."
"That was not the covenant," quoth he. "Do not question me more!
For you've drawn what is due to you, no doubt can you have
        'tis true."
    They laugh, and with voices fair
1400   their merriment pursue,
    and to supper soon repair
    with many dainties new.

4. A thing seized or requisitioned for the king's use or for the use of the garrisons in his castles.

Later by the chimney in chamber they were seated,
abundant wine of the best was brought to them oft,
1405 and again as a game they agreed on the morrow
to abide by the same bond as they had bargained before:
chance what might chance, to exchange all their trade,
whatever new thing they got, when they gathered at night.
They concluded this compact before the courtiers all;
1410 the drink for the bargain was brought forth in jest;
then their leave at the last they lovingly took,
and away then at once each went to his bed.
When the cock had crowed and cackled but thrice,
the lord had leaped from his bed, and his lieges each one;
1415 so that their meal had been made, and the Mass was over,
and folk bound for the forest, ere the first daybreak,
  to chase.
  Loud with hunters and horns
  o'er plains they passed apace,
1420   and loosed there among the thorns
  the running dogs to race.

Soon these cried for a quest in a covert by a marsh;
the huntsman hailed the hound that first heeded the scent,
stirring words he spoke to him with a strident voice.
1425 The hounds then that heard it hastened thither swiftly,
and fell fast on the line, some forty at once.
Then such a baying and babel of bloodhounds together
arose that the rock-wall rang all about them.
Hunters enheartened them with horn and with mouth,
1430 and then all in a rout rushed on together
between a fen-pool in that forest and a frowning crag.
In a tangle under a tall cliff at the tarn's° edges,   *mountain pond*
where the rough rock ruggedly in ruin was fallen,
they fared to the find, followed by hunters
1435 who made a cast round the crag and the clutter of stones,
till well they were aware that it waited within:
the very beast that the baying bloodhounds had spoken.
Then they beat on the bushes and bade him uprise,
and forth he came to their peril against folk in his path.
1440 'Twas a boar without rival that burst out upon them;
long the herd he had left, that lone beast aged,
for savage was he, of all swine the hugest,
grim indeed when he grunted. Then aghast were many;
for three at the first thrust he threw to the ground,
1445 and sprang off with great speed, sparing the others;
and they hallooed on high, and ha! ha! shouted,
and held horn to mouth, blowing hard the rally.
Many were the wild mouthings of men and of dogs,
as they bounded after this boar, him with blare and with din
1450   to quell.

Many times he turns to bay,
and maims the pack pell-mell;
he hurts many hounds, and they
grievously yowl and yell.

1455 Hunters then hurried up eager to shoot him,
aimed at him their arrows, often they hit him;
but poor at core proved the points that pitched on his shields,
and the barbs on his brows would bite not at all;
though the shaven shaft shivered in pieces,
1460 back the head came hopping, wherever it hit him.
But when the hurts went home of their heavier strokes,
then with brain wild for battle he burst out upon them,
ruthless he rent them as he rushed forward,
and many quailed at his coming and quickly withdrew.
1465 But the lord on a light horse went leaping after him;
as bold man on battle-field with his bugle he blew
the rally-call as he rode through the rough thickets,
pursuing this wild swine till the sunbeams slanted.
This day in such doings thus duly they passed,
1470 while our brave knight beloved there lies in his bed
at home in good hap, in housings so costly
       and gay.
   The lady did not forget:
   she came to bid good day;
1475 early she on him set,
   his will to wear away.

She passed to the curtain and peeped at the knight.
Sir Gawain graciously then welcomed her first,
and she answered him alike, eagerly speaking,
1480 and sat her softly by his side; and suddenly she laughed,
and with a look full of love delivered these words:
"Sir, if you are Gawain, a wonder I think it
that a man so well-meaning, ever mindful of good,
yet cannot comprehend the customs of the gentle;
1485 and if one acquaints you therewith, you do not keep them in mind:
thou hast forgot altogether what a day ago I taught
by the plainest points I would put into words!"
"What is that?" he said at once. "I am not aware of it at all.
But if you are telling the truth, I must take all the blame."
1490 "And yet as to kisses," she quoth, "this counsel I gave you:
wherever favour is found, defer not to claim them:
that becomes all who care for courteous manners."
"Take back," said the true knight, "that teaching, my dear!
For that I dared not do, for dread of refusal.
1495 Were I rebuffed, I should be to blame for so bold an offer."
"Ma fay!"° said the fair lady, "you may not be refused;   *"My faith" (Fr.)
you are stout enough to constrain one by strength, if you like,
if any were so ill bred as to answer you nay."

"Indeed, by God," quoth Gawain, "you graciously speak;
1500   but force finds no favour among the folk where I dwell,
and any gift not given gladly and freely.
I am at your call and command to kiss when you please.
You may receive as you desire, and cease as you think
        in place."
1505   Then down the lady bent,
        and sweetly kissed his face.
        Much speech then there they spent
        of lovers' grief and grace.

"I would learn from you, lord," the lady then said,
1510   "if you would not mind my asking, what is the meaning of this:
that one so young as are you in years, and so gay,
by renown so well known for knighthood and breeding,
while of all chivalry the choice, the chief thing to praise,
is the loyal practice of love: very lore of knighthood[5]—
1515   for, talking of the toils that these true knights suffer,
it is the title and contents and text of their works:
how lovers for their true love their lives have imperilled,
have endured for their dear one dolorous trials,
until avenged by their valour, their adversity passed,
1520   they have brought bliss into her bower by their own brave virtues—
and you are the knight of most noble renown in our age,
and your fame and fair name afar is published,
and I have sat by your very self now for the second time,
yet your mouth has never made any remark I have heard
1525   that ever belonged to love-making, lesser or greater.
Surely, you that are so accomplished and so courtly in your vows
should be prompt to expound to a young pupil
by signs and examples the science of lovers.
Why? Are you ignorant who all honour enjoy?
1530   Or else you esteem me too stupid to understand your courtship?
        But nay!
        Here single I come and sit,
        a pupil for your play;
        come, teach me of your wit,
1535   while my lord is far away."

"In good faith," said Gawain, "may God reward you!
Great delight I gain, and am glad beyond measure
that one so worthy as you should be willing to come here
and take pains with so poor a man: as for playing with your knight,
1540   showing favour in any form, it fills me with joy.
But for me to take up the task on true love to lecture,
to comment on the text and tales of knighthood
to you, who I am certain possess far more skill

---

5. The lady compares Gawain's behavior to descriptions of courtly love in romances; the poem is mirrored within itself.

in that art by the half than a hundred of such

1545 as I am, or shall ever be while on earth I remain,
it would be folly manifold, in faith, my lady!
All your will I would wish to work, as I am able,
being so beholden in honour, and, so help me the Lord,
desiring ever the servant of yourself to remain."

1550 Thus she tested and tried him, tempting him often,
so as to allure him to love-making, whatever lay in her heart.
But his defence was so fair that no fault could be seen,
nor any evil upon either side, nor aught but joy
     they wist.

1555   They laughed and long they played;
     at last she him then kissed,
     with grace adieu him bade,
     and went whereso she list.

Then rousing from his rest he rose to hear Mass,
1560 and then their dinner was laid and daintily served.
The livelong day with the ladies in delight he spent,
but the lord o'er the lands leaped to and fro,
pursuing his fell swine that o'er the slopes hurtled
and bit asunder the backs of the best of his hounds,
1565 wherever to bay he was brought, until bowmen dislodged him,
and made him, maugre° his teeth, move again onward,   *despite*
so fast the shafts flew when the folk were assembled.
And yet the stoutest of them still he made start there aside,
till at least he was so spent he could speed no further,
1570 but in such haste as he might he made for a hollow
on a reef beside a rock where the river was flowing.
He put the bank at his back, began then to paw;
fearfully the froth of his mouth foamed from the corners;
he whetted his white tusks. Then weary were all
1575 the brave men so bold as by him to stand
of plaguing him from afar, yet for peril they dared not
    come nigher.
    He had hurt so many before,
    that none had now desire
1580   to be torn with the tusks once more
    of a beast both mad and dire.

Till the knight himself came, his courser spurring,
and saw him brought there to bay, and all about him his men.
Nothing loth he alighted, and leaving his horse,
1585 brandished a bright blade and boldly advanced,
striding stoutly through the ford to where stood the felon.
The wild beast was aware of him with his weapon in hand,
and high raised his hair; with such hate he snorted
that folk feared for the knight, lest his foe should worst him.
1590 Out came the swine and set on him at once,
and the boar and the brave man were both in a mellay°   *struggle*

in the wildest of the water. The worse had the beast,
for the man marked him well, and as they met he at once
struck steadily his point straight in the neck-slot,
1595   and hit him up to the hilts, so that his heart was riven,
and with a snarl he succumbed, and was swept down the water
    straightway.
        A hundred hounds him caught,
        and fiercely bit their prey;
1600   the men to the bank him brought,
        and dogs him dead did lay.

There men blew for the prise in many a blaring horn,
and high and loud hallooed all the hunters that could;
bloodhounds bayed for the beast, as bade the masters,
1605   who of that hard-run chase were the chief huntsmen.
Then one that was well learnéd in woodmen's lore
with pretty cunning began to carve up this boar.
First he hewed off his head and on high set it,
then he rent him roughly down the ridge of the back,
1610   brought out the bowels, burned them on gledes,°   *coals*
and with them, blended with blood, the bloodhounds rewarded.
Next he broke up the boar-flesh in broad slabs of brawn,
and haled forth the hastlets° in order all duly,   *innards*
and yet all whole he fastened the halves together,
1615   and strongly on a stout pole he strung them then up.
Now with this swine homeward swiftly they hastened,
and the boar's head was borne before the brave knight himself
who felled him in the ford by force of his hand
    so great.
1620   Until he saw Sir Gawain
        in the hall he could hardly wait.
        He called, and his pay to gain
        the other came there straight.

The lord with his loud voice and laughter merry
1625   gaily he greeted him when Gawain he saw.
The fair ladies were fetched and the folk all assembled,
and he showed them the shorn slabs, and shaped his report
of the width and wondrous length, and the wickedness also
in war, of the wild swine, as in the woods he had fled.
1630   With fair words his friend the feat then applauded,
and praised the great prowess he had proved in his deeds;
for such brawn on a beast, the brave knight declared,
or such sides on a swine he had never seen before.
They then handled the huge head, and highly he praised it,
1635   showing horror at the hideous thing to honour the lord.
"Now, Gawain," said the good man, "this game is your own
by close covenant we concluded, as clearly you know."
"That is true," he returned, "and as truly I assure you
all my winnings, I warrant, I shall award you in exchange."

1640   He clasped his neck, and courteously a kiss he then gave him
       and swiftly with a second he served him on the spot.
       "Now we are quits," he quoth, "and clear for this evening
       of all covenants we accorded, since I came to this house,
           as is due."
1645   The lord said: "By Saint Gile,[6]
           your match I never knew!
           You'll be wealthy in a while,
           such trade if you pursue."

       Then on top of the trestles the tables they laid,
1650   cast the cloths thereon, and clear light then
       wakened along the walls; waxen torches
       men set there, and servants went swift about the hall.
       Much gladness and gaiety began then to spring
       round the fire on the hearth, and freely and oft
1655   at supper and later: many songs of delight,
       such as canticles of Christmas, and new carol-dances,
       amid all the mannerly mirth that men can tell of;
       and ever our noble knight was next to the lady.
       Such glances she gave him of her gracious favour,
1660   secretly stealing sweet looks that strong man to charm,
       that he was passing perplexed, and ill-pleased at heart.
       Yet he would fain not of his courtesy coldly refuse her,
       but graciously engaged her, however against the grain
           the play.
1665   When mirth they had made in hall
           as long as they wished to stay,
           to a room did the lord them call
           and to the ingle° they made their way.   hearth

       There amid merry words and wine they had a mind once more
1670   to harp on the same note on New Year's Eve.
       But said Gawain: "Grant me leave to go on the morrow!
       For the appointment approaches that I pledged myself to."
       The lord was loth to allow it, and longer would keep him,
       and said: "As I am a true man I swear on my troth
1675   the Green Chapel thou shalt gain, and go to your business
       in the dawn of New Year, sir, ere daytime begins.
       So still lie upstairs and stay at thine ease,
       and I shall hunt in the holt here, and hold to my terms
       with thee truly, when I return, to trade all our gains.
1680   For I have tested thee twice, and trusty I find thee.
       Now 'third time pays for all,' bethink thee tomorrow!
       Make we merry while we may and be mindful of joy,
       for the woe one may win whenever one wishes!"
       This was graciously agreed, and Gawain would linger.

---

6. A hermit and patron saint of woodlands.

1685 Then gaily drink is given them and they go to their beds
             with light.
          Sir Gawain lies and sleeps
          soft and sound all night;
          his host to his hunting keeps,
1690   and is early arrayed aright.

      After Mass of a morsel he and his men partook.
      Merry was the morning. For his mount then he called.
      All the huntsmen that on horse behind him should follow
      were ready mounted to ride arrayed at the gates.
1695 Wondrous fair were the fields, for the frost clung there;
      in red rose-hued o'er the wrack° arises the sun,   *mist*
      sailing clear along the coasts of the cloudy heavens.
      The hunters loosed hounds by a holt-border;°   *grove's edge*
      the rocks rang in the wood to the roar of their horns.
1700 Some fell on the line to where the fox was lying,
      crossing and re-crossing it in the cunning of their craft.
      A hound then gives tongue, the huntsman names him,
      round him press his companions in a pack all snuffling,
      running forth in a rabble then right in his path.
1705 The fox flits before them. They find him at once,
      and when they see him by sight they pursue him hotly,
      decrying him full clearly with a clamour of wrath.
      He dodges and ever doubles through many a dense coppice,
      and looping oft he lurks and listens under fences.
1710 At last at a little ditch he leaps o'er a thorn-hedge,
      sneaks out secretly by the side of a thicket,
      weens he is out of the wood and away by his wiles from the hounds.
      Thus he went unawares to a watch that was posted,
      where fierce on him fell three foes at once
1715   all grey.
          He swerves then swift again,
          and dauntless darts astray;
          in grief and in great pain
          to the wood he turns away.

1720 Then to hark to the hounds it was heart's delight,
      when all the pack came upon him, there pressing together.
      Such a curse at the view they called down on him
      that the clustering cliffs might have clattered in ruin.
      Here he was hallooed when hunters came on him,
1725 yonder was he assailed with snarling tongues;
      there he was threatened and oft thief was he called,
      with ever the trailers at his trail so that tarry he could not.
      Oft was he run at, if he rushed outwards;
      oft he swerved in again, so subtle was Reynard.
1730 Yea! he led the lord and his hunt as laggards behind him
      thus by mount and by hill till mid-afternoon.
      Meanwhile the courteous knight in the castle in comfort slumbered

behind the comely curtains in the cold morning.
But the lady in love-making had no liking to sleep

1735   nor to disappoint the purpose she had planned in her heart;
but rising up swiftly his room now she sought
in a gay mantle that to the ground was measured
and was fur-lined most fairly with fells well trimmed,
with no comely coif° on her head, only the clear jewels   *close-fitting cap*

1740   that were twined in her tressure° by twenties in clusters;   *hairnet*
her noble face and her neck all naked were laid,
her breast bare in front and at the back also.
She came through the chamber-door and closed it behind her,
wide set a window, and to wake him she called,

1745   thus greeting him gaily with her gracious words
            of cheer:
        "Ah! man, how canst thou sleep,
        the morning is so clear!"
        He lay in darkness deep,

1750   but her call he then could hear.

In heavy darkness drowsing he dream-words muttered,
as a man whose mind was bemused with many mournful thoughts,
how destiny should his doom on that day bring him
when he at the Green Chapel the great man would meet,

1755   and be obliged his blow to abide without debate at all.
But when so comely she came, he recalled then his wits,
swept aside his slumbers, and swiftly made answer.
The lady in lovely guise came laughing sweetly,
bent down o'er his dear face, and deftly kissed him.

1760   He greeted her graciously with a glad welcome,
seeing her so glorious and gaily attired,
so faultless in her features and so fine in her hues
that at once joy up-welling went warm to his heart.
With smiles sweet and soft they turned swiftly to mirth,

1765   and only brightness and bliss was broached there between them
            so gay.
        They spoke then speeches good,
        much pleasure was in that play;
        great peril between them stood,

1770   unless Mary for her knight should pray.

For she, queenly and peerless, pressed him so closely,
led him so near the line, that at least he must needs
either refuse her with offence or her favours there take.
He cared for his courtesy, lest a caitiff° he proved,   *coward*

1775   yet more for his sad case, if he should sin commit
and to the owner of the house, to his host, be a traitor.
"God help me!" said he. "Happen that shall not!"
Smiling sweetly aside from himself then he turned
all the fond words of favour that fell from her lips.

1780   Said she to the knight then: "Now shame you deserve,

if you love not one that lies alone here beside you,
who beyond all women in the world is wounded in heart,
unless you have a lemman,° more beloved, whom you like better,   *lover*
and have affianced faith to that fair one so fast and so true
1785   that your release you desire not—and so I believe now;
and to tell me if that be so truly, I beg you.
For all sakes that men swear by, conceal not the truth
  in guile."
  The knight said: "By Saint John,"
1790   and softly gave a smile,
  "Nay! lover have I none,
  and none will have meanwhile."

"Those words," said the woman, "are the worst that could be.
But I am answered indeed, and 'tis hard to endure.
1795   Kiss me now kindly, and I will quickly depart.
I may but mourn while I live as one that much is in love."
Sighing she sank down, and sweetly she kissed him;
then soon she left his side, and said as she stood there:
"Now, my dear, at this parting do me this pleasure,
1800   give me something as thy gift, thy glove it might be,
that I may remember thee, dear man, my mourning to lessen."
"Now on my word," then said he, "I wish I had here
the loveliest thing for thy delight that in my land I possess;
for worthily have you earned wondrously often
1805   more reward by rights than within my reach would now be,
save to allot you as love-token thing of little value.
Beneath your honour it is to have here and now
a glove for a guerdon° as the gift of Sir Gawain   *reward*
and I am here on an errand in unknown lands,
1810   and have no bearers with baggage and beautiful things
(unluckily, dear lady) for your delight at this time.
A man must do as he is placed; be not pained nor aggrieved,"
  said he.
  Said she so comely clad:
1815   "Nay, noble knight and free,
  though naught of yours I had,
  you should get a gift from me."

A rich ring she offered him of red gold fashioned,
with a stone like a star standing up clear
1820   that bore brilliant beams as bright as the sun:
I warrant you it was worth wealth beyond measure.
But the knight said nay to it, and announced then at once:
"I will have no gifts, fore God, of your grace at this time.
I have none to return you, and naught will I take."
1825   She proffered it and pressed him, and he her pleading refused,
and swore swiftly upon his word that accept it he would not.
And she, sorry that he refused, said to him further:
"If to my ring you say nay, since too rich it appears,

and you would not so deeply be indebted to me,
1830   I shall give you my girdle, less gain will that be."
She unbound a belt swiftly that embracing her sides
was clasped above her kirtle under her comely mantle.
Fashioned it was of green silk, and with gold finished,
though only braided round about, embroidered by hand;
1835   and this she would give to Gawain, and gladly besought him,
of no worth though it were, to be willing to take it.
And he said nay, he would not, he would never receive
either gold or jewelry, ere God the grace sent him
to accomplish the quest on which he had come thither.
1840   "And therefore I pray you, please be not angry,
and cease to insist on it, for to your suit I will ever

        say no.
      I am deeply in debt to you
      for the favour that you show,
1845   to be your servant true
      for ever in weal or woe."

"Do you refuse now this silk," said the fair lady,
"because in itself it is poor? And so it appears.
See how small 'tis in size, and smaller in value!
1850   But one who knew of the nature that is knit therewithin
would appraise it probably at a price far higher.
For whoever goes girdled with this green riband,
while he keeps it well clasped closely about him,
there is none so hardy under heaven that to hew him were able;
1855   for he could not be killed by any cunning of hand."
The knight then took note, and thought now in his heart,
'twould be a prize in that peril that was appointed to him.
When he gained the Green Chapel to get there his sentence,
if by some sleight he were not slain, 'twould be a sovereign device.
1860   Then he bore with her rebuke, and debated not her words;
and she pressed him on the belt, and proffered it in earnest;
and he agreed, and she gave it very gladly indeed,
and prayed him for her sake to part with it never,
but on his honour hide it from her husband; and he then agreed
1865   that no one ever should know, nay, none in the world

        but they.
      With earnest heart and mood
      great thanks he oft did say.
      She then the knight so good
1870   a third time kissed that day.

Then she left him alone, her leave taking,
for amusement from the man no more could she get.
When she was gone Sir Gawain got him soon ready,
arose and robed himself in raiment noble.
1875   He laid up the love-lace that the lady had given,
hiding it heedfully where he after might find it.

Then first of all he chose to fare to the chapel,
privately approached a priest, and prayed that he there
would uplift his life, that he might learn better
1880   how his soul should be saved, when he was sent from the world.
There he cleanly confessed him and declared his misdeeds,
both the more and the less, and for mercy he begged,
to absolve him of them all he besought the good man;
and he assoiled him and made him as safe and as clean
1885   as for Doom's Day indeed, were it due on the morrow.[7]
Thereafter more merry he made among the fair ladies,
with carol-dances gentle and all kinds of rejoicing,
than ever he did ere that day, till the darkness of night,
     in bliss.
1890   Each man there said: "I vow
    a delight to all he is!
    Since hither he came till now,
    he was ne'er so gay as this."

Now indoors let him dwell and have dearest delight,
1895   while the free lord yet fares afield in his sports!
At last the fox he has felled that he followed so long;
for, as he spurred through a spinney° to espy there the villain,   *grove*
where the hounds he had heard that hard on him pressed,
Reynard on his road came through a rough thicket,
1900   and all the rabble in a rush were right on his heels.
The man is aware of the wild thing, and watchful awaits him,
brings out his bright brand and at the beast hurls it;
and he blenched at the blade, and would have backed if he could.
A hound hastened up, and had him ere he could;
1905   and right before the horse's feet they fell on him all,
and worried there the wily one with a wild clamour.
The lord quickly alights and lifts him at once,
snatching him swiftly from their slavering mouths,
holds him high o'er his head, hallooing loudly;
1910   and there bay at him fiercely many furious hounds.
Huntsmen hurried thither, with horns full many
ever sounding the assembly, till they saw the master.
When together had come his company noble,
all that ever bore bugle were blowing at once,
1915   and all the others hallooed that had not a horn:
it was the merriest music that ever men harkened,
the resounding song there raised that for Reynard's soul
     awoke.
    To hounds they pay their fees,
1920   their heads they fondly stroke,

---

7. Gawain's confession and absolution are problematic, since he has just accepted the green girdle and resolved to break the covenant of exchange with his host.

and Reynard then they seize,
and off they skin his cloak.

And then homeward they hastened, for at hand was now night,
making strong music on their mighty horns.
1925   The lord alighted at last at his beloved abode,
found a fire in the hall, and fair by the hearth
Sir Gawain the good, and gay was he too,
among the ladies in delight his lot was most joyful.
He was clad in a blue cloak that came to the ground;
1930   his surcoat well beseemed him with its soft lining,
and its hood of like hue that hung on his shoulder:
all fringed with white fur very finely were both.
He met indeed the master in the midst of the floor,
and in gaiety greeted him, and graciously said:
1935   "In this case I will first our covenant fulfil
that to our good we agreed, when ungrudged went the drink."
He clasps then the knight and kisses him thrice,
as long and deliciously as he could lay them upon him.
"By Christ!" the other quoth, "you've come by a fortune
1940   in winning such wares, were they worth what you paid."
"Indeed, the price was not important," promptly he answered,
"whereas plainly is paid now the profit I gained."
"Marry!" said the other man, "mine is not up to't;
for I have hunted all this day, and naught else have I got
1945   but this foul fox-fell—the Fiend have the goods!—
and that is price very poor to pay for such treasures
as these you have thrust upon me, three such kisses
        so good."
        "'Tis enough," then said Gawain.
1950   "I thank you, by the Rood,"
and how the fox was slain
he told him as they stood.

With mirth and minstrelsy and meats at their pleasure
as merry they made as any men could be;
1955   amid the laughter of ladies and light words of jest
both Gawain and the good man could no gayer have proved,
unless they had doted indeed or else drunken had been.
Both the host and his household went on with their games,
till the hour had approached when part must they all;
1960   to bed were now bound the brave folk at last.
Bowing low his leave of the lord there first
the good knight then took, and graciously thanked him:[8]
"For such a wondrous welcome as within these walls I have had,
for your honour at this high feast the High King reward you!

8. Gawain's highly stylized leave-taking is typical of courtly romance and again emphasizes his command of fine manners.

1965   In your service I set myself, your servant, if you will.
        For I must needs make a move tomorrow, as you know,
        if you give me some good man to go, as you promised,
        and guide me to the Green Chapel, as God may permit me
        to face on New Year's day such doom as befalls me."
1970   "On my word," said his host, "with hearty good will
        to all that ever I promised I promptly shall hold."
        Then a servant he assigns him to set him on the road,
        and by the downs to conduct him, that without doubt or delay
        he might through wild and through wood ways most straight
1975   pursue.
           Said Gawain, "My thanks receive,
           such a favour you will do!"
           The knight then took his leave
           of those noble ladies two.

1980   Sadly he kissed them and said his farewells,
        and pressed oft upon them in plenty his thanks,
        and they promptly the same again repaid him;
        to God's keeping they gave him, grievously sighing.
        Then from the people of the castle he with courtesy parted;
1985   all the men that he met he remembered with thanks
        for their care for his comfort and their kind service,
        and the trouble each had taken in attendance upon him;
        and every one was as woeful to wish him adieu
        as had they lived all their lives with his lordship in honour.
1990   Then with link-men and lights he was led to his chamber
        and brought sweetly to bed, there to be at his rest.
        That soundly he slept then assert will I not,
        for he had many matters in the morning to mind, if he would,
               in thought.
1995   There let him lie in peace,
               near now is the tryst he sought.
               If a while you will hold your peace,
               I will tell the deeds they wrought!

Part 4

        Now New Year draws near and the night passes,
2000   day comes driving the dark, as ordained by God;
        but wild weathers of the world awake in the land,
        clouds cast keenly the cold upon earth
        with bitter breath from the North biting the naked.
        Snow comes shivering sharp to shrivel the wild things,
2005   and whistling wind whirls from the heights
        and drives every dale full of drifts very deep.
        Long the knight listens as he lies in his bed;
        though he lays down his eyelids, very little he sleeps:
        at the crow of every cock he recalls well his tryst.

2010 Briskly he rose from his bed ere the break of day,
for there was light from a lamp that illumined his chamber.
He called to his chamberlain, who quickly him answered,
and he bade him bring his byrnie° and his beast saddle.   *chain-mail coat*
The man got him up and his gear fetched him,
2015 and garbed then Sir Gawain in great array;
first he clad him in his clothes to keep out the cold,
and after that in his harness that with heed had been tended,
both his pauncer and his plates° polished all brightly,   *leg armor*
the rings rid of the rust on his rich byrnie:
2020 all was neat as if new, and the knight him thanked
        with delight.
    He put on every piece
    all burnished well and bright;
    most gallant from here to Greece
2025   for his courser called the knight.

While the proudest of his apparel he put on himself:
his coat-armour, with the cognisance of the clear symbol
upon velvet environed with virtuous gems
all bound and braided about it, with broidered seams
2030 and with fine firs lined wondrous fairly within,
yet he overlooked not the lace that the lady had given him;
that Gawain forgot not, of his own good thinking;
when he had belted his brand° upon his buxom haunches,   *sword*
he twined the love-token twice then about him,
2035 and swiftly he swathed it sweetly about his waist,
that girdle of green silk, and gallant it looked
upon the royal red cloth that was rich to behold.
But he wore not for worth nor for wealth this girdle,
not for pride in the pendants, though polished they were,
2040 not though the glittering gold there gleamed at the ends,
but so that himself he might save when suffer he must,
must abide bane without debating it with blade or with brand
        of war.
    When arrayed the knight so bold
2045   came out before the door,
    to all that high household
    great thanks he gave once more.

Now Gringolet was groomed, the great horse and high,
who had been lodged to his liking and loyally tended:
2050 fain to gallop was that gallant horse for his good fettle.
His master to him came and marked well his coat,
and said: "Now solemnly myself I swear on my troth
there is a company in this castle that is careful of honour!
Their lord that them leads, may his lot be joyful!
2055 Their beloved lady in life may delight befall her!
If they out of charity thus cherish a guest,
upholding their house in honour, may He them reward

that upholds heaven on high, and all of you too!
And if life a little longer I might lead upon earth,
2060   I would give you some guerdon° gladly, were I able."   *reward*
Then he steps in the stirrup and strides on his horse;
his shield his man showed him, and on shoulder he slung it,
Gringolet he goaded with his gilded heels,
and he plunged forth on the pavement, and prancing no more
2065   stood there.
        Ready now was his squire to ride
        that his helm and lance would bear.
        "Christ keep this castle!" he cried
        and wished it fortune fair.

2070   The bridge was brought down and the broad gates then
unbarred and swung back upon both hinges.
The brave man blessed himself, and the boards crossing,
bade the porter up rise, who before the prince kneeling
gave him "Good day, Sir Gawain!", and "God save you!"
2075   Then he went on his way with the one man only
to guide him as he goes to that grievous place
where he is due to endure the dolorous blow.
They go by banks and by braes° where branches are bare,[1]   *hillsides*
they climb along cliffs where clingeth the cold;
2080   the heavens are lifted high, but under them evilly
mist hangs moist on the moor, melts on the mountains;
every hill has a hat, a mist-mantle huge.
Brooks break and boil on braes all about,
bright bubbling on their banks where they bustle downwards.
2085   Very wild through the wood is the way they must take,
until soon comes the season when the sun rises
        that day.
        On a high hill they abode,
        white snow beside them lay;
2090   the man that by him rode
        there bade his master stay.

"For so far I have taken you, sir, at this time,
and now you are near to that noted place
that you have enquired and questioned so curiously after.
2095   But I will announce now the truth, since you are known to me,
and you are a lord in this life that I love greatly,
if you would follow my advice you would fare better.
The place that you pass to, men perilous hold it,
the worst wight in the world in that waste dwelleth;
2100   for he is stout and stern, and to strike he delights,
and he mightier than any man upon middle-earth is,
and his body is bigger than the four best men

1. The grimness of this landscape, reminiscent of wastelands in Anglo-Saxon poetry, swiftly returns the poem from the courtly world to the elemental challenge Gawain now faces.

that are in Arthur's house, either Hector[2] or others.
All goes as he chooses at the Green Chapel;
2105 no one passes by that place so proud in his arms
that he hews not to death by dint of his hand.
For he is a man monstrous, and mercy he knows not;
for be it a churl or a chaplain that by the Chapel rideth,
a monk or a mass-priest or any man besides,
2110 he would as soon have him slain as himself go alive.
And so I say to you, as sure as you sit in your saddle,
if you come there, you'll be killed, if the carl has his way.
Trust me, that is true, though you had twenty lives
     to yield.
2115   He here has dwelt now long
    and stirred much strife on field;
    against his strokes so strong
    yourself you cannot shield.

And so, good Sir Gawain, now go another way,
2120 and let the man alone, for the love of God, sir!
Come to some other country, and there may Christ keep you!
And I shall haste me home again, and on my honour I promise
that I swear will by God and all His gracious saints,
so help me God and the Halidom,[3] and other oaths a plenty,
2125 that I will safe keep your secret, and say not a word
that ever you fain were to flee for any foe that I knew of."
"Gramercy!" quoth Gawain, and regretfully answered:
"Well, man, I wish thee, who wishest my good,
and keep safe my secret, I am certain thou wouldst.
2130 But however heedfully thou hid it, if I here departed,
fain in fear now to flee, in the fashion thou speakest,
I should a knight coward be, I could not be excused.
Nay, I'll fare to the Chapel, whatever chance may befall,
and have such words with that wild man as my wish is to say,
2135 come fair or come foul, as fate will allot
    me there.
    He may be a fearsome knave
    to tame, and club may bear;
    but His servants true to save
2140   the Lord can well prepare."

"Marry!" quoth the other man, "now thou makest it so clear
that thou wishest thine own bane to bring on thyself,
and to lose thy life hast a liking, to delay thee I care not!
Have here thy helm on thy head, thy spear in thy hand,
2145 and ride down by yon rock-side where runs this same track,
till thou art brought to the bottom of the baleful valley.
A little to thy left hand then look o'er the green,

2. Chief hero among the defenders of Troy and, like Arthur, one of the "Nine Worthies" celebrated for their heroic valor; or perhaps Arthur's knight Hector De Maris.
3. "By my holy relics."

and thou wilt see on the slope the selfsame chapel,
and the great man and grim on ground that it keeps.

2150   Now farewell in God's name, Gawain the noble!
For all the gold in the world I would not go with thee,
nor bear thee fellowship through this forest one foot further!"
With that his bridle towards the wood back the man turneth,
hits his horse with his heels as hard as he can,

2155   gallops on the greenway, and the good knight there leaves
    alone.
    Quoth Gawain: "By God on high
    I will neither grieve nor groan.
    With God's will I comply,

2160   Whose protection I do own."

Then he puts spurs to Gringolet, and espying the track,
thrust in along a bank by a thicket's border,
rode down the rough brae right to the valley;
and then he gazed all about: a grim place he thought it,

2165   and saw no sign of shelter on any side at all,
only high hillsides sheer upon either hand,
and notched knuckled crags with gnarled boulders;
the very skies by the peaks were scraped, it appeared.
Then he halted and held in his horse for the time,

2170   and changed oft his front the Chapel to find.
Such on no side he saw, as seemed to him strange,
save a mound as it might be near the marge of a green,
a worn barrow[4] on a brae by the brink of a water,
beside falls in a flood that was flowing down;

2175   the burn° bubbled therein, as if boiling it were.   *brook*
He urged on his horse then, and came up to the mound,
there lightly alit, and lashed to a tree
his reins, with a rough branch rightly secured them.
Then he went to the barrow and about it he walked,

2180   debating in his mind what might the thing be.
It had a hole at the end and at either side
and with grass in green patches was grown all over,
and was all hollow within: nought but an old cavern,
or a cleft in an old crag; he could not it name

2185   aright.
    "Can this be the Chapel Green,
    O Lord?" said the gentle knight.
    "Here the Devil might say, I ween,
    his matins about midnight!"

2190   "On my word," quoth Gawain, "'tis a wilderness here!
This oratory looks evil. With herbs overgrown
it fits well that fellow transformed into green

---

4. Perhaps a burial mound, which seems to link the moment to ancient, probably pagan, inhabitants.

to follow here his devotions in the Devil's fashion.
Now I feel in my five wits the Fiend 'tis himself
2195   that has trapped me with this tryst to destroy me here.
This is a chapel of mischance, the church most accursed
that ever I entered. Evil betide it!"
With high helm on his head, his lance in his hand,
he roams up to the roof of that rough dwelling.
2200   Then he heard from the high hill, in a hard rock-wall
beyond the stream on a steep, a sudden startling noise.
How it clattered in the cliff, as if to cleave it asunder,
as if one upon a grindstone were grinding a scythe!
How it whirred and it rasped as water in a mill-race!
2205   How it rushed, and it rang, rueful to harken!
Then "By God," quoth Gawain, "I guess this ado
is meant for my honour, meetly to hail me
            as knight!
        As God wills! Waylaway!
2210   That helps me not a mite.
        My life though down I lay,
        no noise can me affright."

Then clearly the knight there called out aloud:
"Who is master in this place to meet me at tryst?
2215   For now 'tis good Gawain on ground that here walks.
If any aught hath to ask, let him hasten to me,
either now or else never, his needs to further!"
"Stay!" said one standing above on the steep o'er his head,
"and thou shalt get in good time what to give thee I vowed."
2220   Still with that rasping and racket he rushed on a while,
and went back to his whetting, till he wished to descend.
And then he climbed past a crag, and came from a hole,
hurtling out of a hid nook with a horrible weapon:
a Danish axe[5] newly dressed the dint to return,
2225   with cruel cutting-edge curved along the handle—
filed on a whetstone, and four feet in width,
'twas no less—along its lace of luminous hue;
and the great man in green still guised as before,
his locks and long beard, his legs and his face,
2230   save that firm on his feet he fared on the ground,
steadied the haft on the stones and stalked beside it.
When he walked to the water, where he wade would not,
he hopped over on his axe and haughtily strode,
fierce and fell on a field where far all about
2235   lay snow.
        Sir Gawain the man met there,
        neither bent nor bowed he low.

5. A long-bladed ax, associated with Viking raiders.

The other said: "Now, sirrah fair,
I true at tryst thee know!"

2240   "Gawain," said that green man, "may God keep thee!
On my word, sir, I welcome thee with a will to my place,
and thou hast timed thy travels as trusty man should,
and thou hast forgot not the engagement agreed on between us:
at this time gone a twelvemonth thou took'st thy allowance,
2245   and I should now this New Year nimbly repay thee.
And we are in this valley now verily on our own,
there are no people to part us—we can play as we like.
Have thy helm off thy head, and have here thy pay!
Bandy me no more debate than I brought before thee
2250   when thou didst sweep off my head with one swipe only!"
"Nay," quoth Gawain, "by God that gave me my soul,
I shall grudge thee not a grain any grief that follows.
Only restrain thee to one stroke, and still shall I stand
and offer thee no hindrance to act as thou likest
2255   right here."
            With a nod of his neck he bowed,
            let bare the flesh appear;
            he would not by dread be cowed,
            no sign he gave of fear.

2260   Then the great man in green gladly prepared him,
gathered up his grim tool there Gawain to smite;
with all the lust in his limbs aloft he heaved it,
shaped as mighty a stroke as if he meant to destroy him.
Had it driving come down as dour as he aimed it,
2265   under his dint would have died the most doughty man ever.
But Gawain on that guisarm° then glanced to one side,   axe
as down it came gliding on the green there to end him,
and he shrank a little with his shoulders at the sharp iron.
With a jolt the other man jerked back the blade,
2270   and reproved then the prince, proudly him taunting.
"Thou'rt not Gawain," said the green man, "who is so good reported,
who never flinched from any foes on fell or in dale;
and now thou fleest in fear, ere thou feelest a hurt!
Of such cowardice that knight I ne'er heard accused.
2275   Neither blenched I nor backed, when thy blow, sir, thou aimedst,
nor uttered any cavil in the court of King Arthur.
My head flew to my feet, and yet fled I never;
but thou, ere thou hast any hurt, in thy heart quailest,
and so the nobler knight to be named I deserve
2280   therefore."
            "I blenched once," Gawain said,
            "and I will do so no more.
            But if on floor now falls my head,
            I cannot it restore.

2285   But get busy, I beg, sir, and bring me to the point.
        Deal me my destiny, and do it out of hand!
        For I shall stand from thee a stroke and stir not again
        till thine axe hath hit me, have here my word on't!"
        "Have at thee then!" said the other, and heaved it aloft,
2290   and watched him as wrathfully as if he were wild with rage.
        He made at him a mighty aim, but the man he touched not,
        holding back hastily his hand, ere hurt it might do.
        Gawain warily awaited it, and winced with no limb,
        but stood as still as a stone or the stump of a tree
2295   that with a hundred ravelled roots in rocks is embedded.
        This time merrily remarked then the man in the green:
        "So, now thou hast thy heart whole, a hit I must make.
        May the high order now keep thee that Arthur gave thee,
        and guard thy gullet at this go, if it can gain thee that."
2300   Angrily with ire then answered Sir Gawain:
        "Why! lash away, thou lusty man! Too long dost thou threaten.
        'Tis thy heart methinks in thee that now quaileth!"
        "In faith," said the fellow, "so fiercely thou speakest,
        I no longer will linger delaying thy errand
2305   right now."
            Then to strike he took his stance
            and grimaced with lip and brow.
            He that of rescue saw no chance
            was little pleased, I trow.

2310   Lightly his weapon he lifted, and let it down neatly
        with the bent horn of the blade towards the neck that was bare;
        though he hewed with a hammer-swing, he hurt him no more
        than to snick him on one side and sever the skin.
        Through the fair fat sank the edge, and the flesh entered,
2315   so that the shining blood o'er his shoulders was shed on the earth;
        and when the good knight saw the gore that gleamed on the snow,
        he sprang out with spurning feet a spear's length and more,
        in haste caught his helm and on his head cast it,
        under his fair shield he shot with a shake of his shoulders,[6]
2320   brandished his bright sword, and boldly he spake—
        never since he as manchild of his mother was born
        was he ever on this earth half so happy a man:
        "Have done, sir, with thy dints! Now deal me no more!
        I have stood from thee a stroke without strife on this spot,
2325   and if thou offerest me others, I shall answer thee promptly,
        and give as good again, and as grim, be assured,
            shall pay.
            But one stroke here's my due,

---

6. Gawain, who has displayed so much courtly refinement and religious emotion, now shows himself a practiced fighter, swiftly pulling his armor into place.

as the covenant clear did say
2330   that in Arthur's halls we drew.
And so, good sir, now stay!"

From him the other stood off, and on his axe rested,
held the haft to the ground, and on the head leaning,
gazed at the good knight as on the green he there strode.
2335   To see him standing so stout, so stern there and fearless,
armed and unafraid, his heart it well pleased.
Then merrily he spoke with a mighty voice,
and loudly it rang, as to that lord he said:
"Fearless knight on this field, so fierce do not be!
2340   No man here unmannerly hath thee maltreated,
nor aught given thee not granted by agreement at court.
A hack I thee vowed, and thou'st had it, so hold thee content;
I remit thee the remnant of all rights I might claim.
If I brisker had been, a buffet, it may be,
2345   I could have handed thee more harshly, and harm could have done thee.
First I menaced thee in play with no more than a trial,
and clove thee with no cleft: I had a claim to the feint,
for the fast pact we affirmed on the first evening,
and thou fairly and unfailing didst faith with me keep,
2350   all thy gains thou me gavest, as good man ought.
The other trial for the morning, man, I thee tendered
when thou kissedst my comely wife, and the kisses didst render.
For the two here I offered only two harmless feints

to make.
2355   The true shall truly repay,
for no peril then need he quake.
Thou didst fail on the third day,
and so that tap now take!

"For it is my weed that thou wearest, that very woven girdle:
2360   my own wife it awarded thee, I wot° well indeed.   *know*
Now I am aware of thy kisses, and thy courteous ways,
and of thy wooing by my wife: I worked that myself!
I sent her to test thee, and thou seem'st to me truly
the fair knight most faultless that e'er foot set on earth!
2365   As a pearl than white pease is prized more highly,
so is Gawain, in good faith, than other gallant knights.
But in this you lacked, sir, a little, and of loyalty came short.
But that was for no artful wickedness, nor for wooing either,
but because you loved your own life: the less do I blame you."
2370   The other stern knight in a study° then stood a long while,   *thinking*
in such grief and disgust he had a grue° in his heart;   *shudder*
all the blood from his breast in his blush mingled,
and he shrank into himself with shame at that speech.
The first words on that field that he found then to say
2375   were: "Cursed be ye, Coveting, and Cowardice also!

In you is vileness, and vice that virtue destroyeth."
He took then the treacherous thing, and untying the knot
fiercely flung he the belt at the feet of the knight:
"See there the falsifier, and foul be its fate!
2380   Through care for thy blow Cowardice brought me
to consent to Coveting, my true kind to forsake,
which is free-hand and faithful word that are fitting to knights.
Now I am faulty and false, who afraid have been ever
of treachery and troth-breach: the two now my curse
2385   may bear!
    I confess, sir, here to you
    all faulty has been my fare.
    Let me gain your grace anew,
    and after I will beware."

2390   Then the other man laughed and lightly answered:
"I hold it healed beyond doubt, the harm that I had.
Thou hast confessed thee so clean and acknowledged thine errors,
and hast the penance plain to see from the point of my blade,
that I hold thee purged of that debt, made as pure and as clean
2395   as hadst thou done no ill deed since the day thou wert born.
And I give thee, sir, the girdle with gold at its hems,
for it is green like my gown. So, Sir Gawain, you may
think of this our contest when in the throng thou walkest
among princes of high praise; 'twill be a plain reminder
2400   of the chance of the Green Chapel between chivalrous knights.
And now you shall in this New Year come anon to my house,
and in our revels the rest of this rich season
        shall go."
    The lord pressed him hard to wend,
2405   and said, "my wife, I know,
    we soon shall make your friend,
    who was your bitter foe."

"Nay forsooth!" the knight said, and seized then his helm,
and duly it doffed, and the doughty man thanked:
2410   "I have lingered too long! May your life now be blest,
and He promptly repay you Who apportions all honours!
And give my regards to her grace, your goodly consort,
both to her and to the other, to mine honoured ladies,
who thus their servant with their designs have subtly beguiled.
2415   But no marvel it is if mad be a fool,
and by the wiles of women to woe be brought.
For even so Adam by one on earth was beguiled,
and Solomon by several, and to Samson moreoever
his doom by Delilah was dealt; and David was after
2420   blinded by Bathsheba, and he bitterly suffered.[7]

---

7. Gawain suddenly erupts in a brief but fierce diatribe, including this list of treacherous women recognizable from contemporary misogynist texts.

Now if these came to grief through their guile, a gain 'twould be vast
to love them well and believe them not, if it lay in man's power!
Since these were aforetime the fairest, by fortune most blest,
eminent among all the others who under heaven bemused

2425   were too,
    and all of them were betrayed
    by women that they knew,
    though a fool I now am made,
    some excuse I think my due.

2430   "But for your girdle," quoth Gawain, "may God you repay!
That I will gain with good will, not for the gold so joyous
of the cincture, nor the silk, nor the swinging pendants,
nor for wealth, nor for worth, nor for workmanship fine;
but as a token of my trespass I shall turn to it often

2435   when I ride in renown, ruefully recalling
the failure and the frailty of the flesh so perverse,
so tender, so ready to take taints of defilement.
And thus, when pride my heart pricks for prowess in arms,
one look at this love-lace shall lowlier make it.

2440   But one thing I would pray you, if it displeaseth you not,
since you are the lord of yonder land, where I lodged for a while
in your house and in honour—may He you reward
Who upholdeth the heavens and on high sitteth!—
how do you announce your true name? And then nothing further."

2445   "That I will tell thee truly," then returned the other.
"Bertilak de Hautdesert hereabouts I am called,
[who thus have been enchanted and changed in my hue]
by the might of Morgan le Fay[8] that in my mansion dwelleth,
and by cunning of lore and crafts well learned.

2450   The magic arts of Merlin she many hath mastered;
for deeply in dear love she dealt on a time
with that accomplished clerk, as at Camelot runs
      the fame;
    and Morgan the Goddess

2455   is therefore now her name.
    None power and pride possess
    too high for her to tame.

She made me go in this guise to your goodly court
to put its pride to the proof, if the report were true

2460   that runs of the great renown of the Round Table.
She put this magic upon me to deprive you of your wits,
in hope Guinevere to hurt, that she in horror might die

---

8. Morgan is Arthur's half-sister and ruler of the mysterious Avalon; she learned magical arts from Merlin. Her presence can bode good or ill. In some stories she holds a deep grudge against Guinevere, yet she carries off the wounded Arthur after his final battle, perhaps to heal him. The earlier Celtic Morrigan, possibly related, is queen of demons, sower of discord, and goddess of war.

aghast at that glamoury° that gruesomely spake   *enchanted one*
with its head in its hand before the high table.

2465   She it is that is at home, that ancient lady;
she is indeed thine own aunt, Arthur's half-sister,
daughter of the Duchess of Tintagel on whom doughty Sir Uther
after begat Arthur, who in honour is now.[9]
Therefore I urge thee in earnest, sir, to thine aunt return!

2470   In my hall make merry! My household thee loveth,
and I wish thee as well, upon my word, sir knight,
as any that go under God, for thy great loyalty."
But he denied him with a "Nay! by no means I will!"
They clasp then and kiss and to the care give each other

2475   of the Prince of Paradise; and they part on that field
     so cold.
      To the king's court on courser keen
     then hastened Gawain the bold,
     and the knight in the glittering green

2480   to ways of his own did hold.

Wild ways in the world Gawain now rideth
on Gringolet: by the grace of God he still lived.
Oft in house he was harboured and lay oft in the open,
oft vanquished his foe in adventures as he fared

2485   which I intend not this time in my tale to recount.
The hurt was healed that he had in his neck,
and the bright-hued belt he bore now about it
obliquely like a baldric[1] bound at his side,
under his left arm with a knot that lace was fastened

2490   to betoken he had been detected in the taint of a fault;
and so at last he came to the Court again safely.
Delight there was awakened, when the lords were aware
that good Gawain had returned: glad news they thought it.
The king kissed the knight, and the queen also,

2495   and then in turn many a true knight that attended to greet him.
About his quest they enquire, and he recounts all the marvels,
declares all the hardships and care that he had,
what chanced at the Chapel, what cheer made the knight,
the love of the lady, and the lace at the last.

2500   The notch in his neck naked he showed them
that he had for his dishonesty from the hands of the knight
     in blame.
      It was torment to tell the truth:
     in his face the blood did flame;

2505   he groaned for grief and ruth°   *remorse*
     when he showed it, to his shame.

---

9. The poem now recalls an earlier transgression of guest–host obligations, when Uther began to lust for Ygerne while her husband, Gorlois, was at his court; he later killed Gorlois and married Ygerne.
1. A belt for a sword or bugle, worn over one shoulder and across the chest.

"Lo! Lord," he said at last, and the lace handled,
"This is the band! For this a rebuke I bear in my neck!
This is the grief and disgrace I have got for myself
2510 from the covetousness and cowardice that o'ercame me there!
This is the token of the troth-breach that I am detected in,
and needs must I wear it while in the world I remain;
for a man may cover his blemish, but unbind it he cannot,
for where once 'tis applied, thence part will it never."
2515 The king comforted the knight, and all the Court also
laughed loudly thereat, and this law made in mirth
the lords and the ladies that whoso belonged to the Table,
every knight of the Brotherhood, a baldric should have,
a band of bright green obliquely about him,
2520 and this for love of that knight as a livery should wear.
For that was reckoned the distinction of the Round Table,
and honour was his that had it evermore after,
as it is written in the best of the books of romance.
Thus in Arthur his days happened this marvel,
2525 as the Book of the Brut beareth us witness;
since Brutus the bold knight to Britain came first,
after the siege and the assault had ceased at Troy,
        I trow,
many a marvel such before,
2530 has happened here ere now.
To His bliss us bring Who bore
the Crown of Thorns on brow!   AMEN

HONY SOYT QUI MAL PENCE[2]

Peter Abelard and Heloïse
c. 1079–c. 1142   c. 1095–c. 1163

Abelard and Heloïse were the most famous couple of the twelfth century, celebrated as much
for their extraordinary learning as for their tragic love affair. Abelard was a prolific songwriter,
a popular lecturer and debater, and an influential author of works on philosophy and theology.
Heloïse was already regarded as one of France's most learned women before she met Abelard,
who became her tutor; she would later become one of the country's most powerful women as
abbess of the Paraclete hermitage. Their correspondence is representative of an era where scripture and classical literature were recited as if second nature, and where questions of theology
were embraced as passionately as those of love.

---

2. "Let them be ashamed who think ill of it" (French), the English royal motto.

It is difficult to dispute Abelard's claim that his life was wholly governed by the changeable nature of Fortune's wheel. The scholarly life lured him away from the knightly calling to which his birth into the petty nobility of Brittany would have pointed him. He eventually worked his way into a top position as a Paris lecturer in the *trivium:* grammar, rhetoric, and logic, or dialectic, as it was commonly known. Lecturing was part explication of texts, part debate, and part public performance; Abelard excelled in all three aspects, making short work of his main rival (and former teacher) William of Champeaux, to become master of the Cathedral School at Notre Dame. Such positions were closely tied to political connections, and Abelard's star in Paris waxed and waned with the fortunes of his benefactor and William's enemy, the powerful and unscrupulous Stephen de Garlande, who was, on and off, the most powerful man in the court of Louis VI, king of France.

Abelard became Heloïse's tutor when around 1117 he came to lodge at the house of her uncle and guardian, Fulbert, a canon at Notre Dame. Although he portrays her as a naive teenager in his autobiography, *Historia Calamitatum (The Story of My Adversities)*, Heloïse was likely in her early twenties when they met. Abelard was in his thirties, and at the height of his powers. He claimed to have coldheartedly seduced her; she called it love at first sight. Either way, the affair was the talk of Paris, as Abelard's love songs (none of which have survived) were performed all over the city. When Heloïse became pregnant, Abelard spirited her away to his family's estate, where she gave birth to a son, whom they named Astrolabe, after an instrument used by astronomers. On their return to Paris, they were secretly married in the presence of Fulbert and witnesses. Secular clergymen like Abelard were permitted to marry, but the existence of a wife would have precluded his advancement far more than would a mistress. When Heloïse swore publicly that she was not married, Abelard felt compelled to take her away again, disguised as a nun, out of reach of her furious uncle to Argenteuil outside Paris. In retaliation, Fulbert's kinsmen burst in on Abelard at night and castrated him. Abelard chose to take vows as a monk, and compelled Heloïse to take the veil.

There were few paths open to an ambitious woman in twelfth century Europe, and Heloïse appears to have pinned most of her hopes on Abelard. She had adamantly opposed the marriage; she equally resisted becoming a nun. Once forced into the role, she nevertheless excelled, soon becoming abbess at Argenteuil. Ten years after she and Abelard had gone their separate ways, Heloïse and her nuns, in a move that was probably politically motivated, were expelled from Argenteuil on charges of immorality. Abelard had founded the Paraclete, a hermitage near the main road from Paris to Dijon. As he had since left to become abbot of Saint Gildas, a monastery in the far west of Brittany, he offered the Paraclete to Heloïse. She remained there until her death thirty-five years later.

While at Saint Gildas, at a low point in his fortunes, and under threat of death from his unruly charges, Abelard wrote and circulated the *Historia Calamitatum* in hopes of restoring his reputation. When the account found its way to Heloïse, she chose to respond, and their correspondence began. The letters take the form of a passionate debate, as Heloïse musters all of the tools of logic and rhetoric learned from Abelard to challenge his version of their past and his instructions on how she should behave in the present. For Abelard, the past was a series of mistakes, of incorrect actions to be overcome and regretted; for Heloïse, the past remained continuous with the present. As a good Christian, Abelard argued, he had laid their love to rest and married her to Christ. Heloïse retorted that she was a hypocrite, living a life of denial and unfulfilled desire. Abelard succeeded in quieting Heloïse's passionate recriminations; she succeeded in forcing him to stay in contact with her. Abelard provided the Paraclete with a steady stream of devotional writing such as hymns and letters of instruction. In the context of a marriage originally based equally on carnal passion and on the interchange of ideas, this can be regarded as a victory for Heloïse.

While Heloïse remained at the Paraclete, Abelard returned to Paris, where, in another partly political move, he was charged with heresy by a group including his rival William of Champeaux. The case was prosecuted by Bernard of Clairvaux, founder of the reforming Cistercian Order and a staunch opponent of the rational approach to theology and faith represented by Abelard's writings. Bernard's influence with the pope carried the day: Abelard and his followers were excommunicated, his doctrine was condemned, he was sentenced to perpetual silence as a heretic, and his books were consigned to the fire. Abelard found refuge at Cluny with Peter the Venerable, but, his health broken, he died just two years later, in 1142.

Among the most important of Abelard's voluminous writings are *Yes and No (Sic et Non)* where he demonstrated the need of rational analysis to explain doctrine by citing contradictory answers from the Church Fathers to a series of key questions of faith; the *Dialogue Between a Jew, a Philosopher, and a Christian,* in which Abelard judges a debate between three positions on religion; the *Ethics,* in which he argued that a deed was sinful only if the intention was sinful; and his *Theologia,* published in several versions, all of which maintained that the unity of the Trinity was not a mystery which could only be taken on faith, but was a reasonable proposition comprehensible to any intelligent person, Christian or pagan. Abelard has been regarded as the first modern theologian, attempting to reconcile human reason with Christian revelation, and the first intellectual, founder of the university culture of Paris. The life of Heloïse is no less important, not only as a record of professional accomplishment, but as a striking reminder of the complex ways in which religion both controlled and reflected the dictates of individual desire in medieval Europe.

PRONUNCIATIONS:
Heloïse: eh-lo-EEZ
Abelard: AH-be-lahrd

from The Letters of Abelard and Heloïse[1]

from *Letter 1. Heloïse to Abelard*

To her master, or rather her father, husband, or rather brother; his handmaid, or rather his daughter, wife, or rather sister; to Abelard, Heloïse.[2]

Not long ago, my beloved, by chance someone brought me the letter of consolation you had sent to a friend.[3] I saw at once from the superscription that it was yours, and was all the more eager to read it since the writer is so dear to my heart. I hoped for renewal of strength, at least from the writer's words which would picture for me the reality I have lost. But nearly every line of this letter was filled, I remember, with gall and wormwood, as it told the pitiful story of our entry into religion and the cross of unending suffering which you, my only love, continue to bear.

In that letter you did indeed carry out the promise you made your friend at the beginning, that he would think his own troubles insignificant or nothing, in comparison with your own. First you revealed the persecution you suffered from your teachers, then the supreme treachery of the mutilation of your person, and then described the abominable jealousy and violent attacks of your fellow-students, Alberic of Rheims

1. Translated by Betty Radice.
2. The heading of Heloïse's letter manages to encapsulate the entire history of their relationship: as her *magister,* master or teacher; as her spiritual father, founder of the

Paraclete; as her lover first and afterwards as her husband; as her brother under God; and as the individual Abelard to the individual Heloïse.
3. The *Historia Calamitatum.*

and Lotulf of Lombardy. You did not gloss over what at their instigation was done to your distinguished theological work or what amounted to a prison sentence passed on yourself. Then you went on to the plotting against you by your abbot and false brethren, the serious slanders from those two pseudo-apostles, spread against you by the same rivals, and the scandal stirred up among many people because you had acted contrary to custom in naming your oratory after the Paraclete. You went on to the incessant, intolerable persecutions which you still endure at the hands of that cruel tyrant and the evil monks you call your sons, and so brought your sad story to an end.

No one, I think, could read or hear it dry-eyed; my own sorrows are renewed by the detail in which you have told it, and redoubled because you say your perils are still increasing. All of us here[4] are driven to despair of your life, and every day we await in fear and trembling the final word of your death. And so in the name of Christ, who is still giving you some protection for his service, we beseech you to write as often as you think fit to us who are his handmaids and yours, with news of the perils in which you are still storm-tossed. We are all that are left you, so at least you should let us share your sorrow or your joy.

It is always some consolation in sorrow to feel that it is shared, and any burden laid on several is carried more lightly or removed. And if this storm has quietened down for a while, you must be all the more prompt to send us a letter which will be the more gladly received. But whatever you write about will bring us no small relief in the mere proof that you have us in mind. Letters from absent friends are welcome indeed, as Seneca himself shows us by his own example when he writes these words in a passage of a letter to his friend Lucilius:[5]

> Thank you for writing to me often, the one way in which you can make your presence felt, for I never have a letter from you without the immediate feeling that we are together. If pictures of absent friends give us pleasure, renewing our memories and relieving the pain of separation even if they cheat us with empty comfort, how much more welcome is a letter which comes to us in the very handwriting of an absent friend.

Thank God that here at least is a way of restoring your presence to us which no malice can prevent, nor any obstacle hinder; then do not, I beseech you, allow any negligence to hold you back.

You wrote your friend a long letter of consolation, prompted no doubt by his misfortunes, but really telling of your own. The detailed account you gave of these may have been intended for his comfort, but it also greatly increased our own feeling of desolation; in your desire to heal his wounds you have dealt us fresh wounds of grief as well as re-opening the old.[6] I beg you, then, as you set about tending the wounds which others have dealt, heal the wounds you have yourself inflicted. You have done your duty to a friend and comrade, discharged your debt to friendship and comradeship, but it is a greater debt which binds you in obligation to us who can properly be called not friends so much as dearest friends, not comrades but daughters, or any other conceivable name more tender and holy. How great the debt by which you have bound yourself to us needs neither proof nor witness, were it in any doubt; if the whole world kept silent, the facts themselves would cry out. For you after God are the

---

4. At the Paraclete, where Heloïse was then abbess. "Paraclete" (advocate, intercessor) is a name for the Holy Spirit.
5. Cited from the Roman philosopher and tragedian Seneca, *Moral Epistles*, number 70. Here, as throughout,

Heloïse uses Abelard's sources and references in the *Historia Calamitatum* to structure her own letter.
6. Heloïse uses the first-person plural, encompassing both herself and the nuns of the Paraclete, even though the undertone of the letter is extremely personal.

sole founder of this place, the sole builder of this oratory, the sole creator of this community. You have built nothing here upon another man's foundation.[7] Everything here is your own creation. This was a wilderness open to wild beasts and brigands, a place which had known no home nor habitation of men. In the very lairs of wild beasts and lurking-places of robbers, where the name of God was never heard, you built a sanctuary to God and dedicated a shrine in the name of the Holy Spirit. To build it you drew nothing from the riches of kings and princes, though their wealth was great and could have been yours for the asking: whatever was done, the credit was to be yours alone. Clerks and scholars came flocking here, eager for your teaching, and ministered to all your needs; and even those who had lived on the benefices of the Church and knew only how to receive offerings, not to make them, whose hands were held out to take but not to give, became pressing in their lavish offers of assistance.

And so it is yours, truly your own, this new plantation for God's purpose, but it is sown with plants which are still very tender and need watering if they are to thrive. Through its feminine nature this plantation would be weak and frail even if it were not new; and so it needs a more careful and regular cultivation, according to the words of the Apostle: "I planted the seed and Apollos watered it; but God made it grow."[8] The Apostle through the doctrine that he preached had planted and established in the faith the Corinthians, to whom he was writing. Afterwards the Apostle's own disciple, Apollos, had watered them with his holy exhortations and so God's grace bestowed on them growth in the virtues.[9] You cultivate a vineyard of another's vines which you did not plant yourself and which has now turned to bitterness against you, so that often your advice brings no result and your holy words are uttered in vain.[1] You devote your care to another's vineyard; think what you owe to your own. You teach and admonish rebels to no purpose, and in vain you throw the pearls of your divine eloquence to the pigs.[2] While you spend so much on the stubborn, consider what you owe to the obedient; you are so generous to your enemies but should reflect on how you are indebted to your daughters. Apart from everything else, consider the close tie by which you have bound yourself to me, and repay the debt you owe a whole community of women dedicated to God by discharging it the more dutifully to her who is yours alone.

Your superior wisdom knows better than our humble learning of the many serious treatises which the holy Fathers compiled for the instruction or exhortation or even the consolation of holy women, and of the care with which these were composed. And so in the precarious early days of our conversion long ago I was not a little surprised and troubled by your forgetfulness, when neither reverence for God nor our mutual love nor the example of the holy Fathers made you think of trying to comfort me, wavering and exhausted as I was by prolonged grief, either by word when I was with you or by letter when we had parted. Yet you must know that you are bound to me by an obligation which is all the greater for the further close tie of the marriage sacrament uniting us, and are the deeper in my debt because of the love I have always borne you, as everyone knows, a love which is beyond all bounds.

---

7. Compare to Romans 15:20: "thus making it my ambition to preach the gospel, not where Christ has already been named, lest I build on another man's foundation."
8. Corinthians 3:6: "I planted, Apollos watered, but God gave the growth." Like many women writers in the Middle Ages, Heloïse was adept at adapting conventional sayings about women to serve her own arguments.
9. Acts 18:24–28.
1. Compare Jeremiah 2:21: "Yet I planted you a choice vine, wholly of pure seed. How then have you turned degenerate and become a wild vine?"
2. Matthew 7:6: "Do not throw your pearls before swine."

You know, beloved, as the whole world knows, how much I have lost in you, how at one wretched stroke of fortune that supreme act of flagrant treachery robbed me of my very self in robbing me of you; and how my sorrow for my loss is nothing compared with what I feel for the manner in which I lost you. Surely the greater the cause for grief the greater the need for the help of consolation, and this no one can bring but you; you are the sole cause of my sorrow, and you alone can grant me the grace of consolation. You alone have the power to make me sad, to bring me happiness or comfort; you alone have so great a debt to repay me, particularly now when I have carried out all your orders so implicitly that when I was powerless to oppose you in anything, I found strength at your command to destroy myself. I did more, strange to say—my love rose to such heights of madness that it robbed itself of what it most desired beyond hope of recovery, when immediately at your bidding I changed my clothing along with my mind, in order to prove you the sole possessor of my body and my will alike. God knows I never sought anything in you except yourself; I wanted simply you, nothing of yours. I looked for no marriage-bond, no marriage portion, and it was not my own pleasures and wishes I sought to gratify, as you well know, but yours. The name of wife may seem more sacred or more binding, but sweeter for me will always be the word mistress, or, if you will permit me, that of concubine or whore. I believed that the more I humbled myself on your account, the more gratitude I should win from you, and also the less damage I should do to the brightness of your reputation.

You yourself on your own account did not altogether forget this in the letter of consolation I have spoken of which you wrote to a friend; there you thought fit to set out some of the reasons I gave in trying to dissuade you from binding us together in an ill-starred marriage. But you kept silent about most of my arguments for preferring love to wedlock and freedom to chains. God is my witness that if Augustus, Emperor of the whole world,[3] thought fit to honour me with marriage and conferred all the earth on me to possess for ever, it would be dearer and more honourable to me to be called not his Empress but your whore.

 * * * What king or philosopher could match your fame? What district, town or village did not long to see you? When you appeared in public, who did not hurry to catch a glimpse of you, or crane his neck and strain his eyes to follow your departure? Every wife, every young girl desired you in absence and was on fire in your presence; queens and great ladies envied me my joys and my bed.

You had besides, I admit, two special gifts whereby to win at once the heart of any woman—your gifts for composing verse and song, in which we know other philosophers have rarely been successful. This was for you no more than a diversion, a recreation from the labours of your philosophic work, but you left many love-songs and verses which won wide popularity for the charm of their words and tunes and kept your name continually on everyone's lips. The beauty of the airs ensured that even the unlettered did not forget you; more than anything this made women sigh for love of you. And as most of these songs told of our love, they soon made me widely known and roused the envy of many women against me. For your manhood was adorned by every grace of mind and body, and among the women who envied me then, could there be one now who does not feel compelled by my misfortune to sympathize with my loss of such joys? Who is there who was once my enemy, whether

---

3. Caesar Augustus, born Gaius Octavius (63 B.C.E.–14 C.E.), was the first Roman emperor. The contrast between pagan and Christian heightens the rhetorical comparison between wife and whore.

man or woman, who is not moved now by the compassion which is my due? Wholly guilty though I am, I am also, as you know, wholly innocent. It is not the deed but the intention of the doer which makes the crime, and justice should weigh not what was done but the spirit in which it is done.[4] What my intention towards you has always been, you alone who have known it can judge. I submit all to your scrutiny, yield to your testimony in all things.

Tell me one thing, if you can. Why, after our entry into religion, which was your decision alone, have I been so neglected and forgotten by you that I have neither a word from you when you are here to give me strength nor the consolation of a letter in absence?[5] Tell me, I say, if you can—or I will tell you what I think and indeed the world suspects. It was desire, not affection which bound you to me, the flame of lust rather than love. So when the end came to what you desired, any show of feeling you used to make went with it. This is not merely my own opinion, beloved, it is every-one's. There is nothing personal or private about it; it is the general view which is widely held. I only wish that it *were* mine alone, and that the love you professed could find someone to defend it and so comfort me in my grief for a while. I wish I could think of some explanation which would excuse you and somehow cover up the way you hold me cheap.

I beg you then to listen to what I ask—you will see that it is a small favour which you can easily grant. While I am denied your presence, give me at least through your words—of which you have enough and to spare—some sweet semblance of yourself. It is no use my hoping for generosity in deeds if you are grudging in words. Up to now I had thought I deserved much of you, seeing that I carried out everything for your sake and continue up to the present moment in complete obedience to you. It was not any sense of vocation which brought me as a young girl to accept the austeri-ties of the cloister, but your bidding alone, and if I deserve no gratitude from you, you may judge for yourself how my labours are in vain. I can expect no reward for this from God, for it is certain that I have done nothing as yet for love of him. When you hurried towards God I followed you, indeed, I went first to take the veil—perhaps you were thinking how Lot's wife turned back[6] when you made me put on the religious habit and take my vows before you gave yourself to God. Your lack of trust in me over this one thing, I confess, overwhelmed me with grief and shame. I would have had no hesitation, God knows, in following you or going ahead at your bidding to the flames of Hell.[7] My heart was not in me but with you, and now, even more, if it is not with you it is nowhere; truly, without you it cannot exist. See that it fares well with you, I beg, as it will if it finds you kind, if you give grace in return for grace,[8] small for great, words for deeds. If only your love had less confidence in me, my dear, so that you would be more concerned on my behalf! But as it is, the more I have made you feel secure in me, the more I have to bear with your neglect.

---

4. Heloïse uses Abelard's own "ethics of pure intention" to bolster her argument. According to his treatise *Know yourself* (*Scito te ipsum*), actions are inherently neither bad nor good, nor can they be evaluated according to their consequences, but only according to the spirit in which they have been carried out.

5. Here Heloïse distinguishes between Abelard's visits to the Paraclete and more personal attention to herself and her own misery.

6. Genesis 19:26. When Lot, his wife, and two daughters were allowed to flee the destruction of Sodom and Gomorrah, Lot's wife disobeyed the angels' warning. Looking back, she was turned into a pillar of salt.

7. Literally, "Vulcan's region," or Tartarus, the classical underworld, recalling classical myths such as Orpheus's descent to find his beloved Eurydice (see Ovid's *Metamorphoses* in Volume A), or the exchange of the brothers Castor and Pollux.

8. John 1:16, referring to Christ: "And from his fullness have we all received grace upon grace." Throughout the letter, Heloïse has implicitly contrasted her love for Abelard with the love she ought to bear for God.

Remember, I implore you, what I have done, and think how much you owe me. While I enjoyed with you the pleasures of the flesh, many were uncertain whether I was prompted by love or lust; but now the end is proof of the beginning. I have finally denied myself every pleasure in obedience to your will, kept nothing for myself except to prove that now, even more, I am yours. Consider then your injustice, if when I deserve more you give me less, or rather, nothing at all, especially when it is a small thing I ask of you and one you could so easily grant. And so, in the name of God to whom you have dedicated yourself, I beg you to restore your presence to me in the way you can—by writing me some word of comfort, so that in this at least I may find increased strength and readiness to serve God. When in the past you sought me out for sinful pleasures your letters came to me thick and fast, and your many songs put your Heloïse on everyone's lips, so that every street and house echoed with my name. Is it not far better now to summon me to God than it was then to satisfy our lust? I beg you, think what you owe me, give ear to my pleas, and I will finish a long letter with a brief ending: farewell, my only love.

from *Letter 2. Abelard to Heloïse*

To Heloïse, his dearly beloved sister in Christ, Abelard her brother in Christ.[1]

If since our conversion from the world to God I have not yet written you any word of comfort or advice, it must not be attributed to indifference on my part but to your own good sense, in which I have always had such confidence that I did not think anything was needed; God's grace has bestowed on you all essentials to enable you to instruct the erring, comfort the weak and encourage the fainthearted, both by word and example, as, indeed, you have been doing since you first held the office of prioress under your abbess.[2] So if you still watch over your daughters as carefully as you did previously over your sisters, it is sufficient to make me believe that any teaching or exhortation from me would now be wholly superfluous. If, on the other hand, in your humility you think differently, and you feel that you have need of my instruction and writings in matters pertaining to God, write to me what you want, so that I may answer as God permits me. Meanwhile thanks be to God who has filled all your hearts with anxiety for my desperate, unceasing perils, and made you share in my affliction; may divine mercy protect me through the support of your prayers and quickly crush Satan beneath our feet. To this end in particular, I hasten to send the psalter you earnestly begged from me,[3] my sister once dear in the world and now dearest in Christ, so that you may offer a perpetual sacrifice of prayers to the Lord for our many great aberrations, and for the dangers which daily threaten me.[4]

[*In the body of the letter, Abelard recommends prayer as the most efficacious demonstration of faith by Christian women, reminding her of the prayers they would say together at the Paraclete.*]

But if the Lord shall deliver me into the hands of my enemies so that they overcome and kill me, or by whatever chance I enter upon the way of all flesh while

---

1. Abelard reduces Heloïse's elaborate heading to a single relationship, which he spells out: brother and sister "in Christ."
2. At Argenteuil, where Heloïse had first gone after taking the veil and had become prioress in 1118.
3. The request for a psalter, or book of Psalms, was not made in Heloïse's letter, but presumedly by some more public means of communication.
4. The public tone of Abelard's letter contrasts strongly with the private nature of Heloïse's, just as his repetition of Christian language and imagery contrasts with her preference for classical sources and values.

absent from you, wherever my body may lie, buried or unburied, I beg you to have it brought to your burial-ground, where our daughters, or rather, our sisters in Christ may see my tomb more often and thereby be encouraged to pour out their prayers more fully to the Lord on my behalf. There is no place, I think, so safe and salutary for a soul grieving for its sins and desolated by its transgressions than that which is specially consecrated to the true Paraclete, the Comforter, and which is particularly designated by his name. Nor do I believe that there is any place more fitting for Christian burial among the faithful than one amongst women dedicated to Christ. Women were concerned for the tomb of our Lord Jesus Christ, they came ahead and followed after, bringing precious ointments, keeping close watch around this tomb, weeping for the death of the Bridegroom, as it is written: "The women sitting at the tomb wept and lamented for the Lord."[5] And there they were first reassured about his resurrection by the appearance of an angel and the words he spoke to them; later on they were found worthy both to taste the joy of his resurrection when he twice appeared to them, and also to touch him with their hands.[6]

Finally, I ask this of you above all else; at present you are over-anxious about the danger to my body, but then your chief concern must be for the salvation of my soul, and you must show the dead man how much you loved the living by the special support of prayers chosen for him.

Live, fare you well, yourself and your sisters with you,

Live, but I pray, in Christ be mindful of me.

from *Letter 3. Heloïse to Abelard*

To her only one after Christ, she who is his alone in Christ.

I am surprised, my only love, that contrary to custom in letter-writing and, indeed, to the natural order, you have thought fit to put my name before yours in the greeting which heads your letter, so that we have woman before man, wife before husband, handmaid before master, nun before monk, deaconess before priest and abbess before abbot. Surely the right and proper order is for those who write to their superiors or equals to put their names before their own, but in letters to inferiors, precedence in order of address follows precedence in rank.

We were also greatly surprised when instead of bringing us the healing balm of comfort you increased our desolation and made the tears to flow which you should have dried. For which of us could remain dry-eyed on hearing the words you wrote towards the end of your letter: "But if the Lord shall deliver me into the hands of my enemies so that they overcome and kill me . . ."? My dearest, how could you think such a thought? How could you give voice to it? Never may God be so forgetful of his humble handmaids as to let them outlive you; never may he grant us a life which would be harder to bear than any form of death.

* * * I beg you, spare us—spare her at least, who is yours alone, by refraining from words like these. They pierce our hearts with swords of death, so that what comes before is more painful than death itself. A heart which is exhausted with grief cannot find peace, nor can a mind preoccupied with anxieties genuinely devote itself to God. I beseech you not to hinder God's service to which you specially committed

---

5. Mark 16:1, Luke 23:55–56. The Bridegroom is Christ,   6. Matthew 28, John 20:11–18.
in language drawn from the Song of Solomon.

us. Whatever has to come to us bringing with it total grief we must hope will come suddenly, without torturing us far in advance with useless apprehension which no foresight can relieve. This is what the poet has in mind when he prays to God:

> May it be sudden, whatever you plan for us; may man's mind
> Be blind to the future. Let him hope on in his fears.[1]

But if I lose you, what is left for me to hope for? What reason for continuing on life's pilgrimage, for which I have no support but you, and none in you save the knowledge that you are alive, now that I am forbidden all other pleasures in you and denied even the joy of your presence which from time to time could restore me to myself? O God—if I dare say it—cruel to me in everything! O merciless mercy! O Fortune who is only ill-fortune, who has already spent on me so many of the shafts she uses in her battle against mankind that she has none left with which to vent her anger on others. She has emptied a full quiver on me, so that henceforth no one else need fear her onslaughts, and if she still had a single arrow she could find no place in me to take a wound. Her only dread is that through my many wounds death may end my sufferings; and though she does not cease to destroy me, she still fears the destruction which she hurries on.

Of all wretched women I am the most wretched, and amongst the unhappy I am unhappiest. The higher I was exalted when you preferred me to all other women, the greater my suffering over my own fall and yours, when I was flung down; for the higher the ascent, the heavier the fall. Has Fortune ever set any great or noble woman above me or made her my equal, only to be similarly cast down and crushed with grief?[2] What glory she gave me in you, what ruin she brought upon me through you! Violent in either extreme, she showed no moderation in good or evil. To make me the saddest of all women she first made me blessed above all, so that when I thought how much I had lost, my consuming grief would match my crushing loss, and my sorrow for what was taken from me would be the greater for the fuller joy of possession which had gone before; and so that the happiness of supreme ecstasy would end in the supreme bitterness of sorrow.

＊＊＊ For if I truthfully admit to the weakness of my unhappy soul, I can find no penitence whereby to appease God, whom I always accuse of the greatest cruelty in regard to this outrage. By rebelling against his ordinance, I offend him more by my indignation than I placate him by making amends through penitence. How can it be called repentance for sins, however great the mortification of the flesh, if the mind still retains the will to sin and is on fire with its old desires?[3] It is easy enough for anyone to confess his sins, to accuse himself, or even to mortify his body in outward show of penance, but it is very difficult to tear the heart away from hankering after its dearest pleasures.

＊＊＊ In my case, the pleasures of lovers which we shared have been too sweet—they can never displease me, and can scarcely be banished from my thoughts. Wherever I turn they are always there before my eyes, bringing with them awakened

---

1. Lucan, *Pharsalia* 2.14–15. Although Heloïse frames these lines as a prayer to God, they appear in the poem as the narrator's plea for Fortune not to reveal all of Rome's misfortune at one time, as it would be too much to bear.
2. Although she had been adapted to the broader Christian framework of divine Providence, the Roman goddess Fortuna exemplifies a classically Stoic approach to life, a belief that only personal fortitude can protect one from the inevitable bufferings of chance.
3. Heloïse applies again the "ethics of pure intention" she had invoked in her first letter, but here negatively to discount the surface actions of penitence when the mind itself does not repent.

longings and fantasies which will not even let me sleep. Even during the celebration of the Mass, when our prayers should be purer, lewd visions of those pleasures take such a hold upon my unhappy soul that my thoughts are on their wantonness instead of on prayers. I should be groaning over the sins I have committed, but I can only sigh for what I have lost. Everything we did and also the times and places are stamped on my heart along with your image, so that I live through it all again with you. Even in sleep I know no respite. Sometimes my thoughts are betrayed in a movement of my body, or they break out in an unguarded word. In my utter wretchedness, that cry from a suffering soul could well be mine: "Miserable creature that I am, who is there to rescue me out of the body doomed to this death?" Would that in truth I could go on: "The grace of God through Jesus Christ our Lord."[4] This grace, my dearest, came upon you unsought—a single wound of the body by freeing you from these torments has healed many wounds in your soul. Where God may seem to you an adversary he has in fact proved himself kind: like an honest doctor who does not shrink from giving pain if it will bring about a cure. But for me, youth and passion and experience of pleasures which were so delightful intensify the torments of the flesh and longings of desire, and the assault is the more overwhelming as the nature they attack is the weaker.

Men call me chaste; they do not know the hypocrite I am. They consider purity of the flesh a virtue, though virtue belongs not to the body but to the soul. I can win praise in the eyes of men but deserve none before God, who searches our hearts and loins and sees in our darkness. I am judged religious at a time when there is little in religion which is not hypocrisy, when whoever does not offend the opinions of men receives the highest praise. And yet perhaps there is some merit and it is somehow acceptable to God, if a person whatever his intention gives no offence to the Church in his outward behaviour, does not blaspheme the name of the Lord in the hearing of unbelievers nor disgrace the Order of his profession amongst the worldly. And this too is a gift of God's grace and comes through his bounty—not only to do good but to abstain from evil—though the latter is vain if the former does not follow from it, as it is written: "Turn from evil and do good."[5] Both are vain if not done for love of God.

* * *

from *Letter 4. Abelard to Heloïse*

To the bride of Christ, Christ's servant.

[After applying logic and biblical examples to counter the irrational passion he sees in Heloïse's letter, Abelard turns to her inability to break with the past, and her refusal to view the sequence of events as part of the plan of divine Providence.]

I come at last to what I have called your old perpetual complaint, in which you presume to blame God for the manner of our entry into religion instead of wishing to glorify him as you justly should. I had thought that this bitterness of heart at what was so clear an act of divine mercy had long since disappeared. The more dangerous such bitterness is to you in wearing out body and soul alike, the more pitiful it is and distressing to me. If you are anxious to please me in everything, as you claim, and in this at least would end my torment, or even give me the greatest pleasure, you must rid

---

4. Romans 7:24. Heloïse quotes Paul's cry of despair but lacks the conviction to provide his consoling response; the continuation speaks directly of the split which she cannot heal: "So then, I myself serve the law of God with my mind, but with my flesh I serve the law of sin." If the mind is sinful, she argues, there is no hope at all.
5. Psalm 37:27.

yourself of it. If it persists you can neither please me nor attain bliss with me. Can you bear me to come to this without you—I whom you declare yourself ready to follow to the very fires of hell? Seek piety in this at least, lest you cut yourself off from me who am hastening, you believe, towards God; be the readier to do so because the goal we must come to will be blessed, and our companionship the more welcome for being happier. Remember what you have said, recall what you have written, namely that in the manner of our conversion, when God seems to have been more my adversary, he has clearly shown himself kinder. For this reason at least you must accept his will, that it is most salutary for me, and for you too, if your transports of grief will see reason. You should not grieve because you are the cause of so great a good, for which you must not doubt you were specially created by God. Nor should you weep because I have to bear this, except when our blessings through the martyrs in their sufferings and the Lord's death sadden you. If it had befallen me justly, would you find it easier to bear? Would it distress you less? In fact if it had been so, the result would have been greater disgrace for me and more credit to my enemies, since justice would have won them approval while my guilt would have brought me into contempt. And no one would be stirred by pity for me to condemn what was done.

However, it may relieve the bitterness of your grief if I prove that this came upon us justly, as well as to our advantage, and that God's punishment was more properly directed against us when we were married than when we were living in sin. After our marriage, when you were living in the cloister with the nuns at Argenteuil and I came one day to visit you privately, you know what my uncontrollable desire did with you there, actually in a corner of the refectory, since we had nowhere else to go.[1] I repeat, you know how shamelessly we behaved on that occasion in so hallowed a place, dedicated to the most holy Virgin. Even if our other shameful behaviour was ended, this alone would deserve far heavier punishment.

* * * You know too how when you were pregnant and I took you to my own country you disguised yourself in the sacred habit of a nun, a pretence which was an irreverent mockery of the religion you now profess. Consider, then, how fittingly divine justice, or rather, divine grace brought you against your will to the religion which you did not hesitate to mock, so that you should willingly expiate your profanation in the same habit, and the truth of reality should remedy the lie of your pretence and correct your falsity. And if you would allow consideration of our advantage to be an element in divine justice, you would be able to call what God did to us then an act not of justice, but of grace.

* * * You know the depths of shame to which my unbridled lust had consigned our bodies, until no reverence for decency or for God even during the days of Our Lord's Passion,[2] or of the greater sacraments could keep me from wallowing in this mire. Even when you were unwilling, resisted to the utmost of your power and tried to dissuade me, as yours was the weaker nature I often forced you to consent with threats and blows. So intense were the fires of lust which bound me to you that I set those wretched, obscene pleasures, which we blush even to name, above God as above myself; nor would it seem that divine mercy could have taken action except by forbidding me these pleasures altogether, without future hope. And so it was wholly just and merciful, although by means of the supreme treachery of your uncle, for me

---

1. The details that constitute Abelard's proof suggest his memory of the past was as vivid as Heloïse's.

2. The Church forbade all manner of sexual intercourse during Lent (the 40 days of fasting before Easter), during Easter week, and in preparation for other major feasts.

to be reduced in that part of my body which was the seat of lust and sole reason for those desires, so that I could increase in many ways; in order that this member should justly be punished for all its wrongdoing in us, expiate in suffering the sins committed for its amusement, and cut me off from the slough of filth in which I had been wholly immersed in mind as in body. Only thus could I become more fit to approach the holy altars, now that no contagion of carnal impurity would ever again call me from them. How mercifully did he want me to suffer so much only in that member, the privation of which would also further the salvation of my soul without defiling my body nor preventing any performance of my duties! Indeed, it would make me readier to perform whatever can be honourably done by setting me wholly free from the heavy yoke of carnal desire.

So when divine grace cleansed rather than deprived me of those vile members which from their practice of utmost indecency are called "the parts of shame" and have no proper name of their own, what else did it do but remove a foul imperfection in order to preserve perfect purity? Such purity, as we have heard, certain sages have desired so eagerly that they have mutilated themselves, so as to remove entirely the shame of desire. The Apostle too is recorded as having besought the Lord to rid him of this thorn in the flesh, but was not heard.[3] The great Christian philosopher Origen provides an example, for he was not afraid to mutilate himself in order to quench completely this fire within him, as if he understood literally the words that those men were truly blessed who castrated themselves for the Kingdom of Heaven's sake, and believed them to be truthfully carrying out the bidding of the Lord about offending members, that we should cut them off and throw them away;[4] and as if he interpreted as historic fact, not as a hidden symbol, that prophecy of Isaiah in which the Lord prefers eunuchs to the rest of the faithful: "The eunuchs who keep my sabbaths, and choose to do my will I will give a place in my own house and within my walls and a name better than sons and daughters. I will give them an everlasting name which shall not perish."[5] Yet Origen is seriously to be blamed because he sought a remedy for blame in punishment of his body. True, he has zeal for God, but an ill-informed zeal, and the charge of homicide can be proved against him for his self mutilation.[6] Men think he did this either at the suggestion of the devil or in grave error but, in my case, through God's compassion, it was done by another's hand. I do not incur blame, I escape it. I deserve death and gain life. I am called but hold back; I persist in crime and am pardoned against my will. The Apostle prays and is not heard, he persists in prayer and is not answered. Truly the Lord takes thought for me. I will go then and declare how much the Lord has done for my soul.[7]

* * * It was he who truly loved you, not I. My love, which brought us both to sin, should be called lust, not love. I took my fill of my wretched pleasures in you, and this was the sum total of my love. You say I suffered for you, and perhaps that is true, but it was really through you, and even this, unwillingly; not for love of you but under compulsion, and to bring you not salvation but sorrow. But he suffered truly for your salvation, on your behalf of his own free will, and by his suffering he cures all sickness and removes all suffering. To him, I beseech you, not to me, should be directed

---

3. 2 Corinthians 12:7–10.
4. Matthew 19:12, 18:8. The third-century theologian Origen had actually castrated himself so as to eliminate the source of temptation.
5. Isaiah 56:4–5.
6. Compare Romans 10:2: "They have a zeal for God, but it is not enlightened." Self-mutilation had been a capital

crime under Roman law. Self-castration had been prohibited during the 4th century as overzealous behavior, and Paul's treatment of the temptations of the flesh as a thorn to be suffered and overcome (2 Cor. 12:7–10) was the more orthodox attitude.
7. Psalm 40:18, 66:16.

all your devotion, all your compassion, all your remorse. Weep for the injustice of the great cruelty inflicted on him, not for the just and righteous payment demanded of me, or rather, as I said, the supreme grace granted us both. For you are unrighteous if you do not love righteousness, and most unrighteous if you consciously oppose the will, or more truly, the boundless grace of God. Mourn for your Saviour and Redeemer, not for the seducer who defiled you, for the Master who died for you, not for the servant who lives and, indeed, for the first time is truly freed from death. I beg you, beware lest Pompey's reproach to weeping Cornelia is applied to you, to your shame:

> The battle ended, Pompey the Great
> Lives, but his fortune died. It is this you now mourn
> And loved.[8]

Take this to heart, I pray, and blush for shame, unless you would commend the wanton vileness of our former ways. And so I ask you, sister, to accept patiently what mercifully befell us.

* * *

from *Letter 5. Heloïse to Abelard*

God's own in species, his own as individual.[1]

I would not want to give you cause for finding me disobedient in anything, so I have set the bridle of your injunction on the words which issue from my unbounded grief; thus in writing at least I may moderate what it is difficult or rather impossible to forestall in speech. For nothing is less under our control than the heart—having no power to command it we are forced to obey.[2] And so when its impulses move us, none of us can stop their sudden promptings from easily breaking out, and even more easily overflowing into words which are the everready indications of the heart's emotions: as it is written, "A man's words are spoken from the overflowing of the heart."[3] I will therefore hold my hand from writing words which I cannot restrain my tongue from speaking; would that a grieving heart would be as ready to obey as a writer's hand! And yet you have it in your power to remedy my grief, even if you cannot entirely remove it. As one nail drives out another hammered in,[4] a new thought expels an old, when the mind is intent on other things and forced to dismiss or interrupt its recollection of the past. But the more fully any thought occupies the mind and distracts it from other things, the more worthy should be the subject of such a thought and the more important it is where we direct our minds.[5]

---

8. Abelard's final argument uses a classical citation to echo the words Heloïse had quoted when taking the veil, according to the *Historia Calamitatum*. There, she had spoken Cornelia's lament for her part in marrying Pompey and bringing about his death; Abelard here cites the dying Pompey's words rebuking his wife for indulging in sorrow over the tribulations of fate. Not only in Christian but also in classical terms, he implies, her behavior is incorrect, because, just as Pompey lives (although disgraced by defeat), so Abelard lives, although his former life is irrevocably lost.

1. As a species, they are united in God, but only truly exist as unique individuals. The word *dominus* can mean either God, a feudal lord, or a husband; hence the phrase is far more ambiguous than the translation suggests.

2. Heloïse thus concedes only the words of Abelard's plea to be reasonable, reserving a place in her heart beyond the reach of reason, just as mystics such as Bernard of Clairvaux would reserve aspects of faith as existing beyond the apprehension of reason.

3. Matthew 12:34.

4. Cicero, *Tusculan Disputations* 4.35.75.

5. From this point, Heloïse held true to her promise to restrain her heart, and Abelard true to his to maintain contact, and the correspondence focused on problems of running the Paraclete.

Peter Abelard: David's Lament for Jonathan[1]

Low in thy grave with thee
Happy to lie,
Since there's no greater thing left Love to do;
And to live after thee
5   Is but to die,
For with but half a soul what can Life do?

So share thy victory,
Or else thy grave,
Either to rescue thee, or with thee lie:
10   Ending that life for thee,
That thou didst save,
So Death that sundereth might bring more nigh.

Peace, O my stricken lute!
Thy strings are sleeping.
15   Would that my heart could still
Its bitter weeping!

Peter Abelard: from Yes and No[1]

Among the multitudinous words of the holy Fathers some sayings seem not only to differ from one another but even to contradict one another. Hence it is not presumptuous to judge concerning those by whom the world itself will be judged, as it is written, "They shall judge nations" (Wisdom 3:8) and, again, "You shall sit and judge" (Luke 22:30). We do not presume to rebuke as untruthful or to denounce as erroneous those to whom the Lord said, "He who hears you hears me; he who despises you despises me" (Luke 10:16). Bearing in mind our foolishness we believe that our understanding is defective rather than the writing of those to whom the Truth Himself said, "It is not you who speak but the spirit of your Father who speaks in you" (Matthew 10:20).[2] Why should it seem surprising if we, lacking the guidance of the Holy Spirit through whom those things were written and spoken, the Spirit impressing them on the writers, fail to understand them? Our achievement of full understanding is impeded especially by unusual modes of expression and by the different significances that can be attached to one and the same word, as a word is used now in one sense, now in another. Just as there are many meanings so there are many words. Tully says

---

1. Translated by Helen Waddell. Nothing remains of the love songs that were the talk of Paris; Abelard's extant verse consists of the hymns and sequences he wrote for the convent of the Paraclete and six laments in the voices of Old Testament characters. The lament of David for his beloved friend Jonathan, killed in battle with the Philistines (the history is recounted in I Samuel), demonstrates Abelard's skill in investing a religious episode with the passion of a love lyric. The moving lament attributed to David himself is composed of heroic praise, and ends by declaring that "your love to me was wonderful, passing the love of women" (2 Samuel 1:26).

1. Translated by Brian Tierney. In this selection from the prologue, Abelard discusses his influential "dialectical method," which sought the truth about Christian doctrine by presenting over 150 questions, each one followed by apparently conflicting answers from Scripture and different church authorities. Although his intent may have been pious, his method risked subverting the authorities it sought to reconcile.
2. The "Truth Himself" is Jesus Christ. Abelard interprets Jesus's words to his disciples as if they applied to the Church Fathers such as Ambrose, Augustine, and Jerome.

that sameness is the mother of satiety in all things, that is to say it gives rise to fastidious distaste, and so it is appropriate to use a variety of words in discussing the same thing and not to express everything in common and vulgar words.[3] * * *

We must also take special care that we are not deceived by corruptions of the text or by false attributions when sayings of the Fathers are quoted that seem to differ from the truth or to be contrary to it; for many apocryphal writings are set down under names of saints to enhance their authority, and even the texts of divine Scripture are corrupted by the errors of scribes. That most faithful writer and true interpreter, Jerome, accordingly warned us, "Beware of apocryphal writings. . . ."[4] Again, on the title of Psalm 77 which is "An Instruction of Asaph," he commented, "It is written according to Matthew that when the Lord had spoken in parables and they did not understand, he said, 'These things are done that it might be fulfilled which was written by the prophet Isaiah, *I will open my mouth in parables.*' The Gospels still have it so. Yet it is not Isaiah who says this but Asaph." Again, let us explain simply why in Matthew and John it is written that the Lord was crucified at the third hour but in Mark at the sixth hour. There was a scribal error, and in Mark too the sixth hour was mentioned, but many read the Greek *epismo* as *gamma*.[5] So too there was a scribal error where "Isaiah" was set down for "Asaph." We know that many churches were gathered together from among ignorant gentiles. When they read in the Gospel, "That it might be fulfilled which was written by the prophet Asaph," the one who first wrote down the Gospel began to say, "Who is this prophet Asaph?" for he was not known among the people. And what did he do? In seeking to amend an error he made an error. We would say the same of another text in Matthew. "He took," it says, "the thirty pieces of silver, the price of him that was prized, as was written by the prophet Jeremias." But we do not find this in Jeremias at all. Rather it is in Zacharias.[6] You see then that here, as before, there was an error. If in the Gospels themselves some things are corrupted by the ignorance of scribes, we should not be surprised that the same thing has sometimes happened in the writings of later Fathers who are of much less authority. * * *

It is no less important in my opinion to ascertain whether texts quoted from the Fathers may be ones that they themselves have retracted and corrected after they came to a better understanding of the truth as the blessed Augustine did on many occasions;[7] or whether they are giving the opinion of another rather than their own opinion . . . or whether, in inquiring into certain matters, they left them open to question rather than settled them with a definitive solution. * * * In order that the way be not blocked and posterity deprived of the healthy labor of treating and debating difficult questions of language and style, a distinction must be drawn between the work of later authors and the supreme canonical authority of the Old and New Testaments. If, in Scripture, anything seems absurd you are not permitted to say, "The author of this book did not hold the truth"—but rather that the codex[8] is defective or that the interpreter erred or that you do not understand. But if anything seems contrary to truth in the works of later authors, which are contained in innumerable books, the reader or auditor is free to judge, so that he may approve what is pleasing and reject what gives

3. Cicero ("Tully"), *De inventione* 1, 41, 76 (84 B.C.E.), a treatise on rhetorical invention for public speaking.
4. Jerome (c. 347–c. 420) introduced the term "apocrypha" to describe texts he wanted to exclude from his Latin translation of the Bible, the Vulgate, and from the Christian canon. The warning is from Letter 107.12.
5. The ancient Greek symbol for the number 6, episemon, resembles the letter gamma, which could be used to symbolize the number three.
6. Matthew 27:9; Zacharias 11:13.
7. In the years leading up to his death in 430, Augustine read through all of his many writings and composed a volume of *Retractiones,* or reconsiderations and corrections.
8. A manuscript book.

offense, unless the matter is established by certain reason or by canonical authority (of the Scriptures). * * * In view of these considerations we have undertaken to collect various sayings of the Fathers that give rise to questioning because of their apparent contradictions as they occur to our memory. This questioning excites young readers to the maximum of effort in inquiring into the truth, and such inquiry sharpens their minds. Assiduous and frequent questioning is indeed the first key to wisdom. Aristotle, that most perspicacious of all philosophers, exhorted the studious to practice it eagerly, saying, "Perhaps it is difficult to express oneself with confidence on such matters if they have not been much discussed. To entertain doubts on particular points will not be unprofitable."[9] For by doubting we come to inquiry; through inquiring we perceive the truth, according to the Truth Himself. "Seek and you shall find," He says, "Knock and it shall be opened to you."[1] In order to teach us by His example He chose to be found when He was about twelve years old sitting in the midst of the doctors and questioning them, presenting the appearance of a disciple by questioning rather than of a master by teaching, although there was in Him the complete and perfect wisdom of God.[2] Where we have quoted texts of Scripture, the greater the authority attributed to Scripture, the more they should stimulate the reader and attract him to the search for truth. Hence I have prefixed to this my book, compiled in one volume from the sayings of the saints, the decree of Pope Gelasius concerning authentic books, from which it may be known that I have cited nothing from apocryphal books.[3] I have also added excerpts from the Retractions of St. Augustine, from which it will be clear that nothing is included which he later retracted and corrected.

～∞～

RESONANCE

Bernard of Clairvaux: Letters Against Abelard[1]

from LETTER 238: TO THE BISHOPS AND CARDINALS IN CURIA[2]

To the lords and reverend fathers, the Bishops and Cardinals in Curia, from the child of their holiness. * * * The faith of the simple is being held up to scorn, the secrets of God are being reft open, the most scared matters are being recklessly discussed, and the Fathers are being derided because they held that such matters are better allowed to rest than solved. Hence it comes about that, contrary to the law of God, the Paschal Lamb is either boiled or eaten raw, with bestial mouth and manners. And what is left over is not burned with fire, but trodden under foot.[3] So mere human ingenuity is taking on itself to solve everything, and leave nothing to faith. It is trying for things

9. Abelard knew the passage from a citation by Boethius (480–524) in his commentary *On Aristotle's Categories*.
1. Matthew 7:7.
2. Luke 2:41–52 (Volume A).
3. Traditionally attributed to Gelasius I, who was pope from 492–496, the Decree of Gelasius was probably written in the mid-6th century. It lists the writings it considers canonical and virulently rejects those it considers schismatic or heretical.
1. Translated by Bruno Scott James. Bernard of Clairvaux, the brilliant founder of the Cistercian order, was responsible for Abelard's conviction as a heretic in 1140. In this letter, he outlines the case against Abelard: because

Abelard relies solely on reason and leaves nothing to faith, delving into mysteries that must be believed rather than explained, he denies the fundamental tenets of Christianity and risks leading simpler souls astray.
2. The Curia is a group of Vatican officials that aid the Pope in his everyday duties of presiding over the Catholic Church. Among other duties, the Curia was responsible for ruling on the heretical character of books.
3. From the Mosaic law concerning the proper treatment of the Passover Lamb (Exodus 12:9), itself a standard metaphor for the body and blood of Christ, Bernard composes a metaphor for the treatment of Scripture by its interpreters.

about itself, prying into things too strong for it, rushing into divine things, and profaning rather than revealing what is holy. Things closed and sealed, it is not opening but tearing asunder, and what it is not able to force open, that it considers to be of no account and not worthy of belief.

Read, if you please, that book of Peter Abelard which he calls a book of Theology. You have it to hand since, as he boasts, it is read eagerly by many in the Curia. See what sort of things he says there about the Holy Trinity, about the generation of the Son, about the procession of the Holy Spirit, and much else that is very strange indeed to Catholic ears and minds.[4] Read that other book which they call the *Book of Sentences,*[5] and also the one entitled *Know Thyself,* and see how they too run riot with a whole crop of sacrileges and errors. See what he thinks about the soul of Christ, about the person of Christ, about his descent into hell, about the Sacrament of the Altar, about the power of binding and loosing, about original sin, about the sins of human weakness, about the sins of ignorance, about sinful action, and about sinful intention. And if you then consider that I am rightly disturbed, do you also bestir yourselves and, so as not to bestir yourselves in vain, act according to the position you hold, according to the dignity in which you are supreme, according to the power you have received, and let him who has scanned the heavens go down even into hell, and let the works of darkness that have braved the light be shown up by the light, so that while he who sins in public is publicly rebuked, others, who speak evil in their hearts and write it in their books, may restrain themselves from putting darkness for light, and disputing on divine matters at the crossroads. Thus shall the mouth that mutters wickedness be closed.

LETTER 243: TO CARDINAL STEPHEN, BISHOP OF PALESTRINA[1]

To his venerable lord and very dear father, Stephen, by the grace of God Bishop of Palestrina, that he may play the man and keep his courage high, from Brother Bernard, Abbot of Clairvaux.

I tell you of the difficulties and sorrows of the bride of Christ all the more readily for knowing you to be the friend of the Bridegroom and very glad to hear his voice.[2] If I have rightly judged your disposition, I am certain that you do not seek your own interests, but those of Jesus Christ. Peter Abelard proves by his life, by his behaviour, and by his books, which are now issuing from darkness into the light of day, that he is a persecutor of the Catholic Church, and an enemy of the cross of Christ. Outwardly he appears a monk, but within he is a heretic having nothing of the monk about him save the habit and the name. He opens up the old wells and the trodden-in pools of heretics, so that the ox and the ass may fall in.[3] He had long been silent, but while he kept silence in Brittany he conceived sorrow, and now in France he has brought forth iniquity.[4] He has come out of his hole like a twisting snake, and like the hydra when

---

4. The mystery of the Trinity led many philosophers into great difficulties; Bernard enumerates the primary heresies in Letter 243 below.

5. Bernard was probably referring to *Yes and No,* which speaks in its opening lines about "sayings" or *sententiae.*

1. A monk of Clairvaux, Stephen had been promoted to Cardinal and consecrated to the see, or seat, of Palestrina, an ancient Latin city near Rome, in 1141. He died three years later.

2. The metaphor of the Bride and the Bridegroom comes from the Song of Songs (Volume A); as in Bernard's celebrated commentary, the Bride generally was the Church and the Bridegroom was Christ.

3. The metaphor is drawn from a parable told by Jesus in Luke 14:5: "Which of you shall have an ass or an ox fallen into a pit, and will not straightway pull him out on the sabbath day?"

4. Abelard had returned from Brittany to the vicinity of Paris in 1135.

one head is cut off he grows seven more in its place. A single head was cut off, a single heresy of that man, at Soissons;[5] but already seven greater ones have grown up in its place, an example of which I have sent you. Raw and inexperienced listeners hardly finished with their dialectics, and those who can hardly, so to speak, stand the first elements of the faith, are introduced by him to the mystery of the Holy Trinity, to the Holy of Holies, to the chamber of the King, and to him who is "shrouded with darkness."[6] In fine, our theologian has laid down degrees and grades in the Trinity like Arius, with Pelagius he puts free will before grace, and with Nestorius he divides Christ by excluding from association with the Trinity the human nature he assumed.[7] Thus he runs through almost all the sacraments, and "boldly sweeps from world's end to world's end," ordering all things mischievously. Besides this he boasts that he has infected the Roman Curia with the virus of his new ideas, that his books and sayings have found their way into the hands and hearts of the Romans, and he summons to protect his errors those very men by whom he ought to be judged and condemned. May God care for his Church for which he died, so that he may behold it without spot or wrinkle, and so that the perpetual silence should be imposed on that man, "whose mouth overflows with curses, calumny, and deceit."[8]

The Play of Adam
c. 1150

There are two traditions of early medieval theater: the satirical burlesques staged by itinerant mimes, singers, and actors, and the Christian dramas put on by monks as part of services at the great church festivals. Aspects of both traditions are evident in the early twelfth-century *Play of Adam* (*Le Jeu d'Adam*). Intended for production outdoors for a lay audience, it was composed in the language of the Anglo-Norman court of southern England; the work survives in a single paper manuscript from the early thirteenth century. There are three parts, or scenes: the Fall of Adam and Eve, Cain's murder of Abel, and a procession of Prophets foretelling the coming of Christ. Dialogue is written in the Old French dialect of the court; the detailed stage directions and the Gregorian "responds" to be chanted by a choir are in Latin. The first scene fleshes out the mythic figures of Genesis 1–3 (see Volume A) as familiar characters in feudal society: Adam is a good French farmer or burgher, Eve his headstrong wife, God their somewhat domineering lord, and the Devil a good-for-nothing courtier. The success of the play lies in the way it merges this popular material with the awesome severity of the theological lesson of the Fall of Man.

The staging most likely incorporated the cosmological symbolism embodied in the architecture of the medieval church, using the slightly elevated porch and steps of the west end

5. The first version of Abelard's *Theologia* had been formally condemned as heretical and burned by a council held at Soissons in 1121.

6. A series of expressions designed to represent the inaccessibility and elevated status of the "mystery of the Holy Trinity," contrary to Abelard's insistence on exposing it to the harsh light and everyday practice of dialectics.

7. Three major heresies of the early church whose ideas continued to plague Christian orthodoxy. The doctrine of

Arianism, which held that God was the only immutable being in the Trinity, had been declared heretical in 325; Pelagianism and its privileging of free will and asceticism in obtaining salvation had been declared heretical in 417; Nestorianism, which held that the divine and human natures of Christ were independent of one another, had been declared heretical in 431.

8. Psalm 38:12.

(known as the "paradise") to represent the Garden of Eden, with God emerging from and return-ing to his proper domain of the church's interior. Earth is represented by the *platea*, the lower "place" or open ground between the audience and Paradise, with the "house" of Hell off to one side, normally represented as a dragon or monster's head, its jaws and teeth the door, or "hell-mouth." The staging visualizes the theme of the fallen world, as when the devils "run about 'the place,' making appropriate gestures" to the audience, reminding its members of their place in the world, nearer to Satan than to God, with salvation so near and yet so very far away.

The plainsong "responds" freeze the action, recalling the audience to the ingrained rhythms and homilies of the Genesis version of Eden. By contrast, the vernacular dialogues, rendered primarily in eight-syllable rhyming couplets, are colloquial in tone and render the fated events as a series of dramatic encounters in which the participants are fully au-tonomous, even willful in their actions. In the dialogue between Adam and Eve invented by the playwright, for example, we find a miniature psychodrama of persuasion. Satan tempts Eve not just by pointing out the beauty of the fruit, as in Genesis, but by flattering her in courtly terms for her complexion as clear as "Snow in an icebound valley falling," and ap-pealing to her sense of superiority: "You have feelings—*Adam* has none. / All the same, you are the one with sense." Drawn from the types of low comedy—the ambitious wife, the plod-ding husband, the suave con man—the trio are a far cry from the distant protagonists they ap-peared to be in Scripture. Dashing around the stage and playing up to the audience, Satan is the star of the scene, while Adam is the butt of the action, lured by his helpmate into calamity.

Nevertheless, we should not assume that the audience would have lost sight for long of the sacred context of the scenes they were enjoying. Adam himself makes several references to the foreordained role of Christ in his future salvation, reminding the audience of the serious mes-sage wrapped up in the comedy of the presentation. Framed by the proper doctrine of the life to come, *The Play of Adam*, like so much of popular medieval religious writing, finds space to do justice to the sensual and intellectual delights of the earthly life as well.

from The Play of Adam[1]
SCENE 1. ADAM AND EVE

Paradise shall be set up in a fairly high place; curtains and silk cloths shall be hung around it, at such a height that the persons who shall be in Paradise can be seen from the shoulders upwards. Fragrant flowers and leaves shall be planted there; there shall also be various trees with fruit hanging on them, so that it looks a very pleasant place. Then shall come God the Saviour wearing a dalmatic,[2] and Adam and Eve shall be stationed in front of him. Adam shall wear a red tunic, but Eve a woman's garment in white with a white silk scarf[3] and they shall both stand in front of God—Adam, however, nearer to God with a calm countenance, Eve with face lowered. Adam shall be well trained not to answer too quickly nor too slowly, when he has to answer. Not only Adam but all the actors shall be instructed to control their speech and to make their actions appropriate to the matter they speak of; and, in speaking the verse, not to add a syllable, nor to take one away, but to enunciate everything dis-tinctly, and to say everything in the order laid down. Whenever anyone shall speak of Paradise, he shall look towards it and point it out with his hand.

---

1. Translated by Richard Axton and John Stevens. The manuscript title is in Latin, *Ordo representationis Ade* ("Order for the representation of Adam").
2. A bishop's robe with wide sleeves and a slit on each side of the skirt, and two stripes, also worn by kings and emperors at such special events as coronations.
3. The rich clothing suggests that Adam and Eve at the beginning of the play are free vassals rather than the serfs they will become.

[Then shall the lesson begin:]

CHOIR: In principio creavit Deus celum et terram[4]

[After which the choir shall sing:]

CHOIR: Formavit igitur dominus[5]

[And after that God shall say:][6] Adam!

[And Adam shall answer:] My Lord.

GOD: I moulded you
                  From earthly clay.[7]

ADAM: Yes, this I know.

GOD: I've given you a living soul,
                  And formed you like myself in all.[8]

5   Made you from earth in my own form;
                  You never should be my enemy.

ADAM: I never will, but follow your word,
                  Obeying my creator, Lord.

GOD: I've given you a good companion:

10   She is your wife, her name is Eve,
                  She is your wife and partner; you
                  Must stay faithful to her and true.
                  May you love her and in turn she
                  Love you; both will be loved by me.

15   She must answer to your command,
                  The two of you be in my hand.
                  Out of your rib your wife I shaped;
                  She's born from you and is no stranger.
                  Straight from your body I made her:

20   She came from you—not from elsewhere.
                  Govern her by the light of reason;
                  Between you be there no dissension,
                  But mutual comfort, mutual love—
                  Such shall the law of marriage be.

25   And now to you, Eve, will I speak—
                  Attend, and listen carefully:
                  If you desire to take my part,
                  You'll harbour goodness in your heart.

4. "In the beginning God created heaven and earth" (Genesis 1:1; here and below adapted from the New International Version). The Latin chorus incorporates the language of the liturgy, or prescribed services for Septuagesima, the ninth Sunday before Easter and third before Lent and start of the penitential season. A respond adapted from biblical text is answered in a *versus* or verse, then the respond (or part of it) is repeated. The manuscript gives only the first line of the sequence in each case.
5. Genesis 2:7: "And the lord God formed." The *versus* continues: "formed the man from the dust of the ground and breathed into his nostrils the breath of life, and the man became a living being."
6. Throughout the play, the character that stands in and speaks for God (who would not be represented directly) is called "Figura," a living symbol, or "figure" of the way in which God and his words were revealed through the events of history.
7. *De limo terre.* The original Latin repeats the words of the responsory before it.
8. Compare to Genesis 1:27: "So God created man in his own image."

Honour me, Creator, God!
30   Acknowledge me to be your Lord!
My service must be all your thought,
All your wisdom, all your strength.
Love Adam, hold him dear as life—
He is your husband, you his wife.
35   To him remain obedient;
Don't go beyond his government.
Serve him and love him well, then sure
You'll be to keep the marriage law.
If you make him a good help-meet,
40   With him in glory you'll be set.

EVE: I will do, Lord, as you command;
I shall not wish to stray beyond.
I'll recognize your sovereign sway;
As mate and master him obey.
45   I'll always serve him faithfully:
He'll have the best support from me.
Your pleasure and Your service, Lord,
I shall in everything perform.[9]

[Then God shall call Adam nearer and shall speak more particularly to him.]

GOD: Now listen, Adam, and hear what I shall say!
50   I made you, and endow you with this wealth:
You'll live for ever, if you keep my word,
Feel no disease but always have good health;
    No hunger know; nor drink from any need;
Never be cold; nor of the heat complain.
55   You shall be happy, never tired at all,
Full of delight, you never shall know pain.
    In joy the days of all your life you'll lead,
Exist for ever, your life not short but long;
I tell you this, and wish that Eve may hear;
60   If she does not, she does herself a wrong.
    You two have lordship over all the earth—
The birds, the beasts, and all created things.
Of small account is he who envies you,
For over all the world you shall be kings.[1]
65   Within yourselves I put both good and evil;
To give you this is still to leave you free.
Weigh everything in balance fairly now;
Accept this counsel—keep your faith with me!
    Put aside evil, and give your mind to good.

9. Here, as throughout, the relationship between Adam and Eve and their Lord God is defined as a feudal one. Like Adam in lines 7–8, Eve swears an oath of fealty.
1. Compare to Genesis 1:28–30: "God blessed them and said to them, 'Be fruitful and increase in number; fill the earth and subdue it. Rule over the fish of the sea and the birds of the air and over every living creature that moves on the ground.'" "Lordship" (*seignorie*) is a standard feudal term of dominion.

70   Love your good lord, and firmly hold to him.
        For no one else's counsel turn from mine;
        If you observe it, then you'll never sin.
ADAM: Great thanks I give to your benignity,
        The God who made me with such kind intent,
75   That right and wrong you put within my power.
        To serve you, may my will be always bent.
            You are my Lord; I, your created thing;
        You formed me, I'm the product of your art.
        My will shall never be so hard, so set,
80   That serving you shall not take all my heart.

    [*Then shall God point out Paradise to Adam with his hand saying:*]

GOD: Adam!
ADAM: My Lord.
GOD: I'll tell you my design:
        This garden.
ADAM: What's it called?
GOD: Paradise.
ADAM: How fine it is!
GOD: I grew and planted it.
        He who lives here shall always be my friend.
85   I entrust it you, to dwell here and to guard it.

    [*Then shall he lead them into Paradise, saying:*]

        It is for you.
ADAM: Then, can we settle here?
GOD: For all your lives; you need not be afraid.
        Within it neither sickness is, nor death.

    [*The choir shall sing:* Tulit ergo dominus hominem.][2]

    [*Then shall God stretch out his hand towards Paradise, saying:*]

GOD: The nature of this garden I'll recount:[3]
90   No joy is lacking here as you will find;
        Whatever good things men in the world desire
        Here can be found in measure and in kind.
        No woman shall a husband's anger know,
        No husband for his wife feel fear or shame;
95   The act of love is not for man a sin;
        Nor shall a woman here give birth in pain.
        You'll live for ever, in this marvellous place
        And not grow any older. Have no fear

---

2. "The Lord took the man," followed by the rest of Genesis 2:15.

3. Paradise is described in the vocabulary and terms of the medieval *locus amoenus* ("pleasant place") characteristic of courtly romance.

Of death here, for it cannot do you harm.
100   I wish you not to leave; your home is here!

[*The choir shall sing:* Dixit Dominus ad Adam.][4]

[*Then shall God show Adam the trees of Paradise, saying:*]

GOD: Of all *that* fruit, eat as it pleases you.

[*And he shall show him the forbidden tree and its fruit, saying:*]

GOD: *This* is forbidden! Take no comfort here!
    If you eat this, you shall be dead at once;
    My love you'll lose, and change your happy state.
ADAM: I will observe all that you do command;
    Neither my wife nor I will swerve an inch.
    For a single fruit to lose this place of bliss!
    I should deserve to be thrown headlong out.
    If for one apple I reject your love,
110   Then all my life I'll pay for being mad:
    He will be rightly judged as traitors are
    Who breaks his faith and thus betrays his Lord.

[*Then shall God go into the church, while Adam and Eve walk up and down, innocently delighting in Paradise. Meanwhile devils shall run about the "place," making appropriate gestures: and they shall come in turn near to Paradise, pointing out the forbidden fruit to Eve as if persuading her to eat it. Then shall Satan[5] come to Adam and say to him:*]

SATAN: What are you doing, Adam?
ADAM: Enjoying life.[6]
SATAN: All well with you?
ADAM: I feel nothing amiss.
SATAN: It could be better.
ADAM: I can't imagine how.
SATAN: Do you want to know?
ADAM: I've no desire at all.
SATAN: I know, I know *how.*
ADAM: What's that to me?
SATAN: Why not?
ADAM: It means nothing to me.
SATAN: It'll be worth while.
ADAM: I can't see when.
SATAN: I'm in no hurry to let you know.

---

4. "The Lord said to Adam," followed by a rearranged version of the rest of Genesis 16–18: "'Do not eat from the tree that is in the middle of paradise, for when you eat of it you will surely die.' And the Lord commanded the man saying, 'Eat from any tree in the garden; do not eat from the tree of the knowledge of good and evil.'"

5. There is no analogue in Genesis for the Devil's two attempts to seduce Adam, but there is in the c. 7th-century Old English fragment known as "Genesis B."
6. *Ci vif en grant déduit*—literally, "I live here in great pleasure"; *déduit* was a key term for courtly leisure and the *locus amoenus.*

ADAM: Tell me, come on!
SATAN: Certainly not,
           Until you're tired of asking me.
ADAM: I'm really not on fire to know.
SATAN: You don't deserve to have good things;
125   The good you have you don't enjoy.
ADAM: I don't—how?
SATAN: Would you like to hear?
           I'll whisper it quietly in your ear.
ADAM: I certainly would like to know.
SATAN: Listen, then, Adam! Listen to me,
130   For your own good.
ADAM: All right, go on!
SATAN: You *will* believe me?
ADAM: Yes, of course.
SATAN: Absolutely?
ADAM: Except one thing.
SATAN: What thing is that?
ADAM: I'll tell it you.
           I will not act against my God.
SATAN: Are you so afraid?
ADAM: Indeed I am;
           I love and fear him.
SATAN: You're a fool.
           What can he do?
ADAM: Both good and bad.
SATAN: You are a madman, if you think
140   Anything bad can come of this.
           In Paradise!—You cannot die.
ADAM: God said to me that I should die
           If I transgressed his ordinance.
SATAN: What is this great trangression? Come
           I'd like to hear, and no delay.
ADAM: I'll tell you all about it, all.
           He gave me this command to keep:
           All the fruits in Paradise
           I am allowed to eat, he said,
150   Bar one; that is forbidden me—
           I shall not lay a hand upon it.
SATAN: And which is that?

[*Then shall Adam stretch out his hand and show Satan the forbidden fruit, saying:*]

ADAM: You see that there?
           That one he's quite forbidden me.
SATAN: Do you know why?
ADAM: Indeed I don't.
SATAN: I'll tell you what the real cause is.
           He doesn't care about the rest—

[And with his hand let him point to the forbidden fruit, saying to Adam:]

SATAN: Only this fruit that hangs up high:

This is the fruit of Knowledge, this

160   Gives insight into everything.

If you eat this, you will do well.

ADAM: Do well? In what?

SATAN: You will soon see.

At once you will be wide-awake.

The future—? Like an open book!

165   You'll gratify your every whim,

It will be wise to pick it now;

Eat it Adam! and you'll do well.

You'll no more be afraid of God,

But, rather, his equal, equal in all.

170   This is the reason He said no.

Will you believe me? Taste the fruit.

ADAM: I will not.

SATAN: A fine thing to hear!

Why won't you?

ADAM: No!

SATAN: You are a fool.

One day you'll say, "He told me so!"

[Then let the Devil retreat; and he shall go to the other devils and shall run about the "place," and after a little while he shall come back, happy and glad, to tempt Adam, and he shall say to him:]

SATAN: Well, Adam?—will you change your mind?

Are you still set in your stupid ways?

I meant to say the other day,

God has made you a mere dependant,

And put you here to eat his fruit.

180   Do you have any other fun?

ADAM: Certainly. Everything I want.

SATAN: Have you got no ambition, man?

You set a value on yourself

'Cause God has made you his—gardener!

185   God's made you keeper of his garden:

Don't you want anything else from life?

Did he make you just for belly-joys?

Hasn't he anything higher in store?

Now listen, Adam, to what I say.

190   I'll give you some genuine advice—

You can be your very own master

On a level with God himself.

To summarize the whole affair—

If you eat this apple here,

[Then he shall raise his hand towards Paradise:]

195   You shall be king, in majesty,
        Sharing power with God himself.
ADAM: Get out of here!
SATAN: What are you saying?
ADAM: Get out of here! You are the devil,[7]
        The foul-mouthed devil.
SATAN: What do you mean?
ADAM: You want to shove me down in hell,
        And put me in the wrong with God,
        End happiness, start misery.
        I cannot trust you. Out you go!
        And, Satan—don't you have the nerve
205   Ever to come near me again.
        You are a traitor, a faithless thing.

[*Then sadly and with downcast look Satan shall leave Adam and go to the gates of hell, where he shall talk with the other devils. After that he shall run around among the spectators; and then he shall approach Paradise, on Eve's side, and with a pleasant expression on his face suavely address her:*][8]

SATAN: Eve, I've come to talk to you.
EVE: Tell me, Satan, what on earth for?
SATAN: I've come in your best interests.
EVE: God's blessing on it!
SATAN: Don't be afraid.
        I have known for quite a while
        All the secrets of Paradise.
        I'll pass on some of them to you.
EVE: Go on, begin, I'm listening.
SATAN: Will you hear me out?
EVE: Why, certainly.
        I shan't put you in a temper.
SATAN: You'll keep it quiet?
EVE: Of course I will.
SATAN: It'll get out.
EVE: It won't through me.
SATAN: I put myself into your hands;
220   For me your word is good enough.
EVE: You will be safe—I've promised you.
SATAN: You have been very well brought up.
        I've seen Adam—but he's a fool.

7. Here Adam calls him "Sathan" (Satan, "the adversary") for the first time.
8. Compare the scene in Genesis 3:1–3 (there is no encounter between Adam and the serpent in Genesis): "Now the serpent was more crafty than any of the wild animals the Lord God had made. He said to the woman, 'Did God really say, "You must not eat from any tree in the garden"?' The woman said to the serpent, 'We may eat fruit from the trees in the garden, but God did say, "You must not eat fruit from the tree that is in the middle of the garden, and you must not touch it, or you will die."' 'You will surely not die,' the serpent said to the woman. 'For God knows that when you eat of it your eyes will be opened, and you will be like God, knowing good and evil.'"

EVE:	A bit severe.
SATAN:	He'll soften up.
225	Harder than hell he is just now.
EVE:	He's a gentleman.
SATAN:	A menial, rather.[9]
	Even if he neglects himself,
	At least he might look after you.
	You're delicate and sensitive,
230	Sweeter to look at than a rose;
	A crystal-clear complexion (like
	Snow in an icebound valley falling).
	You two! God made a bad match there:
	You have feelings—*Adam* has none.
235	All the same, you are the one with sense,
	Mature and wise to the finger-tips.
	Obviously you're the one to deal with;
	I'd like a word.
EVE:	You can trust me.
SATAN:	No one must know.
EVE:	Why, who should know?
SATAN:	Not even Adam.
EVE:	Not even him.
SATAN:	All right, I'll tell you. Listen now.
	There's no one here except us two.
	And Adam over there—but he can't hear.
EVE:	Speak up, he'll never catch a word.
SATAN:	You are the victims of a trick,
	A trick—worked in this very spot.
	The fruit which God has given you—
	There's hardly any goodness in it;
	The fruit you *aren't* allowed to eat
250	Has in it most amazing power—
	The very gift of life itself,
	Of strength, and of authority,
	Of all knowledge, both good and evil.
EVE:	How does it taste?
SATAN:	It's heavenly.
255	With your figure and your face
	You deserve a chance like this—
	To be first lady in the world
	Queen of heaven and of hell—
	Knowing all that is to be,
260	And being mistress of it all.
EVE:	Is that the fruit?
SATAN:	Yes, that's the one.

---

9. Eve claims Adam is *franc*—literally a free man, but also a courtly man. The Devil responds in kind, calling Adam a "serf," a bondsman or laborer bound to the land he worked or to his lord.

[Then shall Eve look carefully at the forbidden fruit, and having looked for a long time she shall say:]

EVE:	It does me good simply to *see* it.
SATAN:	Well, just imagine *eating* it!
EVE:	I? How can I?
SATAN:	You won't believe me!
265	Pick it first, give Adam some.
	At once you'll have the crown of heaven,
	Be on a par with Him who made you.
	He'll have no secrets from you then.
	As soon as you have eaten the fruit,
270	You'll feel completely different;
	You'll be with God, I guarantee,
	In equal goodness, equal power.
	Taste it and see!
EVE:	I'm thinking of it.
SATAN:	Don't believe Adam.
EVE:	I will do it.
SATAN:	When will you do it?
EVE:	Let me be,
	I'll wait till Adam's having a rest.
SATAN:	Come on, eat it, don't be afraid.
	Only children put things off.

[Then shall Satan leave Eve and go to hell. Adam, however, shall come to Eve, taking it badly that the Devil has been talking with her, and he shall say to her:]

ADAM:	Tell me, Eve, what was he after,
280	That devil Satan? What did he want?
EVE:	He spoke to me of our well-being.
ADAM:	Now—don't believe a word he says,
	He's a traitor.
EVE:	I know he is.[1]
ADAM:	How do you know?
EVE:	I've tried him out.
	What does it matter if I see him?
ADAM:	He'll influence the way you think.
EVE:	He won't, you know. I shan't believe
	A thing he says until *I've* tried it.
ADAM:	Don't let him come near you again!
290	He's not a person one can trust;
	He wanted to betray his master,
	And put himself in the high command.
	I shouldn't like that kind of blackguard
	To come crawling to you for help.

---

1. Some modern editors (including the translators, who have been amended here) assign this and the following several lines differently than the manuscript gives them, but there is no reason to assume that they are inconsistent with the character Eve in the play.

[Then shall a serpent cunningly contrived climb up the trunk of the forbidden tree; Eve shall put her ear up to it as if listening to its advice. Then Eve shall take the apple and offer it to Adam. Adam, however, shall not yet take it, and Eve shall say to him:]

EVE:	Eat it! You don't know what it's like.
	We mustn't lose our opportunity.
ADAM:	Is it so good?
EVE:	You'll see it is.
	You'll never know unless you taste.
ADAM:	I'm not so sure.
EVE:	Well, leave it!
ADAM:	I won't.
EVE:	You're a coward to put it off.
ADAM:	But I *will* take it.
EVE:	Come on, then! Bite!
	Full understanding's in your grasp,—
	Of good and evil. I'll eat it first.
ADAM:	And I will afterwards.
EVE:	That's right.

[Then shall Eve eat part of the apple, and say to Adam:]

EVE:	I've tasted it. Oh, God! The flavour!
	I've never tasted such a sweetness.
	This apple has a taste like . . . like . . .
ADAM:	Like what?
EVE:	Like no one's ever tasted.
	At last my eyes are opened—wide;
310	I feel like God—God, the almighty.
	All past and future circumstance
	I have it all, all in my grasp.
	Eat, Adam, eat—don't hesitate.
	It's the best thing you'll ever do.[2]

[Then shall Adam take the apple from Eve's hand, saying:]

ADAM:	I'll trust in you—you are my wife.
EVE:	Eat! there's nothing for you to fear.

[Then shall Adam eat part of the apple; as soon as it is eaten he shall realize his sin; and, bending down so that the on-lookers cannot see him, he shall take off his fine clothes and put on poor clothes sewn with figleaves. Then simulating the greatest possible grief he shall begin his lament:]

ADAM:	Oh! What wickedness I've done![3]
	No escape left, but death alone.

---

2. Compare to Genesis 3:6–7: "When the woman saw that the fruit of the tree was good for food and pleasing to the eye, and also desirable for gaining wisdom, she took some and ate it. She also gave some to her husband, who was with her, and he ate it. Then the eyes of both of them were opened, and they realized they were naked; so they sewed fig leaves together and made coverings for themselves."

The fleeting but divine vision with which Eve is graced is similar to a longer vision in the English Genesis B manuscript.

3. In Genesis, the only reaction of Adam and Eve is shame; God must explain the consequences of their transgression to them.

No hope of rescue—dead am I.
320   So evil is my destiny:
Evilly changed, good fortune gone;
I had bright hopes, now I've none.
I have betrayed the Lord of life
Through counsel of a wicked wife.
325   I know my guilt; what shall I do?
My Lord, I cannot look on you.
How can I gaze on holiness
Forsaken through my foolishness?
I never made a worse exchange;
330   Now I know truly what sin is.
O, death, why don't you seize on me?
Why cannot earth from guilt be free?
Why do I cumber up° the world?   *burden*
Into hell I must be hurled.
335   In hell shall be my dwelling-place
Until He come who shall me save.[4]
In hell thus shall I lead my life;
Whence to me shall come relief?
Whence shall I assistance gain?
340   Who can release me from this pain?
Why did I as a traitor end?
I am the man without a friend;
There is no one to help me out;
I am lost beyond a doubt.
345   Against my Lord I've done such ill
I cannot plead with him at all,
Since I am wrong and he is right.[5]
Lord! this shall be my cursed plight.
Who'll ever now remember me,
350   Who wronged the King of Majesty?
The King of Glory I've defied,
No trace of reason on my side.
I have no neighbour, have no friend,
Who could reprieve me at the end.
355   Whom shall I call upon for aid,
Now my wife has me betrayed,
The wife God gave to partner me?
She counselled me to misery.
Oh, Eve.

[*Then he shall see Eve his wife, and shall say:*]

ADAM: You wicked woman!

---

4. Adam demonstrates his awareness of the saving structure of history in Christian theology: God's plan to redeem the original sin of Adam and Eve through the incarnation, crucifixion, and resurrection of Jesus. Further allusions to these future events appear later on.
5. According to feudal law, either the lord or the vassal could be responsible for breaking fealty, but Adam is wholly in the wrong, and thus cannot even plead his case.

360   Why were you ever born, you witch?
       I wish that rib had been burnt up,
       The rib that's plunged me in despair.
       It should have been thrown into the fire;
       Look at the terrible things it's brought.
365   When God withdrew it from my side,
       Why didn't he burn it and slaughter me?
       This rib's betrayed the whole body—
       Damaged and ruined from head to foot.
       What shall I say? What shall I do?
370   Unless grace comes to me from heaven
       I shall never find release
       From this excruciating pain.
       Ah, Eve, it was an evil hour,
       A great unhappiness in store,
375   When you were given me for wife.
       Now through your advice I'm damned,
       Utterly ruined because of you—
       Down from the mountains to the shadows.
       No one will come to rescue me,
380   Unless it be mighty God himself.
       What am I saying? Why name Him?
       Will He help, when I've angered Him?
       No one will ever send me aid,
       Except the son of Blessed Mary.
385   I don't know whom to ask for help
       When we've not kept our faith with God.
       Now in God's keeping all must be:
       There's nothing left for me but death.

[*Then shall the chorus begin:* Dum deambularet.]⁶

[*After which God shall come, wearing a stole,*⁷ *and he shall enter Paradise and look around him, as if searching for Adam. But Adam and Eve shall hide in a corner of Paradise, as if acknowledging their wretched state, and God shall say:*]

GOD: Adam, where are you?

[*Then they shall both get up and stand before God, not, however, completely upright, but stooping a little because of the shame of their sin, and very sorrowful; and Adam shall reply:*]

ADAM: I'm here, my Lord.
390   I've hidden to avoid your anger.
       My nakedness makes me ashamed—
       And so I've shut myself away.

---

6. "Then was walking," followed by the rest of Genesis 3:8–10: "God in paradise in the cool of day. He called and said, 'Adam, where are you?' 'I heard your voice, Lord, so I hid. I heard your voice in paradise, and I was afraid because I was naked, so I hid.'"

7. Priest's strip of silk, worn particularly during exorcisms.

GOD: What have you done? How have you sinned?
    Who's snatched you from your happiness?
395   What have you done? Why so ashamed?
    Shall we reckon our accounts?
    There was nothing the other day
    Of which you needed feel ashamed,
    And now I see you sad and grey;
400   There's no joy in such a life.
ADAM: I'm so ashamed before you, Lord;
    That's why I hide.
GOD: You, hide? Now why?
ADAM: I'm so entwined with my disgrace
    I scarcely dare look in your face.
GOD: Why did you go against my ban?
    Have you gained anything at all?
    You are my servant,° I your Lord.   *serf*
ADAM: I cannot contradict the facts.
GOD: I made you in my likeness; why
410   Have you transgressed the law I gave?
    I moulded you in my own image;
    Why have you outraged me thus?
    My interdiction you've not kept;
    You've broken it quite wantonly.
415   You ate the fruit, of which I said
    I plainly had forbidden it.
    Did you think *you* could be my equal?
    I don't think you will boast of it.

[*Then shall Adam extend his hand towards God, and then towards Eve, saying:*]

ADAM: The woman whom you gave to me,
420   She was the first to do this thing;
    She gave it me and then I ate:
    Now, I think, it's turned to gall.
    I meddled wrongly with this fruit;
    I've sinned, and it was due to her.
GOD: You trusted in her more than in me;
    You ate the fruit without my leave,
    Now you shall have your recompense:
    The earth shall henceforth bear a curse
    Where you wish to sow your grain:
430   It'll fail you when it comes to harvest;
    It shall be cursed beneath your hand.
    You shall work the soil in vain:
    Your crop will ripen, certainly—
    Thorns and thistles it will yield!
435   Your farming will not be the same;
    It will be cursed (I pass this sentence):
    With great labour, with great pain,
    You will toil to get your bread;

With great hardship, and with great sweat
440   Both night and day you'll live your life.[8]

[*Then shall God turn to Eve and with threatening face say to her:*]

GOD: And you, Eve, you wicked wife,
        You quickly took up arms against me,
        Lightly regarded my commands.
EVE: The wicked serpent set me a trap.
GOD: Through him you thought to equal me?
        You know now how to prophecy?
        And once you had the mastery
        Over all things that are alive.
        How quickly you have lost it all!
450   I see you sad and miserable:
        Have you won or lost? Now say!
        I wish to render you your due,
        Give it to you as servant's hire:
        You shall be plagued in every way.
455   In pain your children you shall bear;
        In pain they shall to death endure.
        Your children even in birth shall languish,
        And die amidst the greatest anguish.
        You've pledged to deep disquietude
460   Yourself, and all your flesh and blood.
        All, who shall issue from your seed,
        All will lament your sinful deed.

[*And Eve shall reply saying:*]

EVE: I have done wrong; it was my foolishness:
        A single apple brings me great distress.
465   It casts me and my children in deep sorrow;
        A moment's pleasure brings me pain tomorrow.
        If I did wrong, it is no great surprise—
        It was the treacherous serpent closed my eyes.
        He has an evil mind; he is no lamb;
470   The man who takes *his* word is bound for doom.
        I took the apple (I know I was a fool)
        Against your word; this act of mine was cruel.
        A wicked taste! I now live in your hate:
        I lose my life for one small fruit I ate.

[*Then shall God threaten the serpent, saying:*]

GOD: And you, serpent! My curse on you
        Shall rest, till I obtain my due.
        On your belly you shall glide

---

8. Paraphrasing Genesis 3:17–19. As opposed to the account in Genesis, however, Adam had already been warned of this fate, and his curse comes before those of the serpent and Eve, emphasizing his primary responsibility for the Fall.

Till the last days of your life.
The dust shall be your only food,
480 On heath, in field, in wood.
Women will hate you to the core—
An evil thing to have next door.
Even though you bruise her heel,
She can overcome that ill:
485 She'll strike your head a mighty blow
That will bring you pain and woe.
She'll undertake all she can do
To have her just revenge on you.
You chose unwisely for a friend:
490 She will make your neck to bend.
A mighty Root from her shall rise
To shatter all your energies.[9]

[*Then God shall expel them from Paradise, saying:*]

Now, get you gone from Paradise!
Your change of country is for worse.
495 In earth set up your home, for here
You have no right to reappear.
You have no rightful claim to make;
Now, get outside, never come back!
Gone is your privilege—now roam
500 And find elsewhere a place for home.
Exiled from beatitude,
You shall be tired, you shall crave food.
Pain and misery will seek
And find you, seven days in the week.
505 On earth you'll miserably toil
Only for death at end of all;
And then, when you have tasted death,
Go straight away, to hell beneath.
The body's exiled in this world,
510 But there the soul's in peril hurled.
Satan will hold you in his power;
No man can help at that dark hour.
From whom do you expect rescue,
Unless *I* choose to pity you?

[*The choir shall sing the Respond:*]

515 CHOIR: In sudore vultus tui.[1]

[*Meanwhile an angel shall come, clothed in white, bearing a shining sword in his hand, whom God shall station at the gate of Paradise, saying to him:*]

---

9. The "Root" is Jesus, son of the Virgin Mary, whose purity was considered to have removed the blight caused by Eve's transgression. "Root of Jesse" was a common metaphor for Christ.
1. "By the sweat of your brow," followed by part of Genesis 3:19 and 3:17–18.

GOD: Mount guard on Paradise, and bar
            This outlaw ever entering there.
            See that he has no power nor might
            To lay hands on the fruit of Life.
520   Prevent him with your flashing sword
            From setting foot upon this road.

[*When they are outside Paradise, looking sad and cast down, they shall bend down to the earth over their ankles, and God shall point to them with his hand, his face turned towards Paradise. And the choir shall begin: Ecce Adam quasi unus.[2] At the end of which God shall go away to the church. Then Adam shall have a spade and Eve a mattock[3] and they shall begin to cultivate the ground and they shall sow wheat in it. After they have sowed, they shall go and sit somewhere for a little while, as if wearied of work, and, weeping, they shall look back often towards Paradise, striking their breasts. Meanwhile the devil shall come and shall plant thorns and thistles in their plot and go away. When Adam and Eve come to their plot and see the thorns and thistles growing, they shall be seized with violent grief and prostrate themselves on the ground and sitting there they shall beat their breasts and thighs, showing their grief in their actions; and Adam shall begin his lament:*]

ADAM: Alas! Wretched, that ever I saw this hour
            When sins of mine have overwhelmed me so
            That I've forsaken God whom all adore;
525   Who'll intercede with Him to help me now?

[*Here shall Adam look back to Paradise, and shall lift up both his hands towards it and inclining his head devoutly he shall say:*]

ADAM: Ah!—Paradise, our glorious residence,
            Garden of bliss, beautiful to our sense!
            Exiled I am indeed because of sin;
            I've lost all hope of getting back again.
530   I was inside, yet scarcely did enjoy;
            Followed advice which brought me banishment.
            Now it's too late—what use is it to sigh?
            Though I repent, I have my punishment.
              Where was my wisdom, where my memory,
535   That I for Satan left the King of Glory?
            Now, though I labour, it's no use to me:
            My sins will be recounted in man's story.

[*Then he shall raise his hand towards Eve, who shall be a little distant from him, and shaking his head with great indignation he shall say to her:*]

             O evil woman, with a traitor's heart
             Thus did you send me quickly to perdition,
540   When reasoning and sense you did pervert.

---

2. "Behold Adam as one," followed by the rest of Genesis 3:22, "of us has become, knowing good and evil; he must not be allowed to reach out his hand and take also from the tree of life and eat, and live forever."
3. A hoe.

Now I repent, but cannot have remission.
    Unhappy Eve, how prompt you were to sin,
How swiftly followed counsel from the devil!
You brought me death; I lost the life within;
545   Your sin shall be inscribed in every chronicle.
    Do you see the signs of chaos come again?
The earth itself feels our disgraceful curse.
We sowed our wheat; and thistles grow, not grain;
Wearily sweated, but the harvest's worse.
550   You saw the start of this our evil end—
A heavy sorrow, yet greater is in store;
To hell we shall be taken. Understand,
Torment and pain we'll suffer evermore.
    O wretched Eve, what do you say now?
555   These are your winnings, this your heritage.
You'll never have a blessing to bestow—
Unreasonable, perverse, into old age.
    All those who issue from our mutual seed
Will share the punishment for your misdeed.
560   It falls on all, although you did the wrong;
Before the doom's reversed, it will be long.

      [*Then shall Eve reply to Adam:*]

EVE: Adam, my lord, on me reproach you've bent:
You blame me for my crime and castigate.
If I did wrong, I feel the punishment;
565   I am to blame, God is the magistrate.
    Both against God and you it was a crime;
My wickedness men will for long recall.
My sins are hateful to me; great is my blame.
A sinner—there's no good in me at all.
570   I've no excuse; to God how could I defend
Myself? No grounds can clear me of this sin.
Forgive me, since I cannot make amend:
If I were able, I would—with offering
    Sinful, unhappy, wretched that I am
575   Before God's face I'm overcome with shame.
Death, take me now, and let me live no more!
I am in peril, and cannot reach the shore.
    The wicked serpent, evil-hearted snake,
Compelled me of the cursed fruit to take.
580   I gave you some—to do you good, I thought;
Sank you in sin and cannot lift you out.
    Why could I not Creation's Lord obey?
Why did I not accept a husband's care?
You did wrong too; but first I showed the way.
585   The evil done will take an age to cure.
    My wicked deed, my fateful accident,
Will make our offspring pay the highest price.

The fruit was sweet; but stern the punishment;
To eat was wicked, and we were unwise.
590   Nevertheless, my hope in God I place—
For sin there will be reconciliation.
God will bestow His favour and His grace;
His strength from Hell will bring us to salvation.

[*Then shall come the devil, and three or four other devils with him, carrying in their hands iron chains and manacles, which they shall put round the necks of Adam and Eve. And some of the devils shall drive them, and others shall drag them, to hell; yet other devils shall be near hell to meet them as they come, and they shall make a great dance amongst themselves at the damnation of Adam and Eve; and some of the devils shall point to them as they come, and shall receive them and despatch them to hell. From hell they shall make a great smoke to arise, and shall shout to each other in their joy; and they shall bang their cauldrons and kettles together so that they can be heard outside. And after a little while the devils shall emerge and run around the "place"; some, however, shall remain in hell.*]

Dante Alighieri
1265–1321

In the traces of autobiography he wove throughout his writings, Dante made it clear that there were two defining tragedies in his life: the death of his beloved Beatrice in 1290 and his exile from Florence in 1302, condemned to death should he ever return. Much else must have occurred in his life of which we know next to nothing—around 1285, he was married to one Gemma Donati, who bore him four children; he wrote his epic poem the *Commedia* during his peripatetic years of exile, finishing it right around the time of his death in Ravenna in 1321—but in the world of his poetry he chose to epitomize his life by an episode of unrequited love and a moment of high political drama.

DANTE'S FLORENCE
Dante's Florence was an independent republic, and its status as a banking center had made it one of the most important cities in late medieval Europe. It was also, like much of Italy, torn by civil strife. In 1260, two coalitions of noble families had fought for control of the city: the victorious Ghibellines, allied with the Hohenstaufen ruler Manfred, and the defeated Guelfs, allied with the papacy and a group of north-central Italian cities. The Guelfs regained control of Florence seven years later, banishing the Ghibellines and confiscating their property. In 1295, Dante enrolled in one of the professional guilds that constituted the power base of the *popolo,* a popular party which sought to contain the feuding of the aristocratic families, now focused on the drive by Pope Boniface VIII to bring northern Italy under papal control. In 1300, Dante was appointed to a two-month term as one of the city's seven priors (chief magistrates). As the city was rocked with violence, the priors exiled leading members of the new clashing factions of Black and White Guelfs, including Dante's good friend, the poet Guido Cavalcanti, who would die later that year. While an emissary in Rome two years later, Dante was sentenced to death in absentia, probably as revenge for his part in the earlier decision. He spent the last two decades of his life in miserable exile, wandering from city to city and patron to patron, all over Italy and possibly as far as Paris.

Dante's Works

Dante's earliest writings include *Il Fiore* (*The Flower*), a sonnet sequence adapted from *The Romance of the Rose*, a popular allegory of courtly love, and other writings related to the Northern Italian lyric movement of the *dolce stil novo*, or "sweet new style," as he would call it in the *Commedia*. The new Italian lyric was predominantly metaphysical, using Provençal forms and imagery to explore questions of philosophy, theology, and knowledge. Love was seldom sexual and seldom even social; the poet need barely have spoken to an idealized beloved like Dante's Beatrice or Cavalcanti's Giovanna. According to his poetic autobiography, *La Vita nuova* (*The New Life*, 1292–1294), Dante first encountered the Florentine girl, Beatrice Portinari, when she was eight and he was nine years old; she died sixteen years later without Dante having ever exchanged more than a few words with her. While he suffers from her presence (and her absence) just as a courtly lover would have done, he also comes to regard his beloved as nothing less than a manifestation of Christ, descended to earth to inspire him with love in order to lead him to a deeper understanding and a better life.

Much of Dante's writing was concerned with the meaning of what he had already written. *La Vita nuova* placed a series of his most celebrated early lyrics in the context of his obsession with Beatrice, explaining in retrospect how each poem had come to be written and how each reflected a different stage in his love from afar and a different aspect of his divine beloved. In *Il Convivio* (*The Banquet*), written in exile between about 1304 and 1307 and left unfinished, Dante reinterpreted several long love lyrics, this time as allegories about Lady Philosophy. During the same period he wrote but didn't finish *De Vulgari Eloquentia* (*On the Vulgar Tongue*) in which he surveyed the lyric tradition as a defense for composing intellectually ambitious verse in an Italian vernacular rather than in Latin. Dante also spoke about his use of the vernacular in an important letter to his patron Can Grande della Scala, which can be found in Volume C in The Rise of the Vernacular in Europe. Somewhere around 1310, he wrote *De Monarchia* (*On Monarchy*), a treatise on political philosophy arguing that an emperor was necessary to provide political stability to the world. His last and greatest work, the *Commedia* or *Comedy*, widely known as *The Divine Comedy*, incorporates all of Dante's earlier themes; it documents the difficulty of fulfilling his youthful ambitions, and the many ways in which the poet may or may not actually be worthy of doing so.

The *Commedia*

The structure of the *Commedia* is dazzlingly simple and impossibly intricate, an attempt to mirror the essential mystery of the Trinity. Everything is divided into threes and ones, their ideal permutations of nine and ten, and the perfect number seven. The single poem is composed of three parts, or canticles, *Inferno, Purgatorio,* and *Paradiso,* each describing one of the three distinct realms of the afterlife that compose the single universe comprehended by the divine plan. Each canticle is made up of thirty-three cantos, for a total of ninety-nine, except that *Inferno* has one extra to make a perfect hundred. Usually the first canto is considered as a prelude to the rest; this is one example of the ways in which Dante introduced dissymmetry to prevent the overall order of his poem from becoming monotonous. Cantos, for example, range in length from 115 to 160 lines. The meter Dante invented for the *Commedia,* which he called *terza rima* (third rhyme), embodies the poem's tension between order and disorder, stability and change. The eleven-syllable lines are divided into *terzinas,* or triplets, the first and third lines rhyming with each other, the second line introducing the main rhyme for the next *terzina.* So, for example, the first nine lines of the *Commedia:*

> Nel mezzo del cammin di nostra vita
>   mi ritrovai per una selva oscura,

ché la diritta via era smarrita.
Ahi quanto a dir qual era è cosa dura
5   esta selva selvaggia e aspra e forte
che nel pensier rinova la paura!
Tant' è amara che poco è più morte:
ma per trattar del ben ch'i' vi trovai,
diro de l'altre cose ch'i' v'ho scorte.

(Ed. Petrocchi)

When I had journeyed half of our life's way,
I found myself within a shadowed forest,
for I had lost the path that does not stray.
Ah, it is hard to speak of what it was,
5   that savage forest, dense and difficult,
which even in recall renews my fear:
so bitter—death is hardly more severe!
But to retell the good discovered there,
I'll also tell the other things I saw.

Each *terzina* is a self-contained argument, but the overlapping rhymes link one unit to the next, providing both closure and continuity. For example in line 3, *smarrita* ("lost") brings the opening image to a frightening close, but then the next rhymes of *dura* ("hard") and *paura* ("fear") recall and expand the previous description of the *selva oscura* ("dark forest"), while the new rhyme word *forte* ("difficult") looks forward to the next *terzina,* which rounds out the opening argument of all nine verses: he will tell us of the bad so that we will understand the good that came after.

STRUCTURE
The vision the poet recounts encompasses God's plan for the world, from its creation through to the Last Judgment. From the divine perspective, time doesn't exist, for in Dante's theology, as in Augustine's (see Volume A), God existed before time began and will still exist after time ceases. Everything that happens in the world, every thought and action, is known by God beforehand. From the human perspective, however, seeing only at best the deeds of the past, the lessons of history, and the memories of a life, this eternal scheme can hardly be comprehended, much less put into words. The formal structure of the poem is the most fundamental of the many ways in which Dante tries to impart this dual perspective to his readers. The transience, variety, and fascination of human life alternate with the eternity, unity, and fixity of the afterlife. Rather than simply relate what he saw in his vision and explain what it meant, the all-knowing poet slowly reveals it through a first-person persona (referred to in the notes to the poem as "the pilgrim") who is as unfamiliar as we are with what he is seeing. For the medieval Christian, the world and everything in it was a book created by God to be read and interpreted, and this is how Dante conceived the afterlife, as an enormously complex rebus, a puzzle to be deciphered. Each soul the pilgrim encounters presents a mystery; it is often unclear in terms of strict Catholic doctrine why a certain soul has been damned to hell or another saved in purgatory. Even though the poet claims to have been there and to have understood what everything in this plan means, he wants us instead to be confused, intrigued, and even outraged by what we see. The reader is to be converted, taught the way to salvation, but as an active participant.

GUIDES

There are three guides who lead the pilgrim on this journey: the classical Roman poet Virgil (70–19 B.C.E.), who takes him through Hell and Purgatory; Beatrice, who takes him through Paradise; and Saint Bernard of Clairvaux (see page 872), who prepares him for the final momentary union with the godhead. In addition to their historical character, each of these figures can be understood as a personification in an allegory about the conversion of a human soul: Virgil as the role of Reason in comprehending the rational cost of sin, either damnation or expiation; Beatrice as the role of Love and Faith in moving beyond the physical bounds of sin into the heavens; Bernard as the role of mystic vision and theology in achieving a final, perfect fusion with God. Each can be understood also as a personification of letters and study: Virgil as the preparatory ground of the classics; Beatrice as the inspirational role of love poetry; Bernard as the conclusive grasp of theology and mysticism. Further, they personify key influences in Dante's own life, the depth and emotional commitment of his attachment especially to the poetry and legend of Virgil and to the person and memory of Beatrice. For the *Commedia* is also a deeply felt spiritual autobiography, moving from suicidal despair to hope and the fulfillment of the pilgrim's innermost wishes.

GEOGRAPHY

The landscape of this autobiography is an idiosyncratic version of medieval geography and myth. Dante places Hell within the earth, an inverted cone created when Satan fell from heaven through the southern hemisphere directly opposite the future site of Jerusalem. As Satan was lodged in the center of the earth, land fleeing his presence piled up in both directions. The land escaping to the north created the inhabited world and hollowed out the cone of Hell beneath it. To the south, a passage was created leading to the surface of the southern hemisphere, where the mountain of Purgatory arose, its seven terraces analogous to the nine circles of hell. At the top of the mountain of Purgatory sits the earthly paradise, where Adam and Eve first dwelt in Eden before they were banished to the world below. Paradise is located in the fiery Empyrean, beyond the planets and stars above. Dante tells us that the three realms are peopled by innumerable souls, but singles out various individuals as emblematic of each sin or quality. His selection is eclectic: men and women out of classical myth and Roman history, biblical figures, Florentines, other Italians, and Europeans, friends and enemies, poets and politicians, characters from medieval legend, and popes who hadn't even died yet in 1300 when the journey is supposed to occur. Dante chooses to persuade us of the extraordinary bliss of heaven and the intolerable torment of hell by painting them in the vivid colors we know so well from the world in which we live. He invests every one of these characters, every word they say and everything the pilgrim does with enormous significance, a significance that he makes us urgently need to know.

PRONUNCIATIONS:

Beatrice: BAY-ah-TREE-che
Commedia: koh-ME-dee-ah
Contrapasso: kohn-trah-PAH-soh
Dante Alighieri: DAHN-tay ah-lee-ghee-AYR-ee
Francesca: frahn-CHES-kah
Inferno: een-FAYR-noh

Guido Cavalcanti: GWEE-doh kah-vahl-KAHN-tee
La Vita Nuova: lah VEE-tah noo-OH-vah
Paradiso: pah-rah-DEE-soh
Purgatorio: poor-gah-TOR-ee-oh
terza rima: TAYR-tzah REE-mah
Ugolino: oo-goh-LEE-noh

from La Vita Nuova[1]

1

In my Book of Memory, in the early part where there is little to be read, there comes a chapter with the rubric: *Incipit vita nova.*[2] It is my intention to copy into this little book the words I find written under that heading—if not all of them, at least the essence of their meaning.

2

Nine times already since my birth the heaven of light had circled back to almost the same point,[3] when there appeared before my eyes the now glorious lady of my mind, who was called Beatrice even by those who did not know what her name was.[4] She had been in this life long enough for the heaven of the fixed stars to be able to move a twelfth of a degree to the East in her time; that is, she appeared to me at about the beginning of her ninth year, and I first saw her near the end of my ninth year. She appeared dressed in the most patrician of colors, a subdued and decorous crimson, her robe bound round and adorned in a style suitable to her years.[5] At that very moment, and I speak the truth, the vital spirit,[6] the one that dwells in the most secret chamber of the heart, began to tremble so violently that even the most minute veins of my body were strangely affected; and trembling, it spoke these words: *Ecce deus fortior me, qui veniens dominabitur michi.*[7] At that point the animal spirit, the one abiding in the high chamber to which all the senses bring their perceptions, was stricken with amazement and, speaking directly to the spirits of sight, said these words: *Apparuit iam beatitudo vestra.*[8] At that point the natural spirit, the one dwelling in that part where our food is digested, began to weep, and weeping said these words: *Heu miser, quia frequenter impeditus ero deinceps!*[9] Let me say that, from that time on, Love governed my soul, which became immediately devoted to him, and he reigned over me with such assurance and lordship, given him by the power of my imagination, that I could only dedicate myself to fulfilling his every pleasure.[1] Often he commanded me to go and look for this youngest of angels; so, during those early years I often went in search of her, and I found her to be of such natural dignity and worthy of such admiration that the words of the poet Homer suited her perfectly: "She seemed to be the daughter not of a mortal, but of a god."[2] And though her image, which remained constantly with me, was Love's assurance of holding me, it was of such a pure quality that it never allowed me to be ruled by Love without the faithful counsel of reason, in

---

1. Translated by Mark Musa.
2. The phrase is Latin: "Here begins the new life." The idea that memory is like a book was a common medieval image. It reappears in Dante's *Commedia,* as well as in Chaucer's writings and elsewhere.
3. Ancient and medieval astronomers believed the sun ("the heaven of light") circled the earth once a year, rather than vice versa; hence, Dante was nine years old.
4. Beatrice Portinari (see introduction to Dante, page 894). Her name in Latin means "she who blesses."
5. In addition to being a "noble" color, crimson was the color of the Christian virtue of *caritas,* charity or love, as well as, more generally, the color of passion.
6. According to medieval medicine, three "spirits" or

fluids permeated the blood vessels and organs of the human body: the natural originated in the liver, the vital in the heart, and the animal in the brain. Love seizes him in all three.
7. Latin: "Here is a god stronger than I, who is coming to rule over me."
8. Now your bliss [*beatitude*] has appeared (Latin).
9. Alas, wretch that I am, from now on I shall be hindered often (Latin).
1. It was common to personify the power of love in a God of Love adapted from the classical Eros or Cupid, who ruled over the Lover.
2. The quotation alludes to Priam's description of his son, the hero Hector in *Iliad* 24.258–59.

all those things where such advice might be profitable. Since to dwell on my passions and actions when I was so young might seem like recounting fantasies, I shall put them aside and, omitting many things that could be copied from the text which is the source of my present words, I shall turn to those written in my memory under more important headings.[3]

3

After so many days had passed that precisely nine years were ending since the appearance, just described, of this most gracious lady, it happened that on the last one of those days the miraculous lady appeared, dressed in purest white, between two ladies of noble bearing both older than she was; and passing along a certain street, she turned her eyes to where I was standing faint-hearted and, with that indescribable graciousness for which today she is rewarded in the eternal life, she greeted me so miraculously that I seemed at that moment to behold the entire range of possible bliss. It was precisely the ninth hour of that day, three o'clock in the afternoon, when her sweet greeting came to me.[4] Since this was the first time her words had ever been directed to me, I became so ecstatic that, like a drunken man, I turned away from everyone and I sought the loneliness of my room, where I began thinking of this most gracious lady and, thinking of her, I fell into a sweet sleep, and a marvelous vision appeared to me. I seemed to see a cloud the color of fire and, in that cloud, a lordly man, frightening to behold, yet he seemed also to be wondrously filled with joy. He spoke and said many things, of which I understood only a few; one was *Ego dominus tuus*.[5] I seemed to see in his arms a sleeping figure, naked but lightly wrapped in a crimson cloth; looking intently at this figure, I recognized the lady of the greeting, the lady who earlier in the day had deigned to greet me. In one hand he seemed to be holding something that was all in flames, and it seemed to me that he said these words: *Vide cor tuum*.[6] And after some time had passed, he seemed to awaken the one who slept, and he forced her cunningly to eat of that burning object in his hand; she ate of it timidly. A short time after this, his happiness gave way to bitterest weeping, and weeping he folded his arms around this lady, and together they seemed to ascend toward the heavens. At that point my drowsy sleep could not bear the anguish that I felt; it was broken and I awoke. At once I began to reflect, and I discovered that the hour at which that vision had appeared to me was the fourth hour of the night; that is, it was exactly the first of the last nine hours of the night. Thinking about what I had seen, I decided to make it known to many of the famous poets of that time. Since just recently I had taught myself the art of writing poetry, I decided to compose a sonnet addressed to all of Love's faithful subjects; and, requesting them to interpret my vision, I would write them what I had seen in my sleep. And then I began to write this sonnet, which begins: *To every captive soul*.

> To every captive soul and loving heart[7]
> to whom these words I have composed are sent
> for your elucidation in reply,

---

3. Continuing the metaphor of the book of memory, Dante informs us that he has omitted inessential, youthful entries, and chosen only those under "important headings."
4. On the numerological importance of threes and nines, see the introduction to Dante, pages 894–895. The first hour of the day was six in the morning.

5. I am your master (Latin).
6. Behold your heart (Latin).
7. This poem is given in both English and Italian. The loving or noble (*gentil*) heart was a key concept of the *dolce stil novo*, in particular the famous *canzone* of Guido Guinizelli, to which Dante also alludes in *Inferno* 5.100 ff.

greetings I bring for your sweet lord's sake, Love.
The first three hours, the hours of the time
of shining stars, were coming to an end,
when suddenly Love appeared before me
(to remember how he really was appalls me).

Joyous, Love seemed to me, holding my heart
within his hand, and in his arms he had
my lady, loosely wrapped in folds, asleep.
He woke her then, and gently fed to her
the burning heart; she ate it, terrified.[8]
And then I saw him disappear in tears.[9]

A ciascun' alma presa e gentil core
nel cui cospetto ven lo dir presente,
In ciò che mi rescrivan suo parvente,
salute in lor segnor, cioè Amore.
Già eran quasi che atterzate l'ore
del tempo che onne stella n'è lucente,
quando m'apparve Amor subitamente,
(cui essenza membrar mi dà orrore).

Allegro mi sembrava Amor tenendo
meo core in mano, e ne le braccia avea
madonna involta in un drappo dormendo.
Poi la svegliava, e d'esto core ardendo
lei paventosa umilmente pascea.
Appresso gir lo ne vedea piangendo.

This sonnet is divided into two parts. In the first part I extend greetings and ask for a response, while in the second I describe what it is that requires the response. The second part begins: *The first three hours.*

This sonnet was answered by many, who offered a variety of interpretations; among those who answered was the one I call my best friend,[1] who responded with a sonnet beginning: *I think that you beheld all worth.* This exchange of sonnets marked the beginning of our friendship. The true meaning of the dream I described was not perceived by anyone then, but now it is completely clear even to the least sophisticated.

[*Disappointed in something she has heard about Dante, Beatrice refuses him her greeting. After much suffering, he resolves his dilemma by gaining pleasure from writing poetry praising her rather than the unpredictable pursuit of her greeting.*]

19

Then it happened that while walking down a path along which ran a very clear stream, I suddenly felt a great desire to write a poem, and I began to think how I would go about it. It seemed to me that to speak of my lady would not be becoming unless I

---

8. To eat of the lover's heart was a common and powerful image in the poetry of courtly love.
9. The opening sonnet already prefigures the death of Beatrice.
1. The Florentine poet Guido Cavalcanti (c. 1259–1300). See *Inferno* 10.58–111 (pages 938–939).

were to address my words to ladies, and not just to any ladies, but only to those who are worthy, not merely to women. Then, I must tell you, my tongue, as if moved of its own accord, spoke and said: *Ladies who have intelligence of love.* With great delight I decided to keep these words in mind and to use them as the beginning of my poem. Later, after returning to the aforementioned city and reflecting for several days, I began writing a *canzone,* using this beginning, and arranged it in a way that will be seen below in its division. The *canzone* begins: *Ladies who have.*[2]

Ladies who have intelligence of love,
   I wish to speak to you about my lady,
   not thinking to complete her litany,°   *praises*
   but to talk in order to relieve my heart.
I tell you, when I think of her perfection,
Love lets me feel the sweetness of his presence,
   and if at that point I could still feel bold,
   my words could make all mankind fall in love.
I do not want to choose a tone too lofty,
   for fear that such ambition make me timid;
   instead I shall discuss her graciousness,
defectively, to measure by her merit,
   with you, ladies and maidens whom Love knows,
   for such a theme is only fit for you.

The mind of God receives an angel's prayer:[3]
   "My Lord, there appears to be upon your earth
   a living miracle, proceeding from
   a radiant soul whose light reaches us here."
Heaven, that lacks its full perfection only
in lacking her, pleads for her to the Lord,
   and every saint is begging for this favor.
Compassion for His creatures still remains,
   for God, who knows they are speaking of my lady,
   says: "Chosen ones, now suffer happily
that she, your hope, live her appointed time
   for the sake of one down there who fears her loss,
   and who shall say unto the damned in Hell:
   'I have beheld the hope of Heaven's blest.'"

My lady is desired in highest Heaven.
   Now let me tell you something of her power.
   A lady who aspires to graciousness
   should seek her company, for where she goes
Love drives a killing frost into vile hearts
that freezes and destroys what they are thinking;
   should such a one insist on looking at her,
   he is changed to something noble or he dies.

---

2. Adapted from the Provençal *canso,* the *canzone* was composed of multiple stanzas of identical structure. Presented here as the first result of Dante's new resolution to find fulfillment in praising his beloved, this poem would later be cited in *Purgatorio* 24.49–51 as the epitome of *dolce stil novo* poetry.

3. The quasi-divine nature of the beloved was an innovation of the *dolce stil novo;* Dante took it further than any other poet, making the love of Beatrice not merely heavenly but literally an agent of salvation.

And if she finds one worthy to behold her,
that man will feel her power for salvation
when she accords to him her salutation,
which humbles him till he forgets all wrongs.
God has graced her with an even greater gift:
whoever speaks with her shall speak with Him.

Love says of her: "How can a mortal body
achieve such beauty and such purity?"
He looks again and swears it must be true:
God does have something new in mind for earth.
Her color is the pallor of the pearl,
a paleness perfect for a gracious lady;
she is the best that Nature can achieve
and by her mold all beauty tests itself;
her eyes, wherever she may choose to look,
send forth their spirits radiant with love
to strike the eyes of anyone they meet,
and penetrate until they find the heart.
You will see Love depicted on her face,
there where no one dares hold his gaze too long.

My song, I know that you will go and speak
to many ladies when I bid you leave,
and since I brought you up as Love's true child,
ingenuous and plain, let me advise you
to beg of anybody you may meet:
"Please help me find my way; I have been sent
to the lady with whose praise I am adorned."
And so that you may not have gone in vain,
do not waste time with any vulgar people;
do what you can to show your meaning only
to ladies, or to men who may be worthy;
they will direct you by the quickest path.
You will find Love and with him find our lady.
Speak well of me to Love, it is your duty.

[*Beatrice dies on the ninth day of a month and year replete with further permutations of the number nine. Dante is devastated. As he recovers from the shock, he begins to take pleasure in the consolation of another lady, which causes much inner turmoil. A vision of Beatrice cures him of this infatuation. This is the situation in the two chapters that follow, which conclude "La Vita nuova."*]

41

Some time afterward, two gentlewomen sent word to me requesting that I send them some of my poetry. Taking into consideration their noble station, I decided not only to let them have some of my poems but also to write something new to go along with those words—in this way doing their request more honor. So I wrote a sonnet which tells of my condition and sent it to them accompanied by the preceding sonnet and by the one which begins: *Now come to me and listen to my sighs.*

The new sonnet I wrote begins: *Beyond the sphere,* and contains five parts. In the first I tell where my thought is going, naming it after one of its effects. In the second I tell why it goes up there, that is, who causes it to go. In the third I tell what it saw, that is, a lady being honored up there, and I call it a "pilgrim spirit" because it makes the journey upward spiritually and, once there, is like a pilgrim far from home. In the fourth I tell how it sees her to be such, that is of such a nature, that I cannot understand it: that is to say that my thought ascends into the nature of this lady to such a degree that my mind cannot grasp it, for our minds function in relation to those blessèd souls as the weak eye does in relation to the sun, and this the Philosopher tells us in the second book of the *Metaphysics.*[4] In the fifth part I say that, even though I cannot understand what my thought has taken me to see, that is her miraculous nature, at least I understand this much: this thought of mine is entirely about my lady, for many times when it comes to my mind, I hear her name. At the end of this fifth part I say: "dear ladies," so that it be understood that it is to ladies that I speak. The second part begins: *a new intelligence,* the third: *Once arrived,* the fourth: *But when it tries,* the fifth: *This much.* It could be divided and explained more subtly, but since it can pass with this analysis, I do not concern myself with further division.

Beyond the sphere that makes the widest round,[5]
passes the sigh arisen from my heart;
a new intelligence that Love in tears
endowed it with is urging it on high.
Once arrived at the place of its desiring
it sees a lady held in reverence,
splendid in light; and through her radiance
the pilgrim spirit looks upon her being.

But when it tries to tell me what it saw,
I cannot understand the subtle words
it speaks to the sad heart that makes it speak.
I know it tells of that most gracious one,
for I often hear the name of Beatrice.
This much, at least, is clear to me, dear ladies.

42

After I wrote this sonnet there came to me a miraculous vision in which I saw things that made me resolve to say no more about this blessèd one until I would be capable of writing about her in a nobler way. To achieve this I am striving as hard as I can, and this she truly knows. Accordingly, if it be the pleasure of Him through whom all things live that my life continue for a few more years, I hope to write of her that which has never been written of any other woman. And then may it please the One who is the Lord of graciousness that my soul ascend to behold the glory of its lady, that is, of that blessèd Beatrice, who in glory contemplates the countenance of the One *qui est per omnia secula benedictus.*[6]

---

4. The "Philosopher" is Aristotle. Dante knew Aristotle's *Metaphysics* from its translation and commentary by Thomas Aquinas, from which the image of the sun is drawn.

5. This sphere, the Empyrean, is the fiery realm beyond the ninth heaven, the Primum Mobile; it is the realm of God, the angels, and the blessed.

6. Who is through all ages blessed (Latin).

THE DIVINE COMEDY[1]

from Inferno

INFERNO

Hell serves double duty in the *Commedia:* it describes the consequences of a sinful life and it teaches the reader how to read the poem. Although from early on critics began mapping its nine circles (plus the vestibule, or ante-hell) and arguing about who did or didn't deserve to be where, Dante actually reveals the structure of Hell gradually, sometimes only partially, and often in ways a medieval reader would never have expected. This begins with Virgil, the most complex character in the poem. He was renowned for his virtue and considered a prophet of Christianity, and there was no pressing reason to condemn him to Hell at all. As with many of the souls encountered, however, Virgil's fate serves to define his place (Limbo) as a series of debates and dilemmas rather than a simple equation. In God's eyes, sin may be a simple and well-ordered business, but from the human perspective, it is not so easy to judge. Sin can be seductive, like Francesca da Rimini in the circle of the Lustful; it can inspire pity and fear, like Ugolino at the very bottom of Hell. Seldom, however, is it exactly what it seems, for Dante expects his readers to move back and forth through the poem, to compare what he says about a shade to what was known or written about him or her: he challenges his readers to be like himself, so immersed in the classics, the Bible, myth, history and thirteenth-century art and politics that they become emotional, life-and-death concerns. The portraits are striking in their own right, but the more we know about their models the more profound and far-reaching are the moral and ethical dilemmas they embody.

We unravel the meaning of each circle of Hell through the souls we are told it contains, by the dramatic encounters the two pilgrims have with certain of these souls, by the particular guardian (usually a mythological monster) assigned to each, by the particular landscape, by the style of the language, which ranges from the sublimity of epic to the simplicity of lyric to the earthiness of the folk tale, and by the nature of the torment. One soul terms Hell's torments the *contrapasso,* or counter-punishment. The principle of *contrapasso* is poetic justice: each soul receives what he or she most desired or did on earth, but in a perverse and unwanted form—the flatterers drown in excrement; the sowers of discord are split asunder. There is a tension throughout *Inferno* between the moral lessons we are to learn from the damned characters, and the fascination many of them exert on us, both positive and negative, in their quality as stubbornly alive and suffering individuals.

Many of the damned serve to demonstrate that there is a danger in knowing Hell too well. The underworld offers great temptation for rage and revenge, and it contains much of apparent pleasure and beauty as well: the worthies of Limbo, Francesca's love, Dante's mentor Brunetto Latini, the doting father of his friend and fellow poet Cavalcanti. This will also be a dilemma in *Purgatorio,* where the souls, although saved, must suffer much in weaning themselves from their ties to the world they loved, but in the *Inferno* the dilemma takes a starker form. The stakes are very high, not just for individuals but for society, and Dante is also careful to indicate which parts of Hell cause particular trouble, either to him or to his society: sins of desire, which are so close to the love and longing that can lead one to God; the complex and subdivided sins of fraud in the eighth circle, which attack the very bonds of sociability on which community relies. Dante doesn't want us to submit meekly to the journey through Hell; he expects us to go through it kicking and screaming, arguing and cursing, although he also expects that in the end he will win us over, as in the end he has won over himself.

---

1. Translated by Allen Mandelbaum.

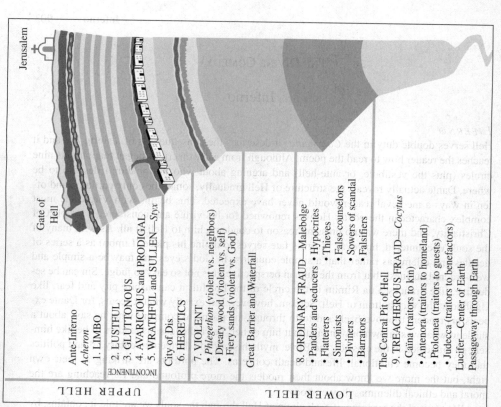

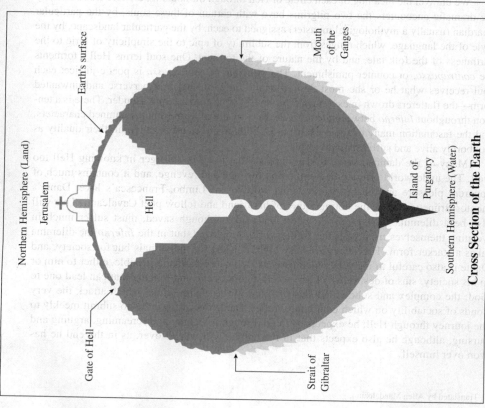

Cross Section of the Earth

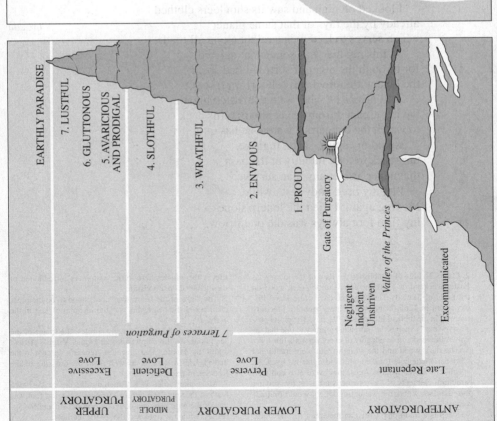

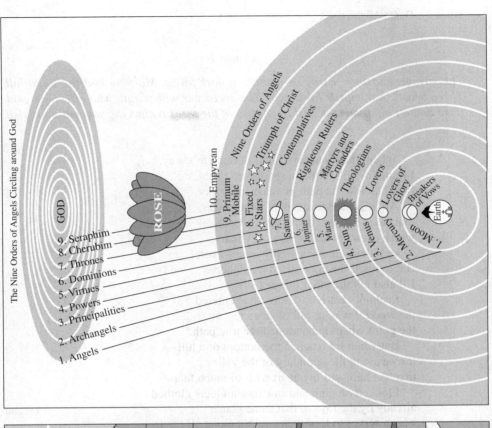

Canto 1

The voyager-narrator astray by night in a dark forest. Morning and the sunlit hill.
Three beasts that impede his ascent. The encounter with Virgil, who offers his guid-
ance and an alternative path through two of the three realms the voyager must visit.

When I had journeyed half of our life's way,[2]
I found myself within a shadowed forest,
for I had lost the path that does not stray.[3]
    Ah, it is hard to speak of what it was,
5   that savage forest, dense and difficult,
which even in recall renews my fear:
    so bitter—death is hardly more severe!
But to retell the good discovered there,
I'll also tell the other things I saw.
10   I cannot clearly say how I had entered
the wood; I was so full of sleep just at
the point where I abandoned the true path.[4]
    But when I'd reached the bottom of a hill—
it rose along the boundary of the valley
15   that had harassed my heart with so much fear—
    I looked on high and saw its shoulders clothed
already by the rays of that same planet°   *the sun*
which serves to lead men straight along all roads.
    At this my fear was somewhat quieted;
20   for through the night of sorrow I had spent,
the lake within my heart felt terror present.[5]
    And just as he who, with exhausted breath,
having escaped from sea to shore, turns back
to watch the dangerous waters he has quit,
25   so did my spirit, still a fugitive,
turn back to look intently at the pass
that never has let any man survive.[6]
    I let my tired body rest awhile.
Moving again, I tried the lonely slope—
30   my firm foot always was the one below.[7]

2. Canto 21.112–14 establishes the date of the journey as Easter weekend of 1300, the entry into the dark wood on the night of Maundy Thursday, the day before Good Friday. Born in 1265, Dante would have been 35, precisely midway in the biblical life span of 70 years. The plural possessive "our" expands the individual journey to one that involves the reader in an allegory of every person's life.
3. The dark wood and the straight path were traditional Christian metaphors for the sinful and righteous lives, respectively. In the Middle Ages, they were also common structural elements of the romance narrative: by straying into the dark wood, the wandering knight would find adventure.
4. Sleep is a traditional Christian metaphor for the sinful

life; it also alludes here to the customary introduction of the medieval dream vision.
5. The "lake of the heart" was understood to be the inner chamber of the heart; this was the location of fear in the body.
6. The first of the poem's many similes: the image of the sea alludes to the shipwreck that begins Virgil's *Aeneid* and to the landfall that precedes Aeneas's descent to the underworld in Book 6, as well as to the crossing of the Red Sea in Exodus.
7. Most likely, this is a Christian allegory of the "two feet" of the soul. The left, or "firmer," dragging foot was that of the will, weighed down by original sin and the appetites, while the right was that of the intellect.

And almost where the hillside starts to rise—
look there!—a leopard, very quick and lithe,
a leopard covered with a spotted hide.[8]

He did not disappear from sight, but stayed;
35 indeed, he so impeded my ascent
that I had often to turn back again.

The time was the beginning of the morning;
the sun was rising now in fellowship
with the same stars that had escorted it

40 when Divine Love first moved those things of beauty;[9]
so that the hour and the gentle season
gave me good cause for hopefulness on seeing

that beast before me with his speckled skin;
but hope was hardly able to prevent
45 the fear I felt when I beheld a lion.

His head held high and ravenous with hunger—
even the air around him seemed to shudder—
this lion seemed to make his way against me.

And then a she-wolf showed herself; she seemed
50 to carry every craving in her leanness;
she had already brought despair to many.

The very sight of her so weighted me
with fearfulness that I abandoned hope
of ever climbing up that mountain slope.

55 Even as he who glories while he gains
will, when the time has come to tally loss,
lament with every thought and turn despondent,

so was I when I faced that restless beast,
which, even as she stalked me, step by step
60 had thrust me back to where the sun is speechless.

While I retreated down to lower ground,
before my eyes there suddenly appeared
one who seemed faint because of the long silence.

When I saw him in that vast wilderness,
65 "Have pity on me," were the words I cried,
"whatever you may be—a shade, a man."

He answered me: "Not man; I once was man.
Both of my parents came from Lombardy,
and both claimed Mantua as native city.

70 And I was born, though late, *sub Julio,*
and lived in Rome under the good Augustus—
the season of the false and lying gods.

I was a poet, and I sang the righteous
son of Anchises who had come from Troy

---

8. Medieval commentaries of the *Inferno* quickly identified the leopard with lust, the lion with pride, and the wolf
with avarice, or cupidity. They parallel the later threefold
division of the sins of hell between those of incontinence,
violence, and fraud in Canto 11.

9. The world was believed to have been created in spring,
when the sun was in the constellation of Ares; Dante's
journey takes place in the same season and under the
same stars.

75   when flames destroyed the pride of Ilium.[1]
            But why do you return to wretchedness?
        Why not climb up the mountain of delight,
        the origin and cause of every joy?"
            "And are you then that Virgil, you the fountain
80   that freely pours so rich a stream of speech?"
        I answered him with shame upon my brow.
            "O light and honor of all other poets,
        may my long study and the intense love
        that made me search your volume serve me now.
85   You are my master and my author, you—
        the only one from whom my writing drew
        the noble style for which I have been honored.
            You see the beast that made me turn aside;
        help me, o famous sage, to stand against her,
90   for she has made my blood and pulses shudder."
            "It is another path that you must take,"
        he answered when he saw my tearfulness,
        "if you would leave this savage wilderness;
            the beast that is the cause of your outcry
95   allows no man to pass along her track,
        but blocks him even to the point of death;
            her nature is so squalid, so malicious
        that she can never sate her greedy will;
        when she has fed, she's hungrier than ever.
100   She mates with many living souls and shall
        yet mate with many more, until the Greyhound
        arrives, inflicting painful death on her.
            That Hound will never feed on land or pewter,
        but find his fare in wisdom, love, and virtue;
105   his place of birth shall be between two felts.[2]
            He will restore low-lying Italy
        for which the maid Camilla died of wounds,
        and Nisus, Turnus, and Euryalus.[3]
            And he will hunt that beast through every city
110   until he thrusts her back again to Hell,
        from which she was first sent above by envy.[4]

1. Virgil (70–19 B.C.E.) was born during the lifetime of Julius Caesar, who was assassinated in 44, too soon to have known the poet's writing. Virgil's patron was Caesar's adopted son, the emperor Augustus. Virgil identifies himself with his final work, the mythical epic of Aeneas, the "righteous son of Anchises," who journeyed from the destruction of Troy ("Ilium") to Italy to found the city of Rome.
2. Virgil explains the she-wolf's sway by means of the first of the poem's many prophecies. The poetical aptness of a Greyhound (veltro) to hunt down and kill the she-wolf is clear; possible identities are many and not mutually exclusive. There is some reference to the redemptive powers of Christ, but also to the desired coming of a secular leader who would be above corruption, seeking neither land nor money ("pewter"), and who would reestablish temporal authority in Christendom: perhaps Dante's benefactor Can Grande della Scala of Verona, whose domain was roughly limited by the two "felts" (Feltros) of Feltre and Montefeltro, perhaps a Holy Roman Emperor, elected by the casting of ballots in the felt-lined urns used at the time.
3. Virgil refers to Italy in terms of his own epic of the founding of the classical Roman empire, alluding to four characters who died in the civil war for the possession of Italy related in the second half of the Aeneid.
4. "But by the envy of the devil, death entered the world" (Wisdom 2:24).

Therefore, I think and judge it best for you
to follow me, and I shall guide you, taking
you from this place through an eternal place,

115   where you shall hear the howls of desperation
and see the ancient spirits in their pain,
as each of them laments his second death;[5]

and you shall see those souls who are content
within the fire,° for they hope to reach—   *of Purgatory*
120   whenever that may be—the blessed people.

If you would then ascend as high as these,
a soul more worthy than I am will guide you;
I'll leave you in her care when I depart,

because that Emperor who reigns above,
125   since I have been rebellious to His law,
will not allow me entry to His city.

He governs everywhere, but rules from there;
there is His city, His high capital:
o happy those He chooses to be there!"

130   And I replied: "O poet—by that God
whom you had never come to know—I beg you,
that I may flee this evil and worse evils,

to lead me to the place of which you spoke,
that I may see the gateway of Saint Peter[6]
135   and those whom you describe as sorrowful."
Then he set out, and I moved on behind him.

Canto 2

The following evening. Invocation to the Muses. The narrator's questioning of his worthiness to visit the deathless world. Virgil's comforting explanation that he has been sent to help Dante by three Ladies of Heaven. The voyager heartened. Their setting out.

The day was now departing; the dark air
released the living beings of the earth
from work and weariness; and I myself

alone prepared to undergo the battle
5   both of the journeying and of the pity,
which memory, mistaking not, shall show.

O Muses, o high genius, help me now;
o memory that set down what I saw,
here shall your excellence reveal itself![1]

10   I started: "Poet, you who are my guide,
see if the force in me is strong enough
before you let me face that rugged pass.

5. Either the condemnation of the soul to hell after death, or the final condemnation to hell and reunion with the body that will occur during the Last Judgment.
6. Either the gate of Purgatory or the entry to Paradise.

1. Echoes of the *Aeneid* continue: the invocation of the classical muses was a staple of the epic style. Dante adds the stress on the poet's memory of what he has seen.

You say that he who fathered Sylvius,
while he was still corruptible, had journeyed
15   into the deathless world with his live body.[2]
    For, if the Enemy of every evil
was courteous to him, considering
all he would cause and who and what he was,
    that does not seem incomprehensible,
20   since in the empyrean heaven he was chosen
to father honored Rome and her empire;
    and if the truth be told, Rome and her realm
were destined to become the sacred place,
the seat of the successor° of great Peter.   *the Pope*
25   And through the journey you ascribe to him,
he came to learn of things that were to bring
his victory and, too, the papal mantle.[3]
    Later the Chosen Vessel travelled there,
to bring us back assurance of that faith
30   with which the way to our salvation starts.[4]
    But why should I go there? Who sanctions it?
For I am not Aeneas, am not Paul;
nor I nor others think myself so worthy.
    Therefore, if I consent to start this journey,
35   I fear my venture may be wild and empty.
You're wise; you know far more than what I say."
    And just as he who unwills what he wills
and shifts what he intends to seek new ends
so that he's drawn from what he had begun,
40   so was I in the midst of that dark land,
because, with all my thinking, I annulled
the task I had so quickly undertaken.
    "If I have understood what you have said,"
replied the shade of that great-hearted one,
45   "your soul has been assailed by cowardice,
    which often weighs so heavily on a man—
distracting him from honorable trials—
as phantoms frighten beasts when shadows fall.
    That you may be delivered from this fear,
50   I'll tell you why I came and what I heard
when I first felt compassion for your pain.[5]
    I was among those souls who are suspended;°   *in Limbo*

---

2. In lines 13–27, Dante retells the story of *Aeneid* 6
(see Volume A) in a Christian context. While still alive,
Aeneas (father of Sylvius, ancestor of the founder of
Rome) descended to the underworld, which included both
a place of punishment and a paradise, in order to meet his
father and learn the fate of his descendants.
3. Aeneas's father gave him advice on the upcoming war
and showed his son a procession of souls of future Romans that forecast the empire of Augustus; in Dante's
version it also forecasts papal Rome.

4. The apostle Paul ("the Chosen Vessel") described in
his second Epistle to the Corinthians (12:2–4) how he was
"caught up into Paradise"; the apocryphal *Vision of
St. Paul* narrates a descent into hell as well.
5. Virgil explains how he came to appear before Dante
and provides a "divine" authorization for the journey (and
the poem) that follows. The language of the account is
less that of the high style of the *Aeneid* than of the lyric of
courtly love.

a lady called to me, so blessed, so lovely
that I implored to serve at her command.

55   Her eyes surpassed the splendor of the star's;
and she began to speak to me—so gently
and softly—with angelic voice. She said:
'O spirit of the courteous Mantuan,
whose fame is still a presence in the world

60   and shall endure as long as the world lasts,
my friend, who has not been the friend of fortune,
is hindered in his path along that lonely
hillside; he has been turned aside by terror.
From all that I have heard of him in Heaven,

65   he is, I fear, already so astray
that I have come to help him much too late.
Go now; with your persuasive word, with
all that is required to see that he escapes,
bring help to him, that I may be consoled.

70   For I am Beatrice who send you on;
I come from where I most long to return;
Love prompted me, that Love which makes me speak.
When once again I stand before my Lord,
then I shall often let Him hear your praises.'

75   Now Beatrice was silent. I began:
'O Lady of virtue, the sole reason why
the human race surpasses all that lies
beneath the heaven with the smallest spheres,
so welcome is your wish, that even if

80   it were already done, it would seem tardy;
all you need do is let me know your will.
But tell me why you have not been more prudent—
descending to this center, moving from
that spacious place where you long to return?'

85   'Because you want to fathom things so deeply,
I now shall tell you promptly,' she replied,
'why I am not afraid to enter here.
One ought to be afraid of nothing other
than things possessed of power to do us harm,

90   but things innocuous need not be feared.
God, in His graciousness, has made me so
that this, your misery, cannot touch me;
I can withstand the fires flaming here.[6]
In Heaven there's a gentle lady—one

95   who weeps for the distress toward which I send you,
so that stern judgment up above is shattered.
And it was she who called upon Lucia,[7]

6. Neither the fires of hell nor the damned have the power physically to harm any of the blessed, nor do their sufferings deserve any compassion—a cornerstone of Catholic doctrine that Dante sorely tests in the *Inferno*.

7. St. Lucy of Syracuse, a late-3rd-century virgin martyr who is patron saint of sight, and a symbol of illuminating grace.

requesting of her: "Now your faithful one
has need of you, and I commend him to you."

100   Lucia, enemy of every cruelty,
arose and made her way to where I was,
sitting beside the venerable Rachel.[8]

She said: "You, Beatrice, true praise of God,
why have you not helped him who loves you so
105   that—for your sake—he's left the vulgar crowd?

Do you not hear the anguish in his cry?
Do you not see the death he wars against
upon that river ruthless as the sea?"

No one within this world has ever been
110   so quick to seek his good or flee his harm
as I—when she had finished speaking thus—

to come below, down from my blessed station;
I trusted in your honest utterance,
which honors you and those who've listened to you.'

115   When she had finished with her words to me,
she turned aside her gleaming, tearful eyes,
which only made me hurry all the more.

And, just as she had wished, I came to you:
I snatched you from the path of the fierce beast
120   that barred the shortest way up the fair mountain.

What is it then? Why, why do you resist?
Why does your heart host so much cowardice?
Where are your daring and your openness

as long as there are three such blessed women
125   concerned for you within the court of Heaven
and my words promise you so great a good?"

As little flowers, which the chill of night
has bent and huddled, when the white sun strikes,
grow straight and open fully on their stems,

130   so did I, too, with my exhausted force;
and such warm daring rushed into my heart
that I—as one who has been freed—began:

"O she, compassionate, who has helped me!
And you who, courteous, obeyed so quickly
135   the true words that she had addressed to you!

You, with your words, have so disposed my heart
to longing for this journey—I return
to what I was at first prepared to do.

Now go; a single will fills both of us:
140   you are my guide, my governor, my master."
These were my words to him; when he advanced,

I entered on the steep and savage path.

8. Beatrice has her seat in heaven next to Rachel, younger sister of Leah in Genesis, and beloved of Jacob.

Canto 3

The inscription above the Gate of Hell. The Ante-Inferno, where the shades of those who lived without praise and without blame now intermingle with the neutral angels. He who made the great refusal. The River Acheron. Charon. Dante's loss of his senses as the earth trembles.

THROUGH ME THE WAY INTO THE SUFFERING CITY,
THROUGH ME THE WAY TO THE ETERNAL PAIN,
THROUGH ME THE WAY THAT RUNS AMONG THE LOST.

JUSTICE URGED ON MY HIGH ARTIFICER;
5 MY MAKER WAS DIVINE AUTHORITY,
THE HIGHEST WISDOM, AND THE PRIMAL LOVE.

BEFORE ME NOTHING BUT ETERNAL THINGS
WERE MADE, AND I ENDURE ETERNALLY.
ABANDON EVERY HOPE, WHO ENTER HERE.[1]

10 These words—their aspect was obscure—I read
inscribed above a gateway, and I said:
"Master, their meaning is difficult for me."

And he to me, as one who comprehends:
"Here one must leave behind all hesitation;
15 here every cowardice must meet its death.

For we have reached the place of which I spoke,
where you will see the miserable people,
those who have lost the good of the intellect."[2]

And when, with gladness in his face, he placed
20 his hand upon my own, to comfort me,
he drew me in among the hidden things.

Here sighs and lamentations and loud cries
were echoing across the starless air,
so that, as soon as I set out, I wept.

25 Strange utterances, horrible pronouncements,
accents of anger, words of suffering,
and voices shrill and faint, and beating hands—

all went to make a tumult that will whirl
forever through that turbid, timeless air,
30 like sand that eddies when a whirlwind swirls.

And I—my head oppressed by horror—said:
"Master, what is it that I hear? Who are
those people so defeated by their pain?"

And he to me: "This miserable way
35 is taken by the sorry souls of those
who lived without disgrace and without praise.

They now commingle with the coward angels,

---

1. The famous inscription on the Gate of Hell announces several key laws of the realm: it is the negative counterpart to the city of God, but also created by divine order, subject to the Lord's authority, and ruled by justice and love. Evil is not independent from, but somehow part of the divine scheme since it was first created by Satan's rebellion at the beginning of time.

2. The rules may be clear, but their meaning is not. Virgil gives a first definition of the state of damnation: those ruled by their appetites rather than their reason. Truth, following Aristotle, is the good of the intellect; for Dante the highest good is God.

the company of those who were not rebels
nor faithful to their God, but stood apart.

40   The heavens, that their beauty not be lessened,
have cast them out, nor will deep Hell receive them—
even the wicked cannot glory in them."[3]

And I: "What is it, master, that oppresses
these souls, compelling them to wail so loud?"

45   He answered: "I shall tell you in few words.

Those who are here can place no hope in death,
and their blind life is so abject that they
are envious of every other fate.

The world will let no fame of theirs endure;

50   both justice and compassion must disdain them;
let us not talk of them, but look and pass."[4]

And I, looking more closely, saw a banner
that, as it wheeled about, raced on—so quick
that any respite seemed unsuited to it.

55   Behind that banner trailed so long a file
of people—I should never have believed
that death could have unmade so many souls.

After I had identified a few,
I saw and recognized the shade of him

60   who made, through cowardice, the great refusal.[5]

At once I understood with certainty:
this company contained the cowardly,
hateful to God and to His enemies.

These wretched ones, who never were alive,

65   went naked and were stung again, again
by horseflies and by wasps that circled them.

The insects streaked their faces with their blood,
which, mingled with their tears, fell at their feet,
where it was gathered up by sickening worms.

70   And then, looking beyond them, I could see
a crowd along the bank of a great river;
at which I said: "Allow me now to know

who are these people—master—and what law
has made them seem so eager for the crossing,

75   as I can see despite the feeble light."

And he to me: "When we have stopped along
the melancholy shore of Acheron,°   *a river of Hell*
then all these matters will be plain to you."

At that, with eyes ashamed, downcast, and fearing

---

3. Dante invented a category of souls who belong neither in Heaven nor in Hell properly speaking: the "lukewarm," grouped with the neutral angels, those who neither rebelled with Satan nor sided with God.
4. Here the poetically apt punishment consists of the complete lack of fame for those who made no choices in life, and of goading insects and speeding banners, since they would not be goaded and chose no banners.
5. The one soul singled out among the lukewarm, fittingly, is not named. Early commentators mostly agreed he was Pope Celestine V, who abdicated ("the great refusal") only five months after his election as pope in 1294, allowing the election of Boniface VIII, pope from 1294 to 1303, one of the arch-villains of the *Commedia.*

80   that what I said had given him offense,
     I did not speak until we reached the river.

        And here, advancing toward us, in a boat,
     an aged man—his hair was white with years[6]—
     was shouting: "Woe to you, corrupted souls!

85   Forget your hope of ever seeing Heaven:
     I come to lead you to the other shore,
     to the eternal dark, to fire and frost.

        And you approaching there, you living soul,
     keep well away from these—they are the dead."

90   But when he saw I made no move to go,

        he said: "Another way and other harbors—
     not here—will bring you passage to your shore:
     a lighter craft will have to carry you."

        My guide then: "Charon, don't torment yourself:

95   our passage has been willed above, where One[7]
     can do what He has willed; and ask no more."

        Now silence fell upon the wooly cheeks
     of Charon, pilot of the livid marsh,
     whose eyes were ringed about with wheels of flame.

100   But all those spirits, naked and exhausted,
     had lost their color, and they gnashed their teeth
     as soon as they heard Charon's cruel words;

        they execrated God and their own parents
     and humankind, and then the place and time

105 of their conception's seed and of their birth.

        Then they forgathered, huddled in one throng,
     weeping aloud along that wretched shore
     which waits for all who have no fear of God.

        The demon Charon, with his eyes like embers,

110 by signaling to them, has all embark;
     his oar strikes anyone who stretches out.

        As, in the autumn, leaves detach themselves,
     first one and then the other, till the bough
     sees all its fallen garments on the ground,[8]

115   similarly, the evil seed of Adam
     descended from the shoreline one by one,
     when signaled, as a falcon—called—will come.[9]

        So do they move across the darkened waters;
     even before they reach the farther shore,

120 new ranks already gather on this bank.

        "My son," the gracious master said to me,
     "those who have died beneath the wrath of God,
     all these assemble here from every country;

---

6. The first figure out of pagan mythology encountered in
Hell, the ferryman Charon was the son of Erebus and
Night.
7. God, Christ, and the Holy Spirit are never named in
Hell directly.

8. The simile of autumn leaves to describe dead souls reworks that of *Aeneid* 6.309–12.
9. A simile from medieval falconry: the moment when the
falcon is lured down by the hunter.

125
and they are eager for the river crossing
because celestial justice spurs them on,
so that their fear is turned into desire.

130
No good soul ever takes its passage here;
therefore, if Charon has complained of you,
by now you can be sure what his words mean."

And after this was said, the darkened plain
quaked so tremendously—the memory
of terror then, bathes me in sweat again.

135
A whirlwind burst out of the tear-drenched earth,
a wind that crackled with a bloodred light,
a light that overcame all of my senses;
and like a man whom sleep has seized, I fell.

Canto 4

*Dante's awakening to the First Circle, or Limbo, inhabited by those who were worthy
but lived before Christianity and/or without baptism. The welcoming of Virgil and
Dante by Homer, Horace, Ovid, Lucan. The catalogue of other great-hearted spirits
in the noble castle of Limbo.*

5
The heavy sleep within my head was smashed
by an enormous thunderclap, so that
I started up as one whom force awakens;
I stood erect and turned my rested eyes
from side to side, and I stared steadily
to learn what place it was surrounding me.

10
In truth I found myself upon the brink
of an abyss, the melancholy valley
containing thundering, unending wailings.
That valley, dark and deep and filled with mist,
is such that, though I gazed into its pit,
I was unable to discern a thing.[1]

15
"Let us descend into the blind world now,"[2]
the poet, who was deathly pale, began;
"I shall go first and you will follow me."
But I, who'd seen the change in his complexion,
said: "How shall I go on if you are frightened,
you who have always helped dispel my doubts?"

20
And he to me: "The anguish of the people
whose place is here below, has touched my face
with the compassion you mistake for fear.
Let us go on, the way that waits is long."
So he set out, and so he had me enter

---

1. The first glimpse of the geography of Hell proper. The pit was a standard component of medieval hells; the cone-like valley the pilgrim will encounter was not.

2. Blind because bereft of sun and stars, and blind because bereft of spiritual clarity.

on that first circle girdling the abyss.[3]

25 Here, for as much as hearing could discover,
there was no outcry louder than the sighs
that caused the everlasting air to tremble.

The sighs arose from sorrow without torments,
out of the crowds—the many multitudes—
30 of infants and of women and of men.

The kindly master said: "Do you not ask
who are these spirits whom you see before you?
I'd have you know, before you go ahead,

they did not sin; and yet, though they have merits,
35 that's not enough, because they lacked baptism,
the portal of the faith that you embrace.

And if they lived before Christianity,
they did not worship God in fitting ways;
and of such spirits I myself am one.

40 For these defects, and for no other evil,
we now are lost and punished just with this:
we have no hope and yet we live in longing."

Great sorrow seized my heart on hearing him,
for I had seen some estimable men
45 among the souls suspended in that limbo.

"Tell me, my master, tell me, lord," I then
began because I wanted to be certain
of that belief which vanquishes all errors,

"did any ever go—by his own merit
50 or others'—from this place toward blessedness?"
And he, who understood my covert speech,[4]

replied: "I was new-entered on this state
when I beheld a Great Lord enter here;
the crown he wore, a sign of victory.[5]

55 He carried off the shade of our first father,°   *Adam*
of his son Abel, and the shade of Noah,
of Moses, the obedient legislator,

of father Abraham, David the king,
of Israel,° his father, and his sons,   *Jacob*
60 and Rachel, she for whom he worked so long,

and many others—and He made them blessed;
and I should have you know that, before them,
there were no human souls that had been saved."

We did not stay our steps although he spoke;

---

3. The first circle of Hell is Limbo, according to doctrine
the place of children who died before baptism and of
righteous Old Testament figures who lived before the
coming of Christ. Dante took the liberty of adding a new
category: the virtuous pagans, whose number includes
Virgil.
4. The pilgrim wants to ask whether Virgil, his guide, can
be saved. He doesn't receive the answer he desires.

5. The apocryphal Gospel of Nicodemus tells that between his crucifixion on Good Friday and his resurrection
on Easter Sunday, Christ descended into Limbo and took
its Old Testament figures with him up to Heaven. The
Harrowing of Hell was proclaimed as dogma during the
13th century. Virgil died in 19 B.C.E.; hence he was newly
arrived when Christ descended in 33 C.E.

65   we still continued onward through the wood—
      the wood, I say, where many spirits thronged.
          Our path had not gone far beyond the point
      where I had slept, when I beheld a fire
      win out against a hemisphere of shadows.
70   We still were at a little distance from it,
      but not so far I could not see in part
      that honorable men possessed that place.
          "O you who honor art and science both,
      who are these souls whose dignity has kept
75   their way of being, separate from the rest?"
          And he to me: "The honor of their name,
      which echoes up above within your life,
      gains Heaven's grace, and that advances them."
          Meanwhile there was a voice that I could hear:
80   "Pay honor to the estimable poet;
      his shadow, which had left us, now returns."
          After that voice was done, when there was silence,
      I saw four giant shades approaching us;
      in aspect, they were neither sad nor joyous.
85   My kindly master then began by saying:
      "Look well at him who holds that sword in hand,
      who moves before the other three as lord.
          That shade is Homer, the consummate poet;
      the other one is Horace, satirist;
90   the third is Ovid, and the last is Lucan.⁶
          Because each of these spirits shares with me
      the name called out before by the lone voice,
      they welcome me—and, doing that, do well."
          And so I saw that splendid school assembled,
95   led by the lord of song incomparable,°   *Homer*
      who like an eagle soars above the rest.
          Soon after they had talked a while together,
      they turned to me, saluting cordially;
      and having witnessed this, my master smiled;
100   and even greater honor then was mine,
      for they invited me to join their ranks—
      I was the sixth among such intellects.
          So did we move along and toward the light,
      talking of things about which silence here
105   is just as seemly as our speech was there.
          We reached the base of an exalted castle,
      encircled seven times by towering walls,

---

6. Dante produces a pantheon of classical poets. Homer was known only by reputation in Dante's time. Virgil's friend and contemporary, Horace (65–8 B.C.E.), is remembered here for his *Satires* and *Epistles.* Ovid (43 B.C.E.–17 C.E.) and Lucan (39–65 C.E.) are the two classical poets Dante cites most frequently after Virgil, from Ovid primarily his epic compilation of myth, the *Metamorphoses,* and from Lucan his violent epic on the civil war between Caesar and Pompey, *De bello civili,* or *Pharsalia.*

defended all around by a fair stream.[7]

We forded this as if upon hard ground;

110 I entered seven portals with these sages;

we reached a meadow of green flowering plants.

The people here had eyes both grave and slow;

their features carried great authority;

they spoke infrequently, with gentle voices.

115 We drew aside to one part of the meadow,

an open place both high and filled with light,

and we could see all those who were assembled.[8]

Facing me there, on the enameled green,

great-hearted souls were shown to me and I

120 still glory in my having witnessed them.

I saw Electra with her many comrades,

among whom I knew Hector and Aeneas,

and Caesar, in his armor, falcon-eyed.[9]

I saw Camilla and Penthesilea

125 and, on the other side, saw King Latinus,

who sat beside Lavinia, his daughter.[1]

I saw that Brutus who drove Tarquin out,

Lucretia, Julia, Marcia, and Cornelia,

and, solitary, set apart, Saladin.[2]

130 When I had raised my eyes a little higher,

I saw the master of the men who know,

seated in philosophic family.[3]

There all look up to him, all do him honor:

there I beheld both Socrates and Plato,

135 closest to him, in front of all the rest;

Democritus, who ascribes the world to chance,

Diogenes, Empedocles, and Zeno,

and Thales, Anaxagoras, Heraclitus;

I saw the good collector of medicinals,

140 I mean Dioscorides; and I saw Orpheus,

and Tully, Linus, moral Seneca;[4]

---

7. The castle's form is allegorically related to the seven liberal arts and the tradition of the House of Fame, suitable for a group distinguished by their achievements in the arts, in heroism, in proper living but not in the faith required by Christian doctrine.

8. The description of the meadow enclosed by the castle walls is reminiscent of the Elysian Fields of Virgil's underworld, as well as of the *locus amoenus,* or "pleasing place" of courtly romances such as *The Romance of the Rose.* The list of "great-hearted souls" he meets blends mythical and historical, classical and medieval personages.

9. The origins and apogee of Rome: Electra was mother of Dardanus, founder of Troy. Hector was the leader of the Trojan forces, the survivors of which Aeneas led to Italy. Caesar founded the imperial line of Rome.

1. Camilla and Penthesilea were female warriors. Latinus was king of Latium; the betrothal of his daughter Lavinia to Aeneas caused Turnus to begin the civil war.

2. Lucius Junius Brutus drove out Tarquin, the last of the legendary Roman kings, in 510 B.C.E. to become one of the first two consuls of the Roman republic. Four female exemplars of Roman virtue are then listed, followed by the Sultan of Egypt from 1171 to 1193, Saladin, who crushingly defeated the Crusaders, but whose magnanimity and generosity were a medieval commonplace.

3. The list of philosophers begins with Aristotle, so influential in Dante's time he need not be named, followed by Socrates, Plato, and seven other celebrated ancient Greek philosophers.

4. Dioscorides was a Greek physician of the 1st century C.E.; Linus and Orpheus were mythical Greek poets; Tully is the Roman orator and philosopher Marcus Tullius Cicero (106–43 B.C.E.), Seneca the moral philosopher and writer of tragedies who committed suicide at the command of Nero in 65 C.E.

and Euclid the geometer, and Ptolemy,
Hippocrates and Galen, Avicenna,
Averroës, of the great Commentary.[5]

145   I cannot here describe them all in full;
my ample theme impels me onward so:
what's told is often less than the event.
The company of six divides in two;
my knowing guide leads me another way,
150   beyond the quiet, into trembling air.
And I have reached a part where no thing gleams.

Canto 5

The Second Circle, where the Lustful are forever buffeted by violent storm. Minos.
The catalogue of carnal sinners. Francesca da Rimini and her brother-in-law, Paolo
Malatesta. Francesca's tale of their love and death, at which Dante faints.

So I descended from the first enclosure
down to the second circle, that which girdles
less space but grief more great,[1] that goads to weeping.
There dreadful Minos stands, gnashing his teeth:
5   examining the sins of those who enter,
he judges and assigns as his tail twines.[2]
I mean that when the spirit born to evil
appears before him, it confesses all;
and he, the connoisseur of sin, can tell
10   the depth in Hell appropriate to it;
as many times as Minos wraps his tail
around himself, that marks the sinner's level.
Always there is a crowd that stands before him:
each soul in turn advances toward that judgment;
15   they speak and hear, then they are cast below.
Arresting his extraordinary task,
Minos, as soon as he had seen me, said:
"O you who reach this house of suffering,
be careful how you enter, whom you trust;
20   the gate is wide, but do not be deceived!"
To which my guide replied: "But why protest?
Do not attempt to block his fated path:
our passage has been willed above, where One
can do what He has willed; and ask no more."

5. The mathematician Euclid lived c. 300 B.C.E.; the geocentric theory of his fellow Alexandrian, the astronomer and geographer Ptolemy, who was active in the 2nd century C.E., was the basis of medieval astronomy. Hippocrates and Galen were Greek physicians. Avicenna (980–1037) and Averroës (1126–1198) were Muslim philosophers, both authors of influential commentaries on Aristotle.
1. Although separated from the rest of Hell by the

guardian and judge Minos, Limbo is called the first circle. The second circle, where the Lustful are punished, "girdles less space" because the cone shape of Hell narrows as it descends.
2. Minos was legendary king of Crete, and with his brother Rhadamanthus judge in Virgil's underworld. The tail, however, is a Dantesque touch that makes Minos more monster and less king, imitating the spiraling structure of Hell.

25   Now notes of desperation have begun
        to overtake my hearing; now I come
        where mighty lamentation beats against me.
            I reached a place where every light is muted,
        which bellows like the sea beneath a tempest,
30   when it is battered by opposing winds.
            The hellish hurricane, which never rests,
        drives on the spirits with its violence:
        wheeling and pounding, it harasses them.
            When they come up against the ruined slope,
35   then there are cries and wailing and lament,
        and there they curse the force of the divine.
            I learned that those who undergo this torment
        are damned because they sinned within the flesh,
        subjecting reason to the rule of lust.
40   And as, in the cold season, starlings' wings
        bear them along in broad and crowded ranks,
        so does that blast bear on the guilty spirits:
            now here, now there, now down, now up, it drives them.
        There is no hope that ever comforts them—
45   no hope for rest and none for lesser pain.
            And just as cranes in flight will chant their lays,
        arraying their long file across the air,
        so did the shades I saw approaching, borne
            by that assailing wind, lament and moan;
50   so that I asked him: "Master, who are those
        who suffer punishment in this dark air?"
            "The first of those about whose history
        you want to know," my master then told me,
        "once ruled as empress over many nations.
55   Her vice of lust became so customary
        that she made license licit in her laws
        to free her from the scandal she had caused.
            She is Semíramis, of whom we read
        that she was Ninus' wife and his successor:
60   she held the land the Sultan now commands.[3]
            That other spirit killed herself for love,
        and she betrayed the ashes of Sychaeus;[4]
        the wanton Cleopatra follows next.[5]
            See Helen, for whose sake so many years
65   of evil had to pass; see great Achilles,

---

3. In Dante's time, Egypt was under the rule of the Sultan.
There is some confusion here because Egypt was fairly
distant from the Mesopotamian kingdom of Assyria, supposedly founded by Ninus and the lustful Semiramis.
4. Curiously, Virgil does not name Dido, whose story he
had related in one of the most celebrated parts of the
Aeneid. Sychaeus was Dido's husband, murdered by her
brother Pygmalion, king of Tyre. Dido fled to North

Africa, where she founded the city of Carthage, and,
according to *Aeneid* 4, was seduced and abandoned by
Aeneas, after which she killed herself in despair.
5. Cleopatra was the queen of Egypt of legendary beauty
who was the lover first of Julius Caesar and then of Marc
Antony, with whom she was defeated at the battle of
Actium in 29 B.C.E. by Augustus. Rather than be taken as
a prisoner to Rome, she killed herself with an asp.

who finally met love—in his last battle.[6]

See Paris, Tristan . . ."—and he pointed out
and named to me more than a thousand shades
departed from our life because of love.

70   No sooner had I heard my teacher name
the ancient ladies and the knights, than pity
seized me, and I was like a man astray.

My first words: "Poet, I should willingly
speak with those two who go together there
75   and seem so lightly carried by the wind."[7]

And he to me: "You'll see when they draw closer
to us, and then you may appeal to them
by that love which impels them. They will come."

No sooner had the wind bent them toward us
80   than I urged on my voice: "O battered souls,
if One does not forbid it, speak with us."

Even as doves when summoned by desire,
borne forward by their will, move through the air
with wings uplifted, still, to their sweet nest,

85   those spirits left the ranks where Dido suffers,
approaching us through the malignant air;
so powerful had been my loving cry.

"O living being, gracious and benign,
who through the darkened air have come to visit
90   our souls that stained the world with blood, if He

who rules the universe were friend to us,
then we should pray to Him to give you peace,
for you have pitied our atrocious state.

Whatever pleases you to hear and speak
95   will please us, too, to hear and speak with you,
now while the wind is silent, in this place.

The land where I was born lies on that shore
to which the Po together with the waters
that follow it descends to final rest.[8]

100   Love, that can quickly seize the gentle heart,
took hold of him because of the fair body
taken from me—how that was done still wounds me.

---

6. The list switches from women to men with two legendary figures of the Trojan War: Helen, wife of Menelaus, king of Sparta, whose abduction by Paris was the origin of the war, and Achilles, the greatest of the Greek heroes. Homer had him killed under the walls of Troy by Paris; according to medieval legend, Paris lured him to his death at the temple of Apollo by promises that he would be given Priam's daughter Polyxena if he changed sides. Tristan was a celebrated figure of medieval romance, lover of Iseult, who was wife of King Mark of Cornwall, his uncle.

7. The first conversation recorded with a condemned soul is also the first appearance of two of Dante's contemporaries,

the lovers Francesca da Rimini and Paolo Malatesta. Daughter of Guido da Polenta, lord of Ravenna, and aunt of Guido Novello, Dante's host at Ravenna at the end of his life, Francesca was married for political reasons to Paolo's older brother Gianciotto some time after 1275. Around 1285, at which time Francesca had a nine-year old daughter and Paolo was around 40 years old, Gianciotto apparently found the lovers out and killed them both. The language of the dialogue is suffused with the language of the *dolce stil novo*, the "sweet new style" of love lyric that first brought fame to Dante.

8. Ravenna is on the Adriatic coast of northern Italy, between the Po River and the Rubicon.

Love, that releases no beloved from loving,
took hold of me so strongly through his beauty
105 that, as you see, it has not left me yet.
    Love led the two of us unto one death.
Caïna waits for him who took our life."[9]
These words were borne across from them to us.
    When I had listened to those injured souls,
110 I bent my head and held it low until
the poet asked of me: "What are you thinking?"
    When I replied, my words began: "Alas,
how many gentle thoughts, how deep a longing,
had led them to the agonizing pass!"
115   Then I addressed my speech again to them,
and I began: "Francesca, your afflictions
move me to tears of sorrow and of pity.
    But tell me, in the time of gentle sighs,
with what and in what way did Love allow you
120 to recognize your still uncertain longings?"
    And she to me: "There is no greater sorrow
than thinking back upon a happy time
in misery—and this your teacher knows.
    Yet if you long so much to understand
125 the first root of our love, then I shall tell
my tale to you as one who weeps and speaks.
    One day, to pass the time away, we read
of Lancelot—how love had overcome him.
We were alone, and we suspected nothing.
130   And time and time again that reading led
our eyes to meet, and made our faces pale,
and yet one point alone defeated us.
    When we had read how the desired smile
was kissed by one who was so true a lover,
135 this one, who never shall be parted from me,
    while all his body trembled, kissed my mouth.
A Gallehault indeed, that book and he
who wrote it, too; that day we read no more."[1]
    And while one spirit said these words to me,
140 the other wept, so that—because of pity—
I fainted, as if I had met my death.
And then I fell as a dead body falls.

---

9. Francesca's speech combines echoes of a famous *canzone* by Dante's friend Guido Guinizelli and its definitions of courtly love with harsh concluding phrases on her own fate. Caïna is the first of the four divisions of the ninth circle of Hell, named after Cain, who killed his brother Abel. This place where those who betray their kin are punished "waits for" Francesca's husband because he was still alive in 1300.

1. The story of Lancelot, "flower of the knighthood of the world," and the love for Queen Guinevere, wife of his lord, King Arthur, that caused him to fail in his quest for the Holy Grail, was one of the most popular medieval romances. In the Old French romance, *Lancelot du lac,* it was Lancelot's friend Gallehault who arranged an interview between the pair and induced them to kiss. The book, as well as its author, are accused of being the "go-between" that led to the death and damnation of Francesca and her silent lover.

Canto 6

Dante's awakening to the Third Circle, where the Gluttonous, supine, are flailed by cold and filthy rain and tormented by Cerberus. Ciacco and his prophecy concerning Florence. The state of the damned after the Resurrection.

Upon my mind's reviving—it had closed
on hearing the lament of those two kindred,
since sorrow had confounded me completely—

I see new sufferings, new sufferers
5   surrounding me on every side, wherever
I move or turn about or set my eyes.

I am in the third circle, filled with cold,
unending, heavy, and accursèd rain;
its measure and its kind are never changed.

10   Gross hailstones, water gray with filth, and snow
come streaking down across the shadowed air;
the earth, as it receives that shower, stinks.

Over the souls of those submerged beneath
that mess, is an outlandish, vicious beast,
15   his three throats barking, doglike: Cerberus.[1]

His eyes are bloodred; greasy, black, his beard;
his belly bulges, and his hands are claws;
his talons tear and flay and rend the shades.

That downpour makes the sinners howl like dogs;
20   they use one of their sides to screen the other—
those miserable wretches turn and turn.

When Cerberus, the great worm, noticed us,
he opened wide his mouths, showed us his fangs;
there was no part of him that did not twitch.

25   My guide opened his hands to their full span,
plucked up some earth, and with his fists filled full
he hurled it straight into those famished jaws.

Just as a dog that barks with greedy hunger
will then fall quiet when he gnaws his food,
30   intent and straining hard to cram it in,

so were the filthy faces of the demon
Cerberus transformed—after he'd stunned
the spirits so, they wished that they were deaf.

We walked across the shades on whom there thuds
35   that heavy rain, and set our soles upon
their empty images that seem like persons.

And all those spirits lay upon the ground,
except for one who sat erect as soon
as he caught sight of us in front of him.

---

1. The mythical three-headed guardian of the underworld, described in *Aeneid* 6.417–23. Dante makes him paradoxically more human and more bestial. The guardian(s) of each circle generally relate to that circle's sin; here, the monster's gluttony is stressed by having his gullets silenced by lumps of earth rather than the honey cakes of the *Aeneid*.

40   "O you who are conducted through this Hell,"
he said to me, "recall me, if you can;
for you, before I was unmade, were made."
      And I to him: "It is perhaps your anguish
that snatches you out of my memory,
45   so that it seems that I have never seen you.
      But tell me who you are, you who are set
in such a dismal place, such punishment—
if other pains are more, none's more disgusting."
      And he to me: "Your city—one so full
50   of envy that its sack has always spilled—
that city held me in the sunlit life.[2]
      The name you citizens gave me was Ciacco;
and for the damning sin of gluttony,
as you can see, I languish in the rain.
55   And I, a wretched soul, am not alone,
for all of these have this same penalty
for this same sin." And he said nothing more.
      I answered him: "Ciacco, your suffering
so weights on me that I am forced to weep;
60   but tell me, if you know, what end awaits
      the citizens of that divided city;
is any just man there? Tell me the reason
why it has been assailed by so much schism."[3]
      And he to me: "After long controversy,
65   they'll come to blood; the party of the woods
will chase the other out with much offense.
      But then, within three suns, they too must fall;
at which the other party will prevail,
using the power of one who tacks his sails.°   *Pope Boniface*
70   This party will hold high its head for long
and heap great weights upon its enemies,
however much they weep indignantly.
      Two men are just, but no one listens to them.
Three sparks that set on fire every heart
75   are envy, pride, and avariciousness."
      With this, his words, inciting tears, were done;
and I to him: "I would learn more from you;
I ask you for a gift of further speech:
      Tegghiaio, Farinata, men so worthy,
80   Arrigo, Mosca, Jacopo Rusticucci,
and all the rest whose minds bent toward the good,
      do tell me where they are and let me meet them;
for my great longing drives me on to learn

---

2. Dante's native city of Florence, which figures prominently in the poem, appears for the first time, and in char-
acteristically negative fashion.

3. The first explicit discussion of contemporary political
events. In spring of 1300, trouble was brewing between
the two Guelf factions, the Whites, led by the Cerchi family, and the Blacks, led by the Donatis.

if Heaven sweetens or Hell poisons them."[4]

85   And he: "They are among the blackest souls;
a different sin has dragged them to the bottom;
if you descend so low, there you can see them.

But when you have returned to the sweet world,
I pray, recall me to men's memory:
90   I say no more to you, answer no more."

Then his straight gaze grew twisted and awry;
he looked at me awhile, then bent his head;
he fell as low as all his blind companions.

And my guide said to me: "He'll rise no more
95   until the blast of the angelic trumpet
upon the coming of the hostile Judge:°   *Christ*

each one shall see his sorry tomb again
and once again take on his flesh and form,
and hear what shall resound eternally."

100   So did we pass across that squalid mixture
of shadows and of rain, our steps slowed down,
talking awhile about the life to come.

At which I said: "And after the great sentence—
o master—will these torments grow, or else
105   be less, or will they be just as intense?"

And he to me: "Remember now your science,
which says that when a thing has more perfection,
so much the greater is its pain or pleasure.

Though these accursed sinners never shall
110   attain the true perfection, yet they can
expect to be more perfect then than now."[5]

We took the circling way traced by that road;
we said much more than I can here recount;
we reached the point that marks the downward slope.

115   Here we found Plutus, the great enemy.[6]

Canto 7

The demon Plutus. The Fourth Circle, where the Avaricious and the Prodigal, in opposite directions, roll weights in semicircles. Fortune and her ways. Descent into the Fifth Circle: the Wrathful and the Sullen, the former besmirched by the muddy Styx, the latter immersed in it.

"Pape Satàn, pape Satàn aleppe!"[1]
so Plutus, with his grating voice, began.

---

4. The pilgrim asks about some famous political figures who lived in Florence before the division between Blacks and Whites. All except Arrigo are found deeper in Hell. 5. "Science" is Aristotelian philosophy as interpreted in Scholasticism. Aquinas held that the soul attains natural perfection only when unified with the body. For the dead, this perfection will be achieved only after the Last Judgment, when their souls will be reunited with their bodies. The pains of the damned will be then be increased ("more

perfect") just as will the pleasure of the blessed.
6. Pluto was mythological god of the underworld; Plutus was the Roman god of wealth. Dante appears to make no distinction between the two, making out of them a minor demon, guardian of the Fourth Circle.
1. A hodgepodge of Latin, Greek, and Hebrew appealing to Plutus's superior: "Oh Satan, oh Satan, the most powerful one!"

The gentle sage, aware of everything,
     said reassuringly, "Don't let your fear
5 defeat you; for whatever power he has,
he cannot stop our climbing down this crag."

     Then he turned back to Plutus' swollen face
and said to him: "Be quiet, cursed wolf!2
Let your vindictiveness feed on yourself.

10   His is no random journey to the deep:
it has been willed on high, where Michael
took revenge upon the arrogant rebellion."3

     As sails inflated by the wind collapse,
entangled in a heap, when the mast cracks,
15 so that ferocious beast fell to the ground.

     Thus we made our way down to the fourth ditch,
to take in more of that despondent shore
where all the universe's ill is stored.

     Justice of God! Who has amassed as many
20 strange tortures and travails as I have seen?
Why do we let our guilt consume us so?

     Even as waves that break above Charybdis,4
each shattering the other when they meet,
so must the spirits here dance their round dance.

25   Here, more than elsewhere, I saw multitudes
to every side of me; their howls were loud
while, wheeling weights, they used their chests to push.

     They struck against each other; at that point,
each turned around and, wheeling back those weights,
30 cried out: "Why do you hoard?" "Why do you squander?"5

     So did they move around the sorry circle
from left and right to the opposing point;
again, again they cried their chant of scorn;

     and so, when each of them had changed positions,
35 he circled halfway back to his next joust.
And I, who felt my heart almost pierced through,

     requested: "Master, show me now what shades
are these and tell me if they all were clerics—
those tonsured ones who circle on our left."6

40   And he to me: "All these, to left and right
were so squint-eyed of mind in the first life—
no spending that they did was done with measure.

     Their voices bark this out with clarity
when they have reached the two points of the circle
45 where their opposing guilts divide their ranks.

---

2. Recalling the cupidity of the she-wolf of Canto 1.
3. Alluding to the Archangel Michael's role as leader of the angels in the battle in heaven that resulted in the casting out of Satan and the rebel angels.
4. A famous whirlpool between the island of Sicily and the Italian coast, described in *Aeneid* 3.420–23 (Dante's source) and Book 12 of the *Odyssey* (Volume A).

5. Here one sin is punished by confrontation with its opposite. In Dante's scheme, the excesses of avarice ("hoarding") and prodigality ("squandering") are equally to be avoided.
6. The tonsure is the shaven crown of the head signifying membership in a monastic or clerical order; the avarice of the clergy was proverbial.

These to the left—their heads bereft of hair—
were clergymen, and popes and cardinals,
within whom avarice works its excess."
    And I to him: "Master, among this kind
50   I certainly might hope to recognize
some who have been bespattered by these crimes."
    And he to me: "That thought of yours is empty:
the undiscerning life that made them filthy
now renders them unrecognizable.
55   For all eternity they'll come to blows:
these here will rise up from their sepulchers
with fists clenched tight; and these, with hair cropped close.
    Ill giving and ill keeping have robbed both
of the fair world° and set them to this fracas—   *Heaven*
60   what that is like, my words need not embellish.
    Now you can see, my son, how brief's the sport
of all those goods that are in Fortune's care,
for which the tribe of men contend and brawl;
    for all the gold that is or ever was
65   beneath the moon could never offer rest
to even one of these exhausted spirits."
    "Master," I asked of him, "now tell me too:
this Fortune whom you've touched upon just now—
what's she, who clutches so all the world's goods?"[7]
70   And he to me: "O unenlightened creatures,
how deep—the ignorance that hampers you!
I want you to digest my word on this.
    Who made the heavens and who gave them guides
was He whose wisdom transcends everything;
75   that every part may shine unto the other,
    He had the light apportioned equally;
similarly, for wordly splendors, He
ordained a general minister and guide
    to shift, from time to time, those empty goods
80   from nation unto nation, clan to clan,
in ways that human reason can't prevent;
    just so, one people rules, one languishes,
obeying the decision she has given,
which, like a serpent in the grass, is hidden.
85   Your knowledge cannot stand against her force;
for she foresees and judges and maintains
her kingdom as the other gods do theirs.
    The changes that she brings are without respite:
it is necessity that makes her swift;
90   and for this reason, men change state so often.

7. Fortune was often pictured blindfolded, turning a wheel at random to distribute her goods. In Virgil's explanation, aimed at reconciling the principles of chance and inequality with those of divine justice and providence, Fortune is one of the Intelligences in the heavenly sphere, in charge of administering the riches of the world.

She is the one so frequently maligned
even by those who should give praise to her—
they blame her wrongfully with words of scorn.
 But she is blessed and does not hear these things;
95 for with the other primal beings, happy,
she turns her sphere and glories in her bliss.[8]
 But now let us descend to greater sorrow,
for every star that rose when I first moved
is setting now;[9] we cannot stay too long."
100 We crossed the circle to the other shore;
we reached a foaming watercourse that spills
into a trench formed by its overflow.
 That stream was even darker than deep purple;
and we, together with those shadowed waves,
105 moved downward and along a strange pathway.
 When it has reached the foot of those malign
gray slopes, that melancholy stream descends,
forming a swamp that bears the name of Styx.
 And I, who was intent on watching it,
110 could make out muddied people in that slime,
all naked and their faces furious.
 These struck each other not with hands alone,
but with their heads and chests and with their feet,
and tore each other piecemeal with their teeth.
115 The kindly master told me: "Son, now see
the souls of those whom anger has defeated;
and I should also have you know for certain
 that underneath the water there are souls
who sigh and make this plain of water bubble,
120 as your eye, looking anywhere, can tell.
 Wedged in the slime, they say: 'We had been sullen
in the sweet air that's gladdened by the sun;
we bore the mist of sluggishness in us:
 now we are bitter in the blackened mud.'
125 This hymn they have to gurgle in their gullets,
because they cannot speak it in full words."
 And so, between the dry shore and the swamp,
we circled much of that disgusting pond,
our eyes upon the swallowers of slime.
130 We came at last upon a tower's base.

Canto 8

Still the Fifth Circle: the Wrathful and the Sullen. The tall tower. Phlegyas and the crossing of the Styx. Filippo Argenti and Dante's fury. Approach to Dis, the lower

8. The Intelligences preside over the revolving heavens and turn the heaven assigned to them, as Fortune turns her sphere. They were commonly referred to as gods and goddesses.

9. The starry heavens make a complete circuit every 24 hours. The stars that were rising when Virgil first set out from Limbo around noon on Good Friday are now setting 12 hours later, after midnight of Holy Saturday.

part of Hell: its moat, its walls, its gate. The demons, fallen angels, and their obstruc-
tion of the poets' entry into Dis.

I say, continuing, that long before
we two had reached the foot of that tall tower,
our eyes had risen upward, toward its summit,

because of two small flames that flickered there,
5 while still another flame returned their signal,
so far off it was scarcely visible.

And I turned toward the sea of all good sense;
I said: "What does this mean? And what reply
comes from that other fire? Who kindled it?"

10 And he to me: "Above the filthy waters
you can already see what waits for us,
if it's not hid by vapors from the marsh."

Bowstring has not thrust from itself an arrow
that ever rushed as swiftly through the air
15 as did the little bark that at that moment
I saw as it skimmed toward us on the water,
a solitary boatman at its helm.
I heard him howl: "Now you are caught, foul soul!"

"O Phlegyas, Phlegyas, such a shout is useless
20 this time," my master said; "we're yours no longer
than it will take to cross the muddy sluice."[1]

And just as one who hears some great deception
was done to him, and then resents it, so
was Phlegyas when he had to store his anger.

25 My guide preceded me into the boat.
Once he was in, he had me follow him;
there seemed to be no weight until I boarded.[2]

No sooner were my guide and I embarked
than off that ancient prow went, cutting water
30 more deeply than it does when bearing others.

And while we steered across the stagnant channel,
before me stood a sinner thick with mud,
saying: "Who are you, come before your time?"

And I to him: "I've come, but I don't stay;
35 but who are you, who have become so ugly?"
He answered: "You can see—I'm one who weeps."

And I to him: "In weeping and in grieving,
accursèd spirit, may you long remain;
though you're disguised by filth, I know your name."[3]

---

1. In ancient myth, Phlegyas was son of Chryse and the war-god Mars, king of the Lapithae, and father of Ixion and Coronis. When Coronis was violated by Apollo, Phlegyas in fury set fire to the god's temple at Delphi. For this sacrilege, according to Virgil in *Aeneid* 6.821–23, he was punished eternally in Tartarus. Dante makes him an infernal boatman in the circle suited to his actions.
2. Reminiscent of Aeneas's crossing of the Styx in *Aeneid*

6.544–46, as Dante too has a real body.
3. Filippo Argenti (identified in line 61 of the canto) was so called because he had his horse shod in silver (*argento*). He was a member of the Adimari clan of Florence, Black Guelfs, and his brother obtained Dante's property from the Commune of Florence when the poet was exiled.

40   Then he stretched both his hands out toward the boat,
     at which my master quickly shoved him back,
     saying: "Be off there with the other dogs!"
         That done, he threw his arms around my neck
     and kissed my face and said: "Indignant soul,
45   blessèd is she who bore you in her womb!
         When in the world, he was presumptuous;
     there is no good to gild his memory,
     and so his shade down here is hot with fury.
         How many up above now count themselves
50   great kings, who'll wallow here like pigs in slime,
     leaving behind foul memories of their crimes!"
         And I: "O master, I am very eager
     to see that spirit soused within this broth
     before we've made our way across the lake."
55   And he to me: "Before the other shore
     comes into view, you shall be satisfied;
     to gratify so fine a wish is right."
         Soon after I had heard these words, I saw
     the muddy sinners so dismember him
60   that even now I praise and thank God for it.
         They all were shouting: "At Filippo Argenti!"
     At this, the Florentine, gone wild with spleen,°   *ill temper*
     began to turn his teeth against himself.
         We left him there; I tell no more of him.
65   But in my ears so loud a wailing pounded
     that I lean forward, all intent to see.
         The kindly master said: "My son, the city
     that bears the name of Dis is drawing near,
     with its grave citizens, its great battalions."[4]
70   I said: "I can already see distinctly—
     master—the mosques that gleam within the valley,
     as crimson as if they had just been drawn
         out of the fire." He told me: "The eternal
     flame burning there appears to make them red,
75   as you can see, within this lower Hell."
         So we arrived inside the deep-cut trenches
     that are the moats of this despondent land:
     the ramparts seemed to me to be of iron.
         But not before we'd ranged in a wide circuit
80   did we approach a place where that shrill pilot
     shouted: "Get out; the entrance way is here."
         About the gates I saw more than a thousand—
     who once had rained from Heaven[5]—and they cried

---

4. Dis was the god of the underworld in the religion of ancient Rome, and by extension the name for the underworld itself. Dante will use the term to refer to Satan; here he means lower Hell, which he depicts as a Muslim city.

5. The rebel angels fallen from Heaven with Lucifer; likened here to Muslim infidels, and for whom the verbal talisman no longer appears to guarantee safe passage. The change in organization and custom introduces the social nature and greater complexity of lower Hell.

in anger: "Who is this who, without death,

85   can journey through the kingdom of the dead?"
And my wise master made a sign that said
he wanted to speak secretly to them.

Then they suppressed—somewhat—their great disdain
and said: "You come alone; let him be gone—
90   for he was reckless, entering this realm.

Let him return alone on his mad road—
or try to, if he can, since you, his guide
across so dark a land, you are to stay."

Consider, reader, my dismay before
95   the sound of those abominable words:
returning here seemed so impossible.

"O my dear guide, who more than seven times
has given back to me my confidence
and snatched me from deep danger that had menaced,

100   do not desert me when I'm so undone;
and if they will not let us pass beyond,
let us retrace our steps together, quickly."

These were my words; the lord who'd led me there
replied: "Forget your fear, no one can hinder
105   our passage; One so great has granted it.

But you wait here for me, and feed and comfort
your tired spirit with good hope, for I
will not abandon you in this low world."

So he goes on his way; that gentle father
110   has left me there to wait and hesitate,
for *yes* and *no* contend within my head.

I could not hear what he was telling them;
but he had not been long with them when each
ran back into the city, scrambling fast.

115   And these, our adversaries, slammed the gates
in my lord's face; and he remained outside,
then, with slow steps, turned back again to me.

His eyes turned to the ground, his brows deprived
of every confidence, he said with sighs:
120   "See who has kept me from the house of sorrow!"[6]

To me he added: "You—though I am vexed—
must not be daunted; I shall win this contest,
whoever tries—within—to block our way.

This insolence of theirs is nothing new;
125   they used it once before and at a gate
less secret—it is still without its bolts[7]—

the place where you made out the fatal text;

---

6. This first of several times when Virgil will be thwarted or deceived in Hell (always by devils) begins a careful development of his strengths and limitations as guide to the afterlife.

7. According to Christian legend, when Christ entered Limbo to harrow Hell, the rebel angels attempted to block his passage. As the Matins of the Office of Holy Saturday have it: "Today our Savior shattered the gates and likewise the bolts of death."

and now, already well within that gate,°   *the gate of Hell*
across the circles—and alone—descends
130   the one who will unlock this realm for us."

Canto 9

The gate of Dis. Dante's fear. The three Furies, invoking Medusa. Virgil's warning to
Dante lest he look at Gorgon, Medusa's head. A heavenly messenger. The flight of the
demons. Entry into Dis, where Virgil and Dante reach the Sixth Circle and its Arch-
Heretics, entombed in red-hot sepulchers.

The color cowardice displayed in me
when I saw that my guide was driven back,
made him more quickly mask his own new pallor.
He stood alert, like an attentive listener,
5   because his eye could hardly journey far
across the black air and the heavy fog.
"We have to win this battle," he began,
"if not . . . But one so great had offered help.
How slow that someone's coming seems to me!"
10   But I saw well enough how he had covered
his first words with the words that followed after—
so different from what he had said before;
nevertheless, his speech made me afraid,
because I drew out from his broken phrase
15   a meaning worse—perhaps—than he'd intended.
"Does anyone from the first circle, one
whose only punishment is crippled hope,
ever descend so deep in this sad hollow?"[1]
That was my question. And he answered so:
20   "It is quite rare for one of us to go
along the way that I have taken now.
But I, in truth, have been here once before:
that savage witch Erichtho, she who called
the shades back to their bodies, summoned me.
25   My flesh had not been long stripped off when she
had me descend through all the rings of Hell,
to draw a spirit back from Judas' circle.[2]
That is the deepest and the darkest place,
the farthest from the heaven that girds all:
30   so rest assured, I know the pathway well.
This swamp that breeds and breathes the giant stench
surrounds the city of the sorrowing,°   *Dis*

---

1. Here the pilgrim probes his guide's knowledge of lower Hell, a realm that, unlike the upper circles, has no direct parallels to the underworld described in the *Aeneid.* 2. Medieval legend had made Virgil a magician, but there is no known source for the strange tale he produces here to establish his expertise. Erichtho was a legendary sorceress who, in an especially gruesome episode in Lucan's *Pharsalia* (6.507–830), is employed to summon the spirit of a dead soldier to learn the outcome of the impending battle of Pharsalia. "Judas' circle" is the lowest part of the last circle of Hell.

which now we cannot enter without anger."

And he said more, but I cannot remember
35   because my eyes had wholly taken me
to that high tower with the glowing summit

where, at one single point, there suddenly
stood three infernal Furies flecked with blood,
who had the limbs of women and their ways

40   but wore, as girdles, snakes of deepest green;
small serpents and horned vipers formed their hairs,
and these were used to bind their bestial temples.[3]

And he, who knew these handmaids well—they served
the Queen of never-ending lamentation[4]—
45   said: "Look at the ferocious Erinyes!

That is Megaera on the left, and she
who weeps upon the right, that is Allecto;
Tisiphone's between them." He was done.

Each Fury tore her breast with taloned nails;
50   each, with her palms, beat on herself and wailed
so loud that I, in fear, drew near the poet.

"Just let Medusa come; then we shall turn
him into stone," they all cried, looking down;
"we should have punished Theseus' assault."[5]

55   "Turn round and keep your eyes shut fast, for should
the Gorgon show herself and you behold her,
never again would you return above,"

my master said; and he himself turned me
around and, not content with just my hands,
60   used his as well to cover up my eyes.

O you possessed of sturdy intellects,
observe the teaching that is hidden here
beneath the veil of verses so obscure.[6]

And now, across the turbid waves, there passed
65   a reboantic° fracas—horrid sound,   *reverberating*
enough to make both of the shorelines quake:

a sound not other than a wind's when, wild
because it must contend with warmer currents,
it strikes against the forest without let,

70   shattering, beating down, bearing off branches,
as it moves proudly, clouds of dust before it,
and puts to flight both animals and shepherds.

He freed my eyes and said: "Now let your optic
nerve turn directly toward that ancient foam,

---

3. The Furies (Greek: Erinyes) were daughters of Night, forces of vengeance feared by gods and men. They were depicted in Virgil's *Aeneid* and elsewhere as monstrous women, with snakes for hair.
4. Hecate or Proserpina, queen of the underworld in classical myth.
5. In mythology, the serpent-haired Gorgon Medusa was so fearful that all who looked upon her head were turned to stone. The legendary Greek hero Theseus descended to Hades to abduct Proserpina.
6. A standard medieval formula for introducing a self-contained allegory, the meaning of which the reader must extract from beneath the "veil" of its surface story.

75   there where the mist is thickest and most acrid."
         As frogs confronted by their enemy,
the snake, will scatter underwater till
each hunches in a heap along the bottom,
         so did the thousand ruined souls I saw
80   take flight before a figure crossing Styx
who walked as if on land and with dry soles.[7]
         He thrust away the thick air from his face,
waving his left hand frequently before him;
that seemed the only task that wearied him.
85   I knew well he was Heaven's messenger,
and I turned toward my master; and he made
a sign that I be still and bow before him.
         How full of high disdain he seemed to me!
He came up to the gate, and with a wand,
90   he opened it, for there was no resistance.
         "O you cast out of Heaven, hated crowd,"
were his first words upon that horrid threshold,
"why do you harbor this presumptuousness?
         Why are you so reluctant to endure
95   that Will whose aim can never be cut short,
and which so often added to your hurts?
         What good is it to thrust against the fates?
Your Cerberus, if you remember well,
for that, had both his throat and chin stripped clean."[8]
100   At that he turned and took the filthy road,
and did not speak to us, but had the look
of one who is obsessed by other cares
         than those that press and gnaw at those before him;
and we moved forward, on into the city,
105   in safety, having heard his holy words.
         We made our way inside without a struggle;
and I, who wanted so much to observe
the state of things that such a fortress guarded,
         as soon as I had entered, looked about.
110   I saw, on every side, a spreading plain
of lamentation and atrocious pain.
         Just as at Arles, where Rhone becomes a marsh,
just as at Pola, near Quarnero's gulf,
that closes Italy and bathes its borders,[9]
115   the sepulchers make all the plain uneven,
so they did here on every side, except
that here the sepulchers were much more harsh;
         for flames were scattered through the tombs, and these

7. The reminiscence of Jesus walking on water at the Sea of Galilee (Matthew 14:21–33) adds to the effect of a repetition of the Harrowing of Hell.
8. The legendary hero Hercules was often regarded as foreshadowing Christ, especially in his Twelve Labors, of which the fetching of Cerberus from the underworld was the final and most difficult.
9. The Provençal town of Arles and the northeastern Italian town of Pola were sites of Roman necropolises.

120   had kindled all of them to glowing heat;
no artisan could ask for hotter iron.
    The lid of every tomb was lifted up,
and from each tomb such sorry cries arose
as could come only from the sad and hurt.
125   And I: "Master, who can these people be
who, buried in great chests of stone like these,
must speak by way of sighs in agony?"
    And he to me: "Here are arch-heretics
and those who followed them, from every sect;
those tombs are much more crowded than you think.
130   Here, like has been ensepulchered with like;
some monuments are heated more, some less."
And then he turned around and to his right;[1]
we passed between the torments and high walls.

Canto 10

Still the Sixth Circle: the Heretics. The tombs of the Epicureans. Farinata degli Uberti. Cavalcante dei Cavalcanti. Farinata's prediction of Dante's difficulty in returning to Florence from exile. The inability of the damned to see the present, although they can foresee the future.

    Now, by a narrow path that ran between
those torments and the ramparts of the city,
my master moves ahead, I following.
    "O highest virtue, you who lead me through
5   these circles of transgression, at your will,
do speak to me, and satisfy my longings.
    Can those who lie within the sepulchers
be seen? The lids—in fact—have all been lifted;
no guardian is watching over them."
10   And he to me: "They'll all be shuttered up
when they return here from Jehosaphat
together with the flesh they left above.[1]
    Within this region is the cemetery
of Epicurus and his followers,
15   all those who say the soul dies with the body.[2]
    And so the question you have asked of me
will soon find satisfaction while we're here,
as will the longing you have hid from me."
    And I: "Good guide, the only reason I
20   have hid my heart was that I might speak briefly,

and you, long since, encouraged me in this."

"O Tuscan, you who pass alive across
the fiery city with such seemly words,
be kind enough to stay your journey here.

25   Your accent makes it clear that you belong
among the natives of the noble city
I may have dealt with too vindictively."[3]

This sound had burst so unexpectedly
out of one sepulcher that, trembling, I
30   then drew a little closer to my guide.

But he told me: "Turn round! What are you doing?
That's Farinata who has risen there—
you will see all of him from the waist up."

My eyes already were intent on his;
35   and up he rose—his forehead and his chest—
as if he had tremendous scorn for Hell.

My guide—his hands encouraging and quick—
thrust me between the sepulchers toward him,
saying: "Your words must be appropriate."

40   When I'd drawn closer to his sepulcher,
he glanced at me, and as if in disdain,
he asked of me: "Who were your ancestors?"[4]

Because I wanted so to be compliant,
I hid no thing from him: I told him all.
45   At this he lifted up his brows a bit,

then said: "They were ferocious enemies
of mine and of my parents and my party,
so that I had to scatter them twice over."[5]

"If they were driven out," I answered him,
50   "they still returned, both times, from every quarter;
but yours were never quick to learn that art."[6]

At this there rose another shade alongside,
uncovered to my sight down to his chin;
I think that he had risen on his knees.[7]

55   He looked around me, just as if he longed
to see if I had come with someone else;
but then, his expectation spent, he said

---

3. The soul has identified Dante because of the Italian dialect he is speaking, from Tuscany, the region of Florence.

4. Farinata, a leader of the Florentine Ghibellines, had died just before Dante was born, so he asks about members of previous generations he would have known, and whether they were known to his illustrious family, the Uberti.

5. Farinata played a prominent role in the expulsion of the Guelfs from Florence in 1248 and in their crushing defeat at Montaperti in 1260, after which he successfully argued for renewed expulsions rather than the destruction of his native city.

6. The Guelfs returned in 1251 after the defeat of the Ghibellines in battle, and again in 1266 after another military

victory. By contrast, the Ghibellines never returned to Florence as a party, and their most powerful families, including the Uberti, were excluded from the city by the terms of the peace of 1280.

7. The speaker is Cavalcante de' Cavalcanti, a notorious Epicurean and father of the famous poet and close friend of Dante, Guido Cavalcanti. An ardent Guelf, Guido was married to Farinata's daughter Beatrice to guarantee peace between the feuding factions. When the priors of Florence (including Dante) put an end to the hostilities in June 1300, the leading Blacks and leading Whites (including Guido) were banished. Guido died of malaria in August of the same year; hence Dante was indirectly responsible for his friend's death.

in tears: "If it is your high intellect
that lets you journey here, through this blind prison,
60   where is my son? Why is he not with you?"

I answered: "My own powers have not brought me;
he who awaits me there, leads me through here
perhaps to one your Guido did disdain."[8]

His words, the nature of his punishment—
65   these had already let me read his name;
therefore, my answer was so fully made.

Then suddenly erect, he cried: "What's that:
He '*did* disdain'? He is not still alive?
The sweet light does not strike against his eyes?"[9]

70   And when he noticed how I hesitated
a moment in my answer, he fell back—
supine—and did not show himself again.

But that great-hearted one, the other shade
at whose request I'd stayed, did not change aspect
75   or turn aside his head or lean or bend;

and taking up his words where he'd left off,
"If they were slow," he said, "to learn that art,
that is more torment to me than this bed.

And yet the Lady who is ruler here
80   will not have her face kindled fifty times[1]
before you learn how heavy is that art.[2]

And so may you return to the sweet world,
tell me: why are those citizens so cruel
against my kin in all of their decrees?"[3]

85   To which I said: "The carnage, the great bloodshed
that stained the waters of the Arbia red
have led us to such prayers in our temple."[4]

He sighed and shook his head, then said: "In that,
I did not act alone, but certainly
90   I'd not have joined the others without cause.

But where I was alone was *there* where all
the rest would have annihilated Florence,
had I not interceded forcefully."[5]

"Ah, as I hope your seed may yet find peace,"
95   I asked, "so may you help me to undo
the knot that here has snarled my course of thought.

8. Guido too was a notorious Epicurean, celebrating "high intellect" as the greatest virtue in his poetry.
9. Guido is not yet dead, but his father misunderstands the meaning of Dante's words.
1. Proserpina is identified with Hecate, goddess of the moon, whose face is fully lit once a month.
2. Farinata foretells Dante's own exile from Florence in 1302, and the difficulty he will have in learning the "art" of returning.
3. The Uberti had been banished from Florence in 1280

and never allowed to return. In 1283, Farinata and his wife had been posthumously excommunicated, their bones exhumed and scattered, and the goods of their heirs confiscated.
4. The hill of Montaperti was on the bank of a small stream near Siena called the Arbia.
5. Farinata recalls his lone opposition to the total destruction of Florence at the council that followed the battle of Montaperti.

It seems, if I hear right, that you can see
beforehand that which time is carrying,
but you're denied the sight of present things."

100   "We see, even as men who are farsighted,
those things," he said, "that are remote from us;
the Highest Lord allots us that much light.

    But when events draw near or are, our minds
are useless; were we not informed by others,
105 we should know nothing of your human state.

    So you can understand how our awareness
will die completely at the moment when
the portal of the future has been shut."[6]

    Then, as if penitent for my omission,
110 I said: "Will you now tell that fallen man
his son is still among the living ones;

    and if, a while ago, I held my tongue
before his question, let him know it was
because I had in mind the doubt you've answered."

115   And now my master was recalling me;
so that, more hurriedly, I asked the spirit
to name the others who were there with him.

    He said: "More than a thousand lie with me:
the second Frederick is but one among them,
120 as is the Cardinal;[7] I name no others."

    With that, he hid himself; and pondering
the speech that seemed to me so menacing,
I turned my steps to meet the ancient poet.

    He moved ahead, and as we made our way,
125 he said to me: "Why are you so dismayed?"
I satisfied him, answering him fully.

    And then that sage exhorted me: "Remember
the words that have been spoken here against you.
Now pay attention," and he raised his finger;

130   "when you shall stand before the gentle splendor
of one whose gracious eyes see everything,
then you shall learn—from her—your lifetime's journey."[8]

    Following that, his steps turned to the left,
leaving the wall and moving toward the middle
135 along a path that strikes into a valley
whose stench, as it rose up, disgusted us.

6. Because time itself will end after the Last Judgment, they will have no more future to see.
7. The Emperor Frederick II (1194–1250), known to his contemporaries as *Stupor Mundi*, "the wonder of the world," was King of Sicily and Naples, and head of the Holy Roman Empire from 1215 until his death. His contemporaries deemed him to be an Epicurean, believing neither in life after death nor in paradise. The Ghibelline Ottaviano degli Ubaldini was made Bishop of Bologna in 1240 and cardinal in 1244. His brother appears in *Purgatorio* and his uncle, Archbishop Ruggieri, in *Inferno* 33.14.
8. Beatrice, who sees all things in the perspective of God, will explain those mysteries which Virgil cannot, as he sees only by the natural light of human reason.

Canto 11

Still the Sixth Circle. Pope Anastasius' tomb. Virgil on the parts of Dis they now will visit, where the modes of malice are punished: violence in the Seventh Circle's Three Rings; "ordinary" fraud in the Eighth Circle; and treacherous fraud in the Ninth Circle. Hell's previous circles, Two through Five, as circles of incontinence. Usury condemned.

Along the upper rim of a high bank
formed by a ring of massive broken boulders,
we came above a crowd more cruelly pent.°   *confined*
          And here, because of the outrageous stench
5   thrown up in excess by that deep abyss,
we drew back till we were behind the lid
          of a great tomb, on which I made out this,
inscribed: "I hold Pope Anastasius,
enticed to leave the true path by Photinus."[1]
10   "It would be better to delay descent
so that our senses may grow somewhat used
to this foul stench; and then we can ignore it."
          So said my master, and I answered him:
"Do find some compensation, lest this time
15   be lost." And he: "You see, I've thought of that."
          "My son, within this ring of broken rocks,"
he then began, "there are three smaller circles;[2]
like those that you are leaving, they range down.
          Those circles are all full of cursed spirits;
20   so that your seeing of them may suffice,
learn now the how and why of their confinement.
          Of every malice that earns hate in Heaven,
injustice is the end; and each such end
by force or fraud brings harm to other men.[3]
25   However, fraud is man's peculiar vice;
God finds it more displeasing—and therefore,
the fraudulent are lower, suffering more.
          The violent take all of the first circle;
but since one uses force against three persons,
30   that circle's built of three divided rings.[4]
          To God and to one's self and to one's neighbor—
I mean, to them or what is theirs—one can
do violence, as you shall now hear clearly.
          Violent death and painful wounds may be
35   inflicted on one's neighbor; his possessions
may suffer ruin, fire, and extortion;

1. Anastasius II was pope from 496 to 498. Tradition appears to have confused him with Anastasius I, Byzantine emperor from 491 to 518, an adherent to the heresy of Photinus, which denied the divine origin of Christ.
2. The seventh, eighth, and ninth, "smaller" because further down in the cone.
3. "Malice" is the blanket term for all the sins of lower

Hell, either by force (seventh circle) or by fraud (eighth and ninth), and distinguishes them from those of upper Hell.
4. "First circle" here means the first of lower Hell, the seventh, subdivided into three rings in order of gravity: the violence against one's neighbor, against self, and against God.

thus, murderers and those who strike in malice,
as well as plunderers and robbers—these,
in separated ranks, the first ring racks.

40   A man can set violent hands against
himself or his belongings; so within
the second ring repents, though uselessly,

    whoever would deny himself your world,
gambling away, wasting his patrimony,
45 and weeping where he should instead be happy.

    One can be violent against the Godhead,
one's heart denying and blaspheming Him
and scorning nature and the good in her;[5]

    so, with its sign, the smallest ring has sealed
50 both Sodom and Cahors and all of those
who speak in passionate contempt of God.[6]

    Now fraud, that eats away at every conscience,
is practiced by a man against another
who trusts in him, or one who has no trust.[7]

55   This latter way seems only to cut off
the bond of love that nature forges;[8] thus,
nestled within the second circle[9] are:

    hypocrisy and flattery, sorcerers,
and falsifiers, simony, and theft,
60 and barrators and panders and like trash.

    But in the former way of fraud, not only
the love that nature forges is forgotten,
but added love that builds a special trust;

    thus, in the tightest circle, where there is
65 the universe's center, seat of Dis,°   *Satan*
all traitors are consumed eternally."

    "Master, your reasoning is clear indeed,"
I said; "it has made plain for me the nature
of this pit and the population in it.

70   But tell me: those the dense marsh holds, or those
driven before the wind, or those on whom
rain falls, or those who clash with such harsh tongues,

    why are they not all punished in the city
of flaming red if God is angry with them?
75 And if He's not, why then are they tormented?"[1]

---

5. Any sin against Nature is considered an injury to God's order of Nature.
6. The Old Testament city of Sodom was identified with the act of sodomy, which in theological discussion was generally called simply "the vice against nature." Cahors is a town in southern France famous as a center of usury, the lending of money with a rate of interest. The third form of violence against God is blasphemy.
7. Fraud is the most complex and dangerous of sins because it is "man's peculiar vice." Dante divides it between simple fraud and treachery, where a bond of trust is broken.

8. In Dante's ethics, humankind is created by love and love is the basis of the natural social bond; hence any act of fraud is a conscious severing of that bond just as the sins of upper Hell pervert (by excess or insufficiency) the innate desire for God's creation.
9. The eighth circle, which contains ten subdivisions in all, is the second circle of lower Hell.
1. The pilgrim's question raises a key tension in the depiction of Hell: do all souls suffer equally because all are damned, or do some suffer more than others? Are all sins equally evil, or are some worse than others?

And then to me, "Why does your reason wander
so far from its accustomed course?" he said.
"Or of what other things are you now thinking?

Have you forgotten, then, the words with which
80   your *Ethics* treats of those three dispositions
that strike at Heaven's will: incontinence

and malice and mad bestiality?[2]
And how the fault that is the least condemned
and least offends God is incontinence?

85   If you consider carefully this judgment
and call to mind the souls of upper Hell,
who bear their penalties outside this city,

you'll see why they have been set off from these
unrighteous ones, and why, when heaven's vengeance
90   hammers at them, it carries lesser anger."

"O sun that heals all sight that is perplexed,
when I ask you, your answer so contents
that doubting pleases me as much as knowing.

Go back a little to that point," I said,
95   "where you told me that usury offends
divine goodness; unravel now that knot."

"Philosophy, for one who understands,
points out, and not in just one place," he said,
"how nature follows—as she takes her course—

100   the Divine Intellect and Divine Art;
and if you read your *Physics* carefully,[3]
not many pages from the start, you'll see

that when it can, your art would follow nature,
just as a pupil imitates his master;
105   so that your art is almost God's grandchild.[4]

From these two, art and nature, it is fitting,
if you recall how *Genesis* begins,
for men to make their way, to gain their living;

and since the usurer prefers another
110   pathway, he scorns both nature in herself
and art, her follower; his hope is elsewhere.[5]

But follow me, for it is time to move;
the Fishes glitter now on the horizon

---

2. In his *Nicomachean Ethics,* known to Dante through the commentaries and translations of Averroës (page 766), Aquinas, and others, Aristotle drew a distinction between three types of immoral practice. Incontinence signifies excess in any passion which, in moderation, is lawful, including all the vices punished in the second through fifth circles. "Mad bestiality" here means violence, and "malice," fraud. Aristotle's classification does not include heresy, and Virgil never mentions the sixth circle in this discussion; nor does he mention the lukewarm souls of Ante-Inferno or the souls of Limbo, whose sins were of omission rather than commission.

3. The *Physics* of Aristotle.
4. Nature, daughter of God, follows his eternal ideas and his art in her own operation; human art and industry, daughter of Nature, ought to follow her and her art in the same way.
5. God's command to Adam and Eve when he expelled them from Eden was that they should gain their living by the sweat of their brows (Genesis 3:19). Because the usurer gains his living from money rather than either from Nature or from her follower, art, he despises her twice over.

and all the Wain is spread out over Caurus;[6]
115   only beyond, can one climb down the cliff."

Canto 12

The Seventh Circle, First Ring: the Violent against their Neighbors. The Minotaur. The Centaurs, led by Chiron, who assigns Nessus to guide Dante and Virgil across the boiling river of blood (Phlegethon). In that river, Tyrants and Murderers, immersed, watched over by the Centaurs.

The place that we had reached for our descent
along the bank was alpine; what reclined
upon that bank would, too, repel all eyes.
Just like the toppled mass of rock that struck—
5   because of earthquake or eroded props—
the Adige on its flank, this side of Trent,
where from the mountain top from which it thrust
down to the plain, the rock is shattered so
that it permits a path for those above:[1]
10   such was the passage down to that ravine.
And at the edge above the cracked abyss,
there lay outstretched the infamy of Crete,[2]
conceived within the counterfeited cow;
and, catching sight of us, he bit himself
15   like one whom fury devastates within.
Turning to him, my sage cried out: "Perhaps
you think this is the Duke of Athens here,
who, in the world above, brought you your death.
Be off, you beast; this man who comes has not
20   been tutored by your sister; all he wants
in coming here is to observe your torments."
Just as the bull that breaks loose from its halter
the moment it receives the fatal stroke,
and cannot run but plunges back and forth,
25   so did I see the Minotaur respond;
and my alert guide cried: "Run toward the pass;
it's better to descend while he's berserk."
And so we made our way across that heap
of stones, which often moved beneath my feet
30   because my weight was somewhat strange for them.
While climbing down, I thought. He said: "You wonder,
perhaps, about that fallen mass, watched over

---

6. The position of the constellations indicates the time: two hours before sunrise, or 4 A.M.

1. The comparison is to the Slavini di Marco, a "toppled mass of rock" resulting from an enormous landslide between Trent and Verona on the Adige River in northeast Italy.

2. The Minotaur, half-man, half-bull, the result of a union

between a bull and queen Pasiphaë of Crete, who hid within an artificial cow to mate with the bull. King Minos of Crete extracted an annual tribute of seven Greek youths and seven maidens to be thrown to the Minotaur in its labyrinth. Theseus, Duke of Athens, traveled to Crete as one of the sacrificial youths and killed the Minotaur.

by the inhuman rage I have just quenched.
Now I would have you know: the other time

35   that I descended into lower Hell,
this mass of boulders had not yet collapsed;[3]
but if I reason rightly, it was just
before the coming of the One who took
from Dis the highest circle's splendid spoils

40   that, on all sides, the steep and filthy valley
had trembled so, I thought the universe
felt love (by which, as some believe, the world
has often been converted into chaos);
and at that moment, here as well as elsewhere,

45   these ancient boulders toppled, in this way.[4]
But fix your eyes below, upon the valley,
for now we near the stream of blood, where those
who injure others violently, boil."
O blind cupidity and insane anger,

50   which goad us on so much in our short life,
then steep us in such grief eternally!
I saw a broad ditch bent into an arc
so that it could embrace all of that plain,
precisely as my guide had said before;

55   between it and the base of the embankment
raced files of Centaurs who were armed with arrows,[5]
as, in the world above, they used to hunt.
On seeing us descend, they all reined in;
and, after they had chosen bows and shafts,

60   three of their number moved out from their ranks;
and still far off, one cried: "What punishment
do you approach as you descend the slope?
But speak from there; if not, I draw my bow."
My master told him: "We shall make reply

65   only to Chiron,[6] when we reach his side;
your hasty will has never served you well."
Then he nudged me and said: "That one is Nessus,
who died because of lovely Deianira
and of himself wrought vengeance for himself.[7]

70   And in the middle, gazing at his chest,
is mighty Chiron, tutor of Achilles;

---

3. Virgil refers to the errand on which Erichtho sent him (Canto 9.22–27), which took place before the crucifixion of Christ and the Harrowing of Hell, mentioned next.

4. According to a theory of the ancient philosopher Empedocles, the alternate supremacy of principles of hate, which keeps things separate, and love, which unites all things, causes periodic destruction and construction in the scheme of the universe; both are required for equilibrium. This is how Virgil understands the earthquake that marked Christ's death (Matthew 27:51), the supreme sacrifice expressing God's love for his creation.

5. In mythology, centaurs are half-man, half-horse, excellent archers, and notorious for their gluttony and violence.

6. An exceptional centaur, Chiron was traditionally depicted as an educator, scientist, and musician who tutored Achilles, Hercules, and other Greek heroes.

7. Dying of a poisoned arrow shot by Hercules after he tried to rape the hero's wife Deianira, Nessus gave Deianira a robe dipped in his blood which he claimed would preserve her husband's love. When she gave Hercules the robe, he was maddened by the poison in the blood, and burned himself to death to end the agony (Ovid, Metamorphoses, 9.127–69).

the third is Pholus, he who was so frenzied.[8]

And many thousands wheel around the moat,
their arrows aimed at any soul that thrusts
75   above the blood more than its guilt allots."

By now we had drawn near those agile beasts;
Chiron drew out an arrow; with the notch,
he parted his beard back upon his jaws.

When he'd uncovered his enormous mouth,
80   he said to his companions: "Have you noticed
how he who walks behind moves what he touches?

Dead souls are not accustomed to do that."
And my good guide—now near the Centaur's chest,
the place where his two natures met—replied:
85   "He is indeed alive, and so alone
it falls to me to show him the dark valley.

Necessity has brought him here, not pleasure.

For she° who gave me this new task was one   *Beatrice*
who had just come from singing halleluiah:
90   he is no robber; I am not a thief.

But by the Power that permits my steps
to journey on so wild a path, give us
one of your band, to serve as our companion;

and let him show us where to ford the ditch,
95   and let him bear this man upon his back,
for he's no spirit who can fly through air."

Then Chiron wheeled about and right and said
to Nessus: "Then, return and be their guide;
if other troops disturb you, fend them off."

100   Now, with our faithful escort, we advanced
along the bloodred, boiling ditch's banks,
beside the piercing cries of those who boiled.

I saw some who were sunk up to their brows,
and that huge Centaur said: "These are the tyrants
105   who plunged their hands in blood and plundering.

Here they lament their ruthless crimes; here are
both Alexander and the fierce Dionysius,
who brought such years of grief to Sicily.[9]

That brow with hair so black is Ezzelino;
110   that other there, the blonde one, is Obizzo
of Este, he who was indeed undone,
within the world above, by his fierce son."[1]

---

8. Pholus was killed during the Centaurs' battle with the
Lapiths at the wedding of Pirithoüs.
9. "Alexander" may be either Alexander the Great of
Macedonia (356–323 B.C.E.) or Alexander of Pherae, a
tyrant of Thessaly of the same period, famed for his cruelty. Dionysius the elder was tyrant of Syracuse in Sicily
during the early 4th century B.C.E.
1. Ezzelino III da Romano (1194–1259) was son-in-law

of Emperor Frederick II, head of the Ghibellines in Upper
Italy, and so infamous for his cruelty that the Pope proclaimed a crusade against him. Obizzo II d'Este
(1247–1293) was an ardent Guelf and supporter of
Charles of Anjou who fought against Manfred, natural
son of Frederick. He was said to have been smothered by
his son, Azzo VIII.

Then I turned to the poet, and he said:
"Now let him be your first guide, me your second."

115   A little farther on, the Centaur stopped
above a group that seemed to rise above
the boiling blood as far up as their throats.

He pointed out one shade, alone, apart,
and said: "Within God's bosom, he impaled
120   the heart that still drips blood upon the Thames."2

Then I caught sight of some who kept their heads
and even their full chests above the tide;
among them—many whom I recognized.

And so the blood grew always shallower
125   until it only scorched the feet; and here
we found a place where we could ford the ditch.

"Just as you see that, on this side, the brook
continually thins," the Centaur said,
"so I should have you know the rivulet,
130   along the other side, will slowly deepen
its bed, until it reaches once again
the depth where tyranny must make lament.

And there divine justice torments Attila
he who was such a scourge upon the earth,
135   and Pyrrhus, Sextus;3 to eternity
it milks the tears that boiling brook unlocks
from Rinier of Corneto, Rinier Pazzo,
those two who waged such war upon the highroads."4
Then he turned round and crossed the ford again.

Canto 13

The Seventh Circle, Second Ring: the Violent against Themselves (Suicides) or against their Possessions (Squanderers). The dreary wood, with the Suicides transformed into strange trees, and the Squanderers, hounded and rent by bitches. Pier della Vigna. Lano and Jacopo da Santo Andrea. The anonymous Florentine suicide.

Nessus had not yet reached the other bank
when we began to make our way across
a wood on which no path had left its mark.

No green leaves in that forest, only black;
5   no branches straight and smooth, but knotted, gnarled;
no fruits were there, but briers bearing poison.

Even those savage beasts that roam between

---

2. Guy, son of Simon de Montfort, killed his first cousin Prince Henry of Cornwall in March 1271 during the assembly of the cardinals to elect a pope, supposedly at the very moment of the elevation of the Host when Henry was on his knees. According to some accounts, Henry's heart was enclosed in a statue on London Bridge over the river Thames, still dripping blood because not yet avenged.

3. Known as "the Scourge of God," Attila was King of the Huns (433–453). Pyrrhus is either the son of Achilles whose savage murder of Priam and other Trojans was recorded in *Aeneid* 2 or a king of Epirus who made war on Rome in the third century B.C.E. Sextus was the son of Pompey and a notorious pirate in Lucan's *Pharsalia*.
4. Two famous highwaymen of Dante's day.

Cécina and Corneto,[1] beasts that hate
tilled lands, do not have holts° so harsh and dense.   *woods*

10   This is the nesting place of the foul Harpies,
who chased the Trojans from the Strophades
with sad foretelling of their future trials.[2]

        Their wings are wide, their necks and faces human;
their feet are taloned, their great bellies feathered;
15   they utter their laments on the strange trees.

        And my kind master then instructed me:
"Before you enter farther know that now
you are within the second ring and shall

        be here until you reach the horrid sand;
20   therefore look carefully; you'll see such things
as would deprive my speech of all belief."[3]

        From every side I heard the sound of cries,
but I could not see any source for them,
so that, in my bewilderment, I stopped.

25   I think that he was thinking that I thought
so many voices moaned among those trunks
from people who had been concealed from us.

        Therefore my master said: "If you would tear
a little twig from any of these plants,
30   the thoughts you have will also be cut off."

        Then I stretched out my hand a little way
and from a great thornbush snapped off a branch,
at which its trunk cried out: "Why do you tear me?"

        And then, when it had grown more dark with blood,
35   it asked again: "Why do you break me off?
Are you without all sentiment of pity?

        We once were men and now are arid stumps:
your hand might well have shown us greater mercy
had we been nothing more than souls of serpents."

40   As from a sapling log that catches fire
along one of its ends, while at the other
it drips and hisses with escaping vapor,

        so from that broken stump issued together
both words and blood; at which I let the branch
45   fall, and I stood like one who is afraid.

        My sage said: "Wounded soul, if, earlier,
he had been able to believe what he
had only glimpsed within my poetry,

1. The river Cecina and the town of Corneto mark the boundaries of the Maremma, a famously dense Tuscan wood.
2. Mythical monsters in the shapes of birds with clawed hands and women's faces, the Harpies, among other deeds, fouled the Trojans' feast and drove Aeneas and his companions from the Strophades, islands in the Ionian Sea, prophesying that they would face starvation and misfortune before reaching Italy (*Aeneid* 3.209–57).
3. This episode closely follows another adventure in *Aeneid* 3. Landed in Thrace, Aeneas tries to tear off a green branch for an altar only to find black blood dripping from it. The tree entombs Polydorus, a son of Priam sent to purchase aid in the Trojan War from the King of Thrace, who murdered him instead, stealing the gold proffered as payment.

50

then he would not have set his hand against you;
but its incredibility made me
urge him to do a deed that grieves me deeply.

But tell him who you were, so that he may,
to make amends, refresh your fame within
the world above, where he can still return."

55

To which the trunk: "Your sweet speech draws me so
that I cannot be still; and may it not
oppress you, if I linger now in talk.[4]

I am the one who guarded both the keys
of Frederick's heart and turned them, locking and

60

unlocking them with such dexterity
that none but I could share his confidence;
and I was faithful to my splendid office,
so faithful that I lost both sleep and strength.

The whore who never turned her harlot's eyes

65

away from Caesar's dwelling, she who is
the death of all and vice of every court,
inflamed the minds of everyone against me;
and those inflamed, then so inflamed Augustus
that my delighted honors turned to sadness.[5]

70

My mind, because of its disdainful temper,
believing it could flee disdain through death,
made me unjust against my own just self.

I swear to you by the peculiar roots
of this thornbush, I never broke my faith

75

with him who was so worthy—with my lord.

If one of you returns into the world,
then let him help my memory, which still
lies prone beneath the battering of envy."

The poet waited briefly, then he said

80

to me: "Since he is silent, do not lose
this chance, but speak and ask what you would know."

And I: "Do you continue; ask of him
whatever you believe I should request;
I cannot, so much pity takes my heart."

85

Then he began again: "Imprisoned spirit,
so may this man do freely what you ask,
may it please you to tell us something more
of how the soul is bound into these knots;
and tell us, if you can, if any one

90

can ever find his freedom from these limbs."

At this the trunk breathed violently, then

---

4. The speaker, Pier della Vigna (c. 1190–1249), was minister and councilor to Emperor Frederick II. Accused (probably falsely) of plotting with the pope to poison Frederick, he was arrested, thrown into prison, and blinded. He soon committed suicide, it is said by dashing his head against a wall. Pier was also a poet and accomplished

letter-writer, as is reflected in the ornamented and mannered style of his speech.
5. The "whore" is envy, which was a sin of the eyes; "Caesar's dwelling" is the imperial court, and "Augustus" is the emperor, after the Roman emperor, Caesar Augustus.

that wind became this voice: "You shall be answered
promptly. When the savage spirit quits
the body from which it has torn itself,

95   then Minos sends it to the seventh maw.
It falls into the wood, and there's no place
to which it is allotted, but wherever

fortune has flung that soul, that is the space
where, even as a grain of spelt, it sprouts.[6]

100   It rises as a sapling, a wild plant;
and then the Harpies, feeding on its leaves,
cause pain and for that pain provide a vent.

Like other souls, we shall seek out the flesh
that we have left, but none of us shall wear it;

105   it is not right for any man to have
what he himself has cast aside. We'll drag
our bodies here; they'll hang in this sad wood,

each on the stump of its vindictive shade."[7]
And we were still intent upon the trunk—

110   believing it had wanted to say more—
when we were overtaken by a roar,
just as the hunter is aware of chase

and boar as they draw near his post—he hears
the beasts and then the branches as they crack.

115   And there upon the left were two who, scratched
and naked, fled so violently that
they tore away each forest bough they passed.

The one in front: "Now come, death, quickly come!"
The other shade, who thought himself too slow,

120   was shouting after him: "Lano, your legs
were not so nimble at the jousts of Toppo!"[8]
And then, perhaps because he'd lost his breath,

he fell into one tangle with a bush.
Behind these two, black bitches filled the wood,

125   and they were just as eager and as swift
as greyhounds that have been let off their leash.
They set their teeth in him where he had crouched;

and, piece by piece, those dogs dismembered him
and carried off his miserable limbs.

130   Then he who was my escort took my hand;
he led me to the lacerated thorn
that wept in vain where it was bleeding, broken.

"O Jacopo," it said, "da Santo Andrea,
what have you gained by using me as screen?

135   Am I to blame for your indecent life?"

---

6. Like other wheats and grains, spelt grows readily and in thick clumps out of a single shoot.

7. Souls are to be rejoined with their bodies after the Last Judgment. Because the shade was unjust ("vindictive") to its own body through suicide, it will not be fully reunited with it.

8. Lano of Siena and Jacopo da Santo Andrea of Padua, two notorious squanderers of 13th-century Italy.

When my good master stood beside that bush,
he said: "Who were you, who through many wounds
must breathe with blood your melancholy words?"[9]
        And he to us: "O spirits who have come
140 to witness the outrageous laceration
that leaves so many of my branches torn,
        collect them at the foot of this sad thorn.
My home was in the city whose first patron
gave way to John the Baptist; for this reason,
145 he'll always use his art to make it sorrow;[1]
and if—along the crossing of the Arno—
some effigy of Mars had not remained,
        those citizens who afterward rebuilt
their city on the ashes that Attila
150 had left to them, would have travailed in vain.[2]
        I made—of my own house—my gallows place."

Canto 14

The Seventh Circle, Third Ring: the Violent against God. The First Zone: Blasphemers, supine on fiery sands. Capaneus. Virgil on the Old Man of Crete, whose streaming tears form the rivers of Hell: Acheron, Phlegethon, Styx, and Cocytus. The sight of Lethe postponed.

        Love of our native city overcame me;
I gathered up the scattered boughs and gave
them back to him whose voice was spent already.
        From there we reached the boundary that divides
5   the second from the third ring—and the sight
of a dread work that justice had devised.
        To make these strange things clear, I must explain
that we had come upon an open plain
that banishes all green things from its bed.
10 The wood of sorrow is a garland round it,
just as that wood is ringed by a sad channel;
here, at the very edge, we stayed our steps.
        The ground was made of sand, dry and compact,
a sand not different in kind from that
15 on which the feet of Cato had once tramped.[1]
        O vengeance of the Lord, how you should be
dreaded by everyone who now can read

9. Generally known as "the anonymous Florentine," this soul appears to represent the general self-destructiveness of his city itself rather than a particular inhabitant.
1. In pagan times, the citizens of Florence had chosen Mars as their special patron; when they switched to Christianity, they incurred the war-god's wrath when they converted his temple to a church dedicated to St. John.
2. According to legend, the statue of Mars was removed to a tower near the river Arno, and it fell into the river

when the city was destroyed by Attila in 450 (confused here with the Ostrogoth king Totila, who had besieged the city in 542). It was said that the retrieval of the statue had permitted the Florentines to rebuild their city (in fact, it was neither destroyed nor rebuilt).
1. Cato of Utica (95–46 B.C.E.), who led the Pompeian forces through the Libyan Desert in 47 B.C.E. (Lucan, *Pharsalia* 9); Dante placed him at the base of the Mountain of Purgatory (*Purgatorio* 1).

whatever was made manifest to me!
    I saw so many flocks of naked souls,
20   all weeping miserably, and it seemed
that they were ruled by different decrees.
    Some lay upon the ground, flat on their backs;
some huddled in a crouch, and there they sat;
and others moved about incessantly.
25   The largest group was those who walked about,
the smallest, those supine° in punishment;   *lying down*
but these had looser tongues to tell their torment.
    Above that plain of sand, distended flakes
of fire showered down;[2] their fall was slow—
30   as snow descends on alps when no wind blows.
    Just like the flames that Alexander saw
in India's hot zones, when fires fell,
intact and to the ground, on his battalions,
    for which—wisely—he had his soldiers tramp
35   the soil to see that every fire was spent
before new flames were added to the old;[3]
    so did the never-ending heat descend;
with this, the sand was kindled just as tinder
on meeting flint will flame—doubling the pain.
40   The dance of wretched hands was never done;
now here, now there, they tried to beat aside
the fresh flames as they fell. And I began
    to speak: "My master, you who can defeat
all things except for those tenacious demons
45   who tried to block us at the entryway,
    who is that giant there, who does not seem
to heed the singeing—he who lies and scorns
and scowls, he whom the rains can't seem to soften?"[4]
    And he himself, on noticing that I
50   was querying my guide about him, cried:
"That which I was in life, I am in death.
    Though Jove wear out the smith from whom he took,
in wrath, the keen-edged thunderbolt with which
on my last day I was to be transfixed;
55   or if he tire the others, one by one,
in Mongibello, at the sooty forge,
while bellowing: 'O help, good Vulcan, help!'[5]—
just as he did when there was war at Phlegra[6]—

2. The rain of fire derives from the fire that fell upon Sodom and Gomorrah (Genesis 19:24) and also from Ezekiel 38:22.
3. The incident comes from an apocryphal letter from Alexander of Macedon to Aristotle; Dante condenses an incident of trampling on heavily falling snow with a rain of fire from the sky.
4. Capaneus was one of the legendary Seven against Thebes, kings who besieged the city; defying Jove as he

scaled the walls, Capaneus was struck down by a thunderbolt.
5. Vulcan, god of fire and of the forge, with his assistants, the Cyclopes, made Jove's thunderbolts. His furnace was thought to be at Mt. Etna in Sicily, called Mongibello in Italian.
6. When the rebellious Giants stormed Olympus, Jove defeated them at the battle of Phlegra (literally "the place of burning") with the help of Hercules.

and casts his shafts at me with all his force,
60 not even then would he have happy vengeance."
    Then did my guide speak with such vehemence
as I had never heard him use before:
"O Capaneus, for your arrogance
    that is not quenched, you're punished all the more:
65 no torture other than your own madness
could offer pain enough to match your wrath."
    But then, with gentler face he turned to me
and said: "That man was one of seven kings
besieging Thebes; he held—and still, it seems,
70   holds—God in great disdain, disprizing° Him;   *scorning*
but as I told him now, his maledictions
sit well as ornaments upon his chest.
    Now follow me and—take care—do not set
your feet upon the sand that's burning hot,
75 but always keep them back, close to the forest."
    In silence we had reached a place where flowed
a slender watercourse out of the wood—
a stream whose redness makes me shudder still.
    As from the Bulicame pours a brook
80 whose waters then are shared by prostitutes,[7]
so did this stream run down across the sand.
    Its bed and both its banks were made of stone,
together with the slopes along its shores,
so that I saw our passageway lay there.
85 "Among all other things that I have shown you
since we first made our way across the gate
whose threshold is forbidden to no one,
    no thing has yet been witnessed by your eyes
as notable as this red rivulet,
90 which quenches every flame that burns above it."
    These words were spoken by my guide; at this,
I begged him to bestow the food for which
he had already given me the craving.[8]
    "A devastated land lies in midsea,
95 a land that is called Crete," he answered me.
"Under its king the world once lived chastely.
    Within that land there was a mountain blessed
with leaves and waters, and they called it Ida;
but it is withered now like some old thing.
100   It once was chosen as a trusted cradle
by Rhea for her son; to hide him better,

---

7. The Bulicame was a famous sulphurous hot spring near Viterbo, north of Rome. Its waters were piped into the houses of prostitutes there.
8. The tale of the Old Man of Crete, used to explain the origin of the waterways of Hell, is a synthesis of Ovid's myth of the four ages—a golden age under Saturn, mythical king of Crete, when "the world once lived chastely," followed in declining order by silver, bronze and iron (*Metamorphoses* 1.89–150), and the prophet Daniel's account of a composite statue in the dream of Nebuchadnezzar (Daniel 2:31–35).

when he cried out, she had her servants clamor.[9]
    Within the mountain is a huge Old Man,
who stands erect—his back turned toward Damietta°—   *in Egypt*

105   and looks at Rome as if it were his mirror.
    The Old Man's head is fashioned of fine gold,
the purest silver forms his arms and chest,
but he is made of brass down to the cleft;
    below that point he is of choicest iron

110   except for his right foot, made of baked clay;
and he rests more on this than on the left.[1]
    Each part of him, except the gold, is cracked;
and down that fissure there are tears that drip;
when gathered, they pierce through that cavern's floor

115   and, crossing rocks into this valley, form
the Acheron and Styx and Phlegethon;
and then they make their way down this tight channel,
    and at the point past which there's no descent,
they form Cocytus; since you are to see

120   what that pool is, I'll not describe it here."
    And I asked him: "But if the rivulet
must follow such a course down from our world,
why can we see it only at this boundary?"
    And he to me: "You know this place is round;

125   and though the way that you have come is long,
and always toward the left and toward the bottom,
    you still have not completed all the circle:
so that, if something new appears to us,
it need not bring such wonder to your face."[2]

130   And I again: "Master, where's Phlegethon
and where is Lethe?[3] You omit the second
and say this rain of tears has formed the first."
    "I'm pleased indeed," he said, "with all your questions;
yet one of them might well have found its answer

135   already—when you saw the red stream boiling.
    You shall see Lethe, but past this abyss,
there where the spirits go to cleanse themselves
when their repented guilt is set aside."
    Then he declared: "The time has come to quit

---

9. Rhea, or Cybele, was mother by Saturn of Jove. In order to avert a prophecy that he would be dethroned by one of his children, Saturn had devoured them one by one as they were born. Only Jove was saved when Rhea retired to Mt. Ida to give birth and substituted a stone for the child. To hide the infant's cries, she had her priests clash their weapons and chant.

1. Nebuchadnezzar's dream imagined a similar statue, broken to pieces by "a stone cut out of a mountain without hands." Dante adds the detail, reminiscent of the pilgrim's aborted climb in Canto 1.30, of the unevenly weighted feet, and the gloss of the statue as an allegory of the four ages.

2. There has been much discussion as to whether Virgil's explanation is consistent with geographical descriptions elsewhere in the canticle, but it is clear enough here: each river is basically level, circling a particular region of Hell, and linked to the others by a descending rivulet such as the one encountered here that leads from Phlegethon down to Cocytus. Because their descent has nearly always been in a leftward direction, the travelers haven't always crossed such connecting streams.

3. Well versed in his classical mythology, the pilgrim is puzzled over the absence of Lethe, the river of forgetting of which the souls in the Elysian Fields drink before returning to the world above (*Aeneid* 6).

140   this wood; see that you follow close behind me;
    these margins form a path that does not scorch,
        and over them, all flaming vapor is quenched."

Canto 15

Still the Seventh Circle, Third Ring: the Violent against God. Second Zone: the Sodomites, endlessly crossing the fiery sands beneath the rain of fire. Brunetto Latini, whom Dante treats as mentor. Priscian, Francesco d'Accorso, and Andrea dei Mozzi, Bishop of Florence.

    Now one of the hard borders bears us forward;
the river mist forms shadows overhead
and shields the shores and water from the fire.
    Just as between Wissant and Bruges, the Flemings,
5   in terror of the tide that floods toward them,
have built a wall of dykes to daunt the sea;
    and as the Paduans, along the Brenta,
build bulwarks to defend their towns and castles
before the dog days fall on Carentana;[1]
10   just so were these embankments, even though
they were not built so high and not so broad,
whoever was the artisan who made them.
    By now we were so distant from the wood
that I should not have made out where it was—
15   not even if I'd turned around to look—
    when we came on a company of spirits
who made their way along the bank; and each
stared steadily at us, as in the dusk,
    beneath the new moon, men look at each other.
20   They knit their brows and squinted at us—just
as an old tailor at his needle's eye.
    And when that family looked harder, I
was recognized by one, who took me by
the hem and cried out: "This is marvelous!"
25   That spirit having stretched his arm toward me,
I fixed my eyes upon his baked, brown features,
so that the scorching of his face could not
    prevent my mind from recognizing him;
and lowering my face to meet his face,
30   I answered him: "Are you here, Ser Brunetto?"[2]
    And he: "My son, do not mind if Brunetto

---

1. Wissant and Bruges are given as the eastern and western boundaries of the Flemish seaboard, lined with great dykes to hold back the North Sea. The melt-off from the Carnic Alps ("Carentana") would swell the northern Italian river Brenta as it flowed down into the city of Padua.
2. "Master" Brunetto, a term of respect. Brunetto Latini (c. 1220–1294) was a celebrated writer and Guelph political figure who was active in Florentine affairs. Author of such works as a French prose encyclopedia and the Italian didactic poem the *Tesoretto*, he was not actually Dante's teacher, but an important influence. He had no reputation as a sodomite, and there has been much debate over whether Dante also intended the sin to be understood, as it often was in the Middle Ages, in terms of a "sterile" or nonproductive use of language and learning.

Latini lingers for a while with you
and lets the file he's with pass on ahead."

I said: "With all my strength I pray you, stay;
35   and if you'd have me rest awhile with you,
I shall, if that please him with whom I go."

"O son," he said, "whoever of this flock
stops but a moment, stays a hundred years
and cannot shield himself when fire strikes.

40   Therefore move on; below—but close—I'll follow;
and then I shall rejoin my company,
who go lamenting their eternal sorrows."

I did not dare to leave my path for his
own level; but I walked with head bent low
45   as does a man who goes in reverence.

And he began: "What destiny or chance
has led you here below before your last
day came, and who is he who shows the way?"

"There, in the sunlit life above," I answered,
50   "before my years were full, I went astray
within a valley. Only yesterday

at dawn I turned my back upon it—but
when I was newly lost, he here appeared,
to guide me home again along this path."

55   And he to me: "If you pursue your star,
you cannot fail to reach a splendid harbor,
if in fair life, I judged you properly;

and if I had not died too soon for this,
on seeing Heaven was so kind to you,
60   I should have helped sustain you in your work.

But that malicious, that ungrateful people
come down, in ancient times, from Fiesole—
still keeping something of the rock and mountain[3]—

for your good deeds, will be your enemy:
65   and there is cause—among the sour sorbs,
the sweet fig is not meant to bear its fruit.[4]

The world has long since called them blind, a people
presumptuous, avaricious, envious;
be sure to cleanse yourself of their foul ways.

70   Your fortune holds in store such honor for you,
one party and the other will be hungry
for you—but keep the grass far from the goat.

For let the beasts of Fiesole find forage
among themselves, and leave the plant alone—
75   if still, among their dung, it rises up—

---

3. The tradition was that Florence was founded following
Caesar's successful siege of the ancient town of Fiesole,
on a hill four miles to the northeast, partly by Romans and
partly by families from the destroyed town.

4. The sorb is related to the apple and the pear; the
metaphor parallels the contrast between Fiesolan and Roman Florentines, with Dante as the fig and his tormenters
as the "sour sorbs."

in which there lives again the sacred seed
of those few Romans who remained in Florence
when such a nest of wickedness was built."
"If my desire were answered totally,"
80 I said to Ser Brunetto, "you'd still be
among, not banished from, humanity.

Within my memory is fixed—and now
moves me—your dear, your kind paternal
image when, in the world above, from time to time
85 you taught me how man makes himself eternal;[5]
and while I live, my gratitude for that
must always be apparent in my words.

What you have told me of my course, I write;
I keep it with another text, for comment
90 by one who'll understand, if I may reach her.

One thing alone I'd have you plainly see:
so long as I am not rebuked by conscience,
I stand prepared for Fortune, come what may.

My ears find no new pledge in that prediction;
95 therefore, let Fortune turn her wheel as she
may please, and let the peasant turn his mattock."°   hoe

At this, my master turned his head around
and toward the right, and looked at me and said:
"He who takes note of this has listened well."

100 But nonetheless, my talk with Ser Brunetto
continues, and I ask of him who are
his comrades of repute and excellence.

And he to me: "To know of some is good;
but for the rest, silence is to be praised;
105 the time we have is short for so much talk.

In brief, know that my company has clerics
and men of letters and of fame—and all
were stained by one same sin upon the earth.

That sorry crowd holds Priscian and Francesco
110 d'Accorso;[6] and among them you can see,
if you have any longing for such scurf,

the one the Servant of His Servants sent
from the Arno to the Bacchiglione's banks,
and there he left his tendons strained by sin.[7]

115 I would say more; but both my walk and words
must not be longer, for—beyond—I see

5. Brunetto wrote in the *Tresor* that "Glory gives the wise man a second life; that is to say, after his death the reputation which remains of his good works makes it seem as if he were still alive" (2.120.1).

6. Priscian (fl. c. 500 C.E.) was a celebrated Latin grammarian whose works were widely used in medieval schools. Francesco d'Accorso (1225–1293) was a renowned lawyer and professor of law at Bologna and Oxford.

7. Andrea de' Mozzi was bishop of Florence (on the Arno) until transferred by Pope Boniface VIII in 1295 to Vicenza (on the Bacchiglione) due to his unseemly living. He died there several months later, leaving a body, according to Brunetto, with muscles "strained" by sodomy. Boniface VIII is referred to, with irony, by the pope's name in official acts, "Servant of Servants."

new smoke emerging from the sandy bed.
    Now people come with whom I must not be.
Let my *Tesoro,* in which I still live,

120   be precious to you; and I ask no more."
    And then he turned and seemed like one of those
who race across the fields to win the green
cloth at Verona; of those runners, he
    appeared to be the winner, not the loser.[8]

Canto 16

Still the Seventh Circle, Third Ring, Second Zone: other Sodomites. Three Floren-
tines, Guido Guerra, Tegghiaio Aldobrandi, Jacopo Rusticucci. The decadence of
Florence. Phlegethon, cascading into the next zone. The cord of Dante, used by Virgil
to summon a monstrous figure from the waters.

    No sooner had I reached the place where one
could hear a murmur, like a beehive's hum,
of waters as they fell to the next circle,
    when, setting out together, three shades ran,

5   leaving another company that passed
beneath the rain of bitter punishment.
    They came toward us, and each of them cried out:
"Stop, you who by your clothing seem to be
someone who comes from our indecent country!"[1]

10   Ah me, what wounds I saw upon their limbs,
wounds new and old, wounds that the flames seared in!
It pains me still as I remember it.
    When they cried out, my master paid attention;
he turned his face toward me and then he said:

15   "Now wait: to these one must show courtesy.
    And were it not the nature of this place
for shafts of fire to fall, I'd say that haste
was seemlier for you than for those three."
    As soon as we stood still, they started up

20   their ancient wail again; and when they reached us,
they formed a wheel, all three of them together.
    As champions, naked, oiled, will always do,
each studying the grip that serves him best
before the blows and wounds begin to fall,

25   while wheeling so, each one made sure his face
was turned to me, so that their necks opposed
their feet in one uninterrupted flow.[2]

---

8. This foot race was instituted in 1207 and run annually
on the first Sunday in Lent outside Verona. According to
Boccaccio, the runners were naked and the prize was a
piece of green cloth.
1. According to the Florentine chronicler Villani, the
dress of his people "was the most beautiful, the most

noble, and the most decorous of that of any nation; it was
in the manner of the togaed Roman."
2. The theme of athletics introduced at the end of the previous canto continues here, referring either to ancient
wrestlers, to the medieval trial by combat to settle judicial
disputes, or to both.

And, "If the squalor of this shifting sand,
together with our baked and barren features,
30   makes us and our requests contemptible,"
one said, "then may our fame incline your mind
to tell us who you are, whose living feet
can make their way through Hell with such assurance.
He in whose steps you see me tread, although
35   he now must wheel about both peeled and naked,
was higher in degree than you believe:
he was a grandson of the good Gualdrada,
and Guido Guerra was his name; in life
his sword and his good sense accomplished much.
40   The other who, behind me, tramples sand—
Tegghiaio Aldobrandi, one whose voice
should have been heeded in the world above.
And I, who share this punishment with them,
was Jacopo Rusticucci; certainly,
45   more than all else, my savage wife destroyed me."[3]
If I'd had shield and shelter from the fire,
I should have thrown myself down there among them—
I think my master would have sanctioned that;
but since that would have left me burned and baked,
50   my fear won out against the good intention
that made me so impatient to embrace them.
Then I began: "Your present state had fixed
not scorn but sorrow in me—and so deeply
that it will only disappear slowly—
55   as soon as my lord spoke to me with words
that made me understand what kind of men
were coming toward us, men of worth like yours.
For I am of your city; and with fondness,
I've always told and heard the others tell
60   of both your actions and your honored names.
I leave the gall and go for the sweet apples
that I was promised by my truthful guide;
but first I must descend into the center."
"So may your soul long lead your limbs and may
65   your fame shine after you," he answered then,
"tell us if courtesy and valor still
abide within our city as they did
when we were there, or have they disappeared
completely;[4] for Guiglielmo Borsiere,
70   who only recently has come to share
our torments, and goes there with our companions,

3. Guido and Tegghiaio were prominent Guelfs of the mid-13th century; Rusticucci a less distinguished neighbor of Tegghiaio and also a Guelf. Dante had asked for news of the latter two in Canto 6. Jacopo blames his wife for his fate.

4. True to the deference with which Dante treats them here, these Florentines are genuinely concerned with the fate of their city which, as in Canto 10, is too close for them to foresee.

has caused us much affliction with his words."[5]

"Newcomers to the city and quick gains
have brought excess and arrogance to you,
75   o Florence, and you weep for it already!"

So I cried out with face upraised; the three
looked at each other when they heard my answer
as men will stare when they have heard the truth.

"If you can always offer a reply
80   so readily to others," said all three,
"then happy you who speak, at will, so clearly.

So, if you can escape these lands of darkness
and see the lovely stars on your return,
when you repeat with pleasure, 'I was there,'
85   be sure that you remember us to men."

At this they broke their wheel; and as they fled,
their swift legs seemed to be no less than wings.

The time it took for them to disappear—
more brief than time it takes to say "amen";
90   and so, my master thought it right to leave.

I followed him. We'd only walked a little
when roaring water grew so near to us
we hardly could have heard each other speak.

And even as the river that is first
95   to take its own course eastward from Mount Viso,
along the left flank of the Apennines

(which up above is called the Acquacheta,
before it spills into its valley bed
and flows without that name beyond Forlì),
100   reverberates above San Benedetto
dell'Alpe as it cascades in one leap,
where there is space enough to house a thousand;[6]

so did we hear that blackened water roar
as it plunged down a steep and craggy bank,
105   enough to deafen us in a few hours.

Around my waist I had a cord as girdle,
and with it once I thought I should be able
to catch the leopard with the painted hide.[7]

And after I had loosened it completely,
110   just as my guide commanded me to do,
I handed it to him, knotted and coiled.

At this, he wheeled around upon his right
and cast it, at some distance from the edge,

5. Guiglielmo Borsiere was a pursemaker known for his courteous manners and bearing; he is the subject of a tale in Boccaccio's *Decameron* (1.8).

6. The roar of the descending Phlegethon is likened to the cascade of the river Acquachete in the eastern Apennine mountains near the Benedictine monastery of San Benedetto dell'Alpe. Below the city of Forlí, its name changes to Montone.

7. The incident of the cord invites an allegorical reading, but a satisfactory one has not yet been found. It would not have been part of the Florentine dress mentioned earlier in the canto; some commentators have suggested the garb of a Franciscan monk (see 27.67), while the leopard hearkens back to the first beast of Canto 1.

straight down into the depth of the ravine.

115   "And surely something strange must here reply,"
I said within myself, "to this strange sign—
the sign my master follows with his eye."
    Ah, how much care men ought to exercise
with those whose penetrating intellect
120 can see our thoughts—not just our outer act!
    He said to me: "Now there will soon emerge
what I await and what your thought has conjured:
it soon must be discovered to your sight."
    Faced with that truth which seems a lie, a man
125 should always close his lips as long as he can—
to tell it shames him, even though he's blameless;
    but here I can't be still; and by the lines
of this my Comedy, reader, I swear[8]—
and may my verse find favor for long years—
130   that through the dense and darkened air I saw
a figure swimming, rising up, enough
to bring amazement to the firmest heart,
    like one returning from the waves where he
went down to loose an anchor snagged upon
135 a reef or something else hid in the sea,
    who stretches upward and draws in his feet.

Canto 17

The monster Geryon. The Seventh Circle, Third Ring, Third Zone: the Violent against Nature and Art (Usurers), each seated beneath the rain of fire with a purse—bearing his family's heraldic emblem—around his neck. Descent to the Eighth Circle on the back of Geryon.

    "Behold the beast who bears the pointed tail,
who crosses mountains, shatters weapons, walls!
Behold the one whose stench fills all the world!"
    So did my guide begin to speak to me,
5 and then he signaled him to come ashore
close to the end of those stone passageways.
    And he came on, that filthy effigy
of fraud, and landed with his head and torso
but did not draw his tail onto the bank.[1]
10   The face he wore was that of a just man,
so gracious was his features' outer semblance;
and all his trunk, the body of a serpent;
    he had two paws, with hair up to the armpits;

8. In a moment of significance in any medieval text, at the midpoint episode of the canticle, Dante names his poem directly for the first time.
1. In classical mythology, Geryon was a giant possessing three bodies and three heads, slain by Hercules when the hero took his prized cattle as one of the Twelve Labors. Dante's description gives Geryon a threefold nature—man, beast and serpent—deriving some of the imagery from biblical sources.

his back and chest as well as both his flanks

15　had been adorned with twining knots and circlets.

No Turks or Tartars ever fashioned fabrics

more colorful in background and relief,

nor had Arachne ever loomed such webs.[2]

As boats will sometimes lie along the shore,

20　with part of them on land and part in water,

and just as there, among the guzzling Germans,

the beaver sets himself when he means war,[3]

so did that squalid beast lie on the margin

of stone that serves as border for the sand.

25　And all his tail was quivering in the void

while twisting upward its envenomed fork,

which had a tip just like a scorpion's.

My guide said: "Now we'd better bend our path

a little, till we reach as far as that

30　malicious beast which crouches over there."

Thus we descended on the right hand side[4]

and moved ten paces on the stony brink

in order to avoid the sand and fire.

When we had reached the sprawling beast, I saw—

35　a little farther on, upon the sand—

some sinners sitting near the fissured rock.

And here my master said to me: "So that

you may experience this ring in full,

go now, and see the state in which they are.

40　But keep your conversation with them brief;

till you return, I'll parley with this beast,

to see if he can lend us his strong shoulders."

So I went on alone[5] and even farther

along the seventh circle's outer margin,

45　to where the melancholy people sat.

Despondency was bursting from their eyes;

this side, then that, their hands kept fending off,

at times the flames, at times the burning soil:

not otherwise do dogs in summer—now

50　with muzzle, now with paw—when they are bitten

by fleas or gnats or by the sharp gadfly.

When I had set my eyes upon the faces

of some on whom that painful fire falls,

I recognized no one; but I did notice

2. Tartar and Turkish cloths were highly valued in the Middle Ages for their richness and intricacy of design; from a dogmatic Christian perspective, their infidel makers were also treacherous. In Greek mythology, the mortal Arachne challenged Minerva to a weaving contest; angry at the result, the goddess transformed her into a spider (Ovid, *Metamorphoses* 6.5–145).

3. According to popular belief, the beaver (common in Germany) caught fish by squirting oily drops while agitating the water with its tail; deceived by the drops, the fish came close enough to be grabbed.

4. The second of the two right-hand turns in Hell (the first was at 9.132); this one suggests the impossibility of approaching fraud in a straightforward manner.

5. The first and only time in the *Inferno* in which the pilgrim moves alone, without Virgil.

55   that from the neck of each a purse was hung
that had a special color and an emblem,
and their eyes seemed to feast upon these pouches.[6]
      Looking about—when I had come among them—
I saw a yellow purse with azure on it
60   that had the face and manner of a lion.
      Then, as I let my eyes move farther on,
I saw another purse that was bloodred,
and it displayed a goose more white than butter.
      And one who had an azure, pregnant sow
65   inscribed as emblem on his white pouch, said
to me: "What are you doing in this pit?
      Now you be off; and since you're still alive,
remember that my neighbor Vitaliano
shall yet sit here, upon my left hand side.
70   Among these Florentines, I'm Paduan;
I often hear them thunder in my ears,
shouting, 'Now let the sovereign cavalier,
      the one who'll bring the purse with three goats, come!'"
At this he slewed his mouth, and then he stuck
75   his tongue out, like an ox that licks its nose.
      And I, afraid that any longer stay
might anger him who'd warned me to be brief,
made my way back from those exhausted souls.
      I found my guide, who had already climbed
80   upon the back of that brute animal,
and he told me: "Be strong and daring now,
      for our descent is by this kind of stairs:
you mount in front; I want to be between,
so that the tail can't do you any harm."
85   As one who feels the quartan fever near
and shivers, with his nails already blue,[7]
the sight of shade enough to make him shudder,
      so I became when I had heard these words;
but then I felt the threat of shame, which makes
90   a servant—in his kind lord's presence—brave.
      I settled down on those enormous shoulders;
I wished to say (and yet my voice did not
come as I thought): "See that you hold me tight."
      But he who—other times, in other dangers—
95   sustained me, just as soon as I had mounted,
clasped me within his arms and propped me up,
      and said: "Now, Geryon, move on; take care to
keep your circles wide, your landing slow;
remember the new weight you're carrying."

---

6. The emblems on the moneylenders' pouches belong to distinguished Florentine and Paduan families well-known for their usury.

7. The quartan fever takes its name from the four-day cycle of shivering fits that accompanies it.

100   Just like a boat that, starting from its moorings,
        moves backward, backward, so that beast took off;
        and when he felt himself completely clear,

        he turned his tail to where his chest had been
        and, having stretched it, moved it like an eel,
105   and with his paws he gathered in the air.

        I do not think that there was greater fear
        in Phaëthon when he let his reins go free—
        for which the sky, as one still sees, was scorched—

        nor in poor Icarus when he could feel
110   his sides unwinged because the wax was melting,
        his father shouting to him, "That way's wrong!"[8]

        than was in me when, on all sides, I saw
        that I was in the air, and everything
        had faded from my sight—except the beast.

115   Slowly, slowly, swimming, he moves on;
        he wheels and he descends, but I feel only
        the wind upon my face and the wind rising.

        Already, on our right, I heard the torrent
        resounding, there beneath us, horribly,
120   so that I stretched my neck and looked below.

        Then I was more afraid of falling off,
        for I saw fires and I heard laments,
        at which I tremble, crouching, and hold fast.

        And now I saw what I had missed before:
125   his wheeling and descent—because great torments
        were drawing closer to us on all sides.

        Just as a falcon long upon the wing—
        who, seeing neither lure nor bird, compels
        the falconer to cry, "Ah me, you fall!"—

130   descends, exhausted, in a hundred circles,
        where he had once been swift, and sets himself,
        embittered and enraged, far from his master;[9]

        such, at the bottom of the jagged rock,
        was Geryon, when he had set us down.
135   And once our weight was lifted from his back,
        he vanished like an arrow from a bow.

Canto 18

The Eighth Circle, called Malebolge ("Evil-Pouches"), with its Ten Pouches, where "ordinary" fraud is punished. The First Pouch, with Panders and Seducers scourged

---

8. Phaëthon was son of Apollo and a mortal woman. Phaëthon persuaded his father to allow him to drive the chariot of the sun for a day, but he couldn't control the horses, and they ran so near to the earth that Jupiter killed Phaëthon with a thunderbolt to save the earth from burning (Ovid, *Metamorphoses* 2.1–138). In another myth, Icarus escaped with his father Daedalus from Crete with wings the inventor had fashioned together with wax.

Ignoring his father's warning, Icarus flew too close to the sun, the wax melted, and he plummeted to his death in the sea (*Metamorphoses* 8.203–35; see Volume A).
9. Trained not to descend until either it sights its prey or is called back by its master whirling a lure, the falcon will remain aloft until compelled by exhaustion to come down.

by horned demons. Venèdico Caccianemico. Jason. The Second Pouch, with Flatterers immersed in excrement. Alessio Interminei. Thais.

There is a place in Hell called Malebolge,
made all of stone the color of crude iron,
as is the wall that makes its way around it.
    Right in the middle of this evil field

5   is an abyss, a broad and yawning pit,
whose structure I shall tell in its due place.
    The belt, then, that extends between the pit
and that hard, steep wall's base is circular;
its bottom has been split into ten valleys.

10   Just as, where moat on moat surrounds a castle
in order to keep guard upon the walls,
the ground they occupy will form a pattern,
    so did the valleys here form a design;
and as such fortresses have bridges running

15 right from their thresholds toward the outer bank,
    so here, across the banks and ditches, ridges
ran from the base of that rock wall until
the pit that cuts them short and joins them all.
    This was the place in which we found ourselves

20 when Geryon had put us down; the poet
held to the left, and I walked at his back.
    Upon the right I saw new misery,
I saw new tortures and new torturers,
filling the first of Malebolge's moats.

25   Along its bottom, naked sinners moved,
to our side of the middle, facing us;
beyond that, they moved with us, but more quickly—
    as, in the year of Jubilee, the Romans,
confronted by great crowds, contrived a plan

30 that let the people pass across the bridge,
    for to one side went all who had their eyes
upon the Castle, heading toward St. Peter's,
and to the other, those who faced the Mount.[1]
    Both left and right, along the somber rock,

35 I saw horned demons with enormous whips,
who lashed those spirits cruelly from behind.[2]
    Ah, how their first strokes made those sinners lift
their heels! Indeed no sinner waited for
a second stroke to fall—or for a third.

40   And as I moved ahead, my eyes met those
of someone else, and suddenly I said:

1. A rarity in medieval times: separate lanes for traffic in each direction. The first Jubilee or Holy Year was proclaimed by Pope Boniface VIII in 1300, granting indulgence (reduction of penance) for all those who visited the basilicas of St. Peter's and San Paolo fuori le Mura; hundreds of thousands of pilgrims came.

2. The reader finally encounters the horned demons familiar from medieval iconography and earlier otherworld visions; in Dante's scheme, they are specific to the realm of fraud.

"I was not spared the sight of him before."
    And so I stayed my steps, to study him;
my gentle guide had stopped together with me
45 and gave me leave to take a few steps back.
    That scourged soul thought that he could hide himself
by lowering his face;[3] it helped him little,
for I said: "You, who cast your eyes upon
    the ground, if these your features are not false,
50 must be Venèdico Caccianemico;[4]
but what brings you to sauces so piquant?"
    And he to me: "I speak unwillingly;
but your plain speech, that brings the memory
of the old world to me, is what compels me;
55   For it was I who led Ghisolabella
to do as the Marquis would have her do—
however they retell that filthy tale.
    I'm not the only Bolognese who weeps here;
indeed, this place is so crammed full of us
60 that not so many tongues have learned to say
    sipa between the Sàvena and Reno;[5]
if you want faith and testament of that,
just call to mind our avaricious hearts."
    And as he spoke, a demon cudgeled him
65 with his horsewhip and cried: "Be off, you pimp,
there are no women here for you to trick."
    I joined my escort once again; and then
with but few steps, we came upon a place
where, from the bank, a rocky ridge ran out.
70   We climbed quite easily along that height;
and turning right upon its jagged back,
we took our leave of those eternal circlings.
    When we had reached the point where that ridge opens
below to leave a passage for the lashed,
75 my guide said: "Stay, and make sure that the sight
    of still more ill-born spirits strikes your eyes,
for you have not yet seen their faces, since
they have been moving in our own direction."
    From the old bridge we looked down at the ranks
80 of those approaching from the other side;
they too were driven onward by the lash.
    And my good master, though I had not asked,
urged me: "Look at that mighty one who comes
and does not seem to shed a tear of pain:
85   how he still keeps the image of a king!

---

3. A change in behavior: the souls this deep in Hell prefer anonymity rather than the fame and salvaged reputation of those higher up.
4. Son of the head of the Guelf party of Bologna. He is said to have been bribed by his ally Obizzo II to gain him entry to his sister Ghisolabella's bedchamber.
5. *Sipa* is the word for "yes" in the old dialect spoken between the Sàvena and Reno streams that form the western and eastern bounds of the territory of Bologna. Dante singles out Bologna for its panders, or pimps.

That shade is Jason, who with heart and head
deprived the men of Colchis of their ram.[6]
He made a landfall on the isle of Lemnos
after its women, bold and pitiless,
90   had given all their island males to death.
With polished words and love signs he took in
Hypsipyle, the girl whose own deception
had earlier deceived the other women.[7]
And he abandoned her, alone and pregnant;
95   such guilt condemns him to such punishment;
and for Medea, too, revenge is taken.
With him go those who cheated so: this is
enough for you to know of that first valley
and of the souls it clamps within its jaws."
100   We were already where the narrow path
reaches and intersects the second bank
and serves as shoulder for another bridge.
We heard the people whine in the next pouch
and heard them as they snorted with their snouts;
105   we heard them use their palms to beat themselves.
And exhalations, rising from below,
stuck to the banks, encrusting them with mold,
and so waged war against both eyes and nose.
The bottom is so deep, we found no spot
110   to see it from, except by climbing up
the arch until the bridge's highest point.
This was the place we reached; the ditch beneath
held people plunged in excrement that seemed
as if it had been poured from human privies.°   *toilets*
115   And while my eyes searched that abysmal sight,
I saw one with a head so smeared with shit,
one could not see if he were lay or cleric.[8]
He howled: "Why do you stare more greedily
at me than at the others who are filthy?"
120   And I: "Because, if I remember right,
I have seen you before, with your hair dry;
and so I eye you more than all: you are
Alessio Interminei of Lucca."[9]
Then he continued, pounding on his pate:
125   "I am plunged here because of flatteries—
of which my tongue had such sufficiency."

6. Jason was leader of the Argonauts on the expedition to Colchis to obtain the golden fleece. Along the way, they landed at Lemnos, where Jason seduced and then abandoned Hypsipyle, daughter of the king, leaving her with twin sons. After Medea, daughter of the king of the Colchians, had helped him to secure the fleece, Jason took her with him as his wife, but later left her for Creusa, daughter of Creon, king of Corinth. In revenge, she killed the two children she had borne him (Ovid,

Metamorphoses 7.1–397).
7. When the women of Lemnos had killed all the other men on the island, Hypsipyle had managed secretly to save her father's life (Statius, *Thebaid* 5.403–85).
8. That is, he couldn't tell if the head was tonsured. Like their hypocrisy (see the sixth pouch), the flattery of clerics was proverbial.
9. Member of a prominent Guelf family of the Tuscan town of Lucca.

At which my guide advised me: "See you thrust
your head a little farther to the front,
so that your eyes can clearly glimpse the face
130   of that besmirched, bedraggled harridan°   *shrew*
who scratches at herself with shit-filled nails,
and now she crouches, now she stands upright.
    That is Thaïs, the harlot who returned
her lover's question, 'Are you very grateful
135   to me?' by saying, 'Yes, enormously.'"[1]
    And now our sight has had its fill of this."

Canto 19

*The Eighth Circle, Third Pouch, where the Simonists are set, heads down, into holes
in the rock, with their protruding feet tormented by flames. Pope Nicholas III.
Dante's invective against simoniacal popes.*

    O Simon Magus! O his sad disciples!
Rapacious ones, who take the things of God,
that ought to be the brides of Righteousness,
    and make them fornicate for gold and silver!
5   The time has come to let the trumpet sound
for you; your place is here in this third pouch.[1]
    We had already reached the tomb beyond
and climbed onto the ridge, where its high point
hangs just above the middle of the ditch.
10   O Highest Wisdom, how much art you show
in heaven, earth, and this sad world below,
how just your power is when it allots![2]
    Along the sides and down along the bottom,
I saw that livid rock was perforated:
15   the openings were all one width and round.
    They did not seem to me less broad or more
than those that in my handsome San Giovanni
were made to serve as basins for baptizing;
    and one of these, not many years ago,
20   I broke for someone who was drowning in it:
and let this be my seal to set men straight.[3]

---

1. Thaïs is a courtesan in *Eunuchus,* a play by the ancient Roman playwright Terence. In fact, the flatterer in the scene referred to is the go-between, a soldier named Gnatho.

1. In the Bible, Simon Magus was a converted sorcerer who attempted to buy the power of conferring the Holy Ghost. He was rebuked by the apostle Peter for presuming that the gift of God might be purchased (Acts 8:9–24). From his name is derived the word "simony," which refers to the buying or selling of spiritual goods and offices. The metaphor of lines 3–4 relates this pouch with the previous one by depicting simonists as pimps of the Church, the Bride of Christ. Town criers would sound a trumpet to announce the public reading of judicial sentences; the word also alludes to the sounding of the angel's trumpet on Judgment Day.

2. The apostrophe to the Lord praises the "art" which he has devoted to the design of hell as much as to that of heaven and earth.

3. Like most Florentine children of the time, Dante was baptized in the famous Baptistery of Florence, San Giovanni. It is possible Dante mentioned his motive in breaking the font to defend himself against accusations of sacrilege; it is certainly noteworthy that he placed it in a canto devoted to the misuse of sacred vessels and offices.

Out from the mouth of each hole there emerged
a sinner's feet and so much of his legs
up to the thigh; the rest remained within.

25   Both soles of every sinner were on fire;
their joints were writhing with such violence,
they would have severed withes° and ropes of grass.   *thin branches*

As flame on oily things will only stir
along the outer surface, so there, too,
30   that fire made its way from heels to toes.

"Master," I said, "who is that shade who suffers
and quivers more than all his other comrades,
that sinner who is licked by redder flames?"

And he to me: "If you would have me lead
35   you down along the steepest of the banks,
from him you'll learn about his self and sins."

And I: "What pleases you will please me too:
you are my lord; you know I do not swerve
from what you will; you know what is unspoken."

40   At this we came upon the fourth embankment;
we turned and, keeping to the left, descended
into the narrow, perforated bottom.

My good lord did not let me leave his side
until he'd brought me to the hole that held
45   that sinner who lamented with his legs.

"Whoever you may be, dejected soul,
whose head is downward, planted like a pole,"
my words began, "do speak if you are able."

I stood as does the friar who confesses
50   the foul assassin who, fixed fast, head down,
calls back the friar, and so delays his death;[4]

and he cried out: "Are you already standing,
already standing there, o Boniface?
The book has lied to me by several years.

55   Are you so quickly sated with the riches
for which you did not fear to take by guile
the Lovely Lady, then to violate her?"[5]

And I became like those who stand as if
they have been mocked, who cannot understand
60   what has been said to them and can't respond.

But Virgil said: "Tell this to him at once:
'I am not he—not whom you think I am.'"
And I replied as I was told to do.

---

4. In the punishment known as "the planting of grapevines," assassins were stuck head downward in a hole that was then filled with dirt, choking them to death.
5. The speaker, Pope Nicholas III, believes he is addressing Boniface VIII, who he knows will die in Rome in 1303, three years after the date of the present encounter, enabling Dante to place a soul in its "proper" place by anticipation. Boniface was surrounded by many accusations of nepotism and simony; as for the charge that he took "by guile the Lovely Lady," that he was elected pope by fraud: he was said to have offered his services to Charles of Anjou in his war in Sicily in return for support of his candidacy.

65   At this the spirit twisted both his feet,
and sighing and with a despairing voice,
he said: "What is it, then, you want of me?
If you have crossed the bank and climbed so far
to find out who I am, then know that I
was one of those who wore the mighty mantle,

70   and surely was a son of the she-bear,
so eager to advance the cubs that I
pursed wealth above while here I purse myself.[6]
Below my head there is the place of those
who took the way of simony before me;

75   and they are stuffed within the clefts of stone.
I, too, shall yield my place and fall below
when he arrives, the one for whom I had
mistaken you when I was quick to question.
But I have baked my feet a longer time,

80   have stood like this, upon my head, than he
is to stand planted here with scarlet feet:
for after him, one uglier in deeds
will come, a lawless shepherd from the west,
worthy to cover him and cover me.[7]

85   He'll be a second Jason, of whom we read
in *Maccabees;* and just as Jason's king
was soft to him, so shall the king of France
be soft to this one."[8] And I do not know
if I was too rash here—I answered so:

90   "Then tell me now, how much gold did our Lord
ask that Saint Peter give to him before
he placed the keys within his care? Surely
the only thing he said was: 'Follow me.'[9]
And Peter and the others never asked

95   for gold or silver when they chose Matthias
to take the place of the transgressing soul.[1]
Stay as you are, for you are rightly punished;
and guard with care the money got by evil

6. The Roman family of Giovanni Orsini, Pope Nicholas III, were commonly referred to as *filii orsae,* cubs of the she-bear, known as a rapacious beast especially fierce in protecting her young. Giovanni was elected pope ("the mighty mantle") in 1277 and died three years later, but his brief tenure was marked by nepotism and intrigue. Line 72 neatly expresses the *contrapasso:* the font in which he is placed is his purse in which he keeps the rewards he sought above.

7. Nicholas has to wait 23 years for Boniface to take the topmost place in the hole, but Boniface will need wait less than 11 for the next simonist pope to replace him: Clement V, who died in 1314 near Avignon. Born in Gascony ("from the west") and elected pope in 1304, Clement saw the Papal See removed from Rome to Avignon in southern France, where it remained for nearly 70 years in what is referred to as the "Babylonian Captivity."

8. While still Archbishop of Bordeaux, Clement had negotiated his election as pope with the powerful King Philip the Fair of France, just as Jason had first been appointed High Priest of the Jews by bribing King Antiochus of Syria, endeavoring afterward to reintroduce Greek customs and pagan worship in place of the Jewish religion (2 Maccabees 4:13–16).

9. The apostle Peter was considered to have been the first pope: "And I say to thee, thou art Peter, and upon this rock I will build my Church. . . . And I will give thee the keys of the kingdom of heaven." (Matthew 16:18–19). "Follow me" were the words with which Jesus first called the brothers Simon (Peter) and Andrew to be his disciples (Matthew 4:18–19).

1. After Judas Iscariot had betrayed Jesus, Matthias was chosen by lot to fill his vacant place among the 12 apostles.

that made you so audacious against Charles.[2]

100   And were it not that I am still prevented
by reverence for those exalted keys
that you had held within the happy life,

I'd utter words much heavier than these,
because your avarice afflicts the world:
105   it tramples on the good, lifts up the wicked.

You, shepherds, the Evangelist had noticed
when he saw her who sits upon the waters
and realized she fornicates with kings,

she who was born with seven heads and had
110   the power and support of the ten horns,
as long as virtue was her husband's pleasure.[3]

You've made yourselves a god of gold and silver;
how are you different from idolaters,
save that they worship one and you a hundred?

115   Ah, Constantine, what wickedness was born—
and not from your conversion—from the dower
that you bestowed upon the first rich father!"[4]

And while I sang such notes to him—whether
it was his indignation or his conscience
120   that bit him—he kicked hard with both his soles.

I do indeed believe it pleased my guide:
he listened always with such satisfied
expression to the sound of those true words.

And then he gathered me in both his arms
125   and, when he had me fast against his chest,
where he climbed down before, climbed upward now;

nor did he tire of clasping me until
he brought me to the summit of the arch
that crosses from the fourth to the fifth rampart.

130   And here he gently set his burden down—
gently because the ridge was rough and steep,
and would have been a rugged pass for goats.

From there another valley lay before me.

Canto 20

The Eighth Circle, Fourth Pouch, where Diviners, Astrologers, Magicians, all have their heads turned backward. Amphiaraus. Tiresias. Aruns. Manto. Virgil on the

2. It was commonly believed that Nicholas had intrigued against Charles of Anjou when Charles had refused to marry Nicholas's niece.
3. In the Book of Revelation, attributed to the Evangelist, St. John, the whore "who sits upon the waters" (17:1–3) was most likely pagan Rome, while Dante interprets her as the Church corrupted by secular interests. The seven heads symbolize the seven sacraments; the ten horns the Ten Commandments.
4. Due to a skillful forgery known as "The Donation of

Constantine," probably composed in the papal court during the 8th century, it was believed that the Emperor Constantine had given to the Church his temporal power in the west when he moved the imperial capital eastward to Constantinople in the 5th century. For Dante, this fraud marked the beginning of the ecclesiastical corruption denounced in this canto. "The first rich father" is Pope Sylvester I, to whom the Donation was said to have been made in exchange for curing Constantine of leprosy.

origin of Mantua, his native city. Eurypylus. Michael Scot and other moderns adept at fraud.

I must make verses of new punishment
and offer matter now for Canto Twenty
of this first canticle—of the submerged.
    I was already well prepared to stare

5   below, into the depth that was disclosed,
where tears of anguished sorrow bathed the ground;
    and in the valley's circle I saw souls
advancing, mute and weeping, at the pace
that, in our world, holy processions take.

10   As I inclined my head still more, I saw
that each, amazingly, appeared contorted
between the chin and where the chest begins;
    they had their faces twisted toward their haunches
and found it necessary to walk backward,

15   because they could not see ahead of them.[1]
    Perhaps the force of palsy[2] has so fully
distorted some, but that I've yet to see,
and I do not believe that that can be.
    May God so let you, reader, gather fruit

20   from what you read; and now think for yourself
how I could ever keep my own face dry
    when I beheld our image so nearby
and so awry that tears, down from the eyes,
bathed the buttocks, running down the cleft.

25   Of course I wept, leaning against a rock
along that rugged ridge, so that my guide
told me: "Are you as foolish as the rest?
    Here pity only lives when it is dead:
for who can be more impious than he

30   who links God's judgment to passivity?
    Lift, lift your head and see the one for whom
the earth was opened while the Thebans watched,
so that they all cried: 'Amphiaraus,
    where are you rushing? Have you quit the fight?'

35   Nor did he interrupt his downward plunge
to Minos, who lays hands on every sinner.[3]
    See how he's made a chest out of his shoulders;
and since he wanted so to see ahead,
he looks behind and walks a backward path.

40   And see Tiresias, who changed his mien

1. In this *bolgia*, diviners and soothsayers are punished for their attempt to see the future by being condemned to see only backward.
2. A condition marked by the paralysis or uncontrollable tremor of a body or a body part.
3. Amphiaraus was a great prophet and hero of Argos and another of the Seven against Thebes consigned to Hell. Foreseeing that he would die there, he had attempted to hide, but his hiding-place was revealed by his wife after she was bribed with a necklace. He and his chariot were swallowed up by the earth as he was fleeing his pursuers at Thebes.

when from a man he turned into a woman,
so totally transforming all his limbs
   that then he had to strike once more upon
the two entwining serpents with his wand

45   before he had his manly plumes again.[4]
   And Aruns is the one who backs against
the belly of Tiresias—Aruns who,
in Luni's hills, tilled by the Carrarese,
   who live below, had as his home, a cave

50   among white marbles, from which he could gaze
at stars and sea with unimpeded view.[5]
   And she who covers up her breasts—which you
can't see—with her disheveled locks, who keeps
all of her hairy parts to the far side,

55   was Manto,[6] who had searched through many lands,
then settled in the place where I was born;
on this, I'd have you hear me now a while.
   When Manto's father took his leave of life,
and Bacchus' city found itself enslaved,[7]

60   she wandered through the world for many years.
   High up, in lovely Italy, beneath
the Alps that shut in Germany above
Tirolo, lies a lake known as Benaco.[8]
   A thousand springs and more, I think, must flow

65   out of the waters of that lake to bathe
Pennino, Garda, Val Camonica.
   And at its middle is a place where three—
the bishops of Verona, Brescia, Trento[9]—
may bless if they should chance to come that way.

70   Peschiera, strong and handsome fortress, built
to face the Brescians and the Bergamasques
stands where the circling shore is at its lowest.[1]
   There, all the waters that cannot be held
within the bosom of Benaco fall,

75   to form a river running through green meadows.
   No sooner has that stream begun to flow
than it is called the Mincio, not Benaco—

4. The famed soothsayer of Thebes, Tiresias, had been changed into a woman when he separated with his staff two coupling serpents. Seven years later, he found the same serpents, struck them, and was changed back to a man. Called upon to mediate a dispute between Jupiter and Juno, he declared that women experience greater pleasure in lovemaking. Jupiter in anger struck him blind; Juno gave him the gift of prophecy in compensation (Ovid, *Metamorphoses* 3.322–31; see Volume A).
5. Aruns was an Etruscan seer who according to Lucan foretold the civil war that ended in Caesar's triumph and Pompey's death (*Pharsalia* 1.585–638). "Luni's hills" are near Carrara in northern Tuscany, famous for its white marble.

6. A prophetess of Thebes, daughter of Tiresias who, by some accounts, settled in Italy where the town of Mantua, Virgil's birthplace, was named after her.
7. Thebes was consecrated to the god Bacchus and tradition made it his birthplace. After the war of the Seven against Thebes, the city came under the tyranny of Creon.
8. To recount the situation of Manua, Virgil begins with a long account of the waters that flow from Lake Garda down into the river Po.
9. That is, an island where the boundaries and jurisdictions of these three dioceses meet.
1. Peschiera was a town and fortress at the southeast shore of the lake, about 20 miles southeast of Brescia and 50 miles from Bergamo.

until Govèrnolo, where it joins the Po.

    It's not flowed far before it finds flat land;

80   and there it stretches out to form a fen

that in the summer can at times be fetid.

    And when she passed that way, the savage virgin

saw land along the middle of the swamp,

untilled and stripped of its inhabitants.

85   And there, to flee all human intercourse,

she halted with her slaves to ply her arts;

and there she lived, there left her empty body.

    And afterward, the people of those parts

collected at that place, because the marsh—

90   surrounding it on all sides—made it strong.

    They built a city over her dead bones;

and after her who first had picked that spot,

they called it Mantua—they cast no lots.[2]

    There once were far more people in its walls,

95   before the foolishness of Casalodi

was tricked by the deceit of Pinamonte.[3]

    Therefore, I charge you, if you ever hear

a different tale of my town's origin,

do not let any falsehood gull° the truth."[4]   *dupe*

100   And I: "O master, that which you have spoken

convinces me and so compels my trust

that others' words would only be spent coals.

    But tell me if among the passing souls

you see some spirits worthy of our notice,

105   because my mind is bent on that alone."

    Then he to me: "That shade who spreads his beard

down from his cheeks across his swarthy shoulders—

when Greece had been so emptied of its males

that hardly any cradle held a son,

110   he was an augur; and at Aulis, he

and Calchas set the time to cut the cables.

    His name's Eurypylus; a certain passage

of my high tragedy has sung it so;

you know that well enough, who know the whole.[5]

115   That other there, his flanks extremely spare,

was Michael Scot,[6] a man who certainly

---

2. An ancient custom was to choose the name of a town by casting lots.

3. The Brescian counts of Casalodi took control of Mantua in 1272. Pinamonte, a native Mantuan, treacherously advised Alberto to appease the populace by expelling many nobles from the city, including his own supporters. With Alberto defenseless, Pinamonte was able to seize power himself.

4. According to the *Aeneid* (10.198–200), Mantua was founded by her son, Ocnus.

5. On the advice of the prophet Calchas, the Greeks sacrificed Agamemnon's daughter Iphigenia to appease the goddess Diana. When they were preparing to return home from Troy, Eurypylus was sent to consult the oracle of Apollo, which advised that their return must also be purchased in blood. *Aeneid* (2.114–24, "my high tragedy") mentions both incidents, but attributes only the second of them to Eurypylus.

6. A famous scientist, philosopher, astrologer, and necromancer from Scotland who served for many years at the court of Frederick II at Palermo in Sicily.

knew how the game of magic fraud was played.

   See there Guido Bonatti; see Asdente,
who now would wish he had attended to
120   his cord and leather, but repents too late.[7]

   See those sad women who had left their needle,
shuttle, and spindle to become diviners;
they cast their spells with herbs and effigies.

   But let us go; Cain with his thorns already
125   is at the border of both hemispheres
and there, below Seville, touches the sea.[8]

   Last night the moon was at its full; you should
be well aware of this, for there were times
when it did you no harm in the deep wood."

130   These were his words to me; meanwhile we journeyed.

Canto 21

The Eighth Circle, Fifth Pouch, with Barrators plunged into boiling pitch and guarded by demons armed with prongs. A newly arrived magistrate from Lucca. Ten demons assigned by Malacoda ("Evil-Tail"), the chief of the Malebranche ("Evil-Claws"), to escort Dante and Virgil. The remarkable signal for their march.

   We came along from one bridge to another,
talking of things my Comedy is not
concerned to sing. We held fast to the summit,
   then stayed our steps to spy the other cleft
5   of Malebolge and other vain laments.
I saw that it was wonderfully dark.[1]

   As in the arsenal of the Venetians,[2]
all winter long a stew of sticky pitch
boils up to patch their sick and tattered ships
10   that cannot sail (instead of voyaging,
some build new keels, some tow and tar the ribs
of hulls worn out by too much journeying;
   some hammer at the prow, some at the stern,
and some make oars, and some braid ropes and cords;
15   one mends the jib, another, the mainsail);
   so, not by fire but by the art of God,
below there boiled a thick and tarry mass
that covered all the banks with clamminess.
   I saw it, but I could not see within it;
20   no thing was visible but boiling bubbles,
the swelling of the pitch; and then it settled.

---

7. Guido Bonatti of Forlí served as astrologer at the court of Guido da Montefeltro (see Canto 27); Asdente ("toothless") was a 13th-century shoemaker of Parma famed as a prophet and soothsayer.
8. Custom held that God had placed Cain in the moon following his murder of Abel; "thorns" refers to the moon spots. For the ideal observer in Jerusalem, the moon is setting in the west ("below Seville"); the time is 6 A.M.
1. Even darker than the other, unlit pouches, because black with boiling pitch.
2. One of the most important shipyards in Europe, and the reason for the Venetian Republic's enduring power at sea.

And while I watched below attentively,
my guide called out to me: "Take care! Take care!"[3]
And then, from where I stood, he drew me near.

25   I turned around as one who is impatient
to see what he should shun but is dashed down
beneath the terror he has undergone,

who does not stop his flight and yet would look.
And then in back of us I saw a black
30   demon as he came racing up the crags.

Ah, he was surely barbarous to see!
And how relentless seemed to me his acts!
His wings were open and his feet were lithe;

across his shoulder, which was sharp and high,
35   he had slung a sinner, upward from the thighs;
in front, the demon gripped him by the ankles.

Then from our bridge, he called: "O Malebranche,
I've got an elder of Saint Zita for you!
Shove this one under—I'll go back for more—

40   his city is well furnished with such stores;
there, everyone's a grafter but Bonturo;
and there—for cash—they'll change a *no* to *yes*."[4]

He threw the sinner down, then wheeled along
the stony cliff: no mastiff's ever been
45   unleashed with so much haste to chase a thief.

The sinner plunged, then surfaced, black with pitch;
but now the demons, from beneath the bridge,
shouted: "The Sacred Face has no place here;[5]

here we swim differently than in the Serchio;[6]
50   if you don't want to feel our grappling hooks,
don't try to lift yourself above that ditch."

They pricked him with a hundred prongs and more,
then taunted: "Here one dances under cover,
so try to grab your secret graft below."

55   The demons did the same as any cook
who has his urchins force the meat with hooks
deep down into the pot, that it not float.

Then my good master said to me: "Don't let
those demons see that you are here; take care
60   to crouch behind the cover of a crag.

No matter what offense they offer me,
don't be afraid; I know how these things go—

---

3. One motivation for the guide's urgency may be that barratry (the buying and selling of public office, the secular equivalent of simony) would be the charge made against Dante when he was sentenced to exile in 1302.
4. St. Zita (1218–c. 1278) was the patron saint of Lucca; the elders were ten citizens holding executive power along with the chief magistrate. Bonturo Dati was the most accomplished barator in a city evidently notorious for the practice. The demon's sarcastic humor is characteristic of their portrayal in the *Inferno*.
5. The Sacred Face of Lucca was a venerated ancient Byzantine crucifix carved in dark wood. The demon's vulgar pleasantry compares it to the pitch-covered rear end of the naked shade.
6. A Tuscan river near Lucca.

I've had to face such fracases before."[7]
 When this was said, he moved beyond the bridgehead.

65 And on the sixth embankment, he had need
to show his imperturbability.

 With the same frenzy, with the brouhaha
of dogs, when they beset a poor wretch who
then stops dead in his tracks as if to beg,

70 so, from beneath the bridge, the demons rushed
against my guide with all their prongs, but he
called out: "Can't you forget your savagery!

 Before you try to maul me, just let one
of all your troop step forward. Hear me out,

75 and then decide if I am to be hooked."

 At this they howled, "Let Malacoda go!"
And one of them moved up—the others stayed—
and as he came, he asked: "How can he win?"

 "O Malacoda, do you think I've come,"

80 my master answered him, "already armed—
as you can see—against your obstacles,

 without the will of God[8] and helpful fate?
Let us move on; it is the will of Heaven
for me to show this wild way to another."

85 At this the pride of Malacoda fell;
his prong dropped to his feet. He told his fellows:
"Since that's the way things stand, let us not wound him."

 My guide then spoke to me: "O you, who crouch,
bent low among the bridge's splintered rocks,

90 you can feel safe—and now return to me."

 At this I moved and quickly came to him.
The devils had edged forward, all of them;
I feared that they might fail to keep their word:

 just so, I saw the infantry when they

95 marched out, under safe conduct, from Caprona;[9]
they trembled when they passed their enemies.

 My body huddled closer to my guide;
I did not let the demons out of sight;
the looks they cast at us were less than kind.

100 They bent their hooks and shouted to each other:
"And shall I give it to him on the rump?"
And all of them replied, "Yes, let him have it!"

 But Malacoda, still in conversation
with my good guide, turned quickly to his squadron

105 and said: "Be still, Scarmiglione, still!"

---

7. Probably referring to the episode with the rebel angels;
the pattern in fact is that the demons generally *do* give
Virgil more trouble than the classical monsters.
8. Literally, "without divine will"; like Christ, the Lord is
never named directly in Hell.
9. A castle in the territory of Pisa, on a hill near the river

Arno. Following the death of Ugolino, leader of the Pisan
Guelfs (see 33.4–75), his party was expelled from the
city, and the castle was taken in 1289 by the Tuscan
Guelfs, led by the Lucchese and Florentines, probably including Dante himself.

To us he said: "There is no use in going
much farther on this ridge, because the sixth
bridge—at the bottom there—is smashed to bits.
Yet if you two still want to go ahead,
110   move up and walk along this rocky edge;
nearby, another ridge will form a path.[1]
Five hours from this hour yesterday,
one thousand and two hundred sixty-six
years passed since that roadway was shattered here.[2]
115   I'm sending ten of mine out there to see
if any sinner lifts his head for air;
go with my men—there is no malice in them."
"Step forward, Alichino and Calcabrina,"
he then began to say, "and you, Cagnazzo;
120   and Barbariccia, who can lead the ten.
Let Libicocco go, and Draghignazzo
and tusky Ciriatto and Graffiacane
and Farfarello and mad Rubicante.[3]
Search all around the clammy stew of pitch;
125   keep these two safe and sound till the next ridge
that rises without break across the dens."
"Ah me! What is this, master, that I see?"
I said. "Can't we do without company?
If you know how to go, I want no escort.
130   If you are just as keen as usual,
can't you see how those demons grind their teeth?
Their brows are menacing, they promise trouble."
And he to me: "I do not want you frightened:
just let them gnash away as they may wish;
135   they do it for the wretches boiled in pitch."
They turned around along the left hand bank:
but first each pressed his tongue between his teeth
as signal for their leader, Barbariccia.
And he had made a trumpet of his ass.

Canto 22

Still the Eighth Circle, Fifth Pouch: the Barrators. The Barrator from Navarre. Fra Gomita and Michele Zanche, two Sardinians. The astuteness of the Navarrese that leads two demons to fall into the pitch.

1. As it turns out, Malacoda is truthful about the nearer bridge, but deliberately deceitful about the farther.
2. The internal dating of the poem hinges on this information. The bridges of Hell crumbled at the moment of Christ's death on the cross. In Dante's reckoning, Christ died at the age of 34, counted from the day of the Incarnation. Matthew gave the time of death as the sixth hour, or noon; Malacoda refers to a moment five hours earlier and one day following this event, that is, 7 A.M. on Holy Saturday, which fell on April 9 in the year 1300. Through other internal signals in the poem,

this places the night in the dark wood on Thursday, April 7, the encounter with the three beasts and Virgil during the next day, and the entry through the Gate of Hell at sunset of Good Friday. It is now just past daybreak in the world above; they have consumed the night in their descent thus far.
3. Some of the devils' names have been coined by Dante: Malacoda ("evil-tail"), Malebranche ("evil-claws"), Cagnazzo ("big dog"). Several were also family names in Lucca.

Before this I've seen horsemen start to march
and open the assault and muster ranks[1]
and seen them, too, at times beat their retreat;
and on your land, o Aretines, I've seen

5   rangers and raiding parties galloping,
the clash of tournaments, the rush of jousts,
now done with trumpets, now with bells, and now
with drums, and now with signs from castle walls,
with native things and with imported ware;[2]

10   but never yet have I seen horsemen or
seen infantry or ship that sails by signal
of land or star move to so strange a bugle!
We made our way together with ten demons:
ah, what ferocious company! And yet

15   "in church with saints, with rotters in the tavern."[3]
But I was all intent upon the pitch,
to seek out every feature of the pouch
and of the people who were burning in it.
Just as the dolphins do, when with arched back,

20   they signal to the seamen to prepare
for tempest, that their vessel may be spared,[4]
so here from time to time, to ease his torment,
some sinner showed his back above the surface,
then hid more quickly than a lightning flash.

25   And just as on the margin of a ditch,
frogs crouch, their snouts alone above the water,
so as to hide their feet and their plump flesh,
so here on every side these sinners crouched;
but faster than a flash, when Barbariccia

30   drew near, they plunged beneath the boiling pitch.
I saw—my heart still shudders in recall—
one who delayed, just as at times a frog
is left behind while others dive below;
and Graffiacane, who was closest to him,

35   then hooked him by his pitch entangled locks
and hauled him up; he seemed to me an otter.
By now I knew the names of all those demons—
I'd paid attention when the fiends were chosen;
I'd watched as they stepped forward one by one.

40   "O Rubicante, see you set your talons
right into him, so you can flay° his flesh!"   *tear off*
So did those cursed ones cry out together.

---

1. The tone of the several cantos of the adventure with the
devils of the fifth *bolgia* is closer to the popular style of
the Italian *novella*, or short tale, than it is to the high,
tragic style of many of the preceding cantos.
2. The Aretines are the people of the Tuscan commune
of Arezzo. Dante is likely to have seen their cavalry in
1289 when the Florentine Guelfs defeated the Aretine

Ghibellines at the Battle of Campaldino, and also later at
Caprona.
3. A popular proverb that also suggests a reason for the
shift in literary style.
4. It was believed that dolphins on the surface of the sea
near a ship were the sign of an imminent storm.

And I: "My master, if you can, find out
what is the name of that unfortunate
who's fallen victim to his enemies."

My guide, who then drew near that sinner's side,
asked him to tell his birthplace. He replied:
"My homeland was the kingdom of Navarre.

My mother, who had had me by a wastrel,
destroyer of himself and his possessions,
had placed me in the service of a lord.

Then I was in the household of the worthy
King Thibault;[5] there I started taking graft;
with this heat I pay reckoning for that."

And Ciriatto, from whose mouth there bulged
to right and left two tusks like a wild hog's,
then let him feel how one of them could mangle.

The mouse had fallen in with evil cats;
but Barbariccia clasped him in his arms
and said: "Stand off there, while I fork him fast."

And turning toward my master then, he said:
"Ask on, if you would learn some more from him
before one of the others does him in."

At which my guide: "Now tell: among the sinners
who hide beneath the pitch, are any others
Italian?" And he: "I have just left

one who was nearby there; and would I were
still covered by the pitch as he is hidden,
for then I'd have no fear of hook or talon."

And Libicocco said, "We've been too patient!"
and, with his grapple, grabbed him by the arm
and, ripping, carried off a hunk of flesh.

But Draghignazzo also looked as if
to grab his legs; at which, their captain wheeled
and threatened all of them with raging looks.

When they'd grown somewhat less tumultuous,
without delay my guide asked of that one
who had his eyes still fixed upon his wound:

"Who was the one you left to come ashore—
unluckily—as you just said before?"
He answered: "Fra Gomita of Gallura,

who was a vessel fit for every fraud;
he had his master's enemies in hand,
but handled them in ways that pleased them all.

He took their gold and smoothly let them off,
as he himself says; and in other matters,
he was a sovereign, not a petty, swindler.

His comrade there is Don Michele Zanche

45
50
55
60
65
70
75
80
85

---

5. King of Navarre in northern Spain and southwestern France.

of Logodoro; and their tongues are never
90 too tired to talk of their Sardinia.[6]
    Ah me, see that one there who grinds his teeth!
If I were not afraid, I'd speak some more,
but he is getting set to scratch my scurf."
    And their great marshal, facing Farfarello—
95 who was so hot to strike he rolled his eyes,
said: "Get away from there, you filthy bird!"
    "If you perhaps would like to see or hear,"
that sinner, terrified, began again,
"Lombards or Tuscans, I can fetch you some;
100   but let the Malebranche stand aside
so that my comrades need not fear their vengeance.
Remaining in this very spot, I shall,
    although alone, make seven more appear
when I have whistled, as has been our custom
105 when one of us has managed to get out."
    At that, Cagnazzo lifted up his snout
and shook his head, and said: "Just listen to
that trick by which he thinks he can dive back!"
    To this, he who was rich in artifice
110 replied: "Then I must have too many tricks,
if I bring greater torment to my friends."[7]
    This was too much for Alichino and,
despite the others, he cried out: "If you
dive back, I shall not gallop after you
115   but beat my wings above the pitch; we'll leave
this height; with the embankment as a screen,
we'll see if you—alone—can handle us."
    O you who read, hear now of this new sport:
each turned his eyes upon the other shore,
120 he first who'd been most hesitant before.
    The Navarrese, in nick of time, had planted
his feet upon the ground; then in an instant
he jumped and freed himself from their commander.
    At this each demon felt the prick of guilt,
125 and most, he who had led his band to blunder;
so he took off and shouted: "You are caught!"
    But this could help him little; wings were not
more fast than fear; the sinner plunged right under;
the other, flying up, lifted his chest:
130   not otherwise the wild duck when it plunges
precipitously, when the falcon nears
and then—exhausted, thwarted—flies back up.

---

6. Two shades of Sardinia, at the time controlled by Pisa (Gallura and Logodoro were two of the four judicial divisions of the island). Fra Gomita was a friar who was hanged for abusing his position of deputy to the judge of Gallura. Little is known for certain about Michel Zanche except that he was father-in-law of his murderer Branca Doria (33.137).

7. Ciampolo thus continues his fraudulent ways in Hell.

But Calcabrina, raging at the trick,
flew after Alichino; he was keen
135   to see the sinner free and have a brawl;
   and once the Navarrese had disappeared,
he turned his talons on his fellow demon
and tangled with him just above the ditch.
   But Alichino clawed him well—he was
140   indeed a full-grown kestrel;° and both fell   *falcon*
into the middle of the boiling pond.
   The heat was quick to disentangle them,
but still there was no way they could get out;
their wings were stuck, enmeshed in glue-like pitch.
145   And Barbariccia, grieving with the rest,
sent four to fly out toward the other shore
with all their forks, and speedily enough
   on this side and on that they took their posts;
and toward those two—stuck fast, already cooked
150   beneath that crust—they stretched their grappling hooks.
We left them still contending with that mess.

Canto 23

*Still the Eighth Circle, Fifth Pouch: the Barrators. Pursuit by the demons, with Virgil
snatching up Dante and sliding down to the Sixth Pouch, where the Hypocrites file
along slowly, clothed in caps of lead. Two Jovial Friars of Bologna, Catalano and
Loderingo. Caiaphas. Virgil's distress at Malacoda's deceitfulness.*

   Silent, alone, no one escorting us,
we made our way—one went before, one after—
as Friars Minor when they walk together.[1]
   The present fracas made me think of Aesop—
5   that fable where he tells about the mouse
and frog; for "near" and "nigh" are not more close
   than are that fable and this incident,
if you compare with care how each begins
and then compare the endings that they share.[2]
10   And even as one thought springs from another,
so out of that was still another born,
which made the fear I felt before redouble.
   I thought: "Because of us, they have been mocked,
and this inflicted so much hurt and scorn
15   that I am sure they feel deep indignation.

---

1. Franciscan monks called themselves Friars Minor because of their devotion to poverty and humility. It was
their custom to travel in bands of two, with the senior
walking ahead of the other.
2. A large collection of animal fables was attributed to
Aesop, a Greek author said to have lived in the early 6th
century B.C.E. In this popular fable, a frog agrees to carry
a mouse across a river. Halfway across, it dives down in

an attempt to kill the mouse, but while the two are fighting, a hawk swoops down and captures either the frog (in
the version of Marie de France), or both the mouse and
the frog. The fable may apply to the end of the previous
canto, with Calcabrina as frog and Alichino as mouse; it
also foreshadows the discovery at the end of this canto
that Malacoda as frog has lied to Virgil and Dante as
mouse about the existence of a bridge.

If anger's to be added to their malice,
they'll hunt us down with more ferocity
than any hound whose teeth have trapped a hare."
    I could already feel my hair curl up

20 from fear, and I looked back attentively,
while saying: "Master, if you don't conceal
    yourself and me at once—they terrify me,
those Malebranche; they are after us;
I so imagine them, I hear them now."

25   And he to me: "Were I a leaded mirror,[3]
I could not gather in your outer image
more quickly than I have received your inner.
    For even now your thoughts have joined my own;
in both our acts and aspects we are kin—

30 with both our minds I've come to one decision.
    If that right bank is not extremely steep,
we can descend into the other moat
and so escape from the imagined chase."
    He'd hardly finished telling me his plan

35 when I saw them approach with outstretched wings,
not too far off, and keen on taking us.
    My guide snatched me up instantly, just as
the mother who is wakened by a roar
and catches sight of blazing flames beside her,

40   will lift her son and run without a stop—
she cares more for the child than for herself—
not pausing even to throw on a shift;
    and down the hard embankment's edge—his back
lay flat along the sloping rock that closes

45 one side of the adjacent moat—he slid.
    No water ever ran so fast along
a sluice to turn the wheels of a land mill,
not even when its flow approached the paddles,[4]
    as did my master race down that embankment

50 while bearing me with him upon his chest,
just like a son, and not like a companion.
    His feet had scarcely reached the bed that lies
along the deep below, than those ten demons
were on the edge above us; but there was

55   nothing to fear; for that High Providence
that willed them ministers of the fifth ditch,
denies to all of them the power to leave it.
    Below that point we found a painted people,
who moved about with lagging steps, in circles,

60 weeping, with features tired and defeated.
    And they were dressed in cloaks with cowls so low

---

3. Lead was the customary backing for mirrors of the time.

4. The mill is situated near a body of water, its paddles turned by water passed through canals or sluices.

they fell before their eyes, of that same cut
that's used to make the clothes for Cluny's monks.[5]

65   Outside, these cloaks were gilded and they dazzled;
but inside they were all of lead, so heavy
that Frederick's capes were straw compared to them.[6]

       A tiring mantle for eternity!
We turned again, as always, to the left,
along with them, intent on their sad weeping;

70   but with their weights that weary people paced
so slowly that we found ourselves among
new company each time we took a step.[7]

       At which I told my guide: "Please try to find
someone whose name or deed I recognize;

75   and while we walk, be watchful with your eyes."

       And one who'd taken in my Tuscan speech
cried out behind us: "Stay your steps, o you
who hurry so along this darkened air!

       Perhaps you'll have from me that which you seek."

80   At which my guide turned to me, saying: "Wait,
and then continue, following his pace."

       I stopped, and I saw two whose faces showed
their minds were keen to be with me; but both
their load and the tight path forced them to slow.

85   When they came up, they looked askance at me
a long while, and they uttered not a word
until they turned to one another, saying:

       "The throbbing of his throat makes this one seem
alive; and if they're dead, what privilege

90   lets them appear without the heavy mantle?"

       Then they addressed me: "Tuscan, you who come
to this assembly of sad hypocrites,
do not disdain to tell us who you are."

       I answered: "Where the lovely Arno flows,

95   there I was born and raised, in the great city;
I'm with the body I have always had.

       But who are you, upon whose cheeks I see
such tears distilled by grief? And let me know
what punishment it is that glitters so."

100   And one of them replied: "The yellow cloaks
are of a lead so thick, their heaviness
makes us, the balances beneath them, creak.[8]

       We both were Jovial Friars, and Bolognese;

---

5. Cluny was a famous Benedictine abbey in Burgundy. In a letter to his nephew, who had left the Cistercian order to join the Cluniacs, Bernard of Clairvaux noted with some sarcasm the luxury of their robes, "made of the finest and most expensive fabrics, with long sleeves and a full hood."
6. Emperor Frederick II was accustomed to punish criminals by fitting them with a leaden cape and then placing them into a cauldron. As the cauldron was heated, the lead would melt, removing the skin piece by piece.
7. This is one of the few parts of Hell in which the pilgrim directly imitates the movements of the damned.
8. Like the words of the hypocrite, the cloaks glitter on the outside but in reality are lead.

105   my name was Catalano, Loderingo
was his, and we were chosen by your city
     together, for the post that's usually
one man's, to keep the peace; and what we were
is still to be observed around Gardingo."9
110   I then began, "O Friars, your misdeeds . . ."
but said no more, because my eyes had caught
one crucified by three stakes on the ground.
     When he saw me, that sinner writhed all over,
and he breathed hard into his beard with sighs;
observing that, Fra Catalano said
115   to me: "That one impaled there, whom you see,
counseled the Pharisees that it was prudent
to let one man—and not one nation—suffer.1
     Naked, he has been stretched across the path,
as you can see, and he must feel the weight
120   of anyone who passes over him.
     Like torment, in this ditch, afflicts both his
father-in-law and others in that council,
which for the Jews has seeded so much evil."2
     Then I saw Virgil stand amazed above
125   that one who lay stretched out upon a cross
so squalidly in his eternal exile.3
     And he addressed the friar in this way:
"If it does not displease you—if you may—
tell us if there's some passage on the right
130   that would allow the two of us to leave
without our having to compel black angels
to travel to this deep, to get us out."
     He answered: "Closer than you hope, you'll find
a rocky ridge that stretches from the great
135   round wall and crosses all the savage valleys,
     except that here it's broken—not a bridge.
But where its ruins slope along the bank
and heap up at the bottom, you can climb."
     My leader stood a while with his head bent,
140   then said: "He who hooks sinners over there

---

9. "Jovial Friars" were members of the Knights of the Blessed Virgin Mary, an order founded in Bologna in 1261 with the object of making peace between the warring factions in Italy's cities. The nickname was given them in reaction to the laxity of their rules. The Guelf Catalano di Guido di Ostia was associated with the Ghibelline Loderingo degli Andalò in founding the order; they were appointed by Pope Clement IV to serve jointly as chief magistrates of Florence, owing allegiance to the pope rather than to their political parties. Their appointment resulted in an uprising of Guelfs and expulsion of Ghibelline nobles along with destruction of their houses, including those of the Uberti, a leading family (Farinata's, see Canto 10), in the neighborhood of Gardingo near the

Palazzo Vecchio.
1. Caiaphas was the high priest under Pontius Pilate who counseled the Pharisees that "one man," Jesus, should die (John 18:13).
2. Caiaphas was supported at the council of the Pharisees by his father-in-law Annas. "Seeded" refers to the Christian belief that the blood of Christ was the "seed" that led to the destruction of Jerusalem and the dispersal of the Jews.
3. All sinners are "exiled" from heaven, but the gibe carries extra weight in the context of the fate of the Jews. Virgil's "amazement" may partly result from the fact that these shades would not have been there on his last passage through Malebolge (9.16–30).

gave us a false account of this affair."

 At which the Friar: "In Bologna, I
once heard about the devil's many vices—
they said he was a liar and father of lies."[4]

145 And then my guide moved on with giant strides,
somewhat disturbed, with anger in his eyes;
 at this I left those overburdened spirits,
  while following the prints of his dear feet.

Canto 24

Still the Eighth Circle, Sixth Pouch: the Hypocrites. Hard passage to the Seventh Pouch: the Thieves. Bitten by a serpent, a thieving sinner who turns to ashes and is then restored: Vanni Fucci. His prediction of the defeat of the Whites—Dante's party—at Pistoia.

 In that part of the young year when the sun
begins to warm its locks beneath Aquarius
and nights grow shorter, equaling the days,
 when hoarfrost mimes the image of his white
5 sister upon the ground—but not for long,
because the pen he uses is not sharp—
 the farmer who is short of fodder rises
and looks and sees the fields all white, at which
he slaps his thigh, turns back into the house,
10 and here and there complains like some poor wretch
who doesn't know what can be done, and then
goes out again and gathers up new hope
 on seeing that the world has changed its face
in so few hours, and he takes his staff
15 and hurries out his flock of sheep to pasture.[1]
 So did my master fill me with dismay
when I saw how his brow was deeply troubled,
yet then the plaster soothed the sore as quickly:
 for soon as we were on the broken bridge,
20 my guide turned back to me with that sweet manner
I first had seen along the mountain's base.[2]
 And he examined carefully the ruin;
then having picked the way we would ascend,
he opened up his arms and thrust me forward.
25 And just as he who ponders as he labors,
who's always ready for the step ahead,
so, as he lifted me up toward the summit
 of one great crag, he'd see another spur,

---

4. The hypocrite maliciously points out Virgil's ignorance of the ways of the devil that led to his deception by Malacoda (21.111), referring to his own experience as well as to the words of the Gospel (John 8:44).

1. The sun is in the sign of Aquarius between late January

and late February. The "white sister" of hoarfrost is snow; both "write" upon the ground, but frost less deeply. The farmer mistakes one for the other, but only for the time it takes the rising sun to melt the frost.

2. When Virgil first appeared to Dante in Canto 1.

30   saying: "That is the one you will grip next,
but try it first to see if it is firm."
That was no path for those with cloaks of lead,[3]
for he and I—he, light; I, with support—
could hardly make it up from spur to spur.
And were it not that, down from this enclosure,
35   the slope was shorter than the bank before,
I cannot speak for him, but I should surely
have been defeated. But since Malebolge
runs right into the mouth of its last well,
the placement of each valley means it must
40   have one bank high and have the other short;
and so we reached, at length, the jutting where
the last stone of the ruined bridge breaks off.
The breath within my lungs was so exhausted
from climbing, I could not go on; in fact,
45   as soon as I had reached that stone, I sat.
"Now you must cast aside your laziness,"
my master said, "for he who rests on down
or under covers cannot come to fame;
and he who spends his life without renown
50   leaves such a vestige of himself on earth
as smoke bequeaths to air or foam to water.
Therefore, get up; defeat your breathlessness
with spirit that can win all battles if
the body's heaviness does not deter it.
55   A longer ladder still is to be climbed;
it's not enough to have left them behind;
if you have understood, now profit from it."[4]
Then I arose and showed myself far better
equipped with breath than I had been before:
60   "Go on, for I am strong and confident."
We took our upward way upon the ridge,
with crags more jagged, narrow, difficult,
and much more steep than we had crossed before.
I spoke as we went on, not to seem weak;
65   at this, a voice came from the ditch beyond—
a voice that was not suited to form words.
I know not what he said, although I was
already at the summit of the bridge
that crosses there; and yet he seemed to move.
70   I had bent downward, but my living eyes
could not see to the bottom through that dark;
at which I said: "O master, can we reach
the other belt? Let us descend the wall,

3. The hypocrites require no other guardian than the robes
they wear.
4. Virgil's words liken the "heaviness" of Dante's body to
the cloaks of the hypocrites, and also remind him that
both fame and salvation will require a much longer climb
later on: the one that leads them out of hell in Canto 34, or
that of the Mountain of Purgatory in the next canticle.

for as I hear and cannot understand,
75 so I see down but can distinguish nothing."
  "The only answer that I give to you
is doing it," he said. "A just request
is to be met in silence, by the act."
  We then climbed down the bridge, just at the end
80 where it runs right into the eighth embankment,
and now the moat was plain enough to me;
  and there within I saw a dreadful swarm
of serpents so extravagant in form—
remembering them still drains my blood from me.[5]
85 Let Libya boast no more about her sands;
for if she breeds chelydri, jaculi,
cenchres with amphisbaena, pareae,
  she never showed—with all of Ethiopia
or all the land that borders the Red Sea[6]—
90 so many, such malignant, pestilences.
  Among this cruel and depressing swarm,
ran people who were naked, terrified,
with no hope of a hole or heliotrope.[7]
  Their hands were tied behind by serpents; these
95 had thrust their head and tail right through the loins,
and then were knotted on the other side.
  And—there!—a serpent sprang with force at one
who stood upon our shore, transfixing him
just where the neck and shoulders form a knot.
100 No *o* or *i* has ever been transcribed
so quickly as that soul caught fire and burned
and, as he fell, completely turned to ashes;
  and when he lay, undone, upon the ground,
the dust of him collected by itself
105 and instantly returned to what it was:
  just so, it is asserted by great sages,
that, when it reaches its five-hundredth year,
the phoenix dies and then is born again;[8]
  lifelong it never feeds on grass or grain,
110 only on drops of incense and amomum;
its final winding sheets are nard and myrrh.[9]
  And just as he who falls, and knows not how—
by demon's force that drags him to the ground
or by some other hindrance that binds man—
115 who, when he rises, stares about him, all

---

5. The fanciful list of serpents comes from Cato's crossing of the Libyan Desert in Lucan's *Pharsalia* 9.711–21.
6. Even if the Libyan Desert is expanded to include Africa south of Egypt as far as Zanzibar and east to the Red Sea.
7. The heliotrope was a stone supposedly found in northern Africa that rendered the wearer invisible.
8. The mythical Arabian phoenix was a bird that burned itself every 500 years on a pyre of incense, rising from the

ashes in the form of a small worm that developed into a full-grown bird by the third day (Ovid, *Metamorphoses* 15.392–402).
9. Amomum and incense, nard and myrrh are fragrant plant extracts and tree resins; the former provide its food, the latter form the phoenix's "winding sheet," the cloth in which its corpse is wrapped.

bewildered by the heavy anguish he
has suffered, sighing as he looks around;
    so did this sinner stare when he arose.
Oh, how severe it is, the power of God
120   that, as its vengeance, showers down such blows!
    My guide then asked that sinner who he was;
to this he answered: "Not long since, I rained
from Tuscany into this savage maw.
    Mule that I was, the bestial life pleased me
125   and not the human; I am Vanni Fucci,
beast; and the den that suited me—Pistoia."[1]
    And I to Virgil: "Tell him not to slip
away, and ask what sin has thrust him here;
I knew him as a man of blood and anger."
130   The sinner heard and did not try to feign
but turned his mind and face, intent, toward me;
and coloring with miserable shame,
    he said: "I suffer more because you've caught me
in this, the misery you see, than I
135   suffered when taken from the other life.
    I can't refuse to answer what you ask:
I am set down so far because I robbed
the sacristy of its fair ornaments,
    and someone else was falsely blamed for that.[2]
140   But lest this sight give you too much delight,
if you can ever leave these lands of darkness,
    open your ears to my announcement, hear:
Pistoia first will strip herself of Blacks,
then Florence will renew her men and manners.
145   From Val di Magra, Mars will draw a vapor
which turbid clouds will try to wrap; the clash
between them will be fierce, impetuous,
    a tempest, fought upon Campo Piceno,
until that vapor, vigorous, shall crack
150   the mist, and every White be struck by it.[3]
    And I have told you this to make you grieve."

Canto 25

Still the Eighth Circle, Seventh Pouch: the Thieves. Vanni Fucci and his obscene figs against God. The Centaur Cacus. Five Florentine Thieves, three of them humans and two of them serpents. The astounding metamorphoses undergone by four of them.

1. The "mule" or illegitimate son of a noble family of Pistoia, northwest of Florence, Vanni Fucci was an ardent Black Guelf. Dante may have known him from the war against Pisa (1289–1293).
2. There are various reports concerning the robbery of the treasury of San Jacopo in the church of San Zeno at Pistoia; an innocent man was nearly executed for the crime.
3. The Blacks of Pistoia were expelled and their houses burned in 1301, but with the help of the ostensible peace-maker, Charles of Valois, they and the Blacks of Florence were able to expel the Florentine Whites, including Dante, in 1302 (lines 143–44). The "vapor" drawn by the war-god from Val di Magra is the Guelf leader Moroello Malaspina. The defeat of the Whites ("the mist" of line 150) may refer to events of 1302 or to the capture of the city in 1306.

When he had finished with his words, the thief
raised high his fists with both figs cocked and cried:
"Take that, o God; I square them off for you!"[1]
      From that time on, those serpents were my friends,
5   for one of them coiled then around his neck,
as if to say, "I'll have you speak no more";
      another wound about his arms and bound him
again and wrapped itself in front so firmly,
he could not even make them budge an inch.
10   Pistoia, ah, Pistoia, must you last:
why not decree your self-incineration,
since you surpass your seed in wickedness?[2]
      Throughout the shadowed circles of deep Hell,
I saw no soul against God so rebel,
15   not even he who fell from Theban walls.[3]
      He fled and could not say another word;
and then I saw a Centaur full of anger,
shouting: "Where is he, where's that bitter one?"
      I do not think Maremma has the number
20   of snakes that Centaur carried on his haunch
until the part that takes our human form.[4]
      Upon his shoulders and behind his nape
there lay a dragon with its wings outstretched;
it sets ablaze all those it intercepts.
25   My master said: "That Centaur there is Cacus,
who often made a lake of blood within
a grotto underneath Mount Aventine.
      He does not ride the same road as his brothers
because he stole—and most deceitfully—
30   from the great herd nearby; his crooked deeds
      ended beneath the club of Hercules,
who may have given him a hundred blows—
but he was not alive to feel the tenth."[5]
      While he was talking so, Cacus ran by
35   and, just beneath our ledge, three souls arrived;
but neither I nor my guide noticed them
      until they had cried out: "And who are you?"
At this the words we shared were interrupted,
and we attended only to those spirits.
40   I did not recognize them, but it happened,
as chance will usually bring about,

---

1. The "fig" is an obscene gesture produced by thrusting out the fist while holding the thumb between the fore-finger and middle finger.

2. According to legend, Pistoia was founded by survivors of the forces of Catiline, the conspirator against the Roman republic defeated nearby in 62 B.C.E.

3. The blasphemer Capaneus in Canto 14.46–72.

4. The beast-filled Tuscan wood of Maremma was referred to already in Canto 13.7–9 to describe the wood of

suicides and squanderers; here, serpents are added to its contents.

5. Cacus was the fire-breathing, half-human son of Vulcan and Medusa who stole cattle from Hercules. In order to conceal his tracks, Cacus dragged the cattle backward into his cave, but their bellowing alerted Hercules, who slew the thief (*Aeneid* 8.193–267). Dante makes Cacus a Centaur, and displaces the fire-breathing to a dragon familiar on its shoulder.

that one of them called out the other's name,[6]
    exclaiming: "Where was Cianfa left behind?"
At this, so that my guide might be alert,

45   I raised my finger up from chin to nose.

    If, reader, you are slow now to believe
what I shall tell, that is no cause for wonder,
for I who saw it hardly can accept it.

    As I kept my eyes fixed upon those sinners,

50   a serpent with six feet springs out against
one of the three, and clutches him completely.

    It gripped his belly with its middle feet,
and with its forefeet grappled his two arms;
and then it sank its teeth in both his cheeks;

55   it stretched its rear feet out along his thighs
and ran its tail along between the two,
then straightened it again behind his loins.

    No ivy ever gripped a tree so fast
as when that horrifying monster clasped

60   and intertwined the other's limbs with its.

    Then just as if their substance were warm wax,
they stuck together and they mixed their colors,
so neither seemed what he had been before;

    just as, when paper's kindled, where it still

65   has not caught flame in full, its color's dark
though not yet black, while white is dying off.

    The other two souls stared, and each one cried:
"Ah me, Agnello, how you change! Just see,
you are already neither two nor one!"[7]

70   Then two heads were already joined in one,
when in one face where two had been dissolved,
two intermingled shapes appeared to us.

    Two arms came into being from four lengths;
the thighs and legs, the belly and the chest

75   became such limbs as never had been seen.

    And every former shape was canceled there:
that perverse image seemed to share in both—
and none; and so, and slowly, it moved on.

    Just as the lizard, when it darts from hedge

80   to hedge, beneath the dog days' giant lash,
seems, if it cross one's path, a lightning flash,

    so seemed a blazing little serpent moving

6. There are five souls involved in the complex action of this canto; all were thieves of noble Florentine families: Cianfa Donati, lost when he became a serpent (50) and eventually fusing (70–78) with Agnello de' Brunelleschi; Francesco Guercio ("squinting") de' Cavalcanti, the "blazing little serpent" (82) that steals the substance of "Buoso" (85), probably Buoso di Forese Donati, nephew of the Buoso Donati mentioned as a victim of counterfeiting in Canto 30.41–44, in the transformation that concludes at line 141; and Puccio Sciancato, "the only soul who'd not been changed" (149).

7. Agnello was reputed to have used disguises to facilitate his thieving. The transformation that follows closely resembles the merging of Salmacis and Hermaphroditus in *Metamorphoses* 4.373–79.

against the bellies of the other two,
as black and livid as a peppercorn.

85   Attacking one of them, it pierced right through
the part where we first take our nourishment;°   *the navel*
and then it fell before him at full length.

The one it had transfixed stared but said nothing;
in fact he only stood his ground and yawned
90   as one whom sleep or fever has undone.

The serpent stared at him, he at the serpent;
one through his wound, the other through his mouth
were smoking violently; their smoke met.

Let Lucan now be silent, where he sings
95   of sad Sabellus and Nasidius,
and wait to hear what flies off from my bow.

Let Ovid now be silent, where he tells
of Cadmus, Arethusa; if his verse
has made of one a serpent, one a fountain,[8]

100   I do not envy him; he never did
transmute two natures, face to face, so that
both forms were ready to exchange their matter.

These were the ways they answered to each other:
the serpent split its tail into a fork;
105   the wounded sinner drew his steps together.

The legs and then the thighs along with them
so fastened to each other that the juncture
soon left no sign that was discernible.

Meanwhile the cleft tail took upon itself
110   the form the other gradually lost;
its skin grew soft, the other's skin grew hard.

I saw the arms that drew in at his armpits
and also saw the monster's two short feet
grow long for just as much as those were shortened.

115   The serpent's hind feet, twisted up together,
became the member that man hides; just as
the wretch put out two hind paws from his member.

And while the smoke veils each with a new color,
and now breeds hair upon the skin of one,
120   just as it strips the hair from off the other,
the one rose up, the other fell; and yet
they never turned aside their impious eyelamps,
beneath which each of them transformed his snout:

he who stood up drew his back toward the temples,
125   and from the excess matter growing there
came ears upon the cheeks that had been bare;

8. Dante invokes (and outdoes) his two primary sources in this canto: the horrific deaths by snakebite of two Roman soldiers in the Libyan Desert in Lucan's *Pharsalia* 9 and the transformations of Ovid's *Metamorphoses,* in this case those of
Thebes' founder Cadmus into a serpent (4.576–89) and of the nymph Arethusa into a fountain (5.572–641).

whatever had not been pulled back but kept,
superfluous, then made his face a nose
and thickened out his lips appropriately.

130 He who was lying down thrust out his snout;
and even as the snail hauls in its horns,
he drew his ears straight back into his head;

his tongue, which had before been whole and fit
for speech, now cleaves; the other's tongue, which had
135 been forked, now closes up; and the smoke stops.

The soul that had become an animal,
now hissing, hurried off along the valley;
the other one, behind him, speaks and spits.

And then he turned aside his new-made shoulders
140 and told the third soul: "I'd have Buoso run
on all fours down this road, as I have done."

And so I saw the seventh ballast change
and rechange;[9] may the strangeness plead for me
if there's been some confusion in my pen.

145 And though my eyes were somewhat blurred, my mind
bewildered, those three sinners did not flee
so secretly that I could not perceive

Puccio Sciancato clearly, he who was
the only soul who'd not been changed among
150 the three companions we had met at first;
the other one made you, Gaville, grieve.[1]

Canto 26

Still the Eighth Circle, Seventh Pouch: the Thieves. Dante's invective against Florence. View of the Eighth Pouch, where Fraudulent Counselors are clothed in the flames that burn them. Ulysses and Diomedes in one shared flame. Ulysses' tale of his final voyage.

Be joyous, Florence, you are great indeed,
for over sea and land you beat your wings;
through every part of Hell your name extends!

Among the thieves I found five citizens
5 of yours—and such, that shame has taken me;
with them, you can ascend to no high honor.

But if the dreams dreamt close to dawn are true,
then little time will pass before you feel
what Prato and the others crave for you.[1]

10 Were that already come, it would not be

---

9. That is, the souls of the seventh *bolgia,* likened to the hold of a ship.
1. Murdered by the inhabitants of the village of Gaville, Francesco de' Cavalcanti was swiftly and savagely avenged by his family.
1. Ancient lore distinguished many sorts of dreams; only

those dreamt near dawn were held to be prophetic, "true." Prato is a Tuscan town between Florence and Pistoia that envied Florentine power; the enigmatic prediction may refer to Cardinal Niccolò da Prato, who placed the city under interdiction after his peacekeeping mission failed in 1304.

too soon—and let it come, since it must be!
As I grow older, it will be more heavy.[2]
      We left that deep and, by protruding stones
that served as stairs for our descent before,
15   my guide climbed up again and drew me forward;
      and as we took our solitary path
among the ridge's jagged spurs and rocks,
our feet could not make way without our hands.
      It grieved me then and now grieves me again
20   when I direct my mind to what I saw;
and more than usual, I curb my talent,
      that it not run where virtue does not guide;
so that, if my kind star or something better
has given me that gift, I not abuse it.
25   As many as the fireflies the peasant
(while resting on a hillside in the season°   *summer*
when he who lights the world least hides his face),
      just when the fly gives way to the mosquito,
sees glimmering below, down in the valley,
30   there where perhaps he gathers grapes and tills—
      so many were the flames that glittered in
the eighth abyss; I made this out as soon
as I had come to where one sees the bottom.
      Even as he who was avenged by bears
35   saw, as it left, Elijah's chariot—
its horses rearing, rising right to heaven—
      when he could not keep track of it except
by watching one lone flame in its ascent,
just like a little cloud that climbs on high:[3]
40   so, through the gullet of that ditch, each flame
must make its way; no flame displays its prey,
though every flame has carried off a sinner.
      I stood upon the bridge and leaned straight out
to see; and if I had not gripped a rock,
45   I should have fallen off—without a push.
      My guide, who noted how intent I was,
told me: "Within those fires there are souls;
each one is swathed in that which scorches him."
      "My master," I replied, "on hearing you,
50   I am more sure; but I'd already thought
that it was so, and I had meant to ask:
      Who is within the flame that comes so twinned
above that it would seem to rise out of

2. The longer he must wait for a retribution to his city that
will be just but bittersweet.
3. After the prophet Elisha was mocked by a group of
boys, two bears came from the woods and killed 42 of

them; he had already witnessed the ascent of his teacher,
the prophet Elijah, to heaven in a fiery chariot (2 Kings
2:23–24).

the pyre Eteocles shared with his brother?"[4]

55 He answered me: "Within that flame, Ulysses
and Diomedes suffer; they, who went
as one to rage, now share one punishment.[5]

And there, together in their flame, they grieve
over the horse's fraud that caused a breach—
60 the gate that let Rome's noble seed escape.

There they regret the guile that makes the dead
Deïdamia still lament Achilles;
and there, for the Palladium, they pay."

"If they can speak within those sparks," I said,
65 "I pray you and repray and, master, may
my prayer be worth a thousand pleas, do not

forbid my waiting here until the flame
with horns approaches us; for you can see
how, out of my desire, I bend toward it."

70 And he to me: "What you have asked is worthy
of every praise; therefore, I favor it.
I only ask you this: refrain from talking.

Let me address them—I have understood
what you desire of them. Since they were Greek,
75 perhaps they'd be disdainful of your speech."[6]

And when my guide adjudged the flame had reached
a point where time and place were opportune,
this was the form I heard his words assume:

"You two who move as one within the flame,
80 if I deserved of you while I still lived,
if I deserved of you much or a little

when in the world I wrote my noble lines,
do not move on; let one of you retell
where, having gone astray, he found his death."

85 The greater horn within that ancient flame
began to sway and tremble, murmuring
just like a fire that struggles in the wind;

and then he waved his flame-tip back and forth
as if it were a tongue that tried to speak,
90 and flung toward us a voice that answered:[7] "When

4. Eteocles and Polynices were twin sons of Oedipus, King of Thebes, and Jocasta. After they forced their father (and brother) to abdicate, he cursed them with enmity. They fought over the kingship, killed each other in single combat, and were burned on a single funeral pyre. So enduring was their hatred that the rising flames divided in two (Statius, *Thebaid* 429ff. and Lucan, *Pharsalia* 1.549–52).

5. Ulysses and Diomedes were Greek heroes of the Trojan War who often acted in tandem. One of their exploits was to steal the Palladium, a wooden image of Pallas Athena said to preserve the walls of Troy. In pretended remorse, they built an enormous, hollow wooden horse in which they and other Greeks hid, and which then led the deceived Trojans to breach their walls in order to bear it

within the city (*Aeneid* 2.18–370). Rome's "noble seed" is Aeneas and his followers, who fled the city's destruction for Italy. Deïdamia was the mother of Pyrrhus; she died of grief after the boy's father, Achilles, sailed to Troy. In *Purgatorio* 22.114, she is said to be among the souls in Limbo.

6. Unlike Dante, Virgil had been fluent in Greek; moreover, his epic, like Homer's, was written in the high, tragic style characteristic of the speech in this encounter. Dante also chooses to stress the greatness and antiquity of the shade being interviewed.

7. There is no known source for this account by Ulysses (the "greater" flame) of his death; it contradicts the prophecy of Tiresias in *Odyssey* 11.134–37 of a peaceful death at sea.

I sailed away from Circe, who'd beguiled me
to stay more than a year there, near Gaeta—
before Aeneas gave that place a name[8]—
neither my fondness for my son nor pity
95 for my old father nor the love I owed
Penelope, which would have gladdened her,
    was able to defeat in me the longing
I had to gain experience of the world
and of the vices and the worth of men.
100   Therefore, I set out on the open sea
with but one ship and that small company
of those who never had deserted me.
    I saw as far as Spain, far as Morocco,
along both shores; I saw Sardinia
105 and saw the other islands that sea bathes.
    And I and my companions were already
old and slow, when we approached the narrows
where Hercules set up his boundary stones
    that men might heed and never reach beyond:
110 upon my right, I had gone past Seville,
and on the left, already passed Ceüta.[9]
    'Brothers,' I said, 'o you, who having crossed
a hundred thousand dangers, reach the west,
to this brief waking-time that still is left
115   unto your senses, you must not deny
experience of that which lies beyond
the sun, and of the world that is unpeopled.
    Consider well the seed that gave you birth:
you were not made to live your lives as brutes,
120 but to be followers of worth and knowledge.'
    I spurred my comrades with this brief address
to meet the journey with such eagerness
that I could hardly, then, have held them back;
    and having turned our stern toward morning,° we   *the east*
125 made wings out of our oars in a wild flight
and always gained upon our left-hand side.
    At night I now could see the other pole
and all its stars; the star of ours had fallen
and never rose above the plain of the ocean.[1]
130   Five times the light beneath the moon had been
rekindled, and, as many times, was spent,[2]

---

8. Circe was an enchantress who transformed Ulysses' men into swine. After forcing her to change them back, Ulysses tarried with Circe for a year before continuing his voyage to his home and family in Ithaca.
9. Ulysses and his men are at the western edge of the known world; on the African and European shores of the Mediterranean, the Pillars of Hercules were twin promontories formed when the hero split a mountain in two

across the Mediterranean, usually identified with the modern promontories of Gibraltar in Spain and Jebel Musa in Morocco. It was thought impossible to sail beyond this boundary and return alive.
1. The "other pole" is Antartica; they have crossed the equator and no longer see the stars of "our" pole, the northern hemisphere.
2. Five months had passed.

since that hard passage faced our first attempt,
 when there before us rose a mountain, dark
because of distance, and it seemed to me
135 the highest mountain I had ever seen.[3]
 And we were glad, but this soon turned to sorrow,
for out of that new land a whirlwind rose
and hammered at our ship, against her bow.
 Three times it turned her round with all the waters;
140 and at the fourth, it lifted up the stern
so that our prow plunged deep, as pleased an Other,°   *God*
until the sea again closed—over us."

Canto 27

*Still the Eighth Circle, Eighth Pouch: the Fraudulent Counselors. Guido da Montefel-
tro, for whom Dante provides a panorama of the state of political affairs in Romagna.
Guido's tale of the anticipatory—but unavailing—absolution given him by Boniface
VIII. The quarrel of a demon and St Francis over Guido's soul.*

The flame already was erect and silent—
it had no more to say. Now it had left
us with the permission of the gentle poet,
 when, just behind it, came another flame
5 that drew our eyes to watch its tip because
of the perplexing sound that it sent forth.
 Even as the Sicilian bull (that first
had bellowed with the cry—and this was just—
of him who shaped it with his instruments)
10 would always bellow with its victim's voice,
so that, although that bull was only brass,
it seemed as if it were pierced through by pain;[1]
 so were the helpless words that, from the first,
had found no path or exit from the flame,
15 transformed into the language of the fire.
 But after they had found their way up toward
the tip, and given it that movement which
the tongue had given them along their passage,
 we heard: "O you to whom I turn my voice,
20 who only now were talking Lombard, saying,
'Now you may leave—I'll not provoke more speech,'[2]
 though I have come perhaps a little late,
may it not trouble you to stop and speak

---

3. This is probably the Mountain of Purgatory; it also resonates with the pilgirm's unsuccessful attempt in Canto 1.
1. The Athenian artisan Perillus fabricated a bronze bull
in which the victims of Phalaris, the 6th-century tyrant of
Agrigentum in Sicily, could be roasted alive, their shrieks
emerging as if the bellowing of a bull. Perillus was chosen to be first to test his apparatus.

2. "Lombardy" in the Middle Ages referred to northern
Italy, including Virgil's birthplace of Mantua where, in
Dante's belief, a version of the Lombard dialect was already spoken in antiquity. Given the focus on "high" language in the previous canto, it is a calculated shock to
suggest to us in retrospect that Virgil was speaking to
Ulysses in Italian (line 3).

with me; see how I stay—and I am burning![3]
25 If you have fallen into this blind world
but recently, out of the sweet Italian
country from which I carry all my guilt,
    do tell me if the Romagnoles have peace
or war; I was from there—the hills between
30 Urbino and the ridge where Tiber springs."
    I still was bent, attentive, over him,
when my guide nudged me lightly at the side
and said: "You speak; he is Italian."[4]
    And I, who had my answer set already,
35 without delay began to speak to him:
"O soul that is concealed below in flame,
    Romagna is not now and never was
quite free of war inside its tyrants' hearts;
but when I left her, none had broken out.
40   Ravenna stands as it has stood for years;
the eagle of Polenta shelters it
and also covers Cervia with his wings.[5]
    The city that already stood long trial
and made a bloody heap out of the French,
45 now finds itself again beneath green paws.[6]
    Both mastiffs of Verruchio, old and new,
who dealt so badly with Montagna, use
their teeth to bore where they have always gnawed.[7]
    The cities on Lamone and Santerno
50 are led by the young lion of the white lair;
from summer unto winter, he shifts factions.[8]
    That city with its side bathed by the Savio,
just as it lies between the plain and mountain,
lives somewhere between tyranny and freedom.[9]
55   And now, I pray you, tell me who you are:
do not be harder than I've been with you,

---

3. The shade is Guido da Montefeltro (c.1220–1298), nick-named the "Fox," who commanded a force of Ghibellines from Romagnola (the region north of Tuscany) and exiles from Bologna and Florence. In his *Convivio,* Dante had re-ferred to the late-life conversion of Guido as exemplary and praised the leader as "our most noble Latin" (4.28.8).
4. By contrast to the previous canto (73–75), where Virgil addressed the Greek shades.
5. The Adriatic cities of Ravenna and Cervia were ruled from 1275 by the Guelf Polenta family, whose coat of arms displayed an eagle. The head of the family from 1275 until his death in 1310 was Guido da Polenta the el-der, father of Francesca da Rimini (5.73–142).
6. Under the leadership of Guido da Montefeltro, Forlì, a central city of Romagna, successfully withstood a year-long siege by French and Guelf troops sent by Pope Martin IV; in 1282 they decimated the attacking force. The following year, the city came to terms with the pope

and drove out Guido. The "green paws" belong to the coat of arms of the Ordelaffi family, new tyrants of Forlì as of 1300.
7. Malatesta, lord of Rimini, had four sons, including Gianciotto, husband of Francesca da Rimini, her lover Paolo, and Malatestino da Verruchio, the "new," or "young mastiff." Both lords were harsh tyrants, killing the head of the Rimini Ghibellines, Montagna de' Parcitati, in 1295.
8. Maghinardo Pagani da Susinana, whose coat of arms displayed a lion on a white ground, ruled the cities of Faenza, on the Lamone, and Imola, on the Santerno River. Ghibelline by birth, he was also loyal to the Florentine Guelfs.
9. Cesena was on the Savio River, midway between Forlì and Rimini. It was a free municipality during this period, but dominated by Guido's powerful cousin, Galasso da Montefeltro.

that in the world your name may still endure."[1]

     After the flame, in customary fashion,
had roared awhile, it moved its pointed tip

60 this side and that and then set free this breath:
     "If I thought my reply were meant for one
who ever could return into the world,
this flame would stir no more; and yet, since none—
if what I hear is true—ever returned

65 alive from this abyss, then without fear
of facing infamy, I answer you.

     I was a man of arms, then wore the cord,°   *of a monk*
believing that, so girt, I made amends;
and surely what I thought would have been true

70 had not the Highest Priest—may he be damned!—
made me fall back into my former sins;
and how and why, I'd have you hear from me.[2]

     While I still had the form of bones and flesh
my mother gave to me, my deeds were not

75 those of the lion but those of the fox.[3]

     The wiles and secret ways—I knew them all
and so employed their arts that my renown
had reached the very boundaries of earth.

     But when I saw myself come to that part

80 of life when it is fitting for all men
to lower sails and gather in their ropes,

     what once had been my joy was now dejection;
repenting and confessing, I became
a friar; and—poor me—it would have helped.

85   The prince of the new Pharisees,° who then   *Pope Boniface*
was waging war so near the Lateran—
and not against the Jews or Saracens,°   *Arabs*

     for every enemy of his was Christian,
and none of them had gone to conquer Acre

90 or been a trader in the Sultan's lands—

     took no care for the highest office or
the holy orders that were his, or for
my cord, which used to make its wearers leaner.[4]

     But just as Constantine, on Mount Soracte,

95 to cure his leprosy, sought out Sylvester,[5]
so this one sought me out as his instructor,

---

1. Guido has been under the misconception that Dante was a shade; Dante doesn't yet know to whom he has been speaking.
2. After leading the Ghibellines, Guido made peace with Boniface VIII and joined the Franciscan order late in life. He died in 1298 at the age of 75. The incident that Dante has him recount here may have been invented.
3. A common distinction between force ("the lion") and guile ("the fox").

4. Rather than waging a holy war—Acre was the principal port of the crusaders in Palestine—Boniface was engaged in a local feud (the Lateran Palace was the papal residence) with the Colonna family.
5. According to legend, the Emperor Constantine was afflicted by leprosy due to his persecution of the Christians. Led by a dream, he sought out Pope Sylvester I on Mt. Soracte north of Rome, who baptized and then cured him.

to ease the fever of his arrogance.
He asked me to give counsel. I was silent—
his words had seemed to me delirious.

100   And then he said: 'Your heart must not mistrust:
I now absolve you in advance—teach me
to batter Penestrino to the ground.[6]

You surely know that I possess the power
to lock and unlock Heaven; for the keys

105   my predecessor did not prize are two.'[7]

Then his grave arguments compelled me so,
my silence seemed a worse offense than speech,
and I said: 'Since you cleanse me of the sin

that I must now fall into, Father, know:

110   long promises and very brief fulfillments
will bring a victory to your high throne.'[8]

Then Francis came, as soon as I was dead,
for me; but one of the black cherubim
told him: 'Don't bear him off; do not cheat me.[9]

115   He must come down among my menials;
the counsel that he gave was fraudulent;
since then, I've kept close track, to snatch his scalp;

one can't absolve a man who's not repented,
and no one can repent and will at once;

120   the law of contradiction won't allow it.'

O miserable me, for how I started
when he took hold of me and said: 'Perhaps
you did not think that I was a logician!'

He carried me to Minos; and that monster

125   twisted his tail eight times around his hide
and then, when he had bit it in great anger,

announced: 'This one is for the thieving fire';
for which—and where, you see—I now am lost,
and in this garb I move in bitterness."

130   And when, with this, his words were at an end,
the flame departed, sorrowing and writhing
and tossing its sharp horn. We moved beyond;

I went together with my guide, along
the ridge until the other arch that bridges

135   the ditch where payment is imposed on those
who, since they brought such discord, bear such loads.

6. The castle at Penestrino southeast of Rome was the stronghold of the Colonna, who surrendered after Boniface had promised complete amnesty (the "long promises" of line 110). He immediately had the castle leveled.
7. The "keys of the kingdom of heaven" (Matthew 16:19) were the symbol of the pope's ultimate power over condemnation and absolution; according to Boniface, his predecessor, Celestine V, who abdicated, "did not prize" them.
8. The pope's promise to Guido to absolve him in advance of whatever evil he may counsel is an extreme version of the abuse of granting indulgences, or reduced penance, for sins not yet committed.
9. Coming for the soul of one of his order, St. Francis takes the place of the customary angel who struggles against the devil ("black cherubim") for possession of a soul.

Canto 28

*The Eighth Circle, Ninth Pouch, where the Sowers of Scandal and Schism, perpetu-
ally circling, are wounded and—after each healing—wounded again by a demon with
a sword. Mohammed and Ali. Warning to Fra Dolcino. Curio. Mosca. Bertran de
Born.*

Who, even with untrammeled° words and many   *unrestrained*
attempts at telling, ever could recount
in full the blood and wounds that I now saw?

    Each tongue that tried would certainly fall short
5   because the shallowness of both our speech
and intellect cannot contain so much.

    Were you to reassemble all the men
who once, within Apulia's fateful land,°   *southern Italy*
had mourned their blood, shed at the Trojans' hands,[1]

10   as well as those who fell in the long war
where massive mounds of rings were battle spoils—
even as Livy writes, who does not err[2]—

    and those who felt the thrust of painful blows
when they fought hard against Robert Guiscard;[3]
15   with all the rest whose bones are still piled up

at Ceperano—each Apulian was
a traitor there—and, too, at Tagliacozzo,
where old Alardo conquered without weapons;[4]

    and then, were one to show his limb pierced through
20   and one his limb hacked off, that would not match
the hideousness of the ninth abyss.

    No barrel, even though it's lost a hoop
or end-piece, ever gapes as one whom I
saw ripped right from his chin to where we fart:

25   his bowels hung between his legs, one saw
his vitals and the miserable sack
that makes of what we swallow excrement.

    While I was all intent on watching him,
he looked at me, and with his hands he spread
30   his chest and said: "See how I split myself!

    See now how maimed Mohammed is![5] And he
who walks and weeps before me is Ali,[6]
whose face is opened wide from chin to forelock.

    And all the others here whom you can see

---

1. The early Romans, descendants of Aeneas and his men, and their wars with the Tarentines (280–274 B.C.E.) and the Samnites (434–290 B.C.E.).

2. Livy (59 B.C.E.–17 C.E.) was the great historian of ancient Rome; his monumental *History* includes an account of the Second Punic War (219–202 B.C.E.), during which Hannibal brought to Carthage a heap of gold rings taken off of the fingers of slain Romans (33.12.1–2).

3. A Norman adventurer (1015–1085) who fought the Greeks and Saracens in Sicily and southern Italy.

4. Sites of bloody battles in the 1260s marked by treachery.

5. The Prophet Mohammed (570–632) was considered in medieval Europe as an apostate Christian; from the same point of view, Islam was a decisive division of religious unity.

6. Mohammed's son-in-law. He was assassinated after only five years as caliph, in 661, leading to the division of Islam into two sects, the Sunnites and the Shiites or Fatimites.

35 were, when alive, the sowers of dissension
and scandal, and for this they now are split.

Behind us here, a devil decks us out
so cruelly, re-placing every one
of this throng underneath the sword edge when

40 we've made our way around the road of pain,
because our wounds have closed again before
we have returned to meet his blade once more.

But who are you who dawdle on this ridge,
perhaps to slow your going to the verdict

45 that was pronounced on your self-accusations?"

"Death has not reached him yet," my master answered,
"nor is it guilt that summons him to torment;
but that he may gain full experience,

I, who am dead, must guide him here below,

50 to circle after circle, throughout Hell:
this is as true as that I speak to you."

More than a hundred, when they heard him, stopped
within the ditch and turned to look at me,
forgetful of their torture, wondering.

55 "Then you, who will perhaps soon see the sun,
tell Fra Dolcino to provide himself
with food, if he has no desire to join me

here quickly, lest when snow besieges him,
it bring the Novarese the victory

60 that otherwise they would not find too easy."[7]

When he had raised his heel, as if to go,
Mohammed said these words to me, and then
he set it on the ground and off he went.

Another sinner, with his throat slit through

65 and with his nose hacked off up to his eyebrows,
and no more than a single ear remaining,

had—with the others—stayed his steps in wonder;
he was the first, before the rest, to open
his windpipe—on the outside, all bloodred—

70 and said: "O you whom guilt does not condemn,
and whom, unless too close resemblance cheats me,
I've seen above upon Italian soil,

remember Pier da Medicina[8] if
you ever see again the gentle plain

75 that from Vercelli slopes to Marcabò.

And let the two best men of Fano know—
I mean both Messer Guido and Angiolello—
that, if the foresight we have here's not vain,

7. In 1300 Fra Dolcino had become head of the reformist sect of the Apostolic Brothers; when the sect was pronounced as heretical in 1305 by Clement V because it believed in holding goods and women in common, thousands of its members fled to the hills between Novara and Vercelli in northwest Italy. Forced by starvation to surrender, many were burned alive, including Fra Dolcino and his companion, Margaret of Trent.
8. Early commentators described Pier da Medicina as a sower of discord in Romagna.

they will be cast out of their ship and drowned,
80   weighed down with stones, near La Cattolica,
because of a foul tyrant's treachery.[9]

Between the isles of Cyprus and Majorca,[1]
Neptune has never seen so cruel a crime
committed by the pirates or the Argives.°   *Greeks*
85   That traitor who sees only with one eye
and rules the land which one who's here with me
would wish his sight had never seen, will call

Guido and Angiolello to a parley,
and then will so arrange it that they'll need
90   no vow or prayer to Focara's wind!"[2]

And I to him: "If you would have me carry
some news of you above, then tell and show me
who so detests the sight of Rimini."

And then he set his hand upon the jaw
95   of a companion, opening his mouth
and shouting: "This is he, and he speaks not.

A man cast out, he quenched the doubt in Caesar,
insisting that the one who is prepared
can only suffer harm if he delays."[3]

100   Oh, how dismayed and pained he seemed to me,
his tongue slit in his gullet: Curio,
who once was so audacious in his talk!

And one who walked with both his hands hacked off,
while lifting up his stumps through the dark air,
105   so that his face was hideous with blood,

cried out: "You will remember Mosca, too,
who said—alas—'What's done is at an end,'
which was the seed of evil for the Tuscans."[4]

I added: "—and brought death to your own kinsmen";
110   then having heard me speak, grief heaped on grief,
he went his way as one gone mad with sadness.

But I stayed there to watch that company
and saw a thing that I should be afraid
to tell with no more proof than my own self—

115   except that I am reassured by conscience,
that good companion, heartening a man

---

9. In c. 1312 Guido del Cassero and Angliolello di Carignano were thrown overboard by henchmen of Malatestino, lord of Rimini (the "new mastiff" of 27.46, and the "foul tyrant" and "one-eyed traitor" here), as they were on their way at his invitation to a meeting at the small coastal town of La Cattolica. Presumedly, Malatestino planned to seize power in their town.
1. The two ends of the Mediterranean.
2. Focara was a proverbially windy and dangerous headland on the Adriatic between Fano and La Cattolica. Guido and Angiolello no longer need to worry about praying for safe passage.

3. While tribune in Rome in 50 B.C.E., Gaius Curio the younger was bought by Julius Caesar away from the Pompeian party. He fled the city after civil war broke out. Dante follows Lucan (*Pharsalia* 1.279–81) by making Curio responsible for Caesar's decision to cross the Rubicon, the stream separating Italy from Cisalpine Gaul; Roman law forbade a general from leading his army beyond the province he controlled.
4. The feuding between the Guelfs and Ghibellines of Florence was viciously renewed in 1215 by the ardent Ghibelline Mosca de' Lamberti.

beneath the breastplate of its purity.
    I surely saw, and it still seems I see,
a trunk without a head that walked just like
120   the others in that melancholy herd;
    it carried by the hair its severed head,
which swayed within its hand just like a lantern;
and that head looked at us and said: "Ah me!"
    Out of itself it made itself a lamp,
125   and they were two in one and one in two;
how that can be, He knows who so decrees.
    When it was just below the bridge, it lifted
its arm together with its head, so that
its words might be more near us, words that said:
130   "Now you can see atrocious punishment,
you who, still breathing, go to view the dead:
see if there's any pain as great as this.
    And so that you may carry news of me,
know that I am Bertran de Born, the one
135   who gave bad counsel to the fledgling king.[5]
    I made the son and father enemies:
Achitophel with his malicious urgings
did not do worse with Absalom and David.[6]
    Because I severed those so joined, I carry—
140   alas—my brain dissevered from its source,
which is within my trunk. And thus, in me
    one sees the law of counter-penalty."

Canto 29

Still the Eighth Circle, Ninth Pouch: the Sowers of Scandal and Schism. Geri del Bello, an unavenged ancestor of Dante. The Tenth Pouch: the Falsifiers. The First Group, Falsifiers of Metals (Alchemists), plagued by scabs, lying on the earth, scratching furiously. Griffolino. Capocchio.

    So many souls and such outlandish wounds
had made my eyes inebriate—they longed
to stay and weep. But Virgil said to me:
    "Why are you staring so insistently?
5   Why does your vision linger there below
among the lost and mutilated shadows?
    You did not do so at the other moats.
If you would count them all, consider: twenty-
two miles make up the circuit of the valley.[1]
10   The moon already is beneath our feet;

5. Bertran de Born (c. 1140–c. 1215) was Lord of Haute-fort, a soldier and a famous troubadour who specialized in political songs. He was said to have urged Prince Henry of England to rebel against his father, Henry II.
6. Achitophel hanged himself after unsuccessfully

encouraging David's son Absalom to rebel against his father (2 Samuel 15–17:23).
1. It is unclear why Dante chose this moment to provide the first exact measurement of any part of Hell.

the time alloted to us now is short,[2]
and there is more to see than you see here."

    "Had you," I answered him without a pause,
"been able to consider why I looked,
15   you might have granted me a longer stay."

    Meanwhile my guide had moved ahead; I went
behind him, answering as I walked on,
and adding: "In that hollow upon which

    just now, I kept my eyes intent, I think
20   a spirit born of my own blood laments
the guilt which, down below, costs one so much."[3]

    At this my master said: "Don't let your thoughts
about him interrupt you from here on:
attend to other things, let him stay there;

25   for I saw him below the little bridge,
his finger pointing at you, threatening,
and heard him called by name—Geri del Bello.

    But at that moment you were occupied
with him who once was lord of Hautefort;°   *Bertran de Born*
30   you did not notice Geri—he moved off."

    "My guide, it was his death by violence,
for which he still is not avenged,"[4] I said,
"by anyone who shares his shame, that made

    him so disdainful now; and—I suppose—
35   for this he left without a word to me,
and this has made me pity him the more."

    And so we talked until we found the first
point of the ridge that, if there were more light,
would show the other valley to the bottom.

40   When we had climbed above the final cloister
of Malebolge, so that its lay brothers[5]
were able to appear before our eyes,

    I felt the force of strange laments, like arrows
whose shafts are barbed with pity; and at this,
45   I had to place my hands across my ears.

    Just like the sufferings that all the sick
of Val di Chiana's hospitals, Maremma's,
Sardinia's,° from July until September   *malarial regions*
    would muster if assembled in one ditch—
50   so was it here, and such a stench rose up
as usually comes from festering limbs.

---

2. If the moon is below them, the sun must be at its zenith above them, in Jerusalem: it is around 2 P.M. Only four hours remain of the 24 allotted to the journey through Hell.

3. This is Geri del Bello degli Alighieri, first cousin to Dante's father. A troublemaker, Geri was murdered by a member of the Sacchetti family; this was avenged by the Alighieri in 1310, and the families apparently continued feuding until 1342.

4. Family feuding and private vendettas were sanctioned by law in Dante's time; hence, Geri still had just cause for complaint against his family in 1300.

5. The cutting metaphor equates the shades of the tenth *bolgia* to working members of a religious house, the "final cloister" of the eighth circle.

And keeping always to the left, we climbed
down to the final bank of the long ridge,
and then my sight could see more vividly

55   into the bottom, where unerring Justice,
the minister of the High Lord, punishes
the falsifiers she had registered.

I do not think that there was greater grief
in seeing all Aegina's people sick[6]

60   (then, when the air was so infected that
all animals, down to the little worm,
collapsed; and afterward, as poets hold
to be the certain truth, those ancient peoples
received their health again through seed of ants)

65   than I felt when I saw, in that dark valley,
the spirits languishing in scattered heaps.

Some lay upon their bellies, some upon
the shoulders of another spirit, some
crawled on all fours along that squalid road.

70   We journeyed step by step without a word,
watching and listening to those sick souls,
who had not strength enough to lift themselves.

I saw two sitting propped against each other—
as pan is propped on pan to heat them up—

75   and each, from head to foot, spotted with scabs;
and I have never seen a stableboy
whose master waits for him, or one who stays
awake reluctantly, so ply a horse
with currycomb, as they assailed themselves

80   with clawing nails—their itching had such force
and fury, and there was no other help.

And so their nails kept scraping off the scabs,
just as a knife scrapes off the scales of carp
or of another fish with scales more large.

85   "O you who use your nails to strip yourself,"
my guide began to say to one of them,
"and sometimes have to turn them into pincers,
tell us if there are some Italians
among the sinners in this moat—so may

90   your nails hold out, eternal, at their work."

"We two whom you see so disfigured here,
we are Italians," one said, in tears.
"But who are you who have inquired of us?"

My guide replied: "From circle down to circle,

95   together with this living man, I am
one who descends; I mean to show him Hell."

---

6. When Jupiter carried off the nymph Aegina to the island of Oenone, their son Aeacus aroused Juno's jealousy by re-
naming the island after his mother. After Juno sent a devastating pestilence as punishment, Jupiter restored the island by
changing its ants into men, called "Myrmidons" after the Greek word for ant (*Metamorphoses* 7.523–657).

At this their mutual support broke off;
and, quivering, each spirit turned toward me
with others who, by chance, had heard his words.

100   Then my good master drew more close to me,
saying: "Now tell them what it is you want."
And I began to speak, just as he wished:

"So that your memory may never fade
within the first world from the minds of men,

105   but still live on—and under many suns—

do tell me who you are and from what city,
and do not let your vile and filthy torment
make you afraid to let me know your names."

One answered me: "My city was Arezzo

110   and Albero of Siena had me burned;
but what I died for does not bring me here.[7]

It's true that I had told him—jestingly—
'I'd know enough to fly through air'; and he,
with curiosity, but little sense,

115   wished me to show that art to him and, just
because I had not made him Daedalus,
had one who held him as a son burn me.

But Minos, who cannot mistake, condemned
my spirit to the final pouch of ten

120   for alchemy I practiced in the world."

And then I asked the poet: "Was there ever
so vain a people as the Sienese?
Even the French can't match such vanity."[8]

At this, the other leper, who had heard me,

125   replied to what I'd said: "Except for Stricca,
for he knew how to spend most frugally;

and Niccolò, the first to make men see
that cloves can serve as luxury (such seed,
in gardens where it suits, can take fast root);

130   and, too, Caccia d'Asciano's company,
with whom he squandered vineyards and tilled fields,
while Abbagliato showed such subtlety.

But if you want to know who joins you so
against the Sienese, look hard at me—

135   that way, my face can also answer rightly—
and see that I'm the shade of that Capocchio
whose alchemy could counterfeit fine metals.
And you, if I correctly take your measure,
recall how apt I was at aping nature."[9]

---

7. Griffolino was an alchemist of Arezzo who promised he could teach Albero of Siena flying, the art of Daedalus (see 17.109–11). Angry at having been fleeced, Albero denounced Griffolino as a magician, and had him burned at the stake.

8. The vanity of the French was proverbial; the young Sienese noblemen listed below all belonged to a group called the "Spendthrift Club" and revelled in squandering their estates.

9. Capocchio was burned alive in 1293 in Siena as an alchemist; apparently, he was acquainted with the young Dante. Because it attempts to create gold out of baser metals, alchemy imitates or "apes" the work of nature.

Canto 30

Still the Eighth Circle, Tenth Pouch: the Falsifiers. Gianni Schicchi and Myrrha in the Second Group, Counterfeiters of Others' Persons. Master Adam in the Third Group, Counterfeiters of Coins. Potiphar's wife and Sinon the Greek in the Fourth Group, Falsifiers of Words, Liars. The quarrel between Adam and Sinon.

When Juno was incensed with Semele
and, thus, against the Theban family
had shown her fury time and time again,
then Athamas was driven so insane
5   that, seeing both his wife and their two sons,
as she bore one upon each arm, he cried:
"Let's spread the nets, to take the lioness
together with her cubs along the pass";
and he stretched out his talons, pitiless,
10   and snatched the son who bore the name Learchus,
whirled him around and dashed him on a rock;
she, with her other burden, drowned herself.[1]
And after fortune turned against the pride
of Troy, which had dared all, so that the king
15   together with his kingdom, was destroyed,
then Hecuba was wretched, sad, a captive;
and after she had seen Polyxena
dead and, in misery, had recognized
her Polydorus lying on the shore,[2]
20   she barked, out of her senses, like a dog—
her agony had so deformed her mind.
But neither fury—Theban, Trojan—ever
was seen to be so cruel against another,
in rending beasts and even human limbs,
25   as were two shades I saw, both pale and naked,
who, biting, ran berserk in just the way
a hog does when it's let loose from its sty.
The one came at Capocchio and sank
his tusks into his neck so that, by dragging,
30   he made the hard ground scrape against his belly.
And he who stayed behind, the Aretine,
trembled and said: "That phantom's Gianni Schicchi,
and he goes raging, rending others so."[3]
And, "Oh," I said to him, "so may the other
35   not sink its teeth in you, please tell me who

---

1. The Theban princess Semele was loved by Jupiter and she bore him the god Bacchus. As part of her vengeance, Jupiter's wife Juno caused Semele's brother-in-law, the king of Thebes, to believe his wife and two sons were a lioness and cubs; to believe his wife and two sons were a lioness and cubs, after he killed one son, his wife drowned herself with the other (*Metamorphoses* 4.512–30).
2. Priam's queen, Hecuba, went mad after the fall of Troy following the killing of her daughter and son. According to Ovid, on seeing her son's unburied body Hecuba howled like a dog and jumped into the sea (*Metamorphoses* 13.404–575).
3. The "Aretine" is Griffolino from the previous canto. Gianni Chicchi (d. 1280) was a Florentine of the Cavalcanti family well known for his skill at mimicry. In one reported incident, he impersonated Buoso Donati at the request of Simone Donati, in order to dictate a new will in Simone's favor that included Buoso's mule, the best in Tuscany.

it is before it hurries off from here."

    And he to me: "That is the ancient soul
of the indecent Myrrha, she who loved
her father past the limits of just love.[4]

40   She came to sin with him by falsely taking
another's shape upon herself, just as
the other phantom who goes there had done,

    that he might gain the lady of the herd,
when he disguised himself as Buoso Donati,

45   making a will as if most properly."

    And when the pair of raging ones had passed,
those two on whom my eyes were fixed, I turned
around to see the rest of the ill-born.

    I saw one who'd be fashioned like a lute

50   if he had only had his groin cut off
from that part of his body where it forks.

    The heavy dropsy, which so disproportions
the limbs with unassimilated humors
that there's no match between the face and belly,

55   had made him part his lips like a consumptive,
who will, because of thirst, let one lip drop
down to his chin and lift the other up.[5]

    "O you exempt from every punishment
in this grim world, and I do not know why,"

60   he said to us, "look now and pay attention
to this, the misery of Master Adam:
alive, I had enough of all I wanted;
alas, I now long for one drop of water.[6]

    The rivulets that fall into the Arno

65   down from the green hills of the Casentino
with channels cool and moist, are constantly

    before me; I am racked by memory—
the image of their flow parches me more
than the disease that robs my face of flesh.

70   The rigid Justice that would torment me
uses, as most appropriate, the place
where I had sinned, to draw swift sighs from me.

    There is Romena, there I counterfeited
the currency that bears the Baptist's seal;

75   for this I left my body, burned, above.

    But could I see the miserable souls
of Guido, Alessandro, or their brother,

---

4. Myrrha conceived a passion for her father Cinyras, king of Cyprus. With the aid of her nurse, she entered her father's bedchamber in disguise and slept with him.
5. Dropsy, or edema, is an abnormal accumulation of watery fluid ("humors") in the body. A "consumptive" here is someone suffering from hectic fever, a wasting disease characterized by hot, dry skin and flushed cheeks.
6. Master Adam counterfeited the gold florin of Florence. Like the florin, his coins bore the seal of John the Baptist, but they were of 21 rather than 24 carats. In 1281 he suffered the penalty of counterfeiters and was burned at the stake.

I'd not give up the sight for Fonte Branda.[7]
And one of them is in this moat already,
80   if what the angry shades report is true.
What use is that to me whose limbs are tied?
Were I so light that, in a hundred years,
I could advance an inch, I should already
be well upon the road to search for him
85   among the mutilated ones, although
this circuit measures some eleven miles
and is at least a half a mile across.
Because of them I'm in this family;
it was those three who had incited me
90   to coin the florins with three carats' dross."
And I to him: "Who are those two poor sinners
who give off smoke like wet hands in the winter
and lie so close to you upon the right?"
"I found them here," he answered, "when I rained
95   down to this rocky slope; they've not stirred since
and will not move, I think, eternally.
One is the lying woman who blamed Joseph;
the other, lying Sinon, Greek from Troy:[8]
because of raging fever they reek so."
100   And one of them, who seemed to take offense,
perhaps at being named so squalidly,
struck with his fist at Adam's rigid belly.
It sounded as if it had been a drum;
and Master Adam struck him in the face,
105   using his arm, which did not seem less hard,
saying to him: "Although I cannot move
my limbs because they are too heavy, I
still have an arm that's free to serve that need."
And he replied: "But when you went to burning,
110   your arm was not as quick as it was now;
though when you coined, it was as quick and more."
To which the dropsied one: "Here you speak true;
but you were not so true a witness there,
when you were asked to tell the truth at Troy."
115   "If I spoke false, you falsified the coin,"
said Sinon; "I am here for just one crime—
but you've committed more than any demon."
"Do not forget the horse, you perjurer,"
replied the one who had the bloated belly,
120   "may you be plagued because the whole world knows it."

---

7. Adam names three of the Conti Guidi family, who in-
stigated his counterfeiting, including Guido II da Romena, who died before 1300. The Fonte Branda is perhaps a
now almost dry fountain near the castle of Romena.
8. After Joseph rejected the advances of Potiphar's wife,

she accused him of attempting to seduce her (Genesis
39:6–20). Sinon was a treacherous Greek who allowed
himself to be captured by the Trojans, persuading them to
take within their walls the wooden horse the Greeks had
left (and hidden inside) (*Aeneid* 2.18–370).

The Greek: "And you be plagued by thirst that cracks
your tongue, and putrid water that has made
your belly such a hedge before your eyes."
And then the coiner: "So, as usual,
125   your mouth, because of racking fever, gapes;
for if I thirst and if my humor bloats me,
you have both dryness and a head that aches;
few words would be sufficient invitation
to have you lick the mirror of Narcissus."[9]
130   I was intent on listening to them
when this was what my master said: "If you
insist on looking more, I'll quarrel with you!"
And when I heard him speak so angrily,
I turned around to him with shame so great
135   that it still stirs within my memory.
Even as one who dreams that he is harmed
and, dreaming, wishes he were dreaming, thus
desiring that which is, as if it were not,
so I became within my speechlessness:
140   I wanted to excuse myself and did
excuse myself, although I knew it not.
"Less shame would wash away a greater fault
than was your fault," my master said to me;
"therefore release yourself from all remorse
145   and see that I am always at your side,
should it so happen—once again—that fortune
brings you where men would quarrel in this fashion:
to want to hear such bickering is base."

Canto 31

*Passage to the Ninth Circle. The central pit or well of Hell, where Cocytus, the last
river of Hell, freezes. The Giants: Nimrod, Ephialtes, Briareus, Antaeus. Antaeus's
compliance with Virgil's request to lower the two poets into the pit.*

The very tongue that first had wounded me,
sending the color up in both my cheeks,
was then to cure me with its medicine—
as did Achilles' and his father's lance,
5   even as I have heard, when it dispensed
a sad stroke first and then a healing one.[1]
We turned our backs upon that dismal valley
by climbing up the bank that girdles it;

---

9. When the nymph Echo's love for the youth Narcissus
was unrequited, she pined away until all that was left was
her voice. In punishment, he was made to fall in love with
his own reflection in a fountain, pining away as well, until
he was transformed into a flower (*Metamorphoses*
3.351–510). To "lick" his mirror thus means to drink.

1. Achilles' father Peleus gave him a spear that by its
mere touch could cure any wound it had caused
(*Metamorphoses* 13.171–2). Medieval poets often used
the image to describe the lady's love, which could be
healed only by opening a new wound in her lover.

we made our way across without a word.

10   Here it was less than night and less than day,
so that my sight could only move ahead
slightly, but then I heard a bugle blast

    so strong, it would have made a thunder clap
seem faint; at this, my eyes—which doubled back
15 upon their path—turned fully toward one place.

    Not even Roland's horn, which followed on
the sad defeat when Charlemagne had lost
his holy army, was as dread as this.[2]

    I'd only turned my head there briefly when
20 I seemed to make out many high towers; then
I asked him: "Master, tell me, what's this city?"

    And he to me: "It is because you try
to penetrate from far into these shadows
that you have formed such faulty images.

25   When you have reached that place, you shall see clearly
how much the distance has deceived your sense;
and, therefore, let this spur you on your way."

    Then lovingly he took me by the hand
and said: "Before we have moved farther on,
30 so that the fact may seem less strange to you,

    I'd have you know they are not towers, but giants,
and from the navel downward, all of them
are in the central pit, at the embankment."

    Just as, whenever mists begin to thin,
35 when, gradually, vision finds the form
that in the vapor-thickened air was hidden,

    so I pierced through the dense and darkened fog;
as I drew always nearer to the shore,
my error fled from me, my terror grew;

40   for as, on its round wall, Montereggioni°   *a hill fortress*
is crowned with towers, so there towered here,
above the bank that runs around the pit,

    with half their bulk, the terrifying giants,
whom Jove still menaces from Heaven when
45 he sends his bolts of thunder down upon them.

    And I could now make out the face of one,
his shoulders and his chest, much of his belly,
and both his arms that hung along his sides.

    Surely when she gave up the art of making
50 such creatures, Nature acted well indeed,
depriving Mars of instruments like these.[3]

    And if she still produces elephants

---

2. A first image of the ninth circle's sin of treachery. In the medieval epic, *The Song of Roland,* after the hero Roland, leader of Charlemagne's rear-guard, has had his forces betrayed to and annihilated by the Saracens at Roncesvalles, he sounds his famous horn so loudly that the emperor returns to avenge his death.

3. Dante equates the Giants of Greek myth with those of the Bible, "expert in war" (Baruch 3:26–28).

and whales, whoever sees with subtlety
holds her—for this—to be more just and prudent;

55   for where the mind's acutest reasoning
is joined to evil will and evil power,
there human beings can't defend themselves.[4]

His face appeared to me as broad and long
as Rome can claim for its St. Peter's pine cone;[5]

60   his other bones shared in that same proportion;

so that the bank, which served him as an apron
down from his middle, showed so much of him
above, that three Frieslanders would in vain

have boasted of their reaching to his hair;

65   for downward from the place where one would buckle
a mantle, I saw thirty spans of him.[6]

"Raphèl maì amècche zabì almi,"
began to bellow that brute mouth, for which
no sweeter psalms would be appropriate.[7]

70   And my guide turned to him: "O stupid soul,
keep to your horn and use that as an outlet
when rage or other passion touches you![8]

Look at your neck, and you will find the strap
that holds it fast; and see, bewildered spirit,

75   how it lies straight across your massive chest."

And then to me: "He is his own accuser;
for this is Nimrod, through whose wicked thought
one single language cannot serve the world.

Leave him alone—let's not waste time in talk;

80   for every language is to him the same
as his to others—no one knows his tongue."

So, turning to the left, we journeyed on
and, at the distance of a bow-shot, found
another giant, far more huge and fierce.

85   Who was the master who had tied him so,
I cannot say, but his left arm was bent
behind him and his right was bent in front,

both pinioned by a chain that held him tight
down from the neck; and round the part of him

90   that was exposed, it had been wound five times.

"This giant in his arrogance had tested
his force against the force of highest Jove,"
my guide said, "so he merits this reward.

---

4. According to Aquinas, "An evil man can do ten thousand times more harm than a beast by his reason which he can use to devise very diverse evils."
5. This bronze pine cone, over 12 feet high, was said to have stood near the Campus Martius in Rome; it was moved to the old basilica of St. Peter's.
6. The inhabitants of Friesland on the North Sea were known for their great height; the giant's top half is about 35 feet.

7. The giant is Nimrod, biblical ruler of Babylon, under whose direction the Tower of Babel was attempted (Genesis 10–11). His incomprehensible words, which no commentator has deciphered, are an apt retribution for his role in causing the confusion of the world's tongues.
8. The hunter's horn derives from the biblical description of Nimrod as a "mighty hunter before the Lord" (Genesis 10:9).

His name is Ephialtes;[9] and he showed
95   tremendous power when the giants frightened
the gods; the arms he moved now move no more."

And I to him: "If it is possible,
I'd like my eyes to have experience
of the enormous one, Briareus."

100   At which he answered: "You shall see Antaeus[1]
nearby. He is unfettered and can speak;
he'll take us to the bottom of all evil.

The one you wish to see lies far beyond
and is bound up and just as huge as this one,
105   and even more ferocious in his gaze."

No earthquake ever was so violent
when called to shake a tower so robust,
as Ephialtes quick to shake himself.

Then I was more afraid of death than ever;
110   that fear would have been quite enough to kill me,
had I not seen how he was held by chains.

And we continued on until we reached
Antaeus, who, not reckoning his head,
stood out above the rock wall full five ells.°   *fifteen feet*
115   "O you, who lived within the famous valley
(where Scipio became the heir of glory
when Hannibal retreated with his men),[2]

who took a thousand lions as your prey—
and had you been together with your brothers
120   in their high war, it seems some still believe
the sons of earth would have become the victors—
do set us down below, where cold shuts in
Cocytus,[3] and do not disdain that task.

Don't send us on to Tityus or Typhon;[4]
125   this man can give you what is longed for here;
therefore bend down and do not curl your lip.

He still can bring you fame within the world,
for he's alive and still expects long life,
unless grace summon him before his time."

130   So said my master; and in haste Antaeus
stretched out his hands, whose massive grip had once
been felt by Hercules, and grasped my guide.

---

9. Son of Neptune; with his brother Otus, he stormed Olympus itself. Virgil placed them both in Tartarus (*Aeneid* 6.771–74).
1. The 100-handed and 50-headed giant Briareus joined the attack of his race against the gods; Jupiter slew him with a thunderbolt and buried him under Mt. Etna. Unlike the enchained giants here, Antaeus was born after the war against the gods. Son of Neptune and Earth, he was invincible while in contact with his mother. He lived in Libya and was said to feed on wild lions. Hercules slew him when he managed to lift Antaeus off the ground and crush

him (*Pharsalia* 4.585–660).
2. The valley of the Bagradas River in north-central Tunisia was site of Scipio's decisive victory over Hannibal's forces in 202 B.C.E. during the Second Punic War between Rome and Carthage.
3. The frozen lake that covers the ninth circle at the bottom of Hell.
4. Two more giants: Tityus was thrown into Tartarus by Apollo and Diana for his attempted rape of their mother Latona; Typhon, incited by his mother, Earth, to attack the Olympian gods, was defeated by Jupiter.

And Virgil, when he felt himself caught up,
called out to me: "Come here, so I can hold you,"
135   then made one bundle of himself and me.

Just as the Garisenda seems when seen
beneath the leaning side, when clouds run past
and it hangs down as if about to crash,[5]
so did Antaeus seem to me as I
140   watched him bend over me—a moment when
I'd have preferred to take some other road.

But gently—on the deep that swallows up
both Lucifer and Judas—he placed us;
nor did he, so bent over, stay there long,
145   but, like a mast above a ship, he rose.

Canto 32

The Ninth Circle, First Ring, called Caïna, where Traitors to their Kin are immersed in the ice, heads bent down. Camiscione dei Pazzi. The Second Ring, called Antenora: the Traitors to their Homeland or Party. Bocca degli Abati's provocation of Dante. Two traitors, one gnawing at the other's head.

Had I the crude and scrannel° rhymes to suit   harsh
the melancholy hole upon which all
the other circling crags converge and rest,
the juice of my conception would be pressed
5   more fully; but because I feel their lack,
I bring myself to speak, yet speak in fear;
for it is not a task to take in jest,
to show the base of all the universe—
nor for a tongue that cries out, "mama," "papa."
10   But may those ladies now sustain my verse
who helped Amphion when he walled up Thebes,
so that my tale not differ from the fact.[1]

O rabble, miscreated past all others,
there in the place of which it's hard to speak,
15   better if here you had been goats or sheep!

When we were down below in the dark well,
beneath the giant's feet and lower yet,
with my eyes still upon the steep embankment,
I heard this said to me: "Watch how you pass;
20   walk so that you not trample with your soles
the heads of your exhausted, wretched brothers."

At this I turned and saw in front of me,
beneath my feet, a lake that, frozen fast,

---

5. One of the leaning towers of Bologna, Garisenda was built in 1110; a cloud passing opposite the direction of the slant gives the illusion of the tower falling out of the sky.
1. The Muses ("ladies") inspired the singer Amphion to charm the stones of Mt. Cithaeron with his lyre into arranging themselves as walls around Thebes (Horace, *Ars Poetica* 394–96; *Thebaid* 10.873–77). The invocation of the Muses marks a new beginning of the poem, and a mixed style of language and diction.

had lost the look of water and seemed glass.

25 The Danube where it flows in Austria,
the Don beneath its frozen sky,° have never   *in Russia*
made for their course so thick a veil in winter

as there was here; for had Mount Tambernic
or Pietrapana's mountain° crashed upon it,   *Italian alps*
30 not even at the edge would it have creaked.

And as the croaking frog sits with its muzzle
above the water, in the season when
the peasant woman often dreams of gleaning,

so, livid in the ice, up to the place
35 where shame can show itself, were those sad shades,
whose teeth were chattering with notes like storks'.

Each kept his face bent downward steadily;
their mouths bore witness to the cold they felt,
just as their eyes proclaimed their sorry hearts.

40 When I had looked around a while, my eyes
turned toward my feet and saw two locked so close,
the hair upon their heads had intermingled.

"Do tell me, you whose chests are pressed so tight,"
I said, "who are you?" They bent back their necks,
45 and when they'd lifted up their faces toward me,

their eyes, which wept upon the ground before,
shed tears down on their lips until the cold
held fast the tears and locked their lids still more.

No clamp has ever fastened plank to plank
50 so tightly; and because of this, they butted
each other like two rams, such was their fury.

And one from whom the cold had taken both
his ears, who kept his face bent low, then said:
"Why do you keep on staring so at us?

55 If you would like to know who these two are:
that valley where Bisenzio descends,
belonged to them and to their father Alberto.[2]

They came out of one body; and you can
search all Caïna,[3] you will never find
60 a shade more fit to sit within this ice—

not him who, at one blow, had chest and shadow
shattered by Arthur's hand;[4] and not Focaccia;
and not this sinner here who so impedes

my vision with his head, I can't see past him;
65 his name was Sassol Mascheroni; if

---

2. The Conti Alberti had two castles in this region west of
Florence. The Guelf Alessandro and the Ghibelline
Napoleone were sons of Alberto degli Alberti; they killed
each other quarreling over the inheritance of the Castle of
Mangano.
3. Caïna, the first of the four subdivisions of Cocytus, is
named after Cain, the first man to betray and kill a kinsman, his brother Abel (Genesis 4).
4. Mordred, the traitorous nephew of King Arthur, slew
his uncle; when Arthur pierced Mordred with a spear in
return, a ray of sunlight passed through the wound.

you're Tuscan, now you know who he has been.[5]
    And lest you keep me talking any longer,
know that I was Camiscion de' Pazzi;
I'm waiting for Carlino to absolve me."[6]

70   And after that I saw a thousand faces
made doglike by the cold; for which I shudder—
and always will—when I face frozen fords.[7]
    And while we were advancing toward the center
to which all weight is drawn—I, shivering

75 in that eternally cold shadow—I
    know not if it was will or destiny
or chance, but as I walked among the heads,
I struck my foot hard in the face of one.
    Weeping, he chided then: "Why trample me?

80 If you've not come to add to the revenge
of Montaperti, why do you molest me?"[8]
    And I: "My master, now wait here for me,
that I may clear up just one doubt about him;
then you can make me hurry as you will."

85   My guide stood fast, and I went on to ask
of him who still was cursing bitterly:
"Who are you that rebukes another so?"
    "And who are you who go through Antenora,
striking the cheeks of others," he replied,

90 "too roughly—even if you were alive?"
    "I am alive, and can be precious to you
if you want fame," was my reply, "for I
can set your name among my other notes."
    And he to me: "I want the contrary;

95 so go away and do not harass me—
your flattery is useless in this valley."
    At that I grabbed him by the scruff and said:
"You'll have to name yourself to me or else
you won't have even one hair left up here."

100   And he to me: "Though you should strip me bald,
I shall not tell you who I am or show it,
not if you pound my head a thousand times."
    His hairs were wound around my hand already,
and I had plucked from him more than one tuft

105 while he was barking and his eyes stared down,
    when someone else cried out: "What is it, Bocca?

5. Foccaccia was the nickname of the White Guelf Vanni de' Cancellieri of Pistoia, guilty of murdering a cousin in 1293. Sassol Mascheroni was a Florentine who murdered a kinsman for the sake of his inheritance.
6. The Ghibelline Camiscion de' Pazzi of the Val d'Arno treacherously killed his kinsman Ubertino. In 1302, his kinsman Carlino would betray the Florentine Whites and Ghibellines in the Castle of Piantravigne to the Blacks. As a traitor against his party, Carlino will "absolve" Camiscion by going to the next, worse ring of Cocytus, where those who betrayed party, country, or city are punished.
7. A subtle transition to the second ring, where the souls hold their heads erect rather than being able to shelter their eyes from the cold. The ring is named Antenora after the Trojan warrior Antenor, who was believed to have betrayed his city to the Greeks.
8. Bocca degli Abati, a Florentine Guelf who betrayed his party at the battle of Montaperti in 1260 when he cut off the hand of the Florentine standard-bearer at the crucial moment of the charge of Manfred's German cavalry.

Isn't the music of your jaws enough
for you without your bark? What devil's at you?"
  "And now," I said, "you traitor bent on evil,
110 I do not need your talk, for I shall carry
true news of you, and that will bring you shame."
  "Be off," he answered; "tell them what you like,
but don't be silent, if you make it back,
about the one whose tongue was now so quick.
115 Here he laments the silver of the Frenchmen;
'I saw,' you then can say, 'him of Duera,
down there, where all the sinners are kept cool.'[9]
  And if you're asked who else was there in ice,
one of the Beccheria is beside you—
120 he had his gullet sliced right through by Florence.
  Gianni de' Soldanieri, I believe,
lies there with Ganelon and Tebaldello,
he who unlocked Faenza while it slept."[1]
  We had already taken leave of him,
125 when I saw two shades frozen in one hole,
so that one's head served as the other's cap;
  and just as he who's hungry chews his bread,
one sinner dug his teeth into the other
right at the place where brain is joined to nape:
130 no differently had Tydeus gnawed the temples
of Menalippus, out of indignation,[2]
than this one chewed the skull and other parts.
  "O you who show, with such a bestial sign,
your hatred for the one on whom you feed,
135 tell me the cause," I said; "we can agree
  that if your quarrel with him is justified,
then knowing who you are and what's his sin,
I shall repay you yet on earth above,
  if that with which I speak does not dry up."

Canto 33

Still the Ninth Circle, Second Ring. Ugolino's tale of his and his sons' death in a Pisan prison. Dante's invective against Pisa. The Third Ring, Ptolomea, where Traitors against their Guests jut out from ice, their eyes sealed by frozen tears. Fra Alberigo and Branca Doria, still alive on earth but already in Hell.

9. In 1265, the Ghibelline leader of Cremona, Buoso da Duera, betrayed Manfred, King of Naples, when he was bribed to allow the French troops to pass through Lombardy unmolested.
1. Tesauro de' Beccheria of Pavia, Abbot of Vallombrosa, was seized and beheaded in 1258 by the Florentine Guelfs on the charge of intriguing with the Ghibellines. Gianni de' Soldanieri was a Florentine Ghibelline who opposed his own party when the populace rose up against it following the defeat and death of Manfred at Benevento in

1266. Tebaldello opened the gates of his city to Guelf enemies in order to avenge a private grudge. As recorded in *The Song of Roland*, Ganelon betrayed the rearguard of Charlemagne at Roncesvalles; his name became synonymous with treachery.
2. King Tydeus was one of the Seven against Thebes. When mortally wounded by Menalippus, whom he slayed in return, the enraged Tydeus gnawed through his enemy's skull and ate part of his brain (*Thebaid* 8.739–62).

That sinner raised his mouth from his fierce meal,
then used the head that he had ripped apart
in back: he wiped his lips upon its hair.

Then he began: "You want me to renew
5   despairing pain that presses at my heart
even as I think back, before I speak.

But if my words are seed from which the fruit
is infamy for this betrayer whom
I gnaw, you'll see me speak and weep at once.[1]

10   I don't know who you are or in what way
you've come down here; and yet you surely seem—
from what I hear—to be a Florentine.

You are to know I was Count Ugolino,
and this one here, Archbishop Ruggieri;
15   and now I'll tell you why I am his neighbor.[2]

There is no need to tell you that, because
of his malicious tricks, I first was taken
and then was killed—since I had trusted him;

however, that which you cannot have heard—
20   that is, the cruel death devised for me—
you now shall hear and know if he has wronged me.

A narrow window in the Eagles' Tower,
which now, through me, is called the Hunger Tower,
a cage in which still others will be locked,[3]

25   had, through its opening, already showed me
several moons, when I dreamed that bad dream
which rent the curtain of the future for me.[4]

This man appeared to me as lord and master;
he hunted down the wolf and its young whelps
30   upon the mountain that prevents the Pisans

from seeing Lucca; and with lean and keen
and practiced hounds, he'd sent up front, before him,
Gualandi and Sismondi and Lanfranchi.

But after a brief course, it seemed to me

1. Several phrases in this speech of Ugolino recall those of Francesca in Canto 5.
2. Count Ugolino della Gherardesca was banished from the traditionally Ghibelline city of Pisa for conspiring with the Guelf leader Giovanni Visconti in 1275, but returned to wealth and position the following year. Following a defeat by Genoa (which he was suspected of abetting) Ugolino was made magistrate of Pisa in 1284. He ceded three castles to Florence and Lucca to assuage the Guelf threat, which his enemies regarded as a betrayal. The following year, Ugolino feuded with his Guelf grandson, Nino Visconti, son of Giovanni, with whom he was sharing the magistracy. The Ghibelline Ruggieri degli Ubaldini was archbishop of Pisa, and magistrate in place of Ugolino in 1288. Ugolino apparently intrigued with Ruggiero against Nino but was betrayed by the archbishop and his Ghibelline allies, who invited the count back into the city only to lock him up with two of his sons

(Gaddo and Uguiccone) and two grandsons (Anselm and a different Nino, nicknamed "Brigata") in the Tower of Gualandi, where they eventually were starved to death. Pisa was now controlled by the Ghibellines, with Guido da Montefeltro (see Canto 27) soon to be made their magistrate.
3. The Tower of Gualandi served as a prison until 1318. According to early commentators, moulting eagles were kept in its Mew, or tower, which became known after Ugolino's death as the Torre della Fame ("Tower of Hunger").
4. In the dream, Ruggieri ("lord and master") hunts down Ugolino and his children on Mt. San Giuliano, between Pisa and Lucca (where the count had political connections). The dogs likely represent the populace roused against Ugolino by Ruggieri; the Gualandi, Sismondi and Lanfranchi were prominent Ghibelline families of Pisa who joined the archbishop.

35 that both the father and the sons were weary;
I seemed to see their flanks torn by sharp fangs.

 When I awoke at daybreak, I could hear
my sons, who were together with me there,
weeping within their sleep, asking for bread.

40 You would be cruel indeed if, thinking what
my heart foresaw, you don't already grieve;
and if you don't weep now, when would you weep?

 They were awake by now; the hour drew near
at which our food was usually brought,

45 and each, because of what he'd dreamed, was anxious;

 below, I heard them nailing up the door
of that appalling tower; without a word,
I looked into the faces of my sons.

 I did not weep; within, I turned to stone.

50 They wept; and my poor little Anselm said:
'Father, you look so . . . What is wrong with you?'

 At that I shed no tears and—all day long
and through the night that followed—did not answer
until another sun had touched the world.

55 As soon as a thin ray had made its way
into that sorry prison, and I saw,
reflected in four faces, my own gaze,

 out of my grief, I bit at both my hands;
and they, who thought I'd done that out of hunger,

60 immediately rose and told me: 'Father,

 it would be far less painful for us if
you ate of us; for you clothed us in this
sad flesh—it is for you to strip it off.'

 Then I grew calm, to keep them from more sadness;

65 through that day and the next, we all were silent;
O hard earth, why did you not open up?

 But after we had reached the fourth day, Gaddo,
throwing himself, outstretched, down at my feet,
implored me: 'Father, why do you not help me?'

70 And there he died; and just as you see me,
I saw the other three fall one by one
between the fifth day and the sixth; at which,

 now blind, I started groping over each;
and after they were dead, I called them for

75 two days; then fasting had more force than grief."[5]

 When he had spoken this, with eyes awry,
again he gripped the sad skull in his teeth,
which, like a dog's, were strong down to the bone.

 Ah, Pisa, you the scandal of the peoples

---

5. This line suggests that Ugolino resorted to cannibalism. Given the allusion to Christ on the cross in line 69 (Matthew 27:46), there is probably a religious overtone as well: Ugolino does not provide his children with spiritual any more than with earthly bread, consuming their hope of salvation.

80   of that fair land where *si* is heard,° because   *Italy*
      your neighbors are so slow to punish you,
          may, then, Caprara and Gorgona° move   *Mediterranean islands*
      and build a hedge across the Arno's mouth,
      so that it may drown every soul in you!

85   For if Count Ugolino was reputed
      to have betrayed your fortresses, there was
      no need to have his sons endure such torment.
          O Thebes renewed,[6] their years were innocent
      and young—Brigata, Uguiccione, and
90   the other two my song has named above!
          We passed beyond, where frozen water wraps—
      a rugged covering—still other sinners,
      who were not bent, but flat upon their backs.
          Their very weeping there won't let them weep,
95   and grief that finds a barrier in their eyes
      turns inward to increase their agony;
          because their first tears freeze into a cluster,
      and, like a crystal visor, fill up all
      the hollow that is underneath the eyebrow.
100   And though, because of cold, my every sense
      had left its dwelling in my face, just as
      a callus has no feeling, nonetheless,
          I seemed to feel some wind now, and I said:
      "My master, who has set this gust in motion?
105   For isn't every vapor quenched down here?"[7]
          And he to me: "You soon shall be where your
      own eye will answer that, when you shall see
      the reason why this wind blasts from above."
          And one of those sad sinners in the cold
110   crust, cried to us: "O souls who are so cruel
      that this last place has been assigned to you,
          take off the hard veils from my face so that
      I can release the suffering that fills
      my heart before lament freezes again."
115   To which I answered: "If you'd have me help you,
      then tell me who you are; if I don't free you,
      may I go to the bottom of the ice."[8]
          He answered then: "I am Fra Alberigo,
      the one who tended fruits in a bad garden,
120   and here my figs have been repaid with dates."[9]
          "But then," I said, "are you already dead?"

6. The ancient city of Thebes was notorious for crime and
bloodshed.
7. The cause of wind was thought to be the heat of the
sun.
8. A deceptive promise, since he is in fact headed to the
"bottom of the ice."
9. Like Catalano and Loderingo (23.103–9), Alberigo was

a member of the order of the Jovial Friars; like Tebaldello
(32.122), he belonged to the Guelf Manfredi family of
Faenza. Alberigo had two of his relatives killed at a banquet at his house in supposed reconciliation. The signal to
the assassins was his order at the end of dinner to bring
the fruit. He believes his punishment overly severe, as a
fig is worth less than a date.

And he to me: "I have no knowledge of
my body's fate within the world above.
   For Ptolomea has this privilege:

125   quite frequently the soul falls here before
it has been thrust away by Atropos.[1]
   And that you may with much more willingness
scrape these glazed tears from off my face, know this:
as soon as any soul becomes a traitor,

130   as I was, then a demon takes its body
away—and keeps that body in his power
until its years have run their course completely.
   The soul falls headlong, down into this cistern;
and up above, perhaps, there still appears

135   the body of the shade that winters here
     behind me; you must know him, if you've just
come down; he is Ser Branca Doria;[2]
for many years he has been thus pent up."
   I said to him: "I think that you deceive me,

140   for Branca Doria is not yet dead;
he eats and drinks and sleeps and puts on clothes."
   "There in the Malebranche's ditch above,
where sticky pitch boils up, Michele Zanche
had still not come," he said to me, "when this one—

145   together with a kinsman, who had done
the treachery together with him—left
a devil in his stead inside his body.
   But now reach out your hand; open my eyes."
And yet I did not open them for him;

150   and it was courtesy to show him rudeness.
   Ah, Genoese, a people strange to every
constraint of custom, full of all corruption,
why have you not been driven from the world?
   For with the foulest spirit of Romagna,
I found one of you such that, for his acts,[3]
in soul he bathes already in Cocytus
   and up above appears alive, in body.

Canto 34

The Ninth Circle, Fourth Ring, called Judecca, where Traitors against their Benefactors are fully covered by ice. Dis, or Lucifer, emperor of that kingdom, his three

---

1. Ptolomea, where betrayers of guests and friends are punished, may be named for the Egyptian king Ptolemy XII (51–47 B.C.E.), murderer of Pompey (*Pharsalia* 8.536–712), or for a governor of Jericho who murdered his father-in-law, the high priest Simon the Maccabee, and two of his sons at a banquet in their honor in 134 B.C.E. (1 Maccabees 16:11–17). Ptolomea is apparently unique among the parts of Hell in that souls can be condemned to it before they are actually dead. (Atropos was

the one of the three Fates responsible for cutting the thread of an individual's life.) The idea is perhaps the most extreme of the many heterodoxies included by Dante in his conception of the afterlife.
2. A Ghibelline of a famous Genoese family who murdered his father-in-law Michel Zanche at a banquet with the aid of another relation.
3. The "foulest spirit of Romagna" is Alberigo; the "Genoese" is Branca Doria.

mouths rending Judas, Brutus, and Cassius. Descent of Virgil and Dante down Lucifer's body to the other, southern hemisphere. Their vision of the stars.

"*Vexilla regis prodeunt inferni*[1]
toward us; and therefore keep your eyes ahead,"
my master said, "to see if you can spy him."

     Just as, when night falls on our hemisphere
5   or when a heavy fog is blowing thick,
a windmill seems to wheel when seen far off,

     so then I seemed to see that sort of structure.
And next, because the wind was strong, I shrank
behind my guide; there was no other shelter.

10   And now—with fear I set it down in meter—
I was where all the shades were fully covered
but visible as wisps of straw in glass.

     There some lie flat and others stand erect,
one on his head, and one upon his soles;
15   and some bend face to feet, just like a bow.

     But after we had made our way ahead,
my master felt he now should have me see
that creature who was once a handsome presence;[2]

     he stepped aside and made me stop, and said:
20   "Look! Here is Dis, and this the place where you
will have to arm yourself with fortitude."

     O reader, do not ask of me how I
grew faint and frozen then—I cannot write it:
all words would fall far short of what it was.

25   I did not die, and I was not alive;
think for yourself, if you have any wit,
what I became, deprived of life and death.

     The emperor of the despondent kingdom
so towered from the ice, up from midchest,
30   that I match better with a giant's breadth

     than giants match the measure of his arms;
now you can gauge the size of all of him
if it is in proportion to such parts.

     If he was once as handsome as he now
35   is ugly and, despite that, raised his brows
against his Maker, one can understand how

     every sorrow has its source in him!
I marveled when I saw that, on his head,
he had three faces: one—in front—bloodred;

40   and then another two that, just above
the midpoint of each shoulder, joined the first;
and at the crown, all three were reattached;

---

1. "The banners of the king of Hell draw closer": modified from a Holy Week hymn, with Hell in place of Heaven, as Lucifer is the negative mirror image of Christ.

2. Lucifer, the "light-bearing" seraph, or angel, was most beautiful of them all before he fell, becoming Satan. Dante identifies him with Dis, the Roman god of the underworld.

the right looked somewhat yellow, somewhat white;
the left in its appearance was like those°   *black Ethiopians*
45   who come from where the Nile, descending, flows.

    Beneath each face of his, two wings spread out,
as broad as suited so immense a bird:
I've never seen a ship with sails so wide.

    They had no feathers, but were fashioned like
50   a bat's; and he was agitating them,
so that three winds made their way out from him—

    and all Cocytus froze before those winds.
He wept out of six eyes; and down three chins,
tears gushed together with a bloody froth.[3]

55   Within each mouth—he used it like a grinder—
with gnashing teeth he tore to bits a sinner,
so that he brought much pain to three at once.

    The forward sinner found that biting nothing
when matched against the clawing, for at times
60   his back was stripped completely of its hide.

    "That soul up there who has to suffer most,"
my master said: "Judas Iscariot—
his head inside, he jerks his legs without.

    Of those two others, with their heads beneath,
65   the one who hangs from that black snout is Brutus—
see how he writhes and does not say a word!

    That other, who seems so robust, is Cassius.[4]
But night is come again, and it is time
for us to leave; we have seen everything."[5]

70   Just as he asked, I clasped him round the neck;
and he watched for the chance of time and place,
and when the wings were open wide enough,

    he took fast hold upon the shaggy flanks
and then descended, down from tuft to tuft,
75   between the tangled hair and icy crusts.

    When we had reached the point at which the thigh
revolves, just at the swelling of the hip,
my guide, with heavy strain and rugged work,

    reversed his head to where his legs had been
80   and grappled on the hair, as one who climbs—
I thought that we were going back to Hell.

---

3. The *contrapasso* of Dis reproduces his rebellion: he is depicted as a false, three-faced Trinity, winged like an angel (the seraph also had six wings), and lord of the realm, but a lord as hideous as he once was beautiful, whose only power is the mechanical beating of wings that freezes Cocytus and confines him in the ice of his own making, and the grinding of teeth that punishes the three traitors in his jaws.
4. The three arch-traitors are Judas Iscariot, who sold Christ (after whom this region of Judecca is named; he is gnawed head-first), and two conspirators against Julius

Caesar, Marcus Junius Brutus and Gaius Cassius Longus (gnawed feet-first) both of whom killed themselves after their defeat at Philippi in 42 B.C.E., two years following Caesar's murder.
5. It is now 6 P.M. on Holy Saturday, 24 hours after the pair entered the Gate of Hell on Good Friday. The anti-climactic nature of Satan and the bottom of Hell shows evil as an empty negation or perversion of good desires and intentions rather than a powerful and independent force of its own.

"Hold tight," my master said—he panted like
a man exhausted—"it is by such stairs
that we must take our leave of so much evil."[6]

85   Then he slipped through a crevice in a rock
and placed me on the edge of it, to sit;
that done, he climbed toward me with steady steps.

I raised my eyes, believing I should see
the half of Lucifer that I had left;

90   instead I saw him with his legs turned up;
and if I then became perplexed, do let
the ignorant be judges—those who can
not understand what point I had just crossed.

"Get up," my master said, "be on your feet:

95   the way is long, the path is difficult;
the sun's already back to middle tierce."[7]

It was no palace hall, the place in which
we found ourselves, but with its rough-hewn floor
and scanty light, a dungeon built by nature.

100   "Before I free myself from this abyss,
master," I said when I had stood up straight,
"tell me enough to see I don't mistake:

Where is the ice? And how is he so placed
head downward? Tell me, too, how has the sun

105   in so few hours gone from night to morning?"

And he to me: "You still believe you are
north of the center, where I grasped the hair
of the damned worm who pierces through the world.

And you were there as long as I descended;

110   but when I turned, that's when you passed the point
to which, from every part, all weights are drawn.

And now you stand beneath the hemisphere
opposing that which cloaks the great dry lands
and underneath whose zenith died the Man

115   whose birth and life were sinless in this world.[8]
Your feet are placed upon a little sphere
that forms the other face of the Judecca.

Here it is morning when it's evening there;
and he whose hair has served us as a ladder

120   is still fixed, even as he was before.
This was the side on which he fell from Heaven;
for fear of him, the land that once loomed here

6. Just as Hell can only be avoided by comprehending
every last part of it, so the only way out of it is through its
very heart, the body of Satan. Because the waist of his
body is placed at the very center of the earth (and of the
universe in Ptolemy's conception), the climb takes the
pair from the northern into the southern hemisphere (held
to be all water), causing the inversion of direction that so
confuses the pilgrim.

7. The reference to the sun—all such references within
Hell were given with respect to the moon and stars—tells
us that in the southern hemisphere it is now 7:30 A.M. The
climb through the southern half of the earth will take 21
or 22 hours, about the same amount of time as the descent
through Hell.

8. Jerusalem was regarded as the center of the northern
hemisphere of land; it was often represented on maps with
the image of Christ hanging on the cross.

made of the sea a veil and rose into
our hemisphere; and that land which appears
125 upon this side—perhaps to flee from him—
left here this hollow space and hurried upward."[9]
There is a place below, the limit of
that cave, its farthest point from Beelzebub,°   *Satan*
a place one cannot see: it is discovered
130   by ear—there is a sounding stream that flows
along the hollow of a rock eroded
by winding waters, and the slope is easy.
My guide and I came on that hidden road
to make our way back into the bright world;
135   and with no care for any rest, we climbed—
he first, I following—until I saw,
through a round opening, some of those things
of beauty Heaven bears. It was from there
that we emerged, to see—once more—the stars.

from Purgatorio

PURGATORIO

The existence of a place in the afterlife where saved souls would purge their earthly sins before entering heaven was still a new idea when Dante created the version of it that would dominate posterity. As befits a temporary space of souls moving from one world to the next, *Purgatorio* resembles the *Inferno* in some respects, the *Paradiso* in others, and in many ways is unique. As in Hell, the souls here suffer poetically suitable torments on a series of levels, and as in Hell, they remain consumed by the worries of their earthly lives. As in Paradise, each level can be seen to correspond to and rectify a circle of Hell, but the divisions are much simpler, and, most importantly, every soul is irrevocably saved rather than damned, and consequently joyful even in suffering. What makes Purgatory unique is that each soul is moving rather than fixed, making his or her way slowly up the mountain, purging a share of each sin along the way. Rather than nine equivalent levels plus an equivocal tenth as in the other two realms, Purgatory is divided into seven terraces purging the seven deadly sins (pride, envy, wrath, sloth, avarice and prodigality, gluttony, and lust at the top), and three parts of Ante-Purgatory at the mountain's base, where souls that were excommunicated, that were indolent in their faith, or that died without last rites must wait before beginning their climb.

Rather than displaying the extremes of *Inferno*, *Purgatorio* is more uniform and often lyric in tone, steeped in the melancholy of the beloved world behind and the hope of the peace to come. The opening cantos introduce this new tension and new tone, while also suggesting the new dilemmas and new dangers of this realm, for the pull of the world is if anything stronger for those who have less to regret in their earthly lives. Canto 22 shows Dante's conception of the order of Purgatory, the punishment of the terrace (here, of Gluttony), the positive and negative examples presented to the souls on each terrace. It also introduces a unique character, Statius (45–96 C.E.), the Roman epic poet, who will accompany Virgil and Dante to the

---

9. In Dante's invention, Lucifer's fall from Heaven provides a geological as well as a theological origin of Hell and Purgatory: when he fell into the southern hemisphere, directly opposite Jerusalem, the land that once filled it fled from him northward. Once he became fixed in the center of the earth, the land around him fled southward, raising the Mountain of Purgatory and hollowing out the cone of Hell.

Earthly Paradise, and who, unlike the countryman whom he eulogizes as the better poet and author of his conversion, has unaccountably been saved. Cantos 29 and 30 are the dramatic climax of the poem: Dante is finally united in the Earthly Paradise with his beloved Beatrice, the first impulse of his journey. Fittingly for Purgatory, his reunion with Beatrice entails leaving his beloved Virgil, adding a poignant note to the difficulty of releasing one's ties to the world and giving a further twist to the conundrum of divine justice.

Canto 1
[ARRIVAL AT MOUNT PURGATORY]

To course across more kindly waters now
my talent's little vessel lifts her sails,
leaving behind herself a sea so cruel;[1]
and what I sing will be that second kingdom,°   *Purgatory*
5   in which the human soul is cleansed of sin,
becoming worthy of ascent to Heaven.
But here, since I am yours, o holy Muses,
may this poem rise again from Hell's dead realm;
and may Calliope rise somewhat here,
10   accompanying my singing with that music
whose power struck the poor Pierides
so forcefully that they despaired of pardon.[2]
The gentle hue of oriental sapphire
in which the sky's serenity was steeped—
15   its aspect pure as far as the horizon—
brought back my joy in seeing just as soon
as I had left behind the air of death
that had afflicted both my sight and breast.
The lovely planet that is patroness
20   of love made all the eastern heavens glad,
veiling the Pisces in the train she led.[3]
Then I turned to the right, setting my mind
upon the other pole,° and saw four stars   *the South Pole*
not seen before except by the first people.[4]
25   Heaven appeared to revel in their flames:
o northern hemisphere, because you were
denied that sight, you are a widower!

---

1. Hell. The water imagery recalls that of *Inferno* 1; poetry-writing as sailing is a classical theme (as is modesty) already used by Dante in the *Convivio* (2.1.1). The combined image is strongly reminiscent of Ulysses' "wild flight" to the South Pole that ended in disaster at the foot of Mount Purgatory (*Inferno* 26.124–42).
2. As in *Inferno* 2, Dante begins this canticle with an invocation to the classical Muses. Calliope was the Muse of heroic poetry; Dante invokes her "somewhat" in comparison to *Paradiso*, where her full powers will be required. When the Pierides, or daughters of Pierus, lost to Calliope in a singing contest, they were transformed into magpies

(Ovid, *Metamorphoses* 5.194–678). The poet's request for divine aid thus goes hand in hand with an implied fear of challenging the gods on their own territory and of using pagan sources in representing the Christian afterlife.
3. It is about two hours before sunrise on Easter morning. Venus is rising in the east, her brightness illuminating the constellation of Pisces.
4. The Earthly Paradise in which Adam and Eve lived before their expulsion to the northern hemisphere is situated at the top of Mount Purgatory. They are the only living persons until Dante and Virgil to have seen the stars of the otherwise uninhabited southern hemisphere.

After my eyes took leave of those four stars,
turning a little toward the other pole,
30   from which the Wain had disappeared by now,[5]
      I saw a solitary patriarch[6]
near me—his aspect worthy of such reverence
that even son to father owes no more.
      His beard was long and mixed with white, as were
35   the hairs upon his head; and his hair spread
down to his chest in a divided tress.
      The rays of the four holy stars so framed
his face with light that in my sight he seemed
like one who is confronted by the sun.
40   "Who are you—who, against the hidden river,[7]
were able to escape the eternal prison?"
he said, moving those venerable plumes.
      "Who was your guide? What served you both as lantern
when, from the deep night that will always keep
45   the hellish valley dark, you were set free?
      The laws of the abyss—have they been broken?
Or has a new, a changed decree in Heaven
let you, though damned, approach my rocky slopes?"
      My guide took hold of me decisively;
50   by way of words and hands and other signs,
he made my knees and brow show reverence.
      Then he replied: "I do not come through my
own self. There was a lady° sent from Heaven;   *Beatrice*
her pleas led me to help and guide this man.
55   But since your will would have a far more full
and accurate account of our condition,
my will cannot withhold what you request.[8]
      This man had yet to see his final evening;
but through his folly, little time was left
60   before he did—he was so close to it.
      As I have told you, I was sent to him
for his deliverance; the only road
I could have taken was the road I took.
      I showed him all the people of perdition;
65   now I intend to show to him those spirits
who, in your care, are bent on expiation.°   *atonement*
      To tell you how I led him would take long;
It is a power descending from above

---

5. Turning his eyes back to the north, the pilgrim notes that the Wain (Ursa Major, or the Great Bear) has sunk below the horizon.
6. In the first great surprise of the canticle, this figure is Cato the Younger of Utica (95–46 B.C.E.), the republican opponent of Julius Caesar in the civil war, who committed suicide at Utica following his defeat; he was renowned for his staunch resolution and morality. Presumably, he was removed from Limbo along with the Old Testament patriarchs at the Harrowing of Hell. As a suicide, an enemy of empire, and a pagan, his presence as the custodian of Purgatory is triply surprising.
7. Either the runoff from the Lethe at the top of Mt. Purgatory, or Hell in general (literally "the blind stream").
8. The proper exercise of the "will" is an integral component of the correction of sin instituted throughout Purgatory.

that helps me guide him here, to see and hear you.

70   Now may it please you to approve his coming;
he goes in search of liberty—so precious,
as he who gives his life for it must know.

You know it—who, in Utica, found death
for freedom was not bitter, when you left
75   the garb that will be bright on the great day.[9]

Eternal edicts are not broken for us;
this man's alive, and I'm not bound by Minos;
but I am from the circle where the chaste
eyes of your Marcia are;[1] and she still prays
80   to you, o holy breast, to keep her as
your own; for her love, then, incline to us.

Allow our journey through your seven realms.[2]
I shall thank her for kindness you bestow—
if you would let your name be named below."

85   "While I was there, within the other world,
Marcia so pleased my eyes," he then replied,
"each kindness she required, I satisfied.

Now that she dwells beyond the evil river,
she has no power to move me any longer,
90   such was the law decreed when I was freed.[3]

But if a lady come from Heaven speeds
and helps you, as you say, there is no need
of flattery; it is enough, indeed,

to ask me for her sake.[4] Go then; but first
95   wind a smooth rush around his waist and bathe
his face, to wash away all of Hell's stains;[5]

for it would not be seemly to approach
with eyes still dimmed by any mists, the first
custodian angel, one from Paradise.

100   This solitary island, all around
its very base, there where the breakers pound,
bears rushes on its soft and muddy ground.

There is no other plant that lives below:
no plant with leaves or plant that, as it grows,
105   hardens—and breaks beneath the waves' harsh blows.[6]

That done, do not return by this same pass;
the sun, which rises now, will show you how

---

9. Cato's body (his "garb") will be restored to him on Judgment Day.
1. Cato's wife Marcia, famed for her virtue, inhabits Limbo along with Virgil and the other virtuous pagans not consigned to the lower depths guarded by Minos (*Inferno* 4.128).
2. The seven terraces in Purgatory, analogous to the seven deadly sins.
3. Cato's ability to separate himself from his earthly love for Marcia introduces a key theme of Purgatory: the difficult task of letting go of earthly ties both good and evil.

4. The rebuke to Virgil is swift and sharp: what counts in this realm are laws rather than words of flattery, a sin punished in the eighth circle of Hell (see *Inferno* 18.125–26).
5. The rush symbolizes humility, reminiscent of the ambivalent use of the monk's cord in *Inferno* 16.106–14 and 27.67–8.
6. Unlike the unbending oak, the pliant reed survives the buffeting of the waves, as humility allows the pious Christian to survive the buffetings of Fortune.

this hillside can be climbed more easily."[7]

With that he vanished; and without a word,
110   I rose and drew in closer to my guide,
and it was on him that I set my eyes.

And he began: "Son, follow in my steps;
let us go back; this is the point at which
the plain slopes down to reach its lowest bounds."

115   Daybreak was vanquishing the dark's last hour,
which fled before it; in the distance, I
could recognize the trembling of the sea.

We made our way across the lonely plain,
like one returning to a lost pathway,
120   who, till he finds it, seems to move in vain.

When we had reached the point where dew contends
with sun and, under sea winds, in the shade,
wins out because it won't evaporate,

my master gently placed both of his hands—
125   outspread—upon the grass; therefore, aware
of what his gesture and intention were,

I reached and offered him my tear-stained cheeks;
and on my cheeks, he totally revealed
the color that Inferno had concealed.

130   Then we arrived at the deserted shore,
which never yet had seen its waters coursed
by any man who journeyed back again.[8]

There, just as pleased another, he girt me.
O wonder! Where he plucked the humble plant
135   that he had chosen, there that plant sprang up
again, identical, immediately.[9]

Canto 2

[The Ship of Souls]

By now the sun was crossing the horizon
of the meridian whose highest point
covers Jerusalem; and from the Ganges,

night, circling opposite the sun, was moving
5   together with the Scales° that, when the length   *the constellation Libra*
of dark defeats the day, desert night's hands;

so that, above the shore that I had reached,
the fair Aurora's° white and scarlet cheeks   *goddess of dawn*

---

7. By descending to the shore before beginning their ascent, the pilgrims will follow the route of the saved soul rather than their unorthodox means of entry to the mountain. It is daybreak on Easter morning; the pilgrim's actions signify a rebirth, the cleansing a new baptism.
8. A strong reminiscence of the "wild flight" of Ulysses

(*Inferno* 26.124–42), who wasn't able to journey back again.
9. Echoing the language used by Virgil in the *Aeneid* (6.190–200) to describe the golden bough plucked by Aeneas to serve as talisman on his journey through the underworld.

were, as Aurora aged, becoming orange.[1]

10   We still were by the sea, like those who think
about the journey they will undertake,
who go in heart but in the body stay.

And just as Mars, when it is overcome
by the invading mists of dawn, glows red
15   above the waters' plain, low in the west,

so there appeared to me—and may I see it
again[2]—a light that crossed the sea: so swift,
there is no flight of bird to equal it.

When, for a moment, I'd withdrawn my eyes
20   that I might ask a question of my guide,
I saw that light again, larger, more bright.

Then, to each side of it, I saw a whiteness,
though I did not know what that whiteness was;
below, another whiteness slowly showed.

25   My master did not say a word before
the whitenesses first seen appeared as wings;
but then, when he had recognized the helmsman,

he cried: "Bend, bend your knees: behold the angel
of God, and join your hands; from this point on,
30   this is the kind of minister you'll meet.

See how much scorn he has for human means;
he'd have no other sail than his own wings
and use no oar between such distant shores.

See how he holds his wings, pointing to Heaven,
35   piercing the air with his eternal pinions,
which do not change as mortal plumage does."

Then he—that bird divine—as he drew closer
and closer to us, seemed to gain in brightness,
so that my eyes could not endure his nearness,

40   and I was forced to lower them; and he
came on to shore with boat so light, so quick
that nowhere did the water swallow it.

The helmsman sent from Heaven, at the stern,
seemed to have blessedness inscribed upon him;[3]
45   more than a hundred spirits sat within.

"In exitu Isräel de Aegypto,"[4]
with what is written after of that psalm,
all of those spirits sang as with one voice.

Then over them he made the holy cross
50   as sign; they flung themselves down on the shore,

---

1. It is sunset (6 P.M.) in Jerusalem, sunrise (6 A.M.) in Purgatory. The river Ganges in India was considered the easternmost point of the known world.
2. That is, may he return to the shores of Mt. Purgatory as a blessed soul.
3. The angelic helmsman bears comparison with the ferryman Charon in *Inferno* 3.82–129, the angel sent from

heaven in *Inferno* 9.64–102, and Ulysses and his crew in *Inferno* 26.124–42.
4. "When Israel went out of Egypt" (Psalm 114), a hymn of thanks for the liberation of the Israelites from their bondage to the Pharaoh. The story of Exodus was seen allegorically as the salvation of the blessed souls from the bondage of the earthly, sinful life.

and he moved off as he had come—swiftly.

The crowd that he had left along the beach
seemed not to know the place; they looked about
like those whose eyes try out things new to them.

55   Upon all sides the sun shot forth the day;
and from mid-heaven its incisive arrows
already had chased Capricorn away,[5]

when those who'd just arrived lifted their heads
toward us and said: "Do show us, if you know,
60 the way by which we can ascend this slope."

And Virgil answered: "You may be convinced
that we are quite familiar with this shore;
but we are strangers here, just as you are;[6]

we came but now, a little while before you,
65 though by another path, so difficult
and dense that this ascent seems sport to us."

The souls who, noticing my breathing, sensed
that I was still a living being, then,
out of astonishment, turned pale; and just

70   as people crowd around a messenger
who bears an olive branch,° to hear his news,   *symbol of peace*
and no one hesitates to join that crush,

so here those happy spirits—all of them—
stared hard at my face, just as if they had
75 forgotten to proceed to their perfection.

I saw one of those spirits moving forward
in order to embrace me—his affection
so great that I was moved to mime his welcome.

O shades—in all except appearance—empty!
80 Three times I clasped my hands behind him and
as often brought them back against my chest.[7]

Dismay, I think, was painted on my face;
at this, that shadow smiled as he withdrew;
and I, still seeking him, again advanced.

85   Gently, he said that I could now stand back;
then I knew who he was, and I beseeched
him to remain awhile and talk with me.

He answered: "As I loved you when I was
within my mortal flesh, so, freed, I love you:
90 therefore I stay. But you, why do you journey?"

"My own Casella,[8] to return again
to where I am, I journey thus;[9] but why,"
I said, "were you deprived of so much time?"

---

5. In the passage of time, the constellation of Capricorn has risen and fallen, "chased" by the sun.
6. The Italian for "stranger" here is *peregrin,* or pilgrim, which has deep resonances with the image of the Christian traveler, with life as a pilgrimage to a celestial goal.
7. Dante recalls the lines with which Virgil described

Aeneas's attempt to embrace his father Anchises' shade in the underworld (*Aeneid* 6.924–27).
8. A musician who may have set lyrics to music and was evidently a close friend of Dante.
9. The pilgrim alludes again to the ultimate goal of his journey: salvation.

And he: "No injury is done to me

95   if he who takes up whom—and when—he pleases

has kept me from this crossing many times,

for his own will derives from a just will.

And yet, for three months now, he has accepted,

most tranquilly, all those who would embark.

100   Therefore, I, who had turned then to the shore

at which the Tiber's waters mix with salt,

was gathered in by his benevolence.[1]

Straight to that river mouth, he set his wings:

that always is the place of gathering

105   for those who do not sink to Acheron."

And I: "If there's no new law that denies

you memory or practice of the songs

of love that used to quiet all my longings,

then may it please you with those songs to solace

110   my soul somewhat; for—having journeyed here

together with my body—it is weary."

"Love that discourses to me in my mind"

he then began to sing—and sang so sweetly

that I still hear that sweetness sound in me.[2]

115   My master, I, and all that company

around the singer seemed so satisfied,

as if no other thing might touch our minds.

We all were motionless and fixed upon

the notes, when all at once the grave old man

120   cried out: "What have we here, you laggard spirits?

What negligence, what lingering is this?

Quick, to the mountain to cast off the slough

that will not let you see God show Himself!"[3]

Even as doves, assembled where they feed,

125   quietly gathering their grain or weeds,

forgetful of their customary strut,

will, if some thing appears that makes them fear,

immediately leave their food behind

because they are assailed by greater care;

130   so did I see that new-come company—

they left the song behind, turned toward the slope,

like those who go and yet do not know where.[4]

And we were no less hasty in departure.

---

1. The three months refer to the proclamation by Pope Boniface VIII of 1300 as a Jubilee year, granting the reduction of penance for sins to all who made the pilgrimage to Rome (see *Inferno* 18.28–33). The souls awaiting purgation are included in the proclamation, having gathered at Ostia on the Tiber near Rome to await transport by the angelic helmsman to the foot of Mount Purgatory.
2. This is a lyric by Dante himself, with which he opened Book 3 of the *Convivio*. The echoes of the word "sweet"

recall *dolce stil nuovo* or "sweet new style" of Dante's lyric poetry.
3. The stern Cato returns to the scene to rebuke the souls for tarrying on the shores rather than beginning immediately their purgatorial ascent of the mountain.
4. Unlike the strict instructions as to where to go in Hell, the souls in Purgatory are guided primarily by their own will and their faith in their own salvation.

[The next seven cantos are occupied with the late-repentant souls lingering in Ante-Purgatory, a division that corresponds to upper Hell. These include those who were excommunicated, those who were negligent, and those who died violent deaths, and the negligent lords who are gathered in the Valley of the Rulers. The Seven Terraces of Purgatory proper are divided, in order of declining severity, according to the seven deadly sins: Pride, Envy, Wrath, Sloth, Avarice and Prodigality, Gluttony, and Lust. The travelers encounter many contemporaries, many relations of souls encountered in Hell, and many poets, musicians and artists.]

Canto 22

[VIRGIL AND STATIUS]

The angel now was left behind us, he
who had directed us to the sixth terrace,
having erased one *P* that scarred my face;[1]
   he had declared that those who longed for justice
5   are blessed, and his voice concluded that
message with *"sitiunt,"*° without the rest.[2]   *they thirst*
   And while I climbed behind the two swift spirits,[3]
not laboring at all, for I was lighter
than I had been along the other stairs,[4]
10   Virgil began: "Love that is kindled by
virtue, will, in another, find reply,
as long as that love's flame appears without;
   so, from the time when Juvenal, descending
among us, in Hell's Limbo, had made plain
15   the fondness that you felt for me,[5] my own
benevolence toward you has been much richer
than any ever given to a person
one has not seen; thus, now these stairs seem short.
   But tell me (and, as friend, forgive me if
20   excessive candor lets my reins relax,
and, as a friend, exchange your words with me):
   how was it that you found within your breast
a place for avarice, when you possessed

---

1. The guardian angel of the gate of Purgatory imprints each soul with seven "P's" (for *Peccatum* or sin) on its brow; one "P" is removed at the exit of each terrace. The pilgrim has already passed through the first five terraces, and passes now into the sixth, where those who were gluttonous purge their sin until their will is ready to pass to the next terrace.

2. The passage through each terrace ends with a suitable song sung by the angel guarding its exit; here the paired sins of avarice and prodigality are countered by the Fourth Beatitude from the Sermon on the Mount (Matthew 5:6): "Blessed are they which do hunger and thirst after righteousness: for they shall be filled." Dante omits "hunger" from the phrase, saving it for the terrace to come.

3. At the previous terrace, Dante and Virgil were joined by the shade of the Roman poet, Statius (45–96 C.E.), author of the *Thebaid* and avowed disciple of Virgil. Statius completed his purgation on the Fifth Terrace and will accompany the pilgrims the rest of their way through Purgatory.

4. Like the shades undergoing purgation, the pilgrim feels lighter with the removal of each "P" from his forehead; his purgation completed, he will feel lighter than air (*Paradiso* 1.94–139).

5. The Roman satirist Juvenal was a younger contemporary of Statius.

the wisdom you had nurtured with such care?"

25   These words at first brought something of a smile
to Statius; then he answered: "Every word
you speak, to me is a dear sign of love.

Indeed, because true causes are concealed,
we often face deceptive reasoning
30 and things provoke perplexity in us.

Your question makes me sure that you're convinced—
perhaps because my circle was the fifth—
that, in the life I once lived, avarice
had been my sin. Know then that I was far
35 from avarice—it was my lack of measure
thousands of months have punished.[6] And if I

had not corrected my assessment by
my understanding what your verses meant
when you, as if enraged by human nature,
40   exclaimed: 'Why cannot you, o holy hunger
for gold, restrain the appetite of mortals?'[7]—
I'd now, while rolling weights, know sorry jousts.[8]

Then I became aware that hands might open
too wide, like wings, in spending; and of this,
45 as of my other sins, I did repent.

How many are to rise again with heads
cropped close, whom ignorance prevents from reaching
repentance in—and at the end of—life![9]

And know that when a sin is countered by
50 another fault—directly opposite
to it—then, here, both sins see their green wither.[1]

Thus, I join those who pay for avarice
in my purgation, though what brought me here
was prodigality—its opposite."

55   "Now, when you sang the savage wars of those
twin sorrows of Jocasta,"[2] said the singer
of the bucolic poems,[3] "it does not seem—

from those notes struck by you and Clio there[4]—
that you had yet turned faithful to the faith
60 without which righteous works do not suffice.

If that is so, then what sun or what candles
drew you from darkness so that, in their wake,

---

6. Two opposed sins are purged on the Fifth Terrace;
Statius was guilty of prodigality rather than avarice.
7. Paraphrasing *Aeneid* 3.56–57.
8. The avaricious and the prodigal are punished in the
Fourth Circle of Hell by rolling weights counter to one
another, clashing at each completed semicircle (*Inferno*
7.25–35).
9. The prodigals in the Fourth Circle of Hell are distinguished by their close-cropped hair (*Inferno* 7.57).
1. As opposed to some sins of excess, avarice and prodigality are opposite extremes of the desired goal of

measure.
2. Statius's epic, the *Thebaid*, recounted the war that resulted from the feuding between Eteocles and Polynices,
the two sons of Jocasta born of her incestuous marriage
with Oedipus.
3. Virgil's "bucolic poems" are the *Eclogues*, the fourth
of which was commonly considered to contain a prophecy
of the coming of Jesus Christ.
4. As he considered his poem to be a history, Statius invoked in it Clio, the muse of history.

you set your sails behind the fisherman?"[5]

    And he to him: "You were the first to send me

65   to drink within Parnassus' caves° and you,   *the Muses' home*

the first who, after God, enlightened me.

    You did as he who goes by night and carries

the lamp behind him—he is of no help

to his own self but teaches those who follow—

70   when you declared: 'The ages are renewed;

justice and man's first time on earth return;

from Heaven a new progeny descends.'[6]

    Through you I was a poet and, through you,

a Christian; but that you may see more plainly,

75   I'll set my hand to color what I sketch.

    Disseminated by the messengers

of the eternal kingdom,° the true faith   *the apostles*

by then had penetrated all the world,

    and the new preachers preached in such accord

80   with what you'd said (and I have just repeated),

that I was drawn into frequenting them.

    Then they appeared to me to be so saintly

that, when Domitian persecuted them,[7]

my own laments accompanied their grief;

85   and while I could—as long as I had life—

I helped them, and their honest practices

made me disdainful of all other sects.

    Before—within my poem—I'd led the Greeks

unto the streams of Thebes, I was baptized;

90   but out of fear, I was a secret Christian

    and, for a long time, showed myself as pagan;

for this halfheartedness, for more than four

centuries, I circled the fourth circle.[8]

    And now may you, who lifted up the lid

95   that hid from me the good of which I speak,

while time is left us as we climb, tell me

    where is our ancient Terence, and Caecilius

and Plautus, where is Varius,° if you know;   *ancient writers*

tell me if they are damned, and in what quarter."

100   "All these and Persius, I, and many others,"

my guide replied, "are with that Greek° to whom   *Homer*

the Muses gave their gifts in greatest measure.

    Our place is the blind prison, its first circle;

and there we often talk about the mountain

---

5. Since there are no traces of Christian sentiment in the *Thebaid* (Statius, unlike Virgil, died in plenty of time to have been exposed to the new religion), Virgil asks when the conversion occurred (the "fisherman" is the apostle Peter).

6. Statius quotes lines 5–7 of Virgil's Fourth Eclogue, long regarded as a prophecy of Christ although Virgil was

referring to the Golden Age of Saturn (see *Inferno* 14.94–6) and to the birth of a son to a powerful Roman consul.

7. Emperor of Rome from 81–96 C.E., Domitian was widely believed to have persecuted practitioners of the new religion.

8. The Terrace of the Slothful.

105   where those who were our nurses always dwell.[9]
         Euripides is with us, Antiphon,
Simonides, and Agathon, as well
as many other Greeks who once wore laurel
         upon their brow; and there—of your own people[1]—
110   one sees Antigone, Deiphyle,
Ismene, sad still, Argia as she was.
         There one can see the woman who showed Langia,
and there, Tiresias' daughter; there is Thetis;
and, with her sisters, there, Deidamia."
115   Both poets now were silent, once again
intent on their surroundings—they were free
of stairs and walls; with day's first four handmaidens°   *hours*
         already left behind, and with the fifth
guiding the chariot-pole and lifting it,
120   so that its horn of flame rose always higher,
         my master said: "I think it's time that we
turn our right shoulders toward the terrace edge,
circling the mountain in the way we're used to."
         In this way habit served us as a banner;
125   and when we chose that path, our fear was less
because that worthy soul gave his assent.[2]
         Those two were in the lead; I walked alone,
behind them, listening to their colloquy,
which taught me much concerning poetry.
130   But their delightful conversation soon
was interrupted by a tree that blocked
our path; its fruits were fine, their scent was sweet,
         and even as a fir-tree tapers upward
from branch to branch, that tree there tapered downward,
135   so as—I think—to ward off any climber.[3]
         Upon our left, where wall enclosed our path,
bright running water fell from the high rock
and spread itself upon the leaves above.
         When the two poets had approached the tree,
140   a voice emerging from within the leaves
cried out: "This food shall be denied to you."
         Then it cried: "Mary's care was for the marriage-
feast's being seemly and complete, not for
her mouth (which now would intercede for you).
145   And when they drank, of old, the Roman women
were satisfied with water; and young Daniel,

---

9. Another reference to Parnassus, whose Muses "nursed" these writers.
1. Euripides and Agathon were ancient Greek tragic poets, Antiphon an orator and statesman, and Simonides a lyric poet. "Your own people": reputedly historical characters appearing in Statius's *Thebaid* and *Achilleid*.
2. Whereas in Hell the travelers nearly always turned to

the left, in Purgatory they always turn to the right; here, they assume that the will of the wholly purged soul is even more trustworthy than "habit."
3. This tree recalls the Tree of the Knowledge of Good and Evil in Eden, but it is impossible to eat from, as the emerging voice attests in line 141, echoing the prohibition of Genesis 2:17.

through his disdain of food, acquired wisdom.

  The first age was as fair as gold: when hungry,
men found the taste of acorns good; when thirsty,
150 they found that every little stream was nectar.

  When he was in the wilderness, the Baptist°   *John the Baptist*
had fed on nothing more than honey, locusts:[4]
for this he was made great, as glorious
as, in the Gospel, is made plain to you."[5]

[*Having passed through the seven Terraces of Purgatory, Dante, Virgil and Statius enter the Earthly Paradise, where they find the river Lethe. A woman, Matilda, a personification of Earthly Felicity, appears to Dante, and tells him that this was the forest imagined by the ancient poets who wrote of the Golden Age.*]

Canto 29

[THE EARTHLY PARADISE]

  Her words were done, but without interruption
she sang—like an enamored woman—thus:
"*Beati quorum tecta sunt peccata!*"[1]

  And just as nymphs who used to walk alone
5 among the woodland shadows, some desiring
to see and some to flee the sun, so she

  moved countercurrent as she walked along
the riverbank; and following her short
footsteps with my own steps, I matched her pace.

10 Her steps and mine together did not sum
one hundred when the banks, still parallel,
so curved about that I was facing east.[2]

  Nor had we gone much farther on that path
when she turned fully round toward me and said:
15 "My brother, look and listen"; and I saw

  a sudden radiance that swept across
the mighty forest on all sides—and I
was wondering if lightning had not struck.

  But since, when lightning strikes, it stops at once,
20 while that light, lingering, increased its force,

4. Each Terrace is bracketed by classical and biblical examples of the contrary virtue and by those of the sin itself. Here, the virtue of temperance is exemplified by Mary at the marriage-feast of Cana. Aquinas asserted that the virtuous women of ancient Rome drank no wine. The prophet Daniel neither drank the king's wine nor ate his meat (Daniel 1:8). In the classical myth of the Golden Age, as in Eden, men lived off what they found in nature. The examples of sin come in Canto 24, accompanied by an offshoot of the tree from which Eve and Adam ate.
5. In the words of Jesus, "among them that are born of women there hath not arisen a greater than John the

Baptist" (Matthew 11:11).
1. Having finished her discourse to the pilgrim, Matilda sings the opening verse of Psalm 32: "Blessed are they whose transgressions are forgiven, whose sins are covered." The description, "She sang—like an enamored woman," is a nearly exact quotation of a ballad by Dante's friend and fellow love-poet Guido Cavalcanti (see *Inferno* 10.52–72).
2. Matilda is across the river Lethe from the pilgrim; both follow the river upstream as it turns eastward, the direction in which the sun rises.

within my mind I asked: "What thing is this?"
    And through the incandescent air there ran
sweet melody; at which, just indignation
made me rebuke the arrogance of Eve

25   because, where earth and heaven were obedient,
a solitary woman, just created,
found any veil at all beyond endurance;
    if she had been devout beneath her veil,
I should have savored those ineffable

30   delights before, and for a longer time.[3]
    While I moved on, completely rapt, among
so many first fruits of eternal pleasure,
and longing for still greater joys, the air
    before us altered underneath the green

35   branches, becoming like an ardent fire,
and now the sweet sound was distinctly song.
    O Virgins, sacrosanct, if I have ever,
for your sake, suffered vigils, cold, and hunger,
great need makes me entreat my recompense.

40   Now Helicon must pour its fountains for me,
Urania must help me with her choir
to put in verses things hard to conceive.[4]
    Not far beyond, we made out seven trees
of gold, though the long stretch of air between

45   those trees and us had falsified their semblance;[5]
    but when I'd drawn so close that things perceived
through mingled senses, which delude, did not,
now they were nearer, lose their real features,
    the power that offers reason matter judged

50   those trees to be—what they were—candelabra,
and what those voices sang to be "Hosanna."[6]
    The upper part of those fair candles flamed
more radiantly than the midmonth° moon   *full*
shines at midnight in an untroubled sky.

55   Full of astonishment, I turned to my
good Virgil; but he only answered me
with eyes that were no less amazed than mine.
    Then I looked at the extraordinary
things that were moving toward us—but so slowly

---

3. Since this Paradise is the Eden in which Adam and Eve first dwelled, Eve's partaking of the forbidden fruit (the "veil" of prohibition she refused to endure) resulted in the exclusion of Dante and the rest of mankind from this wood until after their death and purgation.

4. A new level of wonder requires a new invocation of the virgin Muses in their other dwelling place of the sacred grove on Helicon. Urania was the muse of astronomy and matters celestial.

5. At first glance, the approaching sight appears to be seven golden trees.

6. According to the theory of perception followed by Dante here, brightness and color were always correctly perceived, but objects of perception "common" to several senses could err. Dante may have in mind either branching candelabra or single candlesticks, depending on the translation of the relevant verse of Revelation (1:12), the primary source for much of the imagery to follow. What is now perceived to be a song is the cry with which Christ was greeted by the crowd as he entered Jerusalem, the occasion commemorated by Palm Sunday.

60   that even brides just wed would move more quickly.

The woman° chided me: "Why are you only   *Matilda*
so eager to behold the living lights
and not in seeing what comes after them?"

Then I saw people following those candles,
65   as if behind their guides, and they wore white—
whiteness that, in this world, has never been.

The water, to my left, reflected flames,
and it reflected, too, my left-hand side
if I gazed into it, as in a mirror.

70   When I was at a point along my shore
where all that sundered me from them was water,
I stayed my steps in order to see better,

and I could see the candle flames move forward,
leaving the air behind them colored like
75   the strokes a painter's brush might have described,

so that the air above that retinue
was streaked with seven bands in every hue
of which the rainbow's made and Delia's girdle.[7]

These pennants stretched far back, beyond my vision;
80   as for the width they filled, I judged the distance
between the outer ones to be ten paces.

Beneath the handsome sky I have described,
twenty-four elders moved on, two by two,
and they had wreaths of lilies on their heads.[8]

85   And all were singing: "You, among the daughters
of Adam, *benedicta* are; and may
your beauties blessed be eternally."[9]

After the flowers and the other fresh
plants facing me, along the farther shore,
90   had seen those chosen people disappear,

then—as in heaven, star will follow star—
the elders gone, four animals came on;
and each of them had green leaves as his crown;

each had six wings as plumage, and those plumes
95   were full of eyes; they would be very like
the eyes of Argus, were his eyes alive.[1]

Reader, I am not squandering more rhymes
in order to describe their forms; since I
must spend elsewhere, I can't be lavish here;

---

7. The flame of each candlestick leaves a trail of colored light behind it, making the air above the procession resemble a rainbow or a halo ("girdle") of the moon (the moon-goddess Diana was from Delos, hence "Delia").
8. The procession is usually considered to be an allegorical masque, or pageant, presenting the books of the Bible. The 24 elders, reminiscent of those of Revelation 4:4, would personify the 24 books of the Old Testament. Their white garments and lilies symbolize righteousness, and the lilies faith in the Messiah to come.

9. The elders' song paraphrases the words of the angel to Mary, mother of Christ, "Blessed [*Benedicta*] art thou among women" (Luke 1:28).
1. These are the four creatures around God's throne (Revelation 4:6–8 and Ezekiel 1:4–14), traditionally taken as symbolizing the four Evangelists: Matthew, Mark, Luke, and John. Green was the color of hope. The wings signify knowledge of the past and future, painted with 100 eyes like those of the mythic watchman Argus.

100   but read Ezekiel, for he has drawn
those animals approaching from the north;
with wings and cloud and fire, he painted them.

And just as you will find them in his pages,
such were they here, except that John's with me
105   as to their wings; with him, John disagrees.[2]

The space between the four of them contained
a chariot—triumphal—on two wheels,
tied to a griffin's neck and drawn by him.

His wings, stretched upward, framed the middle band
110   with three bands on each outer side, so that,
though he cleaved air, he left the bands intact.

His wings—so high that they were lost to sight;
his limbs were gold as far as he was bird;
the rest of him was white mixed with bloodred.[3]

115   Not only did no chariot so handsome
gladden Rome's Africanus or Augustus
himself—even the Sun's own cannot match it;

the Sun's—which, gone astray, was burnt to cinders
because Earth offered up her pious prayers,
120   when Jove, in ways not known to us, was just.[4]

Three circling women, then advancing, danced
at the right wheel; the first of them, so red
that even in a flame she'd not be noted;

the second seemed as if her flesh and bone
125   were fashioned out of emerald; the third
seemed to be newly fallen snow. And now

the white one seemed to lead them, now the red;
and from the way in which the leader chanted,
the others took their pace, now slow, now rapid.[5]

130   Upon the left, four other women, dressed
in crimson, danced, depending on the cadence
of one of them, with three eyes in her head.[6]

Behind all of the group I have described
I saw two elders, different in their dress
135   but like in manner—grave and decorous.[7]

---

2. The descriptions of these creatures by John (traditional author of Revelation) and by Ezekiel are in general agreement except in the number of wings.

3. The chariot, similar to those used in triumphal processions in ancient Rome, is drawn by the mythical griffin, with the body of a lion and head and wings of an eagle, its wings reaching up through the streamers of colored light. Because of its dual nature, the griffin was a traditional symbol of Christ, the gold upper part symbolizing his divine nature, the body his human nature, white for his purity and blood-red for the passion. There is general agreement that the chariot personifies the Church.

4. Scipio the Elder (236–143 B.C.E.) and his grandson Scipio the Younger (c. 185–129 B.C.E.) were honored with the title "Africanus" and triumphal processions in Rome for their victories in the Punic Wars against the North African Carthaginians. Virgil described one of the triumphal processions of Caesar Augustus in *Aeneid* 8.929–50. Phaethon was the sun-god's son who drove the Chariot of the Sun too near the earth and was struck down by Jove (*Inferno* 17.107, *Purgatorio* 4.73–5, and *Metamorphoses* 2.47–328).

5. The three Theological Virtues: red for Charity, green ("emerald") for Hope, white ("snow") for Faith.

6. The four Cardinal Virtues, in crimson because they would not exist without Charity: Prudence (with three eyes), Justice, Fortitude, and Temperance.

7. The two Elders personify the book of Acts, authored by the physician Luke ("disciple" of the ancient Greek physician Hippocrates), and St. Paul, whose bright sword exemplifies the combative temperament and spirit of his Epistles.

The first seemed to be one of the disciples
of great Hippocrates, whom nature made
for those who are her dearest living beings;

the other showed an opposite concern—
140   his sword was bright and sharp, and even on
this near side of the river, I felt fear.

Then I saw four of humble aspect; and,
when all the rest had passed, a lone old man,
his features keen, advanced, as if in sleep.[8]

145   The clothes these seven wore were like the elders'
in the first file, except that these had no
garlands of lilies round their brow; instead,

roses and other red flowers wreathed their heads;[9]
one seeing them less closely would have sworn
150   that all of them had flames above their eyebrows.

And when the chariot stood facing me,
I heard a bolt of thunder; and it seemed
to block the path of that good company,

which halted there, its emblems in the lead.

Canto 30

[BEATRICE APPEARS]

When the first heaven's Seven-Stars had halted
(those stars that never rise or set, that are
not veiled except when sin beclouds our vision;[1]

those stars that, there, made everyone aware
5   of what his duty was, just as the Bear
below brings helmsmen home to harbor),[2] then

the truthful band that had come first between
the griffin and the Seven-Stars turned toward
that chariot as toward their peace, and one

10   of them, as if sent down from Heaven, hymned
aloud, *"Veni, sponsa, de Libano,"*
three times, and all the others echoed him.[3]

---

8. James, Peter, John and Jude, authors of the New Testament's shorter epistles, are followed by John, author of the Book of Revelation, visionary and enigmatic rather than historical and moralizing as the previous books.

9. The red garments complete a tableau of the colors of the three theological virtues: the Old Testament elders are crowned with white for their faith in the redemption to come; the four beasts are green for the hope of salvation preached in the Gospels; the seven elders are crowned with red for the spirit of charity with which they spread the word of God after the resurrection.

1. The Seven-Stars are the candelabra of the previous canto, leading the procession. Dante here likens them to the Empyrean, the "first" or outermost heaven, where the blessed dwell with God and which, unlike the other heavens, has no stars of the ordinary kind that rise and set.

2. The Seven-Stars guide the rest of the procession, as the constellation of the Bear lets the helmsman find his bearings. The Seven-Stars thus represent the divine perspective on the book of the world, unchanging, outside of time and aware of its every permutation through to the end of time.

3. Having stopped behind the candelabra, the 24 elders ("the truthful band") follow their lead, turning about to face the chariot, Christ's Church, enacting their prophetic foretelling of "their peace" that was to come. The one who leads the hymn is most likely the Song of Solomon, origin of the lines, "Come with me from Lebanon, my spouse" (4:8). The standard Christian interpretation of the "spouse" of this love song was as the Church, bride of Christ; in the *Convivio,* Dante identified the spouse as Divine Knowledge (2.14.20).

Just as the blessed, at the Final Summons,
will rise up—ready—each out of his grave,
15 singing, with new-clothed voices, Alleluia,[4]
    so, from the godly chariot, eternal
life's messengers and ministers arose:
one hundred stood *ad vocem tanti senis.*[5]
    All of them cried: *"Benedictus qui venis,"*
20 and, scattering flowers upward and around,
"Manibus, oh, date lilia plenis."[6]
    I have at times seen all the eastern sky
becoming rose as day began and seen,
adorned in lovely blue, the rest of heaven;
25   and seen the sun's face rise so veiled that it
was tempered by the mist and could permit
the eye to look at length upon it; so,
    within a cloud of flowers that were cast
by the angelic hands and then rose up
30 and then fell back, outside and in the chariot,
    a woman showed herself to me; above
a white veil, she was crowned with olive boughs;
her cape was green; her dress beneath, flame-red.[7]
    Within her presence, I had once been used
35 to feeling—trembling—wonder, dissolution;
but that was long ago. Still, though my soul,
    now she was veiled, could not see her directly,
by way of hidden force that she could move,
I felt the mighty power of old love.
40   As soon as that deep force had struck my vision
(the power that, when I had not yet left
my boyhood, had already transfixed me),[8]
    I turned around and to my left—just as
a little child, afraid or in distress,
45 will hurry to his mother—anxiously,
    to say to Virgil: "I am left with less
than one drop of my blood that does not tremble:
I recognize the signs of the old flame."[9]

---

4. On Judgment Day ("Final Summons"), the bodies of the righteous will rise from their graves, join with their souls, and proclaim the coming of Christ in judgment.
5. A hundred angels rise out of the chariot, *ad vocem tanti senis*, "at the voice of so venerable an elder"—Dante's Latin rather than a quotation.
6. Two further phrases to signal the advent of Beatrice in judgment over Dante. *Benedictus qui venis* slightly rephrases the words that greeted Jesus' triumphal entry into Jerusalem (see 29.51): "Blessed is he that cometh" becomes "Blessed art thou that cometh"; however, it does not change the gender to feminine, suggesting that Beatrice be understood as an avatar of Christ at the Second Coming. The second phrase, *Manibus date lilia plenis,* "With full hands give me lilies," are the words of the shade of Anchises to his son Aeneas in the Elysian

Fields, mourning the untimely death of Marcellus, nephew and presumed heir to Augustus. Perhaps intended as a final homage to Virgil, the classical citation is striking in such a scriptural context.
7. The olive was the tree sacred to the goddess of wisdom Minerva; the white, green, and red of the clothing are the colors of the three Theological Virtues.
8. According to the *Vita Nuova,* Dante first saw Beatrice, and first felt the symptoms he describes here, at the age of nine. Beatrice died in 1290; hence it was "long ago" that he had last felt her presence.
9. Dante turns to his guide with words translated out of the *Aeneid:* those with which Dido confides to her sister that she after so long has once again felt the pangs of love (4.23).

But Virgil had deprived us of himself,
50   Virgil, the gentlest father, Virgil, he
to whom I gave my self for my salvation;
and even all our ancient mother lost
was not enough to keep my cheeks, though washed
with dew, from darkening again with tears.
55   "Dante, though Virgil's leaving you, do not
yet weep, do not weep yet; you'll need your tears
for what another sword must yet inflict."
Just like an admiral who goes to stern
and prow to see the officers who guide
60   the other ships, encouraging their tasks;[1]
so, on the left side of the chariot
(I'd turned around when I had heard my name—
which, of necessity, I transcribe here),[2]
I saw the lady who had first appeared
65   to me beneath the veils of the angelic
flowers look at me across the stream.
Although the veil she wore—down from her head,
which was encircled by Minerva's leaves°—   *olive boughs*
did not allow her to be seen distinctly,
70   her stance still regal and disdainful,[3] she
continued, just as one who speaks but keeps
until the end the fiercest parts of speech:
"Look here! For I am Beatrice, I am!
How were you able to ascend the mountain?
75   Did you not know that man is happy here?"
My lowered eyes caught sight of the clear stream,
but when I saw myself reflected there,
such shame weighed on my brow, my eyes drew back
and toward the grass; just as a mother seems
80   harsh to her child, so did she seem to me—
how bitter is the savor of stern pity!
Her words were done. The angels—suddenly—
sang, *"In te, Domine, speravi";* but
their singing did not go past *"pedes meos."*[4]
85   Even as snow among the sap-filled trees
along the spine of Italy° will freeze   *the Apennine range*
when gripped by gusts of the Slavonian° winds,   *eastern*
then, as it melts, will trickle through itself—
that is, if winds breathe north from shade-less lands—
90   just as, beneath the flame, the candle melts;
so I, before I'd heard the song of those°   *the angels*

1. The comparison of Beatrice to an admiral heightens the shock felt by the pilgrim, who might have expected a more courtly greeting and behavior.
2. The classical topos of modesty calls attention to the name just given for the first time in the poem.
3. Rather than courtliness, Beatrice's manner recalls that of the angels of *Inferno* 9.88 and *Purgatorio* 2.31.

4. The angels sing the opening verses of Psalm 31, "In thee, O Lord, do I put my trust; let me never be ashamed: deliver me in Thy righteousness"; it continues later on, "I will be glad and rejoice in Thy mercy; for Thou hast considered my trouble; Thou hast known my soul in adversities; and hast not shut me up in the hand of the enemy: Thou hast set my feet [*pedes meos*] in a large room."

whose notes always accompany the notes
of the eternal spheres, was without tears
    and sighs; but when I heard the sympathy
95 for me within their gentle harmonies,
as if they'd said: "Lady, why shame him so?"—
    then did the ice that had restrained my heart
become water and breath; and from my breast
and through my lips and eyes they issued—anguished.
100   Still standing motionless upon the left
side of the chariot, she then addressed
the angels who had been compassionate:
    "You are awake in never-ending day,
and neither night nor sleep can steal from you
105 one step the world would take along its way;
    therefore, I'm more concerned that my reply
be understood by him who weeps beyond,
so that his sorrow's measure match his sin.
    Not only through the work of the great spheres—
110 which guide each seed to a determined end,
depending on what stars are its companions—
    but through the bounty of the godly graces,
which shower down from clouds so high that we
cannot approach them with our vision, he,
115   when young, was such—potentially—that any
propensity innate in him would have
prodigiously succeeded, had he acted.[5]
    But where the soil has finer vigor, there
precisely—when untilled or badly seeded—
120 will that terrain grow wilder and more noxious.[6]
    My countenance sustained him for a while;
showing my youthful eyes to him, I led
him with me toward the way of righteousness.
    As soon as I, upon the threshold of
125 my second age, had changed my life,° he took   had died
himself away from me and followed after
    another; when, from flesh to spirit, I
had risen, and my goodness and my beauty
had grown, I was less dear to him, less welcome:
130   he turned his footsteps toward an untrue path;
he followed counterfeits of goodness, which
will never pay in full what they have promised.[7]

5. The words of Beatrice walk a knife edge between pre-
destination and free will. Destined to a specific end by
"the great spheres" and by the constellation (Gemini) under which he was born, Dante was also given a "bounty of
the godly graces" in a form unapproachable from our low
vantage point. But this was only "potential," enabling him
to succeed "prodigiously" but only through the exercise
of his own free will ("had he acted").
6. The greater the potential for accomplishment, the
greater the potential for failure. The metaphor continues

the image of the seed from line 110.
7. The *Vita Nuova* describes how a *donna gentile* led
Dante to neglect the memory of Beatrice (35–38). This
lady may have been real or allegorical (or both); in the
Convivio, Dante interpreted the poems written for her as
addressed to "Lady Philosophy," opening him up to the
accusation in 33.85–90 that he relied overly much on reason, a likely meaning of the "counterfeits of goodness," or
earthly goods of line 131. The "untrue path" of 130 hearkens back to the "lost path" of *Inferno* 1.3.

Nor did the inspirations I received—
with which, in dream and otherwise, I called
135   him back—help me; he paid so little heed!
He fell so far there were no other means
to lead him to salvation, except this:
to let him see the people who were lost.
For this I visited the gateway of
140   the dead; to him who guided him above
my prayers were offered even as I wept.
The deep design of God would have been broken
if Lethe had been crossed and he had drunk
such waters but had not discharged the debt
145   of penitence that's paid when tears are shed."[8]

[Beatrice hears Dante's confession. He is immersed in the river Lethe by Matilda. Beatrice is unveiled. The Masque continues, enacting the drama of the fall and its atonement by Christ. Dante is then ordered to transcribe what he will see next: an allegorical history and prophecy of the corruption of the Church from the Donation of Constantine to the removal of the papacy to Avignon (see Inferno 19). Beatrice prophesies God's vengeance. Dante and Statius drink of Eunoe, restoring their memory of the good, returning "pure and prepared to climb unto the stars."]

from Paradiso

PARADISO

Of the three realms of Dante's afterlife, Paradise was the most difficult and the most risky to portray, for it was by definition an experience beyond human expression and had traditionally been forbidden territory for Christian poets. Rather than terrestrial in setting as were Hell and Purgatory, Heaven is a spatial paradox, for from the divine perspective it doesn't exist in space or time at all. For us, as for Dante in his vision, it is presented in terms of an earth-centered solar system, with the moon, the sun and the five known planets (Mercury, Venus, Mars, Jupiter, Saturn) corresponding to the circles of Hell and the seven terraces of Purgatory. Beyond them are the Fixed Stars, the Primum Mobile ("heaven's swiftest sphere," where the angels channel movement through the cosmos), and the enigmatic Empyrean, which is both the circumference and the center around which the universe revolves, where all the blessed in fact exist in the form of a celestial rose, and where the pilgrim is granted the final ineffable vision of divinity toward which all mystics strive.

In order to give form to his third canticle and because his theology remained worldly to the end, in *Paradiso* Dante doesn't abandon the tensions and dilemmas of *Inferno* and *Purgatorio*. He does place them in a different perspective, however, showing that even the blessed don't remain detached from the world, although they are no longer affected by it. In the opening cantos, Dante raises the poetic stakes of his *Commedia*, openly protesting the impossibility and the danger of what he will go on to achieve anyway, and warning off those of his readers who may not feel up to the rarified matter of Paradise. Canto 3 shows the way in which Dante establishes multiple parallels on every level between the three canticles, and continues to introduce the divisions of his afterlife as puzzles rather than answers. Piccarda Donati in the moon raises the opposite question of *Inferno*: if all souls are equally blessed, why do they appear categorized as the more and the less blessed? Is it better to be in the eighth heaven or in the

---

8. Tears of repentance are the final purgation Dante must undergo before drinking, like all purged souls, of the river Lethe, erasing the memory of his sins.

first? Can all souls be equally satisfied in a perfect world and still remain individuals? Dante spends all of *Paradiso,* as he did the first two canticles, swinging his reader back and forth between the familiar but flawed perspective of this world and the alien but perfect perspective of the world beyond.

from Paradiso

Canto 1

[ASCENT TOWARD THE HEAVENS]

    The glory of the One who moves all things
permeates the universe and glows
in one part more and in another less.
    I was within the heaven that receives
5   more of His light;[1] and I saw things that he
who from that height descends, forgets or can
    not speak; for nearing its desired end,
our intellect sinks into an abyss
so deep that memory fails to follow it.
10   Nevertheless, as much as I, within
my mind, could treasure of the holy kingdom
shall now become the matter of my song.
    O good Apollo, for this final task
make me the vessel of your excellence,
15   what you, to merit your loved laurel, ask.
    Until this point, one of Parnassus' peaks
sufficed for me; but now I face the test,
the agon that is left; I need both crests.[2]
    Enter into my breast; within me breathe
20   the very power you made manifest
when you drew Marsyas out from his limbs' sheath.[3]
    O godly force, if you so lend yourself
to me, that I might show the shadow of
the blessed realm inscribed within my mind,
25   then you would see me underneath the tree
you love;[4] there I shall take as crown the leaves
of which my theme and you shall make me worthy.
    So seldom, father, are those garlands gathered
for triumph of a ruler or a poet—
30   a sign of fault or shame in human wills—
    that when Peneian° branches can incite   *laurel*

---

1. The Empyrean, the outermost heaven, shines the most with God's light; Dante begins this canticle by telling us where he will be ("I was") at its conclusion.
2. An invocation, more elaborate than those of *Inferno* and *Purgatorio,* summoning the help not only of the Muses, but of Apollo, god of music and poetry.
3. Dante recalls the torment of another challenger of the gods, Marsyas, whose defeat in a musical duel with

Apollo concluded with the challenger being flayed alive, his body drawn out like a sword "from his limbs' sheath."
4. The laurel. Apollo was lover of the nymph Daphne, whose father transformed her into the laurel tree to save her from the god's advances. Apollo thereafter made the laurel his sacred tree, its leaves used to crown both emperors and poets.

someone to long and thirst for them, delight

must fill the happy Delphic deity.°   *Apollo*

35   Great fire can follow a small spark: there may

be better voices after me to pray

to Cyrrha's god for aid—that he may answer.[5]

       The lantern of the world approaches mortals

by varied paths; but on that way which links

four circles with three crosses, it emerges

40   joined to a better constellation and

along a better course, and it can temper

and stamp the world's wax more in its own manner.[6]

       Its entry from that point of the horizon

brought morning there and evening here; almost

45   all of that hemisphere was white—while ours

was dark—when I saw Beatrice turn round

and left, that she might see the sun; no eagle

has ever stared so steadily at it.[7]

       And as a second ray will issue from

50   the first and reascend, much like a pilgrim

who seeks his home again, so on her action,

       fed by my eyes to my imagination,

my action drew, and on the sun I set

my sight more than we usually do.[8]

55   More is permitted to our powers there

than is permitted here, by virtue of

that place, made for mankind as its true home.

       I did not bear it long, but not so briefly

as not to see it sparkling round about,

60   like molten iron emerging from the fire;

       and suddenly it seemed that day had been

added to day, as if the One who can

had graced the heavens with a second sun.

       The eyes of Beatrice were all intent

65   on the eternal circles; from the sun,

I turned aside; I set my eyes on her.

       In watching her, within me I was changed

as Glaucus changed, tasting the herb that made

him a companion of the other sea gods.[9]

70   Passing beyond the human cannot be

5. Cyrrha is the second crest of Parnassus, sacred to Apollo; Dante imagines the imitators that may follow from the "small spark" of his poem.

6. The most favorable point at which the sun can rise is at the vernal equinox, when four astronomical circles form three crosses as they meet: the equator, the ecliptic, the equinoctial colure, and the horizon. "Four" and "three" recall allegorically the three theological and four cardinal virtues encountered in various forms in the Earthly Paradise. The sun is now in the constellation of Aries when, as it is spring, nature, or "the world's wax," is most disposed to be imprinted with its warmth.

7. The eagle was famed for its ability to look directly at the sun, and to fly closest to it of any bird.

8. The word *pilgrim* (Italian, *pelegrin*) refers both to the theme of pilgrimage in the earthly life and to the peregrine falcon, whose powers of sight were almost as fabled as those of the eagle.

9. Glaucus was a fisherman who saw the fish he had caught and set down on the grass resuscitate and jump back into the sea. He ate the grass himself, and was compelled to jump into the sea, where he was transformed into a sea god, passing from human to divine (*Metamorphoses* 13.898–968).

worded; let Glaucus serve as simile—
until grace grant you the experience.
    Whether I only was the part of me
that You created last, You—governing
75   the heavens—know: it was Your light that raised me.[1]
    When that wheel which You make eternal through
the heavens' longing for You drew me with
the harmony You temper and distinguish,[2]
    the fire of the sun then seemed to me
80   to kindle so much of the sky, that rain
or river never formed so broad a lake.[3]
    The newness of the sound and the great light
incited me to learn their cause—I was
more keen than I had ever been before.
85   And she who read me as I read myself,
to quiet the commotion in my mind,
opened her lips before I opened mine
    to ask, and she began: "You make yourself
obtuse with false imagining; you can
90   not see what you would see if you dispelled it.
    You are not on the earth as you believe;
but lightning, flying from its own abode,
is less swift than you are, returning home."°   *to heaven*
    While I was freed from my first doubt by these
95   brief words she smiled to me, I was yet caught
in new perplexity. I said: "I was
    content already; after such great wonder,
I rested. But again I wonder how
my body rises past these lighter bodies."
100   At which, after a sigh of pity, she
settled her eyes on me with the same look
a mother casts upon a raving child,
    and she began: "All things, among themselves,
possess an order; and this order is
105   the form that makes the universe like God.
    Here do the higher beings see the imprint
of the Eternal Worth, which is the end
to which the pattern I have mentioned tends.[4]
    Within that order, every nature has
110   its bent, according to a different station,

---

1. Dante doesn't specify whether only his soul reached heaven or also his body; in this, he echoes Paul's description of being "caught up to the third heaven—whether in the body or out of the body I do not know" (2 Corinthians 12:3).
2. In Dante's cosmology, the heavens' longing for God, who dwells in the outermost sphere, causes them to wheel around. The "harmony" of the spheres was the music made by each sphere as it turned at varying speeds, more swiftly the farther from earth it was.
3. Dante is already rising; the zone of fire may be an expanded vision of the sun, or it may be the "Sphere of Fire," placed by medieval science below the moon.
4. God's divine ordering, the "imprint of the Eternal Worth on the universe," is visible only to "higher beings," angels and blessed souls who see the world through the mind of God.

nearer or less near to its origin.

Therefore, these natures move to different ports
across the mighty sea of being, each
given the impulse that will bear it on.[5]

115 This impulse carries fire to the moon;
this is the motive force in mortal creatures;
this binds the earth together, makes it one.

Not only does the shaft shot from this bow
strike creatures lacking intellect, but those
120 who have intelligence, and who can love.

The Providence that has arrayed all this
forever quiets—with Its light—that heaven
in which the swiftest of the spheres revolves;

to there, as toward a destined place, we now
125 are carried by the power of the bow
that always aims its shaft at a glad mark.

Yet it is true that, even as a shape
may, often, not accord with art's intent,
since matter may be unresponsive, deaf,

130 so, from this course, the creature strays at times
because he has the power, once impelled,
to swerve elsewhere; as lightning from a cloud

is seen to fall, so does the first impulse,
when man has been diverted by false pleasure,
135 turn him toward earth. You should—if I am right—

not feel more marvel at your climbing than
you would were you considering a stream
that from a mountain's height falls to its base.[6]

It would be cause for wonder in you if,
140 no longer hindered, you remained below,
as if, on earth, a living flame stood still."

Then she again turned her gaze heavenward.

[*Dante exhorts those of his readers in "little barks" to turn back from the deep seas
that he now enters. He and Beatrice arrive at the first heaven, the Sphere of the
Moon, where Beatrice corrects Dante's mistaken belief that moon spots are caused
by rarity and density of matter; instead, they result from parts of different worth shining more and less brightly.*]

Canto 3

[THE SOULS APPROACH]

That sun which first had warmed my breast with love
had now revealed to me, confuting, proving,

---

5. There is a hierarchy to creation, with different "natures"
impelled toward different goals in the "sea of being."

6. Dante's rising through the heavens is thus natural in
God's eyes even if implausible from an earthly perspective.

the gentle face of truth, its loveliness;[1]
    and I, in order to declare myself
5   corrected and convinced, lifted my head
as high as my confessional required.
    But a new vision showed itself to me;
the grip in which it held me was so fast
that I did not remember to confess.
10   Just as, returning through transparent, clean
glass, or through waters calm and crystalline
(so shallow that they scarcely can reflect),
    the mirrored image of our faces meets
our pupils with no greater force than that
15 a pearl has when displayed on a white forehead—
    so faint, the many faces I saw keen
to speak; thus, my mistake was contrary
to that which led the man to love the fountain.[2]
    As soon as I had noticed them, thinking
20 that what I saw were merely mirrorings,
I turned around to see who they might be;
    and I saw nothing; and I let my sight
turn back to meet the light of my dear guide,
who, as she smiled, glowed in her holy eyes.
25   "There is no need to wonder if I smile,"
she said, "because you reason like a child;
your steps do not yet rest upon the truth;
    your mind misguides you into emptiness:
what you are seeing are true substances,
30 placed here because their vows were not fulfilled.[3]
    Thus, speak and listen; trust what they will say:
the truthful light in which they find their peace
will not allow their steps to turn astray."[4]
    Then I turned to the shade that seemed most anxious
35 to speak, and I began as would a man
bewildered by desire too intense:
    "O spirit born to goodness, you who feel,
beneath the rays of the eternal life,
that sweetness which cannot be known unless
40   it is experienced, it would be gracious
of you to let me know your name and fate."
At this, unhesitant, with smiling eyes:
    "Our charity will never lock its gates

---

1. The "sun" here is Beatrice, Dante's first love, but also
the sun of reason (the Sphere of the Sun is that of the
wise), for Beatrice argues like a Scholastic, first confuting, or showing the error, and then proving, or demonstrating the truth.
2. The faces of the souls in the Sphere of the Moon are so
faint that Dante mistakes them for their reflections, the
opposite of the error made by Narcissus, who fell in love
with his reflection, believing it was real (*Metamorphoses*

3.351–510).
3. The moon was associated with mutability and inconstancy; consequently, those souls appearing in the lowest
of the spheres are those whom others compelled to break
their vows.
4. Beatrice assures Dante that these, like all blessed souls,
are absolutely trustworthy because their light, however
faint, is that of truth, or God.

against just will; our love is like the Love

45 that would have all Its court be like Itself.[5]

Within the world I was a nun, a virgin;
and if your mind attends and recollects,
my greater beauty here will not conceal me,
and you will recognize me as Piccarda,[6]

50 who, placed here with the other blessed ones,
am blessed within the slowest of the spheres.[7]

Our sentiments, which only serve the flame
that is the pleasure of the Holy Ghost,
delight in their conforming to His order.[8]

55 And we are to be found within a sphere
this low, because we have neglected vows,
so that in some respect we were deficient."

And I to her: "Within your wonderful
semblance there is something divine that glows,

60 transforming the appearance you once showed:
therefore, my recognizing you was slow;
but what you now have told me is of help;
I can identify you much more clearly.

But tell me: though you're happy here, do you

65 desire a higher place in order to
see more and to be still more close to Him?"[9]

Together with her fellow shades she smiled
at first; then she replied to me with such
gladness, like one who burns with love's first flame:

70 "Brother, the power of love appeases our
will so—we only long for what we have;
we do not thirst for greater blessedness.

Should we desire a higher sphere than ours,
then our desires would be discordant with

75 the will of Him who has assigned us here,
but you'll see no such discord in these spheres;
to live in love is—here—necessity,
if you think on love's nature carefully.

The essence of this blessed life consists

80 in keeping to the boundaries of God's will,
through which our wills become one single will;
so that, as we are ranged from step to step
throughout this kingdom, all this kingdom wills

---

5. The soul responds to Dante's courtly phrasing with a metaphor of Heaven as a court of love, with love redefined as the Cardinal Virtue of *caritas,* or charity.
6. Piccarda Donati was sister of a soul Dante has already encountered: his youthful friend Forese Donati, who was among the gluttonous on the Sixth Terrace of Purgatory, and who forecast Piccarda's salvation as well the impending damnation of their brother, Corso Donati, leader of the Black Guelfs of Florence. Dante, a White Guelf, was related to the family through his wife, Gemma Donati.

7. Because the moon revolves closest to earth and is farthest from the Empyrean, it is the "slowest" of the heavenly spheres.
8. Dante presents a key paradox of his Paradise: all the souls are equally blessed because they participate in the Love that moves the universe, but there are multiple degrees of blessedness.
9. The pilgrim asks Piccarda what from an earthly perspective seems an obvious question: doesn't she wish to be "more" blessed than she is?

85   that which will please the King whose will is rule.[1]
        And in His will there is our peace: that sea
       to which all beings move—the beings He
       creates or nature makes—such is His will."[2]
        Then it was clear to me how every place
       in Heaven is in Paradise, though grace

90   does not rain equally from the High Good.
        But just as, when our hunger has been sated
       with one food, we still long to taste the other—
       while thankful for the first, we crave the latter—
        so was I in my words and in my gestures,

95   asking to learn from her what was the web
       of which her shuttle had not reached the end.[3]
        "A perfect life," she said, "and her high merit
       enheaven, up above, a woman whose
       rule governs those who, in your world, would wear

100   nuns' dress and veil, so that, until their death,
       they wake and sleep with that Spouse who accepts
       all vows that love conforms unto His pleasure.[4]
        Still young, I fled the world to follow her;
       and, in her order's habit, I enclosed

105   myself and promised my life to her rule.
        Then men more used to malice than to good
       took me—violently—from my sweet cloister:
       God knows what, after that, my life became.[5]
        This other radiance that shows itself

110   to you at my right hand, a brightness kindled
       by all the light that fills our heaven—she
        has understood what I have said: she was
       a sister, and from her head, too, by force,
       the shadow of the sacred veil was taken.[6]

115   But though she had been turned back to the world
       against her will, against all honest practice,
       the veil upon her heart was never loosed.
        This is the splendor of the great Costanza,
       who from the Swabians' second gust engendered

120   the one who was their third and final power."

1. Paradise functions like an ideal court, with every one of its members content with his or her place within it because the purged will consists in willing freely what the Lord wills.

2. The change in metaphor from the court to the ocean switches perspective from one of hierarchy to one of unity: all the blessed float in the sea of "His will."

3. The question returns to Piccarda, referring either to the interrupted "web" of her story or to that of her broken vows.

4. Piccarda speaks of a follower of St. Francis, St. Clare of Assisi (1194–1253), founder of the order of the Poor Clares. Nuns were considered as brides of Christ, their vows as marriage vows; those that "conform" are vows

undertaken out of charity rather than some other motive. The "rule" of an order was the conduct and activities it required of its members.

5. Piccarda was forcibly removed from the convent by her brother Corso Donati to marry his henchman Rossellino della Tosa.

6. Constance (1154–1198) was daughter of Roger of Hauteville and last heir of the Norman rulers of Sicily. She was forced out of her convent to marry emperor Henry VI (1165–1197), son of Frederick Barbarossa of Swabia (hence, its "second gust"). Their son was Frederick II, "their third and final power," end of the dynasty (with the heretics in *Inferno* 10.119).

This said, she then began to sing *"Ave
Maria"* and, while singing, vanished as
a weighty thing will vanish in deep water.[7]
My sight, which followed her as long as it

125 was able to, once she was out of view,
returned to where its greater longing lay,
and it was wholly bent on Beatrice;
but she then struck my eyes with so much brightness
that I, at first, could not withstand her force;

130 and that made me delay my questioning.

[*As Dante and Beatrice pass through the successive spheres, the souls proper to each
appear to them, first, the flawed souls between the earth and the sun: in Mercury,
those who acted righteously but were overly concerned with honor; in Venus, those
who were overly amorous. From the Sun outward, the spheres are defined positively:
in the Sun, the wise, including Thomas Aquinas; in Mars, warrior spirits, including
Dante's ancestor, Cacciaguida, who explains the dark prophecies about his descendant's exile; in Jupiter, the spirits of the just; in Saturn, the contemplative (the further
planets were not known at the time). In the eighth heaven, the Sphere of the Fixed
Stars, appear those souls who anticipated the coming of Christ or believed in him after his Incarnation; in the Primum Mobile, where the motion of the universe is generated, appear the Angelic Intelligences; in the Empyrean, the Divine Rose of all the
blessed souls appears, and Beatrice takes her place among them after a final condemnation of Pope Boniface VIII.*]

Canto 31

[THE CELESTIAL ROSE]

So, in the shape of that white Rose, the holy
legion was shown to me—the host that Christ,
with His own blood, had taken as His bride.[1]
The other host,° which, flying, sees and sings   *the angels*

5 the glory of the One who draws its love,
and that goodness which granted it such glory,
just like a swarm of bees that, at one moment,
enters the flowers and, at another, turns
back to that labor which yields such sweet savor,

10 descended into that vast flower graced
with many petals, then again rose up
to the eternal dwelling of its love.
Their faces were all living flame; their wings
were gold; and for the rest, their white was so

15 intense, no snow can match the white they showed.

---

7. The souls have appeared to Dante in the sphere that
represents the form and degree of their blessedness; they
now return to their seats in the Empyrean.

1. The "holy legion" are all of the souls of the blessed,
"wedded" to Christ through his sacrifice on the Cross;
wherever they may have appeared earlier in the canticle,
the Rose is their true dwelling place.

When they climbed down into that flowering Rose,
from rank to rank, they shared that peace and ardor
which they had gained, with wings that fanned their sides.
    Nor did so vast a throng in flight, although

20   it interposed between the candid Rose
and light above, obstruct the sight or splendor,
    because the light of God so penetrates
the universe according to the worth
of every part, that no thing can impede it.

25   This confident and joyous kingdom, thronged
with people of both new and ancient times,
turned all its sight and ardor to one mark.
    O threefold Light° that, in a single star   *the Trinity*
sparkling into their eyes, contents them so,

30   look down and see our tempest here below!
    If the Barbarians, when they came from
A region that is covered every day
by Helice, who wheels with her loved son,[2]
    were, seeing Rome and her vast works, struck dumb

35   (when, of all mortal things, the Lateran
was the most eminent),[3] then what amazement
    must have filled me when I to the divine
came from the human, to eternity
from time, and to a people just and sane

40   from Florence came! And certainly, between
the wonder and the joy, it must have been
welcome to me to hear and speak nothing.
    And as a pilgrim, in the temple he
had vowed to reach, renews himself—he looks

45   and hopes he can describe what it was like—
    so did I journey through the living light,
guiding my eyes, from rank to rank, along
a path now up, now down, now circling round.
    There I saw faces given up to love—

50   graced with Another's light and their own smile—
and movements graced with every dignity.
    By now my gaze had taken in the whole
of Paradise—its form in general—
but without looking hard at any part;

55   and I, my will rekindled, turning toward
my lady, was prepared to ask about
those matters that inclined my mind to doubt.

---

2. The nymph Helice, or Callisto, was transformed into a bear by Juno as punishment for her seduction by Jupiter. Arcas, the son from their union, was about to kill her while hunting when Jupiter exalted her to the stars as the constellation of the Great Bear, with Arcas nearby as the Little Bear (*Metamorphoses* 2.401–530). The Bear was visible year round in the homeland of the barbarians in the north of Europe.

3. The Lateran Palace was residence in Rome of the emperors and then the popes.

Where I expected her, another answered:
I thought I should see Beatrice, and saw
60 an elder dressed like those who are in glory.[4]

His gracious gladness filled his eyes, suffused
his cheeks; his manner had that kindliness
which suits a tender father. "Where is she?"
I asked him instantly. And he replied:
65 "That all your longings may be satisfied,
Beatrice urged me from my place. If you
look up and to the circle that is third
from that rank which is highest, you will see
her on the throne her merits have assigned her."
70 I, without answering, then looked on high
and saw that round her now a crown took shape
as she reflected the eternal rays.

No mortal eye, not even one that plunged
into deep seas, would be so distant from
75 that region where the highest thunder forms,
as—there—my sight was far from Beatrice;
but distance was no hindrance, for her semblance
reached me—undimmed by any thing between.

"O lady, you in whom my hope gains strength,
80 you who, for my salvation, have allowed
your footsteps to be left in Hell, in all
the things that I have seen, I recognize
the grace and benefit that I, depending
upon your power and goodness, have received.
85 You drew me out from slavery to freedom
by all those paths, by all those means that were
within your power. Do, in me, preserve
your generosity, so that my soul,
which you have healed, when it is set loose from
90 my body, be a soul that you will welcome."

So did I pray. And she, however far
away she seemed, smiled, and she looked at me.
Then she turned back to the eternal fountain.

And he, the holy elder, said: "That you
95 may consummate your journey perfectly—
for this, both prayer and holy love have sent me
to help you—let your sight fly round this garden;
by gazing so, your vision will be made
more ready to ascend through God's own ray.
100 The Queen of Heaven, for whom I am all
aflame with love, will grant us every grace:

---

4. The shock in the disappearance of Beatrice is minimal in comparison to the parallel replacement of Virgil by Beatrice in the Earthly Paradise (*Purgatorio* 30.43–57). The "elder" is the third and final guide, founder of the Cistercian order and one of the most powerful figures of the 12th century, St. Bernard of Clairvaux.

I am her faithful Bernard."[5] Just as one
   who, from Croatia perhaps, has come
to visit our Veronica—one whose
105   old hunger is not sated, who, as long
   as it is shown, repeats these words in thought:
"O my Lord Jesus Christ, true God, was then
Your image like the image I see now?"[6]—
   such was I as I watched the living love
110   of him who, in this world, in contemplation,
tasted that peace.[7] And he said: "Son of grace,
   you will not come to know this joyous state
if your eyes only look down at the base;
but look upon the circles, look at those
115   that sit in a position more remote,
until you see upon her seat the Queen°   *Mary*
to whom this realm is subject and devoted."
   I lifted up my eyes; and as, at morning,
the eastern side of the horizon shows
120   more splendor than the side where the sun sets,
   so, as if climbing with my eyes from valley
to summit, I saw one part of the farthest
rank of the Rose more bright than all the rest.
   And as, on earth, the point where we await
125   the shaft that Phaethon had misguided glows
brightest, while, to each side, the light shades off,[8]
   so did the peaceful oriflamme[9] appear
brightest at its midpoint, so did its flame,
on each side, taper off at equal pace.
130   I saw, around that midpoint, festive angels—
more than a thousand—with their wings outspread;
each was distinct in splendor and in skill.
   And there I saw a loveliness that when
it smiled at the angelic songs and games
135   made glad the eyes of all the other saints.
   And even if my speech were rich as my
imagination is, I should not try
to tell the very least of her delights.
   Bernard—when he had seen my eyes intent,
140   fixed on the object of his burning fervor—
turned his own eyes to her with such affection
   that he made mine gaze still more ardently.

5. Bernard was well-known for his restoration of the cult of the Blessed Virgin Mary, and thus a suitable candidate for directing Dante's vision of her.

6. Having already likened himself to a barbarian in Rome, Dante now describes his joy at seeing Bernard as akin to that of a pilgrim from the far reaches of Christendom faced with the priceless relic of Veronica's Veil, the image of Christ's face on a piece of cloth, kept in St. Peter's in Rome and said to have been used to wipe his face as he climbed to Calvary.

7. In addition to his temporal power, Bernard was a contemplative who taught the ascetic and mystical way to God.

8. The "shaft" misguided by the sun-god's son, Phaethon, was the chariot of the sun.

9. The ancient royal standard of France, made of red silk split at one end, forming streamers in the shape of flames.

Canto 33

[THE VISION OF GOD][1]

"Virgin mother, daughter of your Son,
more humble and sublime than any creature,
fixed goal decreed from all eternity,

you are the one who gave to human nature
5   so much nobility that its Creator
did not disdain His being made its creature.

That love whose warmth allowed this flower to bloom
within the everlasting peace—was love
rekindled in your womb;[2] for us above,

10   you are the noonday torch of charity,
and there below, on earth, among the mortals,
you are a living spring of hope. Lady,

you are so high, you can so intercede,
that he who would have grace but does not seek
15   your aid, may long to fly but has no wings.

Your loving-kindness does not only answer
the one who asks, but it is often ready
to answer freely long before the asking.[3]

In you compassion is, in you is pity,
20   in you is generosity, in you
is every goodness found in any creature.

This man—who from the deepest hollow in
the universe, up to this height, has seen
the lives of spirits, one by one—now pleads

25   with you, through grace, to grant him so much virtue
that he may lift his vision higher still—
may lift it toward the ultimate salvation.

And I, who never burned for my own vision
more than I burn for his, do offer you
30   all of my prayers—and pray that they may not

fall short—that with your prayers, you may disperse
all of the clouds of his mortality
so that the Highest Joy be his to see.[4]

This, too, o Queen, who can do what you would,
35   I ask of you: that after such a vision,
his sentiments preserve their perseverance.

May your protection curb his mortal passions.[5]

---

1. The final canto of the *Commedia* begins with a long prayer by St. Bernard to the Virgin Mary to grant the pilgrim a final vision of the Godhead.

2. The "flower" is the Incarnation of Christ, the love of God for the human race redeemed ("rekindled") after its first fall.

3. As in the case of the pilgrim, for according to *Inferno* 2.94–99, it was Mary who first initiated the chain of compassion that led Beatrice down into Limbo to ask Virgil to

aid him in the dark wood.

4. Direct vision of God is normally not granted to a living person; it was, however, the goal of any mystic or contemplative, such as Bernard himself.

5. Bernard prays that Dante's vision and memory preserve a record of what he has seen so that he may reproduce it, and that the grace of Mary allow Dante to maintain his faith in the tribulations awaiting him back on earth.

See Beatrice—how many saints with her!
They join my prayers! They clasp their hands to you!"

40   The eyes that are revered and loved by God,
now fixed upon the supplicant, showed us
how welcome such devotions are to her;
        then her eyes turned to the Eternal Light—
there, do not think that any creature's eye
45   can find its way as clearly as her sight.
        And I, who now was nearing Him who is
the end of all desires, as I ought,
lifted my longing to its ardent limit.
        Bernard was signaling—he smiled—to me
50   to turn my eyes on high; but I, already
was doing what he wanted me to do,
        because my sight, becoming pure, was able
to penetrate the ray of Light more deeply—
that Light, sublime, which in Itself is true.
55   From that point on, what I could see was greater
than speech can show: at such a sight, it fails—
and memory fails when faced with such excess.[6]
        As one who sees within a dream, and, later,
the passion that had been imprinted stays,
60   but nothing of the rest returns to mind,
        such am I, for my vision almost fades
completely, yet it still distills within
my heart the sweetness that was born of it.
        So is the snow, beneath the sun, unsealed;
65   and so, on the light leaves, beneath the wind,
the oracles the Sibyl wrote were lost.[7]
        O Highest Light, You, raised so far above
the minds of mortals, to my memory
give back something of Your epiphany,
70   and make my tongue so powerful that I
may leave to people of the future one
gleam of the glory that is Yours, for by
        returning somewhat to my memory
and echoing awhile within these lines,
75   Your victory will be more understood.
        The living ray that I endured was so
acute that I believe I should have gone
astray had my eyes turned away from it.[8]
        I can recall that I, because of this,
80   was bolder in sustaining it until
my vision reached the Infinite Goodness.

---

6. Dante recalls the mystic's difficulty in making memory and speech reproduce the experience of a mystic vision. 7. Two similes to produce the sensation of loss: the melting of snow from the heat of the sun, and a final nod to Virgil, describing the leaves on which the Sibyl inscribes the prophecies of the god, scattered by the wind (*Aeneid* 3.441–51). 8. The word "astray" (*smarrita*) recalls the opening lines of *Inferno*.

O grace abounding, through which I presumed
to set my eyes on the Eternal Light
so long that I spent all my sight on it!

85   In its profundity I saw—ingathered
and bound by love into one single volume—
what, in the universe, seems separate, scattered:[9]
substances, accidents, and dispositions
as if conjoined—in such a way that what
90   I tell is only rudimentary.[1]
I think I saw the universal shape
which that knot takes;[2] for, speaking this, I feel
a joy that is more ample. That one moment
brings more forgetfulness to me than twenty-
95   five centuries have brought to the endeavor
that startled Neptune with the *Argo*'s shadow![3]
So was my mind—completely rapt, intent,
steadfast, and motionless—gazing; and it
grew ever more enkindled as it watched.
100   Whoever sees that Light is soon made such
that it would be impossible for him
to set that Light aside for other sight;
because the good, the object of the will,
is fully gathered in that Light; outside
105   that Light, what there is perfect is defective.[4]
What little I recall is to be told,
from this point on, in words more weak than those
of one whose infant tongue still bathes at the breast.
And not because more than one simple semblance
110   was in the Living Light at which I gazed—
for It is always what It was before[5]—
but through my sight, which as I gazed grew stronger,
that sole appearance, even as I altered,
seemed to be changing. In the deep and bright
115   essence of that exalted Light, three circles
appeared to me; they had three different colors,

---

9. A metaphor to describe the double perspective: what to the mortal point of view is "separate, scattered," is from the divine perspective "ingathered" into a single, coherent volume, "bound by love," the book of the world, already complete from the Creation to the Last Judgment.

1. Here Dante uses the language of Scholasticism to describe the "conjoining," or bringing together, of this volume: a "substance" is that which exists in and of itself, form embodied in matter; an "accident" has no innate existence, but only as an attribute or quality of a substance; the "disposition" is the relationship between the two, the way they are joined. Dante's vision shows him the innate and invisible order of the universe.

2. The metaphor of the "knot" recalls another image-cluster repeated throughout the poem, especially to describe the "knot" of a question which must be unraveled. Here, the "knot" refers to the binding of all the threads of the universe into a single tightly interwoven form whose shape he has finally comprehended.

3. A final, startling, classical reference, and a final use of Ovid's *Metamorphoses* (6.718–21); Dante has forgotten more of this single moment (and there was more in it to forget) than has been forgotten in the 25 centuries since the voyage of Jason and the Argonauts (see *Inferno* 18.82–96). In the popular tradition, their ship, the Argo, was the first to sail the seas, and thus startled the sea god Neptune when its shadow passed over his head.

4. The goal of existence, the "good" toward which every "will" by nature tends, is perfect only within this light; everywhere else it is "defective," only a varying reflection of that light.

5. The Trinity is never less than unified, "always what It was before," but also never less than threefold.

but all of them were of the same dimension;
   one circle seemed reflected by the second,
as rainbow is by rainbow, and the third
120   seemed fire breathed equally by those two circles.[6]
   How incomplete is speech, how weak, when set
against my thought! And this, to what I saw
is such—to call it little is too much.
   Eternal Light, You only dwell within
125   Yourself, and only You know You; Self-knowing,
Self-known, You love and smile upon Yourself!
   That circle—which, begotten so, appeared
in You as light reflected—when my eyes
had watched it with attention for some time,
130   within itself and colored like itself,
to me seemed painted with our effigy,[7]
so that my sight was set on it completely.
   As the geometer intently seeks
to square the circle, but he cannot reach,
135   through thought on thought, the principle he needs,
   so I searched that strange sight: I wished to see
the way in which our human effigy
suited the circle and found place in it[8]—
and my own wings were far too weak for that.
140   But then my mind was struck by light that flashed
and, with this light, received what it had asked.
   Here force failed my high fantasy; but my
desire and will were moved already—like
a wheel revolving uniformly—by
145   the Love that moves the sun and the other stars.

⤬≫

RESONANCES
Dante's Hell

The powerful imagery, memorable characters, and complex structure of Dante's afterlife resonated from the start. Few if any writers have been so often translated, adapted, alluded to, or illustrated (see Color Plate 9). With its endless potential for satirical commentary on the follies of this world, the *Inferno* has been a particular favorite. Like the selections in Translations: Dante's *Inferno* (page 1065), the first selection here shows one figure, Count Ugolino, frozen in the ice of Cocytus in the Ninth Circle of Hell; here, we see Ugolino in the context of Geoffrey Chaucer's *Canterbury Tales* (for more on Chaucer, see page 1087). The second selection demonstrates another form of resonance, the imaginative re-creation of Hell in the terms of mid-twentieth-century Newark, New Jersey.

---

6. Dante's sight has grown stronger, allowing him to see the three circles within the single light: the Father "reflected" by the Son; the Holy Spirit "breathed" by the first two.

7. The second circle, the Second Person of the Trinity, seems "painted" with the image of a human form: the

mystery of the Incarnation, simultaneously human and divine.

8. Dante likens the final effort of his vision—to grasp the role of the human form within the divine—to the proverbially insoluble geometrical puzzle of finding a square that would be equal in area to a given circle.

Geoffrey Chaucer: from *The Canterbury Tales*

from THE MONK'S TALE: OF UGOLINO, COUNT OF PISA[1]

Of Ugolino, Count of Pisa's woe
No tongue can tell the half for hot pity.
Near Pisa stands a tower, and it was so
That to be there imprisoned doomed was he,
5   While with him were his little children three,
The eldest child was scarce five years of age.
Alas, Fortune![2] It was great cruelty
To lock such birds up into such a cage!

Condemned was he to die in that prison,
10   Since Ruggieri, Pisa's bishop, twice
Had lied, intrigued, and egged old passions on,
Whereby the people did against him rise,
And thrust him into prison in such wise
As you have heard; and meat and drink he had
15   So little that it could not long suffice,
And was, moreover, very poor and bad.
And on a day befell it, at the hour
When commonly to him his food was brought,
The gaoler° shut the great doors of the tower.   *jailer*
20   He heard it well enough, but he said naught,
And to his heart anon° there came the thought   *soon*
That they by hunger would leave him to die.
"Alas," said he, "that ever I was wrought!"°   *born*
And thereupon the tears fell from his eye.

25   His youngest son, who three years was of age,
Unto him said: "Father, why do you weep?
When will the gaoler bring us our pottage?°   *soup*
Is there no crumb of bread that you did keep?
I am so hungry that I cannot sleep.
30   Now would God that I might sleep on for aye!°   *ever*
Then should not hunger through my belly creep;
For nothing more than bread I'd rather pray."

Thus, day by day, this little child did cry,
Till on his father's breast at length he lay
35   And said: "Farewell, my father, I must die."
And kissed the man and died that very day.

---

1. Translated by J. U. Nicolson. Chaucer's encounter with Dante's *Commedia* in the 1370s was a formative moment in his conception of the vernacular for addressing an audience that would not be bound to a particular class, estate, or even a particular moment in history. In "The Monk's Tale," Ugolino's fate is one of a litany of tragic stories so repetitive in theme that the teller is finally interrupted by the pilgrims. Dante's Hell is placed firmly in the context of divine retribution and recompense; Chaucer's pilgrims seem less sure where all this suffering may lead, but the Host, at least, is tired of so much *hevynesse*. The passage is based on *Inferno* 33.1–90, although it contains details not in Dante's version. For more about Ugolino and Ruggieri, see note 2 to *Inferno* 33, page 1018.

2. The capriciousness of Fortune is the common theme of the episodes recounted in "The Monk's Tale."

And when the father saw it dead, I say,
For grief his arms gnawed he until blood came,
And said: "Alas, Fortune and welaway,°   *woe*
40   It is thy treacherous wheel that I must blame!"[3]

His children thought that it for hunger was
He gnawed his arms, and not that 'twas for woe,
And cried: "O father, do not thus, alas!
But rather eat our young flesh, even so;
45   This flesh you gave us; take it back and go
And eat enough!" 'Twas thus those children cried,
And after that, within a day or two,
They laid themselves upon his knees and died.

Himself, despairing, all by hunger starved,
50   Thus ended this great count of Pisa's cries;
All his vast riches Fortune from him carved.
Of his fate tragic let thus much suffice.
Whoso would hear it told in longer wise,
Let him read the great bard of Italy
55   Whom men call Dante; seen through Dante's eyes
No point is slurred, nor in one word fails he.

Amiri Baraka (LeRoi Jones): from *The System of Dante's Hell*[1]

THE DIVINERS[2]

Gypsies lived here before me. Heads twisted backwards, out to the yards, stalks. Their brown garages, stocking caps, green Bird suits. Basil suits. 15 feet to the yard, closer from the smashed toilet. Year of The Hurricane. Year of The Plague. Year of The Dead Animals.

                                                                                    Existent.

This is Orlando Davis, who with his curly hair & large ass, steps thru mists everywhere. They caught him stealing on his scooter. They, the cops(?), moralists dropped on him from the skies. The music: Rachmaninoff's 3rd piano glinting.[3] Remarkable thick weather he moved thru. Not as a woman this time, a sultry male. He looked tired, or bewildered. And they mobbed him at the river's edge, yelling their faces at heaven.

---

3. The inexorably turning wheel of blindfolded Fortune meant that whoever was high would inevitably be brought low.

1. LeRoi Jones (b. 1934) burst on the New York scene as an avant-garde jazz critic, poet, playwright, and editor in the early 1960s. By the middle of that decade, he had changed his name to Amiri Baraka, moved back to Newark, New Jersey, and immersed himself in the black arts movement and politics of his hometown. In his first novel, *The System of Dante's Hell* (1961–1965), Baraka used the *Inferno* as a loose framework for a hallucinatory

and partly autobiographical exploration of the inner-city landscape and the people who inhabit it—what he calls here "Hell in the head."

2. This chapter of the novel reworks *Inferno* 20, the encounter with the diviners in the fourth pocket of the eighth circle. Their *contrapasso* is to have their heads facing behind them.

3. The virtuoso Third Piano Concerto by the Russian composer and concert pianist Sergey Rachmaninoff is one of his most celebrated works, composed in 1909 on the occasion of his first U.S. tour.

John Wieners is Michael Scott, made blind by God.[4] Tears for everything. The fruit of his days in the past. Is past, as from a tower, he fell. Simon, dead also. Under various thumbs, our suns will pass.

This is past. Ourselves, under the earth. She made to get away. Thru Lorber's window, we passed ourselves. They were, in all, with me: Arlotta, Strob, Starling(?) and someone else. At the same point, I leave to blaze in the elements. It was a labyrinth. Windows, broken glass in brown weeds. You kicked them as you walked, or rolled heavily if they threw you down.

Sitting across a river, they had fixed themselves with tender faces. Years later I place my fingers on their running skulls.

If anyone ever lived in a closet, it was me. There were tracks, streets, a diner, the dark, all got between me and their strings. "You're going crazy . . . in here with dark green glasses and the light off." It was a yellow bulb tho, and it all sat well on my shoulders. Vague wet air thrashed the stones. It sat well, without those faggots. Or ART, 5 steps up, in a wood house: a true arc.

That, and don't forget the canopied bed. The ugliest green draperies dragged and hooked across the bed. Action as completeness. If I hung out the window, it was warm and people watched.

A guy named powell who is a lawyer. Air pushing. Straight stone streets. A guy named pinckney who is a teacher. (Place again, those fingers, on my strings. Walk in here smiling. Sit yourself down. Rearrange your synods,[5] your corrections, your trees.

Dolores Morgan, who had an illegitimate child. . . .
PROSPEROUS
Calvin Lewis, who gave it to her. . . . PRIDE

Think about that: Michael at a beach, in the warm tide. The figures I saw *were* fucking. "Huge" shadows, sprawling open their cunts.

Big Apple (myth says) knocked down a horse, split open a basketball player's skull.

For him, let us create a new world. Of Sex and cataclysm.

The rest, let them languish on their Sundays. Let them use shadows to sleep.

* * *

There was a pool hall I wondered about, an ugly snarled face, Jacqueline, money was no object for her probable Saturday walks. There were a few trees to circle, the pool hall, and slick Eddie. Also (because Eddie was only a later example) the first *Hipster*. Not Tom Perry in the chinese restaurant. Earlier(?) and in the sun. Saturday morning. It wd be cold & I was learning then to grow tired of the days. Special. I was layed out so flat, and lied, and loved anyone who'd cross my path. A few showed me unbelievable favor. A redhead maid with heavy lips. Worked for an exceptionally respectable faggot. Lived, with some ease, across from the beer barons,

---

4. On the medieval astrologer and scientist Michael Scot, see *Inferno* 20.115–17, page 973–974.

5. Originally referring to a council or assembly of clergy, a synod can be any kind of gathering or group.

IT WAS HERE THAT THE GOLDEN BOYS FLED UP THE STREETS OF ROMANCE. HERE THAT THEY MADE THEIR HEROIC STAND AGAINST ME, ONLY TO SUCCUMB, LATER, TO MACHINATIONS DRAPED ACROSS THE WORLD. HERE, THEY THREW HANDS UP. AS IN CONQUEST, OR FINAL UGLY SUPPLICATION.

REVERE THE GOLDEN BOYS & ALSO LOS CASSEDORES.[6] THEY TRIED.

* * *

You can never be sure of the hour. Someone stands there blocking the light. Someone has his head split open. Someone walks down Waverly Ave.[7] Someone finds himself used.

This is high tragedy. I will be deformed in hell.

Or say this about people. "They breathed & wore plaid pedal pushers." Can you say from that, "I told you so. Look at him, A bebopper."[8]

"Lefty is pretty hip," he said to get me in. To the fag's house. Blonde streak. The Proctors, all interchangeable in the fish truck. Myth shd be broad & rest easily in branch brook lake. It shd rest like the black trestle between Baxter Terrace & The Cavaliers.[9] (Some slight people thot that we, The Cavaliers, were the same as The Caballeros. Some other nuts thot that we were their (The Caballeros) juniors. We came long before them, but they were older and knew all about sex (so they influenced the crowd). We were still mostly masturbators.

Charlie Davis married Dolores Davis. (He cd do a lot of things tolerably well. Third base. 12 pt. basketball game before he got replaced. That was a blow. Beau Furr was much better, but he came from the slums & I knew him very obliquely (except that time he threw me all those passes & Big John said I'd grow up fast & tricky & "be a bitch.") And some of it was wasted on Peggy Ann Davis, i.e., that long weave down the sidelines (abt 45 yards)

PAYDIRT IS THIS:

Ray Simmons, shy & bony, will work in commercial art houses & revere me all his life. (Enough of his missed layups!)

Sess Peoples (it got thru to him, somehow, he sd "Stoneface," "Emperor," "You little dictatorial fart") as dark as he was & embarrassed by what he smelled on my clothes, Give the World. Let him march thru it in September giggling thru his fingers.

(Advanced philosophy wd be more registrations. Get more in. Deep Blue Sea. I, myself, am the debil.

A RANKING OF THE CAVALIERS IN THE ORDER OF THEIR PREPONDERANCE: (Ray & Sess done formal, as they are, floating in for the easy dunk.)

---

6. The Hunters (Spanish). Like the Golden Boys, the Proctors, the Cavaliers, and the Caballeros, these are names of street gangs, cliques of boys, or pick-up sports teams.
7. Like the streets mentioned below, Waverly Avenue is in Newark.
8. Pedal pushers are girls' or women's trousers reaching just below the knee, so-called because originally intended to be worn while cycling. They were popular in the 1950s.

Beboppers are performers or supporters of bebop, a rhythmic, dissonant, and harmonically complex movement that dominated jazz music during the 1950s, performed by artists such as Charlie Parker and Dizzy Gillespie.
9. The 15-acre, 21-building James M. Baxter Terrace Apartments were one of Newark's first public housing projects, in an impoverished part of the city.

Leon Webster (came later, after the decay. My head gone, in new grey flannel suit (Black wool a nigger called it). Away, so far away, wings melted.[1] Rome, if you want metaphor. Use Rome, & Adams calls the turns. The Barbarians had come in.[2] The cultivated & uncultivated alike. Sprawling thru the walls.) Suffice it to say he came from real slums & was as harsh as our enemies.

Morris Hines: As a compact, years ago under the shadows of those grey or brown buildings. Always heavier than his movement. Escape Bolgia in a buick.[3] Left-handed first baseman: "Ingentes."[4] Flatterer, even as whore Beatrice had her prediction, her Georges Sorel.[5] We had our church. Sussex Ave. was rundown & all the negroes from the projects went there (the strivers after righteousness. American ideal, is not Cyrano's death on Lock Street. The poor went to Jemmy's church, but big Morris and his deacon father sat next to Joyce Smith's house every Sunday & their mother wd fan God. Malebolge (for the flatterers) for me, there is all you can imagine. Jehovah *me fecit*.[6]

William Love: eyes are closed. (Was that Hudson St.? Warren?) He cd, after a fashion appear in Adams' class. He had short stubbed fingers he bit for his nerves. A butt. They called him (not our lovely names . . . these bastards like Ora, "Big Shot," called him "Bullet Head" or "Zakong.") I had fashioned something easier for his weakness but killers like Murray ground his face in the tar, & William wd chase him. Goof train. Rebound man, wheeld & for a time, as to the properties of his life, dealed. I'm told (and so fell into disrepute. In hell the sky is black, all see what the other sees. Outside the dark is motionless & dead leaves beat the air.

TRANSLATIONS: DANTE, *INFERNO*

There are many features that an English translator of Dante's work can try to reproduce: the interlocking *terza rima*, or third rhyme, rhyme scheme; the tercet, or three-line divisions that seamlessly match the flow of thought and narration; the word order and sentence structure; the style ranging from classical tragedy to contemporary slang and obscenities. Most translators settle for one of these components; none yet has been able to capture all three. Allen Mandelbaum's translation (page 903) opts for a compromise; the three translations below take a more extreme approach. In the original Italian of Canto 33.55–75,

1. Like Dante, Baraka compares himself here to Icarus, who fell from the sky to his death when the wax binding his artificial wings melted in the heat of the sun (see *Inferno* 17.109–11, page 963).
2. The barbarians (Goths) from the north entered Rome in 410, led by Alaric.
3. *Bolgia* ("pocket") is Dante's word for the ten subdivisions of the eighth circle, *Malebolge,* the circle devoted to punishing sins of fraud.
4. In Spanish and Latin, *ingentes* means literally the immense or great men.
5. The flatterers are punished in the second *bolgia* of the eighth circle. Beatrice was Dante's beloved; in the *Commedia,* she is the inspiration and guiding light of his journey (and, needless to say, not a whore). Georges Sorel (1847–1922) was a French socialist and revolutionary trade-unionist who developed an influential philosophy around the creative and positive value of violence. Among other radical movements, his ideas were influential on the development of German and Italian fascism.
6. "God (Jehovah) made me." *Me fecit* is a traditional tag of authorship; it also appears frequently in the Bible in terms of what God causes someone to do.

part of the Ugolino episode, you can count the regular eleven-syllable lines (consecutive vowels are run into each other) and the complex effect of the *terza rima*:

> Come un poco di raggio si fu messo
> nel doloroso carcere, e io scorsi
> per quattro visi il mio aspetto stesso,
>
> ambo le man per lo dolor mi morsi;
> ed ei, pensando ch'io 'l fessi per voglia
> di manicar, di subito levorsi
>
> e disser: "Padre, assai ci fia men doglia
> se tu mangi di noi: tu ne vestisti
> queste misere carni, e tu le spoglia".
>
> Queta'mi allor per non farli più tristi;
> lo dì e l'altro stemmo tutti muti;
> ahi dura terra, perché non t'apristi?
>
> Poscia che fummo al quarto dì venuti,
> Gaddo mi si gittò disteso a' piedi,
> dicendo: "Padre mio, ché non mi aiuti?".
>
> Quivi morì; e come tu mi vedi,
> vid'io cascar li tre ad uno ad uno
> tra 'l quinto dì e 'l sesto; ond'io mi diedi,
>
> già cieco, a brancolar sovra ciascuno,
> e due dì li chiamai, poi che fur morti.
> Poscia, più che 'l dolor, poté 'l digiuno.

Recounting his own horrible death and that of his sons, Ugolino uses a high, tragic style to evoke sympathy in the listening pilgrim. The final line is famously ambiguous—did Ugolino feed on his sons as they had offered before they died?—and thus presents the translator with the dilemma of leaving it ambiguous or preempting the reader's interpretation.

THOMAS MEDWIN AND PERCY BYSSHE SHELLEY TRANSLATION (1847)

> . . . but when to shine
>
> Upon the world, not us, came forth the light
>
> Of the new sun, and thwart my prison thrown
> Gleamed through its narrow chink, a doleful sight,
> Three faces, each the reflex of my own,
>
> Were imaged by its faint and ghastly ray;
> Then I, of either hand unto the bone,
> Gnawed, in my agony; and thinking they
>
> Twas done from sudden pangs, in their excess,
> All of a sudden raise themselves, and say,
> "Father! our woes, so great, were yet the less

Gustave Doré, 1870 engraving of the Ugolino episode in Dante's *Inferno*.

Would you but eat of us,—twas you who clad
Our bodies in these weeds of wretchedness;
Despoil them." Not to make their hearts more sad,

I hushed myself. That day is at its close,—
Another—still we were all mute. Oh, had
The obdurate earth opened to end our woes!

The fourth day dawned, and when the new sun shone,
Outstretched himself before me as it rose
My Gaddo, saying, "Help, father! hast thou none

For thine own child—is there no help from thee?"
He died—there at my feet—and one by one,
I saw them fall, plainly as you see me.

Between the fifth and sixth day, ere twas dawn,
I found myself blind-groping o'er the three.
Three days I called them after they were gone.

Famine of grief can get the mastery.

Medwin and his cousin and friend Shelley focused their efforts on capturing the effect of terza rima in English (it was a popular form with the Romantic poets). Notice how they do not match the flow of meaning to the tercets; the breaks and pauses have little relation to Dante's. Consequently, the rhyme dominates except for the powerfully isolated final line.

CHARLES SINGLETON TRANSLATION (1970)

As soon as a little ray made its way into the woeful prison, and I discerned by their four faces the aspect of my own, I bit both my hands for grief. And they, thinking I did it for hunger, suddenly rose up and said, "Father, it will be far less painful to us if you eat of us; you did clothe us with this wretched flesh, and do you strip us of it!"

Then I calmed myself in order not to make them sadder. That day and the next we stayed all silent: Ah, hard earth! why did you not open? When we had come to the fourth day Gaddo threw himself outstretched at my feet, saying, "Father, why do you not help me?" There he died; and even as you see me, I saw the three fall, one by one, between the fifth day and the sixth; whence I betook me, already blind, to groping over each, and for two days I called them after they were dead. Then fasting did more than grief had done.

Since it does not have to make any concessions to rhymes or to line length, Dante scholar Charles Singleton's prose translation retains as much as possible the word order and literal meaning of Dante's Italian. In what ways does the lack of any poetic meter or rhyme change the meaning of the poem?

SANDOW BIRK AND MARCUS SANDERS TRANSLATION (2004)

. . . But as soon as the sun came up
again and it got light enough to see the four faces of the
hungry boys suffering with me, I covered my face with
my hands and gnawed on my fist in despair. And then,
seeing me like that and thinking it meant that I was hungry,
my very own little boys said to me, "Don't be like that, Dad.
You're the one who gave us our lives and we'd rather that
you take them from us, if you have to. We'd rather die than
see you go hungry and suffer like this. Take us and kill us,
and then you can eat us. It's better that way. And then you
can decide what's best to be done."

I tried to stay calm from then on so I wouldn't make them
more afraid than they already were. None of us spoke again
for the rest of the day and not even the next. God, how I
wished that the ground would have opened up and
swallowed us all at once and been done with it right then.
By the fourth day, my little Gaddo was so weak that he
collapsed at my feet. "Why don't you help me, Dad?" were
his very last words. As clear as you see me here in front of
you, I had to live to watch my other son and two grandsons
die, one by one, on the fifth night. Finally, blind with
hunger myself, I crawled around the floor of the cell
feeling the cold bodies and faces of those little boys.
I held each one and spoke to them and called their names,
but every one of them was dead. On the eighth day,
the sufferings of my hunger finally overcame my grief.

Artist and surfer Sandow Birk and journalist and surfer Marcus Sanders wrote their version of the *Inferno* to accompany Birk's illustrations. So free and irreverent that they call it an "adaptation" rather than a translation, their language keeps the events and the tone of the original but makes them completely contemporary and colloquial. Do you think they have gone too far? Or do you think that their "slacker verse," as one reviewer called it, lends an immediacy to Dante's Italian lacking in more academic and faithful translations?

There are a number of other translations of Ugolino's tale by poets and translators of note. Geoffrey Chaucer's fourteenth-century version, "De Hugelino Comite de Pize," appears in lines 519–574 of the Monk's Tale in his *Canterbury Tales* (page 1102). The nineteenth-century American poet Henry Wadsworth Longfellow's 1867 translation of Dante's *Commedia* has recently been reissued. In the early twentieth century, at the urging of his poet friend Ezra Pound, Laurence Binyon essayed a translation of the *Commedia* in *terza rima* in 1933; mystery writer and medievalist Dorothy L. Sayers did the same in 1949. And the Nobel prize–winning Irish poet Seamus Heaney included "Ugolino" as the final poem of his collection *Field Work* (1979).

—+—✠—+—

Marco Polo
c. 1254–1324

One of the greatest travelers of his era, the Venetian merchant Marco Polo would be unknown today if he hadn't been thrown into prison in his early forties, following a skirmish at sea between Venice and Genoa in 1295. At that point, Polo had recently returned home from twenty-five years in Asia, brimming over with stories but short on funds—his traveling party had been robbed and stripped of most of their possessions as they neared home. It so happened that a fellow prisoner named Rustichello was a prolific writer of romances, and between them they determined to write a book. Polo dictated his tale to Rustichello, who composed it (apparently with elaborations of his own, especially in the battle scenes at which he excelled), writing in a local dialect, a mixture of French and Italian. The book was an instant hit as it began to circulate in manuscript upon Polo's release from prison, and dozens of copies and translations were soon made. His book achieved printed form in 1477, not long after the invention of printing, and his enthusiastic description of Japan ("Zipangu," as he called it) gave Christopher Columbus a goal for his epochal voyage across the Atlantic in search of a readier trade route than the long and dangerous overland crossing that Polo so vividly described.

Marco Polo had ventured east at the age of fifteen or sixteen in the company of his father Niccolò and his uncle Maffeo, who had earlier established themselves as traders along the Asian Silk Route. They had even visited the Mongol emperor of China, Kubilai (or Kublai) Khan, at his lavish summer residence of Shang-tu—which became known, thanks to Marco's description of it, as the magical Xanadu, dream-palace beloved of Coleridge and other later European writers. When Marco accompanied his father and uncle on their second voyage east in 1271, they traveled through the predominantly Muslim lands of Persia, Afghanistan, and the northern regions of the Indian subcontinent before reaching northern China, arriving at the Mongol court in Shang-tu sometime in around 1275. Kublai Khan liked to employ foreigners, as he was reluctant to rely solely on Chinese courtiers, who weren't necessarily entirely loyal to the Mongols who had conquered them under his grandfather Chinghiz (or Genghis) Khan sixty years before. He welcomed the Polos, who settled at the court for the next sixteen or seventeen years, engaging in trade and probably also in administration of goods (Marco knows a great deal about the government's salt monopoly). Fluent in several languages, Marco served at times as an ambassador for the Khan, making fact-finding missions to distant parts of the empire and outlying regions, including southern China and Burma, before eventually returning to Italy with his father and uncle via the sea route around the Malay Peninsula and India.

In telling Rustichello the remarkable story of his life, Marco probably exaggerated his importance at the Chinese court, but he also gave detailed descriptions of the many lands he had passed through. His account provides sharp, realistic observation of commercially useful facts like the spices and goods produced in each area, while also retailing the many extraordinary customs and marvels he encountered or heard about. His *Travels* stimulated enormous interest in further exploration and trade. The book also produced an ambivalent view of Marco himself: he was seen by some as a bold adventurer and brilliant ambassador, but by others as an unreliable teller of tall tales, suspiciously unshocked by pagan practices and beliefs. In the second Resonance reading given here, the modern Italian novelist Italo Calvino plays on both images in his extraordinary *Invisible Cities,* cast as dialogues between Kublai Khan and his crafty Venetian ambassador. Marco's book, or rather Marco's and Rustichello's book, remains riveting reading today, a compelling blend of factual fiction and astonishing fact.

PRONUNCIATIONS:

Kin-sai: KEEN-sigh
Kublai Khan: COO-blay KAHN
Rustichello: ROOST-ih-CHEL-oh

from The Travels of Marco Polo[1]

[PROLOGUE]

Ye emperors, kings, dukes, marquises, earls, and knights, and all other people desirous of knowing the diversities of the races of mankind, as well as the diversities of kingdoms, provinces, and regions of all parts of the East, read through this book, and ye will find in it the greatest and most marvellous characteristics of the peoples especially of Armenia, Persia, India, and Tartary, as they are severally related in the present work by Marco Polo, a wise and learned citizen of Venice, who states distinctly what things he saw and what things he heard from others. For this book will be a truthful one. It must be known, then, that from the creation of Adam to the present day, no man, whether Pagan, or Saracen, or Christian, or other, of whatever progeny or generation he may have been, ever saw or inquired into so many and such great things as Marco Polo above mentioned. Who, wishing in his secret thoughts that the things he had seen and heard should be made public by the present work, for the benefit of those who could not see them with their own eyes, he himself being in the year of our Lord 1295 in prison at Genoa, caused the things which are contained in the present work to be written by master Rustichello, a citizen of Pisa, who was with him in the same prison at Genoa; and he divided it into three parts.

[THE POLOS SET OUT]

It should be known to the reader that, at the time when Baldwin II was emperor of Constantinople, where a magistrate representing the doge of Venice then resided, and in the year of our Lord 1250, Nicolo Polo, the father of the said Marco, and Maffeo,

---

1. Translated by W. Marsden (slightly revised).

the brother of Nicolo, respectable and well-informed men, embarked in a ship of their own, with a rich and varied cargo of merchandise, and reached Constantinople in safety. After mature deliberation on the subject of their proceedings, it was determined, as the measure most likely to improve their trading capital, that they should extend their voyage into the Black Sea. With this view they made purchases of many fine and costly jewels, and taking their departure from Constantinople, navigated that sea to a port named Soldaia. From there they travelled on horseback many days until they reached the court of a powerful chief of the Western Tartars, named Barka, who dwelt in the cities of Bolgara and Assara, and had the reputation of being one of the most liberal and civilized princes hitherto known amongst the tribes of Tartary. He expressed much satisfaction at the arrival of these travellers, and received them with marks of distinction. In return for which courtesy, when they had laid before him the jewels they brought with them, and perceived that their beauty pleased him, they presented them for his acceptance. The liberality of this conduct on the part of the two brothers struck him with admiration; and being unwilling that they should surpass him in generosity, he not only directed double the value of the jewels to be paid to them, but made them in addition several rich presents.

Having resided a year in the dominions of this prince, the brothers became desirous of revisiting their native country, but were impeded by the sudden breaking out of a war between him and another chief, named Alaù, who ruled over the Eastern Tartars. In a fierce and very bloody battle that ensued between their respective armies, Alaù was victorious. As a result, the roads being rendered unsafe for travellers, the brothers could not attempt to return by the way they came; and it was recommended to them, as the only practicable mode of reaching Constantinople, to proceed in an easterly direction, by an unfrequented route, so as to skirt the limits of Barka's territories. Accordingly they made their way to a town named Oukaka, situated on the confines of the kingdom of the Western Tartars. Leaving that place, and advancing still farther, they crossed the Tigris, one of the four rivers of Paradise, and came to a desert, the extent of which was seventeen days' journey, wherein they found neither town, castle, nor any substantial building, but only Tartars with their herds, dwelling in tents on the plain. Having passed this tract they arrived at length at a well-built city called Bokhara, in a province of that name, belonging to the dominions of Persia, and the noblest city of that kingdom, but governed by a prince whose name was Barak. Here, from inability to proceed farther, they remained three years.

It happened while these brothers were in Bokhara, that a person of consequence and gifted with eminent talents made his appearance there. He was proceeding as ambassador from Alaù before mentioned, to the grand khan, supreme chief of all the Tartars, named Kublai, whose residence was at the extremity of the continent, in a direction between northeast and east. Not having ever before had an opportunity, although he wished it, of seeing any natives of Italy, he was gratified in a high degree at meeting and conversing with these brothers, who had now become proficient in the Tartar language; and after associating with them for several days, and finding their manners agreeable to him, he proposed to them that they should accompany him to the presence of the great khan, who would be pleased by their appearance at his court, which had not hitherto been visited by any person from their country; adding assurances that they would be honourably received, and recompensed with many gifts. Convinced as they were that their endeavours to return homeward would expose them to the most imminent risks, they agreed to this proposal. Recommending themselves to the protection of the Almighty, they set out on their journey in the suite of the ambassador, attended by several Christian servants whom they had brought with them from Venice. The course they took at first was between the northeast and north, and an entire year was consumed before they could reach the imperial residence, in consequence of the extraordinary delays occasioned by the snows and the swelling of the rivers, which obliged them to halt until the snow had melted and the floods had subsided. Many things worthy of admiration were observed by them in the progress of their journey, but they are here omitted, as they will be described by Marco Polo, in the sequel of the book.

Being introduced to the presence of the grand khan, Kublai, the travellers were received by him with the condescension and affability that belonged to his character, and as they were the first Latins who had made their appearance in that country, they were entertained with feasts and honoured with other marks of distinction. Entering graciously into conversation with them, he made earnest inquiries on the subject of the western parts of the world, of the emperor of the Romans, and of other Christian kings and princes. He wished to be informed of their relative importance, the extent of their possessions, the manner in which justice was administered in their several kingdoms and principalities, how they conducted themselves in warfare, and above all he questioned them particularly respecting the Pope, the affairs of the Church, and the religious worship and doctrine of the Christians. Being well instructed and discreet men, they gave appropriate answers upon all these points, and as they were perfectly acquainted with the Tartar (Moghul) language, they expressed themselves always in becoming terms; insomuch that the grand khan, holding them in high estimation, frequently commanded their attendance.

When he had obtained all the information that the two brothers communicated with so much good sense, he expressed himself well satisfied. Having formed in his mind the design of employing them as his ambassadors to the Pope, after consulting with his ministers on the subject, he proposed to them, with many kind entreaties, that they should accompany one of his officers, named Khogatal, on a mission to the see of Rome. His object, he told them, was to make a request to his holiness that he would send to him a hundred men of learning, thoroughly acquainted with the principles of the Christian religion, as well as with the seven arts, and qualified to prove to the learned of his dominions by just and fair argument, that the faith professed by Christians is superior to all others, and founded upon more evident truth than any other; that the gods of the Tartars and the idols worshipped in their houses were only evil spirits, and that they and the people of the East in general were under an error in reverencing them as divinities. He moreover signified his pleasure that upon their return they should bring with them, from Jerusalem, some of the holy oil from the lamp which is kept burning over the sepulchre of our Lord Jesus Christ, whom he professed to hold in veneration and to consider as the true God.

Having heard these commands addressed to them by the grand khan they humbly prostrated themselves before him, declaring their willingness and instant readiness to perform, to the utmost of their ability, whatever might be the royal will. Upon which he caused letters, in the Tartarian language, to be written in his name to the Pope of Rome, and these he delivered into their hands. He likewise gave orders that they should be furnished with a golden tablet displaying the imperial seal, according to the usage established by his majesty; in virtue of which the person bearing it, together with his whole suite, are safely conveyed and escorted from station to station by the governors of all places within the imperial dominions, and are entitled, during the time of their residing in any city, castle, town, or village, to a supply of provisions and everything necessary for their accommodation.

Being thus honourably commissioned they took their leave of the grand khan, and set out on their journey. * * *

Upon their arrival, his holiness received them in a distinguished manner, and immediately despatched them with letters papal, accompanied by two friars of the Order of Preachers, who happened to be on the spot; men of letters and of science, as well as profound theologians. One of them was named Fra Nicolo da Vicenza, and the other, Fra Guielmo da Tripoli. To them he gave licence and authority to ordain priests, to consecrate bishops, and to grant absolution as fully as he could do in his own person. He also provided them with valuable presents, and among these were several handsome vases of crystal, to be delivered to the grand khan in his name, and along with his benediction.

Having taken leave, they again steered their course to the port of Laiassus, where they landed, and from thence proceeded into the country of Armenia. Here they received intelligence that the sultan of Babylonia, named Bundokdari, had invaded the Armenian territory with a numerous army, and had overrun and laid waste the country to a great extent. Terrified at these accounts, and apprehensive for their lives, the two friars determined not to proceed further. Delivering over to the Venetians the letters and presents entrusted to them by the Pope, they placed themselves under the protection of the master of the knights templars, and with him returned directly to the coast. Nicolo, Maffeo, and Marco, however, undismayed by perils or difficulties (to which they had long been inured), passed the borders of Armenia, and continued their journey. After crossing deserts of several days' march, and passing many dangerous regions, they advanced so far, in a direction between northeast and north, that at length they gained information of the grand khan, who then had his residence in a large and magnificent city named Ke-men-fu. Their whole journey to this place occupied no less than three years and a half; but, during the winter months, their progress had been inconsiderable. The grand khan having notice of their approach while still remote, and being aware how much they must have suffered from fatigue, sent forward to have them met at the distance of forty days' journey, and gave orders to prepare in every place through which they were to pass, whatever might be needed for their comfort. By these means, and through the blessing of God, they were conveyed in safety to the royal court.

Upon their arrival they were honourably and graciously received by the grand khan, in a full assembly of his principal officers. When they drew nigh to his person, they paid their respects by prostrating themselves on the floor. He immediately commanded them to rise, and to relate to him the circumstances of their travels, with all that had taken place in their negotiation with his holiness the Pope. He listened with attentive silence to their narrative, which they gave in the regular order of events, and delivered in perspicuous language. The letters and the presents from Pope Gregory were then laid before him, and, upon hearing the letters read, he bestowed much commendation on the fidelity, the zeal, and the diligence of his ambassadors; and receiving with due reverence the oil from the holy sepulchre, he gave directions that it should be preserved with religious care. Upon his observing Marco Polo, and inquiring who he was, Nicolo made answer, "That is your servant, and my son." Upon this the grand khan replied, "He is welcome, and it pleases me much," and he caused him to be enrolled among his attendants of honour. On account of their return he made a great feast and rejoicing; and as long as the brothers and Marco remained in the court of the grand khan, they were honoured even above his own courtiers.

Marco was held in high estimation and respect by all belonging to the court. He learned in a short time and adopted the manners of the Tartars, and acquired a proficiency in four different languages, which he became qualified to read and write. Finding him thus accomplished, his master was desirous of putting his talents for business to the proof, and sent him on an important concern of state to a city named Karazan, situated at a distance of six months' journey from the imperial residence. He conducted himself with so much wisdom and prudence in the management of the affairs entrusted to him, that his services became highly acceptable. On his part, perceiving that the grand khan took a pleasure in hearing accounts of whatever was new to him respecting the customs and manners of people, and the peculiar circumstances of distant countries, he endeavoured wherever he went to obtain correct information on these subjects, and made notes of all he saw and heard, in order to gratify the curiosity of his master. In short, during seventeen years that he continued in his service, he rendered himself so useful that he was employed on confidential missions to every part of the empire and its dependencies; and sometimes also he travelled on his own private account, but always with the consent, and sanctioned by the authority, of the grand khan. Under such circumstances it was that Marco Polo had the opportunity of acquiring a knowledge—either by his own observation, or what he collected from others—of so many things, until his time unknown, respecting the eastern parts of the world. These he diligently and regularly committed to writing, as will appear below. And by this means he obtained so much honour that he provoked the jealousy of the other officers of the court.

[TRAVELS IN CHINA; XANADU]

Departing from the city last mentioned, and proceeding three days' journey in a north-easterly direction, you arrive at a city called Shandu, built by the Grand Khan Kublai, now reigning. In this he caused a palace to be erected, of marble and other handsome stones, admirable both for the elegance of its design and for the skill displayed in its execution. The halls and chambers are all gilt, and very handsome. It presents one front towards the interior of the city, and the other towards the wall; and from each extremity of the building runs another wall to such an extent as to enclose sixteen miles of the adjoining plain, to which there is no access but through the palace. Within the bounds of this royal park there are rich and beautiful meadows, watered by many rivulets, where a variety of animals of the deer and goat kind are pastured, to serve as food for the hawks and other birds employed in the chase, whose mews are also in the grounds. The number of these birds is upwards of two hundred; and the grand khan goes in person at least once a week to inspect them. Frequently, when he rides about this enclosed forest, he has one or more small leopards carried on horseback, behind their keepers; and when he pleases to give direction for their being let loose, they instantly seize a stag, or goat, or fallow deer, which he gives to his hawks, and in this manner he amuses himself. In the center of these grounds, where there is a beautiful grove of trees, he has built a royal pavilion, supported upon a colonnade of handsome pillars, gilt and varnished. Round each pillar a gilded dragon entwines its tail, while its head sustains the projection of the roof, and its talons or claws are extended to the right and left along the entablature. The roof is of bamboo cane, gilded as well, and so well varnished that no wet can injure it. * * *

It is to be understood that his majesty keeps up a stud farm of about ten thousand horses and mares, which are white as snow; and of the milk of these mares no person can presume to drink who is not of the family descended from Gengiz-khan, with the exception only of one other family, named Boriat, to whom that monarch gave the honourable privilege, in reward of valorous achievements in battle, performed in his own presence. So great, indeed, is the respect shown to these horses that, even when they are at pasture in the royal meadows or forests, no one dares to place himself before them, or otherwise to impede their movements.

The astrologers whom he entertains in his service, and who are deeply versed in the diabolical art of magic, having pronounced it to be his duty, annually, on the twenty-eighth day of the moon in August, to scatter in the wind the milk taken from these mares, as an offering to all the spirits and idols whom they adore, for the purpose of propitiating them and ensuring their protection of the people, male and female, of the cattle, the fowls, the grain and other fruits of the earth. This is why his majesty adheres to the rule that has been mentioned, and on that particular day proceeds to the spot where, with his own hands, he is to make the offering of milk. On such occasions these astrologers—or magicians, as they may be termed—sometimes display their skill in a wonderful manner; for if it should happen that the sky becomes cloudy and threatens rain, they ascend the roof of the palace where the grand khan resides at the time, and by the force of their incantations they prevent the rain from falling and stay the tempest; so that the palace itself remains unaffected by the elements while, in the surrounding country, storms of rain, wind, and thunder are experienced.

Those who operate miracles of this nature are persons of Tibet and Kashmir, two classes of idolaters more profoundly skilled in the art of magic than the natives of any other country. They persuaded the common people that these works are effected through the sanctity of their own lives and the merits of their penances; and presuming upon the reputation thus acquired, they exhibit themselves in a filthy and indecent state, disregarding what they owe to their own character as well as the respect due to those in whose presence they appear. They keep their faces always uncleansed by washing and their hair uncombed, living altogether in a squalid style. They are addicted, moreover, to this beastly and horrible practice: when any culprit is condemned to death, they carry off the body, cook it on the fire, and devour it; but they do not eat the bodies of persons who die a natural death. Besides the appellations before mentioned, by which they are distinguished from each other, they are likewise termed *baksi*, which applies to their religious sect or order—as we should say, friars or preachers. So expert are they in their infernal art, they may be said to perform whatever they will; and one instance shall be given, although it may be thought to exceed the bounds of credibility.

When the grand khan sits at meals, in his hall of state (as shall be more particularly described in the following book), the table which is placed in the center is elevated to the height of about a dozen feet, and at a distance from it stands a large buffet, where all the drinking vessels are arranged. Now, by means of their supernatural art, they cause the flagons of wine, milk, or any other beverage to fill the cups spontaneously, without being touched by the attendants, and the cups to move through the air the distance of ten paces until they reach the hand of the grand khan. As he empties them, they return to the place from whence they came; and this is done in the presence of such persons as are invited by his majesty to witness the performance.

These *baksis*, when the festival days of their idols draw near, go to the palace of the grand khan, and thus address him: "Sire, be it known to your majesty, that if the honours of a sacrifice are not paid to our deities, they will in their anger afflict us with bad seasons, with blight to our grain, pestilence to our cattle, and with other plagues. On this account we supplicate your majesty to grant us a certain number of sheep with black heads, together with so many pounds of incense and of aloe wood, so that we can perform the customary rites with due solemnity." Their words, however, are not spoken directly to the grand khan, but to certain great officers, by whom the communication is made to him. Upon receiving it he never fails to comply with the whole of their request; and accordingly, when the day arrives, they sacrifice the sheep, and by pouring out the broth in which the meat has been seethed, in the presence of their idols, perform the ceremony of worship.

In this country there are great monasteries and abbeys, so extensive indeed that they might pass for small cities, some of them containing as many as two thousand monks, who are devoted to the service of their divinities, according to the established religious customs of the people. These are clad in a better style of dress than the other inhabitants; they shave their heads and their beards, and celebrate the festivals of their idols with the utmost possible solemnity, having bands of vocal music and burning candles. Some of this class are allowed to take wives. There is likewise another religious order, the members of which are named *sensim,* who observe strict abstinence and lead very austere lives, having no other food than a kind of bran, which they steep in warm water until the marrow is separated from the husk, and in that state they eat it.

This sect adores fire, and are considered by the others as heretics, not worshipping idols as they do. There is a material difference between them in regard to the rules of their orders, and these last described never marry in any instance. They shave their heads and beards like the others, and wear hempen garments of a black or dull colour; but even if the material were silk, the colour would be the same. They sleep on coarse mats, and suffer greater hardships in their mode of living than any people in the world. We shall now quit this subject, and proceed to speak of the great and wonderful acts of the supreme lord and emperor, Kublai-khan.

[KUBLAI KHAN AND CHRISTIANITY]

In this section we intend to treat of all the great and admirable achievements of the grand khan now reigning, who is styled Kublai-khan; the latter word implying in our language "lord of lords," and with much propriety added to his name; for in respect to number of subjects, extent of territory, and amount of revenue, he surpasses every sovereign that has heretofore been or that now is in the world; nor has any other been served with such implicit obedience by those whom he governs. This will so evidently appear in the course of our work, as to satisfy everyone of the truth of our assertion.

Kublai-khan, it is to be understood, is the lineal and legitimate descendant of Gengiz-khan the first emperor, and the rightful sovereign of the Tartars. He is the sixth grand khan, and began his reign in the year 1256. He obtained the sovereignty by his consummate valour, his virtues, and his prudence, in opposition to the designs of his brothers, supported by many of the great officers and members of his own family. But the succession belonged to him of right. It is forty-two years since he began to reign to the present year, 1298, and he is fully eighty-five years of age. Previously to his ascending the throne he had served as a volunteer in the army, and endeavoured to take a share in every enterprise. Not only was he brave and daring in action, but in point of judgment and military skill he was considered to be the most able and successful commander that ever led the Tartars to battle. From that period, however, he ceased to take the field in person, and entrusted the conduct of expeditions to his sons and his captains. * * * [2]

---

2. Polo now describes a battle the khan took part in, omitted here.

The grand khan, having obtained this signal victory, returned with great pomp and triumph to the capital city of Kanbalu. This took place in the month of November, and he continued to reside there during the months of February and March, in which month was our festival of Easter. Being aware that this was one of our principal rites, he commanded all the Christians to attend him, and to bring with them their Book, which contains the four Gospels of the Evangelists. After causing it to be repeatedly perfumed with incense, in a ceremonious manner, he devoutly kissed it, and directed that the same should be done by all his nobles who were present. This was his usual practice upon each of the principal Christian festivals, such as Easter and Christmas; and he observed the same at the festivals of the Saracens, Jews, and idolaters. Upon being asked his motive for this conduct, he said: "There are four great Prophets who are reverenced and worshipped by the different classes of mankind. The Christians re- gard Jesus Christ as their divinity; the Saracens, Mohammed; the Jews, Moses; and the idolaters, Sogomombar-kan,[3] the most eminent among their idols. I do honour and show respect to all the four, and invoke to my aid whichever among them is in truth supreme in heaven." But from the manner in which his majesty acted towards them, it is evident that he regarded the faith of the Christians as the truest and the best; noth- ing, as he observed, being commanded to its believers that was not replete with virtue and holiness. By no means, however, would he permit them to bear the cross before them in their processions, because upon it so exalted a personage as Christ had been whipped and (ignominiously) put to death.

It may perhaps be asked by some, why, if he showed such a preference to the faith of Christ, he did not conform to it, and become a Christian? His reason for not so doing, he indicated to Nicolo and Maffeo Polo, when he sent them as his ambassadors to the Pope, and they ventured to address a few words to him on the subject of Chris- tianity. "Why," he said, "should I become a Christian? You yourselves must perceive that the Christians of these countries are ignorant, inefficient persons, who do not pos- sess the faculty of performing anything miraculous; whereas you see that the idolaters can do whatever they will. When I sit at table the cups that were in the middle of the hall come to me filled with wine and other drink, spontaneously and without being touched by human hand, and I drink from them. They have the power of controlling bad weather and obliging it to retire to any quarter of the heavens, with many other wonderful gifts of that nature. You are witnesses that their idols have the faculty of speech, and predict to them whatever is required. Should I become a convert to the faith of Christ, and profess myself a Christian, the nobles of my court and other per- sons who do not incline to that religion will ask me what sufficient motives have caused me to receive baptism, and to embrace Christianity. 'What extraordinary pow- ers,' they will say, 'what miracles have been displayed by its ministers? Whereas the idolaters declare that what they exhibit is performed through their own sanctity, and the influence of their idols.' To this I shall not know what answer to make, and I shall be considered by them as labouring under a grievous error; while the idolaters, who by means of their profound art can effect such wonders, may without difficulty com- pass my death.

But return you to your pontiff, and request of him, in my name, to send here a hundred persons well skilled in your law, who being confronted with the idolaters shall have power to coerce them, and showing that they themselves are endowed with similar art—which they refrain from exercising, because it is derived from the agency

---

3. Sakyamuni, a name for the founder of Buddhism.

of evil spirits—shall compel them to desist from practices of such a nature in their presence. When I am witness of this, I shall ban them and their religion, and shall allow myself to be baptized. Following my example, all my nobility will then in like manner receive baptism, and this will be imitated by my subjects in general; so that the Christians of these parts will exceed in number those who inhabit your own country." From this discourse it must be evident that if the Pope had sent out persons duly qualified to preach the gospel, the grand khan would have embraced Christianity, for which it is certain that he had a strong predilection.

[THE KHAN'S CAPITOL CITY, KIN-SAI][4]

Upon leaving Va-giu, in the course of three days' journey you pass many towns, castles, and villages, all of them well inhabited and opulent. The people are idolaters, and the subjects of the grand khan, and they use paper money and have abundance of provisions. At the end of three days you reach the noble and magnificent city of Kin-sai, a name that signifies "the celestial city." It merits this name from its preeminence to all others in the world in point of grandeur and beauty, as well as from its abundant delights, which might lead an inhabitant to imagine himself in paradise. This city was frequently visited by Marco Polo, who carefully and diligently observed and inquired into every circumstance respecting it, all of which he entered in his notes, from whence the following particulars are briefly stated. According to common estimation, this city is a hundred miles in circuit. Its streets and canals are extensive, and there are squares, or market-places, which are very spacious, corresponding in size to the prodigious concourse of people by whom they are frequented.

It is situated between a lake of fresh and very clear water on the one side, and a river of great magnitude on the other, the waters of which are made to run through every quarter of the city by a number of canals, large and small, carrying with them all the filth into the lake, and ultimately to the sea. This network of canals contributes much to the purity of the air, and furnishes a communication by water, in addition to that by land, to all parts of the town. The canals and the streets are of sufficient width to allow of boats on the one, and carriages in the other, conveniently passing, with goods for the inhabitants. It is commonly said that the number of bridges of all sizes amounts to twelve thousand. Those which cross over the principal canals and are connected with the main streets, have arches so high, and built with so much skill, that vessels with their masts can pass under them, even as carts and horses are passing over their heads,—so well is the slope from the street adapted to the height of the arch. If they were not in fact so numerous, there would be no easy way to cross from one place to another.

Beyond the city, and enclosing it on that side, there is a ditch about forty miles in length, very wide, and full of water that comes from the river before mentioned. This was excavated by the ancient kings of the province, in order that when the river should overflow its banks, the superfluous water might be diverted into this channel; and to serve at the same time as a measure of defence. The earth dug out from thence was thrown to the inner side, and has the appearance of many hillocks surrounding the place. There are within the city ten principal squares or market-places, besides innumerable shops along the streets. Each side of these squares is half a mile in length, and in front of them is the main street, forty paces in width, and running in a direct

---

4. Modern Hang-chou, on China's east coast. In Polo's time it had over a million inhabitants.

line from one extremity of the city to the other. It is crossed by many convenient bridges. These market-squares (two miles their whole dimension) are at a distance of four miles from each other. In a direction parallel to that of the main street, but on the opposite side of the squares, runs a very large canal, on the nearer bank of which capacious warehouses are built of stone, for the accommodation of the merchants who arrive from India and other parts, together with their goods and effects, in order that they may be conveniently situated with respect to the market-places. In each of these, three days a week, there is an assemblage of from forty to fifty thousand persons, who attend the markets and supply them with every article of provision that can be desired. There is an abundant quantity of game of all kinds, such as roebucks, stags, fallow deer, hares, and rabbits, together with partridges, pheasants, hawks, quails, common fowls, capons, and such numbers of ducks and geese as can scarcely be expressed; for so easily are they bred and reared on the lake, that, for the value of a Venetian silver groat, you may purchase a couple of geese and two couple of ducks. * * *

In other streets are the habitations of the courtesans, who are here in such numbers as I dare not venture to report; and not only near the squares, which is the situation usually appropriated for their residence, but in every part of the city they are to be found, adorned with much finery, highly perfumed, occupying well-furnished houses, and attended by many female domestics. These women are accomplished, and are perfect in the arts of blandishment and dalliance, which they accompany with expressions adapted to every description of person, insomuch that strangers who have once tasted of their charms remain in a state of fascination, and become so enchanted by their deceptive arts that they can never divest themselves of the impression. Thus intoxicated with sensual pleasures, when they return to their homes they report that they have been in Kin-sai, or the celestial city, and pant for the time when they may be enabled to revisit paradise.

In other streets are the dwellings of the physicians and the astrologers, who also give instructions in reading and writing, as well as in many other arts. They have apartments also among those which surround the market-squares. On opposite sides of each of these squares there are two large edifices, where officers appointed by the grand khan are stationed, to take immediate cognizance of any differences that may happen to arise between the foreign merchants, or among the inhabitants of the place. It is their duty likewise to see that the guards upon the several bridges in their respective vicinities are duly placed, and in cases of neglect, to punish the delinquents at their discretion.

On each side of the principal street, already mentioned as extending from one end of the city to the other, there are houses and mansions of great size, with their gardens, and near to these, the dwellings of the artisans, who work in shops, at their several trades; and at all hours you see such multitudes of people passing and repassing, on their various avocations, that it might seem impossible to provide enough food for them all; but other ideas will be formed when it is observed that, on every market-day, the squares are crowded with tradespeople, who cover the whole space with the articles brought by carts and boats, for all of which they find a sale. The single article of pepper can give some notion of the whole quantity of provisions, meat, wine, groceries, and the like, required for the consumption of the inhabitants of Kin-sai; and of this, Marco Polo learned from an officer employed in the grand khan's customs, the daily amount was forty-three loads, each load being two hundred and forty-three pounds.

[TRAVELS IN INDIA AND THE INDIAN OCEAN]

The kingdom of Guzzerat, which is bounded on the western side by the Indian Sea, is governed by its own king, and has its own language. Here the north star appears to have six fathoms of altitude above the horizon. This country affords harbour to pirates of the most desperate character. When they seize upon a travelling merchant, they immediately oblige him to drink a dose of sea-water, which by its operation on his bowels reveals whether he may not have swallowed pearls or jewels, upon the approach of an enemy, in order to conceal them.

Here there is great abundance of ginger, pepper, and indigo. Cotton is produced in large quantities from a tree that is about six yards in height, and bears for twenty years; but the cotton taken from trees of that age is not good for spinning, but only for quilting. What is taken from trees of twelve years old is suitable for muslins and other manufactures of extraordinary fineness. Great numbers of skins of goats, buffaloes, wild oxen, rhinoceroses, and other beasts are cured here; and vessels are loaded with them, and bound to different parts of Arabia. Coverlets for beds are made of red and blue leather, extremely delicate and soft, and stitched with gold and silver thread; upon these the Mohammedans are accustomed to repose. Cushions also, ornamented with gold wire in the form of birds and beasts, are made in this place; and in some instances their value is so high as six marks of silver. Embroidery is here performed with more delicacy than in any other part of the world. Proceeding further, we shall now speak of the kingdom named Kanan. * * *

Distant from Kesmacoran about five hundred miles towards the south, there are two islands in the ocean within about thirty miles from each other, one of which is inhabited by men, without the company of women, and is called the island of males; and the other by women without men, which is called the island of females. The inhabitants of both are of the same race, and are baptized Christians, but hold the law of the Old Testament. The men visit the island of females, and remain with them for three successive months, namely, March, April, and May, each man occupying a separate habitation along with his wife. They then return to the island of males, where they continue all the rest of the year, without the society of any female. The wives retain their sons with them until they are twelve years old, when they are sent to join their fathers. The daughters they keep at home until they become marriageable, and then they bestow them upon some of the men of the other island. This mode of living is occasioned by the peculiar nature of the climate, which does not allow of their remaining all the year with their wives, unless at the risk of dying. They have their bishop, who is subordinate to the see of the island of Soccotera. The men provide for their wives by sowing the grain, but the women prepare the soil and gather in the harvest. The island likewise produces a variety of fruits. The men live upon milk, meat, rice, and fish. Of these they catch an immense quantity, being expert fishermen. Both when fresh taken and when salted, the fish are sold to the traders resorting to the island, but whose principal object is to purchase ambergris,[5] of which a quantity is collected there.

Upon leaving these islands, and proceeding five hundred miles in a southerly direction, you reach the island of Soccotera, which is very large, and abounds with the necessaries of life. The inhabitants find much ambergris upon their coasts, which is voided from the entrails of whales. As this is an article of merchandise in great demand, they make it a business to take these fish; and this they do by means of a barbed iron, which they strike into the whale so firmly that it cannot be drawn out. To

---

5. A waxy substance produced in whales' intestines, used as an ingredient in perfumes.

the iron (harpoon) a long line is fastened, with a buoy at the end, for the purpose of discovering the place where the fish, when dead, is to be found. They then drag it to the shore, and proceed to extract the ambergris from its belly, while from its head they procure several casks of oil.

All the people, both male and female, go nearly naked, having only a scanty covering before and behind, like the idolaters who have been described. They have no other grain than rice, upon which, with meat and milk, they subsist. Their religion is Christianity, and they are duly baptized, and are under the government, both temporal and spiritual, of an archbishop. He is not in subjection to the pope of Rome, but to a patriarch who resides in the city of Baghdad, by whom he is appointed, or, if elected by the people themselves, by whom their choice is confirmed. Many pirates resort to this island with the goods they have captured, and which the natives purchase of them without any scruple, justifying themselves on the ground of their being plundered from idolaters and Saracens. All ships bound to the province of Aden touch here, and make large purchases of fish and of ambergris, as well as of various kinds of cotton goods manufactured on the spot.

The inhabitants deal more in sorcery and witchcraft than any other people, although forbidden by their archbishop, who excommunicates and condemns them for the sin. Of this, however, they make little account; and if any vessel belonging to a pirate should injure one of theirs, they do not fail to lay him under a spell, so that he cannot proceed on his cruise until he has made satisfaction for the damage. Even if he should have had a fair and leading wind, they have the power of causing it to change, and thereby of obliging him despite himself to return to the island. They can also cause the sea to become calm, and at their will can raise tempests, occasion shipwrecks, and produce many other extraordinary effects, that need not be particularised. We shall now speak of the island of Madagascar.

Leaving the island of Soccotera, and steering a course between south and southwest for a thousand miles, you arrive at the great island of Madagascar, which is one of the largest and most fertile in the world. In circuit it is three thousand miles. The inhabitants are Saracens, or followers of the law of Mohammed. They have four sheikhs, which in our language may be expressed by "elders," who divide the government among them. The people subsist by trade and manufacture, and sell a vast number of elephants' teeth, as those animals abound in the country, as they do also in that of Zanzibar, from whence the export is equally great. The principal food eaten at all seasons of the year is the flesh of camels. That of the other cattle serves them also for food, but the former is preferred, as being both the most wholesome and the most palatable of any to be found in this part of the world. The woods contain many sandalwood trees, and, in proportion to the plenty in which it is found, the price of it is low. There is also much ambergris from the whales; and as the tide throws it on the coast, it is collected for sale. The natives catch lynxes, tigers, and a variety of other animals, such as stags, antelopes, and fallow deer, which afford much sport; as do also birds, which are different from those of our climates.

The island is visited by many ships from various parts of the world, bringing assortments of goods consisting of brocades and silks of various patterns, which are sold to the merchants of the island, or bartered for goods in return; upon all of which they make large profits. Ships do not go to the other numerous islands lying further south, this and the island of Zanzibar alone being frequented. This is the consequence of the sea running with such prodigious velocity in that direction as to render their return impossible. The vessels that sail from the coast of Malabar for this island, perform the voyage in twenty or twenty-five days, but in their returning voyage are obliged to struggle for three months; so strong is the current of water, which constantly runs to the southward.

The people of the island report that at a certain season of the year, an extraordinary kind of bird, which they call a rukh, makes its appearance from the southern region. In form it is said to resemble the eagle, but it is incomparably greater in size; being so large and strong as to seize an elephant with its talons, and to lift it into the air, from whence it lets it fall to the ground, in order that it may prey upon the carcass when dead. Persons who have seen this bird assert that when the wings are spread they measure sixteen paces in extent, from point to point; and that the feathers are eight paces in length, and thick in proportion. Messer Marco Polo, conceiving that these creatures might be griffins, such as are represented in paintings, half birds and half lions, particularly questioned those who reported their having seen them as to this point; but they maintained that their shape was altogether that of birds, or, as it might be said, of the eagle.

Having heard this extraordinary relation, the grand khan sent messengers to the island, on the pretext of demanding the release of one of his servants who had been detained there, but in reality to examine into the circumstances of the country, and the truth of the wonderful things told of it. When they returned to the presence of his majesty, they brought with them (as I have heard) a feather of the rukh, positively affirmed to have measured ninety spans, and the quill part to have been two palms in circumference. This surprising exhibition afforded his majesty extreme pleasure, and upon those by whom it was presented he bestowed valuable gifts. They were also the bearers of the tusk of a wild boar, an animal that grows there to the size of a buffalo, and it was found to weigh fourteen pounds. The island contains likewise camelopards, asses, and other wild animals, very different from those of our country.

~~~

RESONANCES

Samuel Taylor Coleridge: Kubla Khan: Or, A Vision in a Dream A Fragment[1]

In Xanadu did Kubla Khan
A stately pleasure-dome decree:
Where Alph, the sacred river, ran
Through caverns measureless to man
5   Down to a sunless sea.
So twice five miles of fertile ground
With walls and towers were girdled round:

1. The British Romantic poet and critic Samuel Taylor Coleridge (1772–1834) wrote this poem while he was living in a rural farmhouse in the summer of 1797, collaborating with William Wordsworth on the poems that would become their pioneering volume of *Lyrical Ballads*. Coleridge was fascinated with accounts of travels to exotic regions, and he later described "Kubla Khan" as a vision that came to him after he fell asleep while reading an old collection of travel accounts. His vision was assisted by the power of laudanum (opium dissolved in alcohol), which he'd been taking as a treatment for rheumatic pains.

Coleridge claimed that in his sleep he spontaneously composed a complete poem of more than 200 lines; on waking, he began to write it down, but was interrupted by a visitor from a nearby town. Returning to write, he found the rest of the poem "had passed away like images on the surface of a stream into which a stone has been cast." It has often been debated whether the intrusive "person on business from Porlock" really existed or was a fiction invented to account for the poem's fragmentary nature. The poem stands as one of the most powerful evocations of an elusive, enticing East, in which the khan's pleasure-dome becomes an image of transcendent artifice in a wild natural and social world.

And there were gardens bright with sinuous rills
Where blossomed many an incense-bearing tree;
10   And here were forests ancient as the hills,
Enfolding sunny spots of greenery.

But oh! that deep romantic chasm which slanted
Down the green hill athwart a cedarn cover!
A savage place! as holy and enchanted
15   As e'er beneath a waning moon was haunted
By woman wailing for her demon-lover!
And from this chasm, with ceaseless turmoil seething,
As if this earth in fast thick pants were breathing,
A mighty fountain momently was forced:
20   Amid whose swift half-intermitted burst
Huge fragments vaulted like rebounding hail,
Or chaffy grain beneath the thresher's flail:
And 'mid these dancing rocks at once and ever
It flung up momently the sacred river.
25   Five miles meandering with a mazy motion
Through wood and dale the sacred river ran,
Then reached the caverns measureless to man,
And sank in tumult to a lifeless ocean:
And 'mid this tumult Kubla heard from far
30   Ancestral voices prophesying war!
　　The shadow of the dome of pleasure
　　Floated midway on the waves;
　　Where was heard the mingled measure
　　From the fountain and the caves.
35   　It was a miracle of rare device,
　　A sunny pleasure-dome with caves of ice!

　　　A damsel with a dulcimer
　　　In a vision once I saw:
　　　It was an Abyssinian maid,
40   　And on her dulcimer she played,
　　　Singing of Mount Abora.
　　　Could I revive within me
　　　Her symphony and song,
　　　To such a deep delight 'twould win me,
45   　That with music loud and long,
　　I would build that dome in air,
　　That sunny dome! those caves of ice!
　　And all who heard should see them there,
　　And all should cry, Beware! Beware!
50   His flashing eyes, his floating hair!
　　Weave a circle around him thrice,
　　And close your eyes with holy dread,
　　For he on honey-dew hath fed,
　　And drunk the milk of Paradise.

Italo Calvino: from *Invisible Cities*[1]

[PROLOGUE]

Kublai Khan does not necessarily believe everything Marco Polo says when he describes the cities visited on his expeditions, but the emperor of the Tartars does continue listening to the young Venetian with greater attention and curiosity than he shows any other messenger or explorer of his. In the lives of emperors there is a moment which follows pride in the boundless extension of the territories we have conquered, and the melancholy and relief of knowing we shall soon give up any thought of knowing and understanding them. There is a sense of emptiness that comes over us at evening, with the odor of the elephants after the rain and the sandalwood ashes growing cold in the braziers, a dizziness that makes rivers and mountains tremble on the fallow curves of the planispheres where they are portrayed, and rolls up, one after the other, the despatches announcing to us the collapse of the last enemy troops, from defeat to defeat, and flakes the wax of the seals of obscure kings who beseech our armies' protection, offering in exchange annual tributes of precious metals, tanned hides, and tortoise shell. It is the desperate moment when we discover that this empire, which had seemed to us the sum of all wonders, is an endless, formless ruin, that corruption's gangrene has spread too far to be healed by our scepter, that the triumph over enemy sovereigns has made us the heirs of their long undoing. Only in Marco Polo's accounts was Kublai Khan able to discern, through the walls and towers destined to crumble, the tracery of a pattern so subtle it could escape the termites' gnawing.

Cities and Memory: 1

Leaving there and proceeding for three days toward the east, you reach Diomira, a city with sixty silver domes, bronze statues of all the gods, streets paved with lead, a crystal theater, a golden cock that crows each morning on a tower. All these beauties will already be familiar to the visitor, who has seen them also in other cities. But the special quality of this city for the man who arrives there on a September evening, when the days are growing shorter and the multicolored lamps are lighted all at once at the doors of the food stalls and from a terrace a woman's voice cries ooh!, is that he feels envy toward those who now believe they have once before lived an evening identical to this and who think they were happy, that time.

Trading Cities: 1

Proceeding eighty miles into the northwest wind, you reach the city of Euphemia, where the merchants of seven nations gather at every solstice and equinox. The

1. Translated by William Weaver. One of the most inventive writers of the 20th century, Italo Calvino (1923–1985) began writing realistic works based on his experiences in wartime Italy, but then turned increasingly to fantasy and science fiction. *Invisible Cities* (1974) takes the form of a series of dialogues between Marco Polo and Kublai Khan, in which Polo describes a series of unlikely cities in the Khan's far-flung realm. These cities are given under headings—each of which appears several times—like "Cities and Memory," "Trading Cities," and "Thin Cities." Polo's descriptions become meditations on language, desire, and the fate of civilization, as modern Europe increasingly merges with medieval China. In between sets of city descriptions are italicized passages describing the interactions between Polo and the emperor, who finds that Polo's oblique, mysterious descriptions are better clues to the state of his empire than realistic accounts would be. (See also Calvino's entry in Volume F.)

boat that lands there with a cargo of ginger and cotton will set sail again, its hold filled with pistachio nuts and poppy seeds, and the caravan that has just unloaded sacks of nutmegs and raisins is already cramming its saddlebags with bolts of golden muslin for the return journey. But what drives men to travel up rivers and cross deserts to come here is not only the exchange of wares, which you could find, everywhere the same, in all the bazaars inside and outside the Great Khan's empire, scattered at your feet on the same yellow mats, in the shade of the same awnings protecting them from the flies, offered with the same lying reduction in prices. You do not come to Euphemia only to buy and sell, but also because at night, by the fires all around the market, seated on sacks or barrels or stretched out on piles of carpets, at each word that one man says—such as "wolf," "sister," "hidden treasure," "battle," "scabies," "lovers"—the others tell, each one, his tale of wolves, sisters, treasures, scabies, lovers, battles. And you know that in the long journey ahead of you, when to keep awake against the camel's swaying or the junk's rocking, you start summoning up your memories one by one, your wolf will have become another wolf, your sister a different sister, your battle other battles, on your return from Euphemia, the city where memory is traded at every solstice and at every equinox.

Cities and Eyes: 1

The ancients built Valdrada on the shores of a lake, with houses all having verandas one above the other, and high streets whose railed parapets look out over the water. Thus the traveler, arriving, sees two cities: one erect above the lake, and the other reflected, upside down. Nothing exists or happens in the one Valdrada that the other Valdrada does not repeat, because the city was so constructed that its every point would be reflected in its mirror, and the Valdrada down in the water contains not only all the flutings and juttings of the facades that rise above the lake, but also the rooms' interiors with ceilings and floors, the perspective of the halls, the mirrors of the wardrobes.

Valdrada's inhabitants know that each of their actions is, at once, that action and its mirror-image, which possesses the special dignity of images, and this awareness prevents them from succumbing for a single moment to chance and forgetfulness. Even when lovers twist their naked bodies, skin against skin, seeking the position that will give one the most pleasure in the other, even when murderers plunge the knife into the black veins of the neck and more clotted blood pours out the more they press the blade that slips between the tendons, it is not so much their copulating or murdering that matters as the copulating or murdering of the images, limpid and cold in the mirror.

At times the mirror increases a thing's value, at times denies it. Not everything that seems valuable above the mirror maintains its force when mirrored. The twin cities are not equal, because nothing that exists or happens in Valdrada is symmetrical: every face and gesture is answered, from the mirror, by a face and gesture inverted, point by point. The two Valdradas live for each other, their eyes interlocked; but there is no love between them.

Thin Cities: 5

If you choose to believe me, good. Now I will tell how Octavia, the spider-web city, is made. There is a precipice between two steep mountains: the city is over the void, bound to the two crests with ropes and chains and catwalks. You walk on the little wooden ties, careful not to set your foot in the open spaces, or you cling to the hempen strands. Below there is nothing for hundreds and hundreds of feet: a few clouds glide past; farther down you can glimpse the chasm's bed.

This is the foundation of the city: a net which serves as passage and as support. All the rest, instead of rising up, is hung below: rope ladders, hammocks, houses made like sacks, clothes hangers, terraces like gondolas, skins of water, gas jets, spits, baskets on strings, dumb-waiters, showers, trapezes and rings for children's games, cable cars, chandeliers, pots with trailing plants.

Suspended over the abyss, the life of Octavia's inhabitants is less uncertain than in other cities. They know the net will last only so long.

[INTERLUDE]

"Did you ever happen to see a city resembling this one?" Kublai asked Marco Polo, extending his beringed hand from beneath the silken canopy of the imperial barge, to point to the bridges arching over the canals, the princely palaces whose marble doorsteps were immersed in the water, the bustle of light craft zigzagging, driven by long oars, the boats unloading baskets of vegetables at the market squares, the balconies, platforms, domes, campaniles,[2] island gardens glowing green in the lagoon's grayness.

The emperor, accompanied by his foreign dignitary, was visiting Kin-sai, ancient capital of deposed dynasties, the latest pearl set in the Great Khan's crown.[3]

"No, sire," Marco answered, "I should never have imagined a city like this could exist."

The emperor tried to peer into his eyes. The foreigner lowered his gaze. Kublai remained silent the whole day.

After sunset, on the terraces of the palace, Marco Polo expounded to the sovereign the results of his missions. As a rule the Great Khan concluded his day savoring these tales with half-closed eyes until his first yawn was the signal for the suite of pages to light the flames that guided the monarch to the Pavilion of the August Slumber. But this time Kublai seemed unwilling to give in to weariness. "Tell me another city," he insisted.

". . . You leave there and ride for three days between the northeast and east-by-northeast winds . . ." Marco resumed saying, enumerating names and customs and wares of a great number of lands. His repertory could be called inexhaustible, but now he was the one who had to give in. Dawn had broken when he said: "Sire, now I have told you about all the cities I know."

"There is still one of which you never speak."

Marco Polo bowed his head.

"Venice," the Khan said.

Marco smiled. "What else do you believe I have been talking to you about?"

The emperor did not turn a hair. "And yet I have never heard you mention that name."

And Polo said: "Every time I describe a city I am saying something about Venice."

"When I ask you about other cities, I want to hear about them. And about Venice, when I ask you about Venice."

---

2. Italian bell towers.

3. Kin-sai had been the capital of the Ch'in and Sung dynasties centuries before.

"To distinguish the other cities' qualities, I must speak of a first city that remains implicit. For me it is Venice."

"You should then begin each tale of your travels from the departure, describing Venice as it is, all of it, not omitting anything you remember of it."

The lake's surface was barely wrinkled; the copper reflection of the ancient palace of the Sung was shattered into sparkling glints like floating leaves.

"Memory's images, once they are fixed in words, are erased," Polo said. "Perhaps I am afraid of losing Venice all at once, if I speak of it. Or perhaps, speaking of other cities, I have already lost it, little by little."

Geoffrey Chaucer

c. 1340–1400

Like so much else in the world of fourteenth-century England, Chaucer's family name was derived from the French: a maker of *chausses,* shoes or hose. His family had nothing to do with footwear, but Chaucer made his name as a poet with a translation from the French of *Le Roman de la rose,* and he established himself as a valuable servant to three successive English kings partly due to linguistic skills that enabled him to conduct royal business during journeys to France, Spain, and Italy. But what made Chaucer the first great authority of English literature was the way he transformed Continental themes, words, and literary genres into something indelibly and recognizably English. As Dante in his *Commedia* quite consciously created the first epic poem in vernacular Italian rather than Latin, so Chaucer set out in *The Canterbury Tales* to forge a work of poetry for an entire people, in a language—the London dialect that would become modern English—potentially accessible to all citizens, from the highest to the lowest.

Chaucer's ancestors were prosperous vintners and property owners in Ipswich who by the late thirteenth century had moved seventy miles south to settle in London. Chaucer's father served in the household of King Edward III; Geoffrey began his career in 1357 similarly situated, working for the wife of Edward's son, Prince Henry. About ten years later, he made an advantageous marriage to the daughter of a knight of Hainault, and was soon made an *esquier* (esquire), or retainer in the royal household. He traveled frequently around England and abroad in the king's service, not only to nearby France, but to Florence in 1373, where he may have met Boccaccio and Petrarch and certainly learned of their poetry as well as of Dante's. (See Volume C for Boccaccio and Petrarch, early participants in the Renaissance that hadn't yet spread to Chaucer's England.) Chaucer was evidently a skilled courtier; he survived countless power struggles, continued receiving posts and assignments after the accession of Richard II in 1377, and had his annuities confirmed when Henry IV supplanted Richard in 1399.

Unlike the public lives of many medieval writers, Chaucer's lifetime of service was extremely well-documented, but of the nearly 500 items that mention his name only a few allude to his personal affairs and none at all to his poetry. Conversely, Chaucer's poetry rarely mentions the great events of his day, from the Black Death of his childhood to the grand dynastic struggles that must have deeply affected his life. His earlier writings show him immersed in the medieval occupations of translation and popularization. The translation of the foremost authority of medieval romance, *The Romance of the Rose,* was begun before 1372 and that of Boethius's *The Consolation of Philosophy* in the 1380s. *The Book of the Duchess,* which mimics the French genre of the *dits amoureux,* was written to commemorate the death of Blanche, Duchess of Lancaster, in 1369. Like *The Book of the Duchess, The House of Fame* (1378–1380) and *The Parliament of Fowls* (1380–1382) were first-person dream visions dealing with issues of fame, poetry, and love. Here, Chaucer developed a self-deprecating persona that nonetheless voices an ambition to equal Dante, the French romances, and the classical poets, as in this deflation of the grand opening of Virgil's *Aeneid,* "I wol now synge, yif I kan, / The armes and also the man." Up to the middle of the eighteenth century, the most frequently cited of Chaucer's works was a long verse romance, *Troilus and Cressida* (1382–1386), based on a romance by Boccaccio set during the Trojan War, and often considered the first psychological novel due to the depth of its depiction of character.

To write in English was not the obvious choice for a prodigiously learned and ambitious fourteenth-century *esquier,* although its use had increased as the century went on, culminating in Henry V's declared preference for it as the language of literature at his court. French had long been the language of statecraft and civil record-keeping, and of literature in many circles, especially the court. Latin was the language of ecclesiastical and theological discourse, including philosophy, and still an important literary language, especially in Italy. The London dialect adapted by Chaucer would have been primarily a practical language, with limited capacities for meter, rhyme, and vocabulary in comparison to Chaucer's French, Italian, and Latin sources. His genius was to expand the capacities of English without losing its flavor of reality as an everyday language. As with Dante, Chaucer's choice of a local vernacular incorporated the thematic contrast between decorum and plainness, spirit and matter, into the very language of the verse.

THE CANTERBURY TALES

This effect is strongest in *The Canterbury Tales,* parts of which date from as early as the 1370s, but most of which was written in the late 1380s and early 1390s. Chaucer presents the stories told by a diverse collection of twenty-nine pilgrims (more or less) as they make their way from London to the shrine of Saint Thomas à Becket in Canterbury. The pilgrimage was an essential feature of medieval life, whether a brief journey within Kent or a more extended voyage to Santiago de Compostela in Spain or to the Holy Land—and the Wife of Bath has done them all. Undertaken to seek miraculous aid, to visit a famous biblical site, to renounce the world, or to expiate a sin, pilgrimage could also be imposed as penance on criminals, used as a front by charlatans, or undertaken by clergy who had fallen out with parish authorities. The pilgrimage brought together all the estates of society, although rarely involving the extreme social variety of Chaucer's pilgrims, from the devout knight, prioress, and merchant to a range of fairly secular-minded characters to the scurvy Miller and Reeve. Chaucer's pilgrimage is a literary conceit, but a conceit based on a wide and familiar practice.

Chaucer devotes far less time to the motivations behind the characters' decision to take a pilgrimage than he does to the interactions between them and to the many different stories he can tell through their varied persons. In the "General Prologue," he gives a thumbnail sketch of every character except his own stand-in, a self-effacing poet who tells two failed stories; these sketches are noteworthy for their memorable and idiosyncratic detail and for their stylistic range. The procession of characters is based on the estates satire, a comic catalogue of the different estates, or classes of society. Each character represents a type, defined primarily by his or her profession; however, each type is engraved in our memory through tellingly individual touches. We are told of the Miller, for example, that he possesses the strength needed to exercise his profession, but the demonstration of this strength takes a comically unlikely form: he breaks down doors with his head ("Ther was no dore that he nolde heve of harre, / Or breke it rennyng with his head").

In a similar fashion, each tale reflects the milieu of its teller and evokes a literary genre he or she would be familiar with—the Knight tells of chivalry, the Monk of the perils of trusting to Fortune, the Miller and the Reeve bawdy tales (*fabliaux*) about artisans. Yet each tale is constructed with consummate artistry to match the condition of each teller, a feat beyond the capacity of most if not all of Chaucer's characters. In "The Miller's Tale," for example, Chaucer invests the *fabliau* with a doubled and converging seduction plot and a thematic backdrop of mystery plays and courtly love conventions, remaining faithful to the parody and scatological humor of the genre while expanding its scope and heightening its comedy.

The proliferation of narrators and narrative styles often makes it difficult to know how we are meant to evaluate a particular character. Alisoun, the garrulous Wife of Bath, for instance, sums up and embodies centuries of the misogynist clichés and biblical commonplaces of the clerkly tradition and the *querelle des femmes* ("quarrel about women") but she does so with such energy and she travesties her sources with such gusto that the reader is more likely to side with her than against her. In the Prologue to her tale, she recounts the story of her life and five husbands—a prologue that overshadows and doubles the length of her Tale proper, the collection's only version of an Arthurian romance. Even here, digression and anachronism take pride of place over fidelity to her source. The knight's quest for the answer to the question "What thing is it that wommen moost desiren" extends her Prologue's debate over the battle of the sexes, marriage, and desire into the fantasy world of legend: a paradoxically fitting genre for one of Chaucer's most down-to-earth characters.

Unlike Dante, Chaucer left his *magnum opus* unfinished, in ten more or less ordered groupings. There is no numerical perfection, as in the even hundred cantos of the *Commedia* or the ten tellers, ten days and hundred stories of Boccaccio's *Decameron* (see Volume C). Still, the interaction among characters, the sequencing of certain tales, and the repeated themes and motifs create a complex network of comparison. Although he was no stranger to the structures of symmetry so dear to much of medieval poetry, Chaucer prefers here to develop his tales through interruption and disorder, as in the Miller's drunken insistence on telling his tale out of order so that he can "quite," or pay back, the Reeve's insult. Rather than ordering spiritual and secular, courtly and *fabliau,* proper and obscene, Chaucer imagines the multifaceted teeming medieval world all thrown together, with characters looking the other way or staring each other down, reveling in the bickering and bantering in enforced coexistence encapsulated by the pilgrimage setting.

from THE CANTERBURY TALES[1]

The General Prologue

When April with his showers sweet with fruit
The drought of March has pierced unto the root
And bathed each vein with liquor that has power
To generate therein and sire the flower;
5   When Zephyr° also has, with his sweet breath,   *the West Wind*
Quickened again, in every holt° and heath,   *woods*
The tender shoots and buds, and the young sun
Into the Ram one half his course has run,[2]
And many little birds make melody
10   That sleep through all the night with open eye

1. Translated by J. U. Nicolson.

2. The Ram is the zodiacal sign Aries, which lasts from mid-March to mid-April.

(So Nature[3] pricks them on to ramp and rage)—
Then do folk long to go on pilgrimage,
And palmers to go seeking out strange strands,
To distant shrines well known in sundry lands.[4]

15   And specially from every shire's° end   *county's*
Of England they to Canterbury wend,°   *make their way*
The holy blessed martyr there to seek
Who helped them when they lay so ill and weak.[5]

         Befell that, in that season, on a day
20   In Southwark, at the Tabard,[6] as I lay
Ready to start upon my pilgrimage
To Canterbury, full of devout homage,
There came at nightfall to that hostelry
Some nine and twenty in a company

25   Of sundry persons who had chanced to fall
In fellowship, and pilgrims were they all
That toward Canterbury town would ride.
The rooms and stables spacious were and wide,
And well we there were eased, and of the best.

30   And briefly, when the sun had gone to rest,
So had I spoken with them, every one,
That I was of their fellowship anon,°   *soon*
And made agreement that we'd early rise
To take the road, as you I will apprise.

35   But none the less, whilst I have time and space,
Before yet farther in this tale I pace,
It seems to me accordant with reason
To inform you of the state of every one
Of all of these, as it appeared to me,

40   And who they were, and what was their degree,
And even how arrayed° there at the inn;   *dressed*
And with a knight thus will I first begin.

         A knight there was, and he a worthy man,
Who, from the moment that he first began
45   To ride about the world, loved chivalry,
Truth, honour, freedom and courtesy.
Full worthy was he in his liege-lord's° war,   *his feudal lord's*
And therein had he ridden (none more far)
As well in Christendom as heathenesse,°   *pagan lands*
50   And honoured everywhere for worthiness.

---

3. Nature as a creative force was frequently personified as a goddess in the Middle Ages.
4. Pilgrims returning from the Holy Land would carry a palm frond as sign of their achievement; a palmer also designated an itinerant monk.
5. The cathedral town of Canterbury, the ecclesiastical center of England, is about 35 miles southeast of London. It contained the shrine of Archbishop Thomas à Becket, who was murdered by Henry II in 1170 and canonized by the pope three years later. For many centuries it was a primary pilgrimage destination in England.
6. The Canterbury road began in the rather disreputable borough of Southwark, just across London Bridge from London. There was in fact an inn called the Tabard in Southwark at the time.

At Alexandria, he, when it was won;[7]
Full oft the table's roster he'd begun
Above all nations' knights in Prussia.[8]
In Latvia raided he, and Russia,
55 No christened man so oft of his degree.
In far Granada at the siege was he
Of Algeciras,[9] and in Belmarie.°   *Morocco*
At Ayas was he and at Satalye°   *in Turkey*
When they were won; and on the Middle Sea°   *Mediterranean*
60 At many a noble meeting chanced to be.
Of mortal battles he had fought fifteen,
And he'd fought for our faith at Tramissene°   *in Algeria*
Three times in lists, and each time slain his foe.[1]
This self-same worthy knight had been also
65 At one time with the lord of Palatye°   *in Turkey*
Against another heathen in Turkey;
And always won he sovereign fame for prize.
Though so illustrious, he was very wise
And bore himself as meekly as a maid.
70 He never yet had any vileness said,
In all his life, to whatsoever wight.°   *person*
He was a truly perfect, gentle knight.
But now, to tell you all of his array,
His steeds were good, but yet he was not gay.°   *richly dressed*
75 Of simple fustian° wore he a jupon°   *coarse cloth / tunic*
Sadly discoloured by his habergeon;°   *breastplate*
For he had lately come from his voyage
And now was going on this pilgrimage.

With him there was his son, a youthful squire,
80 A lover and a lusty bachelor,[2]
With locks well curled, as if they'd laid in press.
Some twenty years of age he was, I guess.
In stature he was of an average length,
Wondrously active, aye, and great of strength.
85 He'd ridden sometime with the cavalry
In Flanders, in Artois, and Picardy,[3]
And borne him well within that little space
In hope to win thereby his lady's grace.
Prinked out° he was, as if he were a mead,°   *dressed up / meadow*

---

7. The Egyptian city of Alexandria was conquered by
Peter I of Cyprus in 1365 and left behind after a week of
slaughter and plundering.
8. The Baltic region of Prussia was a stronghold of the
Teutonic Knights, a religious order formed in the 12th
century for the purpose of crusading. The Knight has
been granted the place of honor among them.
9. A port city in the Andalusian kingdom of Granada near
Gibraltar. It was conquered by the Christian forces of the
Castilian ruler Alphonso IX in 1344.

1. One-on-one battles between opposing champions were
common features of medieval warfare.
2. Squires were bachelors, or knights of the lowest orders,
and would often serve as attendants or followers of ban-
nerets, more senior knights who had the right to lead under their own banner.
3. Artois and Picardy are regions of northern France near
Belgium, parts of which were controlled by the Counts of
Flanders. The reference is probably to the disastrous
"crusade" led by the bishop of Norwich against Flanders.

90   All full of fresh-cut flowers white and red.
    Singing he was, or fluting, all the day;
    He was as fresh as is the month of May.
    Short was his gown,° with sleeves both long and wide.   *outer robe*
    Well could he sit on horse, and fairly ride.
95   He could make songs and words thereto indite,°   *compose*
    Joust, and dance too, as well as sketch and write.
    So hot he loved that, while night told her tale,
    He slept no more than does a nightingale.
    Courteous he, and humble, willing and able,
100   And carved before his father at the table.[4]

     A yeoman had he, nor more servants, no,
    At that time, for he chose to travel so;[5]
    And he was clad in coat and hood of green.
    A sheaf of peacock arrows bright and keen
105   Under his belt he bore right carefully
    (Well could he keep his tackle yeomanly:
    His arrows had no draggled° feathers low),   *trailing*
    And in his hand he bore a mighty bow.
    A cropped head had he and a sun-browned face.
110   Of woodcraft knew he all the useful ways.
    Upon his arm he bore a bracer gay,°   *bright arm guard*
    And at one side a sword and buckler,° yea,   *small shield*
    And at the other side a dagger bright,
    Well sheathed and sharp as spear point in the light;
115   On breast a Christopher of silver sheen.[6]
    He bore a horn in baldric° all of green;   *shoulder strap*
    A forester he truly was, I guess.[7]

     There was also a nun, a prioress,[8]
    Who, in her smiling, modest was and coy;°   *quiet*
120   Her greatest oath was but "By Saint Eloy!"
    And she was known as Madam Eglantine.°   *briar rose*
    Full well she sang the services divine,
    Intoning through her nose, becomingly;
    And fair she spoke her French, and fluently,
125   After the school of Stratford-at-the-Bow,
    For French of Paris was not hers to know.[9]
    At table she had been well taught withal,°   *as well*
    And never from her lips let morsels fall,
    Nor dipped her fingers deep in sauce, but ate

---

4. One of the squire's customary tasks was to carve the meat for their knights.
5. In addition to his son, the Squire, the Knight is accompanied by a Yeoman, a free servant next in rank below a squire in the feudal order.
6. St. Christopher was the patron saint of travelers; his medallion gave protection on the road.
7. The Yeoman is a gamekeeper, charged with guarding his lord's game from poachers and with conducting the elaborate ceremonies of the hunt.

8. The superior of a religious house or order. The description includes many attributes of the courtly lady of the time, although her own position, and her lack of connection with the court, complicate the portrait.
9. Rather than Parisian French, the Prioress speaks the Anglo-Norman dialect she learned at school in Stratford-at-the-Bow, a village outside London.

130   With so much care the food upon her plate
     That never driblet fell upon her breast.
     In courtesy she had delight and zest.
     Her upper lip was always wiped so clean
     That in her cup was no iota seen
135   Of grease, when she had drunk her draught of wine.
     Becomingly she reached for meat to dine.
     And certainly delighting in good sport,°   *diversions*
     She was right pleasant, amiable—in short.
     She was at pains to counterfeit the look
140   Of courtliness,° and stately manners took,   *court manners*
     And would be held worthy of reverence.
        But, to say something of her moral sense,
     She was so charitable and piteous
     That she would weep if she but saw a mouse
145   Caught in a trap, though it were dead or bled.
     She had some little dogs, too, that she fed
     On roasted flesh, or milk and fine white bread.
     But sore she'd weep if one of them were dead,
     Or if men smote it with a rod to smart:
150   For pity ruled her, and her tender heart.
     Right decorous her pleated wimple° was;   *nun's headdress*
     Her nose was fine; her eyes were blue as glass;
     Her mouth was small and therewith soft and red;
     But certainly she had a fair forehead;
155   It was almost a full span° broad, I own,   *up to nine inches*
     For, truth to tell, she was not undergrown.
     Neat was her cloak, as I was well aware.
     Of coral small about her arm she'd bear
     A string of beads and gauded all with green;
160   And therefrom hung a brooch of golden sheen
     Whereon there was first written a crowned "A,"
     And under, *Amor vincit omnia.*[1]

        Another little nun with her had she,
     Who was her chaplain; and of priests she'd three.[2]
165   A monk there was, one made for mastery,°   *very handsome*
     An outrider, who loved his venery;°   *hunting*
     A manly man, to be an abbot able.[3]
     Full many a blooded° horse had he in stable: *of good breed*
     And when he rode men might his bridle hear
170   A-jingling in the whistling wind as clear,
     Aye, and as loud as does the chapel bell

1. "Love conquers all," a phrase from Virgil's tenth Eclogue. Nuns were generally forbidden to wear brooches.
2. A chaplain was a clergyman or nun who conducted services in a private chapel. Like the Knight's Squire, the Nun serves as attendant and secretary to her superior, the Prioress; like the Yeoman, the Priests (or Priest—there is some dispute over whether Chaucer in the end intended one or three) serve as subordinate attendants.
3. An outrider was a monk whose duties led him outside the confines of his abbey, something that would certainly aid this monk in indulging worldly tastes such as hunting. An abbot is the head of a community of monks.

Where this brave monk was master of the cell.[4]
The rule of Maurus or Saint Benedict,
By reason it was old and somewhat strict,[5]
175 This said monk let such old things slowly pace
And followed new-world manners in their place.
He cared not for that text a clean-plucked hen°   *at all*
Which holds that hunters are not holy men;
Nor that a monk, when he is cloisterless,
180 Is like unto a fish that's waterless;
That is to say, a monk out of his cloister.
But this same text he held not worth an oyster;
And I said his opinion was right good.
What? Should he study as a madman would
185 Upon a book in cloister cell? Or yet
Go labour with his hands and swink° and sweat,   *toil*
As Austin bids? How shall the world be served?[6]
Let Austin have his toil to him reserved.
Therefore he was a rider day and night;
190 Greyhounds he had, as swift as bird in flight.
Since riding and the hunting of the hare
Were all his love, for no cost would he spare.
I saw his sleeves were purfled° at the hand   *fringed*
With fur of grey, the finest in the land;
195 Also, to fasten hood beneath his chin,
He had of good wrought gold a curious pin:
A love-knot in the larger end there was.
His head was bald and shone like any glass,
And smooth as one anointed was his face.
200 Fat was this lord, he stood in goodly case.
His bulging eyes he rolled about, and hot
They gleamed and red, like fire beneath a pot;
His boots were soft; his horse of great estate.
Now certainly he was a fine prelate:°   *church dignitary*
205 He was not pale as some poor wasted ghost.
A fat swan loved he best of any roast.
His palfrey° was as brown as is a berry.   *saddle-horse*

A friar there was, a wanton and a merry,
A limiter, a very festive man.[7]
210 In all the Orders Four is none that can
Equal his gossip and his fair language.

4. A small monastery or nunnery, usually dependent on a larger one.
5. The ascetic Rule of Saint Benedict, brought to France by his disciple, St. Maurus.
6. St. Augustine ("Austin") was reputed author of an early monastic rule and a staunch believer in the need to withdraw one's desires from the things of this world. The ironic question asks who would do the work of the secular world, especially its heavy clerical duties, if not the clergy.

7. A friar was a member of one of the four begging orders instituted in the 13th century. Because they were supposed to own nothing of their own, they were legally permitted to beg within certain limits (hence the word "limiter"). As with the Monk before him, the portrait of the Friar partakes in a tradition of satirical depictions of the clergy.

He had arranged full many a marriage
Of women young, and this at his own cost.
Unto his order he was a noble post.°   *pillar*
215 Well liked by all and intimate was he
With franklins everywhere in his country,[8]
And with the worthy women of the town:
For at confessing he'd more power in gown
(As he himself said) than a good curate,
220 For of his order he was licentiate.°   *licensed confessor*
He heard confession gently, it was said,
Gently absolved too, leaving naught of dread.
He was an easy man to give penance
When knowing he should gain a good pittance;
225 For to a begging friar, money given
Is sign that any man has been well shriven.°   *confessed*
For if one gave (he dared to boast of this),
He took the man's repentance not amiss,
For many a man there is so hard of heart
230 He cannot weep however pains may smart.
Therefore, instead of weeping and of prayer,
Men should give silver to poor friars all bare.
His tippet° was stuck always full of knives   *scarf*
And pins, to give to young and pleasing wives.
235 And certainly he kept a merry note:
Well could he sing and play upon the rote.°   *fiddle*
At balladry he bore the prize away.
His throat was white as lily of the May;
Yet strong he was as ever champion.
240 In towns he knew the taverns, every one,
And every good host and each barmaid too—
Better than begging lepers, these he knew.
For unto no such solid man as he
Accorded it, as far as he could see,
245 To have sick lepers for acquaintances.
There is no honest advantageousness
In dealing with such poverty-stricken curs;
It's with the rich and with big victuallers.°   *food sellers*
And so, wherever profit might arise,
250 Courteous he was and humble in men's eyes.
There was no other man so virtuous.
He was the finest beggar of his house;
A certain district being farmed to him,
None of his brethren dared approach its rim;
255 For though a widow had no shoes to show,
So pleasant was his *In principio,*[9]
He always got a farthing ere he went.

---

8. A franklin was a landowner of free but not noble birth, and of ranking just below the gentry.

9. "In the beginning," the first words of Genesis and of the Gospel According to John in Latin.

He lived by pickings, it is evident.
And he could romp as well as any whelp.°   *pup*
260   On love days¹ could he be of mickle° help.   *great*
For there he was not like a cloisterer,°   *monk*
With threadbare cope° as is the poor scholar,   *cloak*
But he was like a lord or like a pope.
Of double worsted° was his semi-cope,°   *wool / short cloak*
265   That rounded like a bell, as you may guess.
He lisped a little, out of wantonness,
To make his English soft upon his tongue;
And in his harping, after he had sung,
His two eyes twinkled in his head as bright
270   As do the stars within the frosty night.
This worthy limiter was named Hubert.

There was a merchant with forked beard, and girt
In motley° gown, and high on horse he sat,   *multicolored*
Upon his head a Flemish beaver hat;
275   His boots were fastened rather elegantly.²
His spoke his notions out right pompously,
Stressing the times when he had won, not lost.
He would the sea were held at any cost
Across from Middleburgh to Orwell town.³
280   At money-changing he could make a crown.
This worthy man kept all his wits well set;
There was no one could say he was in debt,
So well he governed all his trade affairs
With bargains and with borrowings and with shares.
285   Indeed, he was a worthy man withal,
But, sooth° to say, his name I can't recall.   *truth*

A clerk from Oxford was with us also,
Who'd turned to getting knowledge, long ago.⁴
As meagre was his horse as is a rake,
290   Nor he himself too fat, I'll undertake,
But he looked hollow and went soberly.
Right threadbare was his overcoat; for he
Had got him yet no churchly benefice,°   *employment*
Nor was so worldly as to gain office.⁵
295   For he would rather have at his bed's head
Some twenty books, all bound in black and red,
Of Aristotle and his philosophy

---

1. Days appointed for settling disputes out of court.
2. In keeping with his position ("Merchant" primarily referred to an import-export dealer in such goods as wool, cloth, and furs), the Merchant is dressed very richly.
3. Middleburg was a Dutch port across the Channel from Orwell in England. The Merchant is concerned with piracy en route between the two towns.
4. A clerk was any man ordained to the ministry or the service of the Church; because few except the clergy could read and write, the term was also applied to anyone who could do so, especially one who worked as a scribe, secretary, or keeper of accounts. Education at Oxford or Cambridge was generally intended for those entering the clergy.
5. Employment in secular capacity as a private or government secretary or official.

Than rich robes, fiddle, or gay psaltery.°   *harp*
Yet, and for all he was philosopher,
300   He had but little gold within his coffer;[6]
But all that he might borrow from a friend
On books and learning he would swiftly spend,
And then he'd pray right busily for the souls
Of those who gave him wherewithal for schools.
305   Of study took he utmost care and heed.
Not one word spoke he more than was his need;
And that was said in fullest reverence
And short and quick and full of high good sense.
Pregnant of moral virtue was his speech;
310   And gladly would he learn and gladly teach.

A sergeant of the law,[7] wary and wise,
Who'd often gone to Paul's walk to advise,[8]
There was also, compact° of excellence.   *full*
Discreet he was, and of great reverence;
315   At least he seemed so, his words were so wise.
Often he sat as justice in assize,
By patent or commission from the crown;[9]
Because of learning and his high renown,
He took large fees and many robes could own.
320   So great a purchaser° was never known.   *land-buyer*
All was fee simple° to him, in effect,   *owned outright*
Wherefore his claims could never be suspect.
Nowhere a man so busy of his class,
And yet he seemed much busier than he was.
325   All cases and all judgments could he cite
That from King William's time were apposite.[1]
And he could draw a contract so explicit
Not any man could fault therefrom elicit;
And every statute he'd verbatim quote.
330   He rode but badly° in a medley° coat,   *simply / mixed-colored*
Belted in a silken sash, with little bars,
But of his dress no more particulars.

There was a franklin° in his company;   *large landholder*
White was his beard as is the white daisy.
335   Of sanguine° temperament by every sign,   *optimistic*
He loved right well his morning sop° in wine.   *bread*
Delightful living was the goal he'd won,
For he was Epicurus'° very son,   *Greek philosopher*

---

6. Philosophers were commonly assumed also to be adept in alchemy and other occult matters; the "philosopher's stone" could transmute base metals into gold.
7. Member of a high order of lawyers, equal to knights in prestige.
8. The porch of St. Paul's Cathedral in London, where clients would come to consult with lawyers.

9. Assizes were sessions held in county courts that heard all manner of civil cases; only sergeants of law could preside over them, appointed by the king.
1. This Man of Law supposedly knows all the reports of property transactions dating back to the reign of William the Conqueror (1066–1087).

340 That held opinion that a full delight
  Was true felicity, perfect and right.
  A householder, and that a great, was he;
  Saint Julian[2] he was in his own country.
  His bread and ale were always right well done;
345 A man with better cellars there was none.
  Baked meat was never wanting in his house,
  Of fish and flesh, and that so plenteous
  It seemed to snow therein both food and drink
  Of every dainty that a man could think.
  According to the season of the year
350 He changed his diet and his means of cheer.
  Full many a fattened partridge did he mew,°   *pen*
  And many a bream and pike in fish-pond too.
  Woe to his cook, except° the sauces were   *unless*
  Poignant and sharp, and ready all his gear.
355 His table, waiting in his hall alway,
  Stood ready covered through the livelong day.
  At county sessions was he lord and sire,
  And often acted as a knight of shire.°   *member of Parliament*
  A dagger and a trinket-bag of silk
360 Hung from his girdle, white as morning milk.
  He had been sheriff and been auditor;
  And nowhere was a worthier vavasor.[3]

   A haberdasher and a carpenter,
  An arras°-maker, dyer, and weaver   *tapestry*
365 Were with us, clothed in similar livery.°   *uniform*
  All of one sober, great fraternity.°   *trade guild*
  Their gear was new and well adorned it was;
  Their weapons were not cheaply trimmed with brass,
  But all with silver; chastely° made and well   *purely*
370 Their girdles° and their pouches too, I tell.   *belts*
  Each man of them appeared a proper burgess° *townsman*
  To sit in guildhall on a high dais.[4]
  And each of them, for wisdom he could span,
  Was fitted to have been an alderman;
375 For chattels° they'd enough, and, too, of rent; *possessions*
  To which their goodwives gave a free assent,
  Or else for certain they had been to blame.
  It's good to hear "Madam" before one's name,
  And go to church when all the world may see,
380 Having one's mantle borne right royally.[5]

   A cook they had with them, just for the nonce,° *occasion*
  To boil the chickens with the marrow-bones,

---

2. Patron saint of hospitality.
3. A feudal tenant ranking in nobility below a baron.
4. The guildhall was the meeting-place of a guild, often equivalent to the town hall. On its dais, or high platform, would sit the highest-ranking officials.
5. An alderman's wife was given the title "Madam," allowing her to be treated as if she were nobility.

And flavour tartly and with galingale.°   *aromatic spices*
Well could he tell a draught of London ale.
385   And he could roast and seethe° and broil and fry,   *simmer*
And make a good thick soup, and bake a pie.
But very ill it was, it seemed to me,
That on his shin a deadly sore had he;
For sweet blanc-mange,° he made it with the best.   *stew*

390   There was a sailor, living far out west;
For aught I know, he was of Dartmouth town.[6]
He sadly rode a hackney,° in a gown,   *nag*
Of thick rough cloth falling to the knee.
A dagger hanging on a cord had he
395   About his neck, and under arm, and down.
The summer's heat had burned his visage brown;
And certainly he was a good fellow.
Full many a draught of wine he'd drawn, I trow,°   *believe*
Of Bordeaux vintage, while the trader slept.
400   Nice conscience was a thing he never kept.
If that he fought and got the upper hand,
By water he sent them home to every land.
But as for craft, to reckon well his tides,
His currents and the dangerous watersides
405   His harbours, and his moon, his pilotage,
There was none such from Hull to far Carthage.
Hardy, and wise in all things undertaken,
By many a tempest had his beard been shaken.
He knew well all the havens, as they were,
410   From Gottland to the Cape of Finisterre,
And every creek in Brittany and Spain;[7]
His vessel had been christened *Madeleine*.

        With us there was a doctor of physic;
In all this world was none like him to pick
415   For talk of medicine and surgery;
For he was grounded in astronomy.[8]
He often kept a patient from the pall
By horoscopes and magic natural.
Well could he tell the fortune ascendent
420   Within the houses for his sick patient.
He knew the cause of every malady,
Were it of hot or cold, of moist or dry,
And where engendered, and of what humour;[9]
He was a very good practitioner.

6. A port town on the English Channel.
7. Ports near and far: Hull in northeastern England, Carthage (formerly) in North Africa, Gottland in Scandinavia, Finisterre in Spain.
8. Stars and planets were held to have an important influence on the body.
9. According to classical and medieval medicine, illness was caused by an imbalance in the four elements that composed the body (air, water, fire, earth), as they were manifested in the four humors or fluids: blood (hot and moist), phlegm (cold and moist), yellow bile (hot and dry), and black bile (cold and dry).

425   The cause being known, down to the deepest root,
       Anon he gave to the sick man his boot.°   *remedy*
       Ready he was, with his apothecaries,°   *druggists*
       To send him drugs and all electuaries;°   *medicines*
       By mutual aid much gold they'd always won—
430   Their friendship was a thing not new begun.
       Well read was he in Esculapius,
       And Deiscorides, and in Rufus,
       Hippocrates, and Hali, and Galen,
       Serapion, Rhazes, and Avicen,
435   Averrhoës, Gilbert, and Constantine,
       Bernard, and Gatisden, and John Damascene.[1]
       In diet he was measured as could be,
       Including naught of superfluity,
       But nourishing and easy. It's no libel
440   To say he read but little in the Bible.
       In blue and scarlet he went clad, withal,
       Lined with a taffeta° and with sendal;°
       And yet he was right chary of expense;   *rich silks*
       He kept the gold he gained from pestilence.
445   For gold in physic is a fine cordial,
       And therefore loved he gold exceeding all.

       There was a housewife come from Bath, or near,[2]
       Who—sad to say—was deaf in either ear.
       At making cloth she had so great a bent
450   She bettered those of Ypres and even of Ghent.[3]
       In all the parish there was no good wife
       Should offering make before her, on my life;[4]
       And if one did, indeed, so wroth was she
       It put her out of all her charity.
455   Her kerchiefs were of finest weave and ground;°   *texture*
       I dare swear that they weighed a full ten pound
       Which, of a Sunday, she wore on her head.
       Her hose were of the choicest scarlet red,
       Close gartered, and her shoes were soft and new.
460   Bold was her face, and fair, and red of hue.
       She'd been respectable throughout her life,
       With five churched husbands bringing joy and strife,
       Not counting other company in youth;
       But thereof there's no need to speak, in truth.
465   Three times she'd journeyed to Jerusalem;
       And many a foreign stream she'd had to stem;
       At Rome she'd been, and she'd been in Boulogne,
       In Spain at Santiago, and at Cologne.°   *pilgrimage sites*

1. Famous classical and medieval authorities on medicine
from around the Mediterranean.
2. Named after its ancient Roman baths, Bath was a city
in western England and the center of cloth manufacturing.

3. Trading and manufacturing centers of Flanders, famous
for their cloth.
4. Offerings were given to the priest at the church altar in
order of rank.

She could tell much of wandering by the way:

470 Gap-toothed was she, it is no lie to say.

Upon an ambler° easily she sat,   *easy-riding horse*

Well wimpled, aye, and over all a hat

As broad as is a buckler or a targe;°   *light shield*

A rug was tucked around her buttocks large,

475 And on her feet a pair of sharpened spurs.

In company well could she laugh her slurs.°   *faults*

The remedies of love she knew, perchance,

For of that art she'd learned the old, old dance.

There was a good man of religion, too,

480 A country parson, poor, I warrant you;

But rich he was in holy thought and work.

He was a learned man also, a clerk,

Who Christ's own gospel truly sought to preach;

Devoutly his parishioners would he teach.

485 Benign he was and wondrous diligent.

Patient in adverse times and well content,

As he was ofttimes proven; always blithe,

He was right loath to curse to get a tithe,[5]

But rather would he give, in case of doubt,

490 Unto those poor parishioners about,

Part of his income, even of his goods.

Enough° with little, coloured° all his moods.   *satisfied / harmonized*

Wide was his parish, houses far asunder,

But never did he fail, for rain or thunder,

495 In sickness, or in sin, or any state,

To visit to the farthest, small and great,

Going afoot, and in his hand a stave.

This fine example to his flock he gave,

That first he wrought° and afterwards he taught;   *worked*

500 Out of the gospel then that text he caught.

And this figure he added thereunto—

That, if gold rust, what shall poor iron do?

For if the priest be foul, in whom we trust,

What wonder if a layman yield to lust?

505 And shame it is, if priest take thought for keep,° *is involved*

A shitty shepherd, shepherding clean sheep.

Well ought a priest example good to give,

By his own cleanness, how his flock should live.

He never let his benefice for hire,

510 Leaving his flock to flounder in the mire,

And ran to London, up to old Saint Paul's

To get himself a chantry there for souls.[6]

---

5. Parishioners paid the Church a tithe, or a tenth part of their income.

6. A parish priest was usually granted his church and its lands for life. Some would rent out their post and get well-paid positions with minimal duties, such as saying masses for the dead in London chantries.

Nor in some brotherhood° did he withhold;°   *guild / was he hired*
But dwelt at home and kept so well the fold
515   That never wolf could make his plans miscarry;
He was a shepherd and not mercenary.
And holy though he was, and virtuous,
To sinners he was not impiteous,
Nor haughty in his speech, nor too divine,
520   But in all teaching prudent and benign.
To lead folk into Heaven but by stress
Of good example was his busyness.
But if some sinful one proved obstinate,
Be who it might, of high or low estate,
525   Him he reproved, and sharply, as I know.
There is nowhere a better priest, I trow.
He had no thirst for pomp or reverence,
Nor made himself a special, spiced° conscience,   *dainty*
But Christ's own lore, and His apostles' twelve
530   He taught, but first he followed it himselve.

With him there was a plowman, was his brother,
That many a load of dung, and many another
Had scattered, for a good true toiler, he,
Living in peace and perfect charity.
535   He loved God most, and that with his whole heart
At all times, though he played or plied his art,
And next, his neighbour, even as himself.
He'd thresh and dig, with never thought of pelf,°   *money*
For Christ's own sake, for every poor wight,°   *person*
540   All without pay, if it lay in his might.
He paid his taxes, fully, fairly, well,
Both by his own toil and by stuff he'd sell.
In a tabard° he rode upon a mare.   *smock*
There were also a reeve and miller there;
545   A summoner, manciple and pardoner,
And these, beside myself, made all there were.

The miller was a stout churl,° be it known,   *country man*
Hardy and big of brawn and big of bone;
Which was well proved, for when he went on lam°   *fought*
550   At wrestling, never failed he of the ram.°   *prize*
He was a chunky fellow, broad of build;
He'd heave a door from hinges if he willed,
Or break it through, by running, with his head.
His beard, as any sow or fox, was red,
555   And broad it was as if it were a spade.
Upon the coping° of his nose he had   *bridge*
A wart, and thereon stood a tuft of hairs,
Red as the bristles in an old sow's ears;
His nostrils they were black and very wide.
560   A sword and buckler bore he by his side.

His mouth was like a furnace door for size.
He was a jester and could poetize,
But mostly all of sin and ribaldries.
He could steal corn and full thrice charge his fees;
565 And yet he had a thumb of gold, begad.
A white coat and blue hood he wore, this lad.
A bagpipe he could blow well, be it known,
And with that same he brought us out of town.

There was a manciple from an inn of court,
570 To whom all buyers might quite well resort
To learn the art of buying food and drink;[7]
For whether he paid cash or not, I think
That he so knew the markets, when to buy,
He never found himself left high and dry.
575 Now is it not of God a full fair grace
That such a vulgar man has wit to pace°   *outdo*
The wisdom of a crowd of learned men?
Of masters had he more than three times ten,
Who were in law expert and curious;
580 Whereof there were a dozen in that house
Fit to be stewards of both rent and land
Of any lord in England who would stand
Upon his own and live in manner good,
In honour, debtless (save his head were wood),
585 Or live as frugally as he might desire;
These men were able to have helped a shire
In any case that ever might befall;
And yet this manciple outguessed them all.

The reeve he was a slender, choleric man,
590 Who shaved his beard as close as razor can.[8]
His hair was cut round even with his ears;
His top was tonsured like a pulpiteer's.°   *preacher's*
Long were his legs, and they were very lean,
And like a staff, with no calf to be seen.
595 Well could he manage granary and bin;
No auditor could ever on him win.
He could foretell, by drought and by the rain,
The yielding of his seed and of his grain.
His lord's sheep and his oxen and his dairy,
600 His swine and horses, all his stores, his poultry,
Were wholly in this steward's managing;
And, by agreement, he'd made reckoning°   *settled accounts*
Since his young lord of age was twenty years;
Yet no man ever found him in arrears.°   *behind in payments*

---

7. A manciple was a servant or officer charged with provisioning a college, an inn of court, or a monastery. The inns of court controlled training in the legal profession.

8. The overseer or steward of an estate. Chaucer's Reeve suffers from an excess of the humor of yellow bile, hot and dry, making him choleric, or quick to anger.

605   There was no agent, hind,° or herd° who'd cheat   *servant / herdsman*
    But he knew well his cunning and deceit;
    They were afraid of him as of the death.
    His cottage was a good one, on a heath;
    By green trees shaded with this dwelling-place.
610   Much better than his lord could he purchase.
    Right rich he was in his own private right,
    Seeing he'd pleased his lord, by day or night,
    By giving him, or lending, of his goods,
    And so got thanked—but yet got coats and hoods.
615   In youth he'd learned a good trade, and had been
    A carpenter, as fine as could be seen.
    This steward sat a horse that well could trot,
    And was all dapple-grey, and was named Scot.
    A long surcoat° of blue did he parade,   *overcoat*
620   And at his side he bore a rusty blade.
    Of Norfolk° was this reeve of whom I tell,   *in north England*
    From near a town that men call Badeswell.
    Bundled he was like friar from chin to croup,°   *rump*
    And ever he rode hindmost of our troop.

625   A summoner was with us in that place,[9]
    Who had a fiery-red, cherubic face,
    For eczema he had; his eyes were narrow
    As hot he was, and lecherous, as a sparrow;
    With black and scabby brows and scanty beard;
630   He had a face that little children feared.
    There was no mercury, sulphur, or litharge,
    No borax, ceruse, tartar,[1] could discharge,
    Nor ointment that could cleanse enough, or bite,
    To free him of his boils and pimples white,
635   Nor of the bosses° resting on his cheeks.   *lumps*
    Well loved he garlic, onions, aye and leeks,
    And drinking of strong wine as red as blood.
    Then would he talk and shout as madman would.
    And when a deal of wine he'd poured within,
640   Then would he utter no word save Latin.
    Some phrases had he learned, say two or three,
    Which he had garnered out of some decree;
    No wonder, for he'd heard it all the day;
    And all you know right well that even a jay
645   Can call out "Wat" as well as can the pope.
    But when, for aught else, into him you'd grope,
    'Twas found he'd spent his whole philosophy;
    Just "*Questio quid juris*" would he cry.[2]

---

9. A summoner was a petty court officer who summoned for court appearances and kept track of them.
1. These primarily mineral compounds were different remedies recommended by medieval medicine for the treatment of the Summoner's skin disorder.
2. "The question is, what point of law (applies)?"

He was a noble rascal, and a kind;
650   A better comrade 'twould be hard to find.
Why, he would suffer, for a quart of wine,
Some good fellow to have his concubine
A twelve-month, and excuse him to the full
(Between ourselves, though, he could pluck a gull).
655   And if he chanced upon a good fellow,
He would instruct him never to have awe,
In such a case, of the archdeacon's curse,°   *excommunication*
Except a man's soul lie within his purse;
For in his purse the man should punished be.
660   "The purse is the archdeacon's Hell," said he.
But well I know he lied in what he said,
A curse ought every guilty man to dread
(For curse can kill, as absolution save),
And 'ware° *significavit*³ to the grave.   *beware*
665   In his own power had he, and at ease,
The boys and girls of all the diocese,
And knew their secrets, and by counsel led.
A garland° had he set upon his head,   *wreath*
Large as a tavern's wine-bush on a stake;°   *sign*
670   A buckler had he made of bread they bake.

        With him there rode a gentle pardoner
Of Rouncival, his friend and his compeer;°   *companion*
Straight from the court of Rome had journeyed he.⁴
Loudly he sang "Come hither, love, to me,"
675   The summoner joining with a burden° round;   *bass line*
Was never horn of° half so great a sound.   *made with*
This pardoner had hair as yellow as wax,
But lank it hung as does a strike of flax;
In wisps hung down such locks as he'd on head,
680   And with them he his shoulders overspread;
But thin they dropped, and stringy, one by one.
But as to hood, for sport of it, he'd none,
Though it was packed in wallet° all the while.   *bag*
It seemed to him he went in latest style,
685   Dishevelled, save for cap, his head all bare.
As shiny eyes he had as has a hare.
He had a fine veronica sewed to cap.⁵
His wallet lay before him in his lap,
Stuffed full of pardons brought from Rome all hot.
690   A voice he had that bleated like a goat.

---

3. An ecclesiastical writ for the arrest of an excommunicated person.
4. A pardoner was licensed by the Church (and the Pope, at the "court of Rome") to sell indulgences, or papal pardons for sin. This Pardoner is connected to St. Mary Rouncesval in Charing Cross, London.

5. According to legend, St. Veronica had wiped Christ's face with her kerchief on his way to be crucified. The cloth retained an impression of the face, and was kept as a sacred relic in Rome. Reproductions would be carried by pilgrims as tokens of their pilgrimage.

No beard had he, nor ever should he have,
For smooth his face as he'd just had a shave;
I think he was a gelding° or a mare.°   *eunuch / homosexual*
But in his craft, from Berwick unto Ware,°   *in all of England*
695   Was no such pardoner in any place.
For in his bag he had a pillowcase
The which, he said, was Our True Lady's veil:
He said he had a piece of the very sail
That good Saint Peter had, what time he went
700   Upon the sea, till Jesus changed his bent.[6]
He had a latten° cross set full of stones   *brass*
And in a bottle had he some pig's bones.
But with these relics, when he came upon
Some simple parson, then this paragon
705   In that one day more money stood to gain
Than the poor dupe in two months could attain.
And thus, with flattery and suchlike japes,°   *tricks*
He made the parson and the rest his apes.
But yet, to tell the whole truth at the last,
710   He was, in church, a fine ecclesiast.
Well could he read a lesson or a story,
But best of all he sang an offertory;
For well he knew that when that song was sung,
Then might he preach, and all with polished tongue,
715   To win some silver, as he right well could;
Therefore he sang so merrily and so loud.

       Now have I told you briefly, in a clause,°   *short space*
The state, the array, the number, and the cause
Of the assembling of this company
720   In Southwark, at this noble hostelry
Known as the Tabard Inn, hard by the Bell.°   *another tavern*
But now the time is come wherein to tell
How all we bore ourselves that very night
When at the hostelry we did alight.
725   And afterward the story I engage
To tell you of our common pilgrimage.
But first, I pray you, of your courtesy,
You'll not ascribe it to vulgarity
Though I speak plainly of this matter here,
730   Retailing you their words and means of cheer;
Nor though I use their very terms, nor lie.
For this thing do you know as well as I:
When one repeats a tale told by a man,
He must report, as nearly as he can,
735   Every least word, if he remember it,

---

6. The Pardoner's fake relics include Mary's veil and part of the sail used by Peter as a fisherman before he was called by Jesus to be a disciple.

However rude it be, or how unfit;
Or else he may be telling what's untrue,
Embellishing and fictionizing too.
He may not spare, although it were his brother;
740   He must as well say one word as another.
Christ spoke right broadly out, in holy writ,
And, you know well, there's nothing low in it.
And Plato says, to those able to read:
"The word should be the cousin to the deed."[7]
745   Also, I pray that you'll forgive it me
If I have not set folk, in their degree
Here in this tale, by rank as they should stand
My wits are not the best, you'll understand.[8]

      Great cheer our host gave to us, every one,
750   And to the supper set us all anon;
And served us then with victuals of the best.
Strong was the wine and pleasant to each guest.
A seemly man our good host was, withal,
Fit to have been a marshal in some hall;[9]
755   He was a large man, with protruding eyes,
As fine a burgher as in Cheapside lies;[1]
Bold in his speech, and wise, and right well taught,
And as to manhood, lacking there in naught.
Also, he was a very merry man,
760   And after meat, at playing he began,
Speaking of mirth among some other things,
When all of us had paid our reckonings;
And saying thus: "Now masters, verily
You are all welcome here, and heartily:
765   For by my truth, and telling you no lie,
I have not seen, this year, a company
Here in this inn, fitter for sport than now.
Fain° would I make you happy, knew I how.   *gladly*
And of a game have I this moment thought
770   To give you joy, and it shall cost you naught.
      "You go to Canterbury; may God speed
And the blest martyr soon requite your meed.°   *reward you*
And well I know, as you go on your way,
You'll tell good tales and shape yourselves to play;
775   For truly there's no mirth nor comfort, none,
Riding the roads as dumb as is a stone;
And therefore will I furnish you a sport,

---

7. The saying is taken from Plato's *Timaeus,* but probably cited as a commonplace from a later source. According to the narrator, both Plato and Jesus, in the sayings attributed to him in the Gospels, held a principle of realism: things should be called by their true names, and words should be reported as they were said.

8. Rather than organized according to the social standing ("degree") of their tellers, the tales are given in the order in which they were supposedly told. The pretense of modesty was a standard theme of medieval rhetoric.
9. Master of ceremonies and arrangements at a banquet.
1. A major market area in London.

As I just said, to give you some comfort.
And if you like it, all, by one assent,
780 And will be ruled by me, of my judgment,
And will so do as I'll proceed to say,
Tomorrow, when you ride upon your way,
Then, by my father's spirit, who is dead,
If you're not gay, I'll give you up my head.
785 Hold up your hands, nor more about it speak."
    Our full assenting was not far to seek;
We thought there was no reason to think twice,
And granted him his way without advice,
And bade him tell his verdict just and wise,
790   "Masters," quoth he, "here now is my advice;
But take it not, I pray you, in disdain;
This is the point, to put it short and plain,
That each of you, beguiling the long day,
Shall tell two stories as you wend your way
795 To Canterbury town; and each of you
On coming home, shall tell another two,
All of adventures he has known befall.
And he who plays his part the best of all,
That is to say, who tells upon the road
800 Tales of best sense, in most amusing mode,
Shall have a supper at the others' cost
Here in this room and sitting by this post,
When we come back again from Canterbury.
And now, the more to warrant you'll be merry
805 I will myself, and gladly, with you ride
At my own cost, and I will be your guide.
But whosoever shall my rule gainsay°   *deny*
Shall pay for all that's bought along the way.
And if you are agreed that it be so,
810 Tell me at once, or if not, tell me no,
And I will act accordingly. No more."
    This thing was granted, and our oaths we swore,
With right glad hearts, and prayed of him, also,
That he would take the office, nor forgo
815 The place of governor of all of us,
Judging our tales; and by his wisdom thus
Arrange that supper at a certain price,
We to be ruled, each one, by his advice
In things both great and small; by one assent,
820 We stood committed to his government.
And thereupon, the wine was fetched anon;
We drank, and then to rest went every one,
And that without a longer tarrying.°   *delay*
    Next morning, when the day began to spring,
825 Up rose our host, and acting as our cock,
He gathered us together in a flock,

And forth we rode, a jog-trot° being the pace,   *slow, steady pace*
Until we reached Saint Thomas' watering-place.[2]
And there our host pulled horse up to a walk,
830   And said: "Now, masters, listen while I talk.
You know what you agreed at set of sun.
If even-song and morning-song are one,[3]
Let's here decide who first shall tell a tale.
And as I hope to drink more wine and ale,
835   Whoso proves rebel to my government
Shall pay for all that by the way is spent.
Come now, draw cuts, before we farther win,
And he that draws the shortest shall begin.
Sir knight," said he, "my master and my lord,
840   You shall draw first as you have pledged your word.
Come near," quoth he, "my lady prioress:
And you sir, clerk, put by your bashfulness,
Nor ponder more; out hands, now, every man!"
      At once to draw a cut each one began,
845   And, to make short the matter, as it was,
Whether by chance or whatsoever cause,
The truth is, that the cut fell to the knight,
At which right happy then was every wight.
Thus that his story first of all he'd tell,
850   According to the compact, it befell,
As you have heard. Why argue to and fro?
And when this good man saw that it was so,
Being a wise man and obedient
To plighted° word, given by free assent,   *pledged*
855   He said: "Since I must then begin the game,
Why, welcome be the cut, and in God's name!
Now let us ride, and hearken what I say."
And at that word we rode forth on our way;
And he began to speak, with right good cheer,
860   His tale anon, as it is written here.

* * *

The Miller's Prologue

Now when the knight had thus his story told,
In all the rout° there was nor young nor old   *company*
But said it was a noble story, well
Worthy to be kept in mind to tell;
5   And specially the gentle folk, each one.
Our host, he laughed and swore, "So may I run,
But this goes well; unbuckled is the mail;
Let's see now who can tell another tale:

---

2. A brook located a couple of miles from London.   3. If they still agree this morning (the hour of morning services) what they had agreed the previous evening.

	For certainly the game is well begun.	
10	Now shall you tell, sir monk, if't can be done,	
	Something with which to pay° for the knight's tale."	*recompense*
	The miller, who with drinking was all pale,	
	So that unsteadily on his horse he sat,	
	He would not take off either hood or hat,	
15	Nor wait for any man, in courtesy,	
	But all in Pilate's voice began to cry,[1]	
	And by the Arms and Blood and Bones° he swore,	*of Christ*
	"I have a noble story in my store,	
	With which I will requite° the good knight's tale."	*pay back*
20	Our host saw, then, that he was drunk with ale,	
	And said to him: "Wait, Robin, my dear brother,	
	Some better man shall tell us first another:	
	Submit and let us work on profitably."	
	"Now by God's soul," cried he, "that will not I!	
25	For I will speak, or else I'll go my way."	
	Our host replied: "Tell on, then, till doomsday!	
	You are a fool, your wit is overcome."	
	"Now hear me," said the miller, "all and some!	
	But first I make protestation round	
30	That I'm quite drunk, I know it by my sound:	
	And therefore, if I slander or mis-say,	
	Blame it on ale of Southwark, so I pray;	
	For I will tell a legend and a life	
	Both of a carpenter and of his wife,	
35	And how a scholar set the good wright's cap."°	*tricked him*
	The reeve replied and said: "Oh, shut your trap.	
	Let be your ignorant drunken ribaldry!	
	It is a sin, and further, great folly	
	To asperse any man, or him defame,	
40	And, too, to bring upon a man's wife shame.	
	There are enough of other things to say."	
	This drunken miller spoke on in his way,	
	And said: "Oh, but my dear brother Oswald,	
	The man who has no wife is no cuckold.	
45	But I say not, thereby, that you are one:	
	Many good wives there are, as women run,	
	And ever a thousand good to one that's bad,	
	As well you know yourself, unless you're mad.	
	Why are you angry with my story's cue?°	*set-up*
50	I have a wife, begad, as well as you,	
	Yet I'd not, for the oxen of my plow,	
	Take on my shoulders more than is enow,°	*enough*
	By judging of myself that I am one;	
	I will believe full well that I am none.	
55	A husband must not be inquisitive	

---

1. Loudly, like the character of Pontius Pilate in medieval mystery plays.

Of God, nor of his wife, while she's alive.
So long as he may find God's plenty there,
For all the rest he need not greatly care."
    What should I say, except this miller rare
60 He would forgo his talk for no man there,
But told his churlish tale in his own way:
I think I'll here re-tell it, if I may.
And therefore, every gentle soul, I pray
That for God's love you'll hold not what I say
65 Evilly meant, but that I must rehearse
All of their tales, the better and the worse,
Or else prove false to some of my design.
Therefore, who likes not this, let him, in fine,
Turn over page and choose another tale:
70 For he shall find enough, both great and small,
Of stories touching on gentility,
And holiness, and on morality;
And blame not me if you do choose amiss,
The miller was a churl, you well know this;
75 So was the reeve, and many another more,
And ribaldry they told from plenteous store,
Be then advised, and hold me free from blame;
Men should not be too serious at a game.

The Miller's Tale

Once on a time was dwelling in Oxford
80 A wealthy lout who took in guests to board,
And of his craft he was a carpenter.
A poor scholar was lodging with him there,
Who'd learned the arts, but all his phantasy°   *fancy*
Was turned to study of astrology;
85 And knew a certain set of theorems
And could find out by various stratagems,
If men but asked of him in certain hours
When they should have a drought or else have showers,
Or if men asked of him what should befall
90 To anything—I cannot reckon them all.
    This clerk was called the clever Nicholas;
Of secret loves he knew and their solace;
And he kept counsel, too, for he was sly
And meek as any maiden passing by,
95 He had a chamber in that hostelry,
And lived alone there, without company,
All garnished with sweet herbs of good repute;
And he himself sweet-smelling as the root
Of licorice, valerian, or setwall.
100 His *Almagest*[2] and books both great and small,

2. Treatise by the ancient Greek astronomer Ptolemy.

His astrolabe,° belonging to his art,   *astronomical instrument*
His algorism stones°—all laid apart   *abacus beads*
On shelves that ranged beside his lone bed's head;
His press° was covered with a cloth of red.   *cupboard*
105   And over all there lay a psaltery°   *small harp*
Whereon he made an evening's melody,
Playing so sweetly that the chamber rang;
And *Angelus ad virginem* he sang;
And after that he warbled the *King's Note:*[3]
110   Often in good voice was his merry throat.
And thus this gentle clerk his leisure spends
Supported by some income and his friends.
    This carpenter had lately wed a wife
Whom he loved better than he loved his life;
115   And she was come to eighteen years of age.
Jealous he was and held her close in cage.
For she was wild and young and he was old,
And deemed himself as like to be cuckold.
He knew not Cato,[4] for his lore was rude:
120   That vulgar° man should wed similitude.   *common*
A man should wed according to estate,
For youth and age are often in debate.
But now, since he had fallen in the snare,
He must endure, like other folk, his care,°   *worry*
125   Fair was this youthful wife, and therewithal
As weasel's was her body slim and small.
A girdle wore she, barred and striped, of silk.
An apron, too, as white as morning milk
About her loins, and full of many a gore;°   *flounce*
130   White was her smock, embroidered all before
And even behind, her collar round about,
Of coal-black silk, on both sides, in and out;
The strings of the white cap upon her head
Were, like her collar, black silk worked with thread;
135   Her fillet° was of wide silk worn full high: *head-band*
And certainly she had a lickerish° eye.   *lecherous*
She'd thinned out carefully her eyebrows two,
And they were arched and black as any sloe.°   *plum*
She was a far more pleasant thing to see
140   Than is the newly budded young pear-tree;
And softer than the wool is on a wether,°   *ram*
Down from her girdle hung a purse of leather,
Tasselled with silk, with latten beading sown.
In all this world, searching it up and down,
145   So gay a little doll, I well believe,
Or such a wench, there's no man can conceive,

3. A secular song. "The angel to the virgin" was a medieval song about the Annunciation.

4. Roman statesman whose collected maxims were used to teach elementary Latin.

Far brighter was the brilliance of her hue
Than in the Tower the gold coins minted new.
And songs came shrilling from her pretty head
150 As from a swallow's sitting on a shed.
Therewith she'd dance too, and could play and sham
Like any kid or calf about its dam.°   *mother*
Her mouth was sweet as bragget or as mead°   *honeyed ales*
Or hoard of apples laid in hay or weed.
155 Skittish she was as is a pretty colt,
Tall as a staff and straight as cross-bow bolt.
A brooch she wore upon her collar low,
As broad as boss of buckler did it show;
Her shoes laced up to where a girl's legs thicken.
160 She was a primrose, and a tender chicken
For any lord to lay upon his bed,
Or yet for any good yeoman to wed.
        Now, sir, and then, sir, so befell the case,
That on a day this clever Nicholas
165 Fell in with this young wife to toy and play,
The while her husband was down Osney way,°   *near Oxford*
Clerks being as crafty as the best of us;
And unperceived he caught her by the puss,
Saying: "Indeed, unless I have my will,
170 For secret love of you, sweetheart, I'll spill."
And held her hard about the hips, and how!—
And said: "O darling, love me, love me now,
Or I shall die, and pray you God may save!"
        And she leaped as a colt does in the trave,⁵
175 And with her head she twisted fast away,
And said: "I will not kiss you, by my fay!
Why, let go," cried she, "let go, Nicholas!
Or I will call for help and cry 'alas!'
Do take your hands away, for courtesy!"
180   This Nicholas for mercy then did cry,
And spoke so well, importuned her so fast
That she her love did grant him at the last,
And swore her oath, by Saint Thomas of Kent,°   *Thomas à Becket*
That she would be at his command, content,
185 As soon as opportunity she could spy.
        "My husband is so full of jealousy,
Unless you will await me secretly,
I know I'm just as good as dead," said she.
"You must keep all quite hidden in this case."
190   "Nay, thereof worry not," said Nicholas,
"A clerk has lazily employed his while°   *time*
If he cannot a carpenter beguile."

5. When penned in to be shod.

And thus they were agreed, and then they swore
To wait a while, as I have said before.
195 When Nicholas had done thus every whit°   *bit*
And patted her about the loins a bit,
He kissed her sweetly, took his psaltery,
And played it fast and made a melody.
Then fell it thus, that to the parish kirk,°   *church*
200 The Lord Christ Jesus' own works for to work,
This good wife went, upon a holy day;
Her forehead shone as bright as does the May,
So well she'd washed it when she left off work.
Now there was of that church a parish clerk
205 Whose name was (as folk called him) Absalom.
Curled was his hair, shining like gold, and from
His head spread fanwise in a thick bright mop;
'Twas parted straight and even on the top;
His cheek was red, his eyes grey as a goose;
210 With Saint Paul's windows cut upon his shoes,[6]
He stood in red hose fitting famously.
And he was clothed full well and properly
All in a coat of blue, in which were let
Holes for the lacings, which were fairly set.
215 And over all he wore a fine surplice°   *linen robe*
As white as ever hawthorn spray, and nice.
A merry lad he was, so God me save,
And well could he let blood, cut hair, and shave,
And draw a deed or quitclaim,° as might chance.   *legal release*
220 In twenty manners could he trip and dance,
After the school that reigned in Oxford, though,
And with his two legs swinging to and fro;
And he could play upon a violin;
Thereto he sang in treble voice and thin;
225 And as well could he play on his guitar.
In all the town no inn was, and no bar,
That he'd not visited to make good cheer,
Especially were lively barmaids there.
But truth to tell, he was a bit squeamish
230 Of farting and of language haughtyish.
This Absalom, who was so light and gay,
Went with a censer° on the holy day,   *incense pot*
Censing the wives like an enthusiast;
And on them many a loving look he cast,
235 Especially on this carpenter's good wife.
To look at her he thought a merry life,
She was so pretty, sweet, and lickerous.
I dare well say, if she had been a mouse

---

6. A style of cutting the uppers of the shoes so that they resembled the latticework of the windows of St. Paul's Cathedral.

And he a cat, he would have mauled her some.
240   This parish clerk, this lively Absalom
Had in his heart, now, such a love-longing
That from no wife took he an offering,
For courtesy, he said, he would take none.
The moon, when it was night, full brightly shone,
245   And his guitar did Absalom then take,
For in love-watching he'd intent to wake.°   *stay awake*
And forth he went, jolly and amorous,
Until he came unto the carpenter's house
A little after cocks began to crow;
250   And took his stand beneath a shot-window°   *hinged window*
That was let into the good wood-wright's wall.
He sang then, in his pleasant voice and small,
"Oh now, dear lady, if your will it be,
I pray that you will have some ruth° on me,"   *pity*
255   The words in harmony with his string-plucking.
This carpenter awoke and heard him sing,
And called unto his wife and said, in sum:
"What, Alison! Do you hear Absalom,
Who plays and sings beneath our bedroom wall?"
260   And she said to her husband, therewithal:
"Yes, God knows, John, I hear it, truth to tell."
So this went on; what is there better than well?
From day to day this pretty Absalom
So wooed her he was woebegone therefrom.
265   He lay awake all night and all the day;
He combed his spreading hair and dressed him gay;
By go-betweens and agents, too, wooed he,
And swore her loyal page he'd ever be.
He sang as tremulously as nightingale;
270   He sent her sweetened wine and well-spiced ale
And waffles piping hot out of the fire,
And, she being town-bred, mead for her desire.
For some are won by means of money spent,
And some by tricks, and some by long descent.°   *family name*
275   Once, to display his versatility,
He acted Herod on a scaffold high.[7]
        But what availed it him in any case?
She was enamoured so of Nicholas
That Absalom might go and blow his horn;
280   He got naught for his labour but her scorn.
And thus she made of Absalom her ape,
And all his earnestness she made a jape.
For truth is in this proverb, and no lie,
Men say well thus: It's always he that's nigh°   *near*

---

7. The tyrant Herod was a stock villain in the mystery plays.

285   That makes the absent lover seem a sloth.
         For now, though Absalom be wildly wroth,°   *wrathful*
         Because he is so far out of her sight,
         This handy Nicholas stands in his light.
            Now bear you well, you clever Nicholas!
290   For Absalom may wail and sing "Alas!"
         And so it chanced that on a Saturday
         This carpenter departed to Osney;
         And clever Nicholas and Alison
         Were well agreed to this effect: anon
295   This Nicholas should put in play a wile
         The simple, jealous husband to beguile;
         And if it chanced the game should go a-right,
         She was to sleep within his arms all night,
         For this was his desire, and hers also.
300   Presently then, and without more ado,
         This Nicholas, no longer did he tarry,
         But softly to his chamber did he carry
         Both food and drink to last at least a day,
         Saying that to her husband she should say—
305   If he should come to ask for Nicholas—
         Why, she should say she knew not where he was,
         For all day she'd not seen him, far or nigh;
         She thought he must have got some malady,
         Because in vain her maid would knock and call;
310   He'd answer not, whatever might befall.
            And so it was that all that Saturday
         This Nicholas quietly in chamber lay,
         And ate and slept, or did what pleased him best,
         Till Sunday when the sun had gone to rest.
315   This simple man with wonder heard the tale,
         And marvelled what their Nicholas might ail,
         And said: "I am afraid, by Saint Thomas,
         That everything's not well with Nicholas.
         God send he be not dead so suddenly!
320   This world is most unstable, certainly;
         I saw, today, the corpse being borne to kirk
         Of one who, but last Monday, was at work.
         Go up," said he unto his boy anon,
         Call at his door, or knock there with a stone,
325   Learn how it is and boldly come tell me."
            The servant went up, then, right sturdily,
         And at the chamber door, the while he stood,
         He cried and knocked as any madman would—
         "What! How! What do you, Master Nicholay?
330   How can you sleep through all the livelong day?"
            But all for naught, he never heard a word;
         A hole he found, low down upon a board,
         Through which the house cat had been wont° to creep;   *accustomed*

And to that hole he stooped, and through did peep,
335 And finally he ranged him in his sight.
This Nicholas sat gaping there, upright,
As if he'd looked too long at the new moon.
Downstairs he went and told his master soon
In what array he'd found this self-same man.

340   This carpenter to cross himself began,
And said: "Now help us, holy Frideswide!⁸
Little a man can know what shall betide.
This man is fallen, with his astromy,⁹
Into some madness or some agony;

345 I always feared that somehow this would be!
Men should not meddle in God's privity.°   *secrets*
Aye, blessed always be the ignorant man,
Whose creed is all he ever has to scan!
So fared another clerk with astromy;

350 He walked into the meadows for to pry
Into the stars, to learn what should befall,
Until into a clay-pit he did fall;
He saw not that. But yet, by Saint Thomas,
I'm sorry for this clever Nicholas.

355 He shall be scolded for his studying,
If not too late, by Jesus, Heaven's King!
    "Get me a staff, that I may pry before,
The while you, Robin, heave against the door.
We'll take him from this studying, I guess."

360   And on the chamber door, then, he did press.
His servant was a stout lad, if a dunce,
And by the hasp° he heaved it up at once;   *fastening*
Upon the floor that portal fell anon.
This Nicholas sat there as still as stone,

365 Gazing with gaping mouth, straight up in air.
This carpenter thought he was in despair,
And took him by the shoulders, mightily,
And shook him hard, and cried out, vehemently:
"What! Nicholay! Why how now! Come, look down!

370 Awake, and think on Jesus' death and crown!
I cross you from all elves and magic wights!"°   *creatures*
And then the night-spell said he out, by rights,
At the four corners of the house about,
And at the threshold of the door, without:—

375   "O Jesus Christ and good Saint Benedict,
Protect this house from all that may afflict,
For the night hag the white Paternoster!¹—
Where hast thou gone, Saint Peter's sister?"
And at the last this clever Nicholas

8. The virgin St. Frideswide was patroness of Oxford, which grew around the convent of which she was abbess.

9. The carpenter mistakes the term.

1. A charm against evil spirits.

380   Began to sigh full sore, and said: "Alas!
         Shall all the world be lost so soon again?"
             This carpenter replied: "What say you, then?
         What! Think on God, as we do, men that swink."°   labor
             This Nicholas replied: "Go fetch me drink;
385   And afterward I'll tell you privately
         A certain thing concerning you and me;
         I'll tell it to no other man or men."
             This carpenter went down and came again,
         And brought of potent ale a brimming quart;
390   And when each one of them had drunk his part,
         Nicholas shut the door fast, and with that
         He drew a seat and near the carpenter sat.
             He said: "Now, John, my good host, lief° and dear,   beloved
         You must upon your true faith swear, right here,
395   That to no man will you this word betray;
         For it is Christ's own word that I will say,
         And if you tell a man, you're ruined quite;
         This punishment shall come to you, of right,
         That if you're traitor you'll go mad—and should!"
400   "Nay, Christ forbid it, for His holy blood!"
         Said then this simple man: "I am no blab,
         Nor, though I say it, am I fond of gab.
         Say what you will, I never will it tell
         To child or wife, by Him° that harried Hell!"   Christ
405   "Now, John," said Nicholas, "I will not lie;
         But I've found out, from my astrology,
         As I have looked upon the moon so bright,
         That now, come Monday next, at nine of night,
         Shall fall a rain so wildly mad as would
410   Have been, by half, greater than Noah's flood.
         This world," he said, "in less time than an hour,
         Shall all be drowned, so terrible is this shower;
         Thus shall all mankind drown and lose all life."
             This carpenter replied: "Alas, my wife!
415   And shall she drown? Alas, my Alison!"
         For grief of this he almost fell. Anon
         He said: "Is there no remedy in this case?"
             "Why yes, good luck," said clever Nicholas,
         "If you will work by counsel of the wise;
420   You must not act on what your wits advise.
         For so says Solomon, and it's all true,
         'Work by advice and thou shalt never rue.'°   be sorry
         And if you'll act as counselled and not fail,
         I undertake, without a mast or sail,
425   To save us all, aye you and her and me.
         Haven't you heard of Noah how saved was he,
         Because Our Lord had warned him how to keep
         Out of the flood that covered earth so deep?"

       "Yes," said this carpenter, "long years ago."

430   "Have you not heard," asked Nicholas, "also
       The sorrows of Noah and his fellowship
       In getting his wife to go aboard the ship?
       He would have rather, I dare undertake,
       At that time, and for all the weather black,

435   That she had one ship for herself alone.
       Therefore, do you know what would best be done?
       This thing needs haste, and of a hasty thing
       Men must not preach nor do long tarrying.°   *delaying*
       "Presently go, and fetch here to this inn

440   A kneading-tub, or brewing vat, and win
       One each for us, but see that they are large,
       Wherein we may swim out as in a barge,
       And have therein sufficient food and drink
       For one day only; that's enough, I think.

445   The water will dry up and flow away
       About the prime of the succeeding day.
       But Robin must not know of this, your knave,
       And even Jill, your maid, I may not save;
       Ask me not why, for though you do ask me,

450   I will not tell you of God's privity.
       Suffice you, then, unless your wits are mad,
       To have as great a grace as Noah had.
       Your wife I shall not lose, there is no doubt,
       Go, now your way, and speedily get about,

455   But when you have, for you and her and me,
       Procured these kneading-tubs, or beer-vats, three,
       Then you shall hang them near the roof-tree° high,   ***main beam***
       That no man our purveyance may espy.
       And when you thus have done, as I have said,

460   And have put in our drink and meat and bread,
       Also an axe to cut the ropes in two
       When the flood comes, that we may float and go,
       And cut a hole, high up, upon the gable,
       Upon the garden side, over the stable,

465   That we may freely pass forth on our way
       When the great rain and flood are gone that day—
       Then shall you float as merrily, I'll stake,
       As does the white duck after the white drake.°   ***male duck***
       Then I will call, 'Ho, Alison! Ho John!

470   Be cheery, for the flood will pass anon.'
       And you will say, 'Hail, Master Nicholay!
       Good morrow, I see you well, for it is day!'
       And then shall we be barons all our life
       Of all the world, like Noah and his wife.

475   "But of one thing I warn you now, outright.
       Be well advised, that on that very night
       When we have reached our ships and got aboard,

Not one of us must speak or whisper word,
Nor call, nor cry, but sit in silent prayer;
480   For this is God's own bidding, hence—don't dare!
     "Your wife and you must hang apart, that in
The night shall come no chance for you to sin
Either in looking or in carnal deed.
These orders I have told you, go, God speed!
485   Tomorrow night, when all men are asleep,
Into our kneading-tubs will we three creep
And sit there, still, awaiting God's high grace.
Go, now, your way, I have no longer space
Of time to make a longer sermoning.
490   Men say thus: 'Send the wise and say nothing.'
You are so wise it needs not that I teach;
Go, save our lives, and that I do beseech."
     This silly carpenter went on his way.
Often he cried "Alas!" and "Welaway!"
495   And to his wife he told all, privately
But she was better taught thereof than he
How all this rigmarole° was to apply.   *nonsense*
Nevertheless she acted as she'd die,
And said: "Alas! Go on your way anon,
500   Help us escape, or we are lost, each one;
I am your true and lawfully wedded wife;
Go, my dear spouse, and help to save our life."
     Lo, what a great thing is affection found!
Men die of imagination, I'll be bound,
505   So deep an imprint may the spirit take.
This hapless carpenter began to quake;
He thought now, verily, that he could see
Old Noah's flood come wallowing like the sea
To drown his Alison, his honey dear.
510   He wept, he wailed, he made but sorry cheer,
He sighed and made full many a sob and sough.°   *sigh*
He went and got himself a kneading-trough
And, after that, two tubs he somewhere found
And to his dwelling privately sent round,
515   And hung them near the roof, all secretly.
With his own hand, then, made he ladders three,
To climb up by the rungs thereof, it seems
And reach the tubs left hanging to the beams;
And those he victualled, tubs and kneading-trough,
520   With bread and cheese and good jugged ale, enough
To satisfy the needs of one full day.
But ere he'd put all this in such array,
He sent his servants, boy and maid, right down
Upon some errand into London town.
525   And on the Monday, when it came on night,
He shut his door, without a candle-light,

And ordered everything as it should be.
And shortly after up they climbed, all three;
They sat while one might plow a furlong-way.°   *one-eighth mile*

530   "Now, by Our Father, hush!" said Nicholay,
And "Hush!" said John, and "Hush!" said Alison.
This carpenter, his loud devotions done,
Sat silent, saying mentally a prayer,
And waiting for the rain, to hear it there.

535   The deathlike sleep of utter weariness
Fell on this wood-wright even (as I guess)
About the curfew time, or little more;
For travail of his spirit he groaned sore,
And soon he snored, for badly his head lay.

540   Down by the ladder crept this Nicholay,
And Alison, right softly down she sped.
Without more words they went and got in bed
Even where the carpenter was wont to lie.
There was the revel and the melody!

545   And thus lie Alison and Nicholas,
In joy that goes by many an alias,
Until the bells for lauds began to ring
And friars to the chancel went to sing.[2]

        This parish clerk, this amorous Absalom,
550   Whom love has made so woebegone and dumb,
Upon the Monday was down Osney way,
With company, to find some sport and play;
And there he chanced to ask a cloisterer,°   *monk*
Privately, after John the carpenter.

555   This monk drew him apart, out of the kirk,
And said: "I have not seen him here at work
Since Saturday; I think well that he went
For timber, that the abbot has him sent;
For he is wont for timber thus to go,

560   Remaining at the grange a day or so;
Or else he's surely at his house today;
But which it is I cannot truly say."
        This Absalom right happy was and light,
And thought: "Now is the time to wake all night;

565   For certainly I saw him not stirring
About his door since day began to spring.
So may I thrive, as I shall, at cock's crow,
Knock cautiously upon that window low
Which is so placed upon his bedroom wall.

570   To Alison then will I tell of all
My love-longing, and thus I shall not miss
That at the least I'll have her lips to kiss.

2. Lauds are the first morning prayers, before daybreak.

Some sort of comfort shall I have, I say,
My mouth's been itching all this livelong day;
575   That is a sign of kissing at the least.
All night I dreamed, too, I was at a feast.
Therefore I'll go and sleep two hours away,
And all this night then will I wake and play."
        And so when time of first cock-crow was come,
580   Up rose this merry lover, Absalom,
And dressed him gay and all at point-device,°   *extremely well*
But first he chewed some licorice and spice
So he'd smell sweet, ere he had combed his hair.
Under his tongue some bits of true-love° rare,   *a sweet herb*
585   For thereby thought he to be more gracious.
He went, then, to the carpenter's dark house.
And silent stood beneath the shot-window;
Unto his breast it reached, it was so low;
And he coughed softly, in a low half tone:
590   "What do you, honeycomb, sweet Alison?
My cinnamon, my fair bird, my sweetie,
Awake, O darling mine, and speak to me!
It's little thought you give me and my woe,
Who for your love do sweat where'er I go.
595   Yet it's no wonder that I faint and sweat;
I long as does the lamb for mother's teat.
Truly, sweetheart, I have such love-longing
That like a turtle-dove's my true yearning;
And I can eat no more than can a maid."
600   "Go from the window, jack-a-napes,"° she said,   *monkey*
"For, s'help me God it is not 'come kiss me.'
I love another, or to blame I'd be,
Better than you, by Jesus, Absalom!
Go on your way, or I'll stone you therefrom,
605   And let me sleep, the fiends take you away!"
        "Alas," quoth Absalom, "and welaway!
That true love ever was so ill beset!
But kiss me, since you'll do no more, my pet,
For Jesus' love and for the love of me."
610   "And will you go, then, on your way?" asked she.
"Yes truly, darling," said this Absalom.
"Then make you ready," said she, "and I'll come!"
And unto Nicholas said she, low and still:
"Be silent now, and you shall laugh your fill."
615   This Absalom plumped down upon his knees,
And said: "I am a lord in all degrees;
For after this there may be better still!
Darling my sweetest bird, I wait your will."
        The window she unbarred, and that in haste.
620   "Have done," said she, "come on, and do it fast,
Before we're seen by any neighbour's eye."

This Absalom did wipe his mouth all dry;
Dark was the night as pitch, aye dark as coal,
And through the window she put out her hole,
625 And Absalom no better felt nor worse,
But with his mouth he kissed her naked arse
Right greedily, before he knew of this.
　　Aback he leapt—it seemed somehow amiss,
For well he knew a woman has no beard;
630 He'd felt a thing all rough and longish haired,
And said, "Oh fie, alas! What did I do?"
　　"Teehee!" she laughed, and clapped the window to;
And Absalom went forth a sorry pace.
"A beard! A beard!" cried clever Nicholas,
635 "Now by God's *corpus*° this goes fair and well!"   *body*
This hapless Absalom, he heard that yell,
And on his lip, for anger, he did bite;
And to himself he said, "I will requite!"
　　Who vigorously rubbed and scrubbed his lips
640 With dust, with sand, with straw, with cloth, with chips,
But Absalom, and often cried "Alas!
My soul I give now unto Satanas,
For rather far than own this town," said he,
"For this despite, it's well revenged I'd be.
645 Alas," said he, "from her I never blenched!"°   *flinched*
His hot love was grown cold, aye and all quenched;
For, from the moment that he'd kissed her arse,
For paramours he didn't care a curse,
For he was healed of all his malady;
650 Indeed all paramours he did defy,
And wept as does a child that has been beat.
With silent step he went across the street
Unto a smith whom men called Dan Jarvis,
Who in his smithy forged plow parts, that is
655 He sharpened shares° and coulters° busily.   *plough blades*
　　This Absalom he knocked all easily,
And said: "Unbar here, Jarvis, for I come."
　　"What! Who are you?"
　　　　　　　　　　　"It's I, it's Absalom."
　　"What! Absalom! For Jesus Christ's sweet tree,°   *cross*
660 Why are you up so early? *Ben'cite*°   *bless me*
What ails you now, man? Some gay girl, God knows,
Has brought you on the jump to my bellows;
By Saint Neot,[3] you know well what I mean."
　　This Absalom cared not a single bean
665 For all this play, nor one word back he gave;
He'd more tow on his distaff,° had this knave,   *things on his mind*

---

3. Also known as the Pygmy Saint because he was reportedly only 15 inches tall, this monk and hermit was especially venerated in Cornwall.

Than Jarvis knew, and said he: "Friend so dear,
This red-hot coulter in the fireplace here,
Lend it to me, I have a need for it,
670   And I'll return it after just a bit."
Jarvis replied: "Certainly, were it gold
Or a purse filled with yellow coins untold,
Yet should you have it, as I am true smith;
But eh, Christ's foe! What will you do therewith?"
675   "Let that," said Absalom, "be as it may;
I'll tell you all tomorrow, when it's day"—
And caught the coulter then by the cold steel
And softly from the smithy door did steal
And went again up to the wood-wright's wall.
680   He coughed at first, and then he knocked withal
Upon the window, as before, with care.
This Alison replied: "Now who is there?
And who knocks so? I'll warrant it's a thief."
"Why no," quoth he, "God knows, my sweet roseleaf,
685   I am your Absalom, my own darling!
Of gold," quoth he, "I have brought you a ring;
My mother gave it me, as I'll be saved;
Fine gold it is, and it is well engraved;
This will I give you for another kiss."
690   This Nicholas had risen for a piss,
And thought that it would carry on the jape
To have his arse kissed by this jack-a-nape.
And so he opened window hastily,
And put his arse out thereat, quietly,
695   Over the buttocks, showing the whole bum;
And thereto said this clerk, this Absalom,
"O speak, sweet bird, I know not where thou art."
This Nicholas just then let fly a fart
As loud as it had been a thunder-clap,
700   And well-nigh blinded Absalom, poor chap;
But he was ready with his iron hot
And Nicholas right in the arse he got.
Off went the skin a hand's-breadth broad, about,
The coulter burned his bottom so, throughout,
705   That for the pain he thought that he should die.
And like one mad he started in to cry,
"Help! Water! Water! Help! For God's dear heart!"
This carpenter out of his sleep did start,
Hearing that "Water!" cried as madman would,
710   And thought, "Alas, now comes down Noel's flood!"
He struggled up without another word
And with his axe he cut in two the cord,
And down went all; he did not stop to trade
In bread or ale till he'd the journey made,
715   And there upon the floor he swooning lay.

Up started Alison and Nicholay
And shouted "Help!" and "Hello!" down the street
The neighbours, great and small, with hastening feet
Swarmed in the house to stare upon this man,
720   Who lay yet swooning, and all pale and wan;
For in the falling he had smashed his arm.
He had to suffer, too, another harm,
For when he spoke he was at once borne down
By clever Nicholas and Alison.
725   For they told everyone that he was odd;
He was so much afraid of "Noel's flood,"
Through fantasy, that out of vanity
He'd gone and bought these kneading-tubs, all three,
And that he'd hung them near the roof above;
730   And that he had prayed them, for God's dear love,
To sit with him and bear him company.
    The people laughed at all this fantasy;
Up to the roof they looked, and there did gape,
And so turned all his injury to a jape.
735   For when this carpenter got in a word,
'Twas all in vain, no man his reasons heard;
With oaths impressive he was so sworn down
That he was held for mad by all the town;
For every clerk did side with every other.
740   They said: "The man is crazy, my dear brother."
And everyone did laugh at all this strife.
Thus futtered was the carpenter's good wife,
For all his watching and his jealousy;
And Absalom has kissed her nether eye;
745   And Nicholas is branded on the butt.
This tale is done, and God save all the rout!°   *troop*

* * *

The Wife of Bath's Prologue

"Experience, though no authority
Were in this world, were° good enough for me,   *would be*
To speak of woe that is in all marriage;
For, masters, since I was twelve years of age,
5   Thanks be to God Who is for aye° alive,   *ever*
Of husbands at church door have I had five;
For men so many times have wedded me;
And all were worthy men in their degree.°   *rank*
But someone told me not so long ago
10   That since Our Lord, save once, would never go
To wedding (that at Cana in Galilee),[1]

1. Site of Jesus's first miracle (John 2:1–10). This was a standard passage for arguments in favor of monogamy, dating back to St. Jerome, from whose treatise *Adversus Jovinianum* (393) the bulk of the scriptural argument that follows was drawn.

Thus, by this same example, showed He me
I never should have married more than once.
Lo and behold! What sharp words, for the nonce,
15   Beside a well Lord Jesus, God and man,
Spoke in reproving the Samaritan:
'For thou hast had five husbands,' thus said He,
'And he whom thou hast now to be with thee
Is not thine husband.'[2] Thus He said that day,
20   But what He meant thereby I cannot say;
And I would ask now why that same fifth man
Was not husband to the Samaritan?
How many might she have, then, in marriage?
For I have never heard, in all my age,
25   Clear exposition of this number shown,
Though men may guess and argue up and down.[3]
But well I know and say, and do not lie,
God bade us to increase and multiply;
That worthy text can I well understand.
30   And well I know He said, too, my husband
Should father leave, and mother, and cleave to me;[4]
But no specific number mentioned He,
Whether of bigamy or octogamy;°   *eight marriages*
Why should men speak of it reproachfully?
35   "Lo, there's the wise old king Dan Solomon;
I understand he had more wives than one;[5]
And now would God it were permitted me
To be refreshed one half as oft as he!
Which gift of God he had for all his wives!
40   No man has such that in this world now lives.
God knows, this noble king, it strikes my wit,
The first night he had many a merry fit
With each of them, so much he was alive!
Praise be to God that I have wedded five!
45   Welcome the sixth whenever come he shall.
Forsooth,° I'll not keep chaste for good and all;   *truly*
When my good husband from the world is gone,
Some Christian man shall marry me anon;
Of whom I did pick out and choose the best
50   Both for their nether° purse and for their chest.   *lower*
Different schools make divers perfect clerks,
Different methods learned in sundry works
Make the good workman perfect, certainly.
Of full five husbands tutoring am I.

---

2. John 4:5–30.
3. The Wife of Bath avoids the plain sense of the passage by claiming it must have some obscure mystical meaning.
4. Following standard practice in biblical interpretation, she counters one biblical precept with several others that seem to give the opposite instructions: God's instruction to Adam and Eve to "increase and multiply" (Genesis 1:28) and Jesus's words in Matthew 19:5–6 (in fact arguing against divorce), citing Adam and Eve.
5. King Solomon had a thousand wives and concubines (1 Kings 11:3).

55   For then, the apostle° says that I am free   *Paul*
      To wed, in God's name, where it pleases me.
      He says that to be wedded is no sin;
      Better to marry than to burn within.[6]
      What care I though folk speak reproachfully
60   Of wicked Lamech and his bigamy?
      I know well Abraham was holy man,
      And Jacob, too, as far as know I can;
      And each of them had spouses more than two;
      And many another holy man also.[7]
65   Or can you say that you have ever heard
      That God has ever by His express word
      Marriage forbidden? Pray you, now, tell me;
      Or where commanded He virginity?
      I read as well as you no doubt have read
70   The apostle when he speaks of maidenhead;
      He said, commandment of the Lord he'd none.
      Men may advise a woman to be one,
      But such advice is not commandment, no;
      He left the thing to our own judgment so.[8]
75   For had Lord God commanded maidenhood,
      He'd have condemned all marriage as not good;
      And certainly, if there were no seed sown,
      Virginity—where then should it be grown?[9]
      Paul dared not to forbid us, at the least,
80   A thing whereof his Master'd no behest.°   *injunction*
      The dart° is set up for virginity;   *prize*
      Catch it who can; who runs best let us see.
          "But this word is not meant for every wight,
      But where God wills to give it, of His might.
85   I know well that the apostle was a maid;°   *virgin*
      Nevertheless, and though he wrote and said
      He would that everyone were such as he,
      All is not counsel to virginity;
      And so to be a wife he gave me leave
90   Out of permission; there's no shame should grieve
      In marrying me, if that my mate should die,
      Without exception,° too, of bigamy.   *objection*
      And though 'twere good no woman's flesh to touch,
      He meant, in his own bed or on his couch;
95   For peril 'tis fire and tow to assemble;
      You know what this example may resemble.[1]

---

6. Quoting 1 Corinthians 7:9 and 7:28.
7. Lamech was a descendant of the accursed Cain who was considered to have been the first bigamist (Genesis 4:19–24). By contrast, Abraham and Jacob were biblical patriarchs who also had several wives.
8. According to Paul, "if a virgin marry, she hath not sinned," since there was no commandment against

marriage (1 Corinthians 7:25 and 28), but he did advise even those who had wives to remain celibate (7:29).
9. How would virgins be born unless people have sex?
1. 1 Corinthians 7:1: "It is good for a man not to touch a woman"; Alisoun adds a proverb ("example") that fire and tow (flax or hemp) placed too closely together will burn.

This is the sum: he held virginity
Nearer perfection than marriage for° frailty.   *out of*
And frailty's all, I say, save° he and she   *unless*
100   Would lead their lives throughout in chastity.
    "I grant this well, I have no great envy
Though maidenhood's preferred to bigamy;
Let those who will be clean, body and ghost,°   *soul*
Of my condition I will make no boast.
105   For well you know, a lord in his household,
He has not every vessel all of gold;
Some are of wood and serve well all their days.
God calls folk unto Him in sundry° ways,   *diverse*
And each one has from God a proper gift,
110   Some this, some that, as pleases Him to shift.
    "Virginity is great perfection known,
And continence e'en° with devotion shown.   *equally*
But Christ, Who of perfection is the well,
Bade not each separate man he should go sell
115   All that he had and give it to the poor
And follow Him in such wise going before.[2]
He spoke to those that would live perfectly;
And, masters, by your leave, such am not I.
I will devote the flower of all my age
120   To all the acts and harvests of marriage.
    "Tell me also, to what purpose or end
The genitals were made, that I defend,
And for what benefit was man first wrought?[3]
Trust you right well, they were not made for naught°   *nothing*
125   Explain who will and argue up and down
That they were made for passing out, as known,
Of urine, and our two belongings small
Were just to tell a female from a male,
And for no other cause—ah, say you no?
130   Experience knows well it is not so;
And, so the clerics be not with me wroth,°   *angry*
I say now that they have been made for both,
That is to say, for duty and for ease
In getting,° when we do not God displease.   *procreation*
135   Why should men otherwise in their books set
That man shall pay unto his wife his debt?°   *marital duty*
Now wherewith should he ever make payment,
Except he used his blessed instrument?
Then on a creature were devised these things
140   For urination and engenderings.

2. Matthew 19:21: "If thou wilt be perfect, go and sell
what thou hast, and give to the poor, and thou shalt have
treasure in heaven: and come and follow me."
3. Here, as most of her other arguments in favor of sexual

activity, the Wife of Bath closely echoes Jean de Meun's
continuation of *The Romance of the Rose,* which Chaucer
had translated from the French.

"But I say not that every one is bound,
Who's fitted out and furnished as I've found,
To go and use it to beget an heir;
Then men would have for chastity no care.
145 Christ was a maid, and yet shaped like a man,
And many a saint, since this old world began,
Yet has lived ever in perfect chastity.
I bear no malice to virginity;
Let such be bread of purest white wheat-seed,
150 And let us wives be called but barley bread;
And yet with barley bread (if Mark you scan)
Jesus Our Lord refreshed full many a man.[4]
In such condition as God places us
I'll persevere, I'm not fastidious.
155 In wifehood I will use my instrument
As freely as my Maker has it sent.
If I be niggardly,° God give me sorrow!   *stingy*
My husband he shall have it, eve and morrow,
When he's pleased to come forth and pay his debt.
160 I'll not delay, a husband I will get
Who shall be both my debtor and my thrall°   *slave*
And have his tribulations therewithal
Upon his flesh, the while I am his wife.
I have the power during all my life
165 Over his own good body, and not he.
For thus the apostle told it unto me;
And bade our husbands that they love us well.[5]
And all this pleases me wherof I tell."
        Up rose the pardoner, and that anon.
170 "Now dame," said he, "by God and by Saint John,
You are a noble preacher in this case!
I was about to wed a wife, alas!
Why should I buy this on° my flesh so dear?   *with*
No, I would rather wed no wife this year."
175   "But wait," said she, "my tale is not begun;
Nay, you shall drink from out another tun°   *barrel*
Before I cease, and savour worse than ale.
And when I shall have told you all my tale
Of tribulation that is in marriage,
180 Whereof I've been an expert all my age,
That is to say, myself have been the whip,
Then may you choose whether you will so sip
Out of very tun which I shall broach.
Beware of it ere you too near approach;
185 For I shall give examples more than ten.

4. Jesus made enough food to feed five thousand out of five barley loaves and two small fishes. Bread made from barley was considered very low fare.

5. This is not exactly what Paul intended by his metaphors of debt and subordination (1 Corinthians 7:3–5), which advised husband and wife rather to be sparing in their possession of each other.

Whoso will not be warned by other men
By him shall other men corrected be.
The self-same words has written Ptolemy;
Read in his Almagest and find it there."[6]
190   "Lady, I pray you, if your will it were,"
Spoke up this pardoner, "as you began,
Tell forth your tale, nor spare° for any man,   refrain
And teach us younger men of your technique."
"Gladly," said she, "since it may please, not pique.°   offend
195   But yet I pray of all this company
That if I speak from my own phantasy,°   fancy
They will not take amiss the things I say;
For my intention's only but to play.
"Now, sirs, now will I tell you forth my tale.
200   And as I may drink ever wine and ale,
I will tell truth of husbands that I've had,
For three of them were good and two were bad.
The three were good men and were rich and old.
Not easily could they the promise hold
205   Whereby they had been bound to cherish me.
You know well what I mean by that, pardie!°   indeed
So help me God, I laugh now when I think
How pitifully by night I made them swink;°   toil
And by my faith I set by it no store.°   pay it no heed
210   They'd given me their gold, and treasure more;
I needed not do longer diligence
To win their love, or show them reverence.
They all loved me so well, by God above,
I never did set value on their love!
215   A woman wise will strive continually
To get herself loved, when she's not, you see.
But since I had them wholly in my hand,
And since to me they'd given all their land,
Why should I take heed, then, that I should please,
220   Save it were for my profit or my ease?
I set them so to work, that, by my fay,°   faith
Full many a night they sighed out 'Welaway!'°   woe is me
The bacon was not brought them home, I trow,°   trust
That some men have in Essex at Dunmowe.[7]
225   I governed them so well, by my own law,
That each of them was happy as a daw,°   crow
And fain to bring me fine things from the fair.
And they were right glad when I spoke them fair;°   kindly
For God knows that I nagged them mercilessly.
230   "Now hearken how I bore me properly,

---

6. The *Almagest*, written around 150 C.E. by the Greek astronomer and mathematician Ptolemy.

7. It was long the custom in this town to award a side of bacon to any married couple who managed not to quarrel for at least a year.

All you wise wives that well can understand.
    "Thus shall you speak and wrongfully demand;
For half so brazenfacedly can no man
Swear to his lying as a woman can.
235 I say not this to wives who may be wise,
Except when they themselves do misadvise.
A wise wife, if she knows what's for her good,
Will swear the crow is mad, and in this mood
Call up for witness to it her own maid;[8]
240 But hear me now, for this is what I said.[9]
    "'Sir Dotard,° is it thus you stand today?   *old imbecile*
Why is my neighbour's wife so fine and gay?
She's honoured over all where'er she goes;
I sit at home, I have no decent clo'es.
245 What do you do there at my neighbour's house?
Is she so fair? Are you so amorous?
Why whisper to our maid? *Benedicite!*°   *bless us*
Sir Lecher old, let your seductions be!
And if I have a gossip or a friend,
250 Innocently, you blame me like a fiend
If I but walk, for company, to his house!
You come home here as drunken as a mouse,
And preach there on your bench, a curse on you!
You tell me it's a great misfortune, too,
255 To wed a girl who costs more than she's worth;
And if she's rich and of a higher birth,
You say it's torment to abide her folly
And put up with her pride and melancholy.
And if she be right fair, you utter knave,
260 You say that every lecher will her have;
She may no while in chastity abide
That is assailed by all and on each side.
    "'You say, some men desire us for our gold,
Some for our shape and some for fairness told;
265 And some, that she can either sing or dance,
And some, for courtesy and dalliance;
Some for her hands and for her arms so small;
Thus all goes to the devil in your tale.
You say men cannot keep a castle wall
270 That's long assailed on all sides, and by all.[1]
    "'And if that she be foul, you say that she
Hankers for every man that she may see;
For like a spaniel will she leap on him

---

8. In a common fable, a talking crow informs a husband
of his wife's infidelity; her maid backs up her lies.
9. Alisoun's exhaustive response is composed of passages
from several well-worn misogynist treatises, including
Theophrastus, Jerome, Matheolus, Jean de Meun, and

Eustache Deschamps.
1. In *The Romance of the Rose,* from which these and the
following lines are adapted, the Rose is imprisoned in a
castle which the Lover is determined to take by any
means.

Until she finds a man to be victim;
275 And not a grey goose swims there in the lake
But finds a gander willing her to take.
You say, it is a hard thing to enfold
Her whom no man will in his own arms hold.
This say you, worthless, when you go to bed;
280 And that no wise man needs thus to be wed,
No, nor a man that hearkens unto Heaven.
With furious thunder-claps and fiery levin°   *lightning*
May your thin, withered, wrinkled neck be broke;
"'You say that dripping eaves, and also smoke,
285 And wives contentious, will make men to flee
But of their houses; ah, *benedicite!*
What ails such an old fellow so to chide?
"'You say that all we wives our vices hide
Till we are married, then we show them well;
290 That is a scoundrel's proverb, let me tell!
"'You say that oxen, asses, horses, hounds
Are tried out variously, and on good grounds;
Basins and bowls, before men will them buy,
And spoons and stools and all such goods you try,
295 And so with pots and clothes and all array;
But of their wives men get no trial, you say,
Till they are married, base old dotard you!
And then we show what evil we can do.
"'You say also that it displeases me
300 Unless you praise and flatter my beauty,
And save° you gaze always upon my face   *unless*
And call me "lovely lady" every place;
And save you make a feast upon that day
When I was born, and give me garments gay;
305 And save due honour to my nurse is paid
As well as to my faithful chambermaid,
And to my father's folk and his allies—
Thus you go on, old barrel full of lies!
"'And yet of our apprentice, young Jenkin,
310 For his crisp hair, showing like gold so fine,
Because he squires me walking up and down,
A false suspicion in your mind is sown;
I'd give him naught, though you were dead tomorrow.
"'But tell me this, why do you hide, with sorrow,
315 The keys to your strong box away from me?
It is my gold as well as yours, pardie.
Why would you make an idiot of your dame?
Now by Saint James,[2] but you shall miss your aim,
You shall not be, although like mad you scold,
320 Master of both my body and my gold;

2. Alisoun has made a pilgrimage to the shrine of St. James at Compostela.

One you'll forgo in spite of both your eyes;
Why need you seek me out or set on spies?
I think you'd like to lock me in your chest!
You should say: "Dear wife, go where you like best,
325   Amuse yourself, I will believe no tales;
You're my wife Alis true, and truth prevails."
We love no man that guards us or gives charge
Of where we go, for we will be at large.
      "'Of all men the most blessed may he be,
330   That wise astrologer, Dan Ptolemy,
Who says this proverb in his Almagest;
"Of all men he's in wisdom the highest
That nothing cares who has the world in hand."
And by this proverb shall you understand:
335   Since you've enough, why do you reck° or care   *worry*
How merrily all other folks may fare?
For certainly, old dotard, by your leave,
You shall have cunt all right enough at eve.
He is too much a niggard who's so tight
340   That from his lantern he'll give none a light.
For he'll have never the less light, by gad;
Since you've enough, you need not be so sad.
      "'You say, also, that if we make us gay
With clothing, all in costliest array,
345   That it's a danger to our chastity;
And you must back the saying up, pardie!
Repeating these words in the apostle's° name: *Paul's*
"In habits meet for chastity, not shame,
Your women shall be garmented," said he,
350   "And not with broidered hair, or jewellery,
Or pearls, or gold, or costly gowns and chic";
After your text and after your rubric°   *heading*
I will not follow more than would a gnat.
You said this, too, that I was like a cat;
355   For if one care to singe a cat's furred skin,
Then would the cat remain the house within;
And if the cat's coat be all sleek and gay,
She will not keep in house a half a day,
But out she'll go, ere° dawn of any day,   *before*
360   To show her skin and caterwaul° and play.   *howl like a cat*
This is to say, if I'm a little gay,
To show my rags I'll gad about all day.
      "'Sir Ancient Fool, what ails you with your spies?
Though you pray Argus, with his hundred eyes,
365   To be my body-guard and do his best,[3]

---

3. Argus was a 100-eyed watchman in Greek and Roman myth who never closed all of his eyes at once. He was set by the jealous goddess Juno to guard the mortal woman Io and to prevent her husband Jupiter from sleeping with her. He did not succeed.

Faith, he sha'n't hold me, save I am modest;
I could delude him easily—trust me!
    "'You said, also, that there are three things—three—
The which things are a trouble on this earth,
370   And that no man may ever endure the fourth:
O dear Sir Rogue, may Christ cut short your life!
Yet do you preach and say a hateful wife
Is to be reckoned one of these mischances.
Are there no other kinds of resemblances
375   That you may liken thus your parables to,
But must a hapless wife be made to do?
    "'You liken woman's love to very Hell,
To desert land where waters do not well.
You liken it, also, unto wildfire;
380   The more it burns, the more it has desire
To consume everything that burned may be.
You say that just as worms destroy a tree,
Just so a wife destroys her own husband;
Men know this who are bound in marriage band.'
385   "Masters, like this, as you must understand,
Did I my old men charge and censure, and
Claim that they said these things in drunkenness;
And all was false, but yet I took witness
Of Jenkin and of my dear niece also.
390   O Lord, the pain I gave them and the woe,
All guiltless, too, by God's grief exquisite!
For like a stallion could I neigh and bite.
I could complain, though mine was all the guilt,
Or else, full many a time, I'd lost the tilt.°   *joust*
395   Whoso comes first to mill first gets meal ground;
I whimpered first and so did them confound.
They were right glad to hasten to excuse
Things they had never done, save in my ruse,
    "With wenches would I charge him, by this hand,
400   When, for some illness, he could hardly stand.
Yet tickled this the heart of him, for he
Deemed it was love produced such jealousy.
I swore that all my walking out at night
Was but to spy on girls he kept outright;
405   And under cover of that I had much mirth.
For all such wit is given us at birth;
Deceit, weeping, and spinning, does God give
To women, naturally, the while they live.
And thus of one thing I speak boastfully,
410   I got the best of each one, finally,
By trick, or force, or by some kind of thing,
As by continual growls or murmuring;
Especially in bed had they mischance,
There would I chide and give them no pleasance;

415   I would no longer in the bed abide
     If I but felt his arm across my side,
     Till he had paid his ransom unto me;
     Then would I let him do his nicety.
     And therefore to all men this tale I tell,
420   Let gain who may, for everything's to sell.
     With empty hand men may no falcons lure;
     For profit would I all his lust endure,
     And make for him a well-feigned appetite;
     Yet I in bacon never had delight;
425   And that is why I used so much to chide.
     For if the pope were seated there beside
     I'd not have spared them, no, at their own board.°   *table*
     For by my truth, I paid them, word for word.
     So help me the True God Omnipotent,
430   Though I right now should make my testament,
     I owe them not a word that was not quit.°   *repaid*
     I brought it so about, and by my wit,
     That they must give it up, as for the best,
     Or otherwise we'd never have had rest.
435   For though he glared and scowled like lion mad,
     Yet failed he of the end he wished he had.
        "Then would I say: 'Good dearie, see you keep
     In mind how meek is Wilkin, our old sheep;
     Come near, my spouse, come let me kiss your cheek!
440   You should be always patient, aye, and meek,
     And have a sweetly scrupulous tenderness,
     Since you so preach of old Job's patience, yes.
     Suffer always, since you so well can preach;
     And, save you do, be sure that we will teach
445   That it is well to leave a wife in peace.
     One of us two must bow,° to be at ease;   *submit*
     And since a man's more reasonable, they say,
     Than woman is, you must have patience aye,
     What ails you that you grumble thus and groan?
450   Is it because you'd have my cunt alone?
     Why take it all, lo, have it every bit;
     Peter!° Beshrew° you but you're fond of it!   *By St. Peter / curse*
     For if I would go peddle my *belle chose*,°   *beautiful thing*
     I could walk out as fresh as is a rose;
455   But I will keep it for your own sweet tooth.
     You are to blame, by God I tell the truth.'
        "Such were the words I had at my command.
     Now will I tell you of my fourth husband.
        "My fourth husband, he was a reveller,
460   That is to say, he kept a paramour;
     And young and full of passion then was I,
     Stubborn and strong and jolly as a pie.°   *magpie*
     Well could I dance to tune of harp, nor fail

To sing as well as any nightingale
465   When I had drunk a good draught of sweet wine.
Metellius, the foul churl and the swine,
Did with a staff deprive his wife of life
Because she drank wine;[4] had I been his wife
He never should have frightened me from drink;
470   For after wine, of Venus must I think:
For just as surely as cold produces hail,
A liquorish° mouth must have a lickerish° tail.   *greedy / lecherous*
In women wine's no bar of impotence,
This know all lechers by experience.
475   "But Lord Christ! When I do remember me
Upon my youth and on my jollity,
It tickles me about my heart's deep root.
To this day does my heart sing in salute
That I have had my world in my own time
480   But age, alas! that poisons every prime.
Has taken away my beauty and my pith;°   *vigor*
Let go, farewell, the devil go therewith!
The flour is gone, there is no more to tell,
The bran, as best I may, must I now sell;
485   But yet to be right merry I'll try, and
Now will I tell you of my fourth husband.
        "I say that in my heart I'd great despite
When he of any other had delight.
But he was quit, by God and by Saint Joce![5]
490   I made, of the same wood, a staff most gross;°   *paid him back in kind*
Not with my body and in manner foul,
But certainly I showed so gay a soul
That in his own thick grease I made him fry
For anger and for utter jealousy.
495   By God, on earth I was his purgatory,
For which I hope his soul lives now in glory.
For God knows, many a time he sat and sung
When the shoe bitterly his foot had wrung
There was no one, save God and he, that knew
500   How, in so many ways, I'd twist the screw.
He died when I came from Jerusalem,
And lies entombed beneath the great rood-beam,°   *crossbeam*
Although his tomb is not so glorious
As was the sepulchre of Darius,
505   The which Apelles wrought full cleverly;[6]
'Twas waste to bury him expensively.
Let him fare well. God give his soul good rest,

---

4. Alisoun refers to an ancient Roman incident of a man who beat his wife to death with a staff for drinking wine.
5. St. Jodocus, or Josse, was a Breton king who abdicated after a pilgrimage to Rome and became a hermit.

6. The Persian ruler Darius III was an opponent of Alexander the Great in the 4th century B.C.E. The story of his tomb comes from a medieval romance about Alexander.

He now is in the grave and in his chest.°   *coffin*
   "And now of my fifth husband will I tell.
510 God grant his soul may never get to Hell
And yet he was to me most brutal, too;
My ribs yet feel as they were black and blue,
And ever shall, until my dying day.
But in our bed he was so fresh and gay,
515 And therewithal he could so well impose,
What time he wanted use of my *belle chose,*
That though he'd beaten me on every bone,
He could re-win my love, and that full soon.
I guess I loved him best of all, for he
520 Gave of his love most sparingly to me.
We women have, if I am not to lie,
In this love matter, a quaint fantasy;
Look out a thing we may not lightly have,
And after that we'll cry all day and crave.
525 Forbid a thing, and that thing covet we;
Press hard upon us, then we turn and flee.
Sparingly offer we our goods, when fair;
Great crowds at market make for dearer ware,
And what's too common brings but little price;
530 All this knows every woman who is wise.
   "My fifth husband, may God his spirit bless!
Whom I took all for love, and not riches,
Had been sometime a student at Oxford,
And had left school and had come home to board
535 With my best gossip,° dwelling in our town,   *friend*
God save her soul! Her name was Alison.
She knew my heart and all my privity°   *secrets*
Better than did our parish priest, s'help me!
To her confided I my secrets all.
540 For had my husband pissed against a wall,
Or done a thing that might have cost his life,
To her and to another worthy wife,
And to my niece whom I loved always well,
I would have told it—every bit I'd tell,
545 And did so, many and many a time, God wot,°   *knows*
Which made his face full often red and hot
For utter shame; he blamed himself that he
Had told me of so deep a privity.
   "So it befell that on a time, in Lent[7]
550 (For oftentimes I to my gossip went,
Since I loved always to be glad and gay
And to walk out, in March, April, and May,

---

7. The springtime period of Lent was supposed to be a time of fasting and penitence leading up to Holy Week and Easter.

From house to house, to hear the latest malice),
Jenkin the clerk, and my gossip Dame Alis,
555   And I myself into the meadows went.
My husband was in London all that Lent;
I had the greater leisure, then, to play,
And to observe, and to be seen, I say,
By pleasant folk; what knew I where my face
560   Was destined to be loved, or in what place?
Therefore I made my visits round about
To vigils and processions of devout,
To preaching too, and shrines of pilgrimage,
To miracle plays, and always to each marriage,
565   And wore my scarlet skirt before all wights.
These worms and all these moths and all these mites,
I say it at my peril, never ate;
And know you why? I wore it early and late.°   *all the time*
        "Now will I tell you what befell to me.
570   I say that in the meadows walked we three
Till, truly, we had come to such dalliance,
This clerk and I, that, of my vigilance,°   *in my foresight*
I spoke to him and told him how that he,
Were I a widow, might well marry me.
575   For certainly I say it not to brag,
But I was never quite without a bag
Full of the needs of marriage that I seek.
I hold a mouse's heart not worth a leek
That has but one hole into which to run,
580   And if it fail of that, then all is done.
        "I made him think he had enchanted me;
My mother taught me all that subtlety.
And then I said I'd dreamed of him all night,
He would have slain me as I lay upright,
585   And all my bed was full of very blood;
But yet I hoped that he would do me good,
For blood betokens gold, as I was taught.
And all was false, I dreamed of him just—naught,
Save as I acted on my mother's lore,
590   As well in this thing as in many more.
        "But now, let's see, what was I going to say?
Aha, by God, I know! It goes this way.
        "When my fourth husband lay upon his bier,
I wept enough and made but sorry cheer,
595   As wives must always, for it's custom's grace,
And with my kerchief covered up my face;
But since I was provided with a mate,
I really wept but little. I may state.
        "To church my man was borne upon the morrow
600   By neighbours, who for him made signs of sorrow;
And Jenkin, our good clerk, was one of them.

So help me God, when rang the requiem
After the bier, I thought he had a pair
Of legs and feet so clean-cut and so fair
605   That all my heart I gave to him to hold.
He was, I think, but twenty winters old,
And I was forty, if I tell the truth;
But then I always had a young colt's tooth.°   *youthful tastes*
Gap-toothed I was, and that became me well;
610   I had the print of holy Venus' seal.°   *a birthmark*
So help me God, I was a healthy one,
And fair and rich and young and full of fun;
And truly, as my husbands all told me,
I had the silkiest *quoniam*° that could be.   *you-know-what*
615   For truly, I am all Venusian
In feeling, and my brain is Martian.[8]
Venus gave me my lust, my lickerishness,
And Mars gave me my sturdy hardiness.
Taurus was my ascendant, with Mars therein.[9]
620   Alas, alas, that ever love was sin!
I followed always my own inclination
By virtue of my natal constellation;[1]
Which wrought me so I never could withdraw
My Venus-chamber from a good fellow.
625   Yet have I Mars's mark° upon my face,   *birthmark*
And also in another private place.
For God so truly my salvation be
As I have never loved for policy,
But ever followed my own appetite,
630   Though he were short or tall, or black or white;
I took no heed, so that° he cared for me,   *as long as*
How poor he was nor even of what degree.°   *estate*
      "What should I say now, save, at the month's end,
This jolly, gentle, Jenkin clerk, my friend,
635   Had wedded me full ceremoniously,
And to him gave I all the land and fee°   *goods*
That ever had been given me before;
But later I repented me full sore.
He never suffered me to have my way.
640   By God, he smote me on the ear, one day,
Because I tore out of his book a leaf,°   *folio page*
So that from this my ear is grown quite deaf.
Stubborn I was as is a lioness,
And with my tongue a very jay, I guess,

8. Her feelings are dominated by the planet Venus and ruled by love; her brain is dominated by the planet Mars and ruled by conflict.
9. Alisoun was born under Taurus, the second sign of the zodiac, ruled by Venus. Mars was also passing through Taurus at that time; hence the double influence.
1. By contrast, the proper approach for a medieval Christian would be to accept the influence of the stars and use his or her will to overcome their sinful aspects.

645   And walk I would, as I had done before,
        From house to house, though I should not, he swore.
        For which he often times would sit and preach
        And read old Roman tales to me and teach
        How one Sulpicius Gallus left his wife
650   And her forsook for term of all his life
        Because he saw her with bared head, I say,
        Looking out from his door, upon a day.[2]
             "Another Roman told he of by name
        Who, since his wife was at a summer-game
655   Without his knowing, he forsook her eke,[3]
        And then would he within his Bible seek
        That proverb of the old Ecclesiast[4]
        Where he commands so freely and so fast
        That man forbid his wife to gad about;
660   Then would he thus repeat, with never doubt:
             'Whoso would build his whole house out of sallows,°   *willow branches*
             And spur his blind horse to run over fallows,°   *ploughed land*
             And let his wife alone go seeking hallows,°   *shrines*
             Is worthy to be hanged upon the gallows.'
665   But all for naught, I didn't care a haw°   *at all*
        For all his proverbs, nor for his old saw,°   *saying*
        Nor yet would I by him corrected be.
        I hate one that my vices tells to me,
        And so do more of us—God knows!—than I.
670   This made him mad with me, and furiously,
        That I'd not yield to him in any case.
             "Now will I tell you truth, by Saint Thomas,
        Of why I tore from out his book a leaf,
        For which he struck me so it made me deaf.
675   "He had a book that gladly, night and day,
        For his amusement he would read alway.
        He called it 'Theophrastus' and 'Valerius,'[5]
        At which book would he laugh, uproarious.
        And, too, there sometime was a clerk at Rome,
680   A cardinal, that men called Saint Jerome,
        Who made a book against Jovinian;
        In which book, too, there was Tertullian,
        Chrysippus, Trotula, and Heloïse
        Who was abbess near Paris' diocese;
685   And too, the *Proverbs* of King Solomon,
        And Ovid's *Art,* and books full many a one,

---

2. The *Memorable Deeds and Sayings* of Valerius Maximus (1st century C.E.) recorded this "harsh" but "logical"
choice of the consul Gaius Suspicius Gallus.
3. Valerius Maximus also recorded this anecdote about the
consul Publius Sempronius Sophus divorcing his wife.

4. The author of the biblical book, Ecclesiasticus, a collection of maxims.
5. Authors of two famous Latin tracts against marriage.

And all of these were bound in one volume.[6]
And every night and day 'twas his custom,
When he had leisure and took some vacation
690 From all his other worldly occupation,
To read, within this book, of wicked wives.
He knew of them more legends and more lives
Than are of good wives written in the Bible.
For trust me, it's impossible, no libel,
695 That any cleric shall speak well of wives,
Unless it be of saints and holy lives,
But naught for other women will they do.
Who painted first the lion, tell me who?[7]
By God, if women had but written stories,
700 As have these clerks within their oratories,°   *chapels*
They would have written of men more wickedness
Than all the race of Adam could redress.
The children of Mercury and of Venus
Are in their lives antagonistic thus;
705 For Mercury loves wisdom and science,
And Venus loves but pleasure and expense.
Because they different dispositions own,
Each falls when other's in ascendant shown.
And God knows Mercury is desolate
710 In Pisces, wherein Venus rules in state;
And Venus falls when Mercury is raised;
Therefore no woman by a clerk is praised.[8]
A clerk, when he is old and can naught do
Of Venus' labours worth his worn-out shoe,
715 Then sits he down and writes, in his dotage,
That women cannot keep vow of marriage!
    "But now to tell you, as I started to,
Why I was beaten for a book, *pardieu.*°   *by God*
Upon a night Jenkin, who was our sire,
720 Read in his book, as he sat by the fire,
Of Mother Eve who, by her wickedness,
First brought mankind to all his wretchedness,
For which Lord Jesus Christ Himself was slain,
Who, with His heart's blood, saved us thus again.
725 Lo here, expressly of woman, may you find
That woman was the ruin of mankind.

---

6. Jenkins's volume contains key sources in clerkly misogyny, from the church fathers Jerome and Tertullian, the Bible, and the Roman poet Ovid (Volume A). Unusually, his collection includes the writings of two women: Trotula, a medieval physician who wrote several works on gynecology; and Heloïse (see page 856), who argued against marriage with her lover Abelard, before becoming an abbess.
7. The Wife of Bath refers to a fable first told by Aesop,
and more recently by Marie de France, that recounts the response of a lion when confronted with the image of a peasant killing a lion.
8. Another astrological explanation: the planet Mercury was associated with the learning proper to the clerk, Venus with the qualities they attributed to women. In terms of the zodiac, when one is ascendant, as Venus in Pisces, the other is descendant—hence, for Alisoun, the conflict between clerks and women.

"Then read he out how Samson lost his hairs,
Sleeping, his leman° cut them with her shears;   *lover*
And through this treason lost he either eye.[9]
730   "Then read he out, if I am not to lie,
Of Hercules, and Deianira's desire
That caused him to go set himself on fire.[1]
            "Nothing escaped him of the pain and woe
That Socrates had with his spouses two;
735   How Xantippe threw piss upon his head;
This hapless man sat still, as he were dead;
He wiped his head, no more durst he complain
Than 'Ere the thunder ceases comes the rain.'[2]
            "Then of Pasiphaë, the queen of Crete,
740   For cursedness he thought the story sweet;
Fie! Say no more—it is an awful thing—
Of her so horrible lust and love-liking.
            "Of Clytemnestra, for her lechery,
Who caused her husband's death by treachery,
745   He read all this with greatest zest, I vow.
            "He told me, too, just when it was and how
Amphiaraus at Thebes lost his life;
My husband had a legend of his wife
Eriphyle who, for a brooch of gold,
750   In secrecy to hostile Greeks had told
Whereat her husband had his hiding place,
For which he found at Thebes but sorry grace.[3]
            "Of Livia and Lucia told he me,
For both of them their husbands killed, you see,
755   The one for love, the other killed for hate;
Livia her husband, on an evening late,
Made drink some poison, for she was his foe.
Lucia, lecherous, loved her husband so
That, to the end he'd always of her think,
760   She gave him such a philtre, for love-drink,
That he was dead or ever it was morrow;
And husbands thus, by same means, came to sorrow.[4]
            "Then did he tell how one Latumius
Complained unto his comrade Arrius
765   That in his garden grew a baleful tree
Whereon, he said, his wives, and they were three,
Had hanged themselves for wretchedness and woe.

---

9. The story of Delilah's betrayal of Samson to the Philistines, by cutting off the hair that gave him his great strength, was originally told in the biblical book of Judges. Like the other passages cited here, it had become proverbial.
1. In fact, Deianira's role in the death of her husband, the hero Hercules, was accidental.
2. Jerome is the source for this version of the philosopher Socrates and his proverbially shrewish wife.

3. Episodes from Greek legend: Pasiphaë's passion for a bull, the adulterous Clytemnestra's murder of her husband Agamemnon on his return from Troy, and Eriphyle's betrayal of her husband's hiding place, sending him to a death in Thebes he had already foreseen.
4. Two episodes from Roman history: Livia was said to have murdered her husband with the help of her lover; Lucia (or Lucilla) was said to have killed her husband, the poet Lucretius, accidentally with a love potion.

'O brother,' Arrius said, 'and did they so?
Give me a graft of that same blessed tree
770 And in my garden planted it shall be!'
     "Of wives of later date he also read,
How some had slain their husbands in their bed
And let their lovers shag them all the night
While corpses lay upon the floor upright.
775 And some had driven nails into the brain
While husbands slept and in such wise were slain.
And some had given them poison in their drink.
He told more evil than the mind can think.
And therewithal he knew of more proverbs
780 Than in this world there grows of grass or herbs.
'Better,' he said, 'your habitation be
With lion wild or dragon foul,' said he,
'Than with a woman who will nag and chide.'
'Better,' he said, 'on the housetop abide
785 Than with a brawling wife down in the house;
Such are so wicked and contrarious
They hate the thing their husband loves, for aye.'
He said, 'a woman throws her shame away
When she throws off her smock,' and further, too:
790 'A woman fair, save she be chaste also,
Is like a ring of gold in a sow's nose.'
Who would imagine or who would suppose
What grief and pain were in this heart of mine?
     "And when I saw he'd never cease, in fine,
795 His reading in this cursed book at night,
Three leaves of it I snatched and tore outright
Out of his book, as he read on; and eke
I with my fist so took him on the cheek
That in our fire he reeled and fell right down.
800 Then he got up as does a wild lion,
And with his fist he struck me on the head,
And on the floor I lay as I were dead.
And when he saw how limp and still I lay,
He was afraid and would have run away,
805 Until at last out of my swoon I made:
'Oh, have you slain me, you false thief?' I said,
'And for my land have you thus murdered me?
Kiss me before I die, and let me be.'
     "He came to me and near me he knelt down,
810 And said: 'O my dear sister Alison,
So help me God, I'll never strike you more;
What I have done, you are to blame therefor.
But all the same forgiveness now I seek!'
And thereupon I hit him on the cheek,
815 And said: 'Thief, so much vengeance do I wreak!
Now will I die, I can no longer speak!'

But at the last, and with much care and woe,
We made it up between ourselves. And so
He put the bridle reins within my hand

820 To have the governing of house and land;
And of his tongue and of his hand, also;
And made him burn his book, right then, oho!
And when I had thus gathered unto me
Masterfully, the entire sovereignty,

825 And he had said: 'My own true wedded wife,
Do as you please the term of all your life,
Guard your own honour and keep fair my state'—
After that day we never had debate.
God help me now, I was to him as kind

830 As any wife from Denmark unto Ind,°   *India*
And also true, and so was he to me.
I pray to God, Who sits in majesty,
To bless his soul, out of His mercy dear!
Now will I tell my tale, if you will hear."

835 The friar laughed when he had heard all this.
"Now dame," said he, "so have I joy or bliss
This is a long preamble to a tale!"
    And when the summoner heard this friar's hail,
"Lo," said the summoner, "by God's arms two!

840 A friar will always interfere, mark you.
Behold, good men, a housefly and a friar
Will fall in every dish and matters higher.[5]
Why speak of preambling, you in your gown?
What! Amble, trot, hold peace, or go sit down;

845 You hinder our diversion thus to inquire."
    "Aye, say you so, sir summoner?" said the friar,
"Now by my faith I will, before I go,
Tell of a summoner such a tale, or so,
That all the folk shall laugh who're in this place."

850 "Otherwise, friar, I beshrew° your face,"   *curse*
Replied this summoner, "and beshrew me
If I do not tell tales here, two or three,
Of friars ere I come to Sittingbourne,[6]
That certainly will give you cause to mourn,

855 For well I know your patience will be gone."
    Our host cried out, "Now peace, and that anon!"
And said he: "Let the woman tell her tale.
You act like people who are drunk with ale.
Do, lady, tell your tale, and that is best."

860 "All ready, sir," said she, "as you request,

5. That is, will eat anything and meddle in any business. There was a longstanding dislike between clergy possessing land and goods and mendicants, who did not.

6. On the pilgrimage route, about 40 miles from London and 16 from Canterbury.

If I have license of° this worthy friar."   *permission from*
    "Yes, dame," said he, "to hear you's my desire."

The Wife of Bath's Tale

Now in the olden days of King Arthur,
Of whom the Britons speak with great honour,
865   All this wide land was land of faëry
The elf-queen, with her jolly company,
Danced often times on many a green mead;°   *meadow*
This was the old opinion, as I read.[1]
I speak of many hundred years ago;
870   But now no man can see the elves, you know.
For now the so-great charity and prayers
Of limiters and other holy friars
That do infest each land and every stream
As thick as motes° are in a bright sunbeam,   *dust particles*
875   Blessing halls, chambers, kitchens, ladies' bowers,°   *chambers*
Cities and towns and castles and high towers,
Manors and barns and stables, aye and dairies—
This causes it that there are now no fairies.[2]
For where was wont to walk full many an elf,
880   Right there walks now the limiter himself
In noons and afternoons and in mornings,
Saying his matins and such holy things,
As he goes round his district in his gown.[3]
Women may now go safely up and down,
885   In every copse° or under every tree;   *thicket*
There is no other incubus than he,[4]
And would do them nothing but dishonour.
        And so befell it that this King Arthur
Had at his court a lusty bachelor°   *young knight*
890   Who, on a day, came riding from river;
And happened that, alone as she was born,
He saw a maiden walking through the corn,
From whom, in spite of all she did and said,
Straightway by force he took her maidenhead;
895   For which violation was there such clamour,
And such appealing unto King Arthur,
That soon condemned was this knight to be dead
By course of law, and should have lost his head,
Peradventure,° such being the statute then;   *as it chanced*

1. Although its specific source is unknown, "The Wife of
Bath's Tale" is drawn from the Matter of Britain, a collection of tales and romances about the deeds of the legendary King Arthur and his court. See also the *lais* of
Marie de France (page 785).
2. In her offhand way, Alisoun allows Chaucer to draw
out an important theme of the Matter of Britain: the tension between the ancient pre-Christian Celtic religion,

including its fairies, elves, and magic, and the Christian
belief system that was replacing it.
3. A friar limiter (allowed to beg within certain limits),
like the one who has just finished interrupting her tale.
4. An incubus was an evil spirit who descended on people
in their sleep; with women especially it sought sexual activity. Their existence was recognized by both church and
state during the Middle Ages.

900   But that the other ladies and the queen
       So long prayed of the king to show him grace,
       He granted life, at last, in the law's place,
       And gave him to the queen, as she should will,
       Whether she'd save him, or his blood should spill.

905   The queen she thanked the king with all her might,
       And after this, thus spoke she to the knight,
       When she'd an opportunity, one day:
       "You stand yet," said she, "in such poor a way
       That for your life you've no security.

910   I'll grant you life if you can tell to me
       What thing it is that women most desire.
       Be wise, and keep your neck from iron dire!°   *dreadful iron*
       And if you cannot tell it me anon,
       Then will I give you license to be gone

915   A twelvemonth° and a day, to search and learn   *year*
       Sufficient answer in this grave concern.
       And your knight's word I'll have, ere forth you pace,
       To yield your body to me in this place."

           Grieved was this knight, and sorrowfully he sighed;
920   But there! he could not do as pleased his pride.
       And at the last he chose that he would wend,°   *depart*
       And come again upon the twelvemonth's end,
       With such an answer as God might purvey;°   *provide*
       And so he took his leave and went his way.

925   He sought out every house and every place
       Wherein he hoped to find that he had grace
       To learn what women love the most of all;
       But nowhere ever did it him befall
       To find, upon the question stated here,

930   Two persons who agreed with statement clear.
           Some said that women all loved best riches,
       Some said, fair fame, and some said, prettiness;
       Some, rich array, some said 'twas lust abed
       And often to be widowed and re-wed.

935   Some said that our poor hearts are aye most eased
       When we have been most flattered and thus pleased
       And he went near the truth, I will not lie;
       A man may win us best with flattery;
       And with attentions and with busyness

940   We're often limed,° the greater and the less.   *ensnared*
           And some say, too, that we do love the best
       To be quite free to do our own behest,
       And that no man reprove us for our vice,
       But saying we are wise, take our advice.

945   For truly there is no one of us all,
       If anyone shall rub us on a gall,°   *sore spot*
       That will not kick because he tells the truth.
       Try, and he'll find who does so, I say sooth.°   *truth*

No matter how much vice we have within,
950   We would be held for wise and clean of sin.
            And some folk say that great delight have we
To be held constant, also trustworthy,
And on one purpose steadfastly to dwell,
And not betray a thing that men may tell.
955   But that tale is not worth a rake's handle;
By God, we women can no thing conceal,
As witness Midas. Would you hear the tale?[5]
            Ovid, among some other matters small,
Said Midas had beneath his long curled hair,
960   Two ass's ears that grew in secret there
The which defect he hid, as best he might,
Full cunningly from every person's sight,
And, save his wife, no one knew of it, no.
He loved her most, and trusted her also;
965   And he prayed of her that to no creature
She'd tell of his disfigurement impure.
            She swore him: Nay, for all this world to win
She would do no such villainy or sin
And cause her husband have so foul a name;
970   Nor would she tell it for her own deep shame.
Nevertheless, she thought she would have died
Because so long the secret must she hide;
It seemed to swell so big about her heart
That some word from her mouth must surely start;
975   And since she dared to tell it to no man,
Down to a marsh, that lay hard by, she ran;
Till she came there her heart was all afire,
And as a bittern booms in the quagmire,
She laid her mouth low to the water down:
980   "Betray me not, you sounding water blown,"
Said she, "I tell it to none else but you:
Long ears like asses' has my husband two!
Now is my heart at ease, since that is out;
I could no longer keep it, there's no doubt."
985   Here may you see, though for a while we bide,
Yet out it must; no secret can we hide.
The rest of all this tale, if you would hear,
Read Ovid: in his book does it appear.
            This knight my tale is chiefly told about
990   When what he went for he could not find out,
That is, the thing that women love the best,
Most saddened was the spirit in his breast;
But home he goes, he could no more delay.
The day was come when home he turned his way;

---

5. Ovid recounts the tale in Book 11 of the *Metamorphoses*, although the Wife of Bath has replaced the original version's barber with a wife.

995   And on his way it chanced that he should ride
       In all his care, beneath a forest's side,
       And there he saw, a-dancing him before,
       Full four and twenty ladies, maybe more;
       Toward which dance eagerly did he turn
1000   In hope that there some wisdom he should learn.
       But truly, ere he came upon them there,
       The dancers vanished all, he knew not where.[6]
       No creature saw he that gave sign of life,
       Save, on the greensward sitting, an old wife;
1005   A fouler person could no man devise.
       Before the knight this old wife did arise,
       And said: "Sir knight, hence lies no travelled way.
       Tell me what thing you seek, and by your fay.
       Perchance you'll find it may the better be;
1010   These ancient folk know many things," said she.
           "Dear mother," said this knight assuredly,
       "I am but dead, save I can tell, truly,
       What thing it is that women most desire;
       Could you inform me, I'd pay well your hire."
1015   "Plight me your troth° here, hand in hand," said she,   *promise me*
       "That you will do, whatever it may be,
       The thing I ask if it lie in your might;
       And I'll give you your answer ere the night."
           "Have here my word," said he. "That thing I grant."
1020   "Then," said the crone, "of this I make my vaunt°   *boast*
       Your life is safe; and I will stand thereby,
       Upon my life, the queen will say as I.
       Let's see which is the proudest of them all
       That wears upon her hair kerchief or caul,°   *ornamented hairnet*
1025   Shall dare say no to that which I shall teach;
       Let us go now and without longer speech."
           Then whispered she a sentence in his ear,
       And bade him to be glad and have no fear.
           When they were come unto the court, this knight
1030   Said he had kept his promise as was right,
       And ready was his answer, as he said.
       Full many a noble wife, and many a maid,
       And many a widow, since they are so wise,
       The queen herself sitting as high justice,
1035   Assembled were, his answer there to hear;
       And then the knight was bidden to appear.[7]
           Command was given for silence in the hall,

---

6. The *locus amoenus*, or pleasing place, reached after a long wandering journey, was a central locale in medieval romance.
7. The setting and the type of question recall the "courts of love" of Eleanor of Aquitaine and her daughter Marie, who had been primarily responsible for reviving the Matter of Britain and who were patrons to many of the most important poets and writers of the time, including Marie de France, Andreas Capellanus, and Chrétien de Troyes.

And that the knight should tell before them all
What thing all worldly women love the best.

1040 This knight did not stand dumb, as does a beast,
But to this question presently answered
With manly voice, so that the whole court heard:
"My liege lady, generally," said he,
"Woman desire to have the sovereignty

1045 As well upon their husband as their love,
And to have mastery their man above;°   *over their man*
This thing you most desire, though me you kill
Do as you please, I am here at your will."
        In all the court there was no wife or maid

1050 Or widow that denied the thing he said,
But all held, he was worthy to have life.
        And with that word up started the old wife
Whom he had seen a-sitting on the green.
"Mercy," cried she, "my sovereign lady queen!

1055 Before the court's dismissed, give me my right.
'Twas I who taught the answer to this knight;
For which he did plight troth to me, out there,
That the first thing I should of him require
He would do that, if it lay in his might.

1060 Before the court, now, pray I you sir knight,"
Said she, "that you will take me for your wife;
For well you know that I have saved your life.
If this be false, say nay, upon your fay!"
        This knight replied: "Alas and welaway!

1065 That I so promised I will not protest.
But for God's love pray make a new request,
Take all my wealth and let my body go."
        "Nay then," said she, "beshrew us if I do!
For though I may be foul and old and poor,

1070 I will not, for all metal and all ore
That from the earth is dug or lies above,
Be aught except your wife and your true love."
        "My love?" cried he, "nay, rather my damnation!
Alas! that any of my race and station

1075 Should ever so dishonoured foully be!"
        But all for naught; the end was this, that he
Was so constrained he needs must go and wed,
And take his ancient wife and go to bed.
        Now, peradventure, would some men say here,

1080 That, of my negligence, I take no care
To tell you of the joy and all the array
That at the wedding feast were seen that day.
Make a brief answer to this thing I shall;
I say, there was no joy or feast at all;

1085 There was but heaviness and grievous sorrow;
For privately he wedded on the morrow,°   *the next day*

And all day, then, he hid him like an owl;[8]
So sad he was, his old wife looked so foul.
 Great was the woe the knight had in his thought
1090 When he, with her, to marriage bed was brought;
He rolled about and turned him to and fro.
His old wife lay there, always smiling so
And said: "O my dear husband, *ben'cite!*
Fares every knight with wife as you with me?
1095 Is this the custom in King Arthur's house?
Are knights of his all so fastidious?
I am your own true love and, more, your wife;
And I am she who saved your very life;
And truly, since I've never done you wrong,
1100 Why do you treat me so, this first night long?
You act as does a man who's lost his wit;
What is my fault? For God's love tell me it,
And it shall be amended, if I may."
 "Amended!" cried this knight, "Alas, nay, nay!
1105 It will not be amended ever, no!
Your are so loathsome, and so old also,
And therewith of so low a race were born,
It's little wonder that I toss and turn.
Would God my heart would break within my breast!"
1110 "Is this," asked she, "the cause of your unrest?"
"Yes, truly," said he, "and no wonder 'tis."
"Now, sir," said she, "I could amend all this,
If I but would, and that within days three,
If you would bear yourself well towards me.
1115 "But since you speak of such gentility
As is descended from old wealth, till ye
Claim that for that you should be gentlemen,
I hold such arrogance not worth a hen.
Find him who is most virtuous alway,
1120 Alone or publicly, and most tries aye
To do whatever noble deeds he can,
And take him for the greatest gentleman.
Christ wills we claim from Him gentility,
Not from ancestors of landocracy.°   *landed gentry*
1125 For though they give us all their heritage,
For which we claim to be of high lineage,
Yet can they not bequeath, in anything,
To any of us, their virtuous living,
That made men say they had gentility,
1130 And bade us follow them in like degree.
 "Well does that poet wise of great Florence,
Called Dante, speak his mind in this sentence;
Somewhat like this may it translated be:

8. Owls emerge only at night.

'Rarely unto the branches of the tree
1135   Doth human worth mount up: and so ordains
He Who bestows it; to Him it pertains.'[9]
For of our fathers may we nothing claim
But temporal things, that man may hurt and maim.
      "And everyone knows this as well as I,
1140   If nobleness were implanted naturally
Within a certain lineage, down the line,
In private and in public, I opine,
The ways of gentleness they'd alway show
And never fall to vice and conduct low.
1145   "Take fire and carry it in the darkest house
Between here and the Mount of Caucasus,°   *east of the Black Sea*
And let men shut the doors and from them turn;
Yet will the fire as fairly blaze and burn
As twenty thousand men did it behold;
1150   Its nature and its office it will hold,
On peril of my life, until it die.
      "From this you see that true gentility
Is not allied to wealth a man may own,
Since folk do not their deeds, as may be shown,
1155   As does the fire, according to its kind.
For God knows that men may full often find
A lord's son doing shame and villainy;
And he that prizes his gentility
In being born of some old noble house,
1160   With ancestors both noble and virtuous,
But will himself do naught of noble deeds
Nor follow him to whose name he succeeds,
He is not gentle,° be he duke or earl;   *noble*
For acting churlish makes a man a churl.
1165   Gentility is not just the renown
Of ancestors who have some greatness shown,
In which you have no portion of your own.
Your own gentility comes from God alone;
Thence comes our true nobility by grace,
1170   It was not willed us with our rank and place
      "Think how noble, as says Valerius,
Was that same Tullius Hostilius,
Who out of poverty rose to high estate.[1]
Seneca and Boethius inculcate,°   *urge*
1175   Expressly (and no doubt it thus proceeds),
That he is noble who does noble deeds;[2]

---

9. The passage is translated from *Purgatorio* 7.121–23, where Dante bemoaned the inability of good character to be transmitted as reliably as a good name. For Dante this demonstrated the difference between fallibly human conceptions of fate and inscrutably divine conceptions of justice.
1. The *Memorable Deeds and Sayings* of Valerius Maximus record the legendary life of the herdsman Tullius Hostilius, who rose to become the third king of Rome.
2. Referring to the *Moral Epistles* of Seneca the Younger (d. 65 C.E.) and to the *Consolation of Philosophy* of the Roman philosopher Boethius, which Chaucer had translated during the 1380s.

And therefore, husband dear, I thus conclude:
Although my ancestors mayhap° were rude,°   *peraps / uncultured*
Yet may the High Lord, and so hope I,
1180   Grant me the grace to live right virtuously.
Then I'll be gentle when I do begin
To live in virtue and to do no sin.
       "And when you me reproach for poverty,
The High God, in Whom we believe, say I,
1185   In voluntary poverty lived His life.
And surely every man, or maid, or wife
May understand that Jesus, Heaven's King,
Would not have chosen vileness of living.
Glad poverty's an honest thing, that's plain,
1190   Which Seneca and other clerks maintain.
Whoso will be content with poverty,
I hold him rich, though not a shirt has he.
And he that covets much is a poor wight,
For he would gain what's all beyond his might
1195   But he that has not, nor desires to have,
Is rich, although you hold him but a knave.
       "True poverty, it sings right naturally;
Juvenal gaily says of poverty:³
'The poor man, when he walks along the way,
1200   Before the robbers he may sing and play.'
Poverty's odious good, and, as I guess,
It is a stimulant to busyness;
A great improver, too, of sapience
In him that takes it all with due patience.
1205   Poverty's this, though it seem misery—
Its quality may none dispute, say I.
Poverty often, when a man is low,
Makes him his God and even himself to know.
And poverty's an eye-glass, seems to me,
1210   Through which a man his loyal friends may see.
Since you've received no injury from me,
Then why reproach me for my poverty.
       "Now, sir, with age you have upbraided me;
And truly, sir, though no authority
1215   Were in a book, you gentles° of honour   *gentle folk*
Say that men should the aged show favour,
And call him father, of your gentleness;
And authors could I find for this, I guess.
       "Now since you say that I am foul and old,
1220   Then fear you not to be made a cuckold;
For dirt and age, as° prosperous I may be,   *however*
Are mighty wardens over chastity.

---

3. The Roman satirist Juvenal, in his tenth Satire.

Nevertheless, since I know your delight,
I'll satisfy your worldly appetite.
1225   "Choose, now," said she, "one of these two things, aye,
To have me foul and old until I die,
And be to you a true and humble wife,
And never anger you in all my life;
Or else to have me young and very fair
1230   And take your chance with those who will repair
Unto your house, and all because of me,
Or in some other place, as well may be.
Now choose which you like better and reply."
   This knight considered, and did sorely sigh,
1235   But at the last replied as you shall hear:
"My lady and my love, and wife so dear,
I put myself in your wise governing;
Do you choose which may be the more pleasing,
And bring most honour to you, and me also.
1240   I care not which it be of these things two;
For if you like it, that suffices me."
   "Then have I got of you the mastery,
Since I may choose and govern, in earnest?"
   "Yes, truly, wife," said he, "I hold that best."
1245   "Kiss me," said she, "we'll be no longer wroth,
For by my truth, to you I will be both;
That is to say, I'll be both good and fair.
I pray God I go mad, and so declare,
If I be not to you as good and true
1250   As ever wife was since the world was new.
And, save I be, at dawn, as fairly seen
As any lady, empress, or great queen
That is between the east and the far west,
Do with my life and death as you like best.
1255   Throw back the curtain and see how it is."
   And when the knight saw verily all this,
That she so very fair was, and young too,
For joy he clasped her in his strong arms two,
His heart bathed in a bath of utter bliss;
1260   A thousand times, all in a row, he'd kiss.
And she obeyed his wish in everything
That might give pleasure to his love-liking.
   And thus they lived unto their lives' fair end,
In perfect joy; and Jesus to us send
1265   Meek husbands, and young ones, and fresh in bed,
And good luck to outlive them that we wed.
And I pray Jesus to cut short the lives
Of those who'll not be governed by their wives;
And old and querulous niggards with their pence,
1270   And send them soon a mortal pestilence!

BIBLIOGRAPHY

Medieval China

General • Cyril Birch, ed., *Studies in Chinese Literary Genres*, 1974. • Tse-tsung Chow, ed., *Wen-lin: Studies in Chinese Humanities*, 1968. • Christopher Leigh Connery, *The Empire of the Text: Writing and Authority in Early Imperial China*, 1998. • A. R. Davis, *The Penguin Book of Chinese Verse*, 1971. • Hans Frankel, *The Flowering Plum and the Palace Lady: Interpretations of Chinese Poetry*, 1976. • Donald Holzman, *Chinese Literature in Transition from Antiquity to the Middle Ages*, 1998. • Wu-chi Liu, *An Introduction to Chinese Literature*, 1966. • Wu-chi Liu and Irving Lo, eds., *Sunflower Splendor: Three Thousand Years of Chinese Poetry*, 1976. • Michael Loewe, *Everyday Life in Early Imperial China*, 1968. • Stephen Owen, *Traditional Chinese Poetry and Poetics: Omen of the World*, 1984. • Stephen Owen, *Remembrances: The Experience of the Past in Classical Chinese Literature*, 1986. • Scott Pearce, Audrey Spiro, and Patricia Ebrey, eds., *Culture and Power in the Reconstitution of the Chinese Realm, 200–600*, 2001. • Burton Watson, *Chinese Lyricism*, 1970. • Burton Watson, *The Columbia Book of Chinese Poetry*, 1984. • Pauline Yu, *The Reading of Imagery in the Chinese Poetic Tradition*, 1987.

Perspectives: What Is Literature? • John L. Bishop, ed., *Studies in Chinese Literature*, 1966. • James R. Hightower, *Topics in Chinese Literature*, 1962. • James J. Y. Liu, *Chinese Theories of Literature*, 1975. • Ronald Miao, ed., *Studies in Chinese Poetry and Poetics*, 1981. • Stephen Owen, *Readings in Chinese Literary Thought*, 1992. • Adele Rickett, ed., *Chinese Approaches to Literature from Confucius to Liang Ch'i-ch'ao*, 1978. • Siu-kit Wong, *Early Chinese Literary Criticism*, 1983.

Cao Pi • Howard L. Goodman, *Ts'ao P'i Transcendent: The Political Culture of Dynasty-founding in China at the End of the Han*, 1998.

Liu Xie • Zong-qi Cai, ed., *A Chinese Literary Mind: Culture, Creativity and Rhetoric in Wenxin Diaolong*, 2001. • Vincent Yu-chung Shih, trans., *The Literary Mind and the Carving of Dragons: A Study of Thought and Pattern in Chinese Literature*, 1983. • Ferenc Tokei, *Genre Theory in China in the 3rd–6th Centuries (Liu Hsieh's Theory on Poetic Genres)*, 1971. • Siu-kit Wong, Allan Chung-hang Lo, and Kwong-tai Lam, trans., *The Book of Literary Design*, 1999.

Lu Ji • Tony Barnstone and Chou Ping, trans. and eds., *The Art of Writing: Teachings from the Chinese Masters*, 1996. • Sam Hamill, trans., *The Art of Writing: Lu Chi's Wen Fu*, 2000. • E. R. Hughes, *The Art of Letters: Lu Chi's "Wen fu," A.D. 302, A Translation and Comparative Study*, 1951.

Sikong Tu • Yoon-wah Wong, *Ssu-K'ung T'u: A Poet-Critic of the T'ang*, 1976.

Wang Changling • Richard W. Bodman, *Poetics and Prosody in Early Medieval China*, Ph.D. diss., 1978.

Poetry of the Tang Dynasty • Witter Bynner, *The Jade Mountain*, 1964. • François Cheng, *Chinese Poetic Writing*, 1982. • Arthur Cooper, *Li Po and Tu Fu*, 1973. • David Gordon, *Equinox: A Gathering of T'ang Poets*, 1975. • A. C. Graham, *Poems of the Late T'ang*, 1965. • Shuen-fu Lin and S. Owen, eds. *The Vitality of the Lyric Voice*, 1986. • James J. Y. Liu, *The Art of Chinese Poetry*, 1962. • Stephen Owen, *The Poetry of the Early T'ang*, 1977. • Stephen Owen, *The Great Age of Chinese Poetry: The High T'ang*, 1981. • Stephen Owen, *The End of the Chinese "Middle Ages": Essays in Mid-Tang Literary Culture*, 1996. • Vikram Seth, *Three Chinese Poets*, 1992. • Hugh Stimson, *Fifty-five T'ang Poems*, 1976. • Arthur Wright and Denis Twitchett, *Perspectives on the T'ang*, 1973. • David Young, trans., *Five T'ang Poets*, 1990.

Women in Early China • Kang-i Sun Chang and Haun Saussy, eds., *Women Writers of Traditional China: An Anthology of Poetry and Criticism*, 1999. • Patricia B. Ebrey, *Women* *and the Family in Chinese History*, 2003. • Anna Gerstlacher et al., *Women and Literature in China*, 1985. • Richard W. Guisso and Stanley Johannesen, eds., *Women in China: Current Directions in Historical Scholarship*, 1981. • Bret Hinsch, *Women in Early Imperial China*, 2002. • Lisa Ann Raphals, *Sharing the Light: Representations of Women and Virtue in Early China*, 1998. • Jowen R. Tung, *Fables for the Patriarchs: Gender Politics in Tang Discourse*, 2000. • Ellen Widmer and Kang-i Sung Chang, eds., *Writing Women in Late Imperial China*, 1997.

Ban Zhao • S. L. Baldwin, trans., *The Chinese Book of Etiquette and Conduct for Women and Girls, Entitled: Instruction for Chinese Women and Girls*, 1900. • Nancy Lee Swann, *Pan Chao: Foremost Woman Scholar of China*, 2001.

Bo Juyi • Howard S. Levy, *Translations from Po Chü-i's Collected Works*, 1978. • Arthur Waley, *The Life and Times of Po Chü-i*, 1949.

Du Fu • Rewi Alley, trans., *Tu Fu: Selected Poems*, 1962. • Eva Shan Chou, *Reconsidering Tu Fu: Literary Greatness and Cultural Context*, 1995. • A. R. Davis, *Tu Fu*, 1971. • Sam Hamill, trans., *Facing the Snow: Visions of Tu Fu*, 1988. • David Hawkes, *A Little Primer of Tu Fu*, 1967. • William Hung, *Tu Fu: China's Greatest Poet*, 1952. • David McCraw, *Du Fu's Laments from the South*, 1992.

Han-shan • Robert G. Henricks, *The Poetry of Han-shan: A Complete, Annotated Translation of Cold Mountain*, 1990. • Peter Hobson, *Poems of Hanshan*, 2003. • Dennis Maloney, ed., Arthur Tobias et al., trans., *The View From Cold Mountain: Poems of Han-shan and Shih-te*, 1982. • Gary Snyder, *Riprap, and Cold Mountain Poems*, 1969. • Burton Watson, *Cold Mountain: 100 Poems by the T'ang Poet Han-shan*, 1962.

Li Bo • Rewi Alley, trans., *Li Pai: 200 Selected Poems*, 1980. • Shigeyoshi Obata, *The Works of Li Po*, 1922. • J. P. Seaton and James Cryer, trans., *Bright Moon, Perching Bird: Poems*, 1987. • Arthur Waley, *The Poetry and Career of Li Po*, 1950. • Siu-kit Wong, *The Genius of Li Po*, 1984.

Li Qingzhao • James Cryer, trans., *Plum Blossom: Poems of Li Qingzhao*, 1984. • Sam Hamill,

trans., *The Lotus Lovers: Poems and Songs*, by Zi Ye and Li Qingzhao, 1985. • Kenneth Rexroth and Ling Chung, trans. and ed., *Li Ch'ing-chao, Complete Poems*, 1979.

Liu Xiang • Ida Lee Mei, *Chinese Womanhood*, 1981. • Albert Richard O'Hara, ed., *The Position of Woman in Early China According to the Lieh Nu Chuan, "The Biographies of Eminent Chinese Women,"* 1981.

Li Yu • Daniel Bryant, ed. and trans., *Lyric Poets of the Southern T'ang: Feng Yen-ssu, 903–960, and Li Yu, 937–978*, 1982.

Tao Qian • W. R. B. Acker, *T'ao the Hermit*, 1952. • Kang-i Sun Chang, *Six Dynasties Poetry*, 1986. • A. R. Davis, *T'ao Yuan-ming*, 1983. • James R. Hightower, *The Poetry of T'ao Ch'ien*, 1970. • Charles Yim-tze Kwong, *Tao Qian and the Chinese Poetic Tradition*, 1994.

Voices of Women • Kenneth Rexroth and Ling Chung, *The Orchid Boat: Women Poets of China*, 1972. • Wang Rongpei, trans., *A Pair of Peacocks, the Mulan Ballad*, 1998.

Wang Wei • Tony Barnstone et al., *Laughing Lost in the Mountains—Selected Poems of Wang Wei*, 1989. • Yin-nan Chang and Lewis C. Walmsley, *Poems by Wang Wei*, 1958. • G. W. Robinson, *Poems of Wang Wei*, 1973. • Marsha L. Wagner, *Wang Wei*, 1981. • Lewis C. Walmsley and Dorothy B. Walmsley, *Wang Wei: The Painter-Poet*, 1968. • Eliot Weinberger and Octavio Paz, *Nineteen Ways of Looking at Wang Wei*, 1987. • Wai-lim Yip, *Hiding the Universe: Poems by Wang Wei*, 1972. • Pauline Yu, *The Poetry of Wang Wei: New Translations and Commentary*, 1980.

Yuan Cai • Patricia B. Ebrey, trans., *Family and Property in Sung China: Yuan Ts'ai's Precepts for Social Life*, 1984. • Patricia B. Ebrey, *The Inner Quarters: Marriage and the Lives of Chinese Women in the Sung Period*, 1993.

Yuan Zhen • Yu-Hwa Lee, *Fantasy and Realism in Chinese Fiction: T'ang Love Themes in Contrast*, 1984. • Wang Shifu, *The Story of the Western Wing*, trans. and ed. Stephen H. West and Wilt L. Idema, 1995. • Yang Xianyi and Gladys Yang, trans., *Tang Dynasty Stories*, 1986.

Japan

General • Geoffrey Bownas and Anthony Thwaite, trans. and ed. *The Penguin Book of Japanese Verse,* 1964. • Robert Brower and Earl Miner, *Japanese Court Poetry,* 1961. • Steven D. Carter, trans. and ed. *Traditional Japanese Poetry: An Anthology,* 1991. • William T. de Bary, ed. *Sources of Japanese Tradition,* 1958. • John Whitney Hall, *Japan: From Prehistory to Modern Times,* 1970. • Haruo Shirane, *Early Modern Japanese Literature, An Anthology,* 2001. • Donald Keene, *Japanese Literature: An Introduction for Western Readers,* 1953. • Donald Keene, ed. *Anthology of Japanese Literature: From the Earliest Era to the Mid-Nineteenth Century,* 1955. • Donald Keene, *Seeds in the Heart: Japanese Literature from Earliest Times to the late 16th Century,* 1993. • Donald Keene, *World Within Walls: Japanese Literature of the Pre-Modern Era, 1600–1867,* 1976. • Jin'ichi Konishi, *A History of Japanese Literature,* Vols. 1–3, 1984, 1986 and 1991. • Helen Craig McCullough, ed. *Classical Japanese Prose: An Anthology,* 1990. • Helen Craig McCullough, trans. and ed., *Genji and Heike: Selections from "The Tale of Genji" and "The Tale of the Heike,"* 1994. • Earl Miner, *An Introduction to Japanese Court Poetry,* 1968. • Earl Miner, Hiroko Odagiri, and Robert E. Morrell, *The Princeton Companion to Classical Japanese Literature,* 1985. • Ivan Morris, *The World of the Shining Prince: Court Life in Ancient Japan,* 1964. • Edward Putzar, *Japanese Literature: An Historical Outline,* 1973. • J. Thomas Rimer, *A Reader's Guide to Japanese Literature,* 1988. • George Sansom, *Japan: A Short Cultural History,* 1948. • Conrad Totman, *Japan before Perry: A Short History,* 1981. • Makoto Ueda, *Literary and Art Theories in Japan,* 1967. • H. Paul Varley, *Japanese Culture,* 1984.

Perspectives: Courtly Women • Richard Bowring, *Murasaki Shikibu: Her Diary and Poetic Memoirs,* 1982. • Earl Miner, trans., *Japanese Poetic Diaries,* 1969. • Ivan Morris, trans., *As I Crossed a Bridge of Dreams: Recollections of a Woman in Eleventh-Century Japan,* 1971. • Edith Sarra, *Fictions of Femininity: Literary Conventions of Gender in Japanese Court Women's Memoirs,* 1999.

Mother of Mitchitsuna • Sonja Arntzen, *The Kagero Diary: A Woman's Autobiographical Text From the Tenth Century,* 1997. • Edward Seidensticker, trans., *The Gossamer Years: The Diary of a Noblewoman of Heian Japan,* 1964.

Ono no Komachi • Jane Hirshfield and Mariko Aratani, trans., *The Ink Dark Moon: Love Poems by Ono no Komachi and Izumi Shikibu, Women of the Ancient Court of Japan,* 1988. • Konishi Jin'ichi, "The Genesis of the *Kokinshû* Style," trans. Helen Craig McCullough, *Harvard Journal of Asiatic Studies* 38 (1978): 61–170. • Helen Craig McCullough, *Brocade by Night: Kokin Wakashû and the Court Style in Classical Japanese Poetry,* 1985. • Helen Craig McCullough, trans., *Kokin Wakashû. The First Imperial Anthology of Japanese Poetry, With "Tosa Nikki" and "Shinsen Waka,"* 1985. • Laura Rasplica Rodd and Mary Catherine Henkenius, trans., *Kokinshû: A Collection of Poems Ancient and Modern,* 1984.

Sei Shōnagon • Ivan Morris, trans., *The Pillow Book of Sei Shōnagon,* 2 vols., 1967, 1971. • Arthur Waley, trans., *The Pillow-Book of Sei Shōnagon,* 1957.

Noh: Drama of Ghosts, Memories, and Salvation • Karen Brazell, ed. *Traditional Japanese Theater: An Anthology of Plays,* 1998. • Karen Brazell, ed. *Twelve Plays of the Nô and Kyôgen Theatres,* 1990. • Donald Keene, ed. *Twenty Plays of the Nô Theatre,* 1970. • Donald Keene, *Nô: The Classical Theatre of Japan,* 1966. • Don Kenny, *A Guide to Kyôgen,* 1968. • Kunio Komparu, *The Noh Theater: Principles and Perspectives,* 1983. • Richard N. McKinnon, trans., *Selected Plays of Kyôgen,* 1968. • Nippon Gakujutsu Shinkôkai, *Japanese Noh Drama,* 3 vols. 1955, 1959, and 1960. • Ezra Pound and Ernest Fenollosa, trans., *The Classic Noh Theatre of Japan,* 1959. • Shio Sakanishi, trans., *Japanese Folk-Plays: The Ink-Smeared Lady and Other Kyôgen,* 1960. • Royall Tyler, trans., and ed. *Japanese Nô Dramas,* 1992. • Arthur Waley, *The Nô Plays of Japan,* 1957. • Kenneth Yasuda, *Masterworks of the No Theater,* 1989.

Man'yōshū (Collection of Myriad Leaves) • Edwin Cranston, *A Waka Anthology: The Gem-Glistening Cup,* 1993. • Gary L.

Ebersole, *Ritual Poetry and the Politics of Death in Early Japan*, 1989. ● Ian Hideo Levy, *Hitomaro and the Birth of Japanese Lyricism*, 1984. ● Ian Hideo Levy, *The Ten Thousand Leaves*, 1987. ● Nippon Gakujutsu Shinkōkai. *The Man'yōshū: One Thousand Poems*, 1983.

Murasaki Shikibu ● Norma Field, *The Splendor of Longing in the Tale of Genji*, 1987. ● Edward Kamens, ed. *Approaches to Teaching Murasaki Shikibu's The Tale of Genji*, 1993. ● Ivan Morris, *The Tale of Genji Scroll*, 1971. ● H. Richard Okada, *Figures of Resistance: Language, Poetry, and Narrating in The Tale of Genji and Other Mid-Heian Texts*, 1991. ● Edward Seidensticker, trans., *The Tale of Genji*, 1981. ● Haruo Shirane, *The Bridge of Dreams: A Poetics of "The Tale of Genji,"* 1987. ● Amanda Mayer Stinchecum, "Who Tells the Tale? 'Ukifune': A Study in Narrative Voice." *Monumenta Nipponica* 35 (1980): 375–403. ● Royall Tyler, trans., *The Tale of*

Genji, 2001. ● Arthur Waley, trans., *The Tale of Genji*, 1957.

Tales of the Heike ● Helen Craig McCullough, trans., *The Tale of the Heike*, 1988. ● Barbara Ruch, "The Other Side of Culture in Medieval Japan," in *Cambridge History of Japan*, Vol. 3, ed. John Hall et al., 1988. ● Paul Varley, "Warriors as Courtiers: The Taira in *Heike monogatari*," in *Currents in Japanese Culture: Translations and Transformations*, ed. Amy Vladeck Heinrich, 1997.

Zeami ● Thomas Blenman Hare, *Zeami's Style: The Noh Plays of Zeami Motokiyo*, 1986. ● J. Thomas Rimer and Yamazaki Masakazu, trans., *On the Art of Nô Drama: The Major Treatises of Zeami*, 1984. ● Masakazu Yamazaki, "The Aesthetics of Transformation: Zeami's Dramatic Theories," trans. Susan Matisoff, *Journal of Japanese Studies* 7.2 (1981): 215–257.

Classical Arabic and Islamic Literatures

General ● *The Encyclopaedia of Islam*, 1986. ● *The Cambridge History of Iran*, 1968. ● T. J. Andrae, *Muhammad: The Man and His Faith*, 1936. ● J. Ashtiani et al., eds., *Abbasid Belles-Lettres*, 1988. ● J. Bacharach, *A Middle Eastern Studies Handbook*, 1984. ● A. F. Beeston et al., eds., *Arabic Literature to the End of the Ummayad Period*, 1983. ● R. Blachère, *Histoire de la Littérature Arabe*, 3 vols., 1952–1966. ● C. E. Bosworth, *The Islamic Dynasties*, 1967. ● Peter Brown, *The World of Late Antiquity*, 1971. ● A. J. Butler, *The Arab Conquest of Egypt*, 1902. ● J. M. Cook, *The Persian Empire*, 1983. ● D. Eikelman, *The Middle East: An Anthropological Approach*, 1981. ● H. A. R. Gibb, *Arabic Literature*, 1963. ● H. A. R. Gibb, *Islam*, 1969. ● H. A. R. Gibb, *Muhammadansim*, 1949. ● H. A. R. Gibb, *Studies on the Civilisation of Islam*, 1962. ● G. E. von Grunebaum, *Medieval Islam: A Study in Cultural Orientation*, 1953. ● Sabry Hafez, *The Genesis of Arabic Narrative Discourse*, 1993. ● H. W. Hazard, *Atlas of the Islamic History*, 1957. ● P. M. Holts et al., eds., *The Cambridge History of Islam*, 1970. ● Albert Hourani, *A History of the Arab Peoples*, 1991. ● Albert Hourani, *Syria and Lebanon*, 1946. ● G. F. Hourani, *Arab Seafaring in the Indian Ocean in Ancient and*

Medieval Times, 1951. ● T. Khalidi, *Classical Arab Islam*, 1985. ● S. Lane-Poole, *The Muhammadan Dynasties*, 1925. ● I. M. Lapidus, *A History of Muslim Societies*, 1988. ● Bernard Lewis, *Istanbul and the Civilisation of the Ottoman Empire*, 1963. ● Bernard Lewis, ed. *The World of Islam*, 1976. ● S. Moscati, *The Semites in Ancient History*, 1959. ● J. D. Pearson et al., eds., *Index Islamicus*, 1958. ● F. Rahman, *Islam*, 1979. ● R. Roolvink, *Historical Atlas of the Muslim Peoples*, 1957. ● M. Ruthven, *Islam in the World*, 1984. ● Jean Sargent, *Introduction to the History of the Muslim East*, 1965. ● J. Sauvaget, *Introduction à l'histoire de l'orient musulman*, 1961. ● I. Shahid, *Rome and the Arabs*, 1984. ● L. Udovitch, ed., *The Islamic Middle East 700–1900: Studies in Economic and Social History*, 1981. ● W. M. Watt, *Muhammad: Prophet and Statesman*, 1961. ● W. M. Watt, *Muhammad at Mecca*, 1953. ● W. M. Watt, *Muhammad at Medina*, 1956.

Perspectives: Asceticism, Sufism, and Wisdom
● A. J Arberry, *The Mawaqif and Mukhatabat of al-Niffari*, 1978. ● J. Baldick, *Imaginary Muslims*, 1993. ● M. Bayradkdar, *La Philosophy Mystique*, 1990. ● W. C. Chittick, *The*

Five Divine Presences, 1982. • H. Corbin, *The Man of Light in Iranian Sufism*, 1978. • H. Corbin, *Spiritual Body and Celestial Earth*, 1977. • M. A. K. Danner, *The Key to Salvation*, 1996. • J. T. de Bruijn, *Persian Sufi Poetry*, 1997. • J. W. Drewes, *Directions for Travellers on Mystic Path*, 1977. • Farid al-Din 'Attar, *The Conference of the Birds*, trans. Afkham Darbandi and Dick Davis, 1984. • Farid al-Din 'Attar, *The Conference of the Birds: Mantiq ut-Tair: A Philosophical Religious Poem in Prose*, trans. C. S. Nott, 1993. • Farid al-Din 'Attar, *Mantiq al-Tair*, trans. Badi' Muhammad Jum'ah, 1979. • Farid al-Din 'Attar, *The Speech of the Birds: Concerning Migration to the Real*, trans. English by P. W. Avery, 1998. • Al-Hallaj, *Dîwân Hoceïn Mansûr Hallâj*, trans. Louis Massignon, 1955. • Al-Hallaj, *The Great Sufic Text on the Unity of Reality: The Tawasin*, ed. Louis Massignon, 1978. • Al-Hallaj, *The Tawasin of Mansur al-Hallaj*, trans. Aisha abd ar-Rahman at-Tarjumana, 1974. • Ibn al-'Arabi, *Awrad al-Usbu'*, trans. Pablo Beneito and Stephen Hirtenstein, 2000. • Ibn al-'Arabi, *The Bezels of Wisdom*, trans. R. W. J. Austin, 1980. • Ibn al-'Arabi, *Les Illuminations de la Mecque*, trans. Michel Chodkiewicz, 1988. • Ibn al-'Arabi, *Journey to the Lord of Power: A Sufi Manual on Retreat*, trans. Rabia Terri Harris, 1981. • Ibn al-'Arabi, *Turjuman al-Ashwaq: A Collection of Mystical Odes*, trans. Reynold A. Nicholson, 1978. • T. Izutsu, *Creation and the Timeless Order of Things*, 1994. • H. L. Landolt, *The Legacy of Medieval Persian Sufism*, 1992. • H. L. Landolt, *Le Révélateur des Mysères*, 1986. • L. Lewisohn, *Beyond Faith and Infidelity*, 1995. • Muhyi al-Din Ibn al-'Arabi, *L'Arbre du Monde*, ed. and trans. Maurice Gloton, 1982. • S. Murata, *The Tao of Islam*, 1992. • R. A. Nicholson, *Studies in Islamic Mysticism*, 1921. • R. S. O'Fahey, *Enigmatic Saints*, 1990. • A. M. Schimmel, *Mystical Dimensions in Islam*, 1975. • A. M. Schimmel, *Mystical Poetry in Islam*, 1982. • A. M. Schimmel, *Pain and Grace: A Study of Two Mystical Writers*, 1976. • Margaret Smith, *The Persian Mystics: Attar*, 1932.

Perspectives: Poetry, Wine, and Love • A. J. Arberry, *Poems of Al-Mutanabbi*, 1967. • J. E. Bencheikh, Khamriyya, in *Encyclopaedia of Islam*, 1965. • R. Blachére, *Les Principaux Thémes de la Poésie Érotique*, 1941. • A. Cour, *Un Poète Arabe d'Andalousie*, 1920. • H. G. Farmer, *A History of Arabian Music to*

XIIIth Century, 1929. • Guadefroy-Demomnyne, *Introduction au Livre de la Poésie et des Poètes*, 1947. • R. Guest, *Life and Works of Ibn al-Rumi*, 1944. • W. H. Ingrams, *Abu Nuwas in Life and in Legend*, 1933. • Philip F. Kennedy, *The Wine Song in Classical Arabic Poetry: Abu Nuwas and the Literary Tradition*, 1997. • James L. Kugel, ed., *Poetry and Prophecy*, 1992. • R. A. Nicholson, *Studies in Islamic Poetry*, 1921. • D. J. Rikabi, *La Poésie Profane sous les Ayyubdes*, 1949. • S. M. Stern, *Hispano-Arabic Strophic Poetry*, 1964. • J. Vadet, *La Littérature Courtiose dans les Cinq Primiers Siècles de l'Hégire*, 1973. • Arthur Wormhoudt, *The Diwan of Abu Nuwas al-Hasan ibn Hani al-Hakami*, 1974.

Pre-Islamic Poetry • N. Abbott, *The Rise of the North Arabic Script*, 1939. • A. Arazi, *La Réalité et la Fiction dans la Poésie Arabe Ancienne*, 1989. • A. J. Arberry, *The Seven Odes*, 1957. • A. F. L. Beeston and T. M. Johnston, *Arabic Literature to the End of the Ummayyad Period*, 1983. • Jacques Berque, *Cultural Expression in Arab Society*, trans. Robert W. Stookey, 1974. • M. M. Bravmann, *The Spiritual Background of Early Islam*, 1972. • H. Charles, *Le Christianisme des Arabes Nomades*, 1936. • *The Diwan of Imr'u al Qais ibn Hujr ibn Kinda*, trans. Arthur Wormhoudt, 1974. • T. Fahd, *La Divination Arabe*, 1987. • H. G. Farmer, *The Sources of Arabian Music*, 1940. • Ghani Tengku Jusoh, *A Critical Examination of Five Poems by Imru al-Qays*, 1990. • I. Goldziher, *Muslim Studies*, 2 vols., 1967–1971. • Alan Jones, *Early Arabic Poetry*, 1992. • Khansa' Bint 'Amr, *Diwan al Khansa*, 1974. • M. J. Kister, *Studies in Jahiliyya and Early Islam*, 1990. • H. Lammens, *L'Arabie Occidentale avant l'Hégire*, 1928. • C. J. Lyall, *Ancient Arabian Poetry*, 1930. • R. A. Nicholson, *Literary History of the Arabs*, 1930. • C. Rabin, *Ancient West-Arabian*, 1951. • Suzanne Pinckney Stetkevych, *The Mute Immortals Speak*, 1993. • M. Zwettler, *The Oral Tradition of Classical Arabic Poetry*, 1978.

The Epic of Son-Jara • John William Johnson, *The Epic of Son-Jara: A West African Tradition*, 1992. • D. T. Niane, *Sundiata: An Epic of Old Mali*, 1965.

Firdawsi • Ehsan Yar-e-Shater, *Dastan'ha-yi Shahnamah: Selected Stories from Book of Kings "Shah-nameh,"* 1959. • Abu al-Qasim

Hasan Firdawsi, *The Story of Siyawush from the Shahnamah*, 2 vols., trans. M. Qarib and M. Mada'eni, 1985–1990. ● Firdawsi, *An Abridged Version of Bizhan and Manizha*, 1965. ● Firdawsi, *The Legend of Seyavash*, trans. Dick Davis, 1992. ● Firdawsi, *Roustem et Sohrab: Épisode du Livre des Rois*, trans. Auguste Bricteux, 1938. ● *The Tragedy of Sohrab and Rostam: From the Persian National Epic, the Shahname*, trans. Jerome W. Clinton, 1996. ● Stuart Cary Welch, *Shahnamah: A King's Book of Kings*, 1972.

Hafiz ● A. J. Alston, *In Search of Hafiz: 109 Poems from the Diwan of Hafiz*, 1996. ● A. J. Arberry, *Classical Persian Poetry*, 1958. ● A. J. Arberry, *Hafiz: Fifty Poems*, 1947. ● U. M. Daudpota, *The Influence of Arabic Poetry on the Development of Persian Poetry*, 1939. ● Michael Glünz and J. Christoph Bürgel, eds., *Intoxication: Earthly and Heavenly: Seven Studies on the Poet Hafiz of Shiraz*, 1991. ● Hafiz, *Divan*, trans. Reza Saberi, 1995. ● L. Lewisohn, ed., *Classical Persian Sufism, from Its Origins to Rumi*, 1993. ● Vincent Mansour Monteil, *L'Amour, l'Aimant, l'Aimé: Cent Ballades du Divân Hâfez Shirâzi*, 1989. ● G. Morrison, *History of Persian Literature from the Beginning of the Islamic Period to the Present Day*, 1981. ● C. A. Storey, *Persian Literature*, 1939.

Ibn Battuta ● Rose E. Dunn, *The Adventures of Ibn Battuta, a Muslim Traveler of the Fourteenth Century*, 1986. ● Tim Mackintosh-Smith, *Travels with a Tangerine: A Journey in the Footnotes of Ibn Battutah*, 2001.

The Qur'an ● A. J. Arberry, *The Qur'an Interpreted*, 1955. ● H. Berkeland, *Old Muslim Opposition against Interpretation of the Qur'an*, 1955. ● J. Bowker, *Jesus in the Qur'an*, 1965. ● J. Burton, *The Collection of the Qur'an*, 1977. ● K. Cragg, *The Event of the Qur'an*, 1971. ● K. Cragg, *The Mind of the Qur'an*, 1973. ● Ali Dashti, *Twenty-Three Years: A Study of the Prophetic Career of Muhammad*, 1985. ● F. Gabrieli, *Muhammad and the Conquests of Islam*, 1968. ● H. Gätje, *Qur'an and Its Exegeses*, 1976. ● J. B. Glubb, *The Life and Times of Muhammad*, 1979. ● M. H. Haykal, *The Life of Muhammad*, 1976. ● R. G. Hovannisian, ed., *Islam's Understanding of Itself*, 1983. ● T. Isutsu, *Ethico-Religious Concepts in the Qur'an*, 1966. ● T. Isutsu, *God and Man in the Qur'an*, 1964. ● J. Jansen, *The Interpretation of the Qur'an in Modern Egypt*, 1974. ● A. Jeffery, *Reader on Islam*, 1962. ● J. Jomier, *The Bible and the Qur'an*, 1964. ● M. Lings, *Muhammad: His Life Based on the Earliest Sources*, 1983. ● Henry Mercier and Lucien Tremlett, *The Qur'an*, 1973. ● A. Abul Qaswm, *The Recitation and Interpretation of the Qur'an*, 1979. ● D. Rahbar, *God of Justice: A Study in the Ethical Doctine of the Qur'an*, 1960. ● Fazlur Rahman, *Islam*, 1966. ● M. Rodinson, *Mohammed*, 1971. ● M. S. Seale, *Qur'an and Bible*, 1978. ● S. H. Shamma, *The Ethical System underlying the Qur'an*, 1959. ● W. Montgomery Watt, *Muhammad at Mecca*, 1953. ● W. Montgomery Watt, *Muhammad at Medina*, 1966. ● A. J. Wensinck, *Muhammad and the Jews of Mecca*, 1975.

Jalal al-Din Rumi ● Jalal al-Din Rumi, *Discourses of Rumi*, 1975. ● Jalal al-Din Rumi, *More Tales from the Masnavi*, trans. A. J. Arberry, 1963. ● Jalal al-Din Rumi, *Tales from the Masnavi*, trans. A. J. Arberry, 1961. ● A. J. Arberry, trans. *Mystical Poems of Rumi: First selection, poems 1–200*, 1968. ● A. J. Arberry, trans. *Mystical Poems of Rumi: Second selection, poems 201–400*, 1979. ● Amin Banani and Richard Hovannisian, *Poetry and Mysticism in Islam: The Heritage of Rumi*, 1994. ● Coleman Barks and John Moyne, ed. and trans., *The Essential Rumi*, 2000. ● Deepak Chopra and Fereydoun Kia, eds. and trans., *The Love Poems of Rumi*, 1998. ● James Cowan, *Rumi's Divan of Shems of Tabriz: Selected Odes, a New Interpretation*, 1997. ● Philip Dunn, et al., trans. *The Illustrated Rumi: A Treasury of Wisdom from Poet of the Soul*, 2000. ● Camille and Kabir Helminski, eds. and trans., *Rumi: Daylight: a Daybook of Spiritual Guidance*, 1990. ● L. Lewisohn, ed. *Classical Persian Sufism, from its Origins to Rumi*, 1993. ● Juliet Mabey, trans., *Rumi: A Spiritual Treasury*, 2000. ● Muriel Maufroy, ed., *Breathing Truth: Quotations from Jalaluddin Rumi*, 1997. ● G. Morrison, *History of Persian Literature from the Beginning of the Islamic Period to the Present Day*, 1981. ● John Moyne and Coleman Barks, trans., *Open Secret: Versions of Rumi*, 1999. ● Reynold A. Nicholson, ed. and trans. *Selected Poems from the Divani Shamsi Tabriz*, 1994. ● Annemarie Schimmel, trans., *Look! This Is Love: Poems of Rumi*, 1991. ● Shahram T. Shiva, *Rending the Veil: Literal and Poetic Translations of Rumi*, 1995.

• Muhammad Isa Waley, *The Stanzaic Poems (tarji'at) of Rumi*, 1991.

The Thousand and One Nights • Daniel E. Beaumont, *Slave of Desire: Sex, Love, and Death in The 1001 Nights*, 2002. • Sir Richard F. Burton, trans., *The Arabian Nights: Tales from a Thousand and One Nights*, introduction by A. S. Byatt, 2001. • Peter L. Caracciolo, ed., *The "Arabian Nights" in English Literature*, 1988. • André Clot, *Harun al-Rashid and the World of the Thousand and One Nights*, 1989. • Ferial J. Ghazoul, *Nocturnal Poetics: The Arabian Nights in Comparative Perspective*, 1996. • Husain Haddawy, trans., *The Arabian Nights*, 1990. • Husain Haddawy, trans., *The Arabian Nights II: Sinbad and Other Popular Stories*, 1995. • Robert Irwin, *The Arabian Nights: A Companion*, 1995. • Muhsin Mahdi, ed., *The Thousand and One Nights (Alf Layla wa-Layla) from the Earliest Known Sources*, 3 vols., 1984–1994. • Powys Mathers, trans., *The Book of the Thousand Nights and One Night*, 4 vols., from the French translation of J. C. Mardrus, 1964. • David Pinault, *Story-Telling Techniques in the Arabian Nights*, 1992. • Iqbal 'Ali Shah, *Alone in Arabian Nights*, 1933. • Douglas Brooke Wheelton Sladen, *Oriental Cairo: The City of the "Arabian Nights,"* 1987.

Medieval Europe

General • *The New Cambridge Medieval History*, 1995–2003. • Erich Auerbach, *Literary Language and Its Public in Late Latin Antiquity and in the Middle Ages*, trans. Ralph Manheim, 1993. • Erich Auerbach, *Mimesis: The Representation of Reality in Western Literature*, trans. Willard R. Trask, 1968. • W. R. J. Barron, W. R. J., ed. *The Arthur of the English: The Arthurian Legend in Medieval English Life and Literature*, 2001. • Marc Bloch, *Feudal Society*, trans. L. A. Manyon, 1964. • R. Howard Bloch, *Medieval Misogyny and the Invention of Western Romantic Love*, 1991. • Renate Blumenfeld-Kosinski, *Reading Myth: Classical Mythology and its Interpretations in Medieval French Literature*, 1997. • John Boswell, *Christianity, Social Tolerance, and Homosexuality: Gay People in Western Europe from the Beginning of the Christian Era to the Fourteenth Century*, 1980. • Christopher Brooke, *Europe in the Central Middle Ages, 962-1154*, 2000. • Peter Brown, *The World of Late Antiquity A.D. 150-750*, 1989. • Peter Brown and Jacques Le Goff, eds., *The Rise of Western Christendom: Triumph and Diversity A.D. 200-1000*, 1997. • Carolyn Walker Bynum, *Holy Feast and Holy Fast: The Significance of Food to Medieval Women*, 1987. • Franco Cardini, *Europe and Islam*, trans. Caroline Beamish, 2001. • Mary Carruthers, *The Book of Memory: A Study of Memory in Medieval Culture*, 1990. • Roger Collins, *Early Medieval Europe, 300-1000*, 1999. • Ernst Robert Curtius, *European Literature and the Latin Middle Ages*, trans. Willard Trask, 1973. • Peter Dronke, *Medieval Latin and the Rise of the European Love Lyric*, 1968. • Peter Dronke, *The Medieval Lyric*, 1996. • Peter Dronke, *Women Writers of the Middle Ages: A Critical Study of Texts from Perpetua (203) to Marguerite Porete (1310)*, 1984. • Georges Duby, *France in the Middle Ages 987-1460: From Hugh Capet to Joan of Arc*, trans. Juliet Vale, 1991. • Georges Duby, ed., *Revelations of the Medieval World*. Vol. 2 of *A History of Private Life*, 1987–1991. • Angus Fletcher, *Allegory, the Theory of a Symbolic Mode*, 1964. • Boris Ford, ed., *Medieval Literature: The European Inheritance*, 1983. • Barbara Harvey, ed., *The Twelfth and Thirteenth Centuries, 1066-c. 1280*, 2001. • George Holmes, ed., *The Oxford Illustrated History of Medieval Europe*, 1988. • Bruce Holsinger, *Music, Body, and Desire in Medieval Culture: Hildegard of Bingen to Chaucer*, 2001. • Johan Huizinga, *The Autumn of the Middle Ages*, trans. Rodney J. Payton and Ulrich Mammitzsch, 1996. • W. T. H. Jackson, *The Hero and the King: An Epic Theme*, 1982. • Roberta L. Krueger, *The Cambridge Companion to Medieval Romance*, 2000. • Jacques Le Goff, *Intellectuals in the Middle Ages*, trans. Teresa Lavender Fagan, 1993. • Jacques Le Goff, *The Medieval Imagination*, trans. Arthur Goldhammer, 1988. • Bernard Lewis and Dominique Schnapper, eds., *Muslims in Europe*, 1994. • C. S. Lewis, *The Allegory of Love: A Study in Medieval Tradition*, 1958. • C. S. Lewis, *The Discarded Image: An Introduction to Medieval and Renaissance Literature*, 1994. • María Rosa Menocal, *Shards of Love: Exile and the Origins of the Lyric*, 1994. • William Paden, ed., *Medieval Lyric: Genres in Historical Context*, 2002. • Lee Patterson, *Negotiating the Past: The Historical Understanding of Medieval Literature*, 1987. • James J. Paxson, *The Poetics of Personification*, 1994. • David L. Pike, *Passage through Hell: Modernist Descents, Medieval Underworlds*, 1997. • Michael A. Signer and John Van Engen, eds., *Jews and Christians in Twelfth-Century Europe*, 2001. • J. Riley Smith, ed. *The Oxford Illustrated History of the Crusades*, 1995. • Brian Stock, *The Implications of Literacy: Written Language and Models of Interpretation in the Eleventh and Twelfth Centuries*, 1983. • R. N. Swanson, *The Twelfth-Century Renaissance*, 1999. • Barbara Tuchman, *A Distant Mirror: The Calamitous Fourteenth Century*, 1978.

Perspectives: Iberia, The Meeting of Three Worlds • Samuel Armistead, Mishael M. Caspi, et al., eds., *Jewish Culture and the Hispanic World*, 2001. • Eliahu Ashtor, *The Jews of Moslem Spain*, 1992. • Yitzhak Baer, *A History of the Jews in Christian Spain*, 1992. • Stacy N. Beckwith, *Charting Memory: Recalling Medieval Spain*, 1999. • Gilbert Chase, *The Music of Spain*, 1941. • Richard Fletcher, *Moorish Spain*, 1993. • Daniel Frank, ed., *The Jews of Medieval Islam: Community, Society, and Identity*, 1995. • Jane S. Gerber, *The Jews of Spain: A History of the Sephardic Experience*, 1994. • L. P. Harvey, *Islamic Spain 1250–1500*, 1992. • Salma Khadra Jayyusi, *The Legacy of Muslim Spain*, 2 vols., 1992. • John Esten Keller and Annette Grant Cash, *Daily Life Depicted in the Cantigas de Santa Maria*, 1998. • Hugh Kennedy, *Muslim Spain and Portugal: A Political History of Al-Andalus*, 1997. • Vivian B. Mann, Thomas F. Glick, and Jerrilynn D. Dodds, *Convivencia: Jews, Muslims, and Christians in Medieval Spain*, 1992. • Manuela Marin, Julio Samsó, and Maribel Fierro, *The Formation of Al-Andalus*, 2 vols., 1998. • María Rosa Menocal, *The Arabic Role in Medieval Literary History: A Forgotten Heritage*, 1987. • María Rosa Menocal, *Shards of Love: Exile and the Origins of the Lyric*, 1994. • María Rosa Menocal and Harold Bloom, *The Ornament of the World: How Muslims, Jews, and Christians Created a Culture of Tolerance in Medieval Spain*, 2002. • María Rosa Menocal, Raymond Scheindlin, and Michael Sells, eds., *The Literature of Al-Andalus*, 2000. • Louise Mirrer, *Women, Jews, and Muslims in the Texts of Reconquest Castile*, 1996. • A. R. Nykl, *Hispano-Arabic Poetry and Its Relation to the Old Provençal Troubadours*, 1946. • Bernard F. Reilly, *The Medieval Spains*, 1993. • Julian Ribera, *Music in Ancient Arabia and Spain*, 1929. • Lucy A. Sponsler, *Women in the Medieval Spanish Epic and Lyric Traditions*, 1975. • David Wasserstein, *The Rise and Fall of the Party-Kings: Politics and Society in Islamic Spain 1002–1086*, 1985.

Abelard and Heloïse • M. T. Clanchy, *Abelard: A Medieval Life*, 1999. • Peter Dronke, *Abelard and Heloise in Medieval Testimonies*, 1976. • Peggy Kamuf, *Fictions of Feminine Desire: Disclosures of Heloise*, 1982. • D. E. Luscombe, *The School of Peter Abelard*, 1969. • John Marenbom, *The Philosophy of Peter Abelard*, 1997. • Elizabeth Mary McNamer, *The Education of Heloise: Methods, Content, and Purpose of Learning in the Twelfth Century*, 1991. • Denis Meadows, *A Saint and a Half: A New Interpretation of Abelard and St. Bernard of Clairvaux*, 1963. • Constant J. Mews, *Abelard and His Legacy*, 2001. • Constant J. Mews, *The Lost Love Letters of Heloise and Abelard: Perceptions of Dialogue in Twelfth-Century France*, 1999. • Constant J. Mews, ed., *Reason and Belief in the Age of Roscelin and Abelard*, 2002. • A. Victor Murray, *Abélard and St. Bernard: A Study in Twelfth-Century "Modernism,"* 1967. • Bonnie Wheeler, ed., *Listening to Heloise: The Voice of a Twelfth-Century Woman*, 2000. • Paul L. Williams, *The Moral Philosophy of Peter Abelard*, 1980.

Beowulf • Adrien Bonjour, *The Digressions in Beowulf*, 1950. • R. W. Chambers and C. L. Wrenn, *Beowulf: An Introduction to the Study of the Poem*, 1959. • Craig R. Davis, *Beowulf and the Demise of Germanic Legend in England*, 1996. • Susan E. Deskis, *Beowulf and the Medieval Proverb Tradition*, 1996. • James W. Earl, *Thinking About Beowulf*, 1994. • John Miles Foley, *Traditional Oral Epic: The Odyssey, Beowulf, and the Serbo-Croatian Return Song*, 1990. • Ritchie Girvan and Rupert Bruce-Mitford, *Beowulf and the Seventh Century*, 1971. • John M. Hill, *The Anglo-Saxon Warrior Ethic*, 2000. • Edward B. Irving, *A Reading of Beowulf*, 1968. • J. D. A. Ogilvy, and Donald C. Baker, *Reading Beowulf: An Introduction to the Poem, Its Background, and Its Style*, 1983. • Gillian R. Overing, *Language, Sign, and Gender in Beowulf*, 1990.

• Fred C. Robinson, *Beowulf and the Appositive Style,* 1985. • Kenneth Sisam, *The Structure of Beowulf,* 1965. • J. Michael Stitt, *Beowulf and the Bear's Son: Epic, Saga, and Fairytale in Northern Germanic Tradition,* 1992. • J. R. R. Tolkien, *Beowulf and the Critics,* ed. Michael D.C. Drout, 2002. • Dorothy Whitelock, *The Audience of Beowulf,* 1951.

Castilian Ballads and Traditional Songs • Ingrid Bahler and Katherine Gyékényesi Gatto, *Of Kings and Poets: Cancionero Poetry of the Trastámara Courts,* 1992. • Robert Stevenson, *Spanish Music in the Age of Columbus,* 1960. • Ruth H. Webber, ed., *Hispanic Balladry Today,* 1989.

Geoffrey Chaucer • Malcolm Andrew, *Critical Essays on Chaucer's Canterbury Tales,* 1991. • Peter Beidler, ed., *The Wife of Bath,* 1996. • C. David Benson, *Chaucer's Drama of Style: Poetic Variety and Contrast in The Canterbury Tales,* 1986. • Piero Boitano, *Chaucer and the Italian Trecento,* 1983. • Piero Boitano and Jill Mann, eds., *The Cambridge Chaucer Companion,* 1986. • Muriel Bowden, *A Commentary on the General Prologue to "The Canterbury Tales,"* 1967. • Susan Crane, *Gender and Romance in Chaucer's "Canterbury Tales,"* 1994. • W. A. Davenport, *Chaucer and His English Contemporaries: Prologue and Tale in "The Canterbury Tales,"* 1998. • Alfred David, *The Strumpet Muse: Art and Morals in Chaucer's Poetry,* 1976. • Carolyn Dinshaw, *Chaucer's Sexual Poetics,* 1989. • E. Talbot Donaldson, *Speaking of Chaucer,* 1970. • Sigmund Eisner, *A Tale of Wonder: A Source Study of The Wife of Bath's Tale,* 1969. • John M. Fyler, *Chaucer and Ovid,* 1979. • Jodi-Anne George, ed. *Geoffrey Chaucer: The General Prologue to the "Canterbury Tales,"* 2000. • Warren Ginsberg, *Chaucer's Italian Tradition,* 2002. • John C. Hirsch, *Chaucer and the Canterbury Tales: A Short Introduction,* 2003. • Donald R. Howard, *Chaucer: His Life, His Works, His World,* 1987. • Donald R. Howard, *The Idea of the Canterbury Tales,* 1976. • Peggy Knapp, *Chaucer and the Social Contest,* 1990. • Stephen Knight, *Geoffrey Chaucer,* 1986. • V. A. Kolve, *Chaucer and the Imagery of Narrative,* 1984. • H. Marshall Leicester Jr., *The Disenchanted Self: Representing the Subject in the Canterbury Tales,* 1990. • Kathryn L. Lynch, ed. *Chaucer's Cultural Geography,* 2002. • Jill Mann, *Chaucer and Medieval Estates Satire: The Literature of Social Classes and the General Prologue to the "Canterbury Tales,"* 1973. • Robert P. Miller, ed. *Chaucer: Sources and Backgrounds,* 1977. • A. J. Minnis, *Chaucer and Pagan Antiquity,* 1982. • A. J. Minnis, ed., *Chaucer's Boece and the Medieval Tradition of Boethius,* 1993. • Charles Muscatine, *Chaucer and the French Tradition,* 1957. • Richard Neuse, *Chaucer's Dante: Allegory and Epic Theater in The Canterbury Tales,* 1991. • Paul A. Olson, *The Canterbury Tales and the Good Society,* 1986. • Lee Patterson, *Chaucer and the Subject of History,* 1991. • S. H. Rigby, *Chaucer in Context: Society, Allegory, and Gender,* 1996. • D. W. Robertson, *Chaucer's London,* 1968. • D. W. Robertson, *A Preface to Chaucer,* 1962. • Beryl Rowland, ed., *Companion to Chaucer Studies,* 1979. • Brenda Deen Schildgen, *Pagans, Tartars, Moslems, and Jews in Chaucer's "Canterbury Tales,"* 2001. • Paul Strohm, *Social Chaucer,* 1989. • David Wallace, *Chaucerian Polity: Absolutist Lineages and Associational Forms in England and Italy,* 1997. • Winthrop Wetherbee, *Geoffrey Chaucer: "The Canterbury Tales,"* 1989.

Dante Alighieri • William Anderson, *Dante the Maker,* 1980. • Peter Armour, *Dante's Griffin and the History of the World,* 1989. • Peter Armour, *The Door of Purgatory: A Study of Multiple Symbolism in Dante's Purgatorio,* 1983. • Erich Auerbach, *Dante Poet of the Secular World,* 1961. • Erich Auerbach, "Figura," in *Scenes from the Drama of European Literature,* 1984. • Michele Barbi, *Life of Dante,* 1954. • Teodolinda Barolini, *Dante's Poets: Textuality and Truth in the Comedy,* 1983. • Teodolinda Barolini, *The Undivine Comedy: Detheologizing Dante,* 1992. • Steven Botterill, *Dante and the Mystical Tradition: Bernard of Clairvaux in the Commedia,* 1994. • Patrick Boyde, *Dante, Philomythes and Philosopher: Man in the Cosmos,* 1981. • Patrick Boyde, *Human Vices and Human Worth in Dante's Comedy,* 2000. • Anthony K. Cassell, *Inferno I,* 1989. • A. C. Charity, *Events and Their Afterlife: The Dialectics of Christian Typology in the Bible and Dante,* 1966. • Marc Cogan, *The Design in the Wax: The Structure of the Divine Comedy and Its Meaning,* 1999. • Alison Cornish, *Reading Dante's Stars,* 2000. • Charles Davis, *Dante and the Idea of Rome,* 1957. • Charles Davis, *Dante's Italy and Other Essays,* 1984. • Alessandro Passerin d'Entrèves, *Dante as a*

Political Thinker, 1952. ● Peter Dronke, *Dante and Medieval Latin Traditions,* 1986. ● Robert M. Durling and Ronald L. Martinez, *Time and the Crystal: Studies in Dante's Rime Petrose,* 1990. ● Francis Fergusson, *Dante,* 1966. ● Frances Fergusson, *Dante's Drama of the Mind: A Modern Reading of Purgatorio,* 1953. ● Joan M. Ferrante, *The Political Vision of the Divine Comedy,* 1984. ● Kenelm Foster, *The Two Dantes and Other Studies,* 1977. ● Wallace Fowlie, *A Reading of Dante's Inferno,* 1981. ● William Franke, *Dante's Interpretive Journey,* 1996. ● John Freccero, ed., *Dante: A Collection of Critical Essays,* 1965. ● John Freccero, *Dante: The Poetics of Conversion,* ed. Rachel Jacoff, 1986. ● Eileen Gardiner, trans., *Visions of Heaven and Hell Before Dante,* 1989. ● Etienne Gilson, *Dante and Philosophy,* trans. David Moore, 1963. ● Cecil Grayson, ed., *The World of Dante,* 1980. ● Robert Pogue Harrison, *The Body of Beatrice,* 1988. ● Robert Hollander, *Allegory in Dante's Commedia,* 1969. ● Robert Hollander, *Dante: A Life in Works,* 2001. ● George Holmes, *Dante,* 1980. ● Rachel Jacoff, ed., *The Cambridge Companion to Dante,* 1993. ● Rachel Jacoff and Jeffrey Schnapp, ed., *The Poetry of Allusion: Virgil and Ovid in Dante's Commedia,* 1991. ● Rachel Jacoff and William A. Stephany, *Inferno II,* 1989. ● Robin Kirkpatrick, *Dante's Inferno: Difficulty and Dead Poetry,* 1987. ● John Kleiner, *Mismapping the Underworld: Daring and Error in Dante's Comedy,* 1994. ● Richard Lansing, ed., *Dante: The Critical Complex,* 8 vols., 2003. ● Jacques Le Goff, *The Birth of Purgatory,* 1984. ● Ronald Macdonald, *The Burial Places of Memory: Epic Underworlds in Vergil, Dante, and Milton,* 1987. ● Allen Mandelbaum, et al., eds., *Lectura Dantis: Inferno,* 1998. ● Antonio C. Mastrobuono, *Dante's Journey of Sanctification,* 1990. ● Jerome Mazzaro, *The Figure of Beatrice,* 1981. ● Joseph Anthony Mazzeo, *Structure and Thought in the Paradiso,* 1958. ● Giuseppe Mazzotta, ed., *Critical Essays on Dante,* 1991. ● Giuseppe Mazzotta, *Dante, Poet of the Desert: History and Allegory in the Divine Comedy,* 1979. ● Giuseppe Mazzotta, *Dante's Vision and the Circle of Knowledge,* 1993. ● María Rosa Menocal, *The Arabic Role in Medieval Literary History,* 1987. ● Edward G. Miller, *Sense Perception in Dante's Commedia,* 1996. ● Alison Morgan, *Dante and the Medieval Other World,* 1990. ● Mary A. Orr, *Dante and the Early Astronomers,* 1961.

● Shirley J. Paolini, *Confessions of Sin and Love in the Middle Ages: Dante's Commedia and St. Augustine's Confessions,* 1982. ● Ricardo Quinones, *Dante Alighieri,* 1979. ● Brenda Deen Schildgen, *Dante and the Orient,* 2002. ● Jeffrey Schnapp, *The Transfiguration of History at the Center of Dante's Paradise,* 1986. ● John A. Scott, *Dante's Political Purgatory,* 1996. ● J. E. Shaw, *Essays on the Vita Nuova,* 1929. ● Maria Picchio Simonelli, *Inferno III,* 1993. ● Charles S. Singleton, *Dante's Commedia: Elements of Structure,* 1977. ● Charles S. Singleton, *An Essay on the Vita Nuova,* 1949. ● Charles S. Singleton, *Journey to Beatrice,* 1958. ● Madison U. Sowell, ed., *Dante and Ovid: Essays in Intertextuality,* 1991. ● Jeremy Tambling, ed., *Dante,* 1999. ● Miguel Tasín Palacios, *Islam and the Divine Comedy,* 1968. ● J. F. Took, *Dante, Lyric Poet and Philosopher: An Introduction to the Minor Works,* 1990. ● Paget Toynbee, *Dante Alighieri, His Life and Works,* 1965.

Dom Dinis and Martin Codax ● Sheila R. Ackerlind, *King Dinis of Portugal and the Alfonsine Heritage,* 1990. ● Frede Jensen, *The Earliest Portuguese Lyrics,* 1978.

Sir Gawain and the Green Knight ● Ross Arthur, *Medieval Sign Theory and Sir Gawain and the Green Knight,* 1987. ● W. R. J. Barron, *English Medieval Romance,* 1987. ● Larry D. Benson, *Art and Tradition in Sir Gawain and the Green Knight,* 1965. ● Robert J. Blanch and Julian Wasserman, *From Pearl to Gawain,* 1995. ● Robert J. Blanch et al., eds., *Text and Matter: New Critical Perspectives of the Pearl-Poet,* 1991. ● Marie Borroff, *Sir Gawain and the Green Knight: A Stylistic and Metrical Study,* 1962. ● Derek Brewer, ed., *Studies in Medieval English Romance,* 1988. ● Derek Brewer and Jonathan Gibson, eds. *A Companion to the Gawain-Poet,* 1997. ● Elisabeth Brewer, ed., *Sir Gawain and the Green Knight: Sources and Analogues,* 1992. ● J. A. Burrow, *A Reading of "Sir Gawain and the Green Knight,"* 1966. ● Wendy Clein, *Concepts of Chivalry in "Sir Gawain and the Green Knight,"* 1987. ● Lynn Staley Johnson, *The Voice of the Gawain-poet,* 1984. ● Maldwyn Mills et al., eds., *Romance in Medieval England,* 1991. ● Sandra Pearson Prior, *The Pearl Poet Revisited,* 1994. ● Ad Putter, *An Introduction to the Gawain-Poet,* 1996. ● Lee C. Ramsey, *Chivalric Romances,* 1983. ● A. C. Spearing, *The Gawain-Poet: A Critical Study,* 1970.

Ibn Arabi • A. E. Affifi, *The Mystical Philosophy of Muhyid din-Ibnul 'Arabi,* 1939. • Henri Corbin, *Creative Imagination in the Sufism of Ibn 'Arabi,* trans. Ralph Manheim, 1958. • Seyyed Hossain Nasr, *Three Muslim Sages,* 1969.

Ibn Ḥazm • Lois A. Giffen, "Ibn Ḥazm and the *Ṭawq al-ḥamma.*" *The Legacy of Muslim Spain,* ed. Salma Khadra Jayyusi, 1992. • Eric Ormsby, "Ibn Ḥazm," in *The Literature of Al-Andalus,* ed. Maria Rosa Menocal et al., 2000.

Ibn Rushd (Averroës) • Herbert A. Davidson, *Alfarabi, Avicenna, and Averroës on Intellect: Their Cosmologies, Theories of the Active Intellect, and Theories of Human Intellect,* 1992. • Oliver Leamon, *Averroës and His Philosophy,* 1988. • Dominique Urvoy, *Ibn Rushd, Averroës,* trans. Olivia Stewart, 1991.

Ramon Llull • J. N. Hillgarth, *Raymond Llull and Llullism in Fourteenth-Century France,* 1971. • Mark D. Johnston, *The Evangelical Rhetoric of Ramon Llull: Lay Learning and Piety in the Christian West Around 1300,* 1996. • Mark D. Johnston, *The Spiritual Logic of Ramon Llull,* 1987. • E. Allison Peers, *Ramon Llull: A Biography,* 1969. • Frances A. Yates, *Llull and Bruno: Collected Essays,* Vol. 1, 1982.

Marie de France • R. Howard Bloch, *The Anonymous Marie de France,* 2003. • Margaret M. Boland, *Architectural Structure in the Lais of Marie de France,* 1995. • Glyn S. Burgess, *The Lais of Marie de France: Text and Context,* 1987. • Caroline Walker Bynum, *Metamorphosis and Identity,* 2001. • Paula Clifford, *Marie de France: Lais,* 1982. • Mortimer J. Donovan, *The Breton Lay: A Guide to Varieties,* 1969. • Chantal Maréchal, ed., *In Quest of Marie de France: A Twelfth-Century Poet,* 1992. • Emanuel J. Mickel, Jr., *Marie de France,* 1974.

Mozarabic Kharjas • Samuel G. Armistead, "A Brief History of *Kharja* Studies," *Hispania* 70: 8–15, 1987 • Richard Hitchcock, *The Kharjas: A Critical Bibliography,* 1977. • Alan Jones, *Romance 'Kharjas' in Andalusian Arabic Muwassah Poetry: A Paleographical Analysis,* 1988. • Samuel Stern, *Hispano-Arabic Strophic Poetry: Studies,* 1974. • Otto Zwartjes, *Love Songs from al-Andalus: History, Structure, and Meaning of the Kharja,* 1997.

The Play of Adam • Eric Auerbach, "Adam and Eve" in *Mimesis,* 1954. • Richard Axton, *European Drama of the Early Middle Ages,* 1975. • Joseph A. Dane, *Res / Verba: A Study in Medieval French Drama,* 1985. • Grace Frank, *The Medieval French Drama,* 1954. • Lynette R. Muir, *The Biblical Drama of Medieval Europe,* 1995.

The Poem of the Cid • Simon Barton and Richard Fletcher, trans. and ed., *The World of El Cid: Chronicles of the Spanish Reconquest,* 2000. • Edmund de Chasca, *The Poem of the Cid,* 1976. • A. D. Deyermond, ed., *"Mio Cid" Studies,* 1977. • Joseph J. Duggan, *The 'Cantar de Mio Cid': Poetic Creation in Economic and Social Contexts,* 1989. • Michael Harney, *Kinship and Polity in the Poema de mío Cid,* 1993. • Ramón Menéndez Pidal, *The Cid and His Spain,* trans. Harold Sutherland, 1971. • Thomas Montgomery, *Medieval Spanish Epic: Mythic Roots and Ritual Language,* 1998. • Marjorie Ratcliffe, *Jimena: A Woman in Spanish Literature,* 1992. • Colin Smith, *The Making of the Poema de Mio Cid,* 1983.

Marco Polo • Maurice Collins, *Marco Polo,* 1961. • Henry H. Hart, *Marco Polo, Venetian Adventurer,* 1967. • Li Man Kin, *Marco Polo in China,* 1981. • R. P. Lister, *Marco Polo's Travels in Xanadu with Kublai Khan,* 1976. • Frances Wood, *Did Marco Polo Go to China?,* 1995.

Yehudah ha-Levi and Solomon Ibn Gabirol • Ross Brann, *The Compunctious Poet: Cultural Ambiguity and Hebrew Poetry in Muslim Spain,* 1991. • David Hartman, *Israelis and the Jewish Tradition: An Ancient People Debating Its Future,* 2000. • Rudolf Kayser, *The Life and Time of Jehudah Halevi,* trans. Frank Gaynor, 1949. • Raphael Loewe, *Ibn Gabirol,* 1990. • Arie Schippers, *Spanish Hebrew Poetry and the Arabic Literary Tradition: Arabic Themes in Hebrew Andalusian Poetry,* 1994.

CREDITS

TEXT CREDITS

Abelard and Heloïse: From *The Letters of Abelard and Heloise,* translated by Betty Radice. Copyright © 1974 by Betty Radice. Reproduced with permission of Penguin Books, Ltd.

Abelard, Peter: "Peter Abelard, Yes and No," from *The Middle Ages Volume I: Sources of Medieval History,* Third Edition, edited and translated by Brian Tierney, 1970.

Abelard, Peter: "Lament" from *Medieval Latin Lyrics* by Helen Waddell (London: Constable & Company, Ltd., 1929).

"Abenámar," translated by William M. Davis, from *An Anthology of Medieval Lyrics,* edited by Angel Flores (New York: The Modern Library, 1962). Reprinted by permission of Barbara Dederick c/o The Permissions Company.

Abu-Nuwas: "My Body is racked with sickness, worn out by exhaustion," *Journal of Arabic Literature,* Vol. XXVII, (Leiden: E. J. Brill, 1996) p. 9. Reprinted by permission of Brill Academic Publishers.

Abu-Nuwas: "Splendid young blades, like lamps in the darkness," as appeared in *Journal of Arabic Literature,* Vol. XXV, (Leiden: E. J. Brill, 1994) pp. 117–119. Reprinted by permission of Brill Academic Publishers.

Abu-Nuwas: "Praise wine in its sweetness," "O censor, I satisfied the Imam," "Bringing the cup of oblivion for sadness," "What's between me and the censurers," "He spoke these verses about a girl named Sammaja," and "One possessed with a rosy cheek," translated by Arthur Wormhoudt, from *The Diwan of Abu Nuwas al Hasan ibn Hani al Hakami,* diss., William Penn College, 1974. Reprinted by permission of Arthur Wormhoudt.

Abu 'Uthman ibn Bahr al-Jahiz: From *Approaches to Arabic Literature, No. 2, The Epistle on Singing-Girls of Jahiz,* translated by A. F. L. Beeston. Copyright © 1980 by A. F. L. Beeston. Reprinted by permission of Aris & Phillips, Ltd.

Abu 'Uthman ibn Bahr al-Jahiz: "The Tale of Layla al-Na'itiyyah," "The Tale of Ahmad b. Khalaf," and "The Tale of Tammam b. Ja'far," from *The Book of Misers,* translated by R. B. Serjeant. Reprinted by permission of Garnet Publishing, Ltd. Reading, UK.

Abu 'Uthman ibn Bahr al-Jahiz: "Man is a microcosm," "Prolixity and conciseness," "Doubt and conviction," "Garrulity and indiscretion," and "It is hard to keep a secret" from *The Life and Works of Jahiz,* translations of selected texts by Charles Pellat, translated by D. M. Hawke (London: Routledge and Kegan Paul, 1969). Reprinted by permission of Routledge and Kegan Paul.

Al-Khansa: "In the evening remembrance keeps me awake," from *Early Arabic Poetry, Volume 1: Marathi and Su'luk Poems,* edited and translated by Alan Jones (Reading, England: Ithaca Press, 1992), pp. 254–255, 258–260, 268–270.

Al-Khansa: "A mote in your eye, dust blown in the wind," from *Classical Arabic Poetry, 162 Poems From Imrulkais to Ma'Arri,* translated by Charles Greville Tuetey (London: Kegan Paul, 1985). Reprinted by permission of Kegan Paul International, Ltd.

Al-Tabari: Reprinted from *The History of al-Tabari, Vol. XXX: The Abbasid Caliphate in Equilibrium: The Caliphates of Musa al-Hadi and Harun al-Rashid A.D. 785–809/A.H. 169–193,* translated by C. E. Bosworth. Copyright © 1989 by the State University of New York Press, State University of New York. All rights reserved.

Al-Hallaj: "I have a dear friend whom I visit in solitary places," translated by D. P. Brewster, *Journal of Arabic Literature,* Vol. IX (Leiden: E. J. Brill, 1978), p. 65. Reprinted by permission of Brill Academic Publishers.

Al-Hallaj: "I continued to float on the sea of love," "Painful enough it is that I am ever calling out to You," "Your place in my heart is the whole of my heart," "You who blame me for my love of Him," and "I swear to God, the sun has never risen or set," translated by M. M. Badawi, *Journal of Arabic Literature,* Vol. XIV (Leiden: E. J. Brill, 1983), pp. 46–47. Reprinted by permission of Brill Academic Publishers.

Al-Hallaj: "Ah! I or You? These are the two Gods," "Here am I, here am I," and 'I am not I and I am not He; then who am I and who is He?" translated by Samah Salim, *Journal of Arabic Literature,* Vol. XXI (Leiden: E. J. Brill, 1990), pp. 38–40. Reprinted by permission of Brill Academic Publishers.

Al-Mutanabbi: "On hearing in Egypt that his death had been reported to Saif al-Daula in Aleppo," "Satire on Kafur composed on 9 Dhu'l-Hijja 350 (19 January 962), one day before the poet's departure from Egypt," "Panegyric to 'Adud al-Daula and his sons, Abu 'l-Fawaris and Abu Dulaf" from *The Poems of Al-Mutanabbi,* translated by A. J. Arberry. Copyright © 1967 by Cambridge University Press. Reprinted by permission of Cambridge University Press.

Averroës: "The Decisive Treatise Determining the Nature of the Connection Between Religion and Philosophy," from *Averroës on Harmony of Religion and Philosophy,* translated by G. F. Hourani. Reprinted by permission of the publisher, the E. J. W. Gibb Memorial Trust.

From *The Book of the Thousand Nights and One Night, Vol. II,* "The Tale of Sympathy the Learned" and "An Adventure of the Poet Abu Nuwas," translated by J. C. Mardrus and Powys Mathers (London: Routledge & Kegan Paul Ltd., 1964). Reprinted by permission of Routledge and Kegan Paul.

"Three Moorish Girls" [Tres Morillas], Anonymous, English translation by Angela Buxton.

Urwa b. al-Ward: "Do not be so free with your blame of me," from *Early Arabic Poetry, Volume 1: Marathi and Su'luk Poems,* edited and translated by Alan Jones (Reading: Ithaca Press, 1992), pp. 254–255, 258–260, 268–270.

Wang Changling: "A Discussion of Literature and Meaning," from Richard Wainwright Bodman, *Poetics and Prosody in Early Mediaeval China: A Study and Translation of Kukai's Bunkyo Hifuron,* diss., Cornell University, 1978. Reprinted by permission of Richard Wainwright Bodman.

Wang Shifu: From *The Story of the Western Wing,* translated by Stephen H. West and Wilt L. Idema. Copyright © 1991 by The Regents of the University of California. Reprinted by permission of the University of California Press.

Wang Wei: "Song of the Peach Blossom Spring," "Meng Wall Cove," "Deer Enclosure," "Sophora Path," "Lake Yi," "Bamboo Lodge," "Bird Call Valley," "Farewell," "Farewell to Yuan," "Visiting the Temple," "Zhongnan Retreat," "In Response . . . ," from *The Poetry of Wang Wei: New Translations and Commentary,* translated by Pauline Yu. Copyright © 1980 Indiana University Press. Reprinted by permission of the publisher.

Master Wŏlmyŏng: "Requiem," from *Anthology of Korean Literature: From Early Times to the Nineteenth Century,* edited by Peter H. Lee. Copyright © 1990 University of Hawaii Press. Reprinted by permission.

Xue Tao: "Midnight Songs," from *Brocade River Poems: Selected Works of the Tang Dynasty Courtesan Xue Tao,* translated by Jeanne Larsen. Copyright © 1987 Princeton University Press. Reprinted by permission of Princeton University Press.

Yehuda ha-Levi: "Cups without wine are lowly," translated by William M. Davis, from *An Anthology of Medieval Lyrics,* edited by Angel Flores (New York: The Modern Library, 1962). Reprinted by permission of Barbara Dederick c/o The Permissions Company.

Yehuda ha-Levi: "Your breeze, Western shore, is perfumed" and "My Heart is in the East," from *Hebrew Poems from Spain,* edited and translated by David Goldstein. Reprinted by permission of David Higham Associates Ltd.

Yehuda ha-Levi: "From time's beginning, You were love's abode," from *The Gazelle: Medieval Hebrew Poems on God, Israel, and the Soul,* edited and translated by Raymond Scheindlin. Copyright 1991 by Ramond P. Scheindlin. Reprinted by permission of The Jewish Publication Society.

Yehuda ha-Levi: "Ofra does her laundry with my tears" and "Once when I fondled him upon my thighs," from *Wine, Women, and Death: Medieval Hebrew Poems on the Good Life,* edited and translated by Raymond Scheindlin. Copyright 1986 by The Jewish Publications Society. Reprinted by permission.

Priest Yŏngjae: "Meeting with Bandits" from *Anthology of Korean Literature: From Early Times to the Nineteenth Century,* edited by Peter H. Lee. Copyright © 1990 University of Hawaii Press. Reprinted by permission.

Yuan Cai: "Precepts for Social Life," translated by Patricia Buckley Ebrey, reprinted with permission of The Free Press, a Division of Simon & Schuster, Inc., from *Chinese Civilization and Society: A Sourcebook* by Patricia Buckley Ebrey. Copyright © 1981 by The Free Press.

Yuan Zhen: "The Story of Ying-ying" translated by Arthur Waley, from *Anthology of Chinese Literature,* edited by Cyril Birch. Copyright © 1965 by Grove Press, Inc. Used by permission of Grove/Atlantic, Inc.

Zeami: "Atsumori, A Tale of Heike Play" and "Matsukase, Pining Wind", from *Japanese No Dramas,* translated by Royall Tyler. Translation Copyright © 1992 by Royall Tyler. Reproduced with permission of Penguin Books, Ltd.

Ban Zhao: "Lessons for Women" from *Pan Choa: Foremost Woman Scholar of China,* translated by Nancy Lee Swann, 2001. Copyright © The East Asian Library and the Gest Collection, Princeton University. Used by permission.

ILLUSTRATION CREDITS

Cover image: Detail from *Portrait of Murasaki Shikibu,* c. 978–1014, by Ogata Korin (1658–1716). **Inside front cover image:** Al-Idrisi, *Map of the World.* The Bodleian Library, University of Oxford. **Page xxx:** *King Arthur and His Knights,* from a manuscript of the *Prose Lancelot,* France, 13th century. Yale University, Beinecke Rare Book and Manuscript Library. **Page 10:** Sakyamuni Buddha, Yungang, Shanxi Province, c. 460. Copyright © Wolfgang Kaehler/CORBIS. All Rights Reserved. **Page 16:** The urban plans of imperial Chang'an and of imperial Rome. *Ten Thousand Things: Module and Mass Production in Chinese Art,* by Lothar Lettrose, Princeton, NJ/Princeton University Press, 1999. **Page 21:** Female polo-player, lead-glazed earthenware, Tang dynasty, c. 695–715. With permission of the Royal Ontario Museum © ROM. **Page 24:** *Mencius and His Mother,* from an illustrated version of the *Memoirs of Women,* preface dated 1552, reprinted in a later Qing dynasty. **Page 88:** Liang Kai, *Li Bo Chanting a Poem,* hanging scroll, 13th century. Tokyo National Museum. **Page 124:** Shusetsu Dōjin, landscape painting, Japan, 15th century. © Staatliche Museen zu Berlin Stiftung Preussischer Kulturbesitz, Museum fur Ostasiatische Kunst/Bildarchiv Preussischer Kulturbesitz/Art Resource, NY. **Page 131:** Mutō Shūi, *Portrait of the Monk Musō Soseki*/Shokikuji Temple. **Page. 238:** Japanese court women from *The Tale of Genji Picture Scroll,* late 12th century. The Tokugawa Reimeikai Foundation. **Page 314:** Calligraphy of the name of the

Prophet Muhammad, Turkey, 1827. The Nasser D. Khalili Collection of Islamic Art (CAL 70). © Nour Foundation. **Page 327:** Mosque of Muhammad Ali, Cairo, early 19th century. © Roger Wood/CORBIS. All Rights Reserved. **Page 385:** Medieval portrait of four musicians, accompanying an evening of feasting and poetry recitations/ Concert, Fol. 17 Ottoman, from Turkey, 18th century C.E. Levni/Art Resource, NY. **Page 490:** Page from Husayn Bayqara's *Majalis al-Ushshaq* ("Sessions of the Lovers"), 16th century. Bodleian Library, University of Oxford, England. **Page 518:** *Muhammad Visiting Paradise,* Persian miniature, 15th century. Bibliothèque Nationale de France. **Page 566:** Cathedral of Notre Dame, Paris, 12th century. Bill Bachmann/Index Stock Imagery. **Page 573:** Shrine of the Book of Dimma. Ireland, 12th century. Trinity College Library, University of Dublin. **Page 575:** Saint Benedict writing his rule. Württembergische Landesbibliothek, Stuttgart. **Page 578:** Scenes from the Bayeux Tapestry, France, late 11th century. Musée de la Tapisserie, Bayeux. Copyright © Giraudon/Art Resource, NY. **Page 758:** *Christian and Muslim playing chess,* illuminated manuscript page from King Alfonso X's *Book of Games,* Castile, midthirteenth century. Instituto Amatller de Arte Hispanico, Barcelona, Spain. **Pages 904–905:** Alighieri, Dante. "Diagrams" by C. W. Scott-Giles, from *The Divine Comedy by Dante,* translated by Mark Musa. Copyright © 1971. Used by permission of Penguin, a division of Penguin Group (USA). **Page 1067:** Gustave Doré, 1870 engraving of the Ugolino episode in Dante's *Inferno.* Bodleian Library, University of Oxford.

FONTS CREDIT

The EuroSlavic, AfroRoman, Macron, TransIndic, Semitic Transliterator, and ANSEL fonts used to publish this work are available from Linguist's Software, Inc., PO Box 580, Edmonds, WA 98020-0580 USA, tel (425) 775-1130, www.linguistsoftware.com.

INDEX

1175